The Editors

WAYNE A. MEEKS is Woolsey Professor Emeritus in the Department of Religious Studies, Yale University, where he taught from 1969 until 1999. Earlier, he taught at Indiana University, 1966–69, and Dartmouth College, 1964–65. He has served as president of the two leading professional societies in his field, the Society of Biblical Literature (1985) and *Studiorum Novi Testamenti Societas* (2004–05). He holds an honorary doctorate from the University of Uppsala and is a fellow of the British Academy and of the American Academy of Arts and Sciences. He is best known for his publications on the writings of the apostle Paul and on the Fourth Gospel, for his investigation of the social history of earliest Christianity, and for work on the formation of early Christian morality.

JOHN T. FITZGERALD has been a member of the Department of Religious Studies at the University of Miami since 1981 and has served as a visiting associate professor at Brown University and the Yale Divinity School. He concentrates on the religions and philosophical schools of the ancient Mediterranean world in the period between Alexander the Great (d. 323 BCE) and Constantine (d. 337 CE), highlighting ways in which Jews and Christians interacted with various segments of Greco-Roman culture and appropriated philosophical materials for religious use. He is the founding General Editor of the Society of Biblical Literature's Writings from the Greco-Roman World series.

NORTON CRITICAL EDITIONS IN THE
HISTORY OF IDEAS

AQUINAS • ST. THOMAS AQUINAS ON POLITICS AND ETHICS
translated and edited by Paul E. Sigmund

DARWIN • DARWIN
selected and edited by Philip Appleman (Third Edition)

ERASMUS • THE PRAISE OF FOLLY AND OTHER WRITINGS
translated and edited by Robert M. Adams

HERODOTUS • THE HISTORIES
translated by Walter Blanco, edited by Walter Blanco and Jennifer Tolbert Roberts

HOBBES • LEVIATHAN
edited by Richard E. Flathman and David Johnston

LOCKE • THE SELECTED POLITICAL WRITINGS OF JOHN LOCKE
edited by Paul E. Sigmund

MACHIAVELLI • THE PRINCE
translated and edited by Robert M. Adams (Second Edition)

MALTHUS • AN ESSAY ON THE PRINCIPLE OF POPULATION
edited by Philip Appleman (Second Edition)

MARX • THE COMMUNIST MANIFESTO
edited by Frederic L. Bender

MILL • MILL: THE SPIRIT OF THE AGE, ON LIBERTY, THE SUBJECTION OF WOMEN
edited by Alan Ryan

MORE • UTOPIA
translated and edited by Robert M. Adams (Second Edition)

NEWMAN • APOLOGIA PRO VITA SUA
edited by David J. DeLaura

NEWTON • NEWTON
selected and edited by I. Bernard Cohen and Richard S. Westfall

ROUSSEAU • ROUSSEAU'S POLITICAL WRITINGS
translated by Julia Conaway Bondanella, edited by Alan Ritter

ST. PAUL • THE WRITINGS OF ST. PAUL
edited by Wayne A. Meeks and John T. Fitzgerald (Second Edition)

THOREAU • WALDEN AND RESISTANCE TO CIVIL GOVERNMENT
edited by William Rossi (Second Edition)

THUCYDIDES • THE PELOPONNESIAN WAR
translated by Walter Blanco, edited by Walter E. Blanco and Jennifer Tolbert Roberts

TOCQUEVILLE • DEMOCRACY IN AMERICA
edited by Isaac Kramnick

WATSON • THE DOUBLE HELIX: A PERSONAL ACCOUNT OF THE DISCOVERY OF THE
STRUCTURE OF DNA
edited by Gunther S. Stent

WOLLSTONECRAFT • A VINDICATION OF THE RIGHTS OF WOMAN
edited by Carol H. Poston (Second Edition)

FOR A COMPLETE LIST OF NORTON CRITICAL EDITIONS, VISIT
www.wwnorton.com/college/English/nce_home.htm

A NORTON CRITICAL EDITION

THE WRITINGS OF ST. PAUL

ANNOTATED TEXTS

RECEPTION AND CRITICISM

SECOND EDITION

Edited by

WAYNE A. MEEKS
YALE UNIVERSITY

JOHN T. FITZGERALD
UNIVERSITY OF MIAMI

W • W • NORTON & COMPANY, INC. • *New York* • *London*

Copyright © 2007, 1972 by W. W. Norton & Company, Inc.

All rights reserved.
Printed in the United States of America.
Second Edition.

Scripture taken from Today's New International Version Bible Copyright © 1973, 1978, 1984, 2005 by International Bible Society. The "TNIV" and "Today's New International Version" trademarks are registered in the United States Patent and Trademark Office by International Bible Society. Reprinted by permission of Hodder and Stoughton Limited.

The text of this book is composed in Fairfield Medium
with the display set in Bernhard Modern.
Design by Antonina Krass.
Composition by Binghamton Valley Composition.
Map by Maps.com.
Manufacturing by the Courier Companies—Westford Division.
Production manager: Benjamin Reynolds.

Library of Congress Cataloging-in-Publication Data

The writings of St. Paul: annotated texts, reception and criticism /
edited by Wayne A. Meeks, John T. Fitzgerald.—2nd ed.
p. cm.—(A Norton critical edition)
Includes bibliographical references (p.   ) and index.

ISBN-13: 978-0-393-97280-1 (pbk.)
ISBN-10: 0-393-97280-1 (pbk.)

1. Bible, N.T. Epistles of Paul—Theology. 2. Bible, N.T. Epistles of Paul—Criticism, interpretation, etc. I. Meeks, Wayne A. II. Fitzgerald, John T., 1948–
BS2651.W78 2006
227'.06—dc22
2006047301

W. W. Norton & Company, Inc., 500 Fifth Avenue, New York, N.Y. 10110-0017
www.wwnorton.com

W. W. Norton & Company Ltd., Castle House, 75/76 Wells Street, London W1T 3QT

2 3 4 5 6 7 8 9 0

Contents

Preface

Since the first edition of this Norton Critical Edition appeared in 1972, numerous monographs and articles on the apostle Paul and his letters have been published, and new perspectives on Pauline Christianity have emerged. In order to take account of some of these new developments and emphases in Pauline studies, we have prepared a revised and expanded edition of *The Writings of St. Paul*. Although the basic format of the volume remains the same, we have added new sections, deleted others entirely, and made changes to almost all the sections retained from the first edition.

The Introduction provides an orientation to the man who, next to Jesus, was the most important and the most enigmatic figure in the initial stages of Christianity. The first two parts of the volume contain the complete extant works attributed to Paul in the New Testament. Because some of these are probably the work of Paul's disciples writing in his name, we have divided them, following a common scholarly convention, into the seven letters undoubtedly authentic (Part I) and the six whose authorship is questionable (Part II). Within each group we have endeavored to place the letters in chronological order, though dates in several cases are impossible even to approximate. The reader will thus find the order here different from that in the New Testament, where the letters have been listed since antiquity in order of diminishing length. The introductions and notes are not designed to substitute for the standard reference works named in the Bibliography, but only to give the reader an entrée into the historical milieu of Pauline Christianity. In addition, they point out particularly important elements of form and style that are frequently overlooked.

The text of the Pauline letters is from Today's New International Version (TNIV). It was chosen from the several excellent modern versions now available because its relatively conservative mode of translation enables the reader to recognize certain distinctive features of Paul's style, while still taking account of current discussions in biblical scholarship and aiming for both inclusiveness and accuracy in the representation of gender. The alternate readings indicated in the marginal notes by the TNIV translators have been omitted here, though the most important of these interpretive options are discussed in the notes to the letters. As in every modern translation, paragraphing and sentence divisions follow the translators' understanding of sense units; often they do not coincide with *verse* divisions, which go back to printed Greek texts of the sixteenth century.

Part III is new and contains the major pseudo-Pauline works not included in the New Testament. Part IV has been considerably expanded and gives a variety of views of Paul in the ancient church. This section includes not only depictions and discussions of Paul by ancient authors but also treatments of those writings by modern scholars. The next three parts treat the subjects of "Law versus Grace and the Problem of Ethics"

(V), Paul as "The Second Founder of Christianity" (VI), and "Pauline Christianity and Judaism" (VII). Part VIII is new, illustrating ways in which readings of Romans 7 and 13 have influenced religious and political thought both in antiquity and in later periods. Part IX contains a selection of modern approaches to Paul, and an Epilogue reflects on the remarkable variety of images of Paul revealed in the history of his influence.

The anthology of secondary works contained in this edition has two purposes: (1) to suggest some of the major ways in which these writings and the reactions to them have contributed to the shape of Christianity and of Western thought and (2) to provide representative examples of modern critical studies. The selections could be multiplied endlessly. Specialists will think of essays that they would have wished included, even at the cost of some that we have chosen. But choices had to be made.

Unless otherwise indicated, the translations of essays not originally written in English are ours. In the excerpted materials, only those footnotes are reproduced that are essential for the reader's understanding. For the authors' complete references to other literature and to scholarly debate, the originals must be consulted.

Many teachers and colleagues have contributed, knowingly or unknowingly, to the success of the first edition and to our revisions of the second, but above all our thanks are due to the hundreds of students whose vigorous dialogue in seminars at Indiana, Yale, and Miami has given to both editions of this book its substance and purpose. We are particularly grateful to Carol Bemis of W. W. Norton & Company for her extraordinary patience and good advice as we prepared the present edition.

W. A. M.   J. T. F.
Hamden, Connecticut   Miami, Florida

Introduction

Among the scores of religious sects that offered eternal hope or present ecstasy to the diverse peoples of the Roman Empire in the middle of the first century, Christianity was not conspicuous. Impartial observers, asked which of these cults might someday become the official religion of the empire, even a world religion, would perhaps have chosen Mithraism. They certainly would not have named the inconspicuous followers of a crucified Jew. The obscurity of the factors that would produce its incredible expansion makes the story of Christianity's first three centuries one of the most baffling and fascinating chapters in the history of human civilization. Since the impartial observers of its beginnings provide no solution to the puzzle, we are forced to turn to its partisans, who were certain from the beginning that their "gospel"—the "news" about the crucified and risen Christ—was the means by which God would "have mercy upon all people" (Rom. 11: 32).

The best known of those partisans is the subject of this anthology, because he alone of first-century Christians left a substantial literary bequest. Letters attributed to him comprise a quarter of the New Testament, and another twelfth of its pages—most of the Book of Acts—is devoted to a description of his career. Closest attention has to be paid to the letters, for they are our most direct and earliest primary sources for the beginnings of Christianity. They were not intended as literature. Paul would have been doubly astonished that they should have a place in the "history of ideas," for he had no high opinion of human wisdom, and he thought he was living at the end of history. On the other hand, they are not merely private letters. They are official correspondence, directed to a variety of immediate and urgent problems confronting the newly established Christian congregations in the cities of the eastern Mediterranean. For that reason they afford a most candid glimpse into the character of those congregations as well as of the man who founded them. And indirectly they provide precious hints about the form of Christianity that existed before Paul's conversion and about the special school he shaped, which was destined to survive him.

Early Christianity was never a monolithic society, but a polymorphous movement, the vector constituted by tensions in many directions. Paul himself embodied many of those tensions, and while his influence upon the subsequent history of Christianity, especially in the West, has been enormous, his legacy has been a subject of fierce debate. Of all the early Christians, he was undoubtedly the most controversial, simultaneously evoking feelings of love from his awed admirers and expressions of hostility from his outraged critics. This mixed response to the apostle and the gospel he proclaimed has continued through the centuries. His admirers have included Christians such as Ambrose, who called him "Christ's second eye," and Martin Luther, who testified that "in the scholastics I lost Christ but found him again in Paul." His critics have included John Stuart Mill and Alfred North Whitehead, the former declaring, "I hold St. Paul to have been the first great corrupter of Christianity," and the latter opining, "The man who, I suppose, did more than anybody else to distort and subvert Christ's teaching was Paul." But have either Paul's admirers or his critics correctly understood him? Already an ancient admirer of the apostle lamented that "his letters contain some things that are hard to understand" (2 Pet. 3:16), which is only one of many factors responsible for the diverse interpretations and assessments of his thought. Even Paul's admirers have not agreed upon which letters he wrote, what he meant, or whether Christians must accept his ideas. Abelard, for example, said, "I do not want to be a philosopher if the price of it is that I must rebel against St. Paul." Similarly, Søren Kierkegaard declared that "I have not got to listen to St. Paul because he is clever, or even brilliantly clever; I am to bow before St. Paul because he has divine authority." Bishop James Pike, on the other hand, concluded, "St. Paul was wrong about sex."[1] Perhaps no one has stated the issue more sharply than Franz Overbeck: "Nowadays no one has really understood Paul who thinks that he still can agree with him."[2] Whether Paul had something important to say, and if so, whether one should embrace any or all of his convictions, are issues that readers of his letters will continue to debate for the foreseeable future.

The quest of the historical Paul, like that of the historical Jesus, is an ongoing endeavor. The diverse portraits of Paul that appear in this anthology are both a reflection of this quest and the result of different decisions scholars have reached about the ancient sources and the methods used to interpret them. Because of the complexity of these debates, it may be helpful at the outset to provide a brief introduction to the sources and a short outline of Paul's life.

The Sources

Modern readers have at their disposal three basic sources for reconstructing the life and thought of Paul. The first and primary source is the corpus of thirteen letters attributed to him in the New Testament; in canonical order, these are Romans, 1 and 2 Corinthians, Galatians, Ephesians, Philippians, Colossians, 1 and 2 Thessalonians, 1 and 2 Timothy, Titus, and Philemon. The scholarly consensus is that Paul wrote at least seven of these letters: Romans, 1–2 Corinthians, Galatians, Philippians, 1 Thessalonians, and Philemon. His authorship of the remaining six letters is disputed, largely because they are different in key respects (style, vocabulary, church structure, theological viewpoint, etc.) from the undisputed letters. The most fiercely contested are 2 Thessalonians and Colossians, with some affirming that Paul wrote both letters, others that he wrote only one (usually 2 Thessalonians), and still others that he wrote neither letter.

---

1. The quotations in this paragraph are taken from Malcolm Muggeridge and Alex Vidler, *Paul, Envoy Extraordinary* (New York: Harper, 1972), 11–16, who provide a wide assortment of positive and negative opinions on Paul.
2. The statement appears in both his *Kirchenlexikon* and *Christentum und Kultur* (Basel, 1919), both now conveniently available in Franz Overbeck, *Werke und Nachlass* (7 vols.; Stuttgart: Metzler, 1994–2002), vol. 5, 211; vol. 6/1, 87.

Most contemporary scholars do not believe that Paul wrote Ephesians, and a virtual consensus holds that he did not write any of the so-called "Pastoral Letters" (1–2 Timothy and Titus).

Letters not written by Paul are usually attributed to the "Pauline school," a diverse group of Paulinists who wrote letters in the apostle's name in order to mediate his influence to a new generation of believers and address problems that had arisen in the Christian communities following his death. In writing such "deutero-Pauline" letters, these disciples and admirers of Paul were following the widespread ancient practice of writing pseudonymous documents. Certain Cynics, for example, wrote letters in the names of both Socrates and Diogenes,[3] and one Christian even produced a pseudonymous exchange of letters between King Abgar of Edessa and Jesus.[4] In antiquity these inauthentic documents were typically transmitted along with the genuine works of the person in whose name they were written. The Platonic corpus, for instance, contains some forty-three works; of these, modern classicists universally regard twenty-four as genuine (e.g., the *Republic*), reject seven as undoubtedly spurious (e.g., the *Axiochus*), and debate the authenticity of the rest.[5]

In keeping with common practice, Paul typically dictated his correspondence to a secretary (Rom. 16:22) and added comments in his own hand at the end of the transcribed letter (1 Cor. 16:21; Gal. 6:11; Phlm. 19; 2 Thess. 3:17; Col. 4:18). Their oral style, enhanced by the occasional use of the diatribe,[6] makes them comparable in certain respects to the orations of ancient rhetoricians, whereas the presence of various literary clichés ("absent in body, present in spirit") and devices (such as the *inclusio* to frame a discussion of a topic) shows that they were composed with an awareness of epistolary theory and practice.[7] Carried by Paul's associates, delegates from the churches, or traveling Christians (Rom. 16:1), the letters were read aloud to the assembled community (*ekklēsia*) in liturgical settings (1 Thess. 5:26–27). In some cases, more than one group was the intended recipient, with Galatians sent to several churches in that region (Gal. 1:2) and Romans directed to multiple house churches in the imperial city (Rom. 16:5, 10–11, 14–15). In such cases, the letter carrier may have delivered a copy of the letter to each group or the latter may have transcribed their own copy of the original. The recipients of these letters apparently began to exchange them among themselves at an early stage, possibly already during Paul's lifetime (Col. 4:16). Similarly, from an early time slightly edited versions of some of the longer letters, such as Romans and 1 Corinthians, began to circulate independently in cities other than Rome and Corinth, with the names of the original locales deleted (Rom. 1:7, 15; 1 Cor. 1:2).[8] These exchanges of letters and catholicized editions reflect

3. For texts and translations, see A. J. Malherbe (ed.), *The Cynic Epistles* (Missoula, MT: Scholars, 1977), 91–183, 217–307.
4. See Eusebius, *Hist. eccl.* 1.13.5–10, and H. J. W. Drijvers, "The Abgar Legend," in *New Testament Apocrypha*, ed. by Wilhelm Schneelmelcher (rev. ed.; 2 vols.; Louisville: Westminster John Knox, 1991), vol. 1, 492–500.
5. Plato's thirteen *Letters* are treated here collectively as one work. Assessments of the twelve disputed works generally range from "very probable" to "highly unlikely," with most accepting some of these as genuine and rejecting others.
6. For the diatribe as a conversation with an imagined interlocutor, see S. K. Stowers, *The Diatribe and Paul's Letter to the Romans* (Chico, CA: Scholars, 1981).
7. A. J. Malherbe (ed.), *Ancient Epistolary Theorists* (Atlanta: Scholars, 1988).
8. Harry Gamble, *The Textual History of the Letter to the Romans* (Grand Rapids: Eerdmans, 1977).

the awareness that Paul's letters, though written for particular situations, had a broader applicability,[9] and the pseudonymous letter to the Ephesians, intended from the outset for wide dissemination, was composed without any local address.[1]

The person who made the first collection of Paul's letters is unknown. An older generation of scholars tended to think primarily in terms of the "original" letter that Paul had dispatched to a particular church. The impetus for collecting the letters was correspondingly viewed as coming from the churches or from some prominent individual within them, who formed the corpus by doggedly acquiring copies of the apostle's correspondence. Contemporary scholars, by contrast, increasingly reckon with the probability that Paul followed the ancient practice of retaining copies of his letters, especially since they were official correspondence. Indeed, some believe that Paul himself started the process by producing an edited version of some of his own letters,[2] and that the process was continued by the churches, who produced partial collections by exchanging letters that each had received.[3] Others think in terms of the Pauline school, which, perhaps acting at Paul's behest, used his dossier of letters to produce the first collection.[4] In forming this corpus, the Paulinists did not simply compile the apostle's letters but also added works of their own. In addition, they may also have combined portions of Paul's letters and inserted new material at key points. Many view both 2 Corinthians and Philippians as composite letters, and a number of crucial passages in the undisputed letters (such as Rom. 16:25–27) are widely suspected of being interpolations by later Paulinists.[5] Once again, such activities would not be unique to the redactors of the Pauline corpus. Some of Cicero's letters, for example, are composite,[6] and many of the prophetic books in the Hebrew Bible (such as Isaiah) reflect the activity of later editors who not only compiled the oracles of the prophets and shaped the earliest traditions about them but also added to their content. Eventually, different collections of Paul's letters came into existence, some with ten letters (the letters to the churches, plus Philemon), others with thirteen letters (containing the Pastoral Epistles), and still others with fourteen letters (with Hebrews included).

Decisions that readers make about these issues have important implications for their understandings of Paul and his views on key issues. To give but one example: what was Paul's view of women and their role in the communities he founded? Those who believe that Paul wrote 1 Timothy and that 1 Corinthians contains no interpolations tend to give a largely negative answer that places severe restrictions on women's roles. Those who believe that a later Paulinist wrote 1 Timothy and that 1 Corinthians 14:33b–36 ("women should remain silent in the churches") is an inter-

9. See esp. N. A. Dahl, "The Particularity of the Pauline Epistles as a Problem in the Ancient Church," in *Neotestamentica et Patristica* (Leiden: Brill, 1962), 261–71.
1. The words "in Ephesus" of Eph. 1:1 are a later scribal addition, perhaps reflecting the awareness that Ephesians were among the anticipated readers of the letter.
2. David Trobisch, *Paul's Letter Collection* (Minneapolis: Fortress, 1994).
3. Jerome Murphy-O'Connor, *Paul the Letter-Writer* (Collegeville: Liturgical Press, 1995), 114–30.
4. Harry Gamble, *Books and Readers in the Early Church* (New Haven: Yale University Press, 1995), 99–101.
5. For a comprehensive listing of proposed post-Pauline insertions, see W. O. Walker, *Interpolations in the Pauline Letters* (Sheffield: Sheffield Academic Press, 2001).
6. See Hans-Josef Klauck, "Compilation of Letters in Cicero's Correspondence," in *Early Christianity and Classical Culture*, ed. by J. T. Fitzgerald, T. H. Olbricht, and L. M. White (Leiden: Brill, 2003), 131–55.

polation will paint a more positive picture that emphasizes the importance of women and their freedom during Paul's lifetime to engage in various forms of ministry.

As a reflection of the ancient practice of writing pseudonymous letters and the modern debate about which letters stem directly from Paul, we have divided the thirteen letters into two basic groups: "The Undoubted Letters of St. Paul" and "Works of the Pauline School." Not included in either category is the Letter to the Hebrews, although it was often attributed to Paul between the third and the nineteenth centuries.[7] Inasmuch as Paul did not write this anonymous document nor does it in any sense represent the Pauline school, we have not included it in this volume.[8]

The second source is the Book of Acts, which, starting with Paul's persecution of the nascent church in Jerusalem, traces the story of his subsequent life, including his conversion, activities as a missionary, and various imprisonments. The account ends in Rome, with Paul awaiting trial before the Roman emperor Nero. The Book of Acts is the second part of a two-volume work, with the Gospel of Luke the first part. Because Luke-Acts is anonymous, the identity of its author, the first Christian historian, is unknown. Early Christian tradition identified the author as a physician by the name of Luke, known from the Pauline corpus as one of Paul's associates (Phlm. 24; Col. 4:14; 2 Tim. 4:11). In several instances, the narrator of Acts switches from his usual third person form to the first person. These "we-sections" of Acts (16:10–17; 20:5–15; 21:1–18; 27:1–28:16) traditionally have been viewed as the eyewitness testimony of Luke himself, ostensibly giving these narratives a high degree of historical value. Some modern scholars accept this ancient tradition and view Acts' portrait of Paul as very reliable, whereas other scholars are less confident about the veracity of the tradition and of Acts' historical value. The latter stress the anonymity of Acts' author and point out that the tools and conventions used by ancient writers did not ensure the reliability of their narratives, which often give the appearance of eyewitness testimony even when it is lacking. Ancient historians, for example, were not only dependent on written and oral sources for many of their accounts but also frequently edited their sources or departed from them entirely in order to provide a different or altered version of an event or person. Although they boasted about their access to firsthand information, they often composed the speeches that they attributed to their speakers, giving the sort of speech that would have been appropriate for the occasion and not what was actually said. Similarly, they sometimes switched to a first-person form of narration to make their accounts livelier or more dramatic, not because they were there. It is clear that "Luke" (as we may call him for reasons of convenience rather than conviction) acted in a similar way. Like many other historians and writers

---

7. P[46], the earliest extant manuscript of the *Corpus Paulinum*, already includes Hebrews, placing it immediately after Romans.

8. In recognition of its different style and content, Hebrews was sometimes attributed in antiquity to co-workers or admirers of Paul, such as Luke, Clement of Rome, or Barnabas (Tertullian, *Pud.* 20). Doing so allowed one to say that the thoughts were Paul's but the style and composition belonged to a follower (Eusebius, *Hist. eccl.* 6.25.11–14, quoting Origen). Those who defended Pauline authorship often resorted to fanciful explanations, such as Clement of Alexandria's proposal that Paul wrote in Hebrew and deliberately omitted his name because Jews regarded him with contempt. Because Hebrews was subsequently and most eloquently translated into Greek by Luke, it appeared different from Paul's other letters but was stylistically similar to Acts (Eusebius, *Hist. eccl.* 6.14.2–4; see also Jerome, *Vir. ill.* 5 [cited on pp. 210–11]).

of various technical and professional prose works, he begins his account of the Jesus movement with a preface in which he acknowledges his dependence on works by his predecessors, yet he asserts that his is an accurate account in which competent auditors may have full confidence (Luke 1: 1–4).[9] One of the sources that he used for the first volume was the Gospel of Mark, and even a brief comparison of material common to these two gospels makes clear that Luke felt free to edit Mark's account or depart from it entirely. The same literary freedom is evident in Acts, where Luke gives three similar yet strikingly different accounts of the Christophany on the road to Damascus (9:1–19a; 22:3–21; 26:2–23). Finally, if the preface in Luke 1:1–4 is intended to cover the whole of Luke-Acts and not simply the Gospel of Luke, its author was not an eyewitness to what he narrates about Paul but is drawing on traditions about Paul that were nurtured and transmitted within the Pauline school.[1]

Despite the limitations of Acts as a source, it is of indispensable value and has often exerted more influence in the reconstruction of Paul's life than the apostle's own letters. Each of these two sources sometimes provides unique information not found in the other. Only Paul, for instance, tells us that he was from the tribe of Benjamin (Rom. 11:1; Phil. 3:5), and only Acts says that he was also known as Saul (13:9). At other times, both Paul and Acts provide information about people and events, such as the founding of Christian communities in Philippi, Thessalonica, and Corinth. When Paul and Acts overlap, their accounts sometimes contain the same information, e.g., that Crispus was one of Paul's Corinthian converts (1 Cor. 1:14; Acts 18:8). When they provide different information, the latter is sometimes complementary and sometimes contradictory. That Paul was a Benjaminite and also called Saul is complementary and suggests that he was named after King Saul, the tribe's most famous ancestor (Acts 13:21). An example of two contradictory accounts is Paul's first visit to Jerusalem following Christ's appearance to him. Paul depicts it as a private, two-week visit in which the only apostles he saw were Peter and James the Lord's brother, so that after his departure he was still personally unknown to the churches of Judea (Gal. 1:18–24). Acts, by contrast, depicts his visit as a public one in which he not only had intimate contact with the apostles but also preached openly, entered into debates, and departed the city only when a plot arose against his life (9:26–30).

Given these differences, how should these two basic sources be used? For many centuries priority was given to Acts, with Luke's account used to provide the basic outline of Paul's life and the letters invoked at appropriate places. The logic justifying this approach was that Acts depicted Paul the missionary, whereas the letters showed Paul the pastor, writing letters to the churches that he had founded. Modern scholars, by contrast, uniformly give priority to the letters and use Acts as a secondary source. Yet they vary in their use of Acts. Whereas some functionally ignore Acts in their treatments of Paul, especially in reconstructing a chronology of his life, others (including the editors of this volume) seek to use it judiciously, recognizing that its theological perspective is Luke's, not Paul's.

---

9. For a discussion of Luke's preface in light of the traditions of Greek preface-writing, see Loveday Alexander, *The Preface to Luke's Gospel* (New York: Cambridge University Press, 1993).
1. For Luke's use of traditional material in Acts, see Jacob Jervell, *Luke and the People of God* (Minneapolis: Augsburg, 1972), 19–39.

When Acts is invoked, its evidence is typically cited either to corroborate that provided by the letters or to complement and supplement it. The third basic source for Paul is the non-canonical material transmitted about him by his ancient fans and foes. With certain exceptions, this immense source has played a quite limited role in discussions or depictions of Paul. The most important has been the tradition that he died as a martyr in Rome, which remains the standard view of his death.[2] While the historical value of this non-canonical material varies significantly from document to document, its overall importance is immense as a testimony to Paul's influence on developing Christianity and his significance in the ancient church.

A Short Outline of Paul's Life

Names: Various explanations have been offered for the apostle's two names. Because Acts consistently uses the name "Saul" in conjunction with his persecution of the church (8:3; 9:1, 4; 22:7; 26:14) and "Paul" when describing most of his activities as a believer, many people have thought that Saul was his birth name and Paul his Christian name. But that explanation shatters on the fact that Acts switches from Saul to Paul in narrating his activity as a missionary (13:9), not his conversion (9:1–18). A second suggestion stems from this connection and derives "Paul" from the name of "Sergius Paulus," his first named convert.[3] Yet the incidental way in which Acts makes the switch ("Saul, who was also called Paul") prior to Sergius' conversion makes this improbable. The more likely explanation is that, like many Jews who lived in areas where contact with Gentiles was frequent,[4] he grew up with two names, one Jewish (Saul) and one Roman (Paul).[5] Inasmuch as Acts' switch from "Saul" to "Paul" occurs at the beginning of his first missionary journey into the larger Greco-Roman world and in conjunction with his assumption of the leadership of that mission, the change in names indicates a change in Paul's status. It will be he rather than Barnabas who leads the mission, and he does so using his Roman name (compare 13:1, 7 with 13:13).

Date of Birth: Paul's date of birth is unknown and can only be conjectured from the two instances where his age group is indicated. When writing to Philemon in either the mid-50s or the early 60s, Paul calls himself a *presbytēs* (Phlm. 9). Both the TNIV and NRSV give "an old man" as the meaning, but the term more accurately indicates someone in the final stage of "middle age," before becoming an old man (*gerōn*). Acts (7:58) calls him a "young man" (*neanias*) at the time of Stephen's death in the early 30s. Both terms were somewhat elastic. A highly schematized document cir-

---

2. For Paul's martyrdom in Christian apocryphal and patristic literature, see H. W. Tajra, *The Martyrdom of St. Paul* (Tübingen: Mohr-Siebeck, 1994), 118–97.

3. The suggestion goes back to the early church; see e.g., Jerome, *Vir. ill.* 5.

4. Cf. Peter, who similarly appears to have grown up with the traditional Jewish name Simeon (Acts 15:14; 2 Pet. 1:1 NRSV) and the Greek name Simon (Luke 22:31). Paul, however, calls him by the Aramaic name Cephas (1 Cor. 1:12; 3:22; 9:5; 15:5; Gal. 1:18; 2:9, 11, 14) or its Greek equivalent Peter (Gal. 2:7–8), using the nickname that Jesus bestowed on him (Matt. 16:17–18; John 1:42).

5. N. A. Dahl, *Studies in Paul* (Minneapolis: Augsburg, 1972), 3, offers the plausible conjecture that "one of Paul's ancestors was taken prisoner of war when Pompey conquered Palestine in 63 BCE, that he was sold as a slave, and was eventually emancipated by a Roman citizen belonging to the Roman *gens* Paulus. Such a history would explain both Paul's Latin name and his Roman citizenship."

culating under the name of Hippocrates uses "youth" (*neaniskos*) of people from twenty-two to twenty-eight, and *presbytēs* of individuals from fifty to fifty-six, the latter marking the transitional stage during which one passes from active adulthood (29–49) to the significantly diminished powers of "old age" (57–death). Ancient authors typically distinguish "youth" (*neaniskos*) from "young man" (*neanias*), making the latter follow immediately upon the former, so that it normally indicates someone who is in his late twenties or early thirties (roughly 29–35) and thus has entered the early stage of "manhood." The "Hippocratic" view of a *presbytēs'* age as fifty to fifty-six was by no means typical, for most placed it later. For example, the Athenian lawgiver Solon viewed fifty to fifty-six as the prime of life, when intellectual and rhetorical powers reached their peak, treated fifty-seven to sixty-nine as the age of gentle decline, and set the onset of severe old age at seventy.[6] Jewish tradition tended to use sixty as the age when the prime of life ceased (Lev. 27:2–7; CD 10:7–10) and one became an "elder" (m. *Aboth* 5.21).

In Paul's culture, therefore, a "young man" was typically someone in his late twenties or early thirties, a time of peak physical vitality that corresponds to the ferocity with which Acts depicts Paul's activity as a persecutor (Acts 8:3; 9:1–2; 22:4–5; 26:9–11). A *presbytēs*, on the other hand, was someone who was nearing but had not reached old age. It was roughly applicable as a term to people in their late fifties or sixties, though sometimes it was used of individuals in their early to mid-fifties. Given the cumulative impact of Paul's apostolic afflictions on his physical health, he convincingly could have portrayed himself as a *presbytēs* at an earlier age than many of his contemporaries, and it is a designation that fits well the rhetorical strategy that he adopts in writing to Philemon. Thus, if Paul were in his late twenties or early thirties when he began to persecute the followers of Jesus, he would have been in his mid-fifties or early sixties when he wrote Philemon, his age depending upon the date of the letter. All in all, it is likely that he was born about the beginning of the first century CE, a few years after the birth of Jesus (ca. 4 BCE), though dates both earlier and later are entirely possible.

Early Years: Although some of Paul's later opponents alleged that he was a Gentile by birth and had become a proselyte to Judaism in a failed attempt to marry the daughter of a Jewish priest (see "A False Proselyte" in Part IV), he was certainly "a Hebrew (born) of Hebrews" (Phil. 3:5) who not only boasted that he was an Israelite and descendant of Abraham (Rom. 11:1; 2 Cor. 11:22) but also bragged that his zeal for ancestral traditions enabled him to make greater progress in Judaism than many of his Jewish contemporaries (Gal. 1:14). A member of the tribe of Benjamin (Rom. 11:1; Phil. 3:5), he was circumcised on the eighth day (Phil. 3:5) in strict conformity to Jewish law (Gen. 17:12; 21:4; Lev. 12:3).

According to Acts, he was born in Tarsus of Cilicia (9:11; 21:39; 22:3). Because this datum goes against Acts' tendency to associate Paul as much as possible with Jerusalem, there is every reason to accept Tarsus as his birthplace. How long he remained there is a matter of fierce debate that is reflected in different punctuations of Acts 22:3. Traditionally, the verse has been punctuated as follows: "I am a Jew, born in Tarsus in Cilicia, but

---

6. For the views of "Hippocrates" and Solon, see Philo, *Opif.* 103–5.

brought up in this city [Jerusalem] at the feet of Gamaliel, educated strictly according to our ancestral law" (NRSV). Those who favor this punctuation, which connects his being "brought up" with the training provided by Gamaliel, tend to think that Paul left Tarsus and came to Jerusalem as an adolescent for rabbinical training. The alternative view is based on W. C. van Unnik's contention that Luke uses the common Hellenistic triad of birth, nurture, and education in giving biographical data (e.g., Acts 7:20–22).[7] Within this fixed literary unit, nurture ("brought up") is used regularly of what takes place in the home, especially during the first three years of life. This suggests that Acts 22:3 should be rendered: "I am a Jew, born in Tarsus of Cilicia, but brought up in this city. Under Gamaliel I was thoroughly trained in the law of our fathers" (NIV). Van Unnik thus contends that Luke wishes to indicate that Paul, though born in Tarsus, was in Jerusalem from infancy on. Of the two interpretations of Acts 22:3, van Unnik's is the more likely but is suspect historically inasmuch as it fits Luke's tendency to give Paul close ties to Jerusalem. Therefore the question remains: when Paul embarked on his mission to the Gentiles, was he returning to the syncretistic culture that he had absorbed as a boy or was this his first real exposure to Greek myths and mores outside of the hellenized cities of Syria-Palestine?

Wherever he grew up, his letters show that he was fluent in Greek (the *lingua franca* of the Greco-Roman world) and knew Hebrew, and Acts likely implies that he was also fluent in Aramaic (Acts 21:40; 22:2), though Hebrew may be meant. Letter-writing and rhetoric were taught at the tertiary stage of ancient education using an approach that combined theory and practice, so it is likely that he had received basic training in both fields, though one group of critics was more impressed by his epistolary abilities than his oratorical prowess (2 Cor. 10:10; compare 11:6; Acts 13:16; 14:12; 17:18). A Pharisee (Phil 3:5; Acts 23:6; 26:5) and thus devoted to the oral law (Gal. 1:14), he had also perhaps received scribal training, for his use of midrashic forms and techniques resembles that of later rabbis, though Acts alone makes Gamaliel, the student of the famous Hillel, his teacher (Acts 22:3). Yet when he quoted the Jewish scriptures, it was typically not in the Hebrew of his ancestors, but in the Greek translation (the Septuagint) heard in Hellenistic synagogues of the Diaspora.

In his letters Paul tells us nothing about his family (except that they were Jewish), not even the names of his parents.[8] Acts, however, says that his father was a Pharisee (23:6) and that he had a sister whose son was in Jerusalem at the time of Paul's last visit to the city (23:16). Whether "Uncle Saul" was ever married is unknown. At the time of his letters he certainly was not, and he encouraged other single Christians to remain so (1 Cor. 7:7–8).

Acts portrays Paul's social level as remarkably high, especially for a Jew of that period, making him a citizen of both his native Tarsus (21:39) and Rome (16:37–38; 22:25–29; 23:37), data that cannot be confirmed from the letters. It also portrays him as an ardent opponent of the early Christians, relentlessly persecuting them (8:3; 9:1–2; 22:4–5; 26:9–11). Though

---

7. *Tarsus or Jerusalem? The City of Paul's Youth* (London; Epworth, 1962).
8. According to Jerome (*Vir. ill.* 5; *Comm. Phlm.* 5), Paul and his parents once lived in the town of Gischala in northern Galilee but had migrated (or been deported) to Tarsus when a Roman army invaded and plundered the province.

not as vivid in details, Paul's own portrait depicts a zealot bent on destroying the church (Gal. 1:13; Phil. 3:6). His revulsion appears to have stemmed from the disciples' proclamation of a crucified and thus accursed man (Deut. 21:23; Gal. 3:13) as God's anointed one. That he ties his activity as a persecutor to his zeal for the traditions of his ancestors (Gal. 1:13–14) and to his own success in fulfilling the law's demands (Phil. 3:6) is revealing. It shows that he was not conflicted in mind or troubled by religious failure when he harassed the disciples, but that he did so with great self-confidence, convinced that the Jesus movement posed a dangerous threat to the central legal tradition of Judaism. If that is so, the idea of freedom from the law that we find developed in Paul's letters did not originate with him but was one of the reasons he did his utmost to destroy the new sect.

Acts locates Paul's activity as a persecutor in Jerusalem (8:3), and when the disciples flee the city, he heads to Damascus to arrest them and bring them back to Jerusalem as prisoners (9:1–2). As Heitmüller points out (Part VI: "Hellenistic Christianity before Paul"), Paul's sworn declaration that he was "personally unknown to the churches of Judea" (Gal. 1:22) creates problems for Acts' depiction and suggests that Paul persecuted the church in Damascus rather than Jerusalem. Other scholars, however, limit Paul's declaration to the visit that he is discussing and contend that the report that "the man who formerly persecuted *us*" (Gal. 1:23) has reference to persecution by Paul in Judea.

The Damascus Experience: The central event in Paul's life was Christ's appearance to him and some scholars attempt to explain his entire gospel as an unfolding of the implications of that religious experience. Unfortunately, Paul himself only alludes to this unexpected event and does not describe the occasion when Christ "grabbed" him (Phil. 3:12) and caused a radical reorientation of his life and values. Yet the event was so dramatic that no biographer, even the earliest one, could refrain from romanticizing it.

Viewed collectively, the sources depict this event as having a threefold significance. It marked, in the first place, his conversion to Christ, the inception of a new allegiance to the one whom he formerly persecuted (Acts 9:5; 22:8; 26:15). It was not a change from Judaism to Christianity, which did not yet exist as a religion separate from Judaism, nor did it make Paul any less Jewish. Indeed, Acts portrays Paul as still a Pharisee many years afterward (23:6). He simply added to his existing Jewish beliefs his new conviction that the crucified and risen Jesus was indeed the Messiah, through whom God would fulfill all the promises he had made to Abraham.

Second, the Damascus Christophany constituted Paul's call to be a prophet. Paul (Gal. 1:15–16) uses language drawn ultimately from Jeremiah's account of his prophetic call to describe God's selection of him as a "prophet to the nations" (Jer. 1:5; see also Isa. 49:1). Third, it marked Paul's commission as an apostle. His apostolic credentials rested ultimately on his claim to have seen the risen Jesus (1 Cor. 9:1), and though that appearance happened chronologically much later than similar epiphanies to Peter and James, in his own eyes it made him just as much an apostle as they (1 Cor. 15:5–11). Both during his own lifetime (1 Cor. 9:2) and after his death, his opponents disputed that claim (see Part IV: "Messenger of Satan"), and even Luke typically withholds the title "apostle" from Paul, recognizing that his hero lacked the credentials necessary for apostolic status (Acts 1:21–22).[9]

In short, Paul did not begin as a simple believer, later become a prophet, and ultimately achieve the status of an apostle. For Paul himself, all these things were tremendously important and happened at one fell swoop; he was simultaneously and henceforth "in Christ" (the word "Christian did not yet exist), a prophet, and an apostle. It was with this self-understanding that he began his apostolic labors.

Paul's Apostolic Career: According to Paul's account in Galatians, he left Damascus and went immediately into "Arabia," probably the northwest portion of the Arab kingdom of Nabataea, where he almost certainly began his preaching to Gentiles. At some unspecified time later, he returned to Damascus (Gal. 1:15–17), where, according to Acts (9:19b-22), he preached in the city's synagogues. Both Paul and Acts indicate that his activities aroused considerable hostility against him, though Paul attributes the opposition to the local Nabataean ethnarch and Acts (in typical fashion) to "the Jews." Paul was forced to flee the city at night, being let down in a basket through an opening in the wall (2 Cor. 11:32–33; Acts 9:23–25).

Following his ignominious escape, Paul went to Jerusalem for the first time following the Christophany (Gal. 1:18–24; Acts 9:26–30). Paul's relationship with the Jerusalem church was—and still is—a controversial one. His opponents in Galatia thought that he was a flunky of the Jerusalem apostles and lacked any independent authority,[1] whereas his later Jewish-Christian critics considered him the Jerusalem apostles' arch-enemy (Part IV: "The Messenger of Satan"). Modern Pauline scholarship since the time of F. C. Baur (Part VI: "Hebrews, Hellenists, and Catholics") has tended to stress opposition rather than concord, though the relationship had both elements. Paul himself stressed his independence from Jerusalem, and his letters reflect only three visits to the city: the first took place three years after his Damascus experience (Gal. 1:18), the second some fourteen years later (Gal. 2:1), and the third when he had completed his labors in the Aegean and was making plans to begin missionary work in the West (Rom. 15:25–29). Acts, by contrast, narrates five visits (9:26–30; 11:27–30; 15:1–35; 18:22; 21:17–23:35), has Paul deliver aid to the Jerusalem church at a time of famine (11:27–30), portrays him as endorsing a letter from the Jerusalem church to Gentile converts in which he is praised (15:22–35), and has Paul follow the advice of James and the elders to observe a Jewish purificatory rite (21:20–26). Furthermore, Acts makes his co-worker Barnabas a close and trusted associate of the apostles and a man with solid ties to Jerusalem (4:36–37; 9:27; 11:22–24). Their eventual conflict is decidedly non-theological, involving a difference in judgment about the suitability of John Mark for a missionary journey (15:36–41; see also 12:12, 25; 13:13), not a personal failing on the part of Barnabas (Gal. 2:13). Silas, his major companion on the second missionary journey, is likewise depicted as a man of high standing in the Jerusalem church (15:

9. Acts uses the Greek word *apostolos* of Paul only twice (14:4, 14). Since Acts simultaneously applies it to Barnabas (who is clearly distinguished from the "apostles" elsewhere in the narrative), the use is probably not technical and has reference to the two missionaries as the "envoys" commissioned by the Antioch church (13:1–3).

1. Centuries later, Jerome claimed that Paul "was ordained apostle to the Gentiles by Peter, James, and John," thus separating his apostleship from the Damascus Christophany (*Vir. ill.* 5).

22). A prophet, he becomes Paul's cohort only after being selected by the apostles and elders to expound and enforce their decision (15:25–27, 32, 40). There are never any theological disputes with the leadership of the Jerusalem church, only with individuals or groups within it (15:1–2), and the church greets him warmly when he arrives for his final visit (21:17) and praises God for the success of his ministry (21:19–20). The result is a much more extensive and harmonious relationship than the one indicated in the letters, where Paul does not hesitate to express his utter indifference toward the "pillars" of the Jerusalem church, accusing Peter of hypocrisy and men from James of undermining the truth of the gospel by opposing Antioch's practice of Jewish and Gentile believers dining together (Gal. 2:5–14).

The most important of Paul's Jerusalem visits was for the so-called Apostolic Council (Gal. 2:1–10; Acts 15:1–35). The debate centered on an issue central to Paul's self-understanding as an apostle to the Gentiles: what did God require of Gentiles in order to be part of his people? There was ample precedent for Gentiles embracing Judaism, so the issue was not whether Gentiles might join the Jesus movement, but the terms under which they could do so. The issue had not arisen before, and no saying by the earthly or risen Jesus was deemed decisive in settling the debate. Furthermore, the first preaching of the gospel to Gentiles had been done, not by Jesus' twelve apostles, but by Diaspora Jews, who, like Paul, had no personal contact with Jesus during his ministry (Acts 11:19–21). No one—certainly not the Jerusalem church—had authorized their proclamation. But the decisive step had been taken, raising all kinds of questions (especially about social relations between Jewish and Gentile believers) that now had to be addressed more formally. Some looked on these developments with a jaundiced eye whereas others were ecstatic at the prospects.

Not surprisingly in a patriarchal society, the key issue in the debate was the quintessentially male question about the necessity of circumcision and the concomitant commitment to observe the law. To oversimplify, early Christians defended four basic positions on this issue. The first was the *rigorist* position, which required Gentile men to be circumcised and to observe the whole law (Acts 15:1, 5). That is, Gentiles who desired to worship God as part of his people needed to become proselytes by converting to Judaism. A covenant relationship with the God of Abraham entailed circumcision (Gen. 17) and the duty to keep all the commandments handed down by Moses (Deut. 28). The second position was the *conservative* one, which required circumcision of Gentile males but not their keeping of the law in its entirety. This was the position of Paul's opponents in Galatia, who insisted upon observance of the Jewish festival calendar (Sabbath, etc.) but not the whole law (Gal. 4:10; 5:3). A third position was the *moderate* one, rejecting circumcision as necessary for either a right relationship with God or membership within the church. Yet its advocates insisted upon the necessity of Gentile converts keeping a portion of the law, and Acts presents this as the position adopted by the Apostolic Council (15:20, 28–29; 21:25), at which Paul is depicted as playing only a minor role (15:12).

The fourth position was the *radical* one argued by Paul and his allies, who rejected as essential both circumcision and law observance. Paul was, as Martin Dibelius once observed, "the first radical Christian,"[2] and his radicality consisted above all in his conviction that the whole legal aspect of the Torah had been canceled with the coming of the Messiah. By championing this position, he completely renounced the legal tradition that previously had been central to his life and self-understanding. Embracing the dangerous view that he once attacked, he was a tireless opponent of those who wanted to make that legal tradition a part of the rapidly developing Jesus movement. He vigorously defended his views, arguing from both scripture and religious experience that God accepted Gentiles on the same basis as he accepted Abraham and his descendants—that is, faith. This was the position, he argues, that was adopted by the Apostolic Council (at which, in contrast to Acts' depiction, he played a decisive role) and from which he never wavered despite repeated attacks on both his position and person (Gal. 2:1–10). His opponents charged him with preaching a gospel of "cheap grace" that gutted the gospel of its uncompromising demands and was designed to make it easier to convert Gentiles. They viewed his position on the law as nothing less than a prelude to moral anarchy. According to the traditional Israelite paradigm, the newly emancipated Hebrews had received the Torah at Mt. Sinai. Liberation and law thus went hand-in-hand, and the only enduring freedom was one that was structured by law. Paul, however, shifted the paradigm by equating slavery with Mt. Sinai and freedom with liberation from the law. In his new paradigm, liberty and love were correlates, and believers' death to sin and possession of the Spirit enabled them to live in a manner pleasing to God. Given these diametrically opposite points of view, it is no wonder that Paul's letters are often polemical and that the history of Paulinism has been a history of controversy.

Though the Jesus movement was born in the village culture of Palestine, its future lay in the cities. Paul was preeminently a man of the city—that is apparent whenever he uses an agricultural metaphor. His urgent crisscrossing of the eastern provinces of the empire followed the major roads and sea routes. Two of Paul's three great missionary journeys in Acts are described as taking place after the Apostolic Council, and with the possible but unlikely exception of Galatians, all of his letters were written during this later period. For the first time, his work as an apostle took him to Europe, where he founded churches in population centers and trading hubs strategically located along important thoroughfares, places such as Philippi, Thessalonica, and Corinth. Unlike most Christian missionaries who traversed the ancient Mediterranean area, he refrained from asking his converts for financial remuneration for his preaching and supported himself by means of manual labor, which Acts identifies as making tents (18:3). According to his own testimony, he toiled from dawn to dusk, which means that the workshop was the setting for much of his missionary activity.

His missionary preaching to Gentiles in these urban centers built upon Hellenistic Jewish precedents in addressing Gentiles but focused on the death and resurrection of Jesus. As has often been observed, Paul could freely proclaim Christ's resurrection but had to explain his crucifixion. The

2. "Paulus und die Mystik," in *Botschaft und Geschichte* (2 vols.; Tübingen: Mohr-Siebeck, 1953–56), vol. 2, 159.

latter, as he admits in 1 Corinthians, boggled the ancient mind; a crucified Christ was a scandalous "stumbling block" (*skandalon*) to Jews and "utterly ridiculous" (*mōria*) to Gentiles (1:23). Yet rather than evade the marketing problem by focusing on the wisdom of Jesus' words, he rarely cited the latter and placed emphasis squarely on the cross of Christ, doing so in the conviction that it was the clearest expression of God's wisdom and power (1 Cor. 1:24). Jesus died a vicarious death, and in raising him God not only vindicated him but also inaugurated the climactic events in human history. Christ's resurrection was not for Paul an isolated event, rather "the first fruits" of what would soon be a final eschatological "harvest" (1 Cor. 15:23–24). Consequently, Paul believed that Christ's "coming" (*parousia*) in triumph was imminent, occurring either within his own lifetime or that of his converts. This conviction was a factor in some of the counsel he gave his fellow believers; for example, his advice to the Corinthians regarding sex and marriage reflects his total lack of concern for reproduction (1 Cor. 7).

To those who responded to his message and became part of his faith community, Paul provided additional instruction and transmitted to them various traditions that he himself had received (1 Cor. 11:2, 23–25; 15:1–7; 2 Thess. 2:15). Included within this teaching was instruction in ethics (1 Thess. 4:1), warnings about future afflictions and sufferings (1 Thess. 3:4), and guidance in the proper interpretation of scripture, which many Gentile converts were hearing or reading for the first time. The extent to which this teaching included sayings of Jesus is debated. Paul only occasionally quotes Jesus in his letters (e.g., 1 Cor 7:10–11), which caused Carl G. Jung to lament, "It is frankly disappointing to see how Paul hardly ever allows the real Jesus of Nazareth to get a word in."[3] Yet he may have been more fully informed than his rare explicit quotations suggest. Some of his letters contain both phrases and ideas that are strikingly similar to what is attested of Jesus, so that he may very well be alluding to Jesus' teaching in a number of instances (Luke 6:27–28; Rom. 12:14). In addition to allusions, both the undisputed and disputed letters contain passages where Paul or a Paulinist appears to be drawing on earlier traditional material that was in use in Pauline communities and may have played a part in the instruction the apostle gave his new converts (e.g., Phil. 2:6–11; 1 Tim. 2:5–6; 3:16).

After leaving the churches he had founded, Paul attempted to stay in touch, doing so by occasional return visits, oral messages delivered by his co-workers, and, above all, by letters, which functioned as a substitute for his personal presence. The churches, for their part, did the same, sending envoys to Paul (Phil. 2:25) and writing him letters (1 Cor. 7:1). The Pauline corpus is the result of this occasional and often hurried correspondence, not all of which was preserved (1 Cor. 5:9). No consensus exists concerning the sequence in which the letters were written, though the earliest was quite likely 1 Thessalonians, written ca. 51 CE, and the latest was perhaps Philippians or Philemon, possibly written ca. 62 CE. Composed some two to three decades following his Damascus experience, the letters are not those of a new convert. They represent the mind of a sea-

---

3. Quoted by Muggeridge and Vidler, *Paul, Envoy Extraordinary*, 15.

soned missionary, yet one whose theology never stagnated but continued to develop until his death.

Acts never mentions Paul's letters or the collection for the Jerusalem church (except perhaps obliquely at 24:17), an enterprise to which Paul devoted nearly a decade of his life. The idea apparently originated at the Apostolic Council (Gal. 2:10) and was conceived as a tangible expression of the unity of Jew and Gentile in Christ. In recognition of Jewish priority and spiritual beneficence, Gentile Christians were to make a material contribution to the mother church in Jerusalem. By accepting this gift, the Jewish Christians of Jerusalem would ipso facto accept the uncircumcised Gentiles who gave it and thereby reaffirm the legitimacy of Paul's mission and the torah-free gospel that he proclaimed (Rom. 15:25–27). In order to guard against charges that the collection was a scam operation designed to line Paul's pockets with money fleeced from his converts and to increase the odds of Jerusalem's acceptance of the gift, Gentile representatives of the contributing churches accompanied Paul when he brought it to Jerusalem (1 Cor. 16:1–4; 2 Cor. 8–9). Whether the Jerusalem church accepted the gift is unknown but highly unlikely. The silence of the sources is damning. If Jerusalem had accepted the gift, Acts and the Paulinists (especially the author of Ephesians, who extolled the unity of Jew and Gentile) would surely have celebrated that event. Yet the last reference to the collection occurs in Romans, with Paul already apprehensive about both its fate and his (Rom. 15:30–32).

Paul's premonitions were correct, for his final trip to Jerusalem was a disaster. His passionate, perhaps quixotic determination to bring a token of unity to the Christians of Jerusalem, holy city of his past, brought the last of his many arrests. Transferred to Caesarea Maritima, he was subsequently taken to Rome for trial. Those who accept the authenticity of Colossians and Ephesians usually date them to the two-year period that transpired before the trial (Acts 28:30). The outcome of the trial is a matter of speculation. Although Acts says nothing definite about the trial, it strongly hints that it ended in Paul's death (20:25). The earliest documents do not describe his martyrdom, which later became the subject of legend.[4] Probably Paul died around 64 CE, just before Nero began his well-known general persecution of the Christians of the capital.

The Pastoral Epistles, however, posit a different scenario, with Paul's "first defense" (2 Tim. 4:16) apparently resulting in his release and departure from Rome. These pseudonymous letters either reflect or create a tradition of Paul returning to the East, where he resumed missionary work by going to Nicopolis in western Greece (Tit. 3:12), Crete (Tit. 1:5), Miletus (2 Tim. 4:20), Ephesus (1 Tim. 1:3), Troas (2 Tim. 4:13), and Macedonia (1 Tim. 1:3). Other church legends have him preaching in the West, even realizing his earlier hope of going to Spain (Rom. 15:24, 28).[5]

These divergent accounts converge in having Paul once more incarcerated, then executed. But where? In 2 Timothy, Paul is depicted as incarcerated (1:8; 2:9), but the location is ambiguous. Given the eastern orientation of the other Pastoral Epistles, it is possible that the pseudon-

---

4. See Part IV: "The Martyrdom of Paul."
5. The tradition of Paul preaching in the West is reflected, e.g., in the Muratorian Canon and Jerome, *Vir. ill.* 5.

ymous author presupposes that Paul is still in Macedonia (1 Tim. 1:3), perhaps Philippi. In that case, "Paul" would be asking Timothy to proceed from Ephesus to Troas (2 Tim. 4:13) and on to Macedonia, hoping that he will arrive before the apostle's execution.[6] Yet 2 Timothy may presuppose Rome as the place of this imprisonment (1:17), which would accord well with the ancient tradition that the apostle met his end in the imperial city. Some thirty years later a bishop of that city, after alluding to Paul's martyrdom in words more eloquent than informative, added: "He taught righteousness to all the world" (*1 Clem.* 5:7).

---

6. For the possibility that the Pastoral Epistles reflect a tradition of Paul's martyrdom occurring in Philippi, see the essays by Helmut Koester and A. D. Callahan in *Philippi at the Time of Paul and after His Death*, ed. by Charalambos Bakirtzis and Helmut Koester (Harrisburg, PA: Trinity, 1998).

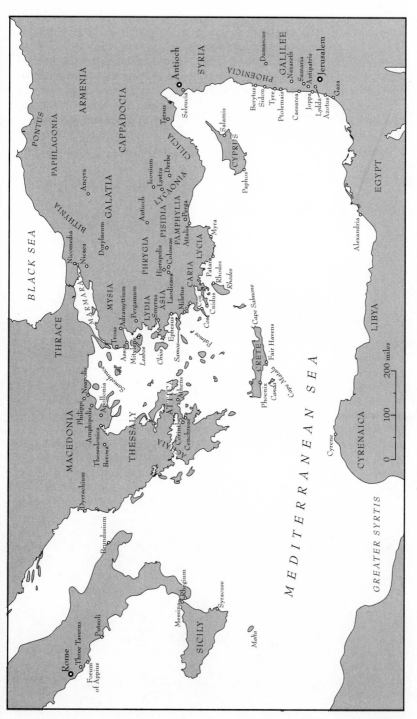

The Eastern Mediterranean in the Time of St. Paul

Abbreviations

A	Page A of Codex I (the Jung Codex) in the Nag Hammadi Library (the line number follows)
ACCS	Ancient Christian Commentary on Scripture
Adv. Haer., AH	Irenaeus, *Against Heresies* // Hippolytus, *Refutation of All Heresies* // Tertullian, *Prescription against Heretics*
Aem.	Plutarch, *Aemilius Paullus*
Aen.	Vergil, *Aeneid*
AJ	Josephus, *Jewish Antiquities*
An.	Tertullian, *The Soul*
ANE	Ancient Near East
Ann.	Tacitus, *Annals*
Ant.	Josephus, *Jewish Antiquities*
AP	*Acts of Paul*
1 Apoc. Jas.	*First Apocalypse of James*
Apoc. Paul	*Apocalypse of Paul*
Apoc. Pet.	*Apocalypse of Peter*
Apoc. Zeph.	*Apocalypse of Zephaniah*
1 Apol.	Justin Martyr, *First Apology*
Apol.	Tertullian, *Apology*
Apos. Con.	*Apostolic Constitutions and Canons*
ASV	American Standard Version
AThR	*Anglican Theological Review*
b.	Babylonian Talmud (name of tractate follows)
Bapt.	Tertullian, *Baptism*
Barn.	*Epistle of Barnabas*
BCE	Before the Common Era (equivalent to B.C.)
Bel	*Bel and the Dragon*
Ben.	Seneca, *On Benefits*
Ber.	Tractate *Berakot* in Mishnah and Talmuds
BJ	Josephus, *Jewish War*
BZNW	Beihefte zur Zeitschrift für die neutestamentliche Wissenschaft
C. ep. Parmen.	Augustine, *Against the Letter of Parmenian*
ca.	circa
Cath.	Prudentius, *Hymns for Every Day*
CD	Cairo Genizah copy of the *Damascus Document*
CE	Common Era (equivalent to A.D.)
Cels., c. Cels.	Origen, *Against Celsus*
cent.	century, centuries
cf.	*confer*, compare
CG	Coptic Gnostic Library = Nag Hammadi Codices (codex number and treatise number follow)
ch., chap., chs.	chapter, chapters
1, 2 Chron.	First, Second Chronicles
CIG	*Corpus inscriptionum graecarum*
CIJ	*Corpus inscriptionum judaicarum*
CIL	*Corpus inscriptionum latinarum*

Civ.	Augustine, *The City of God*
1 Clem.	*1 Clement*
Col.	Colossians
Comm. Dan.	Hippolytus, *Commentary on Daniel*
Comm. Gal.	Jerome, *Commentary on Galatians*
Comm. Phlm.	Jerome, *Commentary on Philemon*
Comm. Rom.	Origen, *Commentary on Romans*
Comm. Tit.	Jerome, *Commentary on Titus*
Cons.	Augustine, *Harmony of the Gospels*
Constit. Monast.	Pseudo-Basil, *The Ascetic Constitutions*
Cor.	Tertullian, *The Crown*
1, 2 Cor.	First, Second Corinthians
3 *Cor.*	Third Corinthians
CSEL	Corpus scriptorum ecclesiasticorum latinorum
Dan.	Daniel
Dessau	H. Dessau, *Inscriptiones latinae selectae*
Deus	Philo, *That God Is Unchangeable*
Deut., Dt.	Deuteronomy
Dial.	Justin Martyr, *Dialogue with Trypho*
Diss.	Epictetus, *Discourses*
Doct.	*Teaching of the Apostles* (= *Doctrina Apostolorum*)
DSS	Dead Sea Scrolls
Eccl.	Ecclesiastes (Qoheleth)
Ecclus.	Ecclesiasticus (Jesus ben Sira = Sirach)
ed.	edited, edition
e.g.	*exempli gratia*, for example
Eloc.	Pseudo-Demetrius, *On Style*
Enchir.	Augustine, *Enchiridion*
Ep., Epist.	*Epistle*
Eph.	Ephesians
Epist. Char.	Pseudo-Libanius, *Epistolary Styles*
1 Esd.	First Esdras
EvT	*Evangelische Theologie*
Ex., Exod.	Exodus
Ex. Thdt.	Clement of Alexandria, *Excerpta ex Theodoto*
exc.	*excerptum*, excerpt(s)
Ezek.	Ezekiel
f., ff.	and the following (ones)
Flora	Ptolemy, *Letter to Flora*
frg., fr.	fragment
Gal.	Galatians
Gal.	Julian, *Against the Galileans*
Gen.	Genesis
Geog.	Strabo, *Geographica*
Gos. Phil.	*Gospel of Philip*
Gos. Thom.	*Gospel of Thomas*
Hab.	Habakkuk
Haer.	*Against Heresies*
Hag.	Tractate *Hagiga* in Mishnah and Talmuds
HB	Hebrew Bible
HE	Eusebius, *Ecclesiastical History*
Heb.	Hebrews, Hebrew
Hier.	Eusebius, *Against Hierocles*
Hippoc. et Plat.	Galen, *On the Opinions of Hippocrates and Plato*
Hist. eccl.	*Ecclesiastical History*

Hom.	*Homily, Homilies* (Pseudo-Clement)
hom. in Heb., Rom.	John Chrysostom, *Homilies on the Epistle to the Hebrews, to the Romans*
Hos.	Hosea
HTR	*Harvard Theological Review*
i.a.	*inter alia*, among other things
ibid.	*ibidem*, in the same place
IG	*Inscriptiones graecae*
in ep. ad Rom. comment. lib.	Origen, *Commentary on Romans*
in Lc.	Ambrose, *Exposition of the Gospel of Luke*
in Titum	Jerome, *Commentary on Titus*
Inst.	Lactantius, *The Divine Institutes* // Quintilian, *The Orator's Education*
Is., Isa.	Isaiah
Jas.	James
JB	*The Jerusalem Bible*
JBL	*Journal of Biblical Literature*
Jdt.	Judith
Jer.	Jeremiah
Jn.	John
Josh.	Joshua
Jov.	Jerome, *Against Jovian*
JRH	*Journal of Religious History*
JRS	*Journal of Roman Studies*
J.W.	Josephus, *Jewish War*
1, 2 Kgs.	First, Second Kings
KJV	The King James Version (Authorized Version)
Lam.	Lamentations
Lat.	Latin
Laud. Paul.	John Chrysostom, *In Praise of St. Paul*
LCL	Loeb Classical Library
Leg. Man.	Cicero, *Oration in Defense of the Manilian Law* (= *On Pompey's Command*)
Lev., Lv.	Leviticus
lit.	literally
Lk.	Luke
LXX	Septuagint (ancient Greek translation of the Hebrew Bible / OT)
m.	Mishnah (name of tractate follows)
1, 2, 3, 4 Macc.	The Books of the Maccabees
Mal.	Malachi
Marc.	Tertullian, *Against Marcion*
Mart. Pal.	Eusebius, *The Martyrs of Palestine*
Mart. Polyc.	*Martyrdom of Polycarp*
Matt., Mt.	Matthew
Med.	Euripides, *Medea*
Mem.	Valerius Maximus, *Memorable Deeds and Sayings*
Met.	Ovid, *Metamorphoses*
Mic.	Micah
Mis.	Julian, *The Beard Hater*
Mk.	Mark
ML	J.-P. Migne, *Patrologia latina*
Mor.	Plutarch, *Moralia*
Mos.	Philo, *The Life of Moses*
MS, MSS	manuscript, manuscripts
NAB	The New American Bible

Nat.	Pliny the Elder, *Natural History*
Nat. d.	Cicero, *On the Nature of the Gods*
n.b.	*nota bene*, note carefully
NEB	The New English Bible
Neh.	Nehemiah
NIV	The New International Version of the Bible
Noct. att.	Aulus Gellius, *Attic Nights*
NRSV	The New Revised Standard Version of the Bible
NT	New Testament
Num.	Numbers
Oct.	Pseudo-Seneca, *Octavia*
Ody.	Homer, *Odyssey*
OL	Old Latin Version of the Bible
Opif.	Philo, *On the Creation of the World*
Or.	*Oration*
OT	Old Testament
p.	Palestinian Talmud (name of tractate follows)
P	Papyrus (number of papyrus follows)
Pan.	Epiphanius, *Refutation of All Heresies*
par.	parallel(s)
1, 2 Pet., Pt.	First, Second Peter
PG	J-P. Migne, *Patrologia graeca*
Phaedr.	Plato, *Phaedrus*
Phil.	Philippians
Phil.	Polycarp, *To the Philippians*
Philoc.	Origen, *Philocalia*
Phlm.	Philemon
PL	J.-P. Migne, *Patrologia latina*
plur.	plural
P.Oxy.	Oxyrhynchus Papyri
Pr. Paul	*Prayer of the Apostle Paul*
Praescr.	Tertullian, *Prescription against Heretics*
Prax.	Tertullian, *Against Praxeas*
Princ.	Origen, *First Principles*
Pro Cael.	Cicero, *For Caelius*
Propos.	Augustine, *Commentary on Statements in the Letter of Paul to the Romans*
Protr.	Clement of Alexandria, *Exhortation to the Greeks*
Prov.	Proverbs
Ps.	Psalm, Psalms
Ps.-	Pseudo-
Ps. Sol.	*Psalms of Solomon*
Pud.	Tertullian, *On Modesty*
1QpHab	The "Commentary on Habakkuk" from Cave 1, Qumran
1QS	The "Manual of Discipline" ("Rule of the Community") from Cave 1, Qumran
4QPB	The "Patriarchal Blessings" scroll from Cave 4, Qumran
11QMelch	"Melchizedek" from Cave 11, Qumran
11QTemple	The "Temple Scroll" from Cave 11, Qumran
Quest. Vet. et Novi Test.	Pseudo-Augustine, *Questions on the Old and New Testament* (now attributed to Ambrosiaster)
Quint.	Quintilian
Recog.	*Recognitions* (Pseudo-Clement)
Ref.	Hippolytus, *Refutation of All Heresies*
rep., rp.	reprinted
Resp.	Plato, *Respublica*

rev.	revised
Rev.	Revelation (The Apocalypse)
Rh. Al.	Pseudo-Aristotle, *Rhetoric to Alexander*
Rh. Her.	*Rhetorica ad Herennium* (once falsely attributed to Cicero)
Rom.	Romans
RSV	The Revised Standard Version of the Bible
RV	Revised Version
1, 2 Sam.	First, Second Samuel
SEÅ	*Svensk exegetisk årsbok*
Sir.	*Sirach (Jesus ben Sira = Ecclesiasticus)*
Smyrn.	Ignatius, *To the Smyrnaeans*
Solin	H. Solin, *Die griechischen Personennamen in Rom*
Song	The Song of Songs (or, Song of Solomon)
Spec. Laws	Philo, *On the Special Laws*
sq., sqq.	*sequens, sequentia,* (and) the following
Strom., Str.	Clement of Alexandria, *Miscellanies*
Symp.	Plato, *Symposim*
T. Abr.	*Testament of Abraham*
T. Dan	*Testament of Dan*
T. Levi	*Testament of Levi*
1, 2 Thess.	First, Second Thessalonians
Tht.	Plato, *Theaetetus*
1, 2 Tim., Tm.	First, Second Timothy
Tit.	Titus
TLZ	*Theologische Literaturzeitung*
TNIV	Today's New International Version
Tob.	Tobit
tr., trans.	translated, translation, translator
Tract. Ev. Jo.	Augustine, *Tractates on the Gospel of John*
Tract. Ps.	Jerome, *Tractate on the Psalms*
Trad. ap.	Hippolytus, *Apostolic Tradition*
Trop.	Tryphon, *On Tropes*
Tusc. Disp.	Cicero, *Tusculan Disputations*
USQR	*Union Seminary Quarterly Review*
v., vv., vs., vss.	verse, verses
VC	*Vigiliae christianae*
Vir. ill.	Jerome, *On Illustrious Men*
v.l.	*varia lectio,* variant reading
vol., vols.	volume, volumes
Völker	W. Völker, *Quellen zur Geschichte der christlichen Gnosis*
VP	Iamblichus, *On the Pythagorean Way of Life*
VS	Eunapius, *Lives of the Sophists*
Wis., Wisd.	The Wisdom of Solomon
Zech.	Zechariah
Zeph.	Zephaniah
ZNW	*Zeitschrift für die neutestamentliche Wissenschaft*

PART I

The Undoubted Letters of St. Paul

The annotated text of the seven letters of Paul whose genuineness is beyond
reasonable doubt.

THE FIRST LETTER TO THE THESSALONIANS
(ca. 50–51)

This is widely regarded as the earliest of the extant letters of Paul and the earliest writing in the NT. It was written from Corinth, probably in late 50 or early 51 CE, just before Paul's appearance before Gallio (Acts 18:12–17). Gallio's proconsulship can be dated, from an inscription found at Delphi, 51–52 CE (less likely, 52–53).

Thessalonica was an important port, the largest city of Macedonia. The Via Egnatia, linking Rome with the eastern provinces, ran through it, and the Romans made it the provincial capital but a free city. There, less than a year prior to the writing of this letter, Paul had established a small but vigorous Christian congregation. That Paul not only supported himself in Thessalonica by manual labor (2:9) but also received financial assistance from the Philippians at least twice while he was there (Phil. 4:16) suggests that he was in the city longer than the three weeks mentioned in Acts 17:2, perhaps two or three months. Forced to leave Thessalonica abruptly (2:15, 17; Acts 17:5–10), he became increasingly anxious over the fate of the new congregation and sent Timothy from Athens to strengthen his converts' faith and ascertain their attitude toward him (3:1–6). Timothy's return brought good news about the church's abiding affection for Paul (3:6) as their model (1:6) and about its general spiritual condition, although it had endured some harassment (2:14; 3:3–4), and the death of some of its members had raised questions about their status at the anticipated coming of Christ (4:13).

According to Acts (17:1–4), the mission began in the synagogue and emphasized Jesus' fulfillment of the OT, but the letter reflects a household-based evangelistic effort aimed directly at Gentiles (1:9), and it contains only a few allusions to the OT and no quotations of it. From the Acts' account we receive the impression that the first Christians in Thessalonica were either Jews or Gentile God-fearers converted from the synagogue (Acts 17:4); their opponents were Jews who made use of pagan ruffians to harass the church (Acts 17:5). In the letter itself, however, the Christians are addressed as Gentiles, converted directly from paganism (1:9), and their suffering at the hands of their "fellow citizens" is clearly distinguished from the analogous persecution by the Jews experienced by Christians in Judea (2:14). Acts also conveys the impression that many of the Thessalonian converts were socially elevated individuals, including a significant number of prominent women (Acts 17:4) and Jason, who owned a house and was able to post bond when accused by rabble from the marketplace who were his social inferiors (Acts 17:5–9). The recipients of the letter, by contrast, appear to be poor (2 Cor. 8:1–2) members of the artisan class (4:11), for whom Paul's own pre-dawn-to-dusk manual labor was intended to be paradigmatic (2:9; 2 Thess. 3:7–9).

In both content and style, 1 Thessalonians is a letter of moral exhortation, called by the Greeks *parainesis*. Like other parenetic letters, it affirms the friendly relations between writer and recipients (1:2–3:13), reminds the latter (2:9; 4:9) of instructions previously given (3:4; 4:2, 6, 9) and of knowledge already possessed (1:2, 5; 2:1–2, 5, 11; 3:3–4; 4:2; 5:2), bestows praise for conduct that is not only exemplary for others but also conforms to recognized models (1:6–7), and encourages the continuation or amplification of current actions (4:1, 10; 5: 11). Even the first part of chapter 2, which reads like an *apologia* by Paul, has a parenetic function. There is no evidence that a personal attack on him had been made by anyone in Thessalonica; the antithetical state-

3

ments are rather typical of those by which Hellenistic philosophers and prophets sought to present themselves as trustworthy moral guides by distinguishing themselves from the numerous charlatans who claimed the same vocations. Paul's extensive use in 1 Thessalonians of the techniques and traditions of the Hellenistic moralists shows that he presupposes that his readers will be sufficiently familiar with the commonplaces of popular philosophy to understand the nuances of his various exhortations and instructions.

The form of the letter is unusual. After the initial greeting(1:1) an extraordinarily large proportion of it is incorporated into the familiar epistolary thanksgiving (1:2–3:13), which rehearses the history of Paul's relationship with the readers: they are exemplary converts (1:2–10), as he has been an exemplary missionary (2:1–12), so that he can be thankful that they, as imitators of himself and of the Palestinian churches, have stood fast under persecution (2:13–16). His personal concern led to the sending of Timothy, whose encouraging report occasions this letter, a temporary substitute for the apostle's own return to visit them, which he prays will be soon (2:17–3:13). The remainder of the content is subsumed under another familiar component of NT epistolary style, the hortatory or *parakalō*-section, so called by the verb that frequently introduces it, "I urge you" (4:1; see also 2:12; 3:2; 4:10; 5:11, 14). This includes a traditional catechetical summary of the way of Christian "holiness" (4:2–8) and a mixture of ad hoc instructions and traditional phraseology under the headings "about your love for one another" (4:9–12), "about those who sleep in death" (4:13–18), "about times and dates" (i.e., the end of days and the return of Christ) (5:1–11), rounded off by an appeal to engage in mutual exhortation and to maintain an orderly but free and charismatic congregational life (5:12–22). Benedictions, greetings, and the adjuration that the letter be read to the assembled congregation bring it to a close (5:23–28).

1 Thessalonians

1 Paul, Silas and Timothy,[1]
    To the church[2] of the Thessalonians in God the Father and the Lord Jesus Christ:
    Grace and peace to you.
2 We always thank God for all of you and continually mention you in our prayers.[3] 3 We remember before our God and Father your work produced by faith, your labor prompted by love,[4] and your endurance inspired by hope in our Lord[5] Jesus Christ.

1. According to Acts 17, Silas and Timothy had been with the apostle when he established the church in Thessalonica. Like Paul, the former is known by two names; the apostle refers to him here and elsewhere (2 Cor. 1:19; 2 Thess.1:1) as Silvanus, a Latin name, but Acts consistently calls him Silas (either a Semitic name or a shortened Greek form: Acts 15:22, 27, 32, [34], 40; 16:19–38; 17:4, 10, 14–15; 18:5). He is probably the same as the writer of 1 Peter (1 Pet. 5:12). For Timothy, see 1 Thess. 3:2, 6; 2 Thess. 1:1; 1 Cor. 4:17; 16:10; 2 Cor. 1:1, 19; Rom. 16:21; Phil. 1:1; 2:19; Phlm. 1; Col. 1:1; 1 Tim. 1:2, 18; 6:20; 2 Tim. 1:2; Acts 16:1–3; 17:14–15; 18:5; 19:22; 20:4.
2. "Church" translates a political term, "assembly" of voting citizens of a Greek city, occasionally used of a "meeting" of a club, but often in the Greek OT of Israel assembled before God. Calling God "Father" (see also 1:3; 3:11, 13; 2 Thess. 1:1) anticipates Paul's extensive use of kinship language in the letter and suggests that the church is a new family to which the recipients belong.
3. A brief prayer of thanks regularly began an ancient letter; Paul develops the form in an unusually free and expansive way, often including liturgical elements (the letter was to be read aloud in the assembly) and signalling the main themes of the letter. This one begins a long autobiographical section written in parenetic style that is intended to strengthen the bond between Paul and the Thessalonians and to lay the foundation for the exhortations and instructions given in 4:1–5:22. Note the resumption of the thanksgiving in 2:13 and 3:9.
4. Note the formula faith, hope, love as in 5:8; Gal. 5:5–6; 1 Cor. 13:13; Col. 1:4–5; see also 1 Thess. 3:6; Rom. 5:1–5.
5. "Inspired by hope in our Lord": literally "of the hope of our Lord."

4 For we know, brothers and sisters loved by God, that he has chosen you, 5 because our gospel came to you not simply with words but also with power, with the Holy Spirit and deep conviction. You know how we lived among you for your sake. 6 You became imitators of us and of the Lord, for you welcomed the message in the midst of severe suffering[6] with the joy given by the Holy Spirit. 7 And so you became a model to all the believers in Macedonia and Achaia.[7] 8 The Lord's message rang out from you not only in Macedonia and Achaia—your faith in God has become known everywhere. Therefore we do not need to say anything about it, 9 for they themselves report what happened when we visited you. They tell how you turned[8] to God from idols to serve the living and true God, 10 and to wait for his Son from heaven, whom he raised from the dead—Jesus, who rescues us from the coming wrath.[9]

2 You know, brothers and sisters, that our visit[1] to you was not without results. 2 We had previously suffered and been treated outrageously in Philippi,[2] as you know, but with the help of our God we dared to tell you his gospel in the face of strong opposition.[3] 3 For the appeal we make does not spring from error or impure motives, nor are we trying to trick you.[4] 4 On the contrary, we speak as those approved by God to be entrusted with the gospel. We are not trying to please people but God, who tests our hearts. 5 You know we never used flattery, nor did we put on a mask to cover up greed—God is our witness. 6 We were not looking for praise[5] from any human being, not from you or anyone else, even though as apostles of Christ we could have asserted our prerogatives. 7 Instead, we were like young children among you.

Just as a nursing mother[6] cares for her children, 8 so we cared for you. Because we loved you so much, we were delighted to share with you not only the gospel of God but our lives as well. 9 Surely you remember, brothers and sisters, our toil and hardship; we worked night and day[7] in

---

6. The translation "severe suffering" reflects the view that Paul is referring to persecution, as in 2:14; more likely Paul has in mind the conflicting emotions of distress and joy characteristically experienced by new converts (v. 9); see notes on 2:2 and 3:3–4.

7. As capital of the Roman province of Macedonia (4:10), Thessalonica was of strategic importance; the congregations there and at Philippi were the first we hear of on European soil (though that at Rome may have been founded a year or two earlier; see Suetonius, *Claudius* 25.3). Achaia was the neighboring province, of which Corinth now served as capital.

8. "Turned": a standard term for religious and moral conversion that stresses the radical reorientation of identity, life, and values that is to distinguish the convert from others (4:5: "not like the heathen"; 4:13: "not like the rest"); see Acts 3:19; 9:35; 14:15; 15:3, 19; 26:20; 1 Pet. 2:25. "Living God" is a Hellenistic Jewish term for God as the creator and sustainer of the universe (Bel 5; Acts 14:15).

9. Vv. 9–10 are a terse summary of missionary preaching to Gentiles, perhaps a pre-Pauline formula; 2:1–12 elaborate on v. 9.

1. Literally "entrance," "arrival" as in 1:9, where the same word is translated "when we visited."

2. See Acts 16:19–24.

3. Paul uses here two words prominent in Hellenistic moral rhetoric. *Parrhēsia*, "bold speech" ("dared to tell") is what distinguishes the true friend from the flatterer (v. 5). *Agōn*, "contest, struggle": what Paul means is debated: external opposition that he faced in Thessalonica; his own emotional turmoil and inward "struggle"; or the "strenuous effort" with which he proclaimed the gospel.

4. The sharp sarcasm of Gal. 1:10, 2 Cor. 2:17, 4:2–12, 12:16–17, where Paul's authority has been directly attacked, is absent here. Paul's self-praise in vv. 3–6 is stereotyped (see introductory note above and the essay by A. J. Malherbe in Part IX) and introduces subjects treated later in the letter, such as pleasing God (v. 4; 4:1; cf. 2:16).

5. Paul rejects here one of Greek society's most powerful sanctions for public morality, namely, "love of honor."

6. Lit., "wet nurse."

7. This suggests that Paul's toil was even longer than an artisan's normal dawn-to-dusk work day. For Paul's pride in his self-support by handwork, which set him apart from propagandists for religious or philosophical cults and from other Christian apostles, see 1 Cor. 9 and 2 Cor. 11:7–11. He did accept money occasionally, however, especially from Philippi: Phil. 4:16; 2 Cor. 11:9.

order not to be a burden to anyone while we preached the gospel of God to you.

10 You are witnesses, and so is God, of how holy, righteous and blameless we were among you who believed. 11 For you know that we dealt with each of you as a father deals with his own children, 12 encouraging, comforting and urging you to live lives worthy of God, who calls you into his kingdom and glory.

13 And we also thank God continually because, when you received the word of God, which you heard from us, you accepted it not as a human word, but as it actually is, the word of God, which is indeed at work in you who believe. 14 For you, brothers and sisters, became imitators of God's churches in Judea, which are in Christ Jesus: You suffered from your fellow citizens[8] the same things those churches suffered from the Jews, 15 who killed the Lord Jesus and the prophets and also drove us out. They displease God and are hostile to everyone[9] 16 in their effort to keep us from speaking to the Gentiles so that they may be saved. In this way they always heap up their sins to the limit. The wrath of God has come upon them at last.[1]

17 But, brothers and sisters, when we were orphaned by being separated from you for a short time (in person, not in thought), out of our intense longing we made every effort to see you. 18 For we wanted to come to you—certainly I, Paul, did, again and again—but Satan[2] blocked our way. 19 For what is our hope, our joy, or the crown in which we will glory in the presence of our Lord Jesus when he comes[3]? Is it not you? 20 Indeed, you are our glory and joy.

3 So when we could stand it no longer, we thought it best to be left by ourselves in Athens.[4] 2 We sent Timothy, who is our brother and co-worker

---

8. Lit., "belonging to the same tribe." This suggests that those formerly closest to the converts now disdain their association with the new cult. Their opposition was likely expressed primarily through social pressure and verbal abuse.

9. The entire verse is in solemn rhetorical style, produced by a series of rhyming words: *apokteinantōn, ekdiōxantōn, mē areskontōn, enantiōn.* "Killed . . . Jesus": The earliest instance of the tendency in Christian literature to put the entire blame for Jesus' execution on "the Jews"; see Acts 2:23, 36; 3:14–15; Luke 23:25; Matt. 27:25; Mark 12:8. The martyrdom of the prophets (see 1 Kings 19:10, quoted by Paul, Rom. 11:3) became a prominent motif in Jewish legend; in the NT see Matt. 23:31–35; Mark 12:5; Luke 13:33–34. Evidently Christian apologetic very early connected Jesus' death with this tradition: see Acts 7:52. Contempt for the gods ("displease God") and hatred of humanity ("hostile to everyone") were charges frequently made by anti-Jewish pamphleteers of Alexandria and Rome; from Paul the statement is astonishing and leads many scholars to the conclusion that vv. 14–16 are either a non-Pauline interpolation or the Pauline school's generalizing reinterpretation of an original reference to specific Jewish opponents.

1. The basis for Paul's hostile statement, which contrasts so severely with his attitude elsewhere, is the opposition by Jews (Judeans? Thessalonian Jews? [see Acts 17:5–9, 11, 13]) to his Gentile mission. The idea of filling up sins "to the limit" belongs to the apocalyptic periodization of history (Dan. 8:33), with the severest punishment reserved for the end (2 Macc. 6:14). "At last": or, "completely," "fully." In Wisd. 16:5; 19:1, a similar phrase contrasts the punishment by God of Israel, "not to the end," with his destruction of the Egyptians, "to the end." "Forever" is also a possible translation, though that would make the contradiction of Rom. 9–11 absolute. On the revelation of the wrath of God against all people, "the Jew first and also the Greek,"see Rom. 1: 18–3:20.

2. "Satan": a Semitic word. Paul does not use the Greek equivalent *diabolos* ("devil"), which appears however in Ephesians (4:27; 6:11) and the Pastorals (1 Tim. 3:6–7; 2 Tim. 2:26). See 1 Cor. 5: 5; 7:5; 2 Cor. 2:11; 11:14; 12:7; Rom. 16:20; 2 Thess. 2:9; 1 Tim. 1:20; 5:15. What empirical circumstances stopped Paul cannot be determined.

3. Greek, "in his *parousia.*" The word had acquired in the Hellenistic period the technical usage "arrival," "visit," "appearance," particularly of divinities and kings. In the NT this technical sense is applied to the return of the exalted Christ, connected with the other events associated with the end of the age in Jewish eschatology, notably the final judgment.

4. Since the 1st person plural (we) is used ambiguously by Paul (often = "I"), it is debated whether Paul and Silvanus or Paul alone stayed in Athens (n.b. v. 5: "I sent"). In Acts neither Silas nor

in God's service in spreading the gospel of Christ, to strengthen and encourage you in your faith, 3 so that no one would be unsettled by these trials. You know quite well that we are destined for them. 4 In fact, when we were with you, we kept telling you that we would be persecuted.[5] And it turned out that way, as you well know. 5 For this reason, when I could stand it no longer, I sent to find out about your faith. I was afraid that in some way the tempter[6] had tempted you and that our labors might have been in vain.

6 But Timothy has just now come to us from you and has brought good news about your faith and love. He has told us that you always have pleasant memories of us and that you long to see us, just as we also long to see you. 7 Therefore, brothers and sisters, in all our distress and persecution we were encouraged about you because of your faith. 8 For now we really live, since you are standing firm in the Lord. 9 How can we thank God[7] enough for you in return for all the joy we have in the presence of our God because of you? 10 Night and day we pray most earnestly that we may see you again and supply what is lacking in your faith.

11 Now may our God and Father himself and our Lord Jesus clear the way for us to come to you. 12 May the Lord make your love increase and overflow for each other and for everyone else, just as ours does for you. 13 May he strengthen your hearts so that you will be blameless and holy in the presence of our God and Father when our Lord Jesus comes with all his holy ones.[8]

4 As for other matters, brothers and sisters, we instructed you[9] how to live in order to please God, as in fact you are living. Now we ask you and urge you in the Lord Jesus to do this more and more. 2 For you know what instructions[1] we gave you by the authority of the Lord Jesus.

3 It is God's will that you should be sanctified:[2] that you should avoid

---

Timothy is with Paul in Athens; both remain in Berea and only rejoin him in Corinth (Acts 17: 14–15; 18:1, 5).

5. As with 1:6, opinions differ as to whether Paul's mention of trials (*thlipsis*: lit., "pressure," "affliction") is a reference to the abuse of the converts by non-Christians (so the TNIV: "persecuted"), their psychic distress at conversion, Paul's anguish at being suddenly separated from his new converts (2:17)—in which case he is worried that his own afflictions might cause them to be unsettled (v. 6)—or to all of the above. That physical and psychological afflictions were destined was a regular part ("we kept telling you") of the instruction of new converts (see 1 Peter *passim*); similar warnings were given to neophytes in philosophy. Also relevant may be the apocalyptic notion that a period of distress would precede the Messiah's coming (see 2 Thess. 2:3–12). For the connection of Christian affliction with the suffering of Jesus, see 1:6; 2 Cor. 4:7–12; Phil. 3: 10–11; 1 Pet. 2:19–24; 3:16–18; 4:1, 12–19.

6. "The tempter" = Satan (see on 2:18), so called also in Matt. 4:3.

7. This third occurrence of the basic thanksgiving formula (vv. 9–10; see 1:2; 2:13) sums up the whole first section of the letter and leads to the prayer in solemn, liturgical style that concludes this portion (vv. 11–13). The rhetorical and liturgical style of the whole section (1:2–3: 13) shows that the letter was dictated with the awareness it would be read in public worship (see 5:27); it is not just private "correspondence," though it is quite personal and connected with a specific occasion.

8. The prayer anticipates the parenesis of 4:1–5:11, with "love . . . for each other and for everyone else" taken up in 4:9–12, "blameless and holy" in 4:3–8, and esp. the "coming" (*parousia*, as in 2: 19 and 5:23) of Jesus in 4:13–5:11. Eschatological notes in Pauline thanksgivings and prayers are common; the number of them here (1:10; 2:19; see also 2:12, 16;3:3–4) points ahead to the questions dealt with in chaps. 4 and 5. "His holy ones": although the OT text lying behind this image, "The Lord my God will come, and all the holy ones with him" (Zech. 14:5, LXX), refers to the angels (see Mark 8:38: 13:27; 2 Thess. 1:7; Jude 14), Paul ordinarily uses the term to mean "Christians."

9. "We instructed you": lit., "you received from us." Paul uses here a technical term indicating the transmission and reception of traditional material.

1. The word refers to ethical "precepts" on proper conduct in particular situations (see note on 4: 11).

2. Vv. 3–8 are an example of a preceptorial tradition, a pithy, hellenized summary of Lev. 18, whose

sexual immorality; 4 that each of you should learn to control your own body[3] in a way that is holy and honorable, 5 not in passionate lust[4] like the pagans, who do not know God; 6 and that in this matter no one should wrong or take advantage of a brother or sister.[5] The Lord will punish all those who commit such sins, as we told you and warned you before. 7 For God did not call us to be impure, but to live a holy life.[6] 8 Therefore, anyone who rejects this instruction does not reject a human being but God, the very God who gives you his Holy Spirit.

9 Now about your love for one another[7] we do not need to write to you, for you yourselves have been taught by God to love each other. 10 And in fact, you do love all the brothers and sisters throughout Macedonia. Yet we urge you, dear friends, to do so more and more, 11 and to make it your ambition to lead a quiet life: You should mind your own business[8] and work with your hands, just as we told[9] you, 12 so that your daily life may win the respect of[1] outsiders and so that you will not be dependent on anybody.·

13 Brothers and sisters, we do not want you to be uninformed about those who sleep in death,[2] so that you do not grieve like the rest, who have no hope. 14 We believe that Jesus died and rose again, and so we believe that God will bring with Jesus those who have fallen asleep in him. 15 According to the Lord's word,[3] we tell you that we who are still alive,

---

key word "holiness" ("sanctified") is used by Paul to bracket his discussion (vv. 3, 7). It was probably adapted by Christians from the diaspora synagogue (n.b. v.5) for pre- or post-baptismal instruction (see 1 Pet. 1:15–16).

3. Greek *skeuos*, "vessel, container, receptacle." The TNIV's translation reflects the view that Paul is referring to the exercise of self-control. The first edition of the NAB expresses this interpretation more directly, treating *skeuos* as the penis ("member"). More probable is the interpretation that Paul is citing a precept on marriage that advised the acquisition of a wife as a prophylactic against illicit sex (see Tobit 4:12; *T. Levi* 9:9–10). Women were commonly viewed as vessels in both Jewish and Greek circles (1 Pet. 3:7), and Paul's androcentric idiom accords with the Hebrew equivalent in rabbinic texts and fits the traditional context here. The idea—so foreign to modern sensibilities and physiology—is that of the woman's womb as essentially a receptacle for the man's semen. The same precept is likely used in the discussion of marriage in 1 Cor. 7:2–3, where, however, it is considerably transformed by Paul.

4. On taking a wife in the proper manner that does not involve lust, see Tobit 8:7.

5. Some see here a change in subject matter from marriage to business, but it is more likely that Paul is using the language of commercial greed ("take advantage of") to describe adultery, which traditionally constituted a violation of the husband's property rights (Exod. 20:17). To "wrong" is lit. "to transgress (the rights of)."

6. "To be impure" is here a metaphor for forbidden sexual activity; monogamy belongs to the "holy life."

7. The topic of brotherly love (*philadelphia*) was frequently discussed by moralists concerned with the proper treatment of one's natural siblings, but it is adapted here by Paul to discuss love within the Christian community and its obligations to non-Christians (vv. 9–12).

8. "To lead a quiet life" and to "mind one's own business" were characteristics of the contemplative life that was commended by some philosophers (esp. Epicureans) but criticized by others as socially irresponsible and conducive to laziness. Paul's insistence on manual labor is intended to foster self-sufficiency (a virtue esp. praised by Stoics, cf. v. 12) and prevent meddlesomeness (2 Thess. 3:11), thereby enabling the Christians to make a positive impression on outsiders (v. 12).

9. The verb is cognate with the noun translated "instructed" ("precepts") in 4:2.

1. Or, "behave with decorum toward." Perhaps a quasi-technical term for a seemly occupation.

2. Presumably the death of some of the Thessalonian Christians has raised difficulties about the nature of the deliverance promised by the Son whom they await (1:10); evidently Paul's preaching, like that of the earliest Christians in general, included Christ's imminent *parousia* (compare 4:17 with Mark 9:1). The concern about the relation of the dead and the living at the time of the end was frequent in Jewish apocalypses (see, e.g., 4 Ezra 5:41–42; 13:16–24; 2 Baruch 51:13), and Paul's parenesis here is in apocalyptic style. "To fall asleep" is a common euphemism for "to die" and says nothing about the specifically Christian or Jewish belief in resurrection.

3. This may refer to a saying of Jesus (see 1 Cor. 7:10, 12, 25) unattested elsewhere, but more likely to an apocalypse of the risen Christ received by a Christian prophet (see Rev. 1:1), perhaps even Paul himself (1 Cor. 15:50–51). V. 15b or vv. 15b-17 may be a direct quotation of this "word"; the particle "that" is frequently equivalent to a quotation mark.

who are left till the coming of the Lord, will certainly not precede those who have fallen asleep. 16 For the Lord himself will come down from heaven, with a loud command, with the voice of the archangel and with the trumpet call of God, and the dead in Christ will rise first. 17 After that, we who are still alive and are left will be caught up[4] together with them in the clouds to meet the Lord in the air. And so we will be with the Lord forever. 18 Therefore encourage one another with these words.

5 Now, brothers and sisters, about times and dates we do not need to write[5] to you, 2 for you know very well that the day of the Lord will come like a thief in the night. 3 While people are saying, "Peace and safety," destruction will come on them suddenly, as labor pains on a pregnant woman, and they will not escape.

4 But you, brothers and sisters, are not in darkness so that this day should surprise you like a thief.[6] 5 You are all children of the light and children of the day. We do not belong to the night or to the darkness.[7] 6 So then, let us not be like others, who are asleep, but let us be awake and sober. 7 For those who sleep, sleep at night, and those who get drunk, get drunk at night. 8 But since we belong to the day, let us be sober, putting on faith and love as a breastplate, and the hope of salvation as a helmet. 9 For God did not appoint us to suffer wrath but to receive salvation through our Lord Jesus Christ. 10 He died for us so that, whether we are awake or asleep,[8] we may live together with him. 11 Therefore encourage one another and build each other up, just as in fact you are doing.[9]

12 Now we ask you, brothers and sisters, to acknowledge those who work hard among you, who care for you in the Lord and who admonish you.[1] 13 Hold them in the highest regard in love because of their work. Live in peace with each other. 14 And we urge you, brothers and sisters, warn those who are idle and disruptive, encourage the disheartened, help the weak, be patient with everyone.[2] 15 Make sure that nobody pays back

---

4. The term translated "caught up" was typically used by mourners to lament how the deceased had been "snatched away" by death; Paul, by contrast, uses it here to console the bereaved (v. 13) by affirming that the living will be "snatched up" to be reunited with the deceased at the parousia. The repeated use of the word "with" is also consolatory (vv. 13, 17; 5:10), emphasizing how the eschatological action overcomes the separation caused by death.
5. Statements about not needing to write are parenetic and presuppose the recipients' knowledge (v. 2) or prior instruction (4:9).
6. A widespread image: Matt. 24:43; Luke 12:39; 2 Pet. 3:10; Rev. 3:3; 16:15.
7. The dualism of "children of light" vs. "children of darkness" is common in the apocalyptic world-view, most clearly attested in the Dead Sea Scrolls; elsewhere in Pauline writings only in 2 Cor. 6:14–7:1 and Eph. 5:3–14; cf. Rom.13:12; Col. 1:13. Apocalyptic language functions here, as elsewhere in Paul, to distinguish members of the sect from others and reinforce their own sense of solidarity and uniqueness. The metaphoric "armor" (v. 8) is closely associated with this dualism: the Dead Sea sect expected a literal "war of the sons of light with the sons of darkness."
8. "Awake or asleep": here and in 4:13–18, "alive or dead"; note the quite different meaning in the apocalyptic admonition of 5:2–9, where only those who "keep awake," i.e., are morally vigilant, are saved, while those who "fall asleep," i.e., are slothful, perish with the sons of darkness (see also 4:6).
9. A transitional sentence that concludes 5:1–10 and introduces 5:12–22, which deals with relationships within the church. Spiritual guidance or pastoral care is envisioned here as an endeavor of the entire community ("one another"), done "one on one" ("each other"; see also 2:11, "each one of you"). Vv. 12–13 discuss the proper attitude toward community caregivers, and vv.14–15 treat the patient manner in which that pastoral care is to be given.
1. The three verbs (participles in Greek)—"work hard," "care for you," "admonish"—do not distinguish three church offices, but three functions of spiritual guidance.
2. The terms here describe various character traits and psychological dispositions, not discrete groups within the church. "Idle": lit., "disorderly" (used of people who refuse to conform to recognized moral standards); "disheartened": or, "discouraged," "despondent." The morally "weak" are those who experience difficulty in living according to the community's norms and thus require special help.

wrong for wrong, but always strive to do what is good for each other and for everyone else.

16 Rejoice always, 17 pray continually, 18 give thanks in all circumstances; for this is God's will for you in Christ Jesus.

19 Do not put out the Spirit's fire. 20 Do not treat prophecies with contempt 21 but test them all; hold on to what is good, 22 reject whatever is harmful.[3]

23 May God himself, the God of peace, sanctify you through and through. May your whole spirit, soul and body be kept blameless at the coming of our Lord Jesus Christ. 24 The one who calls you is faithful, and he will do it.

25 Brothers and sisters, pray for us. 26 Greet all God's people with a holy kiss.[4] 27 I charge you before the Lord to have this letter read to all the brothers and sisters.

28 The grace of our Lord Jesus Christ be with you.

THE LETTER TO THE GALATIANS
(ca. 54)

Identification of "Galatia" hangs on the question whether Paul used the term in its narrow sense, of the area comprised by the old Celtic (*galatai* = *keltai*) tribal kingdom in north central Asia Minor (capital, Ancyra), or more loosely of the Roman province which included that region but extended south to include also Lycaonia and other areas. Evidence favors the former (see note on 3:1), although in that case Paul's founding of the churches goes unmentioned in Acts.

Opinions about the date of Galatians vary widely; it has been called the earliest and the latest of Paul's letters. Thematic similarities with Romans suggest a relatively late date; 4:13 *can* be understood to imply two previous visits by Paul to Galatia, hence written after the journey of Acts 18:23; Ephesus (Acts 19:1 ff.) would be a convenient place from which to communicate with Galatia. Therefore, though none of these or of the other arguments commonly advanced is probative, most recent commentators have placed the writing between 53 and 55, from Ephesus.

Formally the most striking thing about the letter is the absence of the customary thanksgiving (see the note on 1 Thess. 1:2; of the other letters, only 2 Corinthians lacks a thanksgiving, and for it Paul substitutes a blessing in liturgical style). After the normal salutation—which already hints at one of the principal themes—Paul explodes in a rebuke of the Galatian Christians (1:6). This angry tone persists throughout the letter. Anathemas are proclaimed freely, sarcasm abounds—about the "Pillars" in Jerusalem, about the Galatians, about "agitators," even about Paul's own mission among them. At points this sarcasm becomes bitter: "You foolish Galatians! Who has bewitched you?" (3:1); "As for those agitators, I wish they would go the whole way and emasculate themselves!" (5:12); "If you keep on biting and devouring each other, watch out or you will be destroyed by each other" (5:15). There are a number

---

3. Vv. 19–22 illustrate the prevalence of charismatic phenomena in early Christianity—and also Paul's ambivalence toward them (see in detail 1 Cor. 12–14). On "testing" claims made in the Spirit, see 1 John 4:1.
4. See 1 Cor. 16:20; 2 Cor. 13:12; Rom. 16:16; also 1 Pet. 5:14. The "kiss of peace" soon received a fixed place in the liturgy of the Eucharist.

of *anacolutha*—sentences in which Paul pauses in mid-thought and continues with a different grammatical structure (e.g., 2:5–7).

Nevertheless, it would be a mistake to assume that the letter is a disordered outpouring of emotion. Chapters 1–2 develop the theme stated in 1:1, 11 f. ("not from men nor through man") in the rhetorical sequence called *chiasm* (argument in the form of the Greek letter X, thus: a, b, b̄, á). Smaller units also use chiasm (e.g., 4:4 f.), parallelism, and other rhetorical devices. The central example of the promise to Abraham, however obscure it may seem to modern readers, is rather tightly argued; perhaps Paul had worked it out previously. The same may be true of the Hagar–Sarah allegory (4:21–31), and of portions of the hortatory section (5:13–6:10).

Moreover, Paul's replacement of the usual thanksgiving by a paragraph beginning "I am astonished that you are so quickly deserting . . . and are turning" is not unusual in ancient letter-writing. There are numerous surviving examples of letters beginning this way from writers several centuries before and after Paul. One handbook of epistolary style lists two model letters with similar phrases. One, "the ironic letter," begins "I am greatly astonished at your sense of equity, that you have so quickly rushed from a well-ordered life to its opposite." The other, "the letter of reproach," starts with "You have received many favors from us, and I am exceedingly amazed that you remember none of them."[1]

The cause of Paul's anger is clear in general, though some details are baffling. There has been a direct challenge to Paul's apostolate in the Galatian region. In his absence another group of Christian missionaries has visited the churches he founded there, preaching what both Paul and these other apostles regard as "a different gospel" from the one he proclaimed (1:6–9; 4:17; 5:10, 12; 6:12). Like Paul, these apostles believe that these two versions of the gospel are mutually exclusive. They accuse Paul of having watered down the requirements of conversion in order "to win human approval"; Paul in turn claims that "they are trying to pervert the gospel." At issue, then, are both the content of the Christian faith and the legitimacy of Paul's authority.

Some characteristics of the opponents can readily be deduced from the letter, but scholars have not been able to agree on their precise identity (see the essay by J. L. Martyn in Part IV). The Jewish law stands at the forefront of the conflict; Paul's opponents believe that pagan converts to Christianity must submit, in some general way, to being "under the law" (4:21; cf. 2:16 ff.; 3:2–4: 7). They insist that all Christians be circumcised (5:2–12; 6:12–15; cf. 2:3, 12). They observe a festival calendar (4:10). They hold Paul's apostolic credentials in contempt, accusing him of being the purveyor of merely human traditions, lacking independent authority but dependent upon the Jerusalem apostles while deviating from the practice of the latter (chaps. 1–2). Perhaps they even accuse him of preaching circumcision himself, but not drawing appropriate consequences from it (5:11).

As the opposing apostles see the situation, we could compare it to the conversion to Judaism of the royal household of Adiabene, as described by Josephus (*Ant.* 20.34–48). An itinerant Jewish merchant named Ananias had first introduced Judaism to the household. So persuasive was his description of Jewish belief and practice that the entire household was won over, even including the crown prince. When the latter, about to be enthroned as king, asked to be circumcised, however, both his mother, who had herself converted to Judaism, and Ananias, now his private tutor, became alarmed at the possible political consequences. Ananias assured the king that this step was not necessary, for "without circumcision he could worship the Divine, if he had fully

---

1. Ps.-Libanius, *Epist. Char.* 56, 64, trans. by Abraham J. Malherbe, *Ancient Epistolary Theorists*, SBL Sources for Biblical Study (Atlanta: Scholars Press, 1988), 76–77.

made up his mind to be zealous for the traditions of the fathers of the Jews" (*Ant.* 20.41; cf. Gal. 1:14). Then, however, another Jewish itinerant, one Eleazar, arrived at the palace, with a stricter interpretation of the Torah's requirements. Did the king not know that scripture clearly commanded that every son of the covenant must be circumcised? Convinced by this argument, the king forthwith completed his conversion by submitting to circumcision. Similarly Paul's opponents in Galatia must have argued that his allowing mere baptism to substitute for circumcision was a matter of expediency (cf. 1:10). His quasi-converts, if male, must now "finish" their conversion (cf. 3:3) by being circumcised and observing the basic commandments of Judaism.

Paul's outraged response is the letter we have before us. For him the astonishing news ("gospel") that the Messiah of God is none other than the crucified Jesus, a notion so abhorrent (cf. 3:13) that Paul himself had tried to stamp out the sect that was forming around it (1:13), had changed everything. This gospel of the crucified Christ, if it was true, meant that God had acted in the world with such revolutionary love that a faithful response could not be defined by mere rules, that "turning to God from idols to serve the living and true God" (1 Thess. 1:9) was not merely a conversion to any sect, not even the one defined by God's own covenant mediated by Moses (Gal. 3:19). What has happened is nothing less than "a new creation" (6:15); what that creation entails is, before any code of obligations, liberation from every form of slavery (5:1).

Galatians

1 Paul, an apostle—sent not with a human commission nor by human authority,[1] but by Jesus Christ and God the Father, who raised him from the dead— 2 and all the brothers and sisters with me,

To the churches in Galatia:

3 Grace and peace to you from God our Father and the Lord Jesus Christ, 4 who gave himself for our sins to rescue us from the present evil age, according to the will of our God and Father, 5 to whom be glory for ever and ever. Amen.[2]

6 I am astonished that you are so quickly deserting the one[3] who called you by the grace of Christ and are turning to a different gospel— 7 which is really no gospel at all. Evidently some people are throwing you into confusion and are trying to pervert the gospel of Christ. 8 But even if we or an angel from heaven should preach a gospel other than the one we preached to you, let that person be under God's curse! 9 As we have already said, so now I say again: If anybody is preaching to you a gospel other than what you accepted, let that person be under God's curse!

10 Am I now trying to win human approval,[4] or God's approval? Or am

---

1. The issue of Paul's authority is thus joined in the first words of the salutation. With the following prepositional phrases, the word "apostle" retains something of its original verbal character, literally, "sent," in the technical sense of "commissioned as an agent." It had not yet become the title of an office, nor been limited to the circle of "the Twelve."

2. The opening formula, liturgical in style, is somewhat fuller than usual. Like the opening of Romans, it contains a terse summary of the gospel. In Romans, however, the summary defines the basis of Paul's anticipated unity with the congregation; here it defines the gospel which he immediately accuses them of deserting.

3. God, not Paul or even Christ; cf. 1:15; 5:8; 1 Thess. 2:12; 5:24; 1 Cor. 1:9; Rom. 8:30; and elsewhere.

4. Probably this reflects one of the accusations made against Paul by the opponents; cf. 1 Thess. 2:3–6 and the note there. When fundamental issues were not at stake, Paul did try "to please everyone in every way," 1 Cor. 10:33.

I trying to please people? If I were still trying to please people, I would not be a servant[5] of Christ.

11 I want you to know,[6] brothers and sisters, that the gospel I preached is not of human origin. 12 I did not receive it from any human source, nor was I taught it; rather, I received it by revelation from Jesus Christ.[7]

13 For you have heard of my previous way of life in Judaism,[8] how intensely I persecuted the church of God and tried to destroy it. 14 I was advancing in Judaism beyond many of my own age among my people and was extremely zealous for the traditions of my fathers. 15 But when God, who set me apart from birth[9] and called me by his grace, was pleased 16 to reveal his Son in me so that I might preach him among the Gentiles, my immediate response was not to consult any human being. 17 I did not go up to Jerusalem to see those who were apostles before I was, but I went into Arabia.[1] Later I returned to Damascus.

18 Then after three years, I went up to Jerusalem to get acquainted with Cephas[2] and stayed with him fifteen days. 19 I saw none of the other apostles—only James, the Lord's brother. 20 I assure you before God that what I am writing you is no lie.

21 Then I went to Syria and Cilicia. 22 I was personally unknown to the churches of Judea that are in Christ. 23 They only heard the report: "The man who formerly persecuted us is now preaching the faith he once tried to destroy." 24 And they praised God because of me.

2 Then after fourteen years,[3] I went up again to Jerusalem, this time with Barnabas. I took Titus along also.[4] 2 I went in response to a revelation and,

5. "Servant": properly, "slave"; cf. Rom. 1:1; Phil. 1:1. Paul may have used the expression "slave of Christ" as a title analogous to the OT title "servant of the Lord," applied to Moses, David, and certain prophets. See also James 1:1; 2 Pet. 1:1; Jude 1:1; Rev. 1:1; cf. Titus 1:1, "slave of God."

6. With this disclosure formula ("I want you to know," as in 1 Cor. 12:3; 15:1) Paul begins a recounting of his own relevant life story, framed as a defense of both his practice and his understanding of the gospel (1:11–2:21).

7. This statement seems to contradict 1 Cor. 15:1, 3, where "the gospel" is identified with a formula that was "received" and "delivered"—technical terms for the transmission of tradition. But here Paul is concerned with the *authorization* of his message; Paul claims that legitimation did not come through any human agency. Naturally he learned much of the content of his preaching and teaching from those who were Christians before him, though apparently not from Jerusalem. (See the essay by Heitmüller in Part VI.)

8. "Judaism" is a Greek term coined in the Hellenistic period to describe the practices of observant Jews, as in 1 Macc. 8:1, which could also be adopted by non-Jews in varying degrees. For identification of Judaism with "zeal for the traditions of the fathers," compare Josephus, *Ant.* 20:41, quoted in the introductory note above.

9. A clear allusion to Isa. 49:1 and Jer. 1:5; Paul frequently hints that he thinks of himself as a prophet in the classical tradition, even a new Moses (see notes on 2 Cor. 3–4 and Rom. 9:3).

1. "Arabia" was vaguely defined, even including Sinai (4:25); here probably Paul means the northwest portion of the Nabatean kingdom, immediately southeast of Damascus. Modern romantic notions of Paul's meditating in the desert are off the mark; more likely he was preaching in the Hellenized cities like Petra and Bostra—otherwise the hostility of the Nabatean ethnarch, who pursued him back to Damascus (2 Cor. 11:32 f.), is inexplicable. The Acts' account of this period is incomplete, resulting in a distorted picture of Paul's relationship to Jerusalem (Acts 9:19–30).

2. "Cephas": the Aramaic equivalent of Peter (cf. John 1:42).

3. The time periods are ambiguous; they could all be dated from the year of conversion, so that the fourteen–year period would include the three years. More likely they are successive, though the total might still be no more than fourteen full years, since it was common practice to count even a few days of the initial and final years as whole years.

4. The report of Paul's second visit to Jerusalem can hardly be harmonized with the account in Acts. The nature of the matters discussed parallels Acts 15, but that is the *third* visit mentioned by Acts; however, the second visit according to Acts (11:27–30) comes too early in Paul's career. Further, if the "apostolic council" actually produced the legislation quoted in Acts 15:20, 29; 21:25, then Paul's statement in Gal. 1:10 is less than candid. Various solutions have been proposed; probably the inadequacy of the sources used by the author of Acts and the requirements of his literary and theological outline have produced the disparity. For Barnabas, see Acts 4:36; 9:27; 11:22–26, 30; 12:25; 13:1–12, 42–52; 14:12, 14, 20; 15:1–39; 1 Cor. 9:6; Titus: 2 Cor. 2:13; 7:6, 13f.; 8:6, 16, 23; 12:18; 2 Tim. 4:10; Tit. 1:4.

meeting privately with those esteemed as leaders, I set before them the gospel that I preach among the Gentiles. I wanted to be sure I was not running and had not been running my race in vain. 3 Yet not even Titus, who was with me, was compelled to be circumcised, even though he was a Greek. 4 This matter arose because some false believers had infiltrated our ranks to spy on the freedom we have in Christ Jesus and to make us slaves. 5 We did not give in to them for a moment, so that the truth of the gospel might remain with you.[5]

6 As for those who were held in high esteem—whatever they were makes no difference to me; God does not show favoritism—they added nothing to my message. 7 On the contrary, they saw that I had been entrusted with the task of preaching the gospel to the Gentiles, just as Peter had been to the Jews. 8 For God, who was at work in Peter as an apostle to the Jews, was also at work in me as an apostle to the Gentiles. 9 James, Cephas and John, those esteemed as pillars, gave me and Barnabas the right hand of fellowship[6] when they recognized the grace given to me. They agreed that we should go to the Gentiles, and they to the Jews. 10 All they asked was that we should continue to remember the poor,[7] the very thing I had been eager to do all along.

11 When Cephas came to Antioch, I opposed him to his face, because he stood condemned. 12 For before certain people came from James,[8] he used to eat with the Gentiles. But when they arrived, he began to draw back and separate himself from the Gentiles because he was afraid of those who belonged to the circumcision group. 13 The other Jews joined him in his hypocrisy, so that by their hypocrisy even Barnabas was led astray.

14 When I saw that they were not acting in line with the truth of the gospel, I said to Cephas in front of them all, "You are a Jew, yet you live like a Gentile and not like a Jew. How is it, then, that you force Gentiles to follow Jewish customs?[9]

15 "We who are Jews by birth and not sinful Gentiles 16 know that a person is not justified by observing the law, but by faith in Jesus Christ.[1]

---

5. The sentence comprising vv. 3–5 is grammatically incomplete and logically confusing; ancient copyists trying to improve the sense have added to the uncertainty. What happened because of "false believers" (Greek: "pseudo-brothers")? Some commentators argue that because of them Titus after all was circumcised, and some ancient scribes expressed that interpretation by omitting the "not" in v. 5. Such a reading, however, would defeat Paul's whole argument. The circumcision of Timothy (if we are to believe Acts 16:3) forms a startling contrast, even though his case was different (by Jewish law, the child of a Jewish mother is a Jew). The identity of the pseudo-brothers—the term identifies them as members of the Christian movement—is obscure; they are apparently not the same as Paul's opponents in Galatia, and clearly not the leaders of the Jerusalem church. The "spying" and attempted coercion may have taken place in Antioch.
6. A handshake with the right hand often sealed a formal agreement in Roman practice and law; the word translated "fellowship" is often the equivalent of the Latin *societas* in its meaning, "contractual partnership."
7. Some scholars have argued that "the poor" was a self–designation of the whole church in Jerusalem, by analogy with the usage of the Qumran Essenes and of the later Jewish–Christian "Ebionites." NT evidence suggests rather that the term here and in Paul's description elsewhere of the collection for "the poor among the saints in Jerusalem" (Rom. 15:26), which occupied much of Paul's energy in the final years of his ministry (1 Cor. 16:1–4; 2 Cor. 8; 9; Rom. 15:25–28), points to those members of the community who were literally poor.
8. The first mention of James as the patron of a zealous Jewish–Christian party, a role that is emphasized in later Ebionite legend. The "people from James" are probably not to be identified with the opponents in Galatia, since the principal issue here, kosher food practices, is not mentioned elsewhere in the letter. Just what relationship, if any, existed between the Galatian opponents and the leaders of the Jerusalem church remains obscure.
9. On the face-off between Peter and Paul, see the discussion of Porphyry on p. 265 and the excerpt from Victorinus on pp. 325–28.
1. Greek, "faith *of* Jesus Christ"; also in the following clause. The TNIV translation here represents

So we, too, have put our faith in Christ Jesus that we may be justified by faith in Christ and not by observing the law, because by observing the law no one will be justified.

17 "But if, in seeking to be justified in Christ, we Jews[2] find ourselves also among the sinners, doesn't that mean that Christ promotes sin? Absolutely not! 18 If I rebuild what I destroyed, then I really would be a lawbreaker.

19 "For through the law I died to the law[3] so that I might live for God. 20 I have been crucified with Christ and I no longer live, but Christ lives in me. The life I now live in the body, I live by faith in the Son of God, who loved me and gave himself for me. 21 I do not set aside the grace of God, for if righteousness could be gained through the law, Christ died for nothing!"

3 You foolish Galatians![4] Who has bewitched you? Before your very eyes Jesus Christ was clearly portrayed as crucified. 2 I would like to learn just one thing from you: Did you receive the Spirit by observing the law, or by believing what you heard? 3 Are you so foolish? After beginning with the Spirit, are you now trying to finish by human effort[5]? 4 Have you experienced so much in vain—if it really was in vain? 5 Does God give you his Spirit and work miracles among you by your observing the law, or by your believing what you heard[6]? 6 So also Abraham "believed God, and it was credited to him as righteousness."[7]

7 Understand, then, that those who have faith are children of Abraham. 8 Scripture foresaw that God would justify the Gentiles by faith, and announced the gospel in advance to Abraham: "All nations will be blessed through you."[8] 9 So those who rely on faith are blessed along with Abraham, the man of faith.

10 All who rely on observing the law are under a curse, for it is written: "Cursed is everyone who does not continue to do everything written in the Book of the Law."[9] 11 Clearly no one is justified before God by the law,

---

the traditional understanding, especially since the Reformation, which assumes that the believer's faith must be meant. Several recent studies have argued persuasively for a more literal translation: Paul is saying that Christ's faith (or faithfulness) makes possible the faith of believers, which is understood in a communal, not individualistic, sense. See also 3:23–25.

2. "Jews" is not in the text.

3. A puzzling phrase: how did Paul conceive of the law as the means by which he has "died to the law"? Rom. 7:4 says "you also died to the law *through the body of Christ*"; so in the next verse here, Paul says "I have been crucified with Christ." Does Paul think of the law as the instrument of Jesus' execution (cf. John 19:7: "according to the law he ought to die")? In the churches Paul knew, baptism dramatically enacted each believer's incorporation into that death (Rom. 6:3–14).

4. Even the insult would be ineffective if the letter were addressed to congregations from the multicultural southern cities of province Galatia; "You dumb Celts!" would be meaningless to them.

5. Lit., "flesh": perhaps a double entendre, alluding to circumcision, while placing it and all other "works of the law" within the sphere of "flesh," which for Paul is inalterably opposed to "spirit." "Finish" may also be ironic, for the word implies "coming to perfection"; it could satirize the opponents' belief that the law is necessary to "complete" the faith of Gentile Christians.

6. Greek, "hearing (or "message" as in Rom. 10:16 = Isa. 53:1) of faith."

7. Gen. 15:6. Here begins an argument articulated by the ingenious, sometimes obscure, connection of scriptural passages, in the fashion of *midrash aggadah*, the didactic exegesis familiar to us from rabbinic collections of later times.

8. Gen. 12:3.

9. Deut. 27:26. The artificial paragraphing of the translation should not keep us from seeing that vv. 9 and 10 are parallel, and set up the theme of the following verses, how a curse can become a blessing. The most baffling problem with the passage is that the citation from Deut. 27:26 says the exact opposite of what Paul wishes to prove by it; Deut. 28:1 f. in fact pronounces the "blessing" precisely on those who keep the commandments of the law. Possible solutions that have been offered are these: (1) The unstated assumption is that no one in fact can keep all the commandments; therefore, in practice all are cursed. But Paul claimed himself to have kept the law "blamelessly" (Phil. 3:6); here and in Romans the opposite of faith is not failure to keep the law, but the

because "the righteous will live by faith."[1] 12 The law is not based on faith; on the contrary, it says, "Whoever does these things will live by them."[2] 13 Christ redeemed us from the curse of the law by becoming a curse for us, for it is written: "Cursed is everyone who is hung on a pole."[3] 14 He redeemed us in order that the blessing given to Abraham might come to the Gentiles through Christ Jesus, so that by faith we might receive the promise of the Spirit.

15 Brothers and sisters, let me take an example from everyday life. Just as no one can set aside or add to a human covenant[4] that has been duly established, so it is in this case. 16 The promises were spoken to Abraham and to his seed. Scripture does not say "and to seeds," meaning many people, but "and to your seed,"[5] meaning one person, who is Christ. 17 What I mean is this: The law, introduced 430 years later, does not set aside the covenant previously established by God and thus do away with the promise. 18 For if the inheritance depends on the law, then it no longer depends on the promise; but God in his grace gave it to Abraham through a promise.

19 What, then, was the purpose of the law? It was added because of[6] transgressions until the Seed to whom the promise referred had come.[7] The law was given through angels and entrusted to a mediator.[8] 20 A mediator, however, implies more than one party; but God is one.[9]

21 Is the law, therefore, opposed to the promises of God? Absolutely not! For if a law had been given that could impart life, then righteousness would certainly have come by the law.[1] 22 But Scripture has locked up

---

"boasting" and self-righteousness that result in success in keeping it. (2) Paul is emphasizing the "all" of the Deut. text: "all things written in the book" include the prophecies of the Christ and the testimonies to faith which Paul quotes here. (3) Paul is using a familiar technique of midrash in which two verses of scripture produce an impossible dilemma, to be solved by adducing a third text. The dilemma is that, if one fails to "abide by . . . the law," one is cursed by God (Deut. 27: 26), yet if one does abide with the law, one cannot obtain the righteousness that gives life, since that is promised only to faith (Hab. 2:4; Lev. 18:5). The escape from both law and curse is discovered in Deut. 21:23, interpreted by the Christian proclamation of the crucified Messiah.

1. Hab. 2:4 (which will define the theme of the Letter to Romans: Rom. 1:17).
2. Lev. 18:5.
3. Deut. 21:23. The Temple Scroll from Qumran (11QTemple 64.7–12) applies this verse to cases of crucifixion. Some have thought Paul's opponents introduced this verse into the argument, but that would mean they rejected the basic *kerygma* of the Christian movement, namely, the crucified Messiah. It is Paul who introduces the verse, to reduce the legal argument to absurdity.
4. Paul plays on the ambiguity of the Greek word which ordinarily means "will, testament," but occasionally "contract," and in the latter sense was used to translate the Heb. *brit*, "covenant."
5. Paul is of course aware that the word is a collective (see v. 29); to make his christocentric point, he probably depends here on a midrashic tradition that equates "the seed" (from 2 Sam. 7:12, there the seed of David) with the Messiah.
6. "Because of": or perhaps "for the sake of"; cf. Rom. 5:20. The law precipitated transgressions, actualizing and exposing human rebellion against the Creator.
7. "Until [x] should come" is a formula found frequently in Jewish tradition indicating that temporary regulations will be superseded by the advent of some figure of the Endtime: e.g., Ezra 2:63; Neh. 7:65; 1 Macc. 4:46; 14:41; in the Dead Sea Scrolls, 1QS 9:11, "until there shall come the Prophet and the Anointed Ones of Aaron and of Israel" and 4QPB, which interprets Gen. 49:10, "until the Messiah of Righteousness comes, the Branch of David, for to him and to his *seed* has been given the covenant of kingship for his people for everlasting generations." In Talmud and Midrash, disputed judgments are sometimes left unsettled "until Elijah comes." Paul's radicality consists in regarding the whole legal aspect of the Torah as such a temporary ordinance, canceled by the Messiah's advent.
8. That the angels were involved in transmitting the Torah on Sinai is a well-attested Jewish tradition; in the NT, cf. Acts 7:53; Heb. 2:2. The other mediator mentioned here is, of course, Moses.
9. A puzzling sentence. Lit., "The mediator is not of one, but God is one." What Paul wishes to suggest, apparently, is that the promise, given directly by the one God to Abraham, is superior to the law, which came through a multiplicity of mediators. Paul, of course, does not deny that the law came ultimately from God.
1. This terse disclaimer is hardly clear by itself, but see Rom. 7.

everything under the control of sin, so that what was promised, being given through faith in Jesus Christ, might be given to those who believe.

23 Before the coming of this faith, we were held in custody under the law, locked up until the faith that was to come would be revealed. 24 So the law was put in charge of us[2] until Christ came that we might be justified by faith. 25 Now that this faith has come, we are no longer under the supervision of the law.

26 So in Christ Jesus you are all children of God through faith, 27 for all of you who were baptized into Christ have clothed yourselves with Christ. 28 There is neither Jew nor Gentile, neither slave nor free, neither male nor female, for you are all one in Christ Jesus.[3] 29 If you belong to Christ, then you are Abraham's seed, and heirs according to the promise. 4 What I am saying is that as long as heirs are underage they are no different from slaves, although they own the whole estate. 2 They are subject to guardians and trustees until the time set by their fathers. 3 So also, when we were underage, we were in slavery under the elemental spiritual forces of the world.[4] 4 But when the set time had fully come, God sent his Son, born of a woman, born under the law, 5 to redeem those under the law, that we might receive adoption to sonship. 6 Because you are his sons, God sent the Spirit of his Son into our hearts, the Spirit who calls out, "Abba, Father."[5] 7 So you are no longer slaves, but God's children; and since you are his children, he has made you also heirs.

8 Formerly, when you did not know God, you were slaves to those who by nature are not gods. 9 But now that you know God—or rather are known by God—how is it that you are turning back to those weak and miserable forces[6]? Do you wish to be enslaved by them all over again? 10 You are observing special days and months and seasons and years! 11 I fear for you, that somehow I have wasted my efforts on you.

12 I plead with you,[7] brothers and sisters, become like me, for I became like you. You have done me no wrong. 13 As you know, it was because of

2. Greek, "the law was our *paidagōgos*," a slave charged with the general custody, and especially the discipline, of children in a Greek or Roman family between the ages of six and sixteen. The translation "schoolmaster" (KJV) and even the recent "tutor" (NEB) are misleading.

3. Probably quoted from the baptismal liturgy (cf. 1 Cor. 12:13; Col. 3:11); the final pair of terms (lit., "neither male *and* female") makes clear that the underlying notion is the restoration of the lost "image of God" (Gen. 1:26 f.), healing the fundamental divisions of humankind.

4. Lit. "elements of the cosmos," a phrase found also in Col. 2:8, 20. Many commentators, observing the parallel in v. 8, have thought these were conceived as personal beings, perhaps even the stars and planets understood as living beings. The most common use of the phrase is to refer to the four elements, earth, air, fire, and water, of which ancients thought the world was composed, but it is hard to see how that meaning would fit Paul's argument.

5. The Aramaic expression attests the antiquity of this acclamation, which probably occurs at baptism. Cf. Rom. 8:15.

6. "Forces" = "elements" as in v. 3. The contrast between pre-conversion life ("formerly") and life "in Christ" ("but now") is a common pattern in early Christian preaching, and the former life is often described as "not knowing God" or as serving "non-gods" or "idols" (cf. Acts 17:23; 1 Thess. 4:5; 2 Thess. 1:8; 1 Cor. 6:9–11; 12:2; Col. 1:12–21; 2:8–15; Eph. 1:25–2:22; 1 Pet. 1:13–2:10). To "turn" from that world of idols to knowledge of "the true and living God" was a normal way for Jews, including the first Christians (1 Thess. 1:9), to describe conversion. Paul's rhetoric here is thus deliberately shocking: if the Galatian believers heed his opponents and adopt Jewish ritual practices, far from "finishing" their conversion (3:3), they will be "turning again"—in effect "unconverting"—to return to the state of slavery in which they were before.

7. Here Paul, as a careful speaker, "changes his tone"—as he says ironically he wishes he could (v.20)—by describing his first meeting with the Galatians in the same language of endearment that he uses throughout 1 Thessalonians. Rebuking letters, especially those written primarily in an ironic style, were characteristically used between friends whose close relationship had been threatened by some perceived misconduct, and that is the case here. The admonitions that fill the remaining part of this letter (esp. 4:12–20), while still argumentative in part, use more and more the style and language of the parenetic letter of friendship.

an illness that I first preached the gospel to you. 14 Even though my illness was a trial to you, you did not treat me with contempt or scorn.[8] Instead, you welcomed me as if I were an angel of God, as if I were Christ Jesus himself. 15 What has happened to all your joy? I can testify that, if you could have done so, you would have torn out your eyes and given them to me. 16 Have I now become your enemy by telling you the truth?

17 Those people are zealous to win you over, but for no good. What they want is to alienate you from us, so that you may have zeal for them. 18 It is fine to be zealous, provided the purpose is good, and to be so always, not just when I am with you. 19 My dear children, for whom I am again in the pains of childbirth until Christ is formed in you,[9] 20 how I wish I could be with you now and change my tone, because I am perplexed about you!

21 Tell me, you who want to be under the law, are you not aware of what the law says? 22 For it is written that Abraham had two sons, one by the slave woman and the other by the free woman. 23 His son by the slave woman was born as the result of human effort, but his son by the free woman was born as the result of a divine promise.

24 I am taking these things figuratively,[1] for the women represent two covenants. One covenant is from Mount Sinai and bears children who are to be slaves: This is Hagar. 25 Now Hagar stands for Mount Sinai in Arabia[2] and corresponds to the present city of Jerusalem, because she is in slavery with her children. 26 But the Jerusalem that is above is free, and she is our mother. 27 For it is written:

"Be glad, barren woman,
you who never bore a child;
shout for joy and cry aloud,
you who were never in labor;
because more are the children of the desolate woman
than of her who has a husband."[3]

28 Now you,[4] brothers and sisters, like Isaac, are children of promise. 29 At that time the son born by human effort persecuted the son born by the power of the Spirit. It is the same now. 30 But what does Scripture say? "Get rid of the slave woman and her son, for the slave woman's son will never share in the inheritance with the free woman's son." 31 Therefore, brothers and sisters, we are not children of the slave woman, but of the free woman.

---

8. Lit., "You did not spit," a superstitious gesture to ward off the demonic influence thought to emanate from victims of certain diseases, especially epilepsy or insanity. What exactly Paul's illness was (cf. 2 Cor. 12:7–10) it is impossible to say, despite centuries of scholarly and unscholarly speculation.

9. Paul uses the metaphor of his being the "father" or "mother" of his converts elsewhere (1 Cor. 4:15; 2 Cor. 6:13; 1 Thess. 2:7, 11; Phlm. 10), but nowhere else does he develop the metaphor so shockingly as here: he is still in labor pains because the converts have not yet been fully born.

1. Greek *allēgoroumena*, "understood as an allegory." See Part IV for Theodore of Mopsuestia's discussion of vv. 24–31.

2. The text is uncertain, another major group of manuscripts reading, "For Sinai is a mountain in Arabia"; copyists have evidently tried to help out Paul's limping allegory by adding notes. Some critics suggest that the whole sentence may be a gloss. "In Arabia" is perhaps suggested by traditional identification of Ishmael, Hagar's son, as forefather of the Arabs. Identification of Sinai with Jerusalem/Zion is frequent in Jewish tradition. Thus the basic allegory is Hagar = Sinai = Jerusalem = the covenant of law; Sarah = the heavenly Jerusalem = the new covenant of grace.

3. Isa. 54:1 LXX.

4. "We" also has wide manuscript support.

5 It is for freedom that Christ has set us free. Stand firm, then, and do not let yourselves be burdened again by a yoke of slavery. 2 Mark my words! I, Paul, tell you that if you let yourselves be circumcised, Christ will be of no value to you at all. 3 Again I declare to every man who lets himself be circumcised that he is obligated to obey the whole law. 4 You who are trying to be justified by the law have been alienated from Christ; you have fallen away from grace. 5 But by faith we eagerly await through the Spirit the righteousness for which we hope. 6 For in Christ Jesus neither circumcision nor uncircumcision has any value.[5] The only thing that counts is faith expressing itself through love.

7 You were running a good race. Who cut in on you to keep you from obeying the truth? 8 That kind of persuasion does not come from the one who calls you. 9 "A little yeast works through the whole batch of dough."[6] 10 I am confident in the Lord that you will take no other view. The one who is throwing you into confusion will have to pay the penalty, whoever that may be. 11 Brothers and sisters, if I am still preaching circumcision, why am I still being persecuted? In that case the offense of the cross has been abolished. 12 As for those agitators, I wish they would go the whole way and emasculate themselves!

13 You, my brothers and sisters, were called to be free. But do not use your freedom to indulge the sinful nature[7]; rather, serve one another[8] humbly in love. 14 For the entire law is fulfilled in keeping this one command: "Love your neighbor as yourself."[9] 15 If you keep on biting and devouring each other, watch out or you will be destroyed by each other.

16 So I say, walk by the Spirit, and you will not gratify the desires of the sinful nature. 17 For the sinful nature desires what is contrary to the Spirit, and the Spirit what is contrary to the sinful nature. They are in conflict with each other, so that you are not to do whatever you want. 18 But if you are led by the Spirit, you are not under the law.

19 The acts of the sinful nature are obvious: sexual immorality, impurity and debauchery; 20 idolatry and witchcraft; hatred, discord, jealousy, fits of rage, selfish ambition, dissensions, factions 21 and envy; drunkenness, orgies, and the like.[1] I warn you, as I did before, that those who live like this will not inherit the kingdom of God.

22 But the fruit of the Spirit is love, joy, peace, patience, kindness, goodness, faithfulness, 23 gentleness and self-control. Against such things there is no law. 24 Those who belong to Christ Jesus have crucified the sinful nature with its passions and desires. 25 Since we live by the Spirit,

---

5. Cf. 6:15; 1 Cor. 7:19.
6. Probably a proverbial saying quoted by Paul here and in 1 Cor. 5:6.
7. Lit. "flesh," and so also in the following verses. The exhortations that follow are largely traditional and are not grounds for assuming a "libertine" tendency among the Galatians. The use of freedom as license was a danger logically inherent in Paul's position, which he must defend against such a misinterpretation (cf. Rom. 6).
8. For the free person taking on servitude out of love for the other, compare Paul's own example as he presents it in 1 Cor. 9:19.
9. The use of this sentence from Lev. 19:18 to sum up the demands of the law (Rom. 13:9; Matt. 5:43; 22:39; Mark 12:31; Luke 10:27; James 2:8) was commonplace in Judaism as well as early Christianity.
1. Catalogues of virtues (vv. 22 f.) and vices (vv. 19–21) were the simplest of the standard forms of moral teaching in the Greco-Roman world, including Judaism. They were sometimes placed into a dualistic framework, "the way of light" and "the way of darkness" (Qumran, the *Didache*); similarly, here Paul associates them with "flesh" and "Spirit." Some manuscripts add "murder" (*phonoi*) after "envy" (*phthonoi*) in v. 21.

let us keep in step with the Spirit. 26 Let us not become conceited, provoking and envying each other.

6 Brothers and sisters, if someone is caught in a sin, you who live by the Spirit should restore that person gently. But watch yourselves, or you also may be tempted. 2 Carry each other's burdens, and in this way you will fulfill the law of Christ.[2] 3 If any of you think you are something when you are nothing, you deceive yourselves. 4 Each of you should test your own actions. Then you can take pride in yourself, without comparing yourself to somebody else, 5 for each of you should carry your own load. 6 Nevertheless, those who receive instruction in the word should share all good things with their instructor.

7 Do not be deceived: God cannot be mocked. People reap what they sow. 8 Those who sow to please their sinful nature, from that nature will reap destruction; those who sow to please the Spirit, from the Spirit will reap eternal life. 9 Let us not become weary in doing good, for at the proper time we will reap a harvest if we do not give up. 10 Therefore, as we have opportunity, let us do good to all people, especially to those who belong to the family of believers.

11 See what large letters I use as I write to you with my own hand![3]

12 Those who want to impress others by means of the flesh are trying to compel you to be circumcised. The only reason they do this is to avoid being persecuted for the cross of Christ. 13 Not even those who are circumcised keep the law, yet they want you to be circumcised that they may boast about your circumcision in the flesh. 14 May I never boast except in the cross of our Lord Jesus Christ, through which[4] the world has been crucified to me, and I to the world. 15 Neither circumcision nor uncircumcision means anything; what counts is the new creation.[5] 16 Peace and mercy to all who follow this rule—to the Israel of God.[6]

17 From now on, let no one cause me trouble, for I bear on my body the marks of Jesus.[7]

18 The grace of our Lord Jesus Christ be with your spirit, brothers and sisters. Amen.

2. "The law of Christ": a startling phrase after Paul's polemic against the law, but cf. Rom. 8:2; 1 Cor. 9:21. It is perhaps a deliberate oxymoron, for in Paul's sense "the law of Christ" does not consist of legislation at all.
3. Letters were ordinarily dictated. A letter written with the sender's own hand was appreciated as a token of special affection. Cf. 1 Cor. 16:21; Col. 4:18; and the notes on Rom. 16:22 and 2 Thess. 3:17.
4. Or, "through whom."
5. Compare and contrast 1 Cor. 7:19; on the new creation, cf. 2 Cor. 5:17.
6. To invoke peace and mercy upon Israel is traditional in many forms of Jewish prayer (e.g., Ps. 125:5; 128:6; Ps. Sol. 11:9; and the last of the benedictions in the daily prayer). Paul's applying this prayer simultaneously to "the Israel of God" and to "all who follow this rule [of the New Creation]" is both grammatically ambiguous (the Greek text contains an "and," which can either distinguish the two or, more plausibly, as translated here, identify them) and profoundly charged by the issues addressed in the letter. Here he leaves his Galatian audience to work out the relationship; he himself will return more carefully to the question in Romans.
7. "The marks of Jesus": not reproductions of the wounds of crucifixion, as in medieval legends of St. Francis and others—though the Greek word stigmata here provides the usual term for those—but scars received in the rigors of his mission (cf. 2 Cor. 4:8–12; 11:24–28), perhaps regarded as the "brands" identifying him as "Christ's slave."

THE FIRST LETTER TO THE CORINTHIANS
(53–55)

Corinth was located on the isthmus between Attica and the Peloponnesus. Its site, with two harbors, Cenchreae on the Saronian Gulf to the east, Lechaeon on the Gulf of Corinth to the north, assured commercial success. The Romans destroyed it in 146 BCE, during their campaign against the Achaean League, but in 44 BCE Julius Caesar refounded it as a Roman colony. It grew quickly to prominence again. In 27 BCE it was made the capital of the province of Achaia, which in 44 CE became a proconsular "province of the Roman people." The geographer Strabo, writing at the end of the first century BCE, said that the original colonists were mainly freedmen from Italy (*Geog.* 8.6.23), but the commercial opportunities of the new colony soon brought many immigrants of all sorts, including apparently a large community of Jews, although the latter have left little evidence of their existence in either material or literary remains. Thus, while the public face of the colony was Roman in language, government, and architecture, there was a cosmopolitan substructure, revealed for example in the use of Greek that suddenly blossomed in public inscriptions in the time of Hadrian. The circumstances of the refounding, and the prominence of former slaves among the first colonists, made for a kind of social mobility rare in ancient towns. The monuments and inscriptions that stand as markers for the ambitions and successes of the community leaders in Corinth rarely mention ancestors; the top ranks of Corinthian society were newly minted. It is not surprising that questions of status are prominent in Paul's letter.

The church was founded by Paul, probably around 51 CE (Acts 18:1–11). After his initial stay there he carried on an extended correspondence with the Corinthian Christians, writing a total of at least four and possibly five, six, or even seven letters to them (1 Cor. 5:9; 2 Cor. 2:3 f.); visited them himself twice more; sent personal representatives more than once; and received delegations and informal reports from them. Our First Corinthians follows up on an earlier letter, lost early on, which had not had the effects Paul wanted (1 Cor. 5:9–11). The extant letter was written near the end of Paul's stay in Ephesus (16:8; cf. Acts 19) in the spring probably of the year 54 or 55. It is a response to reports which have come to Paul by two means: a letter, brought by an official delegation, Stephanas, Fortunatus, and Achaicus (16:17; cf. 7:1) and information from "Chloe's household" (1:11), otherwise unknown. Although Timothy is already en route overland to Corinth (Paul expects the letter, presumably carried by the returning Stephanas group, to arrive by sea before he does: 4:17; 16:10f.; cf. Acts 19:22), and Paul himself expects to come soon, the problems are urgent enough to require immediate intervention.

The problems are diverse. Paul has heard that there are "factions" or "quarrels" in the church, which stem from invidious comparisons among apostles, Paul, Apollos, and Peter (1:12), some taking special pride in the apostle who baptized them or in whose name they were baptized (vv. 13–17). The Corinthians prize "wisdom and eloquence"—the displays of rhetoric, often laced with stock topics from popular moral philosophy, that made pop stars of many orators. Some Corinthian Christians challenge Paul's authority—apparently they think him lacking in this "wisdom"—and doubt that this unstable missionary will ever be seen again (4:18 f; cf. 16:5–7). There are also less subtle problems. A flagrant case of incest in the congregation (chap. 5) produces "boasting" over this violation of ordinary taboos (5:2, 6). Some Christians are suing one another in pagan courts (6:18). Others defend their patronage of the once-famous Corinthian brothels with a slogan that sounds superficially Pauline (6:9–20). Yet others reject sex altogether (chap. 7). The liberating knowledge, taught by Paul himself, that the pagan gods are not real (cf. 1 Thess. 1:9; Gal. 4:8) leads some to the conviction that they are free to participate in social occasions in pagan shrines or to eat meat "sacrificed to idols"; others are scandalized by this practice (chaps. 8–10). The role of women who prophesy in the assemblies is a matter of contention (11:2–16; 14:34–36), and disorder infects the celebration of the Lord's Supper (11:17–34). Charismatic phenomena—especially ecstatic speech (*glossolalia*)—threaten to divide the community (chaps. 12–14). And some do not believe in the resurrection of the dead (chap. 15).

Modern scholars have sought with great diligence and ingenuity to find some underlying ideology that would explain all the problems Paul takes up in this letter: perhaps a sacramental theology shared with the other initiatory cults that flourished in Corinth as in other eastern cities in the Roman era; or perhaps a kind of proto-Gnosticism, based on myths of creation that inverted the Biblical order of reality and elevated the spiritual in opposition to everything physical; or perhaps a "realized eschatology," radicalizing Paul's own apocalyptic preaching, in which the spirit-endowed initiates could already live "as the angels in heaven," disregarding all social and moral conventions and taboos.

More recently scholars have tended instead to see the problems Paul addresses as the sorts of conflicts that would naturally emerge as a radical messianic sect encountered the ordinary structures of social existence in an eastern Roman colony—the expectations of household order, of social rank and power, of women and men, free persons and slaves, patrons and clients, of differing understandings of power, honor, and social obligation. The theological continuities found in the letter, in this view, are more likely to be Paul's own ad hoc constructions, freely melding biblical examples, personal models from his own and other apostles' lives, Jewish traditions of interpretation, and early Christian formulas, traditions, and ritual practices—all in a framework adapted from Greco-Roman rhetoric and philosophy.

Although the Christian communities in Corinth are several in number, meeting ordinarily in the houses of individual patrons, Paul addresses the letter to the single "*ekklēsia* of God that is in Corinth" (1:2). In everyday speech, *ekklēsia* was a political term (see note 2 on 1 Thess. 1:1), and there are many echoes of political rhetoric in this letter. Paul addresses the "town meeting of God" in Corinth in the way a philosophical speaker might address the assembled voting citizens of a democratic Greek polis. Factions were always the great internal danger to the life of the city, and some of the most treasured speeches from the great orators of Paul's age, like Dio Chrysostom of Prusa, are those that celebrate the concord (*homonoia*) that makes truly civilized life possible and that warn against the discord that factions bring. Paul's letter in its main outlines closely resembles such a speech. It uses some of the favorite metaphors of the orators—the community as a well-founded building, the community as a body in which all the "members" work together in harmony—and many of the typical turns of phrase.

Yet that very "eloquence or human wisdom" (2:5) that Paul uses so adroitly in seeking to address the disorder he hears reported of his Corinthian congregations is, from another angle, a part of the problem, one of the means that served that status-seeking "love of honor" that was so strong in Greco-Roman society and visibly manifest in the daily life of the Corinthian colony. Paul purports to speak of a different kind of wisdom, requiring a different eloquence (2:1–5). So he strives here to find a form of rhetoric, a new range of metaphors that will be adequate to express what he calls "the message of the cross"—in Greek, "the *logos* of the cross," that is, the logic and rational structure not only of an appropriate rhetoric but of a revised sense of reality, of what Paul had called in his Letter to the Galatians "a new creation" (Gal. 6:15; cf. 2 Cor. 5:17).

The letter opens with a formal prescript, in Paul's usual expansive style (1: 1–3), followed by a thanksgiving (1:4–9). There follows immediately an appeal for unity and avoidance of factions (1:10), which serves as the thesis for the argument of the entire letter. Because chapter 7 begins, "Now for the matters you wrote about," some commentators have assumed that in the earlier chapters Paul takes up problems reported by Chloe's household, while treating in the later chapters the matters raised in the letter brought by Stephanas, Fortunatus, and Achaicus, but that is not necessarily the case. Paul chooses the sequence to construct a coherent, if complex, argument. In 1:11–4:21 he reflects on the rivalry between adherents of individual apostles—with himself and Apollos as the primary examples (chaps. 3–4; note esp. 4:6 and the note there)—in the light of what he calls "the *logos* of the cross" (1:18). Chapters 5–7 deal with the purity of the community, beginning with correction of a misunderstanding of his earlier letter, dealing with both sexual matters (5:1–13; 6:12–7:40) and lawsuits (chap. 6). The question of eating meat and its association with pagan sacrifices provokes the larger discussion, in 8:1–11:1, of the difficult balance between freedom—the freedom enjoyed by those possessing knowledge and authority and the unique freedom that is central to Paul's preaching of the gospel—and responsibility for "building up" the community, including those members of the community who are "weak" in the eyes of the ones who take pride in their knowledge and status. The gatherings of the *ekklēsia* for worship expose several sources of division, treated in 11:2–14: 40: the behavior and dress of women who are prophesying (11:2–16); divisions between richer and poorer members at the Lord's Supper (11:17–34); and different kinds of "spiritual gifts" (*charismata*, 12:1–14:40). Chapter 15 discusses the resurrection of the dead. Chapter 16 includes instructions for the collection for Jerusalem (vv. 1–4), travel plans (vv. 5–12), a summary appeal (vv. 13–14) with special commendation for Stephanas and thanks for the delegation he led (vv. 15–18), and epistolary greetings (vv. 19–20). Paul adds a greeting in his own handwriting (v. 21) and concludes with a formal anathema and the Aramaic phrase inviting the Lord's coming, both probably from the eucharistic liturgy, and a benediction (vv. 22–24).

1 Corinthians

1 Paul, called to be an apostle of Christ Jesus by the will of God, and our brother Sosthenes,[1]

2 To the church of God in Corinth,[2] to those sanctified in Christ Jesus and called to be his holy people, together with all those everywhere who call on the name of our Lord Jesus Christ—their Lord and ours:

3 Grace and peace to you from God our Father and the Lord Jesus Christ.

4 I always thank my God for you because of his grace given you in Christ Jesus. 5 For in him you have been enriched in every way—with all kinds of speech and with all knowledge— 6 God thus confirming our testimony

---

1. Acts 18:17 mentions a Sosthenes, president of the synagogue in Corinth, who, after opposing Paul before the proconsul, was beaten for his trouble. Some commentators, assuming that Paul is referring to the same man here, have speculated about Sosthenes' conversion, but that is by no means certain.
2. For the political term *ekklēsia*, translated "church," see note on 1 Thess. 1:1. Here it collectively designates several groups of believers who met in the homes of various members (see 1 Cor. 16: 19 and note on Rom. 16:5), though perhaps occasionally in one place (Rom. 16:23). Paul's use of the singular (contrast the plural in Gal. 1:2) may be significant in view of the central theme of the letter (see the introduction above).

about Christ among you. 7 Therefore you do not lack any spiritual gift as you eagerly wait for our Lord Jesus Christ to be revealed. 8 He will also keep you firm to the end, so that you will be blameless on the day of our Lord Jesus Christ. 9 God is faithful, who has called you into fellowship with his Son, Jesus Christ our Lord.[3]

10 I appeal to you,[4] brothers and sisters, in the name of our Lord Jesus Christ, that all of you agree with one another in what you say and that there be no divisions[5] among you, but that you be perfectly united in mind and thought. 11 My brothers and sisters, some from Chloe's household[6] have informed me that there are quarrels[7] among you. 12 What I mean is this: One of you says, "I follow Paul"; another, "I follow Apollos"; another, "I follow Cephas"; still another, "I follow Christ."[8]

13 Is Christ divided?[9] Was Paul crucified for you? Were you baptized into the name of Paul? 14 I thank God that I did not baptize any of you except Crispus and Gaius, 15 so no one can say that you were baptized into my name. 16 (Yes, I also baptized the household of Stephanas;[1] beyond that, I don't remember if I baptized anyone else.) 17 For Christ did not send me to baptize, but to preach the gospel—not with wisdom and eloquence,[2] lest the cross of Christ be emptied of its power.

18 For the message of the cross is foolishness to those who are perishing, but to us who are being saved it is the power of God. 19 For it is written:

"I will destroy the wisdom of the wise;
the intelligence of the intelligent I will frustrate."[3]

3. The thanksgiving (vv. 4–9), brief as it is, nevertheless alludes to a number of the themes of the letter: "enriched" (v. 5) is used sarcastically in 4:8; *logos* and *gnōsis* (v. 5) are the subject of chaps. 1–4; also 8:1, 7, 10, 11; cf. 12:8; 13:2; "spiritual gifts" (*charismata*, v. 7): chaps. 12–14; cf. 7:7; the eschatological emphasis (v. 7), and especially the implication that the "Day of our Lord" (v. 8) will render present human judgments invalid, forms the underlying tension of the entire letter, explicitly 3:10–17; 4:1–5, reaching its climax in chap. 15; "fellowship" (*koinōnia*, v. 9) suggests Paul's emphasis on the harmony and unity of the community.
4. This verse states the thesis of the entire letter. The form, "I appeal to you," was commonly used in friendly letters of moral admonition (*parainesis*; see the introduction to 1 Thessalonians), but also in official letters in which commands, e.g., by a Hellenistic ruler to a subject city, could thus be stated with deliberate courtesy (cf. Phlm. 8–10). It occurs frequently in NT letters: see esp. 1 Thess. 4:10; 5:14; Rom. 12:1; 15:30; 16:17. The content of the present appeal uses stock phrases of deliberative speeches urging concord (see introduction above): "to say the same thing," "no factions," "the same mind," "the same thought."
5. The "divisions" (*schismata*, from the Greek verb "to tear or split") are not likely organized "parties," as some commentators since the nineteenth century have thought.
6. Chloe is otherwise unknown. Her household, most likely in Corinth, would include slaves and freedpersons (former slaves, now clients), who may be traveling on some business of their mistress or patroness. They are evidently Christians, and the household obviously known to the other Christians of Corinth, but Chloe herself may or may not be a Christian (see the note on Rom. 16: 11).
7. "Quarrels" may be too weak a translation; the Greek *eris* is the opposite of *homonoia*, "concord," and in Homer and Hesiod even the name of a goddess who provokes people to war and domestic strife.
8. There is no need to assume that the factions in the Corinthian house churches actually use the slogans Paul attributes to them here, or even that there are precisely four factions. Paul may be using the common rhetorical ploy of speech-in-character to satirize the implication of their dissensions. In the remainder of the first section of the letter (chaps. 1–4) only the rivalry between adherents of Paul and Apollos figures.
9. By suggesting that the dissensions among his addressees are "dividing" Christ Paul may hint of the trope he will use in chap. 12, the community as Christ's body.
1. Stephanas, one of the delegates from Corinth, was present in Ephesus as Paul wrote (16:15–18); did he remind Paul of the omission while the latter was dictating?
2. "Wisdom and eloquence" (lit. "wisdom of speech" or "rhetorical wisdom," *sophia logou*) are highly valued in Greco-Roman society, signs of sophistication and superior status. Here Paul begins his ironic, even sarcastic, inversion of those values by insisting that the gospel he was commissioned to preach entails a different *logos* and a different wisdom (1:18–4:21).
3. Isa. 29:14.

20 Where are the wise? Where is the teacher of the law? Where is the philosopher of this age? Has not God made foolish the wisdom of the world? 21 For since in the wisdom of God the world through its wisdom did not know him, God was pleased through the foolishness of what was preached to save those who believe. 22 Jews demand signs and Greeks look for wisdom, 23 but we preach Christ crucified: a stumbling block to Jews and foolishness to Gentiles, 24 but to those whom God has called, both Jews and Greeks, Christ the power of God and the wisdom of God. 25 For the foolishness of God is wiser than human wisdom, and the weakness of God is stronger than human strength.[4]

26 Brothers and sisters, think of what you were when you were called. Not many of you were wise by human standards; not many were influential; not many were of noble birth. 27 But God chose the foolish things of the world to shame the wise; God chose the weak things of the world to shame the strong. 28 God chose the lowly things of this world and the despised things—and the things that are not—to nullify the things that are, 29 so that no one may boast before him. 30 It is because of him that you are in Christ Jesus, who has become for us wisdom from God—that is, our righteousness, holiness and redemption. 31 Therefore, as it is written: "Let those who boast boast in the Lord."[5]

2 And so it was with me, brothers and sisters. When I came to you, I did not come with eloquence or human wisdom as I proclaimed to you the testimony[6] about God. 2 For I resolved to know nothing while I was with you except Jesus Christ and him crucified. 3 I came to you in weakness with great fear and trembling. 4 My message and my preaching were not with wise and persuasive words, but with a demonstration of the Spirit's power,[7] 5 so that your faith might not rest on human wisdom, but on God's power.

6 We do, however, speak a message of wisdom among the mature,[8] but not the wisdom of this age or of the rulers of this age,[9] who are coming to

4. Vv 18–25 are highly rhetorical; note the antithetic parallelism (18, 22–25) and the climactic series of four questions (20). The antithesis between Jews and Greeks—a frequent pairing in Paul's letters—set both on the side of those who are unable to penetrate the oxymoron of God's "foolish" wisdom and "weak" power, over against "those whom God has called," transcending these ethnic identities (23 f.) by a new identity. "Calling" has been emphasized already in 1:1, 2, and now will be treated with some irony in Paul's following reminders of how that "calling" took place (1:26–4:21). See also 7:17–24.

5. Vv. 26–29 are a superb example of Paul's fondness of parallelism. The whole section vv. 26–31 satirizes the status-seeking that Paul discerns behind the church's factionalism. The quotation is from Jer. 9:24.

6. "Testimony" (martyrion): "mystery" or "secret" (mysterion) is also very strongly attested; cf. v. 7. Having reminded the Corinthian status-seekers that they were "nothing" in the world's eyes before God "called" them, Paul now uses his own "weakness" and lack of "eloquence or human wisdom" as an example of the paradox of God's power.

7. How God's Spirit and power were demonstrable is one of the points of contention between Paul and those Corinthian Christians who prided themselves in their "spiritual gifts"; here, however, he speaks quite conventionally and may think of the miracles by which apostles and other "divine men" won attention (2 Cor. 12:12; Rom. 15:19; cf. 1 Thess. 1:5).

8. Or, "perfect." The word (teleios) could refer to one who had been "initiated" in the mysteries; also metaphorically for one who was "initiated" into the higher speculations of philosophy. For Philo, for example, the "sage" who had won virtue by self-discipline, mastered the rational means of acquiring truth, and gone on to ecstatic vision became teleios, "neither God nor man, but . . . on the borderline between" the two (On Dreams, ii. 234). The primary meaning of the word for Paul here, however, is simply "adult," because he wants to show the people he is admonishing that their behavior reveals them not as "perfected" "spirituals," but as quite "fleshly" "babies" (3:1–4).

9. Commentators have disagreed whether the "rulers of this age" should be understood as political rulers or as demonic powers: the context speaks for the latter; cf. the "god of this age" (2 Cor. 4:4).

nothing. 7 No, we declare God's wisdom, a mystery that has been hidden and that God destined for our glory before time began.[1] 8 None of the rulers of this age understood it, for if they had, they would not have crucified the Lord of glory. 9 However, as it is written:

"What no eye has seen,

what no ear has heard,

and what no human mind has conceived—

these things God has prepared for those who love him"—[2]

10 for God has revealed them to us by his Spirit.

The Spirit searches all things, even the deep things of God. 11 For who knows a person's thoughts except that person's own spirit within? In the same way no one knows the thoughts of God except the Spirit of God. 12 We have not received the spirit of the world but the Spirit who is from God, that we may understand what God has freely given us. 13 This is what we speak, not in words taught us by human wisdom but in words taught by the Spirit, explaining spiritual realities with Spirit-taught words. 14 The person without the Spirit[3] does not accept the things that come from the Spirit of God but considers them foolishness, and cannot understand them because they are discerned only through the Spirit. 15 The person with the Spirit makes judgments about all things, but such a person is not subject to merely human judgments, 16 for,

"Who has known the mind of the Lord

so as to instruct him?"[4]

But we have the mind of Christ. Mindset that does not seek self PROMOtion

3 Brothers and sisters, I could not address you as spiritual but as worldly—mere infants in Christ. 2 I gave you milk, not solid food, for you were not yet ready for it. Indeed, you are still not ready. 3 You are still worldly. For since there is jealousy and quarreling among you, are you not worldly? Are you not acting like mere human beings?[5] 4 For when one says, "I follow Paul," and another, "I follow Apollos," are you not mere human beings?

5 What, after all, is Apollos?[6] And what is Paul? Only servants, through whom you came to believe—as the Lord has assigned to each his task. 6 I planted the seed, Apollos watered it, but God has been making it grow. 7 So neither the one who plants nor the one who waters is anything, but only God, who makes things grow. 8 The one who plants and the one who waters have one purpose, and they will each be rewarded according to their

---

1. The pattern "formerly hidden/now revealed" was evidently a regular form of preaching in the Pauline school; cf. Rom. 16:25 f.; Col. 1:26 f.; Eph. 3:4 f., 9 f.: similarly 2 Tim. 1:9 f.; Tit. 1:2 f.; 1 Pet. 1:20 f.

2. The source of this quotation cannot be identified; Origen found it in an "Apocalypse of Elijah" which has not survived.

3. "Person without the Spirit": *psychikos*, i.e., having (only) "soul," *psychē*. Three classes of persons are distinguished: the "spirituals" (*pneumatikoi*), the "souled" (*psychikoi*), and the "fleshly" (*sarkikoi, sarkinoi,* translated here "worldly"). The "spirituals" are identical with the "perfect." The same division appears in some later Christian Gnostic systems, perhaps dependent on this passage; Paul uses it here sarcastically.

4. Isa. 40:13, LXX.

5. The simple word "human beings" (*anthrōpoi*) mocks the elitism expressed in the spiritual/souled/fleshly divisions. 3:1–4 forms a classic example of Paul's satire. In 2:6–16 Paul seems to accept the position of the "spirituals," that an apostle is one who imparts an esoteric "wisdom," accessible only to "the perfect." But for him that "hidden" wisdom is identical with the public proclamation, "Christ and him crucified." Therefore the mundane fact of their divisions and arguments shows that they are not "spirituals" but only "people of flesh," not "perfect" (i.e., "adults"), but only "babes."

6. On Apollos' mission to Corinth see Acts 18:24–28. Note that of the factions mentioned in 1:12 only that of Apollos is singled out here, and that not in a hostile fashion. It is doubtful whether Cephas = Peter ever actually visited Corinth.

own labor. 9 For we are God's co-workers; you are God's field, God's building.

10 By the grace God has given me, I laid a foundation as a wise builder, and someone else is building on it. But each one should build with care. 11 For no one can lay any foundation other than the one already laid, which is Jesus Christ. 12 If anyone builds on this foundation using gold, silver, costly stones, wood, hay or straw, 13 their work will be shown for what it is, because the Day[7] will bring it to light. It will be revealed with fire, and the fire will test the quality of each person's work. 14 If what has been built survives, the builder will receive a reward. 15 If it is burned up, the builder will suffer loss but yet will be saved—even though only as one escaping through the flames.

16 Don't you know that you yourselves are God's temple[8] and that God's Spirit dwells in your midst? 17 If anyone destroys God's temple, God will destroy that person;[9] for God's temple is sacred, and you together are that temple.

18 Do not deceive yourselves. If any of you think you are wise by the standards of this age, you should become "fools" so that you may become wise. 19 For the wisdom of this world is foolishness in God's sight. As it is written: "He catches the wise in their craftiness"[1]; 20 and again, "The Lord knows that the thoughts of the wise are futile."[2] 21 So then, no more boasting about human leaders! All things are yours, 22 whether Paul or Apollos or Cephas or the world or life or death or the present or the future—all are yours, 23 and you are of Christ, and Christ is of God.[3]

4 This, then, is how you ought to regard us: as servants of Christ and as those entrusted with the mysteries God has revealed.[4] 2 Now it is required that those who have been given a trust must prove faithful. 3 I care very little if I am judged by you or by any human court; indeed, I do not even judge myself. 4 My conscience is clear, but that does not make me innocent. It is the Lord who judges me. 5 Therefore judge nothing before the appointed time; wait till the Lord comes. He will bring to light what is hidden in darkness and will expose the motives of people's hearts. At that time each will receive their praise from God.

6 Now, brothers and sisters, I have applied these things to myself and

7. I.e., "the day of the Lord," see 1:8. A biblical notion (e.g. Amos 5:18–20; Joel 2:11; Zeph. 1:7–2:3; Isa. 13:6; Ezek. 13:5; 30:2–3), often transferred by early Christians to Jesus, confessed as "Lord," in his capacity as judge at the end-time.
8. In Hellenistic popular philosophy the notion that the individual person is a shrine within which a divine being, i.e., the rational self, dwells is a commonplace (e.g., Epictetus, *Diss.* 2.8.14); Philo applies this cliché to the boy Moses (*Mos.* 1.27). For Paul, however, it is not the individual but the community that is the new temple—an idea that was important also in the sect of the Dead Sea Scrolls. The metaphor of the building (vv. 10–15) is thus particularized into a challenge to the addressees ("don't you know") to act like that sacred edifice which they have been called to be.
9. Sayings in this form ("if any one does *x*, *x* will be done to him") occur several places in early Christian literature (e.g., 1 Cor. 14:38; 2 Cor. 9:6; Rom. 2:12; Matt. 5:19; 6:14 f.; 10:32 f.; Mark 4:24 f.; 8:38; Rev. 22:18). The style is that of ancient sacral law (cf. Gen. 9:6; Deut. 28:1, 15; Aeschylus, *Choephoroe* 312 f.), with an eschatological setting.
1. Job 5:13.
2. Ps. 94:11.
3. Vv. 18–23 are a reprise of the themes introduced in 1:10–25; thus chaps. 1–3 form a rhetorical "circle" or ring-composition. Note also the carefully stylized ending, vv. 21–23. Chap. 4 pointedly draws out the lessons for the addressees before Paul turns, in chap. 5, to the first of the special issues in Corinth.
4. The words *hypēretēs* and *oikonomos*, translated "servants" and "those entrusted," are common titles in civil, cultic, and business bureaucracies, often rendered "assistant" or "secretary" and "manager."

Apollos for your benefit,[5] so that you may learn from us the meaning of the saying, "Do not go beyond what is written."[6] Then you will not be puffed up in being a follower of one of us over against the other. 7 For who makes you different from anyone else? What do you have that you did not receive? And if you did receive it, why do you boast as though you did not?

8 Already you have all you want! Already you have become rich! You have begun to reign[7]—and that without us! How I wish that you really had begun to reign so that we also might reign with you! 9 For it seems to me that God has put us apostles on display at the end of the procession, like those condemned to die in the arena. We have been made a spectacle to the whole universe, to angels as well as to human beings. 10 We are fools for Christ, but you are so wise in Christ! We are weak, but you are strong! You are honored, we are dishonored! 11 To this very hour we go hungry and thirsty, we are in rags, we are brutally treated, we are homeless. 12 We work hard with our own hands. When we are cursed, we bless; when we are persecuted, we endure it; 13 when we are slandered, we answer kindly. We have become the scum of the earth, the garbage of the world—right up to this moment.

14 I am writing this not to shame you but to warn you as my dear children.[8] 15 Even if you had ten thousand guardians in Christ, you do not have many fathers, for in Christ Jesus I became your father through the gospel. 16 Therefore I urge you to imitate me. 17 For this reason I have sent to you Timothy, my son whom I love, who is faithful in the Lord. He will remind you of my way of life in Christ Jesus, which agrees with what I teach everywhere in every church.

18 Some of you have become arrogant, as if I were not coming to you. 19 But I will come to you very soon, if the Lord is willing, and then I will find out not only how these arrogant people are talking, but what power they have. 20 For the kingdom of God is not a matter of talk but of power. 21 What do you prefer? Shall I come to you with a rod of discipline, or shall I come in love and with a gentle spirit?

5. The verb translated "applied" normally means "to transform," perhaps "to speak figuratively." In rhetoric, it pointed to the figure called "covert allusion" by which orators masked their sharp criticisms through irony and metaphor in order to avoid offence or to appeal to shame rather than fear. By explicitly naming what he has been doing—something rhetoricians warn against—Paul makes his argument transparent and puts the addressees, especially the proud lovers of rhetoric, on the spot.

6. A proverb from the way children were taught to write, following carefully an outline traced by their teachers. A modern parallel, in a non-progressive preschool, would be "Don't color outside the lines." Paul is continuing to satirize the childishness of his audience while urging that they follow the real example of those apostles they claim to idolize.

7. It was a commonplace in popular philosophy, especially in Stoicism, that "only the wise person is truly a king." True wealth, also, was only attained by the wise. With his repeated "already," Paul not only exposes the absence of moral progress in these would-be sages who yet remain children, but also signals their failure to understand the importance of the future fulfillment that Christians must await. This leads to the rhetorical climax in which Paul sarcastically contrasts their exalted self-image (vv. 7f.) with the facts of the apostle's life (vv. 9–13). The latter verses are in the form of a "catalogue of circumstances," which appears very often in ancient rhetoric in depictions of the ideal sage. Circumstances, usually hardships, as here, were thought to test the virtue of a person, exposing sham wisdom. Often philosophers attribute their ability to stand firm in the face of hardships to the power of the divine which they served, and so does Paul, though of course his concept of God's power, as he has emphasized in 1:18–25, is quite different from that common in popular philosophy. Paul makes frequent use of this rhetorical pattern: see also 2 Cor. 4:8–9; 6:4–10; 11:23–28; 12:10; Rom. 8:35–39; Phil. 4:11f.

8. Paul's too-transparent denial that he is "writing . . . to shame you," when obviously that is exactly what he is doing, permits him now the turn the childhood metaphor back to the relation of tender affection that is typical of friendly admonitions in ancient moral discourse, as we have seen at length in 1 Thessalonians.

5 It is actually reported that there is sexual immorality among you, and of a kind that even pagans do not tolerate: A man has his father's wife.[9] 2 And you are proud! Shouldn't you rather have gone into mourning and have put out of your fellowship the man who has been doing this? 3 For my part, even though I am not physically present, I am with you in spirit. As one who is present with you in this way, I have already passed judgment in the name of our Lord Jesus on the one who has been doing this. 4 So when you are assembled and I am with you in spirit, and the power of our Lord Jesus is present, 5 hand this man over to Satan for the destruction of the sinful nature so that his spirit may be saved on the day of the Lord.[1]

6 Your boasting is not good. Don't you know that a little yeast leavens the whole batch of dough? 7 Get rid of the old yeast, so that you may be a new unleavened batch—as you really are. For Christ, our Passover lamb, has been sacrificed.[2] 8 Therefore let us keep the Festival, not with the old bread leavened with malice and wickedness, but with the unleavened bread of sincerity and truth.

9 I wrote to you in my letter[3] not to associate with sexually immoral people— 10 not at all meaning the people of this world who are immoral, or the greedy and swindlers, or idolaters. In that case you would have to leave this world. 11 But now I am writing to you that you must not associate with any who claim to be fellow believers[4] but are sexually immoral or greedy, idolaters or slanderers, drunkards or swindlers. With such persons do not even eat.

12 What business is it of mine to judge those outside the church? Are you not to judge those inside? 13 God will judge those outside. "Expel the wicked person from among you."[5]

6 If any of you has a dispute with another, do you dare to take it before the ungodly[6] for judgment instead of before the Lord's people? 2 Or do you not know that the Lord's people will judge the world?[7] And if you are to judge the world, are you not competent to judge trivial cases? 3 Do you not know that we will judge angels? How much more the things of this life! 4 Therefore, if you have disputes about such matters, do you ask for a ruling from those whose way of life is scorned in the church? 5 I say this to shame you. Is it possible that there is nobody among you wise enough to judge a dispute between believers? 6 But instead, one brother goes to law against another—and this in front of unbelievers!

7 The very fact that you have lawsuits among you means you have been completely defeated already. Why not rather be wronged? Why not rather

9. I.e., his stepmother; even if the father is dead, the relationship is forbidden by both Roman and Jewish law (see Lev. 18:8).
1. We cannot be sure what exactly is meant by "destruction of the sinful nature [lit., flesh]," but the most obvious meaning would be the death of the offender. It is not likely that this is the same man mentioned in 2 Cor. 2:5–11.
2. The metaphor is drawn from the Jewish custom that the household must be purged of every trace of leaven before Passover. Although Jesus can be metaphorically identified with a sacrificial lamb elsewhere in the NT (Rev. 5:6, 12; 1 Pet. 1:19), only here is he explicitly called "our Passover lamb" (*pascha*), though that identification may be implied by the chronology of the passion narrative in the Fourth Gospel.
3. This letter is lost; attempts to identify part of it with 2 Cor. 6:14–7:1 are not persuasive.
4. Lit., "anyone calling himself a brother." The following list of vices is conventional, intended to embrace typical faults, not specific problems in Corinth.
5. Deut. 17:7; 22:21, 24; 24:7; cf. 13:5.
6. I.e., in pagan courts; "ungodly" (more accurately, "unjust") here means no more than "unbelievers."
7. The notion comes from Jewish apocalypticism, e.g., in the Dead Sea Scrolls 1QpHab. 5:4 f.; cf. Dan. 7:22; Wisd. 3:8; Matt. 19:28; Luke 22:30.

be cheated? 8 Instead, you yourselves cheat and do wrong, and you do this to your brothers and sisters.[8] 9 Or do you not know that wrongdoers will not inherit the kingdom of God? Do not be deceived: Neither the sexually immoral nor idolaters nor adulterers nor male prostitutes nor practicing homosexuals 10 nor thieves nor the greedy nor drunkards nor slanderers nor swindlers will inherit the kingdom of God. 11 And that is what some of you were. But you were washed, you were sanctified, you were justified in the name of the Lord Jesus Christ and by the Spirit of our God.[9]

12 "I have the right to do anything,"[1] you say—but not everything is beneficial. "I have the right to do anything"—but I will not be mastered by anything.[2] 13 You say, "Food for the stomach and the stomach for food, and God will destroy them both."[3] The body, however, is not meant for sexual immorality but for the Lord, and the Lord for the body. 14 By his power God raised the Lord from the dead, and he will raise us also. 15 Do you not know that your bodies are members of Christ himself? Shall I then take the members of Christ and unite them with a prostitute? Never! 16 Do you not know that he who unites himself with a prostitute is one with her in body? For it is said, "The two will become one flesh."[4] 17 But whoever is united with the Lord is one with him in spirit.

18 Flee from sexual immorality. All other sins people commit are outside their bodies, but those who sin sexually sin against their own bodies. 19 Do you not know that your bodies are temples of the Holy Spirit, who is in you, whom you have received from God?[5] You are not your own; 20 you were bought at a price. Therefore honor God with your bodies.

7 Now for the matters you wrote about: "It is good for a man not to have sexual relations with a woman." 2 But since sexual immorality is occurring, each man should have sexual relations with his own wife, and each woman with her own husband. 3 The husband should fulfill his marital duty to his wife, and likewise the wife to her husband. 4 The wife does not have authority over her own body but yields it to her husband. In the same way, the husband does not have authority over his own body but yields it to his wife.[6] 5 Do not deprive each other except perhaps by mutual consent and for a time, so that you may devote yourselves to prayer. Then come together

---

8. The form of vv. 6 and 8 is parallel, creating a climactic effect.

9. The "once/now" pattern was a regular form of early Christian preaching; cf. Gal. 4:3 f.; 4:8 f.; Rom. 6:17–22; 7:5 f.; 11:30; Col. 1:21 f.; 3:5–10; Eph. 2:1–10, 11–22; Tit. 3:3–7; 1 Pet. 2:10; 4: 3f. When linked, as here, with a catalogue of vices (see note 4 above and the note on Gal. 5:21), it may echo traditional warnings at baptism, which would give more force to Paul's "Do you not know . . . ?" in v. 9.

1. Evidently a slogan of the Corinthian "spirituals"; they may well believe that they are expressing the freedom they learned from Paul (cf. 3:21). Similar phrases are found in the rhetoric of the time to express the absolute freedom of "the divine," of a king, and—in line with the Stoic slogan mentioned above at 4:8—of the truly wise man. The verb (*exestin*) is cognate with the noun *exousia*, "authority," important in chaps. 8–10. Cf. 10:23. Paul's reply is also in the common idiom of political rhetoric; freedom is limited by what is "beneficial" (*sympheron*), i.e., to the community. The slogan, with the same limit, appears again in 10:23.

2. Paul's pun, *exestin/exousiasthēsomai*, can hardly be imitated in English.

3. Whereas the NIV and NRSV make "God will destroy them both" a part of Paul's response to the preceding Corinthian slogan, the TNIV correctly treats these words as part of the slogan, where they support the spiritualists' argument that the body, like the food it consumes, is morally irrelevant. Paul's retort is that God's resurrection of the body (v. 14) proves its moral relevance. Similarly, v. 18b ("every sin a person commits is apart from the body") is perhaps another Corinthian slogan, with v. 18c ("but sexually immoral people sin against their own bodies") a Pauline counter-slogan.

4. Gen. 2:24.

5. A reprise of 3:16, but here focusing on the individual.

6. The carefully balanced clauses about men and women respectively stand in sharp contrast to the traditional, and highly patriarchal, directive that Paul quotes in 1 Thess. 4:3–4, of which this must be a modification.

again so that Satan will not tempt you because of your lack of self-control. 6 I say this as a concession, not as a command. 7 I wish that all of you were as I am. But each of you has your own gift from God; one has this gift, another has that.

8 Now to the unmarried and the widows I say: It is good for them to stay unmarried, as I do. 9 But if they cannot control themselves, they should marry, for it is better to marry than to burn with passion.

10 To the married I give this command (not I, but the Lord): A wife must not separate from her husband. 11 But if she does, she must remain unmarried or else be reconciled to her husband. And a husband must not divorce his wife.[7]

12 To the rest I say this (I, not the Lord): If any brother has a wife who is not a believer and she is willing to live with him, he must not divorce her. 13 And if a woman has a husband who is not a believer and he is willing to live with her, she must not divorce him. 14 For the unbelieving husband has been sanctified through his wife, and the unbelieving wife has been sanctified through her believing husband. Otherwise your children would be unclean, but as it is, they are holy.

15 But if the unbeliever leaves, let it be so. The brother or sister is not bound in such circumstances; God has called us to live in peace. 16 How do you know, wife, whether you will save your husband? Or, how do you know, husband, whether you will save your wife?

17 Nevertheless, each of you should live as a believer in whatever situation the Lord has assigned to you, just as God has called you.[8] This is the rule I lay down in all the churches. 18 Was a man already circumcised when he was called? He should not become uncircumcised. Was a man uncircumcised when he was called? He should not be circumcised. 19 Circumcision is nothing and uncircumcision is nothing.[9] Keeping God's commands is what counts. 20 Each of you should remain in the situation you were in when God called you.

21 Were you a slave when you were called? Don't let it trouble you— although if you can gain your freedom, do so.[1] 22 For those who were slaves when called to faith in the Lord are the Lord's freed people; similarly, those who were free when called are Christ's slaves. 23 You were bought at a price; do not become slaves of human beings. 24 Brothers and sisters, all of you, as responsible to God, should remain in the situation in which God called you.

25 Now about virgins: I have no command from the Lord, but I give a judgment as one who by the Lord's mercy is trustworthy. 26 Because of the present crisis, I think that it is good for a man to remain as he is. 27 Are you pledged to a woman? Do not seek to be released. Are you free from such a commitment? Do not look for a wife. 28 But if you do marry, you have not sinned; and if a virgin marries, she has not sinned. But those who marry will face many troubles in this life, and I want to spare you this.

29 What I mean, brothers and sisters, is that the time is short. From

---

7. Cf. Matt. 5:32; 19:9; Mark 10:11 f.; Luke 16:18. One of Paul's very rare allusions to a saying of Jesus.
8. Vv. 17–24 comprise another short ring-composition, this one on the subject of "calling" which has appeared earlier in 1:1, 2, 9, 24, 26; 7:15.
9. Compare and contrast Gal. 5:6; 6:15.
1. This translation is possible, but the elliptical clause could also mean, "Even if you can gain your freedom, rather make use [of your slavery]."

now on those who are married should live as if they were not; 30 those
who mourn, as if they did not; those who are happy, as if they were not;
those who buy something, as if it were not theirs to keep; 31 those who
use the things of the world, as if not engrossed in them. For this world in
its present form is passing away.

32 I would like you to be free from concern. An unmarried man is concerned about the Lord's affairs—how he can please the Lord. 33 But a
married man is concerned about the affairs of this world—how he can
please his wife— 34 and his interests are divided. An unmarried woman
or virgin is concerned about the Lord's affairs: Her aim is to be devoted to
the Lord in both body and spirit. But a married woman is concerned about
the affairs of this world—how she can please her husband. 35 I am saying
this for your own good, not to restrict you, but that you may live in a right
way in undivided devotion to the Lord.

36 If anyone is worried that he might not be acting honorably toward
the virgin he is engaged to,[2] and if she is getting beyond the usual age for
marrying and he feels he ought to marry, he should do as he wants. He is
not sinning. They should get married. 37 But the man who has settled the
matter in his own mind, who is under no compulsion but has control over
his own will, and who has made up his mind not to marry the virgin—this
man also does the right thing. 38 So then, he who marries the virgin does
right, but he who does not marry her does better.

39 A woman is bound to her husband as long as he lives. But if her
husband dies, she is free to marry anyone she wishes, but he must belong
to the Lord. 40 In my judgment, she is happier if she stays as she is—and
I think that I too have the Spirit of God.

8 Now about food sacrificed to idols:[3] We know that "We all possess knowledge."[4] But knowledge puffs up while love builds up. 2 Those who think
they know something do not yet know as they ought to know. 3 But whoever loves God is known by God.[5]

4 So then, about eating food sacrificed to idols: We know that "An idol
is nothing at all in the world" and that "There is no God but one." 5 For
even if there are so-called gods, whether in heaven or on earth (as indeed
there are many "gods" and many "lords"), 6 yet for us there is but one God,
the Father, from whom all things came and for whom we live; and there
is but one Lord, Jesus Christ, through whom all things came and through
whom we live.

7 But not everyone possesses this knowledge. Some people are still so
accustomed to idols that when they eat sacrificial food they think of it as
having been sacrificed to a god, and since their conscience is weak, it is

---

2. Lit., "his virgin," as also in v. 38. One traditional interpretation, which refers the passage to the
question whether a father should marry off his daughter, is improbable. The case is either of
engaged persons who, misunderstanding the basis of Paul's ascetic practice and recommendations,
are afraid that marriage would be a sin, or of an early form of "spiritual marriage," i.e., without
sexual relations, which is known from the third century on.

3. Chaps. 8:1–11:1 have confused many commentators, who find Paul's position inconsistent and
unclear. In fact they are a carefully unified rhetorical composition, with Paul's own personal
example as the centerpiece (chap. 9, resumed at 10:23–11:1). The confusion results from Paul's
sympathy with both positions and the care with which he tries to restate the concerns of each
faction within a fuller context of biblical teachings, tradition, facts of social life in Corinth, and
above all the possibility that groups with quite different perspectives and interests within the
church can learn to live in mutual responsibility and concord.

4. Another slogan of the Corinthian spiritualists, allowing Paul to reprise his earlier warnings about
worldly knowledge (1:18–4:21), summing up with an antithesis between knowledge and love.

5. Cf. 3:18; 10:12; also Gal. 6:9.

defiled. 8 But food does not bring us near to God; we are no worse if we do not eat, and no better if we do.

9 Be careful, however, that the exercise of your rights does not become a stumbling block to the weak. 10 For if anyone with a weak conscience sees you, with all your knowledge, eating in an idol's temple,[6] won't they be emboldened[7] to eat what is sacrificed to idols? 11 So this weak brother or sister, for whom Christ died, is destroyed by your knowledge. 12 When you sin against them in this way and wound their weak conscience, you sin against Christ. 13 Therefore, if what I eat causes my brother or sister to fall into sin, I will never eat meat again, so that I will not cause them to fall.

9 Am I not free? Am I not an apostle?[8] Have I not seen Jesus our Lord? Are you not the result of my work in the Lord? 2 Even though I may not be an apostle to others, surely I am to you! For you are the seal of my apostleship in the Lord.

3 This is my defense to those who sit in judgment on me. 4 Don't we have the right to food and drink? 5 Don't we have the right to take a believing wife[9] along with us, as do the other apostles and the Lord's brothers and Cephas? 6 Or is it only I and Barnabas who don't have the right not to work for a living?

7 Who serves as a soldier at his own expense? Who plants a vineyard and does not eat of its grapes? Who tends a flock and does not drink of the milk? 8 Do I say this merely on human authority? Doesn't the Law say the same thing? 9 For it is written in the Law of Moses: "Do not muzzle an ox while it is treading out the grain."[1] Is it about oxen that God is concerned? 10 Surely he says this for us, doesn't he? Yes, this was written for us, because when farmers plow and thresh, they should be able to do so in the hope of sharing in the harvest. 11 If we have sown spiritual seed among you, is it too much if we reap a material harvest from you? 12 If others have this right of support from you, shouldn't we have it all the more?

But we did not use this right. On the contrary, we put up with anything rather than hinder the gospel of Christ.

13 Don't you know that those who serve in the temple get their food from the temple, and that those who serve at the altar share in what is offered on the altar? 14 In the same way, the Lord has commanded that those who preach the gospel should receive their living from the gospel.[2]

15 But I have not used any of these rights.[3] And I am not writing this in the hope that you will do such things for me, for I would rather die than allow anyone to deprive me of this boast. 16 For when I preach the gospel, I cannot boast, since I am compelled to preach. Woe to me if I do not

6. Meals in the cult shrine were extremely important in the family, social, and civic life of Hellenistic culture; for many participants most such occasions had scarcely any religious significance except in the sense of civic piety.

7. Lit., "built up," the sarcastic reverse of 8:1b.

8. While chap. 9 seems to interrupt the argument and has been misidentified by many commentators as a self-defense by Paul (because of the word *apologia* in v.3), actually it is a personal example of the principle being developed: Christian freedom includes the freedom to use or to renounce one's "right," depending on the communal situation. The word *exousia*, "right," its verbal form *exestin* (10:23), and its synonym *eleutheros, -ia*, "free," "freedom" (9:1, 19; 10:29), signal the central theme of these chapters.

9. Lit., "a sister [i.e., a Christian] as wife."

1. Deut. 25:4.

2. Another allusion to a saying attributed to Jesus: cf. Luke 10:7; Matt. 10:10; Gal. 6:6; 1 Tim. 5:18.

3. Cf. 1 Thess. 2:9; 2 Cor. 11:7–11.

preach the gospel! 17 If I preach voluntarily, I have a reward; if not voluntarily, I am simply discharging the trust committed to me. 18 What then is my reward? Just this: that in preaching the gospel I may offer it free of charge, and so not misuse my rights as a preacher of the gospel.

19 Though I am free and belong to no one, I have made myself a slave to everyone,[4] to win as many as possible. 20 To the Jews I became like a Jew, to win the Jews. To those under the law I became like one under the law (though I myself am not under the law), so as to win those under the law. 21 To those not having the law I became like one not having the law (though I am not free from God's law but am under Christ's law), so as to win those not having the law. 22 To the weak I became weak, to win the weak. I have become all things to all people so that by all possible means I might save some. 23 I do all this for the sake of the gospel, that I may share in its blessings.

24 Do you not know that in a race all the runners run, but only one gets the prize? Run in such a way as to get the prize. 25 Everyone who competes in the games goes into strict training. They do it to get a crown that will not last; but we do it to get a crown that will last forever. 26 Therefore I do not run like someone running aimlessly; I do not fight like a boxer beating the air. 27 No, I strike a blow to my body and make it my slave so that after I have preached to others, I myself will not be disqualified for the prize.[5]

10 For I do not want you to be ignorant of the fact, brothers and sisters, that our ancestors were all under the cloud and that they all passed through the sea.[6] 2 They were all baptized into Moses in the cloud and in the sea. 3 They all ate the same spiritual food 4 and drank the same spiritual drink; for they drank from the spiritual rock that accompanied them, and that rock was Christ.[7] 5 Nevertheless, God was not pleased with most of them; their bodies were scattered in the wilderness.

6 Now these things occurred as examples to keep us from setting our hearts on evil things as they did. 7 Do not be idolaters, as some of them were; as it is written: "The people sat down to eat and drink and got up to indulge in revelry." 8 We should not commit sexual immorality, as some of them did—and in one day twenty-three thousand of them died.[8] 9 We should not test Christ, as some of them did—and were killed by snakes.[9] 10 And do not grumble, as some of them did—and were killed by the destroying angel.[1]

11 These things happened to them as examples and were written down as warnings for us, on whom the culmination of the ages has come.[2] 12 So,

4. "Slave to everyone" in contemporary political debate identifies a populist kind of leadership, i.e., from the point of view of the upper classes (and the ambitions of "those who have knowledge" whom Paul addresses here) the demagogue. Paul dares to apply this phrase to himself in order to challenge the assumptions about freedom and its responsibilities within the community.

5. Metaphors from athletics were favorites in Greek rhetoric of every school; perhaps the popularity of the Isthmian Games held near Corinth would give them special currency here.

6. 10:1–13 are a homily or *midrash*, in a style found frequently in Jewish literature, on the key passage quoted in v. 7 from Exod. 32:6. Whether Paul is quoting a homily he or someone else previously composed or is constructing it for the occasion, we cannot be sure.

7. The "spiritual food" is the manna (Ex. 16:4–35; Deut. 8:3; Ps. 78:23–25); the "spiritual drink," the water from the rock (Ex. 17:6; Num. 20:2–13). The double account of the water miracle (Ex. 17; Num. 20) led to the legend of a rock that "went up with them to the hills and down to the valleys . . ." (Tosefta, *Sukkah* iii.11 and elsewhere).

8. Num. 25.

9. Num. 21:5 f.

1. Num. 14:2, 36; 16:41–49; Ps. 106:25–27.

2. For the notion that biblical prophecies contained hidden messages for "the culmination of the ages," compare 1QpHab 7.1 (among the Dead Sea Scrolls). Treating biblical stories as "types" ("as

if you think you are standing firm, be careful that you don't fall! 13 No temptation has overtaken you except what is common to us all. And God is faithful; he will not let you be tempted beyond what you can bear. But when you are tempted, he will also provide a way out so that you can endure it.

14 Therefore, my dear friends, flee from idolatry. 15 I speak to sensible people; judge for yourselves what I say. 16 Is not the cup of thanksgiving for which we give thanks a participation[3] in the blood of Christ? And is not the bread that we break a participation in the body of Christ? 17 Because there is one loaf, we, who are many, are one body, for we all partake of the one loaf.

18 Consider the people of Israel:[4] Do not those who eat the sacrifices participate in the altar? 19 Do I mean then that food sacrificed to an idol is anything, or that an idol is anything? 20 No, but the sacrifices of pagans[5] are offered to demons, not to God, and I do not want you to be participants with demons. 21 You cannot drink the cup of the Lord and the cup of demons too; you cannot have a part in both the Lord's table and the table of demons. 22 Are we trying to arouse the Lord's jealousy? Are we stronger than he?

23 "I have the right to do anything," you say—but not everything is beneficial.[6] "I have the right to do anything"—but not everything is constructive. 24 No one should seek their own good, but the good of others.

25 Eat anything sold in the meat market[7] without raising questions of conscience, 26 for, "The earth is the Lord's, and everything in it."[8]

27 If an unbeliever invites you to a meal and you want to go, eat whatever is put before you without raising questions of conscience. 28 But if someone says to you, "This has been offered in sacrifice,"[9] then do not eat it, both for the sake of the one who told you and for the sake of conscience. 29 I am referring to the other person's conscience, not yours. For why is my freedom being judged by another's conscience? 30 If I take part in the meal with thankfulness, why am I denounced because of something I thank God for?

31 So whether you eat or drink or whatever you do, do it all for the glory of God. 32 Do not cause anyone to stumble, whether Jews, Greeks or the church of God— 33 even as I try to please everyone in every way. For I am not seeking my own good but the good of many, so that they may be saved.

11 Follow my example, as I follow the example of Christ.[1]

2 I praise you for remembering me in everything and for holding to the

---

examples" here translates *typikōs*, cf. v. 6, *typoi*) becomes one of the main interpretive strategies of the ancient church; cf. Rom. 5:14.

3. Or, "communion," *koinōnia*.

4. Lit., "Israel according to the flesh."

5. Several important witnesses read "they [Israel] sacrifice." The clause is a quotation from Deut. 32:17, which refers to Israel's apostasy (cf. v. 7). In the Hebrew that apostasy is called a rejection of "the Rock," though the LXX translation is "God."

6. Cf. 6:12.

7. Temples were the source of most meat sold in the market; priests were by profession butchers.

8. Ps. 24:1.

9. Who is this imagined informant, a pagan or one of the "weak" Christians? Use of the common term "sacred sacrifice," *hierothyton* here, rather than the parodistic *eidōlothyton*, "idol sacrifice," which Paul has used earlier, might suggest the former, but then how are we to take v. 29?

1. See 4:16; 1 Thess. 1:6.

traditions just as I passed them on to you.[2] 3 But I want you to realize that the head of every man is Christ, and the head of the woman is man, and the head of Christ is God. 4 Every man who prays or prophesies with his head covered[3] dishonors his head. 5 But every woman who prays or prophesies with her head uncovered dishonors her head[4]—it is the same as having her head shaved. 6 For if a woman does not cover her head, she might as well have her hair cut off; but if it is a disgrace for a woman to have her hair cut off or her head shaved, then she should cover her head.

7 A man ought not to cover his head, since he is the image and glory of God; but woman is the glory of man. 8 For man did not come from woman, but woman from man;[5] 9 neither was man created for woman, but woman for man. 10 It is for this reason that a woman ought to have authority over her own head, because of the angels.[6] 11 Nevertheless, in the Lord woman is not independent of man, nor is man independent of woman. 12 For as woman came from man, so also man is born of woman. But everything comes from God.

13 Judge for yourselves: Is it proper for a woman to pray to God with her head uncovered? 14 Does not the very nature of things teach you that if a man has long hair, it is a disgrace to him, 15 but that if a woman has long hair, it is her glory? For long hair is given to her as a covering.[7] 16 If anyone wants to be contentious about this, we have no other practice—nor do the churches of God.

17 In the following directives I have no praise for you, for your meetings do more harm than good.[8] 18 In the first place, I hear that when you come together as a church, there are divisions among you, and to some extent I believe it. 19 No doubt there have to be differences among you to show which of you have God's approval. 20 So then, when you come together, it is not the Lord's Supper you eat, 21 for when you are eating, some of you go ahead with your own private suppers. As a result, one person remains hungry and another gets drunk. 22 Don't you have homes to eat

2. Vv. 2–16 are one of the most obscure passages in the Pauline letters. Only a few points are relatively clear: (1) The issue is raised by the prophetic movement that flourished briefly, practiced by both men and women, in the early church, and was regarded as a gift of the Spirit and a sign that Christians belonged already to the end of days. (2) One of the "traditions" that Paul "passed on" was the baptismal formula that "in Christ" there is "no 'male and female' " (Gal. 3:28); in Corinth at least one of the factions tried to find practical applications of such statements in the present life of the community (see above on chap. 7). (3) Paul, though "praising" this fundamental position, wishes to limit the enthusiasm that threatens to lapse into fantasy. His rather awkward argument is based on widespread custom (a woman with loose or uncovered hair dishonors her husband) and speculations based on Gen. 1–2.

3. "With his head covered": the opposite "uncovered" in v. 5 seems to require this translation, but both grammar and Jewish custom speak against it. The Greek would normally mean, "having (something: long hair?) hanging down from the head." Perhaps, then, the requirement suggested for the female prophets refers not to veils or head scarves but to having their hair bound up or braided, to avoid the disheveled locks associated with the frenzy of women participating in Dionysiac or other ecstatic cults.

4. "Head" in vv. 4, 5 must be a double entendre (v. 3), alluding to God and the husband, respectively.

5. Gen. 2:21–23.

6. No one knows what this means, though many guesses have been offered. To ward off the demonic powers (cf. Gen. 6:2 and note 2 Cor. 11:3, 14)? Because angels guard the created order? Because angels share in the community's worship (suggested by comparison with the Dead Sea Scrolls)? Because angels transmit prophecy? None of these is convincing.

7. Paul was not the first nor the last to confuse custom with "nature" (*physis*). Similar statements are found in pagan and Jewish moralists of this period; e.g., Pseudo-Phocylides, 210–12.

8. Lit., "It is not for the better but for the worse that you come together." Paul ironically plays the literal meaning of "come together" against its extended meaning, "to unite." Thus v. 18 reiterates the theme of the whole letter, the warning against "divisions" (1:10). That the divisions here have their roots in socioeconomic differences is clear, though neither the details of the situation nor of Paul's remedy are certain.

and drink in? Or do you despise the church of God by humiliating those who have nothing? What shall I say to you? Shall I praise you? Certainly not in this matter!

23 For I received from the Lord what I also passed on to you:[9] The Lord Jesus, on the night he was betrayed, took bread, 24 and when he had given thanks, he broke it and said, "This is my body, which is for[1] you; do this in remembrance of me." 25 In the same way, after supper he took the cup, saying, "This cup is the new covenant in my blood; do this, whenever you drink it, in remembrance of me." 26 For whenever you eat this bread and drink this cup, you proclaim the Lord's death until he comes.

27 So then, whoever eats the bread or drinks the cup of the Lord in an unworthy manner will be guilty of sinning against the body and blood of the Lord. 28 Everyone ought to examine themselves before they eat of the bread and drink of the cup. 29 For those who eat and drink without discerning the body of Christ[2] eat and drink judgment on themselves. 30 That is why many among you are weak and sick, and a number of you have fallen asleep. 31 But if we were more discerning with regard to ourselves, we would not come under such judgment. 32 Nevertheless, when we are judged in this way by the Lord, we are being disciplined so that we will not be finally condemned with the world.

33 So then, my brothers and sisters, when you gather to eat, you should all eat together. 34 Those who are hungry should eat something at home, so that when you meet together it may not result in judgment.

And when I come I will give further directions.

12 Now about the gifts of the Spirit,[3] brothers and sisters, I do not want you to be uninformed. 2 You know that when you were pagans, somehow or other you were influenced and led astray to mute idols. 3 Therefore I want you to know that no one who is speaking by the Spirit of God says, "Jesus be cursed,"[4] and no one can say, "Jesus is Lord," except by the Holy Spirit.

4 There are different kinds of gifts, but the same Spirit distributes them. 5 There are different kinds of service, but the same Lord. 6 There are different kinds of working, but in all of them and in everyone it is the same God at work.

7 Now to each one the manifestation of the Spirit is given for the common good. 8 To one there is given through the Spirit a message of wisdom, to another a message of knowledge by means of the same Spirit, 9 to another faith by the same Spirit, to another gifts of healing by that one Spirit, 10 to another miraculous powers, to another prophecy, to another distinguishing between spirits, to another speaking in different kinds of

---

9. "Received," "passed on" are technical terms for transmission of tradition; hence "from the Lord" here (contrast Gal. 1:11 f.) obviously includes, not excludes, human mediation. To the tradition itself, compare Matt. 26:26–28; Mark 14:22–24; Luke 22:17–19. See also the essay by H.-J. Klauck in Part IX.
1. Some texts read "broken for," a few, "given for."
2. "Of Christ" is not in the Greek, but many manuscripts add "of the Lord."
3. This theme, apparently answering another question of the Corinthians' letter, occupies chaps. 12–14, and continues the discussion of factions that appear when the believers "come together."
4. Various explanations are offered for this startling formula: (1) an allusion to the occasional requirement (attested from the second century) by Roman officers that recanting Christians curse Christ and acclaim Caesar as "Lord" to escape persecution—but nothing in 1 Cor. speaks of persecution; (2) an ecstatic cry by Corinthian "spirituals" or "Gnostics," assumed to distinguish between the physical "Jesus" and the spiritual "Christ"; (3) supposed Jewish curses of the crucified (Deut. 21: 23)—but this would have no connection with the context. More likely, it is merely Paul's hyperbole, formulated as a hypothetical opposite of the normal confession, "Jesus is Lord."

tongues, and to still another the interpretation of tongues. 11 All these are the work of one and the same Spirit, and he distributes them to each one, just as he determines.

12 Just as a body, though one, has many parts, but all its many parts form one body,[5] so it is with Christ. 13 For we were all baptized by one Spirit so as to form one body—whether Jews or Gentiles, slave or free— and we were all given the one Spirit to drink.[6] 14 Even so the body is not made up of one part but of many.

15 Now if the foot should say, "Because I am not a hand, I do not belong to the body," it would not for that reason cease to be part of the body. 16 And if the ear should say, "Because I am not an eye, I do not belong to the body," it would not for that reason cease to be part of the body. 17 If the whole body were an eye, where would the sense of hearing be? If the whole body were an ear, where would the sense of smell be? 18 But in fact God has placed the parts in the body, every one of them, just as he wanted them to be. 19 If they were all one part, where would the body be? 20 As it is, there are many parts, but one body.

21 The eye cannot say to the hand, "I don't need you!" And the head cannot say to the feet, "I don't need you!" 22 On the contrary, those parts of the body that seem to be weaker are indispensable, 23 and the parts that we think are less honorable we treat with special honor. And the parts that are unpresentable are treated with special modesty, 24 while our presentable parts need no special treatment. But God has put the body together, giving greater honor to the parts that lacked it, 25 so that there should be no division in the body, but that its parts should have equal concern for each other. 26 If one part suffers, every part suffers with it; if one part is honored, every part rejoices with it.

27 Now you are the body of Christ, and each one of you is a part of it. 28 And God has placed in the church first of all apostles, second prophets, third teachers, then miracles, then gifts of healing, of helping, of guidance, and of different kinds of tongues. 29 Are all apostles? Are all prophets? Are all teachers? Do all work miracles? 30 Do all have gifts of healing? Do all speak in tongues? Do all interpret? 31 Now eagerly desire the greater gifts.

And yet I will show you the most excellent way.[7]

13 If I speak in human or angelic tongues, but do not have love, I am only a resounding gong or a clanging cymbal. 2 If I have the gift of prophecy and can fathom all mysteries and all knowledge, and if I have a faith that can move mountains, but do not have love, I am nothing. 3 If I give all I possess to the poor and give over my body [to hardship] that I may boast,[8] but do not have love, I gain nothing.

5. The metaphor of body and limbs to describe a society was ancient and very widespread; the fable of Menenius Agrippa, in which hands, mouth, and teeth rebel against the belly, was especially often quoted (Livy 2:32.12–33.1), but many variations were used in political speeches that warned against factions and urged concord. Paul's only innovation is in linking the body metaphor to the baptismal language about "putting on Christ" (v. 13).

6. Cf. Gal. 3:27 f.; Col. 3:11.

7. Some commentators have taken chap. 13 to be a separate composition, inserted here by Paul himself or a later editor (note the repetition of v. 12:31a in 14:1a). It is composed in the style of an encomium on a virtue, a form quite familiar in Greek literature: the praises of Eros in Plato's *Symposium* are the most famous; for a Jewish example, see 1 Esd. 4:33–41. It is very carefully constructed, and Paul might well have written it for some earlier occasion, but it sums up themes that have been important throughout the letter. For Paul as for many Greco-Roman moral philosophers, love is the best cure for discord: "knowledge puffs up while love builds up" (8:1).

8. Ancient texts are divided between *kauthēsōmai*, "to be burned," and *kauchēsōmai*, "that I may boast." In either case the allusion is to martyrdom; cf. Dan. 3:28.

4 Love is patient, love is kind. It does not envy, it does not boast, it is not proud. 5 It does not dishonor others, it is not self-seeking, it is not easily angered, it keeps no record of wrongs. 6 Love does not delight in evil but rejoices with the truth. 7 It always protects, always trusts, always hopes, always perseveres.[9]

8 Love never fails. But where there are prophecies, they will cease; where there are tongues, they will be stilled; where there is knowledge, it will pass away. 9 For we know in part and we prophesy in part, 10 but when completeness comes, what is in part disappears. 11 When I was a child, I talked like a child, I thought like a child, I reasoned like a child. When I became a man, I put the ways of childhood behind me. 12 For now we see only a reflection as in a mirror;[1] then we shall see face to face. Now I know in part; then I shall know fully, even as I am fully known.

13 And now these three remain: faith, hope and love.[2] But the greatest of these is love.

14 Follow the way of love and eagerly desire spiritual gifts, especially the gift of prophecy. 2 For those who speak in a tongue[3] do not speak to other people but to God. Indeed, no one understands them; they utter mysteries by the Spirit. 3 But those who prophesy speak to people for their strengthening, encouragement and comfort. 4 Those who speak in a tongue edify themselves, but those who prophesy edify[4] the church. 5 I would like every one of you to speak in tongues, but I would rather have you prophesy. Those who prophesy are greater than those who speak in tongues, unless they interpret, so that the church may be edified.

6 Now, brothers and sisters, if I come to you and speak in tongues, what good will I be to you, unless I bring you some revelation or knowledge or prophecy or word of instruction? 7 Even in the case of lifeless things that make sounds, such as the pipe or harp, how will anyone know what tune is being played unless there is a distinction in the notes? 8 Again, if the trumpet does not sound a clear call, who will get ready for battle? 9 So it is with you. Unless you speak intelligible words with your tongue, how will anyone know what you are saying? You will just be speaking into the air. 10 Undoubtedly there are all sorts of languages in the world, yet none of them is without meaning. 11 If then I do not grasp the meaning of what someone is saying, I am a foreigner to the speaker, and the speaker is a foreigner to me. 12 So it is with you. Since you are eager for gifts of the Spirit, try to excel in those that build up the church.

13 For this reason those who speak in a tongue should pray that they

9. The list of what love is *not* corresponds rather precisely to Paul's description of the factionalism of the Corinthian Christians: they are jealous (3:3), boast and are "puffed up" (1:29, 31, 3:21; 4:6, 7, 18, 19; 5:2), count up evil and are quick to judge (4:1–5; 6:1–11), and lack the hope promised by the preaching of resurrection (chap. 15). Above all, they are childish (see notes on chaps. 1–4 above and v. 11 below).
1. The mirror metaphor is used in many ways by ancient authors; here it merely emphasizes the indirectness and incompleteness of knowledge in the present world. On knowing vs. being known (by God), cf. 8:3 and Gal. 4:9.
2. For the triad faith, hope, love, cf. 1 Thess. 1:3; 5:8; Rom 5:1–5; Col. 1:4 f.
3. Cf. 13:1. "To speak in a tongue" was, we assume, similar to the ecstatic phenomenon which we know in some modern religious movements and which we call, after the Greek in the NT, "glossolalia." It consists in involuntary utterance of rapid sequences of inarticulate sounds, perhaps in a chanting cadence. In the early church it was interpreted as a "gift of the Spirit," 12:10, 28, 30; 13:1, 8; Acts 2:4–13 (where the author interprets the phenomenon in a more "rational," miraculous, and symbolic way); 10:46; 19:6; elsewhere in early Christian literature only in the spurious ending of Mark, 16:17.
4. "Edify," i.e., "build up," vv. 4, 5, 12, 17, 26; an important metaphor for Paul: 8:1; 10:23; 1 Thess. 5:11.

may interpret what they say. 14 For if I pray in a tongue, my spirit prays, but my mind is unfruitful. 15 So what shall I do? I will pray with my spirit, but I will also pray with my understanding; I will sing with my spirit, but I will also sing with my understanding. 16 Otherwise when you are praising God in the Spirit, how can the others, who are now put in the same situation as an inquirer,[5] say "Amen" to your thanksgiving, since they do not know what you are saying? 17 You are giving thanks well enough, but the others are not edified.

18 I thank God that I speak in tongues more than all of you. 19 But in the church I would rather speak five intelligible words to instruct others than ten thousand words in a tongue.

20 Brothers and sisters, stop thinking like children. In regard to evil be infants, but in your thinking be adults.[6] 21 In the Law it is written:

"With other tongues
and through the lips of foreigners
I will speak to this people,
but even then they will not listen to me,
says the Lord."[7]

22 Tongues, then, are a sign, not for believers but for unbelievers; prophecy, however, is not for unbelievers but for believers. 23 So if the whole church comes together and everyone speaks in tongues, and inquirers or unbelievers come in, will they not say that you are out of your mind? 24 But if an unbeliever or an inquirer comes in while everyone is prophesying, they are convicted of sin and are brought under judgment by all, 25 as the secrets of their hearts are laid bare. So they will fall down and worship God, exclaiming, "God is really among you!"

26 What then shall we say, brothers and sisters? When you come together, each of you has a hymn, or a word of instruction, a revelation, a tongue or an interpretation. Everything must be done so that the church may be built up. 27 If anyone speaks in a tongue, two—or at the most three—should speak, one at a time, and someone must interpret. 28 If there is no interpreter, the speaker should keep quiet in the church; let them speak to themselves and to God.

29 Two or three prophets should speak, and the others should weigh carefully what is said. 30 And if a revelation comes to someone who is sitting down, the first speaker should stop. 31 For you can all prophesy in turn so that everyone may be instructed and encouraged. 32 The spirits of prophets are subject to the control of prophets. 33 For God is not a God of disorder but of peace—as in all the congregations of the Lord's people.

34 Women should remain silent in the churches. They are not allowed to speak, but must be in submission, as the law says.[8] 35 If they want to

---

5. Lit., "One who fills the place of the outsider [Greek *idiōtēs*]."
6. See note on 2:6; Paul may be playing on the various connotations of the word to say that glossolalia is not a sure sign of spiritual "perfection" or "initiation," but may rather, when it produces pride and factiousness, indicate childishness.
7. Isa. 28:11–12.
8. This statement seems flatly to contradict 11:2–16, which presupposes that women are free to prophesy in the church. If 14:33b-35 is taken to refer only to non-ecstatic discussion in the assembly, as v. 35 suggests, then it is not clear why the passage stands in the context of a chapter dealing with ecstasy. Translating "wives" instead of "women," which is perfectly possible, would encounter the same difficulty. Some manuscripts place these verses after v. 10. Some modern commentators regard them as an interpolation by some later, conservative Paulinist; cf. 1 Tim. 2: 11f.

inquire about something, they should ask their own husbands at home; for it is disgraceful for a woman to speak in the church.

36 Or did the word of God originate with you? Or are you the only people it has reached? 37 If any think they are prophets or otherwise gifted by the Spirit, let them acknowledge that what I am writing to you is the Lord's command. 38 Those who ignore this will themselves be ignored.[9]

39 Therefore, my brothers and sisters, be eager to prophesy, and do not forbid speaking in tongues. 40 But everything should be done in a fitting and orderly way.

15 Now, brothers and sisters, I want to remind you of the gospel I preached to you, which you received and on which you have taken your stand. 2 By this gospel you are saved, if you hold firmly to the word I preached to you. Otherwise, you have believed in vain.

3 For what I received I passed on to you[1] as of first importance: that Christ died for our sins according to the Scriptures, 4 that he was buried, that he was raised on the third day according to the Scriptures, 5 and that he appeared to Cephas, and then to the Twelve. 6 After that, he appeared to more than five hundred of the brothers and sisters at the same time, most of whom are still living, though some have fallen asleep. 7 Then he appeared to James, then to all the apostles, 8 and last of all he appeared to me also, as to one abnormally born.[2]

9 For I am the least of the apostles and do not even deserve to be called an apostle, because I persecuted the church of God. 10 But by the grace of God I am what I am, and his grace to me was not without effect. No, I worked harder than all of them—yet not I, but the grace of God that was with me. 11 Whether, then, it is I or they, this is what we preach, and this is what you believed.

12 But if it is preached that Christ has been raised from the dead, how can some of you say that there is no resurrection of the dead?[3] 13 If there is no resurrection of the dead, then not even Christ has been raised.

9. On the form of v. 38, see note on 3:17.
1. On the technical designation of tradition, see notes on 11:23 and Gal. 1:12. The tradition is carefully formulated:

> that Christ died for our sins
>   according to the scriptures
>   and that he was buried
> that he was raised on the third day
>   according to the scriptures
>   and that he appeared
>   to Cephas, then to the Twelve.

Where it ends is not certain, since Paul adds other reports that are also, in a looser sense, tradition.
2. "One abnormally born": lit. an "abortion" or "miscarriage," perhaps a term of abuse used by Paul's opponents; v. 9 can be regarded as interpreting the term.
3. Paul's question, intended to show the logical absurdity of the position held by "some" of the Corinthian believers, also baffles modern interpreters. If this group accepts the basic statement of "the gospel," which Paul has just outlined and of which Christ's resurrection is an essential element, then how *can* they "say that there is no resurrection of the dead"? Some commentators, pointing out that Paul emphasizes the phrase "from the dead," think he confronts Christians like those he addresses in 1 Thess. 4:13–18, who think of resurrection as an exaltation to heaven and fear that those who have already died will be left out. Others point out the emphasis throughout 1 Corinthians on the phenomena of spirit possession and suggest that "some" believe they have already been "spiritually" resurrected in baptism (cf. the second-century *Gos. Phil.* 79, and the position attributed to Hymenaeus and Philetus in 2 Tim. 2:18). It would be possible to read some of the extravagant language of the early baptismal liturgy in such a way: see Col. 2:11f.; Eph. 2: 4–7, which speak of the resurrection of the baptized in the past tense, in contrast to Paul's future tenses in Rom. 6:4f.

14 And if Christ has not been raised, our preaching is useless and so is your faith. 15 More than that, we are then found to be false witnesses about God, for we have testified about God that he raised Christ from the dead. But he did not raise him if in fact the dead are not raised. 16 For if the dead are not raised, then Christ has not been raised either. 17 And if Christ has not been raised, your faith is futile; you are still in your sins. 18 Then those also who have fallen asleep[4] in Christ are lost. 19 If only for this life we have hope in Christ, we are to be pitied more than all others.

20 But Christ has indeed been raised from the dead, the firstfruits of those who have fallen asleep. 21 For since death came through a human being, the resurrection of the dead comes also through a human being. 22 For as in Adam all die, so in Christ all will be made alive. 23 But in this order: Christ, the firstfruits; then, when he comes, those who belong to him. 24 Then the end will come, when he hands over the kingdom to God the Father after he has destroyed all dominion, authority and power. 25 For he must reign until he has put all his enemies under his[5] feet. 26 The last enemy to be destroyed is death. 27 For he "has put everything under his feet." Now when it says that "everything" has been put under him, it is clear that this does not include God himself, who put everything under Christ. 28 When he has done this, then the Son himself will be made subject to him who put everything under him, so that God may be all in all.[6]

29 Now if there is no resurrection, what will those do who are baptized for the dead?[7] If the dead are not raised at all, why are people baptized for them? 30 And as for us, why do we endanger ourselves every hour? 31 I face death every day—yes, just as surely as I boast about you in Christ Jesus our Lord. 32 If I fought wild beasts in Ephesus[8] with no more than human hopes, what have I gained? If the dead are not raised,

"Let us eat and drink,
for tomorrow we die."[9]

33 Do not be misled: "Bad company corrupts good character."[1] 34 Come back to your senses as you ought, and stop sinning; for there are some who are ignorant of God—I say this to your shame.

35 But someone will ask, "How are the dead raised? With what kind of body will they come?" 36 How foolish! What you sow does not come to life unless it dies. 37 When you sow, you do not plant the body that will be, but just a seed, perhaps of wheat or of something else. 38 But God gives it a body as he has determined, and to each kind of seed he gives its own body. 39 All flesh is not the same: Human beings have one kind of

---

4. "Fallen asleep" is a common euphemism for death.
5. Ps. 110:1, with "all" added from Ps. 8:7.
6. Christ's own ultimate submission to God, at the moment of his triumph, is Paul's ultimate example of exercising "rights" for concord rather than discord. Each of Paul's rare uses of language about kingship in this letter makes the same point: 4:8, 20; 15:50.
7. Nothing further is known about the practice of vicarious baptism, though church fathers report similar practices later by Marcionites, Montanists, and Cerinthians (schismatic groups of the second to fourth centuries).
8. In the diatribe style of the philosophical schools, which pervades this passage, the figure of "fighting beasts" frequently refers to the wise person's struggle against passion or pleasure, but also occasionally against opponents who are hedonists, as the Epicureans were commonly said to be. Paul faces "many opponents" in Ephesus (16:9); if his struggle were merely human (see 3:3f. for a similar use of *kata anthrōpon*), i.e., without hope of the future resurrection, his example would be of no significance.
9. Isa. 22:13.
1. Menander, *Thais*, frg. 218.

flesh, animals have another, birds another and fish another. 40 There are also heavenly bodies and there are earthly bodies; but the splendor of the heavenly bodies is one kind, and the splendor of the earthly bodies is another. 41 The sun has one kind of splendor, the moon another and the stars another; and star differs from star in splendor.

42 So will it be with the resurrection of the dead. The body that is sown is perishable, it is raised imperishable; 43 it is sown in dishonor, it is raised in glory; it is sown in weakness, it is raised in power; 44 it is sown a natural[2] body, it is raised a spiritual body.

If there is a natural body, there is also a spiritual body. 45 So it is written: "The first Adam became a living being"[3]; the last Adam, a life-giving spirit. 46 The spiritual did not come first, but the natural, and after that the spiritual. 47 The first man was of the dust of the earth; the second man is of heaven. 48 As was the earthly man, so are those who are of the earth; and as is the heavenly man, so also are those who are of heaven. 49 And just as we have borne the image of the earthly man, so shall we bear the image of the heavenly man.

50 I declare to you, brothers and sisters, that flesh and blood cannot inherit the kingdom of God, nor does the perishable inherit the imperishable. 51 Listen, I tell you a mystery:[4] We will not all sleep, but we will all be changed— 52 in a flash, in the twinkling of an eye, at the last trumpet. For the trumpet will sound, the dead will be raised imperishable, and we will be changed. 53 For the perishable must clothe itself with the imperishable, and the mortal with immortality. 54 When the perishable has been clothed with the imperishable, and the mortal with immortality, then the saying that is written will come true: "Death has been swallowed up in victory."

55 "Where, O death, is your victory?
   Where, O death, is your sting?"[5]

56 The sting of death is sin, and the power of sin is the law. 57 But thanks be to God! He gives us the victory through our Lord Jesus Christ.

58 Therefore, my dear brothers and sisters, stand firm. Let nothing move you. Always give yourselves fully to the work of the Lord, because you know that your labor in the Lord is not in vain.

16 Now about the collection for the Lord's people:[6] Do what I told the Galatian churches to do. 2 On the first day of every week, each one of you should set aside a sum of money in keeping with your income, saving it up, so that when I come no collections will have to be made. 3 Then, when I arrive, I will give letters of introduction to the men you approve and send them with your gift to Jerusalem. 4 If it seems advisable for me to go also, they will accompany me.

5 After I go through Macedonia, I will come to you—for I will be going through Macedonia. 6 Perhaps I will stay with you for a while, or even spend the winter, so that you can help me on my journey, wherever I go. 7 For I do not want to see you now and make only a passing visit; I hope

---

2. "Natural" in this verse and the next translates *psychikon*; see the note on 2:14.
3. Gen. 2:7. Paul is apparently alluding to and rejecting (v. 46) a tradition, attested by Philo and certain later Gnostic texts, that distinguished the "heavenly man" of Gen. 1:26 ff. from the "earthly man" of Gen. 2.
4. Cf. 1 Thess. 4:13–18.
5. The quotation is composite: Isa. 25:8; Hos. 13:14.
6. Cf. 2 Cor. 8, 9; Rom. 15:25–31; Gal. 2:10.

to spend some time with you, if the Lord permits. 8 But I will stay on at Ephesus until Pentecost,[7] 9 because a great door for effective work has opened to me, and there are many who oppose me.

10 When Timothy comes, see to it that he has nothing to fear while he is with you, for he is carrying on the work of the Lord, just as I am. 11 No one, then, should treat him with contempt. Send him on his way in peace so that he may return to me. I am expecting him along with the brothers.

12 Now about our brother Apollos: I strongly urged him to go to you with the brothers. He was quite unwilling[8] to go now, but he will go when he has the opportunity.

13 Be on your guard; stand firm in the faith; be courageous; be strong. 14 Do everything in love.

15 You know that the household of Stephanas were the first converts[9] in Achaia, and they have devoted themselves to the service of the Lord's people. I urge you, brothers and sisters, 16 to submit to such as these and to everyone who joins in the work and labors at it. 17 I was glad when Stephanas, Fortunatus and Achaicus arrived, because they have supplied what was lacking from you. 18 For they refreshed my spirit and yours also. Such men deserve recognition.

19 The churches in the province of Asia send you greetings. Aquila and Priscilla[1] greet you warmly in the Lord, and so does the church that meets at their house. 20 All the brothers and sisters here send you greetings. Greet one another with a holy kiss.[2]

21 I, Paul, write this greeting in my own hand.

22 If anyone does not love the Lord, let that person be cursed! Come, Lord![3]

23 The grace of the Lord Jesus be with you.

24 My love to all of you in Christ Jesus. Amen.

THE SECOND LETTER TO THE CORINTHIANS
(54–56)

Two issues have dominated scholarly discussion of 2 Corinthians for well over a century: (1) Is this a single letter, more or less as Paul dictated it, or is it a composite of several, written on different occasions? (2) Who are the opponents whom Paul so vigorously attacks, particularly in the last four chapters? No consensus has been attained on either question.

The primary reason for doubting the unity of the letter is the stark contrast between the last four chapters and the previous ones. The early chapters are irenic; they speak of a conflict between Paul and the Corinthians which has been happily resolved. Chapters 10–13, on the other hand, portray a congregation in open rebellion against Paul's authority, evidently incited by a group

---

7. Note that Paul can write to the predominantly Gentile congregation off-handedly of the Jewish festival Pentecost-Shavuot; cf. 5:7f.
8. Or possibly, "It was not at all God's will for him."
9. Lit. "firstfruits"; for a similar use of the metaphor, see Rom. 16:5.
1. See Acts 18:2, 18, 26; Rom. 16:3. Paul, here as elsewhere, calls the wife Prisca, not Priscilla.
2. Cf. 1 Thess. 5:26; 2 Cor. 13:12; Rom. 16:16. In ancient cities only family members usually kissed each other; the exchange of kisses by members of the Christian groups was thus a powerful symbol of their being a new family.
3. The Greek transliterates the Aramaic *marana tha*; probably both this and the preceding anathema belong to the early eucharistic liturgy. Cf. Rev. 22:20.

of rival apostles who have come to Corinth from outside. Even in the first part of the letter there are abrupt transitions. The long self-defense, 2:14–7:4, not only carries quite a different tone from 1:1–2:13 and 7:5–16, but also interrupts Paul's report of his trip from Troas to Macedonia (2:13; 7:5). Similarly the appeal of 6:13, "open wide your hearts," is interrupted in mid-sentence, to resume again in 7:2. The intervening admonition is quite different from Paul's usual writing in style, vocabulary, and content. Finally, both chapters 8 and 9 concern the collection that Paul is arranging for the poor in Jerusalem, but they seem quite independent of each other, and they appeal on different grounds for the addressees to participate. Some scholars would explain these anomalies by Paul's use of various rhetorical strategies in one complex letter. Most, however, find it easier to believe that some very early editor stitched together portions of several different letters.

We know of numerous communications in both directions between Paul and the Corinthian Christian groups, but it is not easy to sort them all out. Our 1 Corinthians is at least the second letter written by Paul to Corinth, for it mentions an earlier one (1 Cor. 5:9), lost as far as we know. He had also heard from them, both by a formal delegation which apparently brought a letter from the congregations (7:1), and by information brought by some members of Chloe's household (1:11). In response he not only sent his second letter (1 Corinthians), but also sent Timothy (4:17; 16:10 f.), who, when he returned (2 Cor. 1:1), doubtless brought new information (distressing to Paul, as we may surmise from the next two events). Our 2 Corinthians also mentions a previous letter, written with strong emotion (2 Cor. 1:23–2:4; 7:5–11), which cannot convincingly be identified with our 1 Corinthians. That letter, moreover, was written after Paul had paid a "painful visit" (2:1), during which some individual personally offended him (2:1–11; 7:12). It was most likely Timothy's report that provoked the painful visit and the subsequent "letter of tears." The carrier of that letter was Titus, who also returned with news, this time good (7:6f.). Titus was also charged to go to Corinth with two other emissaries to make arrangements for the Jerusalem collection (8:16–23). This would be Titus's second recorded visit, and he was taking with him at least the directives about the collection that constitute our chapter 8. But how much more, if any, of our 2 Corinthians was in that letter Titus was carrying?

The key piece in the jigsaw puzzle is the angry, sarcastic, argumentative appeal of 10:1–13:10. If the parts of this letter were written at different times, was this the earliest or the latest, or was it written sometime in between? It is in this section, particularly in chapter 11, that we hear about some rival missionaries, whom Paul calls sarcastically "super-apostles" (11:5) and directly "false apostles, deceitful workers, masquerading as apostles of Christ," and even "servants of Satan" (11:13,15). From some of Paul's defensive statements in chapter 10, we may judge that they had said equally derogatory things about him. When did they arrive in Corinth? Were they the ones who stirred up the opposition that Timothy had reported, and who thus provoked both the "painful visit" and the "letter of tears"? In that case, chapters 10–13 might be all or part of that emotional letter. The first part of our 2 Corinthians, then—that is, all or parts of chapters 1–7—would be Paul's reconciling response to the Corinthian congregations' repentance, evoked by their "grief" over the "letter of tears." The sequence of writing the two main sections of 2 Corinthians would then be more or less the reverse of the transmitted order, which uses Paul's final, reconciling letter for the editorial framework of the whole, including the relatively happy ending, 13:11–13.

The main problem with this reconstruction is that the "super-apostles" are not explicitly mentioned in the early chapters. Instead, Paul focuses on a single individual who has wronged him in some way, who has been punished by the congregation in response to Paul's emotional letter, and whom Paul would now like to see forgiven and reinstated (2:5–11; 7:8–13). Another way of reading the evidence, then, would be to suppose that the "letter of tears" dealt solely with that individual and his offense, whatever it was, and that the letter is lost—unless a few scattered paragraphs from it may be found in our transmitted letter. In that case, however, the reconciliation achieved by Paul's subsequent letter and by Titus's intervention was only temporary, for the later arrival of the "super-apostles" would provoke a new crisis, to which our present chapters 10–13 would have been Paul's response. In that case, Paul's expression of confidence in 13:11–14, if it really did end his final letter to the Corinthians, is surprising after the vehemence of chapters 10 and 11 and his ironic "fool's speech" of chapter 12, but perhaps not inexplicable following the strong but confident appeal of 13:1–10.

Further complexity is added when we ask what to make of chapters 8 and 9: one letter or two about the collection? Both addressed to the congregations in Corinth, or perhaps one to a wider circle of congregations in the province? Sent separately, or attached to one of the other letters? And did the project of the Jerusalem collection itself cause part of the ill-feeling toward Paul, which had in part to do with his sometimes refusing, sometimes asking for money?

Finally, the identity of the intrusive apostles remains vague. From Paul's parodies it is probable that they used the titles "apostle," "worker," and "servants (*diakonoi*) of Christ" (11:13–15, 23). Like Paul, they were Jews, proud to be called "Hebrews," "Israelites," "seed of Abraham" (11:22). They tended, at least as Paul saw it, to equate authority with power. Their demands on the Corinthian congregations were direct and assertive (11:20); they scoffed at Paul's "weakness" (11:30; cf. chaps. 3–4), his humble demeanor, unprepossessing appearance, and feeble oratorical skills in person in contrast with the power he asserted in his letters (10:2, 10). Perhaps they made Paul's refusal to accept gifts from the Corinthians a ground for suspecting his legitimacy and motives (11:7–11; 12:13–18). They seem to have put some stock in visible manifestations of spirit-possession, like performance of miracles (12:12) and "visions and revelations" (12:1), as well as in personal appearance and oratorical power (10:1–11; 11:6). But such traits are not uncommon in descriptions of charismatic figures of many kinds in the literature of the time—the Book of Acts describes all the apostles and Paul himself in ways that are not dissimilar. There are no clues strong enough to identify the "super-apostles" with any known group of early Christian missionaries, not even the apostles who caused Paul such trouble earlier in Galatia.

There are a few bits of evidence that the story had a relatively happy outcome: the survival of the letter itself, however it may have been edited, the fact that the Achaeans did join in with the Macedonians (8:1–5; 9:2) to send money to Jerusalem (Rom. 15:26), and the warm greetings that several Corinthians add to Paul's letter to Rome, which he wrote from their city (Rom. 16:21–23). That "third visit" (12:14; 13:1) must have been much more satisfactory than the second.

2 Corinthians

1 Paul, an apostle of Christ Jesus by the will of God, and Timothy[1] our brother,

To the church of God in Corinth, together with all his holy people throughout Achaia:[2]

---

1. Timothy was with Paul when the church was established at Corinth (Acts 18:5; 2 Cor. 1:19) and later returned there as his intermediary (Acts 19:22; 1 Cor. 4:17; 16:10–11).
2. Achaia is the Roman province, of which Corinth had been the capital since 27 BCE.

2 Grace and peace to you from God our Father and the Lord Jesus Christ.

3 Praise be to the God and Father of our Lord Jesus Christ,[3] the Father of compassion and the God of all comfort, 4 who comforts us in all our troubles,[4] so that we can comfort those in any trouble with the comfort we ourselves receive from God. 5 For just as we share abundantly in the sufferings of Christ, so also our comfort abounds through Christ. 6 If we are distressed, it is for your comfort and salvation; if we are comforted, it is for your comfort, which produces in you patient endurance of the same sufferings we suffer. 7 And our hope for you is firm,[5] because we know that just as you share in our sufferings, so also you share in our comfort.

8 We do not want you to be uninformed, brothers and sisters, about the troubles we experienced in the province of Asia.[6] We were under great pressure, far beyond our ability to endure, so that we despaired of life itself. 9 Indeed, we felt we had received the sentence of death. But this happened that we might not rely on ourselves but on God, who raises the dead. 10 He has delivered us from such a deadly peril, and he will deliver us again. On him we have set our hope that he will continue to deliver us, 11 as you help us by your prayers. Then many will give thanks on our behalf for the gracious favor granted us in answer to the prayers of many.

12 Now this is our boast:[7] Our conscience testifies that we have conducted ourselves in the world, and especially in our relations with you, with integrity[8] and godly sincerity. We have done so, relying not on worldly wisdom but on God's grace. 13 For we do not write you anything you cannot read or understand. And I hope that, 14 as you have understood us in part, you will come to understand fully that you can boast of us just as we will boast of you in the day of the Lord Jesus.[9]

15 Because I was confident of this, I wanted to visit you[1] first so that you might benefit twice. 16 I wanted to visit you on my way to Macedonia and to come back to you from Macedonia, and then to have you send me on my way to Judea.[2] 17 Was I fickle when I intended to do this? Or do I make my plans in a worldly manner[3] so that in the same breath I say both "Yes, yes" and "No, no"?[4]

3. Instead of his customary thanksgiving (see Rom. 1:8–15; 1 Cor. 1:4–9), Paul uses here a benediction (vv. 3–4) derived from ancient Jewish liturgical formulas such as "blessed be the Lord" (see Gen. 24:26–27; see also Eph. 1:3–14; 1 Pet. 1:3–9).
4. Affliction and comfort are central themes both of the blessing and of the letter as whole; see 1:3–8; 2:4; 4:8, 17; 6:4; 7:4–7; 8:2, 13.
5. Expressions of Paul's confidence in the Corinthians are frequent, a major element in his appeal for reconciliation: see also 1:24; 7:4, 14, 16; 8:7.
6. The sentence begins with a disclosure formula frequently used by Paul to impart new or important information (Rom. 1:13; 11:25; 1 Cor. 10:1; 12:1; 1 Thess. 4:13). Asia is the Roman province of which Ephesus was the largest city. Nothing certain is known about the event Paul mentions; some conjecture that it was an otherwise unknown imprisonment in Ephesus during which he faced the possibility of execution (v. 9; see also Phil. 1:12–26; cf. Acts 19:23–41).
7. The topic of Paul's "boast" or self-commendation is prominent in the Letters to Corinth, sometimes negatively, sometimes ironically, sometimes as here positively; see 1 Cor. 9:15; 2 Cor. 3:1; 4:2; 5:12; 6:4; 10:8, 12–18; 11:10, 16–18, 30; 12:1, 5–6, 9, 11.
8. The alternative reading "holiness" is also strongly supported.
9. See 1 Cor. 1:8 and the note on 1 Cor. 3:13; 5:5; 1 Thess. 5:2; Phil. 2:16. For Paul's pride in the Corinthians, see also 1 Cor. 15:31; 2 Cor. 7:4, 14; 8:24; 9:2–3; for their pride in him, 5:12.
1. For Paul's various travel plans in regard to Corinth, see also 1 Cor. 4:18–21; 11:34; 16:3–9; 2 Cor. 9:4; 12:14; 13:1.
2. Both Philippi and Thessalonica were in the Roman province Macedonia. The phrase "send me on" implies financial assistance for the journey (see Rom. 15:24; 1 Cor. 16:6, 11; Titus 3:13; 3 John 6–8). For the planned trip to Judea, see also Rom. 15:25; 1 Cor. 16:3.
3. Lit. "according to the flesh."
4. Cf. Matt. 5:37; Jas. 5:12.

18 But as surely as God is faithful, our message to you is not "Yes" and "No." 19 For the Son of God, Jesus Christ, who was preached among you by us—by me and Silas[5] and Timothy—was not "Yes" and "No," but in him it has always been "Yes." 20 For no matter how many promises God has made, they are "Yes" in Christ. And so through him the "Amen"[6] is spoken by us to the glory of God. 21 Now it is God who makes both us and you stand firm in Christ. He anointed us, 22 set his seal of ownership on us, and put his Spirit in our hearts as a deposit,[7] guaranteeing what is to come.

23 I call God as my witness[8]—and I stake my life on it—that it was in order to spare you that I did not return to Corinth. 24 Not that we lord it over your faith, but we work with you for your joy, because it is by faith you stand firm.

2 So I made up my mind that I would not make another painful visit to you.[9] 2 For if I grieve you, who is left to make me glad but you whom I have grieved? 3 I wrote as I did, so that when I came I would not be distressed by those who should have made me rejoice. I had confidence in all of you, that you would all share my joy. 4 For I wrote you out of great distress and anguish of heart and with many tears, not to grieve you but to let you know the depth of my love for you.[1]

5 If anyone[2] has caused grief, he has not so much grieved me as he has grieved all of you to some extent—not to put it too severely. 6 The punishment[3] inflicted on him by the majority is sufficient. 7 Now instead, you ought to forgive and comfort him, so that he will not be overwhelmed by excessive sorrow. 8 I urge you, therefore, to reaffirm your love for him. 9 Another reason I wrote you was to see if you would stand the test and be obedient in everything. 10 Anyone you forgive, I also forgive. And what I have forgiven—if there was anything to forgive—I have forgiven in the sight of Christ for your sake, 11 in order that Satan[4] might not outwit us. For we are not unaware of his schemes.

12 Now when I went to Troas[5] to preach the gospel of Christ and found that the Lord had opened a door for me,[6] 13 I still had no peace of mind,

---

5. Silvanus (1 Thess. 1:1; 2 Thess. 1:1; 1 Pet. 5:12), called by the abbreviated "Silas" only in Acts. He was with Paul and Timothy when the church was established at Corinth (Acts 18:5).

6. A Jewish and Christian liturgical acclamation meaning "So let it be," uttered by the congregation in response to benedictions and thanksgivings (see 1 Cor. 14:16; Gal. 1:5; Phil. 4:20).

7. The same commercial word is used of the Spirit in 5:5 and Eph. 1:14; a cultic term usually translated "firstfruits" is used with similar meaning in Rom. 8:23.

8. Cf. Rom. 1:9; Phil. 1:8; 1 Thess. 2:5, 10.

9. The previous visit, Paul's second, was painful because of the events he alludes to in the following verses. Thematically, joy and pain, grief and consolation in 1:23–2:11 resume Paul's earlier discussion of affliction and consolation (1:3–11).

1. For hypotheses concerning this "letter of tears," see the introduction above.

2. See also 7:12. Both the identity of this individual and the details of his actions are unknown. Earlier critics identified him with the miscreant of 1 Cor. 5, but most modern interpreters think Paul's language here suggests a direct offense against Paul himself. The authority exercised over him by the local congregation makes it likely he was one of them, not one of the outsiders mentioned in chaps. 10–13.

3. Or "strong moral rebuke."

4. Satan is frequently mentioned not only in Paul's Letters to Corinth (1 Cor. 5:5; 7:5; 2 Cor. 6:15; 11:14; 12:7) but also in those written from that city (Rom. 16:20; 1 Thess. 2:18; 2 Thess. 2:9).

5. I.e., Alexandria Troas, a seaport and Roman colony located in the northwest corner of Asia Minor (see Acts 16:8, 11; 20:5–6; 2 Tim. 4:13).

6. Cf. 1 Cor. 16:9; Col 4:3; Rev. 3:8.

because I did not find my brother Titus[7] there. So I said good-by to them and went on to Macedonia.[8]

14 But thanks be to God, who always leads us as captives in Christ's triumphal procession[9] and uses us to spread the aroma of the knowledge of him everywhere. 15 For we are to God the pleasing aroma[1] of Christ among those who are being saved and those who are perishing. 16 To the one we are an aroma that brings death; to the other, an aroma that brings life.[2] And who is equal[3] to such a task? 17 Unlike so many,[4] we do not peddle the word of God for profit. On the contrary, in Christ we speak before God with sincerity, as those sent from God.

3 Are we beginning to commend[5] ourselves again? Or do we need, like some people, letters of recommendation[6] to you or from you? 2 You your-selves are our letter, written on our hearts, known and read by everyone. 3 You show that you are a letter from Christ, the result of our ministry, written not with ink but with the Spirit of the living God, not on tablets of stone but on tablets of human hearts.[7]

4 Such confidence we have through Christ before God. 5 Not that we are competent in ourselves to claim anything for ourselves, but our com-petence comes from God. 6 He has made us competent as ministers of a new covenant[8]—not of the letter[9] but of the Spirit; for the letter kills, but the Spirit gives life.

7 Now if the ministry that brought death,[1] which was engraved in letters on stone, came with glory, so that the Israelites could not look steadily at the face of Moses because of its glory, transitory though it was, 8 will not the ministry of the Spirit be even more glorious? 9 If the ministry that brought condemnation was glorious, how much more glorious is the min-

---

7. Titus (see 7:6 f., 13–15; 8:6, 16–23; 12:18; 2 Tim. 4:10; Tit. 1:4) was apparently the bearer of the letter mentioned in 2:3 f., 9.

8. The travel narrative is resumed in 7:5. Some commentators think that 2:14–6:13; 7:2–4 were originally part of an earlier, apologetic letter.

9. Alluding to the famous Roman military parades in which victorious generals celebrated their tri-umphs along with their soldiers and in which their prisoners of war were compelled to march (see also Col. 2:15), Paul refers to his itinerant apostolic ministry as directed by God.

1. A technical term for an offering acceptable to God (see, e.g., Ex. 29:18, 25, 41; Lev. 1:9, 13, 17; 2:2, 9, 12; 35, 11, 16). Paul uses the metaphor quite freely here, first identifying the aroma with his proclamation of the gospel, which brings knowledge of God (v. 14), then with the sacrifice of Christ (v. 15), which brings opposite reactions from "those who are being saved and those who are perishing."

2. Lit., "from death to death," "from life to life." See further 4:10.

3. This phrase translates the same Greek word that appears with two cognates, translated "compe-tent," "competence," and "made competent," in 3:5f. This question is central to the dispute between Paul and his opponents.

4. Here and in 4:2 Paul is probably referring to those rival apostles whom he attacks so sarcastically in chaps. 10–13, simultaneously denying accusations they have made against him while implying their own lack of sincerity.

5. This verb occurs 8 more times in 2 Corinthians: 4:2, 5:12; 6:4; 7:11; 10:12, 18; 12:11, thus linking thematically parts that some commentators would attribute to originally separate letters. Compare the note on 1:12.

6. Letters of recommendation were widely used in the Greco-Roman world to praise friends and acquaintances and to introduce them to others. Early Christians made frequent use of this ancient convention, especially for traveling missionaries (see Acts 18:27; Rom. 16:1; 1 Cor. 16:10).

7. Paul now mixes the metaphor of the letter with an allusion to the commandments given to Moses (Ex. 24:12; 31:18; Deut. 9:10f.); for the notion of writing on the heart, see Prov. 3:3; 7:3; Jer. 31:33; cf. Ezek. 11:19; 36:26. Thus he begins the contrast between the ministries of the old and new covenants that is the theme of vv. 4–18.

8. Cf. Jer. 31:31–34. The words translated "minister" and "ministry" here are *diakonos, diakonia*; they recur throughout this section (3:7, 8, 9; 4:1; 5:18; 6:3, 4), several times in close proximity to the verb "to commend" (see note on 3:1).

9. "Letter" here translates *gramma*; the word in 3:1–3 is *epistolē*.

1. Cf. Rom. 7:10. Here Paul begins a two-part interpretation of Ex 34:29–35, expounding his thesis statement 3:6 in vv. 7–18.

istry that brings righteousness! 10 For what was glorious has no glory now in comparison with the surpassing glory. 11 And if what was transitory came with glory, how much greater is the glory of that which lasts![2]

12 Therefore, since we have such a hope, we are very bold.[3] 13 We are not like Moses, who would put a veil over his face to prevent the Israelites from seeing the end of what was passing away.[4] 14 But their minds were made dull, for to this day the same veil remains when the old covenant is read.[5] It has not been removed, because only in Christ is it taken away. 15 Even to this day when Moses[6] is read, a veil covers their hearts. 16 But whenever anyone turns to the Lord, the veil is taken away. 17 Now the Lord is the Spirit,[7] and where the Spirit of the Lord is, there is freedom. 18 And we all, who with unveiled faces contemplate the Lord's glory, are being transformed into his image with ever-increasing glory,[8] which comes from the Lord, who is the Spirit.

4 Therefore, since through God's mercy we have this ministry, we do not lose heart.[9] 2 Rather, we have renounced secret and shameful ways; we do not use deception, nor do we distort the word of God. On the contrary, by setting forth the truth plainly we commend ourselves to everyone's conscience in the sight of God. 3 And even if our gospel is veiled,[1] it is veiled to those who are perishing. 4 The god of this age[2] has blinded the minds of unbelievers, so that they cannot see the light of the gospel that displays the glory of Christ, who is the image of God. 5 For what we preach is not ourselves, but Jesus Christ as Lord, and ourselves as your servants[3] for Jesus' sake. 6 For God, who said, "Let light shine out of darkness,"[4] made his light shine in our hearts to give us the light of the knowledge of God's glory displayed in the face of Christ.

7 But we have this treasure in jars of clay to show that this all-surpassing

---

2. In vv. 7–11 Paul uses the common argumentative rule, "from the lesser to the greater," known in later rabbinic exegesis as "light and heavy" (*qal ve homer*). "Glory" is suggested by the LXX translation of the phrase "shone with light" by "became glorious" in Ex. 34:29, 30, 35.

3. This refers to the manner of Paul's speaking, not his state of mind. In both Hellenistic philosophy and Pauline theology, frank speech was based on freedom (v. 17), confidence (v. 4), and competence (vv. 5–6), and it was appropriately used to foster moral improvement.

4. Because Ex. 34:33 does not say explicitly *why* Moses put on a veil whenever he was neither speaking to the Lord nor conveying the Lord's oracles to the people, Paul finds room for this bit of creative midrash. His starting premise is that, if the covenant of which Moses was the minister was replaced, as Jeremiah had prophesied, by a *new* covenant (v.6), then the former must be "transitory" (v. 11; the same word here translated "passing away").

5. This translation is misleading, for there was not yet a *book* called "the old covenant" (or "Old Testament"), as there was not yet a book called "the New Testament." Rather, we should translate the Greek literally, "the same veil is over the reading of [that is, the way of reading that belonged to] the old covenant."

6. I.e., "the book of Moses" (the Torah or Pentateuch); see 2 Chron. 25:4; Neh. 13:1; Mark 12:26; Acts 15:21.

7. An exegetical remark: Paul's midrash takes "the Lord" in Ex. 34:34 to mean "the Spirit." So also in v. 18.

8. This statement reflects the widespread Hellenistic belief that humans are changed as a result of beholding the divine. On the metamorphosis to the divine image, see Rom. 8:29; 1 Cor. 15:49; Col. 3:10; for Christ as the image of God, see 4:4.

9. Repetition of this phrase in 4:16 marks off one step in Paul's argument.

1. Echoing his disquisition on the veil of Moses (3:7–18), Paul probably alludes also to an accusation made by his opponents, who may have believed that he craftily distorted and hid his gospel by using rhetorical devices such as irony and covert allusion (see 1 Cor. 4:6–8), or that Paul's sufferings veiled his message about God and led to its rejection.

2. The only NT reference to Satan as "god." A surprisingly sharp expression of the limited dualism which Paul and much of early Christianity shared with Jewish apocalyptic groups, like the Qumran community; see also 1 Cor. 2:6, 8; John 12:31; 14:30; 16:11; Eph. 2:2. See Part IV for Irenaeus's attempt to avoid this interpretation.

3. Lit., "slaves."

4. Paul is paraphrasing Gen. 1:3; cf. Ps. 112:4; Isa. 9:2; John 1:5.

power is from God and not from us. 8 We are hard pressed on every side, but not crushed; perplexed, but not in despair; 9 persecuted, but not abandoned; struck down, but not destroyed.[5] 10 We always carry around in our body the death[6] of Jesus, so that the life of Jesus may also be revealed in our body. 11 For we who are alive are always being given over[7] to death for Jesus' sake, so that his life may also be revealed in our mortal body. 12 So then, death is at work in us, but life is at work in you.

13 It is written: "I believed; therefore I have spoken."[8] Since we have that same spirit of faith, we also believe and therefore speak, 14 because we know that the one who raised the Lord Jesus from the dead will also raise us with Jesus and present us with you to himself. 15 All this is for your benefit, so that the grace that is reaching more and more people may cause thanksgiving to overflow to the glory of God.[9]

16 Therefore we do not lose heart. Though outwardly we are wasting away, yet inwardly[1] we are being renewed day by day. 17 For our light and momentary troubles are achieving for us an eternal glory that far outweighs them all.[2] 18 So we fix our eyes not on what is seen, but on what is unseen, since what is seen is temporary, but what is unseen is eternal.[3]

5 For we know that if the earthly tent[4] we live in is destroyed, we have a building from God, an eternal house in heaven, not built by human hands. 2 Meanwhile we groan,[5] longing to be clothed with our heavenly dwelling, 3 because when we are clothed, we will not be found naked. 4 For while we are in this tent, we groan and are burdened, because we do not wish to be unclothed but to be clothed with our heavenly dwelling, so that what is mortal may be swallowed up by life. 5 Now the one who has fashioned us for this very purpose is God, who has given us the Spirit as a deposit,[6] guaranteeing what is to come.

6 Therefore we are always confident and know that as long as we are at home in the body we are away from the Lord. 7 We live by faith, not by sight.[7] 8 We are confident, I say, and would prefer to be away from the body and at home with the Lord.[8] 9 So we make it our goal to please him, whether we are at home in the body or away from it. 10 For we must all

---

5. Lists of hardships were commonly used to depict the ideal sage's own victory over adversity (see note on 1 Cor. 4:9–13). Paul claims a similar superiority but consistently attributes it to God rather than himself (v. 7). In the Greek, rhythm and internal rhyme heighten the rhetorical effect. Similar lists appear in 6:4–10; 11:23–28; 12:10; Rom. 8:35–39; 1 Cor. 4:9–13; Phil. 4:11–12; 2 Tim. 3:11.
6. Greek *nekrōsis*, a graphic word used by medical writers of dead or dying tissue. Paul uses it to make more vivid the paradoxical statements that express the center of his theology.
7. Or, "are always giving ourselves over."
8. Ps. 115:1 LXX; cf. Ps. 116:10.
9. See 1:11; 9:11 f.
1. Lit., "our outer person [*anthrōpos*] is wasting away," "our inner person." The contrast was common in Middle Platonism. See also Rom. 7:22; Eph. 3:16; 1 Pet. 3:4. In this section, 4:16b–5:10, commonplaces of popular Hellenistic philosophy—inner/outer person, visible and transient/unseen and eternal, the body as a tent—alternate with notions familiar in Jewish apocalyptic discourse—present affliction/eternal glory; house or temple stored up in heaven; final judgment. Paul's free mixing of dwelling metaphors with clothing metaphors adds to the complexity of the passage.
2. See Rom. 8:18; 2 Thess. 1:5; 1 Pet. 1:6 f.
3. Compare Col. 1:16; Heb. 11:1, 3.
4. See also Wis. 9:15; 2 Pet. 1:13. The tent/building contrast continues the temporary/permanent antithesis of 4:17–18.
5. Again in 5:4; cf. Rom. 8:23, 26.
6. See note on 1:22.
7. See 4:18; Rom. 8:24–25; 1 Cor. 13:12; 1 Pet. 1:8.
8. Cf. Phil. 1:23.

appear before the judgment seat of Christ,[9] that everyone may receive what is due them for the things done while in the body, whether good or bad.

11 Since, then, we know what it is to fear the Lord,[1] we try to persuade people. What we are is plain to God, and I hope it is also plain to your conscience. 12 We are not trying to commend ourselves to you again,[2] but are giving you an opportunity to take pride in us, so that you can answer those who take pride in what is seen rather than in what is in the heart.[3] 13 If we are "out of our mind,"[4] as some say, it is for God; if we are in our right mind, it is for you. 14 For Christ's love compels us, because we are convinced that one died for all, and therefore all died. 15 And he died for all, that those who live should no longer live for themselves but for him who died for them and was raised again.[5]

16 So from now on we regard no one from a worldly point of view.[6] Though we once regarded Christ in this way, we do so no longer. 17 Therefore, if anyone is in Christ, the new creation has come: The old has gone, the new is here![7] 18 All this is from God, who reconciled us to himself through Christ and gave us the ministry of reconciliation: 19 that God was reconciling the world to himself in Christ, not counting people's sins against them. And he has committed to us the message of reconciliation. 20 We are therefore Christ's ambassadors, as though God were making his appeal through us. We implore you on Christ's behalf: Be reconciled to God.[8] 21 God made him who had no sin to be sin for us,[9] so that in him we might become the righteousness[1] of God.

6 As God's co-workers we urge you not to receive God's grace in vain. 2 For he says,

"In the time of my favor I heard you,
and in the day of salvation I helped you."[2]

I tell you, now is the time of God's favor, now is the day of salvation.

3 We put no stumbling block in anyone's path, so that our ministry will not be discredited. 4 Rather, as servants of God we commend ourselves[3]

---

9. See 1 Cor. 3:12–15; 4:5; Rom. 2:6–10, 16; 14:9–10.
1. Lit., "know the fear of the Lord"; see 7:1, where the same word for "fear" is translated "reverence." The phrase "fear of the Lord" occurs many times in Jewish scriptures (39 times in the LXX); e.g., Ps. 19:9; 111:10; Prov. 9:10; Isa. 11:1–3; Sir. 1:11–20.
2. See note on 1:12.
3. Echoing 1 Sam. 16:7, Paul suggests that his opponents' way of seeing is the opposite of God's.
4. The verb used here is the root of the English word "ecstasy." Most interpreters see here a reference to mystical experiences (see 12:1–6), which, though praised by Paul's adversaries, were evaluated by him according to the same standard he applied to speaking in tongues (1 Cor. 14:2, 19, 28). Some think he is referring to the "letter of tears" (2:4).
5. See Rom. 6:1–11; 7:4; 14:7–9; Gal. 2:19–20.
6. Lit., "according to flesh"; see 1:17; 10:2f.; 11:18.
7. See Isa. 43:18–19; 65:17; 66:22; Gal. 6:15; Eph. 2:15; 2 Pet. 3:13; Rev. 21:1–5.
8. In ancient thought, reconciliation between persons or nations involved the removal of enmity and the establishment or restoration of friendship. In the political world this was a task quintessentially entrusted to an ambassador (v. 20). The responsibility for reconciliation normally resided with those who were responsible for rupturing a relationship. Paul not only applies the concept to the divine-human relationship, but in a major paradigm shift presents God as the reconciler (Rom. 5: 10–11; also Col. 1:20–22), not as the object of reconciliation (as in 2 Macc. 1:5; 5:20; 7:33; 8: 29). Consequently, Paul is not humanity's ambassador appealing to God, but God's to the world.
9. Either in the sense that Christ assumed sinful human nature (see Rom. 8:3), or that on the cross God treated the sinless Jesus as a sinner (see Gal. 3:13), or that Jesus became a sacrifice for sin, either a guilt offering or a sin offering (see Isa. 53:10; Rom. 8:3). On his sinlessness, see John 7:18; 8:46; Heb. 4:15; 7:26; 1 Pet. 1:19; 2:22; 3:18; 1 John 3:5.
1. Cf. 1 Cor. 1:30. "Righteousness of God" is a central phrase for Paul, occurring ten times in the letters; see Rom. 1:17; 3:5, 21–22, 25–26; 10:3; Phil. 3:9.
2. Isa. 49:8.
3. See note on 1:12. The self-commendation takes the form of a catalogue of hardships (see the note at 4:8). Adversity and virtue were closely linked in antiquity, so that the nine hardships given in

in every way: in great endurance; in troubles, hardships and distresses; 5 in beatings, imprisonments and riots; in hard work, sleepless nights and hunger; 6 in purity, understanding, patience and kindness; in the Holy Spirit and in sincere love; 7 in truthful speech and in the power of God; with weapons of righteousness in the right hand and in the left; 8 through glory and dishonor, bad report and good report; genuine, yet regarded as impostors; 9 known, yet regarded as unknown; dying, and yet we live on; beaten, and yet not killed; 10 sorrowful, yet always rejoicing; poor, yet making many rich;[4] having nothing, and yet possessing everything.[5]

11 We have spoken freely to you,[6] Corinthians, and opened wide our hearts to you. 12 We are not withholding our affection from you, but you are withholding yours from us. 13 As a fair exchange—I speak as to my children[7]—open wide your hearts also.[8]

14 Do not be yoked together with unbelievers. For what do righteousness and wickedness have in common? Or what fellowship can light have with darkness? 15 What harmony is there between Christ and Belial[9]? Or what does a believer have in common with an unbeliever? 16 What agreement is there between the temple of God and idols? For we are the temple of the living God.[1] As God has said:[2]

> "I will live with them
>   and walk among them,
> and I will be their God,
>   and they will be my people."

17 Therefore,

> "Come out from them
>   and be separate,
>   says the Lord.
> Touch no unclean thing,
>   and I will receive you."

6:4–5 function not only to magnify Paul's great endurance (v. 4) but also to prove that he is virtuous; the list of virtues (vv. 6–7) underscores the point. For other virtue lists, see Gal. 5:22–23; Phil. 4:8; Col. 3:12; 1 Pet. 3:8; 2 Pet. 1:5–7.

4. See 8:9.

5. The seven antithetic clauses that conclude this section (vv. 8–10) contrast the outward appearance with the hidden reality (5:12). In formulating these verses, Paul draws on Ps. 118:17–18 as well as Greco-Roman paradoxes about the ideal sage.

6. Lit., "Our mouth is open to you." On frank speech, see also 7:4 and the note on 3:12. The open mouth and wide heart contrast rhetorically with the "withholding"—lit. "narrowing"—of affection in the following verse. After his long description of his reconciling ministry (2:14–6:10), Paul now appeals to the Corinthian church to be fully reconciled with him (6:11–7:4) and with the one who wronged him (7:5–16).

7. See 1 Cor. 4:14; Gal. 4:19; 1 Thess. 2:11.

8. Because this appeal is resumed in very similar language in 7:2, many commentators have doubted that the digression 6:14–7:1 belongs here. Moreover, this passage contains a number of words not found elsewhere in Paul's letters and exhibits a more starkly dualistic view of the world than we see elsewhere in Paul, reminiscent of the language and use of scripture in the Dead Sea Scrolls. Of the various solutions proposed, five merit mention. The passage could be (1) a fragment from the letter mentioned in 1 Cor. 5:9; (2) a digression in which Paul deliberately uses unusual and highly emotional language for rhetorical effect; (3) a passage, non-Pauline in origin, that Paul himself inserts here to provide moral exhortation and/or warn the Corinthians against associating with his opponents; (4) a non-Pauline passage, perhaps of Essene origin, inserted by a later editor; or even (5) an originally anti-Pauline passage that reflects the theology of Paul's opponents.

9. Hebrew, "worthlessness," one of the various Jewish names for Satan (see 2:11) Most of the Greek manuscripts spell it *Beliar*, a phonetic variant.

1. On the community as temple, see 1 Cor. 3:16 and the note there.

2. Three quotation formulas introduce, connect, and conclude the chain of citations and paraphrases: in v. 16, Lev. 26:11f.; Ezek. 37:27; in v. 17, Isa. 52:11; Ezek. 20:34 LXX; in v. 18, 2 Sam. 7:14; Isa. 43:6. For similar chains see Rom. 3:10–18; 15:9–12.

18 And,

> "I will be a Father to you,
> and you will be my sons and daughters,
> says the Lord Almighty."

7 Therefore, since we have these promises, dear friends, let us purify ourselves from everything that contaminates body and spirit, perfecting holiness out of reverence for God.

2 Make room for us in your hearts. We have wronged no one, we have corrupted no one, we have exploited no one.[3] 3 I do not say this to condemn you; I have said before that you have such a place in our hearts that we would live or die with you.[4] 4 I have spoken to you with great frankness;[5] I take great pride in you. I am greatly encouraged; in all our troubles my joy knows no bounds.

5 For when we came into Macedonia,[6] this body of ours had no rest, but we were harassed at every turn—conflicts on the outside, fears within. 6 But God, who comforts the downcast,[7] comforted us by the coming of Titus, 7 and not only by his coming but also by the comfort you had given him. He told us about your longing for me, your deep sorrow, your ardent concern for me, so that my joy was greater than ever.

8 Even if I caused you sorrow by my letter,[8] I do not regret it. Though I did regret it—I see that my letter hurt you, but only for a little while—9 yet now I am happy, not because you were made sorry, but because your sorrow led you to repentance. For you became sorrowful as God intended and so were not harmed in any way by us. 10 Godly sorrow brings repentance that leads to salvation and leaves no regret, but worldly sorrow brings death. 11 See what this godly sorrow has produced in you: what earnestness, what eagerness to clear yourselves, what indignation, what alarm, what longing, what concern, what readiness to see justice done. At every point you have proved yourselves to be innocent in this matter. 12 So even though I wrote to you, it was neither on account of the one who did the wrong nor on account of the injured party,[9] but rather that before God you could see for yourselves how devoted to us you are. 13 By all this we are encouraged.

In addition to our own encouragement, we were especially delighted to see how happy Titus was, because his spirit has been refreshed by all of you. 14 I had boasted to him about you, and you have not embarrassed me. But just as everything we said to you was true, so our boasting[1] about you to Titus has proved to be true as well. 15 And his affection for you is all the greater when he remembers that you were all obedient,[2] receiving him with fear and trembling. 16 I am glad I can have complete confidence in you.

---

3. See 12:17–18.
4. A Christianized version of a traditional friendship formula (see 2 Sam. 15:21).
5. Frankness is a sign of friendship (see note on 3:12). This verse recalls the major themes of 1:3–14, thus providing a transition to the next section.
6. Here Paul takes up the narrative left off at 2:13. On questions the break raises about the unity of the letter, see the introduction.
7. See 1:3–4; Isa 49:13.
8. See 2:3.
9. Paul himself.
1. See 1:14.
2. See 2:9. On the importance of confidence expressions in this letter, see the note on 1:7. This one sums up the story of restored friendship of vv. 5–15 and also lays the foundation for the requests made in chs. 8–9.

8 And now, brothers and sisters, we want you to know about the grace[3] that God has given the Macedonian churches. 2 In the midst of a very severe trial,[4] their overflowing joy and their extreme poverty welled up in rich generosity. 3 For I testify that they gave as much as they were able, and even beyond their ability. Entirely on their own, 4 they urgently pleaded with us for the privilege of sharing in this service to the Lord's people.[5] 5 And they went beyond our expectations; having given themselves first of all to the Lord, they gave themselves by the will of God also to us. 6 So we urged Titus, just as he had earlier made a beginning, to bring also to completion this act of grace on your part.[6] 7 But since you excel in everything—in faith, in speech, in knowledge, in complete earnestness and in the love we have kindled in you[7]—see that you also excel in this grace of giving.

8 I am not commanding you,[8] but I want to test the sincerity of your love by comparing it with the earnestness of others. 9 For you know the grace of our Lord Jesus Christ, that though he was rich, yet for your sake he became poor, so that you through his poverty might become rich.[9]

10 And here is my judgment about what is best for you in this matter. Last year[1] you were the first not only to give but also to have the desire to do so. 11 Now finish the work, so that your eager willingness to do it may be matched by your completion of it, according to your means. 12 For if the willingness is there, the gift is acceptable according to what one has, not according to what one does not have.

13 Our desire is not that others might be relieved while you are hard pressed, but that there might be equality. 14 At the present time your plenty will supply what they need, so that in turn their plenty will supply what you need. The goal is equality, 15 as it is written: "The one who gathered much did not have too much, and the one who gathered little did not have too little."[2]

16 Thanks be to God, who put into the heart of Titus the same concern

---

3. Paul uses one of his favorite words, "grace" (Greek *charis*) several times and with several nuances of meaning in these chapters: for the beneficence of God and Christ (8:1, 9; 9:14) and for human response to divine action in giving (8:4 [here translated "privilege"], 6–7) and in giving thanks (8: 16; 9:15).
4. See also Phil. 1:29 f.; 1 Thess. 1:6; 2:14; 3:3–4. The contrast Paul sketches in vv. 2–5 between affliction (*thlipsis*) and the joyous response enabled by grace echoes both the principal motifs of 1:3–14 (see note at 1:4) and Paul's own catalogues of difficulties (4:7–18; 6:4–10; see note at 4: 8). Some commentators see this as a sign of continuity in the letter, but others think chap. 8 may originally have been a separate administrative letter, perhaps written not long after 1 Corinthians.
5. Lit. "holy ones," as in 1:1 and frequently in the letters. Here Paul refers to the collection for the poor of the Jerusalem church, intended not only to address economic need but also to ratify the unity between Jewish and Gentile Christians (Rom. 15:25–32; 1 Cor. 16:1–4; Gal. 2:10; also Acts 24:17). The term translated "sharing" here is *koinōnia* (also 9:13; Rom. 15:26), elsewhere used to express participation in Christ (1 Cor. 1:9), especially in his body and blood (1 Cor. 10:16) and in his sufferings (2 Cor. 1:7; Phil. 3:10), communion with the Spirit (2 Cor. 13:13), and partnership in the gospel (Phil. 1:5). "Service" (*diakonia*: see 9:1, 12–13; also 8:19–20; Rom. 15:31).
6. See v. 10 and, for Titus's role, also vv. 16–24; 12:18. The "beginning" of Titus' work on the collection was probably on his former visit, when he brought Paul's "letter of tears." He returns now, either with the reconciling letter (chaps. 1–7 in whole or in part) including this directive about the collection, or on another occasion with this administrative letter alone. Other chronologies are possible: see the introduction.
7. See 1 Cor. 1:5; 12:8–10; 13:1–2, 8.
8. See 1 Cor. 7:6, 25, 40; Phlm. 8f. Accordingly v. 10 is framed as advice.
9. A typically terse summary of the Gospel, framed here to suit the occasion. See 5:21; Rom. 4:25; Phil. 2:6–8, and compare Paul's self-description in 6:10.
1. See 9:2.
2. Ex. 16:18.

I have for you. 17 For Titus not only welcomed our appeal, but he is coming to you with much enthusiasm and on his own initiative. 18 And we are sending along with him the brother[3] who is praised by all the churches for his service to the gospel. 19 What is more, he was chosen by the churches to accompany us as we carry the offering, which we administer in order to honor the Lord himself and to show our eagerness to help. 20 We want to avoid any criticism of the way we administer this liberal gift.[4] 21 For we are taking pains to do what is right, not only in the eyes of the Lord but also in the eyes of others.[5]

22 In addition, we are sending with them our brother who has often proved to us in many ways that he is zealous, and now even more so because of his great confidence in you. 23 As for Titus, he is my partner and co-worker among you; as for our brothers, they are representatives[6] of the churches and an honor to Christ. 24 Therefore show these men the proof of your love and the reason for our pride in you, so that the churches can see it.

9 There is no need for me to write to you about this service to the Lord's people.[7] 2 For I know your eagerness to help, and I have been boasting about it to the Macedonians, telling them that since last year you in Achaia were ready to give; and your enthusiasm has stirred most of them to action. 3 But I am sending the brothers[8] in order that our boasting about you in this matter should not prove hollow, but that you may be ready, as I said you would be. 4 For if any Macedonians come with me and find you unprepared, we—not to say anything about you—would be ashamed of having been so confident. 5 So I thought it necessary to urge the brothers to visit you in advance and finish the arrangements for the generous gift you had promised. Then it will be ready as a generous gift, not as one grudgingly given.

6 Remember this: Whoever sows sparingly will also reap sparingly, and whoever sows generously will also reap generously.[9] 7 Each of you should give what you have decided in your heart to give, not reluctantly or under compulsion, for God loves a cheerful giver.[1] 8 And God is able to bless you abundantly, so that in all things at all times, having all that you need, you will abound in every good work.[2] 9 As it is written:

"They have scattered abroad their gifts to the poor;
their righteousness endures forever."[3]

10 Now he who supplies seed to the sower and bread for food[4] will also supply and increase your store of seed and will enlarge the harvest of your righteousness.[5] 11 You will be made rich in every way so that you can be

3. The identity of the two brothers (vv. 18, 22) who serve as the churches' envoys is unknown (but see 12:18; Acts 20:4–6).
4. See 6:3.
5. See Prov. 3:4.
6. The Greek word is the same as that translated "apostles."
7. This sounds like the introduction of a new topic, odd on the heels of chap. 8. Some commentators believe that chap. 9 was originally part of a separate letter addressed to Christians in other places in Achaia (e.g., at Cenchreae; see Rom. 16:1).
8. See 8:16–23 and the note at 8:18.
9. The idea is widespread in antiquity (see, e.g., Prov. 11:24).
1. Prov. 22:8 LXX. Cf. 8:3; Phlm. 14; also Deut. 15:10.
2. See Eph. 2:10; Col. 1:10; 2 Thess. 2:17; 2 Tim. 3:17; Titus 2:14.
3. Ps. 112:9.
4. See Isa. 55:10.
5. Hos. 10:12 LXX.

generous on every occasion, and through us your generosity will result in thanksgiving to God.

12 This service that you perform[6] is not only supplying the needs of the Lord's people but is also overflowing in many expressions of thanks to God. 13 Because of the service by which you have proved yourselves, people will praise God for the obedience that accompanies your confession of the gospel of Christ, and for your generosity in sharing with them and with everyone else. 14 And in their prayers for you their hearts will go out to you, because of the surpassing grace God has given you. 15 Thanks be to God for his indescribable gift!

10 By the meekness and gentleness of Christ, I appeal to you—I, Paul, who am "timid" when face to face with you, but "bold" toward you when away![7] 2 I beg you that when I come I may not have to be as bold as I expect to be toward some people who think that we live by the standards of this world.[8] 3 For though we live in the world, we do not wage war[9] as the world does. 4 The weapons we fight with are not the weapons of the world. On the contrary, they have divine power to demolish strongholds. 5 We demolish arguments and every pretension that sets itself up against the knowledge of God, and we take captive every thought to make it obedient to Christ. 6 And we will be ready to punish every act of disobedience, once your obedience is complete.

7 You are judging by appearances.[1] If anyone is confident that they belong to Christ, they should consider again that we belong to Christ just as much as they do. 8 So even if I boast somewhat freely about the authority the Lord gave us for building you up rather than tearing you down,[2] I will not be ashamed of it. 9 I do not want to seem to be trying to frighten you with my letters. 10 For some say, "His letters are weighty and forceful, but in person he is unimpressive and his speaking amounts to nothing." 11 Such people should realize that what we are in our letters when we are absent, we will be in our actions when we are present.

12 We do not dare to classify or compare ourselves with some who commend themselves.[3] When they measure themselves by themselves and compare themselves with themselves, they are not wise. 13 We, however, will not boast beyond proper limits, but will confine our boasting to the sphere of service God himself has assigned to us, a sphere that also

6. The Greek combines two terms for service: *diakonia*, frequent in early Christian literature and often translated "ministry," and *leitourgia*, the standard term for an act of public service that private citizens performed at their own expense (see also Rom. 15:27).

7. In diatribal style, Paul ironically repeats an accusation made by his opponents; see also v. 10. The verb "appeal" (also in 2:8; 6:1) and its synonym "beg" in the following verse (also 5:20) indicates that the ultimate goal of chaps. 10–13 is exhortation. On the problems of these chapters, see the introduction.

8. Lit., "according to flesh," and also in the following verse (see 1:17; 5:16; 11:18).

9. Paul takes up military imagery, often used in debates among philosophers, projecting a whole campaign in three successive stages: the demolishing of fortifications (vv. 4–5), the taking of captives (v. 5), and the punishing of resistance (v. 6). He depicts the "strongholds" of his opponents in terms typically used to describe the Stoic sage, who used reason ("arguments," "thought") as a defense. Perhaps they mocked him the way some rigorous Cynics used the image of Odysseus to attack easier-going rivals as duplicitous and underhanded.

1. See 5:12 and the note there.

2. See 10:4; 12:19; 13:10; also Jer 1:10; 24:6.

3. It was a standard laudatory technique to "classify" or "compare" someone with people of superior worth and to "measure" that person's achievements against those of others. For Paul's ironic use of the device, see 11:22–23. V. 18 sums up this paragraph on self-commendation, a topic introduced also at 3:1 (see the note there).

includes you. 14 We are not going too far in our boasting, as would be the case if we had not come to you, for we did get as far as you with the gospel of Christ. 15 Neither do we go beyond our limits by boasting of work done by others. Our hope is that, as your faith continues to grow, our sphere of activity among you will greatly expand, 16 so that we can preach the gospel in the regions beyond you. For we do not want to boast about work already done in someone else's territory.[4] 17 But, "Let those who boast boast in the Lord."[5] 18 For it is not those who commend themselves who are approved, but those whom the Lord commends.

11 I hope you will put up with me in a little foolishness.[6] Yes, please put up with me! 2 I am jealous for you with a godly jealousy. I promised you to one husband, to Christ, so that I might present you as a pure virgin to him.[7] 3 But I am afraid that just as Eve was deceived by the serpent's cunning, your minds may somehow be led astray from your sincere and pure devotion to Christ.[8] 4 For if someone comes to you and preaches a Jesus other than the Jesus we preached, or if you receive a different spirit from the Spirit you received, or a different gospel from the one you accepted,[9] you put up with it easily enough.

5 I do not think I am in the least inferior to those "super-apostles."[1] 6 I may indeed be untrained as a speaker,[2] but I do have knowledge. We have made this perfectly clear to you in every way. 7 Was it a sin for me to lower myself in order to elevate you by preaching the gospel of God to you free of charge? 8 I robbed other churches by receiving support from them so as to serve you. 9 And when I was with you and needed something, I was not a burden to anyone, for the brothers and sisters who came from Macedonia supplied what I needed. I have kept myself from being a burden to you in any way, and will continue to do so. 10 As surely as the truth of Christ is in me, nobody in the regions of Achaia will stop this boasting of mine. 11 Why? Because I do not love you? God knows I do![3]

12 And I will keep on doing what I am doing in order to cut the ground from under those who want an opportunity to be considered equal with us in the things they boast about. 13 For such persons are false apostles, deceitful workers, masquerading as apostles of Christ. 14 And no wonder,

4. Paul had strong views on the "limits" (v. 13) of his mission field; see Rom. 15:17–21. The implication is that the rival apostles have trespassed in Paul's territory.
5. Jer. 9:24 [LXX 23], quoted also in 1 Cor. 1:31.
6. By adopting the persona of a fool, Paul allows himself the kind of boasting and self-laudatory comparisons that he has rejected (10:7–18), while showing up his boastful opponents as fools or worse, and hinting that his audience has been foolish to be taken in by them. This speech, 11:1–12:13, is as deeply ironic as anything we have from Paul.
7. Paul casts himself as father of the bride, the church (1 Cor. 4:14f.), responsible for safeguarding her purity between the time of the betrothal and the wedding to Christ; see Mt. 9:15; 25:1–13; Eph. 5:26–32; Rev. 19:7–9; 21:2, 9.
8. Gen. 3:13 LXX. A legend, based on the puzzling text of Gen. 4:1b (the Heb. of Eve's statement could be translated literally, "I have got as husband the LORD"), said that the serpent (Satan) seduced Eve by pretending to be the angel that bore God's name (Ex. 23:21). Paul alludes to this legend again in v. 14; see also 1 John 3:12; 1 Tim. 2:14.
9. Because Paul does not say specifically what was "different" about the teachings of his opponents, we remain ignorant of their identity, though scholarly speculation has been abundant. See the introduction.
1. Many ancient and some modern commentators think Paul means the Jerusalem apostles, but more likely this is a sarcastic reference to his opponents.
2. See 10:10.
3. By conventions of the day, to refuse a benefaction could be construed as rejection of friendship (while acceptance, on the other hand, could be an admission of dependence), so what Paul sees as an expression of love the opponents could interpret as the opposite. (On his practice, see 1 Cor. 9; 1 Thess. 2:9; 2 Thess. 3:7–9.) Moreover, manual labor (tentmaking, according to Acts 18:3) was widely regarded as demeaning (v. 7; see 10:1, where a cognate word is translated "timid").

for Satan himself masquerades as an angel of light.[4] 15 It is not surprising, then, if his servants also masquerade as servants of righteousness. Their end will be what their actions deserve.

16 I repeat: Let no one take me for a fool. But if you do, then tolerate me just as you would a fool, so that I may do a little boasting. 17 In this self-confident boasting I am not talking as the Lord would,[5] but as a fool. 18 Since many are boasting in the way the world does, I too will boast. 19 You gladly put up with fools since you are so wise! 20 In fact, you even put up with any who enslave you or exploit you or take advantage of you or push themselves forward or slap you in the face. 21 To my shame I admit that we were too weak for that!

Whatever anyone else dares to boast about—I am speaking as a fool— I also dare to boast about. 22 Are they Hebrews? So am I. Are they Israelites? So am I. Are they Abraham's descendants?[6] So am I. 23 Are they servants of Christ? (I am out of my mind to talk like this.) I am more.[7] I have worked much harder, been in prison more frequently, been flogged more severely, and been exposed to death again and again. 24 Five times I received from the Jews the forty lashes minus one. 25 Three times I was beaten with rods, once I was pelted with stones, three times I was shipwrecked, I spent a night and a day in the open sea, 26 I have been constantly on the move. I have been in danger from rivers, in danger from bandits, in danger from my own people, in danger from Gentiles; in danger in the city, in danger in the country, in danger at sea; and in danger from false believers. 27 I have labored and toiled and have often gone without sleep; I have known hunger and thirst and have often gone without food; I have been cold and naked. 28 Besides everything else, I face daily the pressure of my concern for all the churches. 29 Who is weak, and I do not feel weak? Who is led into sin, and I do not inwardly burn?

30 If I must boast, I will boast of the things that show my weakness. 31 The God and Father of the Lord Jesus, who is to be praised forever, knows that I am not lying. 32 In Damascus the governor under King Aretas had the city of the Damascenes guarded in order to arrest me. 33 But I was lowered in a basket from a window in the wall and slipped through his hands.[8]

12 I must go on boasting. Although there is nothing to be gained, I will go on to visions and revelations from the Lord.[9] 2 I know a man[1] in Christ who fourteen years ago was caught up to the third heaven. Whether it was in the body or out of the body I do not know—God knows. 3 And I know that this man—whether in the body or apart from the body I do not know, but God knows— 4 was caught up to paradise and heard inexpressible things, things that no one is permitted to tell. 5 I will boast about someone like that, but I will not boast about myself, except about my weaknesses.

4. See note on v. 3.
5. Lit., "according to the Lord," contrasted in v. 18 with "according to flesh."
6. The opponents, like Paul, are proud of their Jewish heritage; compare Rom. 9:4; 11:1; Phil. 3:5.
7. Once again Paul makes use of a list of hardships (see 4:8f.; 6:4–10 and notes there), summing up the special irony of his point of view in v. 30; 12:5, 9f.
8. In Acts 9:23–25 the attempt to capture Paul in Damascus is blamed on the Jews. Aretas (IV) was king of the Arab kingdom of Nabatea (see Gal. 1:17 and the note there) from 9 BCE until his death (ca. 40 CE).
9. See 1 Cor. 9:1; 15:8; Gal. 1:12; 2:1–2.
1. Paul himself. Heavenly journeys were a popular means of claiming divine authentication and were apparently used by Paul's opponents for this purpose. See Part III for two pseudo-Pauline apocalypses inspired by 2 Cor. 12.

6 Even if I should choose to boast, I would not be a fool, because I would be speaking the truth. But I refrain, so no one will think more of me than is warranted by what I do or say, 7 or because of these surpassingly great revelations. Therefore, in order to keep me from becoming conceited, I was given a thorn[2] in my flesh, a messenger of Satan, to torment me. 8 Three times I pleaded with the Lord to take it away from me. 9 But he said to me, "My grace is sufficient for you, for my power is made perfect in weakness." Therefore I will boast all the more gladly about my weaknesses, so that Christ's power may rest on me. 10 That is why, for Christ's sake, I delight in weaknesses, in insults, in hardships, in persecutions, in difficulties. For when I am weak, then I am strong.

11 I have made a fool of myself, but you drove me to it. I ought to have been commended by you,[3] for I am not in the least inferior to the "super-apostles," even though I am nothing. 12 I persevered in demonstrating among you the marks of a true apostle, including signs, wonders and miracles.[4] 13 How were you inferior to the other churches, except that I was never a burden to you?[5] Forgive me this wrong!

14 Now I am ready to visit you for the third time, and I will not be a burden to you, because what I want is not your possessions but you. After all, children should not have to save up for their parents, but parents for their children.[6] 15 So I will very gladly spend for you everything I have and expend myself[7] as well. If I love you more, will you love me less? 16 Be that as it may, I have not been a burden to you. Yet, crafty fellow that I am, I caught you by trickery![8] 17 Did I exploit you through any of the men I sent to you? 18 I urged Titus to go to you and I sent our brother with him.[9] Titus did not exploit you, did he? Did we not walk in the same footsteps by the same Spirit?

19 Have you been thinking all along that we have been defending ourselves to you? We have been speaking in the sight of God as those in Christ; and everything we do, dear friends, is for your strengthening.[1] 20 For I am afraid that when I come I may not find you as I want you to be, and you may not find me as you want me to be. I fear that there may be quarreling, jealousy, outbursts of anger, factions, slander, gossip, arrogance and disorder. 21 I am afraid that when I come again my God will humble me before you,[2] and I will be grieved over many who have sinned earlier and have not repented of the impurity, sexual sin and debauchery in which they have indulged.

13 This will be my third visit to you. "Every matter must be established by

2. What specifically Paul meant by the "thorn" and "messenger of Satan" remains unclear. Suggestions have included physical or mental illness (often referring to Gal. 4:13f.), spiritual trials, persecution, and opposition by adversaries.

3. See 3:1–3.

4. Three different terms for miracles, which functioned in antiquity to validate the claims of charismatic figures; see Acts 2:22; 14:3; 15:12; Rom. 15:19; Heb. 2:4.

5. By demanding payment for missionary activities as his rivals apparently did; see 11:7–11 and the note there.

6. Cf. Mt. 15:5–6; 1 Tim. 5:4, 8.

7. See Phil. 2:17.

8. Paul was apparently charged with refusing support for himself while deceitfully enriching himself by means of the collection (see chs. 8–9).

9. See 8:16–9:5 and the note on 8:6. Many scholars regard 12:18 as a retrospective reference to the same visit for the collection that is only anticipated in 8:6, 18, but on difficulties of the chronology, see the introduction.

1. Lit., "upbuilding"; see 10:8 with note; 13:10; see also note on 1 Cor. 14:4.

2. "Again" may modify either "come" or "humble"; Paul fears a repetition of what happened at the second visit; see 2:1–4.

the testimony of two or three witnesses."³ 2 I already gave you a warning when I was with you the second time. I now repeat it while absent: On my return I will not spare⁴ those who sinned earlier or any of the others, 3 since you are demanding proof⁵ that Christ is speaking through me. He is not weak in dealing with you, but is powerful among you. 4 For to be sure, he was crucified in weakness, yet he lives by God's power. Likewise, we are weak in him, yet by God's power we will live with him in our dealing with you.

5 Examine yourselves to see whether you are in the faith; test yourselves. Do you not realize that Christ Jesus is in you⁶—unless, of course, you fail the test? 6 And I trust that you will discover that we have not failed the test. 7 Now we pray to God that you will not do anything wrong. Not that people will see that we have stood the test but that you will do what is right even though we may seem to have failed. 8 For we cannot do anything against the truth, but only for the truth. 9 We are glad whenever we are weak but you are strong; and our prayer is that you may be fully restored. 10 This is why I write these things when I am absent, that when I come I may not have to be harsh in my use of authority—the authority the Lord gave me for building you up, not for tearing you down.⁷

11 Finally, brothers and sisters, rejoice! Strive for full restoration, encourage one another, be of one mind, live in peace. And the God of love and peace will be with you.

12 Greet one another with a holy kiss. 13 All God's people here send their greetings.⁸

14 May the grace of the Lord Jesus Christ, and the love of God, and the fellowship of the Holy Spirit be with you all.⁹

THE LETTER TO THE ROMANS
(ca. 57)

Paul wrote this, the longest of his extant letters, from Corinth, during his final, three-month stay there (Acts 20:2 f.). Given the obvious importance of the imperial capital, it is not surprising that Paul should want to preach in Rome (1:15), or that he should send a letter in advance of his visit, since he had not founded the church and hence exercised no direct authority over it (note the careful choice of words in 1:8–15). He intended his visit to be only in passing, however, for he hoped to go on to begin a new mission in Spain (15:24–28). Before that he would complete the collection for Jerusalem, a project with which he had been busy for several years. The Jerusalem trip obviously evoked some anxiety (15:31)—amply justified by subsequent events, for Paul was destined to make his journey from Jerusalem to Rome in chains, there, according to firm early tradition, to die at the hands of an imperial executioner. The

3. Deut. 19:15, used also in Mt. 18:16; 1 Tim. 5:19.
4. See 1:23, where Paul says "it was in order to spare you" that he canceled the previously planned trip.
5. The underlying issue in the dispute. On testing and "proof," see further 1 Cor. 11:28; 16:3; 2 Cor. 8:8, 22; 9:13; and 13:5–7.
6. "You" is plural; see Rom. 8:10; Gal. 2:20; Col. 1:27, and cf. 1 Cor. 3:16.
7. See 10:8.
8. The letter closing is typically Pauline; for the holy kiss, see note on 1 Cor. 16:20; 1 Thess. 5:26; Rom. 16:16.
9. The trinitarian formula is anticipated in 1:21–22; see also Mt. 28:19.

premonition of danger, however, is a very faint note in the letter, which is dominated by a mood of confidence, even triumph. Clearly the trip to Jerusalem and then to the West represents for Paul a decisive turning point in his career. He says that he has "fully proclaimed the gospel" over a vast area in the East (15:19); "there is no more place for [him] to work in these regions" (15:23). He looks to Rome, therefore, as the center of the known world, and his visit there becomes a symbol for the universality of his mission to "all the Gentiles" (1:5, cf. v. 14; 15:16 ff.). Practically speaking, he also asks for (financial) help from the Roman congregations "to . . . assist me on my journey" to Spain (15:24). It may be, as some commentators have suggested, that he hopes the Romans will use their influence, as well as their prayers, to support him in the coming confrontation in Jerusalem (15:25–32).

But why did Paul write *this* kind of letter in order to introduce himself to the Roman Christians? It resembles more a philosophical lecture than an ordinary letter of self-commendation. One might suppose that Paul's reputation as a controversial figure had preceded him to Rome, requiring a defense rather than an introduction to pave the way for his coming. And Paul's preoccupation with his mission was so total that in his case a self-defense would have to take the form of a defense of his proclamation (1:16 f.). Yet the letter is not an apology in form, and it is certainly not a systematic summary of Pauline theology—his Christology, for example, is presupposed, not described. The thematic exposition in chapters 1–11 turns about the single question of the relationship between Jew and Gentile, with the necessary corollary, the place of the law in Christianity. From his other correspondence we would not suspect that this was *the* central concern of Paul's proclamation, for elsewhere only in Galatians does it become the dominant issue. On the other hand, the admonitions in chapters 14 f. recall some of the issues dealt with in the Corinthian correspondence. Thus the Letter to Romans presents no retrospective survey of Paul's thought, but takes up only some of those issues which have been uppermost in his mind during the past two or three years. It contains the fruit of his reflection on the controversies of Galatia and Corinth, with greater emphasis on the problem addressed in the former, of the Jewish law and the radical newness of "the gospel." That issue, it seems, had come for Paul to have such fundamental significance that he wanted to expound it to the church at large and particularly to the household communities of believers in Rome.

Perhaps there were also factors in the Roman congregations that influenced Paul's choice of themes. There is, to be sure, no indication in the letter of any particular crisis in Rome to which Paul is responding, nor was Paul, as a stranger to that city's Christian groups, in any position to speak directly to local problems as he would in one of the churches he had founded. Furthermore, it is uncertain how much Paul would have known about the Roman congregations. Nevertheless certain general facts would certainly have been well known and would call for attention. The Christian sect in Rome evidently originated within the Jewish community, which was quite large. It is known that the emperor Claudius expelled the Jews from the city, probably in the year 49 CE; the historian Suetonius, writing three-quarters of a century later, said that Claudius had done so because of "disturbances at the instigation of Chrestus" (*Claudius* 25.4). Assuming a natural confusion between *Christos* and *Chrēstos* (pronounced identically in Greek of the time), this probably means that the disturbances arose from the first missionary activity of Christians among the Roman Jews. After the accession of Nero in 54, the Claudian decree was annulled, and Jews, very likely including Jewish-Christians, drifted back to Rome. (Aquila and Prisca were probably among the returning exiles: 16:3; Acts 18:2.) In the meantime the church had become preponderantly Gentile—it is evident throughout Paul's letter that he addresses Christian groups principally Gentile but with some former Jews among them. Considering the circumstances of the Claudian expulsion, one can readily imagine that the relationships must have been sensitive both between church and synagogue and between former Jew and former Gentile within the church. Paul's emphasis both on the unity of Jew and Gentile and on the abiding validity of God's promises to Israel would certainly have had immediate relevance to those relationships.

On the other hand, it is very doubtful whether it is possible to deduce from Paul's admonitions the actual problems existing in Rome. For example, the warning against divisiveness and deviant teaching in 16:17–20 is quite general and stereotyped; it by no means indicates that a particular kind of heresy was rampant in Rome at that moment—indeed v. 19 would seem to suggest the contrary. The same is true of the admonitions of chapters 12 and 13, which show signs of having been assembled for catechetical purposes. Even the issue dealt with at length in chapters 14 f.—the mutual responsibilities of "weak" and "strong" Christians in questions of dietary rules and similar regulations—is more likely a generalized paradigm based on experiences in Corinth (1 Cor. 8–10) than response to a present issue in Rome.

The question of the letter's purpose has been further complicated by uncertainties about its original extent. There is manuscript evidence that the letter circulated in three forms of varying lengths: one a text of sixteen chapters as commonly printed today; one equivalent to only the first fourteen chapters; and another to the first fifteen. There also was one version that omitted all reference to Rome (1:7, 15). Several influential scholars in the twentieth century argued that chapter 16 was originally a separate letter of introduction addressed to Ephesus, later attached by error or design to one of the shorter versions of Romans. More recent studies of the style of epistolary conclusions as well as of the full manuscript evidence, however, have added strong support to the view that the longest version, with the Roman address, is the original. Probably either liturgical use or the letter's position at the head of the Pauline collection (in most ancient editions) prompted the abbreviations that made it more like a universal treatise.

The form of the letter is both more orderly and more complex than that of the earlier letters. The basic division is between chapters 1–11, which are didactic, elaborating the theme of 1:16 f., and chapters 12–15, which are hortatory. Systematic outlines of the letter, which may be found in any standard commentary, are not always helpful, for the argument proceeds by stating certain themes that are then elaborated from various sides in turn, returning each time to the theme. Questions are raised along the way that have to be deferred for later discussion. The resultant interlocking structure is pointed out by our notes on key verses.

That structure would not have seemed strange, however unusual its content, to Greek speakers in Rome. The language of Romans, as of all Paul's letters, is Greek, for that was the common language of most of the immigrant population of Rome, including the Jews, as well as the preferred language of philosophy and literature among the more educated classes. In the rhetorical culture of antiquity, many of those gathered in the house churches of Rome to hear the apostle's letter read aloud would have recognized in its lively, conversational style the kind of argument called the *diatribe*, which developed in the philosophical schools of Greece and Rome, especially among Cynic and Stoic teachers. By putting questions and objections into the mouth of imaginary interlocutors, the teachers led their students to explore different sides of issues and to hone their logical skills. Diatribe abounded in rhetorical questions, quoted maxims and proverbs, parodies of other positions, conundrums and paradoxes, speeches in the character of a fictitious person or personification, antitheses, and *reductio ad absurdam*: "What then? Is this what we are saying? Certainly not! For in that case . . ." The diatribal style was especially useful for introducing new students to the distinctive tenets of a school, and Romans has many of the marks of such a *protreptic* speech.

Paul, of course, is not introducing a philosophy, but freely adapting a familiar rhetorical style, as he does in his other letters, here to introduce "the gospel" as he has come to understand it through the confrontations and controversies he has experienced. He uses that introduction, as we suggested above and will see in more detail below, for multiple purposes as he prepares for what will be his final journey, to Jerusalem and to Rome.

Romans

1 Paul, a servant[1] of Christ Jesus, called to be an apostle and set apart for the gospel of God— 2 the gospel he promised beforehand through his prophets in the Holy Scriptures 3 regarding his Son, who as to his earthly life[2] was a descendant of David, 4 and who through the Spirit of holiness was appointed the Son of God in power by his resurrection from the dead: Jesus Christ our Lord. 5 Through him we received grace and apostleship to call all the Gentiles to faith and obedience[3] for his name's sake. 6 And you also are among those Gentiles who are called to belong to Jesus Christ.

7 To all in Rome who are loved by God and called to be his holy people:
Grace and peace to you from God our Father and from the Lord Jesus Christ.

8 First, I thank my God through Jesus Christ for all of you,[4] because your faith is being reported all over the world. 9 God, whom I serve in my spirit in preaching the gospel of his Son, is my witness how constantly I remember you 10 in my prayers at all times; and I pray that now at last by God's will the way may be opened for me to come to you.

11 I long to see you so that I may impart to you some spiritual gift to make you strong— 12 that is, that you and I may be mutually encouraged by each other's faith. 13 I do not want you to be unaware, brothers and sisters, that I planned many times to come to you (but have been prevented from doing so until now) in order that I might have a harvest among you, just as I have had among the other Gentiles.

14 I am obligated both to Greeks and non-Greeks, both to the wise and the foolish.[5] 15 That is why I am so eager to preach the gospel also to you who are in Rome.

---

1. Greek, "slave." Paul names himself alone as sender; the other undoubted letters all have co-senders, but cf. Eph. 1:1. The formal letter opening (vv. 1–7) is unusually long.
2. Lit., "according to flesh." Vv. 3b–4 probably are an early Christian creedal summary (like 1 Cor. 15:3–5) which Paul quotes. Note the antithetic form, "according to the flesh," "according to the Spirit," and parallelism, clearer in the Greek. The Jewish tradition that the Messiah, as "descendant [lit., 'seed'] of David," would be called Son of God, based on 2 Sam. 7:12–14, does not appear elsewhere in Paul, but see note on Gal. 3:16.
3. Lit., "obedience of faith"; this may mean "obedience that consists of faith," or "faithful obedience."
4. As we have seen in the earlier letters, Paul shows how freely and expansively he can adapt the formal thanksgiving (vv. 8–17) that ordinarily opened a Greek friendly letter, seeking to establish friendly relations with the recipients and telegraphing some of the main themes to follow. As in Phil. 1:3–11, the thanksgiving merges into an intercession (v. 10). Here the intercession places the longed-for visit into the context of Paul's mission to "all the Gentiles," and in turn introduces the theme of the entire letter, vv. 16 f. The sentences are linked together in the Greek by repetition of "for" or "because" (*gar*), characteristic of the oral style of this letter (144 times!).
5. "Greeks and non-Greeks [lit., 'barbarians']," "wise and foolish" are Greek clichés, here a periphrastic way of saying "everyone." The thematic statement in vv. 16 f. replaces these formulaic

16 I am not ashamed of the gospel, because it is the power of God that brings salvation[6] to everyone who believes: first to the Jew, then to the Gentile. 17 For in the gospel the righteousness of God is revealed—a righteousness that is by faith from first to last,[7] just as it is written: "The righteous will live by faith."[8] 18 The wrath of God is being revealed[9] from heaven against all the godlessness and wickedness of human beings who suppress the truth by their wickedness, 19 since what may be known about God is plain to them, because God has made it plain to them. 20 For since the creation of the world God's invisible qualities—his eternal power and divine nature—have been clearly seen, being understood from what has been made, so that people are without excuse.

21 For although they knew God, they neither glorified him as God nor gave thanks to him, but their thinking became futile and their foolish hearts were darkened. 22 Although they claimed to be wise, they became fools 23 and exchanged the glory of the immortal God for images made to look like mortal human beings and birds and animals and reptiles.

24 Therefore God gave them over[1] in the sinful desires of their hearts to sexual impurity for the degrading of their bodies with one another. 25 They exchanged the truth about God for a lie, and worshiped and served created things rather than the Creator—who is forever praised. Amen.

26 Because of this, God gave them over to shameful lusts. Even their women exchanged natural sexual relations for unnatural ones.[2] 27 In the same way the men also abandoned natural relations with women and were inflamed with lust for one another. Men committed shameful acts with other men, and received in themselves the due penalty for their error.

28 Furthermore, just as they did not think it worthwhile to retain the knowledge of God, so God gave them over to a depraved mind, so that they do what ought not to be done. 29 They have become filled with every kind of wickedness, evil, greed and depravity. They are full of envy, murder, strife, deceit and malice. They are gossips, 30 slanderers, God-haters, inso-

---

pairs with one much more theologically significant for Paul: "Jew and Gentile" [lit., "Jew and Greek"].

6. Cf. Isa. 50:7 f.

7. Lit., "from faith to faith," perhaps only a rhetorical emphasis, "faith and nothing but faith," or perhaps, as in 3:22, expressing the relational character of faith in the Pauline sense, "from [God's or Christ's] faithfulness to [a person's] faith." "The righteousness of God" is the fundamental concept in Romans. Its precise meaning has been debated for centuries (see Parts V and IX). Originating in the OT and Judaism, the term includes both "the justice of God" (JB) and "God's way of righting wrong" (NEB). See also note on 3.25.

8. Hab. 2:4. The Hebrew text has "*his* [the righteous person's] faithfulness," the Greek, "*my* [God's] faithfulness"; Paul's text has neither. Whether "by faith[fulness]" modifies "the righteous" or "will live" is also ambiguous (some translate, "the one who is righteous by faith will live"), and Paul's exposition in the rest of the letter exploits both ambiguities. Hab. 2:1–4 is a prophetic meditation on the reliability of God's promises to Israel, and that is the theme of Rom. 9–11. Cf. Gal. 3:11.

9. First of two variations of the theme 1:17a which subdivide chaps. 1–3: see 3:21, and note the change of tense as well as subject. Throughout the OT, and especially in the classical prophets, "the wrath of God" is the reaction of God to human provocations against God's holiness and justice. In some Jewish literature in the Hellenistic and Roman periods, notably the Dead Sea Scrolls, the phrase is frequently used for punishment meted out at the last judgment; cf. 2:5; 5: 9; 1 Thess. 1:10. Connection of this eschatological term with the present tense, "is being revealed" (parallelism with v. 17) requires us to understand "in the gospel," sets up a characteristic Pauline paradox. Otherwise, vv. 18–32 read like a typical Hellenistic-Jewish polemic against paganism; Wisd. chaps. 13 f. are a very close parallel both in theme and language. Yet similar language could also be used of Israel's apostasy, especially referring to the Golden Calf episode of Ex. 32: Ps. 106: 20; Jer. 2:11.

1. This phrase is solemnly repeated in vv. 26, 28. Paul's primary focus is not on human actions, but God's.

2. For patristic interpretations of this verse, see the essay by Bernadette J. Brooten in Part IV.

lent, arrogant and boastful; they invent ways of doing evil; they disobey their parents; 31 they have no understanding, no fidelity, no love, no mercy.[3] 32 Although they know God's righteous decree that those who do such things deserve death, they not only continue to do these very things but also approve of those who practice them.

2 You, therefore, have no excuse,[4] you who pass judgment on someone else, for at whatever point you judge another, you are condemning yourself, because you who pass judgment do the same things. 2 Now we know that God's judgment against those who do such things is based on truth. 3 So when you, a mere human, pass judgment on them and yet do the same things, do you think you will escape God's judgment? 4 Or do you show contempt for the riches of his kindness, forbearance and patience, not realizing that God's kindness is intended to lead you to repentance?[5]

5 But because of your stubbornness and your unrepentant heart, you are storing up wrath against yourself for the day of God's wrath,[6] when his righteous judgment will be revealed. 6 God "will repay everyone according to what they have done."[7] 7 To those who by persistence in doing good seek glory, honor and immortality, he will give eternal life. 8 But for those who are self-seeking and who reject the truth and follow evil, there will be wrath and anger. 9 There will be trouble and distress for every human being who does evil: first for the Jew, then for the Gentile; 10 but glory, honor and peace for everyone who does good: first for the Jew, then for the Gentile. 11 For God does not show favoritism.[8]

12 All who sin apart from the law will also perish apart from the law, and all who sin under the law will be judged by the law. 13 For it is not those who hear the law who are righteous in God's sight, but it is those who obey the law who will be declared righteous. 14 (Indeed, when Gentiles, who do not have the law, do by nature things required by the law, they are a law for themselves, even though they do not have the law. 15 They show that the requirements of the law are written on their hearts, their consciences also bearing witness, and their thoughts now accusing, now even defending them.) 16 This will take place on the day when God judges everyone's secrets through Jesus Christ,[9] as my gospel declares.

17 Now you, if you call yourself a Jew; if you rely on the law and boast in God; 18 if you know his will and approve of what is superior because you are instructed by the law; 19 if you are convinced that you are a guide for the blind, a light for those who are in the dark, 20 an instructor of the foolish, a teacher of infants, because you have in the law the embodiment

3. The "vice catalogue" by repetition of similar sounds in Greek achieves a certain rhetorical luxuriance that climaxes the first part of this section. V. 32 provides the transition to his deliberately abrupt irony in chap. 2.

4. This picks up and universalizes the statement of 1:20b, preparing the way for 3:9, 19 f., 23. Who is the hypocritical judge addressed here? Many commentators have assumed Paul that turns here to the imagined Jew addressed in v. 17, but the apostrophe in v. 1 is, perhaps deliberately, ambiguous: "Oh person (Ō anthrōpe)!" The style throughout this part of the letter is typical of the diatribe (see headnote).

5. One of the very rare occurrences of the term "repentance" in Paul's letters; the statement here is typical of Judaism, for which repentance is the way prescribed by God to overcome failure to achieve the righteousness demanded by the Torah.

6. Zeph. 14–18; 2:3; Lam. 1:12; 2:1, 21, 22; Ps. 110:5; Ezek. 22:24; Rev. 6:17.

7. Prov. 24:12; cf. Ps. 62:12. Note the use of parallelism to add solemnity to the following lines, and the chiasm of vv. 7–10 (good/bad//bad/good).

8. A fundamental principle in Judaism: Deut. 10:17; 2 Chron. 19:7; see the Mishnah tractate Aboth, 4:22. However, Paul's use of the principle to deny any distinction between Jew and Gentile is radical.

9. Here Paul mentions Jesus Christ for the first time in his exposition of the letter's theme.

of knowledge and truth— 21 you, then, who teach others, do you not teach yourself? You who preach against stealing, do you steal? 22 You who say that people should not commit adultery, do you commit adultery? You who abhor idols, do you rob temples? 23 You who boast in the law, do you dishonor God by breaking the law? 24 As it is written: "God's name is blasphemed among the Gentiles because of you."[1]

25 Circumcision has value if you observe the law, but if you break the law, you have become as though you had not been circumcised. 26 If those who are not circumcised keep the law's requirements, will they not be regarded as though they were circumcised? 27 The one who is not circumcised physically and yet obeys the law will condemn you who, even though you have the written code and circumcision, are a lawbreaker.

28 A person is not a Jew who is one only outwardly, nor is circumcision merely outward and physical. 29 No, a person is a Jew who is one inwardly; and circumcision is circumcision of the heart, by the Spirit, not by the written code. Such a person's praise is not from other people, but from God. 3 What advantage, then, is there in being a Jew, or what value is there in circumcision? 2 Much in every way! First of all, the Jews have been entrusted with the very words of God.

3 What if some were unfaithful? Will their unfaithfulness nullify God's faithfulness? 4 Not at all![2] Let God be true, and every human being a liar.[3] As it is written:

"So that you may be proved right when you speak
and prevail when you judge."[4]

5 But if our unrighteousness brings out God's righteousness more clearly, what shall we say? That God is unjust in bringing his wrath on us? (I am using a human argument.) 6 Certainly not! If that were so, how could God judge the world? 7 Someone might argue, "If my falsehood enhances God's truthfulness and so increases his glory, why am I still condemned as a sinner?" 8 Why not say—as we are being slanderously reported as saying and as some claim that we say—"Let us do evil that good may result"?[5] Their condemnation is just!

9 What shall we conclude then? Do we have any advantage?[6] Not at all! We have already made the charge that Jews and Gentiles alike are all under the power of sin. 10 As it is written:

"There is no one righteous, not even one;
11 there is no one who understands;
   there is no one who seeks God.
12 All have turned away,
   they have together become worthless;
   there is no one who does good,
   not even one."

1. Isa. 52:5 LXX; cf. Ezek. 36:20–22.
2. Diatribal style dominates chap. 3. Objections voiced by rhetorical questions are rejected here by quick retorts; they receive longer answers later in the letter. Thus the question of v. 3 becomes the topic of chaps. 9–11.
3. The last phrase is biblical: Ps. 116:11 LXX (115:2).
4. Ps. 51:4.
5. This question is dealt with in chap. 6.
6. The meaning of the first half of this verse has been disputed since ancient times, resulting in variations among the manuscripts and differences in punctuation in modern editions. Most recent commentators adopt a translation similar to that in the text, though it requires an unusual construal of the principal verb. More straightforward grammatically, but making the logical connection to what follows a bit less clear, would be, "What then? Are we *disadvantaged*?"

13 "Their throats are open graves;
   their tongues practice deceit."
"The poison of vipers is on their lips."
14 "Their mouths are full of cursing and bitterness."
15 "Their feet are swift to shed blood;
16 ruin and misery mark their ways,
17 and the way of peace they do not know."
18 "There is no fear of God before their eyes."[7]

19 Now we know that whatever the law[8] says, it says to those who are under the law, so that every mouth may be silenced and the whole world held accountable to God. 20 Therefore no one will be declared righteous in God's sight by observing the law; rather, through the law we become conscious of our sin.[9] *law refers back to scrip.*

21 But now apart from the law the righteousness of God has been made known,[1] to which the Law and the Prophets testify. 22 This righteousness is given through faith in Jesus Christ[2] to all who believe. There is no difference between Jew and Gentile, 23 for all have sinned and fall short of the glory of God, 24 and all are justified freely by his grace through the redemption that came by Christ Jesus. 25 God presented Christ as a sacrifice of atonement, through the shedding of his blood—to be received by faith. He did this to demonstrate his justice, because in his forbearance he had left the sins committed beforehand unpunished—[3] 26 he did it to demonstrate his justice at the present time, so as to be just and the one who justifies those who have faith in Jesus.

27 Where, then, is boasting? It is excluded. Because of what law? The law that requires works? No, because of the "law" that requires faith. 28 For we maintain that a person is justified by faith apart from observing the law. 29 Is God the God of Jews only? Is he not the God of Gentiles too? Yes, of Gentiles too, 30 since there is only one God, who will justify the circumcised by faith and the uncircumcised through that same faith. 31 Do we, then, nullify the law by this faith? Not at all! Rather, we uphold the law.[4]

4 What then shall we say that Abraham, the forefather of us Jews, discovered in this matter? 2 If, in fact, Abraham was justified by works, he had something to boast about—but not before God.[5] 3 What does Scrip-

---

7. The chain of quotations includes Eccl. 7:20; Ps. 14:1–3 (or 53:1–3); 5:9; 140:3; 10:7; Isa. 59:7 f. (cf. Prov. 1:16); Ps. 36:1.
8. "The law" here means "Torah" in the broad sense, more or less equivalent to "scripture" (cf. 1 Cor. 14:21), as exemplified in the catena of Psalm and prophetic texts just before.
9. The first clause is from Ps. 143:2 LXX; Paul adds "by observing [lit., 'from works of'] the law" and the epigrammatic statement of the law's function as he now sees it—the statement will be elaborated in 7:7–25.
1. This second restatement of the theme (see 1:17, 18) is a major turning point in the argument.
2. Or, "through the faithfulness of Jesus Christ"; see the note on Gal. 2:16; cf. Gal. 3:22, 26; Phil. 3:9.
3. Vv. 24 f. are a formula which Paul quotes and then comments on to reinforce his argument. The first phrase of v. 26 repeats almost exactly the phrase from v. 25 which Paul wishes to expound. The phrases "by his grace" (v. 24) and "by faith" (v. 25; "to be received" is not in the Greek) are probably also added by Paul to the formula. The word translated "sacrifice of atonement" (*hilastērion*) is used in the LXX for the "atonement cover" (older versions: "mercy seat") of the Ark of the Covenant, and some commentators think Paul is alluding to the ritual described in Lev. 16: 15 f.
4. Here again a quick answer to a question that will receive fuller attention later: see 7:7–25 (and cf. Gal. 3:19–22).
5. Cf. 3:27; chap. 4 can be regarded as a footnote on that statement: "All boasting is excluded—even Abraham's."

ture say? "Abraham believed God, and it was credited to him as right-eousness."[6]

4 Now to anyone who works, their wages are not credited to them as a gift, but as an obligation. 5 However, to anyone who does not work but trusts God who justifies the ungodly,[7] their faith is credited as righteous-ness. 6 David says the same thing when he speaks of the blessedness of those to whom God credits righteousness apart from works:

7 "Blessed are those
   whose transgressions are forgiven,
   whose sins are covered.
8 Blessed are those
   whose sin the Lord will never count against them."[8]

9 Is this blessedness only for the circumcised, or also for the uncircum-cised? We have been saying that Abraham's faith was credited to him as righteousness. 10 Under what circumstances was it credited? Was it after he was circumcised, or before? It was not after, but before! 11 And he received circumcision as a sign, a seal of the righteousness that he had by faith while he was still uncircumcised. So then, he is the father of all who believe but have not been circumcised, in order that righteousness might be credited to them. 12 And he is then also the father of the circumcised who not only are circumcised but who also follow in the footsteps of the faith that our father Abraham had before he was circumcised.

13 It was not through the law that Abraham and his offspring received the promise that he would be heir of the world, but through the right-eousness that comes by faith. 14 For if those who depend on the law are heirs, faith means nothing and the promise is worthless, 15 because the law brings wrath. And where there is no law there is no transgression.

16 Therefore, the promise comes by faith, so that it may be by grace and may be guaranteed to all Abraham's offspring—not only to those who are of the law but also to those who have the faith of Abraham. He is the father of us all. 17 As it is written: "I have made you a father of many nations."[9] He is our father in the sight of God, in whom he believed—the God who gives life to the dead[1] and calls into being things that were not.

18 Against all hope, Abraham in hope believed and so became the father of many nations, just as it had been said to him, "So shall your offspring be."[2] 19 Without weakening in his faith, he faced the fact that his body was as good as dead—since he was about a hundred years old—and that Sarah's womb was also dead. 20 Yet he did not waver through unbelief regarding the promise of God, but was strengthened in his faith and gave glory to God, 21 being fully persuaded that God had power to do what he

---

6. Gen. 15:6; chap. 4 is a midrash on this passage, like Gal. 3:6–29.
7. Contrast Ex. 23:7; the unthinkable notion that God would "justify the ungodly" (the Greek phrase is identical in Ex. 23:7; in Isa. 5:23 it is used of corrupt judges) is stated deliberately by Paul; cf. Rom. 5:6–8.
8. Ps. 32:1 f. The keyword *logizesthai*, "count against," translated "credited" in v. 3 above, provides Paul the springboard of his argument, by a common rule of midrash. The Psalm text permits the inference that "crediting" may take place even where works have failed, while the Genesis passage connects "crediting" with "believing." Note the recurrence of the verb in vv. 9, 10, 11, 22, 23, 24. Contrast the opposite conclusion arrived at in James 2:21–24, a midrash on the same Gen. text.
9. Gen. 17:5.
1. The phrase recalls the second blessing of the Jewish daily prayer, which was frequently associated with Abraham on the basis of a legend that Isaac was actually sacrificed (Gen. 22) and restored to his father only by resurrection (cf. Heb. 11:17–19).
2. Gen. 15:5; cf. 22:16 f.

had promised. 22 This is why "it was credited to him as righteousness."
23 The words "it was credited to him" were written not for him alone,
24 but also for us, to whom God will credit righteousness—for us who
believe in him who raised Jesus our Lord from the dead. 25 He was delivered over to death for our sins and was raised to life for our justification.[3]
5 Therefore, since we have been justified through faith, we[4] have peace
with God through our Lord Jesus Christ, 2 through whom we have gained
access by faith[5] into this grace in which we now stand. And we[6] boast in
the hope of the glory of God. 3 Not only so, but we also glory in our
sufferings, because we know that suffering produces perseverance; 4 perseverance, character; and character, hope. 5 And hope does not put us to
shame, because God's love has been poured out into our hearts through
the Holy Spirit, who has been given to us.

6 You see, at just the right time, when we were still powerless, Christ
died for the ungodly. 7 Very rarely will anyone die for a righteous person,
though for a good person someone might possibly dare to die. 8 But God
demonstrates his own love for us in this: While we were still sinners, Christ
died for us.

9 Since we have now been justified by his blood, how much more shall
we be saved from God's wrath through him! 10 For if, while we were God's
enemies, we were reconciled to him through the death of his Son, how
much more, having been reconciled, shall we be saved through his life![7]
11 Not only is this so, but we also boast in God through our Lord Jesus
Christ, through whom we have now received reconciliation.

12 Therefore, just as sin entered the world through one man, and death
through sin,[8] and in this way death came to all people, because all sinned—[9]

13 To be sure, sin was in the world before the law was given, but sin is
not charged against anyone's account where there is no law. 14 Nevertheless, death reigned from the time of Adam to the time of Moses, even over
those who did not sin by breaking a command, as did Adam, who is a
pattern[1] of the one to come.

15 But the gift is not like the trespass.[2] For if the many died by the

3. Perhaps another quoted formula, though the terse antithesis is also typical of Paul's style.
4. Many manuscripts read, "let us" (the difference in Greek is a single letter), but the context
demands the indicative. The themes of vv. 1–11 are elaborated in chap. 8; chaps. 5–8 are therefore
to be understood as a unit.
5. "By faith" is lacking in several important manuscripts.
6. Or, "let us"; so also in the following verse.
7. V. 10 restates v. 9 with slightly different language, in the form of a typical Pauline antithesis:
"through the death"/ "through his life"; "justified" and "reconciled" thus function as synonyms.
See also note on 2 Cor. 5:18–20.
8. Gen. 2:17; 3:19.
9. Paul begins a more extended version of the analogy between Adam and Christ that he has earlier
used in 1 Cor. 15:21 f.: "Just as in Adam . . . so in Christ"; cf. 15:45–49. But here he interrupts
the thought with important qualifications (vv. 13–17), completing the comparison only in vv. 18f.
How Paul (and some Jewish authors contemporary with him) conceived of the connection between
Adam's sin and death and those of following generations, he does not explain. The phrase translated "because" in v. 12 has been much debated; among the alternative translations that have been
suggested, "with the result that" is especially worth considering. See Part V.
1. Greek *typos*. The notion of "type" and "anti-type" was one way of interpreting present or anticipated
events by scriptural patterns; cf. 1 Cor. 10:6, 11; 1 Pet. 3:20 f. The analogy between the beginning
and the end of human history was particularly cultivated in some Jewish traditions.
2. Paul upsets his own analogy: the "just as . . . so . . ." form that governs the entire section is awk-
wardly disrupted here and in v. 16 by "*not* as . . ." Thus the act of grace does not simply undo the
transgression of Adam—in that case grace would become a kind of magic in which humanity's
automatic fall in Adam would be reversed by automatic salvation in Christ. What breaks the
analogy is the law, whose purpose, Paul claims, was to *increase* transgression! (v. 20, cf. Gal. 3:
19). Confronted with the law's commandments, humanity's potential rebellion against God

trespass of the one man, how much more did God's grace and the gift that came by the grace of the one man, Jesus Christ, overflow to the many! 16 Nor can the gift of God be compared with the result of one man's sin: The judgment followed one sin and brought condemnation, but the gift followed many trespasses and brought justification. 17 For if, by the trespass of the one man, death reigned through that one man, how much more will those who receive God's abundant provision of grace and of the gift of righteousness reign in life through the one man, Jesus Christ!

18 Consequently, just as one trespass resulted in condemnation for all people, so also one righteous act resulted in justification and life for all. 19 For just as through the disobedience of the one man the many were made sinners, so also through the obedience of the one man the many will be made righteous.

20 The law was brought in so that the trespass might increase. But where sin increased, grace increased all the more, 21 so that, just as sin reigned in death, so also grace might reign through righteousness to bring eternal life through Jesus Christ our Lord.

6 What shall we say, then? Shall we go on sinning so that grace may increase?[3] 2 By no means! We are those who have died to sin; how can we live in it any longer? 3 Or don't you know that all of us who were baptized into Christ Jesus were baptized into his death? 4 We were therefore buried with him through baptism into death in order that, just as Christ was raised from the dead through the glory of the Father, we too may live a new life.[4]

5 If we have been united with him in a death like his, we will certainly also be united with him in a resurrection like his. 6 For we know that our old self was crucified with him so that the body ruled by sin might be done away with,[5] that we should no longer be slaves to sin— 7 because anyone who has died has been set free from sin.[6]

8 Now if we died with Christ, we believe that we will also live with him. 9 For we know that since Christ was raised from the dead, he cannot die again; death no longer has mastery over him. 10 The death he died, he died to sin once for all; but the life he lives, he lives to God.

11 In the same way, count yourselves[7] dead to sin but alive to God in

---

becomes actual (cf. 7:5, 7–10); every person disobeys as Adam did (5:12). Note the repetition of "how much more" (vv. 15, 17) and stress on the abundance of grace (v. 17; in v. 20b, the same Greek root is heightened in the verb "increased all the more," lit. "superabounded." Grace superabounds by justifying the multiplicity of human sin and by giving life which overwhelms the death wrought by human rebellion against the Creator.

3. The question follows logically, in diatribe style, as a possible objection to 5:20 f.; it has been raised previously: 3:8.

4. Paul appeals to traditional interpretation of the ritual of baptism. The rite undoubtedly included from the beginning some admonitions to the newly baptized to live the new life which had just been given them, and reminders of baptism are frequently expressed or implied in the admonitions of the Pauline letters and other early Christian writings (e.g., Col. 3; Ephesians *passim*; 1 Peter *passim*). The ritual and its parenetic use became one of the fundamental ways in which Paul and other early followers of Jesus interpreted Jesus' death. The death had meaning as it was vicarious ("died for our sins," 1 Cor. 15:3) and participatory or representative ("with him"; "into his death" as here; cf. Col. 2:12 f.; 3:1; Eph. 2:5 f.; 2 Cor. 5:14 f.). Some forms of the baptismal liturgy probably spoke of resurrection with Christ as something already accomplished in baptism (Col. 3: 1; Eph. 2:1, 5 f.; see note on 1 Cor. 15:12); here Paul carefully stresses its futurity, even while emphasizing its present implications for the moral life.

5. Or, "rendered powerless."

6. In the Talmud a similar saying is attributed to R. Yohanan (third century CE): "As soon as a man dies he is free from the commandments" (b. *Niddah* 61b; *Shabbat* 30a, 151b). The word translated "has been set free" is the one elsewhere translated "is justified."

7. "Count yourselves" (*logizesthe*) recalls the way God "counted" Abraham as righteous (see note on 4:8 above).

Christ Jesus. 12 Therefore do not let sin reign in your mortal body so that you obey its evil desires. 13 Do not offer any part of yourself to sin as an instrument of wickedness, but rather offer yourselves to God as those who have been brought from death to life; and offer every part of yourself to him as an instrument of righteousness. 14 For sin shall no longer be your master, because you are not under the law, but under grace.

15 What then? Shall we sin because we are not under the law but under grace?[8] By no means! 16 Don't you know that when you offer yourselves to someone as obedient slaves, you are slaves of the one you obey— whether you are slaves to sin, which leads to death, or to obedience, which leads to righteousness? 17 But thanks be to God that, though you used to be slaves to sin, you have come to obey from your heart the pattern of teaching that has now claimed your allegiance.[9] 18 You have been set free from sin and have become slaves to righteousness.

19 I am using an example from everyday life because of your human limitations. Just as you used to offer yourselves as slaves to impurity and to ever-increasing wickedness, so now offer yourselves as slaves to right- eousness leading to holiness. 20 When you were slaves to sin, you were free from the control of righteousness. 21 What benefit did you reap at that time from the things you are now ashamed of? Those things result in death! 22 But now that you have been set free from sin and have become slaves of God, the benefit you reap leads to holiness, and the result is eternal life. 23 For the wages of sin is death, but the gift of God[1] is eternal life in[2] Christ Jesus our Lord.

7 Do you not know, brothers and sisters—for I am speaking to those who know the law—that the law has authority over[3] someone only as long as that person lives? 2 For example, by law a married woman is bound to her husband as long as he is alive, but if her husband dies, she is released from the law that binds her to him.[4] 3 So then, if she marries another man while her husband is still alive, she is called an adulteress. But if her husband dies, she is released from that law and is not an adulteress if she marries another man.

4 So, my brothers and sisters, you also died to the law through the body of Christ, that you might belong to another, to him who was raised from the dead, in order that we might bear fruit for God. 5 For when we were controlled by our sinful nature,[5] the sinful passions aroused by the law

8. The question reformulates the beginning point (v. 1) in terms of the argument so far, dividing the chapter into two parts. In the first the contrast death/life dominates; in the latter, slavery/freedom.

9. The grammar of v. 17 is difficult, and commentators offer many ways of reading it. The verb translated here "have come to obey," is the passive of one usually meaning "to hand over"—a tradition (1 Cor. 15:3), a person, e.g., to punishment or to slavery (Rom. 1:24–28), or a possession or status (1 Cor. 15:24). Several scholars have argued that the whole clause "you have come . . . allegiance" is a gloss by some early scribe, but there is no manuscript evidence to support this conjecture.

1. That the "benefit" (lit., "fruit") of ethical conduct is not a reward is now stressed by the charac- teristic Pauline contrast between "wages" and "gift": cf. 4:4 f.

2. Or, "through."

3. Lit., "is master of"; the verb is cognate with *kurios*, "lord"; cf. 6:14. Thus Paul continues the metaphor of slavery, and the discussion of freedom from the law in 7:1–6 runs parallel to the exposition of freedom from sin in 6:12–23.

4. By introducing this illustration, which does not quite fit either the principle just enunciated or the analogy to be drawn in vv. 4 ff., Paul produces a crippled metaphor. But because the point he is trying to make presupposes a resurrection, it is a little hard to find an analogy in ordinary jurisprudence.

5. Lit., "when we were in the flesh."

were at work in us, so that we bore fruit[6] for death. 6 But now, by dying to what once bound us, we have been released from the law so that we serve in the new way of the Spirit, and not in the old way of the written code.[7]

7 What shall we say, then? Is the law sinful?[8] Certainly not! Nevertheless, I would not have known what sin was had it not been for the law.[9] For I would not have known what coveting really was if the law had not said, "You shall not covet."[1] 8 But sin, seizing the opportunity afforded by the commandment, produced in me every kind of coveting. For apart from the law, sin was dead. 9 Once I was alive apart from the law; but when the commandment came, sin sprang to life and I died. 10 I found that the very commandment that was intended to bring life actually brought death. 11 For sin, seizing the opportunity afforded by the commandment, deceived me, and through the commandment put me to death. 12 So then, the law is holy, and the commandment is holy, righteous and good.

13 Did that which is good, then, become death to me? By no means! Nevertheless, in order that sin might be recognized as sin, it used what is good to bring about my death, so that through the commandment sin might become utterly sinful.[2]

14 We know that the law is spiritual; but I am unspiritual, sold as a slave to sin. 15 I do not understand what I do. For what I want to do I do not do, but what I hate I do. 16 And if I do what I do not want to do, I agree that the law is good. 17 As it is, it is no longer I myself who do it, but it is sin living in me. 18 I know that good itself does not dwell in me, that is, in my sinful nature.[3] For I have the desire to do what is good, but I cannot carry it out. 19 For I do not do the good I want to do, but the evil I do not want to do—this I keep on doing. 20 Now if I do what I do not want to do, it is no longer I who do it, but it is sin living in me that does it.

21 So I find this law at work: Although I want to do good, evil is right there with me.[4] 22 For in my inner being I delight in God's law; 23 but I see another law at work in me, waging war against the law of my mind and making me a prisoner of the law of sin at work within me. 24 What a wretched man I am! Who will rescue me from this body of death? 25 Thanks be to God, who delivers me through Jesus Christ our Lord!

---

6. "Bearing fruit" of course still belongs to the marriage metaphor, though it links also with common Christian moral discourse: 6:21, 22; Gal. 5:22; Eph. 5:9.

7. Cf. Gal. 3:23–4:7; 5:1, 18–25.

8. Lit., "Is the law sin?" Paul continues his personification of both sin and law as overmastering powers. Here again he takes up an objection (cf. 6:1, 15), one raised at 3:31 and made more urgent by the subsequent argument (4:15; 5:13, 20; 6:14; 7:5 f.). The section 7:7–25 has been one of the most controversial in the Pauline letters; see Part VIII, pp. 495–538. Particularly problematical has been Paul's use of the first person, "I," which many commentators have taken to be directly autobiographical. More likely he uses the common rhetorical device of "speech-in-character"—but precisely what character does the "I" here represent?

9. See 3:20.

1. Ex. 20:17; Deut. 5:21. The verb chosen by the LXX translators is often used by Greco-Roman moralists, especially those influenced by Stoicism, to represent the vice of "passionate desire," which, they taught, so often subverts human attempts to achieve self-mastery.

2. Cf. 5:20.

3. Lit., "in my flesh"; so also in v. 25.

4. The sentiment expressed here and in vv. 15 and 19 may be compared with Medea's words in Euripides, *Med.* 1078 f., "I understand that what I am about to do is evil, but anger is stronger than my plans," often quoted by philosophical moralists.

So then, I myself in my mind am a slave to God's law, but in my sinful nature a slave to the law of sin.[5]

8 Therefore,[6] there is now no condemnation for those who are in Christ Jesus, 2 because through Christ Jesus the law of the Spirit who gives life has set you[7] free from the law of sin and death. 3 For what the law was powerless to do because it was weakened by the sinful nature,[8] God did by sending his own Son in the likeness of sinful humanity to be a sin offering.[9] And so he condemned sin in human flesh, 4 in order that the righteous requirement of the law might be fully met in us, who do not live according to the sinful nature but according to the Spirit.

5 Those who live according to the sinful nature have their minds set on what that nature desires; but those who live in accordance with the Spirit have their minds set on what the Spirit desires. 6 The mind controlled by the sinful nature[1] is death, but the mind controlled by the Spirit is life and peace. 7 The sinful mind is hostile to God; it does not submit to God's law, nor can it do so. 8 Those controlled by the sinful nature[2] cannot please God.

9 You, however, are not controlled by the sinful nature but are in the Spirit, if indeed the Spirit of God lives in you.[3] And if anyone does not have the Spirit of Christ, they do not belong to Christ. 10 But if Christ is in you, then even though your body is subject to death because of sin, the Spirit gives life because of righteousness.[4] 11 And if the Spirit of him who raised Jesus from the dead is living in you, he who raised Christ from the dead will also give life to your mortal bodies because of[5] his Spirit who lives in you.

12 Therefore, brothers and sisters, we have an obligation—but it is not to the sinful nature, to live according to it. 13 For if you live according to the sinful nature, you will die; but if by the Spirit you put to death the misdeeds of the body,[6] you will live.

14 For those who are led by the Spirit of God are the children of God. 15 The Spirit you received does not make you slaves, so that you live in fear again; rather, the Spirit you received brought about your adoption to sonship. And by him we cry, "Abba, Father."[7] 16 The Spirit himself testifies with our spirit that we are God's children. 17 Now if we are children, then

5. A number of commentators think v. 25b is a later gloss, or that it belongs before v. 24. There is no manuscript evidence for a different text, however, and other interpreters regard it as a summary of the whole chapter.

6. The "therefore" does not link with what immediately precedes, but with 7:6. As 7:7–25 elaborated the negative (past) side of that statement, so 8:1–17 elaborates the positive (future) side.

7. The "you" is singular; many manuscripts read "me," and a few witnesses, "us." There is no difference in meaning; all continue the dialogue style, like the "I" of chap. 7. The surprising phrase "law of the Spirit of life" (here translated "Spirit who gives life") is chosen to contrast with "the law of sin and death" which Paul has discussed in chap. 7.

8. Lit., "by the flesh," as also in vv. 4, 5, 8, 9, 12, 13.

9. Or, "for sin." The pattern of vv. 3b–4 had apparently become common in early Christian preaching and liturgy: "Christ . . . for us, in order that we . . ." Cf. 1 Thess. 5:9 f.; Gal. 3:13 f.; 4:4f.; 2 Cor. 5:14 f., 21; also Phil. 2:6–11.

1. Lit., "way of thinking of the flesh," also in the next verse.

2. Lit., "those in the flesh," and so also in the next verse.

3. Contrast the notion of "sin living in me" in 7:20.

4. Lit., "though the body is dead because of sin, the spirit is life because of righteousness."

5. Some manuscripts read "through."

6. Paul would usually say, "deeds of the flesh," since ordinarily "body" is for him a neutral term, but in the context he has been speaking of "the body of sin" or "body of death." Some manuscripts have corrected "body" to "flesh" here, indicating that copyists were sometimes more consistent than Paul.

7. See note on Gal. 4:6, and compare this whole paragraph with Gal. 3:26–4:7.

we are heirs—heirs of God and co-heirs with Christ, if indeed we share in his sufferings in order that we may also share in his glory.[8]

18 I consider that our present sufferings are not worth comparing with the glory that will be revealed in us. 19 The creation waits in eager expectation for the children of God to be revealed. 20 For the creation was subjected to frustration, not by its own choice, but by the will of the one who subjected it, in hope 21 that[9] the creation itself will be liberated from its bondage to decay and brought into the freedom and glory of the children of God.

22 We know that the whole creation has been groaning as in the pains of childbirth right up to the present time. 23 Not only so, but we ourselves, who have the firstfruits of the Spirit,[1] groan inwardly as we wait eagerly for our adoption, the redemption of our bodies. 24 For in this hope we were saved. But hope that is seen is no hope at all.[2] Who hopes for what they already have? 25 But if we hope for what we do not yet have, we wait for it patiently.

26 In the same way, the Spirit helps us in our weakness. We do not know what we ought to pray for, but the Spirit himself intercedes for us through wordless groans. 27 And he who searches our hearts knows the mind of the Spirit, because the Spirit intercedes for God's people in accordance with the will of God.

28 And we know that in all things God works for the good[3] of those who love him, who have been called according to his purpose. 29 For those God foreknew he also predestined to be conformed to the image of his Son, that he might be the firstborn among many brothers and sisters. 30 And those he predestined, he also called; those he called, he also justified; those he justified, he also glorified.

31 What, then, shall we say in response to these things? If God is for us, who can be against us? 32 He who did not spare his own Son,[4] but gave him up for us all—how will he not also, along with him, graciously give us all things? 33 Who will bring any charge against those whom God has chosen? It is God who justifies. 34 Who then can condemn? No one. Christ Jesus who died—more than that, who was raised to life—is at the right hand of God and is also interceding for us.[5] 35 Who shall separate us from the love of Christ? Shall trouble or hardship or persecution or famine or nakedness or danger or sword? 36 As it is written:

"For your sake we face death all day long;
we are considered as sheep to be slaughtered."[6]

37 No, in all these things we are more than conquerors through him who loved us. 38 For I am convinced that neither death nor life, neither

---

8. The two compound verbs in *sun-* (suffer *with*, be glorified *with*) recall 6:1–11. V.17 announces the theme of vv. 18–39.
9. Or, "in hope. For . . ."
1. Cf. 2 Cor. 1:22; 5:5; Eph. 1:14.
2. Cf. 2 Cor. 4:18; 5:7; 1 Pet. 1:8; Heb. 11:1.
3. Another reading, very well attested, omits "God"; it can be translated either "all things work together for good" or "he [the Spirit, just mentioned in v. 27] works all things for good."
4. An allusion to Abraham's "binding of Isaac," Gen. 22:16. See the essay by N. A. Dahl in Part IX.
5. "No one" is not in the Greek text but interprets the answer implied by the previous questions. But more probably we should punctuate this verse, like all the other clauses in vv. 31–35, as a rhetorical question: "Who then can condemn? Christ Jesus who . . . is also interceding for us?" The questions thus build up to the expansive climax of v. 35 and scripture quotation in v. 36, providing an impressive close to the whole section, chaps. 5–8.
6. Ps. 44:22.

angels nor demons[7] neither the present nor the future, nor any powers, 39 neither height nor depth, nor anything else in all creation, will be able to separate us from the love of God that is in Christ Jesus our Lord.

9 I speak the truth in Christ—I am not lying, my conscience confirms it through the Holy Spirit[8]— 2 I have great sorrow and unceasing anguish in my heart. 3 For I could wish that I myself were cursed and cut off from Christ for the sake of my people, those of my own race,[9] 4 the people of Israel. Theirs is the adoption; theirs the divine glory, the covenants, the receiving of the law, the temple worship and the promises. 5 Theirs are the patriarchs, and from them is traced the human ancestry of the Messiah, who is God over all, forever praised![1] Amen.

6 It is not as though God's word had failed.[2] For not all who are descended from Israel are Israel. 7 Nor because they are his descendants are they all Abraham's children. On the contrary, "It is through Isaac that your offspring will be reckoned."[3] 8 In other words, it is not the natural children who are God's children, but it is the children of the promise who are regarded as Abraham's offspring. 9 For this was how the promise was stated: "At the appointed time I will return, and Sarah will have a son."[4]

10 Not only that, but Rebekah's children were conceived at the same time by our father Isaac. 11 Yet, before the twins were born or had done anything good or bad—in order that God's purpose in election might stand: 12 not by works but by him who calls—she was told, "The older will serve the younger."[5] 13 Just as it is written: "Jacob I loved, but Esau I hated."[6]

14 What then shall we say? Is God unjust?[7] Not at all! 15 For he says to Moses,

"I will have mercy on whom I have mercy,

and I will have compassion on whom I have compassion."[8]

16 It does not, therefore, depend on human desire or effort, but on God's mercy. 17 For Scripture says to Pharaoh: "I raised you up for this very purpose, that I might display my power in you and that my name might

---

7. Rather, "rulers," spiritual powers whether good or evil.

8. This solemn oath (cf. 2 Cor. 11:31; Gal. 1:20) opens a new section (chaps. 9–11), which returns to the theme of chaps. 1–3: both Jew and Gentile are saved by grace, not works prescribed by law. At the same time, these chapters answer the specific question raised in 3:1–4, whether Paul's doctrine of grace does not invalidate God's promises to Israel. The style of the diatribe as well as typical strategies of Jewish midrash both characterize the section, which can be summarized thus: The history of Israel shows God's utter freedom in selecting whomever he will; the Gentile mission is only the latest example of that freedom (9:6–29). Except for a small remnant (those Jews who have joined the Jesus movement) Israel has erred by pursuing righteousness as if it were based on works (9:30–10:21). Nevertheless, God has not *rejected* Israel, since even their disobedience fits his purpose to save all people. Now, however, Israel stands in the same relationship to God as the Gentiles once did, until they learn to receive God's righteousness as a gift (11:1–32). The discussion is bracketed by the opening oath (9:1–5) and a concluding doxology (11:33–36).

9. An informed reader would recognize that here Paul compares himself with Moses, the great intercessor for Israel (Ex. 32:32). In Jewish tradition this was part of the role of every prophet.

1. Because Paul nowhere else calls Christ "God," the punctuation of this verse has been debated since antiquity. The best of the several alternative possibilities is "the Messiah. God who is over all be praised!" See note on Tit. 2:11–15 and the excerpt from Julian in Part IV.

2. Cf. 3:3 f. The problem is not merely Paul's attachment to his own people, but that God's veracity is tied up with the fate of Israel.

3. Gen. 21:12; not only Paul's midrash on Abraham and Isaac (chap. 4; Gal. 3:6–18) but also the Sarah/Hagar allegory (Gal. 4:21–31) are in his mind here.

4. Gen. 18:10, 14.

5. Gen. 25:23.

6. Mal. 1:2 f.

7. Cf. Rom. 3:5.

8. Ex. 33:19.

be proclaimed in all the earth."[9] 18 Therefore God has mercy on whom he wants to have mercy, and he hardens whom he wants to harden.

19 One of you will say to me: "Then why does God still blame us? For who is able to resist his will?" 20 But who are you, a mere human being, to talk back to God? "Shall what is formed say to the one who formed it, 'Why did you make me like this?' " 21 Does not the potter have the right to make out of the same lump of clay some pottery for noble purposes and some for disposal of refuse?

22 What if God, although choosing to show his wrath and make his power known, bore with great patience the objects of his wrath—prepared for destruction? 23 What if he did this to make the riches of his glory known to the objects of his mercy, whom he prepared in advance for glory—[1] 24 even us, whom he also called, not only from the Jews but also from the Gentiles? 25 As he says in Hosea:

"I will call them 'my people' who are not my people;
and I will call her 'my loved one' who is not my loved one,"[2]
26 and,
"In the very place where it was said to them,
'You are not my people,'
they will be called 'children of the living God.' "[3]
27 Isaiah cries out concerning Israel:
"Though the number of the Israelites be like the sand by the sea,
only the remnant will be saved.
28 For the Lord will carry out
his sentence on earth with speed and finality."[4]
29 It is just as Isaiah said previously:
"Unless the Lord Almighty
had left us descendants,
we would have become like Sodom,
we would have been like Gomorrah."[5]

30 What then shall we say? That the Gentiles, who did not pursue righteousness, have obtained it, a righteousness that is by faith; 31 but the people of Israel, who pursued the law as the way of righteousness,[6] have not attained their goal. 32 Why not? Because they pursued it not by faith but as if it were by works. They stumbled over the stumbling stone. 33 As it is written:

"See, I lay in Zion a stone that causes people to stumble
and a rock that makes them fall,
and the one who believes in him will never be put to shame."[7]

10 Brothers and sisters, my heart's desire and prayer to God for the Israelites is that they may be saved.[8] 2 For I can testify about them that they

---

9. Ex. 9:16. The midrashic link between this passage and the one quoted just before is found in the similar phrases in both about proclaiming God's name. The combination then gives Paul the warrant for his negative restatement of the former passage in v. 18.
1. There are several allusions to OT passages in these verses: Isa. 29:16; 45:9; Jer. 18:6; 50:25 (LXX 27:25); Isa. 54:16 f. (LXX). See also Wisd. 12:12; 15:7.
2. Hos. 2:23.
3. Hos. 1:10.
4. Isa. 10:22 f. LXX.
5. Isa. 1:9.
6. Lit., "a law of righteousness."
7. A combination of Isa. 8:14 and 28:16.
8. See Rom. 9:3 and the note there.

are zealous for God, but their zeal is not based on knowledge. 3 Since they did not know the righteousness of God and sought to establish their own, they did not submit to God's righteousness.[9] 4 Christ is the culmination of the law[1] so that there may be righteousness for everyone who believes.

5 Moses writes this about the righteousness that is by the law: "Whoever does these things will live by them."[2] 6 But the righteousness that is by faith says: "Do not say in your heart, 'Who will ascend into heaven?' " (that is, to bring Christ down) 7 "or 'Who will descend into the deep?' " (that is, to bring Christ up from the dead). 8 But what does it say? "The word is near you; it is in your mouth and in your heart,"[3] that is, the message concerning faith that we proclaim: 9 If you declare with your mouth, "Jesus is Lord,"[4] and believe in your heart that God raised him from the dead, you will be saved. 10 For it is with your heart that you believe and are justified, and it is with your mouth that you profess your faith and are saved. 11 As Scripture says, "Anyone who believes in him will never be put to shame."[5] 12 For there is no difference[6] between Jew and Gentile—the same Lord is Lord of all and richly blesses all who call on him, 13 for, "Everyone who calls on the name of the Lord will be saved."[7]

14 How, then, can they call on the one they have not believed in? And how can they believe in the one of whom they have not heard? And how can they hear without someone preaching to them? 15 And how can anyone preach unless they are sent? As it is written: "How beautiful are the feet of those who bring good news!"[8]

16 But not all the Israelites accepted the good news. For Isaiah says, "Lord, who has believed our message?"[9] 17 Consequently, faith comes from hearing the message, and the message is heard through the word about Christ. 18 But I ask: Did they not hear? Of course they did:

"Their voice has gone out into all the earth,
their words to the ends of the world."[1]

19 Again I ask: Did Israel not understand? First, Moses says,

"I will make you envious by those who are not a nation;
I will make you angry by a nation that has no understanding."[2]

20 And Isaiah boldly says,

"I was found by those who did not seek me;
I revealed myself to those who did not ask for me."[3]

21 But concerning Israel he says,

---

9. Failure to "submit to God's righteousness" means for Paul simply failure to accept the "gospel" of Jesus as the crucified Messiah, because that proclamation disrupted the Jewish understanding of fulfillment of the covenant (cf. Galatians, *passim*).

1. Since antiquity scholars have debated whether this should be translated "cessation of the law" or "goal of the law." The Greek word (*telos*) can mean either, but the thrust of Paul's argument, beginning with the racetrack imagery of 9:31 f., supports "goal."

2. Lev. 18:5; cf. Gal. 3:12.

3. Deut. 30:11–14, originally speaking of the Torah. Paul boldly substitutes "Christ" for Torah and, for the "word" of the law, "the message . . . that we proclaim."

4. One of the earliest Christian confessions; cf. 1 Cor. 12:3; Phil. 2:11.

5. Isa. 28:16; returning to one of the verses combined in 9:33, Paul rounds off this stage of his exposition.

6. Better, "no distinction" or "no separation"; cf. 3:22.

7. Joel 2:32.

8. Isa. 52:7.

9. Isa. 53:1.

1. Ps. 19:4.

2. Deut. 32:21.

3. Isa. 65:1.

"All day long I have held out my hands
to a disobedient and obstinate people."[4]

11 I ask then: Did God reject his people?[5] By no means! I am an Israelite myself, a descendant of Abraham, from the tribe of Benjamin.[6] 2 God did not reject his people, whom he foreknew. Don't you know what Scripture says in the passage about Elijah—how he appealed to God against Israel: 3 "Lord, they have killed your prophets and torn down your altars; I am the only one left, and they are trying to kill me"? 4 And what was God's answer to him? "I have reserved for myself seven thousand who have not bowed the knee to Baal."[7] 5 So too, at the present time there is a remnant chosen by grace. 6 And if by grace, then it cannot be based on works; if it were, grace would no longer be grace.

7 What then? What the people of Israel sought so earnestly they did not obtain. The elect among them did, but the others were hardened, 8 as it is written:

"God gave them a spirit of stupor,
eyes that could not see
and ears that could not hear,
to this very day."[8]

9 And David says:

"May their table become a snare and a trap,
a stumbling block and a retribution for them.

10 May their eyes be darkened so they cannot see,
and their backs be bent forever."[9]

11 Again I ask: Did they stumble so as to fall beyond recovery? Not at all! Rather, because of their transgression, salvation has come to the Gentiles to make Israel envious. 12 But if their transgression means riches for the world, and their loss means riches for the Gentiles, how much greater riches will their fullness bring!

13 I am talking to you Gentiles. Inasmuch as I am the apostle to the Gentiles, I make much of my ministry 14 in the hope that I may somehow arouse my own people to envy and save some of them. 15 For if their rejection brought reconciliation to the world, what will their acceptance be but life from the dead? 16 If the part of the dough offered as firstfruits is holy, then the whole batch is holy;[1] if the root is holy, so are the branches.

17 If some of the branches have been broken off, and you, though a wild olive shoot, have been grafted in among the others and now share in the nourishing sap from the olive root, 18 do not consider yourself to be superior to those other branches. If you do, consider this: You do not support the root, but the root supports you. 19 You will say then, "Branches were broken off so that I could be grafted in." 20 Granted. But they were broken off because of unbelief, and you stand by faith. Do not be arrogant, but tremble. 21 For if God did not spare the natural branches, he will not spare you either.

4. Isa. 65:2.
5. Cf. Ps. 94:14; 1 Sam. 12:22; Jer. 31:37; contrast Isa. 2:6.
6. Cf. Phil. 3:5.
7. 1 Kings 19:10, 14, 18.
8. Deut. 29:4; cf. Isa. 29:10.
9. Ps. 69:22 f.
1. Cf. Num. 15:17–21.

22 Consider therefore the kindness and sternness of God: sternness to those who fell, but kindness to you, provided that you continue in his kindness. Otherwise, you also will be cut off. 23 And if they do not persist in unbelief, they will be grafted in, for God is able to graft them in again. 24 After all, if you were cut out of an olive tree that is wild by nature, and contrary to nature were grafted into a cultivated olive tree, how much more readily will these, the natural branches, be grafted into their own olive tree!

25 I do not want you to be ignorant of this mystery,[2] brothers and sisters, so that you may not think you are superior: Israel has experienced a hardening in part until the full number of the Gentiles has come in, 26 and in this way all Israel will be saved. As it is written:

"The deliverer will come from Zion;

he will turn godlessness away from Jacob.

27 And this is[3] my covenant with them

when I take away their sins."[4]

28 As far as the gospel is concerned, they are enemies for your sake; but as far as election is concerned, they are loved on account of the patriarchs,[5] 29 for God's gifts and his call are irrevocable. 30 Just as you who were at one time disobedient to God have now received mercy as a result of their disobedience, 31 so they too have now become disobedient in order that they too may now[6] receive mercy as a result of God's mercy to you. 32 For God has bound everyone over to disobedience so that he may have mercy on them all.[7]

33 Oh, the depth of the riches of the wisdom and knowledge of God!

How unsearchable his judgments,

and his paths beyond tracing out!

34 "Who has known the mind of the Lord?

Or who has been his counselor?"[8]

35 "Who has ever given to God,

that God should repay them?"[9]

36 For from him and through him and to him are all things.

To him be the glory forever! Amen.[1]

12 Therefore, I urge you,[2] brothers and sisters, in view of God's mercy, to offer your bodies as a living sacrifice, holy and pleasing to God—this is

---

2. Paul and his school often use "mystery" in an apocalyptic sense: the secret to be revealed at the end of days; see 1 Cor. 15:51; Col. 1:26; Eph. 3:3; 2 Thess. 2:7.
3. Or, "will be."
4. A composite quotation: Isa. 59:20 f., 27:9.
5. Later rabbinic writings speak of *zakut avot*—the "merit of the fathers," and some commentators suggest that Paul alludes to that notion. The next verse shows, however, that he is not thinking of the fathers' merit, but of God's fidelity to the promises he made to the fathers.
6. Many manuscripts lack "now."
7. Cf. Rom. 3:19–26.
8. Isa. 40:13.
9. Job 41:11.
1. This doxology (vv. 33–36) brings a formal conclusion not only to chaps. 9–11, but to the whole didactic portion of the letter, 1:18–11:32.
2. As in 1 Thess. 4:1; Eph. 4:1 (cf. 1 Pet. 2:11), this appeal or admonition introduces a collection of ethical injunctions (*parainesis*; for the term see the introduction to 1 Thessalonians), 12:3–15:13. Many of these are traditional, some adapted from the Hellenistic synagogue, all shaped by use in the oral instruction of converts in the churches. The individual maxims or brief groups of sayings follow one another without systematic order, occasionally linked together by mnemonic key-words.

true worship.[3] 2 Do not conform to the pattern of this world,[4] but be trans-formed by the renewing of your mind. Then you will be able to test and approve what God's will is—his good, pleasing and perfect will.

3 For by the grace given me I say to every one of you: Do not think of yourself more highly than you ought, but rather think of yourself with sober judgment, in accordance with the faith God has distributed to each of you. 4 For just as each of us has one body with many members, and these members do not all have the same function, 5 so in Christ we, though many, form one body, and each member belongs to all the others.[5] 6 We have different gifts, according to the grace given to each of us. If your gift is prophesying, then prophesy in accordance with your faith; 7 if it is serv-ing, then serve; if it is teaching, then teach; 8 if it is to encourage, then give encouragement; if it is giving, then give generously; if it is to lead, do it diligently; if it is to show mercy, do it cheerfully.

9 Love must be sincere. Hate what is evil; cling to what is good. 10 Be devoted to one another in love. Honor one another above yourselves. 11 Never be lacking in zeal, but keep your spiritual fervor, serving the Lord. 12 Be joyful in hope, patient in affliction, faithful in prayer. 13 Share with the Lord's people who are in need. Practice hospitality.[6]

14 Bless those who persecute you; bless and do not curse.[7] 15 Rejoice with those who rejoice; mourn with those who mourn. 16 Live in harmony with one another. Do not be proud, but be willing to associate with people of low position.[8] Do not think you are superior.[9]

17 Do not repay anyone evil for evil. Be careful to do what is right in the eyes of everyone.[1] 18 If it is possible, as far as it depends on you, live at peace with everyone. 19 Do not take revenge, my dear friends, but leave room for God's wrath, for it is written: "It is mine to avenge; I will repay,"[2] says the Lord. 20 On the contrary:

"If your enemy is hungry, feed him;
if he is thirsty, give him something to drink.
In doing this, you will heap burning coals on his head."[3]
21 Do not be overcome by evil, but overcome evil with good.

13 Let everyone be subject to the governing authorities,[4] for there is no authority except that which God has established. The authorities that exist

---

3. Both in Judaism and in pagan authors of the Hellenistic and Roman eras "living sacrifice" or "rational [here translated 'true'] worship" was often opposed to the "bloody sacrifices" of traditional cults. "Bodies" here means the whole person, as mention of the "mind" in the following verse shows.

4. Or, "age" (Greek, *aiōn*). The contrast between "this age" and "the age to come" is an apocalyptic notion fundamental to Paul's worldview—as to virtually all early Christianity. In chaps. 1–11 he has argued that believers are in the paradoxical situation of having already received the eschato-logical righteousness of God as a gift, even though they must still live in "this age." The Spirit, as "firstfruits" or "down payment" of the age to come, enables them to live the life of the new age in the old. Here they are admonished to manifest the new life they have received in concrete ethical acts.

5. Cf. 1 Cor. 12.

6. The style of vv. 9–13 is remarkably compact; there are no finite verbs, but only adjectives and participles describing the recommended mode of life. The same form for rules of behavior is found in 1 Pet. 2:18; 3:7 ff.; 4:7 ff.; there are parallels also in rabbinic rules, codified much later.

7. Cf. Matt. 5:44; Luke 6:28. Note that Paul does not designate this as a saying of Jesus.

8. Or, "willing to do menial work."

9. Prov. 3:7.

1. Prov. 3:4 (LXX).

2. Deut. 32:35.

3. Prov. 25:21 f.

4. Cf. Tit. 3:1; 1 Pet. 2:13–17. Vv. 1–7 have been important in the development of Western political thought, receiving usually a conservative but occasionally a revolutionary interpretation; see Part VIII, pp. 539–86.

have been established by God. 2 Consequently, whoever rebels against the authority is rebelling against what God has instituted, and those who do so will bring judgment on themselves. 3 For rulers hold no terror for those who do right, but for those who do wrong. Do you want to be free from fear of the one in authority? Then do what is right and you will be commended. 4 For the one in authority is God's servant for your good. But if you do wrong, be afraid, for rulers do not bear the sword for no reason. They are God's servants, agents of wrath to bring punishment on the wrongdoer. 5 Therefore, it is necessary to submit to the authorities, not only because of possible punishment[5] but also as a matter of conscience.

6 This is also why you pay taxes, for the authorities are God's servants, who give their full time to governing. 7 Give to everyone what you owe: If you owe taxes, pay taxes; if revenue, then revenue; if respect, then respect; if honor, then honor.

8 Let no debt remain outstanding,[6] except the continuing debt to love one another, for whoever loves others has fulfilled the law. 9 The commandments, "You shall not commit adultery," "You shall not murder," "You shall not steal," "You shall not covet,"[7] and whatever other command there may be, are summed up in this one command: "Love your neighbor as yourself."[8] 10 Love does no harm to its neighbor. Therefore love is the fulfillment of the law.

11 And do this, understanding the present time. The hour has already come for you to wake up from your slumber, because our salvation is nearer now than when we first believed. 12 The night is nearly over; the day is almost here. So let us put aside the deeds of darkness and put on the armor of light. 13 Let us behave decently, as in the daytime, not in carousing and drunkenness, not in sexual immorality and debauchery, not in dissension and jealousy. 14 Rather, clothe yourselves with the Lord Jesus Christ, and do not think about how to gratify the desires of the sinful nature.[9]

14 Accept those whose faith is weak,[1] without quarreling over disputable matters. 2 One person's faith allows them to eat everything, but another person, whose faith is weak, eats only vegetables. 3 The one who eats everything must not treat with contempt the one who does not, and the one who does not eat everything must not judge the one who does, for God has accepted that person. 4 Who are you to judge someone else's

---

5. Lit., "on account of the wrath," i.e., of God (as in 1:18; 2:5, 8; 3:5; 4:15; 5:9; 9:22; 12:19).

6. The verb represented by this phrase (*opheilete*) is cognate with "what you owe" (*opheilas*) in v. 7; this shows how disparate material was linked together by keywords for oral instruction.

7. Paul quotes the commandments in the order found in the LXX of Deut. 5:17 ff.; some manuscripts complete the list by adding "you shall not bear false witness."

8. Lev. 19:18. The summing up of the law by this commandment is found frequently in Judaism as well as in early Christianity: Mark 12:28–34; Matt. 22:34–40; Luke 10:27; James 2:8; Gal. 5:14. For the rabbis, the specific commandments were expressions of the law of love; for Paul, love *replaced* the commandments.

9. Lit., "of the flesh"; cf. Gal. 5:16. This section, vv. 11–14, reads like a formal conclusion to the preceding admonitions; what follows in 14:1–15:13 is less stereotyped, probably formulated directly on the basis of Paul's Corinthian experience. The eschatological framework is common in early Christian exhortation: cf. especially 1 Thess. 5:2–8. The metaphor of undressing and reclothing brings together several motifs, including removal of vices (v. 12; cf. Col. 3:8; Eph. 4: 22, 25), putting on armor for a spiritual battle (v. 12; cf. Eph. 6:11–17), and clothing oneself with Christ (v.14), once again a reminder of baptism (cf. Gal. 3:27; Col. 3:12; Eph. 4:24).

1. For the problem of the "weak" and the "strong," cf. 1 Cor. 8–10. Here the "weak" is specified as weak "in faith," and in 15:1 the "strong" explicitly called such. Paul has generalized from the problem raised in Corinth; the question of "food sacrificed to idols" is not mentioned, and the examples of "disputable matters" are expressed in quite general terms.

servant[2]? To their own master they stand or fall. And they will stand, for the Lord is able to make them stand.

5 Some consider one day more sacred than another; others consider every day alike. Everyone should be fully convinced in their own mind. 6 Those who regard one day as special do so to the Lord. Those who eat meat do so to the Lord, for they give thanks to God; and those who abstain do so to the Lord and give thanks to God. 7 For we do not live to ourselves alone and we do not die to ourselves alone. 8 If we live, we live to the Lord; and if we die, we die to the Lord. So, whether we live or die, we belong to the Lord. 9 For this very reason, Christ died and returned to life so that he might be the Lord of both the dead and the living.[3]

10 You, then, why do you judge your brother or sister?[4] Or why do you treat your brother or sister with contempt? For we will all stand before God's judgment seat. 11 It is written:

" 'Assuredly as I live,' says the Lord,
'every knee will bow before me;
every tongue will confess to God.' "[5]

12 So then, we will all give an account of ourselves to God.

13 Therefore let us stop passing judgment on one another. Instead, make up your mind not to put any stumbling block or obstacle in the way of a brother or sister. 14 I am convinced, being fully persuaded in the Lord Jesus, that nothing is unclean in itself. But if anyone regards something as unclean, then for that person it is unclean. 15 If your brother or sister is distressed because of what you eat, you are no longer acting in love. Do not by your eating destroy your brother or sister for whom Christ died. 16 Therefore do not let what you know is good be spoken of as evil. 17 For the kingdom of God is not a matter of eating and drinking, but of righteousness, peace and joy in the Holy Spirit, 18 because anyone who serves Christ in this way is pleasing to God and receives human approval.

19 Let us therefore make every effort to do what leads to peace and to mutual edification. 20 Do not destroy the work of God for the sake of food. All food is clean, but it is wrong for a person to eat anything that causes someone else to stumble. 21 It is better not to eat meat or drink wine or to do anything else that will cause your brother or sister to fall.

22 So whatever you believe about these things keep between yourself and God. Blessed are those who do not condemn themselves by what they approve. 23 But those who have doubts are condemned if they eat, because their eating is not from faith; and everything that does not come from faith is sin.[6]

15 We who are strong ought to bear with the failings of the weak and not to please ourselves. 2 We should all please our neighbors for their good, to build them up. 3 For even Christ did not please himself but, as it is written: "The insults of those who insult you have fallen on me."[7] 4 For

---

2. Lit., "house slave." The apostrophe, "who are you to judge?" recalls 2:1, and is resumed in v. 10.

3. Cf. 1 Thess. 5:10.

4. The apostrophe of v. 4 is repeated with the significant change of "someone else's servant" to "your brother [or sister]." Vv. 3–12 thus comprise a kind of "ring-composition." The anticipation of God's ultimate judgment should undercut the temptation to judge each other; cf. 2 Cor. 5:10, and note Paul's use of a similar rhetorical strategy in 1 Cor. 1–4; see esp. 1 Cor. 2:15 and 4:1–5.

5. Isa. 45:23 (plus a phrase from 49:18).

6. Some texts insert here the doxology found at 16:25–27, where it would have concluded one of the shortened versions of the letter (see above, p. 63).

7. Ps. 69:9.

everything that was written in the past was written to teach us,[8] so that through the endurance taught in the Scriptures and the encouragement they provide we might have hope.

5 May the God who gives endurance and encouragement give you the same attitude of mind toward each other that Christ Jesus had, 6 so that with one mind and one voice you may glorify the God and Father of our Lord Jesus Christ.

7 Accept one another, then, just as Christ accepted you,[9] in order to bring praise to God. 8 For I tell you that Christ has become a servant of the Jews[1] on behalf of God's truth, so that the promises made to the patriarchs might be confirmed 9 and, moreover, that the Gentiles might glorify God for his mercy. As it is written:

"Therefore I will praise you among the Gentiles;
I will sing the praises of your name."[2]

10 Again, it says,

"Rejoice, you Gentiles, with his people."[3]

11 And again,

"Praise the Lord, all you Gentiles;
let all the peoples extol him."[4]

12 And again, Isaiah says,

"The Root of Jesse will spring up,
one who will arise to rule over the nations;
in him the Gentiles will hope."[5]

13 May the God of hope fill you with all joy and peace as you trust in him, so that you may overflow with hope by the power of the Holy Spirit.

14 I myself am convinced, my brothers and sisters, that you yourselves are full of goodness, filled with knowledge and competent to instruct one another. 15 Yet I have written you quite boldly on some points to remind you of them again,[6] because of the grace God gave me 16 to be a minister of Christ Jesus to the Gentiles. He gave me the priestly duty of proclaiming the gospel of God, so that the Gentiles might become an offering acceptable to God, sanctified by the Holy Spirit.[7]

17 Therefore I glory in Christ Jesus in my service to God. 18 I will not venture to speak of anything except what Christ has accomplished through me in leading the Gentiles to obey God by what I have said and done— 19 by the power of signs and wonders, through the power of the Spirit of God. So from Jerusalem all the way around to Illyricum, I have fully proclaimed the gospel of Christ. 20 It has always been my ambition to preach the gospel where Christ was not known, so that I would not be building on someone else's foundation.[8] 21 Rather, as it is written:

---

8. Cf. 1 Cor. 10:11.
9. Cf. 14:1. The pattern, "Do [x], as Christ did [x]," was one of the common patterns of early Christian exhortation: cf. Eph. 4:32; 5:2, 25, 29; Col. 3:12 f.; similarly Rom. 15:2 f.; Mark 10:44 f.; 1 Pet. 2:21 ff.
1. Lit., "of circumcision."
2. Ps. 18:49 = 2 Sam. 22:50.
3. Deut. 32:43 LXX.
4. Ps. 117:1.
5. Isa. 11:10 LXX.
6. Paul tactfully hedges his expressions of apostolic authority at the beginning and end of the letter; cf. 1:11 f.
7. The sacrificial imagery is reminiscent of 12:1–3.
8. Cf. 1 Cor. 3:10; 2 Cor. 10:13 ff.

"Those who were not told about him will see,
and those who have not heard will understand."[9]

22 This is why I have often been hindered from coming to you.

23 But now that there is no more place for me to work in these regions, and since I have been longing for many years to visit you, 24 I plan to do so when I go to Spain. I hope to see you while passing through and to have you assist me on my journey there, after I have enjoyed your company for a while. 25 Now, however, I am on my way to Jerusalem in the service of the Lord's people there.[1] 26 For Macedonia and Achaia[2] were pleased to make a contribution for the poor among the Lord's people in Jerusalem. 27 They were pleased to do it, and indeed they owe it to them. For if the Gentiles have shared in the Jews' spiritual blessings, they owe it to the Jews to share with them their material blessings. 28 So after I have completed this task and have made sure that they have received this fruit,[3] I will go to Spain and visit you on the way. 29 I know that when I come to you, I will come in the full measure of the blessing of Christ.

30 I urge you, brothers and sisters, by our Lord Jesus Christ and by the love of the Spirit, to join me in my struggle by praying to God for me. 31 Pray that I may be kept safe from the unbelievers in Judea and that the contribution I take to Jerusalem may be favorably received by the Lord's people there,[4] 32 so that by God's will I may come to you with joy and together with you be refreshed. 33 The God of peace be with you all. Amen.[5]

16 I commend to you our sister Phoebe, a deacon[6] of the church in Cenchreae.[7] 2 I ask you to receive her in the Lord in a way worthy of his people and to give her any help she may need from you, for she has been the benefactor[8] of many people, including me.

3 Greet Priscilla[9] and Aquila, my co-workers in Christ Jesus. 4 They risked their lives for me. Not only I but all the churches of the Gentiles are grateful to them.

5 Greet also the church that meets at their house.[1]

9. Isa. 52:15 LXX.
1. Cf. Gal. 2:10; 1 Cor. 16:1–4; 2 Cor. 8; 9.
2. The Corinthians' (in Achaia) doubts have apparently been assuaged (2 Cor. 8; 9), but what has become of the Galatians (contrast 1 Cor. 16:1)?
3. Lit., "have sealed to them this fruit." This rather obscure metaphor evidently comes from the commercial practice of sealing sacks or jars of produce to protect the contents.
4. The account in Acts 21:17 ff. shows that Paul's fears were well founded. Acts does not mention the collection.
5. One very early manuscript has the doxology (16:25–27) at this point.
6. Or, "minister, assistant" in a broad sense, as in 1 Cor. 3:5; 2 Cor. 3:6; 6:4; 11:23; but for *diakonos* as an office, see Phil. 1:1; 1 Tim. 3:8, 12. On Rom. 16, see the essay by Peter Lampe in Part IX.
7. The eastern port of Corinth.
8. The Greek *prostatis* is equivalent to Lat. *patrona*. Patrons and patronesses were an important social force in Greco-Roman society, and their support was invaluable for the support of early Christian congregations. In 1 Thess. 5:12 the participle of the cognate verb is used for leaders of the congregation, and some commentators would translate "president" here. However, the final phrase, "including me," makes that translation difficult.
9. Here, as in 1 Cor. 16:19; 2 Tim. 4:19, "Prisca," in Acts "Priscilla." She and Aquila had been among the Jews expelled from Rome by Claudius; they had settled first in Corinth, then in Ephesus: Acts 18:2 ff.; 1 Cor. 16:19.
1. For the church meeting in the house of a patron, see 1 Cor. 16:19; Col. 4:15; Phlm. 2. The word translated "church" (*ekklēsia*) means simply a meeting, but most commonly used as a political term for a voting assembly of the citizens of a Greek city-state (*polis*). The Greek translators of the Hebrew Bible used it to translate the term for a solemn assembly of Israel, preëminently that at Mt. Sinai, and the early Jesus movement adopted it. In Romans Paul does not use the word in the letter opening, but only in these final greetings; contrast 1 Thess. 1:1; 1 Cor. 1:2; 2 Cor. 1:1; Gal. 1:2.

Greet my dear friend Epenetus, who was the first convert[2] to Christ in the province of Asia.

6 Greet Mary, who worked very hard for you.

7 Greet Andronicus and Junia,[3] my fellow Jews who have been in prison with me. They are outstanding among the apostles, and they were in Christ before I was.

8 Greet Ampliatus, my dear friend in the Lord.

9 Greet Urbanus, our co-worker in Christ, and my dear friend Stachys.

10 Greet Apelles, whose fidelity to Christ has stood the test.

Greet those who belong to the household of Aristobulus.

11 Greet Herodion, my fellow Jew.

Greet those in the household of Narcissus[4] who are in the Lord.

12 Greet Tryphena and Tryphosa, those women who work hard in the Lord.

Greet my dear friend Persis, another woman who has worked very hard in the Lord.

13 Greet Rufus, chosen in the Lord, and his mother, who has been a mother to me, too.

14 Greet Asyncritus, Phlegon, Hermes, Patrobas, Hermas and the other brothers and sisters with them.

15 Greet Philologus, Julia, Nereus and his sister, and Olympas and all the Lord's people who are with them.

16 Greet one another with a holy kiss.[5]

All the churches of Christ send greetings.

17 I urge you, brothers and sisters, to watch out for those who cause divisions and put obstacles in your way that are contrary to the teaching you have learned. Keep away from them. 18 For such people are not serving our Lord Christ, but their own appetites.[6] By smooth talk and flattery they deceive the minds of naive people. 19 Everyone has heard about your obedience, so I rejoice because of you; but I want you to be wise about what is good, and innocent about what is evil.

20 The God of peace will soon crush Satan under your feet.[7]

The grace of our Lord Jesus be with you.

21 Timothy,[8] my co-worker, sends his greetings to you, as do Lucius, Jason and Sosipater, my fellow Jews.

22 I, Tertius, who wrote down this letter,[9] greet you in the Lord.

23 Gaius, whose hospitality I and the whole church here enjoy, sends you his greetings.

---

2. Lit., "first fruits"; cf. 1 Cor. 16:15.

3. The Greek *Iounian* could be the accusative of the masculine name "Junias," though that name is not actually attested, and many translators have, until quite recently, so translated. Many ancient commentators, however, recognized that the reference must be to "Junia," otherwise unknown, as wife of Andronicus, and expressed admiration that a woman could be an apostle.

4. Possibly the notorious freedman who held enormous power as secretary of the emperor Claudius, no longer alive when Paul writes. As in several of the other instances mentioned by Paul, communities of Christians could meet in a household whose head was not Christian.

5. See the note on 1 Cor. 16:20; cf. 1 Thess. 5:26; 2 Cor. 13:12; also 1 Pet. 5 :14.

6. Lit., "their own belly"; cf. Phil. 3:19.

7. An allusion to Gen. 3:15.

8. See note on 1 Thess. 1:1.

9. Dictating letters (and other documents and literary works) to a professional scribe was common practice; for Paul's practice, see Gal. 6:11 and 1 Cor. 16:21. By exception, Tertius, himself a Christian, sends his own greetings.

Erastus, who is the city's director of public works,[1] and our brother Quartus send you their greetings.[2] 25 Now to him who is able to establish you in accordance with my gospel, the message I proclaim about Jesus Christ, in keeping with the revelation of the mystery hidden for long ages past, 26 but now revealed and made known through the prophetic writings by the command of the eternal God, so that all the Gentiles might come to faith and obedience— 27 to the only wise God be glory forever through Jesus Christ! Amen.[3]

THE LETTER TO THE PHILIPPIANS
(ca. 62? ca. 56?)

The story of Paul's founding of the church at Philippi (ca. 49 CE) is told in Acts 16, replete with miraculous details that appropriately underscore the significance of his first work on European soil. While Philippi was not technically "the leading city of the district of Macedonia" (Acts 16:12: Thessalonica was capital of the province, and Amphipolis capital of the first district in which Philippi lay), it was an important one. Located on the Via Egnatia, this small but densely populated city bore the name of its second founder, Philip of Macedon. The site of Antony and Octavian's victory over the republican forces of Brutus and Cassius in 42 BCE, it was subsequently made a Roman military colony by each of the victors, with the legal prerogatives and the largely Latin population that implied. A center of agriculture, it attracted a large number of Greek-speaking immigrants who, like Lydia (Acts 16:14), were engaged primarily in commerce or crafts. Although the apostle's initial preaching there, according to 1 Thess. 2:2 and Acts, was tumultuous and brief, the church evidently flourished and its relationship with Paul was extraordinarily cordial. Only in the case of Philippi, for example, did Paul break his customary rule of not accepting money from his converts (4:15–16). Such a gift, in fact, was one of factors that occasioned this letter (4:10–20).

Yet Philippians is not only an expression of gratitude for the Philippians' continuing partnership with him in the gospel but also a letter of friendship and exhortation. Paul not only writes in friendly style but also makes copious use of terms drawn from the philosophical and rhetorical topic "On Friendship." His purpose in writing is to shape his Christian friends' *phronēsis*, their practical moral reasoning, so that it will conform to that exhibited by Christ in the liturgical poem that he quotes in 2:6–11. Toward that goal he adduces as a model not only himself (3:17) but also Timothy (2:19–23) and Epaphroditus (2:25–30), who had carried the Philippians' gift and possibly a letter to Paul. He exhorts them to use Christian *phronēsis* in maintaining unity within the Christian community (2:2–4; 4:2–3) and in confronting their adversaries (1: 27–30; 3:2, 18–19).

A different analysis is offered by scholars who think that Philippians is a composite document. Some scholars divide it into two letters (A: 1:1–3:1a; 4:2–7,

---

1. Cf. Acts 19:22; 2 Ti. 4:20. Probably the same Erastus named in an inscription at Corinth, who "in return for his aedileship, laid the pavement [of the court in front of the theater] at his own expense." Whether the office of *aedile* is the same as the Greek *oikonomos* found in this verse or a higher office is debated.
2. Some texts add as v. 24 the benediction given here as v. 20b (with the addition of "all"); a few have it after v. 27.
3. Most critics regard the doxology (vv. 25–27) as a late addition, perhaps composed when the Pauline letters were published as a collection. Paul has brief doxologies elsewhere: 11:36; Gal. 1:5; Phil. 4:20; cf. Eph. 3:20 f.; 1 Tim. 1:17; Jude 24 f. For the pattern "once hidden/now revealed," see note on 1 Cor. 2:7.

10–23; B: 3:1b–4:1, 8–9),whereas others isolate fragments of three letters (A: 4:10–20; B:1:1–3:1 + 4:4–7, 21–23; C: 3:2–4:3 + 4:8–9). The letter does contain some peculiarities, yet these can be adequately if not convincingly explained without recourse to partition theories, and various rhetorical devices and thematic features, such as the pervasive use of friendship language, suggest the letter's integrity.

The place of composition cannot be determined with absolute certainty. Paul was in prison (1:7, 13–14, 17) at the time of writing—at least of 1:1–3:1a. In the ancient church it was universally supposed that the imprisonment was in Rome (Acts 28). Paul was in prison many times, however, and some modern scholars have proposed either Caesarea (Acts 25–26) or, more plausibly, Ephesus. Of the several objections raised against Rome as the place of origin, the most substantial is that the distance between Rome and Philippi (about 800 miles, a trip of five to seven weeks each way) would have made the several communications between Paul and the congregation implied by the letter very difficult. Since, however, Paul was in prison in Rome at least two years, that is not an insuperable difficulty. Furthermore, several elements in the letter, such as mention of the *praetorium* (1:13), "Caesar's household" (4:22), and Paul's conviction that his case is about to be settled, are most natural in Rome, though none of them is impossible in Ephesus (or even Caesarea). Rome, therefore, remains the most likely place of composition for the entire letter. An alternative solution, for those who accept a theory of multiple letters, is to regard 3:1a–4:1 as part of a letter written from Ephesus ca. 56, with the other two written during the Roman imprisonment, ca. 62.

Whatever its history, the letter stands as an example of the finest elements in Paul's thought and style, addressed to a community for whom he had the deepest affection.

Philippians

1 Paul and Timothy, servants[1] of Christ Jesus,

To all God's holy people in Christ Jesus at Philippi, together with the overseers and deacons:[2]

2 Grace and peace to you from God our Father and the Lord Jesus Christ.

3 I thank my God every time I remember you. 4 In all my prayers for all of you, I always pray with joy[3] 5 because of your partnership[4] in the gospel from the first day until now, 6 being confident of this, that he who began a good work in you will carry it on to completion until the day of Christ Jesus.

1. Lit., "slaves," an important motif in the letter; see 2:7, 22.
2. This is the first mention in Christian literature of "overseers" (or "bishops") and "deacons" (or "ministers") as distinct functions and possibly as local church offices (unless this reference is, as some hold, a later interpolation). The two terms were sometimes used interchangeably, along with a third equivalent, "presbyters" ("elders"); "deacon" (*diakonos*) could also be used as a title of an "apostle" (2 Cor. 11:23). Perhaps in Philippi the development toward a more highly structured organization was taking place more rapidly than elsewhere.
3. See 1:18, 25; 2:2, 17–18, 28–29; 3:1; 4:1, 4, 10.
4. An allusion to the concrete expression of their partnership in the gift they had sent him (4:10–20); Paul could use the same term (*koinōnia*) to refer to the collection for Jerusalem (2 Cor. 8:4; 9:13). The referent is also much broader, however, as v. 7 shows (where "share with me" translates *synkoinōnous*); see also 2:1; 3:10. Indeed, *koinōnia* belongs to the ancient vocabulary of friendship, which makes use of a number of commercial metaphors to express aspects of the relationship (see 4:15). Paul's friendship with the Philippians has as its goal the advancement of the gospel (1:7, 12, 16, 27; 2:22; 4:3, 15).

7 It is right for me to feel[5] this way about all of you, since I have you in my heart[6] and, whether I am in chains or defending and confirming the gospel, all of you share in God's[7] grace with me. 8 God can testify how I long for all of you with the affection of Christ Jesus.

9 And this is my prayer: that your love may abound more and more in knowledge and depth of insight, 10 so that you may be able to discern what is best and may be pure and blameless for the day of Christ, 11 filled with the fruit of righteousness[8] that comes through Jesus Christ—to the glory and praise of God.[9]

12 Now I want you to know,[1] brothers and sisters, that what has happened to me has actually served to advance the gospel. 13 As a result, it has become clear throughout the whole palace guard and to everyone else that I am in chains for Christ.[2] 14 And because of my chains, most of the brothers and sisters have become confident in the Lord and dare all the more to proclaim the gospel without fear.

15 It is true that some preach Christ out of envy and rivalry, but others out of goodwill.[3] 16 The latter do so out of love, knowing that I am put here[4] for the defense of the gospel. 17 The former preach Christ out of selfish ambition, not sincerely, supposing that they can stir up trouble for me while I am in chains. 18 But what does it matter? The important thing is that in every way, whether from false motives or true, Christ is preached. And because of this I rejoice.

Yes, and I will continue to rejoice, 19 for I know that through your prayers and God's provision of the Spirit of Jesus Christ what has happened to me will turn out for my deliverance.[5] 20 I eagerly expect and hope that I will in no way be ashamed,[6] but will have sufficient courage[7] so that now as always Christ will be exalted in my body, whether by life or by death. 21 For to me, to live is Christ and to die is gain. 22 If I am to go on living in the body, this will mean fruitful labor for me. Yet what shall I choose?[8] I do not know! 23 I am torn between the two: I desire to depart and be with Christ,[9] which is better by far; 24 but it is more necessary for you that

---

5. Rather, "think (*phronein*)," an important word indicating practical moral reasoning, often within the context of friendship; see 2:5; 3:15, 19; 4:10.
6. Others translate "you have me in your heart."
7. The manuscripts lack "God's."
8. The phrase is biblical: e.g., Prov. 11:30; Amos 6:12. See also Jas. 3:18 and compare Gal. 5:22; Rom. 7:4.
9. See 2:11.
1. This disclosure formula marks the beginning of the body of the letter.
2. Lit., "my bonds have become manifest in (or, by means of) Christ." "Palace guard" translates *praetorium*, a term used both of the official residence of a governor (see Acts 23:35) and of the elite imperial bodyguard. If Paul is writing from Rome, the military personnel are in view.
3. Or, "(God's) good purpose"; see 2:13.
4. Or, "I am destined, appointed (by God)."
5. Job 13:16 LXX, Paul probably intends the quotation as a double entendre, indicating both eternal "salvation" and "deliverance" from prison (vv. 25–26).
6. I.e., "of the gospel" (Rom. 1:16), or, "be put to shame" (by the outcome of his trial).
7. Rather, "with all boldness of speech" (*parrhēsia*)"; compare Acts 4:29–31.
8. The language of decision derives from ancient philosophical discussions of suicide and other instances of voluntary death, where life and death are frequently viewed (esp. by Stoics) as morally indifferent; in harsh circumstances such as prison (v. 13), suicide is often regarded as both a necessity (v. 24) and a rational act done for personal gain (v. 21). Paul's use of such language is not prompted by despair (4:11–13); rather it is rhetorical and connected with his self-portrayal as an ethical paradigm (see note on v. 25).
9. To "be with Christ" seems here to be anticipated immediately upon death, in 1 Thess. 4:14 only at the parousia. If Paul had a clear and consistent picture of what the believer would experience after death, it is not apparent from his letters: see 1 Cor. 15; 2 Cor. 5:1–5; Rom. 8:18–23.

I remain in the body. 25 Convinced of this, I know that I will remain, and I will continue with all of you for your progress and joy in the faith, 26 so that through my being with you again your boasting in Christ Jesus will abound on account of me.[1]

27 Whatever happens, as citizens of heaven live in a manner worthy of the gospel of Christ.[2] Then, whether I come and see you or only hear about you in my absence, I will know that you stand firm in the one Spirit, striving together with one accord for the faith of the gospel 28 without being frightened in any way by those who oppose you. This is a sign to them that they will be destroyed, but that you will be saved[3]—and that by God. 29 For it has been granted to you on behalf of Christ not only to believe on him, but also to suffer for him, 30 since you are going through the same struggle you saw I had, and now hear that I still have.

2 Therefore if you have any encouragement from being united with Christ, if any comfort from his love, if any common sharing in the Spirit, if any tenderness and compassion, 2 then make my joy complete by being likeminded, having the same love, being one in spirit and of one mind.[4] 3 Do nothing out of selfish ambition or vain conceit. Rather, in humility value others above yourselves, 4 not looking to your own interests but each of you to the interests of the others.

5 In your relationships with one another, have the same attitude of mind Christ Jesus had:[5]

6 Who, being in very nature God,[6]
    did not consider equality with God something to be used to his
    own advantage;[7]

---

1. One of the standard functions of a friend or mentor was to aid in moral or spiritual progress by bold speech (v. 20). Paul's willingness to forgo his own advantage (vv. 21, 23) and seek that of the Philippians (v. 24) not only provides a model for their imitation (2:4) but also represents an interesting inversion of the widespread idea about a friend's willingness to die for friends (John 15:13): rather than die for his friends, Paul here chooses to live for them.
2. For the citizenship metaphor, see 3:20; for the notion of life "worthy of the gospel," see 1 Thess. 2:12; Col. 4:1; Eph. 4:1; 3 John 6.
3. See 3:19; 2 Thess. 1:9.
4. Paul's exhortation makes liberal use of friendship language, including "one spirit" (1:27), "one accord" (1:27, "one soul"), "like-minded" (2:2, lit. "think the same thing"), "having the same love" (2:2), and "being one in spirit and of one mind" (2:2, lit.: "fellow souls, thinking one thing"). All are expressions of the harmony essential to friendship and are the antithesis of the envy, rivalry, and selfish ambition displayed by those with improper motives (1:15, 17–18; 2:3), who constitute a negative example of behavior.
5. Lit., "Think this, which in Christ Jesus." The way translators complete the sentence depends upon their understanding of the function of the liturgical poem quoted in vv. 6–11. Most likely we should understand something like this: "Base your practical moral reasoning on what you see in Christ Jesus." It is generally agreed that the hymn depicts the redemptive act of Christ in mythical form, but there have been wide disagreements about the background(s) of the hymn's religious language (Palestinian Judaism, Hellenistic folk religion, or Gnosticism), its function in Christian worship (eucharist or baptism), its allusions to Scripture (Gen. 1–3; Isa. 52:13–53:12; etc.), and its precise literary structure. A more recent debate has centered on whether Jesus is depicted in the hymn as an originally human figure who is exalted after death to divine status or as a divine figure who (as in the Fourth Gospel) invades the world and then returns to heaven. The following notes assume that the latter view is correct, and that the hymn's pattern of descent/exaltation derives from Jewish myths about divine Wisdom.
6. A quite tendentious rendering of "in the form of God." Three terms are used synonymously in vv. 6–8: *morphē* (vv. 6, 7:"form," here trans. "nature"), *schēma* (v. 8: "appearance"), and *homoiōma* (v. 7: "likeness"). An allusion to the "image" and "likeness" of God borne by the first human (Gen. 1:26–27) is likely; this notion was very important in early Christian baptism (see e.g., Col. 1:15; 3:10).
7. The rare word translated by this phrase has been much discussed. It could mean "act of robbery" (see the KJV), or"booty," either to be seized or already possessed and to be clung to. But the whole phrase is in fact a proverbial expression for "treat something as a stroke of luck"; hence the translation in the TNIV here. Some commentators have seen in the phrase an allusion to the Lucifer myth; others, more plausibly, to the Adam myth.

7 rather, he made himself nothing[8]
   by taking the very nature of a servant,[9]
   being made in human likeness.
8 And being found in appearance as a human being,
   he humbled himself
   by becoming obedient to death—
     even death on a cross![1]
9 Therefore God exalted him to the highest place
   and gave him the name[2] that is above every name,
10 that at the name of Jesus every knee should bow,
   in heaven and on earth and under the earth,[3]
11 and every tongue acknowledge that Jesus Christ is Lord,
   to the glory of God the Father.[4]

12 Therefore, my dear friends, as you have always obeyed—not only in my presence, but now much more in my absence—continue to work out your salvation with fear and trembling, 13 for it is God who works in you to will and to act in order to fulfill his good purpose.

14 Do everything without grumbling or arguing, 15 so that you may become blameless and pure, "children of God without fault in a warped and crooked generation."[5] Then you will shine among them like stars in the sky 16 as you hold firmly to[6] the word of life. And then I will be able to boast on the day of Christ that I did not run or labor in vain. 17 But even if I am being poured out like a drink offering on the sacrifice and service coming from your faith, I am glad and rejoice with all of you. 18 So you too should be glad and rejoice with me.

19 I hope in the Lord Jesus to send Timothy[7] to you soon, that I also may be cheered when I receive news about you. 20 I have no one else like him,[8] who will show genuine concern for your welfare. 21 For everyone looks out for their own interests, not those of Jesus Christ. 22 But you know that Timothy has proved himself, because as a son with his father he has served[9] with me in the work of the gospel. 23 I hope, therefore, to send him as soon as I see how things go with me. 24 And I am confident in the Lord that I myself will come soon.[1]

25 But I think it is necessary to send back to you Epaphroditus, my

---

8. Lit., "emptied himself."
9. Lit., "slave." In the Greco-Roman world human life was frequently regarded as enslaved to demonic forces (see Gal. 4:1–9).
1. The appositive phrase "even death on a cross," which interrupts the rhythm of the hymn, was probably added by Paul.
2. God's own name, "Lord" (v. 11).
3. The threefold division of the world (heaven, earth, under the earth) was common in Hellenism; the reference is to superhuman powers, here envisioned as making forced obeisance to the new ruler at his enthronement and as uttering the same confession as Christian converts: "Jesus Christ is Lord" (Rom. 10:9; 1 Cor. 12:3). The hymn's cosmic narrative thus serves to legitimate the church's audacious acclamation.
4. The hymn's final strophe is a Christian expansion of Isa. 45:23.
5. Deut. 32:5 LXX.
6. Better, "hold out [to the world]," i.e., by the example of their communal life.
7. The warm words about Timothy (vv. 19–24; see 1:1 and the note on 1 Thess. 1:1) and Epaphroditus (vv. 25–30; 4:18) function to undergird their roles as intermediaries between Paul and the Philippians, mediating not only information but also close personal relations.
8. Lit., "of equal soul," an expression that combines two ancient definitions of friendship: "friends are of one soul" (1:27) and "friendship is equality."
9. Lit., "was a slave."
1. If Philippians is written from Rome, this statement indicates that Paul has abandoned his plan for a Spanish mission (Rom. 15:24, 28). We do not know whether his hope for either Timothy (vv. 19–23) or himself (v. 24) was fulfilled.

brother, co-worker and fellow soldier, who is also your messenger, whom you sent to take care of my needs.[2] 26 For he longs for all of you and is distressed because you heard he was ill. 27 Indeed he was ill, and almost died.[3] But God had mercy on him, and not on him only but also on me, to spare me sorrow upon sorrow. 28 Therefore I am all the more eager to send him, so that when you see him again you may be glad and I may have less anxiety. 29 Welcome him in the Lord with great joy, and honor people like him, 30 because he almost died for the work of Christ. He risked his life to make up for the help[4] you yourselves could not give me.

3 Further, my brothers and sisters, rejoice[5] in the Lord! It is no trouble for me to write the same things to you again, and it is a safeguard for you. 2 Watch out for those dogs,[6] those evildoers,[7] those mutilators of the flesh.[8] 3 For it is we who are the circumcision,[9] we who serve God by his Spirit, who boast in Christ Jesus, and who put no confidence in the flesh— 4 though I myself have reasons for such confidence.

If others think they have reasons to put confidence in the flesh, I have more:[1] 5 circumcised on the eighth day, of the people of Israel, of the tribe of Benjamin, a Hebrew of Hebrews; in regard to the law, a Pharisee; 6 as for zeal, persecuting the church; as for righteousness based on the law, faultless.

7 But whatever were gains to me I now consider loss for the sake of[2] Christ. 8 What is more, I consider everything a loss because of the surpassing worth of knowing Christ Jesus my Lord, for whose sake I have lost all things. I consider them garbage, that I may gain Christ 9 and be found in him, not having a righteousness of my own that comes from the law, but that which is through faith in Christ[3]—the righteousness that comes from God on the basis of faith. 10 I want to know Christ—yes, to know the power of his resurrection and participation in his sufferings, becoming like him in his death, 11 and so, somehow, attaining to the resurrection from the dead.

2. See 4:10–20. "Fellow soldier" is one of several military metaphors in the letter; others include "stand firm" (1:27; 4:1), "contending" (1:27; 4:3), and "struggle" (*agōn*: 1:30).
3. Paul's double mention of Epaphroditus' near death presents him as one who embodied the story of Christ summed up in the quoted hymn (see v. 8).
4. Greek *leitourgia*, the same word as that rendered "service" in v. 17 and cognate with that translated "to take care of" in v. 25.
5. The Greek term rendered "rejoice" (see also 4:4) is often translated "farewell" by scholars who believe that v. 1b marks the beginning of a fragment of another letter. In that case, v. 1b might have served to connect the following section with its original context, which would have contained the referent of "the same things."
6. The phrase is harsh, but also humorous (*cave canem*, "beware the dog," was found beside ancient doorways). The most famous man of antiquity to be called a dog was Diogenes, whose followers turned the jest into a proudly ironic nickname: "Cynics." It was standard practice to warn friends about those who might do them harm and thwart their moral progress, so the warning here is appropriate to a friendly letter. The nature of the threat in Philippi is debated; some think an anti-Pauline group has already invaded Philippi, causing some in the city to distance themselves from Paul, whereas others think that Paul's words are intended as an inoculation against future harm rather than an attack on a current problem (compare Rom. 16:17f.). The relationship of the opponents of 3:2 (probably Judaizers) to the adversaries of 1:27–30, the spiritual perfectionists of 3:12–16, and the enemies of 3:18–19 is disputed. Some see only one group of opponents, whereas others see two, three, or even four groups.
7. Compare 2 Cor. 11:13.
8. *Katatomē*, "incision" or "mutilation," a pun on *peritomē*, "circumcision" (v. 3). See Gal. 5:12.
9. For metaphorical use of "circumcision," see Rom. 2:25–29; Eph. 2:11.
1. The rhetorical purpose of Paul's glowing self-depiction is to present himself as the perfect embodiment of what his opponents advocate, so that he can effectively discount it as mere "garbage" (v. 8). Compare Gal. 1:13–17 and 2 Cor. 11:21–23.
2. Or, "because of." Paul uses commercial metaphors in this verse to say, in effect, that he was, despite his religious affluence, bankrupted by Christ.
3. Lit., "faith of Christ." See the note on Gal. 2:16.

12 Not that I have already obtained all this,[4] or have already arrived at my goal, but I press on to take hold of that for which Christ Jesus took hold of me. 13 Brothers and sisters, I do not consider myself yet[5] to have taken hold of it. But one thing I do: Forgetting what is behind and straining toward what is ahead, 14 I press on toward the goal to win the prize for which God has called me heavenward[6] in Christ Jesus.

15 All of us, then, who are mature should take such a view of things. And if on some point you think differently, that too God will make clear to you. 16 Only let us live up to what we have already attained.

17 Join together in following my example,[8] brothers and sisters, and just as you have us as a model, keep your eyes on those who live as we do. 18 For, as I have often told you before and now tell you again even with tears, many live as enemies of the cross of Christ. 19 Their destiny is destruction, their god is their stomach,[9] and their glory is in their shame. Their mind is set on earthly things. 20 But our citizenship[1] is in heaven. And we eagerly await a Savior from there, the Lord Jesus Christ, 21 who, by the power that enables him to bring everything under his control, will transform our lowly bodies so that they will be like his glorious body.[2]

4 Therefore, my brothers and sisters, you whom I love and long for, my joy and crown, stand firm in the Lord in this way, dear friends![3]

2 I plead with Euodia and I plead with Syntyche to be of the same mind[4] in the Lord. 3 Yes, and I ask you, my true companion,[5] help these women since they have contended at my side in the cause of the gospel, along with Clement and the rest of my co-workers, whose names are in the book of life.

4 Rejoice in the Lord always. I will say it again: Rejoice![6] 5 Let your gentleness be evident to all. The Lord is near. 6 Do not be anxious about anything, but in every situation, by prayer and petition, with thanksgiving,

4. Or, possibly, "him," and also in the following clause (see 3:8–9). The verbs have no object in the Greek.
5. Most manuscripts, including some of the best and most ancient, omit "yet."
6. Lit., "prize of the upward call of God."
7. See the note on 1 Cor. 2:6. As in 1 Corinthians, Paul is warning against a spiritual perfectionism which regards "resurrection" as a state already attained.
8. Like the drama of Christ's story (2:6–11), Paul's life—as well as that of others, such as Timothy and Epaphroditus—provides a positive "model" for the Philippians to follow; it contrasts with the negative example of those "enemies of the cross," who are probably deviant Christians rather than pagans.
9. See Rom. 16:18. This and the following phrase do not necessarily refer to sensuality or immoral behavior in a narrow sense, but may only imply that Paul regards the motives of the rival missionaries as selfish.
1. Or, "commonwealth" (politeuma). The term was sometimes used of the quasiconstitutional organization of immigrants who resided as aliens within a foreign city; it could also describe a philosophical community.
2. Paul's language echoes the hymn in 2:6–11, yet it also occurs elsewhere (e.g., 1 Cor. 15:51–54; 2 Cor. 3:18; Rom. 8:29); these themes, like the hymn itself, are probably part of the baptismal imagery of early Christianity (cf. Col. 1:15–20; 3:1–11). "Our lowly bodies" and "his glorious body": lit., "the body of our humiliation" and "the body of his glory."
3. Lit., "beloved"; see also 2:12.
4. See 2:2. Whereas it was customary to praise friends publicly but to exhort and rebuke them privately, Paul departs radically here from both the cultural norm and his own practice by mentioning the disputants by name. His boldness in this case is all the more striking because the cultural presumption was that the "fragile female psyche" made it difficult for males to speak candidly to females. Nothing more about these two women or the nature of their controversy is known.
5. Like other anonymous persons mentioned by Paul, the identity of the "true yokefellow" (syzygos) has aroused the wildest ingenuity of generations of commentators. Some have suggested that Paul was using Syzygus as a proper name, and others (as early as Clement of Alexandria) have even thought Paul's wife was meant (see below, p. 213). But the phrase belongs to the ancient vocabulary of friendship and is used here by Paul to address someone as his "genuine friend."
6. See the note on 3:1a.

present your requests to God. 7 And the peace of God, which transcends all understanding, will guard your hearts and your minds in Christ Jesus.

8 Finally, brothers and sisters, whatever is true, whatever is noble, whatever is right, whatever is pure, whatever is lovely, whatever is admirable[7]— if anything is excellent or praiseworthy—think about such things. 9 Whatever you have learned or received or heard from me, or seen in me—put it into practice. And the God of peace will be with you.

10 I rejoiced greatly in the Lord that at last you renewed your concern for me.[8] Indeed, you were concerned, but you had no opportunity[9] to show it. 11 I am not saying this because I am in need, for I have learned to be content whatever the circumstances.[1] 12 I know what it is to be in need, and I know what it is to have plenty. I have learned the secret[2] of being content in any and every situation, whether well fed or hungry, whether living in plenty or in want. 13 I can do all this through him who gives me strength.

14 Yet it was good of you to share in my troubles. 15 Moreover, as you Philippians know, in the early days of your acquaintance with the gospel, when I set out from Macedonia, not one church shared with me in the matter of giving and receiving,[3] except you only; 16 for even when I was in Thessalonica, you sent me aid[4] more than once when I was in need. 17 Not that I desire your gifts; what I desire is that more be credited to your account. 18 I have received full payment and have more than enough. I am amply supplied, now that I have received from Epaphroditus the gifts you sent. They are a fragrant offering, an acceptable sacrifice, pleasing to God. 19 And my God will meet all your needs according to the riches of his glory in Christ Jesus.

20 To our God and Father be glory for ever and ever. Amen.

21 Greet all God's people in Christ Jesus. The brothers and sisters who are with me send greetings. 22 All the Lord's people here send you greetings, especially those who belong to Caesar's household.[5]

23 The grace of the Lord Jesus Christ be with your spirit. Amen.[6]

---

7. See the note on Gal. 5:22–23.
8. Lit., "Your thinking (*phronein*, see note on 1:7) about me bloomed again." Horticultural imagery is frequent in discussions of friendship and especially appropriate in a letter to Philippi, an agricultural center. Some think that vv. 10–20 comprise (part of) a note of thanks sent on an earlier occasion (see the introduction). It is more likely that Paul has reserved his discussion of the gift until the end of the letter so that he could provide the proper context for viewing its significance. Friends often dispensed with the social convention of explicitly thanking one another for gifts received. Thus Paul, rather than formally thanking the Philippians for their gift, expresses his gratitude by emphasizing his joy (v. 12); he does, however, issue them a receipt (v. 18).
9. A socially legitimate reason for a friend to be slow in returning a benefit; the Greek text lacks "to show it."
1. Because the Hellenistic ideal of self-sufficiency stood in logical tension with the practice of friendship, it often evoked comment by those who wanted to affirm both values; thus Paul, though joyfully accepting the Philippians' gift, denies that their friendship is utilitarian or grounded in "need." The list of "circumstances" functions to prove that he is self-sufficient; for similar lists, see the note on 1 Cor. 4:9–12.
2. Lit., "I have been initiated."
3. As a relationship of exchange, ancient friendship entailed "giving and receiving." See 2 Cor. 11: 8–9.
4. The word "aid" is not in the Greek text; others supply "money" or "a gift" (v. 17).
5. "Caesar's household" comprised all who were employed in the imperial administration, mostly slaves and freedmen. While this establishment was particularly large in Rome, it would also be found throughout the empire. Members of this group had greater upward social mobility than did any other non-elite segment of Roman society; that some of this socially prominent group had become Christians was significant and prompts Paul's remark.
6. Though "amen" is original in v. 20, here it is a scribal addition.

THE LETTER TO PHILEMON
(ca. 62? ca. 56?)

Both ancient and modern writers have wondered why this letter, written to an individual about a private matter, should have been preserved and canonized alongside the "official" letters of Paul. Yet the letter is not entirely private. Although the body of the letter is all in the first and second person singular ("I" and "you"), in the salutation Timothy is associated with Paul as a sender and besides Philemon not only Apphia and Archippus but the whole "church that meets in [Philemon's] home" are addressed (vv. 1–2). Moreover, five individuals join Paul in sending their greetings (vv. 23–24), and the request that Paul makes of Philemon may not be quite so private a matter as it appears at first glance.

Traditionally, most commentators have assumed that Onesimus was a runaway slave and that Paul's sending him back to Philemon (v. 12) was in punctilious observance of Roman laws governing fugitive slaves, for these laws—in contrast to biblical law (Deut. 23:15–16)—demanded the return of the runaway and payment of all damages due the master (vv. 18–19). Yet it is by no means certain that this is the correct reconstruction of the situation. Some scholars have argued that Onesimus, having become estranged from Philemon, sought out Paul because he was his owner's friend (*amicus domini*) and asked the apostle to become his intercessor and advocate. In so doing Onesimus had not become a fugitive and Paul was under no strict legal obligation to return him to his master. Other scholars, however, observing that the language of flight is entirely absent from the letter, argue that Onesimus was no thieving runaway but had been sent to Paul by Philemon as his envoy. In that case, the reference to injury or debt in vv. 18–19 is either genuinely hypothetical or a rhetorical device by which Paul seeks to remove any possible objection to Philemon's compliance with his request.

But what was Paul's request? What action did he want Philemon to take? If Onesimus was either a fugitive or an estranged slave, Paul's letter can be viewed simply as a letter of intercession in which the apostle asks Philemon to receive back his slave without punishing him severely. The letter would thus be similar in purpose to a famous second-century letter by the pagan writer Pliny the Younger, who successfully appealed to a friend for clemency toward a freedman who had offended him.[1] A few scholars have suggested, however, that Paul wished Onesimus to be set free (v. 16), while others have argued persuasively that Paul's real desire was that Onesimus, whether manumitted or not, should be sent back to him to serve as his fellow evangelist (v. 13). As the notes to the text will show, Paul's puns and double entendres, his hints and subtle pleas, make this intent almost unmistakable. Indeed, Paul's manipulation of Philemon is perfectly transparent, and carried out so adroitly that the latter could hardly be offended; his freedom of decision is preserved (v. 14), even though Paul is "confident of [his] obedience" (v. 21).

Paul was in prison when he wrote the letter, but again the place of his imprisonment is uncertain. Rome, Caesarea, and Ephesus have been advocated; of these Caesarea is least likely. Since Ephesus was much closer to Colossae, it would be easier for a runaway or estranged slave from Colossae (Col. 4:9) to meet Paul there than in Rome, and more understandable that Paul writes Philemon to prepare a guest room for him (Phlm. 22). Also, a trip

---

1. The Latin text of Pliny's letter to Sabinianus (*Ep.* 9.21) and an English translation are conveniently available in Betty Radice (trans.), *Pliny's Letters and Panegyricus* (LCL; Cambridge: Harvard University Press, 1969), vol. 2, pp. 118–21. The letter is instructive for both its similarities to and differences from Paul's letter.

eastward from Ephesus to Colossae would correspond better with Paul's other movements during the mid-50s, for his intention at a subsequent period was to travel westward from Rome toward Spain (Rom. 15:22–24). On the other hand, the first century was characterized by great physical mobility, so that the long journey to Rome would not have constituted a serious impediment to Onesimus, particularly if he was traveling as Philemon's envoy. Those who take Colossians to be authentic argue further it must have been written very late in Paul's career and at about the same time as the letter to Philemon (compare the greetings at the end of the two letters.). In that case, however, Paul has changed his travel plans from those announced in Romans 15:22–24.

What was the outcome of Paul's letter? The likelihood is that Paul achieved his purpose. The positive reference to Onesimus in Colossians 4:9 probably reflects a post-Pauline tradition about Onesimus' activity in church service that indicates the success of Paul's plea and vindicates his judgment about Onesimus' usefulness and character. John Knox and others have speculated that the Bishop Onesimus of Ephesus to whom Ignatius wrote four or five decades later was the same man. That is an interesting possibility, but no more.

Philemon

1 Paul, a prisoner of Christ Jesus, and Timothy our brother, To Philemon our dear friend and fellow worker— 2 also to Apphia our sister and Archippus our fellow soldier—and to the church that meets in your home:[1]

3 Grace and peace to you from God our Father and the Lord Jesus Christ.

4 I always thank my God as I remember you[2] in my prayers, 5 because I hear about your love for all his people and your faith in the Lord Jesus.[3] 6 I pray that your partnership with us in the faith may be effective in deepening your understanding of every good thing we share for the sake of Christ.[4] 7 Your love has given me great joy and encouragement, because you, brother, have refreshed the hearts of the Lord's people.

8 Therefore, although in Christ I could be bold and order you to do what you ought to do, 9 yet I prefer to appeal to you on the basis of love.[5] It is as none other than Paul—an old man and now also a prisoner[6] of Christ

---

1. Although Apphia and Archippus may have been members of Philemon's family (perhaps his wife and son), Paul here identifies them, like his associate Timothy (the "brother"), in terms of their Christian identity (the "sister") and function ("fellow worker," "fellow soldier"). In the earliest period the Christian congregations naturally had no special buildings erected for their assemblies but met in the home of an affluent Christian; for the "house church," see also 1 Cor. 16:19; Rom. 16:5; Col. 4:15.
2. "You" here and in the following lines is singular; "you" in v. 3 is plural.
3. Elsewhere Paul uses an expression like "hear about your faith" only in the case of those with whom he is unacquainted directly (Rom. 1:8; Col. 1:4; Eph. 1:15). Yet the rest of the letter, especially v. 19b, suggests that Paul knows Philemon rather well.
4. The content of Paul's prayer is undoubtedly related to the concrete request he wishes to make of Philemon. Does he hope that the latter's "partnership in the faith" will take the form of sending back Onesimus as his agent in Paul's work?
5. Throughout the letter Paul deftly uses a combination of both persuasion ("appeal," vv. 9–10; "not . . . without your consent," "not . . . forced," v. 14) and pressure ("what you ought to do," v. 8; "obedience," v. 21) to prompt Philemon to do what is appropriate, yet he never explicitly states what the latter's moral duty is, only making it plain by indirection.
6. By referring to himself as an "old man" and mentioning five times in this brief letter that he is a "prisoner" (see also vv. 1, 10, 13, 23), Paul makes an appeal for sympathy based on two socially recognized conditions of vulnerability and dependence. Some, however, think Paul is referring to himself as an "ambassador" rather than an "old man."

Jesus— 10 that I appeal to you for my son[7] Onesimus, who became my son while I was in chains. 11 Formerly he was useless to you, but now he has become useful[8] both to you and to me. → PUN ON ONESIMUS'S name

12 I am sending him[9]—who is my very heart[1]—back to you. 13 I would have liked to keep him with me so that he could take your place in helping[2] me while I am in chains for the gospel. 14 But I did not want to do anything without your consent, so that any favor you do would not seem forced but would be voluntary.[3] 15 Perhaps the reason he was separated from you for a little while was that you might have him back forever— 16 no longer as a slave, but better than a slave, as a dear brother. He is very dear to me but even dearer to you, both as a fellow man and as a brother in the Lord.

ONESIMUS → PAUL'S HEART

17 So if you consider me a partner, welcome him as you would welcome me. 18 If he has done you any wrong or owes you anything, charge it to me. 19 I, Paul, am writing this with my own hand. I will pay it back—not to mention that you owe me your very self.[4] 20 I do wish, brother, that I may have some benefit from you in the Lord; refresh <u>my heart in Christ.</u>[5] 21 Confident of your obedience, I write to you, knowing that you will do even more than I ask.[6]

22 And one thing more: Prepare a guest room for me, because I hope to be restored to you in answer to your prayers.

23 Epaphras, my fellow <u>prisoner</u> in Christ Jesus, sends you greetings. 24 And so do Mark, Aristarchus, Demas and Luke, my fellow workers.[7]

25 The grace of the Lord Jesus Christ be with your spirit.

---

7. Onesimus became Paul's "son" when the latter converted him; see note on Gal. 4:19. Paul's appeal is not simply on behalf of Onesimus but "for" him.
8. A pun on the name Onesimus, which means "useful."
9. Instead of "sending him back" and "would have liked to keep him with me," some translate "whose case I am referring to you . . . whom I would like to keep with me." This translation reflects the view that Paul is not returning Onesimus to Philemon but asking for permission to retain him.
1. The word "heart" (*splagchna*) was a popular synonym for "child" (v. 10).
2. The word translated "helping" is used elsewhere by Paul for Christian ministry in the service of the gospel.
3. Paul's earlier refusal to "order" Philemon (v. 8) is what makes it possible for Philemon's good deed to be voluntary, not coerced.
4. The debt owed Paul is most readily explained as an allusion to Philemon's conversion, though that is of course denied by commentators who insist that Paul did not know him (see above, v. 5).
5. Paul's desire for some "benefit" (*onaimēn*) is a second pun on "Onesimus." The command to "refresh" Paul's "heart" is probably a third word play. In v. 7 Paul gives thanks that Philemon has previously "refreshed the hearts" of the saints; in v. 12 he says that Onesimus is his "very heart"; now he asks that Philemon "refresh my heart."
6. In the light of the puns and double entendres throughout the letter, the phrase "even more than I ask" is significant.
7. All five of Paul's companions also send greetings in Col. 4:10–14, plus Jesus Justus (Col. 4:11). The latter is not named here, though his name could easily have been omitted by an early copyist, if it originally followed "Christ Jesus."

PART II

Works of
the Pauline School

The annotated text of six letters bearing Paul's name, the authenticity of which is disputed among modern scholars.

THE SECOND LETTER TO THE THESSALONIANS
(ca. 51?)

Until the beginning of the nineteenth century, no one seriously doubted that
2 Thessalonians was just what it appeared to be: a second letter written by the
apostle not long after his first letter to the church in Thessalonica, responding
to some new problems that had arisen there. During the past two centuries,
however, a growing number of scholars have concluded that the puzzles that
everyone finds in this letter could be more easily solved if we assume it to be
the product of someone writing later in Paul's name. Today scholarship is
sharply divided between those who defend the traditional viewpoint and those
who deny Paul's authorship. If authentic, 2 Thessalonians was written within
a few months after 1 Thessalonians. The scholars who think that it was not
written by Paul but by a disciple or even an opponent offer a discouraging
variety of possible dates, mostly around 70, some as late as 100.

The letter's authenticity has been questioned principally on two grounds:
the unusually close similarity in phrase and order of parts of 1 and 2 Thessalonians, which some scholars have taken to be signs of direct copying, and
contradictions that some see between the theological positions represented in
the two letters. In addition, some recent scholarship has emphasized differences in style: several words are used with different nuances in the two letters;
the sentences of 2 Thessalonians tend to be longer than those in the earlier
letter; figurative language abounds in 1 Thessalonians but is rare in 2 Thessalonians; and much of the second letter is formal, even harsh, lacking the
personal warmth that is so characteristic of the first. Most commentators on
the letters, however, point out that these differences are hardly greater than
between any two of the uncontested letters of Paul, and they can easily be
explained by differences of purpose and occasion. The issue of style becomes
important only if one is inclined toward a judgment of inauthenticity on one
or both of the other grounds.

It was the question of theological consistency that first raised doubts about
Paul's authorship. If both letters were genuine, argued J. E. Christian Schmidt
in 1801, then Paul flatly contradicted in the shorter one what he had said in
the longer. In 1 Thessalonians, and in several places in his later letters, Paul
clearly expresses the conviction that the return of Christ, the "day of the Lord,"
was very near (1 Thessalonians 4:15–17). But that is exactly the belief which
2 Thessalonians 2:2 appears to warn against (as Schmidt and others translated
the verse; see below). Others thought the expectation that "the day of the Lord
will come like a thief in the night" (1 Thess. 5:2) contradicted the idea put
forth in 2 Thessalonians 2:3–12 that the day would be heralded by public,
predictable events. Yet, as many subsequent critics have pointed out, the two
notions did not seem contradictory to many apocalyptic writers in antiquity,
for both the suddenness of the End of Days and the signs of its imminence
were found side by side in many Jewish as well as Christian apocalypses, including Mark 13 and its parallels and the Apocalypse of John. Nevertheless, later
critics continued to find a difference in eschatological timetable or emphasis
between the two letters. Some simply found the second much more typically
apocalyptic in its language—more similar, for example, to the language of the
Apocalypse of John, usually dated ca. 95—so they suggested that 2 Thessalonians 2:1–12 might be responding to some specific historical occasion, such
as the death of Nero and the legend of his expected return, or the Judean revolt
of 66–72, or to a supposed general recrudescence of apocalypticism toward

the end of the century. None of these suggestions has proved persuasive. As for the inconsistency of timetable, it may be simply one example of the flexibility with which Paul uses end-time language in several of his letters—in Galatians, for example, compared with 1 Corinthians.

If differences between the two letters in style and in the depiction of Christ's return in glory leave the question of authorship ambiguous, the decision must rest mainly on our answers to two questions: Why was 2 Thessalonians written? What was its relation to 1 Thessalonians? The key passages for any attempt to answer these questions are 2:2; 3:6–16; and 3:17. Is the letter mentioned in 2:2 a forgery, which the author of 2 Thessalonians warns against, reinforced by the exceptional self-authentication of the present letter in 3:17? If so, then such a forgery is more plausible after authentic letters of Paul are in circulation, in which case 2 Thessalonians itself must be late and more probably written by one member of the Pauline school against another. Or does 2:2 refer to 1 Thessalonians itself, in which case either Paul himself is refuting a misinterpretation of it, or someone else is using Paul's name to cast doubt on Paul's own letter? And what exactly is the belief that the questioned letter conveyed to the Thessalonians—that "the day of the Lord has already come" or that it "is imminent"? Ambiguities in the grammar of 2:2 (see notes there) make these convoluted questions even more difficult.

Further, how are we to explain the combination of close similarities in form and language between some parts of the two letters with striking differences in others? Some scholars have seen here the sign of a careful forger, working directly from a copy of the first letter. If we were persuaded that the situation in Thessalonica had changed so much since the first letter that a long time must have passed, this would indeed be a persuasive argument. If only a short time had passed, however, Paul's own memory and epistolary habits would provide a simpler explanation. To have produced a document so similar to 1 Thessalonians in parts yet so different in others, it is argued, the forger would have had to master the Pauline vocabulary and style so thoroughly that he could use it as freely as Paul himself. Furthermore, if one recognizes that traditional, formulaic, and idiomatic elements, including Paul's own habitual phrases, account for most of the parallels, then the copying hypothesis becomes unnecessary. Much depends, then, on our reconstruction of the situation in Thessalonica.

The commands that Paul lays out so rigorously in 3:6–16 pose that question in another way. Are the "disruptive" people whom the author orders the congregation to shun the same as those mentioned in 1 Thessalonians 5:14? If so, why has their behavior become so acute that strict discipline is now needed to control them? Are the changes related to the beliefs about the day of the Lord; for example, do the "idle and disruptive" people refuse to work (3:11 f.) because they think the End is so near that there is no point? Or are they simply taking advantage of the mutual aid that Paul and other early Christian leaders encouraged in the new communities?

The answers must depend on careful reading of both letters in their entirety and, more difficult, on our reconstruction of the history of Pauline Christianity's earliest developments. One particular dimension of the latter is especially relevant to the question. We have seen that the characteristic form of the early Pauline group was a small community that gathered regularly in the house of a patron. Consequently, even when Paul, in order to stress the unity of these groups, addresses his letter to a single "meeting" (*ekklēsia*) in a city, the weekly gatherings would ordinarily be in several separate houses (see 1 Cor. 1:1 f.; 2 Cor. 1:1; 1 Thess. 1:1; 2 Thess. 1:1; contrast Gal. 1:2). Thus a letter from Paul might well be read in each of several meetings—and understood differently, or even interpreted differently by the reader adding his or her oral comments (see note on 2:2). The difficulties Paul has heard about (3:11) might in that case not be the results of some long development, but of differences between one and another of the house communities. The issues are difficult: after two centuries of scholarly debate, there is still no consensus.

Formally 2 Thessalonians is similar to 1 Thessalonians, though somewhat simpler. It begins with a salutation almost identical with that of the first letter (1:1–2). In the place of the very long thanksgiving of the first, it has two thanksgiving periods, the former (1:3–12) developing the theme of God's just judgment, rewarding the oppressed and punishing the oppressors. It is followed by a hortatory section introduced by the typical "we ask you" (2:1–12), warning against premature excitement about the Day of the Lord (the most controversial section of the letter). The second thanksgiving is extremely brief (2:13–17), interrupted by an exhortation (v. 15), but concluding with a benediction exactly in the style of 1 Thessalonians 3:11–13. Appeal for mutual prayers (3:1–5) is followed by a section of commands (3:6–15) dealing with the "idle." The usual benedictions (3:16, 18) bracket an extraordinary authentication in Paul's handwriting (v. 17), which, ironically, many critics have regarded as the over-clever ruse of a forger.

2 Thessalonians

1 Paul, Silas and Timothy,

To the church of the Thessalonians in God our Father and the Lord Jesus Christ:

2 Grace and peace to you from God the Father and the Lord Jesus Christ.[1]

3 We ought always to thank God for you, brothers and sisters,[2] and rightly so, because your faith is growing more and more, and the love all of you have for one another is increasing. 4 Therefore, among God's churches we boast about your perseverance and faith in all the persecutions and trials you are enduring.[3]

5 All this is evidence that God's judgment is right, and as a result you will be counted worthy of the kingdom of God, for which you are suffering.[4] 6 God is just: He will pay back trouble to those who trouble you 7 and give relief to you who are troubled,[5] and to us as well. This will happen when

---

1. The salutation differs from that of 1 Thessalonians only in the addition of "our" in v. 1 and the phrase "from God the Father and the Lord Jesus Christ" in v. 2. Both are standard Pauline phrases, but the result is a repetitiveness in vv. 1 and 2 that is unusual.
2. Address as "brothers and sisters" [Greek "brothers," an inclusive term in the Pauline groups] at the beginning of a thanksgiving period is unusual and may recall the kinship language so characteristic of 1 Thessalonians.
3. A variation of the triad "faith, love, hope" of 1 Thess. 1:3 (see note there), with special emphasis on the addressees' love; the "endurance" connected in the earlier letter with hope is here (translated "perseverance") joined with faith and related specifically to "persecutions" (a word not used in 1 Thessalonians; see note on 1 Thess. 1:6) and "trials."
4. Both the construction and the meaning of v. 5 are difficult. In Greek vv. 3–12 are one sentence, and the grammatical function of "evidence" is ambiguous. The translators add "all this is," in agreement with most commentators, for clarity, but what "this" refers back to remains uncertain. Is the mere fact of persecution evidence of the righteous judgment that is coming, or the "perseverance" of the addressees? For language and thought, compare Phil. 1:28.
5. Assonance of the words (*tois thlibousin . . . thlipsin, . . . tois thlibomenois anesin . . .*) emphasizes the fittingness of reward and punishment. This understanding of the "just judgment" is typically but not exclusively apocalyptic. It is often felt to be un-Pauline, despite such passages as Rom. 2:5–10.

the Lord Jesus is revealed[6] from heaven in blazing fire with his powerful angels. 8 He will punish those who do not know God and do not obey the gospel of our Lord Jesus. 9 They will be punished with everlasting destruction and shut out from the presence of the Lord and from the glory of his might[7] 10 on the day he comes to be glorified in his holy people and to be marveled at among all those who have believed. This includes you, because you believed our testimony to you.

11 With this in mind, we constantly pray for you, that our God may make you worthy of his calling, and that by his power he may bring to fruition your every desire for goodness and your every deed prompted by faith. 12 We pray this so that the name of our Lord Jesus may be glorified in you, and you in him, according to the grace of our God and the Lord Jesus Christ.

2 Concerning the coming[8] of our Lord Jesus Christ and our being gathered to him, we ask you, brothers and sisters, 2 not to become easily unsettled[9] or alarmed by the teaching allegedly from us—whether by a prophecy or by word of mouth or by letter[1]—asserting that the day of the Lord has already come.[2] 3 Don't let anyone deceive you in any way, for [that day will not come][3] until the rebellion[4] occurs and the man of lawlessness[5] is revealed, the man doomed to destruction.[6] 4 He will oppose and will exalt himself over everything that is called God or is worshiped, so that he sets himself up in God's temple, proclaiming himself to be God.[7]

5 Don't you remember that when I was with you I used to tell you these things? 6 And now you know what is holding him back,[8] so that he may

6. Instead of the "advent" (*parousia*) of Jesus (1 Thess. 2:19; 3:13; 4:15; 5:23; cf. 2 Thess. 2:1, 8) this verse speaks of his "revelation" (*apokalupsis*; cf. 1 Cor. 1:7).

7. V. 9 uses a phrase from Isa. 2:10. Vv. 6–10 are in fact saturated with the language of the Greek OT, particularly language that speaks of the theophanies of "the Lord" (Yahweh), here transferred to "the Lord Jesus." See Exod. 3:2; Isa. 66:4, 15; Jer. 10 25; 4 Macc. 10:15; Isa. 2:10, 19, 21; Ps. 67:36 LXX (English 68:35); 88:8 LXX (English 89:8); Isa. 2:11, 17; 66:5,18.

8. *Parousia*; see note on 1 Thess. 2:19.

9. Lit., "shaken out of [your] mind"; the second verb, "to be alarmed," occurs in a similar context in the synoptic apocalypse: Mark 13:7 = Matt. 24:6.

1. Lit., "by spirit, by word, or by letter." For the latter two, cf. 2:15; for "spirit" denoting prophecy, see 1 Thess. 5:19. All three may refer to a copy of 1 Thessalonians carried by a member of one of the house churches of Thessalonica to another and read there with further interpretation by the carrier. If that is the case, then Paul is writing to correct that misinterpretation. Some commentators take the phrase "allegedly from us" to modify only "letter," but that is less likely.

2. See 1 Thess. 5:2; also 1 Cor. 1:8; 5:5 and the note there; 2 Cor. 1:14; 2 Pet. 3:10. A few scholars translate, against the normal grammatical sense, "is coming" or "is imminent," but Paul has other ways of saying that (1 Thess. 5:2; Rom. 13:12; Phil. 4:5).

3. The bracketed clause is lacking in the Greek, but necessary for sense.

4. Use of the definite article marks this as a known quantity, like "the man of lawlessness" (see v. 5). "Rebellion" can mean either political revolt or religious "apostasy" (the Greek word is *apostasia*). The latter is probably meant here (cf. Matt. 24:10–12), but in the sense of pagan opposition (n.b. v. 4) rather than Christian lapses.

5. Many manuscripts and ancient quotations read "the man of sin"; the meaning is the same: the legendary Antichrist—more correctly, the false prophet whose activity was expected to set in motion the last success of the powers of evil before the day of the Lord. Cf. Rev. 13.

6. John 17:12 uses the same term, possibly derived from Isa. 57:4, for Judas.

7. The picture of the tyrant who put himself in the place of God in the temple entered apocalyptic imagery from the desecration of the Jerusalem temple by the Syrian king Antiochus IV (168 BCE) and was reinforced by the attempt of the Roman emperor Gaius Caligula to install his own statue there in 40 CE; see also Ezek. 28:2.

8. "What is holding . . . back" and "the one who holds . . . back" (v. 7) translate participles of the same verb, one neuter, the other masculine. Neither participle has a complement: "him" and "it" are added by the translators. If the original readers "know," as Paul says, the puzzling force of person who holds back the events of the end, the secret died with them, for subsequent commentators have conjectured every possible identification, from Paul's own mission to the Roman Empire to Satan. The notion as such perhaps stems from the myth of a monster bound at creation, to be released at the end of the world: cf. Rev. 20:1–3 for one apocalyptic variation. Paul's purpose here is not to produce a dogmatic description of the last things, however, but, as in other places

be revealed at the proper time. 7 For the secret power of lawlessness is already at work; but the one who now holds it back will continue to do so till he is taken out of the way. 8 And then the lawless one will be revealed, whom the Lord Jesus will overthrow with the breath of his mouth[9] and destroy by the splendor of his coming.[1] 9 The coming of the lawless one will be in accordance with how Satan works. He will use all sorts of displays of power through signs and wonders that serve the lie, 10 and all the ways that wickedness deceives those who are perishing. They perish because they refused to love the truth and so be saved. 11 For this reason God sends[2] them a powerful delusion so that they will believe the lie 12 and so that all will be condemned who have not believed the truth but have delighted in wickedness.

13 But we ought always to thank God for you, brothers and sisters loved by the Lord, because God chose you as firstfruits[3] to be saved through the sanctifying work of the Spirit and through belief in the truth. 14 He called you to this through our gospel, that you might share in the glory of our Lord Jesus Christ.[4]

15 So then, brothers and sisters, stand firm and hold fast to the teachings we passed on to you, whether by word of mouth or by letter.

16 May our Lord Jesus Christ himself and God our Father, who loved us and by his grace gave us eternal encouragement and good hope, 17 encourage your hearts and strengthen you in every good deed and word. 3 As for other matters, brothers and sisters, pray for us that the message of the Lord may spread rapidly and be honored, just as it was with you. 2 And pray that we may be delivered from wicked and evil people, for not everyone has faith. 3 But the Lord is faithful, and he will strengthen you and protect you from the evil one. 4 We have confidence in the Lord that you are doing and will continue to do the things we command. 5 May the Lord direct your hearts into God's love and Christ's perseverance.

6 In the name of the Lord Jesus Christ, we command you, brothers and sisters, to keep away from every believer who is idle and disruptive and does not live according to the teaching you received from us.[5] 7 For you yourselves know how you ought to follow our example.[6] We were not idle when we were with you, 8 nor did we eat anyone's food without paying for

---

where he uses apocalyptic traditions, he has a pastoral aim. He wants to reassure people who are undergoing persecution and stress (1:4) that such evil is presently under restraint and, in God's good time, will end. See Part IV for Theodoret's interpretation.

9. The image is from Isa. 11:4; cf. Job 4:9; Rev. 19:15.

1. Lit., "by the appearance (*epiphaneia*) of his coming (*parousia*)," a pleonasm, since "epiphany" and "parousia" are synonyms.

2. As always in Jewish apocalyptic, the dualism of the myth is circumscribed by the monotheistic insistence that God ultimately controls the whole sequence of events. For the God-sent delusion (lit. "a power of error") cf. 1 Kings 22:21–23.

3. The manuscripts are divided between "from the beginning" (*ap'archēs*) and "firstfruits" (*aparchēn*). The former expression is not used elsewhere by Paul; he uses the latter figuratively in Rom. 16:5 and 1 Cor. 16:15 for "first converts" in an area, but the Philippian, not the Thessalonian church was the first in Macedonia and Europe. Perhaps the meaning is that Christians in general are the "firstfruits" of humankind, as in James 1:18.

4. Vv. 13 f., formulated in contrast to the preceding threats against the unbelieving, recapitulate the thanksgiving of 1:3–12.

5. By using the verb "command," repeated in v. 12 to bracket this section, instead of the parenetic "appeal" or "ask," Paul stresses the seriousness of the issue, raised in friendly parenetic language in 1 Thess. 5:14. For the sanction of shunning people who violate community norms ("keep away," "do not associate," v. 14) see 1 Cor. 5:9–11.

6. For Paul's "example" of earning his own living, see 1 Cor. 9; 2 Cor. 11:7–11, and the note on 1 Thess. 2:9.

it. On the contrary, we worked night and day, laboring and toiling so that we would not be a burden to any of you. 9 We did this, not because we do not have the right to such help, but in order to offer ourselves as a model for you to imitate. 10 For even when we were with you, we gave you this rule: "Anyone who is unwilling to work shall not eat."[7]

11 We hear that some among you are idle and disruptive. They are not busy; they are busybodies.[8] 12 Such people we command and urge in the Lord Jesus Christ to settle down and earn the bread they eat. 13 And as for you, brothers and sisters, never tire of doing what is good.

14 Take special note of those who do not obey our instruction in this letter. Do not associate with them, in order that they may feel ashamed. 15 Yet do not regard them as enemies, but warn them as fellow believers.

16 Now may the Lord of peace himself give you peace at all times and in every way. The Lord be with all of you.

17 I, Paul, write this greeting in my own hand, which is the distinguishing mark in all my letters. This is how I write.[9]

18 The grace of our Lord Jesus Christ be with you all.

THE LETTER TO THE COLOSSIANS
(ca. 65–75?)

Colossae, located on the Lycus River in Phrygia and on the main highway from Ephesus to Tarsus, had once been an important mercantile city. By the first century, however, competition with nearby Laodicea and Hierapolis had reduced it to a minor market town. Paul never visited it, but Epaphras, who had evidently been trained by Paul, founded a vigorous church there. Little is heard of Colossae in later years; the town may have been destroyed by an earthquake which, according to several ancient authors, struck the Lycus valley during the reign of Nero. We would be greatly helped in deciding on the letter's date and authenticity if more precise information about the earthquake were available, but the ancient reports do not agree on either its extent or its date. Since the site of Colossae has unfortunately never been excavated, archaeological confirmation is lacking.

While the letter seems at first glance to have only a general, pastoral character, rehearsing doctrines familiar to the recipients from their liturgy and adding stereotyped ethical instructions, yet chapter 2 reveals that its central purpose is to combat a deviant form of Christianity. The polemic is much more restrained than in the comparable passages of Galatians and 2 Corinthians 10–13. The style is more didactic and admonitory; elements of the diatribe, so typical of Paul elsewhere, are almost entirely missing, except for 2:20–23. The subtlety of the polemic makes the task of reconstructing the opposing position

---

7. An example of the tradition mentioned in v. 6. Whether Paul coined or quoted this "golden rule of work," which sums up a commonplace sentiment in antiquity, he certainly assured its place in Western proverbial wisdom. It is quoted, for example (without attribution), in art. XII of the 1936 Constitution of the Soviet Union.

8. Their behavior runs directly counter to the exhortation in 1 Thess. 4:1 f. "Busybody" was a term of contempt often applied to philosophers or others who thought of themselves as representing higher values than those of the workaday world.

9. Letters and legal documents in antiquity, dictated to a scribe, were frequently signed in the author's own hand; see also 1 Cor. 16:21; Col. 4:18; with a different point, Phlm. 19; more expansively, Gal. 6:11; note also Rom. 16:22. The emphasis here on authentication, however, is unique in the Pauline letters.

excruciatingly difficult—yet without at least a general picture of that position a full understanding of the letter itself is impossible.

The opponents' teaching is called "philosophy" (2:8); the word does not refer in this case to rational inquiry but, as often in the Hellenistic and Roman periods, to occult speculations and practices, depending on a body of "tradition" (*ibid.*). Thus it was concerned with "the elemental spiritual forces of this world" (*ibid.*) and "the worship of angels" (or "the angels' worship," 2:18). It set forth "rules" (*dogmata*, cf. 2:20) requiring adherence to a festival calendar (2:16) and ascetic practices (2:16, 18, 20–23). The key to understanding how these strange elements fit together is probably hidden in 2:18, a verse so difficult that many commentators have despaired of either understanding or translating it.

Colossians was most likely not written by Paul, but by a disciple (perhaps Timothy, 1:1) using his name. Doubts about Pauline authorship were raised as early as 1838, because of the obvious divergences of style and content from the accepted letters. However, the significance of those divergences proved very difficult to measure. There is hardly one of the special stylistic features in Colossians that is totally absent from the undoubted letters; only the quantity of them is unusual. Moreover, recognition in recent years that many peculiarities of style and vocabulary are the result of liturgical influence and of allusions to the "philosophy" combated by the author has invalidated any stylistic studies that do not allow for quoted and stereotyped phrases. Similar questions may be raised about most of the unique ideas in the letter—such as the cosmic dimensions of Christ's work of redemption and the metaphor of "head" and "body."

Perhaps the most important question, however, is whether the relation between sacraments and eschatology in Colossians is one that Paul could have agreed with. Here it is stated, for example, that the believer has already been resurrected (presumably, in baptism) with Christ (3:1). Some scholars say categorically that Paul could never have made such a statement, for he is so careful elsewhere to stress the *future* fulfillment of the Christian hope (see, e.g., the notes on 1 Corinthians). They call attention to the careful way in which he breaks up the obvious parallelism of his statements about baptism into Christ in Romans 6 by using only the future tense to speak of sharing in Christ's resurrection. Others, however, point out that the future dimension of the Christian life is guarded with equal care in Colossians (3:3 f., and the whole of the ethical admonitions), only in different language. It seems likely that the baptismal liturgy in the Pauline (and other Hellenistic) churches spoke of dying *and* rising with Christ in baptism. The author of Colossians is perhaps closer to the language of the liturgy than Paul in 1 Corinthians and Romans, but the difference of emphasis may be dictated by the different situation. The future element, for example, receives hardly any mention in Galatians, where Paul opposes a movement that may have had some things in common with the Colossian opponents.

It was not until 1973 that a comprehensive analysis of the style, rhetorical character, and thought-structure of the entire letter, taking into account all the difficulties mentioned above, persuaded most critical scholars that we hear in Colossians not the voice of Paul himself, but one of those he called his "fellow workers" (e.g., Phlm. 1:24).[1] Not all scholars agree, but perhaps the question is not so important as it once seemed, for once we recognize Paul's indirect relationship with the church addressed, and the extent to which this letter is filled with materials that were common traditions cultivated in the

---

1. Walter Bujard, *Stilanalytische Untersuchungen zum Kolosserbrief als Beitrag zur Methodik von Sprachvergleichen*, Studien zur Umwelt des Neuen Testaments (Göttingen: Vandenhoeck und Ruprecht, 1973).

Pauline churches, then it has to be understood as representative of the Pauline *school*, whoever was its immediate author.

We cannot determine with any confidence just when the letter was written, or from where. It represents Paul as a prisoner (4:18), and, if it were written by Paul, then the traditional locus, his imprisonment in Rome at the time of Nero, would be perfectly plausible—but so would be Ephesus or Caesarea, at an earlier date. Of course an associate of Paul could also have written for him during one of those imprisonments. However, the description of Paul's sufferings and his apostleship (1:24–29) begins to sound almost like posthumous hagiography (cf. the even more exalted language of Eph. 3:2–12). That and the subtle changes in christological and ecclesiological language, in comparison with the undoubted letters, which could be understood as the product of further developments within the Pauline school, persuade some scholars that the letter must have been written after Paul's death. If the earthquake mentioned above was in the early 60s, and if it led to the abandonment of the city, then a date this late would mean that the address to Colossae was fictional and the admonitions of the letter intended for some other city—perhaps neighboring Laodicaea (cf. 4:16).

Formally, the letter exhibits the usual Pauline thanksgiving, 1:3–23, which contains two inlays: vv. 5–8, reflecting on the church's origin, and vv. 15–20, a carefully formed christological statement, which the author has adopted from a liturgical poem or chant. A statement summing up Paul's mission, with special emphasis on the significance of his suffering (1:24–29) and his relationship to the Lycus valley congregations (2:1–5), lays the foundation for his authoritative warnings against heresy (2:6–23). The *parainesis* (3:1–4:6; on the term, see introduction to 1 Thessalonians) contains mostly stereotyped elements, some of which very likely belonged to baptismal catechesis. Here we meet for the first time in Christian literature a form that was very common in Hellenistic moral philosophy, the "household table" (3:18–4:1). A commendation of the bearers of the letter, Tychicus and Onesimus (!), and the usual greetings, followed by Paul's autograph (4:7–18), conclude the letter.

Colossians

1 Paul, an apostle of Christ Jesus by the will of God, and Timothy our brother,

2 To God's holy people in Colossae, the faithful brothers and sisters in Christ: Grace and peace to you from God our Father.[1]

3 We always thank God,[2] the Father of our Lord Jesus Christ, when we pray for you, 4 because we have heard of your faith in Christ Jesus and of the love you have for all his people— 5 the faith and love that spring from the hope[3] stored up for you in heaven and about which you have already heard in the true word[4] of the gospel 6 that has come to you. In the same way, the gospel is bearing fruit and growing throughout the whole world—

---

1. Many manuscripts add "and the Lord Jesus Christ."
2. Vv. 3–8 are a single sentence in Greek, circling around from what the writers have "heard" (v. 4) to what Epaphras has "told" them (v. 8).
3. Note the common early Christian triad, "faith, love, hope"; see the note on 1 Thess. 1:3. Usually in Pauline usage "hope" means the act of hoping; here it is the object of hope. For the notion of a reward "stored up" in heaven, an image found also in Jewish apocalypses of the same period, compare 1 Pet. 1:4.
4. "True word" (lit. "word of truth") was one of the standard synonyms for "gospel": see Eph. 1:13; 2 Tim. 2:15; James 1:18; cf. 2 Cor. 6:7. The phrase was biblical: e.g., Ps. 119:43.

just as it has been doing among you since the day you heard it and truly understood God's grace. 7 You learned it from Epaphras,[5] our dear fellow servant, who is a faithful minister of Christ on our[6] behalf, 8 and who also told us of your love in the Spirit.

9 For this reason, since the day we heard about you, we have not stopped praying for you. We continually ask God to fill you with the knowledge of his will through all the wisdom and understanding that the Spirit gives,[7] 10 so that you may live a life worthy of the Lord and please him in every way: bearing fruit in every good work, growing in the knowledge of God, 11 being strengthened with all power according to his glorious might[8] so that you may have great endurance and patience, 12 and giving joyful thanks to the Father, who has qualified you[9] to share in the inheritance of his people[1] in the kingdom of light. 13 For he has rescued us from the dominion of darkness and brought us into the kingdom of the Son he loves, 14 in whom we have redemption, the forgiveness of sins.

15 The Son is the image of the invisible God, the firstborn over all creation.[2] 16 For in him all things were created: things in heaven and on earth, visible and invisible, whether thrones or powers or rulers or authorities; all things have been created through him and for him.[3] 17 He is before all things, and in him all things hold together.

18 And he is the head of the body, the church;[4] he is the beginning and the firstborn from among the dead, so that in everything he might have the supremacy. 19 For God was pleased to have all his fullness dwell in him, 20 and through him to reconcile to himself all things, whether things on earth or things in heaven, by making peace through his blood, shed on the cross.[5]

---

5. According to Phlm. 23, in prison with Paul. Epaphras is otherwise unknown.
6. Though some manuscripts read "your," the reading in the text is almost certainly correct. Thus Epaphras' authority is backed by that of the apostle.
7. More literally, "all spiritual wisdom and understanding."
8. The accumulation of synonymous expressions, both verbs and nouns, is typical of the style of Col. and Eph.
9. "Us" is also well attested in the manuscripts; there is confusion between the first and second person pronouns (HMEIC was easily mistaken for YMEIC) in the text tradition throughout the letter.
1. Lit. "his holy ones" (as in v. 2), but some commentators take the word to refer to angels (see note on 1 Thess. 3:13), in which case this verse might already allude to the "worship of angels" (2:18). The language of vv. 12 f. has parallels in the Dead Sea Scrolls, where speculations about the angels were also important.
2. Vv. 15–20 are probably adapted from a liturgical poem (some commentators speak of a "hymn," others, a "creed"), of two strophes, each beginning with the relative pronoun "who": (1) "[who] is the image . . . , the firstborn over [lit. of] all creation . . ."; (2) "[who] is the beginning and the firstborn from the dead." If a hymn, an introductory phrase (something like "Praise the Lord," or "Praised be Christ") would have stood originally at the beginning. Some commentators think the second part was not part of the original hymn, but a reinterpretation of it by the author of the letter. The language of the first strophe has many parallels in the Jewish wisdom tradition, especially in Philo, who could speak of the Logos as the image and "firstborn" of God. Other early Christian verse, including the poem incorporated into the prologue of the Gospel according to John, makes use of the same tradition.
3. Stoics used a similar formula of God or Nature; in the NT, it is used of both God and Christ (Rom. 11:36; 1 Cor. 8:6; Eph. 4:6). This statement of Christ's role in creation goes beyond anything in the earlier Pauline letters (though 1 Cor. 8:6 indicates the beginning of such a notion); the closest NT parallel is the prologue to the Fourth Gospel.
4. "The church" is regarded by many commentators as an addition to the hymn by the author of the letter. In the hymn, the "body" would refer to the cosmos, cf. 2:10.
5. For the cosmic dimensions of the activity of Christ, cf. Phil. 2:10 f. The phrase "through his blood, shed on the cross" is probably an addition to the hymn by the letter's author, like Paul's addition of "even death on a cross" in Phil. 2:8.

21 Once you were alienated from God and were enemies in your minds because of your evil behavior. 22 But now he has reconciled you[6] by Christ's physical body through death to present you holy in his sight, without blemish and free from accusation— 23 if you continue in your faith, established and firm, and do not move from the hope held out in the gospel. This is the gospel that you heard and that has been proclaimed to every creature[7] under heaven, and of which I, Paul, have become a servant.

24 Now I rejoice in what I am suffering for you, and I fill up in my flesh what is still lacking[8] in regard to Christ's afflictions, for the sake of his body, which is the church. 25 I have become its servant by the commission God gave me to present to you the word of God in its fullness— 26 the mystery that has been kept hidden for ages and generations, but is now disclosed to the Lord's people.[9] 27 To them God has chosen to make known among the Gentiles the glorious riches of this mystery, which is Christ in you, the hope of glory.

28 We proclaim him, admonishing and teaching everyone with all wisdom, so that we may present everyone fully mature[1] in Christ. 29 To this end I strenuously contend with all the energy Christ so powerfully works in me.

2 I want you to know how hard I am contending for you and for those at Laodicea, and for all who have not met me personally. 2 My goal is that they may be encouraged in heart and united in love, so that they may have the full riches of complete understanding, in order that they may know the mystery of God, namely, Christ, 3 in whom are hidden all the treasures of wisdom and knowledge. 4 I tell you this so that no one may deceive you by fine-sounding arguments. 5 For though I am absent from you in body, I am present with you in spirit and delight to see how disciplined you are and how firm your faith in Christ is.

6 So then, just as you received Christ Jesus as Lord, continue to live your lives in him, 7 rooted and built up in him, strengthened in the faith as you were taught, and overflowing with thankfulness.

8 See to it that no one takes you captive through hollow and deceptive philosophy, which depends on human tradition and the elemental spiritual forces[2] of this world rather than on Christ.

9 For in Christ all the fullness of the Deity lives in bodily form,[3] 10 and in Christ you have been brought to fullness. He is the head over every power and authority. 11 In him you were also circumcised with a circumcision not performed by human hands. Your sinful nature was put off when

---

6. In the final sentence of the thanksgiving (vv. 21–23), the author connects the hymn's imagery of cosmic reconciliation ("all things") with the reconciliation of the human congregation to God. Compare Paul's use of the hymn he quotes in Phil. 2:5–11 in the following verses (12–29). "Reconciliation" is an important concept in the Pauline school: see the note on 2 Cor. 5:18–21; cf. Rom. 5:10 f.; 11:15; Eph. 2:16. In v. 21 "because of your evil behavior" could be translated "as shown by your evil behavior."

7. For the hyperbole, cf. 1 Thess. 1:8; Rom. 15:18–23.

8. The meaning of this expression is obscure. Since the author wishes to emphasize the *completeness* of the victory won by Christ (2:8–15), it would be suprising if he meant to imply here that Christ's sufferings did not accomplish all that was needed. Some commentators point to the Jewish notion of the "woes of the Messiah," shared by the community of the end of days, as a possible source for the notion, but there is nothing in the context to suggest that.

9. For the form of this verse, see note on 1 Cor. 2:7.

1. On the word "mature," see note on 1 Cor. 2:6.

2. See note on Gal. 4:3.

3. This picks up a statement from the poem, 1:19. In second-century Gnosticism, "fullness" (*plērōma*) became a technical term for the whole heavenly world composed of emanations from the highest god.

you were circumcised by Christ,[4] 12 having been buried with him in baptism, in which you were also raised with him through your faith in the working of God, who raised him from the dead.

13 When you were dead in your sins and in the uncircumcision of your sinful nature,[5] God made you alive with Christ. He forgave us all our sins, 14 having canceled the charge of our legal indebtedness, which stood against us and condemned us; he has taken it away, nailing it to the cross. 15 And having disarmed[6] the powers and authorities, he made a public spectacle of them, triumphing over them by the cross.[7]

16 Therefore do not let anyone judge you by what you eat or drink, or with regard to a religious festival, a New Moon celebration or a Sabbath day.[8] 17 These are a shadow of the things that were to come; the reality,[9] however, is found in Christ. 18 Do not let anyone who delights in false humility and the worship of angels disqualify you. Such people also go into great detail about what they have seen, and their unspiritual minds puff them up with idle notions.[1] 19 They have lost connection with the head, from whom the whole body, supported and held together by its ligaments and sinews, grows as God causes it to grow.

20 Since you died with Christ to the elemental spiritual forces of this world, why, as though you still belonged to the world, do you submit to its rules:[2] 21 "Do not handle! Do not taste! Do not touch!"? 22 These rules, which have to do with things that are all destined to perish with use, are based on merely human commands and teachings. 23 Such regulations indeed have an appearance of wisdom, with their self-imposed worship, their false humility and their harsh treatment of the body, but they lack any value in restraining sensual indulgence.

3 Since, then, you have been raised with Christ, set your hearts on things above, where Christ is seated at the right hand of God.[3] 2 Set your minds on things above, not on earthly things. 3 For you died, and your life is now hidden with Christ in God. 4 When Christ, who is your life, appears, then you also will appear with him in glory.

---

4. Lit., "in the circumcision of Christ," perhaps meaning "the Christian equivalent of circumcision," i.e., baptism. The notion that one's "sinful nature" (lit., "body of flesh") was "put off" in baptism is found elsewhere. The use of a change of clothing to symbolize a change of life is found in many forms of initiation rite as well as in metaphors of conversion in popular philosophy. For Christians, removal of clothing before baptism represented removal of "the old human"; reclothing after immersion (from a later period, the use of white robes, "robes of light," is attested) depicted "putting on Christ" = "the new human." See 3:9 f and cf. Gal. 3:27.
5. "Sinful nature": lit. "flesh."
6. Lit., "stripped"; a cognate word is translated "put off" in v. 11b. The picture is that of a triumphal procession in which a returning conqueror exhibits his captives. See note on 2 Cor. 2:14.
7. "By the cross": grammatically possible, but the context supports the alternative translation, "in him."
8. "Festival, New Moon, Sabbath": a stereotyped formula found in biblical and post-biblical Jewish literature to refer to the whole sacrificial cultus.
9. The Platonic contrast "shadow/reality" (lit., "body") is found frequently in Hellenistic literature, including Josephus and Philo; note also the equivalent pair, "shadow/image" in Heb. 10:1. Possibly the opponents themselves called their cultus a "shadow," implying that it was an earthly copy of heavenly worship.
1. This verse is fraught with difficulties. The word translated "go into great detail," is found associated with mystery and oracle cults, but it meant simply "entering"; its most frequent use is "to enter into possession" (of property). Possibly entrance *into heaven* (mystically) is meant. "Worship of angels" could equally well mean "angels' worship."
2. "Submit to . . . rules" (*dogmatizesthe*) is cognate with "legal indebtedness" (*dogmata*), v. 14. The regulations are clearly ascetic; the first, translated "Do not handle," probably means "Do not engage in sexual acts." The third, "Do not touch," could warn against profaning the heavenly mysteries, as in Ex. 19:12 LXX.
3. An allusion to Ps. 110:1, a favorite of early Christian interpreters.

5 Put to death, therefore, whatever belongs to your earthly nature:[4] sexual immorality, impurity, lust, evil desires and greed, which is idolatry. 6 Because of these, the wrath of God is coming.[5] 7 You used to walk in these ways, in the life you once lived. 8 But now you must also rid yourselves of all such things as these: anger, rage, malice, slander, and filthy language from your lips. 9 Do not lie to each other, since you have taken off your old self[6] with its practices 10 and have put on the new self, which is being renewed in knowledge in the image of its Creator. 11 Here there is no Gentile or Jew, circumcised or uncircumcised, barbarian, Scythian, slave or free, but Christ is all, and is in all.[7]

12 Therefore, as God's chosen people, holy and dearly loved, clothe yourselves with compassion, kindness, humility, gentleness and patience. 13 Bear with each other and forgive one another if any of you has a grievance against someone. Forgive as the Lord forgave you. 14 And over all these virtues put on love, which binds them all together in perfect unity.

15 Let the peace of Christ rule in your hearts, since as members of one body you were called to peace. And be thankful. 16 Let the message of Christ dwell among you richly as you teach and admonish one another with all wisdom through psalms, hymns and songs from the Spirit, singing to God with gratitude in your hearts. 17 And whatever you do, whether in word or deed, do it all in the name of the Lord Jesus, giving thanks to God the Father through him.

18 Wives,[8] submit yourselves to your husbands, as is fitting in the Lord.

19 Husbands, love your wives and do not be harsh with them.

20 Children, obey your parents in everything, for this pleases the Lord.

21 Fathers, do not embitter your children, or they will become discouraged.

22 Slaves, obey your earthly masters in everything; and do it, not only when their eye is on you and to curry their favor, but with sincerity of heart and reverence for the Lord. 23 Whatever you do, work at it with all your heart, as working for the Lord, not for human masters, 24 since you know that you will receive an inheritance from the Lord as a reward. It is the Lord Christ you are serving. 25 Those who do wrong will be repaid for their wrongs, and there is no favoritism.

4 Masters, provide your slaves with what is right and fair, because you know that you also have a Master in heaven.

2 Devote yourselves to prayer, being watchful and thankful. 3 And pray for us, too, that God may open a door for our message, so that we may proclaim the mystery of Christ, for which I am in chains. 4 Pray that I may proclaim it clearly, as I should. 5 Be wise in the way you act toward out-

---

4. Lit., "the limbs that are on earth"; cf. 2:11. The admonitions in this section follow a pattern that developed in the baptismal instruction for new Christians. Hence the allusions to "dying," "rising," "putting off," "putting on," "putting to death."

5. Some manuscripts add, "on those who are disobedient."

6. "Self," lit., "person" (*anthrōpos*); also in the following verse.

7. Cf. Gal. 3:28; 1 Cor. 12:13.

8. The following admonitions, 3:18–4:1, are in the form of a "household table" or "household duty code," which, reflecting the pervasive Greco-Roman concern with household management, set out the duties of each member of a patriarchal household. The form is sometimes said to have originated with Zeno, founder of the Stoa, but it was in the clear outline that Aristotle gave it that it became the common property of all schools of Hellenistic moral philosophy, including Hellenistic Judaism. It is Christianized here by only minor features: "in the Lord" and the like. See the essay by E. Schüssler Fiorenza in Part IX.

siders; make the most of every opportunity. 6 Let your conversation be always full of grace, seasoned with salt, so that you may know how to answer everyone.

7 Tychicus[9] will tell you all the news about me. He is a dear brother, a faithful minister and fellow servant[1] in the Lord. 8 I am sending him to you for the express purpose that you may know about our circumstances and that he may encourage your hearts. 9 He is coming with Onesimus,[2] our faithful and dear brother, who is one of you. They will tell you everything that is happening here.

10 My fellow prisoner Aristarchus sends you his greetings, as does Mark,[3] the cousin of Barnabas. (You have received instructions about him; if he comes to you, welcome him.) 11 Jesus, who is called Justus, also sends greetings. These are the only Jews[4] among my co-workers for the kingdom of God, and they have proved a comfort to me. 12 Epaphras, who is one of you and a servant of Christ Jesus, sends greetings. He is always wrestling in prayer for you, that you may stand firm in all the will of God, mature and fully assured. 13 I vouch for him that he is working hard for you and for those at Laodicea and Hierapolis. 14 Our dear friend Luke, the doctor, and Demas send greetings.[5] 15 Give my greetings to the brothers and sisters at Laodicea, and to Nympha and the church in her house.

16 After this letter has been read to you, see that it is also read in the church of the Laodiceans and that you in turn read the letter from Laodicea.[6]

17 Tell Archippus:[7] "See to it that you complete the work you have received in the Lord."

18 I, Paul, write this greeting in my own hand. Remember my chains. Grace be with you.

THE LETTER TO THE EPHESIANS
(ca. 80?)

Despite the antiquity of its traditional title, the Letter to the Ephesians was certainly not written to Ephesus. Several of the oldest and best manuscripts, including the famous Chester Beatty papyrus, omit the words "in Ephesus" usually found in 1:1. The third-century church fathers Tertullian and Origen and the heretic Marcion also used texts that lacked these words, and Marcion identified the letter with the lost Letter to the Laodiceans (see note on Col. 4:

---

9. Both Tychicus and Aristarchus (v. 10) are mentioned among Paul's companions in Acts 20:4; otherwise they are unknown.
1. Greek "slave." Paul can call himself the slave of Christ (Rom. 1:1; Gal. 1:10; Phil. 1:1), and he often speaks of "fellow workers" (Rom. 16:3, 9, 21; 1 Cor. 3:9; 2 Cor. 1:24; 8:23; Phil. 2:25; cf. Phil. 4:3); the phrase "fellow slave" occurs only here and 1:7.
2. See Philemon, *passim.*
3. For Mark, see Acts 12:12, 25; 13:5, 13; 15:37–40.
4. Lit., "who are of circumcision."
5. Compare the list of companions with that in Phlm. 23 f.
6. The letter in question, presumably sent by Paul or in Paul's name to the neighboring city, was lost before the Pauline letters were collected. It can hardly be identified with Phlm., as some have suggested. A spurious Letter to the Laodiceans is extant in some Latin Bible manuscripts; it was obviously forged, perhaps as early as the second century, to supply the missing letter (see "To the Laodiceans" in Part III). Marcion gave the title "to the Laodiceans" to our Letter to Ephesians.
7. Phlm. 2.

16). More important, this letter was written for people who did not know Paul personally (3:2 ff.; cf. 1:15); it could hardly have been intended for Christians in Ephesus, where Paul worked for two years.

In fact there is nothing in the letter to suggest that it was addressed to any particular congregation. There are no references to any local situation, no greetings to or from individuals, and, although the author warns against deviant teachings, the warning lacks any specificity (4:12–14). In all these ways "Ephesians" is strikingly different from Colossians, a letter addressed to a congregation that Paul had not seen personally. On the other hand, in this respect it is very much like the so-called First Letter of Peter, which is specifically designated (1:1) as an encyclical letter, and which, also like Ephesians, contains many echoes both of liturgical language associated with baptism and of the traditional moral admonitions (*parainesis*) that, in the early church, called on the converts to remember their baptism and live a life worthy of their "calling." Already in 1598 Theodor Beza suggested that Ephesians, too, was an encyclical, and recent scholarship has tended more and more to agree. The letter known since the late second century as "Ephesians" was most likely sent to several churches in the southwestern part of the Roman province Asia (the westernmost region of modern Turkey), as a written substitute for a personal address by the apostle. How the words "in Ephesus" came to be written into the prescript in some manuscript that was then copied widely remains a mystery.

The question of who wrote the letter is also difficult to answer, but just as in the case of Colossians, the very complex relationships between this letter and the undoubted letters of Paul and between it and the ongoing traditions of the Pauline school are most satisfactorily explained by the hypothesis that it was written by a close disciple of the apostle after his death. The author seems to have known and used the Letter to the Colossians, yet not in any simple and wooden way that we could describe as copying and revising—like the use of Jude by the author of 2 Peter, or Paul's own reuse of material from Galatians and 1 Corinthians in his Letter to the Romans. Rather, the author of "Ephesians" seems to have gathered up, both from Colossians and perhaps other letters of Paul as well as from the ongoing and growing body of liturgical, parenetic, and interpretive traditions that were regularly used in the congregations founded by Paul and his co-workers, a model letter representing what he thought was the central legacy of the apostle to be passed on to the new generation.

The letter begins with address and greeting (1:1–2) in typical Pauline form (except for the absence of a place name), followed by a blessing in hymnic style (1:3–14), which, as in 2 Corinthians and 1 Peter, takes the place of the more common thanksgiving. The body of the letter consists of two main parts, which are quite clearly defined by formal elements. The first is introduced by thanksgiving (1:15–23), so that this letter, unlike any other in the New Testament, has both an opening blessing and an opening thanksgiving. This first part comprises a meditation on the new status of Gentiles who have become Christians and on the great "mystery" of the unification of Jew and Gentile (chapter 2), an encomium on Paul's own ministry to the Gentiles (3.1–13), an intercession (3:14–19) that resumes the style of the thanksgiving, and a doxology (3:20 f.).

The second part, which consists of admonitions in traditional patterns, begins with the conventional, "I appeal to you . . ." (4:1). The basic exhortation (4:1–16) is to realize and maintain the unity and harmony that, according to chapter 2, were the gift of God accomplished in Christ's death. There follow admonitions based on conversion motifs: separation from the moral world of "Gentile" society (4:17–19) and replacing "the old human" with the new (4:

20–24). Then a special form of the virtue and vice catalogues, in which a vice is paired with its opposite virtue (4:24–5:5), is underscored by the opposition between the "children of light" and of darkness (5:6–14) and between the "wise" and the "foolish" (5:15–20). A version of the "household table" follows (5:21–6:9). An exhortation to arm for the moral battle against spiritual powers of evil rounds off this section, concluding with an appeal for prayer (6:10–20). A word about Tychicus, almost identical with Colossians 4:7 f., followed by a benediction, brings the letter to a close.

Ephesians

1 Paul, an apostle of Christ Jesus by the will of God,

To God's holy people in Ephesus,[1] the faithful in Christ Jesus:

2 Grace and peace to you from God our Father and the Lord Jesus Christ.

3 Praise be to the God and Father of our Lord Jesus Christ, who has blessed us in the heavenly realms[2] with every spiritual blessing in Christ. 4 For he chose us in him before the creation of the world to be holy and blameless in his sight.[3] In love 5 he predestined[4] us for adoption to sonship through Jesus Christ, in accordance with his pleasure and will— 6 to the praise of his glorious grace, which he has freely given us in the One he loves. 7 In him we have redemption through his blood, the forgiveness[5] of sins, in accordance with the riches of God's grace 8 that he lavished on us. With all wisdom and understanding,[6] 9 he made known to us the mystery of his will according to his good pleasure, which he purposed in Christ, 10 to be put into effect when the times reach their fulfillment—to bring unity to all things in heaven and on earth under Christ.[7]

1. The oldest manuscripts omit "in Ephesus" (see introduction). Yet this text, which would have to be translated "to the holy people who are also faithful," can hardly be original, for the construction in Greek is quite awkward. Archbishop Ussher (1654) ingeniously suggested that the encyclical letter might have had a blank space here, to be filled in by Tychicus for each place he visited, but there is no example from antiquity of such a practice. Perhaps someone—in Ephesus?—saw the letter intended for other churches and made a copy for more general use, omitting the name(s). How "in Ephesus" came to be added later, we can only guess.

2. A peculiar phrase occurring only in Eph. (1:20; 2:6; 3:10; 6:12; cf. 2 Tim. 4:18). The blessing (vv. 3–14; cf. 2 Cor. 1:3–7; 1 Pet. 1:3–9) is a single sentence, linked together by relative clauses, participles, and prepositions. It is enriched by word plays ("praise be to" [= "blessed be"], "has blessed us," "blessing"; "in love," "the One he loves"), parallelism ("redemption through his blood" ‖ "forgiveness of sins," "deposit" ‖ "redemption"); chains of synonyms ("pleasure and [lit., of his] will"; "will . . . pleasure . . . purpose"); repetition of the phrase "in him" or "in whom." For a closer approximation of the Greek style, see the KJV—though even the seventeenth-century translators felt obliged to divide the passage into three sentences! The repeated phrase "to the praise of his glory" (v. 6a, "to the praise of his glorious grace") provides a natural division: vv. 3–6a, 6b-12, 13–14. Blessings (or benedictions), usually much shorter and simpler than this, are very common in Jewish scripture and post-canonical literature, and must have been used often in everyday life. Though it is always God who is praised, the benediction frequently also serves to congratulate a person or group: a sage who gives a brilliant exposition of a difficult passage of scripture is congratulated by his teacher with the words, "Blessed be . . . the God of Israel, who has given a son to Abraham our father, who knows how to speculate, to investigate, and to expound" (b. Hag. 14b). So our author congratulates Christians, including the recipients, for the gifts they have received from God.

3. See Part IV for Victorinus's Neoplatonic interpretation of this verse.

4. Or, ". . . in his sight in love. He predestined . . ."

5. In the Pauline letters the word "forgiveness" occurs only here and in the almost identical clause in Col. 1:14. Cf. the connection of "redemption," "blood," "left . . . sins . . . unpunished" in the early formula quoted in Rom. 3:24 f.

6. The sentence break, necessary for English style, is arbitrary. "With all wisdom and understanding" may modify "he lavished" as well as "he made known."

7. Cf. Col. 1:20; Phil. 2:10. The special theme of Eph. is that this ultimate cosmic reunification is

11 In him we were also chosen,[8] having been predestined according to the plan of him who works out everything in conformity with the purpose of his will, 12 in order that we, who were the first to put our hope in Christ, might be for the praise of his glory. 13 And you also[9] were included in Christ when you heard the word of truth, the gospel of your salvation. When you believed, you were marked in him with a seal, the promised Holy Spirit, 14 who is a deposit[1] guaranteeing our inheritance until the redemption of those who are God's possession[2]—to the praise of his glory.

15 For this reason, ever since I heard about your faith in the Lord Jesus and your love for all his people, 16 I have not stopped giving thanks for you,[3] remembering you in my prayers. 17 I keep asking that the God of our Lord Jesus Christ, the glorious Father, may give you the Spirit[4] of wisdom and revelation, so that you may know him better. 18 I pray that the eyes of your heart may be enlightened in order that you may know the hope to which he has called you, the riches of his glorious inheritance in his people, 19 and his incomparably great power for us who believe. That power is the same as the mighty strength 20 he exerted when he raised Christ from the dead and seated him at his right hand in the heavenly realms, 21 far above all rule and authority, power and dominion, and every name that can be invoked, not only in the present age but also in the one to come.[5] 22 And God placed all things under his feet[6] and appointed him to be head over everything for the church, 23 which is his body, the fullness of him who fills everything in every way.[7]

2 As for you, you were dead in your transgressions and sins, 2 in which you used to live when you followed the ways[8] of this world and of the ruler of the kingdom of the air, the spirit who is now at work in those who are disobedient. 3 All of us also lived among them at one time, gratifying the cravings of our sinful nature[9] and following its desires and thoughts. Like

---

foreshadowed on earth in the unity of the church, particularly in the reconciliation of Jew and Gentile. In some respects Rom. 8:18–25 provides a parallel.

8. Or, "were made heirs"; the verb is cognate with the noun translated "inheritance" in v. 14.

9. The shift to the second person from the hymnic first person applies the general statements of the benediction to the readers and provides the transition to what follows in the letter.

1. Cf. 2 Cor. 1:22; 5:5; Rom. 8:23.

2. The Greek reads "until the redemption of the possession." The words "those who are God's" are added by the translators, because the word translated "possession" or its equivalent is often used of Israel as God's elect people (Ex. 19:5; 23:22 LXX; Deut. 7:6; 14:2; Isa. 43:21; Tit. 2:14; 1 Pet. 2:9).

3. Vv. 15–23, a complete epistolary thanksgiving like those in most of Paul's letters, here introduces the first of the two main sections of the letter, rather than the letter as a whole (see introduction). In several of the oldest and generally best manuscripts, the words "and your love" are missing from v. 15, which would thus read, "I heard about your faithfulness in the Lord Jesus toward all his people (lit., 'all his holy ones')."

4. Or, "a spirit."

5. To vv. 20 f., compare Phil. 2:10 f.

6. Imagery from Ps. 110:1, the basic text used in early Christian exposition to support the notion of Christ's exaltation, and the text from Jewish scripture quoted more often than any other in the New Testament, is here combined with a phrase from Ps. 6:8 (cf. 1 Pet. 3:22).

7. Cf. Col. 2:9 f.; 1:18. Two notions are combined here: (1) Christ is the head of the cosmos (represented by angelic or demonic forces), (2) he is head of the church, as his body. Perhaps the myth of the *macroanthropos*, the universe imagined as a gigantic human figure, has played a role in the imagery. "Fullness" is used in a somewhat different sense here from that in Col. 1:19 (see notes on 1:19–20 and 2:9).

8. Greek, *aiōn*; since the style of Eph. suggests that "ruler" and "spirit" are synonyms, this is best understood as a personal designation: "the Aeon." The name Aeon for a god of endless time, probably derived from the Persian *Zurvan*, is found in several Hellenistic religious and magical contexts. In Mithraic inscriptions and magical amulets he was depicted as a lion-headed man surrounded by snakes. Here, however, he appears as the prince of evil forces, like the Belial of the Dead Sea Scrolls. Cf. 2 Cor. 4:4.

9. Lit. "our flesh."

the rest, we were by nature deserving of wrath. 4 But because of his great love for us, God, who is rich in mercy, 5 made us alive with Christ even when we were dead in transgressions—it is by grace you have been saved. 6 And God raised us up with Christ and seated us with him in the heavenly realms in Christ Jesus,[1] 7 in order that in the coming ages he might show the incomparable riches of his grace, expressed in his kindness to us in Christ Jesus. 8 For it is by grace you have been saved, through faith[2]—and this is not from yourselves, it is the gift of God— 9 not by works, so that no one can boast. 10 For we are God's handiwork, created in Christ Jesus to do good works, which God prepared in advance for us to do.

11 Therefore, remember that formerly you who are Gentiles by birth and called "uncircumcised" by those who call themselves "the circumcision" (which is done in the body by human hands)— 12 remember that at that time you were separate from Christ, excluded from citizenship in Israel and foreigners to the covenants of the promise, without hope and without God in the world.[3] 13 But now in Christ Jesus you who once were far away have been brought near[4] by the blood of Christ.

14 For he himself is our[5] peace, who has made the two one and has destroyed the barrier, the dividing wall[6] of hostility, 15 by setting aside[7] in his flesh the law with its commands and regulations. His purpose was to create in himself one new humanity[8] out of the two, thus making peace, 16 and in one body[9] to reconcile both of them to God through the cross, by which he put to death their hostility. 17 He came and preached peace to you who were far away and peace to those who were near. 18 For through him we both have access to the Father by one Spirit.

19 Consequently, you are no longer foreigners and strangers, but fellow citizens with God's people and also members of his household, 20 built on the foundation of the apostles and prophets,[1] with Christ Jesus himself as

---

1. Cf. Col. 3:1, and compare and contrast Rom. 6.
2. Here, as in v. 5 above, the author sums up what would be remembered as the central point of Paul's theology. He captures in a few words the main theme of Galatians and Romans, but nowhere in the undoubted letters do we find so lapidary a formulation. Almost more Pauline than Paul, it shows how Paul's theology was being preserved by the Pauline school (cf. Tit. 3:4–7), while in other circles of the Christian movement it was just such simplifications that provoked opposition (James 2:18–26).
3. To this list of Israel's prerogatives, cf. Rom. 9:4 f.
4. The "far away" and the "near" were terms used in Judaism for Gentiles and faithful Jews, respectively. They are drawn from Isa. 57:18 f., which serves as the basis for the meditation in vv. 14–18 (combined with Isa. 52:7, as in Acts 10:36 f.).
5. Note the shift from second to first person; the style of vv. 14–18 is hymnic or creedal.
6. The image may have been suggested by the wall that separated the court of the Gentiles from the sacred areas of the temple in Jerusalem. Another possible allusion is to a barrier separating heaven and earth, a notion that plays a role in certain later Gnostic texts, though in them the savior's function is sometimes to break, sometimes to restore the wall. In the present passage the wall is identified with the Jewish law—insofar as it consists of "commands and regulations." The rabbinic practice of interpreting the rules of scriptural law for application in everyday situations could be called "making a fence around the Torah" (e.g., Mishnah *Avot* 1.1). Compare the pejorative sense of "rules"(*dogmata*) in Col. 2:14, 20.
7. In the undoubted letters, Paul is careful not to go so far as to speak of "setting aside" the law: see Rom. 3:31; 7:12; but cf. Col. 2:14.
8. Lit., "one new human person [*anthrōpos*]," a baptismal motif connected with the idea of restoring the lost "image of God" according to which the first human was created, only later to be separated into "the two," male and female (Gen. 1:26 f.; 2:20–23). Cf. Gal. 3:28; 1 Cor. 12:13; Col. 3:11.
9. "Body" here has a double meaning:the physical body of Jesus which was crucified and the metaphorical "body of Christ," the church.
1. A surprising metaphor on two counts: In 1 Cor. 3:10 ff. Paul speaks of the apostles as builders, working on the foundation which is Christ. Nowhere else in Paul are the apostles the foundation (but cf. Rev. 21:14). And the pairing of apostles with "prophets" (Christian charismatics are meant, not OT prophets: see 3:5) is unparalleled in the other letters, though found in later Christian literature.

the chief cornerstone.[2] 21 In him the whole building is joined together and rises to become a holy temple in the Lord. 22 And in him you too are being built together to become a dwelling in which God lives by his Spirit.[3]
3 For this reason I, Paul, the prisoner of Christ Jesus for the sake of you Gentiles—[4]
2 Surely you have heard about the administration of God's grace that was given to me for you, 3 that is, the mystery made known to me by revelation, as I have already written briefly. 4 In reading this, then, you will be able to understand my insight into the mystery of Christ, 5 which was not made known to people in other generations as it has now been revealed by the Spirit to God's holy apostles and prophets.[5] 6 This mystery is that through the gospel the Gentiles are heirs together with Israel, members together of one body, and sharers together in the promise in Christ Jesus.

7 I became a servant of this gospel by the gift of God's grace given me through the working of his power. 8 Although I am less than the least of all the Lord's people,[6] this grace was given me: to preach to the Gentiles the boundless riches of Christ, 9 and to make plain to everyone the administration of this mystery, which for ages past was kept hidden in God, who created all things. 10 His intent was that now, through the church, the manifold wisdom of God should be made known to the rulers and authorities in the heavenly realms,[7] 11 according to his eternal purpose that he accomplished in Christ Jesus our Lord. 12 In him and through faith in him we may approach God with freedom and confidence. 13 I ask you, therefore, not to be discouraged[8] because of my sufferings for you, which are your glory.

14 For this reason I kneel before the Father, 15 from whom every family in heaven and on earth derives its name.[9] 16 I pray that out of his glorious riches he may strengthen you with power through his Spirit in your inner being,[1] 17 so that Christ may dwell in your hearts through faith. And I pray that you, being rooted and established in love, 18 may have power, together with all the Lord's people, to grasp how wide and long and high and deep is the love of Christ, 19 and to know this love that surpasses

2. Some would translate "keystone" or "capstone," but there is probably an allusion to Isa. 28:16 (cf. Rom. 9:33; 10:11; 1 Pet. 2:4), the only occurrence of the rare Greek word in the LXX, where it clearly means "cornerstone." The imagery of the whole passage is not entirely transparent, because the metaphor of the building is mixed with that of the body.
3. On the community as the new temple, cf. 1 Cor. 3:16; 2 Cor. 6:16. A motif prominent in the Dead Sea Scrolls as well as in early Christianity; see also 1 Pet. 2:4–10.
4. The sentence is interrupted here, to resume in v. 14. The digression explains the phrase "a prisoner . . . for the sake of you Gentiles."
5. This verse has the "hidden for ages/now revealed" pattern frequent in early Christian preaching (see note on 1 Cor. 2:7), with two surprising elements: (1) usually the "mystery" is revealed to all Christians (cf. Col. 1:26); here it is to "God's holy apostles and prophets" (see note on 2:20); (2) the content of the mystery is here specified as the unification of Jew and Gentile (v. 6).
6. Cf. 1 Cor. 15:9, where Paul refers to himself as "the least of the apostles." "Least of all the Lord's people [lit., 'holy ones']" is surprising; a case of the disciple's image of the apostle being more Pauline than Paul? See 1 Tim. 1:15 f.
7. Again the "hidden/revealed" pattern, now expanded to include the striking thought that through the church the occult powers from whom the mystery was hidden are now enlightened.
8. Or, "I ask that I may not be discouraged."
9. English cannot imitate the word play between "family" (*patria*) and "father" (*patēr*) which explains "its name." Again the allusion is to a cosmic unity—not only of all human clans, but of all classes of angels—of which the unity of Jew and Gentile in the church is, in the author's view, the first crystallization point.
1. For the phrase "inner being [*anthrōpos*]," cf. Rom. 7:22; 2 Cor. 4:16.

knowledge[2]—that you may be filled to the measure of all the fullness of God.

20 Now to him who is able to do immeasurably more than all we ask or imagine, according to his power that is at work within us, 21 to him be glory in the church and in Christ Jesus throughout all generations, for ever and ever! Amen.

4 As a prisoner for the Lord, then, I urge you to live a life worthy of the calling you have received.[3] 2 Be completely humble and gentle; be patient, bearing with one another in love. 3 Make every effort to keep the unity of the Spirit through the bond of peace. 4 There is one body and one Spirit, just as you were called to one hope when you were called; 5 one Lord, one faith, one baptism; 6 one God and Father of all, who is over all and through all and in all.

7 But to each one of us grace has been given as Christ apportioned it. 8 This is why it says:
"When he ascended on high,
he took many captives
and gave gifts to his people."[4]
9 (What does "he ascended" mean except that he also descended to the lower, earthly regions[5]? 10 He who descended is the very one who ascended higher than all the heavens, in order to fill the whole universe.) 11 So Christ himself gave the apostles, the prophets, the evangelists, the pastors and teachers, 12 to equip his people for works of service, so that the body of Christ may be built up 13 until we all reach unity in the faith and in the knowledge of the Son of God and become mature, attaining to the whole measure of the fullness of Christ.

14 Then we will no longer be infants, tossed back and forth by the waves, and blown here and there by every wind of teaching and by the cunning and craftiness of people in their deceitful scheming. 15 Instead, speaking the truth in love, we will in all things grow up into him who is the head, that is, Christ. 16 From him the whole body, joined and held together by every supporting ligament, grows and builds itself up in love, as each part does its work.[6]

17 So I tell you this, and insist on it in the Lord, that you must no longer live as the Gentiles[7] do, in the futility of their thinking. 18 They are darkened in their understanding and separated from the life of God because of the ignorance that is in them due to the hardening of their hearts. 19 Having lost all sensitivity, they have given themselves over to sensuality so as to indulge in every kind of impurity, and they are full of greed.

20 That, however, is not the way of life you learned 21 when you heard

2. In view of the talk of knowledge that fills this chapter, this final mention of "love . . . that surpasses knowledge" (*gnosis*) is significant, and typically Pauline: 1 Cor. 8:1; 12–14 *passim*.
3. Cf. 1 Thess. 2:12. The specific aspect of the "calling" which is here made central, in keeping with the theme of the first three chapters, is "unity" (vv. 3–16).
4. Ps. 68:18, quoted in a form that differs from the standard OT texts. Jewish tradition applied the verse to Moses, who brought the "gift" of the Torah from heaven.
5. Or, "into the depths of the earth." The reference is not likely to the "descent to Hades" that appears in later Christian literature (cf. 1 Pet. 3:19) but to the incarnation.
6. Note the close parallel in Col. 2:19.
7. The Gentiles are described here in language common in Jewish apologetic literature; cf. Rom. 1: 18–31. The converts addressed in the letter, though "Gentiles by birth" (2:11), now "no longer foreigners . . . but fellow citizens with God's people" (2:19), must behave as such (cf. 1 Thess. 4: 5).

about Christ and were taught in him in accordance with the truth that is in Jesus. 22 You were taught, with regard to your former way of life, to put off your old self,[8] which is being corrupted by its deceitful desires; 23 to be made new in the attitude of your minds; 24 and to put on the new self, created to be like God[9] in true righteousness and holiness.

25 Therefore each of you must put off falsehood and speak truthfully to your neighbor,[1] for we are all members of one body. 26 "In your anger do not sin"[2]: Do not let the sun go down while you are still angry, 27 and do not give the devil a foothold. 28 Those who have been stealing must steal no longer, but must work, doing something useful with their own hands, that they may have something to share with those in need.

29 Do not let any unwholesome talk come out of your mouths, but only what is helpful for building others up according to their needs, that it may benefit those who listen. 30 And do not grieve the Holy Spirit of God, with whom you were sealed for the day of redemption. 31 Get rid of all bitterness, rage and anger, brawling and slander, along with every form of malice. 32 Be kind and compassionate to one another, forgiving each other, just as in Christ God forgave you.

5 Follow God's example,[3] therefore, as dearly loved children 2 and walk in the way of love, just as Christ loved us and gave himself up for us as a fragrant offering and sacrifice to God.

3 But among you there must not be even a hint of sexual immorality, or of any kind of impurity, or of greed, because these are improper for the Lord's people. 4 Nor should there be obscenity, foolish talk or coarse joking, which are out of place, but rather thanksgiving. 5 For of this you can be sure: No immoral, impure or greedy person—such a person is an idolater—has any inheritance in the kingdom of Christ and of God.[4] 6 Let no one deceive you with empty words, for because of such things God's wrath comes on those who are disobedient. 7 Therefore do not be partners with them.[5]

8 For you were once darkness, but now you are light in the Lord. Live as children of light 9 (for the fruit of the light consists in all goodness, righteousness and truth) 10 and find out what pleases the Lord. 11 Have nothing to do with the fruitless deeds of darkness, but rather expose them. 12 It is shameful even to mention what the disobedient do in secret. 13 But everything exposed by the light becomes visible—and everything that is illuminated becomes a light. 14 This is why it is said:

"Wake up, sleeper,
rise from the dead,
and Christ will shine on you."[6]

---

8. "Putting off" the old self (*anthrōpos*) and "putting on" the new is a baptismal motif basic to the exposition in chap. 2 (2:15: "one new humanity") and to the exhortations here; cf. Col. 3:1–17.
9. Cf. Gen. 1:26 f. and Col. 3:10.
1. Zech. 8:16.
2. Ps. 4:4.
3. The ideal of resembling God by sharing God's attributes was a commonplace in popular Greco-Roman philosophy; Plato *Theaetetus* 176b is often quoted: "to become like God is to become righteous and holy and wise." Rabbinic Judaism could also speak of imitating God. Paul speaks several times in the undoubted letters of imitating Christ and himself (1 Thess. 1:6; 1 Cor. 11:1; 4:16; 2 Thess. 3:7–9) but not God.
4. Cf. Gal. 5:19–21; 1 Cor. 6:9 f.
5. This admonition and the following use of the metaphors "light" and "darkness" have close parallels in the sectarian language of the Dead Sea Scrolls. Note the limits set to such a sect-consciousness in 1 Cor. 5:9–13.
6. The origin of the quotation is unknown; perhaps it comes from an apocryphal book now lost,

15 Be very careful, then, how you live—not as unwise but as wise, 16 making the most of every opportunity, because the days are evil. 17 Therefore do not be foolish, but understand what the Lord's will is. 18 Do not get drunk on wine, which leads to debauchery. Instead, be filled with the Spirit,[7] 19 speaking to one another with psalms, hymns and songs from the Spirit. Sing and make music from your heart to the Lord, 20 always giving thanks to God the Father for everything, in the name of our Lord Jesus Christ.[8]

21 Submit[9] to one another out of reverence for Christ.

22 Wives, submit yourselves to your own husbands as you do to the Lord. 23 For the husband is the head of the wife as Christ is the head[1] of the church, his body, of which he is the Savior. 24 Now as the church submits to Christ, so also wives should submit to their husbands in everything.

25 Husbands, love your wives, just as Christ loved the church and gave himself up for her 26 to make her holy, cleansing her by the washing with water through the word, 27 and to present her to himself as a radiant church, without stain or wrinkle or any other blemish,[2] but holy and blameless. 28 In this same way, husbands ought to love their wives as their own bodies. He who loves his wife loves himself. 29 After all, people have never hated their own bodies, but they feed and care for them, just as Christ does the church— 30 for we are members of his body. 31 "For this reason a man will leave his father and mother and be united to his wife, and the two will become one flesh."[3] 32 This is a profound mystery—but I am talking about Christ and the church. 33 However, each one of you also must love his wife as he loves himself, and the wife must respect her husband.

6 Children, obey your parents in the Lord, for this is right. 2 "Honor your father and mother"—which is the first commandment with a promise— 3 "so that it may go well with you and that you may enjoy long life on the earth."[4]

4 Fathers, do not exasperate your children; instead, bring them up in the training and instruction of the Lord.

5 Slaves, obey your earthly masters with respect and fear, and with sincerity of heart, just as you would obey Christ. 6 Obey them not only to win their favor when their eye is on you, but as slaves of Christ, doing the will of God from your heart. 7 Serve wholeheartedly, as if you were serving the Lord, not people, 8 because you know that the Lord will reward each one of you for whatever good you do, whether you are slave or free.

---

perhaps from an early Christian hymn used at baptism. Similar strophes occur in the liturgy of the Mandaean Gnostics, in the "Hymn of the Pearl" found in the apocryphal *Acts of Thomas*, and elsewhere, all later in their extant forms than Eph.

7. The notion of "sober intoxication" is frequent in the language of Hellenistic mysticism, but here it is applied to the communal worship rather than to individual experience.

8. Cf. Col. 3:16; 1 Cor. 14:26.

9. In Greek this verb is a participle connected with the previous sentence; the verse is transitional, introducing the "household table" (5:22–6:9). On the form of the latter, see note at Col. 3:18. The remarkable thing about this example of the household table is the Christological reinterpretation of the husband/wife paragraph; cf. 2 Cor. 11:2.

1. Cf. 1 Cor. 11:3.

2. Cf. Song 4:7.

3. Gen. 2:24.

4. Ex. 20:12 = Deut. 5:16. This is the only place in the Pauline letters where one of the Ten Commandments is used to support a rule for the church.

9 And masters, treat your slaves in the same way. Do not threaten them, since you know that he who is both their Master and yours is in heaven, and there is no favoritism with him.

10 Finally, be strong in the Lord and in his mighty power. 11 Put on the full armor of God,[5] so that you can take your stand against the devil's schemes. 12 For our struggle is not against flesh and blood, but against the rulers, against the authorities, against the powers of this dark world and against the spiritual forces of evil in the heavenly realms. 13 Therefore put on the full armor of God, so that when the day of evil comes, you may be able to stand your ground, and after you have done everything, to stand. 14 Stand firm then, with the belt of truth buckled around your waist, with the breastplate of righteousness in place, 15 and with your feet fitted with the readiness that comes from the gospel of peace. 16 In addition to all this, take up the shield of faith, with which you can extinguish all the flaming arrows of the evil one. 17 Take the helmet of salvation and the sword of the Spirit, which is the word of God.

18 And pray in the Spirit on all occasions with all kinds of prayers and requests. With this in mind, be alert and always keep on praying for all the Lord's people. 19 Pray also for me, that whenever I speak, words may be given me so that I will fearlessly make known the mystery of the gospel, 20 for which I am an ambassador in chains. Pray that I may declare it fearlessly, as I should.

21 Tychicus, the dear brother and faithful servant in the Lord, will tell you everything, so that you also may know how I am and what I am doing. 22 I am sending him to you for this very purpose, that you may know how we are, and that he may encourage you.[6]

23 Peace to the brothers and sisters, and love with faith from God the Father and the Lord Jesus Christ. 24 Grace to all who love our Lord Jesus Christ with an undying love.[7]

THE PASTORAL LETTERS
(95–125?)

Three of the letters attributed to Paul in the New Testament are distinguished from the others by being addressed to individuals, rather than to churches (the other apparent exception, Philemon, is in fact addressed "to Philemon . . . and to Apphia our sister and Archippus . . . and to the church that meets in your home"). The individuals are two of Paul's closest associates among the large circle of "co-workers" that made the Pauline mission possible, his "true sons in the faith," Timothy and Titus. Here they appear as Paul's delegates, a role

---

5. "Put on" recalls the "put off" of 4:25; cf. 4:22–24. The idea of a cosmic struggle against evil powers reminds one of the eschatological battle envisioned in the "Rule for the War of the Sons of Light against the Sons of Darkness" found among the Dead Sea Scrolls. In the present passage, however, the warfare is metaphorical. The notion that the moral struggle is ultimately part of a cosmic war also has many parallels in other religions, notably in Mithraism, another new and rapidly growing cult that was especially popular in the middle ranks of the Roman army. The donning of armor as a metaphor for practicing virtues was, however, a commonplace in Hellenistic moral discourse, including Hellenistic Judaism as well as early Christianity. Cf. 1 Thess. 5:8. Several of the specific images here are drawn from Isa. 11:5; 52:7; 59:17.

6. Cf. Col. 4:7 f.

7. Or, "Grace and immortality to all who love our Lord Jesus Christ."

in which we find them mentioned several times in Paul's undoubted letters, but now with full responsibility for ordering the Christian communities in Ephesus and on the island of Crete, seeing to proper administration by well-chosen officers, tending to the fitting relationships among various ranks and groups in the household of faith, upholding high moral standards, and above all resisting deviant versions of Christian doctrine. This array of concerns, expressed in very similar language in all three letters despite the different genre of 2 Timothy, has led interpreters since the eighteenth century to treat the three as a group and to label them "pastoral." The term is clearly appropriate, but it does not name what is different about this group of letters compared with the others, for in recent years we have come to recognize that *all* of Paul's letters are pastoral. However, there are other significant differences, which have led most scholars over the past century to conclude that the Pastorals were written by someone else in Paul's name.

The vocabulary and style of the Pastorals is quite different from that of the other Pauline letters. Of particular importance is the meager use of the particles and other short words so frequent in Paul; these tend to be unconscious aspects of speech not readily changed and not ordinarily variable with subject matter. Also impressive is the difference in technical theological vocabulary. Some of Paul's most distinctive terms are missing altogether, and in their place are words and phrases that are commonplaces in Greek popular religion and in the emperor cult. Some phrases, moreover, are used in a different sense from that which they have in the undoubted letters.

The Pastorals seem to presuppose a more elaborate church organization than in Paul's time: "bishops" (not yet distinguished from "elders") and "deacons" are clearly names for *offices*, not just functions, a development suggested already in Philippians 1:1 and perhaps Romans 16:1 but here regularized for "every town" (Tit. 1:5) with specified qualifications. "Widows" has become an official designation.

It is difficult to fit the epistles into what we know of the final years of Paul's life. To be sure, there is an early tradition, albeit not very well attested, that Paul was released at the end of his first imprisonment in Rome to travel to Spain on a mission. But that "tradition" is probably merely a guess based on Romans 15:28. The silence of Acts on Paul's death cannot be used to support this tradition, because the style of the final chapters of Acts is that of a martyrology, paralleling Luke's account of Jesus' trials. The author would hardly have written in this fashion unless he knew that Paul's imprisonment ended in death. Particularly the "farewell address" of Acts 20 predicts Paul's death (and prophecies in the literary structure of Acts are always fulfilled), or at the very least that he would never return to the eastern regions of the empire. And it is precisely another eastern journey, not a journey to the West, that is presupposed by the Pastorals. In fact the itinerary they assume seems an artificial construction by an author familiar with Acts.

Finally, there are striking differences between the theology of the Pastorals and that of any of the earlier Pauline letters. Particularly important is the shift of focus in the christological formulations: it is not the death and resurrection that are central here, but "epiphany." Like "savior," which is prominent also in the Pastorals, "epiphany" is a technical term of popular Hellenistic religion, particularly of the emperor cult in the eastern parts of the empire. While there are summary statements about salvation as God's gift which sound thoroughly Pauline (e.g., Tit. 3:4 f.), they stand alongside statements about the law and good works which would have satisfied Paul's Galatian opponents (1 Tim. 1:9; Tit. 2:11–14). The notion of tradition in the Pastorals is also a mark of their lateness. While for Paul tradition (*paradosis*) played an important role, it was used very freely and construed quite dynamically (see the notes on Gal. 1:12

and 1 Cor. 15:3–5). In the Pastorals, however, tradition is described as a "deposit" (*parathēkē*, a commercial term), which is only to be "kept" or "guarded," not developed or interpreted. This is a typical mark of the defensive use of tradition; it contrasts not only with Paul's usage, but also with the later Catholic notion of a "living tradition."

If this evaluation of the Pastorals by the majority of today's critical scholarship is correct, then these letters stand on the threshold between those we have previously considered in this section, which were the work of Paul's immediate disciples adapting his distinctive presentation of the gospel for their own situation, and those works included in Parts III and IV below, which represent the wider appropriation and re-presentation of Paul's life and work for later generations.[1] It is important to see that in all these works, including the undoubted letters of Paul, we catch glimpses of an ongoing process. Paul himself stands within multiple streams of tradition—including philosophical, rhetorical, and popular traditions of Greco-Roman culture, Jewish writings and traditional interpretations, and specifically Christian lore and practice. He and his large circle of co-workers creatively used and transformed elements of those multiple traditions, often in dialogue or conflict with other early Christian interpreters. Paul's own immediate disciples and co-workers and then people of other evolving circles of Christianity further adapted the distinctively Pauline traditions, blending them with other currents of interpretation. Among the varied witnesses to this process, the Pastoral Letters stand particularly close to the canonical Acts of the Apostles (excerpted in Part IV below) in their portrayal of Paul's life and work and their appropriation of some features of his distinctive interpretations of Christian life and belief. One scholar has even proposed that they were written by the same author—a hypothesis not finally persuasive, but indicative of the place of both in the evolution of Paul's image in the ancient church.[2]

All three of the Pastorals belong to the broad category "parenetic letter," that is, personal letters of moral advice and exhortation, described in ancient handbooks of epistolary style. We have already found strong parenetic elements in many of the other Pauline letters. 1 Timothy and Titus resemble a special form of the parenetic letter used by officials of various kinds to instruct their subordinates. 2 Timothy is much more personal and, like Acts 20, resembles the farewell discourse or testament found very often in Greco-Jewish literature and occasionally in pagan literature of the Roman period.

The date of the Pastorals is uncertain. The Letter of Polycarp (bishop of Hierapolis, in Asia Minor, d. ca. 155–6) 4.1, citing Paul's collected letters as models for the letters of Ignatius he is transmitting to the church at Philippi, includes two phrases found in 1 Timothy 6:7, 10. Some scholars have argued that these represent only a common tradition, like some parallels between Ignatius and the Pastorals, but the context makes it more likely that Polycarp is actually quoting 1 Timothy and that he takes it to be by Paul. While this suggests that the Pastorals were included in at least one collection of Paul's letters by around 140 CE in Asia Minor, they appear to have won recognition only later in other places. Marcion (fl. 150) did not include the Pastoral Letters in his canon, and, since later Marcionites did use them, it is not likely that he excluded them on dogmatic grounds (Tertullian's remark, *Against Marcion*

---

1. There are mainstream scholars who reject this critical consensus, and who thus find in the Pastorals important evidence for the late stage of Paul's own mission, unreported in the fragmentary narrative of Acts. For a recent and particularly thoughtful example, see Luke Timothy Johnson, *The First and Second Letters to Timothy: A New Translation with Introduction and Commentary*, The Anchor Bible (New York: Doubleday, 2001), 20–99.

2. Jerome D. Quinn, "The Last Volume of Luke: The Relation of Luke-Acts to the Pastoral Epistles," in *Perspectives on Luke-Acts*, ed. by Charles H. Talbert, Perspectives in Religious Studies: Special Studies Series (Danville, VA: Association of Baptist Professors of Religion, 1978), 62–75.

5.21, to the contrary notwithstanding). The earliest extant manuscript of Paul's letters, the Chester Beatty papyrus (early third century) also lacks the Pastorals; its seven missing pages would not have afforded room for them. Most probably, then, the Pastorals were written in the early decades of the second century.

First Timothy

1 Paul, an apostle of Christ Jesus by the command of God our Savior and of Christ Jesus our hope,

2 To Timothy[1] my true son in the faith:

Grace, mercy and peace from God the Father and Christ Jesus our Lord.

3 As I urged you when I went into Macedonia, stay there in Ephesus[2] so that you may command certain persons not to teach false doctrines any longer 4 or to devote themselves to myths and endless genealogies.[3] Such things promote controversial speculations rather than advancing God's work—which is by faith. 5 The goal of this command is love, which comes from a pure heart and a good conscience[4] and a sincere faith. 6 Some have departed from these and have turned to meaningless talk. 7 They want to be teachers of the law,[5] but they do not know what they are talking about or what they so confidently affirm.

8 We know that the law is good[6] if one uses it properly. 9 We also know that the law is made not for the righteous but for lawbreakers and rebels, the ungodly and sinful, the unholy and irreligious, for those who kill their fathers or mothers, for murderers, 10 for the sexually immoral, for those practicing homosexuality,[7] for slave traders and liars and perjurers.[8] And it is for whatever else is contrary to the sound doctrine[9] 11 that conforms to the gospel concerning the glory of the blessed God, which he entrusted to me.

---

1. Timothy: see 1 Thess. 1:1; 3:2, 6: 1 Cor. 4:17; 16:10; 2 Cor. 1:1, 19; Rom. 16:21; Phil. 1:1; 2:19; Phlm. 1; 2 Thess. 1:1; Col. 1:1; Acts 16:1–3; 17:14, 15; 18:5; 19:22; 20:4. Titus, too, is called Paul's "true son in . . . faith" in Tit. 1:4.
2. The situation implied here cannot be fitted into Paul's travels as described in Acts, but it could have been suggested by Acts 20:1 if 19:22 were overlooked.
3. This would be an apt description of Gnostic teaching, whose "myths" often describe the origins of the world by "genealogies" of pairs of gods that emanate from the highest deity. However, the use of these words in 4:7; 2 Tim. 4:4; Tit. 1:14; 3:9 suggests nothing so specific but belongs to the language used in the philosophical schools from Plato on to disparage opposing positions or popular opinion.
4. "Good" or "clear conscience" (3:9; 2 Tim. 1:3; cf. 1 Pet. 3:16, 21) and its opposite, "seared" (4:2) or "corrupted" [or "soiled"] (Tit. 1:15), is a usage from popular speech, found in later Latin Stoics. Paul uses the word "conscience" fairly often, but without an adjective except in 1 Cor. 8:7–12, where conscience may be "weak" or, presumably, "strong," but not "good" or "bad."
5. The writer opposes teachers who evidently have some Jewish connections (cf. Tit. 1:10, 14–16; 3:9), but the description is vague—the point is simply that they claim knowledge they do not really have.
6. A verbal parallel to Rom. 7:16, but the following clause (literally, "if one uses it lawfully") is hardly Pauline.
7. "Homosexuality" is an anachronism, for this modern word presupposes a construction of sexuality unknown in antiquity. The word translated here is literally "those who sleep with men." The list of sinners in vv. 9–10 is a variant of the vice catalog; see the note on Gal. 5:19–21.
8. "Perjury" in the ancient world was a religious offense against the divine name and was not confined to judicial contexts.
9. The phrase "sound [i.e., "healthy"] doctrine [or "words"]," while common in Greek philosophical writings, is not found elsewhere in the NT. It is very important in the Pastorals (6:3; 2 Tim. 1:13; 4:3; Tit. 1:9, 13; 2:1, 2, 8). Note the close connection between "healthy teaching" and morality, and contrast 2 Tim. 2:16–17 ("more and more ungodly . . . gangrene").

12 I thank[1] Christ Jesus our Lord, who has given me strength, that he considered me trustworthy, appointing me to his service. 13 Even though I was once a blasphemer and a persecutor and a violent man, I was shown mercy because I acted in ignorance and unbelief. 14 The grace of our Lord was poured out on me abundantly, along with the faith and love that are in Christ Jesus.

15 Here is a trustworthy saying[2] that deserves full acceptance: Christ Jesus came into the world to save sinners—of whom I am the worst.[3] 16 But for that very reason I was shown mercy so that in me, the worst of sinners, Christ Jesus might display his immense patience as an example for those who would believe in him and receive eternal life. 17 Now to the King eternal, immortal, invisible, the only God, be honor and glory for ever and ever. Amen.

18 Timothy, my son, I am giving you this command in keeping with the prophecies once made about you,[4] so that by recalling them you may fight the battle well, 19 holding on to faith and a good conscience, which some have rejected and so have suffered shipwreck with regard to the faith. 20 Among them are Hymenaeus and Alexander, whom I have handed over to Satan[5] to be taught not to blaspheme.

2 I urge, then, first of all, that petitions, prayers, intercession and thanksgiving be made for everyone— 2 for kings and all those in authority, that we may live peaceful and quiet lives in all godliness and holiness. 3 This is good, and pleases God our Savior, 4 who wants all people to be saved and to come to a knowledge of the truth. 5 For there is one God and one mediator between God and human beings, Christ Jesus, himself human, 6 who gave himself as a ransom for all people. This has now been witnessed to at the proper time.[6] 7 And for this purpose I was appointed a herald and an apostle—I am telling the truth, I am not lying—and a true and faithful teacher of the Gentiles.

8 Therefore I want the men[7] everywhere to pray, lifting up holy hands without anger or disputing. 9 I also want the women to dress modestly, with decency and propriety, adorning themselves, not with elaborate hairstyles or gold or pearls or expensive clothes, 10 but with good deeds, appropriate for women who profess to worship God.

11 A woman should learn in quietness and full submission. 12 I do not permit a woman to teach or to assume authority over a man; she must be

---

1. Here begins the epistolary thanksgiving, a convention which, as we have seen, Paul adapts very flexibly and with strong rhetorical effect in 1 Thessalonians, 1 Corinthians, Romans, Philippians, and Philemon. This one differs somewhat from those in vocabulary and form, though perhaps not more than they differ from one another. Cf. 2 Tim. 1:3–7; Titus lacks a thanksgiving.
2. This phrase or a shorter form occurs five times: 3:1; 4:9; 2 Tim. 2:11; Tit. 3:8.
3. Cf. Gal. 1:13; 1 Cor. 15:8 f.; but especially Eph. 3:8. Paul now appears as the model convert, a role found frequently in contemporary moralizing philosophy; compare the more dramatic portrayals of the forcibly converted persecutor in Acts 9; 22; 26.
4. Cf. 4:14. For participation of prophets in the commissioning of a missionary, cf. Acts 13:1–3.
5. Cf. 1 Cor. 5:5. Hymenaeus is mentioned again, in different company, in 2 Tim. 2:17; an Alexander, in 2 Tim. 4:14.
6. Vv. 5–6 are probably part of a liturgical formula. The last clause is puzzling and was already so to ancient scribes, who produced several variant readings. The text here translates one of the variants; the more difficult and therefore probably earlier reading is: "as the testimony in [God's] own time." *Anthrōpos* ("himself human") occurs occasionally as a christological title, notably in John 19:5, also in Gnostic texts; it could be related to the title "Son of the Human" found in the gospels.
7. Here begins the first variation of the "household table" (note the summary in 3:15), in which "men," "women" (vv. 9–15), "overseers" (3:1–7), and "deacons" (3:8–13) receive general instructions. For other examples of the household table, see Col. 3:18–4:1; Eph. 5:22–6:9; 1 Pet. 2:8–3:7; in the Pastorals, however, the common pattern of the Greco-Roman household is explicitly transferred to the organization of the Christian congregation, "God's household" (3:15).

quiet.[8] 13 For Adam was formed first, then Eve. 14 And Adam was not the one deceived; it was the woman who was deceived and became a sinner.[9] 15 But women[1] will be saved through childbearing—if they continue in faith, love and holiness with propriety.

3 Here is a trustworthy saying: Whoever aspires to be an overseer[2] desires a noble task. 2 Now the overseer is to be above reproach, faithful to his wife,[3] temperate, self-controlled, respectable, hospitable, able to teach, 3 not given to drunkenness, not violent but gentle, not quarrelsome, not a lover of money. 4 He must manage his own family well and see that his children obey him, and he must do so in a manner worthy of full respect. 5 (If anyone does not know how to manage his own family, how can he take care of God's church?) 6 He must not be a recent convert, or he may become conceited and fall under the same judgment as the devil.[4] 7 He must also have a good reputation with outsiders, so that he will not fall into disgrace and into the devil's trap.

8 In the same way, deacons are to be worthy of respect, sincere, not indulging in much wine, and not pursuing dishonest gain. 9 They must keep hold of the deep truths of the faith with a clear conscience. 10 They must first be tested; and then if there is nothing against them, let them serve as deacons.

11 In the same way, the women[5] are to be worthy of respect, not malicious talkers but temperate and trustworthy in everything.

12 A deacon must be faithful to his wife[6] and must manage his children and his household well. 13 Those who have served well gain an excellent standing and great assurance in their faith in Christ Jesus.

14 Although I hope to come to you soon, I am writing you these instructions so that, 15 if I am delayed, you will know how people ought to conduct themselves in God's household, which is the church of the living God, the pillar and foundation of the truth. 16 Beyond all question, the mystery from which true godliness springs is great:[7]

He[8] appeared in a body,
was vindicated by the Spirit,[9]

---

8. Cf. 1 Cor. 14:34 f.
9. Some think the author is referring to Gen. 3, whereas others point to the legend of Eve's sexual seduction (see note on 2 Cor. 11:3). Whereas Paul applies the Eve myth to the entire church (both male and female) in 2 Cor. 11, the author here makes a gender-specific application.
1. Greek "she," but the following verb is plural. This sentence is obscure. Some would translate "by the birth of the child," thinking of an allusion to Gen. 3:15, understood as a prediction of Christ's birth, but the Greek will hardly bear such a translation. See Part IV for Ambrosiaster's treatment of vv. 9–15.
2. "Overseer" translates *episkopos*, whence our word "bishop."
3. Rather, "married only once" (lit. "husband of one wife"); the meaning is made clear by the corresponding phrase used of widows, 5:9.
4. Though the word *diabolos* means "slanderer" and is so used in the plural in the Pastorals (3:11; 2 Tim. 3:3; Tit. 2:3), in the singular it certainly refers to "the devil." It is not so used in the undoubted letters of Paul, but see Eph. 4:27; 6:11.
5. Sometimes taken to refer to the deacons' wives, but the context points to female deacons like Phoebe of Cenchreae (Rom. 16:1).
6. "Husband of one wife"; see note on 3:1.
7. Greek "confessedly great is the mystery of godliness." Some ancient scribes "corrected" "confessedly" to "we confess as"; what follows is clearly a credal formula or chant. "Godliness" translates *eusebeia*, "religion" or "piety"; it is not used in the undoubted letters of Paul, but frequent in the Pastorals (2:2; 4:7f.; 6:3, 5, 6, 11; 2 Tim. 3:5; Tit. 1:1; the cognate verb in 1 Tim. 5:4).
8. Greek "Who"; cf. the beginning of the hymns in Phil. 2:6; Col. 1:15. The relative pronoun has no grammatical connection here; some manuscripts therefore substitute "God" or "which." The six lines have only a rough meter; they can be construed as three strophes of two lines each in the pattern ab/ba/ab or as two strophes of three lines each, abc/a'b'c'.
9. Or "in spirit" or "in the Spirit."

was seen by angels,
was preached among the nations,
was believed on in the world,
was taken up in glory.

4 The Spirit clearly says[1] that in later times some will abandon the faith and follow deceiving spirits and things taught by demons. 2 Such teachings come through hypocritical liars, whose consciences have been seared as with a hot iron. 3 They forbid people to marry[2] and order them to abstain from certain foods, which God created to be received with thanksgiving by those who believe and who know the truth. 4 For everything God created is good, and nothing is to be rejected if it is received with thanksgiving, 5 because it is consecrated by the word of God and prayer.

6 If you point these things out to the brothers and sisters, you will be a good minister[3] of Christ Jesus, nourished on the truths of the faith and of the good teaching that you have followed. 7 Have nothing to do with godless myths and old wives' tales; rather, train yourself to be godly. 8 For physical training is of some value, but godliness has value for all things, holding promise for both the present life and the life to come. 9 This is a trustworthy saying that deserves full acceptance. 10 That is why we labor and strive,[4] because we have put our hope in the living God, who is the Savior of all people, and especially of those who believe.

11 Command and teach these things. 12 Don't let anyone look down on you because you are young, but set an example for the believers in speech, in conduct, in love, in faith and in purity. 13 Until I come, devote yourself to the public reading of Scripture, to preaching and to teaching.[5] 14 Do not neglect your gift, which was given you through prophecy when the body of elders laid their hands on you.[6]

15 Be diligent in these matters; give yourself wholly to them, so that everyone may see your progress. 16 Watch your life and doctrine closely. Persevere in them, because if you do, you will save both yourself and your hearers.

5 Do not rebuke an older man[7] harshly, but exhort him as if he were your

---

1. The allusion may be to a written prophecy or one delivered by a prophet in a Christian meeting; the notion of false teachings and apostasy as signs of the "later times" is common in apocalyptic texts and in "testamentary" contexts in the NT, e.g., Acts 20:29; 2 Pet. 2:1–3; 3:3; 2 Tim. 3:1–9; 4:3 f.; 2 Thess. 2:3.

2. There were a number of movements in the early church that opposed marriage, including the Encratites and the followers of Marcion (see Part IV). These movements sometimes claimed the authority of Paul, and some would have seen the Pastorals as aimed primarily at one of them, perhaps specifically at the image of Paul in the *Acts of Paul and Thecla.* Compare also the errors combated in Colossians.

3. The word translated "minister" is the same as that translated elsewhere as "deacon." Here the older usage, referring to a missionary (e.g., 1 Cor. 3:5; 2 Cor. 11:23) persists alongside the new technical usage for a local office.

4. Some manuscripts read, "suffer reproach."

5. These are apparently three cardinal elements in public worship. The word translated "preaching" means "admonition" or "exhortation"; homilies to the congregation, not missionary proclamation, are meant.

6. "Body of elders" suggests that governance in the groups addressed by the Pastorals is still like that attested in Acts and similar to that in many Jewish synagogues of the time; thus the "overseers" or "bishops" mentioned in these letters are not yet the "monarchical" bishops that would soon become standard, but members of that corporate body, the *presbuterion.* For the ritual of "laying on of hands" to convey authority, found already in the Hebrew Bible (Num. 8:10; 27:18–23; Deut. 34:9), cf. 5:22; 2 Tim. 1:6; Acts 6:6; 13:3.

7. Here in the ordinary sense; elsewhere (e.g., v. 17) the same word refers to the office of "elder." Vv. 1 f. reflect an ancient Greek ideal for behavior of a person in authority; Plato already used very similar language to describe relationships among the "guardians" of his ideal republic (*Resp.* 463c).

father. Treat younger men as brothers, 2 older women as mothers, and younger women as sisters, with absolute purity.

3 Give proper recognition to those widows[8] who are really in need. 4 But if a widow has children or grandchildren, these should learn first of all to put their religion into practice by caring for their own family and so repaying their parents and grandparents, for this is pleasing to God. 5 The widow who is really in need and left all alone puts her hope in God and continues night and day to pray and to ask God for help. 6 But the widow who lives for pleasure is dead even while she lives. 7 Give the people these instructions, so that no one may be open to blame. 8 Anyone who does not provide for their relatives, and especially for their own household, has denied the faith and is worse than an unbeliever.

9 No widow may be put on the list of widows unless she is over sixty, has been faithful to her husband,[9] 10 and is well known for her good deeds, such as bringing up children, showing hospitality, washing the feet of the Lord's people, helping those in trouble and devoting herself to all kinds of good deeds.

11 As for younger widows, do not put them on such a list. For when their sensual desires overcome their dedication to Christ, they want to marry. 12 Thus they bring judgment on themselves, because they have broken their first pledge. 13 Besides, they get into the habit of being idle and going about from house to house. And not only do they become idlers, but also busybodies who talk nonsense, saying things they ought not to. 14 So I counsel younger widows to marry, to have children, to manage their homes and to give the enemy no opportunity for slander.[1] 15 Some have in fact already turned away to follow Satan.

16 If any woman who is a believer has widows in her care, she should continue to help them and not let the church be burdened with them, so that the church can help those widows who are really in need.

17 The elders[2] who direct the affairs of the church well are worthy of double honor,[3] especially those whose work is preaching and teaching. 18 For Scripture says, "Do not muzzle an ox while it is treading out the grain,"[4] and "Workers deserve their wages."[5] 19 Do not entertain an accusation against an elder unless it is brought by two or three witnesses. 20 But those elders who are sinning you are to reprove before everyone, so that the others may take warning. 21 I charge you, in the sight of God and Christ Jesus and the elect angels, to keep these instructions without partiality, and to do nothing out of favoritism.

---

8. Vv. 3–16 are a surprisingly elaborate set of regulations for the enrollment of widows eligible for church support. The special concern for widows (and orphans) had long been characteristic of Judaism; here their support is apparently becoming a financial burden. A similar set of rules, but much shorter, is found in the Letter of Polycarp (d. 155/6) 4.3, and later books of church order deal with the same problem. Ignatius of Antioch (d. ca. 117?) had mentioned "virgins who are called widows" (*Smyrn.* 13.1). See the essay by Jouette M. Bassler in Part IX.
9. Greek, "wife of one husband"; cf. the corresponding rule for bishops (3:2) and deacons (3:12).
1. Cf. 1 Cor. 7:8 f.
2. "Elders" here has the official sense, identical with "overseers" (see Tit. 1:5–7).
3. Or, "double pay"—as clearly implied by v. 18. But does this mean that one group of elders, as executives, are distinguished from others who receive lesser pay? Possibly the elders receive twice the stipend of widows.
4. Deut. 25:4; cf. 1 Cor. 9:9.
5. Quoted as a saying of Jesus in Luke 10:7 (cf. Matt. 10:10), and alluded to by Paul in 1 Cor. 9:14. If "scripture says" is to be taken strictly as referring to both quotations, then this would be the earliest instance of one of the gospels (or a prior collection of Jesus' sayings: "Q") being placed on a par with what Christians would later call "the Old Testament."

22 Do not be hasty in the laying on of hands, and do not share in the sins of others. Keep yourself pure.[6]

23 <u>Stop drinking only water, and use a little wine because of your stomach and your frequent illnesses.</u>

24 The sins of some are obvious, reaching the place of judgment ahead of them; the sins of others trail behind them. 25 In the same way, good deeds are obvious, and even those that are not obvious cannot remain hidden forever.

6 All who are under the yoke of slavery[7] should consider their masters worthy of full respect, so that God's name and our teaching may not be slandered. 2 Those who have believing masters should not show them disrespect just because they are fellow believers. Instead, they should serve them even better because their masters are dear to them as fellow believers and are devoted to the welfare of their slaves.[8]

These are the things you are to teach and insist on. 3 If anyone teaches otherwise and does not agree to the sound instruction of our Lord Jesus Christ and to godly teaching,[9] 4 they are conceited and understand nothing. They have an unhealthy interest in controversies and quarrels about words that result in envy, strife, malicious talk, evil suspicions 5 and constant friction between people of corrupt mind, who have been robbed of the truth and who think that godliness is a means to financial gain.[1]

6 But godliness with contentment[2] is great gain. 7 For we brought nothing into the world, and we can take nothing out of it.[3] 8 But if we have food and clothing, we will be content with that. 9 Those who want to get rich fall into temptation and a trap and into many foolish and harmful desires that plunge people into ruin and destruction. 10 For the love of money is a root of all kinds of evil.[4] Some people, eager for money, have wandered from the faith and pierced themselves with many griefs.

11 But you, man of God,[5] flee from all this, and pursue righteousness, godliness, faith, love, endurance and gentleness. 12 Fight the good fight of the faith. Take hold of the eternal life to which you were called when you made your good confession in the presence of many witnesses. 13 In the sight of God, who gives life to everything, and of Christ Jesus, who while testifying before Pontius Pilate made the good confession,[6] I charge

---

6. Vv. 24 f. are more closely connected with v. 22 than this verse; typical of the loose topical arrangement of much hortatory literature. V. 23 sets a limit to the last clause of v. 22: "keep yourself pure," a necessary limit in view of ascetic tendencies combated elsewhere in the Pastorals (e.g., 4:3).

7. A fragment of the more conventional type of "household table"; note the concern with the church's reputation in the larger society.

8. Or, "because their masters . . . benefit from their service."

9. Greek, "teaching according to godliness"; on the term translated "godliness," see the note on 3:16.

1. The accusation that the teaching of new doctrines was motivated by desire for profit is very common in polemical literature of the philosophical schools, of the satirists, and of Christian antiheretical literature from this point on. Note the author's inversion of the common meaning by repeating the word in the next verse.

2. "Contentment," more literally, "self-sufficiency," was a fundamental virtue in the Stoic tradition, from which it became a common topic in popular moral philosophy. Note Paul's use of the term in Phil. 4:11.

3. A commonplace in both Greek and Jewish sources; cf. Job 1:21; Eccl. 5:15; Philo, *Spec. Laws* 1.294 f.; Seneca, *Moral Epistles* 102.25.

4. Another cliché of popular moralizing.

5. An OT title, used there of exceptional charismatics (Deut. 33:1; Josh. 14:6; 1 Sam. 9:6 f.; 1 Kings 17:18; 2 Kings 4:7; Neh. 12:24). Vv. 11–16 seem a self-contained unit, perhaps drawn from an exhortation used at baptism or ordination.

6. The description of Jesus as the model martyr who, by his fortitude, encourages followers to "keep

you 14 to keep this command without spot or blame until the appearing of our Lord Jesus Christ, 15 which God will bring about in his own time— God, the blessed and only Ruler, the King of kings and Lord of lords, 16 who alone is immortal and who lives in unapproachable light, whom no one has seen or can see. To him be honor and might forever. Amen.

17 Command those who are rich in this present world not to be arrogant nor to put their hope in wealth, which is so uncertain, but to put their hope in God, who richly provides us with everything for our enjoyment. 18 Command them to do good, to be rich in good deeds, and to be generous and willing to share. 19 In this way they will lay up treasure for themselves as a firm foundation for the coming age, so that they may take hold of the life that is truly life.

20 Timothy, guard what has been entrusted to your care.[7] Turn away from godless chatter and the opposing ideas of what is falsely called knowledge,[8] 21 which some have professed and in so doing have departed from the faith.

Grace be with you all.

Second Timothy

1 Paul, an apostle of Christ Jesus by the will of God, in keeping with the promise of life that is in Christ Jesus,

2 To Timothy, my dear son:

Grace, mercy and peace from God the Father and Christ Jesus our Lord.

3 I thank God, whom I serve, as my ancestors did, with a clear conscience, as night and day I constantly remember you in my prayers. 4 Recalling your tears, I long to see you, so that I may be filled with joy. 5 I am reminded of your sincere faith, which first lived in your grandmother Lois and in your mother[1] Eunice and, I am persuaded, now lives in you also.

6 For this reason I remind you to fan into flame the gift of God, which is in you through the laying on of my hands.[2] 7 For the Spirit God gave us does not make us timid, but gives us power, love and self-discipline. 8 So do not be ashamed of the testimony about our Lord or of me his prisoner. But join with me in suffering for the gospel,[3] by the power of God, 9 who

---

the faith" is foreign to Paul but increasingly important in subapostolic Christianity. A similar theology of martyrdom developed in Jewish literature around the figures of the Maccabees.

7. Lit., "the deposit," a commercial term here applied to the authoritative tradition; cf. 2 Tim. 1:12, 14.

8. The first attestation for the use of the word *gnōsis* as what may be a technical designation for an esoteric movement, but cf. 1 Cor. 8: 1, 7, 10; 13:2; 14:6. Later Irenaeus (ca. 180) would use this phrase in the title of his five-volume work, "On the Exposé and Overthrow of the Falsely Called Knowledge." His principal opponent was Valentinus, who, Irenaeus said, had adapted the myths of a school who called themselves, using a Platonic word, "the Knowing Ones" (*Gnōstikoi*). Some have found in the word translated here "opposing ideas" (*antitheseis*) a reference to Marcion's work, "The Antitheses" (see Part IV), but that would require an improbably late date for this letter.

1. Cf. Acts 16:1.

2. See note on 1 Tim. 4:14.

3. Vv. 6–12 present one of the principal themes of the letter, Paul's suffering as a personal example. Vv. 9 f. are a carefully formulated summary of the gospel, following a pattern frequently found in early Christian preaching: "hidden for ages/now revealed" (cf. note on 1 Cor. 2:7 ff). The typically Pauline terms "mystery" and "hidden" are wanting here, and the terms "appearing" (epiphany)and "savior," so important in the Pastorals, are central. The latter were stock expressions in many forms

has saved us and called us to a holy life—not because of anything we have done but because of his own purpose and grace. This grace was given us in Christ Jesus before the beginning of time, 10 but it has now been revealed through the appearing of our Savior, Christ Jesus, who has destroyed death and has brought life and immortality to light through the gospel. 11 And of this gospel I was appointed a herald and an apostle and a teacher. 12 That is why I am suffering as I am. Yet this is no cause for shame,[4] because I know whom I have believed, and am convinced that he is able to guard what I have entrusted to him[5] until that day.

13 What you heard from me, keep as the pattern of sound teaching, with faith and love in Christ Jesus. 14 Guard the good deposit that was entrusted to you—guard it with the help of the Holy Spirit who lives in us.

15 You know that everyone in the province of Asia[6] has deserted me, including Phygelus and Hermogenes.

16 May the Lord show mercy to the household of Onesiphorus, because he often refreshed me and was not ashamed of my chains. 17 On the contrary, when he was in Rome, he searched hard for me until he found me. 18 May the Lord grant that he will find mercy from the Lord on that day! You know very well in how many ways he helped me in Ephesus.[7]

2 You then, my son, be strong in the grace that is in Christ Jesus. 2 And the things you have heard me say in the presence of many witnesses entrust to reliable people who will also be qualified to teach others. 3 Join with me in suffering,[8] like a good soldier of Christ Jesus. 4 No one serving as a soldier gets involved in civilian affairs; rather, they try to please their commanding officer. 5 Similarly, anyone who competes as an athlete does not receive the victor's crown except by competing according to the rules. 6 The hardworking farmer should be the first to receive a share of the crops. 7 Reflect on what I am saying, for the Lord will give you insight into all this.

8 Remember Jesus Christ, raised from the dead, descended from David.[9] This is my gospel, 9 for which I am suffering even to the point of being chained like a criminal. But God's word is not chained. 10 Therefore I endure everything for the sake of the elect, that they too may obtain the salvation that is in Christ Jesus, with eternal glory.

11 Here is a trustworthy saying:[1]

If we died with him,
we will also live with him;

---

of Hellenistic religion, including healing cults and the cult of the emperors.(One inscription describes Caesar as "the son of Ares and Aphrodite, god manifest [*epiphanē*] and universal savior of mankind.")

4. Cf. Rom. 1:16.

5. Lit., "my deposit," the same word used in v. 14; cf. 1 Tim. 6:20 and the note there.

6. The Roman province, roughly the western half of Asia Minor, of which Ephesus was the capital.

7. Such personal notes, with those of chap. 4, are taken by many commentators as signs of authenticity. Some suggest that fragments of an authentic letter have been used by the pseudonymous author. The persons mentioned here are not otherwise known, until the late apocryphal *Acts of Paul* (see Part IV), which mentions Hermogenes and gives a few more details about Onesiphorus.

8. Cf. 1:8; 4:5. The metaphor of the "good soldier" is common in Hellenistic moralizing rhetoric, and not infrequent in the Pauline corpus: cf. 1 Tim. 1:18; 1 Cor. 9:7; 2 Cor. 10:3 f.; Phil. 2:25; Phlm. 1:2.

9. Another creedal or liturgical fragment; cf. Rom. 1:3 f.

1. For the phrase "Here is a trustworthy saying," see the note on 1 Tim. 1:15. The style of the following quotation is striking; it may be part of a baptismal hymn: note fragmentary parallels in Rom. 6:5, 8; Col. 3:1. Polycarp quotes similar lines (Polycarp 5:2). The *style* is found in the concluding hymn of the Qumran "Rule of the Community."

12 if we endure,
we will also reign with him.
If we disown him,
he will also disown us;
13 if we are faithless,
he remains faithful,
for he cannot disown himself.
14 Keep reminding God's people of these things. Warn them before God against quarreling about words; it is of no value, and only ruins those who listen. 15 Do your best to present yourself to God as one approved, a worker who does not need to be ashamed and who correctly handles[2] the word of truth. 16 Avoid godless chatter, because those who indulge in it will become more and more ungodly. 17 Their teaching will spread like gangrene. Among them are Hymenaeus and Philetus, 18 who have departed from the truth. They say that the resurrection has already taken place,[3] and they destroy the faith of some. 19 Nevertheless, God's solid foundation stands firm, sealed with this inscription: "The Lord knows those who are his,"[4] and, "Everyone who confesses the name of the Lord must turn away from wickedness."[5]

20 In a large house there are articles not only of gold and silver, but also of wood and clay; some are for noble purposes and some for disposal of refuse. 21 Those who cleanse themselves from the latter will be instruments for noble purposes, made holy, useful to the Master and prepared to do any good work.

22 Flee the evil desires of youth and pursue righteousness, faith, love and peace, along with those who call on the Lord out of a pure heart. 23 Don't have anything to do with foolish and stupid arguments, because you know they produce quarrels. 24 And the Lord's servant must not be quarrelsome but must be kind to everyone, able to teach, not resentful. 25 Opponents must be gently instructed, in the hope that God will grant them repentance leading them to a knowledge of the truth, 26 and that they will come to their senses and escape from the trap of the devil,[6] who has taken them captive to do his will.

3 But mark this: There will be terrible times in the last days.[7] 2 People will be lovers of themselves, lovers of money, boastful, proud, abusive, disobedient to their parents, ungrateful, unholy, 3 without love, unforgiving, slanderous, without self-control, brutal, not lovers of the good, 4 treacherous, rash, conceited, lovers of pleasure rather than lovers of God— 5 having a form of godliness but denying its power. Have nothing to do with such people.

---

2. The unusual word translated "correctly handles" is found elsewhere only in Prov. 3:6; 11:5, where it refers to clearing a straight road. For "word of truth," a common expression for the gospel, see note on Col. 1:5.
3. On the possibility of an earlier appearance of this notion, see notes on 1 Cor. 15; for a later instance, see *Gos. Phil.* 56 and the *Treatise on the Resurrection* (both in the Nag Hammadi horde).
4. Num. 16:5 LXX.
5. This quotation is not found in the OT, but cf. Sirach 17:26 and Isa. 26:13.
6. For the "trap of the devil," see 1 Tim. 3:7.
7. A typical formulation in the genre "Testament" or "Farewell Discourse"; see 1 Tim 4:1 and the note there. In the NT, cf. Mark 13:3ff. and parallels; Acts 20:29; 2 Thess. 2:3; 2 Pet. 2:1–3; 3:3; in the OT, the testaments of Jacob (Gen. 49) and Moses (Deut. 33; 34); in the Pseudepigrapha, the *Testaments of the Twelve Patriarchs.* "Paul" thus predicts the time when the Pastorals were written, but subsequent generations have often thought that their own time period was being foretold (see, e.g., Theodoret in Part IV).

6 They are the kind who worm their way into homes and gain control over gullible women, who are loaded down with sins and are swayed by all kinds of evil desires, 7 always learning but never able to come to a knowledge of the truth. 8 Just as Jannes and Jambres opposed Moses,[8] so also these teachers oppose the truth. They are men of depraved minds, who, as far as the faith is concerned, are rejected. 9 But they will not get very far because, as in the case of those men, their folly will be clear to everyone.

10 You, however, know all about my teaching, my way of life, my purpose, faith, patience, love, endurance, 11 persecutions, sufferings—what kinds of things happened to me in Antioch, Iconium and Lystra, the persecutions I endured.[9] Yet the Lord rescued me from all of them. 12 In fact, everyone who wants to live a godly life in Christ Jesus will be persecuted, 13 while evildoers and impostors will go from bad to worse, deceiving and being deceived. 14 But as for you, continue in what you have learned and have become convinced of, because you know those from whom you learned it, 15 and how from infancy you have known the Holy Scriptures, which are able to make you wise for salvation through faith in Christ Jesus. 16 All Scripture is God-breathed and is useful[1] for teaching, rebuking, correcting and training in righteousness, 17 so that all God's people may be thoroughly equipped for every good work.

4 In the presence of God and of Christ Jesus, who will judge the living and the dead,[2] and in view of his appearing and his kingdom, I give you this charge: 2 Preach the word; be prepared in season and out of season; correct, rebuke and encourage—with great patience and careful instruction. 3 For the time will come when people will not put up with sound doctrine. Instead, to suit their own desires, they will gather around them a great number of teachers to say what their itching ears want to hear. 4 They will turn their ears away from the truth and turn aside to myths. 5 But you, keep your head in all situations, endure hardship, do the work of an evangelist, discharge all the duties of your ministry.

6 For I am already being poured out like a drink offering,[3] and the time for my departure is near. 7 I have fought the good fight, I have finished the race, I have kept the faith. 8 Now there is in store for me the crown of righteousness,[4] which the Lord, the righteous Judge, will award to me on that day—and not only to me, but also to all who have longed for his appearing.

9 Do your best to come to me quickly, 10 for Demas, because he loved this world, has deserted me and has gone to Thessalonica. Crescens has gone to Galatia, and Titus to Dalmatia. 11 Only Luke is with me. Get Mark and bring him with you, because he is helpful to me in my ministry. 12 I

---

8. Legend gave these names to the "magicians of Egypt" who, according to Ex. 7:11, contended with Moses in Pharaoh's presence. They are prototypes for opponents of the truth "at the end of days" also in the Dead Sea Scrolls (CD 5:17–19).

9. Cf. 2 Cor. 11:23–29, and the note on 2 Cor. 6:4. See also Acts 13–14.

1. Or, "all God-breathed scripture is useful . . ." "Scripture," as in the previous verse, does not yet include the "New Testament," but refers to the Jewish scriptures (of varying extent, not yet "canonized") taken by the early Christians (mostly reading them in Greek) as authoritative and soon to be called "the Old Testament."

2. Acts 17:31; Rom. 2:16; 2 Cor. 5:10; cf. 1 Cor. 4:5.

3. Cf. Phil. 2:17. The sudden shift of mood has lent color to the hypothesis that fragments of a genuine letter have been used; see note on 1:18.

4. The "crown" is the wreath awarded the victor in an athletic contest, a frequent metaphor in hellenistic moral rhetoric, including much of the New Testament; cf. 2:5; 1 Cor. 9:25; Jas. 1:12; Rev. 2:10; 3:11.

sent Tychicus to Ephesus.[5] 13 When you come, bring the cloak that I left with Carpus at Troas, and my scrolls, especially the parchments.[6]

14 Alexander[7] the metalworker did me a great deal of harm. The Lord will repay him for what he has done. 15 You too should be on your guard against him, because he strongly opposed our message.

16 At my first defense,[8] no one came to my support, but everyone deserted me. May it not be held against them. 17 But the Lord stood at my side and gave me strength, so that through me the message might be fully proclaimed and all the Gentiles might hear it. And I was delivered from the lion's mouth.[9] 18 The Lord will rescue me from every evil attack and will bring me safely to his heavenly kingdom. To him be glory for ever and ever. Amen.

19 Greet Priscilla and Aquila and the household of Onesiphorus. 20 Erastus stayed in Corinth, and I left Trophimus sick in Miletus.[1] 21 Do your best to get here before winter. Eubulus greets you, and so do Pudens, Linus, Claudia and all the brothers and sisters.

22 The Lord be with your spirit. Grace be with you all.

Titus

1 Paul, a servant[1] of God and an apostle of Jesus Christ to further the faith of God's elect and their knowledge of the truth that leads to godliness— 2 in the hope of eternal life, which God, who does not lie, promised before the beginning of time, 3 and which now at his appointed season he has brought to light through the preaching entrusted to me by the command of God our Savior,

4 To Titus, my true son[2] in our common faith:

Grace and peace from God the Father and Christ Jesus our Savior.

5 The reason I left you in Crete[3] was that you might put in order what

---

5. Demas: see Phlm. 24; Col. 4:14; also *Acts of Paul* 1; 14 (in Part IV). Crescens (or Crescas): otherwise unknown. Titus: 2 Cor. 13; 7:6, 13f.; 8:6, 16, 23; 12:18; Gal. 2:1, 3; Tit. 1:4. Luke: Phlm. 1:24; Col. 4:14. Mark: Phlm. 1:24; Col. 4:10; Acts 12:12, 25; 15:37, 38; 1 Pet. 5:13. Tychicus: Acts 20:4; Col. 4:7; Eph. 6:21; Tit. 3:12.

6. "Parchments" may refer to blank sheets for writing.

7. 1 Tim. 1:20; otherwise Alexander is unknown; there is no reason to identify him with the Alexander of Acts 19:33 or of Mark 15:21.

8. Traditionally this has been taken to refer to Paul's first Roman imprisonment, on the assumption that, after a brief period of freedom, he now writes during a second imprisonment. More likely, however, "first defense" refers to a preliminary hearing; the Pastorals throughout seem to presuppose only one imprisonment.

9. Jerome (Part IV) thought the reference was specifically to Nero, but it is to be understood both generally and figuratively (cf. 1 Cor. 15:32 and note); the lion is proverbial for power and danger. The story of Daniel 6 made "delivered from the lion's mouth" an especially pregnant notion in Jewish and early Christian discourse; the phrase used here is very close to 1 Macc. 2:60, referring to Daniel (cf. also Ps. 22:21[LXX 21:22]). For more imaginative dramatizations of Paul and a lion, see the excerpts from the *Acts of Paul* in Part IV.

1. For "Priscilla" (rather, "Prisca," as always in the Pauline letters) and Aquila, see 1 Cor. 16:19; Rom. 16:3; Acts 18:2 f., 18 f., 26. Erastus, Rom. 16:23; Acts 19:22; Trophimus, Acts 20:4; 21: 29. The names in the following verse, Pudens, Linus, and Claudia, are otherwise unknown. Eubulus is mentioned in the pseudonymous correspondence between Paul and the Corinthians (Part III).

1. "Slave," as in Rom. 1:1; Phil. 1:1; cf. 1 Cor. 9:19.

2. Titus: 2 Cor. 13; 7:6, 13f.; 8:6, 16, 23; 12:18; Gal. 2:1, 3; 2 Tim. 4:10. The epithet "my true son" is applied also to Timothy, 1 Tim. 1:2.

3. The only other mention of Crete in the NT is Acts 27:7–13, where the ship bearing Paul as prisoner to Rome is said to have touched briefly at a Cretan harbor. The foundation of a church there is unrecorded.

was left unfinished and appoint elders[4] in every town, as I directed you. 6 An elder must be blameless, faithful to his wife, a man whose children believe and are not open to the charge of being wild and disobedient. 7 Since an overseer manages God's household, he must be blameless—not overbearing, not quick-tempered, not given to drunkenness, not violent, not pursuing dishonest gain. 8 Rather, he must be hospitable, one who loves what is good, who is self-controlled, upright, holy and disciplined. 9 He must hold firmly to the trustworthy message as it has been taught, so that he can encourage others by sound doctrine and refute those who oppose it.

10 For there are many rebellious people, full of meaningless talk and deception, especially those of the circumcision group. 11 They must be silenced, because they are disrupting whole households by teaching things they ought not to teach—and that for the sake of dishonest gain. 12 One of Crete's own prophets has said it: "Cretans are always liars, evil brutes, lazy gluttons."[5] 13 He has surely told the truth! Therefore rebuke them sharply, so that they will be sound in the faith 14 and will pay no attention to Jewish myths or to the merely human commands of those who reject the truth. 15 To the pure, all things are pure, but to those who are corrupted and do not believe, nothing is pure. In fact, both their minds and consciences are corrupted. 16 They claim to know God, but by their actions they deny him. They are detestable, disobedient and unfit for doing anything good.

2 You, however, must teach what is appropriate to sound doctrine. 2 Teach the older men[6] to be temperate, worthy of respect, self-controlled, and sound in faith, in love and in endurance.

3 Likewise, teach the older women to be reverent in the way they live, not to be slanderers or addicted to much wine, but to teach what is good. 4 Then they can urge the younger women to love their husbands and children, 5 to be self-controlled and pure, to be busy at home, to be kind, and to be subject to their husbands, so that no one will malign the word of God.

6 Similarly, encourage the young men to be self-controlled. 7 In everything set them an example by doing what is good. In your teaching show integrity, seriousness 8 and soundness of speech that cannot be condemned, so that those who oppose you may be ashamed because they have nothing bad to say about us.

9 Teach slaves to be subject to their masters in everything, to try to please them, not to talk back to them, 10 and not to steal from them, but to show that they can be fully trusted, so that in every way they will make the teaching about God our Savior attractive.[7]

11 For the grace of God has appeared[8] that offers salvation to all people.

4. "Elders" and "overseers" (or "bishops") are used interchangeably, as in 1 Timothy. The form of the rule for the officers' qualifications is the same as in 1 Tim. 3:2–7 (simply parallel lists of virtues and vices), though there are a number of variations in detail. In many respects Tit. reads like an abbreviated version of 1 Tim.4.

5. Clement of Alexandria reported that this quotation came from a book by Epimenides, a teacher and miracle worker of Crete (fl. 500 BCE). The line had become proverbial.

6. 2:1–10 is a "household table" (see the notes at Col. 3:18 and 1 Tim. 2:8) for older men, older women, young women, young men, and slaves.

7. Here and in 1 Tim. 6:1–2 (also 1 Pet. 2:18–25) there is no corresponding admonition to the masters; contrast Col. 4:1; Eph. 6:9.

8. Vv. 11–15 provide the theological basis for the style of morality urged in the "household table." The language, which has elements of liturgical style, is paralleled in many statements of Hellenistic

12 It teaches us to say "No" to ungodliness and worldly passions, and to live self-controlled, upright and godly lives in this present age, 13 while we wait for the blessed hope—the appearing of the glory of our great God and Savior, Jesus Christ, 14 who gave himself for us to redeem us from all wickedness and to purify for himself a people that are his very own, eager to do what is good.

15 These, then, are the things you should teach. Encourage and rebuke with all authority. Do not let anyone despise you.[9]

3 Remind the people to be subject to rulers and authorities,[1] to be obedient, to be ready to do whatever is good, 2 to slander no one, to be peaceable and considerate, and always to be gentle toward everyone.

3 At one time we too were foolish, disobedient, deceived and enslaved by all kinds of passions and pleasures. We lived in malice and envy, being hated and hating one another. 4 But when the kindness and love of God our Savior appeared, 5 he saved us, not because of righteous things we had done, but because of his mercy. He saved us through the washing of rebirth and renewal by the Holy Spirit, 6 whom he poured out on us generously through Jesus Christ our Savior, 7 so that, having been justified by his grace, we might become heirs having the hope of eternal life.[2] 8 This is a trustworthy saying. And I want you to stress these things, so that those who have trusted in God may be careful to devote themselves to doing what is good. These things are excellent and profitable for everyone.

9 But avoid foolish controversies and genealogies and arguments and quarrels about the law, because these are unprofitable and useless. 10 Warn divisive people once, and then warn them a second time. After that, have nothing to do with them. 11 You may be sure that such people are warped and sinful; they are self-condemned.[3]

12 As soon as I send Artemas[4] or Tychicus to you, do your best to come to me at Nicopolis,[5] because I have decided to winter there. 13 Do everything you can to help Zenas the lawyer and Apollos on their way and see that they have everything they need. 14 Our people must learn to devote themselves to doing what is good, in order to provide for urgent needs and not live unproductive lives.

15 Everyone with me sends you greetings. Greet those who love us in the faith.

Grace be with you all.

Jewish apologetics, in which God's saving act (primarily the Exodus and Sinai revelation) procured for him "a people that are his very own" (v. 14; cf. Ex. 19:5), to be "taught" (v. 12) by his commandments and thus marked out by its superior morality. The terms used here to describe this morality come mainly from the Stoic tradition, and, as throughout the Pastorals, the notion of the "appearing" (*epiphaneia*, vv. 11, 13) of the divine among humans, common in the language of Hellenistic ruler cults, is central. For Jesus as "God," see the note on Rom. 9:5 and the excerpt from Julian in Part IV.

9. Cf. 1 Tim. 4:12.

1. Cf. Rom. 13:1–7; 1 Pet. 2:13–17.

2. The formal character of vv. 4–7 suggests that these verses may again echo the language of liturgy or creed (note the allusion to baptism in v. 5), summarizing some of the distinctive beliefs of Paul and his school. Cf. Rom. 3:9–26; 5:20–21; 1 Cor. 6:9–11; Eph. 2:8 f.

3. A brief return to the teachings and teachers to be avoided (cf. 1:10–16), characterized in terms similar to those found in 1 Tim. 1:4, 7–9; 6:4; 2 Tim. 2:14, 23 f. The command to give but one or two warnings and then shun the deviants is new.

4. Artemas and Zenas are otherwise unknown; for Tychicus, see Col. 4:7; Eph. 6:21; 2 Tim. 4:12; Acts 20:4; Apollos: 1 Cor. 1:12; 3:4 f.; 4:6; 16:12; Acts 18:14–28.

5. A number of cities bearing the name Nicopolis could be meant; perhaps the most likely is in Epirus, on the western coast of the Greek mainland.

PART III

Pseudo-Pauline Works

The Deutero-Pauline letters of the New Testament are deeply anchored in the thought of Paul and represent attempts to adapt the apostle's message to new generations of believers. The pseudo-Pauline works included in this section are quite different and have no such firm mooring. Written for a variety of purposes, these works are clear forgeries.[1] Not all of the Pauline pseudepigrapha are extant.[2] The author of the Muratorian Canon (lines 64–65), for example, refers to a now lost letter of Paul to the Alexandrians but rejects it as a Marcionite composition (for Marcion, see Part IV). Similarly, Ps.-Cyprian, *On Rebaptism* 17, mentions a *Preaching of Paul* that he claims was forged by heretics in support of their theology. The most striking feature of this putative work was its depiction of Jesus confessing his sins (contrast 2 Cor. 5:21), but it also supposedly portrayed Peter and Paul as apostles who only came to know each other in Rome, "as if for the first time" (contrast Gal. 2:1–21).

This section contains the five extant Pauline pseudepigrapha. The first is the *Correspondence of Paul and the Corinthians.* The apostle Paul himself carried on an extensive correspondence with the Christians of Corinth, writing at least four letters to them and receiving one letter from them. The two letters included here purport to be additional instances of this epistolary exchange. According to this correspondence, the arrival of two false teachers in Corinth prompts Stephanas (1 Cor. 1:16; 16:15, 17) and four presbyters to write to Paul, who responds by writing the letter known as 3 *Corinthians.* Whereas the *Epistle to the Alexandrians* and the *Preaching of Paul* were written by heretics to advance their cause, these two letters are orthodox forgeries designed to combat heresy by presenting Paul as the defender of the early Catholic creed. Written in the early or middle part of the second century,[3] these letters were later incorporated into the *Acts of Paul* (late second cent.), which Tertullian (*Bapt.* 17) says was written by a presbyter in Asia Minor "out of love for Paul." The correspondence was part of the Armenian NT and probably also of the fourth-century Pauline canon in Syria, for Aphraates (Aphrahat) cited passages from 3 *Corinthians* as the words of Paul, and Ephraem treated the letters in his commentary on the Pauline epistles. The selection given here is from the *Acts of Paul* and includes the introductory narrative and the report of Paul's receipt of the Corinthians' letter.[4]

Whereas 3 *Corinthians* uses both Pauline and non-Pauline language to address doctrinal issues of the second century, the *Epistle to the Laodiceans* is

---

1. In addition to the Pauline pseudepigrapha, there are works falsely associated in antiquity with the names of some of Paul's associates. It is debated whether these works were written under a pseudonym or were originally anonymous and only later attributed to a member of the Pauline circle. The most famous of these is the *Epistle of Barnabas*, written between 70 and 135, which deals with the issue of whether the covenant belongs to Jews or Christians. Just as Tertullian (*Pud.* 20) attributes the Epistle to the Hebrews to Barnabas, Clement of Alexandria (*Strom.* 2.6, 7) does the same with the *Epistle of Barnabas*. Yet this treatise is hardly Pauline in thought; its author neither mentions Paul by name nor quotes him. There are at most some passages where the sources that the author uses may have been influenced by Paul (cf. esp. *Barn.* 13:7 and Rom. 4:11). Viewed by some ancient Christians as canonical, it was included with the entire NT in the fourth-century biblical codex Sinaiticus. Another work linked to one of Paul's co-workers is the *Epistle of Titus*, a Latin treatise on celibacy from the fourth or fifth century. In striking contrast to the *Epistle of Barnabas*, it frequently quotes Paul and calls him the Lord's vicar and "the impregnable wall among the disciples." An English translation is available in Wilhelm Schneemelcher, ed., *New Testament Apocrypha* (ed. R. McL. Wilson; 2 vols.; Louisville: Westminster/John Knox, 1991), 2:53–74.
2. A Pauline letter to the Macedonians occasionally has been posited on the basis of Clement of Alexandria, *Protr.* 9, but this is a dubious inference. Similarly, based on Lactantius, *Inst.* 4.21, some scholars have conjectured a *Preaching of Peter and Paul* that predicted Jewish sufferings connected with the Roman-Jewish war of 66–70. Others think that Lactantius is referring to an early second century apologetic work known as the *Preaching of Peter* (*Kerygma Petrou*).
3. Some scholars think that 3 *Cor.* combats the teachings of Saturninus (late first century; see Irenaeus, *Haer.* 1.24.1–2) and date the letters to the first half of the second century. Others believe that Marcion (d. ca. 154) and his followers are the real target and date the letters later in the century. Still others think that the description of the heretics is either too generic to permit a specific identification or was intended to cover several groups.
4. The narrative material introducing and linking the two letters was probably written by the author of the *Acts of Paul*.

largely a cento of Pauline phrases drawn principally from passages in Philippians. Although false teachers are mentioned, no concrete information about their "vain talk" is provided. Unlike the polemical 3 *Corinthians*, this letter is pastoral, with the imprisoned Paul chiefly offering words of exhortation and warning. Only with great difficulty can one identify this work with the pseudo-Pauline *Laodiceans* mentioned in the Muratorian Canon (lines 64–65), for that letter was written to foster the cause of Marcion. The current letter is so bland and theologically unobjectionable that it was frequently included in Latin manuscripts of the Bible (most often after Colossians or at the end of the NT), even when it was recognized that Jerome rejected it.[5] The primary aim of the person who wrote this letter was to replace the letter mentioned in Col. 4:16, where the writer exhorts the Colossians to "read the letter from Laodicea." Although some ancient commentators (such as Theodore of Mopsuestia and Theodoret of Cyrus) argued that the reference was to a letter written *by* the Laodiceans to Paul and others thought that the apostle was referring to a letter that he had written *from* Laodicea (John of Damascus suggested 1 Timothy), almost all modern scholars think the reference is to a letter that Paul wrote *to* the Laodiceans. Occasionally this letter is equated with an extant letter (such as Ephesians[6] or Philemon) but more often the letter is viewed as either lost (like the one mentioned in 1 Cor. 5:9) or nonexistent (with the putative letter only a literary device to link Colossians to the Pauline ambit). In any case, the document printed below is certainly not the one referred to in Colossians 4:16; it is rather a pseudonymous work written between the second and fourth century.

Long before the *Correspondence of Paul and Seneca* was written in the fourth century, Christians had noted similarities between the thought of the apostle Paul and the philosopher Seneca.[7] For example, Tertullian (*An.* 20) quotes the famous Stoic thinker with approval, calling him "often our Seneca." The apocryphal exchange of private letters between these two moralists built upon this recognized affinity and led ultimately to the legend that Seneca was a convert to Christianity.[8] The correspondence itself, written in Latin, comprises fourteen letters, eight by Seneca and six by Paul.[9] It was this set of letters that led Jerome to include "our Seneca" (*Jov.* 1.49) in his *On Illustrious Men*, and his words about Seneca were, in turn, inserted in many medieval manuscripts as a preface to the correspondence.[1] Paul and Seneca are depicted as close friends,[2] with Seneca not only reading some of the apostle's letters to Nero but also declaring that the Holy Spirit is in Paul. Seneca's friendship with Paul

---

5. Jerome, *Vir. ill.* 5.11. The oldest and most accurate copy of the apocryphon is found, with no indication of the dispute about its authenticity, in codex Fuldensis, transcribed in 546–547. In later centuries various theologians defended its inclusion in the Bible by claiming that it was written by Paul, though acknowledging that it did not have canonical status. Prior to Luther, *Laodiceans* was customarily included in German Bibles.

6. Tertullian, *Marc.* 5.11, 17, says that the Marcion regarded Ephesians as *Laodiceans* and emended its title accordingly.

7. Seneca (ca. 4 BCE–65 CE) is not mentioned in the NT, but his elder brother L. Junius Gallio is the proconsul of Achaia (ca. 51–53) before whom Paul appears in Acts 18:12–17.

8. In his extant works, Seneca never mentions Christianity. Lactantius, writing before the letters were forged, laments that Seneca could have become a Christian if someone had only instructed him (*Inst.* 6.24). Augustine, who knows of the private correspondence between Paul and Seneca (*Ep.* 153.14) but views the philosopher as a hypocrite, attempts to explain this silence by suggesting that any praise of the Christians would have been counter to Roman tradition and any censure perhaps would have been involuntary (*Civ.* 6.10–11).

9. The final two letters may stem from a different forger than the first twelve, and some scholars also regard *Ep.* 11 as coming from a different hand.

1. "Lucius Annaeus Seneca of Cordova, disciple of the Stoic Sotion and uncle of the poet Lucan, led a most temperate life. I would not place him in the catalog of saints were I not prompted to do so by Paul's letters to Seneca and Seneca's to Paul, which are read by many people. Although he was Nero's tutor and the most powerful man of his time, he says in these letters [in *Ep.* 12] that he would like to hold the same place among his own people as Paul held among Christians. He was put to death by Nero two years before Peter and Paul were crowned as martyrs."

2. Noted already by Ps.-Linus in the seventh century (*Martyrdom of St. Paul the Apostle*, ch. 1).

also allows him, at the same time, to speak candidly to Paul about his deficiencies in style, which he seeks to improve by sending him a rhetorical treatise
on facility in the use of words. Paul, for his part, exhorts Seneca to become a
"new herald of Jesus Christ" and use his oratorical abilities to proclaim the
word of God to Caesar and the imperial household.

Quite different from the preceding Pseudo-Pauline letters are the two apocalypses associated with the name of Paul. Both are based on 2 Corinthians 12:
1–4, where Paul recounts his experience of being caught up to the third
heaven. In that narrative, he says that he heard things that no mortal is permitted to divulge (v. 4). In the first of these apocryphal works, the *Apocalypse
of Paul*, a distinction is introduced between those aspects of the revelation that
must not be repeated and the other parts of his vision that ought to be disclosed
(21).[3] The apocalypse proper begins only in chapter 3 and purports to give
what Paul was permitted, indeed, compelled, to record. According to the Syriac
version,[4] Paul records his vision but does not disclose it while he is alive.
Instead, he buries it under the house of the believer with whom he is staying
in Tarsus. After his death, the Lord prompts him to disclose the revelation.[5]
According to the introductory narrative (1–2), which is best preserved in Latin,
this happens about 388 CE. An angel appears to a nobleman who is residing
in the house and compels him to break open the house's foundation. Having
done so, he discovers a marble box, sealed with lead, and gives it to a judge,
who sends it to the emperor Theodosius (379–395 CE).[6] The latter sends a
copy to Jerusalem, undoubtedly for its dissemination to the world.[7] In short,
Paul's apocalypse, hidden for more than three centuries, is now purportedly
revealed through Theodosius, the imperial enforcer of the Nicene Creed and
founder of the orthodox Christian state![8] As that connection suggests, there is
little if anything heretical about the theology of this apocalypse,[9] which consists
primarily of the apostle's visions of the dead, both the blessed and the damned.
The work was extremely popular in the medieval period in the West and was
one of the inspirations for Dante's *Inferno*.[1]

The *Gnostic Apocalypse of Paul*, on the other hand, was unknown to the
modern world until its discovery in 1945–1946 near the town of Nag Hammadi
in Upper Egypt. Presumably composed in Greek, it survives in a Coptic translation, preserved in a single lacunose papyrus codex. The preserved portion of
the work begins with Paul making a journey to Jerusalem. But before he
reaches the city, he encounters a small child, who is soon identified as the

3. Cf. Rev. 10:4, where John is not permitted to record part of what he has otherwise been commanded to write in a book (1:11).
4. The work was originally composed in Greek, with the first edition probably dating from the mid-
   third century and the second edition from the fourth. Unfortunately, the text in extant Greek
   manuscripts is essentially a synopsis of the original and thus is usually inferior to the Latin. Both
   the Greek and the Latin end in ch. 51, but the Coptic and the Syriac continue, though they
   provide completely different endings.
5. In the Coptic version, the apocalypse ends with Paul being brought to the Mount of Olives, where
   he tells the gathered apostles about his vision. They command Paul and his two disciples, Mark
   and Timothy, to record the revelation. Christ subsequently appears, tells Paul that he has revealed
   to him the entire mystery of his deity, and pronounces eternal blessings on those who give heed
   to the revelation's contents.
6. Sozomen, *Hist. eccl.* 7.19, cites an aged presbyter in Tarsus who says that the church there knows
   nothing about the alleged discovery of the book and that the work's claim is fraudulent.
7. In the Greek text, Theodosius sends the original to Jerusalem and retains a copy for himself. The
   Syriac makes no mention of Jerusalem.
8. For the anti-heretical tendencies of the author, see esp. chs. 41–42; for his ascetic leanings, see
   ch. 22.
9. Augustine, *Tract. Ev. Jo.* 98.8, lambastes the presumptuousness of the authors in claiming to
   reveal what was intended to be unutterable and dismisses the work as a forgery. But even he
   (*Enchir.* 112–113) later adopts a fairly tolerant attitude to the work's most controversial claim,
   viz. that the damned receive a periodic respite from pain in hell, and Prudentius (*Cath.* 5.125–
   136) unreservedly endorses the idea.
1. All or portions of chs. 22–24, 29, and 31–44 are printed below. For a translation of the entire
   work, see J. K. Elliott, *The Apocryphal New Testament* (Oxford: Clarendon, 1993), 620–44.

Holy Spirit. The latter identifies the place where they are conversing as the mountain of Jericho. At the Spirit's beckoning, Paul lifts up his eyes and sees the twelve apostles greeting him. At that point, the Spirit catches him up and carries him to the third heaven (2 Cor. 12:2). Whereas that is as high as Paul ascends in the apocryphal *Apocalypse of Paul*, Paul in the Gnostic apocalypse immediately passes through the third and enters the fourth heaven. Instead of narrating what Paul hears in the third heaven, it recounts Paul's journey from the fourth to the tenth heaven, where he greets his fellow spirits, i.e., that is, his fellow Gnostics. It is precisely this kind of innovative speculation that the Gnostics' proto-orthodox opponents such as Irenaeus, Tertullian, and Hippolytus as well as later heresiologists like Epiphanius sought to discredit,[2] and this ascent apocalypse may well have been written as early as the last half of the second century.[3] For Gnostic readers, however, the ascent of Paul not only demonstrates his superiority as an apostle but also provides a paradigm for their own return to the true divine world.

Finally, not included in this section is the *Prayer of the Apostle Paul*, another Gnostic work found in the Nag Hammadi library. Despite the work's title, the prayer is probably not a Pauline pseudepigraphon, but a petition that invokes Paul as an authority and refers to him as the "evangelist" (A.21). It also makes use of Philippians 2:9 (A.12–13) and the saying that Paul quotes in 1 Corinthians 2:9 (A.25–29; cf. *Gos. Thom.* 17). Although it may have originated in other circles, the prayer in its current form is a product of the school of Valentinus, a Gnostic who, it was said, had been taught by Theudas, a disciple of Paul.[4]

ANONYMOUS

[Correspondence of Paul and the Corinthians] (second century)†

. . . The Corinthians were in great distress about Paul because he was going to die before his time. For men, Simon and Cleobius,[1] had come to Corinth who said, 'There is no resurrection of the flesh but only of the spirit, and the body of man is not created by God, and God did not create

2. From patristic references to Gnostic treatments of Paul, it is certain that there were several Gnostic versions of Paul's ascent. Whether Irenaeus (ca. 185) is aware of such speculations is debated. Many scholars think that he is, whereas others claim that he is arguing preemptively, using Gnostic claims about Paul to prove that they conflict with 2 Cor. 12. In either case, there are certain intriguing similarities between his statements in *Haer.* 2.30.7 and the *Gnostic Apocalypse of Paul*. Tertullian (*Praescr.* 24.5–6) and Hippolytus (*Ref.* 5.8), on the other hand, are undoubtedly aware of Gnostic interpretations of Paul's ascent, yet these seem to have little in common with the Nag Hammadi apocalypse. The same is true for Epiphanius (*Pan.* 38.2.5), who refers to a pseudonymous work known as the *Ascension of Paul* that purports to give the unutterable words the apostle heard when he ascended to the third heaven. Given this description, it cannot be the same work as that found at Nag Hammadi, which says nothing about what happens to Paul in the third heaven. For the claim that Paul wrote enigmatically about his rapture, see the *Cologne Mani Codex* (62.5–6).
3. The Coptic codex in which the work is recorded dates from the mid-fourth century, so the original Greek composition could be as late as the early fourth century, but an earlier date is much more likely.
4. A translation, with a brief introduction, is available in Bentley Layton, *The Gnostic Scriptures* (New York: Doubleday, 1987), 303–5.
† From the *Acts of Paul*, tr. by J. K. Elliott, *The Apocryphal New Testament* (Oxford: Clarendon, 1993), 379–82. Reprinted by permission of Oxford University Press.
1. Simon Magus (Acts 8:9–24) is often depicted by orthodox writers as the founder of Christian Gnosticism. Cleobius is first mentioned by Hegesippus (2nd cent.) in an excerpt quoted by Eusebius, *Hist. eccl.* 4.22.5. The two heretics are depicted in *Apos. Con.* 6.8, 16 as false apostles who work together and forge "poisonous books in the name of Christ and his disciples."

the world and does not know the world, nor has Jesus Christ been crucified but only in appearance, and he was not born of Mary nor of the seed of David.' In a word, they taught many things in Corinth, deceiving many others and deceiving themselves. When therefore the Corinthians heard that Paul was at Philippi they sent a letter to Paul in Macedonia by the hand of Threptus and Eutychus, the deacons. The letter was as follows:

[A. Letter of the Corinthians to the Apostle Paul]

I

1. Stephanus and his fellow-presbyters Daphnus and Eubulus and Theophilus[2] and Zeno to Paul, the brother in the Lord—greeting! 2. Two individuals have come to Corinth, named Simon and Cleobius, who overthrow the faith of some[3] through pernicious words. 3. These you shall examine yourself. 4. For we never heard such things either from you or from the other apostles. 5. But we keep what we have received from you[4] and from the others. 6. Since the Lord has shown us mercy, while you are still in the flesh[5] we should hear this from you once more. 7. Come to us or write to us. 8. For we believe, as it has been revealed to Theonoe, that the Lord has delivered you from the hands of the godless.[6] 9. What they say and teach is as follows: 10. They assert that one must not appeal to the prophets (11) and that God is not almighty, (12) there is no resurrection of the body,[7] (13) man has not been made by God, (14) Christ has neither come in the flesh, nor was he born of Mary, (15) and the world is not the work of God but of angels. 16. Wherefore we beseech you, brother, be diligent to come to us[8] that the Corinthian church may remain without stumbling and the foolishness of these men be confounded.[9] Farewell in the Lord!

II

1. The deacons, Threptus and Eutychus,[1] took the letter to Philippi (2) and Paul received it, being himself in prison[2] because of Stratonike,[3] the wife of Apollophanes; and he became very sad, (3) and exclaimed saying, 'It would have been better had I died and were with the Lord[4] than to abide in the flesh and to hear such words so that sorrow comes upon sorrow,[5] (4) and to be in prison in the face of such great distress and behold such mischief where the wiles of Satan[6] are busy!' 5. And in great affliction Paul wrote the answer to the letter.[7]

2. Eubulus (2 Tim. 4:21) and Theophilus (Luke 1:3; Acts 1:1) are mentioned in the NT but not in connection with Corinth. A Daphnus is mentioned by Ignatius at *Smyrn.* 13:2. For Stephanus [-as] see 1 Cor. 1:16; 16:15–18.
3. Cf. 2 Tim. 2:18.
4. Cf. 1 Cor. 11:2.
5. Cf. Phil. 1:24.
6. The Greek text reads "the lawless one"; cf. 2 Thess. 2:8.
7. Cf. 1 Cor. 15:12.
8. Cf. 2 Tim. 4:9.
9. Cf. 2 Tim. 3:9.
1. Cf. Acts 20:7–12.
2. Cf. Acts 16:22–24.
3. Apparently because she had embraced Paul's proclamation of sexual continence, a major theme in the *Acts of Paul*. See Part IV for the *Acts of Paul and Thecla*, a part of the larger work.
4. Cf. Phil. 1:23.
5. Cf. Phil. 2:27.
6. Cf. Eph. 6:11.
7. Cf. 2 Cor. 2:4.

[B. Paul's Epistle to the Corinthians[8] = 3 Corinthians]

III

1. Paul, the prisoner of Jesus Christ,[9] to the brethren at Corinth—greeting! 2. Being in many afflictions, I marvel not[1] that the teachings of the evil one had such rapid success. 3. For my Lord Jesus Christ will quickly come, since he is rejected by those who falsify his teaching. 4. For I delivered to you first of all what I received[2] from the apostles before me[3] who were always with Jesus Christ,[4] (5) that our Lord Jesus Christ was born of Mary of the seed of David,[5] the Father having sent the spirit from heaven into her (6) that he might come into this world and save[6] all flesh by his own flesh and that he might raise us in the flesh from the dead as he has presented himself to us as our example. 7. And since man is created by his Father, (8) for this reason was he sought by him when he was lost, to become alive by adoption.[7] 9. For the almighty God, maker of heaven and earth, sent the prophets first to the Jews to deliver them from their sins, (10) for he wished to save the house of Israel; therefore he took from the spirit of Christ and poured it out upon the prophets who proclaimed the true worship of God for a long period of time. 11. For the wicked prince[8] who wished to be God himself[9] laid his hands on them and killed them[1] and bound all flesh of man to his pleasure. 12. But the almighty God, being just, and not wishing to repudiate his creation had mercy (13) and sent his Spirit[2] into Mary the Galilean,[3] (15) that the evil one might be conquered by the same flesh by which he held sway, and be convinced that he is not God. 16. For by his own body Jesus Christ saved all flesh, (17) presenting in his own body a temple of righteousness (18) through which we are saved. 19. They who follow them are not children of righteousness but of wrath,[4] who despise the wisdom of God and in their disbelief assert that heaven and earth and all that is in them are not a work of God. 20. They have the accursed belief of the serpent. 21. Turn away from them and keep aloof from their teaching.[5] 24. And those who say that there is no resurrection of the flesh shall have no resurrection, (25) for they do not believe him who had thus risen. 26. For they do not know, O Corinthians, about the sowing of wheat or some other grain that it is cast naked into the ground and having perished rises up again by the will of

---

8. The Greek ms. adds "concerning the flesh."
9. Cf. Phlm. 1; Eph. 3:1.
1. Contrast Gal. 1:6.
2. Cf. 1 Cor. 15:3.
3. Cf. Gal. 1:17.
4. Cf. Acts 1:21.
5. Cf. Rom. 1:3.
6. Cf. 1 Tim. 1:15.
7. Rom. 8:15, 23; 9:4; Gal. 4:5; Eph. 1:5.
8. Probably another name for Satan, the "evil one" of vv. 2 and 15.
9. Cf. 2 Thess. 2:4.
1. Instead of blaming Satan, Luke–Acts levels the charge of killing the prophets against the Jewish people (Luke 11:47–51; 13:34; Acts 7:52).
2. The Greek text adds "through fire."
3. Latin mss. add v. 14: "who believed with all her heart and conceived by the Holy Spirit that Jesus could come into the world."
4. Cf. Eph. 2:3.
5. Some mss. add vv. 22–23: "22. For you are not children of disobedience but of the beloved church. 23. Therefore is the time of resurrection preached to all." Cf. Eph. 2:2; 5:6.

God in a body and clothed.[6] 27. And he not only raises the body which is sown, but blesses it manifold. 28. And if one will not take the parable of the seeds (29) let him look at Jonah, the son of Amathios who, being unwilling to preach to the Ninevites, was swallowed up by the whale. 30. And after three days and three nights God heard the prayer of Jonah out of deepest hell,[7] and nothing was corrupted, not even a hair nor an eyelid. 31. How much more will he raise you up, who have believed in Christ Jesus, as he himself was raised up. 32. When a corpse was thrown on the bones of the prophet Elisha by one of the children of Israel the corpse rose from death;[8] how much more shall you rise up on that day with a whole body, after you have been thrown upon the body and bones and Spirit of the Lord.[9] 34. If, however, you receive anything else let no man trouble me, (35) for I have these bonds on me that I may win Christ, and I bear his marks that I may attain to the resurrection of the dead.[1] 36. And whoever accepts this rule which we have received by the blessed prophets and the holy gospel, shall receive a reward,[2] (37) but for whomsoever deviates from this rule fire shall be for him and for those who preceded him therein (38) since they are Godless men, a generation of vipers.[3] 39. Resist them in the power of the Lord. 40. Peace be with you.

ANONYMOUS

To the Laodiceans (second–fourth century)†

1. Paul, an apostle not of men and not through man, but through Jesus Christ,[1] to the brethren who are in Laodicea:[2] 2. Grace to you and peace from God the Father and the Lord Jesus Christ.[3]

　　3. I thank Christ[4] in all my prayer[5] that you continue in him and persevere in his works, in expectation of the promise at the day of judgement.[6]

---

6. Cf. 1 Cor. 15:37–38.
7. Cf. Matt. 12:40.
8. 2 Kgs. 13:21, a story that was later used to prove the power of relics (*Apos. Con.* 6.30).
9. Some mss. add v. 33: "Also Elijah the prophet: he raised up the widow's son from death: how much more shall the Lord Jesus raise you up from death at the sound of the trumpet, in the twinkling of an eye? For he has shown us an example in his own body." See 1 Kgs. 17:17–24; 1 Cor. 15:52.
1. Cf. Gal. 6:16–17; Phil. 3:8, 11; 1 Cor. 3:14.
2. Some mss. add: "and when he is raised from the dead shall obtain eternal life."
3. Cf. Matt. 3:7; 12:34; 23:33.
† Tr. by J. K. Elliott, *The Apocryphal New Testament* (Oxford: Clarendon, 1993), 546. Reprinted by permission of Oxford University Press.
1. Gal. 1:1.
2. Col. 2:1; 4:13, 15–16; cf. Rev. 1:11; 3:14–22. Laodicea, along with Colossae and Hierapolis, was one of the tri-cities of the Lycus River valley. An important commercial center, it was named after Laodice, the wife of the Seleucid ruler Antiochus II (261–246 BCE). Although severely damaged by an earthquake during the reign of Nero (ca. 60–61 CE), it soon recovered. That it did so out of its own resources, without any subvention by Rome (Tacitus, *Ann.* 14.27.1), was a mark of its affluence. The founder of the Laodicean church was probably Epaphras, who appears to have evangelized the entire Lycus valley (Col. 1:7–8; 4:12–13; Phlm. 23).
3. Gal. 1:3; Phil. 1:2.
4. Cf. Phil. 1:3, though all Pauline thanksgivings are offered to God, not Christ.
5. Phil. 1:4.
6. Cf. 2 Pet. 2:9; 3:7.

4. And may you not be deceived[7] by the vain talk[8] of some people who tell tales[9] that they may lead you away from the truth of the gospel[1] which is proclaimed by me.[2] 5. And now may God grant that those who come from me[3] for the furtherance of the truth of the gospel[4] (. . .)[5] may be able to serve and to do good works for the well-being of eternal life.

6. And now my bonds are manifest,[6] which I suffer in Christ, on account of which I am glad and rejoice.[7] 7. This to me leads to eternal salvation, which itself is brought about through your prayers and by the help of the Holy Spirit,[8] whether it be through life or through death.[9] 8. For my life is in Christ and to die is joy.[1]

9. And his mercy will work in you, that you may have the same love and be of one mind.[2] 10. Therefore, beloved, as you have heard in my presence, so hold fast and work in the fear of God, and eternal life will be yours.[3] 11. For it is God who works in you.[4] 12. And do without hesitation what you do.[5] 13. And for the rest, beloved, rejoice in Christ[6] and beware of those who are out for sordid gain.[7] 14. May all your requests be manifest before God,[8] and be steadfast[9] in the mind of Christ.[1] 15. And do what is pure, true, proper, just and lovely.[2] 16. And what you have heard and received, hold in your heart, and peace will be with you.[3]

17. Salute all the brethren with the holy kiss.[4] 18. The saints salute you.[5] 19. The grace of the Lord Jesus Christ be with your spirit.[6] 20. And see that (this epistle) is read to the Colossians[7] and that of the Colossians to you.[8]

---

7. Cf. Col. 2:4.
8. 1 Tim. 1:6; 2 Pet. 2:18.
9. 2 Tim. 4:4.
1. Gal. 2:5, 14; Col. 1:5.
2. Gal. 1:11.
3. Phil. 1:12 ("what has happened to me") appears to have been changed here to "those who come from me," perhaps recalling a similar expression in Gal. 2:12 of people who "come from James."
4. Phil. 1:12.
5. The text, likely written in Greek but preserved only in Latin, is corrupt at this point.
6. Phil. 1:13.
7. Matt. 5:12; cf. Phil. 1:18.
8. Phil. 1:19.
9. Phil. 1:20.
1. Cf. Phil. 1:21.
2. Phil. 2:2.
3. Cf. Phil. 2:12.
4. Phil. 2:13.
5. Cf. Phil. 2:14; Col. 3:17, 23.
6. Cf. Phil. 3:1.
7. Cf. 1 Tim. 3:8; 6:10; Tit. 1:7; Rev. 3:17.
8. Phil. 4:6.
9. 1 Cor. 15:58.
1. 1 Cor. 2:16; Phil. 2:5.
2. Phil. 4:8.
3. Phil. 4:9.
4. V. 17 is absent from some mss. and is likely an addition drawn from 1 Thess. 5:26; cf. 1 Cor. 16:20.
5. Phil. 4:22.
6. Phil. 4:23; Gal. 6:18.
7. Some mss. omit "to the Colossians" as well as "this epistle."
8. Cf. Col. 4:16.

ANONYMOUS

The Correspondence of Paul and Seneca
(fourth century)†

1. Seneca to Paul greeting

I believe that you have been informed, Paul, of the discussion which my friend Lucilius[1] and I held yesterday concerning the apocrypha[2] and other matters: for some of the followers of your teachings were with me. We had retired to the gardens of Sallust,[3] and it was our good fortune that these disciples whom I have mentioned saw us there and joined us, although they were on their way elsewhere. You may be sure that we wished that you, too, had been present,[4] and I also want you to know this:[5] when we had read your book, that is to say one of the many letters of admirable exhortation to an upright life which you have sent to some city or to the capital of a province, we were completely refreshed. These thoughts, I believe, were expressed not by you, but through you;[6] though sometimes they were expressed both by you and through you; for they are so lofty and so brilliant with noble sentiments that in my opinion generations of men could hardly be enough to become established and perfected in them. I wish you good health, brother.

2. To Annaeus Seneca Paul greeting

I was extremely glad to receive your letter yesterday, and I could have answered it immediately if I had had with me the young man whom I intended to send to you. You know when and by whom and at what time and to whom a thing should be given or entrusted. Therefore I ask you not to think yourself neglected, while I pay attention to the qualities of the messenger. But you write somewhere that you are pleased with my letter, and I count myself fortunate in the approval of a man who is so great. For you, a critic, a philosopher, the teacher of so great a ruler,[7] nay even of everyone, would not say this unless you speak the truth. I hope that you may long be in good health.

3. Seneca to Paul greeting

I have arranged some of my works and set them in order according to their proper divisions. I also intend to read them to Caesar. If only fate is kind

† Tr. by J. K. Elliott, *The Apocryphal New Testament* (Oxford: Clarendon, 1993), 549–53. Reprinted by permission of Oxford University Press.
1. The recipient of Seneca's *Moral Epistles*, to whom he also dedicated his *On Providence* and *Causes of Natural Phenomena*.
2. Or, "hidden things."
3. A Roman historian (ca. 86–35 BCE) who created a large pleasure garden that included parts of the Pincio and Quirinal hills—two of the famous Seven Hills of Rome (Rev. 17:9)—and of the valley that lay between them (in what is today the Via Veneto section). The gardens passed into imperial hands during the Julio-Claudian period, and subsequent emperors enlarged and embellished the gardens, making them among Rome's most beautiful and important.
4. Cf. Gal. 4:20.
5. Cf. Phil. 1:12; Col. 2:1.
6. That is, the thoughts are not Paul's but those of the Holy Spirit (*Ep.* 7) expressed through the apostle.
7. Seneca was Nero's tutor from 49 to his pupil's accession to the throne in 54, thereafter serving as the emperor's adviser until his retirement in 62.

enough to cause him to show renewed interest, perhaps you will be there also; if not, I will at some other time set a day on which we may examine this work together. I could not show him this writing without first conferring with you, if only it were possible to do so without risk, so that you may know that you are not being forgotten. Farewell, dearest Paul.

4. To Annaeus Seneca Paul greeting

Whenever I hear your letters, I think that you are present and I imagine nothing else than that you are continually with us.[8] As soon, therefore, as you begin to come, we shall see each other face to face.[9] I hope that you are in good health.

5. Seneca to Paul greeting

We are distressed at your exceedingly long retirement. What is the matter? What makes you stay away? If it is the displeasure of our empress[1] because you have withdrawn from your old rite and creed and are a convert, then you will be given an opportunity of asking her to believe that you acted reasonably, not lightly.[2] A kind farewell.

6. To Seneca and Lucilius Paul greeting

I may not speak with pen and ink[3] concerning what you have written to me, for the one marks a thing down and defines it, while the other makes it all too clear—especially since I am certain that there are some among your number, with you and in your midst, who are able to understand me.[4] We must show respect to everyone, the more so as they are apt to find cause for offence.[5] If we are patient with them we shall overcome them in every way and on every side—that is, if only they are the kind of people who can be sorry for what they have done.[6] A kind farewell.

7. Annaeus Seneca to Paul and Theophilus[7] greeting

I admit that I enjoyed reading your letters to the Galatians, to the Corinthians, and to the Achaeans,[8] and may our relations be like that religious awe which you manifest in these letters. For the holy spirit that is in you and high above you expresses with lofty speech thoughts worthy of rever-

8. One of many epistolary clichés in the correspondence, this statement reflects the commonplace that letters, as a substitute for personal presence, provide a means for separated friends to be together and converse. Cf. Seneca, *Ep.* 75.1–2.
9. Cf. 2 John 12; 3 John 14.
1. Poppaea Sabina, Nero's former mistress whom he married in 62 and one of the main characters in Ps.-Seneca's *Octavia*. She died in 65, a victim of domestic violence (Tacitus, *Ann.* 16.6; Suetonius, *Nero* 35.2). Josephus depicts her as having Jewish sympathies (*Life* 16; *Ant.* 20.195), though her success in having Gessius Florus appointed procurator of Judea in 64 backfired when his outrages provoked the Jewish-Roman war of 66–70 (*Ant.* 20.252–258; *J.W.* 2.285–296). The author may be attempting here to link the tradition of Nero persecuting Christians as "a new and wicked superstition" (Suetonius, *Nero* 16.2) to his wife's resentment of the apostle's "apostasy" from Judaism.
2. Cf. 2 Cor. 1:17.
3. Cf. 2 John 12; 3 John 13.
4. Cf. 2 Cor. 1:13.
5. Cf. 2 Cor. 6:4.
6. Cf. Acts 17:30; 26:20.
7. Luke 1:3; Acts 1:1.
8. 2 Corinthians; cf. 2 Cor. 1:1.

ence. Therefore since you have such excellent matters to propose I wish that refinement of language might not be lacking to the majesty of your theme. And in order that I may not keep anything secret from you,[9] brother, and burden my conscience, I confess that Augustus[1] was affected by your sentiments. When your treatise on the power that is in you[2] was read to him, this was his reply: he was amazed that one whose education had not been normal could have such ideas. I answered him that the gods are accustomed to speak through the mouths of the innocent and not through those who pride themselves on their learning.[3] When I gave him the example of Vatienus, a farmer to whom appeared in the territory of Reate two men who later were found to be Castor and Pollux,[4] he seemed thoroughly enlightened. Farewell.

8. To Seneca Paul greeting

Even though I am not unaware that our Caesar is now fond of wonders, although he may sometimes lapse, still he allows himself not to be rebuked, but to be informed. I think that it was a very serious mistake on your part to wish to bring to his notice what is against his practice and training. Inasmuch as he worships the gods of the heathen, I do not see what you had in mind wishing him to know this, unless I am to think that you are doing this from your great love for me. I beg you not to do this in the future. You must also be careful not to offend our empress while showing affection for me. Her displeasure, to be sure, cannot harm us if it lasts, nor can we be helped if it never happens. As a queen she will not be insulted; as a woman she will be angry. A kind farewell.

9. Seneca to Paul greeting

I know that it was not so much for your own sake that you were disturbed when I wrote to you that I had read my letters to Caesar as by the nature of things, which withholds the minds of men from all upright pursuits and practices,—so that I am not astonished today, particularly because I have learned this well from many clear proofs. Therefore let us begin anew, and if in the past I have been negligent in any way, you will grant pardon. I have sent you a book on elegance of expression.[5] Farewell, dearest Paul.

9. The ethics of ancient friendship required full disclosure of secrets to a friend; cf. Seneca, *Ep.* 3.2–3.
1. Nero, whose full official name was Nero Claudius Caesar Augustus Germanicus.
2. If the translation is correct, a probable reference to 2 Corinthians (4:7; 6:7; 10:4; 12:9; 13:4; cf. 1 Cor. 2:4). Less likely is the view that this is a reference to an exordium by Seneca on Paul's virtue.
3. Cf. 1 Cor. 1:18–31; Matt. 11:25; Luke 10:21; Plato, *Ion* 534d–e.
4. The divine twins known as the Dioscuri ("sons of Zeus"), who are mentioned in Acts 28:11. From early times they were regarded as savior deities because of their eagerness to help humans in times of crisis, and the Romans in 484 BCE erected a temple in their honor in the Forum to commemorate their intervention in the battle of Lake Regillus. The epiphany mentioned here occurred during the Third Macedonian War (171–167 BCE) and was characteristic of their saving interventions. Castor and Pollux appeared to Vatienus and announced that Perseus, the Macedonian king, had been taken prisoner that very day (in 168). When Vatienus brought the news to the Senate, his report was dismissed and he was thrown in jail. Later, when Perseus' capture was confirmed, Vatienus was vindicated and rewarded (Cicero, *Nat. d.* 2.2.6; 3.5.11–13; Valerius Maximus, *Mem.* 1.8.1; Lactantius, *Inst.* 2.7; cf. Plutarch, *Aem.* 24.3).
5. The forger of this letter may be confusing Seneca the Younger with his father, Seneca the Elder, who wrote treatises on rhetoric. In any case, there is no work *On Abundance of Words* (*De verborum copia*) in the extant works of either Seneca, though there is one with that title among the apocrypha of the philosopher. Quintilian, *Inst.* 12.10.11, speaks of abundance (*copia*) as Seneca's distinctive stylistic quality.

10. To Seneca Paul greeting

Whenever I write to you and place my name after yours, I commit a serious fault and one incompatible with my status.[6] For[7] I ought, as I have often claimed, to be all things to all men[8] and to observe towards you what the Roman law has granted for the honour of the senate[9]—namely, to choose the last place when I have finished my letter, lest I desire to perform in an inadequate and disgraceful manner what is my own will. Farewell, most devoted of teachers. Written 27 June in the consulship of Nero III and Messala [= 58 CE].

11. Seneca to Paul greeting

Greetings, my dearly beloved Paul. Do you think I am not saddened and grieved because you innocent people are repeatedly punished? Or because the whole populace believes you so implacable and so liable to guilt, thinking that every misfortune in the city is due to you?[1] But let us endure it calmly and take advantage of whatever opportunity fortune allots to us, until invincible happiness gives us release from our troubles. Earlier ages endured the Macedonian, the son of Philip,[2] the Cyruses,[3] Darius,[4] Dionysius;[5] our own age endured Gaius Caesar;[6] all of them were free to do whatever they pleased. The source of the frequent fires which the city of Rome suffers is plain. But if lowly people had been allowed to tell the reason, and if it were permitted to speak safely in these times of ill-fortune, everyone would now understand everything. Christians and Jews, charged with responsibility for the fire—alas!—are being put to death, as is usually the case.[7] That ruffian, whoever he is, whose pleasure is murdering and

---

6. It was customary for writers of letters to give their names first, followed by that of the recipient. Seneca does this in all eight of his letters to Paul (*Seneca Paulo salutem*, "Seneca to Paul, greeting") but Paul, following a practice common in Christian letters from the second century on, puts his name in the second position (*Senecae Paulus salutem*, "To Seneca, Paul, greeting"). Although this practice was regarded as a mark of Christian humility (cf. Mark 9:35), Paul here acknowledges that, given his status in the church, it is a mistake to do so. Yet he proceeds to defend his practice by citing his principle of adaptability and his deference for the Roman Senate. Seneca responds in *Ep.* 12 by encouraging Paul to put his name in the first position, and in Paul's final letter (*Ep.* 14), he does so (*Paulus Senecae salutem*, "Paul to Seneca, greeting").
7. The following sentence gives the justification for Paul's practice of placing his name last.
8. 1 Cor. 9:22.
9. Seneca was a senior senator, having served as suffect consul for six months in 55 or 56 CE. Placing the names of senators in the first position in letters was probably a matter of custom rather than law.
1. Cf. Tertullian's complaint (*Apol.* 40) that animosity and violence against Christians were rooted in the belief that they were public enemies and the cause of every calamity: "If the Tiber rises as high as the city walls, . . . if the sky gives no rain, if there is an earthquake, if there is a famine, if there is a plague, immediately it is shouted out, ' 'The Christians to the lion!' ' " To which the apologist gave the sarcastic response, "So many people to a single lion?"
2. Alexander the Great (d. 323 BCE), son of Philip of Macedon.
3. Cyrus the Great, who conquered the Babylonians in 539 BCE, and, most likely, Cyrus the Younger, whose financial support enabled Sparta to defeat Athens in the Peloponnesian War and who led a band of Greek mercenaries and Asiatic troops in a failed attempt (401 BCE) to supplant Artaxerxes II as ruler of Persia (see Xenophon's *Anabasis* for the story of the Greek mercenaries). If, however, the author is drawing on the list of tyrants in Seneca, *Ben.* 7.3.1, he may be thinking of Cambyses, the son and successor of Cyrus the Great, rather than Cyrus the Younger.
4. Darius I, who immortalized his achievements on the rock of Bisitun in Media but whose army was defeated by the Greeks at the Battle of Marathon in 490 BCE.
5. The ruler of Sicily (d. 367 BCE) who was often portrayed in antiquity as the archetypal ruthless tyrant.
6. The emperor Caligula (37–41 CE).
7. To quash rumors that he had instigated the great fire of 64 (Suetonius, *Nero* 38; Ps.-Seneca, *Oct.* 831) and divert blame from himself, Nero made scapegoats of the Christians, subjecting many to torture and execution (Tacitus, *Ann.* 15.44). There is no reliable evidence that Jews were also

whose refuge is lying, is destined for his time of reckoning, and just as the best is sacrificed as one life for many,[8] so he shall be sacrificed for all and burned by fire. One hundred and thirty-two private houses and four thousand apartment-houses burned in six days; the seventh day gave respite.[9] I hope that you are in good health, brother. Written 28 March[1] in the consulship of Frugi and Bassus [= 64 CE].

12. Seneca to Paul greeting

Greetings, my dearly beloved Paul. If such a great man as you and one who is beloved of God is to be, I do not say joined, but intimately associated in all respects with me and my name, then your Seneca will be wholly satisfied. Since, therefore, you are the peak and crest of all the most lofty mountains, do you not, then, wish me to rejoice if I am so close to you as to be considered a second self[2] of yours? Therefore do not think that you are unworthy of having your name in first place in your letters, or else you may seem to be tempting me rather than praising me, especially since you know that you are a Roman citizen.[3] For I wish that my position were yours, and that yours were as mine.[4] Farewell, my dearly beloved Paul. Written 23 March in the consulship of Apronianus and Capito [= 59 CE].

13. Seneca to Paul greeting

Many writings composed by you are throughout allegorical and enigmatic,[5] and for that reason you must adorn that powerful gift of truth and talent which has been bestowed upon you not so much with embellishment of words as with a certain amount of refinement. And do not fear, as I remember I have frequently said, that many who affect such things spoil the thoughts and emasculate the force of their subject-matter.[6] I do wish you would obey me and comply with the pure Latin style,[7] giving a good appearance to your noble utterances, in order that the granting of this excellent gift may be worthily performed by you. A kind farewell. Written 6 July in the consulship of Lurco and Sabinus [= 58 CE].

---

charged with the conflagration, though the insinuation that Christians set fire to the city because they were misanthropic (*ibid.*) was a charge frequently leveled against Jews.

8. Cf. Vergil, *Aen.* 5.815: "one life shall be given for many."

9. According to other accounts, the fire, which probably burned for nine days, damaged ten of Rome's fourteen regions, reducing three of them to rubble. Some think that the forger is drawing his information from an otherwise unknown source.

1. Tacitus, *Ann.* 15.41, places the fire nearly four months later, on July 19.

2. A friend was commonly regarded as a second self.

3. Acts 16:37–38; 22:25–29; 23:27.

4. Cf. Gal. 4:12.

5. Ancient epistolary theory recognized both allegorical and enigmatic types of letters, and from the very beginning, readers of Paul's letters found parts of them to be cryptic. Some lamented the resulting difficulty of understanding his letters, noting the potential for fallacious interpretations (2 Pet. 3:16; cf. 1 Cor. 5:9–11). Others defended this style (often citing 1 Cor. 2:6–16), arguing that "the prophetic style is everywhere sprinkled with figures and riddles" and that the same is true of the apostolic epistles and other Scriptures (Origen, *Princ.* 4.2; see also *Cels.* 3.45; 7.10; *Philoc.* 9.3). Of Paul's letters, Romans was often viewed as the hardest to understand (Origen, *Comm. Rom.* preface 1).

6. Cf. Seneca, *Ep.* 115.1–2, where he tells Lucilius to give less attention to style and more to substance.

7. Ironically, Quintilian, *Inst.* 10.1.125–131, sharply criticizes Seneca's own style, arguing that his *sententiae* are worth reading on moral grounds but that his style is decadent.

14. Paul to Seneca greeting

Things have been revealed to you in your reflections which the Godhead
has granted to few. Therefore I am certain that I am sowing a rich seed in
a fertile field, not a corruptible matter, but the abiding word of God,[8]
derived from him who is ever-increasing and ever-abiding. The determination which your good sense has attained must never fail—namely, to
avoid the outward manifestations of the heathens and the Israelites. You
must make yourself a new herald of Jesus Christ by displaying with the
praises of rhetoric that blameless wisdom which you have almost achieved
and which you will present to the temporal king and to the members of
his household and to his trusted friends, whom you will find it difficult or
nearly impossible to persuade, since many of them are not at all influenced
by your presentations. Once the word of God has inspired the blessing of
life within them it will create a new man, without corruption,[9] an abiding
being,[1] hastening thence to God. Farewell, Seneca, most dear to us. Written 1 August in the consulship of Lurco and Sabinus [= 58 CE].

ANONYMOUS

The Apocalypse of Paul (third century?)†

[PAUL'S VISION OF THE RIGHTEOUS DEAD][1]

Chapters 22–24 and 29

22. And I looked around upon that land,[2] and I saw a river flowing with
milk and honey,[3] and there were trees planted by the bank of that river, full
of fruit; moreover, each single tree bore twelve fruits in the year, having
various and diverse fruits; and I saw the created things which are in that
place and all the work of God, and I saw there palms of twenty cubits,[4] but
others of ten cubits; and that land was seven times brighter than silver. And
there were trees full of fruits from the roots to the highest branches, of ten
thousand fruits of palms upon ten thousand fruits. The grape-vines had ten
thousand plants. Moreover in the single vines there were ten thousand
thousand bunches and in each of these a thousand single grapes; moreover

8. Cf. 1 Pet. 1:23, 25.
9. The same phrase (*sine corruptela*) occurs in 1 Cor. 15:42 OL.
1. Or, "an animal ever in motion" (*perpetuum animal*). In Platonic thought, the immortality of the soul (*anima*) is proved by its being perpetually in motion (Plato, *Phaedr.* 245c).
† Tr. by J. K. Elliott, *The Apocryphal New Testament* (Oxford: Clarendon, 1993), 629–39. Reprinted by permission of Oxford University Press.
1. Whereas earlier cosmic tours contain glimpses of the righteous dead (e.g., *Apoc. Zeph.* 9, 11; *Apoc. Pet.* 13–14), the *Apocalypse of Paul* is the first extant work to develop this brief view into a full vision of the blessed.
2. The cosmic geography reflected in this work is not clear, consistent, or complete, so that tensions in the narrative are not always resolved. For example, whereas in ch. 14 the souls of the righteous enter Paradise, which is located in the third heaven, in ch. 21 they are sent after death to the "promised land," which is situated just outside of heaven, apparently on or above the great river that encircles the earth. Although this land already exists, it will appear only when the current earth (the "first earth" of Rev. 21:1) is dissolved (ch. 21).
3. The imagery here continues the biblical description of the holy land as "flowing with milk and honey" (Exod. 3:8; Deut. 6:3; etc.).
4. The cubit was the standard linear measure used in the ANE, ca. 17.5 to 20 inches.

these single trees bore a thousand fruits.[5] And I said to the angel,[6] 'Why does each tree bear a thousand fruits?' The angel answered and said to me, 'Because the Lord God gives an abounding profusion of gifts to the worthy and because they of their own will afflicted themselves when they were placed in the world doing all things on account of his holy name.' And again I said to the angel, 'Sir, are these the only promises which the Most Holy God makes?' And he answered and said to me, 'No! There are seven times greater than these. But I say to you that when the just go out of the body they shall see the promises and the good things which God has prepared for them. Till then, they shall sigh and lament, saying, "Have we uttered any word from our mouth to grieve our neighbor even on one day?" I asked and said again, 'Are these alone the promises of God?' And the angel answered and said to me, 'These whom you now see are the souls of the married and those who kept the chastity of their nuptials, controlling themselves. But to the virgins and those who hunger and thirst after righteousness[7] and those who afflicted themselves for the sake of the name of God, God will give seven times greater than these,[8] which I shall now show you.'

And then he took me up from that place where I saw these things and behold, a river,[9] and its waters were much whiter than milk,[1] and I said to the angel, 'What is this?' And he said to me, 'This is the Acherusian Lake[2] where is the City of Christ, but not every man is permitted to enter that city; for this is the journey which leads to God, and if anyone is a fornicator and impious, and is converted and shall repent and bear fruits worthy of repentance, at first when he has gone out of the body, he is brought and worships God, and thence by command of the Lord he is delivered to the angel Michael[3] and he baptizes him in the Acherusian Lake—then he leads him into the City of Christ alongside those who have never sinned.[4] But I marvelled and blessed the Lord God for all the things which I saw.

23. And the angel answered and said to me, 'Follow me, and I will lead you into the City of Christ.' And he was standing on the Acherusian Lake and he put me into a golden ship[5] and about three thousand angels were singing a hymn before me till I arrived at the City of Christ. Those who inhabited the City of Christ greatly rejoiced over me as I went to them,

5. Abundance of food as a traditional apocalyptic motif signifying divine pleasure (1 Enoch 10:19; 2 Baruch 29.5; contrast Isa. 5:10) is attributed to Jesus in Irenaeus, Haer. 5.33.3–4.
6. Paul's tour guide and interpreter; cf. Rev. 1:1; 17:1–18; 21:9–22:5; 22:6–11.
7. Matt. 5:6.
8. Cf. ch. 40 for punishments "seven times greater than these."
9. Acheron, a river of Hades. The following draws heavily on the Greek geography of the underworld, esp. as imagined by Plato in the Phaedo.
1. The description of Acheron's waters as white is based on the etiological myth that derives the river's name from the white poplar tree that Heracles found growing on its banks. The comparison with milk (gala in Greek) may be intended to suggest the heavenly realms of the galaxy (cf. "the Milky Way").
2. The body of water separating the area inhabited by the recently deceased from the City of Christ, which here replaces the Elysian fields as the abode of the blessed.
3. The patron angel of Israel (Dan. 10:13, 21; 12:1), he is mentioned in several non-biblical texts, including the DSS. The NT depicts him as contending with the devil for the body of Moses (Jude 9) and warring against the dragon (Rev. 12:7). In the Apocalypse of Paul he is the angel of the covenant, presenting the souls of the righteous to God and leading them into Paradise (ch. 14) and/or the City of Christ (22, 25–27), baptizing sinners (22), and interceding for the human race (chap. 43, 46).
4. Salvation for some sinners is made possible by post-mortem repentance and baptism in Lake Acherusian. In the Greek Life of Adam and Eve 37, Adam is depicted as one of these; he is washed three times by a seraph in the lake and taken by Michael into Paradise. One of the Pauline apocalypse's likely sources, the Apocalypse of Peter, also depicts a baptism in the lake, which is given to those for whom the righteous make intercession (cf. Apoc. Paul 24).
5. An adaptation of the Greek tradition in which Hermes leads the souls of the dead to Charon, who ferries them in his skiff down the Acheron and across the lake.

and I entered and saw the City of Christ,[6] and it was all of gold, and twelve walls encircled it, and twelve interior towers, and there was a stade[7] between each of the encircling walls. And I said to the angel, 'Sir, how much is a stadium?' The angel answered and said to me, 'As much as there is between the Lord God and the men who are on the earth, for the City of Christ alone is great.' And there were twelve gates in the circuit of the city, of great beauty, and four rivers[8] which encircled it. There was a river of honey, and a river of milk, and a river of wine, and a river of oil. And I said to the angel, 'What are these rivers surrounding that city?' And he said to me, 'These are the four rivers which flow abundantly for those who are in this land of promise; the names are these: the river of honey is called Pison, and the river of milk Euphrates, and the river of oil Gion, and the river of wine Tigris. When they were in the world they did not use their power over these things, but they hungered and afflicted themselves for the sake of the Lord God, so that when they enter this city the Lord will assign them these things above all measure.'

24. When I entered the gate I saw trees great and very high before the doors of the city, having no fruit but leaves only, and I saw a few men scattered in the midst of the trees, and they lamented greatly when they saw anyone enter the city. And those trees were sorry for them and humbled themselves and bowed down and again erected themselves. And I saw it and wept with them, and I asked the angel and said, 'Sir, who are these who are not admitted to enter into the City of Christ?' And he said to me, 'These are they who zealously abstained day and night in fasts, but they had a proud heart above other men, glorifying and praising themselves and doing nothing for their neighbours. They gave some people friendly greeting, but to others they did not even say "Hail!" And, indeed, they showed hospitality only to those whom they wished, and if they did anything whatever for their neighbour they were immoderately puffed up.' And I said, 'What then, sir? Did their pride prevent them from entering into the City of Christ?' And the angel answered and said to me, 'Pride is the root of all evils.[9] Are they better than the Son of God who came to the Jews with much humility?' And I asked him and said, 'Why is it that the trees humble themselves and erect themselves again?' And the angel answered and said to me, 'The whole time which these men passed on earth, they zealously served God, but on account of the shame and reproaches of men for a time they blushed and humbled themselves, but they were not saddened, nor did they repent that they should desist from the pride which was in them. This is why the trees humble themselves, and again are raised up.' And I asked and said, 'For what reason were they admitted to the doors of the city?' The angel answered and said to me, 'Because of the great goodness of God, and because this is the entrance of his saints entering this

---

6. For what follows, cf. John's vision of the new Jerusalem in Rev. 21:9–22:5.

7. The stade or stadium was equal to six hundred Greek or Roman feet or one-eighth of a Roman mile (1618.5 yards), thus a little more than two hundred yards. But the angel's response makes clear that human measurements are inadequate to describe Christ's City.

8. The four branches of the river said to flow out of Eden (Gen. 2:10–14) encircle the City of Christ. The land of Pison (Pishon) is the dwelling place of the prophets (ch. 25), both major (Isaiah, Jeremiah, Ezekiel) and minor (Amos, Micah, Zechariah). The land around the Euphrates is the abode of the Bethlehem infants massacred by Herod (ch. 26; cf. Matt. 2:16–18). Abraham, Isaac, Jacob, Lot, Job, and others who have given hospitality to strangers reside in the land of Tigris (ch. 27), and Gion (Gihon) is the habitation of those who devoted themselves wholly to God (ch. 28).

9. Contrast 1 Tim. 6:10.

city: for this reason they are left in this place, but when Christ the King Eternal enters with his saints, all the righteous may pray for them, and then they may enter into the city along with them; yet none of them is able to have the same confidence as those who humbled themselves, serving the Lord God all their lives.'

* * *

29. And he carried me into the midst of the city near the twelve walls. But there was in this place a higher wall, and I asked and said, 'Is there in the City of Christ a wall which exceeds this place in honour?' And the angel answered and said to me, 'There is a second better than the first, and similarly a third better than the second, as each exceeds the other up to the twelfth wall.' And I said, 'Tell me, sir, why one exceeds another in glory.' And the angel answered and said to me, 'All who have in themselves even a little slander or zeal or pride, something of his glory would be made void even if they were in the City of Christ: look behind you.'

And turning round I saw golden thrones placed in each gate, and on them men having golden diadems and gems; and I looked and I saw inside between the twelve men thrones placed in another rank which appeared to be of greater glory, so that no one is able to recount their praise. And I asked the angel and said, 'My lord, who is on the throne?' And the angel answered and said to me, 'Those thrones belong to those who had goodness and understanding of heart, yet made themselves fools for the sake of the Lord God, as they knew neither Scripture nor psalms, but mindful of one chapter of the commands of God, and hearing what it contained, they acted with much diligence and had a true zeal before the Lord God, and the admiration of them will seize all the saints in the presence of the Lord God, for talking with one another they say, "Wait and see how these unlearned men who know nothing more have merited so great and beautiful a garment and so great glory on account of their innocence." '

And I saw in the midst of this city a great altar, very high, and there was someone standing near the altar whose countenance shone as the sun, and he held in his hands a psaltery and harp, and he sang saying, 'Alleluia!' And his voice filled the whole city; at the same time, when all they who were on the towers and gates heard him, they responded, 'Alleluia!' so that the foundations of the city were shaken; and I asked the angel and said, 'Sir, who is this of so great power?' And the angel said to me, 'This is David; this is the city of Jerusalem,[1] for when Christ the King of Eternity shall come with the assurance of his kingdom, he again shall go before him that he may sing psalms, and all the righteous at the same time shall sing responding "Alleluia!" ' And I said, 'Sir, how did David alone above the other saints make a beginning of psalm-singing?' And the angel answered and said to me, 'Because Christ the Son of God sits at the right hand of his Father, and this David sings psalms before him in the seventh heaven, and as it is done in the heavens so also below, because a sacrifice may not be offered to God without David, but it is necessary that David should sing psalms in the hour of the oblation of the body and blood of Christ: as it is performed in heaven, so also on earth.'[2]

1. Cf. Rev. 21:2.
2. One of the liturgical controversies of the fourth century involved a debate as to whether the Psalms of David were to be used at the Eucharist. By depicting David as singing psalms in heaven when

* * *

[PAUL'S VISION OF THE DAMNED][3]

Chapters 31–41, 42b–44

31. When he had ceased speaking to me, he led me outside the city through the midst of the trees and far from the places of the land of the good, and put me across the river of milk and honey; and after that he led me over the ocean[4] which supports the foundations of heaven.

The angel answered and said to me, 'Do you understand why you go hence?' And I said, 'Yes, sir.' And he said to me, 'Come and follow me, and I will show you the souls of the godless and sinners, that you may know what manner of place it is.' And I went with the angel, and he carried me towards the setting of the sun, and I saw the beginning of heaven founded on a great river of water, and I asked, 'What is this river of water?' And he said to me, 'This is the ocean which surrounds all the earth.' And when I was at the outer limit of the ocean I looked, and there was no light in that place, but darkness and sorrow and sadness; and I sighed.

And I saw there a river boiling with fire, and in it a multitude of men and women immersed up to the knees, and other men up to the navel, others even up to the lips, others up to the hair. And I asked the angel and said, 'Sir, who are those in the fiery river?' And the angel answered and said to me, 'They are neither hot nor cold,[5] because they were found neither in the number of the just nor in the number of the godless. For those spent the time of their life on earth passing some days in prayer, but others in sins and fornications, until their death.' And I asked him and said, 'Who are these, sir, immersed up to their knees in fire?' He answered and said to me, 'These are they who when they have gone out of church occupy themselves with idle disputes. Those who are immersed up to the navel are those who, when they have taken the body and blood of Christ, go and fornicate and do not cease from their sins till they die. Those who are immersed up to the lips are those who slander each other when they assemble in the church of God; those up to the eyebrows are those who nod to each other and plot spite against their neighbour.'

32. And I saw to the north a place of various and diverse punishments full of men and women, and a river of fire ran down into it. I observed and I saw very deep pits and in them several souls together, and the depth of that place was about three thousand cubits,[6] and I saw them groaning and weeping and saying, 'Have pity on us, O Lord!', and no one had pity on

---

the Eucharist is celebrated on earth, the author is attempting to use Paul's vision to settle the issue.

3. Although a future resurrection is expected when souls will once again inhabit the bodies out of which they have departed (chs. 14–15), Paul's tour of hell reflects the belief that, following a preliminary judgment, the punishment of wicked humans commences immediately after death (cf. Luke 16:19–31), not after a final eschatological judgment; the latter was the earlier apocalyptic idea (Matt. 25:31–46; 2 Thess. 1:7–10; *Apoc. Pet.* 1–6; etc.), though it sometimes included the belief that the wicked in the intermediate state suffered in anticipation of future pain (4 Ezra 7: 75–87). The tour also reflects the belief in specific penalties for specific sins rather than a generic form of torment in which all share. Both ideas likely reflect the influence of Greek and Roman accounts of descents to Hades on Jewish and Christian apocalyptic.

4. Oceanus, the "Great Outer Sea" that in ancient geography surrounds and waters the entire earth (ch. 21).

5. Cf. Rev. 3:15–16.

6. Another Latin ms. reads "30,000 stadia," a much greater distance.

them. And I asked the angel and said, 'Who are these, sir?' And the angel answered and said to me, 'These are they who did not hope in the Lord, that they would be able to have him as their helper.' And I asked and said, 'Sir, if these souls remain for thirty or forty generations thus one upon another, I believe the pits would not hold them unless they were dug deeper.' And he said to me, 'The Abyss[7] has no measure, for beneath it there stretches down below that which is below it; and so it is that if perchance anyone should take a stone and throw it into a very deep well[8] after many hours it would reach the bottom, such is the abyss. For when the souls are thrown in there, they hardly reach the bottom in fifty years.'

33. When I heard this, I wept and groaned[9] over the human race. The angel answered and said to me, 'Why do you weep? Are you more merciful than God? For though God is good, he knows that there are punishments, and he patiently bears with the human race, allowing each one to do his own will in the time in which he dwells on the earth.'

34. I observed the fiery river and saw there a man being tortured by Tartaruchian angels[1] having in their hands an iron instrument with three hooks with which they pierced the bowels of that old man; and I asked the angel and said, 'Sir, who is that old man on whom such torments are imposed?' And the angel answered and said to me, 'He whom you see was a presbyter who did not perform his ministry well: when he had been eating and drinking and committing fornication he offered the host to the Lord at his holy altar.'

35. And I saw not far away another old man led on by evil angels running with speed, and they pushed him into the fire up to his knees, and they struck him with stones and wounded his face like a storm, and did not allow him to say, 'Have pity on me!' And I asked the angel, and he said to me, 'He whom you see was a bishop and did not perform his episcopate well, who indeed accepted the great name but did not enter into the witness of him who gave him the name all his life, seeing that he did not give just judgement and did not pity widows and orphans,[2] but now he receives retribution according to his iniquity and his works.'

36. And I saw another man in the fiery river up to his knees. His hands were stretched out and bloody, and worms proceeded from his mouth and nostrils, and he was groaning and weeping, and crying he said, 'Have pity on me! For I am hurt more than the rest who are in this punishment.' And I asked, 'Sir, who is this?' And he said to me, 'This man whom you see was a deacon who devoured the oblations and committed fornication and did not do right in the sight of God; for this cause he unceasingly pays this penalty.'

And I looked closely and saw alongside of him another man, whom they delivered up with haste and cast into the fiery river, and he was in it up to the knees; and the angel who was set over the punishments came with a

---

7. The bottomless pit (Rev. 9:1–11; 20:1–3) that is the abode of the dead (Rom. 10:7). Cf. also Tob. 13:2; Sir. 24:5, 29.
8. The shaft of the abyss terminates in the watery deep. Thus the beast of Revelation can be said to ascend from both the abyss (11:7; 17:8) and the sea (13:1).
9. Paul's weeping (cf. chs. 39, 40, 42) contrasts markedly with that of John in Revelation, who never weeps over the suffering that he sees.
1. The guardians of Tartarus (ch. 40), traditionally the deepest region of the underworld where the vilest of humans are unceasingly tortured. Whereas good souls are entrusted to Michael (14), evil souls are handed over to the angel Tartaruchus (16; cf. 18).
2. Cf. Job 22:9; Tob. 1:8; Jas. 1:27.

great fiery razor, and with it he cut the lips of that man and the tongue likewise. And sighing, I lamented and asked, 'Who is that, sir?' And he said to me, 'He whom you see was a reader and read to the people, but he himself did not keep the precepts of God; now he also pays the proper penalty.'

37. And I saw another multitude of pits in the same place, and in the midst of it a river full with a multitude of men and women, and worms consumed them. But I lamented, and sighing asked the angel and said, 'Sir, who are these?' And he said to me, 'These are those who exacted interest on interest and trusted in their riches[3] and did not hope in God that he was their helper.'

And after that I looked and saw another place, very narrow, and it was like a wall, and fire round about it. And I saw inside men and women gnawing their tongues,[4] and I asked, 'Sir, who are these?' And he said to me, 'These are they who in church disparage the Word of God, not attending to it, but as it were making naught of God and his angels; for that reason they now likewise pay the proper penalty.'

38. And I observed and saw another pool[5] in the pit and its appearance was like blood, and I asked and said, 'Sir, what is this place?' And he said to me, 'Into that pit stream all the punishments.' And I saw men and women immersed up to the lips, and I asked, 'Sir, who are these?' And he said to me, 'These are the magicians who prepared for men and women evil magic arts and did not cease till they died.'

And again I saw men and women with very black faces in a pit of fire, and I sighed and lamented and asked, 'Sir, who are these?' And he said to me, 'These are fornicators and adulterers who committed adultery, having wives of their own; likewise also the women committed adultery, having husbands of their own; therefore they unceasingly suffer penalties.'

39. And I saw there girls in black raiment, and four terrifying angels having in their hands burning chains, and they put them on the necks of the girls and led them into darkness; and I, again weeping, asked the angel, 'Who are these, sir?' And he said to me, 'These are they who, when they were virgins, defiled their virginity[6] unknown to their parents; for which cause they unceasingly pay the proper penalties.'

And again I observed there men and women with hands cut and their feet placed naked in a place of ice and snow,[7] and worms devoured them. Seeing them I lamented and asked, 'Sir, who are these?' And he said to me, 'These are they who harmed orphans and widows and the poor,[8] and did not hope in the Lord, for which cause they unceasingly pay the proper penalties.'

And I observed and saw others hanging over a channel of water, and their tongues were very dry, and many fruits were placed in their sight,

---

3. Cf. Ps. 49:6; Prov. 11:28; Sir. 5:1.
4. Here, as is frequently the case in this and other visions of hell, there is a correlation between the sin and the punishment. Thus those who have used their tongues to disparage the word of God are punished by gnawing their tongues.
5. The Latin text here is defective, reading "old man." The Greek reads "hole."
6. Whereas punishment for adultery (chap. 39) in Greco-Roman depictions of Hades is not uncommon, torment for loss of virginity prior to marriage appears almost exclusively in Christian visions of hell.
7. For the anomaly of unmelted snow and ice in a place of fire, cf. Wis. 16:22. In *Apoc. Paul* 42, however, Paul is shown a place in the underworld where there is no fire, only cold and snow.
8. Cf. Zech. 7:10.

and they were not permitted to take of them,[9] and I asked, 'Sir, who are these?' And he said to me, 'These are they who broke their fast before the appointed hour; for this cause they unceasingly pay these penalties.'

And I saw other men and women hanging by their eyebrows and their hair,[1] and a fiery river drew them, and I said, 'Who are these, sir?' And he said to me, 'These are they who join themselves not to their own husbands and wives but to whores, and therefore they unceasingly pay the proper penalties.'[2]

And I saw other men and women covered with dust, and their countenance was like blood, and they were in a pit of pitch and sulphur running in a fiery river, and I asked, 'Sir, who are these?' And he said to me, 'These are they who committed the iniquity of Sodom and Gomorrah,[3] the male with the male, for which reason they unceasingly pay the penalties.'

40. And I observed and saw men and women clothed in bright garments, but with their eyes blind, and they were placed in a pit, and I asked, 'Sir, who are these?' And he said to me, 'These are heathen who gave alms, and knew not the Lord God, for which reason they unceasingly pay the proper penalties.' And I observed and saw other men and women on a pillar of fire, and beasts were tearing them in pieces, and they were not allowed to say, 'Lord have pity on us!' And I saw the angel of torments[4] putting heavy punishments on them and saying, 'Acknowledge the Son of God; for this was prophesied to you when the divine Scriptures were read to you, and you did not attend; for which cause God's judgement is just, because your actions have apprehended you and led you into these punishments.' But I sighed and wept, and I asked and said, 'Who are these men and women who are strangled in the fire and pay their penalties?' And he answered me, 'These are women who defiled the image of God by bringing forth infants out of the womb, and these are the men who lay with them. And their infants addressed the Lord God and the angels who were set over the punishments, saying, "Avenge us of our parents, for they defiled the image of God, having the name of God but not observing his precepts; they gave us for food to dogs and to be trodden on by swine; others they threw into the river." But the infants were handed over to the angels of Tartarus who were set over the punishments, that they might lead them to a spacious place of mercy; but their fathers and mothers were tortured in a perpetual punishment.'[5]

And after that I saw men and women clothed with rags full of pitch and fiery sulphur, and dragons were coiled about their necks and shoulders and feet, and angels with fiery horns restrained them and smote them, and closed their nostrils, saying to them, 'Why did you not know the time in which it was right to repent and serve God, and did not do it?' And I asked, 'Sir, who are these?' And he said to me, 'These are they who seemed to

---

9. An adaptation of the famous myth of Tantalus (Homer, *Ody.* 11.582–592). Inability to maintain a fast is here punished by inability to eat and drink.
1. Adulterous men hang by their eyebrows because their looking at women lustfully has led to their infidelity (Matt. 5:27–29), whereas unfaithful women hang by their hair since they are presumed to have beautified it to entice men (cf. Jdt. 10:3–4; 16:7–9).
2. The Coptic text here contains a condemnation of adulterous women who use "the devil's cosmetics" to beautify themselves before going to church in order to elicit an affair.
3. Gen. 19:1–11.
4. In Coptic, the name of the angel of torment is Aftemelouchos.
5. It is debated whether these individuals are punished for abortion or infanticide or both. In any case, they are torn by beasts because they threw their children to beasts, viz. dogs and swine (ch. 40).

renounce the world, putting on our garb, but the impediments of the world made them wretched, so that they did not maintain a single Agape,[6] and they did not pity widows and orphans; they did not receive the stranger and the pilgrim, nor did they offer an oblation and they did not show mercy to their neighbour. Moreover not even on one day did their prayer ascend pure to the Lord God, but many impediments of the world detained them, and they were not able to do right in the sight of God, and the angels enclosed them in the place of punishments. And those who were in punishments saw them and said to them, "We indeed neglected God when we lived in the world and you also did likewise; when we were in the world we indeed knew that we were sinners, but of you it was said, 'These are just and servants of God.' Now we know that in vain you were called by the name of the Lord, for which cause you pay the penalties." '

And sighing I wept and said, 'Woe unto men, woe unto sinners! Why were they born?'[7] And the angel answered and said to me, 'Why do you lament? Are you more merciful than the Lord God who is blessed forever, who established judgement and sent forth every man to choose good and evil in his own will and do what pleases him?' Then I lamented again very greatly, and he said to me, 'Do you lament when as yet you have not seen greater punishments? Follow me and you shall see seven times greater than these.'

41. And he carried me to the north and placed me above a well, and I found it sealed with seven seals;[8] and the angel who was with me said to the angel of that place, 'Open the mouth of the well that Paul, the well-beloved of God,[9] may see, for authority is given him that he may see all the torments of hell.' And the angel said to me, 'Stand far off that you may be able to bear the stench of this place.' When the well was opened, immediately there arose from it a disagreeable and evil stench, which surpasses all punishments; and I looked into the well, and I saw fiery masses glowing on all sides and anguish, and the mouth of the well was narrow so as to admit one man only. And the angel answered and said to me, 'If any man has been put into this well of the abyss and it has been sealed over him, no remembrance of him shall ever be made in the sight of the Father and his Son and the holy angels.' And I said, 'Who are these, sir, who are put into this well?' And he said to me, 'They are those who do not confess that Christ has come in the flesh[1] and that the Virgin Mary brought him forth, and those who say that the bread and cup of the Eucharist of blessing are not the body and blood of Christ.'[2]

* * *

But hearing these things I stretched out my hands and wept, and sighing again I said, 'It were better for us if we had not been born, all of us who are sinners.'

43. But when those who were in that place saw me weeping with the

---

6. The love-feast (Jude 12) celebrated by early Christians, usually in connection with the Eucharist. Since one of its social purposes was to alleviate the needs of the poor (Tertullian, *Apol.* 39), it is mentioned here in connection with failure to pity the widows and orphans.
7. Similar laments occur in chs. 15 and 42; cf. Job 3:3; Jer. 15:10; 20:14.
8. Cf. Rev. 5:1, 5; 6:1.
9. The author's favorite epithet for Paul: ch. 43, 44 (2x); cf. ch. 20; Acts 15:25; 2 Pet. 3:15.
1. 2 John 7; cf. 1 John 4:2–3.
2. 1 Cor. 10:16.

angel, they cried out and wept saying, 'Lord God have mercy upon us!' And after these things I saw the heavens open, and Michael the archangel descending from heaven, and with him was the whole army of angels, and they came to those who were placed in punishment, and seeing him, again weeping, they cried out and said, 'Have pity on us! Michael the archangel, have pity on us and on the human race for because of your prayers the earth continues. We now see the judgement and acknowledge the Son of God! It was impossible for us before these things to pray for this, before we entered into this place; for we heard that there was a judgement before we went out of the world, but impediments and the life of the world did not allow us to repent.' And Michael answered and said, 'Hear Michael speaking! I am he who stands in the sight of God every hour. As the Lord lives, in whose sight I stand, I do not stop one day or one night praying incessantly for the human race, and I indeed pray for those who are on the earth; but they do not cease committing iniquity and fornications, and they do not do any good while they are placed on earth; and you have consumed in vanity the time in which you ought to have repented. But I have always prayed thus, and I now beseech that God may send dew and send forth rains upon the earth, and now I continue to pray until the earth produce its fruits, and I say that if anyone has done but a little good I will strive for him, protecting him till he escapes the judgement of punishments. Where are your prayers? Where are your penances? You have lost your time contemptibly. But now weep, and I will weep with you and the angels who are with me with the well-beloved Paul, if by chance the merciful God will have pity and give you refreshment.' But hearing these words they cried out and wept greatly, and all said with one voice, 'Have pity on us, Son of God!' And I, Paul, sighed and said, 'O Lord God! Have pity on your creation, have pity on the sons of men, have pity on your own image.'

44. And I looked and saw the heaven move like a tree shaken by the wind. Suddenly, they threw themselves on their faces before the throne. And I saw twenty-four elders[3] and the four beasts[4] adoring God, and I saw an altar and veil and throne, and all were rejoicing; and the smoke of a good odour rose near the altar of the throne of God, and I heard the voice of one saying, 'For what reason do our angels and ministers intercede?' And they cried out, saying, 'We intercede seeing your many kindnesses to the human race.' And after these things I saw the Son of God descending from heaven,[5] and a diadem was on his head. And seeing him, all those who were placed in punishment exclaimed with one voice saying, 'Have pity, Son of the High God! It is you who have granted rest for all in the heavens and on earth, and on us likewise have mercy, for since we have seen you we have refreshment.' And a voice went out from the Son of God through all the punishments, saying, 'And what work have you done that you demand refreshment from me? My blood was poured out for your

---

3. Rev. 4:4, 10; 5:8; 11:16; 19:4.
4. The translation renders *animalia*, seeing here a reference to the four living creatures of Rev. 4:6–9; 5:6, 8, 11; etc. They are cherubim (ch. 14) and can also be called "beasts" because three of them have animal forms (Rev. 4:7).
5. Christ sits at the right hand of God in the seventh heaven (ch. 29), but Paul is never taken higher than the third heaven. At most he hears the voice of God pronounce judgment (chs. 14, 16–17) and catches a long-distance glimpse of that realm (ch. 44). Thus it is striking that when Paul finally sees Christ, he does not do so in either the third or seventh heaven, or in Christ's City, but in the very bowels of hell, where Christ, appropriately, shows mercy. Christ, it should be noted, only speaks of Paul, not to him.

sakes,[6] and even so you did not repent; for your sakes I wore the crown of thorns on my head;[7] for you I received buffets on my cheeks,[8] and you did not repent. I asked for water[9] when hanging on the cross, and they gave me vinegar mixed with gall,[1] with a spear they opened my right side,[2] for my name's sake they slew my prophets and just men,[3] and in all these things I gave you the chance for repentance and you would not. Now, however, for the sake of Michael the archangel of my covenant and the angels who are with him, and because of Paul the well-beloved, whom I would not grieve, for the sake of your brethren who are in the world and offer oblations, and for the sake of your sons, because my commandments are in them, and more for the sake of my own kindness, on the day on which I rose from the dead, I give to you all who are in punishment a night and a day of refreshment forever.' And they all cried out and said, 'We bless you, Son of God, that you have given us a night and a day of respite.' * * * When they had said this, the evil angels of torment were angered with them, saying, * * * 'You received this great grace of a day and a night's refreshment on the Lord's Day[4] for the sake of Paul the well-beloved of God who descended to you.'[5]

ANONYMOUS

The Gnostic Apocalypse of Paul (second century?)†

[. . .] **18** the road. And [he spoke to him], saying, "[By which] road [shall I go] up to [Jerusalem]?"[1] The little child[2] [replied, saying], "Say your name, so that [I may show] you the road." [The little child] knew [who Paul was].

6. Matt. 26:28; Mark 14:24; Luke 22:20.
7. Matt. 27:29; Mark 15:17; John 19:2, 5.
8. Matt. 26:67; John 18:22; 19:3.
9. Cf. John 19:28.
1. Matt. 27:34; cf. Mark 15:23.
2. John 19:34.
3. Cf. Matt. 5:11–12; 10:21; John 15:20–21; 16:2.
4. On Sundays the damned henceforth enjoy a respite from their tortures (see the introduction to this section). The idea of a "Sabbath rest" from punishment was likely derived from rabbinic tradition.
5. Once the tour of hell is complete, Paul is granted a second vision of Paradise, where he sees the tree of the knowledge of good and evil as well as the tree of life (ch. 45), the Virgin Mary (46), Abraham, Isaac, Jacob, the twelve patriarchs (47), Moses (48), Isaiah, Jeremiah, Ezekiel, Lot, Job, the Devil (49), Noah (50), Elijah, Elisha, Enoch, Zechariah, John the Baptist, Abel, and Adam (51). With most of these individuals Paul also converses, and some of them he has seen earlier in his vision (20, 27). The Coptic text has a third vision of Paradise, but this is doubtless a later addition.
† Found in Nag Hammadi Codex 5, 17–24; tr. by George W. MacRae and William R. Murdock, as edited by Douglas M. Parrott, in James M. Robinson, ed., *The Nag Hammadi Library in English* (3rd ed.; San Francisco: HarperSanFrancisco, 1988), 257–59. Copyright © 1978, 1988 by E. J. Brill. Reprinted by permission of HarperCollins Publishers and Brill Academic Publishers. The numbers in boldface indicate the page numbers of the codex.
1. The beginning of the work is lost, but the preserved portion commences with Paul in the midst of a journey to Jerusalem, probably from Damascus. Although some scholars believe that Paul's conversion is presupposed, it is more likely that the following narrative is a Gnostic depiction of the experience Paul recounts in Gal. 1:13–17. The author, who shows no knowledge of the Acts tradition that Paul was well acquainted with Jerusalem, has inferred from Gal. 1:17 that Paul was on his way to Jerusalem when Christ appeared to him. Paul's ignorance about the way to Jerusalem shows that he is still devoid of *gnōsis* (knowledge).
2. Later identified as the Holy Spirit, in keeping with Paul's statement that hidden things are revealed through the Spirit (1 Cor. 2:7–10). Since, however, some Gnostic texts, such as the *Acts of John* (88) and the *Gospel of Judas*, depict Jesus as appearing to some disciples as a child and other texts may refer to Christ as "the Spirit" (*Pr. Paul* A.17; cf. 2 Cor. 3:17–18), most scholars identify the heavenly child as the risen Christ (cf. Gal. 1:12, 16).

He wished to make conversation with him through his words [in order that] he might find an excuse for speaking with him.

The little child spoke, saying, "I know who you are, Paul. You are he who was blessed from his mother's womb.[3] For I have [come] to you that you may [go up to Jerusalem][4] to your fellow [apostles. And] for this reason [you were called. And] I am the [Spirit who accompanies] you. Let [your mind awaken,[5] Paul], with, [. . .]. 19 For [. . .] whole which [. . .] among the [principalities and] these authorities [and] archangels and powers[6] and the whole race of demons, [. . .] the one[7] that reveals bodies to a soul-seed."

And after he brought that speech to an end, he spoke, saying to me,[8] "Let your mind awaken, Paul, and see that this mountain upon which you are standing is the mountain of Jericho,[9] so that you may know the hidden things in those that are visible.[1] Now it is to the twelve apostles that you shall go, for they are elect spirits, and they will greet you." He raised his eyes and saw them greeting him.

Then the Holy [Spirit] who was speaking with [him] caught him up[2] on high to the third heaven,[3] and he passed beyond to the fourth [heaven]. The [Holy] Spirit spoke to him, saying, "Look and see your [likeness] upon the earth."[4] And he [looked] down and saw those [who were upon] the earth. He stared [and saw] those who were upon the [. . . . Then 20 he] gazed [down and] saw the [twelve] apostles [at] his right [and] at his left in the creation;[5] and the Spirit was going before them.

But I[6] saw in the fourth heaven according to class—I saw the angels resembling gods, the angels bringing a soul out of the land of the dead. They placed it at the gate of the fourth heaven. And the angels were whipping it.[7] The soul spoke, saying, "What sin was it that I committed in the world?" The toll-collector who dwells in the fourth heaven replied, saying, "It was not right to commit all those lawless deeds that are in the world of

---

3. Gal. 1:15.
4. Inasmuch as the small child does not direct Paul to the physical city of Jerusalem, this is a hint that Paul is going to ascend to the heavenly Jerusalem (cf. Gal. 4:25–26).
5. Paul's knowledge of his identity and destiny thus come directly from the Heavenly Revealer, who proceeds to give two wake-up calls that emphasize the importance of the following revelation and of setting his mind on what the Spirit says (cf. Rom. 8:5).
6. Cosmic powers (cf. Rom. 8:38; Col. 1:16; Eph. 1:21; 6:12) that strive to keep the soul trapped in the body and prevent its ascent. Spiritual liberation comes through the revealed knowledge that the soul is inalterably divine and destined to return to the divine realm from where it came.
7. Given the context, another hostile power (possibly the Demiurge) that is responsible for the soul's corporeal imprisonment.
8. The narrative at this point switches from third to first person; at the end of the paragraph it reverts to third person.
9. Jericho was the city close to where Elijah was taken up into heaven (2 Kgs. 2:4–18).
1. The visible/invisible contrast appears in Col. 1:16 and is a common feature in Gnostic texts.
2. In 2 Cor. 12:2, Paul dates his heavenly journey to "fourteen years ago" (ca. 41–42 CE), thus making it distinct from his Damascus experience. The author, however, makes the rapture follow immediately upon his apostolic call.
3. Cf. 2 Cor. 12:2, which also ignores the first two heavens. That nothing is said about the third heaven may be due to the prohibition given in 2 Cor. 12:4 or to it being treated in a separate work, like the *Ascension of Paul* mentioned in Epiphanius, *Pan.* 38.2.5.
4. He sees his physical body, proving that his rapture was "out of the body" (2 Cor. 12:2–3). Similarly, the author of the *Cologne Mani Codex* says that Paul was "outside of himself" during his rapture (61.23).
5. Although the twelve are elect spirits and Paul's fellow apostles, he is superior to them, as his place in the center demonstrates (cf. Matt. 20:21; Mark 10:37). See also the sixth heaven, where Paul is led by the Spirit before them.
6. The narrative at this point switches from third to first person for the rest of the work.
7. The fourth heaven is a place of interrogation and judgment. The whips are not so much an instrument of torture as a means that the angels use to herd souls before the judge (toll-collector). See the scene in the fifth heaven.

the dead." The soul replied, saying, "Bring witnesses! Let them [show] you in what body I committed lawless deeds. [Do you wish] to bring a book [to read from]?"

And the three witnesses[8] came. The first spoke, saying, "Was I [not in] the body the second hour [. . .]? I rose up against you **21** until [you fell] into anger [and rage] and envy." And the second spoke, saying, "Was I not in the world? And I entered at the fifth hour, and I saw you and desired you. And behold, then, now I charge you with the murders you committed." The third spoke, saying, "Did I not come to you at the twelfth hour of the day when the sun was about to set? I gave you darkness until you should accomplish your sins." When the soul heard these things, it gazed downward in sorrow. And then it gazed upward. It was cast down. The soul that had been cast down [went] to [a] body which had been prepared [for it.[9] And] behold [its] witnesses were finished.

[Then I gazed] upward and [saw the] Spirit saying [to me], "Paul, come! [Proceed toward] me!" Then as I [went], the gate opened, [and] I went up to the fifth [heaven]. And I saw my fellow apostles [going with me][1] **22** while the Spirit accompanied us. And I saw a great angel in the fifth heaven holding an iron rod[2] in his hand. There were three other angels with him, and I stared into their faces. But they were rivalling each other, with whips in their hands, goading the souls on to the judgment. But I went with the Spirit and the gate opened for me.

Then we went up to the sixth heaven. And I saw my fellow apostles going with me, and the Holy Spirit was leading[3] me before them. And I gazed up on high and saw a great light[4] shining down on the sixth heaven. I spoke, saying to the toll-collector[5] who was in the sixth heaven, "[Open] to me and the [Holy] Spirit [who is] before [me]."[6] He opened [to me].

[Then we went] up to the seventh [heaven and I saw] an old man[7] [. . .] light [and whose garment] was white. [His throne],[8] which is in the seventh heaven, [was] brighter than the sun by [seven] times. **23** The old man spoke, saying to [me], "Where are you going, Paul, O blessed one and the one who was set apart from his mother's womb?"[9]

But I looked at the Spirit, and he was nodding his head, saying to me,

---

8. Cf. Deut. 19:15; 2 Cor. 13:1.
9. The wicked soul is punished for the sins it committed in the body, but instead of being eternally tormented, is returned to earth to inhabit a new body.
1. The role of the apostles is unclear; here and in the sixth heaven Paul sees them accompanying him, whereas they are already present in the eighth heaven to greet him when he arrives.
2. Cf. Ps. 2:9; Rev. 2:27; 12:5; 19:15.
3. For the leading of the Spirit, see Rom. 8:14; Gal. 5:18.
4. The great light is coming from the throne in the seventh heaven and is later described as being seven times brighter than the sun.
5. The offices of tax collectors were typically located at the gates of ancient cities, where they collected revenue from those passing through (cf. toll booths on certain modern highways). The individuals who staffed such booths were the subordinates of those responsible for collecting taxes, just as the principalities and powers were the underlings of the Demiurge. These powers are also called tax collectors in the *First Apocalypse of James* (33.8), another Gnostic ascent apocalypse.
6. This is the first time that Paul has spoken since his question to the little child at the start of the narrative. It is also the first time that he meets any resistance in his ascent.
7. The Demiurge, whose depiction as an old man (cf. Dan. 7:9, 13, 22) contrasts sharply with the Spirit's appearance as a little child. In Gnosticism, the Creator of the material world is both distinct from and inferior to the Father. Whereas the former inhabits the traditional seventh heaven, the latter is presumed to be in the tenth, transcending both Creator and creation.
8. The absence of visual description in this throne scene is typical of Gnosticism but stands in stark contrast to texts such as Dan. 7:9–10 and Rev. 4–5. Similarly, the Spirit who transports and leads Paul never explains anything that the apostle sees (contrast the *Apocalypse of Paul*, where the angelic guide is constantly identifying people and things in Paul's vision).
9. The Creator uses the same epithet as the Spirit and makes the same allusion to Gal. 1:15.

"Speak with him!" And I replied, saying to the old man, "I am going to the place[1] from which I came." And the old man responded to me, "Where are you from?"[2] But I replied, saying, "I am going down to the world of the dead in order to lead captive the captivity that was led captive in the captivity of Babylon."[3] The old man replied to me, saying, "How will you be able to get away from me? Look and see the principalities and authorities."[4] [The] Spirit spoke, saying, "Give him [the] sign that you have, and [he will] open for you."[5] And then I gave [him] the sign. He turned his face downwards to his creation and to those who are his own authorities.

And then the <seventh> heaven opened and we went up to [the] **24** Ogdoad.[6] And I saw the twelve apostles. They greeted me, and we went up to the ninth heaven. I greeted all those who were in the ninth heaven, and we went up to the tenth heaven. And I greeted my fellow spirits.

---

1. The divine realm.
2. The same question occurs in *1 Apoc. Jas.* 33.15.
3. The Gnostic Paul alludes to Eph. 4:8–9, but whereas that text applies Ps. 68:18 to Christ, Paul here applies it to himself. Once his ascent is complete, he will return to the earth to carry out his ministry of liberating captive souls.
4. The Creator's initial friendliness, probably feigned, now turns into hostility as he points to himself and his minions as impeding powers.
5. Whereas Paul spoke to the toll-collector of the sixth heaven without any prompting, the Spirit plays a crucial role in helping Paul pass through the seventh heaven by encouraging him to speak to the Creator and to show him the decisive sign.
6. The eighth heaven, the beginning of the transcendent sphere known as the "Fullness" (*Plērōma*) of Divine Being, which lies beyond the domain of the Demiurge. This sphere, consisting of the eighth, ninth, and tenth heavens, was the focus of much Gnostic speculation, but very little is said about it here.

PART IV

Views of Paul in the
Ancient Church

The ambivalent history of Paulinism begins within the pages of the New Testament. If the consensus of critical scholars is correct, some time after Paul's death his followers wrote several of the letters attributed to him. That suggests that Paul founded a "school" that continued to develop a distinctively Pauline tradition. His method of missionary activity, in close association with Timothy, Titus, Silvanus, Apollos, and others, points in the same direction. Especially in the Pastoral Letters there is clearly visible an effort to make Paul into the *founder* of reliable tradition, the guarantor of the "deposit" of correct church organization, morality, and "sound doctrine," as well as the model of Christian conversion (1 Tim. 1:12–16).

Of the images of Paul that appear in the New Testament, the most important are those provided by the Paulinists in their letters and by the Acts of the Apostles. Fully two-thirds of the latter is devoted to Paul. Indeed, the ordinary picture of the apostle's career owes more to Acts than to data that can be extracted from the letters.[1] The vivid descriptions of the Damascus road Christophany and Paul's subsequent conversion are found only in Acts. The "three missionary journeys" are part of Luke's systematic plan; we could never reconstruct them from the letters alone. The dramatic speech on the Areopagus in Athens, the confrontation between Paul and his fellow Jews in synagogue after synagogue, the poignant farewell speech, Paul's continuing dedication to Jewish law and piety, the tumult in Jerusalem, the series of trials leading to Rome—all these would be missing from the standard biography of Paul but for the art of the unknown historian, whom Irenaeus and other early Christians identify as none other than Luke, Paul's companion. Probably writing toward the end of the first century, "Luke" constructs a history of the Jesus movement that depicts its unstoppable growth and justifies its dramatic transformation from a small and exclusively Jewish sect centered in Jerusalem to a geographically expansive church comprising both Jews and Gentiles. Within that history Paul plays a key role not only as the chief agent in this demographic and geographic shift but also as the central bridge figure standing between the apostolic eyewitnesses, who belong to the "beginning" (Luke 1:2), and Luke's own generation, when the movement has become predominantly Gentile.

In addition to depicting Paul's relationship with Jerusalem as close and congenial, the author of Acts constructs certain parallels between the careers of Peter and Paul. Both, for example, are filled with the Holy Spirit (4:8; 9:17; 13:9), who plays a crucial role in each one's ministry (10:19; 11:12; 13:2, 4; 16:6–7; 20:22–23; 21:4), and both men impart the Spirit to others through the laying on of hands (8:14–17; 19:1–6). Both are instrumental in the conversion of Gentiles (10:1–11:18; 13:47; 15:7–12) and must prevent Gentiles from worshiping them (10:25–26; 14:13–15). Both are effective speakers and proclaim the same kerygmatic message (2:14–42; 13:16–41). Both are miracle-workers, healing the lame (3:1–10; 14:8–10) and raising the dead (9:36–43; 20:9–12) as well as confronting magicians (8:9–24; 13:6–11). When they stand trial before the Sanhedrin, Pharisees intervene on their behalf (5:27–39; 22:30–23:10), and both experience divine intervention while they are in prison (12:3–11; 16:24–26). Similarly, the author of Luke-Acts constructs various parallels between Jesus' fate and that of Paul. Both make a fateful final trip to Jerusalem (Luke 9:51–19:27; Acts 20:1–21:16), fully aware that suffering awaits them (Luke 13:31–34; 17:25; 18:31–33; Acts 20:22–23; 21:10–

1. Given the importance of Acts in shaping the modern portrait of Paul, it is surprising that it was a relatively neglected work prior to the Reformation. Indeed, only twenty or so treatments of Acts survive from the ancient and medieval periods, and most of these are quite fragmentary. The most substantial of the earliest extant treatments are Ephraem's commentary, John Chrysostom's homilies, and Arator's epic poem *On the Acts of the Apostles*. At the same time, one should not exaggerate its neglect. Chrysostom's famous statement at the beginning of his *Homilies on Acts*—that Acts is so little known that many Christians are unaware of its existence—is not so much a lament as a rhetorical ploy to create interest in the sermons he will deliver.

13). Upon arrival, each is initially accorded a warm welcome (Luke 19:37–38; Acts 21:17–20a), subsequently enters the temple (Luke 19:45–48; Acts 21: 26), is seized (Luke 22:54; Acts 21:30), and undergoes a sequence of four trials (Jesus: Sanhedrin, Pilate, Herod Antipas, Pilate; Paul: Sanhedrin, Felix, Herod Agrippa, Festus). During the trials each is slapped (Luke 22:63–64; Acts 23:2), thrice declared innocent (Luke 23:4, 14, 22; Acts 23:9; 25:25; 26: 32), has a hostile crowd shout, "Away with him" (Luke 23:18; Acts 21:36), and is praised or treated kindly by a Roman centurion (Luke 23:47; Acts 27:3, 43). By partly using the same mold to cast his three great heroes, "Luke" shows that Paul is a faithful follower of Jesus and a legitimate counterpart to the apostle Peter. Given the importance of Acts in shaping subsequent treatments of Paul, we provide excerpts from three different discussions of the Lukan Paul (by Daniel Schwartz, Jacob Jervell, and Susan Garrett).

To varying degrees, Pauline influence from time to time has been suspected in other NT documents, especially those that either mention his co-workers by name or were traditionally written by them. These include the pseudonymous letter of 1 Peter, which gives Silvanus as either the amanuensis or the letter-carrier (5:12), the anonymous Letter to the Hebrews, which mentions Timothy (13:23), and the Second and Third Gospels, which early church tradition attributed to Mark and Luke (Phlm. 24; 2 Tim. 4:11). In addition, the Apocalypse of John, with its famous seven letters to the churches (Rev. 2–3), has been thought by some to reflect the ancient idea that Paul wrote to seven churches (Rome, Corinth, Galatia, Ephesus, Philippi, Colossae, and Thessalonica) and that his letters provided an epistolary model that John adapted (Rev. 1:4–5a; 22:21).[2] In all such cases, any real or substantive indebtedness to Pauline ideas and letters remains conjectural. Similarities in thought and expression are more plausibly explained in most cases by other factors, such as joint reliance on early Christian traditions and practices or mutual engagement with the same or similar problems.

On the other hand, some wariness about Paulinism is also expressed in certain NT passages. The author of 2 Peter, perhaps the latest work in the canon, could already apply the term "scriptures" (though perhaps not in the full technical sense) to Paul's letters, yet in the same breath he warned that "his letters contain some things that are hard to understand, which ignorant and unstable people distort . . . to their own destruction" (3:16). Because Paul's ideas frequently differ from those of other NT authors, some of the latter have been suspected of being his covert critics. The two most frequently mentioned in this regard are the authors of the Gospel of Matthew and the Letter of James. Matthew's attitude toward the law (Matt. 5:17–19) conflicts sharply with Paul's perspective (Rom. 7:1–6; Gal. 3:23–26), but it is debated whether the evangelist has Paul and his partisans in mind when he makes disparaging remarks about those who practice and teach a different view of the law (Matt. 5:19). On balance, that seems unlikely. A much stronger case can be made for anti-Paulinism in the Letter of James, whose view of faith and works is dramatically different (Jas. 2:14–26) from Paul's. Furthermore, both Paul and James regard Abraham as paradigmatic, but whereas Paul argues that Abraham was justified when he believed (Gen. 15:6; Rom. 4:3; Gal. 3:6), James follows Jewish tradition by connecting Abraham's justification with the Akedah (the binding of Isaac) in Gen. 22 (Jas. 2:21–23; 1 Macc. 2:52; Philo, Deus 4). Because the formulations of Paul and James are so similar yet the differences in perspective so sharp, at least parts of James can hardly be understood in any other way than as an attack upon a caricatured or poorly understood Paulinism.

---

2. The Muratorian Canon reverses the relationship by making Paul follow John's lead and write to only seven churches.

But who is James and does his anti-Pauline polemic extend to other parts of the letter? Whereas most contemporary scholars regard "James" as the pseudonym used by an author writing after the deaths of both Paul and James, Martin Hengel argues that James is none other than the historical James of Jerusalem, the Lord's brother, and that his letter is replete with criticisms of Paul and his theology. Although we regard Hengel's discussion as more provocative than persuasive, we include an excerpt of his essay to show how an unsympathetic contemporary of Paul could have criticized him.

During the early centuries of Christianity, polar views of Paul continued to be expressed. At one extreme were the Jewish-Christian groups such as the Ebionites who, because of their own continued devotion to the Law of Moses, were more concerned than the "catholics" with Paul's rejection of the law as a way of salvation, and who therefore rejected Paul. In certain ways they were continuing the opposition to Paul mounted by his opponents in Galatia and his critics in Jerusalem. Along with the ancient expressions of hostility to Paul, we thus include modern reconstructions of Paul's opponents in Galatians (J. Louis Martyn) and Jerusalem (David Flusser). But Paul's critics were not limited to Jewish Christians. They included pagan intellectuals whose objections to Christianity sometimes included polemical statements against Paul and his theology. Excerpts from two of these critics, Julian and an anonymous Hellene, illustrate the contempt in which they held the apostle.

At the opposite extreme was the perplexing and fascinating figure of Marcion, who became convinced that Paul was the *only* true apostle of Christ, all the rest having been victims or perpetrators of a conspiracy against the truth. In addition to Marcion, various Gnostics, especially the followers of Valentinus, championed Paul and interpreted his letters in a way that was congenial to their theology. Both ends of the theological spectrum were ultimately pushed out or left the mainstream of the church, so that very little of what these champions and critics of Paul said about him has survived. For the most part, their thoughts have to be represented by fragments picked out of more orthodox documents, typically written by their unsympathetic opponents. In addition to giving some of these fragments, we also include discussions of both Marcion's theology (by Adolf von Harnack) and Gnostic exegesis (by Elaine Pagels).

Paul was a model to many in the early church. Because he had died a martyr's death, Christian martyrs viewed him as a paradigm. Indeed, Paul himself was sometimes the subject of discussion when pagan authorities interrogated Christians. For example, the discussion between Phileas, the bishop of Thmuis, and Culcianus, the prefect of Egypt, involved Paul, as the excerpt given below indicates.

Paul's influences upon ascetic movements in Western Christianity, and the influence in turn of ascetic Christianity upon the common picture of Paul, are important enough to merit special attention. The apocryphal *Acts of Paul and Thecla* shows clearly how Encratite Christians pictured Paul's mission; it is prefaced by a historical sketch of Paul's place in the development of early asceticism, and followed by an essay by Dennis R. MacDonald that explores possible links between the *Acts of Paul and Thecla* and the Pastoral Epistles of the NT.

Alongside these rather exotic portraits of Paul must be set the picture of the apostle that appears in the writings of the major catholic fathers. We include several examples of how they sought to interpret Paul, as well as an essay by Bernadette Brooten on how patristic exegetes understood Rom. 1:26. Part IV is concluded by David Rensberger's judicious survey of the use of Paul's letters in the second century, which demonstrates that Paul's orthodox interpreters battled to preserve his legacy even as they struggled to interpret the more difficult portions of his letters and apply his message to their own time.

Luke's Portrait of Paul

"LUKE"

[The Chosen Instrument] (ca. 95)†

6 7 So the word of God spread. The number of disciples in Jerusalem increased rapidly, and a large number of priests became obedient to the faith.

8 Now Stephen, a man full of God's grace and power, performed great wonders and signs among the people. 9 Opposition arose, however, from members of the Synagogue of the Freedmen (as it was called)—Jews of Cyrene and Alexandria as well as the provinces of Cilicia and Asia—who began to argue with Stephen. 10 But they could not stand up against the wisdom the Spirit gave him as he spoke.

11 Then they secretly persuaded some men to say, "We have heard Stephen speak blasphemous words against Moses and against God."

12 So they stirred up the people and the elders and the teachers of the law. They seized Stephen and brought him before the Sanhedrin. 13 They produced false witnesses, who testified, "This fellow never stops speaking against this holy place and against the law. 14 For we have heard him say that this Jesus of Nazareth will destroy this place and change the customs Moses handed down to us."

15 All who were sitting in the Sanhedrin looked intently at Stephen, and they saw that his face was like the face of an angel.

7 Then the high priest asked Stephen, "Are these charges true?" 2 To this he replied: "Brothers and fathers, listen to me!"

* * *

51 "You stiff-necked people! Your hearts and ears are still uncircumcised. You are just like your ancestors: You always resist the Holy Spirit! 52 Was there ever a prophet your ancestors did not persecute? They even killed those who predicted the coming of the Righteous One. And now you have betrayed and murdered him—53 you who have received the law that was given through angels but have not obeyed it."

54 When the members of the Sanhedrin heard this, they were furious and gnashed their teeth at him. 55 But Stephen, full of the Holy Spirit, looked up to heaven and saw the glory of God, and Jesus standing at the right hand of God. 56 "Look," he said, "I see heaven open and the Son of Man standing at the right hand of God."

† From The Acts of the Apostles 6:7–7:2; 7:51–8:3; 9:1–31; 11:19–30; 12:25–28:31, TNIV. The author of this work, the first volume of which is the Gospel according to Luke, has traditionally been identified with the Luke who is mentioned in Phlm. 24; Col. 4:14; 2 Tim. 4:11 as "the physician" and a companion of Paul. See further the introduction to Part IV and the excerpt from Irenaeus (pp. 186–87).

57 At this they covered their ears and, yelling at the top of their voices, they all rushed at him, 58 dragged him out of the city and began to stone him. Meanwhile, the witnesses laid their coats at the feet of a young man named Saul.

59 While they were stoning him, Stephen prayed, "Lord Jesus, receive my spirit." 60 Then he fell on his knees and cried out, "Lord, do not hold this sin against them." When he had said this, he fell asleep. 8 And Saul approved of their killing him.

On that day a great persecution broke out against the church in Jerusalem, and all except the apostles were scattered throughout Judea and Samaria. 2 Godly men buried Stephen and mourned deeply for him. 3 But Saul began to destroy the church. Going from house to house, he dragged off both men and women and put them in prison.

* * *

9 Meanwhile, Saul was still breathing out murderous threats against the Lord's disciples. He went to the high priest 2 and asked him for letters to the synagogues in Damascus, so that if he found any there who belonged to the Way, whether men or women, he might take them as prisoners to Jerusalem. 3 As he neared Damascus on his journey, suddenly a light from heaven flashed around him. 4 He fell to the ground and heard a voice say to him, "Saul, Saul, why do you persecute me?"

5 "Who are you, Lord?" Saul asked.

"I am Jesus, whom you are persecuting," he replied. 6 "Now get up and go into the city, and you will be told what you must do."

7 The men traveling with Saul stood there speechless; they heard the sound but did not see anyone. 8 Saul got up from the ground, but when he opened his eyes he could see nothing. So they led him by the hand into Damascus. 9 For three days he was blind, and did not eat or drink anything.

10 In Damascus there was a disciple named Ananias. The Lord called to him in a vision, "Ananias!"

"Yes, Lord," he answered.

11 The Lord told him, "Go to the house of Judas on Straight Street and ask for a man from Tarsus named Saul, for he is praying. 12 In a vision he has seen a man named Ananias come and place his hands on him to restore his sight."

13 "Lord," Ananias answered, "I have heard many reports about this man and all the harm he has done to your people in Jerusalem. 14 And he has come here with authority from the chief priests to arrest all who call on your name."

15 But the Lord said to Ananias, "Go! This man is my chosen instrument to proclaim my name to the Gentiles and their kings and to the people of Israel. 16 I will show him how much he must suffer for my name."

17 Then Ananias went to the house and entered it. Placing his hands on Saul, he said, "Brother Saul, the Lord—Jesus, who appeared to you on the road as you were coming here—has sent me so that you may see again and be filled with the Holy Spirit." 18 Immediately, something like scales fell from Saul's eyes, and he could see again. He got up and was baptized, 19 and after taking some food, he regained his strength.

Saul spent several days with the disciples in Damascus. 20 At once he began to preach in the synagogues that Jesus is the Son of God. 21 All those who heard him were astonished and asked, "Isn't he the man who raised havoc in Jerusalem among those who call on this name? And hasn't he come here to take them as prisoners to the chief priests?" 22 Yet Saul grew more and more powerful and baffled the Jews living in Damascus by proving that Jesus is the Messiah.

23 After many days had gone by, there was a conspiracy among the Jews to kill him, 24 but Saul learned of their plan. Day and night they kept close watch on the city gates in order to kill him. 25 But his followers took him by night and lowered him in a basket through an opening in the wall.

26 When he came to Jerusalem, he tried to join the disciples, but they were all afraid of him, not believing that he really was a disciple. 27 But Barnabas took him and brought him to the apostles. He told them how Saul on his journey had seen the Lord and that the Lord had spoken to him, and how in Damascus he had preached fearlessly in the name of Jesus. 28 So Saul stayed with them and moved about freely in Jerusalem, speaking boldly in the name of the Lord. 29 He talked and debated with the Hellenistic Jews, but they tried to kill him. 30 When the believers learned of this, they took him down to Caesarea and sent him off to Tarsus.

31 Then the church throughout Judea, Galilee and Samaria enjoyed a time of peace and was strengthened. Living in the fear of the Lord and encouraged by the Holy Spirit, it increased in numbers.

✳   ✳   ✳

11 19 Now those who had been scattered by the persecution that broke out when Stephen was killed traveled as far as Phoenicia, Cyprus and Antioch, spreading the word only among Jews. 20 Some of them, however, men from Cyprus and Cyrene, went to Antioch and began to speak to Greeks also, telling them the good news about the Lord Jesus. 21 The Lord's hand was with them, and a great number of people believed and turned to the Lord.

22 News of this reached the ears of the church in Jerusalem, and they sent Barnabas to Antioch. 23 When he arrived and saw what the grace of God had done, he was glad and encouraged them all to remain true to the Lord with all their hearts. 24 He was a good man, full of the Holy Spirit and faith, and a great number of people were brought to the Lord.

25 Then Barnabas went to Tarsus to look for Saul, 26 and when he found him, he brought him to Antioch. So for a whole year Barnabas and Saul met with the church and taught great numbers of people. The disciples were called Christians first at Antioch.

✳   ✳   ✳

[A trip to Jerusalem with famine relief for the church there sets the stage for Paul's "first missionary journey," which is described in chapters 13–14. It takes him and Barnabas as far as Pisidia, in Asia Minor.]

14 24 After going through Pisidia, they came into Pamphylia, 25 and when they had preached the word in Perga, they went down to Attalia.

26 From Attalia they sailed back to Antioch, where they had been committed to the grace of God for the work they had now completed. 27 On

arriving there, they gathered the church together and reported all that God had done through them and how he had opened a door of faith to the Gentiles. 28 And they stayed there a long time with the disciples.

15 Certain individuals came down from Judea to Antioch and were teaching the believers: "Unless you are circumcised, according to the custom taught by Moses, you cannot be saved." 2 This brought Paul and Barnabas into sharp dispute and debate with them. So Paul and Barnabas were appointed, along with some other believers, to go up to Jerusalem to see the apostles and elders about this question. 3 The church sent them on their way, and as they traveled through Phoenicia and Samaria, they told how the Gentiles had been converted. This news made all the believers very glad. 4 When they came to Jerusalem, they were welcomed by the church and the apostles and elders, to whom they reported everything God had done through them.

5 Then some of the believers who belonged to the party of the Pharisees stood up and said, "The Gentiles must be circumcised and required to keep the law of Moses."

6 The apostles and elders met to consider this question. 7 After much discussion, Peter got up and addressed them: "Brothers, you know that some time ago God made a choice among you that the Gentiles might hear from my lips the message of the gospel and believe. 8 God, who knows the heart, showed that he accepted them by giving the Holy Spirit to them, just as he did to us. 9 He did not discriminate between us and them, for he purified their hearts by faith. 10 Now then, why do you try to test God by putting on the necks of Gentiles a yoke that neither we nor our ancestors have been able to bear? 11 No! We believe it is through the grace of our Lord Jesus that we are saved, just as they are."

12 The whole assembly became silent as they listened to Barnabas and Paul telling about the signs and wonders God had done among the Gentiles through them. 13 When they finished, James spoke up. "Brothers," he said, "listen to me. 14 Simon has described to us how God first intervened to choose a people for his name from the Gentiles. 15 The words of the prophets are in agreement with this, as it is written:

16 " 'After this I will return
     and rebuild David's fallen tent.
     Its ruins I will rebuild,
     and I will restore it,
17 that the rest of humanity may seek the Lord,
     even all the Gentiles who bear my name,
     says the Lord, who does these things'—
18 things known from long ago.

19 "It is my judgment, therefore, that we should not make it difficult for the Gentiles who are turning to God. 20 Instead we should write to them, telling them to abstain from food polluted by idols, from sexual immorality, from the meat of strangled animals and from blood. 21 For the law of Moses has been preached in every city from the earliest times and is read in the synagogues on every Sabbath."

22 Then the apostles and elders, with the whole church, decided to choose some of their own men and send them to Antioch with Paul and Barnabas. They chose Judas (called Barsabbas) and Silas, who were leaders among the believers. 23 With them they sent the following letter:

The apostles and elders, your brothers,

To the Gentile believers in Antioch, Syria and Cilicia:

Greetings.

24 We have heard that some went out from us without our authorization and disturbed you, troubling your minds by what they said. 25 So we all agreed to choose some men and send them to you with our dear friends Barnabas and Paul— 26 men who have risked their lives for the name of our Lord Jesus Christ. 27 Therefore we are sending Judas and Silas to confirm by word of mouth what we are writing. 28 It seemed good to the Holy Spirit and to us not to burden you with anything beyond the following requirements: 29 You are to abstain from food sacrificed to idols, from blood, from the meat of strangled animals and from sexual immorality. You will do well to avoid these things.

Farewell.

30 So they were sent off and went down to Antioch, where they gathered the church together and delivered the letter. 31 The people read it and were glad for its encouraging message. 32 Judas and Silas, who themselves were prophets, said much to encourage and strengthen the believers. 33– 34 After spending some time there, they were sent off by the believers with the blessing of peace to return to those who had sent them. 35 But Paul and Barnabas remained in Antioch, where they and many others taught and preached the word of the Lord.

36 Some time later Paul said to Barnabas, "Let us go back and visit the believers in all the towns where we preached the word of the Lord and see how they are doing." 37 Barnabas wanted to take John, also called Mark, with them, 38 but Paul did not think it wise to take him, because he had deserted them in Pamphylia and had not continued with them in the work. 39 They had such a sharp disagreement that they parted company. Barnabas took Mark and sailed for Cyprus, 40 but Paul chose Silas and left, commended by the believers to the grace of the Lord. 41 He went through Syria and Cilicia, strengthening the churches.

16 Paul came to Derbe and then to Lystra, where a disciple named Timothy lived, whose mother was Jewish and a believer but whose father was a Greek. 2 The believers at Lystra and Iconium spoke well of him. 3 Paul wanted to take him along on the journey, so he circumcised him because of the Jews who lived in that area, for they all knew that his father was a Greek. 4 As they traveled from town to town, they delivered the decisions reached by the apostles and elders in Jerusalem for the people to obey. 5 So the churches were strengthened in the faith and grew daily in numbers.

* * *

[*Directed by a vision, Paul enters Macedonia, where, in Philippi, he soon wins converts. The cure of a demoniac prophetess, however, leads to his arrest for disturbing the peace. After miraculous signs and the conversion of the jailer, Paul and Silas are released, but forced to leave town.*]

17 When Paul and his companions had passed through Amphipolis and Apollonia, they came to Thessalonica, where there was a Jewish synagogue. 2 As was his custom, Paul went into the synagogue, and on three Sabbath days he reasoned with them from the Scriptures, 3 explaining and proving

that the Messiah had to suffer and rise from the dead. "This Jesus I am proclaiming to you is the Messiah," he said. 4 Some of the Jews were persuaded and joined Paul and Silas, as did a large number of God-fearing Greeks and not a few prominent women.

5 But other Jews were jealous; so they rounded up some bad characters from the marketplace, formed a mob and started a riot in the city. They rushed to Jason's house in search of Paul and Silas in order to bring them out to the crowd. 6 But when they did not find them, they dragged Jason and some other believers before the city officials, shouting: "These men who have caused trouble all over the world have now come here, 7 and Jason has welcomed them into his house. They are all defying Caesar's decrees, saying that there is another king, one called Jesus." 8 When they heard this, the crowd and the city officials were thrown into turmoil. 9 Then they made Jason and the others post bond and let them go.

10 As soon as it was night, the believers sent Paul and Silas away to Berea. On arriving there, they went to the Jewish synagogue. 11 Now the Berean Jews were of more noble character than those in Thessalonica, for they received the message with great eagerness and examined the Scriptures every day to see if what Paul said was true. 12 Many of them believed, as did also a number of prominent Greek women and many Greek men.

13 But when the Jews in Thessalonica learned that Paul was preaching the word of God at Berea, some of them went there too, agitating the crowds and stirring them up. 14 The believers immediately sent Paul to the coast, but Silas and Timothy stayed at Berea. 15 Those who escorted Paul brought him to Athens and then left with instructions for Silas and Timothy to join him as soon as possible.

16 While Paul was waiting for them in Athens, he was greatly distressed to see that the city was full of idols. 17 So he reasoned in the synagogue with both Jews and God-fearing Greeks, as well as in the marketplace day by day with those who happened to be there. 18 A group of Epicurean and Stoic philosophers began to debate with him. Some of them asked, "What is this babbler trying to say?" Others remarked, "He seems to be advocating foreign gods." They said this because Paul was preaching the good news about Jesus and the resurrection. 19 Then they took him and brought him to a meeting of the Areopagus, where they said to him, "May we know what this new teaching is that you are presenting? 20 You are bringing some strange ideas to our ears, and we would like to know what they mean." 21 (All the Athenians and the foreigners who lived there spent their time doing nothing but talking about and listening to the latest ideas.)

22 Paul then stood up in the meeting of the Areopagus and said: "People of Athens! I see that in every way you are very religious. 23 For as I walked around and looked carefully at your objects of worship, I even found an altar with this inscription: TO AN UNKNOWN GOD. So you are ignorant of the very thing you worship—and this is what I am going to proclaim to you.

24 "The God who made the world and everything in it is the Lord of heaven and earth and does not live in temples built by hands. 25 And he is not served by human hands, as if he needed anything. Rather, he himself gives everyone life and breath and everything else. 26 From one man he made all the nations, that they should inhabit the whole earth; and he marked out their appointed times in history and the boundaries of their

lands. 27 God did this so that they would seek him and perhaps reach out for him and find him, though he is not far from any one of us. 28 'For in him we live and move and have our being.' As some of your own poets have said, 'We are his offspring.'

29 "Therefore since we are God's offspring, we should not think that the divine being is like gold or silver or stone—an image made by human design and skill. 30 In the past God overlooked such ignorance, but now he commands all people everywhere to repent. 31 For he has set a day when he will judge the world with justice by the man he has appointed. He has given proof of this to everyone by raising him from the dead."

32 When they heard about the resurrection of the dead, some of them sneered, but others said, "We want to hear you again on this subject." 33 At that, Paul left the Council. 34 Some of the people became followers of Paul and believed. Among them was Dionysius, a member of the Areopagus, also a woman named Damaris, and a number of others.

* * *

[*The following chapters tell of Paul's work in Corinth, Ephesus, and elsewhere, and a brief visit to Jerusalem (18:22). His trial before Gallio, proconsul of Achaia (18:12–17) provides the one occasion in Paul's life that can be rather precisely dated by modern scholarship.*]

19 21 After all this had happened, Paul decided to go to Jerusalem, passing through Macedonia and Achaia. "After I have been there," he said, "I must visit Rome also."

* * *

[*The artisans and worshipers of Artemis, disturbed by Paul's success, provoke a near riot in Ephesus. Paul departs for Macedonia. After working there until after Passover, he begins his final journey to Jerusalem, pausing en route in Miletus.*]

20 17 From Miletus, Paul sent to Ephesus for the elders of the church. 18 When they arrived, he said to them: "You know how I lived the whole time I was with you, from the first day I came into the province of Asia. 19 I served the Lord with great humility and with tears and in the midst of severe testing by the plots of the Jews. 20 You know that I have not hesitated to preach anything that would be helpful to you but have taught you publicly and from house to house. 21 I have declared to both Jews and Greeks that they must turn to God in repentance and have faith in our Lord Jesus.

22 "And now, compelled by the Spirit, I am going to Jerusalem, not knowing what will happen to me there. 23 I only know that in every city the Holy Spirit warns me that prison and hardships are facing me. 24 However, I consider my life worth nothing to me; my only aim is to finish the race and complete the task the Lord Jesus has given me—the task of testifying to the good news of God's grace.

25 "Now I know that none of you among whom I have gone about preaching the kingdom will ever see me again. 26 Therefore, I declare to you today that I am innocent of the blood of everyone. 27 For I have not

hesitated to proclaim to you the whole will of God. 28 Keep watch over yourselves and all the flock of which the Holy Spirit has made you over-seers. Be shepherds of the church of God, which he bought with his own blood. 29 I know that after I leave, savage wolves will come in among you and will not spare the flock. 30 Even from your own number some will arise and distort the truth in order to draw away disciples after them. 31 So be on your guard! Remember that for three years I never stopped warning each of you night and day with tears.

32 "Now I commit you to God and to the word of his grace, which can build you up and give you an inheritance among all those who are sanc-tified. 33 I have not coveted anyone's silver or gold or clothing. 34 You yourselves know that these hands of mine have supplied my own needs and the needs of my companions. 35 In everything I did, I showed you that by this kind of hard work we must help the weak, remembering the words the Lord Jesus himself said: 'It is more blessed to give than to receive.' "

36 When Paul had finished speaking, he knelt down with all of them and prayed. 37 They all wept as they embraced him and kissed him. 38 What grieved them most was his statement that they would never see his face again. Then they accompanied him to the ship.

*   *   *

21 7 We continued our voyage from Tyre and landed at Ptolemais, where we greeted the believers and stayed with them for a day. 8 Leaving the next day, we reached Caesarea and stayed at the house of Philip the evan-gelist, one of the Seven. 9 He had four unmarried daughters who proph-esied.

10 After we had been there a number of days, a prophet named Agabus came down from Judea. 11 Coming over to us, he took Paul's belt, tied his own hands and feet with it and said, "The Holy Spirit says, 'In this way the Jewish leaders in Jerusalem will bind the owner of this belt and will hand him over to the Gentiles.' "

12 When we heard this, we and the people there pleaded with Paul not to go up to Jerusalem. 13 Then Paul answered, "Why are you weeping and breaking my heart? I am ready not only to be bound, but also to die in Jerusalem for the name of the Lord Jesus." 14 When he would not be dissuaded, we gave up and said, "The Lord's will be done."

15 After this, we started on our way up to Jerusalem. 16 Some of the disciples from Caesarea accompanied us and brought us to the home of Mnason, where we were to stay. He was a man from Cyprus and one of the early disciples.

17 When we arrived at Jerusalem, the believers received us warmly. 18 The next day Paul and the rest of us went to see James, and all the elders were present. 19 Paul greeted them and reported in detail what God had done among the Gentiles through his ministry.

20 When they heard this, they praised God. Then they said to Paul: "You see, brother, how many thousands of Jews have believed, and all of them are zealous for the law. 21 They have been informed that you teach all the Jews who live among the Gentiles to turn away from Moses, telling them not to circumcise their children or live according to our customs. 22 What shall we do? They will certainly hear that you have come, 23 so do what

we tell you. There are four men with us who have made a vow. 24 Take these men, join in their purification rites and pay their expenses, so that they can have their heads shaved. Then everyone will know there is no truth in these reports about you, but that you yourself are living in obedience to the law. 25 As for the Gentile believers, we have written to them our decision that they should abstain from food sacrificed to idols, from blood, from the meat of strangled animals and from sexual immorality."

26 The next day Paul took the men and purified himself along with them. Then he went to the temple to give notice of the date when the days of purification would end and the offering would be made for each of them.

27 When the seven days were nearly over, some Jews from the province of Asia saw Paul at the temple. They stirred up the whole crowd and seized him, 28 shouting, "People of Israel, help us! This is the man who teaches everyone everywhere against our people and our law and this place. And besides, he has brought Greeks into the temple and defiled this holy place." 29 (They had previously seen Trophimus the Ephesian in the city with Paul and assumed that Paul had brought him into the temple.)

30 The whole city was aroused, and the people came running from all directions. Seizing Paul, they dragged him from the temple, and immediately the gates were shut. 31 While they were trying to kill him, news reached the commander of the Roman troops that the whole city of Jerusalem was in an uproar. 32 He at once took some officers and soldiers and ran down to the crowd. When the rioters saw the commander and his soldiers, they stopped beating Paul.

33 The commander came up and arrested him and ordered him to be bound with two chains. Then he asked who he was and what he had done. 34 Some in the crowd shouted one thing and some another, and since the commander could not get at the truth because of the uproar, he ordered that Paul be taken into the barracks. 35 When Paul reached the steps, the violence of the mob was so great he had to be carried by the soldiers. 36 The crowd that followed kept shouting, "Get rid of him!"

*   *   *

[Paul makes a speech to the mob, recounting the story of his conversion. His defense before the council and chief priests the next day cleverly exploits the division between Pharisees and Sadducees on belief in resurrection. Transferred to Caesarea to avoid a plot to lynch him, Paul is next tried before the procurator Felix, who delays Paul's case for two years, until Porcius Festus succeeds to the governorship.]

25 Three days after arriving in the province, Festus went up from Caesarea to Jerusalem, 2 where the chief priests and the Jewish leaders appeared before him and presented the charges against Paul. 3 They requested Festus, as a favor to them, to have Paul transferred to Jerusalem, for they were preparing an ambush to kill him along the way. 4 Festus answered, "Paul is being held at Caesarea, and I myself am going there soon. 5 Let some of your leaders come with me, and if the man has done anything wrong, they can press charges against him there."

6 After spending eight or ten days with them, Festus went down to Caesarea. The next day he convened the court and ordered that Paul be brought before him. 7 When Paul came in, the Jews who had come down

from Jerusalem stood around him. They brought many serious charges against him, but they could not prove them.

8 Then Paul made his defense: "I have done nothing wrong against the Jewish law or against the temple or against Caesar."

9 Festus, wishing to do the Jews a favor, said to Paul, "Are you willing to go up to Jerusalem and stand trial before me there on these charges?"

10 Paul answered: "I am now standing before Caesar's court, where I ought to be tried. I have not done any wrong to the Jews, as you yourself know very well. 11 If, however, I am guilty of doing anything deserving death, I do not refuse to die. But if the charges brought against me by these Jews are not true, no one has the right to hand me over to them. I appeal to Caesar!"

12 After Festus had conferred with his council, he declared: "You have appealed to Caesar. To Caesar you will go!"

13 A few days later King Agrippa and Bernice arrived at Caesarea to pay their respects to Festus. 14 Since they were spending many days there, Festus discussed Paul's case with the king. He said: "There is a man here whom Felix left as a prisoner. 15 When I went to Jerusalem, the chief priests and the elders of the Jews brought charges against him and asked that he be condemned.

16 "I told them that it is not the Roman custom to hand over anyone before they have faced their accusers and have had an opportunity to defend themselves against the charges. 17 When they came here with me, I did not delay the case, but convened the court the next day and ordered the man to be brought in. 18 When his accusers got up to speak, they did not charge him with any of the crimes I had expected. 19 Instead, they had some points of dispute with him about their own religion and about a dead man named Jesus who Paul claimed was alive. 20 I was at a loss how to investigate such matters; so I asked if he would be willing to go to Jerusalem and stand trial there on these charges. 21 But when Paul made his appeal to be held over for the Emperor's decision, I ordered him held until I could send him to Caesar."

22 Then Agrippa said to Festus, "I would like to hear this man myself."

He replied, "Tomorrow you will hear him."

23 The next day Agrippa and Bernice came with great pomp and entered the audience room with the high-ranking military officers and the prominent men of the city. At the command of Festus, Paul was brought in. 24 Festus said: "King Agrippa, and all who are present with us, you see this man! The whole Jewish community has petitioned me about him in Jerusalem and here in Caesarea, shouting that he ought not to live any longer. 25 I found he had done nothing deserving of death, but because he made his appeal to the Emperor I decided to send him to Rome. 26 But I have nothing definite to write to His Majesty about him. Therefore I have brought him before all of you, and especially before you, King Agrippa, so that as a result of this investigation I may have something to write. 27 For I think it is unreasonable to send a prisoner on to Rome without specifying the charges against him."

26 Then Agrippa said to Paul, "You have permission to speak for yourself."

So Paul motioned with his hand and began his defense: 2 "King Agrippa, I consider myself fortunate to stand before you today as I make my defense against all the accusations of the Jews, 3 and especially so because you are well acquainted with all the Jewish customs and controversies. Therefore, I beg you to listen to me patiently.

4 "The Jewish people all know the way I have lived ever since I was a child, from the beginning of my life in my own country, and also in Jerusalem. 5 They have known me for a long time and can testify, if they are willing, that I conformed to the strictest sect of our religion, living as a Pharisee. 6 And now it is because of my hope in what God has promised our ancestors that I am on trial today. 7 This is the promise our twelve tribes are hoping to see fulfilled as they earnestly serve God day and night. King Agrippa, it is because of this hope that the Jews are accusing me. 8 Why should any of you consider it incredible that God raises the dead?

9 "I too was convinced that I ought to do all that was possible to oppose the name of Jesus of Nazareth. 10 And that is just what I did in Jerusalem. On the authority of the chief priests I put many of the Lord's people in prison, and when they were put to death, I cast my vote against them. 11 Many a time I went from one synagogue to another to have them punished, and I tried to force them to blaspheme. I was so obsessed with persecuting them that I even hunted them down in foreign cities.

12 "On one of these journeys I was going to Damascus with the authority and commission of the chief priests. 13 About noon, King Agrippa, as I was on the road, I saw a light from heaven, brighter than the sun, blazing around me and my companions. 14 We all fell to the ground, and I heard a voice saying to me in Aramaic, 'Saul, Saul, why do you persecute me? It is hard for you to kick against the goads.'

15 "Then I asked, 'Who are you, Lord?'

" 'I am Jesus, whom you are persecuting,' the Lord replied. 16 'Now get up and stand on your feet. I have appeared to you to appoint you as a servant and as a witness of what you have seen and will see of me. 17 I will rescue you from your own people and from the Gentiles. I am sending you to them 18 to open their eyes and turn them from darkness to light, and from the power of Satan to God, so that they may receive forgiveness of sins and a place among those who are sanctified by faith in me.'

19 "So then, King Agrippa, I was not disobedient to the vision from heaven. 20 First to those in Damascus, then to those in Jerusalem and in all Judea, and then to the Gentiles, I preached that they should repent and turn to God and demonstrate their repentance by their deeds. 21 That is why some Jews seized me in the temple courts and tried to kill me. 22 But God has helped me to this very day; so I stand here and testify to small and great alike. I am saying nothing beyond what the prophets and Moses said would happen— 23 that the Messiah would suffer and, as the first to rise from the dead, would bring the message of light to his own people and to the Gentiles."

24 At this point Festus interrupted Paul's defense. "You are out of your mind, Paul!" he shouted. "Your great learning is driving you insane."

25 "I am not insane, most excellent Festus," Paul replied. "What I am saying is true and reasonable. 26 The king is familiar with these things, and I can speak freely to him. I am convinced that none of this has escaped his notice, because it was not done in a corner. 27 King Agrippa, do you believe the prophets? I know you do."

28 Then Agrippa said to Paul, "Do you think that in such a short time you can persuade me to be a Christian?"

29 Paul replied, "Short time or long—I pray to God that not only you but all who are listening to me today may become what I am, except for these chains."

30 The king rose, and with him the governor and Bernice and those sitting with them. 31 After they left the room, they began saying to one another, "This man is not doing anything that deserves death or imprisonment."

32 Agrippa said to Festus, "This man could have been set free if he had not appealed to Caesar."

27 When it was decided that we would sail for Italy, Paul and some other prisoners were handed over to a centurion named Julius, who belonged to the Imperial Regiment. 2 We boarded a ship from Adramyttium about to sail for ports along the coast of the province of Asia, and we put out to sea. Aristarchus, a Macedonian from Thessalonica, was with us.

3 The next day we landed at Sidon; and Julius, in kindness to Paul, allowed him to go to his friends so they might provide for his needs. 4 From there we put out to sea again and passed to the lee of Cyprus because the winds were against us. 5 When we had sailed across the open sea off the coast of Cilicia and Pamphylia, we landed at Myra in Lycia. 6 There the centurion found an Alexandrian ship sailing for Italy and put us on board.

* * *

[*The omitted portions describe the voyage, including a shipwreck on Malta. Paul's prescience and his miraculous recovery from the bite of a viper, as well as other miracles, are important aspects of the Acts' portrait.*]

28 11 After three months we put out to sea in a ship that had wintered in the island—it was an Alexandrian ship with the figurehead of the twin gods Castor and Pollux. 12 We put in at Syracuse and stayed there three days. 13 From there we set sail and arrived at Rhegium. The next day the south wind came up, and on the following day we reached Puteoli. 14 There we found some believers who invited us to spend a week with them. And so we came to Rome. 15 The believers there had heard that we were coming, and they traveled as far as the Forum of Appius and the Three Taverns to meet us. At the sight of these people Paul thanked God and was encouraged. 16 When we got to Rome, Paul was allowed to live by himself, with a soldier to guard him.

17 Three days later he called together the local Jewish leaders. When they had assembled, Paul said to them: "My brothers, although I have done nothing against our people or against the customs of our ancestors, I was arrested in Jerusalem and handed over to the Romans. 18 They examined me and wanted to release me, because I was not guilty of any crime deserving death. 19 The Jews objected, so I was compelled to make an appeal to Caesar. I certainly did not intend to bring any charge against my own people. 20 For this reason I have asked to see you and talk with you. It is because of the hope of Israel that I am bound with this chain."

21 They replied, "We have not received any letters from Judea concerning you, and none of our people who have come from there has reported or said anything bad about you. 22 But we want to hear what your views are, for we know that people everywhere are talking against this sect."

23 They arranged to meet Paul on a certain day, and came in even larger

numbers to the place where he was staying. He witnessed to them from morning till evening, explaining about the kingdom of God, and from the Law of Moses and from the Prophets he tried to persuade them about Jesus. 24 Some were convinced by what he said, but others would not believe. 25 They disagreed among themselves and began to leave after Paul had made this final statement: "The Holy Spirit spoke the truth to your ancestors when he said through Isaiah the prophet:

26 " 'Go to this people and say,
      "You will be ever hearing but never understanding;
      you will be ever seeing but never perceiving."
27 For this people's heart has become calloused;
      they hardly hear with their ears,
      and they have closed their eyes.
      Otherwise they might see with their eyes,
      hear with their ears,
      understand with their hearts
      and turn, and I would heal them.'
28 "Therefore I want you to know that God's salvation has been sent to the Gentiles, and they will listen!"

30 For two whole years Paul stayed there in his own rented house and welcomed all who came to see him. 31 He proclaimed the kingdom of God and taught about the Lord Jesus Christ—with all boldness and without hindrance!

IRENÆUS

[Luke as Paul's Companion and Biographer] (ca. 180)†

*   *   *

Luke also, the companion of Paul, recorded in a book the Gospel preached by him.

*   *   *

But that this Luke was inseparable from Paul, and his fellow-labourer in the Gospel, he himself clearly evinces, not as a matter of boasting, but as bound to do so by the truth itself. For he says that when Barnabas, and John who was called Mark, had parted company from Paul, and sailed to Cyprus, "we came to Troas;"[1] and when Paul had beheld in a dream a man of Macedonia, saying, "Come into Macedonia, Paul, and help us," "immediately," he says, "we endeavoured to go into Macedonia, understanding that the Lord had called us to preach the Gospel unto them. Therefore, sailing from Troas, we directed our ship's course towards Samothracia." And then he carefully indicates all the rest of their journey as far as Philippi, and how they delivered their first address: "for, sitting down," he says, "we spake unto the

---

† From *Haer.* 3.1 and 3.14, tr. by W. H. Rambaut, in *The Ante-Nicene Fathers*, Vol. I (New York: Scribner's, 1885; rp. Grand Rapids; Eerdmans, 1951). Irenaeus (ca. 115–ca. 202) was Bishop of Lyons.
1. Acts 16:8.

women who had assembled;"[2] and certain believed, even a great many. And again does he say, "But we sailed from Philippi after the days of unleavened bread, and came to Troas, where we abode seven days."[3] And all the remaining [details] of his course with Paul he recounts, indicating with all diligence both places, and cities, and number of days, until they went up to Jerusalem; and what befell Paul there, how he was sent to Rome in bonds; the name of the centurion who took him in charge; and the signs of the ships, and how they made shipwreck; and the island upon which they escaped, and how they received kindness there, Paul healing the chief man of that island; and how they sailed from thence to Puteoli, and from that arrived at Rome; and for what period they sojourned at Rome.[4] As Luke was present at all these occurrences, he carefully noted them down in writing, so that he cannot be convicted of falsehood or boastfulness, because all these [particulars] proved both that he was senior to all those who now teach otherwise, and that he was not ignorant of the truth. That he was not merely a follower, but also a fellow-labourer of the apostles, but especially of Paul, Paul has himself declared also in the Epistles, saying: "Demas hath forsaken me, . . . and is departed unto Thessalonica; Crescens to Galatia, Titus to Dalmatia. Only Luke is with me."[5] From this he shows that he was always attached to and inseparable from him. And again he says, in the Epistle to the Colossians: "Luke, the beloved physician, greets you."[6] But surely if Luke, who always preached in company with Paul, and is called by him "the beloved," and with him performed the work of an evangelist, and was entrusted to hand down to us a Gospel, learned nothing different from him (Paul), as has been pointed out from his words, how can these men, who were never attached to Paul, boast that they have learned hidden and unspeakable mysteries?

DANIEL R. SCHWARTZ

[Paul in the Canonical Book of Acts] (1990)†

There are two ways to approach the topic of Acts' portrayal of Paul: from the side of Paul and from the side of Luke-Acts. The first—from the side of Paul and his epistles—is the approach with which the modern debate on the subject began. Philip Vielhauer's article "On the 'Paulinism' of Acts," published in 1950, initiated a tradition that Werner Georg Kümmel was to call "Luke as Accused by Contemporary Theologians." This tradition, as Kümmel notes, was primarily theological in character, represented by theologians who took their point of departure from the New Testament theologian par excellence, Paul, and found Luke's rendition of him want-

2. Acts 16:13.
3. Acts 20:5 f.
4. Acts 21–28.
5. 2 Tim. 4:10 f.
6. Col. 4:14.
† From "The End of the Line: Paul in the Canonical Book of Acts," in *Paul and the Legacies of Paul*, ed. William S. Babcock (Dallas: SMU Press, 1990), 3–24. Reprinted by permission of the author and Southern Methodist University Press. Schwartz is professor of Jewish history at the Hebrew University of Jerusalem.

ing. For everyone—or almost everyone—agrees that Luke's Paul does not sound like Paul's Paul. On this score, the only arguments that usually come into play concern just how irreconcilable the two versions of Paul are.

The second approach is from the side of Luke-Acts: one can study Luke-Acts as a whole and then attempt to discover the meaning and function, within this context, of the material relating to Paul. This approach, it seems, has come more and more to be preferred in recent years. This shift in orientation reflects not only the fact that Pauline scholars are again relegating Acts to the sidelines of their discussions, but also the effect of certain other works that appeared at about the same time as Vielhauer's article and set in motion an opposing tradition dedicated to clarifying Lucan theology in its own right (something that many previous scholars, taken up with form-critical and source-critical studies, did not admit existed). The pioneers of this other approach, usually termed *redaction criticism* or *composition criticism*, were Hans Conzelmann, whose *Die Mitte der Zeit* appeared in 1954 (it was based on his 1952 dissertation and *Habilitationsschrift*), and Martin Dibelius, whose *Aufsätze zur Apostelgeschichte* appeared in 1951 (and included a previously unpublished essay, "Paulus in der Apostelgeschichte"). If pre-World War II scholarship had tended either to neglect Acts or to treat it only as history, the work of these two scholars—and of their many followers—served to focus attention on the Lucan work as a whole, raising questions about the meaning that Luke attached to the events he reported—or distorted or failed to report—and the methods he used in doing so. This point of view became dominant with the publication of Ernst Haenchen's and Hans Conzelmann's commentaries on Acts, both of which show only relatively minor interest in history per se and are devoted rather to such topics as apologetics and kerygma.

Now it is true that this approach can go much too far. One occasionally has the feeling that some German scholars would be quite pleased if it were established beyond doubt that everything in Acts is historically false, for then it would be clear that Luke wrote his work only for kerygmatic or apologetic reasons. And although it is true that viewing the study of Acts only as a preface to the historical study of early Christianity—as in the case of the largest pre-World War II collaborative effort on Acts—leaves out much of importance, it is no less troubling to note that the largest postwar collaborative effort on Acts, published in 1979, leaves history entirely out of its purview. Nevertheless it is in this direction—from Luke-Acts to Paul—that we must proceed here, for our concern lies not in deciding whether Acts may be used to amplify our knowledge of Paul but rather in clarifying Luke's understanding of Paul and his legacy and in tracing the use to which he put Paul.

Luke-Acts and the Lucan Paul

Acts tells the story of the transformation of Christianity from a community that is (a) Palestinian, (b) Jewish, and (c) Torah-observing into a movement that is, for the most part, (a) diasporan, (b) gentile, and (c) nonobservant of the Torah. In short, whether one regards "being Jewish" as a matter of territory, of race, of religion, or of some combination of these factors, Acts describes how Christianity came to be something non-Jewish. The adjectives *schematic*, *pragmatic*, and *apologetic* seem to me to capture the most salient aspects of this narrative and therefore provide useful headings for characterizing Acts' account of Paul (the Pauline material takes up roughly two-thirds of the book, chiefly chapters 9 and 13–28). After seeing just how well Luke's portrayal of Paul corresponds with (Luke)-Acts in general, we will turn to Luke's presentation of Paul's kerygmatic teachings in particular.

SCHEMATIC

Acts is *schematic* in that it organizes events not, or not always, according to their historical order but rather according to their meaning for the story as the author wishes to present it. Perhaps this is what Luke meant in promising to tell his story *kathexes* (Lk. 1:3). Already in his gospel, for example, Luke had moved the Nazareth pericope forward to the very beginning of Jesus' mission, thus giving the impression of a linear progression from Nazareth to Jerusalem. Similarly, in Acts 11:19ff., we are told that those who were scattered by the persecution that arose in connection with Stephen reached Antioch and began to preach there to non-Jews. These happenings are obviously more or less contemporary with the events recorded in Acts 8 regarding other such refugees, but Luke postponed the story so as to locate it after the account of God's and the church's decision, in Jerusalem, to accept gentile converts (Acts 10–11). If in the gospel everything must progress neatly toward Jerusalem, in Acts things must progress just as neatly in the other direction, outward from Jerusalem.

In a more encompassing way too, Acts exhibits a quite schematic structure with regard to the departures of Christianity from Jewish land, race, and law. In the first six chapters, Christianity is limited to Jerusalem alone; those from outside who would associate themselves with it must come "centripetally" to the capital. It is only after a speech (Acts 7) focusing on God's transcendence and lack of specific interest in Palestine or the temple (along with some other themes) that the movement begins to expand geographically (Acts 8). Having thus broken with the territorial criterion, Luke next takes up the ethnic one, which he had left untouched in the earlier chapters. After telling of some missionizing in what has been called a *Zwischenbereich* of those whose Jewish descent is unclear (the Samaritans and the Ethiopian eunuch of Acts 8) and after Christianizing Paul (Acts 9)—the man who will be the main apostle to the Gentiles, as Luke's readers may already have known and would read a few chapters later—Luke fully and formally recounts how God opened the church to the Gentiles (Acts 10–11). At this point, Luke proceeds to show how the church came to be composed of increasing numbers of Gentiles, due both to the activities of missionaries and to rejection by Jews (Acts 11:19–14:28), thus making it necessary for the next topic to emerge: what obligations of the Torah, if any, devolve upon gentile Christians? And this is, in fact, the next topic addressed head on in Acts, just as programmatically as were Stephen's speech regarding territory and the Cornelius episode regarding race. The consequent discussion (Acts 15)—in which all participants, apart from the original troublemakers, are said to have agreed—results in the emancipation of Christianity from the last specific mark distinguishing Jews from non-Jews. And just as the postponement of the missionizing to Gentiles (to Acts 11:19ff.) was, as we noted, the result of such Lucan schematization, so too the postponement of the question of "the Gentiles and the law" (to Acts 15) reflects a similar concern. The question should have been raised immediately upon the baptism of Cornelius in chapter 10, but Luke postponed it so that it would follow the successful missionizing of the man who was known to be the great missionary to the Gentiles and the great anti-legalist.

Having moved from Lucan schematization in general to Lucan schematization in relation to Paul in particular and having intimated that here too Luke has arranged his materials other than chronologically, I want now to explain why I believe that most of the Pauline material prior to chapter 15 is in fact out of place and that its placement is therefore a legitimate—and in fact an imperative—object for exegesis. The situation with regard to chapters 13–14 is rather simple. Since Galatians 1–2 indicate that Paul visited Jerusalem only once between his call and the so-called apostolic conference, whereas Acts reports two such visits (9:25–30; 11:27–30 [with 12:25]), it is clear that something must be done to account for the discrepancy. I shall do what is usually done; that is, I shall assume that 11:27–30 (with 12:25) and chapter 15 refer to one and the same visit but report different aspects of it. Note, for example, that "both" visits begin with Judaean Christians coming to Antioch and Paul and Barnabas being sent back to Jerusalem in response.

The next question, however, is more difficult: once we have decided to equate the two visits reported separately in chapters 11 and 15, should we then move 11:27–30 forward in time or Acts 15 back in time to combine them into one? That is, did Paul's journeys of chapters 13–14 come before the famine visit and apostolic conference or after? The latter seems far more likely to me. Placing the events of Acts 15 prior to the journeys would bring the question of the Gentiles' obligations into immediate juxtaposition with that of their acceptance into the church—which, as noted above, is where it belongs. Furthermore, this placing eliminates another problem raised by the current order of Acts and left unresolved by the other option (i.e., moving 11:27–30 forward in time): why does the apostolic decree (Acts 15:23) address the Christians of Antioch, Syria, and Cilicia alone—all of whom are mentioned in Acts 11—but ignore the many places Paul is said to have visited and successfully evangelized in chapters 13–14? Instead of supposing that Paul, as the narrative of Acts would have it, interrupted his journey of Acts 13–14 to return to Jerusalem and then went back to the same places to give them a decree not addressed to them at all (16:4), would it not be simpler to assume that the decree was in fact issued before Paul began his major missionary work in Asia Minor? Then it would seem that Luke, assuming that the squabble arose and the decision was made with regard to Paul's work, postponed his account of the conference until after Paul had begun his missionizing in Asia Minor and taken his "turn to the Gentiles" and thus had Paul interrupt his journey to come back for the conference.

The situation is quite similar with regard to Acts 9, the other main block of Pauline material prior to chapter 15. We note first that in the material preceding chapter 9, Paul is mentioned only in reference to the persecution following Stephen's speech; but as has often been recognized, these references are redactional: the *Wiederaufnahme* at the beginning of 7:59 clearly marks the brief allusion to Saul the persecutor in 7:58 as a secondary insertion; and the redundance of 8:1 and 8:3 just as clearly does the same for the former of these two verses. Furthermore, the only other New Testament reference to Paul's participation in the persecution at the time of Stephen comes in a Lucan addition to one of his versions of Paul's call (22:20). Thus, on the one hand, we have no solid reason to assume that Paul was still unconverted at the time of Stephen's martyrdom and the subsequent persecution. On the other hand, we have good reason to believe that Paul was in fact a Christian by the time of that persecution. As several scholars have argued, the Jewish initiative and the complete lack of Roman presence in the story of Stephen apparently indicate that the episode occurred during a break in Roman administration in Judaea following the removal of Pilate and the death of Tiberius. Tiberius died in March of 37, and Pilate was removed from office only shortly before. Given the data of Galatians 1:18 and 2:1, where Paul dates his conversion fourteen (plus three?) years before the apostolic conference, and given the common dating of the latter (and of the famine as well) to around 48 C.E., it follows that Paul was already a Christian by the time of the death of Stephen and the attendant persecution.

It is difficult to determine whether Luke knew that his chronology was wrong. As a fellow historian, I would prefer to give him the benefit of the doubt; and in fact, in at least one case, we are in a good position to see how Luke may have been misled. According to all scholars, the death of Agrippa I is out of place in Luke's narrative, for Josephus locates the famine of Acts 11:27–30 not under Agrippa but during the term of Tiberius Julius Alexander, the second governor of Judaea after Agrippa's death (*Ant.* 20.101). When we note that Acts calls Agrippa "Herod," a name that is never used of him elsewhere in ancient literature, we may suspect, however, that Luke thought the reference was to Herod of Chalcis, Agrippa's brother. And this Herod, according to Josephus (*Ant.* 20.104), did in fact die right after the famine. Thus, if Luke's source termed Agrippa "Herod" —perhaps because of the negative associations of that name for Christians—Luke may diligently have searched for a ruler of that name and found the only possible candidate in the relevant time frame. Similarly, if Luke had a tradition that Paul participated in the persecution of Christians and if the only persecution known to him was the one related to Stephen, he could have inserted Paul there in complete good conscience. And if he had two sources reporting a trip by Saul and Barnabas to Jerusalem and what they did there, he might well have been hard put—as modern scholars frequently are in similar cases—to decide whether the two sources referred to different trips or to the same one.

Nevertheless, whether intentionally misplaced or not, these episodes function eminently well in the structure of Luke's narrative. We have already noted that Paul's call in chapter 9 serves, along with the reports in chapter 8 about the Samaritans and the Ethiopian eunuch, to help prepare the way for the admission of the Gentiles in chapters 10–11. Now we are in a position to note that the persecution of chapter 12 is supported by the whole Jewish people (Acts 12:3, 4, 11). Such a generalization is possible only after the decision has been taken to open the church to others; otherwise the universal hostility of the Jewish people would simply spell failure on the church's part. Again, although we have already noted that chapters 13–14 prepare us for the urgency with which the question of Gentiles' legal obligations is raised in chapter 15, we may now add that it is only in chapter 13, in all of Acts, that Paul criticizes the law (13:38–39) and only here that he (or anyone else in Acts) speaks of "justification," and that by "faith." In other words, when we note that it is not only the place-ment of this chapter but also the specific contents of its sermon that help to prepare us for chapter 15, we realize that we are not dealing with a simple cut-and-paste job but rather with a carefully considered scheme in which Paul has his role to play.

PRAGMATIC

Having thus arrived at a point of Pauline theology, we shall now turn to the second adjective that we applied to Acts: *pragmatic*. In Acts, history moves because things happen or fail to happen, not because of ideas alone. The many unfinished or shrugged-off speeches in Acts testify that Luke realized that most people share Gallio's attitude toward "words and names" (18:15). In contrast, miracles, including Paul's miracles, are very effica-cious; and it is thus no surprise that this aspect of Paul is very prominent in Acts, far beyond anything that his epistles would have led us to expect. Again, in Paul's criticism of the law (13:38–39), the point seems to be less theoretical or theological (works or law and justification are inherently incompatible) than empirical: the law did not grant you justification because you could not fulfill it. The same point is made much more clearly by Peter and James and their colleagues in 15:10, 21, 28. It is therefore not surprising—however disconcerting or contemptible it may be for some readers of Paul's epistles—that a sharp distinction between faith and works is unknown to Luke's Paul, who rather demands "works worthy of repen-tance" (26:20), just as Luke's John the Baptist had done (Lk. 3:8).

The most important pragmatic aspect of the Lucan portrayal of Paul, however, is that it was only pragmatic considerations that led Luke's Paul, against his wishes, to break with Judaea and the Jews. It was only Jewish misunderstanding and hostility that forced Paul out of the temple and out of Jerusalem (9:28–30; 21ff.); it was only as a prisoner and to save his life that Paul was sent away from Jerusalem to Caesarea (Rome's local repre-sentative); and it was only to vindicate himself in the face of hostile Jewish accusations that Paul was eventually transferred to Rome. Thus, as Paul is made to tell us three times in Acts (13:46; 18:6; 28:28 [cf. 19:9]), it was only because the Jews rejected him that he turned away. What then of the promise to Abraham that figures so prominently in Romans and Galatians? And what, for that matter, of Romans 9–11 and the theologically attractive, if unpragmatic, notion that Israel retains its primacy and that God will eventually return to it? Nothing of this sort is to be found in Acts as I read it. Instead we have the simple notion that the gospel is to be preached to those who will accept it. Although the gospel indeed began with the Jews, they rejected it—and there is no reason to bang one's head interminably against a stone wall. Note especially in this regard that of the three versions of Paul's call in Acts, only the last two, which come after Paul has twice announced his break with the Jews (13:46; 18:6), report that Jesus charged Paul to evangelize Gentiles (22:15, 21; 26:17). In the first version, which comes before the Jewish rejection of the gospel, Gentiles figure only among those before whom Paul (like Jesus before him) will have to suffer (9:15–

16; cf. 4:25–28 regarding Jesus). Indeed, whereas it is almost universally held that Acts portrays Paul as fulfilling Jesus' mandate to the apostles to be his witnesses to the end of the earth (1:8)—including to the Gentiles—it seems instead to be the case, as I have argued elsewhere, that the mandate refers to the end of the *land* (of Israel)—to Jews alone—and that Luke depicts Paul, in the wake of Jewish rejection of his message, as having reinterpreted *land* as *earth* with the aid of Isaiah 49: 6 (Acts 13: 47). Below, in our review of Luke's version of Paul's kerygma, we will return to this matter.

APOLOGETIC

This last aspect of Luke's pragmatism with regard to Paul—that is, his claim that Paul left Judaea and the Jews only because they forced him away—leads us to our final adjective for Acts: *apologetic*. The claim that the Jews drove Paul away is the first of the two major features of Luke's apologetics in Acts. It puts the blame for the schism on the hostility and misunderstanding of others. Specifically, in the first eleven chapters of Acts the opponents of the gospel are only certain segments of the Jewish people, mainly the high-priestly aristocracy. Given the association of that aristocracy with the Sadducees (which Luke emphasizes in Acts 5:17), who denied resurrection (as stressed in Lk. 20:27 and Acts 23:8), this identification of the gospel's enemies coheres well with Luke's focus, in Acts, on the resurrection as the heart of the gospel (to which we will return below). The "people," in contrast, are generally said to be favorably disposed toward the church; and it was, of course, from their ranks that new converts came in great numbers (who else was there?) But after the events of chapters 10–11 made it possible to turn away from the Jewish people, Acts suddenly begins to claim in chapter 12, as we have noted, that the whole Jewish people was hostile to the church. And in the account of Paul that follows, this claim is often repeated, even when the details of Acts itself reveal that the matter was not so clear-cut. Thus Acts 13:43 informs us that many Jews were among those who received Paul's message favorably, but 13:45 reports that "the Jews" jealously attacked Paul (so also 14: 1–4; 17:4–5). Paul, for his part, is time and again forced to suffer due to Jewish hostility; and his wanderings are to a certain extent simply a matter of perpetual flight. Nevertheless he continually returns to the synagogues to preach to the Jews; and as we have noted, he even twice overlooks his formal decision to give up the Jewish mission and preach to Gentiles alone.

It is in this context that Paul's strict adherence to the law, according to Acts' repeated testimony, is to be understood. For this portrayal of Paul is just as efficient apologetically as it is difficult for readers of the epistles to accept. Whether or not Acts was also intended for Roman eyes, as an appeal for recognition of Christianity as true Judaism and thus as a licit religion, it is certain that the work was intended to be read by Christians. For such readers, the claim that the Jews rejected the gospel and Paul, and not vice versa, would serve to explain the need for God's intervention and for charting a new course. Luke makes this point very artistically in chapter 22, in the second account of Paul's calling, where—as is appropriate for a speech made in response to being arrested in the temple—a temple scene is included, which is not to be found in the other two versions of the call (Acts 9; 26). Here Paul is said to have been praying in the temple, as the apostles were wont to do (Acts 3:1; 5:12, 42), when Jesus appeared to him and told him to flee Jerusalem immediately, since the Jews would not accept his testimony. Paul did not want to go and remonstrated, pointing out that the Jews knew that he used to persecute the Christians energetically. This reply is either a response to the admonition to flee (Paul means that the Jews, out of consideration for his former "merit," will overlook his current heresy) or a response to the prediction that the Jews will not accept his message (Paul means that his message will be especially convincing, coming as it does from a former persecutor). But Jesus ends the debate with a sovereign command: "Go, for I am sending you far away to the Gentiles" (22:21, NEB). But—and this point is unmistakable—Luke here has Paul telling the story after he had again returned to worship in the temple and demonstrate his loyalty to it (Acts 21:26ff.). In other words, just as Paul twice ignored his own decision to give up on the Jews, so too he first disputed and later ignored Jesus' command to leave Jerusalem. It was only that exasperating Jewish hostility, combining misunderstanding and calumny into an attempt on Paul's life (Acts 21:27ff.), that compelled his departure. And although Paul is said to have been willing to die rather than stay away from Jerusalem (21:11–14), the Romans tear him away from the city to save his life (23:12–35) and also, as Luke reminds us just before the Romans take action (23:11), to fulfill Jesus' command that Paul leave Jerusalem to testify about him to the distant Gentiles (22:21). Despite all this, when Paul gets to Rome he again begins with the Jews; it is only when here too they reject him that he finally reaches the end of the line and, for the third and final time, turns away from them to the Gentiles. This is the Q.E.D. of the entire work, which is the reason the narrative may end here. But Luke took his time in coming to this point; and he took his time in order to make it quite clear that there was ample justification for the transformation of Christianity into something non-Jewish: no one could demand more patience or persistence, but the time had now come to move on.

This theme brings us to the other main focus of Luke's apologetics: Rome. Acts is concerned to show its readers that the Christian religion posed no threat to Rome and that Christians had, on the contrary, always honored Rome and been respected and protected by it. It has been debated whether this apologetic is addressed to Roman officialdom (as is usually assumed) to win toleration for the church or rather to Christian readers to conciliate them with the Empire or even to bring them to ascribe to it a positive role in the fulfillment of God's plans or perhaps to supply them with a model for self-defense in times of persecution. I doubt, however, that it is necessary or justified to settle on any one such alternative. The case is much the same as that regarding the "apologetic" literature of hellenistic Judaism: when one side in a potential conflict portrays the other favorably, readers on both sides will, if convinced, be less disposed to hostility. And indeed once a book is written—especially if, as in the case of Acts, it is written in the vernacular and in a familiar genre—there is no telling who might read it. Authors must bear both internal and external readerships in mind. Thus, when Paul is portrayed as a Roman citizen (Acts 16:37; 22:25–29) who depends on the Roman legal system and is repeatedly found by that system to be innocent of all wrongdoing (25:25;

26:30–32; 28:18), and when Paul's gospel is found to be of no concern to the Roman Empire (18:12–17; 25:19–20; 28:31) and is even accepted by some Roman officials (13:12; cf. 16:25–34; 24:24; 26:28[?]), Luke is quite obviously being apologetic—just as he was in his similar claims about Jesus and the charges (phrased much more politically than in the other gospels) brought against him (Lk. 23, especially 23:2).

In summary, then, we may conclude that Luke fits Paul into his schematic account of "the events that have happened among us" (Lk. 1:1) just as freely and deftly as he usually handles his material; that as a historian he focuses on events, not ideas; and that his depiction of Paul is just as apologetic vis-à-vis the Jews and Rome as is the rest of his work. We will be less than surprised, therefore, to find that the message Luke's Paul teaches is also a very Lucan message.

The Lucan Paul's Kerygma

Paul's preaching, according to Acts, has two foci: resurrection and the kingdom of God. Resurrection, on the one hand, is quite to be expected, for Paul was a Christian preacher whose only direct experience of Jesus Christ is said to have come after Christ's resurrection.

* * *

Acts 28:20, the final instance of "national" hope ("the hope of Israel") turns out to be very similar to the case of chapter 13: since the Jews, or most of them, reject Paul's message, an exasperated Paul tells them that "this salvation of God has now been sent to the Gentiles, and they will listen" (28: 28; cf especially ἀκούοντα δὲ τά ἔθνη in 13:48). If this same salvation can be offered to Gentiles, as it was to Jews, it must be that there is nothing specifically Jewish about it.

Now Acts 28:28, as we have just seen, says that salvation is something to which one may "listen"; it is, therefore, a message. But the message is that there is resurrection of the dead. How is that a saving message? The answer is, quite simply, that the fact that there is resurrection—a fact to which Paul can bear witness because, as Acts tells us repeatedly and at length, he has met a resurrected person—means that none can escape judgment. Those who believe Paul and take resurrection seriously will therefore repent and be saved. It is this repentance, this turning to God before death and resurrection to judgment, that Paul preaches (14:15; 17: 30–31; 26:18, 20; 28:27; see also 15:19 of Paul's converts and 24:16 of his own behavior: *because* he believes in the resurrection of the just and the unjust, *therefore* [ἐν τούτῳ] he strives always to keep his conscience clear). This is what it means to say that forgiveness of sins and justification are proclaimed through the resurrected Jesus and that all who believe therein will be saved (13:38–39). The Lucan Paul's message is that of Jonah, of John the Baptist, and of Jesus, except that Paul is not thinking of the coming judgment of a single city or nation but rather of every individual.

Conclusion: Luke on Paul and Jesus

This call for repentance before the coming judgment corresponds exactly, as we have just hinted, with the way in which Luke's story begins, with the preaching of John the Baptist. Indeed there is a noteworthy correlation between Paul's call for works worthy of repentance (26:20) and John's (Lk. 3:8); and in much the same way, it seems that the perplexing demonstrative pronoun *this* in Paul's final conclusion that "this salvation from God has been sent to the Gentiles" (Acts 28:28) refers back to the only other occurrences of the word *sōterion* in Luke-Acts, both of which come at the very beginning of the gospel. In the "Nunc dimittis," Simeon, holding the baby Jesus, praises God for letting him see "your deliverance which you made ready in full view of all the nations, a light that will be a revelation to the heathen and glory to your people Israel" (Lk. 2:30–32). And at the outset of John's mission, Luke, alone among the gospels, not only cites Isaiah 40:3 but continues the quotation to 40:5: "and all flesh shall see God's deliverance" (Lk. 3:6; contrast Mt. 3:3; Mk. 1:3; Jn. 1:34).

There are, however, two important differences between Simeon and John the Baptist at the beginning of Luke-Acts and Paul at its end, and both differences point to the thrust of Paul's function in Acts. In the first place, both Simeon and John remain within the framework of the Jewish people. Simeon speaks of a deliverance that brings glory to Israel alone, revealing its special status in God's eyes (cf. Dt. 28:10; Is. 52:10). John too, whatever criticism he may have for those who depend on their Israelite descent alone (Lk. 3:8), still considers the Gentiles as only an audience that will view God's deliverance. But Paul claims God's salvation has been sent to the Gentiles.

The other difference between Simeon and John, on the one hand, and Paul, on the other, concerns not the beneficiaries of salvation but its timing. According to Paul, this salvation has been sent to the Gentiles. Nothing else need happen; they must only listen. Paul, it seems from the end of Acts, is not waiting for any further divine intervention in history. Why not? The answer, I believe, goes hand in hand with our preceding observation. Paul, like John and Jesus, looks forward to a coming judgment and urges his listeners to repent so as to survive this judgment and be deemed worthy of eternal life. But whereas Simeon and John and even Jesus can only believe and hope that it will happen, Paul knows it will. The former, Luke says, were looking forward to a restoration of the people of Israel. They had promises but no empirical proof that it would happen. By the time Luke wrote, after more than a century of Herodian-Roman rule and after the destruction of the temple, it was clear that it would not happen; and Luke's apologetic point with respect to Rome is, as we have seen, the surrender of this hope. This surrender, however, leaves only the resurrection of the dead (as in Daniel 12) as the context of judgment; and of resurrection Luke's Paul has ample empirical experience, as the thrice-repeated story of his call laboriously demonstrates.

In other words, by the end of Acts, Jesus is important for Luke's Paul not for anything special he was (son of God or man or David or the like), nor for anything he taught (as in the gospel), nor for anything salvific accomplished by his death (as in Paul's epistles), but rather for what happened to him after he died: he was resurrected. That fact means that resurrection is real and judgment inescapable. As already in Acts 4:2 ("proclaiming in Jesus the resurrection"), so also in 17:31 and 26:23 ("first to rise from the dead") the resurrection of Christ is proof of the reality of resurrection. In these three verses—and in 17:18, 32; 23:6; 24:14, 21; 26:

8, 22–23 as well—the issue is not the resurrection of Jesus but rather the resurrection of the dead in general. The resurrection of Jesus is only a case in evidence. In Athens, Paul's teaching of "Jesus and resurrection" is misunderstood as referring to two things (17:18) but in fact means "resurrection as evidenced by Jesus" (see 17:31). By the same token, when in the very last verse of Acts, Paul's activity is summarized as *proclaiming* the kingdom of God and *teaching* about Jesus, the denationalized and depoliticized kingdom of God means no more than resurrection to judgment, and Jesus is simply the concrete example that Paul may confidently adduce.

We come, then, to our final point. The topic most frequently discussed regarding Luke's "Paulusbild" is the question of Luke's view of Paul's relation to the apostles. Does Luke try to "domesticate" Paul and subordinate him to the twelve apostles, as Günter Klein argued in *Die zwölf Apostel?* Or does he rather put Paul on a par with the apostles, as maintained especially by Christoph Burchard in *Der dreizehnte Zeuge?* Or does he make Paul the disciple of the apostles, as claimed, for example, by Eckhard Plümacher? Or should we agree, on the contrary, with Jacob Jervell, who in his most recent work on the subject argued that Luke portrayed Paul as an "Überapostel"? This argument is perennial, fueled as it is not only by historical and philological considerations but also by debates over spiritualism, apostolic succession, and "early Catholicism" in the canonical New Testament, which may have implications for churches today.

For my part, I would say that the inability to achieve clarity on this point, which is so important for exegetes today, probably indicates that it was not so important for Luke. If he gave three accounts of Paul's call and yet did not raise or settle the question of Paul's relation to the twelve apostles, the point must have been either clear or uninteresting to him. In fact, the manifold and frequently noted parallels in Luke-Acts between Paul and Jesus, between Peter and Paul, or between Jesus and Stephen and Paul seem to indicate rather that Luke was interested in telling a story and that the articulation of the different personalities in the story was not a dominant preoccupation for him. The characters in the story each have a role to play; when that role is completed, Luke's interest in them ceases: if they do not die (John, Jesus, Stephen), they simply disappear (Philip, Peter) or are left hanging in the midst of their own stories, which hold no further interest for Luke (Paul).

Consequently, instead of saying that Luke sees Paul as fulfilling Jesus' mandate to the apostles—and therefore worrying about whether he considered Paul an apostle, or more or less than an apostle—we should leave Jesus out and say that Luke sees Paul as bringing to perfection the transformation of salvation history that began with John the Baptist. John, who saw himself as a forerunner; Jesus, whose apostles saw him as a messiah and who preached repentance and comforted the poor but nevertheless saw himself only as God's agent for Israel; Stephen and Philip, who, as might be expected of diasporan Jews, undercut the territorial and ethnic limits of Judaism; Peter, whom God directed to overstep the ethnic limits altogether: these represent the preceding steps and stages of that transformation. Now it is Paul's turn to continue this line and to take it to its consistent end: if Stephen and Philip were anti-territorialists in Palestine and if Peter baptized a non-Jew there, then Paul would preach to Jews and non-Jews abroad and would eventually concentrate on non-Jews alone. If this transformation required viewing Jesus' messiahship as a primitive conception discarded along the way—together with the bounds of the Jewish land and nation—and required treating him as one of the links in the chain of history rather than its focus (his body a proof of God's miraculous powers, just as other miracles gave similar testimony at other points of the story), then so be it. We must remember, after all, that unlike Mark and Matthew and even John in his own way, Luke never claimed that his gospel was the story of Jesus Christ.

JACOB JERVELL

Paul in the Acts of the Apostles (1979)†

The historical value of and truth in the Lukan picture of Paul is the main point in this paper. Insofar as this problem cannot be isolated from the question of the possible tradition, or rather traditions, that the author of Acts had at his disposal, I will give some attention to this question as well. And the questions of tradition and history are dependent on a third important question: What kind of a picture of Paul do we actually have in Acts? The task advertised in the heading of this essay could have been substantially lightened if we could rely on an agreement among exegetes on this point. The limit set for this essay forbids me to go into a lengthy presentation of the discussion of what the Lukan Paul actually is. On the other hand it is impossible, taking the status of current study of Acts into consideration, simply to drop the question. The problem is there and we will have to say something about it, even if it can be done only by the help of catchwords and superficially treated texts.

*   *   *

In order to evaluate the Lukan Paul we must have an idea of the Pauline Paul first of all. When we compare the Lukan Paul with the Pauline Paul, as it is regularly done, is it actually the Pauline Paul we are dealing with? There are of course even here blind alleys. Philipp Vielhauer says in his stimulating essay on the Lukan Paul that greater parts of the Lukan portrait of Paul can be found in the Pauline letters. The reason for this, according to Vielhauer, is that Paul could adapt himself practically to various conditions, so to say, in spite of his theology. The older theological term for this is "accommodation." The alternative then is theology or practice. Paul could practically behave and do things which he could not do in "theology," if the word is allowed. Examples here are that he could live according to the Mosaic law—live as a Jew.

In my opinion, an understanding like Vielhauer's in this respect overlooks Paul's background in Jewish orthopraxy. By analogy to a Jewish-

† From an essay first published in *Les Actes des Apôtres*, ed. J. Kremer (Gembloux: Duculot, 1979), 297–306, and included in Jervell's *The Unknown Paul* (Minneapolis: Augsburg, 1984), 68–76. Reprinted by permission of Augsburg Fortress Press. Jervell is professor emeritus of New Testament at the University of Oslo.

rabbinical idea I am tempted to reverse Vielhauer's statement: Paul had more freedom in theology than in practice. This is an important point which we will return to below.

More about the question of the Pauline Paul: I am inclined to assert that the versatility and complexity of Paul in his character, personality, and theology at times are absent when we compare the Lukan Paul with the Pauline one. Are we really aware of the charismatic, miracle-believing, visionary, and ecstatic Paul from the first century? And it must not be forgotten methodologically that Paul's letters, thanks to their specific purpose and character, keep back what Paul had in common with nearly all Christians and with the leaders in Jerusalem.

The question whether we deal with the historical Luke when analyzing the Lukan Paul has already been touched upon. Is Acts really a document of Gentile Christianity (which always should be treated as a multifarious phenomenon!), expressing the views of the established church at the end of the first century? And is there anything that justly may be called an established church in a Christendom capable of producing such diverse writings at that time as the gospel of John, the Pastorals, the letter of James, Hebrews, and last but not least, the Revelation?

Vielhauer is right. You may actually find greater parts of Luke's picture of Paul in the Pauline letters. I think we can trace the Lukan Paul, the material connected with that Paul, back to Paul himself. I can exaggerate this point by saying that we can extract the Lukan Paul from the Pauline letters, if not in detail, yet to a great extent. But still, as we can realize, the Lukan Paul is not the Pauline Paul. It goes without saying that there are differences and not only small ones. This is our problem.

My thesis is as follows: The Lukan Paul, the picture of Paul in Acts, is a completion, a filling up of the Pauline one, so that in order to get at the historical Paul, we cannot do without Acts and Luke. By this I do not mean that we in Acts can discover how the contemporaries of Paul saw him, his successors, followers, co-workers, companions, disciples—if I am allowed, his *Wirkungsgeschichte* (historical impact). Nor do I talk about the way the next generation could tolerate and "swallow" him, whereas we in the Pauline letters find Paul as he saw himself. I mean on the contrary that Luke's picture completes partly what lies in seclusion or restrained in Paul's own letters, thanks to their specific purpose, and partly what can be found in the "outskirts" or in the margin of his former and first letters, and partly what we detect, when we realize what became of Paul in the end theologically; I am thinking of Romans 9–11. We could say regarding the Lukan Paul that that which lies in the shadow in Paul's letters Luke has placed in the sun in Acts.

Now we can turn to the question of the historical value of Luke's Paul. In order to present a sketch of Luke's Paul I will confine myself to two features.

The main theme is Paul the Jew, the Jewish-Christian Paul. Luke presents him as the Pharisee Paul who remains a Pharisee after his conversion and never becomes an ex-Pharisee. We find this Paul in a number of scenes, *expressis verbis* in Acts 23:6ff. The story in Acts 21:23ff. of Paul and the (Nazirite) vow, is therefore never meant as accommodation, pragmatism, or tactics, but gives us theological consistency. The vow story in Acts 21 emphasizes that Paul is a Jewish Christian, and as such is a venerator of the Mosaic torah. According to 21:22–24 the story of the vow illustrates not only what Paul personally could do, but also what he teaches Jews and Jewish Christians in the diaspora, namely, to circumcise their children and observe the law. This is not—as Luke sees it—a question of tactics or practice; it has to do with the promises to Israel which shall be given to the people if they repent. The passage in question tells us indirectly that Paul predominantly is a missionary among the Jews in the diaspora; recall the synagogue scenes in the second part of Acts (13:14ff., 44ff.; 14:1 [16:13]; 17:1ff., 10ff., 17; 18:4, 19; 19:8ff.). The synagogue is above all the place for Paul's missionary work. Paul preaching to Gentiles is within the composition of Acts an exception to the rule, as is clearly to be seen in Chapters 14 and 17. When preaching in the synagogue Paul demonstrates that the promises to Israel shall be fulfilled upon Israel (Acts 13:17ff., esp. vv. 17, 23, 26, and 32f.). That the Gentiles too according to the Scriptures shall participate in this salvation of the chosen people is nothing but part of the promises to Israel (Acts 15:15ff.; Luke 24:47; Acts 3:25; 14:47).

The second theme, when treating the picture of Luke's Paul, is Paul as a visionary, charismatic preacher, healer and miracle worker (Acts 13:8ff.; 14:2ff.; 16:16ff.; 19:11ff.; 20:7ff.; 28:1ff.). The given passages show in different ways Paul's life and work encompassed with exorcisms, healings, raisings of the dead, and other miracles of various kinds. Throughout Acts as a whole we realize how Paul's activity is guided directly from heaven, by God, by Jesus, or the Spirit with the help of visions, auditions, different ecstatic experiences, heavenly inspiration, etc.

I am in this context not looking for various pieces of the Lukan picture of Paul, so to say, separately. This would not be of any great help insofar as it will take us only to hunting up the same kind of pieces in the Pauline letters. Important on the contrary is the coherence we realize in Luke's dealing with the worshiping Jewish Pharisee and the charismatic missionary Paul. Luke does not separate πνεῦμα and νόμος, charismatic life and observance of the law. This does not only apply to Paul in Acts, but is in Luke's opinion a characteristic feature within the primitive Christian communities and groups in general. Two examples must suffice: (1) The charismatic, glossolalia-practicing church in Jerusalem with Peter in the van, is a gathering of Jews maintaining and venerating the torah (Acts 2:1ff., 46; 3:1; 5:12, 42; etc.) We have the same combination in the exordium to Luke's gospel, the combination of Spirit, prophecy, and law (Luke 1:11, 41, 66, 67, 80; 2:21, 22, 25ff., 39, 42ff.) (2) Stephen is characterized as an adherent of the law and as a charismatic-ecstatic prophet (6:8–15; 7: 51–53, 54–60). Suggestive are verses 7:51–53: The nonbelieving Jews resist the Spirit, which means that they do not keep the law! In Luke's work the combination of νόμος and πνεῦμα is all-important. And Paul is within this frame portrayed as the charismatic gifted Pharisee.

We will now turn to the Pauline Paul and compare him with the Lukan one. In the debates at the turn of the century about the question of the authorship of Acts it was maintained that the author could not possibly be the companion of Paul by the name Luke; this is how the Lukan Paul could have an attitude towards Jewish faith and Jewish Christians that contradicted Paul's personal and actual behavior. Adolf von Harnack in particular opposed this opinion, but was not too successful, partly because the time was up for Harnack as a theologian. At the same time some of the very valuable insights of Harnack got lost. We will refrain from the question whether Paul's companion Luke is the author of Acts or not. But I do not for a moment doubt that the author of Acts knew Paul well, if not personally.

My starting point in this context is that opinions differed on what Paul actually preached and taught. It is not merely that opponents of Paul inferred from his preaching and teaching anything else than Paul himself could and would do. I am here thinking of passages like Rom. 3:8, "Why not do evil that good may come?" and Gal. 2:17, "Christ, the agent of sin." Our question is how Paul could possibly be accused of preaching circumcision (Gal. 5:11) and at the same time be blamed for annulling the law, declare it as sin, etc. (Rom. 3:31; 7:7ff.; etc.). I see this question as a parallel to our main question: how is the Lukan portrait of Paul historically possible?

The answer is in the first place simply that the Christian Paul lived as a practicing Jew. This is said clearly in the most cited passage, 1 Cor. 9: 19–21. Paul lived among Jews unto the Jews as a Jew. However you interpret this in detail, it should go without saying that it has to do with the ceremonial law, because this was the sign of true Jewishness. We know how Paul makes out this particular behavior of his. The catchwords are "gain" (κερδαίνω) and "for the gospel's sake." But one more important question in our context is how Paul's behavior must be understood and perceived. Taking into consideration what orthopraxy meant to Jews it is clear that Paul is one who maintains the law of Moses in life and practice, even proclaims the law. He confesses his faith in the law simply by doing it. To Jewish Christians it was obvious and confusing(!) that Paul had a positive attitude to the torah, that is, not only to the law in a Christian interpretation, but the torah, so to say, as perceived by Jews.

At the same time it is clear that Paul repeatedly, and not only when as in 2 Corinthians 11 he "speaks as a fool," emphasizes that he himself is a Jew and not a sinner of the Gentiles (Gal. 2:15; 2 Cor. 11:27; Phil. 3:4; Rom. 11:1–5). It is not sufficient to say that he has been a Jew—he is one. Invariably he sticks to the traditions of the fathers. He is accused of preaching circumcision to the Gentiles, something he strongly denies (Gal. 5:11). We should, however, not overlook the fact that he in one particular way exhorts Jewish Christians to adhere to circumcision (see 1 Cor. 7:18). This last mentioned passage differs from the one in 1 Corinthians 9, where we find Paul's personal, and perhaps individual attitude as a missionary. 1 Corinthians 7:18 shows what he teaches others to do. The term περιπατεῖν in this context makes it clear that 1 Corinthians 7 not only gives a warning against undergoing an operation in order to remove the marks of circumcision; rather, the Jewish Christians ought to live, περιπατεῖν, the way which the circumcision of the torah prescribes. Correspondingly, we must infer from Gal. 5:3 that Paul assumed that Jewish Christians should do the whole law, which evidently means to include the various precepts.

We are now dealing with elements lying in the shadow of Paul's letters, but placed in the sun by Luke. And we are approaching the main point in the picture of the Lukan Paul, namely, the missionary to the Jews, the Paul who preaches in the synagogue insofar as this is the true place for the gospel. There is no reason to doubt that Paul even saw himself, primarily and at long sight, as a missionary to the Jews. In his capacity as an apostle to the Gentiles, he has the Jews in mind. 1 Cor. 9:20 tells us that he wanted to "gain" (κερδαίνω) the Jews. Rom. 11:14 discloses how Paul wants to provoke to emulation his people in order to save some of them. The two groups of people in the normal, Pauline churches, Jews and Gentiles, demonstrate Pauline mission as mission among the Jews. We find many Jewish names among his companions and assistants. He knew many Jews in the churches personally, something which is evident from Romans 16. Yet I have not mentioned Romans 9–11 where it is beyond question that Paul's mission among Gentiles has the salvation of Israel in view (Rom. 11:17ff., 25ff.).

I have so far refrained from explaining why Romans 9–11 in my opinion contain the last stage in Paul's thinking, theology, and prophetic preaching. 1 Corinthians 9 and other passages tell us about Paul's life after the law, his adhering to the traditions of the fathers, etc., based upon the principle, "for the sake of the gospel," that is, in order to "gain" some. He is talking of individuals (9:19–23). In Romans it is different. Paul has in Romans a series of sayings disclosing a very positive attitude to the Mosaic law (3:1ff.; 4 passim; 7:7ff.; etc.). The point of view is not the salvation of individuals, of some, and he is not using the principle, "for the sake of the gospel." Here the problem is the whole of Israel (11:26) and the principle is "for the sake of the Scriptures" (9:6) or "God's faithfulness and trustworthiness" (11:1ff., 29ff., etc.). The problem concerns the promises given to the unholy people, to Israel "after the flesh." This line of thought A. v. Harnack denounced as breaking away from universalism, something that created confusion and destroyed the theology of Paul. Others reject it as a lapse into *Heilsgeschichte* (salvation history), not true theology anymore, and some designate the same chapters a separate treatise, a long interpolation, an excursus, etc. We are, however, in Romans 9–11 confronted with that part of Paul which above all is the basis and foundation of the Lukan Paul: the destiny of Israel, now, in the future, and for ever; the salvation of the people; the fulfillment of the promises to God's people—all these elements are of vital importance for Paul and his preaching especially in that critical phase of his life and work when he wrote "The Letter to Jerusalem," as Romans may be called. In this context a positive attitude to Israel κατὰ σάρκα is unavoidable and necessary, merely in order to be able to see, recognize, and know those persons belonging to the unholy people elected for salvation. We have in Rom. 11: 17ff., the passage about the olive tree and the branches, a way of thinking on a par with the Lukan one about Israel as the people of God and the joining in of the Gentiles with that same people. The destiny of Israel occupies the Lukan Paul, and this very theme becomes decisive for the Pauline Paul. They have not the same solution. To Paul, Israel will be saved in the future (Romans 11); for Luke, Israel is saved now or in the past, namely, in the church. And insofar as the problem "Israel" becomes decisive for Paul in the way we see it in Romans, we have the explanation of the fact that Paul in Romans has a more positive attitude to the law than in Galatians.

I am therefore inclined to assert that what Luke writes on the subject of Paul is historically correct, even if not in detail—and we have in Luke of course not the whole of Paul. But the practicing Jew Paul, the missionary of Israel and to Israel, the theologian for whom Israel's salvation is the goal of his work—all these important Lukan views can be found in Paul's letters.

We mentioned above another feature in Acts, namely, Paul as performer of miracles, as a believer in miracles as part of the gospel, and as an ecstatic, visionary charismatic. These phenomena are nothing but illustrations of things merely mentioned by Paul himself, but of considerable importance in his life and work. The gospel, τὸ εὐαγγέλιον, consists of word and power (δύναμις), of preaching and miracles (2 Cor. 12:12; Rom. 15:19; 1 Thess. 1:5; etc.). Luke knows that Paul is a charismatic personality, but he fails to tell us that Paul is a weak and sick charismatic—so according to Paul himself (2 Corinthians 11–12). The tension in Paul, with the inseparable elements of power and weakness, Luke has not grasped.

We have no possibility within the limitations of this essay to deal with this topic, but I will still make one point. Luke and Paul, both of them, are working with the same set of theological questions and subjects, at least partly. A regular complaint against Luke is that he is not familiar with the Pauline concept of justification of the ungodly, with the righteousness of God, with the idea of faith and law. That is evidently correct. Luke has these subjects, but only as rudiments. And Luke is not—even as others were not—capable of perceiving the Pauline doubleness, that is, heterogenous views on the law in dealing with its intention and purpose. Luke has no, or only rudimentary, thoughts about atonement. But at the same time Luke deals thoroughly with the question of the torah, as this is a serious part of his theology. He is eager to demonstrate that the charismatic, spiritual church maintains, lives after, and fulfills the law of Moses, ethically and ceremonially. Obviously the Christian churches had to stand up on this point against serious complaints from the synagogue. Luke's answer to this is that especially those who are led by the Spirit are the ones who in work and life maintain the law as opposed to the synagogue that is without the Spirit.

This particular problem is Paul's problem too. He too is eager to show the positive connection between πνεῦμα and νόμος. Rom. 7:14 tells us that the law is πνευματικός; Rom. 8:4 that the law is being fulfilled in those whose conduct is directed by the Spirit. The error of the synagogue is that the Jews cannot be subject to the law of God and therefore are not able to please God and obey him (Rom. 8:7–8; 9:31). We have the same idea in Gal. 5:23; 2 Cor. 11:22; and Phil. 3:3. Luke gives us a lengthy and broad narrative description of the pious, law-upholding church, whereas Paul has brief and compact statements; the object is the same for both, and certainly so if the whole letter to the Romans is included.

I am not asserting that Luke is, so to say, copying and writing down Paul "himself," his theology, doing this mechanically and dependently. Luke is independent and very much so. He is an excellent historian. He is not able (or willing!) to talk about justification by faith as Paul does. This is, however, not the whole of Paul, not the historical Paul. So far we ought to grant that what our fathers, e.g., A. v. Harnack, said was right, namely, that Paul did not fully and to the end stick to his intentions—if he so wanted! Paul is interpreter of the Scriptures; he is a prophet and not a systematic theologian. The very character of his letters is an obstacle to forcing him into a system. And not only so. Paul himself, as a charismatic, gifted exegete and prophet, as interpreter of the God who acts in history

and today, makes this impossible. In his letters, what we can call the Jewish
Paul lies in the shadow, and we exegetes have not focused that part of
Paul. Luke has done it, and so his impression of Paul is indispensable,
that is, if we want to get at the historical Paul—in his letters and outside
them. He was certainly more multifaceted than we are inclined to think.

SUSAN R. GARRETT

Paul and Bar Jesus (1989)†

Commentators have not quite known what to do with the story of Paul
and Bar Jesus. Even Arthur Darby Nock, one of its most competent interpreters, characterized the story as "lame." First, the problem of the alternation and incorrect translation of the magician's names appears to be
insoluble on either source- or text-critical grounds. Second, the whole episode is historically implausible and literarily unbalanced: if so famous a
person as Sergius Paulus had converted to Christianity (which does not
seem very likely), more should have been made of it. But as Nock states,
"the proconsul's conversion . . . is just stated as though it were that of a
washer-woman." Third, the significance of Paul's curse of the magician is
not readily apparent. If, as some contend, one of Luke's reasons for relating
the incident was to contrast Christianity with magic, his storytelling strategy seems to be inappropriate: to the modern reader Paul's curse of Bar
Jesus looks as "magic-like" as anything the magus himself might have done.
In short, the narrative appears to be full of unlikelihoods and inconsistencies. But Luke was not as inept a narrator as these observations would
suggest. Analysis of the mythological background to the Bar Jesus account
and of its literary function within the narrative of Luke-Acts will suggest
that the story made a definite and important point, and tied in nicely with
other incidents in the two-volume account.

Mission on Cyprus

The incident is the first significant event on Paul's first missionary journey.
Saul and Barnabas had been consecrated by prophets in Antioch and had
then departed from the port of Seleucia for Cyprus. Luke mentions whistle
stops at the Jewish synagogues in Salamis (13:5), and then without further
delay transports the characters to the city of Paphos, on the western end
of the island. Haenchen points out that for the missionaries to cross the
island would have taken at least a week; Luke's silence about other mission
stops along the way indicates that the Paul/Bar Jesus incident is the only
one that interests the evangelist. Saul (alias Paul) and Bar Jesus (alias
Elymas) are the central human characters in the narrative. Paul's companions Barnabas and John play distinctly subsidiary roles, and even the
character of the proconsul, Sergius Paulus, functions primarily as a foil
for the confrontation between Paul and Bar Jesus. Thus in 13:6 it is

† From *The Demise of the Devil* (Minneapolis: Fortress, 1989), 79–87. Reprinted by permission of
  Augsburg Fortress Press. Garrett is professor of New Testament at Louisville Presbyterian Theological Seminary.

reported that when the Christians came to Paphos they found "a certain man, a magician, a Jewish false prophet named Bar Jesus." Sergius Paulus is mentioned almost as an afterthought, in v. 7.

The human combatants Paul and Bar Jesus in turn represent superhuman figures. On the one hand, Paul acts under the power of the Holy Spirit. In the introduction to the episode, Luke has noted that the Spirit set Barnabas and Saul aside for the entire first missionary journey (13:2) and dictated to them their itinerary (v. 4). Furthermore, just before Bar Jesus is rebuked (v. 9) Luke describes Paul as "filled with the Holy Spirit." On the other hand, Bar Jesus is closely linked with the figure of Satan. Paul calls the magician-false prophet a "son of the devil" and "enemy of all righteousness." Paul also accuses Bar Jesus of being "full of all deceit and all fraud" (*plērēs pantos dolou kai pasēs radiourgias*). The proximity of this vitriolic charge (v. 10a) to Luke's description of Paul as "filled with the Holy Spirit" (v. 9) serves to contrast these characters in the sharpest terms possible; Luke would have us see Bar Jesus as controlled by Satan, the very antithesis of the Holy Spirit. Thus the confrontation between Bar Jesus and Paul is also a confrontation between the Holy Spirit and the devil.

Nock was surely mistaken when he suggested that Luke's description of Bar Jesus as a "magician-false prophet" (*magos pseudoprophētēs*) was "almost intentionally vague" and perhaps used merely "like *goēs*, humbug, of a practitioner of another and hostile religion." First, Bar Jesus is not a member of "another and hostile religion," but a Jew, who by practicing magic commits what Luke regarded as the worst sort of idolatry. Second, Luke does not here use the designations "magician" and "false prophet" casually, but on the contrary, emphasizes both roles. The label "magician" occurs twice in close succession (vv. 7,8), and although the designation "false prophet" is explicitly mentioned just once, Paul also charges Bar Jesus with "making crooked the straight paths of the Lord" (v. 10), which is the opposite of what the true prophet John the Baptist had done (Luke 3:4). By making straight paths crooked—in other words, by interfering with Paul's efforts to preach to Sergius Paulus that he might believe and be saved—Bar Jesus acted according to the devil's word-obstructing designs (cf. Luke 8:11–15). Through this indirect promotion of idolatry Bar Jesus filled the classic role of the magician-false prophet as exhibited in contemporaneous Jewish and Christian literary traditions * * *, according to which false teachers or false prophets would arise and lead the people astray into idolatry. In light of such eschatological traditions it seems likely that Bar Jesus' composite identity as magician, false prophet and satanic stand-in was neither fortuitous nor insignificant; these three roles were thought to belong together. The designation "false prophet" (*pseudoprophētēs*), together with Paul's accusation of deceitfulness, would have tipped off many ancient readers that Bar Jesus was something other than what he seemed. Indeed he had a *double* "double identity": he was Bar Jesus and also Elymas; he was a magus serving the esteemed Sergius Paulus and also a false prophet serving Satan. Bar Jesus' position as court magician and his diabolical effort to impede the proclamation of the word provide ample proof of the illegitimacy of any claim to prophetic status.

Paul's Curse of Bar Jesus (Acts 13:11)

On the very first leg of Paul's very first mission to the Gentiles, he proclaims that "the hand of the Lord" is upon Bar Jesus, with the result that "mist and darkness" fall upon the false prophet. Perhaps the most striking point about this action is that it is the opposite of what Paul had been commissioned to do on his journeys to the Gentiles: namely, to "open their eyes" and to cause them "to turn from darkness to light, and from the authority of Satan to God" (Acts 26:18). Why would Luke portray Paul as doing something so blatantly contrary to the directions given him?

In answering this question it will be helpful to begin by looking at Deut. 28:28–29, which has been suggested as a possible model for Luke's composition of the story of Bar Jesus' blindness. In this passage, Moses tells the Israelites that the Lord shall strike those who forsake him (v. 20), so that they "shall grope at noonday, as the blind grope in darkness." This punishment is but one in a long list of curses (katarai) to be inflicted on those who disobey the voice of the Lord by "going after other gods and serving them" (28:14–15); Peter's rebuke of Simon had alluded to another portion of this lengthy discussion in Deuteronomy of the curses falling upon those who disobey the covenant * * *. Luke likely saw Bar Jesus as guilty of such disobedience, since magic and false prophecy were regarded as akin to idolatry. Therefore it is possible that Luke shaped his depiction of the punishment of Bar Jesus to bring it into line with the punishment of idolaters described in Deut. 28:28–29.

Evidence from the Community Rule indicates that the Qumran sectarians employed the curse language of this section of Deuteronomy in their own condemnation of idolatry. Specifically, 1QS 2:11–19 incorporates portions of Deut. 29:20–21 (LXX vv. 19–20), which is an exceptionally harsh malediction against any who commit idolatry but bless themselves in their heart, and who are therefore labelled as "a root bearing poisonous and bitter fruit" (LXX v. 17: riza anō phyousa en cholē kai pikria; cf. Acts 8:23). The Qumran elaboration of this Deuteronomic curse occurs within a series of imprecations to be pronounced against members of the "lot of Belial," and uses light and darkness imagery similar to that employed in the Bar Jesus account:

> And the Priests and Levites shall continue, saying: "Cursed be the man who enters this Covenant while walking among the idols of his heart, who sets up before himself his stumbling-block of sin so that he may backslide! Hearing the words of this Covenant, he blesses himself in his heart and says, 'Peace be with me, even though I walk in the stubbornness of my heart' (Deut. 29:18–19), whereas his spirit, parched (for lack of truth) and watered (with lies), shall be destroyed without pardon. God's wrath and His zeal for His precepts shall consume him in everlasting destruction. All the curses of the Covenant shall cling to him and God will set him apart for evil. He shall be cut off from the midst of all the sons of light, and because he has turned aside from God on account of his idols and his stumbling-block of sin, his lot shall be among those who are cursed for ever." And after them, all those entering the Covenant shall answer and say, "Amen, Amen!"

Thus shall they do, year by year, for as long as the dominion of Satan endures.

1QS 2:11–19

The similarity to Paul's curse of Bar Jesus is notable. Those who enter the Qumran covenant community under false pretexts—feigning obedience to the law of Moses while secretly practicing idolatry—are to be cut off from the children of light and punished forever. So too in Acts, Bar Jesus the Jew—deceitfully pretending to be a prophet, but actually an idolatrous magician—is cut off from the light. The Qumran curse certifies that at the judgment the idolater will be subjected to eternal punishment; Paul's curse brings instant retribution, but may also have an eschatological component.

The consignment of Bar Jesus to "mist and darkness" is a consignment to the authority of his master, Satan (cf. Acts 26:18; Luke 22:53). In Acts as in some contemporaneous writings, the punishment for being a "child of darkness" is darkness itself: Satan and his servants will be banished eternally from the light and life of the Kingdom (Matt. 8:12; 22:13; 25:30; 2 Pet. 2:17; 1QS 4:12–14; cf. Rev. 22:5, 14–15; *Barnabas* 20.1). Though somewhat later than the canonical Acts, *Acts of Peter* includes a curse against the devil and his servants which illustrates this "tit-for-tat" rationale. Peter exclaims:

> "Upon thee may thy blackness be turned and upon thy sons, that most wicked seed; upon thee be turned thy misdeeds, upon thee thy threats, and upon thee and thine angels be thy temptations, thou source of wickedness and abyss of darkness! May thy darkness which thou hast be with thee and with thy vessels whom thou dost possess. Depart therefore from these who shall believe in God, depart from the servants of Christ and from them who would fight for him."

Acts of Peter 4.8

The last sentence vents the further conviction, shared by Luke, that the servants of Satan and the servants of Christ are as divorced from one another as east is from west, as night is from day (cf. 1 Thess. 5:5).

The blinding of Bar Jesus exposes the magician as a fraud. Bar Jesus claimed to be a prophet (or so Luke implies): as such he would have been a source of divine light and leadership, one who made paths straight so that others could follow. But Luke shows that the magician was, despite his claim, a fount of darkness and corruption (cf. 2 Cor. 11:13–15). The curse of blindness communicates this true identity in terms consistent with Luke's symbolism elsewhere. The evangelist has already told his reader that the eye is the lamp of the body: "when your eye is pure [*haplous*], then your whole body has light; but if it is bad [*poneros*], then your body is in darkness" (Luke 11:34; parallel Matt. 6:22–23). Those in the former category have nothing whatever to do with darkness (cf. 2 Cor. 6:14–15). Bar Jesus, on the other hand, belongs to the latter category because he is allied with none other than the Prince of Darkness. Employing the logic of Luke 11:34, when Bar Jesus' "eye" goes "bad," the true state of his "whole body" is revealed. Thus Paul's curse is not only efficacious but also expressive.

The parallels to Paul's own experience are remarkable: both Paul and Bar Jesus had been obstructing the work of the Church when blinded, and both must then be "led about by the hand." Bar Jesus is a "son of the devil," and Paul—like the devil—has "authority to bind" (9:14), tries to make Christians blaspheme (26:11), and repeatedly casts them into prison. The parallels suggest that Luke saw Paul, too, as a one-time servant of the devil. But there are also differences between the experiences of Paul and of Bar Jesus: (1) Bar Jesus is said to "make straight paths crooked" but Paul is led to "a street called straight" (9:11); (2) Bar Jesus is blinded by mist and darkness (13:11), but Paul had been blinded by an intensely bright light (22:11; 26:13); (3) whereas Paul eventually made the transition from darkness to light, Bar Jesus' blindness is not relieved within the context of the narrative. The differences in experience signify the diverging paths or "ways" of their lives.

The reason Luke placed the story in such a prominent position—at the outset of the endeavor to which Paul had been called by Jesus himself—can now be discerned. Jesus had commissioned Paul to open the eyes of the Gentiles, that they might turn from darkness to light and from the authority of Satan to God. But if people's eyes have been "blinded" by Satan's control over their lives, how can Paul open them? Or, to use Luke's other metaphor (Luke 8:11–15), if the devil desires to snatch away the newly planted word, how can Paul stop him? The answer is that *Paul must himself be invested with authority that is greater than Satan's own.* In depicting Paul's successful unmasking and punishment of Bar Jesus, Luke is saying that Paul could do the work to which he had been called because he possessed authority over all the power of the Enemy (cf. Luke 10:19). Ironically, this superiority of Paul to the devil is expressed by the infliction of blindness, which Paul himself had suffered at the hand of the Lord: thus Paul, in spite of his own "dark" past, now shows himself to be one of the devil's staunchest foes. Paul's triumph confirms the change that has taken place in his own life, and brings him a new external status to match the new internal one: he departs from Paphos as the leader of the mission.

*   *   *

Was Paul's curse of Bar Jesus final and irrevocable, or was there still hope for the magician? The question may be of interest to modern readers, but it is slightly out of kilter with Luke's presuppositions, because (as with Simon Magus) Luke is interested in Bar Jesus as a representative or servant of Satan rather than as an individual. Thus to raise the question is like asking "Is there any hope for Satan?" Of course the answer to *that* question is a resounding No! Satan's death knell had tolled long before, in the earthly ministry of Jesus (Luke 10:18; 11:21–22). Luke does imply that the blinding is only temporary: Bar Jesus will not see the sun "for a while" (v. 11). But the temporal reference is meant to underscore the decisive (i.e., not instantly fleeting) quality of Paul's victory over Satan, and so points only incidentally, if at all, to a reprieve for Bar Jesus. Satan had clearly been humbled; his once-powerful servant Bar Jesus must be "led about by the hand" like a small child. Whether or not this particular servant would eventually escape from Satan's power does not appear to be an issue for Luke. If anything, Bar Jesus' consignment to darkness may signify that this shall also be his fate at the judgment.

Summary and Analysis

*   *   *

In Luke and Acts the labels "magic" and "false prophecy" help the reader to sort characters and their actions into the appropriate categories; the categories themselves are defined and delimited not only by cultural precedent but also in part by the placement of each discussion within a larger literary framework. The critic must interpret the parts in relationship to the whole and vice versa, showing how an action performed or word spoken in one place articulates, replicates, or confirms what is depicted elsewhere. Bar Jesus' behavior replicates that of the unrepentant Jews, who likewise oppose the word by refusing to allow the Gospel to be heard, who persecute true prophets, follow false prophets, practice idolatry, and do not keep the law. Jesus bewails a "faithless and perverse [*diestrammenē*] generation" of Jews (Luke 9:41); Bar Jesus is a Jew who "perverts" or "makes crooked" the straight paths of the Lord (*diastrephein*; Acts 13:8, 10). Bar Jesus epitomizes for Luke the tragic situation of all unrepentant Jews, and the blinding of Bar Jesus illustrates not only Christian authority over Satan, but also the sad fate of all unrepentant Jews, who, though they indeed see, do not perceive, for their eyes have closed (28:26,27). In the Bar Jesus incident one can discern a pattern of conflict between good and evil, between the purposes of God and the purposes of Satan, and between the repentant and the uncircumcised in heart which characterizes much of Christian existence as portrayed in Luke-Acts. It is a conflict that will continue in the incident involving the seven sons of Sceva.

The Apocryphal Paul: Some Early Christian Traditions and Legends

Long after Paul's death, various reminiscences of him and legends about his activities continued to circulate. Some of these, such as the story of his martyrdom, became a fixed part of Christian tradition, whereas others were quickly forgotten. Many magnified his importance or the scope of his work, such as Jerome, who boasted that "Paul subjugated the whole world, from the Ocean to the Red Sea" through his missionary work (*Tract. Ps.* 81). To give some indication of these diverse portraits of the apocryphal Paul, we provide a small florilegium from a variety of ancient Christian sources.

JEROME

[Paul at the End of the Fourth Century] (393)†

Paul, formerly called Saul, an apostle outside the number of the twelve apostles, was of the tribe of Benjamin and the town of Giscalis in Judea.[1] When this was taken by the Romans he removed with his parents to Tarsus in Cilicia. Sent by them to Jerusalem to study law he was educated by Gamaliel a most learned man whom Luke mentions. But after he had been present at the death of the martyr Stephen and had received letters from the high priest of the temple for the persecution of those who believed in Christ, he proceeded to Damascus, where constrained to faith by a revelation, as it is written in the Acts of the Apostles, he was transformed from a persecutor into an elect vessel. As Sergius Paulus Proconsul of Cyprus was the first to believe on his preaching, he took his name from him because he had subdued him to faith in Christ, and having been joined by Barnabas, after traversing many cities, he returned to Jerusalem and was ordained apostle to the Gentiles by Peter, James and John. And because a full account of his life is given in the Acts of the Apostles, I only say this, that the twenty-fifth year after our Lord's passion, that is the second of Nero, at the time when Festus Procurator of Judea succeeded Felix, he was sent bound to Rome, and remaining for two years in free custody, disputed daily with the Jews concerning the advent of Christ. It ought to be said that at the first defence, the power of Nero having not yet been

---

† From *Vir. ill.* 5, tr. by E. Richardson in *The Nicene and Post-Nicene Fathers*, Second Series, Vol. 3 (Edinburgh, 1882; rp. Grand Rapids: Eerdmans, 1983), 362–63. Jerome (ca. 347–419/20) is best known as the translator of the Vulgate. For the first seventy-eight lives of his *On Illustrious Men*, Jerome draws heavily on Eusebius, though not all of his statements about Paul are present in Eusebius.

1. Giscalis of Judea appears to be an error for Giscala (Gischala = Gush Halav), a town in Upper Galilee that was the home of John, a prominent Jewish leader during the war against Rome.

confirmed, nor his wickedness broken forth to such a degree as the histories relate concerning him, Paul was dismissed by Nero, that the gospel of Christ might be preached also in the West. As he himself writes in the second epistle to Timothy, at the time when he was about to be put to death dictating his epistle as he did while in chains: "At my first defence no one took my part, but all forsook me: may it not be laid to their account. But the Lord stood by me and strengthened me; that through me the message might be fully proclaimed and that all the Gentiles might hear, and I was delivered out of the mouth of the lion"—clearly indicating Nero as lion on account of his cruelty. And directly following he says "The Lord delivered me from the mouth of the lion" and again shortly "The Lord delivered me from every evil work and saved me unto his heavenly kingdom," for indeed he felt within himself that his martyrdom was near at hand, for in the same epistle he announced "for I am already being offered and the time of my departure is at hand." He then, in the fourteenth year of Nero on the same day with Peter, was beheaded at Rome for Christ's sake and was buried in the Ostian way, the twenty-seventh year after our Lord's passion. He wrote nine epistles to seven churches: *To the Romans* one, *To the Corinthians* two, *To the Galatians* one, *To the Ephesians* one, *To the Philipians* one, *To the Colossians* one, *To the Thessalonians* two; and besides these to his disciples, *To Timothy* two, *To Titus* one, *To Philemon* one. The epistle which is called the *Epistle to the Hebrews* is not considered his, on account of its difference from the others in style and language, but it is reckoned, either according to Tertullian to be the work of Barnabas, or according to others, to be by Luke the Evangelist or Clement afterwards bishop of the church at Rome, who, they say, arranged and adorned the ideas of Paul in his own language, though to be sure, since Paul was writing to Hebrews and was in disrepute among them he may have omitted his name from the salutation on this account. He being a Hebrew wrote Hebrew, that is his own tongue and most fluently while the things which were eloquently written in Hebrew were more eloquently turned into Greek and this is the reason why it seems to differ from other epistles of Paul. Some read one also to the Laodiceans but it is rejected by everyone.

TERTULLIAN

[Jacob Foresees the Two Phases of Paul's Life] (ca. 212)†

For even Genesis promised me Paul long ago. Indeed, when Jacob was pronouncing those well-known figures and prophetic blessings over his sons, he turned to Benjamin and said, "Benjamin is a ravenous wolf; in the morning he shall devour his prey, and in the evening he shall bestow food."[1] He foresaw that Paul would spring forth from the tribe of Benjamin,

† From *Marc.* 5.1. Tertullian (ca. 160–ca. 222) was the first major Christian author to write in Latin. Jacob's last words to his sons in Genesis 49 envisage the future history of the twelve tribes of Israel. Tertullian's fanciful reading of Jacob's prophecy concerning Benjamin (the ancestor of Paul) is an example of anti-Marcionite exegesis, intended to prove that the very book rejected by Marcion contained a prophecy of his beloved apostle.

1. Gen. 49:27. The final clause of the quotation is a Latin rendering of the LXX's translation of the Hebrew.

a ravenous wolf devouring in the morning, that is, in early life he would devastate the Lord's flocks as a persecutor of the churches; then in the evening he would bestow food, that is, in his declining years he would educate Christ's sheep as a teacher of the nations."

ANONYMOUS

[The Risen Christ Foretells Paul's Conversion and Mission] (ca. 150?)†

31. 'And look, you will meet a man whose name is Saul, which being interpreted means Paul. He is a Jew, circumcised according to the command of the law, and he will hear my voice from heaven with terror, fear, and trembling; and his eyes will be darkened and by your hand be crossed with spittle. And do all to him as I have done to you. Deliver him to others! And this man—immediately his eyes will be opened, and he will praise God, my heavenly Father. And he will become strong among the nations and will preach and teach, and many will be delighted when they hear and will be saved. Then will he be hated and delivered into the hand of his enemy, and he will testify before (mortal and perishable) kings, and upon him will come the completion of the testimony to me; because he had persecuted and hated me, he will be converted to me and preach and teach, and he will be among my elect, a chosen vessel and a wall that does not fall. The last of the last will become a preacher to the gentiles, perfect in (*or*, through) the will of my Father. As you have learned from the scriptures that your fathers the prophets spoke concerning me, and it is fulfilled in me'—this certain thing he said—'so you must become a leader to them. And every word which I have spoken to you and which you have written concerning me, that I am the word of the Father and the Father is in me, so you must become also to that man, as it befits you. Teach and remind (him) what has been said in the scriptures and fulfilled concerning me, and then he will be for the salvation of the gentiles.'

ANONYMOUS

[Paul's Physical Appearance] (ca. 190?)‡

Paul [was] a man small in size, bald-headed, bandy-legged, of noble mien, with eyebrows meeting, rather hook-nosed, full of grace. Sometimes he seemed like a man, and sometimes he had the face of an angel.

† From the *Epistle of the Apostles* 31, tr. by J. K. Elliott, *The Apocryphal New Testament* (Oxford: Clarendon, 1993), 576–77. Reprinted by permission of Oxford University Press. This apocryphal work relates a dialogue that ostensibly takes place between Jesus and the apostles after the resurrection. In it the risen Jesus foretells Paul's conversion and ministry, and gives the apostles instructions regarding Paul.

‡ From the *Acts of Paul and Thecla* 3:5, tr. by J. K. Elliott, *The Apocryphal New Testament* (Oxford: Clarendon, 1993), 364. Reprinted by permission of Oxford University Press. Whereas previous generations of scholars tended to think that this description was derived from oral tradition and

CLEMENT OF ALEXANDRIA

[Paul's Wife] (ca. 215)†

Even Paul did not hesitate in one letter to address his consort.[1] The only reason why he did not take her about with him was that it would have been an inconvenience for his ministry. Accordingly he says in a letter: "Have we not a right to take about with us a wife that is a sister like the other apostles?"[2] But the latter, in accordance with their particular ministry, devoted themselves to preaching without any distraction, and took their wives with them not as women with whom they had marriage relations, but as sisters, that they might be their fellow-ministers in dealing with housewives. It was through them that the Lord's teaching penetrated also the women's quarters without any scandal being aroused.

AMBROSIASTER

[Paul's Daily Schedule] (late fourth century)‡

The other apostles labored, but not as much as Paul. He used to earn his living with his own hands, from early morning until about eleven o'clock, and from then until four in the afternoon he would engage in public disputation with such energy that he would usually persuade those who spoke in opposition to him.

---

provided an essentially reliable portrait of the historical Paul, most contemporary scholars believe that it is a literary creation (based partly on the description of Stephen in Acts 6:8, 15) and should be interpreted in light of ancient physiognomic manuals, which assume that bodily (especially facial) characteristics and dispositions are intimately related. Some have suggested that Paul is being depicted here as a general, others that he is being portrayed as a Christian Herakles, and still others that his physical features are derived from ways in which the apostle is characterized in his letters, esp. 2 Corinthians (e.g., "weakness" is portrayed as "smallness of stature"). Christian art begins in the third century, with portraits of Paul as an iconographically distinct figure emerging at least by the early fourth century. Eusebius (*Hist. eccl.* 7.18.4) claims to have seen images of Paul, and the earliest surviving portraits depict him with Christ among the twelve apostles, in the scene known as the *traditio legis* (in which Christ is shown handing over the divine law to Peter and Paul), and on passion sarcophagi (which depict Paul's arrest and martyrdom). In these scenes Paul is typically portrayed along with Peter and depicted as thin, with a dark pointed beard, high forehead, fine features, and at least partly bald (see, for example, the cover illustration of this book). For the depiction of Paul in fourth-century Roman art, see S. A. Cooper, *Marius Victorinus' Commentary on Galatians* (New York: Oxford University Press, 2005), 41–87.

† From *Strom.* 3.53, tr. by J. E. L. Oulton and H. Chadwick, *Alexandrian Christianity* (Philadelphia: Westminster, 1954), 64–65. Copyright © 1954 by SCM Press. Reprinted by permission of Library of Christian Classics. Book 3 of Clement's *Stromateis* (*Miscellanies*) is devoted to marriage, which he defends by giving a short list of the "apostles" who were married: Peter (Mark 1:30; 1 Cor. 9:5), Philip (Acts 21:8–9), and Paul.

1. Clement understands "my true companion" in Phil. 4:3 as a reference to Paul's spouse (see note there).

2. 1 Cor. 9:5.

‡ From Ambrosiaster's commentary on 2 Cor. 11:23 (CSEL 81.292–93), tr. in Gerald Bray (ed.), *1–2 Corinthians* (ACCS, NT 7; Downers Grove: InterVarsity Press, 1999), 297. Reprinted by permission of InterVarsity Press. "Ambrosiaster" (i.e., pseudo-Ambrose) is the name Erasmus gave to the unknown author of a commentary on the thirteen letters of Paul, which had been attributed throughout the Middle Ages to Ambrose of Milan. The earliest complete commentary on the Pauline letters, it was written at Rome in the late fourth century. It helped spark a revival of interest in Paul and influenced later Latin writers on Paul, including Pelagius, Augustine, and Jerome.

ANONYMOUS

[Paul and the Baptized Lion] (ca. 190?)†

[Paul is on his way to Jericho, accompanied by a widow named Lemma and her daughter Amnia.]

There came a great and terrible lion out of the valley of the burial ground[1] . . . But when I (= Paul) finished praying, the beast cast himself at my feet. I was filled with the Spirit and looked at him, and said, 'Lion, what do you want?' He said, 'I wish to be baptized.' I glorified God, who had given speech to the beast and salvation to his servants.

Now there was a great river in that place; I went down into it and he followed me. As doves in terror before eagles fly into a house in order to escape, so it was with Lemma and Amnia, who did not cease to pray humbly, until I had praised and glorified God. I myself was in fear and wonderment, in that I was about to lead the lion like an ox and baptize him in the water. But I stood on the bank, men and brethren,[2] and cried out, saying, 'You who dwell in the heights, who looked upon the humble, who gave rest to the afflicted, who with Daniel shut the mouths of the lions,[3] who sent to me our Lord Jesus Christ, grant that we escape the beast, and accomplish the plan, which you appointed.'

When I had prayed thus, I took the lion by the mane and in the name of Jesus Christ immersed him three times.[4] When he came up out of the water he shook out his mane and said to me, 'Grace be with you!' And I said to him, 'And likewise with you.'[5]

---

† The story of Paul baptizing the lion is preserved only in an unpublished Coptic fragment, whereas the account of the subsequent meeting of Paul and the lion in the stadium at Ephesus is preserved in Greek. Both stories belong to the *Acts of Paul*, and we give the selections translated in J. K. Elliott, *The Apocryphal Jesus* (New York: Oxford University Press, 1996), 140–42. Reprinted by permission of Oxford University Press. The biblical basis for this delightful piece of early Christian fiction is 1 Corinthians 15:32, where Paul refers to fighting with wild beasts at Ephesus. Although Paul almost certainly was speaking figuratively here (cf. 2 Tim. 4:17, "delivered from the lion's mouth"), the author of this tale has used it to create a Christian version of the story of Androclus and the lion (preserved in Aulus Gellius, *Noct. att.* 5.14; cf. Seneca, *Ben.* 2.19.1). George Bernard Shaw was later to use that same story as the basis of his famous play "Androcles and the Lion." Although no one today takes seriously the story of a talking lion (cf. the story of Balaam's talking donkey in Num. 22) and already in the fourth century Jerome (*Vir. ill.* 7) called it a "fable," many early Christians did accept it as historical. Hippolytus, for example, used his readers' belief in the story as a warrant for urging them to accept the story of Daniel in the lions' den (*Comm. Dan.* 3.29). Similarly, when the Latin Christian poet Commodian gives a list of instances in which God has caused the dumb to speak, he includes the following two instances involving the apostle: "For Paul when he preached, he [= God] caused mules to speak of him; he made a lion speak to the people with God-given voice" (*Carmen apologeticum* 627–628, tr. by Elliott, *The Apocryphal New Testament*, 351–52). An adaptation of the story of Paul and the lion occurs in the Ethiopic *Epistle of Pelagia*.

1. Perhaps an allusion to Ezek. 37's "valley of dry bones." In any case, the lion will be depicted as going symbolically from death to life.
2. Paul is depicted as telling this story to Christians assembled in the house of Aquila and Priscilla at Ephesus (cf. Acts 18:18–19).
3. Dan. 6:22.
4. Triple immersion was common by the end of the second century (Hippolytus, *Trad. ap.* 21; Tertullian, *Cor.* 3; *Prax.* 26), but already in the *Didache* (7.3) pouring water three times on the head is permitted when there is insufficient water for immersion.
5. A variant of the liturgical passing of peace (*pax tecum*).

The lion ran off to the country rejoicing (for this was revealed to me in my heart). A lioness met him, but he did not yield to her and ran off.[6]

[Later at Ephesus, Paul is condemned to the beasts by the proconsul Hieronymous, whose anger toward Paul increases when the wife of Hieronymous subsequently becomes a Christian.][7]

At dawn there was a cry from the citizens, 'Let us go to the spectacle! Come, let us see the man who possesses God fighting with the beasts!' Hieronymous himself joined them; he commanded Diophantes[8] and the other slaves to bring Paul into the stadium. He was dragged in, saying nothing but bowed down and groaning because he was led in triumph by the city. And when he was brought out he was immediately flung into the stadium. Everybody was angry at Paul's dignified bearing. Hieronymus ordered a very fierce lion,[9] which had but recently been captured, to be set loose against him. . . . But the lion looked at Paul, and Paul at the lion. Then Paul recognized that this was the lion which had come and been baptized. And borne along by faith Paul said, 'Lion, was it you whom I baptized?' And the lion in answer said to Paul, 'Yes.'[1] Paul spoke to it again and said, 'And how were you captured?' The lion said with its own voice, 'Just as you were, Paul.'[2] After Hieronymus had sent many beasts so that Paul might be slain, and archers that the lion too might be killed, a violent and exceedingly heavy hail-storm fell from heaven, although the sky was clear: many died and all the rest took to flight. But it did not touch Paul or the lion although the other beasts perished under the weight of the hail, which was so heavy that Hieronymus' ear was hit and torn off, and the people cried out as they fled, 'Save us, O God, save us, O God of the man who fought with the beasts!' And Paul took leave of the lion, which spoke no more, and went out of the stadium and down to the harbour and embarked on the ship which was sailing for Macedonia, for there were many who were sailing as if the city were about to perish. So he embarked too like one of the fugitives, but the lion went away into the mountains as was natural for it.[3]

6. According to Pliny the Elder (*Nat.* 8.42), the lion's mane is symbolic of its sexual prowess. But now that the lion has died in baptism (Rom. 6), it—in good encratite fashion—renounces its sexuality and forgoes coitus with the lioness.
7. In the Ethiopic version, the setting of the story is Caesarea, where Paul is condemned by the king because his daughter Pelagia has become a Christian, renounced her husband, and is following the apostle's exhortations (cf. the story of Paul and Thecla, pp. 296–303).
8. A freedman of Hieronymous, whose wife is a disciple of Paul.
9. Earlier, the lion's great size and ferocious roar have been emphasized. In the version of the story found in the Ethiopic *Epistle to Pelagia*, the lion is twelve cubits tall and the size of a horse.
1. Instead of this exchange, the Ethiopic *Epistle of Pelagia* has both Paul and the lion pray and glorify God, then exchange compliments.
2. The Ethiopic version adds, "Didn't they realize that we are dear to each other? We are our Lord's servants."
3. In the Ethiopic version, Paul and the lion are released, but Pelagia is cast into a brazen cow. She is spared when rain extinguishes the fire, but her husband commits suicide.

CLEMENT OF ALEXANDRIA

[Paul's Use of Pagan Oracles] (ca. 215)†

* * *

For that, as God wished to save the Jews by giving to them prophets, so also by raising up prophets of their own in their own tongue, as they were able to receive God's beneficence, He distinguished the most excellent of the Greeks from the common herd, in addition to *"Peter's Preaching,"* the Apostle Paul will show, saying: "Take also the Hellenic books, read the Sibyl, how it is shown that God is one, and how the future is indicated. And taking Hystaspes, read, and you will find much more luminously and distinctly the Son of God described, and how many kings shall draw up their forces against Christ, hating Him and those that bear His name, and His faithful ones, and His patience, and His coming." Then in one word he asks us, "Whose is the world, and all that is in the world? Are they not God's?"[1]

* * *

JOHN CHRYSOSTOM

[Paul as the Paragon of Virtue] (ca. 390)‡

5.1 [230]. Where now are those who accuse death, and say that this passible and corruptible body is for them an impediment to virtue? Let them listen to Paul's virtuous acts and cease from this wicked slander. For what harm has death caused the human race? What impediment has corruptibility caused to virtue? Consider Paul, and you will see that our being mortal brings us the greatest benefits. For if he were not mortal, then he would not have been able to say, or, rather, would not have been able to demonstrate what he said through his deeds, that, "every single day I die, by the boast about you which I have in Christ Jesus" (1 Cor. 15:31). For

† From *Strom.* 6.5, tr. by W. Wilson in *The Ante-Nicene Fathers* (Edinburgh, 1885; rep. Grand Rapids: Eerdmanns, 1986), Vol. 2, 490. Clement of Alexandria (ca. 160–215) was a theologian who sought to harmonize Christian thought and pagan culture. The source of his quotation is unknown, though some have suggested that it may come from an otherwise unknown *Preaching of Paul*, whereas others assign it to either the *Acts of Paul* or the *Preaching of Peter* (understood to have contained the preaching of both Peter and Paul).

1. The tradition of appealing to the *Sibylline Oracles* and the *Oracles of Hystaspes* to prove the truth of Christian claims—which is here traced back to Paul—goes back to at least Justin Martyr (*1 Apol.* 1.20.1; 44.12). Both works were regarded as pagan prophetic books, though the extant *Sibylline Oracles* are largely Jewish and Christian imitations of the pagan oracles. Little is known of the pseudograph that circulated under the name of Hystaspes. Lactantius makes extensive use of this apocalypse and says that Hystaspes was an ancient king of the Medes who handed down to posterity a prophecy of the destruction of the Roman Empire; the prophecy was putatively made before the Trojan race was even founded (*Inst.* 7.15).

‡ From *In Praise of St. Paul* 5, tr. by M. M. Mitchell, *The Heavenly Trumpet* (Tübingen: Mohr Siebeck, 2000), 468–74. Reprinted by permission of Mohr-Siebeck (Tübingen) and Westminster John Knox Press. John Chrysostom (ca. 347–407) was one of the great preachers of the ancient church. In addition to preaching more than 250 sermons on the Pauline letters, he delivered seven panegyrics on Paul, calling on his listeners "to imitate this archetype of virtue" (*Laud. Paul.* 2).

everywhere we just need a soul and the desire to act, and there will be nothing to hinder our being placed in the front ranks. Was not this man, Paul, mortal? Was he not unskilled? Was he not poor and earning his [232] bread from daily labor? Did he not have a body endowed with all the constraints of nature? Then what prevented him from becoming such a man as he was? Nothing. Therefore let no one be disheartened to be poor, let no one be displeased to be unskilled, nor suffer pain for being among the lowest ranks, but only those who have a weakened soul and an enfeebled mind. For this alone is a hindrance to virtue—wickness of soul and weakness of purpose—and apart from this there is no other obstacle. And this is made clear by the example of this blessed man who has now brought us together. For just as these circumstances did him no harm, so also their opposites—rhetorical skill, abundant riches, renowned ancestry, fine reputation, being in a position of power—none of these benefitted the outsiders in the least.

5.2 [232]. Why should I speak of human beings? Indeed, should I confine my speech to the earth when it is possible to speak of the powers above, the dominations, the authorities, and the rulers of this dark age (Eph. 6: 12)? For how did their possessing so lofty a nature benefit them? Are not all the powers coming to be judged by Paul and those in his likeness? "Don't you know," he says, "that we shall judge angels, much less matters of daily life" (1 Cor. 6:3)? Therefore let us not suffer pain for any other reason than wickedness alone, nor rejoice and be made glad for any other reason than virtue alone. If we are zealous for virtue, there is nothing to hinder us from becoming like Paul.

5.3 [234]. For he did not become such as he was from grace alone, but also from his own fervent will. And this is why it was from grace, since it was also from his will. He had both sets of qualities abundantly, the things of God breathed into him, and those he possessed from his own free will. Do you wish to learn about "the things of God"? Demons were frightened by his garments (Acts 19:12). But I don't marvel at this * * * but I marvel because, before he received divine grace, from the very starting gate and beginnings, he appeared doing such amazing things as the following: without possessing this power, nor having received the laying on of hands, he was so inflamed with zeal for Christ that he roused the entire Jewish populace against himself (Acts 9:19–23). And, seeing that he was in such grave dangers and that the city was blockaded, he was lowered down the wall through a window (Acts 9:25; 2 Cor. 11:31–33). Yet after he was lowered down he did not fall into timidity, nor into cowardice and fright, but from the experience he received a greater will to act [236]. Paul gave way to the dangers on account of the divine plan, but he gave way to no one when it came to the teaching. Snatching up the cross again, he followed its path (Mk. 8:34 and pars.), although he still had close at hand the example of what had happened to Stephen, and he saw Jews breathing murder (Acts 9:1) against him more than the others, and how they desired to taste of his very flesh. Therefore, he neither fell into dangers precipitantly, nor when he fled them did he become in turn more weak. He loved the present life exceedingly because of the gain to be had from it, and just as exceedingly he disdained it, because of the philosophical perspective he gained from this disdain, or [perhaps] because he was in a hurry to go off to Jesus (Phil. 1:23).

5.4 *[236]*. As I always say about him, and never shall stop saying, no one falling into contradictory actions has practiced both so accurately. For example, no one so desired the present life as he, not even those with a passionate love for their lives; no one so disdained it, not even those dying the worst death. This is how pure of desire Paul was: he was not devoted to a single thing in the present life, but always determined his own desire by the will of God *[238]*. At one time he said living was more necessary than communion and conversation with Christ (Phil. 1:24), but at another that it was so grievous and burdensome that he groaned and hastened to leave it (2 Cor. 5:4; Phil. 1:23). He desired only those things that would bring him godly gain, even if they happened to be contradictory to what he had done before. For he was a variable and many-sorted man, not acting hypocritically, of course (God forbid!), but becoming all things that were required for the needs of the gospel and the salvation of humanity. And in doing this he was imitating his own Lord.

5.5 *[238]*. For God also appeared, even as a human being, when it was necessary for him to appear that way, and in fire once long ago when the time required it. One time he appeared in the form of a foot-soldier and army man, at another in the image of an old man, now in a cool breeze, then as a traveler, now in the form of a human being, nor did he even beg off from dying. But when I say, "this was necessary," let no one think it was a logical necessity, for it was only so because of his love for humanity. And sometimes God sits on the throne, and other times on the *[240]* Cherubim. He has done all these things with a view to his underlying providential designs. Hence he said through the prophet: "I have multiplied visions, and have been given likenesses by the hands of the prophets" (Hos. 12:11).

5.6 *[240]*. Therefore Paul should not be condemned if, in imitation of his own Lord, at one time he was as a Jew, and at another as one not under the Law; now was keeping the Law, then despising it; at one time was cleaving to the present life, at another condemning it; now was demanding money, then rejecting what was offered; sometimes he was sacrificing and shaving his head, and other times anathematizing those who did such things; once he circumcized, at another time he cast out circumcision. For the deeds were contradictory, but the mind and intention from which they arose were very much in agreement and united with one another. *[242]* He continually sought one thing—the salvation of those hearing his words and seeing his actions. That is why at one time he exalts the Law and at another destroys it. For not only in what he did, but also in what he said, he was variable and many-sorted. However, he did not change his mind, nor become someone else, but he remained the very man that he was, and made use of each of the courses of action I mentioned for the present need. Therefore, don't reproach him for these things, but for them all the more proclaim his praises and crown him.

5.7 [242]. Take the case of a physician. When you see him at one time cauterizing, at another feeding, now using an iron implement, then giving a medicinal remedy, once withholding food and drink, and another time providing the sick their fill of these things, sometimes completely covering up a person with a fever, and at other times ordering him to drink a full cup of cold water, you do not condemn his variability, nor his constant changing. But instead you praise his craft especially when you see that it introduces with confidence treatments which seem contradictory and harmful to us, and guarantees that they are safe. For this is a man who is an expert craftsman. If we accept a physician who does these contradictory things, how much more [244] should we proclaim the praises of Paul's soul, which in the same way attends to the sick? For those who are sick in their souls have no less need of concoction and treatment than those who are are ill in the body. Indeed, if you should approach them with straight-forwardly consistent measures, all the efforts for their salvation will be undone.

5.8 [244]. If human beings do these things, why is it a surprise that God, who is able to do everything, has adopted this principle of healing, and doesn't always deal with us in a straightforward fashion? Since God wished us to be virtuous willingly, and not by compulsion and force, he had need of this approach; not because it was impossible for him (banish the thought!), but because of our weakness. For he is able merely by nodding, or, rather, only wanting it, to make everything just as he wishes. But we, having at one time become our own masters, refuse to obey him in every-thing. But if he were to draw us along unwillingly, then he would destroy precisely what he gave us—the freedom of control, I mean. Hence, so that this might not happen, God had need of many forms of approach. I have not said these things to you frivolously, but to show the variability and cleverness of the blessed Paul. Therefore, when you see him fleeing dan-gers [246], marvel the same as when you see him rushing forward to meet them. For just as the latter is proof of bravery, the former is of wisdom. When you see him telling his magnificent exploits, marvel the same as when you see him speaking modestly. For just as the latter shows humility, the former indicates magnanimity of soul. When you see him boasting, marvel the same as when you see him refusing praise. For the latter shows an uninflated character, and the former compassion and love for others. This is because he was doing all these things to administer the salvation of the many.

5.9 [246]. Hence he said, "if we are out of our minds, it is for God; if we are rightminded, it is for you" (2 Cor. 5:13). No one else had such com-pelling reasons for madness, nor was anyone else so pure of boastfulness. Consider this: "Knowledge puffs up" (1 Cor. 8:1). We would all say this with him. Yet he had knowledge of a caliber not found in any of the human beings ever born, but nevertheless he did not exalt himself, but spoke mod-estly even about this. Thus he says, "we know in part, and we prophesy in part" (1 Cor. 13:9), and again, "Brothers, I do not yet consider myself to have yet apprehended it" (Phil. 3:13), and, "if any think they know some-thing, not yet do they know anything" (1 Cor. 8:2). Or another example:

fasting puffs up. This *[248]* is made clear by the Pharisee who says, "I fast twice a week" (Lk. 18:12). But Paul, not merely fasting, but even starving, called himself a "miscarriage" (1 Cor. 15:8).

5.10 *[248]*. Why should I speak of fasting and knowledge, when he had so many and such continual moments of converse with God as were shared by none of the prophets or apostles, and nevertheless he used to humble himself for them? Now don't tell me that these experiences were written down [in the letters]. For he hid the majority of them, and didn't tell all, so that he not confer great glory on himself; nor did he keep silent about them all, so as not to open the mouths of the false apostles. For that man did nothing frivolously, but did all in conjunction with a just and reasonable cause. And he pursed contradictory actions with such great wisdom that he has attained the same praises from all directions. Such is my point: it is a great good not to boast about oneself. But the person who does it when the moment requires is more to be praised for speaking than for having remained silent. And if he had not done this, then he would be more worthy of blame than those who offer praise for others, but at the wrong time. For if he had not boasted, then he would have lost and abandoned everything, and advanced the cause of his enemies. Thus he knew how to employ it always in the right circumstance, and how to do this forbidden thing with a right purpose—to confer such benefits that he earns no less esteem for it than he would receive for following what is prescribed. Indeed, Paul was more esteemed in the moment of boasting *[250]* than anyone else would be when hiding his good deeds; for no one has done such good deeds in concealing his actions as Paul has done in proclaiming his.

5.11 *[250]*. And what is still more marvelous is the fact that, not only did he speak out, but he stopped precisely at the point of present need. For he did not employ the practice of boasting immoderately, under the pretext that the circumstance gave him license to do so, but he knew how far one should go. And even this did not satisfy him, but, lest he corrupt the others and make them praise themselves frivolously, he calls himself a fool (2 Cor. 12:11). After all, he did this when the need called for it, but the others, seeing him do it, would likely take up the practice by his example, yet do it frivolously and in vain. This is what happens in the case of doctors, as well, for often the physician applies a medicine in a timely fashion, and someone else, by applying it at the wrong time, causes injury and obscures the potency of the medicine.

5.12 *[250]*. Therefore, lest this happen here too, observe how he corrects himself in advance when he is about to boast, not once or twice, but repeatedly shrinks away from doing it. For, he says, "I wish you would put up with a little foolishness from me" (2 Cor. 11:1), and again, "What I speak I do not speak according to the Lord, but as though in foolishness. In whatever respect someone dares to speak in foolishness, I dare, too" (2 Cor. 11:17, 21). And even though he had expressed such strong hesitation, he was not satisfied even at that, but when about to embark on encomia again, he hides himself, saying, "I know *[252]* a man," and again, "On behalf of such a man I shall boast, but on behalf of myself I shall not boast." And after all these statements, he says, "I have been a fool, you compelled me" (2 Cor. 12:2, 5, 11). Who, therefore, is so foolish and extremely stupid as not to flee from the practice of superfluous boasting, and engage in it only when a timely circumstance rendered it necessary? How could one not flee it when one sees that saint, even when a severe necessity befell him, hesitate and shrink away from boasting like a horse coming to a precipice and rearing back continually, even though he was destined to administer such important matters?

5.13 [252]. Do you wish me to offer another such proof of his behavior? This is what is marvelous: that he was not satisfied with his own conscience, but also taught us how we should pursue each of these strategies. Not only was he defending himself by taking recourse to the necessity of the times, but he was also teaching the others, so that when the time befell them, they would neither flee from the practice entirely, nor again pursue it at the wrong moment. Indeed through the comments he made it is almost as if he were saying: "It is a great evil to tell something great and marvelous about oneself." And this is the height of craziness [254], beloved, to adorn oneself with encomia when there is no need, as though there were some compelling need. This is not "speaking according to the Lord" (2 Cor. 11:17), but instead is a proof of madness, and it nullifies the entire reward of our deeds, after much exertion and labors. For Paul told everyone all these things, and more besides that he begged off from telling, when necessity befell him. But, even more than this, not even when necessity befell him did he continually pour out all his virtuous deeds in public, but he hid the most and the best of them. For, he said, "I shall go on to visions and revelations of the Lord. I fear lest someone might consider me to be above what they see or hear from me" (2 Cor. 12:1, 6). He spoke these things to teach us all that not even when there is a necessity should we bring out into the public eye all the good deeds we are conscious of in ourselves, but only what will be useful for the listeners.

*　　*　　*

To say the very things which would be necessary for the present need is the part of one who loves humanity and looks to the advantage of the many. Which is precisely what Paul did. For the slanders being brought against him were that he was not a proven apostle, nor did he have any power. Consequently, because of those charges it was a necessity that he go into the matters which especially would prove his dignified position.

5.15 [256]. Do you see how many means he employed to instruct his hearer not to boast frivolously? First, by showing that he did this from necessity. Second, by calling himself a fool, and repeatedly begging off from engaging in it. Third, by not telling everything, but hiding his greater deeds—and this was when there *was* a necessity. Fourth, by assuming another persona and saying "I know a man" (2 Cor. 12:2). Fifth, by not publicizing every other virtue, but only that portion for which the present time had special need.

5.16 [256]. But it was not only in boasting that he was like this, but also in insulting. Although it had been forbidden to insult a brother (Mt. 5:22),

Paul used this practice, too, in such a fitting manner that he is more esteemed for it than are those who speak in praise *[258]*. Notice how for this reason he calls the Galatians stupid, not once, but twice (Gal. 3:1, 3) and Cretans lazy bellies and wicked beasts (Tit. 1:12), and is awarded praise for it. For he gave us a limit and a standard, so that we might not employ too much solicitation with those who are neglectful of God, but practice a more startling form of speech. The proper measure of all things resides in him. Indeed, for this reason Paul is highly esteemed in everything he does and says, in both insulting and praising, abandoning and soliciting, exalting himself and speaking modestly, boasting and lowering himself. And why should you be surprised if insult and reviling receive esteem, when murder and deceit and guile were esteemed in both the Old and the New Testaments?

5.17 *[258]*. Therefore, now that we have studied all these things accurately, let us marvel at Paul, let us glorify God, and let us deal with him in such a way that also we ourselves might attain the eternal goods, by the grace and beneficence of our Lord Jesus Christ, to whom be the glory and the power, now and always, and forever and ever. Amen.

ANONYMOUS

[Paul's Missionary Journey to Spain]
(late second century)†

1. When Paul was at Rome confirming many in the faith, it also happened that a certain woman named Candida, wife of Quartus the prison warder, heard Paul and listened to his words and became a believer. And when she had instructed her husband he became a believer. Quartus persuaded Paul to leave the city and to go wherever he pleased. Paul said to him, 'If such be the will of God, he will reveal it to me.' And Paul fasted three days and besought the Lord to grant what was good for him, and in a vision he saw the Lord who said to him, 'Paul, arise, and be a physician to the Spaniards!' At this he related to the brethren what God had commanded him, and without hesitation he made ready to leave the city. When Paul was preparing to leave, there was a great lamentation among the brethren because they thought they would never see Paul again; they even tore their garments, bearing in mind that Paul often quarrelled with the teachers of the Jews and had confounded them by saying, 'Christ, on whom your fathers laid their hands, abrogated their Sabbath and their fasting and festivals and circumcision and abolished the teaching of men and other traditions.' And the brethren adjured Paul, by the coming of our Lord Jesus

† From the *Acts of Peter*, tr. by J. K. Elliott, *The Apocryphal New Testament* (Oxford: Clarendon, 1993), 399. Reprinted by permission of Oxford University Press. In Rom. 15:24, 28, Paul indicates that he plans to go to Spain after spending some time in Rome. Nothing more about such a trip is mentioned in the NT, not even in the Pastoral Letters, which presuppose that Paul returned to the East rather than journeying toward the West. Nevertheless, reports of such a trip occasionally occur. The author of the Muratorian Canon, for example, suggests that Luke omitted the story of Paul's journey to Spain because he was not an eyewitness to the trip. The excerpt given here provides a narrative version of Paul's call to undertake the trip to Spain as well as an indication that Paul would return to Rome and be martyred at the hands of Nero.

Christ, not to stay away more than a year saying, 'We know your love for your brethren; forget us not when you come to Spain and do not desert us like children without a mother.' And while they were beseeching him with tears a sound was heard from heaven and a very loud voice, saying, 'Paul, the servant of God, is chosen to the ministry for the rest of his life; under the hands of Nero, the wicked and bad man, he will be perfected before your eyes.' And there was a great fear among the brethren because of the voice, which had come from heaven, and they were the more confirmed in the faith.

The Martyrdom of Paul

The New Testament does not record Paul's death, but Christian tradition places it firmly in Rome, where it also places the death of Peter. The deaths of these two apostles are already mentioned by Clement of Rome toward the end of the first century (see below), and later writers give elaborate accounts of their demise. Peter plays no role in the *Martyrdom of Paul* given below, and Paul is equally absent from the *Martyrdom of Peter* that forms part of the *Acts of Peter*, but later authors sought to unite the two more closely in their deaths. Augustine, for example, believed that Peter and Paul suffered martyrdom on the same day (*Cons.* 10.16; see also Jerome, *Vir. ill.* 5 on p. 211), and the later *Passion of Peter and Paul* (sixth or seventh century), following earlier traditions, has Paul beheaded on the road to Ostia and Peter crucified upside down.

Where Paul was buried is debated; indeed, since there was not yet an interest in martyrs in the 60s of the first century, his remains may well have been lost. But two sites in Rome have been claimed as his burial place. The first is on the Via Ostiensis, where the Roman presbyter Gaius (ca. 200) claimed the "trophy" (memorial) of Paul was located (in Eusebius, *Hist. eccl.* 2.25.7). Similarly, Gaius located Peter's trophy at the Vatican. The second is the double memorial to both Peter and Paul (*memoria apostolorum*), located on the Via Appia in the covered cemetery beneath the church of St. Sebastian. This, according to an epigram by Pope Damasus (366–384), was the resting place of Peter and Paul, and modern excavations have confirmed the ancient veneration of the apostles at this site. Why there were individual sites for each apostle as well as a joint memorial is a puzzle that has elicited various solutions and will doubtless continue to spark debate in the future.

CLEMENT OF ROME

[Pillar of the Church and Example of Endurance]
(ca. 96)†

1. But, to cease from the examples of old time, let us come to those who contended in the days nearest to us; let us take the noble examples of our own generation. 2. Through jealousy and envy the greatest and most righteous pillars of the Church were persecuted and contended unto death. 3. Let us set before our eyes the good apostles: 4. Peter, who because of unrighteous jealousy suffered not one or two but many trials, and having thus given his testimony went to the glorious place which was his due. 5. Through jealousy and strife Paul showed the way to the prize of endurance; 6. seven times he was in bonds, he was exiled, he was stoned, he was

---

† *1 Clem.* 5, tr. by K. Lake, *The Apostolic Fathers*, Vol. 1 (London: Heinemann, 1912), 17. According to the dominant ecclesiastical tradition, Clement was the third bishop of Rome, though Tertullian (*Praescr.* 32) states that the Roman church claimed he was ordained by Peter. The excerpt is from his letter to the church at Corinth.

a herald both in the East and in the West, he gained the noble fame of his faith, 7. he taught righteousness to all the world, and when he had reached the limits of the West he gave his testimony before the rulers, and thus passed from the world and was taken up into the Holy Place,—the greatest example of endurance.

ANONYMOUS

[Paul Is Beheaded and Appears to Nero] (ca. 190?)†

1. Luke, who had come from Gaul, and Titus, who had come from Dalmatia, expected Paul at Rome. When Paul saw them he rejoiced and rented a barn outside Rome where he and the brethren taught the word of truth. He became famous and many souls were added to the Lord, so that it was noised about in Rome and a great many from the house of the emperor came to him and there was much joy.

A certain Patroclus, a cupbearer of the emperor, who had come too late to the barn and could not get near to Paul on account of the throng of the people sat on a high window, and listened as he taught the word of God. But Satan, being wicked, became jealous of the love of the brethren and Patroclus fell down from the window and died; speedily it was reported to Nero. Paul, however, having learned it by the Spirit said, 'Brethren, the evil one has obtained a way to tempt you; go forth and you will find a boy who has fallen down and is dying. Lift him up and bring him here.' This they did. When the people saw him they were frightened. Paul said to them, 'Now, brethren, show your faith. Come, let us mourn to our Lord Jesus Christ, that the boy might live and we remain unharmed.' When all began to lament, the boy took breath and, having put him on an animal, they sent him away alive with all those who were of the emperor's house.

2. And Nero, having heard of Patroclus' death, became very sad, and as he came out from his bath he ordered another to be appointed for the wine. But his servants said, 'Emperor, Patroclus is alive and stands at the sideboard.' When the emperor heard that Patroclus was alive he was frightened and would not come in. But when he came in and saw Patroclus he cried out, 'Patroclus, are you alive?' He answered, 'I am alive, Caesar.' But he said, 'Who is he who made you alive?' And the boy, uplifted by the confidence of faith, said, 'Christ Jesus, the king of the ages.' The emperor asked in dismay, 'Is he to be king of the ages and destroy all kingdoms?' Patroclus said to him, 'Yes, he destroys all kingdoms under heaven, and he alone shall remain in all eternity, and there will be no kingdom which escapes him.' And he struck his face and cried out, 'Patroclus, are you also fighting for that king?' He answered, 'Yes, my lord and Caesar, for he has raised me from the dead.'

And Barsabas Justus the flat-footed and Urion the Cappadocian and Festus of Galatia, the chief men of Nero, said, 'And we, too, fight for him,

† The Martyrdom of Paul, tr. by J. K. Elliott, The Apocryphal New Testament (Oxford: Clarendon, 1993), 385–88. Reprinted by permission of Oxford University Press. This account of Paul's martyrdom was originally part of the Acts of Paul but was separated from it very early and circulated independently, achieving great popularity during the Middle Ages.

the king of the ages.' After having tortured those men whom he used to love he imprisoned them and ordered that the soldiers of the great king be sought, and he issued an edict that all Christians and soldiers of Christ that were found should be executed.

3. And among the many Paul also was brought in fetters. Those who were imprisoned with him looked at him, so that the emperor observed that he was the leader of the soldiers. And he said to him, 'Man of the great king, now my prisoner, what induced you to come secretly into the Roman empire and to enlist soldiers in my territory?' But Paul, filled with the Holy Spirit, said in the presence of all, 'Caesar, we enlist soldiers not only in your territory but in all lands of the earth. For thus we are commanded to exclude none who wishes to fight for my king. If it seems good to you serve him, for neither riches nor the splendours of this life will save you; but if you become his subject and beseech him you shall be saved. For in one day he will destroy the world.'

Having heard this Nero commanded all the prisoners to be burned with fire, but Paul to be beheaded according to the law of the Romans. But Paul was not silent and communicated the word to Longus the prefect and Cestus the centurion. And Nero, being instigated by the evil one, raged in Rome and had many Christians executed without trial, so that the Romans stood before the palace and cried, 'It is enough, Caesar; these men are ours. You destroy the strength of the Romans.' Being thus convinced, he desisted and commanded that no Christian was to be touched till his case had been investigated.

4. After the issuing of the edict Paul was brought before him, and he insisted that he should be executed. And Paul said, 'Caesar, I live not merely for a short time for my king; and if you have me executed I shall do the following: I will rise again and appear to you, for I shall not be dead but alive to my king, Christ Jesus, who shall come to judge the earth.'

And Longus and Cestus said to Paul, 'Whence have you this king that you believe in him without changing your mind even at point of death?' And Paul answered and said, 'You men, who are now ignorant and in error, change your mind and be saved from the fire which comes over the whole earth. For we fight not, as you suppose, for a king who is from the earth but for one who is from heaven: he is the living God who comes as judge because of the lawless deeds which take place in this world. And blessed is he who will believe in him and live in eternity when he shall come with fire to purge the earth.' And they besought him and said, 'We entreat you, help us, and we will release you.' But he answered, 'I am not a deserter from Christ but a faithful soldier of the living God. If I knew that I should die I would still have done it, Longus and Cestus, but since I live to God and love myself I go to the Lord that I may come again with him in the glory of his Father.' And they said to him, 'How can we live after you have been beheaded?'

5. And while they were speaking Nero sent a certain Parthenius and Pheretas to see whether Paul had already been beheaded. And they found him still alive. He summoned them beside him and said, 'Believe in the living God who will raise me, as well as all those who believe in him, from the dead.' But they said, 'We will now go to Nero but when you have died and have been raised up we will believe in your God.'

But when Longus and Cestus continued to ask about salvation he said to them, 'In the early dawn come quickly to my grave and you will find two men at prayer, Titus and Luke; they will give you the seal in the Lord.'

And turning toward the east, Paul lifted up his hands to heaven and prayed at length; and after having conversed in Hebrew with the fathers during prayer he bent his neck, without speaking any more. When the executioner cut off his head milk splashed on the tunic of the soldier. And the soldier and all who stood near by were astonished at this sight and glorified God who had thus honoured Paul. And they went away and reported everything to Caesar.

6. When he heard of it he was amazed and did not know what to say. While many philosophers and the centurion were assembled with the emperor Paul came about the ninth hour, and in the presence of all he said, 'Caesar, behold, here is Paul, the soldier of God; I am not dead but live in my God. But upon you, unhappy one, many evils and great punishment will come because you have unjustly shed the blood of the righteous not many days ago.' And having spoken this Paul departed from him. When Nero had heard he commanded that the prisoners be released, Patroclus as well as Barsabas with his friends.

7. And, as Paul had told them, Longus and Cestus, the centurion, came in fear very early to the grave of Paul. And when they drew near they found two men in prayer and Paul with them, and they became frightened when they saw the unexpected miracle, but Titus and Luke, being afraid at the sight of Longus and Cestus, turned to run away.

But they followed and said to them, 'We follow you not in order to kill you, blessed men of God, as you imagine, but in order to live, that you may do to us as Paul promised us. We have just seen him in prayer beside you.' Upon hearing this Titus and Luke gave them joyfully the seal in the Lord, glorifying God and the Father of our Lord Jesus Christ to whom be glory for ever and ever. Amen.

Paul as Satan's Apostle: Jewish-Christian Opponents

Paul's letter to Galatians attests to a vigorous conflict between the apostle and certain rival missionaries who insisted that Gentile Christians must be circumcised and must adhere to the Law of Moses. While Paul's vehement self-defense was apparently successful at that time in Galatia, the opposition was not silenced. Again and again in the writings of the church fathers, we hear of Jewish-Christian groups who were incensed by Paul's strictures against circumcision and the law and who refused to acknowledge the authority of his writings. The Elkesaites were one such group, who appear to have traced their origin to a prophet named Elkesai (fl. 101). According to Origen (cited in Eusebius, *Hist. eccl.* 6.38), they rejected Paul entirely. It is ironic that Mani (216–276), the founder of Manichaeism, grew up in this baptismal sect. At the age of twenty-four, he received his heavenly call, became "an apostle of light," was expelled from the Elkesaites, and began to spread "the religion of light" with Pauline missionary zeal. Like Paul, Mani typically referred to himself as an "apostle of Jesus Christ."

The precise nature of the Jewish-Christian groups is as difficult to determine as is the precise character of those earlier opponents in Galatia. The most important of them are called Ebionites, from the Semitic word for "poor," and on the basis of passages such as Romans 15:26 and Galatians 2:10 they have been identified as descendants of the original disciples in Jerusalem.[1] That is improbable, although it is clear that some of the Ebionites themselves labored to establish such a connection in the second and third centuries.[2] The orthodox heresiologists classified the Ebionites with the Gnostics. While that guilt-by-association is to be taken with a grain of salt, it is true that the groups we know most about were quite syncretistic. The Jewishness of the group that produced the *Kerygmata Petrou* excerpted below, for instance, would seem bizarre from the perspective of rabbinic Judaism; it could more readily be compared with such esoteric groups as the Essenes.[3]

Not surprisingly, the picture of Paul represented by these sources is a very flat caricature.[4] The originators of these traditions seem to have had no substantial information about Paul. The main points are drawn from the letters and Acts. Stories are concocted, apparently, out of thin air (as in *The Ascents of James*) or adapted from existing legends (as in the curious story of Paul's attack on James, which has some connection with the legend of James' mar-

---

1. An important element in F. C. Baur's scheme of early Christian development (see below pp. 399–408), revived in the twentieth century by H. J. Schoeps, *Theologie und Geschichte des Judenchristentums* (Tübingen: Mohr-Siebeck, 1949); *Jewish Christianity: Factional Disputes in the Early Church* (Philadelphia: Fortress, 1969); S. G. F. Brandon, *The Fall of Jerusalem and the Christian Church* (London: SPCK, 1951); and others.
2. See Leander E. Keck, "The Poor among the Saints in Jewish Christianity," ZNW 57 (1966): 54–78.
3. On the history of Jewish-Christianity, see, besides the works cited above, Jean Daniélou, *Theology of Jewish Christianity* (Chicago, 1964), Marcel Simon, *Recherches d'histoire judéo-chrétienne* (Paris: Mouton, 1962) and *Verus Israel* (New York: Oxford, 1986), and A. F. J. Klijn and G. J. Reinink, *Patristic Evidence for Jewish-Christian Sects* (Leiden: Brill, 1973).
4. See esp. Gerd Lüdemann, *Opposition to Paul in Jewish Christianity* (Minneapolis: Fortress, 1989).

tyrdom recounted by Hegesippus[5]). Even on the central point of contention, Paul's rejection of the law, there is no clarity. The Jewish-Christian groups had, of course, no interest in repeating the subtleties of Paul's argument; Paul's supporters had trouble enough with those. In fact there is little indication that specifically Pauline attitudes toward the law were under discussion. They attacked the Paul depicted by the slowly solidifying main stream of catholic Christianity, all now practically more or less free of the law, at least in its ceremonial aspects. The intricately nuanced argument of the Letter to the Romans was hardly understood by either side, nor was there much incentive to try.

AMBROSIASTER

[The Non-Apostle] (late fourth century)†

Those Jewish believers who nevertheless continued to observe the law of Moses denied that Paul was an apostle because he taught that it was no longer necessary to be circumcised or to observe the sabbath. Even the other apostles thought that he was teaching something different because of this, and they denied that he was an apostle. But to the Corinthians Paul was an apostle, because they had seen the signs of God's power in him.

ANONYMOUS

[A False Proselyte] (third century?)‡

They [sc. the Ebionites] invoke other acts of apostles, in which are many things full of impiety, which they use primarily to arm themselves against the truth. They also produce certain pilgrimages[1] and expositions, namely in "The Ascents of James," pretending that James spoke against the Temple and the sacrifices and against the fire of the altar, and many other things full of empty talk. So also, in the same place, they are not ashamed to slander Paul, using certain charges trumped up by the malice and error of their pseudo-apostles. They say that he was not only a citizen of Tarsus, as he himself admits and does not deny, but also of Greek origin, basing this on the passage in which Paul candidly says, "I am a Tarsan, citizen of no mean city" [Acts 21:39]. Then they declare that he was a Greek, child

---

5. See below, and compare Eusebius, *Ecclesiastical History*. 2.23.4–18; cf. Josephus, *Ant*. 20.200.
† From Ambrosiaster's commentary on 1 Cor. 9:2 (CSEL 81.97), tr. in Gerald Bray (ed.), *1–2 Corinthians* (ACCS, NT 7; Downers Grove: InterVarsity, 1999), 80. Copyright © 1998 by the Institute of Classical Studies, Thomas Oden, and Gerald Bray. Used with permission of InterVarsity Press. On "Ambrosiaster" and his commentary, see note on p. 213.
‡ From "The Ascents of James" (*anabathmoi Iakobou*), of uncertain date, here as paraphrased by Epiphanius (ca. 315–403, bishop of Salamis), *Pan*. 30.16.6–9. We translate the critical edition by Karl Holl (Leipzig, 1915).
1. The word *anabathmos* ordinarily means staircase or the like; hence it was once wrongly suggested that the book was the same as the "Ladder of Jacob" extant in Slavonic. The context shows that not the patriarch but the "brother of the Lord" Jacob (= "James") is meant. *Anabathmos* is evidently used here as a synonym of *anabasis*, "ascent," referring to James' ascents or pilgrimages to Jerusalem. (See Holl's note *ad loc*. in his edition of Epiphanius and G. Strecker, *Das Judenchristentum in den Pseudoklementinen* [Berlin, 1958], p. 252.)

of a Greek mother and a Greek father. He went up to Jerusalem, they say, and when he had spent some time there, he was seized with a passion to marry a daughter of the priest. For this reason he became a proselyte and was circumcised. Then, when he failed to get the girl, he flew into a rage and wrote against circumcision and against Sabbath and Law.

EPIPHANIUS

[The Cerinthians] (ca. 375)†

For they use the Gospel according to Matthew—in part, because of the human genealogy, but not all of it—and they adduce this proof-text from the Gospel: "It is enough for the disciple to be like his teacher" [Matt. 10: 25]. What then, they say—Jesus was circumcised; be circumcised yourself. Christ lived according to the Law, they say, and you must do the same. Hence some of these, like men seized by poisonous drugs, are convinced by the specious arguments based on Christ's having been circumcised. They break with Paul because he does not accept circumcision, but they also reject him because he said, "You who would be justified by the law have fallen away from grace" [Gal. 5:4] and "If you receive circumcision, Christ will be of no advantage to you" [Gal. 5:2].

ANONYMOUS

[Messenger of Satan] (ca. 200?)‡

The Letter of Peter to James

1 Peter to James the lord and bishop of the holy church. By the Father of all things through Jesus Christ (may you be) in peace always.

2 Knowing that you, my brother, eagerly pursue what is of common benefit to us all, I request and implore you not to impart the books of my preachings which I am sending you to any of the Gentiles, nor even to a fellow Jew before he is tested. But if someone, upon examination, is found worthy, then to him you may hand them over, in the same way as Moses

---

† From *Panarion, haer.* 28.5.1–3. Epiphanius says he is describing the beliefs of followers of the Gnostic Cerinthus, but there is some evidence that he has confused them with the Ebionites.

‡ From *The Preachings of Peter* (*Kerygmata Petrou*), introduced by a cover letter from Peter to James. The Jewish-Christian group that produced the original form of this fiction was concerned to demonstrate that their tradition came straight from Peter via James the brother of Jesus, who is described as the first bishop of Jerusalem. Since Paul's interpretation of Christianity depended upon a mere vision it could not stand against this authentic tradition. Moreover, the document inserts Paul into a dualistic framework to show that he belonged to a long series of false prophets. *The Preachings of Peter* was incorporated, with much later material, into a novel that has survived in two major versions, both falsely ascribed to Pope Clement I. (For the problems involved in isolating the different constituents of this literature, see the introduction by G. Strecker in Hennecke's *New Testament Apocrypha*, ed. W. Schneemelcher, trans. by R. McL. Wilson, [rev. ed.; Louisville, 1992], Vol. 2, 483–93; other scholars are less confident about the existence of this work.) In the novel, which has undergone catholic editing, Peter's enemy is the rival religious founder Simon Magus, but it was clearly Paul who played that role in the original. We translate the critical Greek text of the *Homilies*, ed. by Bernhard Rehm (Berlin: Akademie, 1969).

handed on (the tradition) to the seventy who succeeded to his chair. 3 Because of this, the fruit of his precaution is apparent until the present. For his fellow nationals everywhere hold to the same rule of monotheism and the same moral constitution, since they cannot be led by the ambiguities of scripture to adopt any other viewpoint. 4 Rather they try to correct the disagreements of the scriptures according to the norm handed down to them, in case anyone who chances not to know the traditions should be shocked by the ambiguous statements of the prophets. 5 For this reason they permit no one to teach until he has learned how the scriptures ought to be used. Thus among them there is one God, one Law, one Hope.

2 In order then that the same situation may obtain among us, hand over the books of my preachings to our seventy brothers with similar secrecy, that they may prepare those who want to take up the office of teacher. 2 Otherwise, if this is not done, our word of truth will be divided into many opinions. It is not as a prophet that I know this; rather I already see the beginning of this evil. 3 For some of those of Gentile origin have rejected my lawful proclamation, accepting rather a lawless and silly teaching of "the enemy."[1] 4 And even while I am still alive some have undertaken to distort my words, by certain intricate interpretations, into an abolition of the law, as if I myself thought such a thing, but did not preach it openly— God forbid! 5 For to take such a position is to act against the Law of God which was spoken through Moses and whose eternal endurance was attested by our Lord. For he said: "Heaven and earth will pass away; not an iota, not a dot, will pass from the law." 6 And he said this, "that everything might come to pass."[2] But these people who have my mind at their disposal, I know not how, undertake to interpret the words which they heard from me more intelligently than I who spoke them. They tell those who are taking instruction from them that this is my opinion—something I never dreamed of. 7 If they dare to fabricate this kind of lies while I am still alive, how much more will they dare to do who come after me?

* * *

(Homily II, 16–17)

16 As in the beginning God, who is one, created first the heaven, then the earth, like a right and left hand, so he also arranged all the pairs in sequence. In the case of men, however, he no longer does this, but reverses all the pairs. 2 For while from him the first things are better, the second inferior, in the case of men we find the opposite: the first things are worse, the second better. 3 Thus from Adam, who was made in the image of God, came first the unjust Cain, second the just Abel. 4 Again, from the one whom you call Deucalion symbols of two spirits were sent forth, an impure and a pure, that is the black raven and the white dove second. 5 And from the founder of our nation, Abraham, two different ones[3] were born, first Ishmael, then Isaac who was blessed by God. 6 In the same way again two issued from Isaac, Esau the impious and Jacob the pious. 7 Thus in order

---

1. "The enemy," lit., "the hostile man"; the phrase is probably suggested by Matt. 13:25, 28. As *Recog.* I, 71:3 (below) makes plain, Paul was meant in the original version of *The Preachings.*
2. Cf. Matt. 5:18, where however the last clause reads "until everything comes to pass."
3. Accepting Wieseler's emendation; the text reads "two first."

came first, as firstborn in the world, the High Priest [sc. Aaron], then the Lawgiver [sc. Moses].

17 In the same way—for the pair pertaining to Elijah, which ought to come (next), was deliberately postponed until another time, to take it up according to plan at another, appropriate moment— 2 therefore he who is "among those born of women"[4] came first, then he who is among the sons of men appeared second. 3 By following this sequence anyone can understand to whom "Simon" [i.e., Paul] belongs, who first went to the Gentiles, before me, and to whom I [sc. Peter] belong, who came after him, appearing as light after darkness, as knowledge after ignorance, as healing after sickness. 4 Thus, as the True Prophet told us, first a false gospel must come through a certain deceiver, and then, after the destruction of the holy place, a true gospel must be propagated secretly in order to rectify the existing heresies.

* * *

(Homily XI, 35, 3–6)

35 * * * 3 Our Lord and Prophet who commissioned us explained to us how the evil one, having disputed with him without success for forty days, promised to send apostles from his retinue for the purpose of deception. 4 Therefore remember above all not to receive any apostle or prophet or teacher who has not first presented his gospel to James—who is called the brother of the Lord and to whom the direction of the church of the Hebrews in Jerusalem was entrusted—and comes to you with witnesses.[5] 5 Otherwise the wickedness that disputed with the Lord for forty days and could do nothing, and which later "fell like lightning from heaven" to earth,[6] would send against you a herald, as now he has sent "Simon" against us, preaching, under pretext of the truth, in the name of our Lord,[7] but actually sowing error. 6 For this reason the one who commissioned us said, "Many shall come to you in sheep's clothing, but inwardly they are ravenous wolves; by their fruits you shall know them."[8]

(Homily XVII, 13–19)

* * *

13 When "Simon" heard this, he interrupted [Peter] to say, "* * * You assert that you thoroughly understand your teacher's concerns because, in his physical presence, you saw and heard him directly, but no one else could gain such understanding by means of a dream or a vision. 2 But I shall show that this is false. One who hears something directly cannot be quite certain about what was said, for the mind must consider whether,

---

4. Cf. Matt. 11.11 = Luke 7.28.
5. So the Greek; the parallel passage in the *Recognitions* reads "testimonials." The *Recognitions* passage adds, in a sentence that may well go back to the original *Kerygmata*, a comparison of the twelve apostles with the twelve months of the year, thus tacitly declaring any "thirteenth" claimant to apostolicity, such as Paul, to be inauthentic.
6. Luke 10:18; probably understood here as an allusion to Paul's Damascus vision: see Acts 9:3 and below, *Hom.* XVII, 14,5.
7. This phrase shows that Simon Magus could not have been meant by the original *Kerygmata*, for Simon, who regarded himself as a manifestation of the Supreme Power, did not preach "in the name of (the) Lord."
8. Matt. 7:15 f.

being merely human, he has been deceived by the sense impression. But the vision, by the very act of appearing, presents its own proof to the seer that it is divine. First give me an answer to this."

14 And Peter said, "* * * 3 The prophet, once he has proved that he is a prophet, is infallibly believed in the matters which are directly spoken by him. Also, when his truthfulness has been previously recognized, he can give answers to the disciple, however the latter may wish to examine and interrogate him. But one who puts his trust in a vision or an apparition or dream is in a precarious position, for he does not know what it is he is trusting. 4 For it is possible that it is an evil demon or a deceitful spirit, pretending in the speeches to be what he is not. 5 Then if anyone should wish to inquire who it was who spoke, he could say of himself whatever he chose. Thus, like an evil flash of lightning,[9] he stays as long as he chooses and then vanishes, not remaining with the inquirer long enough to answer his questions. * * *"

16 And Peter said, "* * *We know * * * 2 that many idolaters and adulterers and all kinds of sinners have seen visions and true dreams, while others have seen appearances of demons. For I assert that it is not possible to see the incorporeal form of Father or Son, because mortal eyes are dazzled by the great light. 3 Therefore it is not because God is jealous, but because he is merciful that he remains invisible to flesh-oriented man. For no one who sees can survive.[1] 4 For the extraordinary light would dissolve the flesh of the beholder, unless the flesh were changed by the ineffable power of God into the nature of light, so that it could see the light—or unless the light-substance were changed into flesh, so that it could be seen by flesh. For the Son alone is able to see the Father without being transformed. The case of the righteous is different: in the resurrection of the dead, when their bodies, changed into light, become like angels, then they will be able to see. Finally, even if an angel is sent to appear to a man, he is changed into flesh, that he can be seen by flesh. For no one can see the incorporeal power of the Son or even of an angel. But if someone *sees a vision*, let him understand this to be an evil demon.

17 But it is obvious that impious people also see true visions and dreams, and I can prove it from scripture [The cases of Abimelech (Gen. 20:3 ff.), the Egyptian Pharaoh (Gen. 41), and Nebuchadnezzar (Dan. 2) are adduced.] * * * 5 Thus the fact that one sees visions and dreams and apparitions by no means assures that he is a religious person. Rather, to the pure and innate religious mind the truth gushes up, not eagerly courted by a dream, but granted to the good by intelligence.

18 It was in this way that the Son was revealed to me by the Father. Therefore I know what the nature of revelation is, since I learned it myself. [The following passage discusses Peter's Confession, as recounted in Matt. 16:13–16, then cites Num. 2:6–8.] * * * 6 You see how revelations of anger are through visions and dreams, while those to a friend are 'mouth to mouth,'[2] by sight and not by puzzles and visions and dreams, as they are to an enemy.

19 So even if our Jesus did appear in a dream to you, making himself known and conversing with you, he did so in anger, speaking to an oppo-

9. This may be another allusion to Acts 9:3; see above, *Hom.* XI, 35, 5.
1. Cf. Exod. 33:20.
2. Exod. 33:11; Num. 12:8; Deut. 34:10.

nent. That is why he spoke to you through visions and dreams—through revelations which are external. 2 But can anyone be qualified by a vision to become a teacher? And if you say it is possible, then why did the Teacher remain for a whole year conversing with those who were awake? 3 How can we believe even your statement that he appeared to you? How could he have appeared to you, when your opinions are opposed to his teaching? 4 No, if you were visited and taught by him for a single hour and thus became an apostle, proclaim his utterances, interpret his teachings, love his apostles—and do not strive against me, who was his companion. For you have 'opposed' me,[3] the firm Rock, foundation of the church.[4] 5 If you were not an enemy, you would not slander me and disparage what is preached by me, as if I were obviously 'condemned'[5] and you were approved. 6 If you call me 'condemned,' you are accusing God who revealed the Christ to me, and are opposing the one who blessed me because of the revelation. 7 Rather, if you really want to work together for the truth, first learn from us what we learned from him. Then, having become a disciple of the truth, become our fellow-worker."

ANONYMOUS

[Persecutor of the Faith] (date unknown)†

[The preceding chapters describe a debate in Jerusalem between the apostles and the leaders of each of the Jewish sects.] * * * And when matters were at that point that they should come and be baptized, some one of our enemies,[1] entering the temple with a few men, began to cry out, and to say, 'What mean ye, O men of Israel? Why are you so easily hurried on? Why are ye led headlong by most miserable men, who are deceived by a magician?' While he was thus speaking, and adding more to the same effect, and while James the bishop was refuting him, he began to excite the people and to raise a tumult, so that the people might not be able to hear what was said. Therefore he began to drive all into confusion with shouting, and to undo what had been arranged with much labour, and at the same time to reproach the priests, and to enrage them with revilings and abuse, and like a madman, to excite every one to murder, saying, 'What do ye? Why do ye hesitate? Oh, sluggish and inert, why do we not lay hands upon them, and pull all these fellows to pieces?' When he had said this, he first, seizing a strong brand from the altar, set the example of smiting. Then others also, seeing him, were carried away with like madness. Then ensued a tumult on either side, of the beating and the beaten. Much blood is shed; there is a confused flight, in the midst of which that enemy attacked James, and threw him headlong from the top of the steps; and

---

3. Cf. Gal. 2:11.
4. Cf. Matt. 16:18.
5. Gal. 2:11.
† From the *Recognitions of Clement*, Bk. I, chaps. 70–71, tr. by Thomas Smith, in *The Ante-Nicene Fathers*, Vol. VIII (New York, 1899; rp. Grand Rapids, 1951). The Pseudo-Clementine novelist has here used a different source, stemming from the Jewish-Christian community that fled from Jerusalem to Pella at the time of the Jewish revolt in 68 CE.
1. This "enemy" is Paul. The same phrase is applied to him in the Letter of Peter to James (above).

supposing him to be dead, he cared not to inflict further violence upon him.

But our friends lifted him up, for they were both more numerous and more powerful than the others; but, from their fear of God, they rather suffered themselves to be killed by an inferior force, than they would kill others. But when the evening came the priests shut up the temple, and we returned to the house of James, and spent the night there in prayer. Then before daylight we went down to Jericho, to the number of 5000 men. Then after three days one of the brethren came to us from Gamaliel, whom we mentioned before, bringing us secret tidings that that enemy had received a commission from Caiaphas, the chief priest, that he should arrest all who believed in Jesus, and should go to Damascus with his letters, and that there also, employing the help of the unbelievers, he should make havoc among the faithful; and that he was hastening to Damascus chiefly on this account, because he believed that Peter had fled thither. And about thirty days thereafter he stopped on his way while passing through Jericho going to Damascus. At that time we were absent, having gone out to the sepulchres of two brethren which were whitened of themselves every year, by which miracle the fury of many against us was restrained, because they saw that our brethren were had in remembrance before God. * * *

J. LOUIS MARTYN

[Paul's Opponents in Galatia] (1985)†

A Widely Accepted Portrait of Early Christian Missions

That the early church was passionately evangelistic is clear to every reader of the New Testament. Equally clear, or so it would seem, is the scholarly consensus that when Christian evangelists—notably Paul and his co-workers—took the step of reaching beyond the borders of the Jewish people, they did so without requiring observance of the Jewish Law. The work of these evangelists, in turn, is said to have sparked a reaction on the part of firmly observant Christian Jews, who, seeing the growth of the Gentile mission, sought to require observance of the Law by its converts. Struggles ensued, and the outcome, to put the matter briefly, was victory for the mission to the Gentiles, for the Law-free theology characteristic of that mission, and for the churches produced by it. In broad terms such is the standard portrait of early Christian missions. That portrait was codified at the beginning of the twentieth century by the great historian Adolf von Harnack (1851–1930). However varied the Gentile mission may have been in minor regards, in respect to the Jewish Law all *primary, evangelistic* efforts toward Gentiles were the same: *The* Gentile mission was the mission loosed from observance of the Law.

This portrait is not arbitrary. Harnack and his successors drew it on the

† From "A Law-Observant Mission to Gentiles," first published in *Scottish Journal of Theology* 38 (1985): 307–24; revised and reprinted in Martyn, *Theological Issues in the Letters of Paul* (Nashville: Abingdon, 1997), 7–24. Reprinted by permission. Martyn is Edmund Robinson Professor of Biblical Theology Emeritus, Union Theological Seminary in New York.

basis of primary evidence in the letters of Paul, traditions and editorial material in the Acts of the Apostles, and other traditions scattered throughout the New Testament, notably in the gospels. The evidence in Paul's letters is basic, because those letters were written during the sixth decade of the first century, in the midst of what is termed the Gentile mission. Most influential is a paragraph in Paul's letter to the churches of Galatia, in which, speaking of the leaders of the Jewish-Christian church in Jerusalem Paul says, ' . . . they saw clearly that I had been entrusted by God with the gospel as it is directed to those who are not circumcised, just as Peter had been entrusted with the gospel to those who are circumcised' (Gal. 2:7). From Paul's own mouth, therefore, we have a picture that presents two distinguishable missions proceeding along two parallel lines. The context of the quotation makes it clear that one of the lines is Law observant, while the other is not: Peter pursues *the* mission to the Jews (Law observant); Paul pursues *the* mission to the Gentiles (Law free). Thus, the standard portrait of *the* unified, Law-free mission to the Gentiles is drawn on the basis of primary evidence stemming from that mission itself.

Doubt

Is that portrait also fully accurate? Reading between the lines of Paul's letters, we may be assailed by doubt. Here and there, we find hints that at least some early Christian preachers directed their evangelistic message to Gentiles without surrendering observance of the Law. Could it be, in fact, that Galatians, the major witness to the existence of a single, Pauline Law-free mission to Gentiles, proves, upon inspection, to reflect a picture rather more complex than is customarily assumed?

We have only to consider the persons whose coming into Paul's Galatian churches compelled him to write the letter. Is their work entirely secondary to Paul's labors, in the sense that they have no Gentile mission of their own? An affirmative answer is reflected in the custom of referring to these persons as Paul's 'opponents,' for in that usage we imply that their identity is given in their opposition to Paul. True, Paul makes it clear that he views them as opponents, and there are indications that to a considerable extent they view him in the same manner. There is, however, one good reason for considering that nomenclature somewhat reductionistic. As Paul himself makes clear, he is certain that, in their basic identity, these persons are opponents of *God*, not merely of himself (Gal. 1:6–9). Could he be implying that they oppose God quite fundamentally by carrying out their own Law-observant mission to Gentiles? As we focus our attention on that question, we will avoid a premature answer by referring to these persons neutrally as 'the Teachers,' thus taking care not to identify them solely on the basis of their relationship with Paul.

Do the data available to us offer clues sufficient in number and clarity to enable us to draw a reliable picture of the Teachers? There are solid grounds for confidence, even though we have nothing from the hands of the Teachers themselves.

Data in Galatians Itself

Most important are several explicit and highly revealing references to the Teachers in Galatians itself: 1:6–9; 3:1–2, 5; 4:17; 5:7–12; 6:12–14. From these passages alone we can arrive at a sensible portrait. But there is also the helpful fact that, because Paul composes no sentence of the letter without thinking of the Teachers, his explicit references to them are accompanied by numerous allusions to them and to their work. As we will see below, carefully interpreted, these allusions fill out in important ways Paul's explicit references.

Pertinent Jewish and Christian-Jewish Traditions

Data in Galatians show the Teachers to have connections both with Diaspora Judaism and with Palestinian, Christian Judaism. Whatever their birthplace and locale of education, the Teachers are messianic Jews, at home among Gentiles, in the sense of being able not only to live among them, but also to make effective, apologetic contact with them. Several motifs that Paul connects with the Teachers—the view that Gentiles worship the elements of the cosmos, for example—find significant parallels in the apologetic literature of Diaspora Judaism. * * * We can enrich our portrait of the Teachers, therefore, by relating some aspects of their message, as reflected in Galatians, to passages in some of the literature of Diaspora Judaism, such as Wisdom, the writings of Philo and Josephus, *Aristobulus*, and *Joseph and Asenath*.

From Galatians itself, we can also see that the Teachers are in touch with—indeed understand themselves to represent—a powerful circle of Christian Jews in the Jerusalem church, a group utterly zealous for the observance of the Law. * * * Seeking to reconstruct the Teachers' message, then, we will find pertinent data in such Palestinian Jewish traditions as those preserved in Sirach and the Dead Sea Scrolls. There are even good reasons for thinking that certain traditions current in the Jerusalem church of the first century were in fact preserved and shaped in two second-century communities of Christian Jews, known to us from the *Epistle of Peter to James* and the *Ascents of James* [see above, pp. 229–31], not to mention Christian-Jewish traditions in the canonical epistle of James and in the gospel of Matthew. With caution, then, we can further enrich our portrait of the Teachers by noting certain passages in these Christian-Jewish sources.

In short, then, the picture that emerges from Paul's own references to the Teachers' work shows considerable internal coherence *and* a number of motifs for which there are significant parallels in traditions connected with Diaspora Jews, Palestinian Jews, and Christian Jews of various locales. We have reason, then, to think that a trustworthy picture can be drawn.

A Sketch of the Teachers and Their Message

1. Outsiders

Paul consistently differentiates the Teachers from the members of his Galatian congregations. He addresses the Galatians quite directly as 'you,' whereas he always refers to the Teachers by such terms as 'some persons,' 'they,' 'these people.' The Teachers are outsiders who have only recently come into the Galatian churches.

2. Jews

Paul almost certainly knows the Teachers' names, or at least some of the epithets by which they identify themselves (cf. 2 Cor. 11:22–23). We can conclude, then, that, instead of using their names and epithets, he employs such colorless expressions as 'some persons' in order to indicate disdain. We also note, however, that he does employ three descriptive terms in his direct references:

(a) those who are frightening you (1:7, cf. 5:10);
(b) those who are troubling your minds (5:12);
(c) those who are circumcised (6:13).

We shall return to the first two of these below. The third almost certainly tells us that the Teachers are Jews. We thus have a group of Jews who have come into the Galatian churches from somewhere else.

3. Christian-Jewish Evangelists

What, precisely, are they doing in these congregations? In his initial reference to the Teachers (1:6–9), Paul says that, under their influence, the Galatians are turning their allegiance to 'another *gospel*.' Then, having said that, he corrects himself by insisting that in reality there is no 'other gospel.' Does Paul take the route that requires self-correction only for the sake of rhetorical emphasis? Probably not. It would have been easier to avoid associating the Teachers with the term 'gospel,' by saying that, under their influence, the Galatians are turning *away from* the gospel, in that they are giving their allegiance to a *false teaching* (cf. 'the teaching of Balaam' in Rev. 2:14) or to an *impotent philosophy* (cf. 'philosophy . . . according to human tradition' in Col. 2:8). It seems highly probable that Paul takes the path requiring self-correction because he knows that the Teachers are in fact referring to their message as 'the gospel.' It follows that, no less than the Apostle himself, the Teachers are in the proper sense of the term evangelists, probably finding their basic identity not as persons who struggle against Paul, but rather as those who preach 'the good news of God's Messiah.' They are, then, Jews who have come into Galatia proclaiming what they call the gospel, God's good news. And what do they consider that good news to be?

4. The Law as the Good News

Although they themselves speak of the good news as the gospel of Christ, Paul repeatedly portrays them as those who find in the Law the absolute point of departure for their theology (e.g., 5:3–4). Whatever they may be saying about Christ (see below), the Law is itself both the foundation and the essence of their good news.

5. The Law as the Good News for Gentiles

For whom is the Law good news? In the Teachers' view, the Law is good news for the whole of the world, and specifically for Gentiles. For that reason the Teachers' evangelistic vision is, in its scope, no less universalistic than that of Paul (3:8). Just as we do well not to speak of the Teachers simply as Paul's opponents, so we shall not refer to them as 'Judaizers,' as has so frequently been done. For in modern parlance the term 'Judaizer' usually refers to someone who wishes to hem in Gentile Christians by requiring them to live according to 'narrow' Jewish practices. In their own time and place, the Teachers are embarked on an ecumenical mission. They are Christian Jews active in the Diaspora, who preach their nomistic gospel in Greek, quote the Law in Greek, and interpret the Law in ways understandable to persons of Greek culture. Moreover, the Teachers carry out their mission under the genuine conviction—shared, for example, by the author of Wisdom—that the Law of Moses is the cosmic Law, in the sense that it is the divine wisdom for *all* human beings. From the vocabulary employed by Paul in Gal. 4:24–25, we can surmise that, in issuing their evangelistic invitation, the Teachers spoke explicitly of 'the covenantal Law of Sinai.'

6. *The Motivation for a Law-Observant Mission to Gentiles*

Beyond indicating that the Teachers are greatly concerned to correct what they see as the Law-less evangelism of Paul, the letter shows that they are carrying out their Law-observant mission to Gentiles in order to keep on good terms with some persons of considerable power (Gal. 6:12). But their concentration on the expression 'descendants of Abraham' (see below) raises the additional possibility that they see their mission in thoroughly positive terms, perhaps understanding it to be the means by which God is filling out the infinite number of progeny he had promised to the patriarch. One notes the motivation for the Law-observant mission to Gentiles portrayed in the *Ascents of James*:

> It was necessary, then, that the Gentiles be called . . . so that the number [of descendants] which was shown to Abraham would be satisfied; thus the preaching of the kingdom of God has been sent into all the world.

7. *The Law as the Source of the Spirit*

God's readiness to invite Gentiles into his own people is marked by the fact that God bestows his Spirit even on communities of Gentiles, if their communal life is ordered by correct exegesis of scripture and thus by true observance of his Law. In Gal. 3:1–5 there are several hints that Paul is contrasting the type of worship service the Galatians first knew under his direction with the type of worship service they are now experiencing at the hands of the Teachers. Both services have about them certain aspects of the theater. In his preaching, Paul clearly portrayed before the Galatians' eyes the dramatic picture of Christ, as he suffered crucifixion (3:1). Presented with this theater, the Galatians found that the message of the cross elicited their faith, and that the Spirit fell upon them.

Now a new acting company has arrived on the scene, presenting a novel and highly effective drama. In the services of worship conducted by the Teachers, the Galatians see extraordinarily masterful exegetes who quote and interpret the Scriptures with the firm conviction that out of true exegesis will flow mighty manifestations of the Spirit (Gal. 3:5). And, indeed, developments in Galatia seem to confirm this conviction. In their dramatic services, the Teachers somehow manage to demonstrate to the Galatians the impressive connection between their interpretation of the Law and the miraculous dispensation of the Spirit. It follows that God is to be known as the one who supplies the Spirit to those who are both true exegetes of his Law and faithful observers of it.

8. *The Threat of Exclusion*

This laying down of a strict condition for the dependable granting of the Spirit is a token for the conditional nature of the whole of the Teachers' good news. We return, then, to the fact that Paul twice characterizes the

Teachers as persons who frighten the Galatians (1:7; 5:10). How are we to understand these two references? Help comes from Paul's comment in Gal. 4:17, where, employing the image of a gate, he says that the Teachers threaten to shut the Galatians out of salvation. Encountering Gentiles they consider to have been badly misled by Paul, the Teachers feel they must issue a sharp warning: 'Only if you pass through the gate of repentance into the genuine observance of God's Law, will you be included in God's people Israel, thus being saved on the day of judgment.'

9. The Necessity of Circumcision as the Commencement of Law Observance
How is a Gentile to pass through the gate to salvation? One of the major foci of the Teachers' preaching is the subject of circumcision (e.g., Gal. 6: 12). It is a subject that properly belongs to proselytizing, for, in most cases, a Gentile passes into the people of the Law by belonging to a family, the males of which submit to circumcision. Circumcision is the commandment par excellence, the commandment which signifies full participation in the people of God. The Teachers, then, are circumcised, Christian Jews who preach circumcision to Gentiles as the act appropriate to the universal good news of God's Law, the observance of which is the condition for God's pouring out his Holy Spirit. They also preach the necessity of the observance of holy times (Gal. 4:10) and the keeping of dietary regulations (2: 11–14).

10. The Christ of the Law
We may further summarize the motifs we have mentioned thus far by asking what the Teachers say about Christ, the Messiah. However difficult it may be to answer this question with the detail we would desire, and however uncertain we remain as to how the Teachers are successfully communicating their christology to the Galatian Gentiles, five points can be stated with some degree of confidence. (*a*) The Teachers view Christ much as do the members of the strictly observant circumcision party in the Jerusalem church, perhaps seeing him as the savior who brought to completion the ministry of Moses. (*b*) In any case, they view God's Christ in the light of God's Law, rather than the Law in the light of Christ. This means that, in their christology, Christ is secondary to the Law. (*c*) Paul is emphatic, when he says that the Teachers avoid taking their theological bearings from the cross (e.g., Gal. 6:12). They must be including references to Christ's death, however, presumably understanding it to have been a sacrifice for sins, perhaps emphatically for the sins of Gentiles. In short, the Teachers must see Christ's death as a redemptive sacrifice enacted in harmony with God's Law * * *. (*d*) We can be sure, above all, that they consistently avoid every suggestion that God's Law and God's Christ could be even partially in conflict with one another. (*e*) In their own terms, they are presumably certain that Christ came in order to fulfill the Law and the prophets (cf. Matt. 5:17–18), perhaps even to complete Moses' ministry by bringing the Law to the Gentiles. For them, the Messiah is the Messiah of the Law, deriving his identity from the fact that he confirms—and perhaps normatively interprets—the Law. If Christ is explicitly involved in the Teachers' commission to preach to the Gentiles, that must be so because he has deepened their passion to take to the nations God's gift of gifts, the Spirit-dispensing Law that will guide them in their daily life.

These ten points would seem to encapsulate most of what Paul reveals about the Teachers and their gospel in his direct references. As noted earlier, however, there are other data quite revealing of the Teachers' gospel, allusions which, carefully interpreted, fill out in important ways the picture we receive of these evangelists, and especially of their gospel.

11. The Descendants of Abraham; the Blessing of Abraham
The character of Paul's argument in Gal. 3:6–29 shows that he refers to 'the descendants of Abraham' because the Teachers are already doing that in their own way. Specifically, the Teachers are designating themselves as Abraham's descendants, and they are telling the Galatians that they can claim that identity for themselves if they submit to circumcision. Indeed, the Teachers seem also to be speaking at some length about 'the blessing of Abraham,' indicating that when God blessed the patriarch, he did so in such a way as eventually to bless those Gentiles who, by circumcision and Law observance, become 'Abraham's true descendants.' We thus find solid confirmation of the suggestion of Holtzmann that 'descendants of Abraham' is one of the Teachers' favorite catchwords.

12. 'Jerusalem Is Our Mother'
[There is] good reason to think that, in addition to identifying themselves and their Law-observant Gentile converts as 'descendants of Abraham,' the Teachers speak of Jerusalem as their 'mother,' referring thereby to the Jerusalem church. We cannot say with certainty that the Teachers have come to Galatia from Jerusalem, but there are grounds for thinking that they claim to be the true representatives of the Jerusalem church, and that, in making that claim, they are confident of the support of a powerful group in that church.

13. Israel
The way in which Paul employs the word 'Israel' in his final blessing (Gal. 6:16) suggests that, in inviting the Galatians to claim Abraham as their father and the Jerusalem church as their mother, the Teachers are promising the Galatians that they will thereby enter the company of God's people Israel. It is even conceivable that the Teachers are emphasizing the antique superiority of Israel by noting—at least in effect—that Plato and Pythagoras imitated the Law of Moses.

14. Victory over the Impulsive Desire of the Flesh
Finally, horrified at the continuation of various Gentile patterns of life among the Galatian churches (cf. 5:20–21a), the Teachers are taking up the matter of the Galatians' daily behavior. Here, in addition to attacking Paul for leaving the Galatians without potent ethical guidance—an unfaithful student of the Jerusalem apostles, Paul does not teach his Gentile converts what the Law means for the church's daily life—they voice a crucial promise: 'If you Galatians will become observant of the Law, we can promise you that you will not fall prey to the Impulsive Desire of the Flesh (cf. Gal. 5:16; 4 Macc. 1). In this regard, as in others, the Teachers are likely to have portrayed Abraham as the model to be emulated. For, by keeping God's commandments, the patriarch was said to have avoided walking in the path of the Impulsive Desire of the Flesh.

* * *

MARTIN HENGEL

The Letter of James as Anti-Pauline Polemic (1987)†

The Letter of James poses quandaries that until now have still not been satisfactorily solved. On this point, substantially little has changed for the reader in some 150 years of critical exegetical history. To a certain extent, the letter seems to constitute a self-contradiction.

First, it is the only New Testament letter in the form of a writing *to all Christians* (outside of the Holy Land). This is the only interpretation of the addressees, "the twelve tribes in the Dispersion," that makes sense to me. This fact makes it an "encyclical" to all Christians who are living dispersed among the "nations" and who are predominantly "Gentile Christians." It is the first, indeed, the only early Christian letter that opens with the outrageous claim that it is intended to be heard by all.

On the other hand, *why* this "letter" was written in such a loose form and with such a general "parenetic" content remains unclear. Its content (whose character, in part, strikes one as almost trivial) appears—at least outwardly—quite unspecific. In the commentaries, therefore, the details regarding the letter's occasion are accordingly vague.

* * *

German research is dominated even today by Martin Dibelius's grand commentary, now sixty-five years old. Not only did Dibelius assume a basically indeterminable date of composition between 80 and 130, which is in my opinion too late (the only somewhat reliable point of reference is the Letter of Jude, which presupposes James in its opening address), but he was also of the opinion that a compiler of modest gifts, without theological expertise, arranged an anthology of individual parenetic sayings interspersed with some larger collections of sayings; or, more likely, that he assembled it from traditional material. For "the entire work lacks rational coherence." Consequently, according to the logic of Dibelius's entire argument, the question "cui bono" [For whose benefit is it?] could no longer be answered. Even the new key term "parenesis" did not solve the riddle of this letter because, for Dibelius, the rationale for making the selection from this vast traditional material can in no way be satisfactorily explained.

* * *

A. von Harnack—quite contrary to Dibelius—had clearly perceived the "paradoxical" character of the text: "Even the means of expression, the language and the wording of the individual passages, are paradoxical. Some parts seem like a true reproduction of the sayings of Jesus and probably are . . . , other parts are also conceived of hebraically but in the spirit of the ancient prophets . . . , still other parts can be compared in power, correctness, and elegance in the means of expression to good products of

---

† Translated from Hengel's "Der Jakobusbrief als antipaulinische Polemik," in *Tradition and Interpretation in the New Testament*, ed. by G. F. Hawthorne and Otto Betz (Grand Rapids: Eerdmans and Tübingen: Mohr-Siebeck, 1987), 248–78. Copyright © 1987 by Wm. B. Eerdmans Publishing Company. Reprinted by permission of the publisher. All rights reserved. We have retained Hengel's original italics. Hengel is Professor Emeritus of New Testament and Early Judaism at Tübingen.

Greek rhetoric. . . . Other parts are the product of a theological polemicist. Therefore there is no mistaking the fact—and this is the most paradoxical of the paradoxical—that a certain unity of moral conviction as well as of language exists, which, in spite of the lack of connection, lends an internal unity to the whole, similar to certain Old Testament prophetic books. We lack the means, however, to explain these observations *with certainty*." These sentences—written approximately twenty-four years before Dibelius—show that the attempt at interpretation in the latter's commentary is too narrow. He sees only one side and represses the other.

*   *   *

The dilemma of Dibelius's commendable—and for its time revolutionary—commentary consists not least in the fact that the text, with the help of the key word "parenesis," becomes less meaningful, indeed, basically a superfluous "conglomeration," and that the motivations behind its inception largely disappear in the dark. The designations "collection" and "parenesis" are not at all sufficient to explain the significance of its distinctive, quite artistic form.

*   *   *

[*Arguments that the letter was a late, pseudonymous composition are no longer convincing.*]

But even assuming the letter's authenticity, the question remains: Why does James write—presumably to Jewish Christians—such a letter, with so little specificity and such general content, using seemingly disconnected individual exhortations which, in part, often sound quite simple? This is especially so if one does not wish to recognize in 2:14–26 any anti-Pauline polemic since the letter was written before the "Apostolic Council." Here, too, the letter becomes largely incomprehensible. As with the solution proposed by Dibelius, this explanation offers no meaningful reason for the inception of the letter.

This quandary remains even if one discovers in the writing a stronger theological connection or sees in it an original "sermon" of James. Before which community—and with such skill—was such a "speech" delivered, and why did it seem so important to the author that he conveyed it as an "encyclical" to all Christians in the "Diaspora"? If a student edited the letter after James' martyrdom in 62, one must ask: Didn't this student have anything more significant to convey from the mouth of his master, the [Lord's] brother, than this peculiar "mélange"? Why doesn't he go into his martyr's death rather than leave this task to Josephus and the incredible later legend of a Hegesippus? Is one supposed to see in 5:6 a reference to his martyrdom and in 5:16b an allusion to James the "Just" as a charismatic person of prayer?

If James himself, however, conceives the letter directly as a circular writing, the occasion becomes even more opaque. One could perhaps even say: the writer supports in a general way a Christianity of deeds as opposed to a deedless one of bogus faith, one of poverty as opposed to one of an *eo ipso* [by that very fact] wanton wealth. But why does he utilize precisely here such far-fetched examples as the plans of the traveling big businessman (4:13–16), the rhetorically ornate perils of the unbridled tongue, the exploitatively rich big landowner, and, finally, even the exhortation regarding the anointing of the sick and the prayer of the elders, which promises healing if someone confesses his sins? For a call to action, doesn't this sound in part rather far-fetched? Was this the parenesis that the "twelve tribes" in the Diaspora needed—be they Jewish or Gentile Christians?

Solving the Quandary

The following will attempt to solve this quandary through a *hypothesis*. Since our discipline has always been, because of the relatively narrow source-basis, a "science of conjecture"—in any case more than is readily admitted—and has become in the last decades even more so, a *conjecture*—in my view not completely unfounded—ought to be developed. My hypothesis (and it cannot be more than a matter of a hypothetical attempt at a solution) goes in the following direction:

The letter could perhaps *in fact* stem from James the Just, Jesus' brother (or from a secretary under his commission) and have been written as a circular to the communities lying outside of Jewish Palestine, which were predominantly Gentile, some time after the arrest of Paul or his transfer to Rome as a defendant between 58 and 62.

As regards content, * * * in its essential passages the letter contains *anti-Pauline polemic*, naturally—as is often the case with ancient polemic—in an *indirect form* and without mentioning the name of the opponent. Paul's personal behavior as well as his theological view is criticized, and indeed—that is what is remarkable about the letter—in a "parenetic," seemingly generally applicable manner. This makes the letter still readable, comprehensible, and—within certain limits—"edifying" for the communities that were not affected by or informed of the disagreement with Paul. Those who knew Paul, however, must very well have known against whom this letter was directed in the first place and why it was written.

Following from this hypothesis, I am almost inclined to designate the letter a masterpiece of early Christian polemic. The sharpness in the letter's polemic has always struck exegetes, but its actual intention was not understood because of its supposed "generality" (and the vagueness that resulted from it). One could compare the anti-Pauline polemic with Galatians and 2 Corinthians 10–13, where Paul similarly does not mention his opponents by name. James, however, in contrast to the apostle to the Gentiles, does not fight openly. Instead, he consciously does so indirectly, by means of generally formulated admonitions, and he can only be recognized as a critic of Paul by those affected by the dispute. Within the New Testament canon Paul's polemic in Galatians against the Judaizers and in 2 Corinthians against the Palestinian envoys from Peter's mission (?) opposes an outwardly concealed example of anti–Pauline polemic. Irenaeus (*adv. haer.* 1.26.2), the traditions standing behind the pseudo-Clementines, and the reports in Epiphanius attest to the fact that the Ebionites—forced out of the church in the second century—inveighed against Paul in a most severe manner.[1] Compared with that, there appears here an artful, more subtle polemic, which, in a manner different from

---

1. For the anti-Pauline traditions preserved in the *Pseudo-Clementine Homilies and Recognitions* and in Epiphanius's reports about the Ebionites and Cerinthians, see the excerpts given above on pp. 229–35 [Editors' note].

the later massive slanders, at least partly attempts to argue theologically.

1. Research widely acknowledges the anti-Pauline tendency of 2:14–23. It should no longer be disputed, for the conflict or contrast between "faith and works" with a view to salvation is a basic Pauline problem, which *prior to* Paul cannot be attested anywhere, neither in Judaism nor with Jesus and in earliest Christianity. Over against the Pauline thesis of the justification of the godless by faith without works of the law, James sets forth the postulate of the necessity of the performance of works in addition to faith. Indeed, he gives precedence to this necessity in the attainment of salvation.

This outlook becomes apparent at the latest in 1:22, in fact, basically already in 1:2f., where the testing of faith during trials leads to the ἔργον τέλειον ["perfect work"]. In contrast to the Pauline sequence: word (or preaching/gospel)—faith—salvation (cf. Rom. 10:9ff., 17; 1:16f; Gal. 3: 1ff.), fundamental for James is the sequence: word (royal law of liberty or the love commandment)—act of love—justification at the judgment. We find in Paul in Romans 2:5–12 a nexus that in part is linguistically quite similarly formulated. It is of course found within the universal *indictment* of Romans 1:18–3:20, which is preparatory to the saving revelation of the righteousness of God in the atoning death of Jesus. What Paul rejects as a particular human possibility appears—in an almost naive way—in James as a prerequisite for salvation. The pious person can of his own accord persistently (1:25 καὶ παραμείνας ["and continuing"]) fulfill the "perfect law of liberty" (1:25), "the royal law" of Leviticus 19:18 (2:8). His own works of mercy save him at the judgment (2:13). This means, however, that already on the basis of the entire preceding complex of arguments (1: 18–2:13), the following discussion in 2:14–26 about the deficiency of a "mere faith without works" possesses an internal consistency, in fact a necessity, and it represents the polemical climax of the confrontation. James 2:24 is formulated in a directly anti-Pauline way: "You see that on the basis of works a person is justified *and not by faith alone.*" James' concept of faith is essentially that of Judaism, where faith could be understood as a work or virtue; on this score, it is close to that of Hebrews. It thus does not fit in with the "early Catholicism" of the Apostolic Fathers; rather it is still attached to its Jewish roots. In this sense, A. Lindemann's assertion is valid: "James' understanding of πίστις [faith] is already as such anti-Pauline."

But 2:14–26 is not by far the only text in James that criticizes Pauline sayings and behavior. There are, in my estimation, still considerably more such places.

Already in the polemic beginning with 1:13ff., which has older wisdom parallels (Sir. 15:11–20), an anti-Pauline tone could possibly be detected. James refutes any thought that God tempts man, traces back all temptation to man's own sinful desire, and in that connection professes that only good, perfect gifts come from God, and that there is with him "no variation or shadow due to change" (1:17). Paul, on the other hand, was able to say that God had hardened Pharaoh's heart (Rom. 9:17f.), that he "creates vessels of wrath, prepared for destruction," indeed that he gave Israel "a spirit of stupor" (Rom. 11:8 citing Isa. 29:10; cf. Deut. 29:3). That God enables believers "to will and to work" (Phil. 2:13) is completely foreign to James. For him, in keeping with the Jewish—Old Testament tradition, the following is true: ἐγγίσατε τῷ θεῷ καὶ ἐγγιεῖ ὑμῖν ["Come near to God and he will come near to you"] (4:8).

Of course, one can hardly assume with James an in-depth study of Paul's letters; he argues on the basis of an oral knowledge of Pauline theology, which to him is altogether strange and suspect. There is thus a *barrier to understanding* between the two—obviously extremely different—great figures of primitive Christianity. * * *

When in James, however, the center of Pauline theology is attacked in such a direct way, one might assume in this letter *even further attempts at a criticism of Paul*. This criticism, occurring in a writing that argues in a predominantly parenetic-practical and "undogmatic" way, could naturally also be directed *against the personal behavior* of the apostle, and against the dangers arising from it, given that the leading missionary to the Gentiles was certainly wide open to attack as a passionate, multi-faceted personality. * * *

2. In the earliest Christianity of the first century, *big businessmen*, with commercial interests spanning cities and provinces and thus with extensive and lengthy business trips, hardly play a role. The wealthy shipowner, Marcion of Sinope, points to a new epoch in the church's history, which begins with the Antonines. According to a well-known text by Cicero, *De officiis* 1,151, "trade . . . , if it is large and extensive, if it procures many goods from everywhere and distributes to many without deception," is prestigious, whereas small trade appears despicable. These small tradesmen and merchants, who offered their often self-produced wares for sale in the shops, may have been more common in the urban Christian communities of the earliest period, whereas we hardly hear anything about traveling Christian entrepreneurs. The parenetic sense of the argument of James 4:13–16, referring to "Christian (big) businessmen" and their profitable business trips to distant cities, with longer stays, appears against this backdrop to be rather doubtful, for reference is made here to a phenomenon that was hardly yet of any *essential* significance in the communities of the later first century. The letter, however, addresses itself to all Christians and not to a few individual members having close links to the gentile upper class. What is the point of such a polemic in an "ecumenical circular letter"? There were certainly better examples to warn against the danger of "worldliness" (1:27; 4:4). We do find, however, *a comprehensive, long-term, planned "global" travel strategy encompassing metropolises and provinces, with month-long, even year-long stays in several large cities, with the goal of "gaining" Gentiles and Jews. We find it, first and at the same time uniquely in Paul* (and his missionary helpers like Prisca and Aquila, who obviously had bound together missionary work and economic endeavors in singular fashion). In this strategy which encompasses whole provinces, Paul knows himself to be superior to all missionary competitors. In the later period, however, we hear nothing more of comparable plans and strategies. Already for Luke, Paul is therefore the "world missionary," traveling from city to city, from province to province. Does the so peculiar "entrepreneurial" plan of James 4:13: σήμερον ἢ αὔριον πορευσόμεθα εἰς τήνδε τὴν πόλιν καὶ ποιήσομεν ἐκεῖ ἐνιαυτὸν καὶ ἐμπορευσόμεθα καὶ κερδήσομεν ["Today or tomorrow we will go to this or that city, spend a year there, carry on business and make money"], which fits no scheme of Christian parenesis, perhaps point in this direction? The entire plan sounds like a

missionary metaphor. In Acts' description of the Pauline mission, and also in Paul himself, we find numerous parallels to analogous travel plans with temporal details of stay. We encounter the verb κερδαίνειν ["to gain"] four times in 1 Corinthians 9:19–22 *in the sense of the missionary "gaining" of people*. Paul's entire existence is oriented toward that. One could further refer to 1 Peter 3:1, the gaining of the unbelieving spouse, and Matthew 18:15, the (re)gaining of the errant brother. On this point C. Spicq notes: "κερδαίνειν has become a religious, indeed, an apostolic and missionary term." Even the verb ἐμπορεύεσθαι ["to carry on business," "to buy or sell"] can acquire in a polemical context a religious-missionary connotation. 2 Peter 2:3 inveighs against the false teachers: "And in their greed they will buy (ἐμπορεύσονται) you with skillful words." Regarding this point, K. H. Schelkle writes, "Paul, too, must have heard this reproach, and he defends himself fiercely against it," and he refers to 1 Thessalonians 2:5; 2 Corinthians 7:2 and 8:20. The Didache later calls the Christian traveler, who sponges off others and is unwilling to work, a χριστέμπορος ["Christ-monger"] and adds that one ought to be on one's guard against such travelers. Paul's own use demonstrates just how likely was the use of the polemical metaphor of "doing business" in missionary work and in the travel plans associated with it: "Unlike the many, we do not peddle a trade with the word of God. . . ." The reproach of "καπηλεύειν [peddling] with spiritual goods" (Lietzmann on 2 Cor. 2:17) was, as the parallels in Wettstein and later commentators and now especially the thorough investigation by S. J. Hafemann demonstrate, extremely current. While καπηλεύειν here suggests Cicero's "dirty" small trade, the verb ἐμπορεύεσθαι indicates in the context of James 4:13 a missionary "profiteering" in grand style, as one could very well accuse Paul and his assistants of doing.

In other words: The travel plans, encompassing great geographical and temporal space, which Paul himself outlines in his letters, not least in connection with his combined Jerusalem—Rome—Spain project (cf. Rom. 15:14ff.; 2 Cor. 10:13ff.), come suspiciously close to the intentions that James imputes to his plan-forging "businessmen" traveling to (large) cities. In Paul's case, one must speak of an extensive "missionary strategy," which was prepared over a lengthy period with a view to the individual loci of activity, and which must also have been bound up with *economic* considerations. In this way his friends Prisca and Aquila, who were probably themselves successful businesspeople with various domiciles, pave the way for his activity in Ephesus and later also in Rome. That is, Paul was dependent in his strategy upon the assistance of well-to-do friends, among other things perhaps in order to raise money for the relatively high rent of the "School of Tyrannus" in Ephesus (Acts 19:9), for passages by ship with several participants, or for lodging in Rome (Acts 28:30). * * * The verb προπέμπειν several times used by Paul had, according to W. Bauer, not only the meaning "to accompany," but more concretely "*to help on one's journey* with food, money, by arranging for companions, means of travel, etc., *to send on one's way, to transport further*." Without this kind of assistance, Paul's missionary work would have been impossible—even if he himself *demanded* no support from the communities that had just been founded. If it was rendered without being asked for, he gladly accepted it, as Philippians shows.

There is hardly any doubt that Paul's very successful missionary planning and work at the same time strengthened his apostolic sense of mission and that his reference to the fact that he had worked more successfully than all the other apostles, that is, that as a missionary he was superior to all of these, could also be misinterpreted and condemned as "self-glorification." The references to his apostolic deeds and intentions can be found in fact in almost all the letters. 2 Corinthians 10:8, 13–15 shows that Paul, in reference to his missionary success and travel plans, was directly accused of such καυχᾶσθαι [boasting]. The harsh censure of James 4:16 (νῦν δὲ καυχᾶσθε ἐν ταῖς ἀλαζονείαις ὑμῶν· πᾶσα καύχησις τοιαύτη πονηρά ἐστιν ["As it is, you boast in your arrogant schemes. All such boasting is evil."]) is therefore, in my opinion, directed not so much against early Christian big businessmen traveling from city to city—there were hardly any of these—as against missionaries like Paul who planned in an expansive way and boasted of their success. He was the first one to introduce this missionary style, and it also basically ends with him.

*   *   *

The *conditio Jacobaea* (ἐὰν ὁ κύριος θελήσῃ καὶ ζήσομεν καὶ ποιήσομεν τοῦτο ἢ ἐκεῖνο, "if the Lord wills, we will live and do this or that") fits superbly into the context of missionary planning and its imponderables. Paul himself could use the introduction "if the Lord wills." Obviously the opponents of Paul had accused him of obstinacy in his travel planning, and also of fear and other human motives. He, on the other hand, refers to the will of God. Also in Luke this conflict becomes apparent. * * * Should Luke have defended the apostle with his intensifying *vaticinia* [prophecies], while the obvious failure of Paul's worldwide plans and his imprisonment beginning in Jerusalem was understood in many Jewish-Christian circles as a punishment for his unseemly boasting? Although Luke, as Acts 19:21 shows, very well knew the apostle's additional plan of traveling to Rome, he deems it important to emphasize again and again that Paul traveled to Jerusalem in the firm, ever more strongly corroborated certainty of his arrest. Luke also takes the greatest trouble to portray Paul's way to Rome and the open missionary proclamation of the prisoner there as *God's will*. One could also see it completely differently: Doesn't that judgment in James 4:14 (ἀτμὶς γάρ ἐστε ἡ πρὸς ὀλίγον φαινομένη, ἔπειτα καὶ ἀφανιζομένη ["You are a mist that appears for a little while and then vanishes"]) apply to Paul, who had been taken to Rome as a prisoner and had to await there the emperor's final judgment, and whose haughty missionary plans extending to Spain were shattered? Doesn't it apply to him, the greatest Christian "plan-smith"? Isn't the question posed in regard to him, the one threatened with the verdict of death, not just the ζήσομεν ["we will live"] but also the ποιήσομεν ["we will do"]? Luke intends to demonstrate exactly the opposite through his διδάσκων . . . μετὰ πάσης παρρησίας ἀκωλύτως [Acts 28:31, "taught . . . with all boldness and without hindrance"].

James 4:13–16 becomes, in my opinion, most understandable in its enigmatic quality as a unique parenetic document in early Christian literature through the fact that it refers to the sudden shattering of the apostle's missionary plans through his arrest and his subsequent long period of imprisonment with the threatening death penalty. The letter would then have originated in the final days of both rivals, during Paul's imprisonment

in Caesarea or perhaps more likely in Rome (i.e., between 58 and 62).
* * * Paul and James possibly were martyred in the same year 62 CE, each
in his own way as a "breaker of the law." The Letter of James would then
have above all the purpose of calling the attention of the predominantly
Gentile Christian missionary communities of the Greek-speaking Diaspora, which were unsettled by the criminal trial against their hero and
founder, to the perils of a—certainly misunderstood—Pauline theology,
which according to the opinion of Paul's opponents could lead to a libertinistic lawlessness, to a faith without works. At the same time it was
intended to expose certain questionable tendencies in the behavior of the
venerated teacher.

3. The *"various trials"* mentioned at the beginning of the letter (1:2ff.)
represent only a means of testing for genuine faith (through works). Abraham, who was justified by works (2:21ff.)—a view completely different
from Paul's—represents the first and greatest model of this. The opening
discussion (1:2ff.) made perfect sense in this light: The communities
affected, in fact, shaken by the fate of their founder, ought to rejoice in
the test justly imposed by God and, following the (not undeserved) arrest
of their teacher, acquire that steadfastness that alone leads to the "perfect
work" demanded by God (1:2ff.).

The *"wisdom"* required for this, which in James appears in the place of
the Pauline πνεῦμα [Spirit], will of course be achieved through prayer (1:
5ff.). The prerequisite for this is a praying faith that is still wholly oriented
toward the old Jesus-tradition, a faith that is free from all doubts and
absolutely certain. This peaceful, friendly, obedient, and loving wisdom
from above has nothing in common with that demonic, earthly wisdom
from below (3:13–18), which awakens evil desires (4:1f.) and through envy
or jealousy and selfishness (3:14ff.), causes only *disorder* (ἀκαταστασία)
and disputes (πόλεμοι καὶ μάχαι) (4:1f.), as we know all too well from the
Pauline communities through the apostle's letters. The person who is illuminated and enlightened (3:13f.) by divine wisdom demonstrates the possession of this gift, which is only obtained through prayer from an
undivided heart (1:17), on the basis of a peaceful change and the fruit of
righteousness resulting from it (3:18). Did the letter's author miss precisely
this gift in the so contentious apostle to the Gentiles and his partisans, so
that the condition of his communities reflects upon the founder?

4. A highly rhetorical warning about the *endangering of the teacher
through the misuse and the power of the tongue* (3:1–12) follows immediately upon the clearly anti-Pauline remarks about faith and works, even
before coming to terms with the quarrelsome and dogmatic wise man in
3:13ff. and to a certain extent as a lead-in to the latter. First there is a
warning against the ambition of becoming a teacher (3:1a). Was Paul, who
in his own judgment was not endangered by such ambition, forced into
the office of apostolic teacher? In fact, hadn't he forced himself, in the
judgment of his opponents, into this office? Did his apostleship—in spite
of Galatians 2:9—not remain contested? At the beginning (3:1) as well as
at the end (3:12)—one could almost speak of an *inclusio*—there is the
warning about God's judgment in the last days. The teacher who cannot
hold his tongue in check and can cause the greatest damage with it (3:
5ff.) as well as the one who abuses and disgraces or even curses his brothers, must answer before God (3:1b and 4:ff.; cf. 3:9). One could refer here

to the not negligible *boundlessness of Pauline polemic*, in which the apostle, because of his passion, can get carried away—to be sure for the sake of "the truth of the gospel" (Gal. 2:5,14)—into the harshest invectives against his adversaries. In his verbal confrontations Paul could certainly become even harsher than in his letters, where he is silent regarding the names of his opponents. In this connection, one would have to ask the question, how the τίνες ἀπὸ Ἰακώβου [Gal. 2:12, "certain people from James"] whose appearance in Antioch caused the incident between Peter, Barnabas and the Jewish Christians on the one hand and Paul on the other, likely portrayed the behavior of the apostle to the Gentiles upon their return to Jerusalem. Given Paul's emotionalism, the κατὰ πρόσωπον αὐτῷ ἀντέστην, ὅτι κατεγνωσμένος ἦν ["I opposed him to his face, because he stood condemned"], certainly necessary for the sake of "the truth of the gospel" (2:14), would have been bound up with injurious attacks on their persons, which could hardly be justified in view of the first antithesis in Matthew 5:21f. Indeed, the Matthean Jesus does not say that in the struggle for the truth of the faith his teaching no longer applies. We do not know how the representatives of the opposition received invectives such as Galatians 5:12, which bordered on the obscene. Doesn't an answer like that in James 1:20—under the alienating echoes of Pauline language—suggest itself: ὀργὴ γὰρ ἀνδρὸς δικαιοσύνην θεοῦ οὐκ ἐργάζεται ["because our anger does not produce the righteousness that God desires"]? The annoyances were correspondingly enduring, and they continue to show their painful effect in the great letters of the apostle, above all in 1 and 2 Corinthians. James, Peter, and the Antiochenes accepted the compromise of the Apostolic Decree, which solved the rift, obviously without, indeed, perhaps against Paul, who never recognized it as far as we know. History did not give the other side the chance to preserve its image of Paul. The few late and completely distorted traces preserved for us in the pseudo-Clementines and in Epiphanius' brief reference to the Ebionite polemical work Ἀναβαθμοὶ Ἰακώβου [*Ascents of James*][2] can perhaps still be supplemented by the much older and, in our opinion, original evidence in the Letter of James.

In addition to the warning about transgressions with the tongue, the *prohibition against swearing* enters in 5:12, once again in connection with the warning about the judgment. Its form is more original than the closely related version of Matthew 5:34–37. We find in no early Christian work of the first and second centuries so many oath-like asseverations (and curses) as in the letters of Paul. For example, he defends himself against attacks due to unkept plans for travel and visits by calling upon God as witness (Rom. 1:9; 2 Cor. 1:23). Such things obviously flowed rather easily from the apostle's pen. The drastic scene in Acts 23:3 gives the requisite proof of this. Perhaps Luke did in fact know the apostle better than is generally assumed. As a result, research has from time to time postulated that Paul would not have known the Sermon on the Mount's prohibition against swearing. Here, too, the apostle's ardor emerges again, which he himself describes in 2 Corinthians 11:29 with the concise sentence: τίς

---

2. On the *Ascents of James* as paraphrased by Epiphanius, see above, pp. 229f [Editors' note].

σκανδαλίζεται καὶ οὐκ ἐγὼ πυροῦμαι; ["Who is led into sin, and I do not inwardly burn?"]

5. It is understandable that the orphaned Gentile Christian communities—in the uncertain and harried circumstances after Paul's arrest—could well use the concluding *admonition to be patient in the hope of the imminent parousia of the Lord* (5:7ff.). In this connection, the warning about grumbling against one another and the reference to "the endurance of Job" were appropriate. In view of the Judge who is near, who "is standing at the door" (5:9), the constant quarrels and accusations have lost all relevance. With this the letter could actually have concluded. In addition, however, to the completely unexpected reference to the prohibition against swearing—which, however, is understandable with a view towards Paul—there follows a further peculiarity: What is the meaning of this strange, likewise completely unmotivated reference toward the end to the proper *behavior of the sick*? The latter is supposed to call the elders of the community—the office of bishop is obviously still unknown—to pray over him and anoint him with oil in the name of the Lord so that he may become healthy (5:13–16). For prayer that proceeds from genuine faith and is unaffected by doubt (1:6f.; 4:2)—here too it is once more a matter of an *inclusio*—and especially the "prayer of the righteous" have great effect. Of course, the sinner must in this connection confess his sins. Illness, authoritative prayer, anointing with oil, confession of sins, and healing are directly connected; 15b thereby presupposes the confession of sins, even if it is first mentioned in the generalizing summary of v. 16. * * * But perhaps it should also be remembered—after noting that scarcely anything of a severe or incurable illness among Christians is reported to us from early Christianity—that we have from Paul alone his very personal testimony that he suffered from a dreadful illness not better known to us, "the thorn (or splinter) in the flesh," "the messenger of Satan who beats me with his fists," which is imposed by the Lord himself "so that I would not vaunt myself" (!). This suffering—surely oppressive—was not taken from him despite three prayers. He must bear with it further according to the will of the Lord. The communities knew about this illness. Must it not have been interpreted—above all by Jewish Christian opponents—in the traditional Jewish sense as a punishment from God? Is this reference at the end of the Letter of James to the sick who should call the "elders of the church" so that they may heal him with prayer and the anointing of oil after he has confessed his sins—as may be assumed on the basis of the following sentence—just pure coincidence? * * * Or are the Gentile Christian communities here told how even a "hopelessly ill person" (such as Paul), if he only wanted, could have been freed from his demonic illness, had he entrusted himself to prayer together with exorcistic anointing by the elders (or even the prayer of the "Just" [James]: 5:16?) and confessed his sins?

* * *

6. The letter's conclusion is *conciliatory*. He who has turned away from the truth should be won back. Whoever does this saves a soul from death and "will cover a multitude of sins." According to the early Christian view, it was Christ who takes away human sins (John 1:29; 1 John 2:2f.; 1 Cor.

15:3, etc.). The Letter of James has nothing to say about this. Significantly, Christ is mentioned only twice: in the opening address and in 2:1. There the "belief in our Lord Jesus Christ, (the Lord) of glory" refers to the expectation of the coming Lord and Judge in his heavenly glory (2:1). For James it is the good deed that has saving effect and lessens his own and others' offenses (5:20 and 2:13,16).

Here, too, at the closing exhortation of 5:19f., which is supposed to sound peaceful after all the threats of judgment and hard polemic, one can once again ask: Is this simply meant for one and all? Or at the same time doesn't an entirely unique case stand behind it, a model that the Gentile Christian communities should take to heart? A "sinner" against whose "wandering" one is to be warned and for whose salvation one must strive? Is it perhaps even about him who relates the word solely to faith, who expects salvation not from the law but from the Gospel, who proclaims that God justifies solely through faith without works of the law, and for that dares to name Abraham as witness, who considers himself quite a great teacher, who however in extreme polemic is unable to hold his tongue in check, who considers himself wise, with whom however there is little trace of peaceful heavenly wisdom, who rather causes conflict and struggles in the communities and who all too quickly judges others? Who boasts of worldwide missionary travels and success and makes ever more far-reaching plans, who now however has foundered in his boasting and as a prisoner awaits execution, who is also ill yet does not want to be helped by the elders of the mother-church of all Christians?

7. Even the *harsh polemic against the "rich"* without any curtailment and adjustment can be worked in here superbly. As I said before, Paul, in his "worldwide" missionary strategy and his founding of communities, was ever dependent upon the assistance of relatively well-off Christians and their willingness to make sacrifices. Only with their help could "house churches" be founded, lecture halls and apartments be rented, the costs of expensive journeys by ship be paid, letters be delivered, and encroachments from unknown quarters be repulsed. In the letters of Paul and even more so in the Acts of Luke, the "theologian of the poor," we have numerous examples of well-to-do Christians and their help. Active missions cost a lot of money, even when one did without the demand for personal support by the communities. In addition, the collection for "the poor" in Jerusalem had to be gathered. As the organizer of a missionary movement stretching across the entire Roman Empire, Paul could not afford any social-revolutionary experiments and fundamental aversions against those who were economically better off. Precisely on this point James is *inexorable*. His hatred of the rich shows no trace of any willingness to compromise. This already distinguishes him from Luke, the Pastoral Epistles, or the Shepherd of Hermas. The rich, even if they are Christians, seem to be excluded from salvation. A rich man cannot really be a Christian. This corresponds to the situation of the community of the poor in Jerusalem and Judea, which from the beginning was oppressed and sometimes bloodily persecuted by the Sadducean upper class consisting of the high-priestly elite and large landowners, who dominated the Sanhedrin.

* * *

In sum: The Letter of James is according to this *hypothesis* not a late, meager product of chance. It is conceived with deliberation and composed with rhetorical skill. The world of thought standing behind it is that of Jewish wisdom, linked with prophetic pathos and inextricably tied to the Jesus-tradition as we encounter it in Q, Matthew, and Mark.

The author thereby stands in such close relation to his corporeal brother that he doesn't deem it necessary to refer to him constantly or to cite him at all. The complete lack of a reference to "words of the Lord" is a sign of its early origin and of the author's prophetic authority. His letter, as well as his word, is at the same time the "word of the Lord." He speaks as the authority instituted by him, that is, as δοῦλος θεοῦ καὶ κυρίου Ἰησοῦ Χριστοῦ [2:1, "a servant of God and of the Lord Jesus Christ"] and *eo ipso* [by that very fact] in his name, in which δοῦλος [servant] is to be understood here fully in the sense of the Hebrew *'ebed* [servant]. One is almost tempted to speak of a "representative." In such a capacity he turns to the Christians in the Greek-speaking Diaspora. Theologically, one can recognize the problem of the letter, in which a "simplified" Jesus-tradition is reduced to ethos, if one wants to play it off against the Pauline doctrine of justification. By the providence of God, the early church saw in Paul and not in James *the* ἀπόστολος [apostle]. One can also very well understand the hesitation of the church in the third—even in the fourth—century in canonizing [this letter].

The peculiarity of the letter results from its double character. It speaks—in a masterful way—on *two levels* and presupposes to a certain extent two groups of recipients.

1. It appears as a loose, sapientially-rhetorically stylized hortatory speech with different, at least partly traditional themes, which emerge and disappear again in the letter like threads of a tapestry, but which still stand in a certain inner connection to each other. It means to address all Christians, yet appears enigmatic through the choice of motifs and organization of material. Since the actual intention of the letter remains unclear, it has been impossible to this day for exegetes to put the letter in its proper historical place.

2. Nevertheless, the letter contains in its sapiential-parenetic vestment and manifold variations a pointed anti-Pauline polemic, which comes to terms with the personal behavior of Paul, his missionary practice, and the dangerous tendencies of his theology. The author presupposes that the communities that know Paul or were even founded by him understand this polemic quite well and are warned by it. Under the assumptions of this hypothesis it is perhaps still possible to form a better understanding of this peculiar writing with a view to its historical place and its content, and to fit it in historically.

DAVID FLUSSER

[Paul's Jewish-Christian Opponents in Jerusalem and in the *Didache*] (1987)†

The aim of the present paper is not to clarify the various facets of enmity between so called "Jewish Christianity" and Paul. The real purpose of our study is to show that *Didache* 6:2–3 reflects the position of the majority in the Mother Church towards the Gentile Christian believers while Paul's attitude was more unusual and therefore revolutionary. Both positions represent two genuine interpretations of the necessary obligations of Gentile God-fearers. We believe that both factions based their claims upon the Apostolic Decree. Paul's view became victorious but even so it is not without interest to learn what was the opposite view with the help of *Didache* 6:2–3, a position which was held, among others, by the apostle Peter. The text of *Didache* 6:2–3, it will be recalled, runs as follows: "If you can bear the whole yoke of the Lord (i.e., of the Law), you will be perfect; but if you cannot, do what you can. Concerning the food, bear what you will be able to bear. But be sure to refrain completely from meat which has been sanctified before idols, for it represents the worship of dead gods."

The Apostolic Decree is quoted three times in the Acts of the Apostles (15:20, 28–29 and 21:25). Already from the beginning of modern scholarship, the question was asked concerning the actual point of contact between the Apostolic Decree and the so called Noachic precepts in Judaism, because both contain a list of religious and moral obligations for non-Jews. The Noachic precepts were thus a Jewish non-Christian parallel to the Apostolic Decree, which was issued by a community of Jews believing in Jesus in order to lay upon the Gentile no greater burden than that which is necessary. The first step towards the solution of the problem was taken by the German scholar Adolf Resch already in 1905. He rightly recognized the eminent value of the so called Western text of the Apostolic Decree. In contrast to the common text, where Gentiles are obliged to abstain from what has been sacrificed to idols, from blood, from what is strangled and from unchastity, in the Western text the prohibition to eat what is strangled is missing. Resch also succeeded in showing that for the most important of the Church Fathers only the three prohibitions—not including the one concerning that which is strangled—formed the text of the Apostolic Decree and that these three prohibitions were originally identical with the three capital sins in early patristic literature, namely idolatry, bloodshed and fornication. He also rightly argued that Paul in reality fulfilled the obligations of the original text and meaning of the Apostolic Decree.

It is not our task here to treat fully the problems of the text and the historical development of the Apostolic decision. This we have already done in another study. Here we only have to mention the fact that the three capital sins, idolatry, bloodshed and fornication, are often mentioned

---

† From "Paul's Jewish-Christian Opponents in the *Didache*," first published in *Gilgul: Essays on Transformation, Revolution and Permanence in the History of Religions*, ed. by S. Shaked, D. Shulman, and G. G. Stroumsa (Leiden: Brill, 1987), 71–90; reprinted in *The* Didache *in Modern Research*, ed. by J. A. Draper (Leiden: Brill, 1996), 195–211. Reprinted by permission of Brill Academic Publishers. Flusser (1917–2000) was professor of Early Christianity and Judaism of the Second Temple Period at the Hebrew University of Jerusalem.

in rabbinic literature and that, according to a decision from the beginning of the second century CE, a Jew must choose death rather than let himself be coerced to transgress one of these three prohibitions. Some decades later, at the end of the second century CE, perpetrators of these sins were excluded from the church and their penitence was not accepted. Here the main point which pertains to the present study is that idolatry, bloodshed and fornication are also three of the extant seven Noachic precepts. As has been demonstrated by Resch, the prohibition of the same three crimes formed the original content of the Apostolic Decree. The whole list of seven Jewish Noachic precepts is attested only from the mid-second century CE. If so, it is more than probable that in the Apostolic Age the official Jewish position was to require the Noachites, the God-fearing Gentiles, to abstain from idolatry, bloodshed and fornication. Hence quite naturally this same rule was accepted by the Apostolic Church. I hope to show here that even if the basic rule was then accepted by the church, new problems arose in the interpretation of the Apostolic Decree. The two divergent approaches concerning the application and interpretation of the famous decree are represented by the Petrine and Pauline parties. Moreover one discovers some strong indications that the same problem—albeit probably not in such an earnest and clear formulation—also existed among Jews in the politics pertaining to God-fearing Gentiles.

Does *Didache* 6:2–3 express a "conservative" Jewish interpretation of the Noachic laws or does the passage represent an analogous Christian position concerning the Apostolic Decree? I think that the function of our passage in the context of the *Didache* dispels all doubts about the Christian origin of *Didache* 6:2–3. The passage clearly reflects the Jewish-Christian understanding of the obligations of Gentile Christians towards Judaism, a position which was utterly unacceptable for Paul.

Almost as soon as the text of the *Didache* was published in 1882 from a Greek manuscript, it was recognized that the first six chapters of the work are actually a Jewish treatise christianized by the author of the *Didache*; from chapter seven on, the book is of Christian provenance. It was only as a consequence of the discovery of the Dead Sea Scrolls that it was recognized that the Jewish treatise contained in the first six chapters of the *Didache* is indeed extant in an old Latin translation. Its real title was *de doctrina Apostolorum*, but today it is commonly referred to as The Two Ways. This Jewish tractate—and not the Christian *Didache*—was used by the author of the apocryphal Epistle of Barnabas of the first half of the second century CE. All this can lead only to one conclusion: the Jewish treatise The Two Ways was already considered to be a manual of Christian ethics in the first decades of Christianity and often it was even viewed as the teaching of the Apostles. Whether the Didachist was aware of the original provenance of his source is not possible to determine with absolute precision. However it would seem that he was convinced that The Two Ways was a Christian work, and even one of "apostolic" authority because he did not permit himself to change the wording of his source very much. It is reasonable to believe that the *Didache* was written before the end of the first century CE. The Two Ways was written earlier; there are indications that this Jewish treatise was known to Philo of Alexandria.

The Jewish tractate ended originally with an admonition. Although the Didachist (6:1) abbreviated it, the text is more complete in the Latin version of the Jewish source (*Doct.* 6:1–6). Nonetheless it is difficult to recon-struct the precise original wording of the admonition. Even so, it is evident that the Latin translation of the ending reflects the original content of the conclusion of The Two Ways: "Beware lest anyone cause you to abandon this teaching, otherwise you will be taught apart from the (true) instruc-tion. If you do these things daily with deliberation, you will be near to the living God. But if you fail to do them, you will be far from the truth. Store up all these things in your soul and you will not be beguiled from your hope."

This concluding admonition fits admirably well the ethical imperative and the dualistic vein of the Jewish Two Ways, and is an appropriate con-clusion of the work. Neither in the Latin *Doctrina Apostolorum* nor in the paraphrastic *Epistle of Barnabas* was any other new precept added. Here the *Didache* differs. After the abbreviated form of the original conclusion and before the Christian "Manual of Discipline" that follows, in *Didache* 6:2–3 an addition to The Two Ways was inserted.

As has already been noted, the passage was absent from the original tractate of The Two Ways, but the appendix already existed in the copy of the treatise used by the Didachist. Theoretically the passage under ques-tion could have been a Jewish addition to the Jewish tractate, but this is highly improbable. We hope to show further that, although *Didache* 6:2–3 was not composed by the Didachist, it was a Christian work, written by a man whose Christian Weltanschauung differed from the approach of the Didachist. On the other hand, the addition differs also from the preceding Jewish text. While the Two Ways is an inner-Jewish ethical treatise, only *Didache* 6:2–3 is addressed to Gentile believers.

Though The Two Ways is of Jewish origin, it was regarded as apostolic instruction not only by the Didachist, but also by the *Doctrina Apostolo-rum*. If the apostolic ascription appears from the text's very beginnings in all the witnesses without any exceptions, it follows that from the first decades of Christianity, the Two Ways was considered a product of the Apostolic Mother Church. As such, the tractate began to be read also by Gentile believers in Christ, and thus it is no wonder that an appendix was added, reflecting the spirit of the majority of the Jewish Mother Church which sought to stipulate the obligations of Gentile Christian believers.

At this stage the tractate reached the Didachist. For him *Didache* 6:2–3 belonged to the Vorlage and was an authentic apostolic teaching that carried all the authority of his source. Did he notice that the passage was a child of a spirit different from his own? Even if he had some suspicions, the authority of his Vorlage dissipated them. One passage begins with the words: "If you can bear the whole yoke of the Lord, you will be perfect. . . ." The "yoke of the Lord" means here the "yoke of the Law," but as we will see later, the term "the yoke of the Lord" is also Jewish and has the same meaning. The Didachist could understand the expression as describing common Christian duties.

*   *   *

In order to proceed further in our investigation, we must make a few remarks concerning some philological questions. Our passage speaks about the bearing of the whole yoke of the Lord (or of the Law). It is evident that this terminology alludes to the atmosphere of the so called

Apostolic Decree. According to Acts 15:10 it was Peter who said in this connection: "Now therefore why do you make trial of God by pulling a yoke upon the neck of the disciples which neither our fathers nor we have been able to bear?" And according to Acts 15:28 in the letter which announced the decisions of the Apostolic Church it was written: "For it has seemed good to the Holy Spirit and to us to lay upon you no greater burden than these necessary things," namely, the restrictions of the Apostolic Decree. And it was already recognized that a similar terminology appears also in the message to the church of Thyatira in Rev. 2:24–25. "I do not lay upon you any other burden; only hold fast what you have, until I come." According to *Didache* 6:2–3 those who are able to bear the whole yoke are perfect, but if anyone is not able to reach perfection, it does not matter: he shall bear what he is able to bear. This implies that those who are unable to fulfill all the commandments are somehow imperfect. I do not know any other good parallel for the use of the term "perfect," but perhaps the closest text is Mt. 19:21. I will try to explain the strange attitude of our passage later.

As we have seen, although it was recognized that the intended audience of *Didache* 6:2–3 was the believing Gentiles, the relevance of his unique text to this complex problem has not, as far as I know, been fully appreciated until now. The proposal contained in *Didache* 6:2–3 is one of the possible solutions to the question regarding the status of believing Gentiles, a problem which was then common to both Judaism and Christianity. The proposed solution is astonishing, but it makes good sense in the context of various trends within Judaism and the early Christian Church. Although the situation was already known in its broad outlines, *Didache* 6:2–3 throws light upon it, and thus the passage becomes a substantial help for understanding both Judaism and primitive Christianity.

It is surely not our task to describe the strong attraction of the Jewish faith among the Gentiles. "The masses have long since shown a keen desire to adopt our religious observances and there is not one city, Greek or barbarian, not a single nation to which our custom of abstaining from work on the seventh day has not spread, and where the fasts and the lighting of lamps and many of our prohibitions in the matter of food are not observed" (Josephus, *Contra Apion* 2:282–3; cf. ibid. 2:123). Many Gentiles were fascinated not only by the theological spirituality and the ethical values of Judaism, but also by its "ceremonial law." We know from the sources that levels of observing the Jewish way of life as embraced by Gentiles varied from one person to another; it seems that the Gentile God-fearers were more and more eager to accept and follow further Jewish obligations as they proceeded in learning. Since it was impossible in practice, and from the Jewish point of view even undesirable, for all the God-fearing Gentiles to become full proselytes, the Gentile "Judaizers" had to decide how great a burden they desired to assume. In their decisions they necessarily depended upon the advice and the instructions of their Jewish friends.

In this connection the story of the gradual progress of the royal family of Adiabene towards full proselytism (Josephus, *AJ* 20:17ff) is instructive, but at the same time clearly atypical. The obstacles to becoming full proselytes were far more restrictive for persons of a high social position such as sovereigns of a state than for other Gentiles who were not exposed to public censure. One should moreover not forget that the story is narrated by Josephus from the standpoint of his Gentile readers.

In the process of the full proselytization of the royal house of Adiabene at least two Jews were involved. The first was a certain Jewish merchant, named Ananias: "He taught them to worship God after the manner of the Jewish tradition" (AJ 20:34), and it happened, moreover, that the Queen, Helena, "had likewise been instructed by another Jew and had been brought over to their laws" (ibid 35). Finally Izates came to the conclusion, "that he would not be genuinely a Jew unless he was circumcised and therefore he was ready to act accordingly" (Ibid 38). Then Ananias tried to dissuade the king from this last step. "The king could, he said, worship God even without being circumcised if he had fully decided to be a devoted adherent of Judaism, for it was this that counted more than circumcision" (ibid 41). The final decision to complete the process of proselytism was caused by "another Jew, named Eleazar, who came from Galilee and who had the reputation of being extremely strict when it came to the ancestral laws" (ibid 43). The Greek wording that describes Eleazar's Jewish way of life shows that he was a Pharisee. In Greek sources the technical term *akribeia* serves as a definition of Pharisaic piety: the Pharisees "are believed to interpret the laws with strictness" (*met' akribeias*, Josephus, *BJ* 2.162). According to Acts 22:3 Paul was brought up in Jerusalem at the feet of Gamaliel the Pharisee (see Acts 5:34), "according to the strict manner of the law of our fathers" (*kata akribeian tou patroou nomou*). And in Acts 26:5 Paul says that he has lived as a Pharisee, "according to the strictest (*akribestate*) party of our religion." But even if his Eleazar was a Pharisee, this does not mean that his approach represented the opinion of the majority within rabbinic Judaism.

In reality it should be well known already that in general, ancient Judaism neither wished nor required that all the Gentile God-fearers should become full proselytes. On the other hand, the Jews had no choice but to try and find, for the sake of the Gentiles, a formula which would establish the minimum of obligations indispensable for the Gentiles to be saved together with the Jews who were required to observe the whole Law. Today the obligations for the Gentiles are the so called seven Noachic precepts and we have shown elsewhere that these seven obligations are the result of a long development. We also tried to show that in the earliest stage of development, these seven Noachic precepts originally consisted of only three commandments, the same ones as contained in the better reading of the Apostolic Decree.

Today the Jewish code strictly forbids a non-Jew to observe any Jewish commandment, no matter how minor. A Gentile has to live only according to the Noachic prescriptions and nothing more is required, unless he decides to "become a Jew." Only after passing all the prescribed ceremonies of proselytism and becoming legally Jewish, does he have to observe the whole Law. What happened in later Judaism is a historical paradox: medieval Judaism finally reached a solution not dissimilar to that which Paul more or less endeavored to enforce in Gentile Christian communities, i.e. Gentiles were not permitted to observe the Jewish commandments, but if they became Jews, then they were obliged to observe the whole law of Moses. In both cases, a similar approach led to similar results. Both Paul and the medieval Rabbis wanted to separate the Jews from non-Jews and the most dangerous obstacle in the way of achieving this aim was when Gentiles began to fulfill, even partially, the Jewish law. Such a constellation makes a complete separation of Jews from Gentiles and vice versa quite impracticable. Thus Gentile "Judaizers" became non desirable for both sides. The question is how far the medieval Jewish separatist solution was stimulated by the ecclesiastical politics of the Church which punished Judaizers and strictly prohibited all proselytism. Gentile Judaizers and possible proselytes were then a menacing danger for the very existence of the Jewish communities. Thus we cannot completely exclude the possibility that the parallelism between the Church and the Synagogue in their wish to achieve complete mutual separatism also had a hidden, hideous dimension.

*   *   *

The Apostolic Decree was evidently no more than a confirmation and reinforcement of the Noachic prescriptions as they were then commonly understood. But this did not unequivocally solve the whole "Gentile question." Are these prescriptions the minimum obligations of the Gentiles or are they indeed the maximum rules for the God-fearers, as Paul and later the medieval rabbinism decided? In a famous Jewish homily from the second century CE [*Sifra* to Lev. 18:5], we read that a Gentile who does the (Mosaic) Law is considered to be in the same category as the Jewish High Priest himself. It is not written that God's ordinances and statutes are destined for the priests, Levites and Israelites; it is rather said: "You shall keep my statutes and my ordinances which the man (adam) shall do" (Lev. 18:5). In 2 Sam. 7:19, the Law is not given only for the priests, Levites and Israelites, but rather, "This is the Law for man (adam)." Moreover, the prophet Isaiah does not say that God's gates are open for the priests, Levites and Israelites, but he says: "Open the gates that the righteous nation (Hebrew: *goy*, the Gentile) which keeps faith may enter in" (Is. 26: 2). So we see that even a Gentile who practices the (Mosaic) Law is considered to be like the High Priest.

The author of our homily believes that in principle, the Mosaic Law is destined to be observed by all mankind. Therefore he considers a Gentile who 'does the Law' as having great merit, and it is undoubtedly not a proselyte who is meant. Thus there is no doubt that the circles to which the tradent belonged saw in the Noachic precepts no more than an indispensable prerequisite, a minimal obligation for the pious Gentiles. According to the spirit of the saying, a God-fearing Gentile is to be praised if he fulfills many commandments of the Mosaic Law. On the other hand, according to Paul and to later medieval Jewish legislation, a believing Gentile should not accept upon himself more obligations than the Noachic precepts. Did such a Jewish view exist already in Paul's day at least as a recommended suggestion? Until now I have not found any decisive Jewish text which would explicitly confirm this approach, but this position fits admirably well the divergent tendencies within Judaism of antiquity.

This 'dialectical' unity in Judaism is often inaccurately described as its universalism and particularism. It was an expression of the genuine Jewish universalistic tendency which regarded the Law as destined for all of mankind and thus came to hold the opinion that it is preferable for a pious Gentile to accept upon himself the Jewish obligations. It is superfluous to repeat here that Judaism was not and is not a missionary religion; however, as it also has a universal message, Judaism in antiquity mostly welcomed proselytes, but logically this approach was not without some ambivalence. The open mindedness of the school of Hillel towards proselytes, and the reserve shown by the school of Shammai against them are well known. No wonder that the prominent disciple of the school of Shamai, Rabbi Eleazar ben Hyrcanos thought that proselytes tended to possess a bad character. Moreover, if sometimes one had to be careful even of full proselytes, how could one ever trust the Godfearing Gentiles? Rabbi Shimeon ben Yochai was pessimistic. When Pharaoh decided to pursue the children of Israel, he "took six hundred chosen chariots" (Ex. 14:7) but where did he get the beasts to pull the chariots? The beasts of the Egyptians and those of Pharaoh had already died during the ten plagues, and the cattle of the children of Israel remained with them (see Ex. 10:26). To whom did they belong? The cattle belonged to the God-fearing Gentiles among the servants of Pharaoh. Their cattle were spared, since they had heeded the warning of Moses. We learn this fact from another biblical verse: "He who *feared the word of the Lord* among the servants of Pharaoh, made his slaves and his cattle flee into the house" (Ex. 9:20). So Pharaoh used these beasts which belonged to the God-fearers among his servants against the children of Israel. We thus learn that the God-fearing Gentiles constitute a snare for Israel.

Rabbi Eleazar ben Hyrcanos thought that a proselyte did not cease to be attracted by his pagan past. In addition, Rabbi Shimeon ben Yochai believed the God-fearing Gentiles possessed an unstable and weak character and that they presented a danger for the Jewish people because one could not be sure that when Israel was persecuted they would not join their Gentile compatriots. The exaggerated suspicions of the two Jewish sages resulted from the basic ambivalent theological and psychological structure of Judaism which we have already mentioned. As to the God-fearing Gentiles, it is easy to imagine that besides those who welcomed their zeal for Jewish commandments, there were also many Jews in whose hearts the multitude of "half-Jews" evoked an uneasy feeling. Do these Gentiles observe parts of the Mosaic Law because they understand the Jewish call, or perhaps they perform Jewish customs as an act of superstition? Where is the line separating proselytes from God-fearing Gentiles? All who have experienced modern parallels to these ancient Gentile "Judaizers" will surely understand the ambivalent feelings concerning practising Gentiles: on the one hand, the high appreciation of a Gentile who "does the Law"—and on the other, the negative attitude of Rabbi Shimeon ben Yochai against the Godfearing Gentiles. In such a state of affairs, it is plausible to imagine that already in antiquity there existed among the Jews a tendency to recommend that Gentiles restrict themselves in their observance only to those prescriptions which are indispensable, namely the Noachic precepts. It is not too far-fetched even to suppose that Paul's warning to the Gentiles as regards the observance of the Law was not merely a consequence of his conversion. It is possible that the point of departure for this component of his theology lies in Paul's "Pharisaic" past. But as we have already stated, the restriction calling on the Gentiles not to observe more than the Noachic precepts is not explicitly attested in ancient Jewish sources. Nevertheless, the view that the believing and already practising Gentiles should be permitted to perform specifically Jewish commandments is also unattested in ancient Judaism.

Shall we therefore accept the view that *Didache* 6:2–3 is a purely Jewish passage in which an anonymous Jewish maximalist appeals to the God-fearing Gentiles to observe the Mosaic Law as far as they can? This seems to me to be almost impossible. Already at first glance one has the impression that, if the passage is purely Jewish, its content is a very clumsy proposal. However, if the passage is Christian, then it is a directive addressed to the Gentile Christians and inspired by the position of the right wing of the Mother Church and in that case, *Didache* 6:2–3 makes good sense. There are two reasons why the passage is Christian and not purely Jewish. The first is decisive, namely the setting of the passage in the midst of the development of the *Didache* from the Jewish Two Ways towards our actual *Didache*. The second reason why *Didache* 6:2–3 has to be considered as a Christian work is that although the question of the Believing Gentiles was also a Jewish problem, it really became an urgent matter in the primitive Church, whose future and very nature depended upon the manner in which this decisive issue would be resolved.

Let us first requote the passage itself. "If you can bear the whole yoke of the Lord (i.e. of the Law) you will be perfect; but if you cannot, do what you can. Concerning the food, bear what you will be able to bear. But be sure to refrain completely from meat which has been sanctified before idols, for it represents the worship of dead gods." The views expressed in the passage are indeed possible within the framework of ancient Judaism, but it is extremely difficult to imagine that a Jew, or a Jewish authority of the period, would address God-fearing Gentiles and beg them to be perfect and to observe the whole Jewish Law, or at least to observe as much as they can and recommend that their food should be as kosher as possible. I admit that the passage remains somehow grotesque even if it is Christian, but as a Christian composition it becomes far less strange and incredible. Both Jews and Christians are sure that Gentiles will be saved under certain conditions, but as soon as Gentiles accepted the faith in Jesus Christ, the question of their unity with the Christian Jews in one Church was no more essentially identical with the original Jewish religious view about the pious Gentiles. Christians believe that the Messiah has already come and that his expiatory death saves all who believe in him and in this central point there is no difference between Jews believing in Christ and Gentiles. Moreover Christ unites the Jews who believe in him with Christian Gentiles and removes the Christian Jews from the rest of Jewry.

It is necessary to state these truisms in order to understand that a fast and unequivocal solution of the problem of the Christian Gentiles for the Church became from its very beginnings unavoidable. There were two possible kinds of solutions for the Gentile problem in the Church, and both were proposed. The points of departure were naturally the Noachic precepts, for which the Gentiles are held responsible. The first solution was obvious. In order to strengthen the ties of Gentile Christianity with the Jews believing in Christ who were "all zealous of the Law" (Acts 21: 20), it was desirable for the Gentile Christian believers to observe all the Mosaic Law as far as they were able to do so. In this manner the difference between the Jewish believers and their Gentile brethren would be minimized. We have already seen that this solution was based upon Jewish patterns. The other solution was evidently dictated by the suspicion that if Gentile Christians "did the Law," the common bond with the non-Christian Jews would be so great that there would be a danger that Gentile Christians would finally become Jewish (non-Christian) proselytes. Therefore Gentile Christians should not be required to observe the special Jewish prescriptions. Although no explicit Jewish parallel from antiquity is available to authenticate this approach, this Pauline solution fits certain tendencies in Judaism. This has become evident, among other things, from the fact noted above, that Paul's position conforms to the later Jewish legislation concerning Gentiles.

Anyone reading Paul even once knows that he always warns Gentiles not to observe Jewish commandments. During the period, some God-fearing Gentiles evidently underwent circumcision without becoming full proselytes, because they thought that circumcision was only one important component of the Jewish way of life. To those who would adhere to this approach Paul answered, "I testify again to every man who receives circumcision that he is bound to keep the whole law" (Gal. 5:3) Here Paul repeats the current Jewish position. However one cannot be sure that at the time some of the Jewish doctors did not think that for the Gentiles, as for Jews, circumcision was only one of the obligations of the Law. Therefore circumcision would not bind the Gentiles to keep the whole Mosaic Law. If such a view ever existed, it expressed the position of those who thought that Gentile God-fearers were permitted and even encouraged to live at least partially in the same manner as Jews. Such a demand was probably adopted by the majority of the Jewish Mother Church, because it evidently seemed to its members that it was the easiest solution to the urgent problem of the Gentile Christians. If they observed the Jewish commandments as far as possible, the ties between the Jewish and Gentile members of the Church would be strengthened. Such "Church-politics" did not contradict the so called Apostolic Decree, as it agreed with the Jewish viewpoint concerning the Noachic precepts.

Our considerations are based upon the general situation in the Apostolic Church. All its members accepted the authority of the Apostolic Decree but its application depended on two possible interpretations of the indispensable obligations of Gentile believers. The question was whether these obligations constituted a minimum or a maximum. Now we should understand Paul's vehement opposition to such Gentiles who wanted to take upon themselves a heavier Jewish burden. On the other hand, the approach of the faction to which Peter belonged no longer looks as absurd as it often used to do. They adhered to another interpretation of the Apostolic Decree, identical with the Jewish view that the "doing of the Law" by a Gentile is meritorious. Those who tried to persuade Gentile Christians to live more or less like the Jews wanted to reach a high goal, namely the creation of a single Church, composed of both Jews and Gentiles.

Now we can understand the incident which happened in Antioch (Gal. 2:11–14). "For before a certain man came from James, he (Peter) ate with the Gentiles; but when he came he drew back and separated himself, fearing the circumcision party. . . . I said to Cephas (Peter) before them all, 'If you, though a Jew, live like a Gentile and not like a Jew, how can you compel the Gentiles to live like Jews?' " Paul did not blame Peter because he had never before "eaten anything that is common or unclean" (Acts

10:14) but because he now makes concessions to the Gentiles and at the same time he compels them to live like Jews. We have tried to explain what it meant for Peter and the faction to which he belonged to "compel" the Gentiles to live according to the manner of the Jews. Peter and his tried to persuade the Gentile Christians not to become full proselytes but to do some "works of the law" (see Gal. 3:1–5). The argumentation of this faction of the Jewish Mother Church was approximately as follows: "If you (i.e. Gentile Christians) can bear the whole yoke of the Lord, you will be perfect; but if you cannot, do what you can. Concerning the food, bear what you will be able to bear. But be sure to refrain completely from meat which has been sanctified before idols for it represents the worship of dead gods" (*Didache* 6:2–3). Incidentally, one of the points that prove that the passage is indeed Christian is the reference to "what has been sacrificed to idols" which is mentioned in the Apostolic Decree (see also 1 Cor. 8 and 10:25–29 and Rev. 2:14, 20).

We are sure that *Didache* 6:2–3 is of Christian and not Jewish origin. It is a precious document from the first years of Christianity. The passage fits the meagre and incomplete information about the tendencies and aims of the group in the Apostolic Church which Paul opposed, and thus it enlarges and supplements our knowledge about this trend which was once named the "Petrine" faction. I believe that with the help of our passage one can learn also something about Paul, since it casts light upon the tendencies against which Paul was constrained to fight. If, however, some doubts remain about the Christian origin of *Didache* 6:2–3, it is the position of this passage within the final arrangement of the *Didache* which unequivocally decides the question.

We should like at this stage to repeat the main points of this argument: (1) *Didache* 6:2–3 is addressed to Gentiles while the preceding tractate the Two Ways is an inner-Jewish ethical treatise. (2) *Didache* 6:2–3 did not belong to the Jewish treatise, as it can be seen i.a. from the old Latin translation of this Jewish source, where this addition is still absent. (3) Already in the first decades of Christianity the Two Ways was considered to be a product of the Apostolic Mother Church. The apostolic ascription of the Jewish source appears in all witnesses without exception. (4) Under such circumstances it is plausible that at the end of the treatise an appendix was added which regulated the obligations of the Gentile believers in the spirit of the majority of the Apostolic Mother Church. (5) The tractate together with the addition reached the Didachist who also believed in the apostolic origin of his *Vorlage*. He interpolated his source and adjoined it, from chapter 7 on, to his own Christian "Manual of Discipline." (6) The Didachist was a Gentile Christian similar to the author(s) of the Pastoral Epistles and his pastoral work concerns Gentile Christian Churches. On the other hand, the author of *Didache* 6: 2–3 is a Christian Jew. *Didache* 6:2–3 is a child of a different spirit from the following Christian "Manual of Discipline." But as the Didachist believed that both the Two Ways and the addition are a product of the Apostolic Church, he did not pay attention to the different tendencies represented in *Didache* 6:2–3. (7) The progressive development of the text of the *Didache* shows that *Didache* 6: 2–3 was written in a period between the Jewish Two Ways and the Gentile Christian treatise of the Didachist. Also in this respect, *Didache* 6:2–3 is not a Jewish but a Christian composition.

We have come to the end of our journey, which has led us through the birth pangs which finally produced the "historical" Christian church. There is no doubt that the plan of Paul's opponents was well meant, but in reality it was impractical. How could such a Gentile Christian Church have survived in the long run when it contained a membership of Gentile Christians on various levels of Jewish perfection? Paul was capable of imposing his solution upon the Church. But even the best human decision is potentially dangerous and tends to lead to strange consequences if no strong will exists to avoid the impending evil. So Paul's reasonable arrangement succeeded more or less in keeping Gentile Christians from observing the Jewish way of life. Later on, however, not only were Gentiles who observed the smallest Jewish commandment cruelly punished, but also Jews who became Christians were forbidden by the Christian Church to live according to the Law of Moses.

Paul and His Pagan Critics

Paul's critics also included various pagans, who, beginning in the latter half of the second century, began to mount a systematic and sometimes sophisticated intellectual attack on the Christian movement.[1] The first of these scholarly polemicists was Celsus, who attacked Christians for their credulity in his *True Doctrine*, faulting them for rejecting wisdom in favor of foolishness (1.9, 13; 6.12; cf. 1 Cor. 1:18–25; 3:18–20).[2] The first pagan critic to focus on Paul was perhaps Porphyry, a Neoplatonist philosopher who wrote an immense fifteen-volume work entitled *Against the Christians*. Condemned by Constantine in 325 and ordered burned in 448 by Theodosius II and Valentinian III, the work is known today only from references to it by Christians who cited it in order to refute it.[3] In the certain fragments of Porphyry, he identified the humans with whom Paul did not consult (Gal. 1:16) as the Jerusalem apostles, arguing that after being instructed by God, Paul did not deign to confer with mere flesh and blood (frg. 20). Porphyry also seized upon the "childish fight" of Peter and Paul in Antioch (Gal. 2:11–14) to attack both apostles, charging the former with error and the latter with "impudence" (*procacitas*). "Paul," he argued, "burned with envy at Peter's virtues" and attacked Peter for doing what he himself had done; furthermore, he claimed that Paul wrote boastfully of things that either he had not done or had done "impudently" (frg. 21a–b). Porphyry may also have claimed that Paul "secretly lacerated" Peter in Galatians 5:10 ("the one who is throwing you into confusion"), making him by means of this "impudent curse" (*procaci maledicto*) the one who was ultimately responsible for the disturbance in Galatia (frg. 22).[4]

1. In addition to combating Christianity, pagans also responded by pillaging believers' assertions about Christ in order to advance similar claims about their own heroes. Iamblichus, for instance, says that some people regarded Pythagoras as an Olympian god who had "appeared in human form" (*VP* 6.30). Similarly, he also narrates that when Abaris the Scythian saw Pythagoras and believed that the philosopher was none other than Apollo himself, Pythagoras took him aside, confirmed that he was right, and told him that "he had come for the care and benefit of the human race, and for that reason was in human form" (19.91–92; cf. Phil. 2:6–7). Julian makes a similar claim about Asclepius being the son of Zeus, who, having visited the earth from the sky, appeared "in human form" (*Gal.* 200a).

2. About 70 years after Celsus wrote (ca. 178–180), Origen gave a response to his criticisms of Christianity in his *Against Celsus*, and it is only from Origen's quotations of Celsus' treatise that its contents are partially known. Whether Celsus had read any of Paul's letters (esp. 1 Cor.) is debated, though some aspects of Christianity that he finds objectionable have a clear Pauline basis and he is aware of Gnostic Christians who have been influenced by Paul's thoughts and vocabulary (*Cels.* 5.65 [Gal. 6:14]; 6.53 [Phil. 3:8]). Origen (*Cels.* 3.20) says that Celsus would deny that Paul knew anything of the wisdom that he claimed to speak among the mature (1 Cor. 2:6–8) and affirms that anyone who agreed with Celsus would ridicule the Pauline claim about Christ found in Phil. 2:10–11 (*Cels.* 8.59).

3. Porphyry wrote his work at some point after 271 CE, with some scholars preferring a date as late as the early fourth century. According to the church historian Socrates, Porphyry wrote his work in "unrestrained rage" after a gang of Christians in Caesarea gave him a thorough thrashing (*Hist. eccl.* 3.23). Modern scholars who date the work to the reign of Diocletian (284–305) often suspect a political motive, with the attack helping to fan the flames of the emperor's Great Persecution that began in 303. Others think that his *Philosophy from Oracles*—which included a treatment of Jesus and an attack on the disciples—was written at Diocletian's urging. According to a fairly recent hypothesis, *Against the Christians* was not a separate work but only part of his *Philosophy from Oracles* (as was perhaps also his *Ascent of the Soul*), with the attack on Christianity concentrated in three of the fifteen books.

4. Almost certainly including Paul among the missionaries whom he criticized, Porphyry also explained Christian evangelistic success as due to the use of magic, with the aim being that of

In a similar way, Hierocles Sossianus, governor of Bithynia in 303 and a persecutor of the Christians, railed against both Peter and Paul as "disseminators of deceit" in a two-book pamphlet entitled *A Truth-Loving Discourse*, calling them both "liars, uneducated, and wizards."[5] Another pagan critic of Paul was the Roman emperor Julian (361–363), who denounced him and other Christians in his *Against the Galileans* (363),[6] arguing that Paul "surpassed all wizards and deceivers of every time and place" (100a). Yet the most extensive and sustained critique of the apostle was delivered by the anonymous Hellene in Macarius Magnes' *Monogenes* (= *Apocriticus*).[7] Excerpts from the invectives of both Julian and the Hellene are given below.[8]

JULIAN

[Pauline Double Talk: Is the God of Israel Really the God of the Gentiles?] (363)[†]

But that from the beginning God cared only for the Jews and that He chose them out as his portion, has been clearly asserted not only by Moses

---

receiving money from wealthy converts (frg. 4). The basic collection of Porphyry's fragments is that of A. von Harnack, ed., *Porphyrius, "Gegen die Christen," 15 Bücher* (Berlin: Königliche Akademie der Wissenschaften, 1916), though many of the fragments he attributes to Porphyry are conjectures. Among these is frg. 37, where a critic denounces Paul's curse in Gal. 5:12, citing laws against castration and charging that the curse proves that Paul "was not able to control himself because of a Jewish rage and a certain unrestrained insanity." For a recent translation of fragments and testimonia, see Robert M. Berchman, *Porphyry Against the Christians* (Leiden: Brill, 2005), 123–221.

5. Lactantius, *Inst.* 5.2, and Eusebius, *Hier.* 2. Hierocles' knowledge of Scripture was so extensive that Lactantius wondered whether he might once have been a Christian, though Eusebius (traditionally the famous Christian historian but possibly an otherwise unknown sophist with the same name) alleged that most of his work had been pilfered from previous critics such as Celsus. What prompted Eusebius' response to Hierocles was the latter's unfavorable comparison of Christ to Apollonius of Tyana. In *Mart. Pal.* 5, Eusebius of Caesarea depicts Hierocles, now prefect of Egypt, as ruthless in his persecution of Christians, even consigning virgins to brothels.

6. Julian's work has been partially reconstructed from the portions cited by Cyril of Alexandria in his *Against Julian* (ca. 440) and by a few other Christian writers. "Galileans" is Julian's term for Christians, whom he describes in 43a as "neither Greeks nor Jews" (cf. Gal. 3:28; Col. 3:11).

7. Macarius Magnes is usually identified as the Bishop of Magnesia who participated in the Synod of the Oak in 403, although that is far from certain. The anonymous Hellene is depicted as a Neoplatonist philosopher and orator whose critique of the NT is the most extensive to survive from antiquity. The primary source which Macarius used for the Hellene's objections is debated. The three major candidates are Porphyry, Hierocles, and Julian.

8. Paul's name also appears in connection with various pagan allegations, such as the claim that Christ was a magician (cf. Mark 3:22) who had written books on the magical arts. According to some pagans, these books were in the form of letters addressed to Peter and Paul (Augustine, *Cons.* 1.9.14–10.16), as though Jesus were handing over to his successors the secrets of his success as a magician.

† From *Against the Galileans* 106a–c, trans. by W. C. Wright, *The Works of the Emperor Julian* (LCL; 3 vols.; London: W. Heinemann; New York: Macmillan, 1913–23), Vol. 3,343. Julian was reared as a Christian, but he subsequently renounced the faith and enthusiastically embraced the paganism of classical culture. As a result, he became known in Christian tradition as "the Apostate." Unlike other pagan opponents, he attacks Christianity and Paul with an insider's knowledge of the religion. In the portions not included here, Julian denounces Christianity as an apostasy from Judaism. As part of that attack, he assails Paul as the one whose views were largely responsible for Christians not keeping circumcision and the rest of the Mosaic laws (319e; 351a). He also says (206a) that Paul was content to have deluded handmaids and slaves and people such as Sergius Paulus (Acts 13:6–12), pointing to 1 Cor 6:9–10 as evidence of the moral inferiority of Paul's converts (245c). In that connection, Julian also faulted Paul's language in 1 Corinthians, charging that Paul ought to have blushed for his use of the vile language of 1 Cor. 6:9–10 and saying that his praises of the Corinthians amounted to lecherous flattery and slavish pandering if they were not true (245b). In addition, he refers to Paul's discussion of idol meat in 1 Cor. 8 (229c), quotes the phrase "the firstborn over all creation" from Col. 1:15 (262d), and attacks Christian violence against pagans and their holy places by pointing out that Paul never commanded his readers to raze temples and altars or to slaughter religious opponents (206a).

and Jesus but by Paul as well; though in Paul's case this is strange. For according to circumstances he keeps changing his views about God, as the polypus changes its colours to match the rocks,[1] and now he insists that the Jews alone are God's portion, and then again, when he is trying to persuade the Hellenes to take sides with him, he says: "Do not think that he is the God of Jews only, but also of Gentiles: yea of Gentiles also."[2] Therefore it is fair to ask of Paul why God, if he was not the God of the Jews only but also of the Gentiles, sent the blessed gift of prophecy to the Jews in abundance and gave them Moses and the oil of anointing, and the prophets and the law and the incredible and monstrous elements in their myths? For you hear them crying aloud: "Man did eat angels' food."[3] And finally God sent unto them Jesus also, but unto us no prophet, no oil of anointing, no teacher, no herald to announce his love for man which should one day, though late, reach even unto us also.

JULIAN

[Whether Paul Called Jesus "God" and the Secret Worship of Paul's Tomb] (363)†

But you are so misguided that you have not even remained faithful to the teachings that were handed down to you by the apostles. And these also have been altered, so as to be worse and more impious, by those who came after. At any rate neither Paul nor Matthew nor Luke nor Mark ventured to call Jesus God.[1] But the worthy John, since he perceived that a great number of people in many of the towns of Greece and Italy had already been infected by this disease, and because he heard, I suppose, that even the tombs of Peter and Paul were being worshipped[2]—secretly, it is true, but still he did hear this,—he, I say, was the first to venture to call Jesus God.

AN ANONYMOUS HELLENE

[An Attack on Paul] (late fourth century?)‡

[Acts 16.3]

How is it that Paul says, "Being free, I have made myself the slave of all so that I might win all" [1 Cor. 9.19]; how, even though he called circum-

---

1. Julian alludes here to a widespread maxim concerning adaptability (cf. 1 Cor. 9:19–23) that goes back to the archaic poetry of the Theognidea (215–216). He refers to it again in *Mis.* 349d.
2. Rom. 3:29.
3. Ps. 78:25, LXX.
† From *Against the Galileans* 327a–b, trans. by Wright, 3:413.
1. See the notes on Rom. 9:5 and Tit. 2:11–14.
2. Julian elsewhere lambastes Christian veneration of the relics of the martyrs (335b–c), which pagans often equated with worship (Eunapius, *VS* 472).
‡ From excerpts in Macarius Magnes' *Monogenes* (= *Apocriticus* or *Response*) 3.30–36, trans. by R. Joseph Hoffmann, *Porphyry's Against the Christians: The Literary Remains* (Amherst: Prometheus Books, 1994), 58–65. Copyright © R. Joseph Hoffmann. Reprinted by permission. Macarius'

cision "mutilation,"[1] he nevertheless circumcised a certain man named Timothy, as the Acts of the Apostles [16.3] instructs us. Ah! the asinine nature of all this. Such scenes are used in the theater in order to get a laugh. Jugglers give exhibitions like this! For how can a free man be everyone's slave?

How can someone so dependent as this gain anything? If he is an outlaw among the lawless who goes about with Jews as a Jew and with others as he pleases,[2] then his slavery was service to his corruptness of nature, and he was a stranger to freedom. He is actually a slave and minister to the wrong-doing of others; he is an advocate of unhealthy things[3] if he regularly squanders himself in serving people who have no law or accepts their actions as being the same as his own.

These are not the teachings of a healthy mind. This is not [the teaching] of unimpaired reason. The words indeed suggest someone who is mentally feeble and deficient in reasoning powers. And if he lives among the lawless yet accepts the religion of the Jews with an open heart, taking [as it were] a piece from each, then he is confused by each. He participates in their worst shortcomings and makes himself everyone's companion.

Anyone who makes circumcision the dividing line between believers and outsiders and then performs the ritual himself is his own worst accuser—as he says himself: "If I build again the things that I tore down, I make myself a transgressor."[4]

[Acts 22.3; Acts 22.27–9]

Paul also seems to forget himself frequently, as when he tells the captain of the guard that he is not a Jew but a Roman, even though he had said on another occasion, "I am a Jew, born in Tarsus of Cilicia and raised up at the feet of Gamaliel, educated in accordance with the strict manner of

---

treatise answers pagan objections to Christianity and its Scriptures; the work he excerpts is the most extensive extant attack on Paul by a pagan critic. The title of Hoffmann's book reflects his view that Porphyry was its author. If Macarius is indeed the individual who served as the Bishop of Magnesia, the work was likely written in Asia Minor during the last quarter of the fourth century; if not, an earlier or later date is possible. The work contains a dialogue between an anonymous Greek philosopher-orator and a Christian apologist that ostensibly takes place over five days. The debate itself is almost certainly a fiction, with the philosopher a literary construct whose objections are gleaned from the work or works of critics such as Porphyry, Hierocles, and Julian, or possibly from an anthology of pagan objections or even a Christian treatise against one or more of these critics (such as Apollinarius' treatise against Porphyry). Whatever his source(s) may have been, Macarius has reworked them, as the linguistic similarities between the objections and the answers demonstrate.

In the portions of the critique not included here, the Hellene maintained that Paul not only condemned Peter in Gal. 2:11–13 but also included him in his denunciation of "false apostles" and "deceitful workers" in 2 Cor. 11:13 (3.22). Paul's apocalyptic statement that "this world in its present form is passing away" (1 Cor. 7:31) utterly contradicted the Hellene's Neoplatonic assumption that the universe was indestructible, and the latter argued that any change to the world, even for the better, could only imply that its Creator (Demiurge) had not created it perfectly at the outset (4.1). Similarly, he saw Paul's statement about people being caught up into the air in 1 Thess. 4:15–17 as a blatant lie that had been revealed as such by the passage of time since Paul wrote (4.2). Paul had not been caught up into the air but executed in Rome, which the Hellene thought contradicted the promise of protection that Paul had received in Acts 18:9–10 (4.4). Finally, he viewed Paul's understanding of Christian baptism (1 Cor. 6:11) as one that would encourage people to sin (4.19; cf. Rom. 3:8; 6:1–23). In attacking Paul, the Hellene showed himself to be as much an orator as a philosopher, making full use of all the rhetorical means at his disposal, especially vituperation.

1. Phil. 3:2.
2. Cf. 1 Cor. 9:20–22.
3. Whereas the Pastoral Epistles use medical imagery to attack heretics, the Hellene uses it to attack Paul. See 2 Tim. 2:17 and the note on 1 Tim. 1:10.
4. Gal. 2:18

the law of our fathers." * * * But anyone saying [both] "I am a Jew" and "I am a Roman" is neither, even if he would like to be.

The man who hypocritically pretends to be what he is not makes himself a liar in everything that he does. He disguises himself in a mask. He cheats those who are entitled to hear the truth. He assaults the soul's comprehension by various tactics, and like any charlatan he wins the gullible over to his side.

Whoever accepts such principles as a guide for living cannot but be regarded as an enemy of the worst kind—the kind who brings others to submission by lying to them, who reaches out to make captives of everyone within earshot with his deceitful ways. And if, therefore, this Paul is a Jew one minute and the next a Roman, [or a student] of the [Jewish] law now, but at another time [an enemy of the law]—if, in short, Paul can be an enemy to each whenever he likes by burglarizing each, then clearly he nullifies the usefulness of each [tradition] for he limits their worthwhile distinctions with his flattery.

We may conclude that [Paul] is a liar. He is the adopted brother of everything false, so that it is useless for him to declaim, "I speak the truth in Christ, I do not lie" [Rom. 9.1]; for a man who one day uses the law as his rule and the next day uses the gospel is either a knave or a fool in what he does in the sight of others and even when hidden away by himself.

[1 Cor. 9.7]

[Paul] also misrepresents the gospel as his conceit requires, and uses the law for his own benefit: "Who serves as a soldier at his own expense, or who tends a herd without getting some of the milk?" And to get his portion, Paul invokes the law in support of his greed when he says, "Does not the law say the same, for it is written in the law of Moses, 'You shall not muzzle an ox when it is treading out the grain' " [1 Cor. 9.9].

He adds next a piece of foolishness designed to limit God's providence to humanity and to deprive animals of the divine care: "Does God care about the oxen? Does he not speak entirely for our sake? It was written for our sake" [1 Cor. 9.10]. When he says such things, I think he makes the creator—who ages ago brought these [creatures] into being—look ridiculous, as though he had no concern [for his own creation].

For if it is true that God cares nothing for the oxen, why does scripture record, "He has made all things, sheep and oxen and beasts and birds and fishes, subject to him" [Ps. 8.8–9]. If [God] is concerned for fishes, then he must be all the more concerned for the toil of oxen! I am astonished at this man's pious regard for the law, since it is occasioned by his need to get donations from those who listen to his words.

[Rom. 7.12, 14]

Paul next turns around like a man startled awake by a nightmare, screaming, "I, Paul, testify that if a man keeps any bit of the law then he is indebted to the whole law." [Gal. 5.3, paraphrased; cf. James 2.10]. He says this rather than simply asserting that it is wrong to keep the commandments set down in the law.

A man whose intellectual powers are worthy of admiration—one instructed in the specifics of the law of his fathers, one who frequently invokes the authority of Moses—is also one, it seems, so sotted with wine that his wits have abandoned him. Does [Paul] not erase the law for the sake of the Galatians when he says, "Who bewitched you? How is it that you do not obey the truth," which is the gospel [Gal. 3.1]? And as if to press the point and make it an offense for anyone to heed the law he says, "Those who are under the law are under a curse" [Gal 3.10].

The same man who writes, "The law is spiritual" to the Romans, and "The law is holy and the commandment holy and just" now puts a curse upon those who obey what is holy! Then, as if to confuse the point further, he turns everything around and throws up a fog so dense that anyone trying to follow him inevitably gets lost, bumping up against the gospel on the one side, against the law on the other, stumbling over the law and tripping over the gospel—all because the guide who leads them by the hand has no idea where he is headed!

[Rom. 5.20]

Look again at this charlatan's record. Following any number of references to the law which he used to find support [for his case], he nullifies his argument by saying "The law entered so that the offense might increase" and previous to this, "The goad of death is sin and the power of sin is the law" [1 Cor. 15.56].

With a tongue sharp as a sword, [Paul] mercilessly cuts the law into little pieces. But this is [nevertheless] the man who tends to keep the law and finds it virtuous to obey its commandments. By clinging to inconsistency, as he does apparently by habit, he overturns his judgments in all other cases.

[1 Cor. 10.20–26; 8.4, 8]

Further, when Paul talks about eating what has been sacrificed to idols, his advice is essentially that it's all indifferent:[5] [he tells his inquirers] not to ask too many questions, and that even though something has been a sacrifice to an idol, it can be eaten—just as long as no one tells them about it in advance! He says, in effect, "What they sacrifice they sacrifice to demons and I would not wish you to associate with demons."

But then he says, with indifference as to their dietary habits, "We know that an idol is nothing real, and that there is no God but one." Still later, "Food will not endear us to God: we are no worse off if we do not eat, and no better off if we do." Then following this prattle, [Paul] mutters like a man on his deathbed, "Eat whatever's sold in the meatmarket without raising questions on the basis of conscience, for the earth is the Lord's and everything in it."

How ridiculous this farce, based on nothing but the unparalleled inconsistency of his rantings! His sayings undercut each other as if by a sword. O brave new archery! that makes a target of the man who draws the bow!

[1 Tim. 4.1; 1 Cor. 7.25]

In letters written by him [Paul] gives us to believe that virginity is to be praised. Then he turns around and says, "In these last days some will

---

5. *Adiaphoron*, a Stoic term used of actions that are morally neutral, neither virtuous nor vicious.

depart from the faith and will find themselves swayed by seducing spirits who forbid them to marry and command them to abstain from meat" [1 Tim 4.1, 3]. But then, in his letter to the Corinthians, he says, "But with regard to virgins I have no commandment of the Lord."

Thus, anyone who remains single is not doing the right thing—and anyone who refrains from marriage as though it were evil is not acting in accordance with [the commandments of Jesus], since there is no record of Jesus' words concerning virginity. What about those people who brag of being virgins as if they were singled out to be filled with the holy spirit, as was the mother of Jesus?

Valentinus and the Gnostic Paul

The enemies of Paul were much less of a problem for the emerging catholic consensus than were some of his friends. In the second century and even later several of the movements that claimed most enthusiastically to be Paul's true interpreters were very far out of that stream of Christianity that would succeed in the contest for dominance and therefore gain the crown of "orthodoxy." The distinction between heresy and orthodoxy, always very relative, was very fluid in the first four centuries of Christianity. Many differing groups appealed to "apostolic" origins, to special oral traditions allegedly stemming from the apostles, to true interpretation of the scriptures. If for nothing else than the bulk of his writings and the notoriety of his missionary efforts, Paul was named *the* apostle in groups that differed radically from one another in their interpretation of his teachings. Indeed, Tertullian once referred to Paul as "the apostle of the heretics" (*haereticorum apostolus*) because of his opponents' fondness for him and their frequent appeal to his writings in support of their theology (*Marc.* 3.5.4).

The very same things that made Paul abhorrent for the Jewish Christians may have evoked the special sympathy for Paul that existed among certain of the Christian Gnostic groups. For Gnosticism exhibits an almost schizophrenic relationship to Judaism. Frequently engaged, sometimes obsessed, with the Jewish scriptures and traditions, yet it despises the Jewish God and his world.[1] Paul, the ex-Pharisee who uses the law against legalism, naturally held a peculiar fascination for them. His understanding of the Christian gospel, like that of all Gnostics, concentrated on the question of human redemption. His sharp dichotomies between works and faith, flesh and spirit, his emphasis on freedom, his use of traditional myths to depict a heavenly Christ who comes down to take the "form of a human being," his talk of "inexpressible mysteries," his asceticism—all these points, if taken out of Paul's basically Jewish context and placed into an anticosmic dualism, were fertile soil for Gnostic mythmaking.[2]

1. On the "metaphysical anti-Semitism" of Gnosticism, see Hans Jonas, "Response to G. Quispel's 'Gnosticism and the New Testament,' " in *The Bible in Modern Scholarship*, ed. by Philip Hyatt (Nashville: Abingdon, 1965), 286–93, and "Delimitation of the Gnostic Phenomenon—Typological and Historical," *The Origins of Gnosticism*, ed. by Ugo Bianchi (Leiden: Brill, 1967), 100–3. Jewish traditions are particularly prominent in Sethian Gnosticism, on which see Bentley Layton (ed.), *The Rediscovery of Gnosticism*, vol. 2: *Sethian Gnosticism* (Leiden: Brill, 1981). It is important to remember that "Gnosticism" is a modern word, coined in the seventeenth century, and applied by modern scholars to a variety of phenomena in antiquity. "Gnostic," on the other hand, was a technical philosophical term coined by Plato and widely used in later philosophical circles, but never used of persons. Sometime in the second century CE a group of Christians began calling themselves "the Gnostics" [*gnōstikoi*], "the Knowing Ones." On these developments, see especially Bentley Layton, "Prolegomena to the Study of Ancient Gnosticism," in *The Social World of the First Christians: Essays in Honor of Wayne A. Meeks*, ed. by L. Michael White and O. Larry Yarbrough (Minneapolis: Fortress Press, 1995), 336–52, and, at greater length, Karen L. King, *What Is Gnosticism?* (Cambridge, MA; London: Harvard University Press, 2003). See also Kurt Rudolph, *Gnosis: The Nature and History of Gnosticism* (ed. and trans. by R. M. Wilson; San Francisco: Harper & Row, 1983), and Christoph Markschies, *Gnosis: An Introduction* (London; New York: T & T Clark, 2003).
2. Eva Aleith, *Paulusverständnis in der alten Kirche* (Berlin: Töpelmann, 1937), 39–49. This is not the place to pursue the question of influence in the opposite direction, i.e., whether there were predecessors or early forms of the Gnostic movements older than Christianity, which may have influenced Paul himself, as well as the Hellenistic Christianity before and alongside him. An affirmative answer to this question was a major working hypothesis of Rudolf Bultmann and of all

Valentinus (fl. 120–160), perhaps the most creative of the individual Gnostic teachers known to us by name, claimed, according to Clement of Alexandria,[3] that his teacher Theodas had been a personal disciple of Paul. Passages from the Pauline letters are frequently employed in Gnostic allegory, not least in the horde of documents found near Nag Hammadi, Egypt, in 1945, many of which are, at least in the broad sense, Gnostic.[4] The excerpt below from Theodotus illustrates the special place Paul held for some Valentinians. The essay by Elaine Pagels provides a brief overview of how Valentinus and his followers interpreted Paul's letters. It is followed by Irenaeus' reaction to their exegesis of Scripture.[5]

THEODOTUS

[Paul as Paraclete] (second century)†

The followers of Valentinus say that Jesus is the Paraclete,[1] because he has come full of the Aeons, having come forth from the whole. For Christ left behind Sophia, who had put him forth, and going into the Pleroma, asked for help for Sophia, who was left outside; and Jesus was put forth by the good will of the Aeons as a Paraclete for the Aeon which had passed. In the type of the Paraclete, Paul became the Apostle of the Resurrection. Immediately after the Lord's Passion he also was sent to preach.[2] Therefore he preached the Saviour from both points of view: as begotten and passible for the sake of those on the left, because, being able to know him, they are afraid of him in this position, and in spiritual wise from the Holy Spirit and a virgin, as the angels on the right know him. For each one knows the Lord after his own fashion, and not all in the same way.[3]

---

the continental and American scholars who were heavily influenced by him: see below, pp. 593–603. Serious objections have been raised, especially to a tendency to perceive "the Gnostic religion" as a unitary movement: see e.g., Carsten Colpe, *Die religionsgeschichtliche Schule* (Göttingen: Vandenhoeck & Ruprecht, 1961); A. D. Nock, "Gnosticism," *HTR* 57 (1964): 255–79. Still, while important qualifications are necessary, the hypothesis of a "pre-Christian gnosis" or "incipient gnosticism" is still regarded by many specialists as a necessary one. See the attempts at definition of "gnosis" and "Gnosticism" by the Messina Colloquy on *The Origins of Gnosticism* (n. 1 above).

3. *Strom.* 7.17.106f. Many scholars believe that Valentinus is the author of the *Gospel of Truth*, one of the most important treatises from Nag Hammadi. It contains allusions to at least five letters in the Pauline corpus.

4. See esp. Bentley Layton (ed. and trans.), *The Gnostic Scriptures* (Garden City: Doubleday, 1987), and J. M. Robinson (ed.), *The Nag Hammadi Library in English* (3rd ed.; San Francisco: HarperCollins, 1988).

5. See also the discussion of Gnostic Paulinism by David Rensberger on pp. 341–41.

† Tr. by R. P. Casey, *The Excerpta ex Theodoto of Clement of Alexandria* (London: Christophers, 1934), *exc.* 23. Theodotus was a follower of Valentinus. Extracts from his writings are preserved among the works of Clement of Alexandria, who sometimes summarizes Theodotus' words instead of quoting them.

1. The Greek *paraklētos* refers to a helper, especially in a legal context; e.g., an advocate or defense attorney. The term is important in the Johannine literature: John 14:16, 26; 15:26; 16:7; 1 John 2:1.

2. Since Theodotus places Paul's commission right after the resurrection, there is no reference to Paul as persecutor.

3. Paul thus preaches two different messages, one for the psychics and another for the pneumatics. The angels are also mentioned in *exc.* 22, where they are identified as those who are baptized for the dead (1 Cor. 15:29).

ELAINE H. PAGELS

The Gnostic Paul (1975)†

Whoever knows contemporary New Testament scholarship knows Paul as the opponent of gnostic heresy. Paul writes his letters, especially the Corinthian and Philippian correspondence, to attack gnosticism and to refute the claims of gnostic Christians to "secret wisdom"—so Schmithals declares in his recent studies (*Gnosticism in Corinth*, 1971; *Paul and the Gnostics*, 1972). Paul preaches the kerygma of "Christ crucified" (1 Cor. 2:2), warns of the coming judgment, proclaims the resurrection of the body, insists on the priority of love over gnosis; in all these he demonstrates his "genuinely Christian attitude" over against his gnostic opponents. Bultmann (*Theology of the New Testament*, 1947) has explained that "to Paul, the apostles who have kindled a pneumatic-gnostic movement in Corinth are interlopers . . . it is perfectly clear that to the church they have the status of Christian apostles, but to Paul they are 'ministers of Satan' disguising themselves as apostles of Christ" (2 Cor. 11:13) Bornkamm (*Paul*, 1969) says that Paul, much like Luther, regards the "spirit-filled people" as "fanatics," the "really dangerous element" he confronts in his churches. The apostle himself, Bornkamm adds, "utterly repudiates" the secret wisdom and gnosis they teach.

Yet if this view of Paul is accurate, the Pauline exegesis of second-century gnostics is nothing less than astonishing. Gnostic writers not only fail to grasp the whole point of Paul's writings, but they dare to claim his letters as a primary source of *gnostic* theology. Instead of repudiating Paul as their most obstinate opponent, the Naassenes and Valentinians revere him as the one of the apostles who—above all others—was himself a gnostic initiate. The Valentinians, in particular, allege that their secret tradition offers direct access to Paul's *own* teaching of wisdom and gnosis. According to Clement, "they say that Valentinus was a hearer of Theudas, and Theudas, in turn, a disciple of Paul." When Valentinus' disciple Ptolemy tells Flora of "apostolic tradition" that "we too have received from succession," he refers, apparently, to this secret tradition about the savior received through Paul. Valentinus himself often alludes to Paul (in the extant fragments, and very often in the Gospel of Truth, if, as H. Ch. Puech and G. Quispel suggest, Valentinus is its author) his disciples Ptolemy, Heracleon, and Theodotus—no less than Irenaeus, Tertullian, and Clement—revere Paul and quote him simply as "the apostle."

Texts now becoming available from Nag Hammadi offer extraordinary new evidence for *gnostic* Pauline tradition.

* * *

Previous studies of Valentinian hermeneutics, lacking these resources, have relied primarily on the heresiological accounts. G. Henrici (*Die Valentinianische Gnosis und die heilige Schrift*, 1871) concludes from his analysis that although the Valentinians "attempt to place gnosis on biblical

† From *The Gnostic Paul* (Philadelphia: Fortress, 1975; rep. Philadelphia: Trinity Press International, 1992). Copyright © 1975 by Elaine Pagels. Reprinted by permission of Trinity Press International. Pagels is the Harrington Spear Paine Foundation Professor of Religion at Princeton University.

soil" they fail to reckon seriously with scripture as the primary source of revelation. Gnosis itself, and not scripture, remains their primary hermeneutical presupposition. C. Barth (*Die Interpretation des NT in der Valentinianischen Gnosis*, 1911) concludes that "the basic concepts of Valentinian teaching, as of any gnosis, clearly were older than Christianity itself. . . . The Christian element in it was only the most recent powerful element that was introduced into the synthesis. . . . Powerful conflicts and contradictions between gnosis and the NT writers were—in view of the unbiblical origin of the teaching—unavoidable." N. Brox and H. Jonas basically concur with Henrici that gnosis itself serves the gnostics as their hermeneutical principle.

Examination of the newly available resources, however, places both the heresiological accounts and the research based upon them into a different perspective. It suggests that the scholars cited above, besides taking *information* from the heresiologists, also have adopted from them certain value judgments and interpretations of the gnostic material. Each of these scholars, for example, accepts Irenaeus' observation that the gnostics base their exegesis upon unwritten sources—sources not contained in the scriptures themselves. Each of them also accepts, apparently, Irenaeus' judgment that these secret sources, however conceived, are alien to the NT and hence to "authentically Christian" tradition. Henrici, Barth, and Brox, consequently, share the conviction of Irenaeus, Tertullian, and Hippolytus: namely, that gnostic exegesis of Paul's letters projects a pre-Christian (or non-Christian) mythological system into Paul's writings.

Yet Irenaeus himself admits that the Valentinians not only reject the charge of false exegesis, but go on to criticize their opponents on two counts. First, they accuse the "orthodox" of using source materials uncritically; second, of being ignorant of the secret traditions which alone offer the true interpretation of the scriptures. Above all, the Valentinians insist that their own unwritten sources are nothing less than Paul's own secret wisdom tradition—the key to hermeneutical understanding. Irenaeus notes that when they are refuted from the scriptures:

> They turn and accuse these same scriptures as if they were not accurate nor authoritative, and claim that they are ambiguous, and that truth cannot be derived from them by those who are ignorant of tradition. For they allege that truth was not transmitted by means of written documents, but in living speech; and that for this reason Paul declares, "we speak wisdom among the perfect (*telioi*) but not the wisdom of this cosmos" (1 Cor. 2:6).

Irenaeus and Tertullian consider the Valentinian view an insult to Paul. Characterizing their own struggle against the gnostics as that of true exegesis against false, they insist that the gnostic method totally distorts the apostle's meaning. Irenaeus says that he recounts their exegesis only "to demonstrate the method which they use to deceive themselves, abusing the scriptures, trying to support from them their own invention (*plasma*)." Tertullian agrees with Irenaeus that the gnostics practice false exegesis, yet he acknowledges that they defend themselves with Paul's own injunction to "test all things" (1 Thess. 5:21). He accuses them of "taking his words in their own way" when they cite such passages as 1 Cor. 11:19 ("there must be heresies among you, so that those who are approved may be revealed among you"). Tertullian

himself, having debated such issues with self-professed "Pauline" Christians, agrees with the author of 2 Peter that certain "unlearned and
unstable" brethren have "distorted" the letters of "our beloved brother
Paul" (2 Pet. 3:16–17).

Tertullian and Irenaeus both attest that these controversies over Pauline
exegesis extended to controversies over Pauline authorship. Both accuse
the Valentinians of arbitrarily selecting certain texts and rejecting others.
Noting that the heretics have dared to impugn the validity of the Pastoral
Letters, Tertullian insists that the "same Paul" who wrote Galatians also
wrote Titus. Irenaeus, strikingly, opens his great treatise claiming "the
apostle's" authority to oppose the gnostics—citing 1 Tim. 1:4 and Tit. 3:9
from the Pastoral Letters.

When we compare the heresiological accounts with the newly available
evidence, we can trace how two antithetical traditions of Pauline exegesis
have emerged from the late first century through the second. Each claims
to be authentic, Christian, and Pauline: but one reads Paul *antignostically*,
the other *gnostically*. Correspondingly, we discover two conflicting images
of Paul: on the one hand, the antignostic Paul familiar from church tradition, and, on the other, the gnostic Paul, teacher of wisdom to gnostic
initiates!

The Pastoral Letters take up the former tradition, interpreting Paul as
the antagonist of "false teachers" who "set forth myths and endless genealogies" seducing the gullible with the lure of "falsely so-called gnosis."
Irenaeus and Tertullian continue this tradition. Assuming the authenticity
of the Pastorals (both in terms of authorship and of interpretation of Paul
as antignostic polemicist), they claim Paul as their ally against the gnostics.
Valentinian exegetes, adhering to the latter tradition, either bypass or
reject the Pastorals, and cite as Pauline only the following: Romans, 1–2
Corinthians, Galatians, Ephesians, Philippians, Colossians, 1 Thessalonians, and Hebrews (a list that corresponds exactly to the earliest known
Pauline collection attested from Alexandria). These exegetes offer to teach
the same secret wisdom that Paul taught "to the initiates": evidence of
their exegesis occurs in such texts as the Epistle to Rheginos, the Prayer
of the Apostle Paul, and The Interpretation of the Gnosis.

How can gnostic exegetes and theologians make this astonishing claim?
Theodotus explains that Paul, having become "the apostle of the resurrection" through his experience of revelation, henceforth "taught in two ways
at once." On the one hand he preached the savior "according to the flesh"
as one "who was born and suffered," the kerygmatic gospel of "Christ crucified" (1 Cor. 2:2) to those who were psychics, "because this they were
capable of knowing, and in this way they feared him." But to the elect he
proclaimed Christ "according to the spirit, as one born from the spirit and
a virgin" (cf. Rom. 1:3) for the apostle recognized that "each one knows
the Lord in his own way: and not all know him alike."

Paul communicated his pneumatic teaching to his disciple Theudas, and
Theudas, in turn, to Valentinus; and Valentinus to his own initiated disciples (cf. 1 Cor. 2:6). In this way the Valentinians identify Paul himself
as the source of their own esoteric tradition: only those who have received
initiation into this secret, oral tradition are capable of understanding the
true meaning of the scriptures—which include Paul's own letters. Irenaeus' statement that the Valentinians derive their insights "from unwritten

sources" may refer not to a generalized gnosis or gnostic myth but to an allegedly Pauline doctrine of the "mystery of Sophia" (cf. 1 Cor. 2:6) which may have included the myth of Sophia's fall and redemption.

The Valentinians claim that most Christians make the mistake of reading the scriptures only literally. They themselves, through their initiation into gnosis, learn to read his letters (as they read all the scriptures) on the *symbolic* level, as they say Paul intended. Only this pneumatic reading yields "the truth" instead of its mere outward "image."

The Valentinians agree with other Christians, for example, that Paul intends in Romans to contrast that salvation effected "by works," "according to the law," with the redemption that the elect receive "by grace." But most Christians read the letter only in terms of the outward image—in terms of the contrast between the revelation to the Jews and the revelation extended through Christ to the Gentiles. They fail to see what Paul himself clearly states in Rom. 2:28f, that the terms ("Jew/Gentile") are not to be taken literally:

> He is not a Jew, who is one outwardly, nor is circumcision what is outward in the flesh; (but) he is a Jew who is one inwardly, and circumcision is of the heart, pneumatic, not literal.

The Valentinians take this passage as Paul's injunction to symbolic exegesis. While on the literal level he discusses the relation of Jews to Gentiles, simultaneously he intends his words to be read on a pneumatic (that is, symbolic) level. According to such exegesis, Paul's discussion of Jews and Gentiles in Romans refers allegorically to different groups of Christians—to *psychic* and *pneumatic* Christians respectively.

Practice of such exegesis enables the Valentinians to interpret Paul's letters in an entirely new way. They consider the "literal" question of the relation between Jews and Gentiles to be already (c. 140–160) a dated issue, limited to a specific historical and cultural situation. What concerns them in the present is a different issue: how they themselves, as pneumatic Christians initiated into the secret mysteries of Christ, are related to the mass of "simple-minded," "foolish" believers. They perceive that this problem (i.e., the relation of the "few" to the "many," the "chosen" to the "called") has characterized Christian communities from the first—from the time when the savior chose to initiate only a few into the secret meaning of his parables, and deliberately let them remain obscure "to those outside" (Mk. 4:11). They conclude that it is this perennial problem (i.e., the relation of the "chosen few," the elect, to the "many psychics" who are "called") that Paul intends to expound in his letter to the Romans.

Yet Paul, like the savior himself, chooses not to disclose his theme openly. Instead he follows Christ's example and hides his meaning in parables. In writing his letter to the Romans for example, he uses a simple, everyday situation—the relationship between Jews and Gentiles—*as a parable* for the relation between the *called* and the *elect*, between psychic and pneumatic Christians.

Valentinian exegetes attempt systematically to disclose to the initiate the hidden "logos" of Paul's teaching, separating it from the metaphors that serve to conceal it from uninitiated readers. For as Paul indicates in Rom. 2:28, those called "Jews inwardly," "Jews in secret," the "true Israel" are (Theodotus says) the pneumatic elect. They alone worship the "one God"

(Rom. 3:29), the Unengendered Father. But because their affinity with the Father is hidden, a secret from those who are "Jews outwardly" (the psychics) and from the demiurgic god ("the god of the Jews," Rom. 3:29), Paul more often calls the elect in his parable the "uncircumcised," the "Gentiles," or "the Greeks."

The initiated reader could recognize Paul's meaning when he proclaims himself "apostle to the Gentiles" (Rom. 1:5). The Valentinians note how Paul contrasts his own mission to the pneumatic Gentiles with Peter's mission to the psychic Jews (Gal. 2:7). Paul says that he, as apostle to the Gentiles, longs to share with them his "pneumatic charisma" (Rom. 1:11), but acknowledges his obligation "both to the Greeks and to the barbarians," that is, as he says, both "to the wise (*pneumatics*) and to the foolish (*psychics*)" (Rom. 1:14).

This sense of dual responsibility, the Valentinians infer, impels Paul to write his letters, as he preaches, "in two ways at once." As he proclaims the savior to psychics in terms they can grasp, so he addresses to them the outward, obvious message of his letters. But to the initiates, who discern "the truth" hidden there in "images," he directs his deeper communication: they alone interpret pneumatically what psychics read only literally.

*   *   *

Investigation of gnostic exegesis discloses traces of the process whereby Paul became known in the second century as the "apostle of the heretics." Irenaeus, Tertullian, Hippolytus, and Origen, through the energy they devote to its refutation, pay unwilling tribute to the power and appeal of such Valentinian appropriation of Paul. Irenaeus deplores the fact that many bishops and deacons themselves have become convinced by Valentinian propaganda; Tertullian admits that some of the most faithful and outstanding members of his community ("even bishops, deacons, widows, and martyrs") have sought initiation into the Valentinian circle. Both consider the Valentinians far more insidious than the Marcionites or any others who openly criticize the church. For, as Irenaeus says, "outwardly such persons seem to be sheep, for they appear to be like us, from what they say in public, repeating the same words (of confession) as we do; but inwardly, they are wolves." While insisting that they accept and agree with the whole of church confession and doctrine, privately they offer to remedy the "deficiencies" of that faith through their own "apostolic tradition." Irenaeus expresses outrage that they claim Paul's own authority for their violations and contradictions of church doctrine and proceed to defend their views through arguments from scripture!

Analysis of gnostic exegesis indicates, indeed, how "wiley and deceptive" Irenaeus must have found these heretics who reply to ecclesiastical critics with exegeses that even Irenaeus admits sound plausible, and who defend their practices by citing Paul's example. The heresiologists recognize, for example, the obvious allure that the promise of hearing "hidden mysteries" exerts over the curious. Tertullian compares the Valentinian initiation to the Eleusinian: both, he says, prolong the process in order to arouse the candidate to a state of suspenseful anticipation for what follows; both flatter and fascinate the naive with their invitation to join the inner circle of those "in the know." Nevertheless, what Irenaeus and Tertullian denounce as a manipulative technique undoubtedly appears quite different to the

Valentinians themselves. They can claim both the Lord himself (cf. Mark 4) and the apostle Paul as examples of those who recognize that only a few select members of their audience were ready to receive the "wisdom of God hidden in a mystery."

The Valentinians also invoke Paul's example to defend a second element of their teaching that Irenaeus condemns: the gnostic offer of liberation from specific restrictions on their conduct. Irenaeus complains that Valentinian Christians ignore what he himself, as bishop of the Lyons community, considers to be minimal standards of practice incumbent upon all believers: namely, to abstain from eating meat offered to idols, to avoid public feasts and entertainments, and to abhor deviation from monogamy in matters of sexual behavior. These Valentinians (and other gnostic Christians) interpret their own freedom not as libertine but as libertarian, exemplifying the liberty of those who "have gnosis," who are "strong"; the liberty of the pneumatics who, like Paul, celebrate their release from the curse of the law.

When Irenaeus and Tertullian charge that the Valentinians resist church discipline, the latter could reply that they, like Paul, acknowledge only the authority of "the pneumatics" among them. Accused of undermining church sacraments by offering in addition the sacrament of apolytrosis, they could reply that the apostle himself not only endorses their practice, but has himself taught the sacrament that echoes liturgically his own words. Even the psychic Christians, they say, acknowledge unwittingly the aions above as they recite the eucharistic liturgy.

Heresiologists and gnostics both acknowledge that the Valentinians' greatest appeal (or greatest deception, depending on one's viewpoint) lies in their theological teaching. Heracleon describes how the person gifted with pneumatic nature finds ecclesiastical teaching to be "unnourishing, stagnant" water, inadequate to satisfy spirtual thirst; the pneumatic must discover through gnosis the "living water" Christ offers to the elect. Ptolemy apparently considers Flora to be such a person, a believer frustrated by seeming contradictions in scripture: he offers her a new hermeneutical framework to resolve these contradictions, and encourages her to seek further theological enlightenment from esoteric "apostolic tradition." Origen realizes that his friend and student Ambrose became a Valentinian initiate out of genuine concern to understand the "deeper mysteries" of scripture.

The Valentinians offer such seekers of enlightenment an explanation for their condition. Such persons, they say, need to recognize that they are among the elect, of pneumatic nature, and thus are impelled by the spirit to seek the "deep things of God." Those so gifted could not be satisfied with the teaching Jesus offers "to those outside" or with the doctrine that Paul admits he directs to those who are "still sarkic," and who remain incapable of receiving the "wisdom hidden in a mystery" that he would prefer to offer them. This "hidden wisdom," which apparently relates the myth of Sophia, reveals the secret of their election through grace, and teaches the "deeper interpretation" of the scriptures.

So, while the author of 2 Peter warns that "the ignorant and unstable" distort Paul's wisdom, teaching as they do the "other scriptures" (3:16), Valentinian exegetes read in Galatians Paul's proclamation of his independence of Peter. They infer that, since Paul declares that he received his

gospel neither "from men nor through man" (Gal. 1:1; 1:12), certainly he
did not receive it from Peter or the Jerusalem apostles, who remained
"under the influence of Jewish opinions." Instead he received it from Jesus
Christ and from God the Father (1:1) "through revelation" (1:12) that
liberates the elect from the demiurgic law binding upon "the Jews." In
Romans the Valentinians read how God's elect are justified "by faith, apart
from works" (3:28). Nevertheless, they claim to recognize in chapter 9 his
concern for [the situation of those not included among the elect, i.e., for
the psychics]. For although the Father elects only "a remnant" from Israel,
he has not rejected the rest of the Jews: the apostle discloses that their
present "hardness," their blindness to his purpose, contains a mystery to
be resolved only when "all Israel" (the totality of the psychics who are
saved) shall be raised and joined with the "Gentiles" (11:5–26).

The Valentinian reader sees in 1 Corinthians how Paul contrasts the
secret wisdom teaching he discloses "to the initiates" with the "foolishness
of the kerygma" that he offers to psychic believers (2:6–3:4). In 1 Corinthians 7 Valentinian exegetes see Paul's "veiled" discussion of human conjunction in marriage. This, they claim, suggests a double signification: first,
the conjunction of Christ with his elect, celebrated in the apolytrosis sacrament; second, the relation of the elect with psychic believers, the "marriage in the cosmos," which the elect enact in the baptism they perform
"for the dead" (psychics). Finally, they continue, Paul reveals in 1 Corinthians 15 the "mystery of the resurrection," disclosing that those who are
"dead" shall be raised, the psychic transformed and changed, so that "God
shall be all in all."

For the duration of the present age, however, they consider that Paul
counsels those who, like himself, have gnosis to modify their expression
of pneumatic freedom for the sake of "the weak" (Romans 14–15; 1 Cor.
2:15, 8, 9). In Philippians he urges the elect to "become as I am" (Phil. 3:
17), indeed, to become like Christ, who voluntarily yielded up his divine
prerogatives in order to "take on the form of a slave," the "likeness of
human form" (2:6–8). In Ephesians and Colossians the Valentinians see
Paul's praise for the pneumatic Christ, who heads the whole body of his
ecclesia: this is the "mystery revealed among the Gentiles," which the elect
recognize as "Christ in us" (1:27). Finally, the Valentinians claim to discern
in Hebrews Paul's contrast between Moses, the demiurgic "servant" and
Levitical priests who worship him "in the outer tent, which is a parable of
the present age," that is, the psychics, and the pneumatic elect who worship God "spiritually" in the holy of holies. In this epistle "the apostle"
urges those who are enlightened to leave behind them the "elementary
doctrines" and to go on to attain the initiation (teleiōsis) offered to those
who are pneumatic (Heb. 6:1–6).

As we learn to recognize basic patterns and themes of Valentinian exegesis, simultaneously we can appreciate more clearly the danger they presented to those in the church who were attempting to unite the Christian
communities and to consolidate them against the threat of political persecution. Certainly Irenaeus considers them as men whom Satan inspired
to divide the church internally. He condemns their teaching on election
as one that effectively splits the church into factions, encouraging arrogance and contempt among the initiates, and evoking envy, resentment,

or false admiration from those excluded from their circle. So long as their presence is tolerated, Irenaeus warns, they incite confusion and controversy; they call into question the authority of church leaders, and disturb the faith of simple believers. They raise doubts, for example, concerning the efficacy of the sacraments, causing many to wonder whether the baptism they received is, after all, genuinely efficacious, or whether it is only a preparation for the "higher" sacrament of apolytrosis.

* * *

What perspectives can such analysis offer—if any—on the question of Paul's own relation to gnostics? Much of the discussion, as B. Pearson notes, has focused on alledgedly "gnostic terminology" in Paul's letters. How are we to account for this?

R. Reitzenstein, observing parallels between Paul's terminology and that of the second-century gnostics, has argued that Paul himself was a gnostic. Such scholars as U. Wilckens and W. Schmithals object to this theory: they insist instead that where such parallels occur, the apostle is adopting the language of "gnostic" opponents in order to refute them. Both theories, however, share a methodological premise: both attempt to read first-century Pauline material primarily in terms of second-century gnostic evidence. H. Koester has pointed out that such investigation applies criteria for distinguishing between true and false belief which emerge from the works of the second-century heresiologists—criteria which may not at all apply to the theological situations and problems of the first generations of Christians:

> The question is not whether we should characterize Paul's opponents as gnostic heretics. . . . The danger of this way of setting the question is clear: one falls into the error of equating theological questions of the Pauline era with cliches of the second and third century controversies.

Certainly it is not impossible, as proponents on both sides of the argument assume, that extant written materials which date from the second century may represent tradition known to the apostle himself some sixty to eighty years earlier (whether one argues that Paul endorsed or condemned it). Nevertheless, this remains largely an argument from silence, or, at any rate, from later sources. What the sources can document, however, is that the opposing positions more recently debated between Reitzenstein, Lügert, and others, each found defenders in the second-century hermeneutical debate—the gnostics themselves contending that Paul was a gnostic, and the heresiologists taking the opposite stand, arguing that if Paul seems to use gnostic language, he only does so in order to contravert what "he himself" calls "falsely so-called gnostics." Nevertheless, H. Conzelmann, assessing the latter theory, has declared (and indeed, in his own commentary, has demonstrated) that "one does not need this hypothesis in order to explicate the text."

The present study of gnostic exegesis lends support to Conzelmann's view. It seems that we can account for allegedly "gnostic terminology" in Paul's letters if we assume that Paul's theological language subsequently is appropriated and developed by the Valentinians (and other gnostics) into a technical theological vocabulary. (Wilckens, Pearson, and others agree that Paul seems to have adapted his theological language from Jewish and other religious traditions available to him in the first century.)

A survey of the historical evidence reminds us that after Paul's death (c. 60 A.D.) traditions concerning the apostle (like those concerning Jesus) developed in several different directions. The author of Acts (c. 80–90 A.D.) describes Paul as an "apostle" and teacher who was involved in controversy, but agreed to compromise and to work with the Jerusalem Christians in fraternal accord, and who subsequently was sent as a prisoner to Rome. The Pastoral Letters (c. 100–110 A.D.) stress Paul's role as an organizer of ecclesiastical congregations, a mainstay of church discipline, and unswerving antagonist of all heretics. Ephesians, Colossians, and Hebrews (c. 70–95 A.D.), on the other hand, virtually ignore Paul's organizational activity, in order to elaborate and extend the theological conceptions expressed in his letters. These various deutero-Pauline materials—the Pastorals, on the one hand, and Ephesians, Colossians, and Hebrews on the other—although divergent in theological and ecclesiological conception, later are accepted into the canonical collection as basically non-contradictory.

Nevertheless, the tensions in Pauline interpretation which they evince apparently broke into open conflict during the generations following their composition. While Marcion sought to exclude elements of the texts he considered inauthentic, Valentinus tended instead to accept the full texts available to him, interpreting them esoterically. Valentinus' followers accepted, apparently, the full texts of Paul's own letters; and while they virtually ignored the Pastorals, they willingly included (and, indeed, highly revered) Ephesians, Colossians, and Hebrews as sources of Pauline tradition. Often, in fact, they used the latter epistles to interpret the former: the followers of Ptolomy, for example, refer to Eph. 5:32 to interpret Paul's teaching on sexuality and marriage (cf. 1 Corinthians 7) as symbolic references to the "ineffable marriages of syzygies" and the marriage of the pneumatic Christ with Sophia, his bride. Similarly, the author of The Interpretation of Knowledge (CG II, 1) interprets Paul's image of the "body of Christ" (cf. Romans 12, 1 Corinthians 12) in the direction indicated in Ephesians and Colossians. Other Valentinians apply the language of Colossians, which describes the believer's ascent with Christ, to the baptismal teaching of Romans.

Some of what has been described as "gnostic terminology" in the Pauline letters may be explained more plausibly instead as Pauline (and deutero-Pauline) terminology in the *gnostic* writings. This reconstruction not only fits the chronological evidence without distortion, but also accords with the Valentinians' own witness: their reverence for Paul as their great teacher, and their claim that his letters have served as a primary source for their own theology. Tertullian notes that Valentinus, unlike Marcion, developed his theology independently of the ecclesiastical community by means of "different emendations and expositions" of the scriptural texts. His followers, convinced that his hermeneutical method derives directly from Paul's own wisdom tradition, insist that far from contradicting church tradition, such exegesis complements and completes it.

By studying gnostic exegesis, the NT scholar may recognize how ecclesiastical tradition since Irenaeus has directed the course of Pauline interpretation: even today the "antignostic Paul" predominates in the contemporary debate. Yet for the historical theologian to attempt to decide between gnostic and orthodox exegesis would be to accept a false alternative. Each of these opposing images of Paul (and each of the hermeneutical systems they imply) to some extent distorts the reading of the texts. To read Paul either way—as hypergnostic or hyperorthodox—is to read unhistorically, attempting to interpret the apostle's theology in terms of categories formulated in second-century debate. On the other hand, whoever takes account of the total evidence may learn from the debate to approach Pauline exegesis with renewed openness to the texts.

IRENÆUS

[On the Valentinian Interpretation of Scripture]
(ca. 180)†

Such, then, is their system, which neither the prophets announced, nor the Lord taught, nor the apostles delivered, but of which they boast that beyond all others they have a perfect knowledge. They gather their views from other sources than the Scriptures; and, to use a common proverb, they strive to weave ropes of sand, while they endeavour to adapt with an air of probability to their own peculiar assertions the parables of the Lord, the sayings of the prophets, and the words of the apostles, in order that their scheme may not seem altogether without support. In doing so, however, they disregard the order and the connection of the Scriptures, and so far as in them lies, dismember and destroy the truth. By transferring passages, and dressing them up anew, and making one thing out of another, they succeed in deluding many through their wicked art in adapting the oracles of the Lord to their opinions. Their manner of acting is just as if one, when a beautiful image of a king has been constructed by some skillful artist out of precious jewels, should then take this likeness of the man all to pieces, should re-arrange the gems, and so fit them together as to make them into the form of a dog or of a fox, and even that but poorly executed; and should then maintain and declare that *this* was the beautiful image of the king which the skillful artist constructed, pointing to the jewels which had been admirably fitted together by the first artist to form the image of the king, but have been with bad effect transferred by the latter one to the shape of a dog, and by thus exhibiting the jewels, should deceive the ignorant who had no conception what a king's form was like, and persuade them that that miserable likeness of the fox was, in fact, the beautiful image of the king. In like manner do these persons patch together old wives' fables, and then endeavour, by violently drawing away from their proper connection, words, expressions, and parables whenever found, to adapt the oracles of God to their baseless fictions.

† From *Haer.* 1.8.1, tr. by Alexander Roberts, in *The Ante-Nicene Fathers*, Vol. I (New York: Scribner's, 1885; rp. Grand Rapids: Eerdmans, 1951).

The Only True Apostle:
Marcion's Radical Paul

While the Valentinians and other Gnostics emphasized Paul, there was no one in the ancient church, either "heretic" or "orthodox," who made such serious and exclusive claims on Paul and Paul alone as did Marcion. Born some twenty or thirty years after Paul's death, Marcion became convinced that salvation by grace alone was the purest essence of the Christian gospel. But carried to its logical conclusion, he believed this would mean that the God of grace manifested in Jesus Christ was distinct from the God of the Old Testament. The creation and the law were the products of the God of justice, but humanity's hope lay in the God of pure love, unknown before Christ and totally unrelated to this world. Catholic Christianity's insistence on the identity of the two Gods was in Marcion's eyes a devilish mixture of opposites, the result of a Judaizing conspiracy in which all the apostles except Paul had engaged. They had even dared to corrupt the text of Paul's letters, which must therefore be expurgated of references to the Creator and his prophets. Marcion produced his own "critical" New Testament, which some scholars have claimed was the first strictly defined Christian canon of scripture.[1] To it he added his single original writing, *The Antitheses*, portions of which are quoted below.[2]

When Marcion's teaching of the two rival gods got him expelled from the church in Rome—according to one report he had been excommunicated years earlier from his home church in Sinope, Pontus, of which his own father was bishop[3]—he set about to reform the church from without, establishing independent parishes and dioceses, tightly disciplined and organized on lines parallel to the catholics. His reformer's zeal was prodigious—for good reason Harnack has seen in him a second-century Luther—and his success was so great that his churches were serious contenders for dominance over the catholics in many parts of the empire for two centuries. "Tracts 'Against Marcion' were still being written," notes Bardenhewer, "when the name of Valentinus had long since faded away."[4]

Marcion was not a Gnostic. True, some elements of his thought are shared

---

1. See, for example, Hans von Campenhausen, *The Formation of the Christian Bible* (Philadelphia: Fortress, 1972), 148, who argues that "the idea and the reality of a Christian Bible were the work of Marcion." Other scholars argue that Marcion's role in the formation of the NT has been greatly exaggerated. It is extremely unlikely, for example, that he was the first to make a collection of Paul's letters; it is much more probable that he edited an existing corpus, and his textual readings are often less important for their future influence than they are as a witness to the pre-Marcionite Pauline textual tradition. In any case, his Pauline corpus—the so-called *Apostolikon*—consisted of ten letters, all but the Pastoral Epistles, which he either did not know or rejected. The most important recent study of the text of Marcion's *Apostolikon* is that of Ulrich Schmid, *Marcion und sein Apostolos* (Berlin: De Gruyter, 1995).
2. The so-called Marcionite Prologues, which precede the Pauline letters in most of the best manuscripts of the Vulgate, frequently have been claimed to derive, in whole or in part, from Marcionite circles. That claim has now been persuasively refuted by N. A. Dahl, "The Origin of the Earliest Prologues to the Pauline Letters," *Semeia* 12 (1978): 233–77.
3. For a careful analysis of the ancient ecclesiastical traditions about Marcion's pre-Roman period, see Jürgen Regul, *Die antimarcionitischen Evangelienprologe* (Freiburg: Herder, 1969), 177–95.
4. Otto Bardenhewer, *Geschichte der altchristlichen Literatur* (Freiburg i. Br., 1912; rp. Darmstadt: Wissenschaftliche Buchgesellschaft, 1962) I, 371.

by Gnostics[5] and his hatred of the world resembles the Gnostic's existential nausea,[6] but he rejected allegory as an interpretative method, denied that any form of oral tradition (especially esoteric secret tradition) was authoritative, and repudiated cosmogonic mythology—all of which were characteristic of Gnosticism. Above all, his doctrine of grace was fundamentally anti-Gnostic. For the Gnostic, salvation of the spiritual part of humanity is possible only because that part is consubstantial with the saving deity. For Marcion the essence of grace is that the good God is totally other; he has no relationship with humans before his absolutely free decision to save them. In this radical notion of grace, Marcion is not Gnostic, but ultimately Pauline. Yet it is a perversely one-sided (one might say with Harnack, perversely consistent) Paulinism which, in its very zeal to be truly Pauline, has demolished the dialectic that is most characteristic of Paul's genius. Marcion was the only one in the second century who understood Paul, said Harnack, and he misunderstood him.[7]

Since no connected work by Marcion survived the final suppression of his schism, he must be represented here only by a few hostile but revealing words from two of his orthodox opponents,[8] by conjectured fragments of his *Antitheses*, and by excerpts from a modern description of his thought which has become a scholar's classic.[9]

IRENÆUS

[Marcion] (ca. 180)†

Marcion of Pontus . . . increased the [Gnostic] school through his unblushing blasphemy against Him who was proclaimed as God by the law and the prophets, declaring that He was the cause of evils, desirous of war, changeable in opinion and the author of inconsistent statements. He says that Jesus came from the Father, who is above the Creator, to Judaea in the time of Pontius Pilate the governor, who was the procurator of Tiberius Caesar, and in the form of a man was manifested to the people who were then in Judaea. He says that he rendered null and void the prophets and the law and all the works of the Creator God, whom they call Cosmocrator. He used an expurgated edition of the Gospel of Luke, removing all the passages that referred to the birth of our Lord, and many things from his

---

5. Irenaeus (*Haer.* 1.27.1–2) regarded Marcion as a Gnostic and linked him with a Syrian Gnostic teacher in Rome named Cerdo, and several modern scholars have either classified Marcion as a Gnostic or emphasized his closeness to Gnostic thought. See, e.g., Hans Jonas, *The Gnostic Religion* (2nd ed.; Boston: Beacon, 1963), 137–39; Barbara Aland, "Marcion: Versuch einer neuen Interpretation," *ZTK* 20 (1973): 420–47; and Kurt Rudolph, *Gnosis* (San Francisco: HarperCollins, 1983), 313–17.

6. Hans Jonas, "Delimitation of the Gnostic Phenomenon—Typological and Historical," in *The Origins of Gnosticism*, ed. by Ugo Bianchi (Leiden: Brill, 1967), 104.

7. This witticism, made famous by Harnack, was coined by Franz Overbeck, as he says in *Christentum und Kultur* (Basel: B. Schwabe, 1919), 218f.

8. Not included here are excerpts from Clement of Alexandria, who depicts Marcion as a radical Platonist (*Strom.* 3.12.1–25.4, esp. 3.21.2) and thus as someone whose starting point was the philosopher rather than the apostle.

9. The reference is to Adolf von Harnack's magisterial *Marcion: Das Evangelium vom fremden Gott* (Leipzig: Hinrichs, 1921). The second edition of that work (1924) is now available in English: *Marcion: The Gospel of the Alien God*, trans. by J. E. Steely and L. D. Bierma (Durham: Labyrinth, 1990).

† From *The Treatise of Irenaeus of Lugdunum against the Heresies*, tr. by F. R. Montgomery Hitchcock (London: SPCK, 1916), I. 41 i. (= I.25.1 in Harvey's ed. of Irenaeus, I.27.2 in Massuet's). Irenaeus (ca.130–ca.200), a native of Asia Minor, was bishop of Lyons.

teaching in which he very plainly referred to the creator of this universe as his Father. In the same way he mutilated the Epistles of Paul, cutting out all that the Apostle said about the God who made the world, and which went to show that he was the Father of our Lord Jesus Christ, and also passages bearing on the advent of our Lord, which that Apostle had quoted from the prophets.

TERTULLIAN

[Marcion's Special Work] (207)†

* * * Marcion's special and principal work is the separation of the law and the gospel; and his disciples will not deny that in this point they have their very best pretext for initiating and confirming themselves in his heresy. These are Marcion's "Antitheses," or contradictory propositions, which aim at committing the gospel to a variance with the law, in order that from the diversity of the two documents which contain them, they may contend for a diversity of gods also. * * *

MARCION

The Antitheses (ca. 140?)‡

1. The Creator was known to Adam and to the following generations, but the Father of Christ is unknown, as Christ himself said of him in these words: "No one has known the Father except the Son" [Luke 10:22].

2. The Creator did not even know where Adam was, so he cried, "Where are you?" But Christ knew even the thoughts of men [cf. Luke 5:22; 6:8; 9:47].

3. Joshua conquered the land with violence and terror; but Christ forbade all violence and preached mercy and peace.

4. The God of Creation did not restore the sight of the blinded Isaac, but our Lord, because he is good, opened the eyes of many blind men [Luke 7:21].

5. Moses intervened unbidden in the brothers' quarrel, chiding the offender, "Why do you strike your neighbor?" But he was rejected by him with the words, "Who made you master or judge over us?" Christ, on the contrary, when someone asked him to settle a question of inheritance between him and his brother, refused his assistance even in so honest a

† From *Against Marcion*, I.19, tr. by Peter Holmes in the *Ante-Nicene Christian Library* (Edinburgh, 1868), VII, 34. Tertullian (ca. 160—ca.220), a native of Carthage, was the first important Christian theologian to write in Latin.

‡ The epigrammatic antitheses reproduced here are those which Adolf von Harnack reconstructed (*Marcion: Das Evangelium vom fremden Gott* [Leipzig: J. C. Hinrichs, 1924; rp. 1960], 89–92; sources, 266*–296*). It is not certain that all go back to Marcion; several are quoted in a form attributed to Marcion's disciple Megethius in the fourth-century Dialogues of Adamantius. As Harnack showed, "The Antitheses" contained, besides such epigrams, a more systematic theological part, which is impossible to reconstruct.

cause—because he is the Christ of the Good, not of the Just God—and said, "Who made me a judge over you?" [Luke 12:13 f.]

6. At the time of the Exodus from Egypt, the God of Creation commanded Moses, "Be ready, your loins girded, your feet shod, staffs in your hands, knapsacks on your shoulders, and carry off gold and silver and everything that belongs to the Egyptians" [cf. Exod. 3:22; 11:2; 12:35]. But our Lord, the good, said to his disciples as he sent them into the world: "Have no sandals on your feet, nor knapsack, nor two tunics, nor coppers in your belts" [cf. Luke 9:3].

7. The prophet of the God of Creation, when the people was engaged in battle, climbed to the mountain peak and extended his hands to God, imploring that he kill as many as possible in the battle. [cf. Exod. 17:8 ff.]. But our Lord, the good, extended his hands [on the cross] not to kill men, but to save them.

8. In the Law it is said, "An eye for an eye, a tooth for a tooth" [Exod. 21:24; Deut. 19:21]. But the Lord, being good, says in the Gospel: "If anyone strikes you on the cheek, offer him the other as well" [cf. Luke 6:29].

9. In the Law it is said, "A coat for a coat." [Where?] But the good Lord says, "If anyone takes your coat, give him your tunic as well" [Luke 6:29].

10. The prophet of the God of Creation, in order to kill as many as possible in battle, kept the sun from going down until he finished annihilating those who made war on the people [Josh. 10:12 ff.]. But the Lord, being good, says: "Let not the sun go down on your anger" [Eph. 4:26].

11. David, when he besieged Zion, was opposed by the blind who sought to prevent his entry, and he had them killed. But Christ came freely to help the blind.

12. The Creator, at the request of Elijah, sent the plague of fire [2 Kings 1:9–12]; Christ however forbids the disciples to beseech fire from heaven [Luke 9:51 ff.].

13. The prophet of the God of Creation commanded bears to come from the thicket and devour the children who had opposed him [2 Kings 2:14]; the good Lord, however, says, "Let the children come to me and do not forbid them, for of such is the Kingdom of Heaven" [Luke 18:16].

14. Elisha, prophet of the Creator, healed only one of the many Israelite lepers, and that a Syrian, Naaman. But Christ, though himself, "the alien," healed an Israelite, whose own Lord did not want him healed. Elisha used material for the healing, namely water, and seven times; but Christ healed through a single, bare word. Elisha healed only one leper; Christ healed ten, and this contrary to the Law. . . .

15. The prophet of the Creator says: "My bow is strung and my arrows are sharp against them" [Isa. 5:28]; the Apostle says: "Put on the armor of God, that you may quench the fiery arrows of the Evil One" [Eph. 6:11, 16].

16. The Creator says, "Hear and hear, but do not understand" [Isa. 6:9]; Christ on the contrary says, "He who has ears to hear, let him hear" [Luke 8:8, etc.].

17. The Creator says, "Cursed is everyone who hangs on the tree" [Deut. 21:23,] but Christ suffered the death of the cross [cf. Gal. 3:13 f.].

18. The Jewish Christ was designated by the Creator solely to restore

the Jewish people from the Diaspora; but our Christ was commissioned by the good God to liberate all mankind.

19. The Good is good toward all men; the Creator, however, promises salvation only to those who are obedient to him. The Good redeems those who believe in him, but he does not judge those who are disobedient to him; the Creator, however, redeems his faithful and judges and punishes the sinners.

20. Cursing characterizes the Law; blessing, the faith.

21. The Creator commands to give to one's brothers; Christ, however, to all who ask [Luke 6:30].

22. In the Law the Creator said, "I make rich and poor [cf. Prov. 22: 2]; Jesus calls the poor blessed [Luke 6:20].

23. In the Law of the Just [God] fortune is given to the rich and misfortune to the poor; but Christ calls [only] the poor blessed.

24. In the Law God says, "Love him who loves you and hate your enemy [cf. Lv. 19:18 and Matt. 5:43]; our Lord, the good, says: "Love your enemies and pray for those who persecute you" [cf. Luke 6:1 ff.].

25. The Creator established the Sabbath; Christ abolishes it [cf. Luke 6:1 ff.].

26. The Creator rejects the tax collectors as non-Jews and profane men; Christ accepts the tax collectors [Luke 5:27 ff.]

27. The Law forbids touching a woman with a flow of blood; Christ not only touches her, but heals her [Luke 8:45].

28. Moses permits divorce [Deut. 24:1], Christ forbids it [Luke 16:18; 1 Cor. 7:10].

29. The Christ [of the Old Testament] promises to the Jews the restoration of their former condition by return of their land and, after death, a refuge in Abraham's bosom in the underworld. Our Christ will establish the Kingdom of God, an eternal and heavenly possession.

30. Both the place of punishment and that of refuge of the Creator are placed in the underworld for those who obey the Law and the Prophets. But Christ and the God who belongs to him have a heavenly place of rest and a haven, of which the Creator never spoke.

ADOLF von HARNACK

[Marcion's Starting Point] (1924)†

* * * The starting point for Marcion's criticism of the tradition is unmistakable. It lay in the Pauline opposition of Law and Gospel—on the one side malicious, narrow, and vindictive justice; on the other, merciful love. Marcion immersed himself in the basic thought of the Letters to Galatians and Romans, and in them he discovered the full explanation of the nature of Christianity, the Old Testament, and the world. It must have been for him a day of brilliant light, but also a day of trembling over the darkness

† From *Marcion: Das Evangelium vom fremden Gott* (Leipzig: J. C. Hinrichs, 1924; rp. Darmstadt: Wissenschaftliche Buchgesellschaft, 1960), 30–35. Translated by the editors of this Norton Critical Edition. Adolf von Harnack (1851–1930) was a distinguished church historian who taught in Leipzig, Giessen, Marburg, and Berlin. His study of Marcion remains unequaled.

that had eclipsed this light in Christianity, when he recognized that Christ presented and proclaimed a quite new God. Moreover, he saw that religion itself is nothing else than the faith that abandons itself to this Redeemer-God who transforms man, while the whole of previous world history is the evil and repulsive drama of a deity who possesses no higher value than the dull and nauseating world itself, of which he is the creator and governor.

All of Paul's religious antitheses were brought to the sharpest possible expression through this discovery—though this exaggeration moves very far from the apostle's intentions. Marcion remained true to those intentions only in his enthusiastic certainty of *gratia gratis data* (grace freely given) in contrast to the *justitia ex operibus* (righteousness based on works), as well as in the consciousness of a liberation, surpassing all reason, from a terrifying state of perdition. This conviction included the universality of redemption, in contrast to its restriction to a single people. The religious principle that summed up all higher truth in the opposition between Law and Gospel is also the principle which for Marcion explains the whole of nature and history.

In Marcion's new awareness, the religion of redemption and subjectivity is incomparably heightened to an ethical metaphysics that determines everything. The inexorable result was the abandonment of the Old Testament. * * *

* * *

The Old Testament was abandoned—in that moment, however, the new religion stood naked, uprooted and defenseless. One must renounce all proof from antiquity, indeed every historical and literary proof. Yet a deeper speculation taught Marcion that this defenselessness and lack of proof was demanded by the Gospel itself, which therefore they actually supported. Grace is *gratis data*—so taught both Christ and Paul—and that is the entire content of the religion. But how could grace be *gratis data* if he who gave it had also the least obligation to prove it? Yet if he were the creator of mankind, and their tutor and lawgiver from the beginning, then he would be *obliged* to accept them. Only a miserable and groveling sophistry could save the deity from this obligation! Hence God must have no natural or historical connection with the men whom he loved and redeemed—that is, he cannot be the Creator and Lawgiver. * * * The Redeemer-God—the only true God—has never encountered man in any revelation of any kind before his appearance in Christ: that is the necessary consequence of the nature of his act of redemption. He could be understood only as the absolutely alien. Thence it follows also that the Enemy, from which one is redeemed through Christ, can be nothing less than the world itself, together with its Creator. Now since Marcion remained true to the Jewish-Christian tradition insofar as he identified the Creator with the Jewish God, and in the Old Testament saw not a false book, but the true depiction of actual history (a remarkable limitation to his religious anti-Judaism!), he had to regard the Jewish God together with his charter, the Old Testament, as the real Enemy.

* * *

But only after Marcion achieved clarity about the basic principle and basic antinomy did his new task begin. He must now expound for faith and life the true content, so drastically misunderstood, of Jesus' and Paul's proclamation. * * * Marcion must begin his great task for Christianity as critic and restorer, for the Gospel and the testimonies were deeply obscured. In fact, no Christian critic has ever had such a difficult task: to prove from the New Testament scriptures that mankind must be redeemed and had been redeemed from their God and Father. Marcion was not daunted; over against the old books, the Law and the Prophets, he placed new books: the book of the Gospel and the letters of Paul.

To Marcion, certain that the authentic Pauline faith was his own, all seemed lost in the inner constitution of the mainline Christianity around him. While he was convinced that Christ had abolished the Old Testament and its God and had proclaimed an alien God, the Church more and more identified the two Gods and founded itself upon the Old Testament. It became, that is, thoroughly "Jewish." Moreover, books which bore the celebrated names of the first apostles obviously helped and undergirded this error by their narratives. Finally and worst, even in the letters of Paul there were many passages that unambiguously supported the heresy that Christ was the Son of the Creator and that he had advanced the will of this Father.

How had that happened, and how could it happen, when the truth in some major passages in the Pauline letters was so unambiguous and clear? A massive conspiracy against the truth must have begun immediately after Christ left the world and have achieved its goals with decisive success. * * * Marcion seized on this explanation. But he had no means of proving it other than the recollection of the struggle that Paul had had with his Judaizing opponents. Moreover, he knew nothing of this struggle but what he read in the Apostle's letters. * * *

The Model Ascetic

One aspect of Marcion's version of Paulinism has not been mentioned: his asceticism. In order to be baptized into the Marcionite church, one had to take a vow of celibacy. If already married, one was not permitted divorce (Marcion retained Luke 16:18 and perhaps 1 Cor. 7:10 in his canon; see Antithesis 28 above), but must abstain from intercourse after baptism. That Marcion thought he was following the intention of his master is indicated by his "restoration" of the text of Ephesians 5:21–33, the famous allegory on marriage. According to Harnack's reconstruction of Marcion's text, he altered vv. 28 f. to read: "He loves his flesh who loves his wife as Christ (loved) the church [i.e., asexually]"; while v. 31 is made to say, "For the sake of her [sc. the church] a man shall leave his father and mother, and the two [sc. man and the church] shall be one flesh."[1]

Marcion was by no means alone in his belief that Pauline Christianity was ascetic Christianity. That was the conclusion drawn by some of Paul's own converts during his lifetime,[2] and he has been praised and blamed ever since for having introduced the ideal of celibacy into the Christian ethic. It is significant, however, that Marcion and other ascetics who appealed to Paul had to alter or ignore some passages from the Pauline letters in order to make their tutor speak unequivocally on the subject. Paul's teaching was in fact quite complex, as a glance even at the single chapter 1 Corinthians 7 makes plain. Paul obviously did regard sexual continence as desirable—yet not because sex was immoral or marriage a metaphysical trap in an evil world, but only because "this world in its present form is passing away" and "the time is short" (1 Cor. 7:31, 29). Paul's heightened eschatology, which he shared with most of early Christianity, made marriage seem a distraction from the intensely urgent task at hand (1 Cor. 7:32–35), but not evil. Indeed, while the Old Testament commandment "Be fruitful and multiply" had in Paul's eyes been superseded (like all commandments!) by the coming of Christ, yet in practice the implicit mutual obligations between husband and wife were still valid so long as the world endured (1 Cor. 7:1–6). It is not surprising that not only the advocates of a thoroughgoing asceticism but also their opponents were able to appeal to Paul for support. And their debate about Paul's perspective on marriage was carried out in an intellectual context in which philosophers debated whether the sage would marry or remain single.[3]

Apart from Marcion, there were a number of groups in early Christianity who insisted upon rigorous asceticism; wealth, food and drink, and sex were the principal areas of concern.[4] 1 Timothy 4:1–5 combats those "who forbid

---

1. Adolf von Harnack, *Marcion: Das Evangelium vom fremden Gott* (Leipzig: J. C. Hinrichs, 1924), 119* f., cf. p. 50. A different perspective on the textual tradition is offered by Ulrich Schmid, *Marcion und sein Apostolos* (Berlin: De Gruyter, 1995), 69–70, 144–48.
2. See notes on 1 Cor. 7.
3. See esp. O. Larry Yarbrough, *Not Like the Gentiles: Marriage Rules in the Letters of Paul* (Atlanta: Scholars, 1985), and Will Deming, *Paul on Marriage and Celibacy: The Hellenistic Background of 1 Corinthians 7* (2nd ed.; Grand Rapids: Eerdmans, 2004).
4. See Hans von Campenhausen, "Early Christian Asceticism," in *Traditions and Life in the Church* (Philadelphia: Fortress, 1968), 90–122; Henry Chadwick, "The Ascetic Ideal in the History of the Church," in *Monks, Hermits and the Ascetic Tradition*, ed. by W. J. Sheils (Oxford: Blackwell's, 1985), 1–23; Peter Brown, *The Body and Society: Men, Women, and Sexual Renunciation in Early*

people to marry and order them to abstain from certain foods" and the self-abasement insisted on by some Colossian Christians (Col. 2:18, 21 f.) doubtless referred to similar requirements.[5] The heresiologists of the second, third, and fourth centuries applied to such movements the label "Encratites," from the Greek word meaning "self-control." Irenaeus of Lyons (ca. 180 CE) typically traces the heresy back to one teacher, "a certain Tatian," who had been a disciple of Justin Martyr (d. ca. 165 in Rome). Rejected by the churches of the West, Tatian migrated to Eastern Syria, where the extent of his influence is suggested by his composite version of the four gospels, the Diatessaron, becoming *the* gospel in the Syriac New Testament until the fifth century. Whether directly as a result of Tatian's influence or, more likely, because of underlying social factors affecting the origins of Christianity in Mesopotamia, the dominant tendencies of the Eastern Syrian churches were toward an extreme asceticism.[6] Some scholars have argued that a vow of celibacy was actually a requirement for baptism in the earliest Syrian Christianity,[7] since "the fundamental conception around which the Christian belief centered was the doctrine that the Christian life is unthinkable outside the bounds of virginity."[8] Others have vigorously disputed both the early date and the extent of this severe discipline.[9] In any case, numerous documents from the Syriac-speaking church exalt virginity as the proper state for Christians, and occasionally these documents represent Paul as preaching this doctrine. We have to face the question, therefore, to what extent Encratism may have been an outgrowth of Paulinism.

Tatian's own use of the Pauline letters affords one test, which can be applied because Tatian's *Oration to the Greeks* and fragments of other writings have survived. From these it is "plain that Tatian knows Paul well and that in part, at least, his theology is based on the Pauline epistles, including Hebrews."[1] Two examples will demonstrate the way in which Tatian used Paul: First, Paul's advice that husband and wife should "not deprive each other except perhaps by mutual consent and for a time, so that you may devote yourselves to prayer" (1 Cor. 7:5) is thus interpreted by Tatian:

> While agreement to be continent makes prayer possible, intercourse of corruption destroys it. By the very disparaging way in which he [Paul] allows it, he forbids it. For although he allowed them to come together again because of Satan and the temptation to incontinence, he indicated that the man who takes advantage of this permission will be serving two masters, God if there is "agreement," but, if there is no such agreement, incontinence, fornication, and the devil.[2]

Second, we are told by St. Jerome that Tatian took Paul's statement, "Those who sow to please their sinful nature, from that nature will reap destruction" (Gal. 6:8), to refer to sexual intercourse.[3] There is no way to be sure how

Christianity (New York: Columbia University Press, 1988); Vincent L. Wimbush (ed.), *Ascetic Behavior in Greco-Roman Antiquity: A Sourcebook* (Minneapolis: Fortress, 1990); J. Francis, *Subversive Virtue: Asceticism and Authority in the Second-Century Pagan World* (University Park, PA: Pennsylvania University Press, 1995).

5. See the notes on Colossians.

6. See, e.g., Susan Ashbrook Harvey, *Asceticism and Society in Crisis* (Berkeley: University of California Press, 1990).

7. Karl Müller, *Die Forderung der Ehelosigkeit für alle Getauften in der alten Kirche* (Tübingen: Mohr-Siebeck, 1927); Arthur Vööbus, *Celibacy, a Requirement for Admission to Baptism in the Early Syrian Church* (Stockholm: Estonian Theological Society in Exile, 1951), and *History of Asceticism in the Syrian Orient* (CSCO 184, 197, 500; Louvain: CSCO, 1958, 1960, 1988).

8. Vööbus, *History*, Vol. 1, 69.

9. E.g., A. F. J. Klijn, *The Acts of Thomas* (Leiden: Brill, 1962), 50, n. 2, and further references there.

1. Robert M. Grant, "Tatian and the Bible," in *Studia Patristica*, 1 (Berlin: Akademie, 1957), 303.

2. From "On Perfection According to the Savior," quoted by Clement of Alexandria, *Strom.* 3.81, tr. by Henry Chadwick in *Alexandrian Christianity* (Philadelphia: Westminster, 1968), 77 f.

3. *Comm. Gal.*, col. 640; cited by Vööbus, *History*, 1, vol. 1, 3 36; cf. Grant, "Tatian and the Bible," 302.

important these arguments were for Tatian, but they appear rather isolated in his extant works. The style of his argument, moreover, is not that of a man who has discovered a new and compelling idea in the text itself; Tatian would hardly have found these implications in these two texts had he not brought them to the texts from elsewhere. The whole tradition about Tatian suggests rather that he was preoccupied with the gospels and with the picture of Jesus as the paradigmatic ascetic that he found there. The Pauline letters he used quite selectively and freely only to the extent that they could support his major concerns. To confirm this judgment, note that Tatian almost certainly rejected 1 Timothy altogether because of its antiascetic statement (4:1–5, quoted above), but accepted the letter to Titus, presumably because it contained the word "continent" (*enkratē*, "disciplined," 1:8).[4] In only one respect the Encratite's doctrine seems related essentially to Paul's: "Tatian felt strongly that the concept of the Christian life is adequately depicted only by the term 'cross.' "[5] But while Paul draws analogies from the Crucifixion and Resurrection to the apostle's joyful acceptance of suffering encountered in the rigors of his missionary task, Tatian refers to self-chosen and self-inflicted suffering. A fundamentally different atmosphere is present in the writings of the two men. Tatian was not a Paulinist, however much he may have depicted Paul as an Encratite.[6]

As a matter of fact, some of the strongest arguments by opponents of Encratism were based on Paul. Hippolytus of Rome (ca. 170–ca. 236), for example, quotes 1 Tim. 4:1–5 *in extenso* against those "who call themselves Encratites," and concludes, "Thus this voice of the blessed Paul is sufficient to refute those who live this way and who pride themselves in their righteousness, and to show that this, too, is a heresy."[7] His older and more learned contemporary, Clement of Alexandria, derives his refutation of the ascetics very largely from 1 Corinthians 7. On the whole, he is an accurate interpreter of Paul's doctrine of freedom in the realm of sexuality—the "as if not" of 1 Corinthians 7:29–31 appears several times—even though Clement has a much more positive place for the law and a much more schematic position.[8] While Clement is more "liberal" toward sex than most of his contemporaries even in the catholic mainstream, his view would still seem ascetic in ordinary Hellenistic society: sexual relations were to be permitted only in monogamous marriage, and then only for procreation.[9] Moreover, Clement is representative of the emerging catholic position in his approval of celibacy for those given the special grace for this state, while regarding it as not at all superior to "chaste marriage."[1] This double standard, which is clearly derived directly from 1 Corinthians 7, was destined for extensive development and significant influence in the moral teachings of Western Christianity. It could be applied, as Clement interpreted it and as Paul doubtless intended, to enhance the freedom of individual Christians to undertake different forms of discipline without disparaging others. But it was a very short step to the conclusion that, while both married and celibate were

4. Jerome, *Comm. Tit.*, *praef.* (PL 26.590B), cited by Grant, "Tatian and the Bible," 301. Jerome, whose information was likely derived from Origen, says that Tatian rejected several of the Pauline letters but does not specify which ones. That 1 Timothy was among these rejected letters is virtually certain.
5. Vööbus, *History*, vol. 1, 44.
6. In *Haer.* 3.23.8, Irenaeus, who generally regards Tatian as "the amalgamation of all heretics," singles him out as instigating the notion that Adam was not saved, an idea that Tatian saw taught in 1 Cor. 15:22.
7. *Haer.* 8.20.2 (our trans.).
8. *Strom.* Book 3, *passim*. Clement must have had some success in reclaiming Paul for his "liberal" view of sex, as his pupil Origen reported that the Encratites in his time refused to accept the letters of Paul as scripture (*Cels.* 5.65); see also Eusebius, *Hist. eccl.* 4.29.5, and Epiphanius, *Pan.* 47.2.3.
9. *Strom.* 3.96 and elsewhere. It is interesting that Paul himself, in his discussion of the sexual rights and obligations of husband and wife to each other (1 Cor. 7:1–7), never mentions procreation.
1. See especially *Strom.* 3.105.

Christian, the celibate were more so. When Chrysostom (ca. 347–407) distinguished between "that which is good and far more excellent" and that which is merely "safe and suited to assist your weakness," he could still appeal to the same passage of Paul's Corinthian letter. The medieval limitation of the Pauline word *vocatio* to the calling to monastic discipline as the only perfect Christian life was the ultimate outgrowth of this development, in which Paul's distinction between command and concession (1 Cor. 7:6) played a fateful role.[2]

If we are to believe the antiheretical writers of the early church, many of the Gnostics were not ascetics, but libertines. It is tempting to suppose that Paul's "antinomian" passages may have contributed to such a view, just as his proclamation of freedom in the spirit at Corinth may have contributed to the excesses he had later to combat in 1 Corinthians 6. There is a certain Pauline resonance, for example, to the statement by which Carpocrates, according to Irenaeus, defended his insistence that "souls ought to experience every kind of life and action":

> For through faith and love we are saved; all else is indifferent after the opinion of men, and is sometimes considered good, sometimes bad. Nothing is evil by nature.[3]

If Irenaeus describes the Carpocrateans correctly, however, the real basis for their program was an anthropological dualism in which actions of body and soul were radically antithetical—just the kind of dualism that Paul rejects in 1 Corinthians 6:12–20. Here again, as in the case of Tatian, Pauline slogans have been used selectively to gain "apostolic" support for positions arrived at independently of any authentic Pauline tradition.

One could more readily make a case for the Pauline origins of another very curious tradition, one that equates salvation with the restoration of the lost unity of male and female.[4] This very widespread belief, especially but not only in Gnostic circles, presupposes that the separation of male from female constitutes the most fundamental instance of human self-alienation: "In the days when Eve was [in] Adam death did not exist. When she was separated from him, death came into existence."[5] Ultimately, that separation would be overcome in heaven, but already in the church it is overcome sacramentally, either in baptism or, in certain Gnostic groups of the Valentinian school, in a special "sacrament of the bridal chamber."[6] The earliest witness to such sacramental reunification is Paul, who says to those who have "put on Christ" in baptism, "There is neither Jew nor Greek, neither slave nor free, neither 'male and female,' for you are all one in Christ Jesus" (Gal. 3:28).[7] This does not mean, however, that Paul introduced this notion; he is probably quoting here an element of an early baptismal liturgy. There is no evidence that the later writers who elaborate on the reunification of male and female are citing Paul; they represent rather a tradition with which Paul was acquainted, but which developed further quite independently of his influence. Paul, in fact, seems not to have been particularly interested in the male/female aspect of baptismal reu-

---

2. On the early development see Maurice F. Wiles, *The Divine Apostle* (London: Cambridge University Press, 1967), 128–30.

3. Irenaeus, *Haer.* 1.25.5 (= Harvey's ed. 1.20.3), tr. by Robert M. Grant in *Gnosticism: A Source Book of Heretical Writings from the Early Christian Period* (New York: Harper, 1961), 38. For other instances of Gnostic appeals to Paul, see above pp. 272–83.

4. See W. A. Meeks, "The Image of the Androgyne: Some Uses of a Symbol in Earliest Christianity," *HR* 13 (1974): 165–208; rep. in Meeks, *In Search of the Early Christians*, ed. by A. R. Hilton and H. G. Snyder (New Haven: Yale University Press, 2002), 3–54.

5. *The Gospel of Philip* 68: 22–24, tr. by Bentley Layton, *The Gnostic Scriptures* (Garden City, NY: Doubleday, 1987), 342.

6. The sacrament or "mystery" of the bridal chamber, mentioned in Irenaeus' description of the Marcosian Gnostics (*Haer.* 1.13.3 = Harvey 1.7.2; also Epiphanius, *Pan.* 34.2.6–11), is now better known through the *Gospel of Philip* and other documents from the Nag Hammadi library, though its precise nature and meaning are still debated.

7. We have modified the TNIV translation to bring out the Greek's clear allusion to Gen. 1:27; see note *in loc.*

nification, for in the other places where he and his immediate followers allude to the baptismal formula, that aspect is omitted (1 Cor. 12:15; Col. 3:11; cf. Eph. 2:14–16; 6:8). It is the reunification of Jew and Gentile that occupies Paul's primary attention.

Despite the polar tendencies of the interpreters of Paul's teachings on marriage, perhaps the dominant impression of Paul in the ancient church was that of the celibate who by "treading down and subjugating the body" made himself "a beautiful example and pattern to believers."[8] That is certainly the way he is depicted in the apocryphal Acts—those miracle-filled novels of apostolic exploits that were written in the second and third centuries. One of those, the *Acts of Paul*, contains our only physical description of Paul, one that strongly influenced the depiction of the apostle in painting and sculpture.[9] The whole *Acts of Paul* has not survived except in fragments of varying extent, but the portion reprinted here, which circulated separately, has come down in numerous manuscripts and translations.[1] The story principally of Thecla, a virgin saved by Paul from the terrible fate of marriage, it gives a clear picture of the way the apostle's mission was conceived in Encratite circles.[2] Whether the *Acts of Paul* was itself written by an Encratite is doubtful; Encratite ideology appears in fact only in the Thecla cycle, suggesting that these stories originated in such circles, but were adapted into a more "orthodox" novel about Paul by the compiler of the *Acts*. Tertullian (ca. 200) attributes the compilation to "a presbyter in Asia," who lost his position when he confessed his forgery.[3] It is commonly argued that Tertullian must have meant the compiler of the whole *Acts of Paul*, but that is by no means certain, since he mentions Thecla, and his language suggests that the book was issued under the pseudonym of Paul. Erik Peterson has proposed that the *Acts of Paul* was a mediating work, modeled after the *Acts* of Peter, of Thomas, of Andrew, and of John, which are rather clearly of Encratite or related origins. The new work was intended to commend Paul to the ascetics.[4] That is plausible, despite objections that have been raised,[5] but the precise situation that produced these *Acts* is far from being clarified. Their relationship to the Pastoral Epistles is a similarly contested issue; one possible connection is explored here in the essay by Dennis R. MacDonald.[6]

8. From "The First Epistle Concerning Virginity" of pseudo-Clement, chap. 9, tr. by M. B. Riddle in *The Ante-Nicene Fathers* (Grand Rapids: Eerdmans, 1951), Vol. 8, 58.
9. See *AP* 3 and the note on p. 212. On the portrayal of Paul in the visual arts, see also Ernst von Dobschütz, *Der Apostel Paulus*, vol.2: *Seine Stellung in der Kunst* (Halle: Buchhandlung des Weisenhauses, 1928).
1. The *Acts of Paul* contains three blocks of material that also circulated separately: the *Acts of Paul and Thecla*, which is the portion excerpted here; the *Correspondence of Paul and the Corinthians* (see pp. 144–47 above); and the *Martyrdom of Paul* (see pp. 224–27 above). For a recent collection of essays on this composite document, see Jan N. Bremmer (ed.), *The Apocryphal Acts of Paul and Thecla* (Kampen: Kok Pharos, 1996).
2. For women and asceticism, see esp. R. S. Kraemer, "The Conversion of Women to Ascetic Forms of Christianity," *Signs* 6 (1980): 298–307; E. A. Clark, *Ascetic Piety and Women's Faith: Essays on Late Antique Christianity* (Lewiston, NY: Mellen, 1986); and J. Simpson, "Women and Asceticism in the Fourth Century: A Question of Interpretation," *JRH* 15 (1988): 38–60.
3. *Bapt.* 17.
4. "Einige Beobachtungen zu den Anfangen der christlichen Askese," and "Einige Bemerkungen zum Hamburger Papyrusfragment der Acta Pauli," both reprinted in *Frühkirche, Judentum and Gnosis* (Rome, Freiburg, Vienna: Herder, 1959), 183–220. A modified version of Peterson's position is argued by H. J. W. Drijvers, "Der getaufte Löwe und die Theologie der Acta Pauli," in *Carl-Schmidt-Kolloquium 1988*, ed. by P. Nagel (Halle, 1990), 181–89; rep. in his *History and Religion in Late Antique Syria* (Aldershot: Variorum, 1994), chap. 10.
5. P. Devos, "Actes de Thomas et Actes de Paul," in *Analecta Bollandiana* 69 (1951): 119–30; W. Schneemelcher in *New Testament Apocrypha* (rev. ed.; Cambridge: J. Clarke and Louisville: Westminster John Knox, 1992), vol. 2, 213–37.
6. See also two treatments by Willy Rordorf, "In welchem Verhältnis stehen die apokryphen Paulusakten zur kanonischen Apostelgeschichte und zu den Pastoralbriefen?" in *Text and Testimony*, ed. by T. Baarda et al. (Kampen: Kok, 1988), 225–41, and "Nochmals: Paulusakten und Pastoralbriefe," in *Tradition and Interpretation in the New Testament*, ed. by G. F. Hawthorne and O. Betz (Grand Rapids: Eerdmans; Tübingen: Mohr-Siebeck, 1987), 225–41. Both essays are reprinted in his *Lex orandi—Lex credendi* (Freiburg: Universitätsverlag, 1993), 449–65, 466–74. He argues

ANONYMOUS

The Acts of Paul and Thecla (ca. 190?)†

[3:]1. As Paul was going to Iconium after his flight from Antioch, his fellow-travellers were Demas and Hermogenes,[1] the copper-smith, who were full of hypocrisy and flattered Paul as if they loved him. Paul, looking only to the goodness of Christ, did them no harm but loved them exceedingly so that he made sweet to them all the words of the Lord and the interpretation of the gospel concerning the birth and resurrection of the Beloved; and he gave them an account, word for word, of the great deeds of Christ as they were revealed to him.

2. And a certain man, by name Onesiphorus,[2] hearing that Paul was to come to Iconium, went out to meet him with his children Simmias and Zeno and his wife Lectra, in order that he might entertain him. Titus had informed him what Paul looked like, for he had not seen him in the flesh, but only in the spirit.

3. And he went along the royal road to Lystra and kept looking at the passers-by according to the description of Titus. And he saw Paul coming, a man small in size, bald-headed, bandy-legged, of noble mien, with eye-brows meeting, rather hook-nosed, full of grace. Sometimes he seemed like a man, and sometimes he had the face of an angel.

4. And Paul, seeing Onesiphorus, smiled; and Onesiphorus said, 'Hail, O servant of the blessed God.' And he said, 'Grace be with you and your house.' And Demas and Hermogenes were jealous and showed greater hypocrisy, so that Demas said, 'Are we not of the blessed God that you have not thus saluted us?' And Onesiphorus said, 'I do not see in you the fruit of righteousness, but if such you be, come also into my house and refresh yourselves.'

5. And after Paul had gone into the house of Onesiphorus there was great joy and bowing of knees and breaking of bread and the word of God about abstinence and the resurrection. Paul said, 'Blessed are the pure in heart, for they shall see God;[3] blessed are those who have kept the flesh chaste, for they shall become a temple of God; blessed are the continent, for God shall speak with them; blessed are those who have kept aloof from this world, for they shall be pleasing to God; blessed are those who have wives as not having them, for they shall experience God;[4] blessed are those who have fear of God, for they shall become angels of God.

6. 'Blessed are those who respect the word of God, for they shall be comforted;[5] blessed are those who have received the wisdom of Jesus

---

that the compiler of the *Acts of Paul* knew neither the canonical Acts of the Apostles nor the Pastoral Epistles but makes use of some of the same traditions as the authors of these writings. Others argue that he knew both; see, e.g., Richard Bauckham, "The *Acts of Paul* as a Sequel to Acts," in *The Book of Acts in Its Ancient Literary Setting*, ed. by B. W. Winter and A. D. Clarke (Grand Rapids: Eerdmans, 1993), 105–54.

† Tr. by J. K. Elliott, *The Apocryphal New Testament* (Oxford: Clarendon, 1993), 364–72. Reprinted by permission of Oxford University Press.

1. Demas: Phlm. 24; Col. 4:14; 2 Tim. 4:10. Hermogenes: 2 Tim. 1:15.
2. 2 Tim. 1:16–18; 4:19.
3. Matt. 5:8.
4. I Cor. 7:29; Rom 8:17.
5. Matt. 5:4.

Christ, for they shall be called the sons of the Most High;[6] blessed are those who have kept the baptism, for they shall be refreshed by the Father and the Son; blessed are those who have come to a knowledge of Jesus Christ, for they shall be in the light; blessed are those who through love of God no longer conform to the world, for they shall judge angels, and shall be blessed at the right hand of the Father; blessed are the merciful, for they shall obtain mercy[7] and shall not see the bitter day of judgement; blessed are the bodies of the virgins, for they shall be well pleasing to God and shall not lose the reward of their chastity. For the word of the Father shall become to them a work of salvation in the day of the Son, and they shall have rest for ever and ever.'

7. And while Paul was speaking in the midst of the church in the house of Onesiphorus a certain virgin named Thecla, the daughter of Theoclia, betrothed to a man named Thamyris, was sitting at the window close by and listened day and night to the discourse of virginity, as proclaimed by Paul. And she did not look away from the window, but was led on by faith, rejoicing exceedingly. And when she saw many women and virgins going in to Paul she also had an eager desire to be deemed worthy to stand in Paul's presence and hear the word of Christ. For she had not yet seen Paul in person, but only heard his word.

8. As she did not move from the window her mother sent to Thamyris. And he came gladly as if already receiving her in marriage. And Thamyris said to Theoclia, 'Where, then, is my Thecla ⟨that I may see her⟩?'[8] And Theoclia answered, 'I have a strange story to tell you, Thamyris. For three days and three nights Thecla does not rise from the window either to eat or to drink; but looking earnestly as if upon some pleasant sight she is devoted to a foreigner teaching deceitful and artful discourses, so that I wonder how a virgin of her great modesty exposes herself to such extreme discomfort.

9. 'Thamyris, this man will overturn the city of the Iconians and your Thecla too; for all the women and the young men go in to him to be taught by him. He says one must fear only one God and live in chastity. Moreover, my daughter, clinging to the window like a spider, lays hold of what is said by him with a strange eagerness and fearful emotion. For the virgin looks eagerly at what is said by him and has been captivated. But go near and speak to her, for she is betrothed to you.'

10. And Thamyris greeted her with a kiss, but at the same time being afraid of her overpowering emotion said, 'Thecla, my betrothed, why do you sit thus? And what sort of feeling holds you distracted? Come back to your Thamyris and be ashamed.' Moreover, her mother said the same, 'Why do you sit thus looking down, my child, and answering nothing, like a sick woman?' And those who were in the house wept bitterly, Thamyris for the loss of a wife, Theoclia for that of a child, and the maidservants for that of a mistress. And there was a great outpouring of lamentation in the house. And while these things were going on Thecla did not turn away but kept attending to the word of Paul.

11. And Thamyris, jumping up, went into the street, and watched all who went in to Paul and came out. And he saw two men bitterly quarrelling

6. Matt. 5:9.
7. Matt. 5:7.
8. Words bracketed are absent in Greek MSS.

with each other and he said to them, 'Men, who are you and tell me who is this man among you, leading astray the souls of young men and deceiving virgins so that they should not marry but remain as they are? I promise you money enough if you tell me about him, for I am the chief man of this city.'

12. And Demas and Hermogenes said to him, 'Who he is we do not know. But he deprives the husbands of wives and maidens of husbands, saying, "There is for you no resurrection unless you remain chaste and do not pollute the flesh." '

13. And Thamyris said to them, 'Come into my house and refresh yourselves.' And they went to a sumptuous supper and much wine and great wealth and a splendid table. And Thamyris made them drink, for he loved Thecla and wished to take her as wife. And during the supper Thamyris said, 'Men, tell me what is his teaching that I also may know it, for I am greatly distressed about Thecla, because she so loves the stranger and I am prevented from marrying.'

14. And Demas and Hermogenes said, 'Bring him before the Governor Castellius because he persuades the multitude to embrace the new teaching of the Christians, and he will destroy him and you shall have Thecla as your wife. And we shall teach you about the resurrection which he says is to come, that it has already taken place in the children[9] and that we rise again, after having come to the knowledge of the true God.'

15. And when Thamyris heard these things he rose up early in the morning and, filled with jealousy and anger, went into the house of Onesiphorus with rulers and officers and a great crowd with batons and said to Paul, 'You have deceived the city of the Iconians and especially my betrothed bride so that she will not have me! Let us go to the governor Castellius!' And the whole crowd cried, 'Away with the sorcerer for he has misled all our wives!', and the multitude was also incited.

16. And Thamyris standing before the tribunal said with a great shout, 'O proconsul, this man—we do not know where he comes from—makes virgins averse to marriage. Let him say before you why he teaches thus.' But Demas and Hermogenes said to Thamyris, 'Say that he is a Christian and he will die at once.' But the governor kept his resolve and called Paul, saying, 'Who are you and what do you teach? For they bring no small accusation against you.'

17. And Paul, lifting up his voice, said, 'If I today must tell any of my teachings then listen, O proconsul. The living God, the God of vengeance, the jealous God, the God who has need of nothing, who seeks the salvation of men, has sent me that I may rescue them from corruption and uncleanness and from all pleasure, and from death, that they may sin no more. On this account God sent his Son whose gospel I preach and teach, that in him men have hope, who alone has had compassion upon a world led astray, that men may be no longer under judgement but may have faith and fear of God and knowledge of honesty and love of truth. If then I teach the things revealed to me by God what harm do I do, O proconsul?' When the governor heard this he ordered Paul to be bound and sent to prison until he had time to hear him more attentively.

18. And Thecla, by night, took off her bracelets and gave them to the

9. 2 Tim. 2:18.

gatekeeper; and when the door was opened to her she went into the prison. To the jailer she gave a silver mirror and was thus enabled to go in to Paul and, sitting at his feet, she heard the great deeds of God. And Paul was afraid of nothing, but trusted in God. And her faith also increased and she kissed his bonds.

19. And when Thecla was sought for by her family and Thamyris they were hunting through the streets as if she had been lost. One of the gatekeeper's fellow slaves informed them that she had gone out by night. And they examined the gatekeeper who said to them, 'She has gone to the foreigner in the prison.' And they went and found her, so to say, chained to him by affection. And having gone out from there they incited the people and informed the governor what had happened.

20. And he ordered Paul to be brought before the tribunal, but Thecla was riveted to the place where Paul had sat whilst in prison. And the governor ordered her also to be brought to the tribunal, and she came with an exceedingly great joy. And when Paul had been led forth the crowd vehemently cried out, 'He is a sorcerer. Away with him!' But the governor gladly heard Paul speak about the holy works of Christ. And having taken counsel, he summoned Thecla and said, 'Why do you not marry Thamyris, according to the law of the Iconians?' But she stood looking earnestly at Paul. And when she gave no answer Theoclia, her mother, cried out saying, 'Burn the wicked one; burn her who will not marry in the midst of the theatre, that all the women who have been taught by this man may be afraid.'

21. And the governor was greatly moved, and after scourging Paul he cast him out of the city. But Thecla he condemned to be burned. And immediately the governor arose and went away to the theatre. And the whole multitude went out to witness the spectacle. But as a lamb in the wilderness looks around for the shepherd, so Thecla kept searching for Paul. And having looked into the crowd she saw the Lord sitting in the likeness of Paul and said, 'As if I were unable to endure, Paul has come to look after me.' And she gazed upon him with great earnestness, but he went up into heaven.

22. And the boys and girls brought wood and straw in order that Thecla might be burned. And when she came in naked the governor wept and admired the power that was in her. And the executioners arranged the wood and told her to go up on the pile. And having made the sign of the cross she went up on the pile. And they lighted the fire. And though a great fire was blazing it did not touch her. For God, having compassion upon her, made an underground rumbling, and a cloud full of water and hail overshadowed the theatre from above, and all its contents were poured out so that many were in danger of death. And the fire was put out and Thecla saved.

23. And Paul was fasting with Onesiphorus and his wife and his children in a new tomb on the way which led from Iconium to Daphne. And after many days had been spent in fasting the children said to Paul, 'We are hungry.' And they had nothing with which to buy bread, for Onesiphorus had left the things of this world and followed Paul with all his house. And Paul, having taken off his cloak, said, 'Go, my child, sell this and buy some loaves and bring them.' And when the child was buying them he saw Thecla their neighbour and was astonished and said, 'Thecla, where

are you going?' And she said, 'I have been saved from the fire and am following Paul.' And the child said, 'Come, I shall take you to him; for he has been mourning for you and praying and fasting six days already.'

24. And when she had come to the tomb Paul was kneeling and praying, 'Father of Christ, let not the fire touch Thecla but stand by her, for she is yours'; she, standing behind him, cried out, 'O Father who made the heaven and the earth, the Father of your beloved Son Jesus Christ, I praise you that you have saved me from the fire that I may see Paul again.' And Paul, rising up, saw her and said, 'O God, who knows the heart, Father of our Lord Jesus Christ, I praise you because you have speedily heard my prayer.'

25. And there was great love in the tomb as Paul and Onesiphorus and the others all rejoiced. And they had five loaves and vegetables and water, and they rejoiced in the holy works of Christ. And Thecla said to Paul, 'I will cut my hair off and I shall follow you wherever you go.' But he said, 'Times are evil and you are beautiful. I am afraid lest another temptation come upon you worse than the first and that you do not withstand it but become mad after men.' And Thecla said, 'Only give me the seal in Christ, and no temptation shall touch me.' And Paul said, 'Thecla, be patient; you shall receive the water.'

26. And Paul sent away Onesiphorus and all his family to Iconium and went into Antioch, taking Thecla with him. And as soon as they had arrived a certain Syrian, Alexander[1] by name, an influential citizen of Antioch, seeing Thecla, became enamoured of her and tried to bribe Paul with gifts and presents. But Paul said, 'I know not the woman of whom you speak, nor is she mine.' But he, being of great power, embraced her in the street. But she would not endure it and looked about for Paul. And she cried out bitterly, saying, 'Do not force the stranger; do not force the servant of God. I am one of the chief persons of the Iconians and because I would not marry Thamyris I have been cast out of the city.' And taking hold of Alexander, she tore his cloak and pulled off his crown and made him a laughing-stock.

27. And he, although loving her, nevertheless felt ashamed of what had happened and led her before the governor; and as she confessed that she had done these things he condemned her to the wild beasts. The women of the city cried out before the tribunal, 'Evil judgement! impious judgement!' And Thecla asked the governor that she might remain pure until she was to fight with the wild beasts. And a rich woman named Queen Tryphaena,[2] whose daughter was dead, took her under her protection and had her for a consolation.

28. And when the beasts were exhibited they bound her to a fierce lioness, and Queen Tryphaena followed her. And the lioness, with Thecla sitting upon her, licked her feet; and all the multitude was astonished. And the charge on her inscription was 'Sacrilegious.' And the women and children cried out again and again, 'O God, outrageous things take place in this city.' And after the exhibition Tryphaena received her again. For her dead daughter Falconilla had said to her in a dream, 'Mother, receive this stranger, the forsaken Thecla, in my place, that she may pray for me and I may come to the place of the just.'

1. Cf. 1 Tim. 1:19–20; 2 Tim. 4:14–15.
2. Cf. Rom. 16:12. She is later identified as a kinswoman of the emperor (3:36).

29. And when, after the exhibition, Tryphaena had received her she was grieved because Thecla had to fight on the following day with the wild beasts, but on the other hand she loved her dearly like her daughter Falconilla and said, 'Thecla, my second child, come, pray for my child that she may live in eternity, for this I saw in my sleep.' And without hesitation she lifted up her voice and said, 'My God, Son of the Most High, who are in heaven, grant her wish that her daughter Falconilla may live in eternity.' And when Thecla had spoken Tryphaena grieved very much, considering that such beauty was to be thrown to the wild beasts.

30. And when it was dawn Alexander came to her, for it was he who arranged the exhibition of wild beasts, and said, 'The governor has taken his seat and the crowd is clamouring for us; get ready, I will take her to fight with the wild beasts.' And Tryphaena put him to flight with a loud cry, saying, 'A second mourning for my Falconilla has come upon my house, and there is no one to help, neither child for she is dead, nor kinsman for I am a widow. God of Thecla, my child, help Thecla.'

31. And the governor sent soldiers to bring Thecla. Tryphaena did not leave her but took her by the hand and led her away saying, 'My daughter Falconilla I took away to the tomb, but you, Thecla, I take to fight the wild beasts.' And Thecla wept bitterly and sighed to the Lord, 'O Lord God, in whom I trust, to whom I have fled for refuge, who did deliver me from the fire, reward Tryphaena who has had compassion on your servant and because she kept me pure.'

32. And there arose a tumult: the wild beasts roared, the people and the women sitting together were crying, some saying, 'Away with the sacrilegious person!', others saying, 'O that the city would be destroyed on account of this iniquity! Kill us all, proconsul; miserable spectacle, evil judgement!'

33. And Thecla, having been taken from the hands of Tryphaena, was stripped and received a girdle and was thrown into the arena. And lions and bears were let loose upon her. And a fierce lioness ran up and lay down at her feet. And the multitude of the women cried aloud. And a bear ran upon her, but the lioness went to meet it and tore the bear to pieces. And again a lion that had been trained to fight against men, which belonged to Alexander, ran upon her. And the lioness, encountering the lion, was killed along with it. And the women cried the more since the lioness, her protector, was dead.

34. Then they sent in many beasts as she was standing and stretching forth her hands and praying. And when she had finished her prayer she turned around and saw a large pit full of water and said, 'Now it is time to wash myself.' And she threw herself in saying, 'In the name of Jesus Christ I baptize myself on my last day.' When the women and the multitude saw it they wept and said, 'Do not throw yourself into the water!'; even the governor shed tears because the seals were to devour such beauty. She then threw herself into the water in the name of Jesus Christ, but the seals, having seen a flash of lightning, floated dead on the surface. And there was round her a cloud of fire so that the beasts could neither touch her nor could she be seen naked.

35. But the women lamented when other and fiercer animals were let loose; some threw petals, others nard, others cassia, others amomum, so that there was an abundance of perfumes. And all the wild beasts were

hypnotized and did not touch her. And Alexander said to the governor, 'I have some terrible bulls to which we will bind her.' And the governor consented grudgingly, 'Do what you will.' And they bound her by the feet between the bulls and put red-hot irons under their genitals so that they, being rendered more furious, might kill her. They rushed forward but the burning flame around her consumed the ropes, and she was as if she had not been bound.

36. And Tryphaena fainted standing beside the arena, so that the servants said, 'Queen Tryphaena is dead.' And the governor put a stop to the games and the whole city was in dismay. And Alexander fell down at the feet of the governor and cried, 'Have mercy upon me and upon the city and set the woman free, lest the city also be destroyed. For if Caesar hear of these things he will possibly destroy the city along with us because his kinswoman, Queen Tryphaena, has died at the theatre gate.'

37. And the governor summoned Thecla out of the midst of the beasts and said to her, 'Who are you? And what is there about you that not one of the wild beasts touched you?' She answered, 'I am a servant of the living God and, as to what there is about me, I have believed in the Son of God in whom he is well pleased; that is why not one of the beasts touched me. For he alone is the goal of salvation and the basis of immortal life. For he is a refuge to the tempest-tossed, a solace to the afflicted, a shelter to the despairing; in brief, whoever does not believe in him shall not live but be dead forever.'

38. When the governor heard these things he ordered garments to be brought and to be put on her. And she said, 'He who clothed me when I was naked among the beasts will in the day of judgement clothe me with salvation.' And taking the garments she put them on.

And the governor immediately issued an edict saying, 'I release to you the pious Thecla, the servant of God.' And the women shouted aloud and with one voice praised God, 'One is the God, who saved Thecla', so that the whole city was shaken by their voices.

39. And Tryphaena, having received the good news, went with the multitude to meet Thecla. After embracing her she said, 'Now I believe that the dead are raised! Now I believe that my child lives. Come inside and all that is mine I shall assign to you.' And Thecla went in with her and rested eight days, instructing her in the word of God, so that many of the maidservants believed. And there was great joy in the house.

40. And Thecla longed for Paul and sought him, looking in every direction. And she was told that he was in Myra. And wearing a mantle that she had altered so as to make a man's cloak, she came with a band of young men and maidens to Myra, where she found Paul speaking the word of God and went to him. And he was astonished at seeing her and her companions, thinking that some new temptation was coming upon her. And perceiving this, she said to him, 'I have received baptism, O Paul; for he who worked with you for the gospel has worked with me also for baptism.'

41. And Paul, taking her, led her to the house of Hermias and heard everything from her, so that he greatly wondered and those who heard were strengthened and prayed for Tryphaena. And Thecla rose up and said to Paul, 'I am going to Iconium.' Paul answered, 'Go, and teach the word of God.' And Tryphaena sent her much clothing and gold so that she could leave many things to Paul for the service of the poor.

42. And coming to Iconium she went into the house of Onesiphorus and fell upon the place where Paul had sat and taught the word of God, and she cried and said, 'My God and God of this house where the light shone upon me, Jesus Christ, Son of God, my help in prison, my help before the governors, my help in the fire, my help among the wild beasts, you alone are God and to you be glory for ever. Amen.'

43. And she found Thamyris dead but her mother alive. And calling her mother she said, 'Theoclia, my mother, can you believe that the Lord lives in heaven? For if you desire wealth the Lord will give it to you through me; or if you desire your child, behold, I am standing beside you.'

And having thus testified, she went to Seleucia and enlightened many by the word of God; then she rested in a glorious sleep.

DENNIS R. MacDONALD

The Pastoral Epistles against "Old Wives' Tales" (1983)†

Even though each of the Pastoral Epistles bears Paul's name, they are pseudonymous; their author is anonymous. But if not by Paul, then where, when, and by whom were they written?

We have no external evidence of the letters before the last quarter of the second century; therefore, they could have been written as late as the middle of that century but more probably sometime between 100 and 140. Whatever their date, they undoubtedly were written from Asia Minor, for the letters are saturated with personal and place names identified with the subcontinent. Two of the letters are addressed to Timothy, who, according to the Acts of the Apostles, was a native of Lystra, was known to the church in Iconium, and accompanied Paul through Phrygia, Galatia, and provincial Asia (Acts 16:1–11). According to 1 Tim. 1:3, Paul left Timothy in Ephesus to lead the church there. Furthermore, in 2 Tim. 1:15 we find a reference to Asia; in 1:18 to Ephesus; in 3:11 to Antioch, Iconium, and Lystra; in 4:10–13 to Galatia, Ephesus, and Troas; and in 4:20 to Miletus.

To be sure, the mere concentration of Asia Minor place-names is no guarantee of their Asian origin, but several other factors contribute to make this judgment almost certain. Hans von Campenhausen has demonstrated that the ecclesiastical organization, the theological postures, and the social issues addressed in the Pastoral Epistles were all present when Polycarp, bishop of Smyrna, wrote his letter to the Philippians. In fact, so impressed was Von Campenhausen by these similarities that he claimed Polycarp wrote the Pastoral Epistles as well. Even though this thesis goes far beyond the evidence, Von Campenhausen's sharp eye for similarities between Polycarp and the Pastoral Epistles has helped to establish their second-century Asia Minor setting.

† From *The Legend and the Apostle* (Philadelphia: Westminster Press, 1983), 54–77. Copyright © 1983 by Dennis Ronald MacDonald. Reprinted by permission of Westminster John Knox Press. MacDonald is John Wesley Professor of New Testament and Christian Origins at the Claremont School of Theology and serves as the director of the Institute for Antiquity and Christianity at Claremont Graduate University.

Several other scholars have tried to peek behind the author's mask and have claimed the author was not Polycarp but was the same person who wrote Luke-Acts. Ironically, some of the most telling arguments against this theory are the special conditions given by those who defend it in order to make it plausible. But even if one granted these conditions—which I do not—one still could not account for other differences between Luke-Acts and the Pastoral Epistles, such as their contradictory assessments of celibacy (cf. Luke 20:34–35 and 1 Tim. 4:3). We shall probably never know the identity of the author. He must remain masked and unnamed. But the very fact that he chose to mask himself as Paul reveals much about what he hoped his letters would accomplish.

Pseudonymity, or writing in another's name, was a widespread early Christian practice, especially in the Pauline tradition. In addition to the Pastoral Epistles we know of correspondence between Paul and Seneca, an *Epistle to the Laodiceans*, a third letter to the Corinthians, a *Prayer of the Apostle Paul*, and an *Apocalypse of Paul*. [Editors' Note: See Part III.] The New Testament books Ephesians, Colossians, and 2 Thessalonians also probably are pseudonymous. But while there is little doubt that pseudonymity was a popular early Christian literary exercise, there remains a vigorous debate over its legitimacy. To some it simply was a means by which unoriginal minds attempted to give authority to writings otherwise devoid of it, and as such, pseudonymity was a deceptive and deleterious development in the history of the church. Even in antiquity some rejected pseudonymity as a despicable deception, though there were still times when they recognized it as legitimate. In the Hellenistic world, pseudonymity was a school exercise whereby a student attempted to demonstrate a mastery of the style, vocabulary, and philosophical perspectives of a venerated author.

Other scholars have argued that pseudonymity not only was a legitimate literary activity but was consistent with the very nature of early Christian experience. According to some, authors who wrote under a pseudonym did so as the result of ecstatic inspiration in which they became identified with the spirit of another. Others suggest that pseudonymity was the "logical conclusion of the presupposition that the Spirit himself [sic!] was the real author." Out of deference to "the authentic witness, the Holy Spirit, the Lord, and the apostles" the author chose not to write in his own name. According to others, pseudonymity reflects an author's belief that he had been sent out on his mission in the name of an apostle and therefore was justified in writing in that name. Recently several German scholars have championed yet another explanation of pseudonymity: the author recognized the normative value of a certain period in the past for the self-understanding of his community, and by writing in the name of someone from that period he attempted to "personalize the tradition." Pseudonymity, therefore, represents a kind of "transsubjectivity" in that it reclaims the foundational period by identifying with one important figure of that time, and by translating the perspective of that figure into the new situation of the church.

Each of these positive evaluations of pseudonymity downplays the relevance of intra-Christian disputes over the legacy of the apostles which characterized the church of the first two centuries. Paul was a hero not only in that tradition of the church which ultimately became dominant but also among Christian Gnostics, Marcionites, and Montanists. The author of 2 Peter, writing around 150, complains about opponents who twist Paul's letter to support their own positions and who apparently were successful in carrying away many people from the author's religious community (2 Peter 3:15–17).

Consequently, some interpreters have preferred to explain the Pauline facade of the Pastoral Epistles as a literary device for convincing readers that the author's understanding of Paul was the correct one. This explanation accounts for the insistence throughout the letters that they were indeed from Paul's own hand. More than any other pseudo-Pauline document—canonical or noncanonical—the letters struggle to pass themselves off as authentic. Over and over again the author alludes to places, people, and events traditionally identified with the apostle; for example, we find twenty-seven different names of Paul's associates compressed into these three short letters. But if we are to be more precise about the function of this Pauline disguise, we must identify the false teachers against whom the letters were written.

Fully one fifth of the Pastoral Epistles directly refutes false teachers, and many other passages do so indirectly. From this quantity of material one might assume that identifying these opponents would be easy, but the contrary is true. Few issues in the interpretation of these letters have proved as baffling or controversial as describing these elusive foes. The confusion is due to two factors: first, only once does the author engage his opponents in direct theological discourse (1 Tim. 4:1–5); otherwise he resorts to name-calling. Second, it is difficult to identify all the refutations with the characteristics of a single opponent. Those who do so frequently create some unnatural hybrid, like Werner Georg Kümmel's limping centaur: "Jewish-Christian, Gnostic." John J. Gunther lists nineteen different scholarly hypotheses for the identification of these opponents.

Probably it is more nearly correct to think that the Pastoral Epistles oppose false teachers of various kinds: Gnostics (1 Tim. 6:20; cf. 1:3–11; 2 Tim. 2:14–19), Jewish Christians (Titus 1:10–16), and perhaps Marcionites. But there is yet another opponent denounced in the letters who seldom has been identified: Paul himself as depicted in the legend tradition.

The False Teachers and the Legendary Paul

Many characteristics of the false teachers are identical with those of Paul in the legends. For example, in 2 Tim. 3:6–7 Paul commands Timothy to avoid those

> who make their way into households and capture weak women, burdened with sins and swayed by various impulses, who will listen to anybody and can never arrive at a knowledge of the truth.

The word rendered by the Revised Standard Version as "capture" more literally means "to take prisoner of war." The imagery therefore is of missionaries who, like soldiers, enter households and carry off "little women" (gynaikaria) as prisoners. This is precisely what Paul does with Thecla, Artemilla, and Eubula in the Acts of Paul, all of whom leave their lovers to follow the apostle. But in the Pastoral Epistles such women must not leave their households to follow teachers, for they will never comprehend the truth. Instead of responding rationally, they are driven about by base impulses and are burdened down with unnecessary guilt—presumably guilt related to sexual activity and desires.

This concern for the welfare of the household also appears in Titus 1: 10–15, where the opponents are accused of "upsetting whole households by teaching for base gain what they have no right to teach" (v. 11). In v. 15 we see that one aspect of their teaching was asceticism: "To the pure all things are pure, but to the corrupt and unbelieving nothing is pure; their very minds and consciences are corrupted."

In 1 Timothy 4 we find another passage objecting to the asceticism of the false teachers:

> Now the Spirit expressly says that in later times some will depart from the faith by giving heed to deceitful spirits and doctrines of demons, through the pretentions of liars whose consciences are seared, who forbid marriage and enjoin abstinence from foods which God created to be received with thanksgiving by those who believe and know the truth. (1 Tim. 4:1–3)

Obviously the author would have had little sympathy with the Paul of the *Acts of Paul* for whom chastity was a requirement for resurrection (*AP* 3: 12; cf. 3:5). But this passage also contradicts the Paul of the *Acts of Paul* at two other points.

First, in the *Acts of Paul* the apostle is a vegetarian and a teetotaler. Even the Eucharist consists of bread and water instead of wine. The author of the Pastorals, on the other hand, opposes such abstinence from foods and in fact tells Timothy, "No longer drink only water, but use a little wine for the sake of your stomach" (1 Tim. 5:23).

Second, the author claims that the opponents' teaching of asceticism was inspired by "deceitful spirits and doctrines of demons," and not by the Holy Spirit, whom he enlists for his own position: "The Spirit expressly says. . . ." Presumably, the opponents legitimated their asceticism by claims of inspiration, or their inspiration by their asceticism. Both are closely related in the *Acts of Paul* and in the communities in which they most likely were told. In the Thecla story we are told that it is to the continent that God will speak (*AP* 3:5). Thus, throughout the legends those who see visions or speak in the Spirit are the continent, like Paul, Thecla, and the prophetess Myrta.

This association of celibacy with revelation characterizes Montanism. According to the prophetess Priscilla: "[Sexual] purity is harmonious, and they see visions; and, turning their face downward, they even hear manifest voices." Presumably, this is why Montanus annulled marriages at the outbreak of the New Prophecy in central Asia Minor early in the second half of the second century. Both Maximilla and Priscilla deserted their husbands after they received their prophetic gifts, and the Montanist prophet Proclus maintained his virginity until his death. Epiphanius says that Quintillian assemblies commenced with a procession of prophesying virgins.

The author of the Pastorals tries to break this bond between prophecy and celibacy in three ways. First, as we have seen, the Spirit condemns such celibacy as demonic. Second, celibacy and dietary restrictions, instead of attesting a strong and sensitive conscience, attest a conscience either cauterized and thus insensitive to right and wrong, or branded and thus owned by demonic powers. Third, the author accuses the opponents of lying, which may mean nothing more than that they claimed divine approval for their asceticism when in fact they had none. But it could also mean that these opponents told legends about Paul which depicted him as an ascetic. Notice that this passage against celibate prophets continues through vs. 7 and 8, where the author warns Timothy to avoid "old wives' tales."

> Avoid the profane tales told by old women. Rather train yourself toward godliness. For training of the body profits little, but piety is profitable in every way.

If, as many interpreters have suggested, the bodily training opposed here refers to ascetic disciplines, it would confirm our thesis that the liars in v. 2 who forbid marriage should be identified with the women in v. 7 who told stories. To the women these stories were sacred legends; to the author of the Pastorals they were sinister lies.

Nowhere is the disagreement between our legends and the Pastorals more apparent than in 1 Tim. 2:11–15:

> Let a woman learn in silence with all submissiveness. I permit no woman to teach or to have authority over men; she is to keep silent. For Adam was formed first, then Eve; and Adam was not deceived, but the woman was deceived and became a transgressor. Yet woman will be saved through bearing children, if they continue in faith and love and holiness, with modesty.

In the legends, Paul commissions a woman to teach, here he forbids it. In the legends, Paul tells women that only the continent will be saved, here he tells women they shall be saved by bearing children. Instead of luring Thecla away from her lover and encouraging her to teach the word of God, the author of the Pastorals indicates that Paul would have had her marry, be submissive to her husband, raise lots of children, and live happily—in silent domestication—ever after.

In addition to these obvious disagreements between the legends and the Pastoral Epistles there also are many similarities which make it likely that the author knew our legends at some stage in their oral transmission.

The Acts of Paul *and the Pastoral Epistles*

Certain references to Paul's associates and experiences in the Pastoral Epistles cannot be accounted for in terms of independent historical reminiscences of events in Paul's life, nor in terms of dependence on the Acts of the Apostles or on Paul's own letters. Therefore, unless the author fabricated these names and episodes, he probably learned of them through oral channels. I shall attempt to show that because many of these names and episodes appear in the *Acts of Paul* as well as in the Pastoral Epistles, and because literary dependence of one of these documents on the other must be ruled highly unlikely, it would appear that both authors knew the same oral legends about Paul.

In the Thecla story Paul travels with Demas and Hermogenes to Iconium, where they are entertained by Onesiphorus and his family. Later, Demas and Hermogenes desert Paul for a bribe, but the household of Onesiphorus remains faithful to Paul, even though he is imprisoned. Compare these events with 2 Tim. 1:15–18, where the two devious fellow missionaries are not Demas and Hermogenes but Phygelus and Hermogenes:

> You are aware that all who are in *Asia* turned away from me, and among them Phygelus and *Hermogenes*. May the Lord grant mercy to the household of *Onesiphorus*, for he often refreshed me; he was not ashamed of my chains, but when he arrived in Rome he searched for me eagerly and found me—may the Lord grant him to find mercy from the Lord on that Day—and you well know all the service he rendered at Ephesus. (Italics added)

Only in the *Acts of Paul* and the Pastorals in all of early Christian literature do we find a reference to Onesiphorus, and in both he is identified with Asia Minor, in both he befriends Paul during a time of imprisonment, and in both he always appears with his family. Likewise, only in the *Acts* and in the Pastorals do we find a reference to Hermogenes, and in both he is twinned with a companion and deserts Paul in Asia Minor. Even though in the Pastorals Hermogenes is not accompanied by Demas, the author also knows of Demas' desertion: "Demas, in love with this present world, has deserted me" (2 Tim. 4:10a). Philemon, v. 24 and Colossians 4:14 also mention Demas, but only in the *Acts of Paul* and the Pastorals does he desert Paul, and in both his motivation for doing so is greed. In the *Acts of Paul*, Demas and Hermogenes tell Thamyris that the resurrection already has taken place. The only other place in all of early Christian literature where two persons make this claim is in the Pastorals, where Hymenaeus and Philetus are said to have "swerved from the truth by holding that the resurrection is past already. They are upsetting the faith of some" (2 Tim. 2:17–18).

In the *Acts of Paul*, Paul and Thecla leave Iconium, travel toward Lystra, and arrive in Antioch, where Alexander opposes Paul and tries to kill Thecla. The only other reference to an Alexander opposing Paul is in the Pastorals:

> Alexander the coppersmith did me great harm; the Lord will requite him for his deeds. Beware of him yourself, for he strongly opposed our message. (2 Tim. 4:14–15; cf. 1 Tim. 1:19–20)

It would appear that here, as in the *Acts of Paul*, Alexander is a threat to the Pauline mission in Asia Minor, for Timothy is warned to watch out for him in Ephesus.

Further evidence that the author knew of these events in Iconium, Lystra, and Antioch comes from 2 Tim. 3:10–11:

> Now you have observed my teaching, my conduct, my aim in life, my faith, my patience, my love, my steadfastness, my persecutions, my sufferings, what befell me at Antioch; at Iconium, and at Lystra, what persecutions I endured; yet from them all the Lord rescued me.

The Acts of the Apostles also mentions Paul's persecutions in these three cities; therefore, one might argue, the parallels between the *Acts of Paul* and the Pastorals could be explained in terms of a shared knowledge of the canonical Acts. However, the Acts and the *Acts of Paul* share nothing in common regarding the circumstances of Paul's persecutions. Likewise, in the Pastorals, Paul reminds Timothy that he "has observed" these persecutions, but in Acts they all take place prior to Paul meeting Timothy (Acts 16:1–3). If the authors of the *Acts of Paul* and of the Pastorals knew the canonical Acts, they certainly did not take efforts to make their accounts conform with it. Probably we should explain these parallels between the *Acts of Paul* and the Pastorals as we would the others which obviously cannot be attributed to a shared knowledge of Acts.

[Earlier] we saw the similarities between the story of the baptized lion and the Pastorals. According to the *Acts of Paul*, while Paul was staying with Priscilla and Aquila in Ephesus, "all the house of Ammia turned against Paul, that he might die." Without any comrade to lend support, Paul gives a bold witness before the governor and a crowd of spectators. The governor condemns him to be eaten by a ferocious lion, but the lion miraculously refuses to eat him, and both flee the scene unharmed. [Editors' note: See pp. 214–15.] Compare this with 2 Tim. 4:16–19:

> At my first defense no one took my part; all deserted me. May it not be charged against them! But the Lord stood by me and gave me strength to proclaim the message fully, that all the Gentiles might hear it. So I was rescued from the lion's mouth. The Lord will rescue me from every evil and save me for his heavenly kingdom. To him be the glory for ever and ever. Amen. Greet Prisca and Aquila, and the household of Onesiphorus.

Three features are common to both accounts: Paul's friends in Ephesus include Priscilla and Aquila; Paul gives his defense alone before a crowd of Gentiles; and he is saved from a lion.

It is more difficult to find evidence of some genetic connection between the Pastoral Epistles and the martyrdom story, but there does appear to be one point of contact. 2 Timothy 4:10–11a reads: "For Demas, in love with this present world, has deserted me and gone to Thessalonica; Crescens has gone to Galatia [several texts read "Gaul"], Titus to Dalmatia. Luke alone is with me." Compare this with the *Acts of Paul*, where we are told that when Paul arrived in Rome: "There were awaiting Paul at Rome Luke from Gaul and Titus from Dalmatia" (11:1). In both the *Acts of Paul* and the Pastoral Epistles, Luke and Titus accompany Paul in Rome; in both, Titus is associated with Dalmatia; and, if one prefers the reading "Gaul" in 2 Tim. 4:10, in both, one of Paul's companions is a missionary to Gaul. In no other early Christian document do we find a mission of Paul's associates to either Dalmatia or Gaul. Nowhere else is Titus related to Dalmatia or present with Paul in Rome.

Surely this large number of parallels between the *Acts of Paul* and the Pastoral Epistles is not coincidental. The first scholars to recognize these similarities assumed they were best explained as independent reminiscences of historical events. In the fifth century an unknown Christian author (later called Ambrosiaster) wrote a commentary on 2 Timothy in which he notes that the characters Alexander, Demas, and Hermogenes are mentioned in "other scriptures," no doubt referring to the *Acts of Paul*. Five or six centuries later another unknown scholar added to his copy of 2 Timothy, after "what befell me in Antioch," in 3:11 the words "those things he suffered on Thecla's behalf." Again in 4:19 he added the names of Onesiphorus' family members ("Lectra his wife and Simmias and Zeno his children"), which must have come from the *Acts of Paul.*

Modern scholars, however, agree that the similarities between the *Acts of Paul* and the Pastoral Epistles cannot be explained as independent testimonies to historical events, but they do not agree as to which of three basic models best explains the relationship: (1) the author of the *Acts of Paul* knew and used the Pastorals; (2) the author of the Pastorals knew and used a written source behind the *Acts of Paul;* or (3) both authors knew and used the same oral traditions.

MODEL ONE: THE AUTHOR OF THE *ACTS OF PAUL* KNEW AND USED THE PASTORALS

This has been the overwhelmingly favorite model of the persons who have addressed themselves to the question. Into this category fall most of those who attribute the Pastorals to Paul himself or who date them to the first century, but this also has been the model chosen by some of the finest critical students of Christian antiquities. At first glance this judgment would seem quite justified inasmuch as the *Acts of Paul* almost certainly was written after the Pastorals. But a closer investigation reveals that even though this model can account for the similarities between the documents, it makes little sense of the differences.

*   *   *

MODEL TWO: THE AUTHOR OF THE PASTORALS USED A WRITTEN SOURCE BEHIND THE *ACTS OF PAUL*

Many scholars, including both Lipsius and Corssen, have argued that behind the *Acts of Paul* lay an earlier written version of the story of Thecla. In fact, one scholar goes so far as to suggest that this hypothetical text is "the earliest Christian document we possess." Corssen seems to have thought that if indeed there were such a document, the author of the Pastorals may well have known it and consequently may have written in Paul's name to oppose it. Unfortunately, he never developed this hypothesis systematically. The only scholar who did so was Hans Helmut Mayer.

*   *   *

MODEL THREE: THE AUTHORS KNEW THE SAME ORAL LEGENDS

Since, as we have seen, the *Acts of Paul* is heavily dependent on oral legends known in Asia Minor early in the second century, it certainly is possible that they also were known to the author of the Pastoral Epistles, and if so, he certainly would have objected to their depiction of Paul. Apparently he saw in them what one folklorist has called "the doctrinally polluting substance of oral traditions," and wrote in Paul's name to correct them.

Obviously, this hypothesis can account for the different depictions of Paul in the *Acts of Paul* and the Pastorals without conjecturing earlier written sources, but it also can better account for the similarities than either of the other models. Those who attempt to explain the parallels in terms of literary dependence must somehow explain why they are not exact. For example, in the *Acts of Paul*, Hermogenes is associated with Demas; in the Pastorals, with Phygelus. In the *Acts of Paul*, Onesiphorus' home is in Iconium; in the Pastorals, in Ephesus. Rohde tries to solve this problem simply by claiming that the author of the *Acts of Paul* was arbitrary and imprecise in his use of the Pastorals. But if one explains the relationship in terms of a common knowledge of oral tradition, these variations can be attributed to the vagaries of the storytelling process. Substitutions of personal and place names are characteristic of oral transmission, inasmuch as names are epiphenomena to the story: they can be interchanged without fundamentally altering its texture or meaning.

Furthermore, if we assume that this third model is the most adequate, we are able to see how the author of the Pastorals brilliantly exploited the epistolary genre. That is, it would appear that in order to combat the image of Paul in the legend tradition he incorporated into his epistles three rhetorical features heretofore foreign to the genre. First, the author wrote 2 Timothy as though it were Paul's last testament. Shortly before his death Paul reflects on his life, foresees the state of the church in the future, and interprets the circumstances of his death. Second, the author has Paul write to two individuals and by so doing can develop these characters as well as Paul; hence, some scholars speak of "double pseudonymity" in the Pastorals. Third, he incorporates into 1 Timothy and Titus lists of qualifications for bishops, presbyters, deacons, and widows by means of which he presents his idealizations of church leaders in his own day. The author uses each of these three rhetorical devices in order to bend Pauline tradition toward social conservatism.

Bogus Letters and Social Compliance

PAUL: THE SUBMISSIVE MARTYR

In 2 Timothy the epistle provides the literary occasion for the author's version of Paul's final testament. The apostle is in a Roman jail (2 Tim. 1: 17), knows his death is near (4:6–8), and therefore writes his "son" Timothy his final instructions. Paul is accompanied only by Luke (4:11). Demas had deserted Paul, and Crescens, Titus, Tychicus, Erastus, and Trophimus are on missions elsewhere (4:10, 12, 20). Onesiphorus had come to Rome, sought Paul out, and ministered to him (1:16–17), but now was back home in Ephesus (4:19). Paul therefore asks that Timothy come quickly and bring with him Mark, books, parchments, and a misplaced cloak, apparently to make his last days more stimulating and comfortable (4:11, 13).

Why this preoccupation with Paul's situation in Rome? It appears that the author wanted to draw an alternative image of the dying Paul to that drawn by the martyrdom story in the *Acts of Paul*, which bristles with anti-Roman hostility. That story depicts Nero as the archetypal Antichrist, and the empire as the diabolical counterpart to the kingdom of God. No one serves two masters in the story; they cannot serve both Christ and Caesar.

In 2 Timothy, on the other hand, we hear not so much as a whisper of criticism for Rome. Of course, the author considers Paul's execution a wicked act, but he adroitly prevents Paul's execution from becoming an anti-Roman symbol which could be used to stimulate political hostilities. We find no reference to Nero, to soldiers, or to the legal charges or proceedings against Paul. It almost appears that Rome was merely a passive instrument of God's will. God had rescued Paul in the past and could do so easily now if that were God's desire (3:10–11; 4:17–18). But sensing that his end is providentially near, he accepts it with stoic resignation:

> For I am already on the point of being sacrificed; the time of my departure has come. I have fought the good fight, I have finished the race, I have kept the faith. (4:6–7)

Even though Paul is "wearing fetters like a criminal," his imprisonment is not the result of antisocial conduct or of political opposition but of his preaching the gospel (1:8; 11–12; 2:9). Such sufferings are inevitable for anyone wishing to live a godly life (3:12). Nowhere do we find evidence that Paul had caused the Romans difficulty or that they were culpable for his death.

Confirmation of our claim concerning the ameliorating political sentiments behind 2 Timothy comes from passages in the other two Pastoral Epistles. In Titus 3:1–2, Paul commands Titus:

> Remind them to be submissive to rulers and authorities, to be obedient, to be ready for any honest work, to speak evil of no one, to avoid quarreling, to be gentle, and to show perfect courtesy toward all people.

Even more telling is 1 Tim. 2:1–2:

> First of all, then, I urge that supplications, prayers, intercessions, and thanksgivings be made for all people, on behalf of kings [i.e., emperors] and all who are in positions of authority so that we may lead a quiet and peaceful life in all piety and dignity.

The words "first of all" can indicate either that the injunction is of prime importance or that it is the first in a list of commands for the church which continue to 3:13. Even if one prefers the second meaning, the very fact that the author places the command to pray for authorities at the beginning of the list underlines its importance.

The author sees a relationship between these prayers and the tranquillity of the church, but it is not clear what that relationship is. Some have suggested that, as in a prayer for pagan authorities in 1 Clement 61, believers are to pray that the authorities may govern wisely and as a result of this wise governance the church would naturally be at peace. Notice, however, that our passage includes, among other forms of prayer, thanksgiving for the authorities. This expression of appreciation for Rome suggests that the peace of the church depends not on the prayer for wise administration as much as on the act of prayer itself as a demonstration of goodwill toward the empire. This seems to be the idea behind Polycarp's command that Christians "pray also for kings and potentates and rulers and for those who persecute and hate you . . . that your fruit may be manifest to all" (Polycarp, *Philippians* 12:3). Likewise in 1 Peter we are told that by honoring and being subject to the emperor believers will put "to silence the ignorance of foolish" people (1 Peter 2:15). Tertullian and Justin Martyr, both with links to Asia Minor, cite prayers for the emperors as proofs of political cooperation. So too in 1 Timothy: by praying and giving thanks for emperors, rulers, and all humankind Christians demonstrate to outsiders their respect for society at large. This cooperation with political power is epitomized in 2 Timothy by the depiction of Paul as a submissive martyr, resigned to his fate, and reconciled with Rome.

TIMOTHY AND TITUS: THE GUARDIANS OF THE TRADITION

Timothy and Titus are necessary links for establishing the continuity between Paul's authority and the authority of bishops in the author's own day. Six times in the Pastoral Epistles, Paul defends his apostleship by claiming that he was appointed to the office by God or Christ (1 Tim. 1: 1, 12–16; 2:7; 2 Tim. 1:1, 11–12; Titus 1:1–3). The author did not include these repetitious defenses of Paul's apostleship in order to convince those doubting it. Rather, by establishing the divine origin of Paul's apostleship, and by having Paul transmit that authority to Timothy, Titus, and through them to later presbyter-bishops the author demonstrates the genealogical divine origin of the offices. As Werner Stenger has expressed it:

> The author projects the . . . function of the church official of his time in the images of Timothy and Titus—who function as "representatives" of the apostle already in the authentic Paulines—in order to make the apostle present when he himself cannot come. Thereby the author succeeded in building a literary bridge over the gap in time between Paul and the post-Pauline church, and to assert the presence of the apostle himself in the activity of church officers.

Perhaps this is why Paul is the only apostle mentioned in the letters; it is through Paul alone that the authority of the presbyter-bishop is derived.

Timothy and Titus of all of Paul's associates mentioned in his undisputed letters are the best suited for expressing the author's idealization of the authentic Pauline lineage, but in the Pastoral Epistles these two characters are further developed so as to epitomize the perfect church leader.

Timothy is presented as a weak, shy, and fearful youth whom the apostle must encourage to use his rightful authority and to be brave in the shadow of persecution (1 Tim. 4:12; 5:23; 2 Tim. 1:8; 2:1–7). But even though he is young, he is no neophyte. His mother and grandmother were both believers and taught him about the faith as a lad (2 Tim. 1:5; 3:15). Paul was present at Timothy's ordination when his divine selection was revealed to all: prophetic utterances pointed to him, God gave him a special gift, he gave a true confession, and the presbyters laid their hands on him (1 Tim. 1:18–20; 4:14; 6:12; 2 Tim. 1:5–7). Both Timothy and Titus were fellow missionaries with Paul until the apostle decided that for the benefit of local churches Timothy should stay in Ephesus and Titus in Crete, where they would ensure the dominance of true teaching and appoint other clergy (1 Tim. 1:3–4; Titus 1:5). In other words, Timothy and Titus are apostles who have become presbyter-bishops, itinerants who have become resident clergy, missionaries once dependent on Paul who are now independent.

Paul tells Titus that because he now has full independent authority he must be neither disregarded nor drawn into theological disputes (Titus 2: 15; cf. 1:10–11). If someone disagrees with him and continues to be uncompliant after two rebukes, Titus must "have nothing more to do with him, knowing that such a person is perverted and sinful" (3:10–11). Likewise Timothy is told not to become embroiled in arguments but simply to pronounce the truth as he received it: "Have nothing to do with stupid, senseless controversies; you know that they breed quarrels" (2 Tim. 2:23). The author of the Pastorals apparently thought this imperious authority was necessary for ensuring the transmission of "sound doctrine" and the rejection of the insubordinate "who reject the truth" (Titus 1:9 to 2:1). Timothy is all the more capable of "guarding the truth" (2 Tim. 1:14) because he is educated, especially in the Scriptures (2 Tim. 3:15–17; cf. 1 Tim. 1:7; 4:13).

Timothy and Titus also have obligations outside the church in that they must be paradigms of social respectability. As Paul tells Titus:

> Show yourself in all respects a model of good deeds, and in your teaching show integrity, gravity, and sound speech that cannot be censured, so that an opponent may be put to shame, having nothing evil to say of us. (Titus 2:7–8)

How do these characterizations of Timothy and Titus relate to our thesis that the Pastorals were written to counteract the legend tradition? In the legends we find no mention whatever of bishops, presbyters, deacons, or other officers. This silence is striking when we recall that the author of the *Acts of Paul* was himself a presbyter and subject to the authority of a bishop. Furthermore, in the Philippi section of the *Acts of Paul* is a letter from the Corinthians to Paul written by a bishop Stephanus and four presbyters, and delivered to Paul by two deacons (*Acts of Paul* 8:1.1 and 2.1). In the legends, however, ecclesiastical authority is charismatic, itinerant, and relatively democratic, in contrast to the genetic, resident, and hierarchical authority of the Pastoral Epistles.

The letters of Ignatius allow us to see that the two rival models for ecclesiastical leadership were related to actual conditions in Asia Minor churches. Ignatius stayed for a period in Smyrna on his way to Rome for execution, and during this stay he was visited by bishops from Ephesus, Magnesia, and Tralles (*Ephesians* 21:1; *Magnesians* 2:1; *Trallians* 1:1). Later while in Troas he was visited by the bishop of Philadelphia (*Philadelphians* 1:1). Ignatius sent each of these bishops home with a letter which in every case attempted to secure the position of the bishop in the church and to scold the insubordinate. To the Ephesians he wrote that they "should live in harmony with the will of the bishop" (*Ephesians* 4:1). To the Trallians he wrote: "Let all respect the deacons as Jesus Christ, even as the bishop is also a type of the Father, and the presbyters as the council of God and the college of apostles. Without these the name 'Church' is not given" (*Trallians* 3:1). To the Philadelphians he wrote: "For as many as belong to God and Jesus Christ,—these are with the bishop" (*Philadelphians* 3:2). Ignatius' instructions to the Magnesians are especially interesting because their bishop, Damas, was very young—like the Timothy of the Pastorals—and some seem to have presumed on his youth (*Magnesians* 3:1). Even though he is young, Ignatius says, all in the church must be in harmony "with the bishop presiding in the place of God, and the presbyters in the place of the council of the Apostles, and the deacons . . . entrusted with the service of Jesus Christ" (*Magnesians* 6:1). Likewise, to the Smyrneans Ignatius writes: "Let no one do any of the things appertaining to the church without the bishop" (*Smyrneans* 8:1). And when he writes to Polycarp, the bishop of Smyrna, Ignatius commands him to be a strong leader: "Stand firm as an anvil which is smitten" (*Polycarp* 3:1; cf. 2:3; 4:1). Apparently Polycarp was in fact an adamantine leader, for Ignatius' letter to him begins with a reference to his "godly mind which is fixed as if on an immoveable rock" (1:1). This repeated emphasis on the adamance and authority of the bishop in letters often brought to the churches by the bishops themselves suggests that not everyone was in fact obedient to them.

Perhaps now we can understand the importance of the characterizations of Timothy and Titus for counteracting the legend tradition. First, Timothy and Titus, as itinerants who became resident clergy, symbolize the full authority of resident leaders. It is the author's way of saying what the *Didache* says directly: "Do not despise them [i.e., bishops and deacons], for they are your honourable men together with the prophets and teachers" (*Didache* 15:2). Second, the author gives divine sanction to the church officials and thereby limits charismatic authority. Surely this is why he emphasized the role of the Holy Spirit in the ordination of Timothy, who was selected by prophetic utterance and was given a spiritual gift (1 Tim. 1:18; 4:14; 2 Tim. 1:6). Third, by giving authority to a local leader to settle disputes the author hopes both to guarantee the transmission of "sound doctrine" and to minimize theological controversies which to outsiders might appear senseless, trivial, and unnecessarily disruptive. Fourth, Timothy and Titus are models of social respectability. In them the author expresses the ideal to be desired of all other leaders. Needless to say, social respectability is not characteristic of Christian leaders in the legend tradition.

BISHOPS, PRESBYTERS, AND DEACONS: THE RESPECTABLE HOUSEHOLDERS

In addition to presenting Timothy and Titus as the original and ideal resident clergy, the author guarantees the good character of ecclesiastical leaders by altering the epistolary genre to include lists of qualifications for bishops (1 Tim. 3:1–7 and Titus 1:7–9), one short list for presbyters (Titus 1:5–6 and perhaps 2:2), one list for deacons (1 Tim. 3:8–13), and the longest list, including detailed instructions, pertains to the widows (1 Tim. 5:3–16). Because the office of widows presented the author with a particular problem, we shall analyze this passage in detail later. In the present context we shall refer to the widows only when their qualifications are germane to those for other offices.

Most of the qualifications are interchangeable from office to office; therefore, it would appear that instead of lists of set qualifications for particular offices we have lists of stereotypical virtues and vices used to indicate in general terms the character of ecclesiastical leaders. Furthermore, most of the virtues are not distinctively Christian but are those recognized by society at large. Some commentators have illustrated the public nature of these virtues by showing how similar they are to qualifications for Roman generals. The purpose of these lists of qualifications is to ensure the social respectability of leaders in the church.

The most important qualification is a good reputation in society. For example, the bishop "must be well thought of by outsiders, or he may fall into reproach." By their conduct widows must "give the opponent no opportunity to revile us." Leaders must be without blame, and hospitable to outsiders. Twice the author requires bishops to be *sōphrōn*, or "mod-

erate," and in both instances the word clearly implies social prudence, or
savoir faire. Likewise, he requires bishops, deacons, and the wives of deacons to be *semnos*, or "dignified," which one scholar has explained as "the
manner of living which honors the rules [*Ordnungen*] of society."

This idealization of church leaders stands in stark contrast to the Paul
of the legend tradition. Nothing in the legends suggests that Paul or any
other Christian could be characterized as moderate or dignified; rather,
they are proudly presented as socially deviant, impudent, and incorrig-
ible. Against this background it appears that the author of the Pastoral
Epistles wanted to replace the obstreperous prophet with the obsequious
bishop.

Nowhere is this emphasis on social respectability more in conflict with
the legends than in the requirement that every leader have demonstrated
dedication to and competence in leading the *oikia*, or household. In fact,
the most concrete requirement for those holding any office is the demand
that they be "the husband of one wife" (bishops in 1 Tim. 3:2; presbyters
in Titus 1:6; deacons in 1 Tim. 3:12), or in the case of widows, "the
wife of one husband" (1 Tim. 5:9). Most interpretations of this requirement focus on the word "one" and therefore claim that the author is primarily opposing second marriages, but in the light of his opposition to
celibacy it would seem that the author intended this requirement to
exclude not only the twice married but also the never married. This interpretation is consistent with other requirements for the offices. For example, the bishop must "manage his own household well, keeping his
children submissive and respectful in every way; for if someone does not
know how to manage his own household, how can he care for God's
church?" (1 Tim. 3:4–5). A presbyter too must be "the husband of one
wife, having children who are believers, and who are not under judgment
for debauchery or insubordination" (Titus 1:6). Deacons must be "the
husband of one wife, managing well their children and their households"
(1 Tim. 3:12). According to the author, women in the order of widows
must in fact be widows—not virgins pledged to celibacy—and they must
have proven themselves capable in raising children (1 Tim. 5:10).
Whereas the legends pit the household and the church against each other
as competing social institutions, the Pastorals identify the strength of the
church with that of the household. Irresponsibility to one's family is worse
than apostasy.

This concern for the welfare of the household also lies behind the
author's arguments against teachers who told slaves they had a right to
expect manumission from their Christian masters:

> Let all who are under the yoke of slavery regard their masters as wor-
> thy of all honor, so that the name of God and the teaching may not
> be defamed. Those who have believing masters must not be disre-
> spectful on the ground that they are brethren; rather they must serve
> all the better since those who benefit by their service are believers
> and beloved.
>
> Teach and urge these duties. If any one teaches otherwise and does
> not agree with the sound words of our Lord Jesus Christ and the
> teaching which accords with godliness, he is puffed up with conceit,
> he knows nothing; he has a morbid craving for controversy and for
> disputes about words, which produce envy, dissension, slander, base

suspicions, and wrangling among men who are depraved in mind and bereft of the truth. (1 Tim. 6:1–5a)

Titus 2:9 also requires slaves to be submissive to their masters. By reading these two passages together we can reconstruct the events behind the author's objections.

Some slaves were despising and disobeying their masters. They believed that since they were fellow believers, they should no longer be slaves (1 Tim. 6:2; cf. Titus 2:10). Disillusioned and in great pain, some slaves had even abandoned the faith (1 Tim. 6:9–10). As a result of this conflict, the teaching of the church was maligned (1 Tim. 6:1; cf. Titus 2:10), and churches themselves were in turmoil (1 Tim. 6:4–5a).

The author opposes those teachers by calling them arrogant, ignorant, and simply interested in causing disturbances (1 Tim. 6:3–5). Slaves who heed them are using piety as a means of financial advantage in a thirst for wealth (vs. 6–9), but piety has advantage only when it is accompanied by stoiclike contentment with nothing more than food and clothing—the minimal provisions for a slave (v. 8). Therefore, slaves must not treat their masters with envy or contempt but with respect, obedience, and good faith, serving them all the better since they are fellow believers (vs. 1–2; Titus 2:9–10).

Similarly, Ignatius counsels Polycarp to refuse the requests of slaves that the church provide payments for their manumission, lest they become "slaves of lust." The repeated statements in Christian documents from Asia Minor that slaves remain in subjection suggests that these churches were indeed embroiled in controversies over slavery—with the legends and the Pastoral Epistles on opposing sides and both appealing to the authority of Paul.

Thus far we have seen how the author used his depictions of the false teachers, of the dying Paul, of Timothy and Titus, and of bishops, presbyters, and deacons to dissociate Paul from his legendary memory. But it is also possible to show that he attempted to silence the storytellers by restricting the influence of the order of widows.

Silencing the Storytellers

From 1 Tim. 5:3–16 it is clear that the institution of widows was thriving in the communities from which the Pastoral Epistles came. Women in the order included the young as well as the old; they had pledged themselves to celibacy; they were supported by the community at large; and they were responsible for intercessory prayer, acts of mercy, and visitation. The church in Smyrna also supported the order of widows, which included some women who had never married. Apparently, the order presented Polycarp with some difficulties. Ignatius commands him: "Do not let the widows be neglected. After the Lord, you yourself be their manager. Let nothing be done without your approval" (Ignatius, *Polycarp* 4:1). Some have understood this passage to mean that Polycarp must care for the widows' material needs, but from other passages it would appear that Polycarp must keep the widows under control. In other words, make sure *widows* do nothing "without your approval." In his letter to the Philippians, Polycarp sets standards for widows and virgins lest they cause the community to be scorned by outsiders, and among these standards are warnings against slander and lying (Polycarp, *Philippians* 4:3; 5:3). No one is permitted to boast about continence (Ignatius, *Polycarp* 5:2), and widows must not encourage other women to leave their husbands for the sake of pursuing celibacy. Presumably, this is why Ignatius commands Polycarp: "Speak to my sisters that they may love the Lord, and be content with their husbands in flesh and spirit" (Ignatius, *Polycarp* 5:1; cf. Polycarp, *Philippians* 4:2).

The author of the Pastoral Epistles also had problems with the order of widows, and he wanted to decimate the office by denying eligibility to any woman under sixty years of age, to any whose character was questionable, and to any who could have found support from relatives or friends.

The author gives three reasons for his limitations of the order: (1) the church is financially burdened; (2) some of the younger widows have broken their pledges to celibacy; and (3) some of the widows are going from house to house saying things they should not. When one examines each of these objections individually, it appears that the author's primary objection was to their itinerant communication.

* * *

In Titus 2:3b–5 the author says that if women are to teach at all, they must "teach what is good, and so train the young women to love their husbands and children, to be sensible, chaste, domestic, kind, and submissive to their husbands, that the word of God may not be discredited." Presumably, the widows in their housecalls had taught the opposite: they taught celibacy and not domestication, independence and not submission. As we have seen in our discussion of the false teachers, there seems to be a relationship between "the profane tales told by old women" and the rejection of marriage. The author of the Pastorals clearly assumes that the Christian message would be discredited if women were not submissive to their husbands. Over and over again in the legends we are told that a primary source of antagonism against the church was the refusal of women to comply with the desires of their husbands and lovers. It would appear that the author of the Pastorals wanted to soften such tensions by insisting on the domestication of women and by silencing them.

Nowhere is the relationship between silencing women and returning them to diapers and aprons more apparent than in 1 Tim. 2:11–15, where Paul tells women to be silent, submissive, and domestic, for their very salvation depends on their bearing children and bringing them up in the faith.

It is reasonable to conclude that the author of the Pastoral Epistles had two primary purposes in disguising his letters in Pauline garb. First, he wanted to show that the socially radical Paul of the legends was a distortion. Even on the eve of his execution Paul bears no animus for Rome, encourages a conciliatory posture toward society, and emphasizes the value of the household for the success of the church. Second, he wanted to silence those who were telling the stories. In order to do this he forbade women to teach—except to teach younger women how to be content and efficient housewives—he decimated the order of widows, and scorned their stories as so many "old wives' tales."

* * *

Paul and Christian Martyrs

Because pagan criticism of Christianity was often linked with harassment and persecution, Paul was sometimes a point of discussion in some authorities' interrogations of accused Christians. The earliest reference appears in the *Acts of the Scillitan Martyrs*, which gives the trial of twelve Christians prior to their execution (180 CE). When the proconsul Saturninus asks Speratus, the group's spokesman, what items are in his satchel, he replies, "Books and letters of Paul, a just man." The most extensive exchange involving Paul appears in the *Acts of Phileas*, which gives the trial and execution of Phileas, the bishop of Thmuis, in the first decade of the fourth century CE. The relevant portion of the dialogue between Phileas and Clodius Culcianus, the prefect of Egypt, is given below.

ANONYMOUS

[A Martyr's Understanding of Paul] (early fourth century)†

Culcianus said: 'Now sacrifice.'
Phileas said: 'I will not. I never learned how.'
'Did not Paul offer sacrifice?' asked Culcianus.
'No,' replied Phileas; 'God forbid!'

*   *   *

'Did not Paul deny the faith?' said Culcianus.[1]
'God forbid!' said Phileas.
'Who did?' said Culcianus.
'I shall not tell you,' said Phileas.
'I adjure you,' said Culcianus, 'Paul was the one who denied the faith.'
'God forbid,' said Phileas; 'the apostle of my Lord did not deny it.'

*   *   *

---

† Extracts of the dialogue between Clodius Culcianus, the prefect of Egypt, and Phileas, the bishop of Thmuis, are taken primarily from the Latin recension of the *Acts of Phileas*, with the Greek recension used in one place. The translation is that of Herbert Musurillo, *The Acts of the Christian Martyrs* (Oxford: Clarendon, 1972), 333, 335, 345, 347, 349, 351. Reprinted by permission of Oxford University Press. The dialogue begins with Culcianus commanding Phileas to sacrifice to the gods and the latter refusing to do so.
1. In the Greek recension cited here, the prefect appears to be confusing Paul with Peter, whose three denials of Jesus (Matt. 26:69–75) were well known to pagan critics of Christianity. In the Latin recension, Culcianus asks, "Wasn't Paul a persecutor?" But instead of affirming Paul's activities as a persecutor prior to his conversion, Phileas denies that Paul was a persecutor. This inexplicable response is usually taken as evidence that the text is corrupt at this point.

Culcianus said: 'Was not Paul a common man? Was he not a Syrian, and did he not hold his discussions in Aramaic?'

Phileas replied: 'Yes, he was a Jew. But he also spoke Greek, and had deeper wisdom than anyone.'[2]

Culcianus said: 'Perhaps you will say that he was even superior to Plato.'

'Not only Plato', answered Phileas. 'He was more profound than any man. He convinced even philosophers. If you like, I shall quote him for you.'

*   *   *

Culcianus said: 'Was Paul God?'[3]

'No,' answered Phileas.

'Who was he then?'

Phileas replied: 'He was a man like ourselves, but the Spirit of God was in him; and so he performed signs and wonders and acts of virtue in the Spirit.'

*   *   *

---

2. In the Greek recension, Phileas says that Paul was "the first of the apostles [lit., heralds] and he spoke Greek as the first of the Greeks."

3. Or, "Was Paul a god?" In the *Passion of St. Dioscorus*, Culcianus is depicted as asking the same question to the Egyptian martyr Dioscorus prior to his execution.

Claiming Paul for "Orthodoxy": A Sampler of Patristic Interpretations

For many scholars of an earlier generation, especially Protestants, it seemed that Paul had been widely misunderstood or ignored by the earliest of those interpreters who would be numbered among the "Fathers" of the Catholic West and the Orthodox East. In the early centuries, according to the prevailing view, it was not the Christians of the mainstream who made Paul their own, but just those groups who would eventually be marginalized by the emerging consensus—or power centers. Tertullian's sarcastic remark about his Marcionite opponents was taken as a blanket assessment: Paul was *haereticorum apostolus*, the apostle of those who would become the "heretics" in the retrospective history of catholic Christianity.

Over the past two or three decades, that view of Paul's reception in the early church has undergone a searching reassessment.[1] That reassessment was driven in part by our greater awareness of the variety of early Christian thought and practice, evoked especially by the rediscovery of such lost ancient sources as those in the Nag Hammadi horde and by changing methods in the study of patristic literature. Equally important were our growing awareness of the variety to be found in the letters of Paul himself and of his followers, and our recognition that the Paul who seemed to be ignored by so much of the ancient church was to some extent the construct of post-Reformation and modern scholarship. (The emergence and revisions of that modern Paul are documented in Parts V through IX below.) The Christian writers of late antiquity saw Paul through different eyes, and found in the letters attributed to him different answers to their own problems.

We see now that the impact of the Pauline letters on the emerging catholic synthesis was too vast and too varied to be fully represented here. We offer only a sampler of the many ways in which the church's leading interpreters deployed Paul's thought and example and wrestled with the "things difficult to understand" in his letters.

---

1. Representative of that reassessment and influential in its further development were two doctoral dissertations produced almost simultaneously, one in Germany, the other in the United States: Andreas Lindemann, *Paulus im ältesten Christentum: Das Bild des Apostels und die Rezeption der paulinischen Theologie in der frühchristlichen Literatur bis Marcion* (Tübingen: Mohr-Siebeck, 1979); and David K Rensberger, *As the Apostle Teaches: The Development of the Use of Paul's Letters in Second-Century Christianity*, Ph.D. dissertation, Yale University (1981). Rensberger's dissertation was unfortunately never published in print form; an excerpt from it is included below, pp. 341–51.

ORIGEN

[The Multiple Meanings of "Law" in Paul's Letters] (ca. 246)†

The Gentiles need not keep the sabbaths or the new moons or the sacrifices which are written down in the law.[1] For this law[2] is not what is written on the hearts of the Gentiles.[3] Rather it is that which can be discerned naturally, e.g., that they should not kill or commit adultery, that they should not steal nor bear false witness, that they should honor father and mother, etc.[4] It may well be that since God is the one Creator of all, these things are written on the hearts of the Gentiles. . . . For the natural law may agree with the law of Moses in the spirit, if not in the letter. For how would anyone understand by nature that a child should be circumcised on the eighth day?[5]

* * *

[I]t seems to me that those who have thought that the law of nature is the law of God and that the law of Moses is merely the written law are correct. If Paul was speaking of the written law, the law of Moses, when he said: *Sin is not imputed when there is no law,*[6] neither Cain nor those who perished in the flood nor those who were burnt with fire at Sodom would have had their sins imputed to them.[7] But since we see that not only did they have their sins imputed to them, they also suffered retribution for them, it is clear that Paul was speaking here of the natural law, which with the exception of the early years of childhood, is present in all men. For this reason he was quite right to say that all are under the power of sin. Whence it seems to me that the philosophers were right when they said that every mortal being on coming to the age of discretion, when by the entry of the natural law it might distinguish between good and evil, first of all discovers what is evil and afterward combats it by means of instructions, precepts and warnings, so as to move on to virtue. I think that Paul was agreeing with them when he said: *But when the commandment came, sin sprang to life.*[8]

* * *

---

† From Origen's commentary on Rom. 2:14; 3:9, 19–21, tr. in Gerald Bray (ed.), *Romans* (Downers Grove: InterVarsity, 1998), 67, 89, 94–95, 98. Copyright © 1998 by the Institute of Classical Christian Studies, Thomas Oden, and Gerald Bray. Reprinted by permission of InterVarsity Press. Origen (185–254) was probably the most prodigious scholar of the pre-Constantinian church. His commentary on Romans, written while he was in Caesarea, reflects his mature thought. In it he grapples with the issue of how Paul uses the word *nomos* (usually translated "law," though the meaning of the Greek word, like the Hebrew *torah*, is much broader in meaning than the English term). In opposition to other interpreters, Origen insists that Paul not only refers to many kinds of laws but also that he can speak of the Mosaic law under different aspects.

1. Col. 2:16.
2. The law of Moses.
3. Rom. 2:15.
4. Exod. 20:12–16; Deut. 5:16–20.
5. Lev. 12:3.
6. Rom. 5:13.
7. Gen. 4:1–16; 6:5–9:17; 18:16–19:29.
8. Rom. 7:9.

Here we must consider carefully what this law is that speaks to those who are under the law. By what it says to them it deprives them of every excuse, so that they can find no hiding place for their sins. It is this which stops every mouth and makes the whole world accountable to God.[9] Now if we want to take this as referring to the law of Moses, which without doubt spoke only to those who had been circumcised from their mother's womb and had learned what the law was, how is it possible that by that law, which applies to only one nation, every mouth should be stopped and the whole world should be held accountable to God? What have the other nations to do with that law, and why does it affect the entire world? And how is it that a knowledge of sin is said to have originated with the law of Moses, when there were many before his time who were well aware of their sins?

From this it appears that the apostle Paul is not speaking here about the law of Moses but about the natural law which is written on the hearts of men.[1]

*   *   *

Let us see in what way knowledge of sin comes through the law.[2] It comes insofar as we learn through the law what to do and what not to do, what is sin and what is not sin. It is not, as the heretics claim, that God's law is a bad root or a bad tree through which a knowledge of sin comes. Rather the law is like a medicine through which we perceive the true nature of our disease. . . . The medicine itself is good, not least because it enables us to isolate the disease and seek to cure it.

*   *   *

We have just said that in the above verses[3] Paul was speaking about the natural law and not about the law of Moses, but now it appears that there can be no doubt that he is referring to the law of Moses.[4]

*   *   *

Does this mean that the apostle has contradicted himself? There are plenty of people who would like to think so! * * * We have often said, * * * that the apostle mentions many different kinds of law in this epistle, and only the most attentive reader will be able to detect when he is shifting from one to another. . . . The law of nature was able to explain the nature of sin and give us some knowledge of it, but the righteousness of God is above and beyond this, and the human mind is unable to attain it by its natural senses. . . . For this the law of Moses was required, to teach us what God's righteousness is. Do not be surprised that the word *law* is used here in two different senses! . . .

Moreover, there is a way to tell which meaning of the word *law* is intended. The Greek language uses articles in front of proper names. Thus when the law of Moses is intended, the article is used, but when the natural law is meant, the article is omitted.

9. Rom. 3:19.
1. Rom. 2:15.
2. Rom. 3:20.
3. Rom. 3:19–20.
4. Rom. 3:21 ("the Law and the Prophets testify").

IRENÆUS

[On "the god of this world"] (ca. 180)†

1. As to their affirming that Paul said plainly in the Second [Epistle] to the Corinthians, "In whom the god of this world hath blinded the minds of them that believe not," and maintaining that there is indeed one god of this world, but another who is beyond all principality, and beginning, and power, we are not to blame if they, who give out that they do themselves know mysteries beyond God, know not how to read Paul. For if any one read the passage thus—according to Paul's custom, as I show elsewhere, and by many examples, that he uses transposition of words—"In whom God," then pointing it off, and making a slight interval, and at the same time read also the rest [of the sentence] in one [clause], "hath blinded the minds of them of this world that believe not," he shall find out the true [sense]; that it is contained in the expression, "God hath blinded the minds of the unbelievers of this world." And this is shown by means of the little interval [between the clause]. For Paul does not say, "the God of this world," as if recognising any other beyond Him; but he confessed God as indeed God. And he says, "the unbelievers of this world," because they shall not inherit the future age of incorruption. I shall show from Paul himself, how it is that God has blinded the minds of them that believe not, in the course of this work, that we may not just at present distract our mind from the matter in hand, [by wandering] at large.

2. From many other instances also, we may discover that the apostle frequently uses a transposed order in his sentences, due to the rapidity of his discourses, and the impetus of the Spirit which is in him. An example occurs in the [Epistle] to the Galatians, where he expresses himself as follows: "Wherefore then the law of works? It was added, until the seed should come to whom the promise was made; [and it was] ordained by angels in the hand of a Mediator."[1] For the order of the words runs thus: "Wherefore then the law of works? Ordained by angels in the hand of a Mediator, it was added until the seed should come to whom the promise was made,"—man thus asking the question, and the Spirit making answer. And again, in the Second to the Thessalonians, speaking of Antichrist, he says, "And then shall that wicked be revealed, whom the Lord Jesus Christ shall slay with the Spirit of His mouth, and shall destroy him with the presence of his coming; [even him] whose coming is after the working of Satan, with all power, and signs, and lying wonders."[2] Now in these [sentences] the order of the words is this: "And then shall be revealed that wicked, whose coming is after the working of Satan, with all power, and signs, and lying wonders, whom the Lord Jesus shall slay with the Spirit of His mouth, and shall destroy with the presence of His coming." For he

---

† From *Haer.* 3.7, tr. by W. H. Rambaut, in *The Ante-Nicene Fathers*, Vol. I (New York: Scribner's, 1885; rp. Grand Rapids: Eerdmans, 1951), 420–21. Paul's reference to "the god of this world" (2 Cor. 4:4) provided a biblical basis for the dualistic systems of Irenaeus's adversaries. The bishop of Lyons seeks to counter their exegesis of this passage by explaining it as an instance of hyperbaton, a figure of speech involving the transposition of words. By connecting the phrase "of this world" with "the unbelievers" rather than with "god," Irenaeus is able to safeguard the monotheism of the "rule of faith" (*regula fidei*).
1. Gal. 3:19. The initial portion of Irenaeus's text differs from that of most ancient manuscripts.
2. 2 Thess. 2:8–9. Instead of "after," the TNIV renders "in accordance with."

does not mean that the coming of the Lord is after the working of Satan; but the coming of the wicked one, whom we also call Antichrist. If, then, one does not attend to the [proper] reading [of the passage], and if he do not exhibit the intervals of breathing as they occur, there shall be not only incongruities, but also, when reading, he will utter blasphemy, as if the advent of the Lord could take place according to the working of Satan. So therefore, in such passages, the *hyperbaton* must be exhibited by the reading, and the apostle's meaning following on, preserved; and thus we do not read in that passage, "the god of this world," but, "God," whom we do truly call God; and we hear [it declared of] the unbelieving and the blinded of this world, that they shall not inherit the world of life which is to come.

VICTORINUS

[The Conflict of Peter and Paul at Antioch] (ca. 365)†

But when Peter came to Antioch, I opposed him to his face, because he had been reprimanded (2: 11).[1] Not only was my gospel approved, says Paul, on the part of the apostles who were in Jerusalem; not only was I charged to be mindful of the poor (a light, albeit necessary obligation that we fulfilled, something I was very concerned to do), but also I did not keep quiet about Peter's sin, he says. In this, Paul shows his freedom and boldness concerning his gospel—if indeed he reprimanded something being done in a contrary fashion by Peter. There is also the point that Peter, having been reprimanded, would in turn more readily burst out to reprimand Paul. If there were any fault in me, if I were not carrying on properly with the gospel, Peter would uncover the fact and, having suffered a reproach himself, not spare me. When Peter came to Antioch, says Paul, I did not address him at church and among the congregation, rather *I opposed him to his face*—that is, I spoke out against him publicly. Where did Paul get this confidence? Paul alone did not reprimand him; rather, after Peter had been reprimanded by everyone, Paul criticized and accused him, *because he had been reprimanded*. In the judgement of the congre-

---

† From Victorinus's commentary on Gal. 2:11–14, trans. by Stephen A. Cooper, *Marius Victorinus' Commentary on Galatians* (Oxford and New York: Oxford University Press, 2005). Reprinted by permission of Oxford University Press. Victorinus was a pagan rhetorician who became a Christian in old age (ca. 355) and wrote the first Latin commentaries on Paul's letters. The face-off between Peter and Paul at Antioch presented orthodox theologians with a host of exegetical and apologetic problems, for Marcion had used the event to exalt Paul at Peter's expense and pagan critics such as Porphyry and the anonymous Hellene had used it to attack both apostles (see above, p. 265 and the note on p. 268). Victorinus's interpretation is remarkable because he sees here not only a genuine conflict between Peter and Paul but also an indictment of James the Lord's brother. He thus anticipates some ideas later to be developed by F. C. Baur (see below, pp. 399–408). Victorinus's interpretation certainly did not settle the issue of how the text was to be interpreted. Less than fifty years later Jerome and Augustine debated whether Peter and Paul had a real confrontation or had merely engaged in a "fake fight" (*simulata contentio*), with Jerome arguing that Peter had not sinned and that Paul's rebuke of him was feigned. Centuries later, Luther was to agree with Augustine that this was a genuine conflict and used the episode as a warrant for him, like Paul, to rebuke "Peter" (the church hierarchy) for the sake of "the truth of the gospel" (Gal. 2:14).

1. Victorinus's Latin reads *reprehensus erat*, which he interprets as a perfect participle in the passive voice ("he was reprimanded") and understands "the congregation" as the entity taking Peter to task. Paul's public rebuke of Peter thus follows that of the congregation. Ambrosiaster, by contrast, thought Peter was reprimanded "by the truth of the gospel." Many modern scholars regard the Greek participle as being in the middle voice (thus the NRSV: "he was self-condemned").

gation Peter sinned and was therefore accused. And if there were some sin in me, the congregation would in an equal manner be reprimanding me just as they did him.

For before certain people from James came, Peter was eating with Gentiles; but once they came, Peter withdrew, fearing those who were of the circumcision. And the other Jews also went along with him, with the result that even Barnabas went along with their pretence (2: 12–13). Paul forthrightly explains what sort of sin it was Peter had committed. At this point, perhaps, he could have omitted telling what the sin was he claims to have reprimanded in Peter. It was sufficient that Peter had been set straight by the congregation's reprimand and by Paul's public accusation. But because it is beneficial and really necessary for the letter, he therefore relates the story in order to drive two points home. First, that no fault was found with Paul's own gospel; and that although Paul reprimanded Peter, he heard nothing in the way of a reprimand from Peter. Now, secondly, there is that matter which I said was really necessary. Because the Galatians, disregarding the gospel and even the rule of the gospel, were supposing that additions were to be made to their way of life, to the effect that they should observe the sabbath and circumcision and live just like Jews. Because the Galatians were doing this, the letter was written to them. Whence the point is well made that the very thing reprimanded in Peter by Paul was what the congregation reprimanded as well. From there it follows that the Galatians too are sinning.

Now, Paul has included in the narrative how Peter allowed this, or what guilt he incurred. For earlier, he says, *before certain people from James came, Peter was eating with Gentiles*, holding fast to the full gospel and its rule: that the gospel about Christ be preached equally to Jews and Gentiles; and that the food laws of the Jews not be observed but one live simply, according to the manner of the Gentiles. Peter was doing this earlier, Paul says, before there came certain people from James. For the brother of the Lord, James, who is the progenitor of the Symmachians,[2] was the first at Jerusalem to maintain that this was to be taken upon himself: both to preach Christ and to live like the Jews, doing all the things which the Law of the Jews teaches—meaning the things which the Jews understood were to be observed for themselves. Therefore, since certain people from James had come to Peter, Peter was intimidated, Paul says, and he fearfully withdrew so as not to eat with Gentiles. But this Paul reprimanded, as previously Peter *was eating with Gentiles,* and then he withdrew, *fearing those who were of the circumcision*—meaning the people who came from James. Yet what Peter did was a small thing. Where did the major sin come in? Others were also going along with him: *And the other Jews also went along with him.* Let us take *Jews* here in such wise to indicate the Jews who had none the less already accepted Christ, that those people went along in accepting both Christ and Jewish teaching and observance. For unless we take this to be the sense, what will *they went along* mean, if those people had continued to live in the traditional manner according to the Jewish

---

2. In his commentary on Gal. 1:19, Victorinus argues that James was not an apostle and that he had a different understanding of the gospel, which included the observance of Judaism. He thus links James with a Jewish-Christian group called the Symmachians, probably so-named because they used Symmachus' Greek translation of the Hebrew Bible rather than the Septuagint. Victorinus appears to have been influenced by the depiction of James in Jewish-Christian writings such as the *Pseudo-Clementines* (see above, pp. 230–35).

teaching? Rather, the passage is talking about the Jews who had already received the gospel by believing in Christ; and how Peter himself, although he had been eating with Gentiles, later withdrew, fearing those who came from James—surely, men from the circumcision whom Peter feared. This was how the other Jews as well went along with him, so as to live no longer with the Gentiles but with the circumcision. This means that those who had also been Jews beforehand went off and lived with Jews.

With the result that even Barnabas went along with their pretence. Thus, once the Gentiles had been sent off, they dishonestly pretended to live only with Jews, says Paul, *with the result that Barnabas went along* with them. It was stated above that Barnabas was Paul's fellow-worker and held to the full gospel. None the less, he went along with those people and their pretence. So what do we understand *with their pretence* to mean? Could it be that Barnabas, the other Jews, and even Peter had really gone over to living life according to Jewish teaching? Or was it rather that for a while they pretended to do so on account of those present?[3] Was this the reason that *even Barnabas*—Paul says—went along with their pretence? This is how it must be taken. For neither Peter nor any of the others had gone over to the Jewish teaching, but they did go along with it for a while, as indeed from time to time pretended agreement was deemed acceptable. Even so, where in this were Peter and the others sinning? Because they put on this show of going along with them, though not in order to draw in those Jews, which Paul himself had done. He even boasts of having done so in order to get along with the Jews, although he did this to win them over. But because Peter also put on a pretence, he none the less sinned in so doing, because *Peter withdrew, fearing those who were of the circumcision.* Therefore, because Peter put on the pretence from fear, and from fear held himself aloof from the Gentiles, and because Barnabas too went along with that pretence, for that reason, says Paul, I openly opposed him and accused Peter of having made a pretence in this matter from fear. Next Paul follows up the point in this way:

But because I had seen that they were not proceeding straightforwardly in the truth of the gospel (2: 14). Indeed, they had been holding to the gospel, holding it fully, and they understood that life was not to be led the way those of the circumcision live. But since they were engaged in a pretence, they were therefore interpreting the gospel badly, getting badly off track on the way to the truth of the gospel. So because I saw this, *I spoke to Peter in the presence of everyone*—which is what *I opposed him to his face* means. I spoke openly and said in the presence of everyone, *If you, though a Jew, live Gentile-style, how are you compelling the Gentiles to Judaize?* Paul clearly understood that it was on account of his timorousness that Peter made a pretence of not living with Gentiles. And so he does not charge him with this, as Peter could claim 'I was making a pretence'. What, then, does Paul charge him with? You have been living with Gentiles, and you do live with Gentiles. When you have a temporary agreement, there is no question but that you do live Gentile-style. Still, because your pretence is deceiving many people, you are sinning. For you are compelling the Gentiles to Judaize. In saying this, Paul shows that he also understood Peter to have gone along with the Jews only by way of a pretence, but that

---

3. The "pretense" theory is grounded in the Latin word *simulatio* (Gal. 2:13), which, like the Greek *hypokrisis*, can mean either "hypocrisy" or "pretense."

he was none the less sinning. First, because he feared the men who came on the scene; in the next place, because others were deceived and the Gentiles compelled to Judaize, not understanding that Peter was making a pretence. So Paul puts it together, and he recalls having said, Why do you, Peter, although you are a Jew, live Gentile-style? That is to say, why do you live with Gentiles? How now are you compelling these same Gentiles to Judaize—that is, to carry out the Jewish teaching both in diet and religious observances?

THEODORE OF MOPSUESTIA

[The Allegory of Hagar and Sarah] (early fifth century)†

4:21 Tell me, you who desire to be subject to the law, do you not hear the law?

Changing his words to them was appropriate and something right for him to do, since he had been provoked by what had actually happened. For in all these respects the apostle seems to put up with frequent changes of his subject because of his anger at what was carried out. And he is indignant now at these, now at those; but for others he grieves [72] as for lost sons. And altogether if someone were willing to make a careful examination, he would find a great alternation of emotions in his writings, the kind of alternation that the situation itself compelled Paul to make. He preached with such great enthusiasm so that he might be eager to offer all people to Christ, because he wanted all to join Christ because of the immense affection he had for him. And what he means is: "You who have promised to obey the law are paying no attention to what the law says." He adds what this is in what follows:

4:22–23 For it is written that Abraham had two sons, one by a slave woman and the other by a free woman. One, the child of the slave, was born according to the flesh; the other, the child of the free woman, was born through the promise.

Above he demonstrated that the law could have nothing in common with the promises because the law required that its ordinances be fulfilled, while the promise ratified the generosity of the one who gave it. In all respects, however, he was eager to establish the principle of grace; and so he mentioned faith and the promise together with what we hope to be ours. And he placed the law in contrast to all of these, because it plainly offered righteousness in a certain order. It promises to offer these goods, at any rate to those who have first fulfilled the law. But it deceives many, or to speak more truly probably all, because those who strive to fulfill the law are unable to do so. For this reason he said that the righteousness that comes from grace is to the greatest extent better than that which comes

† From Theodore's commentary on Gal. 4:21–30, tr. by Rowan A. Greer, who renders the Latin text found in H. B. Swete, *Theodori episcopi Mopsuesteni in epistolas B. Pauli commentarii* (Cambridge, Cambridge University Press, 1880), Vol. I, 71–87 [page numbers in Swete are included in the translation in brackets]. Reprinted by permission of the Society of Biblical Literature. Theodore (ca. 350–428) wrote commentaries on all of Paul's letters while he was bishop of Mopsuestia (392–428). His commentary on Paul's famous allegory is the best extant evidence for the Antiochene antipathy to this method of interpretation, which was favored by Alexandrian exegetes. Greer's translation will appear in the series "Writings from the Greco-Roman World," published by the Society of Biblical Literature.

from the law, since God bestows it by his own generosity with no one excluded because of natural weakness. And demonstrating the same conclusions as in what preceded on the basis of the illustration about Abraham, he reminded them that Abraham had two sons, one born according to the order of nature, but the other through grace. About this the law [73] says that *Abraham had two sons, one by a slave woman and the other by a free woman. One, the child of the slave, was born according to the flesh,* that is, he was born by the natural order. He calls this *according to the flesh* since childbirth by nature belongs to the flesh. And Ishmael was born by the natural order of the flesh both by Abraham and by Hagar. But *the child of the free woman was born through the promise,* that is, according to grace. For every promise customarily takes place through grace. Now Isaac is said by no means to have been born in the order of nature, because Sarah was unable to give birth for two reasons. For one thing she was barren, and for another she was prevented from giving birth by her great age. And Abraham himself was far advanced in old age. Yet Isaac was born beyond all hope and beyond the order of nature only because of the power as much as the generosity of the one who promised. So he refers to the story of Abraham as it appears written in the divine scriptures. But since he wishes to show why he employed it, he adds:

4:24a *Now this is by an allegory.*

There are people who have great zeal for overturning the meaning of the divine scriptures, and by breaking up everything placed there they fabricate from themselves certain foolish fictions and give their folly the name of allegory. They use this term of the apostle's so as to take from it the right to dismiss the entire meaning of divine scripture by depending on the apostle's expression *by an allegory.* But they fail to understand how great the difference is between their view and what the apostle says in this passage. For the apostle does not do away with the narrative, nor [74] does he get rid of what happened long ago. Instead, he put it down as what had actually taken place at that time, but in such a way that he also used the narrative of what had actually happened for his own interpretation, as when he says *she corresponds to the present Jerusalem* (4:23), or when he says *just as at that time the child who was born according to the flesh persecuted the child who was born according to the Spirit* (4:29). In this way he acknowledged the narrative in all these matters. Otherwise he would not have said that what concerned Hagar corresponds *to the present Jerusalem,* which he acknowledges exists at the present time. Nor would he have put down *just as* to refer to someone he did not think existed. For when he said *just as,* he was doubtless making a comparison; and no comparison can be made unless the terms of the comparison continue to exist. Furthermore, when he said *at that time,* though he supposes it to be unspecified, he meant to indicate a definite time. And the distinction of times would be meaningless if what happened had nevertheless not taken place.

* * *

And it is clear in many passages that the apostle employed the narrative of things of old as true in all respects. [76] And in this passage it is on the basis of events that actually took place and of those traditions acknowledged by the Jews as true that he strives to prove his own claim, which he sets forth from the outset. But what is that claim? He wants to demonstrate that Christ's dispensation is greater than that of the law and that our righteousness should be perceived as far more excellent than that found in the law.

＊　＊　＊

Therefore, with good reason he called both dispensations alike *testaments*, because grace by its guidance was putting into effect those very teachings of the law, namely, the love of God and the neighbor. For the law kept on commanding the keeping of these same commandments, emphasizing them and teaching the duty of not sinning in any way. But grace brings this to fulfillment by the resurrection and that immortality which will then be ours through the Spirit, since when we shall then be guided by him, we shall by no means sin.

Justification, then, is both in the law and with Christ. But in the law it would in fact be acquired only by the person able to acquire it by much toil and sweat. This would prove extremely difficult, indeed to speak more truly impossible, if at any rate one wanted to judge according to a scrupulous keeping of the laws. For it is impossible that any human existing would be completely sinless. Indeed, this is acquired only by grace, for we shall be incapable of sinning any longer at that time when apart from all toil we shall obtain the justification that comes from Christ. [78] Thus, Paul mentioned Hagar and Sarah, the first of whom gave birth according to the order of nature, but the other, since she could not give birth, bore Isaac according to grace. Of the two sons the one born according to grace was found far and away much the more distinguished. Paul mentioned them so that by such a comparison he might demonstrate that now, as well, justification according to Christ is far better than that other justification because it is acquired by grace. He rightly took the woman who gave birth by the order of nature as standing for the justification that is in the law, and he set down the woman seen to have given birth beyond hope as standing for justification which is by grace. He does this because living according to the law is relevant for those who are in the present, but for those who have once risen again and been made incorruptible, circumcision is useless as well as the offering of sacrifices, to say nothing of the observance of days.

＊　＊　＊

Therefore, this is why he said *Now this is by an allegory*. He calls an allegory that comparison which can be made between events that happened long ago and present circumstances.

Then he adds:

4:24b And they are two testaments, one in fact from Mount Sinai, giving birth for slavery, which is Hagar.

"They" refers to the two women. He alludes to what he said, *this is by an allegory*, as though the verse read: "For these women are the two testaments spoken of by an allegory." And what he means is that by allegory one can compare the two testaments to those two, that is to Hagar and Sarah, so that Hagar may be ranked in the law's commands, because the law was given on Mount Sinai and gives birth to slavery. For those who live their lives under the law are so ranked as slaves, and they accept both the commands and the law. [80] But they are punished without any excuse if they are found to have sinned, while they are praised if with all scrupulous care they are willing to observe the law. This is extremely difficult and is accomplished with great toil. And it is appropriate for slaves and not for free people to be held under the law in this way. Then, to demonstrate that the comparison made from Hagar is not foreign to the Old Testament, he adds:

4:25 *Now Hagar is Mount Sinai in Arabia and corresponds to the present Jerusalem, and is in slavery with its sons.*

In times of old Arabia was not only the region that now has that name, but included the entire desert and the places that were inhabited round about the desert, not least of which was the part of Egypt [81] in which there was also the place the Israelites inhabited during their stay in Egypt. For this was the way that place was spoken of, as we learn from divine scripture: *they dwell in the land of Goshen in Arabia.*[1] Therefore, he wanted to demonstrate from this that Hagar and Mount Sinai pertain to Arabia. Consequently, the comparison of Hagar to the Old Testament is suitable because it was given in the place belonging to the nation from which Hagar came.[2]

Now by saying *corresponds to the present Jerusalem* he refers to Hagar, so that he means "that Jerusalem which is with us, [82] that is, which is seen to exist in this age, has the same worth as Hagar, since the present Jerusalem retains for us the system in which the legal ordinances of that testament are fulfilled in contrast to what was expected, what we also hope to enjoy in the age to come." And what Hagar plainly included is contrasted with Sarah. For he said *and is in slavery with its sons* not of Hagar, but he harks back to the testament given on Sinai in order to establish what he had said (4:23): *one from Mount Sinai, bearing children for slavery.* He said that those who live their lives under that testament are its sons. And he rightly said that it *is in slavery with its sons.* For the character of the testament is certainly recognized in those who have received it. For it is not described by its own substance, and so it is in slavery when those who follow it are plainly in slavery.

It would be right for those devoted to allegory to pay attention to what he said: *she corresponds to the present Jerusalem.* For it is quite clearly not a question of breaking up the account of Hagar, but what he wanted to show is that Hagar and the present Jerusalem have a like worth because they have the same meaning. Blessed Paul speaks of the first testament and then makes another statement:

4:26 *But the Jerusalem above is free; she is the mother of us all.*

[83] The apostle does not say *Jerusalem above* by concocting dreams as those people do who suppose that everything must be tossed into allegory. Rather, he uses the expression since he knows how to designate the second testament as the resurrection which those who attained it were awaiting, those who were also hoping to attain the privilege of dwelling in heaven freed from all sin. Therefore, he used the expression *which is the Jerusalem above* in relation to this, pointing out in this way that form of life of ours which we have in the heavens because we shall dwell and live there together with Christ and shall conduct ourselves with perfect diligence. At

1. See Gen 45:10 and 46:34 in LXX.
2. According to Genesis 16:1 Hagar was an Egyptian.

any rate, he used the expression *Jerusalem above* in this way to refer to the heavenly dwelling, since even the Jews who dwelt in the environs of Jerusalem used to think they were dwelling with God. Jerusalem was where they hastened to discharge the slavery they owed to God, since they thought this the right place for them, because they could nowhere else accomplish sacrifice or whole burnt offering or anything else according to the law. This is why that *Jerusalem which is above is free, which is the mother of us all.* What he means is that "by attaining the resurrection and by it also discerning the glorious new birth by which we shall also dwell in heaven, and by thinking that to be our Jerusalem, we shall be at the same time in the greatest freedom, since we shall no longer need to fulfill the law's ordinances or anything else of this kind. And we shall dwell there with great confidence because we shall no longer be capable of submitting to sin." And he employs a scriptural testimony (Isa 54:1):

[84] 4:27 *For it is written, "Rejoice, you barren one, you who bear no children, burst into song and shout, you who endure no birth pangs; for the sons of the desolate woman are more numerous than of the one who has a husband."*

He did not cite this verse as though it were spoken prophetically of the resurrection, but he employed the testimony because of the word *barren,* since he takes Sarah as the barren woman in the rank of the second testament. What he means is that "all that will be beyond hope. For we who have died will rise again so that we shall be found more numerous than those others. For we who come together in this testament shall be much more numerous. Those, however, who are in the testament under the law are a single nation. But we who hold fast to our attainment of the testament of the resurrection shall all be sons." This is why he adds:

4:28 *Now we, brothers, are sons of the promise, like Isaac.*

When he said *like Isaac,* he meant "we shall be like Isaac, not according to nature, but according to grace. For just as Isaac was born beyond all hope, [so it is for us] because the resurrection is by grace and not by nature." And since he has proved by what is found in divine scripture the difference between the two testaments, he shows that the dispensation of grace is much better than that of nature. Therefore, following this train of thought, he also makes full use of the present circumstances:

4:29 *But just as at that time he who was born according to the flesh persecuted the one born according to the Spirit, so it is now also.*

[85] Of those who are according to Christ he uses not only the words faith and promise (as we have already demonstrated above), but also the word Spirit. In many passages he makes special use of this word, as one can clearly see in Romans, because we await our reception of the good things to come by participation in the Spirit. Therefore, in this way he also speaks of those who are according to the law in reference to what belongs to the body, because the law can be useful in this present life. Moreover, the fact that he speaks of flesh as temporal and something easily destroyed when he speaks of our nature is something we have demonstrated in many passages in interpreting the apostle's writings. Our fuller discussion has clearly demonstrated this, at least to those willing to examine his words with the greatest care. And since Hagar, who plainly gave birth by natural order, is driven out, she held the type of the Old Testament because it was capable of keeping a system in the present life for those born in the order

of nature, as we have just said. Therefore, *just as at that time he who was born* by the order of nature *persecuted the one born* by promise, *so also* those who *now* present themselves as champions of the law strive to hunt out what belongs to grace.

[86] And he rightly said *according to the Spirit*, so as to mean that Isaac was according to the promise, because he was about to describe our position by comparing it to the likeness of Isaac's. The word Spirit was truthfully used of both because of what was believed because of them. I should like to ask those most excellent allegorists whether in this passage divine scripture records for us that Ishmael persecuted Isaac because it really means that there would be certain people from the circumcision who in the most recent times would try to hand over those Galatian Christians to the law. Who would ever be able to make enough fun of such an idea? And so if nothing else, it would at least be right for them to recognize that the apostle put the narrative in his discussion as one of events that really happened and one handed down acknowledged as such, and that he did so to establish what he had said. He did indeed want to display the narrative by comparison with its likeness. This is why he plainly employed what had actually happened in reference to circumstances foreign to those events. He adds inconsistently but at the same time splendidly:

4:30 But what does the scripture say? "Drive out the slave and her son; for the son of the slave will not be the heir with the son of the free woman."

He means that "toiling profits them nothing, just as it did not profit him at that time. For neither is there anything in common between the present and the future, nor can the ordinances of the law have a place in our way of life, which we accomplish according to the type of the resurrection.

* * *

VICTORINUS

[Paul and the Pre-Existence of Souls] (ca. 365)†

1,4. *Even as he chose us in him before the foundation of the world that we might be holy.* This is a discourse about divinity and a short explanation of the whole Mystery, in which the following is established: that Christ existed before the world; that the world has been made; that there were souls before the world; that the world exists by God's dispensation; that souls both came into the world and are being freed from the world by God's dispensation; that all that is done is the will of God; and that for those living in accordance with Christ there is a reward so that sins may be forgiven and we may participate in the glory of God. * * *

Though these [elements of the teaching] are esoteric they are nonetheless very true. * * * *God chose us.* This implies that God chose us when we already existed, and God chose us in Christ. So we were and Christ was

† From Victorinus's commentary on Eph. 1:4, trans. by Stephen A. Cooper, *Metaphysics and Morals in Marius Victorinus' Commentary on the Letter to the Ephesians* (New York: Lang, 1995). Reprinted by permission of Stephen A. Cooper. Victorinus's exegesis of Ephesians is an example of full-blown, pre-Augustinian Neoplatonist Paulinism, replete with a doctrine of the pre-existence of souls.

before. But what does this *before* mean? Surely from eternity. For this is what Paul said: *before the foundation of the world; God chose [us]*, he makes the point, *before the foundation of the world*. God did not choose except from among the things that existed. Consequently when he says *in Christ* (this is what *in him* means), we can gather that Christ had existed and that we were in Christ. If God chose us in Christ himself, it cannot be that Christ would have existed and we would not have existed as well. Therefore we were spiritual beings, if we were in Christ. And if we were in Christ and were spiritual beings, we existed—as Paul adds afterward—before the foundation of the world.

✻   ✻   ✻

THEODORET OF CYRUS

[The Man of Sin] (ca. 445)†

Having thus consoled them with the hope of future goods, he shifts his focus to instruction on the consummation. *Now, we ask you, brethren, in connection with the coming of our Lord Jesus Christ and our being gathered to him, not to be hastily diverted from your purpose or be troubled, not by spirit or word or letter as though from us saying that the day of the Lord is at hand* (vv.1–2). He always uses *we ask* to mean we urge. The meaning of the phrase *our being gathered to him* he indicated more clearly in the first letter: he said we would be caught up in the air on the clouds to meet the Lord, and thus we would be with the Lord forever.[1] The Lord also said as much in the sacred Gospels: "He will send his angels, and they will gather his elect from the four winds, from one end of heaven to the other."[2] So the divine apostle recommends them not believe those saying the time of the consummation is at hand and the Lord will come immediately, not even if they pretend to utter oracles and to prophesy (the meaning of *by spirit*), nor if they claim to display a letter written by him, nor if they say he had spoken without writing.

Then in turn he says the same thing concisely: *Let no one deceive you in any way* (v.3). In the one word he rejected all the forms of deception. He teaches them, and through them all of us, the clearest sign of the Lord's coming. *Because unless the defection comes first, and the man of sin is revealed, the son of perdition, who opposes and exalts himself above every so-called god or object of worship so that he takes his seat as God in the temple of God, proclaiming himself to be God* (vv.3–4). By *defection* he referred to the Anti-Christ in person, making a title out of the event. He called him *the man of sin*[3] since he is a man by nature, receiving all the devil's activity in himself, and *son of perdition* as being ruined himself and

---

† From Theodoret's commentary on 2 Thess. 2:1–12, tr. by Robert Charles Hill, *Theodoret of Cyrus, Commentary on the Letters of St. Paul* (Brookline: Holy Cross Orthodox Press, 2001), Vol. 2, 127–30. Reprinted by permission of Holy Cross Orthodox Press. Theodoret (ca. 393–ca. 457) was bishop of Cyrus (about 100 km northeast of Antioch) and wrote commentaries on all of Paul's letters.

1. 1 Thess. 4:17.
2. Matt. 24:31.
3. Manuscripts vary between "man of lawlessness" and "man of sin."

proving the source of ruin to others. In fact, human beings' avenging spirit mimics the Incarnation of our God and Savior; as the latter by assuming human nature procured our salvation, so the former by selecting a human being capable of receiving all his activity will endeavor through him to deceive all human beings, calling himself Christ and God, and betraying the falsity of the so-called gods, which he himself practiced in times past. By *temple of God* he referred to the churches, in which he will arrogate to himself pride of place, striving to declare himself God. The divine Daniel also prophesied this in the words, "He will not recognize him over gods of his ancestors, and will glorify Maozim as god in his own place,"[4] that is, he will name himself powerful god.

Then to emphasize that he is not proposing to them any new teaching, he went on, *Do you not recall that when I was with you I told you this?* (v.5). He also mentions why on earth it is delayed and does not appear immediately. *You know what the restraint is now, so that he may be revealed in his own good time* (v.6). Some commentators took *the restraint* to be the Roman empire, others the grace of the Spirit, implying that with the grace of the Spirit being restrained that person does not come. But it is out of the question that the grace of the Spirit would cease completely: how would it be possible for those deprived of spiritual assistance to prevail over that person's wiles? Yet neither will another empire succeed the Roman empire; the most divine Daniel hinted at the Roman empire in the fourth beast: the small horn grew on it, waging war against the saints.[5] He is the one to whom the divine apostle applied the prophecies. In my opinion the divine apostle is speaking of neither: I suspect the truth lies in what is said by other commentators: the God of all decided he would appear at the time of the consummation. It is God's decree, then, that impedes his appearing now. In my view the verse has a further meaning as well: on learning that the Lord had said that the Gospel must be preached to all the nations and then the end would come,[6] the divine apostle saw that the worship of idols was still flourishing, and in fidelity to the Lord's teaching he said that the power of superstition would first be overthrown and the saving message would shine forth everywhere, and only then would the adversary of truth appear.

The mystery of iniquity is in fact already at work (v.7). Some commentators claimed that to Nero is given the name *mystery of iniquity*, and that he had become a worker of godlessness. It is my view, on the contrary, that the apostle is indicating the heresies that had sprung up: by leading many from the truth through them, the devil causes in advance the ruin of deceit. These people he referred to as *mystery of iniquity* for keeping the snares of iniquity hidden; the devil openly draws people away from God. Hence the apostle referred to his coming as *revelation*: he will then openly and plainly proclaim what he has constantly been working at in secret. *Only until the one who is restraining it is taken away*: the deception of superstition must be brought to an end, and the Gospel be preached.

And then the iniquitous one will be revealed, whom the Lord Jesus will consume by the spirit of his mouth, and will destroy with the manifestation of his coming (v.8). He brought out to the extent possible the magnitude of the

4. Dan. 11:38 (Theodotion's version).
5. Dan. 7:7–8, 19–27.
6. Matt. 24:14.

Lord's power: Coming from above, he is saying, he will simply speak, and will consign to destruction the guilty one. The prophet Isaiah also foretold this: after saying, "A shoot will come forth from the root of Jesse," and giving a description of him, he went on, "and with the breath of his lips he will destroy the godless."[7] The divine apostle explains by whose activity it is that he performs all this: *Whose coming is by the activity of Satan, with all power, signs, and false marvels, and with all deception of injustice among those on the way to ruin* (vv.9–10): he will not have power over all—only those deserving of ruin, who would have deprived themselves of salvation even without his coming. He says as much also in what follows. He explains that even what happens will not be true miracles; even those who get names from pebbles do likewise: they show as gold what is not really gold, and other such things, which shortly after appear in their true colors.

For the reason that they did not accept the love of truth with a view to being saved, and hence God will send on them the working of error so that they believe in falsehood, and so all will be judged who do not believe in the truth but take pleasure in iniquity (vv.10–12). By *love of truth* he referred to the Lord for loving us truly and sincerely. The Lord himself also said as much to the Jews, "I came in the name of my Father, and you do not receive me; another person comes in his own name, and him you will receive."[8] So to the Jews in particular no grounds for excuse will be left: refusing to believe in the Lord as though anti-God, they believe in the other. Admittedly, the Lord did not openly call himself God; but he said he was sent by the Father, received his command, and was doing what was pleasing to the God and Father. The other, by contrast, will call himself God of all; yet the Jews will wait for him and will believe in him when he comes. The phrase, *God will send on them the working of error*, he employed with the meaning, He will allow error to appear so that the lovers of wickedness will be shown up: he will not send it himself, but he will consume it with a word of his mouth.

AMBROSIASTER

[On the Attire, Subordination, and Salvation of Women] (late fourth century)†

[2.9] Also that the women should dress themselves modestly and decently in suitable clothing, not with their hair braided, or with gold, pearls, or expensive clothes, [10] but with good work, as is proper for women who profess reverence for God.

The women should pray in simple clothing, not ostentatiously. She who wishes to be heard should divest herself of luxury and humble herself, so that she may call forth God's mercy. For pretentious clothing does not obtain results, nor does it lead one to think highly of her. What prudent

---

7. Isa. 11:1, 4.
8. John 5:43.
† From Ambrosiaster's commentary on 1 Tim. 2:9–15 (CSEL 81), tr. by David G. Hunter, Stephen Cooper, and Theodore de Bruyn, to appear in the series "Writings from the Greco-Roman World," published by the Society of Biblical Literature. Reprinted by permission of the Society of Biblical Literature. On the identity of "Ambrosiaster," see note on p. 213 above.

person is not horrified at the sight of a woman dressed in ostentatious fashion? How much more is God the creator revolted at the sight of the body, which he created to be free, bound by metal chains! For simple clothing corresponds with the decision to lead a good life, so that a woman's true value cannot be determined apart from her appearance. But if a woman prefers to be seen dressed luxuriously in the house of God, it is clear that she is more interested in attracting the praise of men than of God. Such a woman will acquire nothing from God but blame. For the more splendid one appears before human beings, the more one is despised by God.

[2.11] Let a woman learn in silence with full submission. [12] I permit no woman to teach or to have authority over a man; she is to keep silent.

Not only does he command that a woman should wear simple clothing, but he also states that she must have no authority over a man and that she should be subject to him. Thus both in her clothing and in her obedience she will be under the power of the man, from whom she derived her origin.

[2.13] For Adam was formed first, then Eve; [14] and Adam was not deceived, but the woman was deceived and became a transgressor. [15] Yet she will be saved through childbearing, provided they continue in faith and love and holiness, with modesty.

(1) He places the man over the woman because the man was created first; thus the woman is subordinate because she was created after the man and from the man. Furthermore, he adds that the devil did not seduce the man, but rather the woman; and the man was deceived by means of the woman. Because of this the woman has no warrant for arrogant behavior, but she must be humble, since death entered the world through her. (2) *But she will be saved through childbearing*, he says, if they continue in faith and love and a pure life. He is speaking of those children who are born again through faith in Christ. If they persevere in their rebirth, she will be set free along with them, when she rises from the dead. Not that she will be set free by them, but rather by giving birth to them. When those who are destined for eternal life come to believe, the resurrection of the dead will occur, and she will be saved because they believe and live a chaste life. [For the resurrection has been deferred until all who are predestined to salvation believe.][1]

THEODORET OF CYRUS

[The "Last Days"] (ca. 445)†

Then he foretells the coming ruin of most members of the churches, teaching him[1] not to be upset by the indifference of some, as those coming later will be in a far worse plight. *Be aware of this, that in the last days there*

---

1. The bracketed material occurs in only one recension of the text.
† From Theodoret's commentary on 2 Tim. 3:1–8, tr. by Robert Charles Hill, *Theodoret of Cyrus, Commentary on the Letters of St. Paul* (Brookline: Holy Cross Orthodox Press, 2001), Vol. 2, 243–44. Reprinted by permission of Holy Orthodox Press. In a rare departure from his typical Antiochene method of explicating Scripture, Theodoret gives here a moralizing interpretation in which he sees his own age as the one predicted by Paul. The history of Christianity is replete with instances of such contemporizing exegesis.
1. Timothy.

will be the threat of difficult times: there will be people who are lovers of themselves, lovers of money, arrogant, blasphemous, disobedient to parents, ungrateful, unholy, loveless, implacable, slanderous, licentious, unfeeling, uninterested in the good, treacherous, reckless, conceited, in love with pleasure rather than God, bearing the semblance of piety but denying its efficacy (vv.1–5). In my view he has this age in mind in his prophecy: our lifetime is full of these vices, and though we don the trappings of piety, we are building the idol of wickedness in our works. I mean, we have become attached to money rather than devoted to God, we embrace the slavery of the passions, and to put it in a nutshell, you could find in us all the other vices the divine apostle cited. In what follows he bade those entrusted to Timothy's care to avoid associating with these people, saying, *Give them a wide berth.* And persisting with the accusation he goes on to say, *Among them, in fact, are those who gain entrance to families and captivate silly women carrying a load of sins and under the influence of lusts and pleasures of many kinds, always on the lookout for something new but never managing to arrive at a knowledge of the truth* (vv.6–7). We see the fulfilment of this prophecy: great numbers of people, not even suspecting the apostolic prediction, brazenly commit this lawlessness. Then, to those disheartened at this he offers encouragement with stories of people in former times. *In the same way that Jannes and Jambres opposed Moses, so too these people oppose the truth, being corrupt in mind and false as far as the faith is concerned* (v.8). Weeds normally grow up with grain, he is saying: the preachers of the truth have always had their adversaries. What could be a more famous example of piety than Moses? Yet even he had those men who were sorcerers openly arrayed against the truth. The divine apostle, of course, got their names not from the divine Scripture but from the unwritten tradition of the Jews.[2] It was likely that the grace of the Spirit also revealed them to him.

BERNADETTE J. BROOTEN

Patristic Interpretations of Romans 1:26 (1985)†

*   *   *

Interpretations of Rom. 1:26 occur only rarely in the patristic sources. When the verse is quoted at all, it is usually the first half, 'God gave them up to dishonorable passions,' which is quoted without comment (e.g., Origen often does this). The interpretations which do occur fall into two categories. According to the one, Paul is referring here, not to lesbians, but rather to unnatural heterosexual intercourse. According to the other lesbians are indeed meant. Anastasius and Augustine are examples of the unnatural heterosexual intercourse interpretation, while John Chrysostom and Clement of Alexandria would be examples of the second category.

According to scholia found in two manuscripts of the *Paedagogus* of

2. See the note on 2 Tim. 3:8.
† Published originally in *Studia Patristica XVIII*, Vol. I (Kalamazoo: Cistercian, 1985), 287–91. Reprinted by permission. Brooten is the Kraft-Hiatt Professor of Christian Studies at Brandeis University.

Clement of Alexandria, Anastasius interpreted the verse as follows: 'Clearly they do not go into one another * * *, but rather offer themselves to the men.' He thus seems to dispute the possibility of sexual relations between women at all. Augustine also took the verse as referring to unnatural heterosexual intercourse. For him unnatural means that which does not allow for procreation, such as anal intercourse: 'But as regards any part of the body which is not meant for generative purposes, should a man use even his own wife in it, it is against nature and flagitious.' Augustine sees sexual intercourse with a prostitute as less evil than nonprocreative forms of marital intercourse, because the former is at least not contrary to nature.

How is it possible to interpret the verse as not referring to sexual relations between women? It is the case that, with respect to the women, Paul speaks only of their having 'exchanged natural relations for unnatural.' Thus, one inclined to overlook the existence of lesbians could take vss. 26 and 27 as not parallel to each other, in spite of the ὁμοίως, 'similarly,' of v. 27.

One should note, however, that Augustine does not totally dispute the possibility of love relations between women. In fact, he specifically warns nuns about lesbian existence: 'The love which you bear to each other must be not carnal, but spiritual.'

According to the second category of interpretation, Rom. 1:26 does refer to lesbians. John Chrysostom, in his commentary on Romans, writes that the women in question were without excuse, because they did have access to lawful intercourse, making unnecessary this 'monstrous depravity.' Chrysostom further notes that it is 'more disgraceful that the women should seek this type of intercourse, since they ought to have a greater sense of shame than men.' Thus, for Chrysostom, lesbian existence and male homosexuality are not parallel to each other, for women and men are not meant to be alike. The man was designed to be the teacher of the woman, the woman the helpmate of the man. Gender roles and a polarization of the sexes are essential to his interpretation of Rom. 1:26–27. Homosexual men become, in essence, women and cease to be men or rather blur the differences between women and men. A similar concern with the blurring of gender role distinctions occurs in Chrysostom's tractates on spiritual marriage.

Moving behind Chrysostom to an earlier historical stage, we find that Clement of Alexandria similarly devotes much greater attention to male homosexuality than to lesbian existence. Like Chrysostom, he is concerned that through homosexuality men become like women. Clement emphasizes that men's hair and clothing should not resemble women's hair and clothing. Men should wear a beard as a sign of their stronger nature and their right to rule. Women should be veiled and with covered faces. It is in the context of the necessity of gender differentiation with respect to clothing and hair that Clement discusses homosexuality: 'men passively play the role of women, and women behave like men * * * in that women, contrary to nature, are given in marriage and marry'.

Augustine is likewise concerned about gender distinction with respect to hair, writing that monks should not believe that celibacy means they are no longer men. Monks should avoid long hair, which could create the impression that they are available to be bought. Women should veil themselves, for woman, unlike man, does not through her body show that she is made in the image of God. Man is meant to rule and woman to be subordinate * * *.

To sum up * * *, neither those commentators who interpret Rom 1:26 as referring to heterosexual intercourse, nor those who take it as referring to lesbians interpret v. 26 (on women) as parallel to v. 27 (on men). This is in keeping with these authors' view that the very deep differences between women and men which they posit must be preserved.

* * *

The Second-Century Paul

DAVID K. RENSBERGER

[The Use of Paul's Letters in Second-Century Christianity] (1981)†

* * *

GEOGRAPHICAL SURVEY

There seem to have been two main early centers of interest in the letters of Paul. Not surprisingly, one of these is Asia Minor, the scene of much of Paul's own work. The Pastorals are there, and (evidently in the same milieu) Polycarp. The latter did not yet cite the epistles as normative writings, but obviously recognized Paul's authority and did make respectful use of quotations from him. The source in *AH* 5.5.1; 36.2, whether it is Papias or not, is also significant. Though isolated and difficult to date, it shows that Marcion did not appear in a setting where appeal to Paul was without precedent. That there was some preparation in Asia for his use of the epistles is also clear from the untroubled answering use made by the Presbyter whom Irenaeus quotes, who seems to feel nothing novel about the practice. This in no way detracts from Marcion's originality in the breadth and exclusiveness of his Pauline program; but it is helpful to see it in its local context, among other Paul-related phenomena. In later decades it was there again that the *Acts of Paul* were created, and it is worth recalling that Irenaeus too had Asia Minor as his homeland.

The second geographical center is more problematic, namely, Alexandria. The origins of Christianity there are extremely obscure, and how, when, and in what form the letters of Paul arrived utterly unknown. Yet it was apparently in Alexandria that Paul was first cited in a systematic way alongside other normative texts and used to prove a point, by Basilides. The Carpocrateans may well be placed there too, as well as Basilides' son Isidore and other followers, and probably also Julius Cassianus. If Cassianus was once a Valentinian (Clement, *Strom.* 3.[13].92.1), he evidently was so no longer when we meet with him; but the school of Valentinus had its representative here, and a ready interpreter of Paul, in the person of Theodotus. In fact, Valentinus himself is said to have been of Egyptian birth and Alexandrian education (Ephiphanius, *haer.* 31.2.3). What his position may have been in the history of the canonization of Paul's letters we will consider below, and Alexandria itself as the place where the letters

---

† From *As the Apostle Teaches: The Development of the Use of Paul's Letters in Second-Century Christianity* (unpublished Ph.D. Diss., Yale University, 1981), 354–81. Reprinted by permission of the author. Rensberger is professor of New Testament at the Interdenominational Theological Center in Atlanta.

341

first appear in tandem with other authoritative writings must also figure in our final discussions.

Interest in the letters at Rome was also present early, but developed more slowly. Paul himself had written to Rome and had died there. The author of *1 Clement* knew 1 Corinthians as well as Romans, and epistles of Paul were no doubt familiar in Roman churches well before the middle of the second century, though Justin speaks of the formal weekly reading only of gospels and Old Testament (*1 Apol.* 67.1). Thus while it is tempting to think simply of Asian and Alexandrian uses of Paul converging on Rome in the persons of Marcion and Valentinus, the evidence will not quite allow it. If Marcionites were active there and Valentinus' pupil Ptolemy calls to mind Basilides' procedures, there was also Justin's disciple Tatian, neither Marcionite nor Valentinian, whose use of Paul likewise seems independent of either of these two followings. Though nothing in Justin suggests that Tatian's approach to the Apostle derived from him, and despite the uncertainty about where much of Tatian's work was accomplished, it seems permissible to see in him at the least a further indication of what was possible at Rome. The evidence of Irenaeus, another immigrant from Asia, may be credited to the Roman sphere as well, since he interested himself in affairs there from nearby Gaul (Eusebius, *HE* 5.3.4–4.1; 20.1; 24.11). We may also recall the two exact, if unsignalled, quotations from Paul in the letter regarding the martyrs of Lyons and Vienne.

There are two other geographical points to be noted. The first is also in the West, where the considerable acquaintance with Paul displayed by Tertullian is prepared for in Latin Africa by the testimony of the Scillitan martyrs, though we are again left in the dark as to when and how the letters first came there. In the East it is worth speaking of Antioch, whose early bishop Ignatius certainly knew one or two of the epistles and something of Paul's history as well, and whose later bishop Theophilus was well acquainted with the letters and their author. If the *Odes of Solomon* were not composed in Greek-speaking Antioch, they may at least show some kinship to Ignatius' milieu, Syrian but not without Pauline and Johannine characteristics. Thus though parts of Syria may, in early times at least, have been unfamiliar with or uninterested in Paul (the *Didache*), the whole region was by no means closed to him.

SUMMARY

The picture that results from our investigation is of a leading tendency that runs through the whole period, surrounded by widely diverse specific phenomena. Overall the trend was toward greater and more explicit use of the Pauline epistles as time went on. Confessional and theological differences seem to have had little to do with this. Only Marcion made an issue of the apostle he favored, and his opponents evidently insisted only on including others, not on excluding Paul, as we shall see below. For the rest, gnostics, catholics, and encratites made increasing and increasingly adroit use of the letters throughout the second century, unhindered by anything their adversaries may have been doing with the same writings. Within this framework, there was great variety. Writers in some genres felt no need to use the letters at all, unless prompted by specific circumstances such as the composition of a story about Paul himself or the generally increasing attention to the letters in the later decades. Works written for the instruction of other Christians, such as commentaries, doctrinal treatises, and polemical tracts, on the whole show a larger and earlier engagement with the epistles than those addressed to outsiders. Even so, it remained possible for many writers, gnostics included, to take no notice of them, and only very rarely did Paul's own theological concerns bear fruit in those who excerpted or invoked him. More commonly, Pauline language is found in the service of new ideas suited to new situations, or is even mediated to second-century writers by common Christian tradition, without thought of its source. Beginning in Alexandria and in Asia Minor, and growing with the passage of time, we also find the letters quoted, interpreted, and adduced in support of a broad range of positions in theology, spiritual cosmogony, ethics, ecclesiology, and exegesis. Increasingly, they enter the controversies of the time and are numbered among the resources available to all sides in the debates, so that the correct understanding of particular passages in them becomes an issue itself.

Gnostic Paulinism and the Canonization of the Epistles

These conclusions run counter to the common critical interpretation according to which Paul was ignored and mistrusted during the second century because of the use made of his letters by Marcion and the gnostics. In fact, if our study has one certain result, it is that this view is not merely exaggerated but incorrect. In order to sustain our judgement, we must briefly consider the evidence from this aspect, and then finally go on to take up the much-discussed questions of a special gnostic affinity for Paul expressed in a persistent appeal to his letters, and the influence of such an affinity on the growing regard for the letters as normative writings.

APOSTLE OF THE HERETICS?

That not only Marcion but many prominent gnostic teachers and groups did appeal to Paul is beyond doubt. We have seen this in the case of the Basilideans, Carpocrateans, Valentinians, Naassenes, and others.

* * *

As we have noted, there are considerable tracts of second-century Christian literature that make no use of the epistles at all. Yet we also found no reason to think of this silence as inspired by fear of gnosticism—the more so since it is shared by quite a number of gnostic works, such as the *Baruch* of Justin and many texts from Nag Hammadi. Two specific cases have attracted special attention in the history of scholarship. The first of these is Papias, whose "silence" is in fact quite meaningless, as J. B. Lightfoot demonstrated long ago. The second is Justin Martyr. Our study showed that one can be confident neither that he did nor that he did not use the letters of Paul, making his "silence" also a precarious one from which to argue. Certainly there is nothing positive to suggest hostility to Paul, and since Justin derives heresy from sources which do not include a deviant apostle, while the apologetic genre and his own method in both of his preserved works would not necessitate any allusion to the letters, there is no reason to ascribe his failure to use them (if such is the case) to anxieties about Marcion or gnosticism. Any such interpretation remains purely hypothetical, and quite arbitrary as well, since it has neither a basis in the works of Justin nor parallel in the procedure of other anti-Marcionite and antignostic writers, as we shall see momentarily.

Is there any evidence at all of a negative evaluation of the Apostle and his letters? We have eliminated Hegesippus in this regard. The author of 2 Peter certainly shows some emabrrassment at the way his opponents (whoever they may be) make use of Paul. But since it is he himself who appeals to the letters for support, we can hardly suspect him of mistrust or disapprobation of their author, so that a general antignostic hesitancy about Paul can in no way be extrapolated from the evidence of 2 Peter. The only soundly attested anti-Paulinism in the second century is that of Jewish Christians, for even the encratites spoken of by Origen are of quite uncertain date. No positive evidence exists that gnostic and Marcionite use of Paul provoked a widespread reaction against him.

There is a fair amount of positive evidence concerning the approaches to Paul actually taken by those who opposed gnosticism or Marcionism, and it tells quite a different story. The Pastoral Epistles and 3 *Corinthians* mount their assaults under the Apostle's patronage, and give no indication that their opponents caused them any chagrin by their own use of his writings. Polycarp opposed more than one sort of false teaching during his long career; his preserved letters make free use of Paul's epistles, honor his name, and draw no connection between him and the false teachers. Theophilus of Antioch wrote a book against Marcion, but regarded Paul's letters as "the divine Word" and saw the essence of Paul's lifework as the abolition of the Law. Tatian, who was the pupil and teacher of prominent anti-Marcionites, devoted great energy to gaining Pauline support for his ideas. Any response to gnostic or Marcionite exegesis of the epistles is made in the form of counterexegesis, never of repudiation. Thus the Presbyter cited by Irenaeus in *AH* 4.27–32 opposed Marcion with arguments based on Paul, and even set up Pauline "syntheses" against Marcion's antitheses. The author of the Pseudo-Justin *De resurrectione* placed his own interpretation of 1 Cor 15:50 and its context against those who used it to disprove the resurrection of the flesh. Irenaeus too offered alternatives to his opponents' understandings of Pauline texts, and made even more use of the letters as offensive weapons against them. Given these examples, if we must speculate about Justin's reaction to the use of Paul by Marcion and other adversaries, the most plausible hypothesis would be that he studied the letters and explained them, not that he thrust them into a corner.

The pattern that emerges, then, is one in which gnostics and Marcionites are opposed on matters of substance, but not for the authorities they invoke. Paul himself—like Jesus and like other apostles—is never the issue; no one disavows his authority or doubts his orthodoxy when opponents appeal to him. Only 2 Peter displays any form of self-consciousness or embarrassment about him, and even this is very far from amounting to distaste or rejection. Instead, the letters are *increasingly* echoed and referred to, precisely at the height of the struggle against heresy, and even made a weapon in that struggle. Paul's authority is always accepted without question, the only exception occurring among Jewish Christians. The reaction to gnostic and Marcionite use of Paul, where there was any, consisted of a countering use, not of antagonism or even of neglect. The hypothesis of an anti-Paulinism in the second century occasioned by gnostic and Marcionite appeals to the Apostle must be regarded as definitely disproved.

GNOSTIC PAULINISM

It has not been our purpose to measure the theologies of the second century against a standard of "Paulinism" derived from the letters, nor do we mean to do that for the gnostics here. We must, however, consider a number of positions that others have taken regarding gnostic Paulinism in the light of our own investigation, our purpose being to understand this Paulinism particularly as it relates to the use of the Pauline letters and their rise to authoritative status.

We may begin with Basilides, the first Christian teacher, it appears, to cite Paul alongside the Old Testament and the gospels in order to prove a point. One question does arise concerning the evidence for this, based on the fact that the Valentinians and other groups described by Hippolytus are said to make a rather similar use of the letters. Might it not be that Hippolytus (or his source) simply depicted Basilides according to a fixed "gnostic" pattern; or that Basilides did not originate but simply shared a particular way of employing passages from Paul? Yet there is some differentiation among Hippolytus' accounts in this regard. Certain heretics, such as Justin, are not reported as making any reference to the Apostle at all, and others (e.g., the Peratae) as making much less than is attributed to Basilides. We noted, moreover, the very unusual style especially of the beginning of Hippolytus' report as an indication that it may be based on Basilides' own writing, and also observed that the fragment given by Origen coincides closely with the use of Paul in Hippolytus. It remains possible that Basilides was not the inventor of this approach to the letters, but simply wrote in a milieu in which it was familiar, yet even in that case we would have to locate the milieu in Alexandria in the days of Hadrian, and would still be justified in speaking of Basilides as its first historically identifiable representative.

The question is whether this practice was linked to any special sympathy or understanding for Paul's theology on the part of Basilides. In spite of the power and depth of H. Langerbeck's attempts to prove such a deliberate development of Pauline thought by Basilides, I do not believe he succeeded in showing anything more than that certain of the fragments can be interpreted by means of Pauline categories.[1] If there was any such Paulinism at the root of Basilides' thought as Langerbeck supposed, it simply is not apparent in any extant texts. If we consider the statements about martyrdom taken by Clement from the *Exegetica*, just where "Pauline" predestinationism and universality of sin may seem to be present we find conclusions drawn that are not merely not Pauline but may be said to run quite counter to Paul's theology. According to Basilides, God always punishes the sinfulness of individuals, the only mercy being that it is not publicly exposed, and Christian suffering is always a punishment for sin. The cross of Christ is not brought to bear on either aspect of the problem;

---

1. "Die Anthropologie der alexandrinischen Gnosis," in *Aufsätze zur Gnosis*, ed. by H. Dörries (Göttingen: Vandenhoeck & Ruprecht, 1967), 54–56, 77–82. * * *

of Pauline thought, still less of Pauline writings, there is not the slightest trace. However willingly Basilides may have made use of the letters, there is no way of seeing in him a continuator and expositor of Paul's own ideas.

Much more than Basilides, however, it is Valentinus and the Valentinians who are regularly said to have regarded themselves as "the true Pauline theologians."[2] They, along with the Marcionites, are commonly regarded as *the* heretical thinkers whose Paulinism deeply influenced the feelings of catholic Christians toward the Apostle. Langerbeck claimed that Valentinus and his followers developed their conception of human nature as an elaboration of Paul's ideas about the inner conflict of good and evil and about divine election,[3] and E. H. Pagels has similarly derived Valentinian anthropology from Paul's theology of grace and election.[4] H.-F. Weiss finds an inner connection to exist between Paul's understanding of resurrection and that of the Valentinians, in that both viewed it as a present reality, though he regards the Valentinian position as a onesided, and so erroneous, interpretation of Paul.[5] H. von Campenhausen likewise sees in this understanding a sign of Valentinian engagement with Pauline ideas.[6]

Yet it is noteworthy that such claims of theological influence and affinity are mostly raised apart from any consideration of the actual Valentinian use of Pauline *texts*, which has often been viewed rather differently.[7] C. F. G. Heinrici regarded the Valentinians' connection of scripture to gnosis as superficial and arbitrary, seeing the pneumatic self-consciousness that allowed artificial interpretative combinations to be made as the true authority.[8] T. Zahn, though he stated that "ohne die Briefe des Paulus ist Valentins Lehre . . . undenkbar [without Paul's letters the teaching of Valentinus is . . . inconceivable]," meant by this the use of Pauline words and phrases in mythological construction without concern for Paul's own main ideas.[9] Recently, B. Layton has declared Valentinian exegesis of Paul to be "symbolic and extremely distant from the ordinary sense of the text," and the *Treatise on the Resurrection* in particular "a quite non Pauline theology in a thin and tattered Pauline garb."[1] Likewise Lindemann, acknowledging that "die valentinianische Schule sich paulinischer Aussagen durchaus zu bedienen wusste," finds that "dass die Theologie des Paulus für ihr Denken aber konstitutiv gewesen wäre, kann man nicht behaupten [The Valentinian school definitely knew how to make use of Pauline statements, yet one cannot assert that Paul's theology would have been constitutive for its thought]."[2]

2. Hans von Campenhausen, *The Formation of the Christian Bible*, trans. by J. A. Baker (Philadelphia: Fortress, 1972), 177.

3. Langerbeck, "Anthropologie," 64, 79 f.

4. "The Valentinian Claim to Esoteric Exegesis of Romans as Basis for Anthropological Theory," VC 26 (1972): 254–57.

5. H.-F. Weiss, "Paulus und die Häretiker," in *Christentum und Gnosis*, ed. by W. Eltester (BZNW 37; Berlin: Töpelmann, 1969), 119–25.

6. *Formation*, 145.

7. The exception is Pagels, on whose work see below [and the excerpt on pp. 274–83 above, Editors]

    * * *

8. *Die valentinianische Gnosis und die heilige Schrift* (Berlin: Wiegandt & Grieben, 1871), 46f., 61f., 182f.

9. *Geschichte des neutestamentlichen Kanons* (Erlangen and Leipzig: Deichert [Böhme], 1888–1889), vol. 1/2, 758, 755f.

1. "Vision and Revision: A Gnostic View of Resurrection" (paper read at the International Colloquium on the Texts of Nag Hammadi, Quebec, 1978), 27, 46.

2. *Paulus im ältesten Christentum: das Bild des Apostels und die Rezeption der paulinischen Theologie in der frühchristlichen Literatur bis Marcion* (Tübingen: Mohr-Siebeck, 1979), 300.

Perhaps what is needed is some sorting out of what it means to speak of "Valentinian Paulinism." The term could, in the first place, refer to the influence on Valentinus and his school of some leading elements in Paul's theology, a conscious endeavor to interpret them, to explore and expand them. With respect to the thesis of Langerbeck, we may repeat what was said in the case of Basilides, that while Langerbeck may have succeeded in giving some texts of Valentinus a Pauline reading, he did not show that Valentinus himself derived his ideas from Paul. Langerbeck's work was further weakened by his intentional omission of the Valentinian cosmo-logical myths from his study, in favor of the more "psychological" material transmitted by Clement (in the pursuit of *his* particular interests). The fragments in Clement are undoubtedly the most valuable information that we possess, but on their own they cannot suffice to reconstruct a whole and nonmythological Valentinus. The importance and general similarity of cosmology in all the Valentinian schools, and the fact that the fragments themselves are by no means "pure" in this regard * * * preclude this. Results obtained by leaving aside the mythological aspect of Valentinus' thought simply cannot be accepted as showing that Paul was somehow essential to the construction of Valentinian Christianity. As for the bond between Pauline and Valentinian thinking about the resurrection which Weiss and others have posited, we have just quoted one verdict on the "Paulinism" of the *Treatise on the Resurrection*. We may recall too that participation in the resurrection of Christ as taught in the *Treatise* has no relation to the baptismal context stressed by Weiss as indicating continuity with Paul. Theodotus, indeed, may connect baptism and realized resur-rection, in *Ex. Thdt.* 22.3 (where however the Pauline reference is a pecu-liar interpretation of the peculiar text 1 Cor 15:29, not exactly the center of Paul's thought on the subject), and as one topic in the extended reflec-tions on baptism in *Ex. Thdt.* 67–85. Here 1 Cor 15:49 is in fact alluded to (*Ex. Thdt.* 80.3), but precisely in the service of the "misunderstanding" Weiss points out; where baptism and new life are connected (*Ex. Thdt.* 77.1; 80.2), no reference to Paul is made and no textual allusions are present. The likely explanation is that an understanding of baptism known and alluded to by Paul for his own purposes in Romans 6 remained current in some circles and was eventually appropriated among Valentinians. We have here simply another instance of early Christian tradition, the context of Paul's thought, feeding the theology of a later generation. It is not even the specifically Pauline form of the tradition that is in question. * * * Thus even here it seems impossible to speak of "Paulinism" in the sense under discussion.

On the other hand, however, "Valentinian Paulinism" might simply refer to the fact that Valentinian writers invoked the Apostle as confirmation for their doctrine. If not all Valentinians necessarily "appealed to him con-stantly,"[3] there is in many of them a significant amount of Pauline allusion and citation. Paul was unquestionably a high authority for them, and they found his words as fit for authorizing their statements and stimulating their reflection as the sayings of Jesus. The Valentinians were certainly "Paulin-ists," if this means that they revered the Apostle and sought support for their teachings in his letters. Yet this is not at all the same as saying that

---

3. Von Campenhausen's phrase (*Formation*, 177).

their theology was "Pauline" in the sense that it was an extension or interpretation of Paul's own teachings, or even that they had an especial desire
to be or to appear specifically "Pauline" Christians. It is certainly a well-
established fact that high regard for the Apostle is not necessarily accompanied by deep sympathy or congruence with his theological concerns in
the second century. It is also entirely misleading to discuss the Valentinians' appeal to Paul as if he were somehow their sole authority and guiding light. Zahn already presented ample evidence that Valentinus and his
followers, unlike Marcion, were prepared to support their ideas from the
Old Testament, the gospels, and other "apostolic" writings, not just Paul,
and we have seen that precisely "apostolicity," not "Paulinicity," was their
aim. Indeed, Valentinus can speak of the commonalities shared by Christian writings and things "in ordinary books" (ἐν ταῖς δημοσίαις βίβλοις,
Clement, Str. 6.[6].52.4; fr. 6 Völker). An accurate account of Valentinian
"Paulinism" cannot be given without taking into consideration the relevant
context, that is, the entire constellation of authorities appealed to, and
without at least acknowledging the philosophical sources of Valentinian
ideas.

Pagels seeks to bridge the gap between the Valentinians' use of Paul and
the constitutive levels of their theology by acknowledging that their exegesis is a nonliteral one and characterizing it as "pneumatic." By this she
means that the Valentinians deliberately passed over the literal or natural
sense as superficial and fit only for "psychics" who could penetrate no
deeper, while they themselves sought out Paul's symbolic or "pneumatic"
meaning, perhaps by appealing to a secret tradition.[4] Unfortunately,
though Pagels refers constantly to the practice of "Valentinian exegetes,"
the latter themselves never tell us that this is what they are doing. Theodotus, of course, says that Paul preached the Savior as born and passible
for "those on the left," in accordance with their capacity, and also pneumatically as of the Holy Spirit and the Virgin, as the angels on the right
know him (Ex. Thdt. 23.3). This suggests that a dual apostolic kerygma
was in fact envisioned (cf. Ex. Thdt. 66, speaking of Jesus and the Apostles); but neither here nor elsewhere does Theodotus or any other Valentinian betray any expectation that in the Pauline epistles there is a "literal"
sense apprehended by psychics and differing from his own proposed explanations. The references to aeons and apolytrosis, to Sophia's veiling and
angelic baptism,[5] do not seem to presuppose that there exists any other
more literal and less valid meaning to the texts in question. Though some
gnostics held that knowledge of an oral tradition was necessary to the
understanding of scripture (Irenaeus, AH 3.2.1), Ptolemy evidently did not
regard his proofs from Paul (and others) for the nature of the Law as based
on that tradition, since he said that Flora was not yet ready for it (Flora
7.9). In fact no instance of actual appeal to the tradition for an exegesis
of Paul is known. Perhaps if we had more than Clement's excerpts, Theodotus would make himself more explicit; and perhaps not. In the present
state of the evidence it cannot be said that Valentinian interpretation is
deliberately nonliteral, if this means that a different, "literal" sense is
acknowledged but passed by. Some other explanation for the use of apostolic texts in this way must be found.

---

4. The Gnostic Paul (Philadelphia: Fortress, 1975), 5–7, 159f., and passim.
5. AH 1.3.1; 21.2; 8.1 (= Ex. Thdt. 44.2); Ex. Thdt. 22.1–4.

What has been said of the Valentinians is applicable to gnostics in general. They exhibit no special preference for the writings or the figure of Paul (cf. the Naassenes and the Nag Hammadi documents), and there is no direct connection between the use of Pauline letters and any supposed theological "Paulinism." If Paul—as distinct from beliefs traceable to the first-century Christian milieu in which he lived—exerted any foundational influence on gnostic thought, it is at least not evident in the citation of Pauline texts. Gnostics (some gnostics) certainly intended to represent "Paulinism," i.e., to be interpreters of Paul, just as did Theophilus of Antioch, Tatian, and Irenaeus. But the second century in general read Paul in situations utterly changed from his own and in the service of a variety of theological constructions with many sources other than "pure Paulinism." The letters were approached on every hand through completely new presuppositions, needs, and convictions, and a scientific or "objective" exegesis was not yet on the agenda. That gnostics were part of this is no surprise and certainly no disgrace. The uses to which they put the Apostle and the atmosphere in which they read him were in many respects all their own, but shared the general characteristics of their time and its treatment of normative texts as well.

CANONIZATION OF THE EPISTLES.

For the conclusion of the present discussion, the appropriate question thus appears to be not "Among whom did Paul's theology first bear fruit?"—since "Paul's theology" was not the object of anyone's attention—but "Among whom were Paul's letters first treated as normative texts, and why?"

If Basilides, or at any rate the milieu in which he taught, represents this "first," then he is the one to whom the question must be put. We have seen that his use of the letters is not related to any special concern for Pauline thought, and he, like the Valentinians, seems not to claim to be giving an esoteric interpretation in preference to some other, more literal one. The arrival of Pauline letters in Alexandria remains obscure for us, but at any rate there is nothing to suggest a deeply rooted tradition of interest specifically in Paul there, as there was, for instance, in Asia Minor. On the other hand, for both Greeks and Jews Alexandria was a center of learning and of the interpretation of texts, from Homer to the Septuagint. Certainly there if anywhere we would expect to find Christians treating a variety of writings as authoritative. It is at least not surprising, then, if the writings of the Apostle Paul appear alongside those of Moses and the Psalms and gospels as texts to be consulted and appealed to. That this occurs in a gnostic writer may be, in part at least, a function of the fact that only gnostics are known in Alexandria at this time. Thus I find myself in agreement with R. M. Grant (though for different reasons) that Alexandria was the first locus of the treatment of Paul as a normative text alongside the Old Testament, though we cannot know if any but Basilides engaged in this practice at first. Perhaps the Alexandrian environment was responsible not only for his readiness to handle the Apostle so, but also for his specific procedures. This, however, would be the subject of a different investigation.

According to Grant, the evidence of Basilides casts doubt on Marcion's widely posited influence on the canonization of the New Testament writings.[6] But the question is, what influence did Basilides himself exert on this process? This brings up a fact we have noted more than once, that Basilides' use of Paul is most closely paralleled in Valentinus' disciples, though similar phenomena are found in other gnostic groups. Is it possible that Valentinus brought with him from Alexandria Basilides' way of correlating myth and authoritative text, and passed it on to his followers? We cannot be sure of this, since no comparable material from Valentinus himself survives; but there are one or two factors pointing in this direction. The first is that both Theodotus in Alexandria and Ptolemy in Rome follow similar procedures, suggesting that they learned them from their master. The second is that though there are only a very few cases in which two Valentinian authors use the same text in the same way, there *are* these few, and it may be that they represent interpretations created by Valentinus himself. Most of them are related to the myth. Conclusions from pupil to teacher can be problematic—to suppose that Justin used the epistles in a manner similar to Tatian would almost certainly be wrong. Nevertheless, enough circumstantial evidence does exist to make it at least possible that alongside the very different practice in the fragments and the *Gospel of Truth* Valentinus made use of the letters in a way similar to Basilides and his own disciples. Whether through his agency or not, however, clearly the practice of using Paul to support both mythological and doctrinal points did not remain confined to Alexandria or to Basilidean circles.

As for Marcion, there is no denying that the exclusiveness and the intensity of his argumentation from Paul (and the gospel) represent a new departure. He has therefore often been seen as the great factor in the canonization of the epistles. Certainly we would expect him to have had some impact, given the effort his opponents devoted to refuting him. Nevertheless it is true that in questions of the use and evaluation of New Testament writings the evidence as it stands makes it surprisingly difficult to be certain of any single individual's effect on the development. There may be a good deal that is *post Marcionem* that is not necessarily *propter Marcionem* [due to Marcion]. Nor does his employment of the letters lack all preparation or analogy in his Asian homeland. Other evidence there, however slight, forbids us to think of him as an absolute innovator, and if the literary atmosphere of Alexandria may lie in the background of Basilides' undertaking, then certainly the Pauline heritage of Asia must be counted among the elements that gave the impetus to Marcion.

The fact remains, however, that just as Basilides' use of the epistles alongside the Old Testament in Alexandria is something new, Marcion's use of them instead of the Old Testament in Asia also presents us with a new development. These are the two obvious foci to speak of as the beginning of a truly "canonical" or "scriptural" use of the Pauline letters. Yet it does not do to say that before Irenaeus only gnostics and Marcionites took an exegetical interest in Paul. Aside from other Asian evidence, we have the Presbyter in Irenaeus and Pseudo-Justin, both of whom are responding to positions that have already appealed to Paul, to be sure, but with nothing to suggest that they would otherwise have ignored him, any more than they would have ignored the words of Jesus they also discuss. Above all,

---

6. Robert M. Grant, *The Formation of the New Testament* (New York: Harper & Row, 1965), 123–24.

there are Tatian and Julius Cassianus. Clearly they—especially Tatian—represent a further option alongside gnostics, Marcionites, and catholics. Their exegesis (again particularly clearly in the case of Tatian) is vigorous and subtle, and much more than a matter of catchwords and happy coincidences.

Like the overall development of the use of the letters, their coming to be treated as normative texts must be viewed as a general and really inevitable process throughout second-century Christianity. Forceful and creative personalities—a Basilides, a Marcion, a Tatian—can be seen to take leading roles in the development, and conditions in Alexandria and in Asia Minor may have favored the first advances being made there. If Marcion (who had real interests at stake) and certain gnostics were in the forefront, that does not make their activities a *sine qua non* for the ultimate recognition of the epistles' authoritative status. In part, indeed, their apparent position in the vanguard of Pauline canonization may be only an illusion due to the loss of nearly all of both their opponents' original exposition and their own labors at counterexegesis. Had there never been a Marcion, there would have been a Pauline canon; not a negative factor in the establishment of the Pauline letters among Christianity's scriptures, the gnostics and Marcion were likewise not the decisive positive factor. They may have provided significant impulses; but just here our evidence falls short.

Indeed it falls short at a great many places. We have attempted to reconstruct a development within early Christianity on the basis of the slender remains of a crucial period. There is precedent in that age for a great many ways of using the letters of Paul, some more and some less commendable by modern standards. Never in question except among Jewish Christians, Paul's authority increased throughout the second century, and as his writings gained general recognition as norms of Christian teaching, correspondingly authoritative uses were found for them. Under the pressure of this development even literature that formerly had no occasion to notice them made room for Pauline citations. Yet citing Paul was not at once the same as being taught by Paul, nor was it always to be so in later times. If it is not novel it is nonetheless true to say that Christianity, when it peers into the books it has elected as sacred scripture, is ever and again shocked to discover that the face it sees is not its own.

PART V

Law versus Grace and the Problem of Ethics

By the end of the second century, catholic Christians had something approaching a "Bible" as we know it, comprising both those sacred scriptures that, rejecting the radicalism of Marcionists and the various "Gnostic" movements, they shared with the Jews and a developing collection of new documents, which would soon be known as the scriptures of the "New Covenant" or "New Testament." The letters attributed to Paul were a very large part of the latter. Those letters, with their many parenetic passages that had been aimed at the problems and dilemmas of new congregations, seemed now fine examples of "exhortations to a virtuous life" and "advice concerning what men ought to do," addressed to a universal church.[1]

Many in the church, however, saw that those Pauline letters were much more than that. Their presence in the emerging canon had a profound effect on the way in which the whole of the Christian Bible was to be read. Paul's own reading of scripture seemed to imply a sweeping, even cosmic narrative, in which the crucifixion of Jesus and his subsequent exaltation by God was the climactic episode. The story began "in the beginning," sketched the origins of the human family with its paradisal hopes, its primal disobedience, and the fated history of that fall's consequence, focused on the tumultuous history of a single people, God's own, Israel, and pointed forward to the final moment when all nations and peoples must appear before the great judgment seat of God. Interpreters like Valentinus and Marcion had constructed their brilliant but eccentric versions of the story—which shocked those of the emergent center for whom, as for Paul, the Jewish scriptures spoke authoritatively and positively. Responding to the challenge of the "heretics," Irenaeus, writing in the 180s, set out for the first time, to our knowledge, that whole master narrative which would become, with many variations, the authoritative framework of subsequent Christian orthodoxy. Paul's letters provided key concepts for Irenaeus' narrative: the unity of God, the unity of Christ, and the unity of the history of salvation.[2]

That all-encompassing master narrative, and particularly the uniquely Pauline emphases within it, enormously complicated the church's understanding of "a virtuous life" and "what men ought to do." It seemed to run counter to some of the most cherished insights of the great philosophers. Surely there could be no virtue without the freedom to choose the good; yet Paul seemed to say that the only way one could be liberated from a slavery to sin, the predicament of all humanity, was by becoming a "slave of Christ," submitting to the irresistible will of God. Moreover, if the role of God in the final act of this drama was that of judge, then surely he must be fair and even-handed in rewarding virtue and punishing iniquity—how, then, could faith in "the God who justifies the ungodly" (Rom. 4:5) promote virtue? "Justifying the ungodly" was the very phrase used in the Old Testament itself to define a *corrupt* judge (Exod. 23:7; Isa. 5:23; Sir. 42:2). How could our sin have anything to do with the sin of Adam and Eve in the high and far-off times? And how could the death of Jesus make amends for it? What could Paul have meant in connecting the two (Rom. 5:12–19)? In what sense was Christ "the last Adam" (1 Cor. 15:45)? The brief excerpts below from Origen, Ambrosiaster, and Theodoret show how careful exegetes of the Pauline texts sought answers to these questions.

Toward the end of the fourth century an ardent Christian layman named Pelagius arrived in Rome from Britain. For twenty years or so, until forced with

---

1. The quotations are from a preface to Paul's letters, probably composed near the end of the fourth century and so popular in the Eastern churches that it was incorporated into scores of medieval manuscripts of the NT, trans. by Louis Charles Willard, "A Critical Study of the Euthalian Apparatus" (unpub. Ph.D. diss., Yale University, 1970), 198.
2. Richard A. Norris, Jr., "Irenaeus' Use of Paul in His Polemic against the Gnostics," in *Paul and the Legacies of Paul*, ed. by William S. Babcock (Dallas: Southern Methodist University Press, 1990), 79–98.

many others to flee from the invading Alaric, he took part in the free-wheeling theological debates conducted by well-educated laypeople like himself as well as clerics and monks from many parts of the empire. Though we know little for certain about Pelagius, he appears to have lived a moderately ascetic life himself, and to have become the mentor, or at least the figurehead, for a growing circle of ascetics, all of whom were determined to defend a heroic ideal of Christian morality against an easy, undemanding notion of grace that, in their view, some people were reading into Paul's letters. What was essential to their understanding of the faithful human response to God's grace was the freedom of the human will. Any notion that some primeval Fall of the human ancestor could bind subsequent generations was abhorrent to them. Every person must be free to respond to the Gospel's demand, "You must be perfect as your Father in heaven is perfect." And a commonsense reading of Paul's letters would show that Paul believed the same, as Pelagius undertook to demonstrate in his *Commentary on Thirteen Pauline Epistles*, one of the few writings reliably attributed to him which has survived. The excerpts below from his exposition of Romans illustrate some of his main concerns and his way of reading.

Soon after the sack of Rome a young follower of Pelagius named Caelestius arrived in Carthage and applied to be ordained a priest. In nearby Hippo Regius bishop Augustine, now in late middle age, had already acquired a reputation beyond his provincial see as one of the great minds of the church—and his teaching about grace seemed to Caelestius to strike at the very heart of the central values of the Christian life as Pelagius had taught him. It is not quite clear how the ensuing controversy began; apparently Caelestius fired the first verbal rounds. In any case, some of the most vivid writing we have from Augustine is found in his counterattacks against Caelestius, Caelestius' teacher, and the other Pelagians. All those writings are essentially expositions of Paul's letters. Caelestius' application to become a priest was rejected, and a synod at Carthage in 411 condemned six propositions the bishops culled from his writings—all representing beliefs diametrically opposed to that form of the history of salvation that Augustine was now driven to set forth clearly.

On appeal to Rome, Caelestius was first rebuffed, then vindicated, then, after intervention by the emperor, finally condemned and banished. The ultimate fate of Pelagius himself is unknown. Pelagianism did not disappear, however. Indeed, it could be said that henceforth, in varying degrees, Christian doctrine in the West moved between the two poles of Augustine's doctrine of grace and Pelagius' doctrine of human freedom. By and large, the churches of the East were not much affected by these controversies or their aftermath.

In the West, it was an Augustinian monk, Martin Luther, who in the sixteenth century found in his reading of Paul's words about the justification of the sinner by grace alone the definitive answer to his own and his generation's most fundamental religious question: How could one be found innocent before the bar of God's final judgment? For Luther, Paul's attack on the law became the warrant for his own attack upon the dogmas and structures of the medieval church. The selection below, from Luther's "Lectures on Galatians," shows clearly the way in which he found Paul a comrade in arms, identifying his own struggles and his own enemies with those of the apostle.

In the twentieth century, the young Karl Barth brought Paul once again into the center of controversy, calling him to arms against the prevailing Protestant liberalism in western Europe. Liberalism had come to terms with Paul as the missionary who founded a Christian civilization, as a thinker who released Christianity from the historically limited chrysalis of Judaism to develop into a universal religion of humanity, and especially as a *homo religiosus*, the model of deep religious experience. In this framework, "justification" was understood primarily as forgiveness, the expression of God's eternal quality of fatherly

mercy and his will to unite with the upward-striving human spirit. Paul's doctrines of sin, judgment, and justification were often treated as mere relics of
his Jewish heritage, implicitly broken by his universalism and therefore to be
ignored. But Barth read in the signs of his times, in the collapse of Europe in
World War I, the fatal weakness of that benign "culture-Protestantism," with
its naive optimism and its helplessness before the unanticipated demonism of
"modern" institutions. Barth's massive assault upon that cultural religion took
the form of a commentary on Paul's letter to the Romans.

If the Pauline doctrine of grace has maintained its explosive potential within
Western Christendom, the objections raised against it in the ancient church
have also reasserted themselves repeatedly. First, it is frequently objected that
if salvation is understood as entirely God's work, then the ultimate sanction
for human morality is removed. If all humans are sinners and God's choice
among them depends, not on their attempts to be good, but only on *his* goodness, then there is hardly any reason left to try to be good. There were people
in Paul's lifetime already who thought that was the implication of his teaching;
his replies are found in Romans 3:8; 6:1–7:6; Galatians 5; 1 Corinthians 10,
and elsewhere. It was the underlying concern voiced by Pelagius, and it has
been raised anew whenever and wherever the Pauline attack on "the law" has
been recalled. Does not the categorical rejection of law imply the elimination
of any rules for ethical behavior? This concern has frequently led to attempts
to limit the force of Paul's strictures against the law. For example, in the
ancient church it was regularly assumed that he meant to disparage only the
"ceremonial," not the moral commandments, although Augustine demonstrated clearly that Paul did not make that distinction. Luther taught that the
law remained valid in the kingdom of the world, being radically displaced only
within the church. Calvinists believed that Christians still needed the law for
governing both church and society, although they agreed with Paul that *salvation* could not be accomplished by law. Others, however, have found Paul's
doctrine attractive just because its ethical implications seemed radical. It would
surely not be a mistake to see here the basis for Kierkegaard's opposition
between the ethical stage and the religious stage of life,[3] as well as the framework for several recent controversies over the appropriate shape of a Christian
ethic.

Second, does not the expression of the gospel in forensic terms have fateful
consequences for the understanding of God? Some have blamed Paul for the
retention in Christianity of the "Jewish" picture of God as arbitrary, omnipotent, and judgmental (see the selection from Nietzsche in Part VI, pp. 408–
14). The most extreme forms of this attack came from the prophets of Aryan
racial purity, from Paul de Lagarde in the nineteenth century to Alfred Rosen-
berg and the "German Christians" in the 1930s. But milder statements in the
same direction have been heard rather frequently both within and without
Christian circles. Even so devoted a student of Paul as the late John Knox asks
whether Paul did not introduce a fatal split into the conception of God's character, setting his justice at odds with his mercy.[4] Yet the opposite complaint
has also been made: that Paul has, by attacking the law, severed Christianity's
roots in Judaism. By cutting away the historic center of Jewish commitment,
Paul, these opponents argue, de-historicized Christianity, leaving it subject to
unchecked mythmaking and prey to all kinds of romanticism.

Third, both kinds of anti-Paulinists have tended to agree that Paul's concept
of God as utterly transcendent and holy (either because this concept is "too
Jewish" or not Jewish enough, depending on the point of view) results in a

3. Søren Kierkegaard, *Stages on Life's Way*, ed. and trans. by Howard V. Hong and Edna H. Hong,
Kierkegaard's Writings, vol. 11 (Princeton: Princeton University Press, 1988).
4. *Chapters in a Life of Paul* (Nashville: Abingdon, 1950), 141–55.

perverse view of human powers. Paul seems preoccupied, it is frequently asserted, with sin, with human nothingness, with the "total depravity" of humankind (see the excerpts from both Nietzsche and George Bernard Shaw in Part VI, pp. 408–19). Does not this doctrine of grace reduce human beings to passive lumps in the hand of an arbitrary God? Does not the pernicious doctrine of predestination follow? Is it not true that the most ardent Paulinists in the history of the West have been the advocates of predestinarianism in its most fatalistic form, with its eternally unalterable registers of the Elect and the Damned? The discussion by Karl Barth of "the new man" presents a novel way of responding to some of these questions, in the belief that Paul's doctrine of grace lays the foundation for a new humanism and a new universalism.

ORIGEN

[Human Works and Divine Judgment] (ca. 246)†

The judgment of God[1] is to be expected . . . not only for those who do the things which are listed above[2] but for all who have in any way done anything good or evil. What Paul wants to show here is that only God can judge rightly. For there are some crimes committed in which the deed is evil but the intention is not, e.g., when someone accidentally kills someone else. And there are other cases in which the deed may be good but the thought behind it is not, e.g., if someone shows pity not because God has commanded it but in order to win praise from men.[3] And there are still other cases in which thought and deed are so interfused that one cannot distinguish which is good or evil. Given that only God knows the hearts of men[4] and only he can discern the secrets of the mind, only he has the power to judge rightly.

God has judged rightly in the case of those whose iniquities have been forgiven by the grace of baptism, whose sins have been covered by repentance and whose sin has not been imputed to them[5] because of the glory of martyrdom. Rightness of judgment presupposes that the evil person will receive bad things and the good person good ones. Although the gifts and generosity of God do not allow of any dispute, nevertheless we shall show just how right the divine judgment is. It is commonly accepted that a good man should not be punished and that an evil man should not be rewarded with good. Suppose a man has at some point done evil. It is certain that at the time he was doing it he was evil. But if he repents of his previous deeds, turns his mind to the good and does what is right, says what is right, thinks what is right, desires what is right—does not that person seem good to you, and worthy to receive good things? Likewise, if someone is turned from what is good to what is evil, he will be judged now not to be good (which he was but is no longer) but rather evil, which he is now. For the

† From Origen's commentary on Rom. 2:2, 9–10, 3:10, tr. in Gerald Bray (ed.), *Romans* (Downers Grove: InterVarsity, 1998), 53, 61–62, 90. Copyright © 1998 by the Institute of Classical Christian Studies, Thomas Oden, and Gerald Bray. Reprinted by permission of InterVarsity Press. Intervening material is sometimes omitted without indication by the translator.
1. Rom. 2:2.
2. Rom. 1:18–2:1.
3. Cf. Matt. 6:2.
4. Cf. 1 Kings 8:39.
5. Cf. Rom. 4:7–8, citing Ps. 32:1–2.

deeds of both a good and an evil man pass away, but they shape and construct the mind of the doer according to their respective quality and leave it either good or bad and accordingly destined to receive either punishment or rewards. Therefore it will be unjust either for a good mind to be punished for evil deeds or for an evil mind to be rewarded for good deeds.

* * *

Given that Paul puts the Jews first and the Greeks second, both for punishment and for reward,[6] we have to ask who is meant by these terms. If he meant by Jews those who are still under the law and who have not come to Christ, and by Greeks those who are Christians from among the Gentiles, it is clear that he would be going completely against the meaning of the gospel.[7]

It seems to me that the apostle has distinguished three types of people in this passage. First of all, he talks about those who are looking for glory and honor and immortality by patience in well-doing, whom God will reward with eternal life.[8] Patience in well-doing is something which is certainly to be found in those who have endured suffering and struggle for the sake of godliness, and therefore, as we have already explained above, this must be said about Christians, among whom the martyrs are found.

But as I understand it, when Paul mentions Jews and Greeks he is talking about people who in neither case have become believers in Christ. It may happen that among those who are still under the law there will be someone who, because of pressure from his family and friends, has not believed in Christ but nevertheless does what is good, upholds righteousness, loves mercy,[9] preserves chastity and continence, guards modesty and meekness, and does every good work. Although this person does not have eternal life—because despite the fact that he believes that there is only one true God he has not believed in his Son Jesus Christ, whom God has sent[1]—nevertheless it may be that the glory of his works and the peace and honor which they bring may not perish.

But the Greek, that is the Gentile, if he does not have the law, is a law to himself, showing the work of the law in his heart,[2] and motivated by natural reason, as we see that quite a few Gentiles are, either because they uphold righteousness or preserve chastity or maintain prudence, temperance and modesty. Although such a man is cut off from eternal life because he has not believed in Christ, and cannot enter the kingdom of heaven because he has not been born again of water and the Spirit,[3] yet it appears from what the apostle says that he cannot entirely lose the glory, honor and peace of good works. For if it appears * * * that the apostle condemned the Gentiles on the ground that although they knew God by their natural intelligence they did not glorify him as God,[4] how can we not think that he can and must praise them if they recognize God by their behavior and glorify him? Therefore I do not think it can be doubted that someone who

6. Rom. 2:9 f.
7. Lit., "mystery."
8. Rom. 2:7.
9. Cf. Mic. 6:8.
1. Cf. John 17:3.
2. Rom. 2:14.
3. John 3:5.
4. Rom. 1:21.

deserves to be condemned because of his evil deeds will also be considered worthy of the reward of good works if he does something good. Consider what the apostle says: *For we must all appear before the judgment seat of Christ, so that each one may receive good or evil, according to what he has done in the body.*[5]

* * *

That no one has done good, not even one,[6] is a hard saying and difficult to understand. How is it possible that no one, Jew or Greek, has ever done anything good? Are we supposed to believe that nobody has ever shown hospitality, fed the hungry, clothed the naked, delivered the innocent from the hands of the powerful or done anything similar? It does not seem possible to me that Paul was intending to assert anything as incredible as that. I think that what he meant must be understood as follows. If someone lays the foundation for a house and puts up one or two walls or transports some building materials to the site, can he be said to have built the house, just because he has set to work on it? The man who will be said to have built the house is the one who has finished off each and every part of it. So I think that here the apostle is saying that no one has done good in the sense that no one has brought goodness to perfection and completion. If we ask ourselves who is truly good and who has done good perfectly, we shall find only him who said: *I am the good shepherd,* and again: *The good shepherd lays down his life for the sheep.*[7]

AMBROSIASTER

[Adam's Sin and Ours] (late fourth century)†

Paul said that all have sinned in Adam[1] even though in fact it was Eve who sinned because he was not referring to the particular but to the universal. For it is clear that all have sinned in Adam as though in a lump. For, being corrupted by sin himself, all those whom he fathered were born under sin. For that reason we are all sinners, because we all descend from him. He lost God's blessing because he transgressed and was made unworthy to eat

5. 2 Cor. 5:10; cf. Rom. 14:10.
6. Rom. 3:10; cf. Eccl. 7:20.
7. John 10:11.
† From Ambrosiaster's commentary on Rom. 5:12–14 (CSEL 81:165–79), tr. in Gerald Bray (ed.), *Romans* (ACCS, NT 6; Downers Grove: InterVarsity, 1998), 136, 138–39, 141–42. Copyright © 1998 by the Institute of Classical Christian Studies, Thomas Oden, and Gerald Bray. Reprinted by permission of InterVarsity Press. For the identity of "Ambrosiaster," see note on p. 213 above. Central to the patristic discussion of Rom. 5 and the development of the doctrine of Original Sin was the translation of 5:12. Whereas the Greek text says that all people died "because" (*eph' hō*) they all sinned, both the Old Latin translation and the Vulgate state that death came to all people *in quo* they all sinned. The Latin fathers differed on how they understood this crucial phrase, with some interpreting it to mean "in whom," so that Paul was understood to have said that "all sinned in Adam" (cf. the famous Puritan rhyme "In Adam's fall sinned we all"). Others, however, such as Pelagius, took *in quo* conditionally (if we sin as he did, we also die), and still others took it, like the Greek, in a causal sense. Ambrosiaster, whose commentary on Romans influenced Pelagius and Augustine in quite different ways, interpreted the phrase as a relative clause ("in whom"), affirming that all sinned in Adam "as it were in a mass" (*quasi in massa*). But for him, the consequences of Adam's sin, though profound, were limited: physical death is the result of Adam's sin, but spiritual death and damnation are the consequence of our own sin.
1. Rom. 5:12 Latin.

of the tree of life. For that reason he had to die. Death is the separation of body and soul. There is another death as well, called the second death, which takes place in Gehenna.[2] We do not suffer this death as a result of Adam's sin, but his fall makes it possible for us to get it by our own sins. Good men were protected from this, as they were only in hell, but they were still not free, because they could not ascend to heaven. They were still bound by the sentence meted out in Adam, the seal of which was broken by the death of Christ. The sentence passed on Adam was that the human body would decompose on earth, but the soul would be bound by the chains of hell until it was released.

*   *   *

Before the law was given, men thought that they could sin with impunity before God but not before other men. For the natural law, of which they were well aware, had not completely lost its force, so that they knew not to do to others what they did not want to suffer themselves. For sin was certainly not unknown among men at that time.

How is it then that sin was not imputed, when there was no law?[3] Was it all right to sin, if the law was absent? There had always been a natural law, and it was not unknown, but at that time it was thought to be the only law, and it did not make men guilty before God. For it was not then known that God would judge the human race, and for that reason sin was not imputed, almost as if it did not exist in God's sight and that God did not care about it. But when the law was given through Moses, it became clear that God did care about human affairs and that in the future wrong-doers would not escape without punishment, as they had done up to then.

*   *   *

Although sin was not imputed before the law of Moses was given, death nevertheless reigned in the supremacy of its own seizure of power,[4] knowing those who were bound to it. Therefore death reigned in the security of its dominion both over those who for a time escaped punishment and over those who suffered punishment for their evil deeds. Death claimed everyone as its own, because whoever sins is the servant of sin.[5] Imagining they would get away with it, people sinned all the more and were more prone to wrongdoing because the world abetted it as if it were legal. Because of all this Satan rejoiced, knowing that he was secure in his possession of man, who because of Adam's sin had been abandoned by God. Thus it was that death reigned.

Some Greek manuscripts say that death reigned even in those who had not sinned in the way that Adam had.[6] If this is true, it is because Satan's

2. Rev. 2:11; 20:6, 14; 21:8.
3. Rom. 5:13.
4. Rom. 5:14.
5. John 8:34.
6. The Latin manuscripts known to Ambrosiaster did not contain the word *non* ("not"), so that his version of Rom. 5:14 stated that death reigned over those whose sin was "in the likeness of Adam's transgression" (i.e., they sinned in the same way that Adam did). Yet there were other Latin manuscripts that did have the word *non*, and both Pelagius and Augustine will presuppose this reading. The Greek manuscripts also offer both readings, and Origen offers interpretations for each textual option. Despite Ambrosiaster's claim that only "some" Greek manuscripts have the word *mē* ("not"), the vast majority do have it, and almost all modern scholars accept it as the original reading (TNIV: "death reigned . . . even over those who did not sin").

jealousy was such that death, that is, dissolution, held sway over even those who did not sin. . . . Here there is a textual difference between the Latin version and some of the Greek manuscripts. The Latin says that death reigned over those whose sins were like the sin of Adam, but some Greek manuscripts say that death reigned even over those whose sins were *not* like Adam's. Which of the two readings is the correct one?

What has happened is that somebody who could not win his argument altered the words of the text in order to make them say what he wanted them to say, so that not argument but textual authority would determine the issue.[7] However, it is known that there were Latin-speakers who translated ancient Greek manuscripts which preserved an uncorrupted version from earlier times. But once these problems were raised by heretics and schismatics who were upsetting the harmony of the church, many things were altered so that the biblical text might conform to what people wanted. Thus even the Greeks have different readings in their manuscripts. I consider the correct reading to be the one which reason, history and authority all retain. For the reading of the modern Latin manuscripts is also found in Tertullian, Victorinus and Cyprian. Thus it was in Judea that the destruction of the kingdom of death began, since God was made known in Judea.[8] But now death is being destroyed daily in every nation, since many who once were sons of the devil have become sons of God. Therefore, death did not reign in everyone but only in those who sinned in the same way that Adam had sinned.

PELAGIUS

[Faith, Grace, and Works] (ca. 407)†

3:28 For we deem that a person is justified through faith without the works of the law. 'We are sure' or 'we judge'. Some misuse this verse to do away with works of righteousness, asserting that faith by itself can suffice [for one who has been baptized], although the same apostle says elsewhere: 'And if I have complete faith, so that I move mountains, but do not have love, it profits me nothing' (1 Cor. 13:2); and in another place declares that in this love is contained the fullness of the law, when he says: 'The fullness of the law is love' (Rom. 13:10). Now if these verses seem to contradict the sense of the other verses, what works should one suppose the apostle meant when he said that a person is justified through faith without the works [of the law]? Clearly, the works of circumcision or the sabbath and others of this sort, and not without the works of righteousness,

---

7. Orthodox interpreters tended to assume that heretics emended the text to fit their theology, yet there is good evidence that the orthodox did the same. Each side presumed that the other had corrupted the text and endeavored to restore the original reading through emendation.
8. Cf. Ps. 76:1.
† From Pelagius's commentary on Rom. 3:28; 5:12–21, tr. by Theodore de Bruyn, *Pelagius's Commentary on St. Paul's Epistle to the Romans* (Oxford: Clarendon, 1993), 83, 92–96. Reprinted by permission of Oxford University Press. Pelagius (ca. 350–ca. 425) was a moderate ascetic who was born in Britain and taught in Rome during the late fourth and early fifth century. During the period 405 to 409 he wrote a commentary on the thirteen letters of Paul (excluding Hebrews), stressing free will and good works in opposition to Manichean determinism. His famous dispute with Augustine centered on anthropology but involved quite different understandings of divine grace and human freedom, which both exegetes affirmed.

about which the blessed James says: 'Faith without works is dead' (Jas. 2:
26). But in the verse we are treating he is speaking about that person who
in coming to Christ is saved, when he first believes, by faith alone. But by
adding 'the works of the law' he indicates that there is [also] a [work] of
grace [which those who have been baptized ought to perform].

* * *

5:12 *Therefore, just as through one person sin came into the world, and
through sin death.* By example or by pattern. Just as through Adam sin
came at a time when it did not yet exist, so in the same way through Christ
righteousness was recovered at a time when it survived in almost no one.[1]
And just as through the former's sin death came in, so also through the
latter's righteousness life was regained. *And so death passed on to all people,
in that all sinned.* As long as they sin the same way, they likewise die. For
death did not pass on to Abraham and Isaac [and Jacob], [concerning
whom the Lord says: 'Truly they are all living' [Luke 20:38]. But here he
says all are dead because in a multitude of sinners no exception is made
for a few righteous. So also, elsewhere: 'There is not one who does good,
not even one' (Ps. 13: 1; cf. Rom. 3:12), [and 'every] one a liar' (Rom. 3:
4).[2] Or: Death passed on to all who lived in a human, [and] not a heavenly,
fashion. 13 *For before the law sin was in the world.* [The law] came as a
punisher of sin. Before its coming sinners enjoyed the length of at least
this present life with less restraint. There was indeed sin before the law,
but it was not reckoned to be sin because [natural] knowledge had already
been almost wiped out. *But sin is not counted against one when the law
does not exist.* How did death reign, if sin [was] not counted against one?
Unless you understand: it was not counted against one 'for the present
time'. 14 *But death reigned from Adam to Moses, even over those who did
not sin after the manner of Adam's transgression.* Either: As long as there
was no one who distinguished beforehand between the righteous and the
unrighteous, death imagined that it was lord over all. Or: Death reigned
not only over those who, like Adam, transgressed a commandment—such
as the sons of Noah, who were ordered not to eat the life in the blood (cf.
Gen. 9:4), [and] the sons of Abraham, for whom circumcision was enjoined
(cf. Gen. 17:10)—but also over those who, lacking the commandment,
showed contempt for the law of nature. *Who is a type of the one to come.*
Either: He was a type of Christ because, just as Adam was made by God
without sexual intercourse, so Christ issued from a virgin by the work of
the Holy Spirit. [Or, as] some say: An antithetical type: that is, as Adam
is the source of sin, so too Christ is the source of righteousness. 15 *But
the gift is not like the trespass.* In case one grants equal value to the type.
*For if many died by the trespass of the one, how much more has God's grace
and the gift in the grace of the one person Jesus Christ overflowed to more.*
Righteousness had more power in bringing to life than sin in putting to
death, because Adam killed only himself and his own descendants, but
Christ freed both those who at that time were in the body and the following

---

1. As Pelagius's subsequent remarks make clear, he understands Paul to be referring here and in the
following verses to spiritual death. Yet the latter is not the result of inherited sin—a notion that
he staunchly repudiated—but the consequence of an individual's own sins.
2. "All have sinned" is thus interpreted to mean that "many" have done so (cf. Paul's use of "many"
in Rom. 5:15, 19).

generations. But those who oppose the transmission of sin try to assail it as follows: 'If Adam's sin', they say, 'harmed even those who were not sinners, then Christ's righteousness helps even those who are not believers. For he says that in like manner, or rather to an even greater degree are people saved through the one than had previously perished through the other.' Secondly, they say: 'If baptism washes away that ancient sin, those who have been born of two baptized parents should not have this sin, for they could not have passed on to their children what they themselves in no wise possessed. Besides, if the soul does not exist by transmission, but the flesh alone, then only the flesh carries the transmission of sin and it alone deserves punishment.' [Thus,] declaring it to be unjust that a soul which is born today, not from the lump of Adam, bears so ancient a sin belonging to another, they say that on no account should it be granted that God, who forgives [a person] his own sins, imputes to him another's. 16 *Again, the effect of the gift is not the same as that of the one sinner.* Rather, it is greater. *For the judgement from the one person is to condemnation.* From one [righteous] person who sinned has proceeded a judgement of death. *But grace is from many transgressions to justification.* Because Adam did not come by as much righteousness as he destroyed [by his example], but Christ by his grace discharged the sins of many; and because Adam became only the model for transgression, but Christ [both] forgave sins freely and gave an example of righteousness. 17 *For if by the sin of one person death reigned through one person, how much more shall those who have received an abundance of grace and of the gift and of righteousness reign in life through the one person Jesus Christ.* By which he has forgiven many sins; and an abundance of the gift of the Holy Spirit, because there are many gifts (cf. 1 Cor. 12:4); and also righteousness is given through baptism, and is not gained by merit. 18 *Therefore, just as through one person's transgression in all people to condemnation, so also through one person's righteousness in all people to justification of life.* Death reigned, is understood; 'so also grace reigned through justification'. 19 *For just as through one person's disobedience many were made sinners, so also through one person's obedience many will be made righteous.* Just as by the example of Adam's disobedience many sinned, so also many are justified by Christ's obedience. Great, therefore, is the crime of disobedience that kills so many. 20 *For the law stole in so that transgression abounded.* In case they say, 'But the law forgave us our sins', he says, 'It did not come to forgive transgressions, but to point them out, and when it is transgressed knowingly, transgression begins to abound.' It is as [if] he were saying, as I see it, that the law did not take away sins, but added to them, and not because of its own fault, but because of theirs.[3] Now it 'stole in'—that is, it entered unexpectedly—and so it turned out that transgression abounded. *But where transgression abounded, grace abounded all the more.* Just as the Saviour says: 'One who is forgiven more loves more' (Luke 7:47). For the amount of sin has been revealed so that the greatness of grace might be known and so that we might pay back a corresponding debt of love. 21 *So that, just as sin reigned in death, so also grace reigns through righteousness*

---

3. The *hina*-clause of Rom. 5:20 has been interpreted in terms of both purpose (TNIV) and result (NRSV). Likewise, the Latin translation (*ut abundaret delictum*) was also interpreted both ways. Pelagius, wishing to emphasize the human responsibility for sin and to avoid any implication that the law is the catalyst for sin, takes the clause in terms of result.

in eternal life, through Jesus Christ our Lord. [So that,] just as the reign of sin was abundantly established through contempt for the law, so also the reign of grace is established through the forgiveness of many sinners and thereafter through the doing of righteousness without cease.

AURELIUS AUGUSTINE

On Grace and Free Will (426 or 427)†

Chap. 19—How is Eternal Life Both a Reward for Service and a Free Gift of Grace?

* * * If eternal life is rendered to good works, as the Scripture most openly declares: "Then He shall reward every man according to his works:"[1] how can eternal life be a matter of grace, seeing that grace is not rendered to works, but is given gratuitously, as the apostle himself tells us: "To him that worketh is the reward not reckoned of grace, but of debt;"[2] and again: "There is a remnant saved according to the election of grace;" with these words immediately subjoined: "And if of grace, then is it no more of works; otherwise grace is no more grace"?[3] How, then, is eternal life by grace, when it is received from works? Does the apostle perchance not say that eternal life is a grace? Nay, he has so called it, with a clearness which none can possibly gainsay. It requires no acute intellect, but only an attentive reader, to discover this. For after saying, "The wages of sin is death," he at once added, "The grace of God is eternal life through Jesus Christ our Lord."[4]

Chap. 20—The Question Answered. Justification is Grace Simply and Entirely. Eternal Life is Reward and Grace.

This question, then, seems to me to be by no means capable of solution, unless we understand that even those good works of ours, which are recompensed with eternal life, belong to the grace of God, because of what is said by the Lord Jesus: "Without me ye can do nothing."[5] And the apostle himself, after saying, "By grace are ye saved through faith; and that not of

---

† St. Augustine (354–430) was bishop of Hippo Regius in North Africa and, because of his extensive writings, the most important of the early Western "Doctors of the Church." This treatise from his later years was less directly involved in the polemic against Pelagius than such earlier works as "On the Spirit and the Letter" and "On Nature and Grace," but it does present in brief compass the mature fruit of Augustine's involvement in that controversy. The immediate occasion was a debate among certain monks at Hadrumetum, which had been provoked by Augustine's anti-Pelagian writings. The first few chapters of the treatise, omitted here, reject both poles of the logical dichotomy that had divided the monks: either the denial of human free will, in order to preserve the Pauline concept of grace, or the reduction of grace to God's mere cooperation with humanity's natural good, in order to preserve free will. Scripture, says Augustine, with heavy use of Pauline texts, clearly teaches *both* God's free grace *and* the free responsibility of every person. Chapter 19 begins with the paradox thus stated. The translation is by Peter Holmes, revised by Benjamin B. Warfield, in *A Select Library of Nicene and Post-Nicene Fathers of the Christian Church*, ed. by Philip Schaff (New York: The Christian Literature Company, 1886–90; reprinted Wm. B. Eerdmans, 1980) vol. 5, 451–64.

1. Matt. 16:27.
2. Rom. 4:4.
3. Rom. 11: 5, 6.
4. Rom. 6:23.
5. John 15:5.

yourselves, it is the gift of God: not of works, lest any man should boast;"[6] saw, of course, the possibility that men would think from this statement that good works are not necessary to those who believe, but that faith alone suffices for them; and again, the possibility of men's boasting of their good works, as if they were of themselves capable of performing them. To meet, therefore, these opinions on both sides, he immediately added, "For we are His workmanship, created in Christ Jesus unto good works, which God hath before ordained that we should walk in them."[7] What is the purport of his saying, "Not of works, lest any man should boast," while commending the grace of God? And then why does he afterwards, when giving a reason for using such words, say, "For we are His workmanship, created in Christ Jesus unto good works"? Why, therefore, does it run, "Not of works, lest any man should boast"? Now, hear and understand. "Not of works" is spoken of the works which you suppose have their origin in yourself alone; but you have to think of works for which God has moulded (that is, has formed and created) you. For of these he says, "We are His workmanship, created in Christ Jesus unto good works." Now he does not here speak of that creation which made us human beings, but of that in reference to which one said who was already in full manhood, "Create in me a clean heart, O God;"[8] concerning which also the apostle says, "Therefore, if any man be in Christ, he is a new creature: old things are passed away; behold, all things are become new. And all things are of God."[9] We are framed, therefore, that is, formed and created, "in the good works which" we have not ourselves prepared, but "God hath before ordained that we should walk in them." It follows, then, dearly beloved, beyond all doubt, that as your good life is nothing else than God's grace, so also the eternal life which is the recompense of a good life is the grace of God; moreover it is given gratuitously, even as that is given gratuitously to which it is given. But that to which it is given is solely and simply grace; this therefore is also that which is given to it, because it is its reward;—grace is for grace, as if remuneration for righteousness; in order that it may be true, because it is true, that God "shall reward every man according to his works."[1]

*　　*　　*

Chap. 22—Who is the Transgressor of the Law? The Oldness of its Letter. The Newness of its Spirit.

Therefore, brethren, you ought by free will not do evil but do good; this, indeed, is the lesson taught us in the law of God, in the Holy Scriptures— both Old and New. Let us, however, read, and by the Lord's help understand, what the apostle tells us: "Because by the deeds of the law there shall no flesh be justified in His sight; for by the law is the knowledge of sin."[2] Observe, he says "the knowledge," not "the destruction," of sin. But when a man knows sin, and grace does not help him to avoid what he knows, undoubtedly the law works wrath. And this the apostle explicitly

6. Eph. 2:8–9.
7. Eph. 2:10.
8. Ps. 51:12.
9. 2 Cor. 5:17–18.
1. Matt. 16:27; Ps. 62:12; Rev. 22:12.
2. Rom. 3:20.

says in another passage. His words are: "The law worketh wrath."[3] The reason of this statement lies in the fact that God's wrath is greater in the case of the transgressor who by the law knows sin, and yet commits it; such a man is thus a transgressor of the law, even as the apostle says in another sentence, "For where no law is, there is no transgression."[4] It is in accordance with this principle that he elsewhere says, "That we may serve in newness of spirit, and not in the oldness of the letter;"[5] wishing *the law* to be here understood by "the oldness of the letter," and what else by "newness of spirit" than *grace*? Then, that it might not be thought that he had brought any accusation, or suggested any blame, against the law, he immediately takes himself to task with this inquiry: "What shall we say, then? Is the law sin? God forbid." He then adds the statement: "Nay, I had not known sin but by the law;"[6] which is of the same import as the passage above quoted: "By the law is the knowledge of sin."[7] Then: "For I had not known lust," he says, "except the law had said, 'Thou shalt not covet.'"[8] But sin, taking occasion by the commandment, wrought in me all manner of concupiscence. For without the law sin was dead. For I was alive without the law once; but when the commandment came, sin revived, and I died. And the commandment, which was ordained to life, I found to be unto death. For sin, taking occasion by the commandment, deceived me, and by it slew me. Wherefore the law is holy; and the commandment holy, just, and good. Was, then, that which is good made death unto me? God forbid. But sin, that it might appear sin, worked death in me by that which is good,—in order that the sinner, or the sin, might by the commandment become beyond measure."[9] And to the Galatians he writes: "Knowing that a man is not justified by the works of the law, except through faith in Jesus Christ, even we have believed in Jesus Christ, that we might be justified by the faith of Christ, and not by the works of the law; for by the works of the law shall no flesh be justified."[1]

Chap. 23—The Pelagians Maintain That the Law is the Grace of God Which Helps Us Not to Sin.

Why, therefore, do those very vain and perverse Pelagians say that the law is the grace of God by which we are helped not to sin? Do they not, by making such an allegation, unhappily and beyond all doubt contradict the great apostle? He, indeed, says, that by the law sin received strength against man; and that man, by the commandment, although it be holy, and just, and good, nevertheless dies, and that death works in him through that which is good, from which death there is no deliverance unless the Spirit quickens him, whom the letter had killed,—as he says in another passage, "The letter killeth, but the Spirit giveth life."[2] And yet these obstinate persons, blind to God's light, and deaf to His voice, maintain that the letter which kills gives life, and thus gainsay the quickening Spirit. "There-

3. Rom. 4:15.
4. Ibid.
5. Rom. 7:6.
6. Rom. 7:6–7.
7. Rom. 3:20.
8. Ex. 20:17.
9. Rom. 7:7–13.
1. Gal. 2:16.
2. 2 Cor. 3:6.

fore, brethren" (that I may warn you with better effect in the words of the apostle himself), "we are debtors not to the flesh, to live after the flesh; for if ye live after the flesh ye shall die; but if ye through the Spirit do mortify the deeds of the body, ye shall live."[3] I have said this to deter your free will from evil, and to exhort it to good by apostolic words; but yet you must not therefore glory in man,—that is to say, in your own selves,—and not in the Lord, when you live not after the flesh, but through the Spirit mortify the deeds of the flesh. For in order that they to whom the apostle addressed this language might not exalt themselves, thinking that they were themselves able of their own spirit to do such good works as these, and not by the Spirit of God, after saying to them, "If ye through the Spirit do mortify the deeds of the flesh, ye shall live," he at once added, "For as many as are led by the Spirit of God, they are the sons of God."[4] When, therefore, you by the Spirit mortify the deeds of the flesh, that you may have life, glorify Him, praise Him, give thanks to Him by whose Spirit you are so led as to be able to do such things as show you to be the children of God; "for as many as are led by the Spirit of God, they are the sons of God."

Chap. 24—Who May be Said to Wish to Establish Their Own Righteousness. "God's Righteousness," So Called, Which Man Has from God.

As many, therefore, as are led by their own spirit, trusting in their own virtue, with the addition merely of the law's assistance, without the help of grace, are not the sons of God. Such are they of whom the same apostle speaks as "being ignorant of God's righteousness, and wishing to establish their own righteousness, who have not submitted themselves to the righteousness of God."[5] He said this of the Jews, who in their self-assumption rejected grace, and therefore did not believe in Christ. Their own righteousness, indeed, he says, they wish to establish; and this righteousness is of the law,—not that the law was established by themselves, but that they had constituted their righteousness in the law which is of God, when they supposed themselves able to fulfil that law by their own strength, ignorant of God's righteousness,—not indeed that by which God is Himself righteous, but that which man has from God. And that you may know that he designated as *theirs* the righteousness which is of the law, and as *God's* that which man receives from God, hear what he says in another passage, when speaking of Christ: "For whose sake I counted all things not only as loss, but I deemed them to be dung, that I might win Christ, and be found in Him—not having my own righteousness, which is of the law, but that which is through the faith of Christ, which is of God."[6] Now what does he mean by "not having my own righteousness, which is of the law," when the law is really not his at all, but God's,—except this, that he called it his own righteousness, although it was of the law, because he thought he could fulfil the law by his own will, without the aid of grace which is through faith in Christ? Wherefore, after saying, "Not having my own righteousness, which is of the law," he immediately subjoined, "But that which is

3. Rom. 8:12–13.
4. Rom. 8:14.
5. Rom. 10:3.
6. Phil. 3:8, 9.

through the faith of Christ, which is of God." This is what they were ignorant of, of whom he says, "Being ignorant of God's righteousness,"—that
is, the righteousness which is of God (for it is given not by the letter, which
kills, but by the life-giving Spirit), "and wishing to establish their own
righteousness," which he expressly described as the righteousness of the
law, when he said, "Not having my own righteousness, which is of the
law;" they were not subject to the righteousness of God,—in other words,
they submitted not themselves to the grace of God. For they were under
the law, not under grace, and therefore sin had dominion over them, from
which a man is not freed by the law, but by grace. On which account he
elsewhere says, "For sin shall not have dominion over you; because ye are
not under the law, but under grace."[7] Not that the law is evil; but because
they are under its power, whom it makes guilty by imposing commandments, not by aiding. It is by grace that any one is a doer of the law; and
without this grace, he who is placed under the law will be only a hearer of
the law. To such persons he addresses these words: "Ye who are justified
by the law are fallen from grace."[8]

Chap. 25—As the Law is Not, so Neither is Our Nature Itself That Grace by Which we are Christians.

Now who can be so insensible to the words of the apostle, who so fool-
ishly, nay, so insanely ignorant of the purport of his statement, as to venture to affirm that the law is grace, when he who knew very well what he
was saying emphatically declares, "Ye who are justified by the law are fallen
from grace"? Well, but if the law is not grace, seeing that in order that the
law itself may be kept, it is not the law, but only grace which can give help,
will not nature at any rate be grace? For this, too, the Pelagians have been
bold enough to aver, that grace is the nature in which we were created, so
as to possess a rational mind, by which we are enabled to understand,—
formed as we are in the image of God, so as to have dominion over the
fish of the sea, and over the fowl of the air, and over every living thing that
creepeth upon the earth. This, however, is not the grace which the apostle
commends to us through the faith of Jesus Christ. For it is certain that we
possess this nature in common with ungodly men and unbelievers; whereas
the grace which comes through the faith of Jesus Christ belongs only to
them to whom the faith itself appertains. "For all men have not faith."[9]
Now, as the apostle, with perfect truth, says to those who by wishing to
be justified by the law have fallen from grace, "If righteousness come by
the law, then Christ is dead in vain;"[1] so likewise, to those who think that
the grace which he commends and faith in Christ receives, is nature, the
same language is with the same degree of truth applicable: if righteousness
come from nature, then Christ is dead in vain. But the law was in existence
up to that time, and it did not justify; and nature existed too, but it did not
justify. It was not, then, in vain that Christ died, in order that the law
might be fulfilled through Him who said, "I am come not to destroy the
law, but to fulfil it;"[2] and that our nature, which was lost through Adam,

7. Rom. 6:14.
8. Gal. 5:4.
9. 2 Thess. 3:2.
1. Gal. 2:21.
2. Matt. 5:17.

might through Him be recovered, who said that "He was come to seek and to save that which was lost;"[3] in whose coming the old fathers likewise who loved God believed.

* * *

Chap. 28—Faith is the Gift of God.

I have already discussed the point concerning faith, that is, concerning the will of him who believes, even so far as to show that it appertains to grace,—so that the apostle did not tell us, "I have obtained mercy because I was faithful;" but he said, "I have obtained mercy in order to be faithful."[4] And there are many other passages of similar import,—among them that in which he bids us "think soberly, according as God hath dealt out to every man the proportion of faith;"[5] and that which I have already quoted: "By grace are ye saved through faith; and that not of yourselves; it is the gift of God;"[6] and again another in the same Epistle to the Ephesians: "Peace be to the brethren, and love with faith, from God the Father, and the Lord Jesus Christ;"[7] and to the same effect that passage in which he says, "For unto you it is given in the behalf of Christ not only to believe on Him, but also to suffer for His sake."[8] Both alike are therefore due to the grace of God,—the faith of those who believe, and the patience of those who suffer, because the apostle spoke of both as *given*. Then, again, there is the passage, especially noticeable, in which he says, "We, having the same spirit of faith,"[9] for his phrase is not *"the knowledge of faith,"* but *"the spirit of faith;"* and he expressed himself thus in order that we might understand how that faith is given to us, even when it is not sought, so that other blessings may be granted to it at its request. For "how," says he, "shall they call upon Him in whom they have not believed?"[1] The spirit of grace, therefore, causes us to have faith, in order that through faith we may, on praying for it, obtain the ability to do what we are commanded. On this account the apostle himself constantly puts faith before the law; since we are not able to do what the law commands unless we obtain the strength to do it by the prayer of faith.

Chap. 29—God is Able to Convert Opposing Wills, and to Take Away from the Heart its Hardness.

Now if faith is simply of free will, and is not given by God, why do we pray for those who will not believe, that they may believe? This it would be absolutely useless to do, unless we believe, with perfect propriety, that Almighty God is able to turn to belief wills that are perverse and opposed to faith. Man's free will is addressed when it is said, "To-day, if ye will hear His voice, harden not your hearts."[2] But if God were not able to remove from the human heart even its obstinacy and hardness, He would not say,

3. Matt. 18:11; Luke 19:10.
4. 1 Cor. 7:25.
5. Rom. 12:3.
6. Eph. 2:8.
7. Eph. 6:23.
8. Phil. 1:29.
9. 2 Cor. 4:13.
1. Rom. 10:14.
2. Ps. 95:7–8.

through the prophet, "I will take from them their heart of stone, and will give them a heart of flesh."[3] That all this was foretold in reference to the New Testament is shown clearly enough by the apostle when he says, "Ye are our epistle, . . . written not with ink, but with the Spirit of the living God; not in tables of stone, but in fleshly tables of the heart."[4] * * * Now can we possibly, without extreme absurdity, maintain that there previously existed in any man the good merit of a good will, to entitle him to the removal of his stony heart, when all the while this very heart of stone signifies nothing else than a will of the hardest kind and such as is absolutely inflexible against God? For where a good will precedes, there is, of course, no longer a heart of stone.

* * *

Chap. 31—Free Will has its Function in the Heart's Conversion; but Grace too has its.

Lest, however, it should be thought that men themselves in this matter do nothing by free will, it is said in the Psalm, "Harden not your hearts;"[5] and in Ezekiel himself, "Cast away from you all your transgressions, which ye have impiously committed against me; and make you a new heart and a new spirit; and keep all my commandments. For why will ye die, O house of Israel, saith the Lord? for I have no pleasure in the death of him that dieth, saith the Lord God: and turn ye, and live."[6] We should remember that it is He who says, "Turn ye and live," to whom it is said in prayer, "Turn us again, O God."[7] We should remember that He says, "Cast away from you all your transgressions," when it is even He who justifies the ungodly. We should remember that He says, "Make you a new heart and a new spirit," who also promises, "I will give you a new heart, and a new spirit will I put within you."[8] How is it, then, that He who says, "Make you," also says, "I will give you"? Why does He command, if He is to give? Why does He give if man is to make, except it be that He gives what He commands when He helps him to obey whom He commands? There is, however, always within us a free will,—but it is not always good; for it is either free from righteousness when it serves sin,—and then it is evil,—or else it is free from sin when it serves righteousness,—and then it is good. But the grace of God is always good; and by it it comes to pass that a man is of a good will, though he was before of an evil one. By it also it comes to pass that the very good will, which has now begun to be, is enlarged, and made so great that it is able to fulfil the divine commandments which it shall wish, when it shall once firmly and perfectly wish. This is the purport of what the Scripture says: "If thou wilt, thou shalt keep the commandments;"[9] so that the man who wills but is not able knows that he does not yet fully will, and prays that he may have so great a will that it may suffice for keeping the commandments. And thus, indeed, he receives assistance to perform what he is commanded. Then is the will of use when

3. Ezek. 11:19.
4. 2 Cor. 3:2–3.
5. Ps. 95:8.
6. Ezek. 18:31–32.
7. Ps. 80:3.
8. Ezek. 18:26.
9. Ecclus. 15:15.

we have ability; just as ability is also then of use when we have the will. For what does it profit us if we will what we are unable to do, or else do not will what we are able to do?

Chap. 32—In What Sense it is Rightly Said That, If We Like, We May Keep God's Commandments.

The Pelagians think that they know something great when they assert that "God would not command what He knew could not be done by man." Who can be ignorant of this? But God commands some things which we cannot do, in order that we may know what we ought to ask of Him. For this is faith itself, which obtains by prayer what the law commands.* * *

Chap. 33—A Good Will May be Small and Weak; an Ample Will, Great Love. Operating and Co-operating Grace.

He, therefore, who wishes to do God's commandment, but is unable, already possesses a good will, but as yet a small and weak one; he will, however, become able when he shall have acquired a great and robust will. When the martyrs did the great commandments which they obeyed, they acted by a great will,—that is, with great love. Of this love the Lord Himself thus speaks: "Greater love hath no man than this, that a man lay down his life for his friends."[1] In accordance with this, the apostle also says, "He that loveth his neighbour hath fulfilled the law. For this: Thou shalt not commit adultery, Thou shalt not kill, Thou shalt not steal, Thou shalt not covet; and if there be any other commandment, it is briefly comprehended in this saying, namely, Thou shalt love thy neighbour as thyself.[2] Love worketh no ill to his neighbour: therefore love is the fulfilling of the law."[3] This love the Apostle Peter did not yet possess, when he for fear thrice denied the Lord.[4] "There is no fear in love," says the Evangelist John in his first Epistle, "but perfect love casteth out fear."[5] But yet, however small and imperfect his love was, it was not wholly wanting when he said to the Lord, "I will lay down my life for Thy sake;"[6] for he supposed himself able to effect what he felt himself willing to do. And who was it that had begun to give him his love, however small, but He who prepares the will, and perfects by His co-operation what He initiates by His operation? Forasmuch as in beginning He works in us that we may have the will, and in perfecting works with us when we have the will. On which account the apostle says, "I am confident of this very thing, that He which hath begun a good work in you will perform it until the day of Jesus Christ."[7] He operates, therefore, without us, in order that we may will; but when we will, and so will that we may act, He co-operates with us. We can, however, ourselves do nothing to effect good works of piety without Him either working that we may will, or co-working when we will. Now, concerning His working that we may will, it is said: "It is God which worketh in you,

1. John 15:13.
2. Lev. 19:18.
3. Rom. 13:8–10.
4. Matt. 26:69–75.
5. 1 John 4:18.
6. John 13:37.
7. Phil. 1:6.

even to will."[8] While of His co-working with us, when we will and act by willing, the apostle says, "We know that in all things there is co-working for good to them that love God."[9] What does this phrase, "all things," mean, but the terrible and cruel sufferings which affect our condition? That burden, indeed, of Christ, which is heavy for our infirmity, becomes light to love. For to such did the Lord say that His burden was light,[1] as Peter was when he suffered for Christ, not as he was when he denied Him.

* * *

Chap. 37—The Love which Fulfils the Commandments is not of Ourselves, But of God.

All these commandments, however, respecting love or charity (which are so great, and such that whatever action a man may think he does well is by no means well done if done without love) would be given to men in vain if they had not free choice of will. But forasmuch as these precepts are given in the law, both old and new (although in the new came the grace which was promised in the old, but the law without grace is the letter which killeth, but in grace the Spirit which giveth life), from what source is there in men the love of God and of one's neighbour but from God Himself? For indeed, if it be not of God but of men, the Pelagians have gained the victory; but if it come from God, then we have vanquished the Pelagians. Let, then, the Apostle John sit in judgment between us; and let him say to us, "Beloved, let us love one another." Now, when they begin to extol themselves on these words of John, and to ask why this precept is addressed to us at all if we have not of our own selves to love one another, the same apostle proceeds at once, to their confusion, to add, "For love is of God."[2] It is not of ourselves, therefore, but it is of God. Wherefore, then, is it said, "Let us love one another, for love is of God," unless it be as a precept to our free will, admonishing it to seek the gift of God? Now, this would be indeed a thoroughly fruitless admonition if the will did not previously receive some donation of love, which might seek to be enlarged so as to fulfil whatever command was laid upon it. When it is said, "Let us love one another," it is law; when it is said, "For love is of God," it is grace. For God's "wisdom carries law and mercy upon her tongue."[3] Accordingly, it is written in the Psalm, "For He who gave the law will give blessings."[4]

* * *

Chap. 41—The Wills of Men are so Much in the Power of God, that He can Turn them Whithersoever it Pleases Him.

I think I have now discussed the point fully enough in opposition to those who vehemently oppose the grace of God, by which, however, the human will is not taken away, but changed from bad to good, and assisted

8. Phil. 2:13.
9. Rom. 8:28.
1. Matt. 11:30.
2. 1 John 4:7.
3. Prov. 3:16.
4. Ps. 84:6.

when it is good. I think, too, that I have so discussed the subject that it is
not so much I myself as the inspired Scripture which has spoken to you,
in the clearest testimonies of truth; and if this divine record be looked into
carefully, it shows us that not only men's good wills, which God Himself
converts from bad ones, and, when converted by Him, directs to good
actions and to eternal life, but also those which follow the world are so
entirely at the disposal of God, that He turns them whithersoever He wills,
and whensoever He wills,—to bestow kindness on some, and to heap punishment on others, as He Himself judges right by a counsel most secret to
Himself, indeed, but beyond all doubt most righteous. For we find that
some sins are even the punishment of other sins, as are those "vessels of
wrath" which the apostle describes as "fitted to destruction;"[5] as is also
that hardening of Pharaoh, the purpose of which is said to be to set forth
in him the power of God;[6] as, again, is the flight of the Israelites from the
face of the enemy before the city of Ai, for fear arose in their heart so that
they fled, and this was done that their sin might be punished in the way
it was right that it should be; by reason of which the Lord said to Joshua
the son of Nun, "The children of Israel shall not be able to stand before
the face of their enemies."[7] What is the meaning of, "They shall not be
able to stand"? Now, why did they not stand by free will, but, with a will
perplexed by fear, took to flight, were it not that God has the lordship even
over men's wills, and when He is angry turns to fear whomsoever He
pleases? Was it not of their own will that the enemies of the children of
Israel fought against the people of God, as led by Joshua, the son of Nun?
And yet the Scripture says, "It was of the Lord to harden their hearts, that
they should come against Israel in battle, that they might be extermi-
nated."[8] And was it not likewise of his own will that the wicked son of Gera
cursed King David? And yet what says David, full of true, and deep, and
pious wisdom? What did he say to him who wanted to smite the reviler?
"What," said he, "have I to do with you, ye sons of Zeruiah? Let him alone
and let him curse, because the Lord hath said unto him, Curse David.
Who, then, shall say, Wherefore hast thou done so?"[9] And then the
inspired Scripture, as if it would confirm the king's profound utterance by
repeating it once more, tells us: "And David said to Abishai, and to all his
servants, Behold, my son, which came forth from my bowels, seeketh my
life: how much more may this Benjamite do it! Let him alone, and let him
curse; for the Lord hath bidden him. It may be that the Lord will look on
my humiliation, and will requite me good for his cursing this day."[1] Now
what prudent reader will fail to understand in what way the Lord bade this
profane man to curse David? It was not by a command that He bade him,
in which case his obedience would be praiseworthy; but He inclined the
man's will, which had become debased by his own perverseness, to commit
this sin, by His own just and secret judgment. Therefore it is said, "The
Lord said unto him." Now if this person had obeyed a command of God,
he would have deserved to be praised rather than punished, as we know

5. Rom. 9:22.
6. Ex. 7:3; 10:1.
7. Josh. 7:4, 12.
8. Josh. 11:20.
9. 2 Sam. 16:9–10.
1. 2 Sam. 16:11–12.

he was afterwards punished for this sin. Nor is the reason an obscure one why the Lord told him after this manner to curse David. "It may be," said the humbled king, "that the Lord will look on my humiliation, and will requite me good for his cursing this day." See, then, what proof we have here that God uses the hearts of even wicked men for the praise and assistance of the good. Thus did He make use of Judas when betraying Christ; thus did He make use of the Jews when they crucified Christ. And how vast the blessings which from these instances He has bestowed upon the nations that should believe in Him! He also uses our worst enemy, the devil himself, but in the best way, to exercise and try the faith and piety of good men,—not for Himself indeed, who knows all things before they come to pass, but for our sakes, for whom it was necessary that such a discipline should be gone through with us. Did not Absalom choose by his own will the counsel which was detrimental to him? And yet the reason of his doing so was that the Lord had heard his father's prayer that it might be so. Wherefore the Scripture says that "the Lord appointed to defeat the good counsel of Ahithophel, to the intent that the Lord might bring all evils upon Absalom."[2] It called Ahithophel's counsel *"good,"* because it was for the moment of advantage to his purpose. It was in favour of the son against his father, against whom he had rebelled; and it might have crushed him, had not the Lord defeated the counsel which Ahithophel had given, by acting on the heart of Absalom so that he rejected this counsel, and chose another which was not expedient for him.

* * *

Chap. 43—God Operates on Men's Hearts to Incline Their Wills Whithersoever He Pleases.

From these statements of the inspired word, and from similar passages which it would take too long to quote in full, it is, I think, sufficiently clear that God works in the hearts of men to incline their wills whithersoever He wills, whether to good deeds according to His mercy, or to evil after their own deserts; His own judgment being sometimes manifest, sometimes secret, but always righteous. This ought to be the fixed and immoveable conviction of your heart, that there is no unrighteousness with God. Therefore, whenever you read in the Scriptures of Truth, that men are led aside, or that their hearts are blunted and hardened by God, never doubt that some ill deserts of their own have first occurred, so that they justly suffer these things. Thus you will not run counter to that proverb of Solomon: "The foolishness of a man perverteth his ways, yet he blameth God in his heart."[3] Grace, however, is not bestowed according to men's deserts; otherwise grace would be no longer grace.[4] For grace is so designated because it is given gratuitously. Now if God is able, either through the agency of angels (whether good ones or evil), or in any other way whatever, to operate in the hearts even of the wicked, in return for their deserts,— whose wickedness was not made by Him, but was either derived originally

2. 2 Sam. 17:14.
3. Prov. 19:3.
4. Rom. 11:6.

from Adam, or increased by their own will,—what is there to wonder at if, through the Holy Spirit, He works good in the hearts of the elect, who has wrought it that their hearts become good instead of evil?

Chap. 44—Gratuitous Grace Exemplified in Infants.

Men, however, may suppose that there are certain good deserts which they think are precedent to justification through God's grace; all the while failing to see, when they express such an opinion, that they do nothing else than deny grace. But, as I have already remarked, let them suppose what they like respecting the case of adults, in the case of infants, at any rate, the Pelagians find no means of answering the difficulty. For these in receiving grace have no will, from the influence of which they can pretend to any precedent merit. We see, moreover, how they cry and struggle when they are baptized, and feel the divine sacraments. Such conduct would, of course, be charged against them as a great impiety, if they already had free will in use; and notwithstanding this, grace cleaves to them even in their resisting struggles. But most certainly there is no prevenient merit, otherwise the grace would be no longer grace. Sometimes, too, this grace is bestowed upon the children of unbelievers, when they happen by some means or other to fall, by reason of God's secret providence, into the hands of pious persons; but, on the other hand, the children of believers fail to obtain grace, some hindrance occurring to prevent the approach of help to rescue them in their danger. These things, no doubt, happen through the secret providence of God, whose judgments are unsearchable, and His ways past finding out. These are the words of the apostle; and you should observe what he had previously said, to lead him to add such a remark. He was discoursing about the Jews and Gentiles, when he wrote to the Romans—themselves Gentiles—to this effect: "For as ye, in times past, have not believed God, yet have now obtained mercy through their unbelief; even so have these also now not believed, that through your mercy they also may obtain mercy; for God hath concluded them all in unbelief, that He might have mercy upon all."[5] Now, after he had thought upon what he said, full of wonder at the certain truth of his own assertion, indeed, but astonished at its great depth, how God concluded all in unbelief that He might have mercy upon all,—as if doing evil that good might come,—he at once exclaimed, and said, "O the depth of the riches both of the wisdom and knowledge of God! how unsearchable are His judgments, and His ways past finding out!"[6] Perverse men, who do not reflect upon these unsearchable judgments and untraceable ways, indeed, but are ever prone to censure, being unable to understand, have supposed the apostle to say, and censoriously gloried over him for saying, "Let us do evil, that good may come!" God forbid that the apostle should say so! But men, without understanding, have thought that this was in fact said, when they heard these words of the apostle: "Moreover, the law entered, that the offence might abound; but where sin abounded, grace did much more abound."[7] But grace, indeed, effects this purpose—that good works should now be wrought by those who previously did evil; not that they should

5. Rom. 11:30–32.
6. Rom. 11:33.
7. Rom. 5:20.

persevere in evil courses and suppose that they are recompensed with good. Their language, therefore, ought not to be: "Let us do evil, that good may come;" but: "We have done evil, and good has come; let us henceforth do good, that in the future world we may receive good for good, who in the present life are receiving good for evil." Wherefore it is written in the Psalm, "I will sing of mercy and judgment unto Thee, O Lord."[8] When the Son of man, therefore, first came into the world, it was not to judge the world, but that the world through Him might be saved.[9] And this dispensation was for mercy; by and by, however, He will come for judgment—to judge the quick and the dead. And yet even in this present time salvation itself does not eventuate without judgment—although it be a hidden one; therefore He says, "For judgment I am come into this world, that they which see not may see, and that they which see may be made blind."[1]

Chap. 45—The Reason Why One Person is Assisted By Grace, and Another is Not Helped, Must Be Referred to the Secret Judgments of God.

You must refer the matter, then, to the hidden determinations of God, when you see, in one and the same condition, such as all infants unquestionably have,—who derive their hereditary evil from Adam,—that one is assisted so as to be baptized, and another is not assisted, so that he dies in his very bondage; and again, that one baptized person is left and forsaken in his present life, who God foreknew would be ungodly, while another baptized person is taken away from this life, "lest that wickedness should alter his understanding;"[2] and be sure that you do not in such cases ascribe unrighteousness or unwisdom to God, in whom is the very fountain of righteousness and wisdom, but, as I have exhorted you from the commencement of this treatise, "whereto you have already attained, walk therein,"[3] and "even this shall God reveal unto you,"[4]—if not in this life, yet certainly in the next, "for there is nothing covered that shall not be revealed."[5] When, therefore, you hear the Lord say, "I the Lord have deceived that prophet,"[6] and likewise what the apostle says: "He hath mercy on whom He will have mercy, and whom He will He hardeneth,"[7] believe that, in the case of him whom He permits to be deceived and hardened, his evil deeds have deserved the judgment; whilst in the case of him to whom He shows mercy, you should loyally and unhesitatingly recognise the grace of the God who "rendereth not evil for evil; but contrariwise blessing."[8] Nor should you take away from Pharaoh free will, because in several passages God says, "I have hardened Pharaoh"; or, "I have hardened or I will harden Pharaoh's heart;"[9] for it does not by any means follow that Pharaoh did not, on this account, harden his own heart. For this, too, is said of him, after the removal of the fly-plague from the Egyptians, in these

8. Ps. 101:1.
9. John 3:17.
1. John 9:39.
2. Wisd. 4:11.
3. Phil. 3:16.
4. Phil. 3:15.
5. Matt. 10:26.
6. Ezek. 14:9.
7. Rom. 9:18.
8. 1 Pet. 3:9.
9. Ex. 4:21; 7:3; 14:4.

words of the Scripture: "And Pharaoh hardened his heart at this time also; neither would he let the people go."[1] Thus it was that both God hardened him by His just judgment, and Pharaoh by his own free will. Be ye then well assured that your labour will never be in vain, if, setting before you a good purpose, you persevere in it to the last. For God, who fails to render, according to their deeds, only to those whom He liberates, will then "recompense every man according to his works."[2] God will, therefore, certainly recompense both evil for evil, because He is just; and good for evil, because He is good; and good for good, because He is good and just; only, evil for good He will never recompense, because He is not unjust. He will, therefore, recompense evil for evil—punishment for unrighteousness; and He will recompense good for evil—grace for unrighteousness; and He will recompense good for good—grace for grace.

THEODORET OF CYRUS

[Sin, Sex, and Death] (ca. 445)†

On creating Adam and dignifying him with the gift of reason, the Lord God gave the single commandment of exercising his reason; it was impossible that, sharing in reason and enjoying the discernment of good and its opposite, he should live his life apart from any law. He was deceived and broke the law; and from the beginning the lawgiver linked the threat of punishment to the commandment. Becoming subject to the rule of death, then, Adam begot Cain, Seth and the others. All of them, therefore, on the grounds of their lineage from this man, had a nature subject to death; such a nature is in need of many things—food and drink, clothing and habitation, and diverse skills. Use of these things, however, often stimulates the passions to intemperance, and intemperance generates sin. Consequently, the divine apostle means that, since Adam had sinned and death had occurred through sin, both spread to the race: *death spread to all human beings for the reason that all sinned.*[1] In other words, it is not because of the sin of the first parent but because of their own that each person is liable to the norm of death.

---

1. Ex. 8:32.
2. Matt. 16:27.
† From Theodoret's commentary on Rom. 5:12, tr. by Robert Charles Hill, *Theodoret of Cyrus, Commentary on the Letters of St. Paul* (Brookline: Holy Cross Orthodox Press, 2001), Vol. 1, 72. Reprinted by permission of Holy Orthodox Press. Unlike some of their Latin counterparts, the early Greek fathers prior to John of Damascus (ca. 655–ca. 750) consistently interpreted *eph'hō* in Rom. 5: 12 to mean "because" or something quite similar, and Theodoret is typical in that regard. He is also representative when he argues that all humans, as the descendants of Adam, inherit his mortal nature through the process of procreation. At the same time, he affirms that death is the consequence of each person's own sins, not that of Adam.
1. Rom. 5: 12.

MARTIN LUTHER

[Death to the Law] (1535)†

* * *

I have referred earlier in this epistle to the occasion for St. Paul's discussion of Christian righteousness, namely, that right after he had gone away false teachers among the Galatians had destroyed what he had built up so painstakingly. These false apostles, adherents of Judaism and of Pharisaism at that, were men of great prestige and authority. Among the people they boasted that they belonged to the holy and elect race of the Jews, that they were Israelites of the seed of Abraham, that the promises and the patriarchs belonged to them, finally that they were ministers of Christ and pupils of the apostles, whom they had known personally and whose miracles they had witnessed. They may even have performed some signs or miracles themselves, for Christ declares (Matt. 7:22) that the wicked also perform miracles. When men with such authority come into any country or city, the people immediately develop great admiration for them; and they fool even those who are educated and quite steadfast in the faith. They subvert the Galatians by saying: "Who is Paul anyway? After all, was he not the very last of those who were converted to Christ? But we are the pupils of the apostles, and we knew them intimately. We saw Christ perform miracles, and we heard Him preach. But Paul is a latecomer and is our inferior. It is impossible that God should permit us to fall into error, us who are His holy people, who are the ministers of Christ, and who have received the Holy Spirit. Besides, we are many, while Paul is only one. He did not know the apostles, nor has he seen Christ. In fact, he persecuted the church of Christ. Do you imagine that on account of Paul alone God would permit so many churches to be deceived?"

In our time, whenever the pope does not have the authority of the Scriptures on his side, he always uses this same single argument against us: "The church, the church! Do you suppose that God is so offended that for the sake of a few heretical Lutherans He will reject His whole church? Do you suppose that He would leave His church in error for so many centuries?" With might and main he insists that the church can never be destroyed or overthrown. This argument persuades many people. With these and similar arguments these false apostles impressed the Galatians, so that Paul lost his authority among them and his doctrine came under suspicion.

In opposition to this boasting of the false apostles Paul boldly and with great *parrhēsia* pits his apostolic authority, commends his calling, and defends his ministry. Although he does not do this anywhere else, he refuses to yield to anyone, even to the apostles themselves, much less to any of their pupils. To counteract their pharisaical pride and insolence, he refers to the events that took place in Antioch, where he withstood Peter

† Martin Luther (1483–1546) was the initiator of the German Reformation. These comments on Galatians, which he once called "my epistle, to which I am betrothed," are drawn from his lectures on Galatians, delivered in 1531, first published in 1535, then in a somewhat revised form in 1538. The translation is by Jaroslav Pelikan, in *Luther's Works*, ed. Jaroslav Pelikan and Walter A. Hansen (St. Louis: Concordia, 1963), vols. 26, 27. Volume 26 Copyright © 1963, 1991; Volume 27 Copyright © 1964, 1992 by Concordia Publishing House. Reprinted by permission. All rights reserved.

himself. In addition, he pays no attention to the possible offense but says plainly in the text that he took it upon himself to reprove Peter himself, the prince of the apostles, who had seen Christ and had known Him intimately. "I am an apostle," he says, "and one who does not care what others are. Indeed, I did not shrink from reproving the very pillar of the other apostles."

*　*　*

[Comment on Gal. 1:11]

*　*　*

Peter, the prince of the apostles, lived and taught contrary to the Word of God. Therefore he was in error. And because he was at fault, Paul "opposed him to the face" (Gal. 2:11), attacking him because he was not in conformity with the truth of the Gospel. Here you see that Peter, the most holy apostle, erred. Thus I will not listen to the church or the fathers or the apostles unless they bring and teach the pure Word of God.

Today, too, this argument makes quite a telling point against us. For if we are to believe neither the pope nor the fathers nor Luther nor anyone else unless they teach us the pure Word of God, whom are we to believe? Who will give our consciences sure information about which party is teaching the pure Word of God, we or our opponents? For they, too, claim to have and to teach the pure Word of God. On the other hand, we do not believe the papists, because they neither teach nor can teach the Word of God. They again hate us bitterly and persecute us as the vilest heretics and seducers of the people. What is to be done here? Is every fanatic to have the right to teach whatever he pleases, since the world refuses to listen to or tolerate our teaching? With Paul we boast that we teach the pure Gospel of Christ. Not only should the pope, the sectarians, the fathers, and the church submit to this Gospel; they should receive it with open arms, accept it gratefully, embrace it, and propagate it to others. But if anyone teaches otherwise, whether the pope or St. Augustine or an apostle or an angel from heaven, let him and his gospel be accursed. Still we do not make any progress but are forced to hear that our boasting is not only vain, brazen, and arrogant but blasphemous and demonic. And yet, if we lower ourselves and yield to the ravings of our opponents, both the papists and the sectarians will become proud. The sectarians will brag that they are bringing some strange new doctrine never before heard of by the world, and the papists will reestablish their old abominations. Therefore let everyone take care to be most certain of his calling and doctrine, so that he may boldly and surely say with Paul (Gal. 1:8): "Even if we, or an angel from heaven, etc."

*　*　*

[Comment on Gal. 2:4f.]

*　*　*

The truth of the Gospel is this, that our righteousness comes by faith alone, without the works of the Law. The falsification or corruption of the

Gospel is this, that we are justified by faith but not without the works of the Law. The false apostles preached the Gospel, but they did so with this condition attached to it. The scholastics do the same thing in our day. They say that we must believe in Christ and that faith is the foundation of salvation, but they say that this faith does not justify unless it is "formed by love."[1] This is not the truth of the Gospel; it is falsehood and pretense. The true Gospel, however, is this: Works or love are not the ornament or perfection of faith; but faith itself is a gift of God, a work of God in our hearts, which justifies us because it takes hold of Christ as the Savior. Human reason has the Law as its object. It says to itself: "This I have done; this I have not done." But faith in its proper function has no other object than Jesus Christ, the Son of God, who was put to death for the sins of the world. It does not look at its love and say: "What have I done? Where have I sinned? What have I deserved?" But it says: "What has Christ done? What has He deserved?" And here the truth of the Gospel gives you the answer: "He has redeemed you from sin, from the devil, and from eternal death." Therefore faith acknowledges that in this one Person, Jesus Christ, it has the forgiveness of sins and eternal life. Whoever diverts his gaze from this object does not have true faith; he has a phantasy and a vain opinion. He looks away from the promise and at the Law, which terrifies him and drives him to despair.

Therefore what the scholastics have taught about justifying faith "formed by love" is an empty dream. For the faith that takes hold of Christ, the Son of God, and is adorned by Him is the faith that justifies, not a faith that includes love. For if faith is to be sure and firm, it must take hold of nothing but Christ alone; and in the agony and terror of conscience it has nothing else to lean on than this pearl of great value (Matt. 13:45–46). Therefore whoever takes hold of Christ by faith, no matter how terrified by the Law and oppressed by the burden of his sins he may be, has the right to boast that he is righteous. How has he this right? By that jewel, Christ, whom he possesses by faith. Our opponents fail to understand this. Therefore they reject Christ, this jewel; and in His place they put their love, which they say is a jewel. But if they do not know what faith is, it is impossible for them to have faith, much less to teach it to others. And as for what they claim to have, this is nothing but a dream, an opinion, and natural reason, but not faith.

God is Love

*　*　*

[Comment on Gal. 2:16]

*　*　*

Now the true meaning of Christianity is this: that a man first acknowledge, through the Law, that he is a sinner, for whom it is impossible to perform any good work. For the Law says: "You are an evil tree. Therefore everything you think, speak, or do is opposed to God. Hence you cannot deserve grace by your works. But if you try to do so, you make the bad even worse; for since you are an evil tree, you cannot produce anything except evil fruits, that is, sins. 'For whatever does not proceed from faith

---

1. On the meaning of *fides charitate formata* cf. Thomas Aquinas, *Summa Theologica*, II–II, Qu. 4, Art. 3 [Translator's note].

is sin' (Rom. 14:23)." Trying to merit grace by preceding works, therefore, is trying to placate God with sins, which is nothing but heaping sins upon sins, making fun of God, and provoking His wrath. When a man is taught this way by the Law, he is frightened and humbled. Then he really sees the greatness of his sin and finds in himself not one spark of the love of God; thus he justifies God in His Word and confesses that he deserves death and eternal damnation. Thus the first step in Christianity is the preaching of repentance and the knowledge of oneself.

[margin note: main christian principle]

The second step is this: If you want to be saved, your salvation does not come by works; but God has sent His only Son into the world that we might live through Him. He was crucified and died for you and bore your sins in His own body (1 Pet. 2:24). Here there is no "congruity" or work performed before grace, but only wrath, sin, terror, and death. Therefore the Law only shows sin, terrifies, and humbles; thus it prepares us for justification and drives us to Christ. For by His Word God has revealed to us that He wants to be a merciful Father to us. Without our merit—since, after all, we cannot merit anything—He wants to give us forgiveness of sins, righteousness, and eternal life for the sake of Christ. For God is He who dispenses His gifts freely to all, and this is the praise of His deity. But He cannot defend this deity of His against the self-righteous people who are unwilling to accept grace and eternal life from Him freely but want to earn it by their own works. They simply want to rob Him of the glory of His deity. In order to retain it, He is compelled to send forth His Law, to terrify and crush those very hard rocks as though it were thunder and lightning.

This, in summary, is our theology about Christian righteousness, in opposition to the abominations and monstrosities of the sophists about "merit of congruity and of condignity" or about works before grace and after grace. Smug people, who have never struggled with any temptations or true terrors of sin and death, were the ones who made up these empty dreams out of their own heads; therefore they do not understand what they are saying or what they are talking about, for they cannot supply any examples of such works done either before grace or after grace. Therefore these are useless fables, with which the papists delude both themselves and others.

* * *

[2:]19. *For I through the Law died to the Law, that I might live to God.*

This is amazing language and unheard-of speech which human reason simply cannot understand. It is spoken briefly but very emphatically. Paul seems to be speaking from a fervent and ardent spirit, with great zeal, as though he were indignant. It is as though he were saying: "Why do you boast so much about the Law, about which I do not want to know anything? Why do you din this into me so often? But if there must be a Law, I have a Law of my own." As though he were speaking by the indignation of the Holy Spirit, he calls grace itself "Law." He stamps the content of grace with a new name, as an expression of contempt for the Law of Moses and for the false apostles, who claimed that it was necessary for justification. Thus he opposes the Law to the Law. This is most delicious language. In Scripture, especially in Paul, Law is often opposed to Law, sin to sin, death to death, captivity to captivity, the devil to the devil, hell to hell, altar to altar, lamb to lamb, Passover to Passover.

Rom. 8:3: "For sin He condemned sin"; Ps. 68:18 and Eph. 4:8: "He led captivity captive"; Hos. 14:14: "O death, I will be your death. O hell, I will be your destruction." Thus he says here that through the Law he has died to the Law. It is as though he were saying: "The Law of Moses accuses and damns me. But against that accusing and damning Law I have another Law, which is grace and freedom. This Law accuses the accusing Law and damns the damning Law." Thus death killed death, but this death which kills death is life itself. But it is called the death of death, by an exuberant indignation of the spirit against death. So also righteousness takes the name "sin," because it damns sin; and this damning sin is true righteousness.

Here Paul is the most heretical of heretics; and his heresy is unheard-of, because he says that, having died to the Law, he lives to God. The false apostles taught: "Unless you live to the Law, you do not live to God. That is, unless you live according to the Law, you are dead in the sight of God." But Paul teaches the opposite: "Unless you are dead to the Law, you do not live to God." The doctrine of the fanatics today is the same as that of the false apostles at that time. "If you want to live to God," they say, "that is, to be alive in the sight of God, then live to the Law, or according to the Law." But we say in opposition: "If you want to live to God, you must completely die to the Law." Human reason and wisdom do not understand this doctrine. Therefore they always teach the opposite: "If you want to live to God, you must observe the Law; for it is written (Matt. 19:17): 'If you would enter life, keep the Commandments.' " This is a principle and maxim of all the theologians: "He who lives according to the Law lives to God." Paul says the exact opposite, namely, that we cannot live to God unless we have died to the Law. Therefore we must climb up to this heavenly altitude, in order that we may establish for certain that we are far above the Law, in fact, that we are completely dead to the Law. Now if we are dead to the Law, then the Law has no jurisdiction over us, just as it has no jurisdiction over Christ, who has liberated us from the Law in order that in this way we may live to God. This supports the declaration that the Law does not justify, but that only faith in Christ justifies.

Paul is not speaking about the Ceremonial Law here. He sacrificed in the temple, circumcised Timothy and cut his hair at Cenchreae. He would not have done these things if he had died to the Ceremonial Law. But he is speaking about the entire Law. For the Christian, therefore, the entire Law has been completely abrogated—whether it be the Ceremonial Law or the Decalog—because he has died to it. This does not mean that the Law is destroyed; for it remains, lives, and rules in the wicked. But the godly man is dead to the Law as he is dead to sin, the devil, death, and hell, all of which still remain, and all of which the world and the wicked will inherit. Therefore when the sophist takes Paul to mean that only the Ceremonial Law is abrogated, you understand that for Paul and for every Christian the entire Law is abrogated, and yet that the Law still remains.

For example, when Christ arises from the dead, He is free from the grave; and yet the grave remains. Peter is liberated from prison, the paralytic from his bed, the young man from his coffin, the girl from her couch; nevertheless, the prison, the bed, the coffin, and the couch remain. So also the Law is abrogated when I am freed from it, and the Law dies when I have died to it; and yet the Law still remains. But because I die to it, it also dies to me. Thus Christ's grave, Peter's prison, the girl's couch—all remain. But by His resurrection Christ dies to the grave; by his deliverance Peter is freed from the prison; by her restoration to life the girl is delivered from the couch.

* * *

[Comment on Gal. 2:20]

* * *

Nevertheless, I live; yet not I, but Christ lives in me.

When he says: "Nevertheless, I live," this sounds rather personal, as though Paul were speaking of his own person. Therefore he quickly corrects it and says: "Yet not I." That is, "I do not live in my own person now, but Christ lives in me." The person does indeed live, but not in itself or for its own person. But who is this "I" of whom he says: "Yet not I"? It is the one that has the Law and is obliged to do works, the one that is a person separate from Christ. This "I" Paul rejects; for "I," as a person distinct from Christ, belongs to death and hell. This is why he says: "Not I, but Christ lives in me." Christ is my "form,"[2] which adorns my faith as color or light adorns a wall. (This fact has to be expounded in this crude way, for there is no spiritual way for us to grasp the idea that Christ clings and dwells in us as closely and intimately as light or whiteness clings to a wall.) "Christ," he says, "is fixed and cemented to me and abides in me. The life that I now live, He lives in me. Indeed, Christ Himself is the life that I now live. In this way, therefore, Christ and I are one."

Living in me as He does, Christ abolishes the Law, damns sin, and kills death; for at His presence all these cannot help disappearing. Christ is eternal Peace, Comfort, Righteousness, and Life, to which the terror of the Law, sadness of mind, sin, hell, and death have to yield. Abiding and living in me, Christ removes and absorbs all the evils that torment and afflict me. This attachment to Him causes me to be liberated from the terror of the Law and of sin, pulled out of my own skin, and transferred into Christ and into His kingdom, which is a kingdom of grace, righteousness, peace, joy, life, salvation, and eternal glory. Since I am in Him, no evil can harm me.

Meanwhile my old man (Eph. 4:22) remains outside and is subject to the Law. But so far as justification is concerned, Christ and I must be so closely attached that He lives in me and I in Him. What a marvelous way of speaking! Because He lives in me, whatever grace, righteousness, life, peace, and salvation there is in me is all Christ's; nevertheless, it is mine as well, by the cementing and attachment that are through faith, by which we become as one body in the Spirit. Since Christ lives in me, grace, righteousness, life, and eternal salvation must be present with Him; and

---

2. That is, Christ, not charity, is the *forma* of faith [Translator's note].

the Law, sin, and death must be absent. Indeed, the Law must be crucified, devoured, and abolished by the Law—and sin by sin, death by death, the devil by the devil. In this way Paul seeks to withdraw us completely from ourselves, from the Law, and from works, and to transplant us into Christ and faith in Christ, so that in the area of justification we look only at grace, and separate it far from the Law and from works, which belong far away.

Paul has a peculiar phraseology—not human, but divine and heavenly. The evangelists and the other apostles do not use it, except for John, who speaks this way from time to time. If Paul had not used this way of speaking first and prescribed it for us in explicit terms, no one even among the saints would have dared[3] use it. It is unprecedented and insolent to say: "I live, I do not live; I am dead, I am not dead; I am a sinner, I am not a sinner; I have the Law, I do not have the Law." But this phraseology is true in Christ and through Christ. When it comes to justification, therefore, if you divide Christ's Person from your own, you are in the Law; you remain in it and live in yourself, which means that you are dead in the sight of God and damned by the Law. For you have a faith that is, as the sophists imagine, "formed by love." I am speaking this way for the sake of illustration. For there is no one who has such a faith; therefore what the sophists have taught about "faith formed by love" is merely a trick of Satan. But let us concede that a man could be found who had such a faith. Even if he had it, he would actually be dead, because he would have only a historical faith about Christ, something that even the devil and all the wicked have (James 2:19).

But faith must be taught correctly, namely, that by it you are so cemented to Christ that He and you are as one person, which cannot be separated but remains attached to Him forever and declares: "I am as Christ." And Christ, in turn, says: "I am as that sinner who is attached to Me, and I to him. For by faith we are joined together into one flesh and one bone." Thus Eph. 5:30 says: "We are members of the body of Christ, of His flesh and of His bones," in such a way that this faith couples Christ and me more intimately than a husband is coupled to his wife. Therefore this faith is no idle quality; but it is a thing of such magnitude that it obscures and completely removes those foolish dreams of the sophists' doctrine—the fiction of a "formed faith" and of love, of merits, our worthiness, our quality, etc. I would like to treat this at greater length if I could.

*   *   *

[3:]24. *So that the Law was our custodian until Christ came.*

When Paul says that "the Law was our custodian until Christ came," he once more joins Law and Gospel together in feeling, even though in themselves they are as far apart as possible. This analogy of the custodian is truly outstanding; therefore it must be considered carefully. Although a schoolmaster is very useful and really necessary for the education and training of boys, show me one boy or pupil who loves his schoolmaster! For example, did the Jews love Moses warmly and willingly do what he commanded? Their love and obedience toward Moses was such, as the

---

3. The Weimar text has *fuisses* here, but we have read *fuisset* [Translator's note].

history shows, that at times they would have been willing to stone him. Therefore it is impossible for a pupil to love his schoolmaster. For how could he love the one by whom he is being detained in prison, that is, by whom he is being forbidden to do what he would like to do? If he commits something that is against his schoolmaster's orders, he is denounced and scolded by him; what is more, he is forced to embrace and kiss his whip.[4] How wonderful the pupil's righteousness is, that he obeys a threatening and harsh schoolmaster and even kisses his whip! Does he do this willingly and joyfully? When the schoolmaster is absent, he will break the whip or throw it into the fire. And if he had authority over the schoolmaster, he would not let himself be beaten by the schoolmaster's whips but would order that the schoolmaster be whipped. Nevertheless, a schoolmaster is extremely necessary for a boy, to instruct and chastise him; for otherwise, without this instruction, good training, and discipline, the boy would come to ruin.

Therefore the schoolmaster gives the boy the impression of being his taskmaster and executioner and of holding him captive in prison. To what end and for how long? So that this severe, hateful authority of the school-master and the slavery of the boy will last forever? No, but for a predetermined time, so that this obedience, prison, and discipline may work for the boy's good and so that in due time he may become the heir and the king. For it is not the father's intention that the son be subject to the schoolmaster forever and be whipped by him, but that through the instruction and discipline of the schoolmaster the son may be made fit for accession to his inheritance.

* * *

By means of this fine illustration, therefore, Paul shows the true use of the Law: that it does not justify hypocrites, because they remain outside Christ in their presumptuousness and smugness; on the other hand, if those who have been frightened use the Law as Paul teaches, it does not leave them in death and damnation but drives them to Christ. Those who continue in these terrors and in their faintheartedness and do not take hold of Christ by faith despair utterly. With his allegory of the custodian, therefore, Paul clearly portrays the true use of the Law. For just as the custodian scolds, drives, and troubles his pupils, not with the intention that this custody should last forever, but that it should come to an end when the pupils have been properly educated and trained and that they should then eagerly and freely enjoy their liberty and their inheritance without the constraint of their custodian, so those who are frightened and crushed by the Law should know that these terrors and blows will not be permanent, but that by them they are being prepared for the coming of Christ and the freedom of the Spirit.

* * *

4. From other references in Luther it seems that it was customary for a child to have to kiss the whip after he had been punished [Translator's note].

[*Comments on Gal. 5:1*]

* * *

Every word is emphatic. "Stand fast," he says, "in freedom." In what freedom? Not in the freedom for which the Roman emperor has set us free but in the freedom for which Christ has set us free. The Roman emperor gave—indeed, was forced to give—the Roman pontiff a free city and other lands, as well as certain immunities, privileges, and concessions. This, too, is freedom; but it is a political freedom, according to which the Roman pontiff with all his clergy is free of all public burdens. In addition, there is the freedom of the flesh, which is chiefly prevalent in the world. Those who have this obey neither God nor the laws but do what they please. This is the freedom which the rabble pursues today; so do the fanatical spirits, who want to be free in their opinions and actions, in order that they may teach and do with impunity what they imagine to be right. This is a demonic freedom, by which the devil sets the wicked free to sin against God and men. We are not dealing with this here although it is the most widespread and is the only goal and objective of the entire world. Nor are we dealing with political freedom. No, we are dealing with another kind, which the devil hates and attacks most bitterly.

This is the freedom with which Christ has set us free, not from some human slavery or tyrannical authority but from the eternal wrath of God. Where? In the conscience. This is where our freedom comes to a halt; it goes no further. For Christ has set us free, not for a political freedom or a freedom of the flesh but for a theological or spiritual freedom, that is, to make our conscience free and joyful, unafraid of the wrath to come (Matt. 3:7). This is the most genuine freedom; it is immeasurable. When the other kinds of freedom—political freedom and the freedom of the flesh—are compared with the greatness and the glory of this kind of freedom, they hardly amount to one little drop. For who can express what a great gift it is for someone to be able to declare for certain that God neither is nor ever will be wrathful but will forever be a gracious and merciful Father for the sake of Christ? It is surely a great and incomprehensible freedom to have this Supreme Majesty kindly disposed toward us, protecting and helping us, and finally even setting us free physically in such a way that our body, which is sown in perishability, in dishonor, and in weakness, is raised in imperishability, in honor, and in power (1 Cor. 15:42–43). Therefore the freedom by which we are free of the wrath of God forever is greater than heaven and earth and all creation.

From this there follows the other freedom, by which we are made safe and free through Christ from the Law, from sin, death, the power of the devil, hell, etc. For just as the wrath of God cannot terrify us—since Christ has set us free from it—so the Law, sin, etc., cannot accuse and condemn us. Even though the Law denounces us and sin terrifies us, they still cannot plunge us into despair. For faith, which is the victor over the world (1 John 5:4), quickly declares: "Those things have nothing to do with me, for Christ has set me free from them." So it is that death, which is the most powerful and horrible thing in the world, lies conquered in our conscience through this freedom of the Spirit. Therefore the greatness of Christian freedom should be carefully measured and pondered. The words "freedom from the

Free from the law [handwritten annotation in left margin]

wrath of God, from the Law, sin, death, etc.," are easy to say; but to feel the greatness of this freedom and to apply its results to oneself in a struggle, in the agony of conscience, and in practice—this is more difficult than anyone can say.

* * *

[Comment on Gal. 5:3]

* * *

What I am saying here on the basis of the words of Paul I learned from my own experience in the monastery about myself and about others. I saw many who tried with great effort and the best of intentions to do everything possible to appease their conscience. They wore hair shirts; they fasted; they prayed; they tormented and wore out their bodies with various exercises so severely that if they had been made of iron, they would have been crushed. And yet the more they labored, the greater their terrors became. Especially when the hour of death was imminent, they became so fearful that I have seen many murderers facing execution die more confidently than these men who had lived such saintly lives.

Thus it is certainly true that those who keep the Law do not keep it. The more men try to satisfy the Law, the more they transgress it. The more someone tries to bring peace to his conscience through his own righteousness, the more disquieted he makes it. When I was a monk, I made a great effort to live according to the requirements of the monastic rule. I made a practice of confessing and reciting all my sins, but always with prior contrition; I went to confession frequently, and I performed the assigned penances faithfully. Nevertheless, my conscience could never achieve certainty but was always in doubt and said: "You have not done this correctly. You were not contrite enough. You omitted this in your confession." Therefore the longer I tried to heal my uncertain, weak, and troubled conscience with human traditions, the more uncertain, weak, and troubled I continually made it. In this way, by observing human traditions, I transgressed them even more; and by following the righteousness of the monastic order, I was never able to reach it. For, as Paul says, it is impossible for the conscience to find peace through the works of the Law, much less through human traditions, without the promise and the Gospel about Christ.

* * *

[Comment on Gal. 5:13]

* * *

This evil is very widespread, and it is the worst of all the evils that Satan arouses against the teaching of faith: that in many people he soon transforms the freedom for which Christ has set us free into an opportunity for the flesh. Jude complains of this same thing in his epistle (ch. 4): "Admission has been secretly gained by some ungodly persons who pervert the grace of our God into licentiousness." For the flesh simply does not understand the teaching of grace, namely, that we are not justified by works but by faith alone, and that the Law has no jurisdiction over us, Therefore when it hears this teaching, it transforms it into licentiousness and immediately draws the inference: "If we are without the Law, then let us live as we please. Let us not do good, let us not give to the needy; much less do we have to endure anything evil. For there is no Law to compel or bind us."

Thus there is a danger on both sides, although the one is more tolerable than the other. If grace or faith is not preached, no one is saved; for faith alone justifies and saves. On the other hand, if faith is preached, as it must be preached, the majority of men understand the teaching about faith in a fleshly way and transform the freedom of the spirit into the freedom of the flesh. This can be discerned today in all classes of society, both high and low. They all boast of being evangelicals and boast of Christian freedom. Meanwhile, however, they give in to their desires and turn to greed, sexual desire, pride, envy, etc. No one performs his duty faithfully; no one serves another by love. This misbehavior often makes me so impatient that I would want such "swine that trample pearls underfoot" (Matt. 7:6) still to be under the tyranny of the pope. For it is impossible for this people of Gomorrah to be ruled by the Gospel of peace.

What is more, we ourselves, who teach the Word, do not perform our own duty with as much care and zeal here in the light of truth as we used to in the darkness of ignorance. The more certain we are about the freedom granted to us by Christ, the more unresponsive and slothful we are in presenting the Word, praying, doing good works, enduring evil, and the like. And if Satan were not troubling us inwardly with spiritual trials and outwardly with persecution by our enemies and with the contempt and ingratitude of our own followers, we would become utterly smug, lazy, and useless for anything good; thus in time we would lose the knowledge of Christ and faith in Him, would forsake the ministry of the Word, and would look for some more comfortable way of life, more suitable to our flesh. This is what many of our followers are beginning to do, motivated by the fact that those who labor in the Word not only do not get their support from this but are even treated shamefully by those whom their preaching of the Gospel has set free from the miserable slavery of the pope. Forsaking the poor and offensive figure of Christ, they involve themselves in the business of this present life; and they serve, not Christ but their own appetites (Rom. 16:18), with results that they will experience in due time.

We know that the devil lies in wait especially for us who have the Word—he already holds the others captive to his will—and that he is intent upon taking the freedom of the Spirit away from us or at least making us change it into license. Therefore we teach and exhort our followers with great care and diligence, on the basis of Paul's example, not to think that this freedom of the Spirit, achieved by the death of Christ, was given[5] to them as an opportunity for the flesh or, as Peter says, "to use as a pretext for evil" (1 Pet. 2:16), but for them to be servants of one another through love.

As we have said, therefore, the apostle imposes an obligation on Christians through this law about mutual love in order to keep them from abusing their freedom. Therefore the godly should remember that for the sake of Christ they are free in their conscience before God from the curse of

---

5. For the reading *donatum* in the Weimar text we have substituted *donatam* [Translator's note].

the Law, from sin, and from death, but that according to the body they
are bound; here each must serve the other through love, in accordance
with this commandment of Paul. Therefore let everyone strive to do his
duty in his calling and to help his neighbor in whatever way he can. This
is what Paul requires of us with the words "through love be servants of
one another," which do not permit the saints to run free according to the
flesh but subject them to an obligation.

*   *   *

KARL BARTH

[The New Man] (1952)†

*   *   *

*Jesus Christ is the secret truth about the essential nature of man, and even
sinful man is essentially related to Him. That is what we have learned from
Rom. 5:12–21.*

Now we shall try to summarize our conclusions: We have seen how,
according to vv. 1–11, Jesus Christ is a sharply-defined individual, and
how, as such, He is clearly the representative of an undetermined multitude of other men. In His life and destiny He represents and anticipates
their life and their destiny so that they, without ceasing to be distinct
individuals, must make their life an image and reflection of His life and
must work out the destiny that overtook them in Him. They have to identify
themselves with Him, because He has already identified Himself with
them. There is no question of any merging or any confusion between Him
and them, but neither can there be any question of any abstraction or
separation. He in His individuality is theirs, and so they in their individuality can only be His. The ineffaceable distinction between Him and them
is the guarantee of their indissoluble unity with Him. They as receivers are
subordinated and yet indissolubly related to Him as Giver; they as members are subordinated and yet indissolubly united to Him as Head.

But vv. 1–11 only speak of Jesus Christ and those who *believe* in Him.
If we read that first part of the chapter by itself, we might quite easily come
to the conclusion that for Paul Christ's manhood is significant only for
those who are united to Him in faith. We would then have no right to
draw any conclusion about the relationship between Christ and *man as
such*, from what Paul says about the "religious" relationship between
Christ and Christians. We could not then expect to find in the manhood
of Christ the key to the essential nature of man.

But in vv. 12–21 Paul does not limit his context to Christ's relationship

† This selection is Barth's own summary of his book *Christ and Adam*, a discussion of Romans 5 published in German in 1952, translated into English by T. A. Smail (New York, 1980), 107–17. Translation copyright 1956 by Thomas Allan Smail, renewed 1984; copyright © 2004 Wipf and Stock.
Reprinted by permission of Wipf and Stock and HarperCollins Publishers. The influence of Barth
(1886–1969) on twentieth-century Protestant and ecumenical thought, especially through his
epoch-making commentary on Romans (1919) and his multi-volume *Church Dogmatics*, was
inestimable.

to believers but gives fundamentally the same account of His relationship to all men. The context is widened from Church history to world history, from Christ's relationship to Christians to His relationship to all men. It should be noted that in these verses there is no further mention of faith or even of the gift of the Holy Spirit, and that the first person plural which is continually used in vv. 1–11 is here (with the exception of the last phrase of v. 21) replaced by a quite general third person plural. What is said here applies generally and universally, and not merely to one limited group of men. Here "religious" presuppositions are not once hinted at. The fact of Christ is here presented as something that dominates and includes all men. The nature of Christ objectively conditions human nature and the work of Christ makes an objective difference to the life and destiny of all men. Through Christ grace overflows upon them, bringing them pardon and justification and opening before them a prospect of life with God. In short, "grace rules," as it is put in v. 21. And all that is an exact correspondence to what happens to human nature in its objective relationship to Adam. There sin rules, in exactly the same way, and all men become sinners and unrighteous in Adam, and as such must die. The question about what is the special mark of the *Christian* is just not raised at all. What we are told is what it means for man as such that his objective relationship to Adam is subordinate to and dependent upon and included in his objective relationship to Christ. The question raised here—as distinct from vv. 1–11— concerns the relationship between Christ and all men.

Paul had obviously no intention of fathering an idle and arbitrary speculation when in this passage he passed on to this further account of the same subject. If we have understood the *dia touto* (therefore) of v. 12 rightly, his intention was rather to consolidate the special account he had already given of the relationship between Christ and faith, by placing it in this wider and more general context. Our standing as believers is as vv. 1–11 have described it, because our standing as men is as vv. 12–21 describe it. Our relationship to Christ as believers is based upon our prior relationship to Him as Adam's children and heirs. For even when we were, in the words of vv. 1–11, weak, sinners, godless, and enemies, Christ died for us and so brought us into His Kingdom and under His power.

We have come *to* Christ as believers and Christians, because we had already come *from* Christ, so that there was nothing else for us to do but believe in Him. What is said in vv. 1–11 is not just "religious" truth that only applies to specially talented, specially qualified, or specially guided men; it is truth for *all* men, whether they know it or not, as surely as they are all Adam's children and heirs. The assurance of Christians, as it is described in vv. 1–11, has as its basis the fact that the Christian sphere is not limited to the "religious" sphere. What is *Christian* is secretly but fundamentally identical with what is *universally human*. Nothing in true human nature can ever be alien or irrelevant to the Christian; nothing in true human nature can ever attack or surpass or annul the objective reality of the Christian's union with Christ. Much in true human nature is unrelated to "religion," but nothing in true human nature is unrelated to the Christian faith. That means that we can understand true human nature only in the light of the Christian gospel that we believe. For Christ stands above and is first, and Adam stands below and is second. So it is Christ that reveals the true nature of man. Man's nature in Adam is not, as is usually assumed, his true and original nature; it is only truly human at all in so far as it reflects and corresponds to essential human nature as it is found in Christ. True human nature, therefore, can only be understood by Christians who look to Christ to discover the essential nature of man. Vv. 12–21 are revolutionary in their insistence that what is true of Christians must also be true of all men. That is a principle that has an incalculable significance for all our action and thought. To reject this passage as empty speculation is tantamount to denying that the human nature of Christ is the final revelation of the true nature of man.

What Rom. 5:12–21 is specially concerned to make clear is that man as we know him, man in Adam who sins and dies, has his life so ordered that he is both a distinct individual and, at the same time, the responsible representative of humanity and of all other men. In the same way there are no other responsible representatives of humanity than individual men. We are what Adam was and so are all our fellow men. And the one Adam is what we and all men are. Man is at once an individual and only an individual, and, at the same time, without in any way losing his individuality, he is the responsible representative of all men. He is always for himself and always for all men. That being so, can we build on this foundation? Is it true that essential human nature must always be the existence of the man in humanity and of humanity in the man? We recognize that, first, only in relation to Adam and the many who are like him, and so only in relation to sinful and dying men like ourselves. But have we understood man correctly when we understand him in that way? Could not all that be quite wrong? Might not humanity be a corporate personality of which individuals are only insignificant manifestations or fragmentary parts? Or might not the whole notion of humanity be a fiction, and the reality consist only of a collection of individuals each essentially unrelated to the others and each responsible only for himself? Rom. 5:12–21 points in neither of these directions. If we base our thinking on this passage, we can have nothing to do with either collectivism on the one hand or individualism on the other. It understands the true man in neither of these ways.

But how does this passage come to be so definite about its own interpretation of the true man? For it is dealing expressly with Adam and so with corrupt man, and it might seem questionable to base such definite statements about the true nature of man upon our knowledge of him. What is Paul's authority for basing a categorical conclusion about the structure of human nature upon nothing sounder than his knowledge of fallen man? We have seen that Paul dares to draw this conclusion because he sees Adam not in isolation but in his relationship to Christ. And for him Christ and Adam do not represent two conflicting interpretations of human nature. For in that case the doubt as to which was ultimately valid would still arise—and the tone of vv. 1–11 shows that Paul has no doubts at all. The answer is in vv. 13–14 and 20, where it is shown that the formal correspondence and identity between Adam and Christ is based upon their material disparity. In the encounter between them Christ has more right and power, and Adam less. It is only in this disparity of status and in this disproportion that they can be compared. Adam is subordinate to Christ, and not Christ to Adam. And if Adam is subordinate to Christ, then Adam represents true and genuine human nature in so far as he shows us the man in humanity and humanity in the man.

Whatever else in his representation of human nature may have to be accounted for by its later corruption and ruin, this ordering principle at least belongs to its condition and character as created and untouched by sin. For the subordinate representation of human nature in Adam here corresponds to its primary representation in Christ. In Christ also, the man is in humanity and humanity is in the man. With one important difference: Adam is not God's Son become man, and so he cannot, like Him, be man, and at the same time be *over* all men. Adam, as the one, can represent the many; he as man can represent humanity—but only as one among others. Thus he can represent all the others only in the same way that each of them can represent him. Adam has no essential priority of status over other men. He cannot be their lord and head; he cannot determine their life and their destiny. He can anticipate their life and destiny in himself, only in so far as he is the first man among many others, only in so far as he is *primus inter pares* [first among equals]. The *pollō mallon* (much more) of vv. 15–17 marks this difference. Where it is taken into account, what remains of the identity between Adam and Christ is the unity of the one and the many on both sides, of his deeds and their deeds, of his condition and theirs. In this unity Christ is, like Adam, man. In this unity of the one and the many Adam is the type and likeness of Christ, although formally he differs from Christ because he is not lord and head in this unity, and materially he differs from Him, because his nature is perverted by sin. But this unity, as such, belongs not to the perversion of his nature but to its original constitution. And so Paul makes no arbitrary assertion, and he is not deceiving himself when he presupposes this unity as simply given even in Adam. He does so because he has found it given first and primarily in Christ.

Christ is not only God's Son; He is also a man who is not a sinner like Adam and all of us. He is true man in an absolute sense, and it is in His humanity that we have to recognize true human nature in the condition and character in which it was willed and created by God. To it there certainly belongs this unity of man and humanity. When we inquire about the true nature of man and seek an answer in terms of this unity, we are on firm ground, in so far as even sinful man, whom alone we know, reflects back, as far as this unity is concerned, the human nature of Christ and so has not ceased to be true man and has not ceased to show man's true nature to us.

PART VI

"The Second Founder of Christianity"

The discussion of Paul in the second half of the nineteenth century was defined by the question of his place in the evolution of early Christianity. That was a distinctly post-Enlightenment question. It meant that now people were seeking to understand Christianity as one historical phenomenon among others, subject to the same laws of change as other human institutions or systems of thought. It meant also that the important role of conflict in the formation of early Christianity was being painfully rediscovered. So long as the Bible was read as a sourcebook of systematic theology, a treasury of eternally true propositions—and the post-Reformation defensive postures of Roman Catholics and Protestants alike had led by and large to a flat and rigid view of scripture—then it was hardly possible for the divergent points of view within the Bible to be acknowledged. The Enlightenment revolt against church institutions and dogmatic traditions assured that they would be recognized, and not only recognized but savored.

Perhaps *the* characteristic focus of modern intellectual history has been preoccupation with the processes of change. The nineteenth century produced two massive theories of evolution which were to alter our picture of the world: on the Continent, the abstract, metaphysical dialectic of Hegel; in the English-speaking world, Darwin's empirically grounded construct of biological history. These theories were symptoms—as in turn they became also causes of further acceleration—of a widespread awareness of development and a concern for the understanding of origins and of the ways in which the process of change takes place.

In the study of early Christianity the obsessive question was how to explain the evolution of the world church—replete with metaphysical dogmas, sacramental system, and powerful hierarchy—out of the tiny band of Galilean peasants, artisans, and fishermen taught by Jesus. One of the most curious aspects of the post-Enlightenment critique of Christianity is the strange attraction that the figure of Jesus still exerted over the most diverse schools that were outspokenly hostile to Christianity, from the Deists to Nietzsche to the *Deutsche Christen*. To be sure, these different critics had quite divergent pictures of what the real Jesus had been like. To some he appeared as a simple prophet or rabbi, startling the world with the charming directness and austerity of his ethical maxims. To others he might, by the directness of his talk about God and the fearlessness of his demeanor in the face of death, show that "he had denied every cleft between God and man; he lived this unity of God and man . . ." (Nietzsche). In any case, it was very difficult to harmonize the pictures one might reasonably draw of the historical Jesus with the *Cosmocrator* enthroned in the mosaic dome of a Byzantine basilica, or with the Second Person of the Trinity, consubstantial with the Father, of the Nicene Creed. Any one who read the gospels with a historian's eye would have to observe that Jesus had not taught any of the great ontological systems associated with the fundamental dogmas of the church. How then had these doctrines arisen?

A simple though deceptive way of putting the question was, How had Greek philosophical theology replaced the teachings of Jesus? For it was evident that the Christian theologians of the second and third centuries had used the language of Greek philosophical schools to speak of God, Christ, and salvation. And a simple answer to the question was, Paul was the one who hellenized Christianity. On the face of it this answer had an immediate plausibility. As one moves in the New Testament from the synoptic gospels to Paul's letters (and the naive reader might assume that was a move from earlier to later), one finds a decisive shift from Jesus' teachings about the kingdom of God to Paul's teachings about Christ. And the latter have virtually nothing to say about Jesus' life and teachings, but speak of him as a divine, pre-existent being, the Son of God, who by his death and resurrection accomplished the atonement of humanity with God.

397

Paul might be either praised or blamed for the hellenization of Christianity, depending on one's point of view. If one thought that the essence of Christianity was the ethical teachings of Jesus, or his directly perceptible personality, then Paul might appear to have perverted that simple truth into something complex and sterile. Such a radical separation between Jesus and Paul, however, created more problems for a serious student of Christian origins than it solved, so it was not widely represented save in popular tracts. Moreover, most of the modernizing interpreters of early Christianity's development were not interested in emphasizing the Jewishness of Jesus. For idealists, what was essential in Jesus had by definition to be universal, not limited to the contingencies of a particular time and place. In this discussion "Jewish" became virtually a code word for "particular," "limited," "historically conditioned," while "Greek" came to mean "universal," "rational," and "ideal." Thus for F. C. Baur, as for certain of the English Deists before him, Jesus lived and taught within the thought world of Palestinian Judaism, but his life and message implied a rational, universal religious outlook that far transcended his Jewishness. While Jesus' immediate successors, the Jerusalem apostles, obscured the universal implications of their Master by their narrow Jewishness, Paul was enabled through his conflict with the Jewish Christians to realize the universal potential of Jesus and to free his spirit from the Jewish matrix.

Of course, the picture could be stood on its head. The orientalist Paul de Lagarde, recognizing that many of the essential doctrines of Paul, notably the atonement by Jesus' death, were by no means "Greek," insisted that Paul was the *Judaizer* of Christianity, binding the universal, human religion of Jesus into the straitjacket of "rabbinic" myth. A rather similar position was adopted by Friedrich Nietzsche, particularly in his later works (note the differences between his aphorism about Paul in *The Dawn of Day* and his bitter tirade in the later *The Antichrist*, excerpted below). In the same category also are George Bernard Shaw's remarks about Paul (see below), except of course that they preserve a sense of humor and are free from the dark metaphysical and racial trappings of Teutonic anti-Paulinism.

The Baur proposals received intense criticism from students of early Christian history. Adolf von Harnack agreed that Paul had removed the Jewish "husk" from Jesus' message, but insisted that the development from Jesus to the Jerusalem church to the Gentile mission to Paul was direct and linear, not dialectical. The hellenization of Christianity, with its fateful accretion of dogmas to be believed, did take place, according to Harnack, but only *after* Paul, among the Apologists of the second century.

Quite a new dimension was added to the discussion by the sober exegetical study of Wilhelm Heitmüller, who showed that the "hellenization" of Christianity had already taken place *before* Paul, and that Paul in fact was converted to a "hellenistic" form of Christianity, complete with sacraments, cultus, and atonement doctrine. That put the entire debate in a new light, as one can readily see by examining the subsequent work of religious historians such as Wilhelm Bousset[1] or of New Testament scholars such as Rudolf Bultmann, particularly the plan of the latter's *New Testament Theology* (see his essay in Part IX [pp. 593–603] on Paul's use of myth).

The outcome of the debate was that Paul's Jewishness and his Hellenism were thoroughly established (see the selections in Parts VIII and IX). More recent detailed investigations, some of which have been as one-sided as last century's arguments, have eventually reinforced this conclusion. Moreover, the artificiality of the separation and opposition of the two has been glaringly revealed. In this connection the significance of hellenistic Judaism in paving

---

1. Wilhelm Bousset, *Kyrios Christos: A History of Belief in Christ from the Beginnings of Christianity to Irenaeus*, trans. by John E. Steely (Nashville: Abingdon Press, 1970 [German original published in 1913]).

the way for Paul and, even before him, for the earlier hellenistic Christian congregations, has been recognized. The study of Paul within the context of comparative religious phenomena has been fully vindicated, but not at the cost of denying the significance of Paul as a thinker. At the same time, his theology can never again be conceived of in the dogmatic categories of pre-Baur scholarship, nor of the rationalistic, idealist constructions of the Tübingen school itself. His thought was in the context of the community, not individualistic; practical, not speculative; intensely personal and existential, not abstract; and always in the service of his faith and his mission.

FERDINAND CHRISTIAN BAUR

[Hebraists, Hellenists, and Catholics] (1860)†

* * *

It is a proof of the strong faith of the disciples, and of the great confidence they had already gained in the cause of Jesus, that during the period immediately succeeding his death they neither dispersed about the country nor agreed to meet at any more distant spot, but made Jerusalem itself their permanent centre. Here it was that the first Christian church was formed, and the Church of Jerusalem continued to be regarded by all Jewish believers in Jesus as the headquarters of their religion. Recent critical investigations show that the statements given in the Acts of the Apostles afford but a dim and confused picture of this early community of believers, and yield little to the historian in the way of trustworthy or consistent materials. It is not till we come to the appearance of Stephen and the persecution of which he was the occasion (Chap. vi. and vii.) that we stand on firmer historical ground. Here there are two things to be remarked. The charge brought against Stephen, which is strikingly similar to that brought against Jesus at his trial, and cannot in the latter case any more than that of Stephen have been an entirely baseless statement on the part of the false witnesses, shows us the early beginnings of an opposition which could only find its further development in Paulinism. The more spiritual worship of God which Stephen opposed to the externalism of the existing temple worship, could not fail to lead beyond Judaism. The whole appearance of Stephen suggests that the cause he pleaded was one which would justify us in calling him the forerunner of the apostle Paul. It is important, however, to notice, that this opposition to Judaism to which Stephen was the first to draw public attention, seems to have existed in the Church of Jerusalem for some time, and to have divided the church into two different parties. Stephen was a Hellenist, and it cannot be thought accidental that this more liberal tendency appeared in one who was a Hellenist. The fact of which he is an example, that the primitive church at Jerusalem numbered Hellenists among its members, is confirmed by the express statement of the Acts (viii. 4, xi. 19, *sq.*) When the members of the Church fled from the persecution to which Stephen fell a martyr, and were scattered abroad

† From *The Church History of the First Three Centuries*, English translation ed. by Allan Menzies (London: Williams & Norgate, 1878), I, 44–66, 75–77. The translation is from the 3d German ed., 1863, identical with the 2d, 1860. F. C. Baur (1792–1860) was professor of theology at Tübingen and founder of the "Tübingen School," which was long a center of controversy.

throughout the regions of Judea and Samaria, not only did these fugitives carry Christianity to Samaria, to the towns of the sea-coast, and even to Cyprus and Antioch, but at Antioch some of them, men from Cyprus and Cyrene, and of course Hellenists, took the important step in advance of preaching the Gospel to the Gentiles. Antioch thus became the seat of the first church of Gentile Christians, as Jerusalem was the mother church of the Jewish Christians. It is stated in the Acts (viii. 1) that only the apostles stayed in Jerusalem at this persecution; but this is improbable. If we may judge from the occasion out of which it arose, this persecution was not aimed at the Church as a whole, but rather at the Hellenists who sympathised with Stephen in his more liberal views and his consequent hostility to Judaism. Thus the history of Stephen affords clear evidence to show that the Church of Jerusalem had all along consisted of two parties, the Hebraists and the Hellenists, who now effected a complete separation from each other. From this time forth the Church of Jerusalem consisted entirely of Hebraists. The Hellenists, however, were widely diffused even before this time; and though the more liberal tendency only found its first expression in Stephen, yet we cannot be wrong in thinking that it had been at work before, and that it was due to its influence that Hellenism was already giving birth to Gentile Christianity. It was the apostle Paul, however, in whom Gentile Christianity found in the course of these same movements, of which the proto-martyr Stephen is the centre, its true herald, and logical founder and expositor.

The history of the development of Christianity dates of course from the departure of Jesus from the world. But in Paul this history has a new beginning; from this point we are able to trace it not only in its external features, but also in its inner connection.

What the Acts tell us of the conversion of the apostle can only be regarded as the outward reflection of an inner spiritual process. The explanation of this process is to be found in the apostle's own individuality as we have it set before us in his Epistles. * * * It is true that no analysis, either psychological or dialectical, can detect the inner secret of the act in which God revealed his Son in him. Yet it may very justly be asked whether what made the transition possible can have been anything else than the great impressiveness with which the great fact of the death of Jesus came all at once to stand before his soul. From the moment of the revelation in which the Son of God was revealed in him, he lives only in contemplation of the Crucified One: he knows no other, he is crucified with him, his whole system of thought turns on this one fact. The death which was to the Jews a stumbling-block, and to the Greeks foolishness, for him contains and expresses all salvation, and that as no ideal death, but in its most obvious and material aspect as a fact, as the death on the cross from which Christianity itself is named the word, the preaching of the cross. In what other way can he have overcome his hatred and repugnance towards Christianity but by being plunged, almost against his will, in a high-wrought and intense frame of spirit, into contemplation of this death? To the Jewish imagination a crucified Messiah was the most intolerable of ideas. His mind, however, accustomed as it was to deeper thinking, came to see that even what was most repugnant to man's natural feelings might yet prove to be the most profoundly and essentially true, and so the idea ceased to be intolerable. Death, he came to see, can be transfigured into life. A Messiah who has died in the flesh cannot indeed be a *Christos kata sarka* [Christ according to the flesh] in the sense of the Jewish national ideas. Yet all the more surely may he be discerned as one who has died to the flesh and been transfigured to a higher life and stands as a Redeemer high above all the limitations of Judaism. A death which ran so directly counter to all the facts and presuppositions of the Jewish national consciousness, could not be confined in its significance to the Jewish nation, it must have a scope far transcending the particularism of Judaism. There can be no doubt that this was the thought in which the apostle first discerned the truth of Christianity. It was certainly the thought which lay at the root of his view of the person of Christ, and from which the whole dialectical development of Pauline Christianity proceeded. Now the Christian universalism which thus became a certainty to the apostle before any other of the disciples had reached it implied from the first a much deeper breach with Judaism than we might have supposed. This is the only possible explanation of the fact, that from the time of his conversion the apostle Paul went his own independent way, and avoided intentionally and on principle all contact with the older apostles.

* * *

But the apostle takes up an attitude of so great freedom and independence not only towards the older apostles, but towards the person of Jesus himself, that one might be inclined to ask whether a view of his relation to the person of Christ can be the right one which would make the apostle Paul the originator and first exponent of that which constitutes the essence of Christianity as distinguished from Judaism. Is there not too great a distance between the founder of Christianity and one who made his first appearance altogether outside the circle of the first apostles? The difficulty is great if we are to suppose that this apostle derived no assistance from the original apostles, but did of himself what no one had done before,— introduced Christianity to its true destination as a religion for the world, and enunciated, with a full sense of its vast significance, the principle of Christian universalism. Here, however, we shall do well to attend to the two elements which we found in the person of Jesus, and to their relation to each other. First, there was the moral universal in him, the unconfined humanity, the divine exaltation, which gave his person its absolute significance. On the other side there was the cramping and narrowing influence of the Jewish national Messianic idea. The latter was the form which the person of Jesus was obliged to assume if the former element was to have a point of vantage from which to go forth into the stream of history, and to find the way on which it could pass into the general consciousness of mankind. What, then, could be more natural than that one set of his followers should hold to the national side of his appearance, and attach themselves to it so firmly as never to surmount the particularism of Judaism at all, while the other of the two elements, which in the person of Jesus were combined in a simple unity, found in another quarter a much more distinct and energetic expression than the first set of his followers ever could have given it? In this way the natural starting-point of each party is found in the life and work of the founder. The only question comes to be how the apostle Paul appears in his Epistles to be so indifferent to the historical facts of the life of Jesus. He seldom appeals to any traditions on the subject, though his apostolic activity, as well as that of the other apostles, would have been meaningless without them. He bears himself but little like a disciple who has received the doctrines and the principles which he preaches from the Master whose name he bears. But this only shows us how large and how spiritual his conception of Christianity was. The special and particular vanish for him in the contemplation of the whole. Christianity stands before him as a great historical fact which can be understood and grasped only in its unity and its immediateness as a divine revelation. The great facts of the death and resurrection of Jesus make it what it is. Around these facts his whole Christian consciousness revolves; his whole Christian consciousness is transformed into a view of the person of Jesus which stands in need of no history to elucidate it. Why should he go to eye-witnesses and ear-witnesses of Christ's life to ask what he was according to the flesh, when he has seen himself in the spirit? Why should he ask whether what he is teaching agrees with the original teaching of Jesus, and with the discourses and sayings which have been handed down from him, when in the Christ who lives and works in him he hears the voice of the Lord himself? Why should he draw from the past what the Christ who is present in him has made to be the direct utterance of his own consciousness?

⁂ ⁂ ⁂

As the number of converts from heathenism increased, and as the efforts of these who carried the Gospel to the Gentiles diffused it more and more widely throughout the Gentile world, the Christians of Jerusalem became alarmed. They could not look on with indifference, when they saw a Gentile Christian Church arising over-against the Church of Jerusalem in utter disregard of the ordinances and privileges of Judaism, and yet putting forth a claim to equal place and dignity with themselves. Members of the Church of Jerusalem came to Antioch, as the apostle himself tells us (Gal. ii. 1, sq.) He calls them false brethren, intruders, who jealously spied out the liberty that was enjoyed and claimed as a Christian right at Antioch, and made it their aim to bring the Christians there into bondage under the law. The matter appeared so important to the apostle that he felt he must himself go to Jerusalem and have the question discussed on the spot where it had arisen, and where alone it could be decided. The direct practical issue of the question which had been raised was whether or not Gentile Christians required to be circumcised. The apostle therefore took with him not only Barnabas but also Titus, an uncircumcised Gentile Christian, that there might be a case before the Church at Jerusalem, in which the strength of the resistance to the demand that had been made there might be visibly demonstrated. But who were the opponents to whom Paul and Barnabas had to offer so strenuous a resistance? Who else than the elder apostles themselves? We should have a strange conception of the Church at Jerusalem and the position the apostles occupied in it, if we thought that a question of such importance as this could arise in it, and that the apostles took no part in the discussion, the originators of the dispute being merely certain extreme Judaists, with whose assertions and demands the apostles themselves did not agree. Had such been the case, how easy would it have been to arrive at an understanding! This view is clearly contrary, not only to the nature of the case, but to the plain meaning of the apostle's own words. It has often been repeated, but it can never amount to anything more than an unwarrantable claim to set aside the original account, which bears the direct impress of the facts as they occurred, and to set above it a narrative which is inconsistent with it, and is manifestly governed by the writer's desire to give a new version of what had occurred. We need only consider the phrases which Paul selects to describe his opponents, and which are carefully designed to indicate only their own view of the position which they held. He calls them *hoi dokountes* [TNIV: "those esteemed as leaders"], *dokountes einai ti* [TNIV: "those who were held in high esteem"], *hoi dokountes styloi einai* [TNIV: "those esteemed as pillars"], thus showing us that the older apostles themselves were the authorities for the view with which he had to contend. Then we may remember how deliberately and with how full a sense of the independence of his own position he confronted the apostle Peter himself (ii. 7, *sq.*), and lastly, what the result of the whole conference was. The three principal representatives of the Church of Jerusalem did indeed give to Paul and Barnabas the right hand of fellowship, but the agreement which was arrived at consisted simply in recognising that each party had a right to go his own way, separate from, and independent of the other. Thus there were now two Gospels, a Gospel of the circumcision and a Gospel of the uncircumcision, a mission to the Jews and a mission to the Gentiles. The two were to go on side by side, separate and independent, without crossing each other's paths. The only bond to connect the Gentile with the Jewish Christians was to be the care for the support of the poor of the parent Church. So decided an attitude of opposition did the two standpoints now assume: on the one side was the apostle Paul refusing with immovable firmness to be shaken even for a moment in any point which his principles required him to maintain, or to yield any compliance to the proposals addressed to him: on the other side were the older apostles clinging tenaciously to their Judaism.

*   *   *

We have seen that at the very outset of the controversy, as soon as the question of circumcision had arisen, men once and again appeared on the scene who had come from the Church at Jerusalem, and openly sought to bring about a reaction (Gal. ii. 4, 12). We meet with the same phenomenon in the Gentile Christian Churches planted by Paul. Judaists of the same stamp appeared in these churches, and made it their business to bring Pauline Christianity into discredit, and to destroy what the apostle had founded and built up as his own work, without the law and in opposition to the law, in order to rear it up again on the basis of the law. The first actual proof of this systematic opposition to the apostle Paul appears in the Epistle to the Galatians, which was occasioned by that very opposition. * * * The opponents who had taken the field against him in the Churches of Galatia were but a new detachment of the opposition with which he had had to contend before. * * * No other Epistle affords us so deep an insight into the grave significance of the rapidly widening struggle, and into the religious motives which operated on each side. The Judaists maintained it to be the absolute privilege of Judaism that only by the law and circumcision could any man be saved; while the apostle Paul set up the counter-proposition, that whoever was circumcised, Christ would profit him nothing (v. 2). According to the former it is in vain to be a Christian without being a Jew also. According to the latter it is in vain to be a Christian if, as a Christian, one chooses to be a Jew as well. And as it is impossible to be a Jew without accepting circumcision, and with circumcision the obligation to keep the whole law in all its particulars, it is evident at once how the man who takes this road must contradict himself, and be divided in his own mind. But the apostle is not content with exposing this contradiction to the Galatians, and showing them how unjustifiable and irrational the step was which they were about to take. He goes to the root of the matter, and attacks Judaism itself, showing that its being a religion based on law, far from giving it any distinction, reduces it to a subordinate and secondary place in the history of the religious development of mankind. Even within the sphere of Jewish religious history, the law is not the primary and original element. Above it stands the promise given to Abraham, which points forward to a time when the same faith which was counted to Abraham for righteousness will become the blessing of all nations. This promise can only be fulfilled when the law, whose curse passes upon all who do not continue in all things that are written in the law to do them, gives away to faith. By faith, faith that is to say in him who has redeemed us from the curse of the law, we receive that which was the object of the promise made to Abraham, namely, the spirit. * * *

Thus Judaism is nothing more than the religion of the law in contradistinction to Christianity, which is the religion of the spirit. Both its position in the world and its inner constitution declare that the function of Judaism is that of effecting a transition, of filling up an interval. The object it is there to serve is to exercise the stern severity of a watcher set to mark transgressions, and to keep the promise and the fulfilment apart, till the period which God has fixed for this event in the order of the world arrive (the *plerōma tou chronou* [lit., "the fullness of time"], Gal. iv. 4), and the promise reach its fulfilment. * * * Not only does he repudiate, as utterly unjustifiable, the demand which they had made with regard to circumcision, he denies that the law possessed that absolute right which the Jew ascribed to it. He places Judaism and Christianity together under the light of a great religio-historical contemplation, and of a view of the course of the world before the universal idea of which the particularism of Judaism must disappear. The demand of circumcision which was made upon the Gentile Christians amounted to a claim that, in submitting to that rite, they should acknowledge the absolute superiority which the Jewish nation as God's chosen people possessed over all the other nations of the world. This claim the apostle's wide and comprehensive view of history sufficiently disposed of. The cardinal point of his dialectical polemic, however, is to be found in the passage where he draws the conclusion from the previous discussion regarding the law and the promise, that all who are baptized into Christ enter at once, in that very act, into a new community, in which all the causes of division between man and man, which are to be found in the outward circumstances of life, are at once removed, so that there is no difference any longer between the Jew and the Greek, between circumcision and uncircumcision, but all may regard themselves as children of Abraham. All are one in Christ, in the same faith which manifests itself by love.

* * * Whatever may have been the result of Paul's Epistle to the Galatians, and of his controversy with his opponents in the Galatian Churches,

the dispute did not end there. Not long after that Epistle was written, we meet with opponents of the apostle in a different quarter of his sphere of labour, whose attacks upon him seem to be dictated by the same motives, and to be carried on in the same spirit. There can be no doubt that the Epistle to the Galatians was written in the earlier period of the apostle's residence at Ephesus, which is to be placed in the years 54–57. The composition of our first Epistle to the *Corinthians* belongs to the latter part of his residence there. It was occasioned by news from Corinth which showed him that he had to expect a renewal of his Galatian experiences in the Corinthian Church. Judaizing teachers had made their way into this Church also, and had unsettled the faith of the apostle's converts in his Gospel. Several divisions and parties had arisen; but the main controversy about which they were ranged originated in a party which bore the name of Peter, although there can be no doubt that Peter never was at Corinth at all, and set itself in opposition to those members of the Corinthian Church who remained faithful to the principles of Pauline Christianity. The party-interests which now came to operate in various ways on the Corinthian Church arose undoubtedly out of the same great controversy which forms the subject of the Epistle to the Galatians. It is very remarkable, however, that in the two Corinthian Epistles the subjects of the law and of circumcision, which formerly occupied the forefront of the battle, have completely disappeared. A very personal question has now come to the front, a question which could not fail to be raised sooner or later, namely, the apostolic authority of Paul. What authority could he claim?

* * *

If he appealed to the inner certainty which he possessed regarding his vocation by Christ, and to his apostolic consciousness, they, on the other hand, stood on the historical ground of their actual connection with Christ. Thus principle stood opposed to principle; and only the future development of Christianity could decide which of the two principles would acquire the predominance over the other. In the meantime, the attacks made upon the person of the apostle, and on his apostolic authority, form a new and a noteworthy epoch in the controversy in which Judaism and Paulinism had now come to be engaged. The deep earnestness which the apostle throws into his contendings with these opponents is enough to show the importance they had in his eyes. We should have a very mistaken notion of them did we hold their movement to have been a mere isolated phenomenon, the undirected and arbitrary action of certain individuals who were stirred up by merely fortuitous and personal motives to create disturbance and throw obstacles in the apostle's way in his own sphere of labour. Everything combines to show that they had a great party behind them, and knew themselves to have a right to appear as the agents and emissaries of that party. Not only was the name of the apostle Peter the standard under which their efforts were carried on,—a name which showed what spirit they were of, and made their cause appear to be the common cause of all Jewish Christians. We learn from the apostle himself (2 Cor. iii. 1) that they had brought letters of recommendation with them, which left no doubt as to the party they belonged to. From whom could such letters of recommendation proceed but from men who had such a position in the mother Church, that they could count on their authority being recognised in foreign Churches too? These letters prove to us how party spirit was growing, how the two parties were being ranged in a position of antagonism to each other, how efforts were being made by each party to counteract the other locally. They also represent to us, in a new and striking way, the radical difference between the two principles which are here contending with each other. They exhibited to the Corinthians the contrast between the two conflicting principles of authority. The authority of the one party, having been outwardly communicated, was capable of being delegated by such credentials. Against this outward authority the apostle had nothing to affirm when it came to the point but his own independent self-consciousness. This is his position in the passage where he speaks of these letters of commendation of his opponents (2 Cor. iii. 1–18).

In dealing with his opponents at Corinth, he takes up, as he did in the Epistle to the Galatians, the standpoint of the higher religio-historical contemplation. Judaism and Christianity are related to each other as the old and the new *diathēkē* [covenant]; the old one is antiquated and extinct, but the new one is bright and luminous. In this distinction between the two dispensations, and in the spirit as the principle of the Christian consciousness, is to be found the justification of his apostolic authority. The character of Judaism is that of a religion of concealment and restraint, the religious consciousness which belongs to it is narrow and finite, but Christianity is the opposite of this; in it the religious consciousness has opened up to perfect clearness and self-certainty, and does not need to rely on any material aids. And this is the principle of his apostolic authority too. With those who refuse to recognise him as an apostle he can use no other argument than that their religious consciousness is imperfect, that they are at a standpoint at which the veil, the symbol of Mosaism, still lies upon their Jewish consciousness, and does not allow them to perceive the fact that the end of the old religion is now come. The principle of Paulinism could not be expressed more simply and accurately than is done by the apostle in this same passage, when he sums up his argument against the old covenant and those who had gained the Christian consciousness, and yet remained standing under it, in the words (2 Cor. iii. 17): The Lord is the spirit: and the spirit is liberty. That is to say, the principle and essence of Paulinism is the emancipation of the consciousness from every authority that is external or exercised through human means, the removal of all confining barriers, the elevation of the spirit to a standpoint where everything lies revealed and open in luminous clearness to its eye, the independence and immediateness of the self-consciousness.

Thus the apostle meets the opponents of his doctrine and of his apostolic authority by demonstrating the imperfection, the narrowness, the finiteness of the religion of the Law. But to get rid altogether of that particularism which was so closely interwoven with Judaism, that national pride which led the Jew to think that because he was a Jew he was better and more highly privileged than all other men, it was necessary to attack it more directly, to lay the axe more sharply to its root. This could not be done without a profounder and more searching appeal to the moral consciousness than could be made by a discussion which after all belonged to the sphere of abstract and theoretical contemplation. It is in the Epistle to the Romans that we see the apostle proceed to this, the third and most important stage of the long and hard struggle which his principle had to support as it forced its way through all the forms of opposition it encountered. Regarded from this point of view, the Epistle to the Romans appeared in the light not merely of a compendium of Pauline dogmatics, but as a historical source of the first importance.

*   *   *

It is not necessary to enter in detail into the circumstances under which the apostle met his well-known fate at Jerusalem. There is one question, however, which possesses special interest, namely, who were the authors of those tumults in which the Roman military authorities had to interfere in order to rescue the apostle from the rage of his opponents? Were these tumults caused by Jews, or by Jewish Christians? They were zealots for the law, men who saw in the apostle a transgressor of the law, an apostate, a declared enemy of the national religion. But not only the Jews were zealots of this description, the Jewish Christians also shared this spirit, and carried it even further than the Jews. In their case the mission to the Gentiles had raised the question of the law into a matter of the keenest party interest. And accordingly we can discern, even in the narrative of the Acts, in which the true state of the case is as far as possible concealed, that the Jewish Christians were by no means so unconcerned in the outbreaks of hatred to which the apostle fell a victim, as is generally supposed. Protected by his Roman citizenship the apostle was removed to Rome, after two years' imprisonment at Caesarea. According to the Acts his imprisonment at Rome lasted for a further period of two years: but we are not told when or how it terminated. Even assuming the genuineness of the Epistles which profess to have been written by the apostle during his captivity at Rome, we have no certain or noteworthy information about this period. The most remarkable fact is that the termination of these two years coincides with the date of the great Neronian conflagration, and the persecution of the Christians to which it led. Nothing can be more probable, than that the apostle did not survive this fatal period.

Up to the time when the apostle disappears from the scene of the history, we have before us nothing but differences and oppositions, between which no certain way of compromise or reconciliation yet appears. It was upon that side, from which the great division had proceeded, which broke in upon the common religious consciousness, which Jews and Jewish Christians had hitherto enjoyed together, that a certain need was first felt for approximation and reconciliation between the two parties. But the advance did not meet with such a response as might have been expected from the other party. There were as yet only Jewish Christians and Gentile Christians, with divergent tendencies and interests. There was no ecclesiastical association to combine the two. Nor has history been able as yet to point to any considerable cause which can be said to have effected the filling up of the great gulf which since the events at Antioch had continued to exist between Peter and Paul, the heads of the two parties. All we can say is, that there must have been reconciling elements in the Church of Rome. This was the case before, and the influence which Paul had over this Church, both by his Epistle and by his personal residence there afterwards, must have strengthened this tendency. And how could the martyrdom with which the great apostle of the Gentiles certainly in one way or another finished his work in that city, fail to leave behind it a healing influence for the future of the Church? A legend of much significance, which however arose at a much later time, connects the brotherly unity of the two apostles with this death. This is accordingly a fixed point in the history of the further development of these relations. But the interval which elapsed between the death of the apostle Paul and that point contains many movements in many different directions, and the development of the history will conduct us to that goal by a longer road than might have been supposed.

* * *

FRIEDRICH NIETZSCHE

[The First Christian] (1880)†

The whole world still believes in the literary career of the "Holy Ghost," or is still influenced by the effects of this belief: when we look into our Bibles we do so for the purpose of "edifying ourselves," to find a few words of comfort for our misery, be it great or small—in short, we read ourselves into it and out of it. But who—apart from a few learned men—know that it likewise records the history of one of the most ambitious and importunate souls that ever existed, of a mind full of superstition and cunning: the history of the Apostle Paul? Nevertheless, without this singular history, without the tribulations and passions of such a mind, and of such a soul, there would have been no Christian kingdom; we should scarcely have even heard of a little Jewish sect, the founder of which died on the Cross. It is true that, if this history had been understood in time, if we had read, *really read*, the writings of St. Paul, not as the revelations of the "Holy Ghost," but with honest and independent minds, oblivious of all our personal troubles—there were no such readers for fifteen centuries—it would have been all up with Christianity long ago: so searchingly do these writings of the Jewish Pascal lay bare the origins of Christianity, just as the French Pascal let us see its destiny and how it will ultimately perish. That the ship of Christianity threw overboard no inconsiderable part of its Jewish ballast, that it was able to sail into the waters of the heathen and actually did do so: this is due to the history of one single man, this apostle who was so greatly troubled in mind and so worthy of pity, but who was also very disagreeable to himself and to others.

This man suffered from a fixed idea, or rather a fixed question, an ever-present and ever-burning question: what was the *meaning* of the Jewish Law? and, more especially, *the fulfilment of this Law?* In his youth he had done his best to satisfy it, thirsting as he did for that highest distinction which the Jew could imagine—this people, which raised the imagination of moral loftiness to a greater elevation than any other people, and which

---

† From *The Dawn of Day,* Aphorism 68, tr. by J. M. Kennedy in *The Complete Works of Friedrich Nietzsche,* ed. Oscar Levy (New York: Macmillan, 1909–14, and reprinted), IX, 66–71. Nietzsche (1844–1900), the son of a German pastor, taught classics in Basel until forced by health problems to retire in 1879. His most provocative works were published after that, though he suffered increasing isolation and, after 1889, irreversible mental disorder.

alone succeeded in uniting the conception of a holy God with the idea of sin considered as an offence against this holiness. St. Paul became at once the fanatic defender and guard-of-honour of this God and His Law. Ceaselessly battling against and lying in wait for all transgressors of this Law and those who presumed to doubt it, he was pitiless and cruel towards all evildoers, whom he would fain have punished in the most rigorous fashion possible.

Now, however, he was aware in his own person of the fact that such a man as himself—violent, sensual, melancholy, and malicious in his hatred—*could* not fulfil the Law; and furthermore, what seemed strangest of all to him, he saw that his boundless craving for power was continually provoked to break it, and that he could not help yielding to this impulse. Was it really "the flesh" which made him a trespasser time and again? Was it not rather, as it afterwards occurred to him, the Law itself, which continually showed itself to be impossible to fulfil, and seduced men into transgression with an irresistible charm? But at that time he had not thought of this means of escape. As he suggests here and there, he had many things on his conscience—hatred, murder, sorcery, idolatry, debauchery, drunkenness, and orgiastic revelry,—and to however great an extent he tried to soothe his conscience, and, even more, his desire for power, by the extreme fanaticism of his worship for and defence of the Law, there were times when the thought struck him: "It is all in vain! The anguish of the unfulfilled Law cannot be overcome." Luther must have experienced similar feelings, when, in his cloister, he endeavoured to become the ideal man of his imagination; and, as Luther one day began to hate the ecclesiastical ideal, and the Pope, and the saints, and the whole clergy, with a hatred which was all the more deadly as he could not avow it even to himself, an analogous feeling took possession of St. Paul. The Law was the Cross on which he felt himself crucified. How he hated it! What a grudge he owed it! How he began to look round on all sides to find a means for its total annihilation, that he might no longer be obliged to fulfil it himself! And at last a liberating thought, together with a vision—which was only to be expected in the case of an epileptic like himself—flashed into his mind: to him, the stern upholder of the Law—who, in his innermost heart, was tired to death of it—there appeared on the lonely path that Christ, with the divine effulgence on His countenance, and Paul heard the words: "Why persecutest thou Me?"

What actually took place, then, was this: his mind was suddenly enlightened, and he said to himself: "It is unreasonable to persecute this Jesus Christ! Here is my means of escape, here is my complete vengeance, here and nowhere else have I the destroyer of the Law in my hands!" The sufferer from anguished pride felt himself restored to health all at once, his moral despair disappeared in the air; for morality itself was blown away, annihilated—that is to say, *fulfilled*, there on the Cross! Up to that time that ignominious death had seemed to him to be the principal argument against the "Messiahship" proclaimed by the followers of the new doctrine: but what if it were necessary for doing away with the Law? The enormous consequences of this thought, of this solution of the enigma, danced before his eyes, and he at once became the happiest of men. The destiny of the Jews, yea, of all mankind, seemed to him to be intertwined with this instantaneous flash of enlightenment: he held the thought of thoughts, the key of keys, the light of lights; history would henceforth revolve round him! For from that time forward he would be the apostle of the *annihilation of the Law!* To be dead to sin—that meant to be dead to the Law also; to be in the flesh—that meant to be under the Law! To be one with Christ— that meant to have become, like Him, the destroyer of the Law; to be dead with Him—that meant likewise to be dead to the Law. Even if it were still possible to sin, it would not at any rate be possible to sin against the Law: "I am above the Law," thinks Paul; adding, "If I were now to acknowledge the Law again and to submit to it, I should make Christ an accomplice in the sin"; for the Law was there for the purpose of producing sin and setting it in the foreground, as an emetic produces sickness. God could not have decided upon the death of Christ had it been possible to fulfill the Law without it; henceforth, not only are all sins expiated, but sin itself is abolished; henceforth the Law is dead; henceforth "the flesh" in which it dwelt is dead—or at all events dying, gradually wasting away. To live for a short time longer amid this decay!—this is the Christian's fate, until the time when, having become one with Christ, he arises with Him, sharing with Christ the divine glory, and becoming, like Christ, a "Son of God." Then Paul's exaltation was at its height, and with it the importunity of his soul— the thought of union with Christ made him lose all shame, all submission, all constraint, and his ungovernable ambition was shown to be revelling in the expectation of divine glories.

Such was the first Christian, the inventor of Christianity! before him there were only a few Jewish sectaries.

FRIEDRICH NIETZSCHE

[The Jewish Dysangelist] (1888)†

*   *   *

—I will retrace my steps, and will tell you the *genuine* history of Christianity.—The very word "Christianity" is a misunderstanding,—truth to tell, there never was more than one Christian, and he *died* on the Cross. The "gospel" *died* on the Cross. That which thenceforward was called "gospel" was the reverse of that "gospel" that Christ had lived: it was "evil tidings," a *dysangel.* It is false to the point of nonsense to see in "faith," in the faith in salvation through Christ, the distinguishing trait of the Christian: the only thing that is Christian is the Christian mode of existence, a life such as he led who died on the Cross. . . . To this day a life of this kind is still possible; for certain men, it is even necessary: genuine, primitive Christianity will be possible in all ages. . . . *Not* a faith, but a course of action, above all a course of inaction, non-interference, and a different life. . . . States of consciousness, any sort of faith, a holding of certain things for true, as every psychologist knows, are indeed of absolutely no consequence, and are only of fifth-rate importance compared with the value of the instincts: more exactly, the whole concept of intellectual causality is

† From *The Antichrist, An Attempted Criticism of Christianity,* §§39–43, tr. by Anthony M. Ludovici in *The Complete Works of Friedrich Nietzsche,* ed. Oscar Levy (New York: Macmillan, 1909–14 and reprinted), XVI, 178–87.

false. To reduce the fact of being a Christian, or of Christianity, to a holding of something for true, to a mere phenomenon of consciousness, is
tantamount to denying Christianity. *In fact there have never been any
Christians.* The "Christian," he who for two thousand years has been called
a Christian, is merely a psychological misunderstanding of self. Looked at
more closely, there ruled in him, *notwithstanding* all his faith, only
instincts—and *what instincts!*—"Faith" in all ages, as for instance in the
case of Luther, has always been merely a cloak, a pretext, a *screen*, behind
which the instincts played their game,—a prudent form of *blindness* in
regard to the dominion of *certain* instincts. . . . "Faith" I have already char-
acterised as a piece of really Christian cleverness; for people have always
spoken of "faith" and acted according to their instincts. . . . In the Christian's world of ideas there is nothing which even touches reality; but I have
already recognised in the instinctive hatred of reality the actual motive
force, the only driving power at the root of Christianity. What follows
therefrom? That here, even *in psychologicis*, error is fundamental,—that is
to say capable of determining the spirit of things,—that is to say, *substance*.
Take one idea away from the whole, and put one realistic fact in its stead,—
and the whole of Christianity tumbles into nonentity!—Surveyed from
above, this strangest of all facts,—a religion not only dependent upon
error, but inventive and showing signs of genius only in those errors which
are dangerous and which poison life and the human heart—remains a
spectacle for gods, for those gods who are at the same time philosophers
and whom I met for instance in those celebrated dialogues on the island
of Naxos. At the moment when they get rid of their *loathing* (—*and we do
as well!*), they will be thankful for the spectacle the Christians have offered:
the wretched little planet called Earth perhaps deserves on account of this
curious case alone, a divine glance, and divine interest. . . . Let us not
therefore underestimate the Christians: the Christian, false *to the point of
innocence in falsity*, is far above the apes,—in regard to the Christians a
certain well-known theory of Descent becomes a mere good-natured
compliment.

40

—The fate of the gospel was decided at the moment of the death,—it
hung on the "cross." . . . It was only death, this unexpected and ignominious death; it was only the cross which as a rule was reserved simply for
the *canaille*,—only this appalling paradox which confronted the disciples
with the actual riddle: *Who was that? what was that?*—The state produced
by the excited and profoundly wounded feelings of these men, the suspicion that such a death might imply the *refutation* of their cause, and the
terrible note of interrogation: "why precisely thus?" will be understood only
too well. In this case everything *must* be necessary, everything must have
meaning, a reason, the highest reason. The love of a disciple admits of no
such thing as accident. Only then did the chasm yawn: "who has killed
him?" "who was his natural enemy?"—this question rent the firmament
like a flash of lightning. Reply: *dominant* Judaism, its ruling class. Thenceforward the disciple felt himself in revolt *against* established order; he
understood Jesus, after the fact, as one in *revolt against established order*.
Heretofore this warlike, this nay-saying and nay-doing feature in Christ

had been lacking; nay more, he was its contradiction. The small primitive community had obviously understood *nothing* of the principal factor of all, which was the example of freedom and of superiority to every form of *resentment* which lay in this way of dying. And this shows how little they understood him altogether! At bottom Jesus could not have desired anything else by his death than to give the strongest public *example* and *proof* of his doctrine. . . . But his disciples were very far from *forgiving* this death—though if they had done so it would have been in the highest sense evangelical on their part,—neither were they prepared, with a gentle and serene calmness of heart, to *offer* themselves for a similar death. . . . Precisely the most unevangelical feeling, *revenge*, became once more ascendant. It was impossible for the cause to end with this death: "compensation" and "judgment" were required (—and forsooth, what could be more unevangelical than "compensation," "punishment," "judgment"!) The popular expectation of a Messiah once more became prominent; attention was fixed upon one historical moment: the "Kingdom of God" descends to sit in judgment upon his enemies. But this proves that everything was misunderstood: the "Kingdom of God" regarded as the last scene of the last act, as a promise! But the Gospel had clearly been the living, the fulfillment, the *reality* of this "Kingdom of God." It was precisely a death such as Christ's that was this "Kingdom of God." It was only now that all the contempt for the Pharisees and the theologians, and all bitter feelings towards them, were introduced into the character of the Master,—and by this means he himself was converted into a Pharisee and a theologian! On the other hand, the savage veneration of these completely unhinged souls could no longer endure that evangelical right of every man to be the child of God, which Jesus had taught: their revenge consisted in *elevating* Jesus in a manner devoid of all reason, and in separating him from themselves: just as, formerly, the Jews, with the view of revenging themselves on their enemies, separated themselves from their God, and placed him high above them. The Only God, and the Only Son of God:—both were products of resentment.

41

—And from this time forward an absurd problem rose into prominence: "how *could* God allow it to happen?" To this question the disordered minds of the small community found a reply which in its absurdity was literally terrifying: God gave his Son as a *sacrifice* for the forgiveness of sins. Alas! how prompt and sudden was the end of the gospel! Expiatory sacrifice for guilt, and indeed in its most repulsive and barbaric form,—the sacrifice of the *innocent* for the sins of the guilty! What appalling Paganism!—For Jesus himself had done away with the concept "guilt,"—he denied any gulf between God and man, he *lived* this unity between God and man, it was this that constituted *his* "glad tidings." . . . And he did not teach it as a privilege!—Thenceforward there was gradually imported into the type of the Saviour the doctrine of the Last Judgment, and of the "second coming," the doctrine of sacrificial death, and the doctrine of *Resurrection*, by means of which the whole concept "blessedness," the entire and only reality of the gospel, is conjured away—in favour of a state *after* death! . . . St Paul, with that rabbinic impudence which characterises all his doings, rationalised this conception, this prostitution of a conception, as follows: "if Christ did not rise from the dead, our faith is vain."—And, in a trice, the most contemptible of all unrealisable promises, the *impudent* doctrine of personal immortality, was woven out of the gospel. . . . St Paul even preached this immortality as a reward.

42

You now realise what it was that came to an end with the death on the cross: a new and thoroughly original effort towards a Buddhistic movement of peace, towards real and *not* merely promised *happiness on earth*. For, as I have already pointed out, this remains the fundamental difference between the two religions of *decadence*: Buddhism promises little but fulfils more, Christianity promises everything but fulfils nothing.—The "glad tidings" were followed closely by the absolutely *worst* tidings—those of St Paul. Paul is the incarnation of a type which is the reverse of that of the Saviour; he is the genius in hatred, in the standpoint of hatred, and in the relentless logic of hatred. And alas what did this dysangelist not sacrifice to his hatred! Above all the Saviour himself: he nailed him to *his cross*. Christ's life, his example, his doctrine and death, the sense and the right of the gospel—not a vestige of all this was left, once this forger, prompted by his hatred, had understood in it only that which could serve his purpose. *Not* reality: *not* historical truth! . . . And once more, the sacerdotal instinct of the Jew perpetrated the same great crime against history,—he simply cancelled the yesterday, and the day before that, out of Christianity; he *contrived of his own accord a history of the birth of Christianity*. He did more: he once more falsified the history of Israel, so as to make it appear as a prologue to *his* mission: all the prophets had referred to *his* "Saviour." . . . Later on the Church even distorted the history of mankind so as to convert it into a prelude to Christianity. . . . The type of the Saviour, his teaching, his life, his death, even the sequel to his death—nothing remained untouched, nothing was left which even remotely resembled reality. St Paul simply transferred the centre of gravity of the whole of that great life, to a place *behind* this life,—in the *lie* of the "resuscitated" Christ. At bottom, he had no possible use for the life of the Saviour,—he needed the death on the cross, *and* something more. To regard as honest a man like St Paul (a man whose home was the very headquarters of Stoical enlightenment) when he devises a proof of the continued existence of the Saviour out of a hallucination; or even to believe him when he declares that he had this hallucination, would amount to foolishness on the part of a psychologist: St Paul desired the end, consequently he also desired the means. . . . Even what he himself did not believe, was believed in by the idiots among whom he spread *his* doctrine.—What he wanted was power; with St Paul the priest again aspired to power,—he could make use only of concepts, doctrines, symbols with which masses may be tyrannised over, and with which herds are formed. What was the only part of Christianity which was subsequently borrowed by Muhamed? St Paul's invention, his expedient for priestly tyranny and to the formation of herds: the belief in immortality—*that is to say, the doctrine of the "Last Judgment."* . . .

43

When the centre of gravity of life is laid, *not* in life, but in a beyond—
in nonentity,—life is utterly robbed of its balance. The great lie of personal
immortality destroys all reason, all nature in the instincts,—everything in
the instincts that is beneficent, that promotes life and that is a guarantee
of the future, henceforward aroused suspicion. The very meaning of life is
now construed as the effort to live in such a way that life no longer has
any point. . . . Why show any public spirit? Why be grateful for one's origin
and one's forebears? Why collaborate with one's fellows, and be confident?
Why be concerned about the general weal or strive after it? . . . All these
things are merely so many "temptations," so many deviations from the
"straight path." "One thing only is necessary." . . . That everybody, as an
"immortal soul," should have equal rank, that in the totality of beings, the
"salvation" of each individual may lay claim to eternal importance, that
insignificant bigots and three-quarter-lunatics may have the right to suppose that the laws of nature may be persistently *broken* on their account,—
any such magnification of every kind of selfishness to infinity, to *insolence*,
cannot be branded with sufficient contempt. And yet it is to this miserable
flattery of personal vanity that Christianity owes its *triumph*,—by this
means it lured all the bungled and the botched, all revolting and revolted
people, all abortions, the whole of the refuse and offal of humanity, over
to its side. The "salvation of the soul"—in plain English: "the world revolves
around me." . . . The poison of the doctrine *"equal* rights for all"—has been
dispensed with the greatest thoroughness by Christianity: Christianity,
prompted by the most secret recesses of bad instincts, has waged a deadly
war upon all feeling of reverence and distance between man and man—
that is to say, the *prerequisite* of all elevation, of every growth in culture;
out of the resentment of the masses it wrought its *principal weapons*
against us, against everything noble, joyful, exalted on earth, against our
happiness on earth. . . . To grant "immortality" to every St Peter and St
Paul, was the greatest, the most vicious outrage upon *noble* humanity that
has ever been perpetrated.—And do not let us underestimate the fatal
influence which, springing from Christianity, has insinuated itself even
into politics! Nowadays no one has the courage of special rights, of rights
of dominion, of a feeling of self-respect and of respect for his equals,—of
pathos of distance. Our politics are diseased with this lack of courage!—
The aristocratic attitude of mind has been most thoroughly undermined
by the lie of the equality of souls; and if the belief in the "privilege of the
greatest number" creates and will continue *to create revolutions*,—it is
Christianity, let there be no doubt about it, and Christian values, which
convert every revolution into blood and crime! Christianity is the revolt of
all things that crawl on their bellies against everything that is lofty: the
gospel of the "lowly" *lowers*. . . .

GEORGE BERNARD SHAW

[The Monstrous Imposition upon Jesus] (1913)†

* * *

Paul

Suddenly a man of genius, Paul, violently anti-Christian, enters on the scene, holding the clothes of the men who are stoning Stephen. He persecutes the Christians with great vigor, a sport which he combines with the business of a tentmaker. This temperamental hatred of Jesus, whom he has never seen, is a pathological symptom of that particular sort of conscience and nervous constitution which brings its victims under the tyranny of two delirious terrors: the terror of sin and the terror of death, which may be called also the terror of sex and the terror of life. Now Jesus, with his healthy conscience on his higher plane, was free from these terrors. He consorted freely with sinners, and was never concerned for a moment, as far as we know, about whether his conduct was sinful or not; so that he has forced us to accept him as the man without sin. Even if we reckon his last days as the days of his delusion, he none the less gave a fairly convincing exhibition of superiority to the fear of death. This must have both fascinated and horrified Paul, or Saul, as he was first called. The horror accounts for his fierce persecution of the Christians. The fascination accounts for the strangest of his fancies: the fancy for attaching the name of Jesus Christ to the great idea which flashed upon him on the road to Damascus, the idea that he could not only make a religion of his two terrors, but that the movement started by Jesus offered him the nucleus for his new Church. It was a monstrous idea; and the shock of it, as he afterwards declared, struck him blind for days. He heard Jesus calling to him from the clouds, "Why persecute me?" His natural hatred of the teacher for whom Sin and Death had no terrors turned into a wild personal worship of him which has the ghastliness of a beautiful thing seen in a false light.

The chronicler of the Acts of the Apostles sees nothing of the significance of this. The great danger of conversion in all ages has been that when the religion of the high mind is offered to the lower mind, the lower mind, feeling its fascination without understanding it, and being incapable of rising to it, drags it down to its level by degrading it. Years ago I said that the conversion of a savage to Christianity is the conversion of Christianity to savagery. The conversion of Paul was no conversion at all: it was Paul who converted the religion that has raised one man above sin and death into a religion that delivered millions of men so completely into their dominion that their own common nature became a horror to them, and the religious life became a denial of life. Paul had no intention of surrendering either his Judaism or his Roman citizenship to the new moral world (as Robert Owen called it) of Communism and Jesuism. Just as in our own

† From "Preface on the Prospects of Christianity" to *Androcles and the Lion* (copyright 1913, 1941 by George Bernard Shaw). Shaw's prefaces are almost as famous as his plays themselves. Born in Dubin in 1856, he died in 1950.

time Karl Marx, not content to take political economy as he found it, insisted on rebuilding it from the bottom upwards in his own way, and thereby gave a new lease of life to the errors it was just outgrowing, so Paul reconstructed the old Salvationism from which Jesus had vainly tried to redeem him, and produced a fantastic theology which is still the most amazing thing of the kind known to us. Being intellectually an inveterate Roman Rationalist, always discarding the irrational real thing for the unreal but ratiocinable postulate, he began by discarding Man as he is, and substituted a postulate which he called Adam. And when he was asked, as he surely must have been in a world not wholly mad, what had become of the natural man, he replied "Adam *is* the natural man." This was confusing to simpletons, because according to tradition Adam was certainly the name of the natural man as created in the garden of Eden. It was as if a preacher of our own time had described as typically British Frankenstein's monster, and called him Smith, and somebody, on demanding what about the man in the street, had been told "Smith *is* the man in the street." The thing happens often enough; for indeed the world is full of these Adams and Smiths and men in the street and average sensual men and economic men and womanly women and what not, all of them imaginary Atlases carrying imaginary worlds on their unsubstantial shoulders.

The Eden story provided Adam with a sin: the "original sin" for which we are all damned. Baldly stated, this seems ridiculous; nevertheless it corresponds to something actually existent not only in Paul's consciousness but in our own. The original sin was not the eating of the forbidden fruit, but the consciousness of sin which the fruit produced. The moment Adam and Eve tasted the apple they found themselves ashamed of their sexual relation, which until then had seemed quite innocent to them; and there is no getting over the hard fact that this shame, or state of sin, has persisted to this day, and is one of the strongest of our instincts. Thus Paul's postulate of Adam as the natural man was pragmatically true: it worked. But the weakness of Pragmatism is that most theories will work if you put your back into making them work, provided they have some point of contact with human nature. Hedonism will pass the pragmatic test as well as Stoicism. Up to a certain point every social principle that is not absolutely idiotic works: Autocracy works in Russia and Democracy in America; Atheism works in France, Polytheism in India, Monotheism throughout Islam, and Pragmatism, or No-ism, in England. Paul's fantastic conception of the damned Adam, represented by Bunyan as a pilgrim with a great burden of sins on his back, corresponded to the fundamental condition of evolution, which is, that life, including human life, is continually evolving, and must therefore be continually ashamed of itself and its present and past. Bunyan's pilgrim wants to get rid of his bundle of sins, but he also wants to reach "yonder shining light"; and when at last his bundle falls off him into the sepulchre of Christ, his pilgrimage is still unfinished and his hardest trials still ahead of him. His conscience remains uneasy; "original sin" still torments him; and his adventure with Giant Despair, who throws him into the dungeon of Doubting Castle, from which he escapes by the use of a skeleton key, is more terrible than any he met whilst the bundle was still on his back. Thus Bunyan's allegory of human nature breaks through the Pauline theology at a hundred points. His theological allegory, The Holy War, with its troops of Election Doubters, and its cavalry of "those that rode Reformadoes," is, as a whole, absurd, impossible, and, except in passages where the artistic old Adam momentarily got the better of the Salvationist theologian, hardly readable.

Paul's theory of original sin was to some extent idiosyncratic. He tells us definitely that he finds himself quite well able to avoid the sinfulness of sex by practising celibacy; but he recognizes, rather contemptuously, that in this respect he is not as other men are, and says that they had better marry than burn, thus admitting that though marriage may lead to placing the desire to please wife or husband before the desire to please God, yet preoccupation with unsatisfied desire may be even more ungodly than preoccupation with domestic affection. This view of the case inevitably led him to insist that a wife should be rather a slave than a partner, her real function being, not to engage a man's love and loyalty, but on the contrary to release them for God by relieving the man of all preoccupation with sex just as in her capacity of housekeeper and cook she relieves his preoccupation with hunger by the simple expedient of satisfying his appetite. This slavery also justifies itself pragmatically by working effectively; but it has made Paul the eternal enemy of Woman. Incidentally it has led to many foolish surmises about Paul's personal character and circumstances, by people so enslaved by sex that a celibate appears to them a sort of monster. They forget that not only whole priesthoods, official and unofficial, from Paul to Carlyle and Ruskin, have defied the tyranny of sex, but immense numbers of ordinary citizens of both sexes have, either voluntarily or under pressure of circumstances easily surmountable, saved their energies for less primitive activities.

Howbeit, Paul succeeded in stealing the image of Christ crucified for the figure-head of his Salvationist vessel, with its Adam posing as the natural man, its doctrine of original sin, and its damnation avoidable only by faith in the sacrifice of the cross. In fact, no sooner had Jesus knocked over the dragon of superstition than Paul boldly set it on its legs again in the name of Jesus.

The Confusion of Christendom

Now it is evident that two religions having such contrary effects on mankind should not be confused as they are under a common name. There is not one word of Pauline Christianity in the characteristic utterances of Jesus. When Saul watched the clothes of the men who stoned Stephen, he was not acting upon beliefs which Paul renounced. There is no record of Christ's having ever said to any man: "Go and sin as much as you like: you can put it all on me." He said "Sin no more," and insisted that he was putting up the standard of conduct, not debasing it, and that the righteousness of the Christian must exceed that of the Scribe and Pharisee. The notion that he was shedding his blood in order that every petty cheat and adulterator and libertine might wallow in it and come out whiter than snow, cannot be imputed to him on his own authority. "I come as an infallible patent medicine for bad consciences" is not one of the sayings in the gospels. If Jesus could have been consulted on Bunyan's allegory as to that business of the burden of sin dropping from the pilgrim's back when he caught sight of the cross, we must infer from his teaching that he would have told Bunyan in forcible terms that he had never made a greater mistake in his life, and that the business of a Christ was to make self-satisfied sinners feel the burden of their sins and stop committing them instead of assuring them that they could not help it, as it was all Adam's fault, but that it did not matter as long as they were credulous and friendly about himself. Even when he believed himself to be a god, he did not regard himself as a scapegoat. He was to take away the sins of the world by good government, by justice and mercy, by setting the welfare of little children above the pride of princes, by casting all the quackeries and idolatries which now usurp and malversate the power of God into what our local authorities quaintly call the dust destructor, and by riding on the clouds of heaven in glory instead of in a thousand-guinea motor car. That was delirious, if you like; but it was the delirium of a free soul, not of a shame-bound one like Paul's. There has really never been a more monstrous imposition perpetrated than the imposition of the limitations of Paul's soul upon the soul of Jesus.

The Secret of Paul's Success

Paul must soon have found that his followers had gained peace of mind and victory over death and sin at the cost of all moral responsibility; for he did his best to reintroduce it by making good conduct the test of sincere belief, and insisting that sincere belief was necessary to salvation. But as his system was rooted in the plain fact that as what he called sin includes sex and is therefore an ineradicable part of human nature (why else should Christ have had to atone for the sin of all future generations?) it was impossible for him to declare that sin, even in its wickedest extremity, could forfeit the sinner's salvation if he repented and believed. And to this day Pauline Christianity is, and owes its enormous vogue to being, a premium on sin. Its consequences have had to be held in check by the worldly-wise majority through a violently anti-Christian system of criminal law and stern morality. But of course the main restraint is human nature, which has good impulses as well as bad ones, and refrains from theft and murder and cruelty, even when it is taught that it can commit them all at the expense of Christ and go happily to heaven afterwards, simply because it does not always want to murder or rob or torture.

It is not easy to understand why the Christianity of Jesus failed completely to establish itself politically and socially, and was easily suppressed by the police and the Church, whilst Paulinism overran the whole western civilized world, which was at that time the Roman Empire, and was adopted by it as its official faith, the old avenging gods falling helplessly before the new Redeemer. It still retains, as we may see in Africa, its power of bringing to simple people a message of hope and consolation that no other religion offers. But this enchantment is produced by its spurious association with the personal charm of Jesus, and exists only for untrained minds. In the hands of a logical Frenchman like Calvin, pushing it to its utmost conclusions, and devising "institutes" for hard-headed adult Scots and literal Swiss, it becomes the most infernal of fatalisms; and the lives of civilized children are blighted by its logic whilst negro piccaninnies are rejoicing in its legends.

Paul's Qualities

Paul, however, did not get his great reputation by mere imposition and reaction. It is only in comparison with Jesus (to whom many prefer him) that he appears common and conceited. Though in The Acts he is only a vulgar revivalist, he comes out in his own epistles as a genuine poet, though by flashes only. He is no more a Christian than Jesus was a Baptist; he is a disciple of Jesus only as Jesus was a disciple of John. He does nothing that Jesus would have done, and says nothing that Jesus would have said, though much, like the famous ode to charity, that he would have admired. He is more Jewish than the Jews, more Roman than the Romans, proud both ways, full of startling confessions and self-revelations that would not surprise us if they were slipped into the pages of Nietzsche, tormented by an intellectual conscience that demanded an argued case even at the cost of sophistry, with all sorts of fine qualities and occasional illuminations, but always hopelessly in the toils of Sin, Death, and Logic, which had no power over Jesus. As we have seen, it was by introducing this bondage and terror of his into the Christian doctrine that he adapted it to the Church and State systems which Jesus transcended, and made it practicable by destroying the specifically Jesuist side of it. He would have been quite in his place in any modern Protestant State; and he, not Jesus, is the true head and founder of our Reformed Church, as Peter is of the Roman Church. The followers of Paul and Peter made Christendom, whilst the Nazarenes were wiped out.

ADOLF von HARNACK

[The Founder of Christian Civilization] (1900)†

*   *   *

It was Paul who delivered the Christian religion from Judaism. We shall see how he did that if we consider the following points:—

It was Paul who definitely conceived the Gospel as the message of the redemption already effected and of salvation now present. He preached the crucified and risen Christ, who gave us access to God and therewith righteousness and peace.

It was he who confidently regarded the Gospel as a new force abolishing the religion of the law.

It was he who perceived that religion in its new phase pertains to the individual and therefore to all individuals; and in this conviction, and with a full consciousness of what he was doing, he carried the Gospel to the nations of the world and transferred it from Judaism to the ground occupied by Greece and Rome. Not only are Greeks and Jews to unite on the basis of the Gospel, but the Jewish dispensation itself is now at an end. That the Gospel was transplanted from the East, where in subsequent ages it was never able to thrive properly, to the West, is a fact which we owe to Paul.

---

† From *What Is Christianity?* tr. by Thomas Bailey Saunders (New York: Harper, 1901). Torchbook edition, 173–89. On Harnack, see above, p. 288.

It was he who placed the Gospel in the great scheme of spirit and flesh, inner and outer existence, death and life; he, born a Jew and educated a Pharisee, gave it a *language*, so that it became intelligible, not only to the Greeks but to all *men* generally, and united with the whole of the intellectual capital which had been amassed in previous ages.

These are the factors that go to make the Apostle's greatness in the history of religion. On their inner connexion I cannot here enter in any detail. But, in regard to the first of them, I may remind you of the words of the most important historian of religion in our day. Wellhausen declares that "Paul's especial work was to transform the Gospel of the kingdom into the Gospel of Jesus Christ, so that the Gospel is no longer the prophecy of the coming of the kingdom, but its actual fulfilment by Jesus Christ. In his view, accordingly, redemption from something in the future has become something which has already happened and is now present. He lays far more emphasis on faith than on hope; he anticipates the sense of future bliss in the present feeling of being God's son; he vanquishes death and already leads the new life on earth. He extols the strength which is made perfect in weakness; the grace of God is sufficient for him, and he knows that no power, present or future, can take him from His love, and that all things work together for good to them that love God." What knowledge, what confidence, what strength, was necessary to tear the new religion from its mother earth and plant it in an entirely new one! Islam, originating in Arabia, has remained the Arabian religion, no matter where it may have penetrated. Buddhism has at all times been at its purest in India. But this religion, born in Palestine, and confined by its founder to Jewish ground, in only a few years after his death was severed from that connexion. Paul put it in competition with the Israelitish religion: "Christ is the end of the law." Not only did it bear being thus rooted up and transplanted, but it showed that it was meant to be thus transplanted. It gave stay and support to the Roman empire and the whole world of western civilisation. If, as Renan justly observes, anyone had told the Roman Emperor in the first century that the little Jew who had come from Antioch as a missionary was his best collaborator, and would put the empire upon a stable basis, he would have been regarded as a madman, and yet he would have spoken nothing but the truth. Paul brought new forces to the Roman empire, and laid the foundations of western and Christian civilisation. Alexander the Great's work has perished; Paul's has remained. But if we praise the man who, without being able to appeal to a single word of his master's, ventured upon the boldest enterprise, by the help of the spirit and with the letter against him, we must none the less pay the meed of honour to those personal disciples of Jesus who after a bitter internal struggle ultimately associated themselves with Paul's principles. That Peter did so we know for certain; of others we hear that they at least acknowledged their validity. It was, indeed, no insignificant circumstance that men in whose ears every word of their master's was still ringing, and in whose recollection the concrete features of his personality were still a vivid memory—that these faithful disciples should recognise a pronouncement to be true which in important points seemed to depart from the original message and portended the downfall of the religion of Israel. What was kernel here, and what was husk, history has itself showed with unmistakeable plainness, and by the shortest process. Husk were the whole of the Jewish limitations attaching to Jesus' message; husk were also such definite statements as "I am not sent but unto the lost sheep of the house of Israel." In the strength of Christ's spirit the disciples broke through these barriers. It was his personal disciples—not, as we might expect, the second or third generation, when the immediate memory of the Lord had already paled—who stood the great test. That is the most remarkable fact of the apostolic age.

Without doing violence to the inner and essential features of the Gospel—unconditional trust in God as the Father of Jesus Christ, confidence in the Lord, forgiveness of sins, certainty of eternal life, purity and brotherly fellowship—Paul transformed it into the universal religion, and laid the ground for the great Church. But whilst the original limitations fell away, new ones of necessity made their appearance; and they modified the simplicity and the power of a movement which was from within. Before concluding our survey of the apostolic age, we must direct attention to these modifications.

In the first place: the breach with the Synagogue and the founding of entirely independent religious communities had well-marked results. Whilst the idea was firmly maintained that the community of Christ, the "Church," was something suprasensible and heavenly, because it came from within, there was also a conviction that the Church took visible shape in every separate community. As a complete breach had taken place, or no connexion been established, with the ancient communion, the formation of entirely new societies was logically invested with a special significance, and excited the liveliest interest. In his sayings and parables Jesus, careless of all externals, could devote himself solely to the all-important point; but *how and in what forms* the seed would grow was not a question which occupied his mind; he had the people of Israel with their historical ordinances before him and was not thinking of external changes. But the connexion with their people was now severed, and no religious movement can remain in a *bodiless* condition. It must elaborate *forms* for a common life and common public worship. Such forms, however, cannot be improvised; some of them take shape slowly out of concrete necessities; others are derived from the environment and from existing circumstances. It was in this way that the "Gentile" communities procured themselves an organism, a body. The forms which they developed were in part independent and gradual, and in part based upon the facts with which they had to deal.

But a special measure of value always attaches to forms. By being the means by which the community is kept together, *the value of that to which they minister is insensibly transferred to them*; or, at least, there is always a danger of this happening. One reason for this is that the observance of the forms can always be controlled or enforced, as the case may be; whilst for the inner life there is no control that cannot be evaded.

When the breach with the Jewish national communion had once taken place, there could be no doubt about the necessity for setting up a new community in opposition to it. The self-consciousness and strength of the Christian movement was displayed in the creation of a Church which knew itself to be the true Israel. But the founding of churches and "the Church" on earth brought an entirely new interest into the field; what came from within was joined by something that came from without; law, discipline, regulations for ritual and doctrine, were developed, and began to assert a position by a logic of their own. The measure of value applicable to religion itself no longer remained the only measure, and with a hundred invisible threads religion was insensibly worked into the net of history.

In the second place: we have already referred to the fact that it was above all in his Christology that Paul's significance as a teacher consisted. In his view—we see this as well by the way in which he illuminated the death on the cross and the resurrection, as by his equation, "the Lord is a Spirit"—the Redemption is already accomplished and salvation a present power. "God hath reconciled us to himself through Jesus Christ"; "If any man be in Christ, he is a new creature"; "Who shall separate us from the love of God?" The absolute character of the Christian religion is thus made clear. But it may also be observed in this connexion that every attempt to formulate a theory has a logic of its own and dangers of its own. There was one danger which the apostle himself had to combat, that of men claiming to be redeemed without giving practical proof of the new life. In the case of Jesus' sayings no such danger could arise, but Paul's formulas were not similarly protected. That men are not to rely upon "redemption," forgiveness of sin, and justification, if the hatred of sin and the imitation of Christ be lacking, inevitably became in subsequent ages a standing theme with all earnest teachers. Who can fail to recognise that the doctrines of "objective redemption" have been the occasion of grievous temptations in the history of the Church, and for whole generations concealed the true meaning of religion? The conception of "redemption," which cannot be inserted in Jesus' teaching in this free and easy way at all, became a snare. No doubt it is true that Christianity is the religion of redemption; but the conception is a delicate one, and must never be taken out of the sphere of personal experience and inner reformation.

But here we are met by a second danger closely connected with the first. If redemption is to be traced to Christ's person and work, everything would seem to depend upon a right understanding of this person together with what he accomplished. The formation of a correct theory of and about Christ threatens to assume the position of chief importance, and to pervert the majesty and simplicity of the Gospel. Here, again, the danger is of a kind such as cannot arise with Jesus' sayings. Even in John we read:—"If ye love me, keep my commandments." But with the way in which Paul defined the theory of religion, the danger can certainly arise and did arise. No long period elapsed before it was taught in the Church that the all-important thing is to know how the person of Jesus was constituted, what sort of physical nature he had, and so on. Paul himself is far removed from this position—"Whoso calleth Christ Lord speaketh by the Holy Ghost"—but the way in which he ordered his religious conceptions, as the outcome of his speculative ideas, unmistakeably exercised an influence in a wrong direction. That, however great the attraction which his way of ordering them may possess for the understanding, it is a perverse proceeding to make Christology the fundamental substance of the Gospel, is shown by Christ's teaching, which is everywhere directed to the all-important point, and summarily confronts every man with his God. This does not affect Paul's right to epitomise the Gospel in the message of Christ crucified, thus exhibiting God's power and God's wisdom, and in the love of Christ kindling the love of God. There are thousands today in whom the Christian faith is still propagated in the same manner, namely, through Christ. But to demand assent to a series of propositions about Christ's person is a different thing altogether.

There is, however, another point to be considered here. Under the influence of the Messianic dogmas, and led by the impression which Christ made, Paul became the author of the speculative idea that not only was God in Christ, but that Christ himself was possessed of a peculiar nature of a heavenly kind. With the Jews, this was not a notion that necessarily shattered the framework of the Messianic idea; but with the Greeks it inevitably set an entirely new theory in motion. Christ's *appearance* in itself, the entrance of a divine being into the world, came of necessity to rank as the chief fact, as itself *the real redemption*. Paul did not, indeed, himself look upon it in this light; for him the crucial facts are the death on the cross and the resurrection, and he regards Christ's entrance into the world from an ethical point of view and as an example for us to follow: "For our sakes he became poor"; he humbled himself and renounced the world. But this state of things could not last. The fact of redemption could not permanently occupy the second place; it was too large. But when moved into the first place it threatened the very existence of the Gospel, by drawing away men's thoughts and interests in another direction. When we look at the history of dogma, who can deny that that was what happened? * * *

In the third place: the new church possessed a sacred book, the Old Testament. Paul, although he taught that the law had become of no avail, found a means of preserving the whole of the Old Testament. What a blessing to the church this book has proved! As a book of edification, of consolation, of wisdom, of counsel, as a book of history, what an incomparable importance it has had for Christian life and apologetics! Which of the religions that Christianity encountered on Greek or Roman ground could boast of a similar book? Yet the possession of this book has not been an unqualified advantage to the church. To begin with, there are many of its pages which exhibit a religion and a morality other than Christian. No matter how resolutely people tried to spiritualize it and give it an inner meaning by construing it in some special way, their efforts did not avail to get rid of the original sense in its entirety. There was always a danger of an inferior and obsolete principle forcing its way into Christianity through the Old Testament. This, indeed, was what actually occurred. Nor was it only in individual aspects that it occurred; the whole aim was changed. Moreover, on the new ground religion was intimately connected with a political power, namely, with nationality. How if people were seduced into again seeking such a connexion, not, indeed, with Judaism, but with a new nation, and not with ancient national laws, but with something of an analogous character? And when even a Paul here and there declared Old Testament laws to be still authoritative in spite of their having undergone an allegorical transformation, how could anyone restrain his successors from also proclaiming other laws, remodelled to suit the circumstances of the time, as valid ordinances of God? This brings us to the second point. Although whatever was drawn from the Old Testament by way of authoritative precept may have been inoffensive in substance, it was a menace to Christian freedom of both kinds. It threatened the freedom which comes from within, and also the freedom to form church communities and to arrange for public worship and discipline.

* * *

When the great apostle ended his life under Nero's axe in the year 64, he could say of himself what a short time before he had written to a faithful comrade: "I have finished my course; I have kept the faith." What missionary is there, what preacher, what man entrusted with the cure of souls, who can be compared with him, whether in the greatness of the task which he accomplished, or in the holy energy with which he carried it out? He worked with the most living of all messages, and kindled a fire; he cared for his people like a father and strove for the souls of others with all the forces of his own; at the same time he discharged the duties of the teacher, the schoolmaster, the organiser. When he sealed his work by his death the Roman empire from Antioch as far as Rome, nay, as far as Spain, was planted with Christian communites. There were to be found in them few that were "mighty after the flesh" or of noble degree, and yet they were as "lights in the world," and on them the progress of the world's history rested. They had little "illumination," but they had acquired the faith in the living God and in a life eternal; they knew that the value of the human soul is infinite, and that its value is determined by relation to the invisible; they led a life of purity and brotherly fellowship, or at least strove after such a life. Bound together into a new people in Jesus Christ, their head, they were filled with the high consciousness that Jews and Greeks, Greeks and barbarians, would through them become one, and that the last and highest stage in the history of humanity had then been reached.

WILHELM HEITMÜLLER

[Hellenistic Christianity before Paul] (1912)†

A certain peace and quiet has settled over the discussion of the problem "Paul and Jesus." One can hardly say that the question has been settled. Nevertheless, even where the problem has been taken seriously, it now seems to be recognized that Paul and Jesus belong together as religious personages, that Paul is somehow dependent upon Jesus through the medium of the primitive community, and that the great Apostle of the Gentiles does not begin a new series, but is a link in a chain that begins with Jesus.

Yet the very recognition of these facts raises a question that urgently requires an answer. Assuming that Jesus influenced Paul, assuming both phenomena belong together, how—especially in view of the proximity by which they are joined in space and time—can one explain the extraordinarily great differences that undeniably exist between them? These are differences not merely between Paul's theology and Jesus' preaching, but at many points also between Paul's religion and the religion of Jesus. * * *

---

† From "Zum Problem Paulus und Jesus," *Zeitschrift für die neutestamentliche Wissenschaft* 13 (1912): 320–37. Heitmüller (1869–1926) was professor of New Testament in Marburg, Bonn, and Tübingen.

I

* * * No one can contest the surprising rarity of the apostle's references to the historical Jesus. I have the impression that in theological circles people shut their eyes to this fact far too much or at least soften its impact all too much and too quickly. Arthur Drews has, as we know, again pointed it out emphatically in his "Christ-myth."[1] The deduction which he draws from it, to be sure, is simply untenable: Paulinism without the existence of a man Jesus is utterly incomprehensible. But the fact lies incontestably before us, and we must face it undiminished and unveiled: Jesus, the historical personality Jesus, does not appear in the letters as the factor that essentially determines and shapes Paulinism.

*   *   *

* * * "Even though we have (or, had) known Christ according to the flesh, we know (him) thus no longer" (2 Cor. 5:8). Quite decisively Paul says here that the earthly Jesus, the human personality Jesus, has no meaning whatever for his religious life, for him as one who is "in Christ" and thereby belongs to a higher reality than the earth. The whole thing upon which his opponents place so much weight and which they boast as the superiority of the earlier apostles, the knowledge of Jesus, is for Paul irrelevant. And that means that the tradition about Jesus is also irrelevant. Paul knows the exalted Lord, the "Christ according to spirit"; he lives in Paul and Paul in him; by him Paul is filled. How could the earthly Jesus, the "Christ according to flesh," be important for him? * * *

This attitude of Paul toward the historical Jesus, i.e., naturally also toward the Jesus-tradition, was rooted also in the historical situation in which he found himself—or in any case sharpened by it—namely, his struggle for the rights and independence of his law-free mission. In this struggle the knowledge of the historical Jesus, by which the earlier apostles were distinguished, played a major role. Thus Paul was actually forced to oppose a high evaluation of the tradition. * * *

*   *   *

II

*   *   *

It was the apostle's sacred conviction and great pride that he had not received his gospel "from man and not through a man," but "through Jesus Christ and God" (Gal. 1:1). That does not affect the obvious fact that Pauline Christianity does not really stand in immediate proximity to Jesus' preaching and that it is not independent of human and historical mediation. Paul knows himself to be autonomous and yet he is at the same time dependent upon another form of Christianity. Precisely this fact is a second important element in understanding Paul's distance from Jesus.

Naturally the apostle had become acquainted with the gospel before his conversion, even if perhaps only in outline, for he had persecuted the "church of God." He had obtained impressions of the Jesus-faith and of

1. *Die Christusmythe* (Jena, 1909; new ed. 1924). [*Editors*]

its adherents. We must take for granted that these impressions are of decisive importance for the origin and the form of Pauline Christianity. Furthermore, even if Paul "did not confer with flesh and blood" (and according to the whole tenor of the context, this note is directed in the first instance, if not entirely, against his alleged dependence on *those* men whose authority was thrown up to him, upon whom he was said to be dependent: the earlier apostles), nevertheless he did contact a Christian congregation after his conversion, probably the one in Damascus. Gal. 1:17, 18 does not say that he spent the entire "three years" in Arabia. Even though his conversion was, as far as he was aware, an original, unprepared experience, still the more precise formation of his faith and experience could not remain untouched and independent of the Christianity that surrounded him and within which he lived. How was that Christianity constituted of which he had obtained the first and decisive impressions, and the Christianity by which he was then surrounded for a time later on?

In the debate over Paul and Jesus, it was of great importance, as has been impressively urged,[2] that Paul not be placed immediately beside Jesus, but rather beside the primitive church. It is my opinion, however, that this observation must be further developed or modified. The Christianity which Paul joins and from which he is to be understood, is not really the primitive church in the strict sense, i.e., the Christianity of the earliest Jesus-group on Jewish soil in Jerusalem and Judea, to which the immediate disciples and friends of Jesus belonged. It is rather a *form already further developed*: if one can use an expression and rightly understand it, a *Hellenistic Christianity*.

The dominant view of Paul's introduction to the new messianic sect in Jerusalem is determined by the report of Acts. According to Acts he was in Jerusalem when the first storm, occasioned by Stephen's activity, burst over the church (Acts 7:58 ff.). The future apostle to the Gentiles thus received his first impressions from the oldest form of Christianity, the Jerusalem church. He had first persecuted it, before extending his work of desolation abroad (8:3).

In Gal. 1:22 ff. Paul says that he was personally unknown (prior to the Apostolic Council) to the Christian congregations in Judea, to which the Jerusalem church belonged. As long as I have known the Letter to Galatians I have found it incomprehensible that so little weight is commonly given to this, Paul's own statement, in comparison with the report of Acts. If Paul had been in Jerusalem at that time and if he had persecuted the church there (Acts 8:3), then he could not say in Gal. 1:22 that he was personally unknown to the "churches in Judea." Those two assertions are mutally exclusive. The tenor of the whole argument in Gal. 1:15 ff. comes to this: Paul wants to prove here that every possibility of his contact with, and therefore his dependence upon, the Jerusalem circles is excluded. If he had been in Jerusalem at the time of the Stephen incident, he would have had to defend this fact against misinterpretation. The "we" in Gal. 1: 23 ("he who once persecuted us") can no more be used to prove that Paul persecuted the Judean churches than the "you" of 2:5 can demonstrate that the Galatian congregations already existed at the time of the Apostolic Council.

2. Cf. Adolf Jülicher, *Paulus und Jesus* (1907).

The book of Acts as such cannot claim validity against the clear state-ment of Paul himself. What is more, its nature makes it easy for us to attribute to it an error at this point. As a consequence of an inadequate perspective and at the same time probably because of the use of sources, the author reports *two* journeys of Paul to Jerusalem between his conver-sion and the Apostolic Council, while it is notorious from Paul's own account that there was only one. But we must also take into account the singular viewpoint of the author and the presentation of history that fol-lows therefrom. The author of Acts is convinced that the magnificent expansion of the gospel from Jerusalem to Rome, borne by the Holy Spirit, was achieved under the direction of Jerusalem and especially of the College of Apostles. Thus he proceeds involuntarily to show the connection also of the Gentile mission with this central authority, and to bring its major bearer, Paul, into contact and agreement with Jerusalem and the Twelve. One sees this intention with particular clarity in the historically untenable depiction of the converted Paul's first stay in Jerusalem (9:26–30; cf. Gal. 1:18, 19). From there we can understand that the author, without ade-quate historical foundation, brings Paul to Jerusalem and his conversion into causal connection with a movement of the primitive community that was already becoming sacrosanct. To that can be added a literary-critical fact which has long been observed: the sentences in the Stephen report which refer to Paul (7:58–8:3) appear to be secondarily pasted on or patched into an existing account which originally did not contain them. Finally we may observe that the assertion in Acts 9:1, 2; 22:5; 26:12 that Paul obtained letters from the high priest to the synagogues in Damascus, authorizing him to bring any Christians found there in bonds to Jerusalem, very probably contradicts the actual competence of the sanhedrin. Thus we need have no qualms about consigning to the realm of legend the report of the apostle's presence at the persecution of Stephen.

If that is the case, however, then the tradition no longer gives us any right or occasion to assume that Paul first became acquainted with the Christian sect in Jerusalem and persecuted the community there. We no longer have any express statement that tells where that may have taken place. We must stick to Paul himself. From his own reports we derive the certain information that he experienced his conversion near or in Damas-cus, probably in the midst of his activity as a persecutor. After having been in Arabia, he returned to Damascus: therefore we may conclude that at that time he was a resident of Damascus. And we may further *suppose* that he there first came into contact with the Christian sect.

What is certain and valuable, first of all, is the *negative* observation that Paul did not come to know Christianity in Jerusalem and did not receive his first decisive impressions of Christianity from the Jerusalem primitive church. And by the same token it was not the Christianity of the primitive community, let alone the immediate disciples of Jesus, who influenced the formation of his faith and theology after his conversion. Apart from the one visit to Peter, three years after his conversion, the Christian Paul con-sciously and intentionally kept his distance from Jerusalem and the leaders of the oldest congregations.

On the *positive* side, we learn that Paul became acquainted with the gospel on the soil of *diaspora Judaism* and therefore received the decisive impressions from a diaspora Jewish Christianity. That is of great importance. It is clear that the gospel on the soil of diaspora Judaism could and must receive a different nuance from that on specifically Jewish soil like Jerusalem. One could guess a priori what pressures, impulses, and tendencies lay hidden in diaspora Judaism and would quickly unfold when it encountered the gospel. But we can see them quite clearly and reliably in the figure of the "Hellenist," i.e., the Greek-speaking, diaspora Jew Stephen, and in the external and internal development within early Christianity that emerged from his activity. "Hellenists" first seized upon the germ of universalism that lay in Jesus' preaching; they sensed that something new, beckoning out beyond Judaism, was given with faith in Jesus as the Christ. Hellenists first consciously undertook a mission among Gentiles, probably, initially among proselytes (Acts 8 and 11). Presumably a serious missionary endeavor beyond Judea began first in consequence of the Stephen uproar. Probably one may further assume that the persecution affected only the Hellenistic believers who deprecated the temple cult or the law, who then, having been driven out of Jerusalem, extended their mission also to the non-Jews. This mission movement borne by diaspora Jewish Christians will have spread as far as Damascus; by that means Paul became acquainted with Christianity, persecuted it, and received the unconscious impetus to his conversion.

The gospel first came to the Apostle to Gentiles as *Hellenistic Christianity*. By that I mean a Christianity that was carried by diaspora Jews and which already carried on a mission to the Gentiles. Hellenistic Christianity was involved in the *origin* of the Pauline faith, and Hellenistic Christianity influenced the *formation* of Paulinism. The converted Paul lived among Hellenistic Christians. Hellenistic Christianity comprised the foil and the foundation of his missionary activity. The picture that apparently emerges from the Pauline letters, as if the missionary Paul had carried on his work free-lance, entirely by his own power, is very likely false. The book of Acts at this point provides a good and necessary corrective. As others carried on a Gentile mission before Paul and alongside him (the anonymous Cypriots and Cyreneans, Acts 11:20; Barnabas; Andronicus and Junias? Rom. 16:7), so also his mission was supported by the church, at least before the Apostolic Council, which seems to have meant a turning point in his missionary style. Antioch may have furnished the principal base of operations in this period (Acts 13:1 ff.). From this matrix of his missionary work Paul naturally also drew power and stimulus for his Christianity. He not only gave; he also received.

Accordingly, if we are to solve the problem "Paul and Jesus" correctly, we must take this Hellenistic Christianity into account. Paul was separated from Jesus not only by the primitive church, but by yet a further link. The developmental series reads: Jesus—primitive church—Hellenistic Christianity—Paul. And even if the *genesis* of Pauline Christianity were to be thought of as quite independent of this Hellenistic form of primitive Christianity, it would still remain certain that the piety and theology of the missionary Paul who encounters us in the letters—written more than 14 (17?) years after his conversion—the only Paul we know—could only be understood in light of his constant contact with the Hellenistic Christianity of a congregation like Antioch, which first supported his mission and which was in part Gentile Christian.

This much is clear: if we knew this Hellenistic Christianity that was

before and alongside Paul, then we would have the best key for understanding Paul. What was the nature of this Hellenistic Christianity? How
did it look? Even if we could no longer identify this form of Christianity,
what we have shown so far would not be without value. For from now on,
in any account of Paulinism, we would have to figure in this unknown but
present factor. We would always have to weigh in this *x*, and, at least more
than previously, we would have recognized that we cannot regard Paulinism as a phenomenon conjured up out of thin air, a purely original creation. Rather we must assume a previous stage to which perhaps many
things belong that appear to us now as original Pauline creations.

However, even though we are condemned here to a large measure of
resignation, still we do not remain totally and absolutely helpless. To be
sure we have no direct sources for this phenomenon, but some indirect
and weak sources can be pointed out:

1. First the book of Acts, in the recognized good Hellenistic sources,
chaps. 6, 7, 8, and 11. Here we obtain a few important hints about the
Hellenistic diaspora Jewish Christianity that formed the bridge to the Gentile mission.

2. Above all, however, we must uncover in the Pauline letters themselves sources for this previous stage. That is a little-travelled, difficult,
and dangerous path, but we must venture upon it.

a) We can certainly use 1 Cor. 15:1 ff. Here Paul gives the central
content of his gospel and actually designates it as "received," as tradition.
If the above argument is correct, if he did not become acquainted with the
gospel in Jerusalem, but outside Palestine, perhaps in Damascus, then
strictly speaking what he gives here is not, as is always assumed, what he
received from the primitive church in the strict sense, but what he found
at hand as a tradition of *Hellenistic* Christianity (see above) and took over.
These are the main points of Hellenistic Christianity. To be sure, Paul
expressly points to the earlier apostles in 15:11: they preach the same
thing. But even though it is certainly correct that they also proclaimed
Jesus' atoning death for sins and the Resurrection, yet we have every reason
to doubt that the leaders of the earliest Jerusalem primitive congregation
would have been satisfied to take as the core of the gospel that which Paul
in 15:1 ff. calls its main points. It is not just a question of the individual
statements, but above all of the position they acquired and of what things
were connected or not connected with them. This passage itself, 1 Cor.
15:1 ff., suggests that Paul did not receive his tradition directly from the
primitive church. Restriction to the bare scheme of death, burial, resurrection as the chief content of the gospel is not comprehensible for the
church to which we owe the sayings source and the basic structure of the
Markan gospel. That restriction is only explicable in a circle that was further separated from the historical reality of Jesus' life and its wealth than
was the Jerusalem congregation. We become acquainted here with the
chief content of the *preaching* of Hellenistic Christianity.

But elsewhere as well, apart from 1 Cor. 15:1–11, we must seek to
obtain material by inference from the letters of Paul. The attempt is successful to a certain extent. I believe that we can make use of the passages
in which Paul alludes to acknowledged presuppositions of his arguments
and argues *e concessis*. That is, we must attempt to separate the specifically
Pauline from the common Christian material.

b) In our case the letter to Romans is particularly to be considered. For it is written to a congregation that was not founded by Paul, but may have originated in a way similar to Antioch, independently of Pauline Christianity. "Hellenists" who believed in Jesus must originally have carried out the mission, winning especially proselytes. Then in time it became an essentially Gentile Christian congregation. The dominant Christianity there will have been closely related to the Hellenistic Christianity that Paul came to know and which was his starting point. We shall be able to utilize with confidence that which we can deduce from the letter about the Roman congregation's views.

c) With less confidence, only with reservations, will we use what we recognize from the remaining Pauline letters as common Christian, i.e., as the views of the respective congregations. For here we are confronted with congregations which were brought into the world by Paul (or his pupils) and which received their stamp from him: their Christianity is therefore in any case dependent upon Paul.

The more or less certain material of 1 and 2a-b produces results that can be summarized as follows:

This Hellenistic Christianity began to separate itself inwardly more and more from Judaism and to position itself freely over against Judaism, at least over against the cultus, though not yet so clearly over against observance. The first bearers of this form of Christianity were, as said above, diaspora Jews. These Jews had naturally, from the ground up, a somewhat freer attitude towards the cultic and the rigorously particularistic elements of the patriarchal religion. They were the ones most likely able to grasp the universal powers of Jesus's preaching and to break through the particularistic and national limits. Stephen recognized the religious meaninglessness of the temple and its cultus; thereby an important part of the law also collapsed. Accordingly it was only fitting that one should preach the gospel also to Gentiles—naturally without having first to lead them through Judaism; otherwise it would have been nothing out of the ordinary. Thus in any case the congregation at Antioch originated—and others like it. In Antioch Christians did not think of themselves as bound to the Jewish law. We know that from the fact that they did not observe the Jewish dietary laws (Gal. 2:12). We cannot regard that as only a consequence of Paul's preaching; rather Paul must have found this situation already at hand. For the judgment of Pauline Christianity and of the place of Paul in the history of early Christianity it is of highest significance to note that he found at hand and proceeded from a Christianity that already conducted a Gentile mission and had actually already freed itself to a certain extent from the Jewish law and the Jewish nation.

The preaching of this Hellenistic Christianity is cited by Paul in its chief points in 1 Cor. 15:1 ff.: Christ dead for our sins, buried, risen. That scheme began already to take the place of the wealth of historical reality. That which we recognized in Paul as his conscious, fundamental position (see 1) had de facto already been prepared in this Christianity and had taken shape in his beginnings. The Christ-idea began already at this point to crowd out the historical Jesus. Christology stepped to the foreground.

Corresponding to this content of the gospel, which climaxed in the death and resurrection of Jesus Christ, was the position which was accorded to Jesus. It is subsumed in the title "Lord." This title for Jesus Christ could

be called characteristic of our Hellenistic Christianity and probably originated in it. To be sure we arrive at this conclusion not from those sources
alone which were expressly mentioned above, but from the early Christian
writings in general. Paul did not himself create in the place of *Christos* the
designation *ho kyrios* [the Lord], which was obviously native to Gentile
Christian circles and especially frequent in Paul, but found it at hand and
took it over. That should be obvious even from the self-evident way in
which he employs this name in his letters. Now the traditional opinion is
that the primitive church already called Jesus Lord. The favorite evidence
for that opinion is the *maranatha* of 1 Cor. 16:22. I cannot really convince
myself of the probability of this assumption. That *maranatha* is indeed
proof that in Aramaic-speaking Christian circles, from which the gospel
came to Greek-speaking people, the cry or prayer "Our Lord, come" was
much used, a kind of shibboleth. Thus the designation "Lord" for Jesus
was common in those circles. But to surmise that the same was true for
the Jerusalem primitive church would be to jump to conclusions. From 1
Cor. 16:22 can be deduced initially only that where Paul learned of the
gospel, i.e., in the Christianity of diaspora Judaism, perhaps in Damascus,
or where his Christian missionary base was, perhaps in Antioch, this prayer
was often heard. If we take one step at a time, we can initially get no further
than that. We can add that many considerations make it unlikely that in
the primitive church of purely Jewish origins the designation "Lord" for
Jesus would have arisen or have been common. The attitude of the basic
stratum of gospel literature in relation to the name *ho kyrios* is significant.
Mark never uses it of Jesus in the third person[3] (contrast Mark 16:9, 10!
[Part of the spurious ending found only in late manuscripts]), nor does
Matthew. Even as an address to Jesus the title *Kyrios* has no place yet in
Mark; *kyrie* in the vocative serves for him only as a polite form of address.
The same is true—and that is especially interesting—in the sayings—
source; only in one passage, Matt. 7:21 f. (cf. Luke 6:46) can one ask
whether "Lord" should be interpreted in the sacral or religious sense.[4] If
that should be the case, it would be the only passage, and a quite isolated
one, in this, our best source of information about the primitive community's religion. It is further to be noted (1) that, so far as I know, in the
genuine Jewish literature the Messiah is never called "Lord," so that Jewish
believers would not find this a natural way of naming Jesus as the Messiah;
(2) that for the Jews the name "Lord" was the specific designation for God
himself. On pure Jewish soil, therefore, the prerequisites for origin of the
title "Lord" for Jesus were not present. All that leads to the presumption
that this designation, so pregnant with consequences, must not have arisen
in the primitive church. There remains then only our Hellenistic Christianity. Here the prerequisites for the development of the Messiah Jesus
into the "Lord" Jesus Christ were present: the message of the Messiah
Jesus, dead, exalted, imminently to come, and the fact that the name
"Lord" in pagan circles was a common designation for the deity from whom
one expected salvation and whose fate—that was true of some few—in
violent death and in exaltation reminded one of the fate of the Messiah

---

3. In keeping with the evangelist's usage elsewhere, the expression *ho kyrios* in 11:3 is not to be
understood in the sacral, technical sense.
4. In the material peculiar to Matthew one can think of the technical expression "Lord" in passages
like 14:30; 15:22, 25; 20:30, 31; 25:37, 44.

Jesus. Here now, at least on pagan soil, the floodgates were opened for Hellenistic-Oriental elements. The proclamation of the death and resurrection of Jesus Christ is not a product of the myth of the dying and "rising" God; nevertheless, when it reached Hellenistic soil it could and must immediately enter in pagan minds into an amalgamation with similar-sounding stories of the violent death and exaltation of gods.

By this name "Lord" Jesus was ipso facto given a divine status. With that step was linked unavoidably the cultus, divine worship in some, even if only germinal, form. Though we undoubtedly perceive in Paul the beginnings of the Christ-cult, still we know now that at this point also he was not the creator but the recipient. He had to accommodate himself to what was given; perhaps he even attenuated what was there.

Further, as a rather certain feature of this Hellenistic Christianity, a belief in sacraments has to be recognized. In the Letter to Romans Paul argues (6:1 ff.) on the basis of the readers' customary view of the meaning of baptism. According to this, the Romans know baptism as a sacrament; they connect the conception of dying and new life with the act of baptism. One can hardly contest the fact that Hellenistic ways of thought have been at work here. Thus Paul did not create the singular conception of baptism present here, but received it from the Christianity which he learned and within which he lived—he is not creator but user. It will scarcely be too bold to draw implications from here also for the conception of the Lord's Supper in this pre- and extra-Pauline Hellenistic Christianity. It must have been equally a sacramental conception. And perhaps we can localize here the thought-complex of 1 Cor. 10:1 ff., 14 ff. * * * There the meal is supernatural food and supernatural drink; communion with the exalted Lord is established by bread and wine. We can assume, with appropriate reserve about certainty, that this view belonged to the pre- and extra-Pauline Hellenistic form of Christianity, upon which Paul was dependent. The influence of Hellenistic syncretism that is present in this thought-complex was therefore not first accomplished by Paul. Rather he had to accommodate himself to a sacramental concept that was essentially complete. The way in which he, for his part, works out another aspect of the Supper, corresponding more to his own conception, is shown by 1 Cor. 11:17 ff., where the meal appears primarily as the celebration of Jesus' death and its saving significance.

Finally I should like to single out as a characteristic of this movement, although with somewhat less confidence, the beginnings of Christ-mysticism. The presupposition of the conception in Rom. 6:1 ff., that the baptized person has died and has a new life, is the other notion that he has been baptized "into Christ." Thereafter the baptized person is "in Christ" (cf. Gal. 3:27). Because he is in Christ, he experiences together with Christ the latter's death and resurrection. Thus we must assume that the Christ-mysticism also was present in its initial stages, even if Paul was the first to develop it.

* * *

One could recognize still other features of the picture of the Hellenistic Christianity we have been pursuing, but I will stop here. It was my intention only to indicate the way to be travelled, not to pursue it to the end.

To be sure, much of the path will remain uncertain. But that does not excuse us from the task.

It is at least certain that we cannot place Paul immediately next to the primitive church. Rather he allied himself with a form of Christianity that was already farther from Jesus and under Hellenistic influence. It is also certain that this discovery provides an important factor for understanding the distance, which in fact is very great, between Pauline Christianity and Jesus.

But not only that problem received important light from this knowledge (developed under 2 above). Paulinism appears, when placed alongside Jesus and the primitive church, to have an almost baffling originality. If the argument above is principally correct, then we see that many of the stones in the imposing structure were already quarried and hewn and were only taken over by Paul. Paul's greatness is not thereby lessened; it only becomes historically somewhat more understandable for us.

Further, dissonances and disharmonies have long been discovered in the conceptual and intellectual world of the apostle, which seemed hard to understand, because the apostle was regarded as the free creator of this world. This phenomenon becomes again more understandable, if we recognize how much Paul took over, inherited, and received as ballast.

Moreover, we can in this way know more clearly that which is specifically Pauline, the uniqueness of Paulinism. It was *not* that which Paul had in common with Hellenistic Christianity.

And finally, on this basis we understand somewhat better the peculiar phenomenon that emerges if we inquire about the effects and after-effects of Paulinism in the development of Christianity: the elements of Paulinism that were genuinely peculiar to the apostle were the ones that only later were understood and had their effect.

PART VII

Pauline Christianity and Judaism

The relationship between Christianity and Judaism has been at best sensitive and ambivalent, at worst hostile, often deadly. Long before "Christianity" became the name of what, looking back, we think of as a new religion, the followers of Jesus had to ponder the question of their connection with the other Jewish sects and movements as well as with the settled, organized communities of Jews living in the Greco-Roman world. It was a question that galvanized the Greek-speaking Pharisee Paul, who first tried to destroy the new movement, then became its best-known apostle—not among his fellow Jews, but among the Gentiles. Conflicts over the requirements to be laid on those Gentile converts, between Paul and rival apostles of the new cult of Messiah Jesus, brought forth both the impassioned rhetoric of the Letter to the Galatians and the long, complex, protreptic exposition of the Letter to the Romans. In both letters the central issues were the relation between Jew and Gentile in the plan of God to restore and reconcile all humanity and all creation to himself and the role of the Sinai Covenant and the Law of Moses in that plan. Those letters would inevitably be at the center of the debate whenever the church pondered its connection with the Israel of its scriptures and with the Jews down the street.

We saw in Part IV that in the early centuries Paul was the subject of extreme interpretations. On one side, some Christians rejected Paul altogether, believing like the original opponents in Galatia that Christians must define themselves as other Jews did, by strict keeping of the commandments. At the opposite pole, Marcion drew what he thought was the logical conclusion of Paul's arguments by rejecting both Israel's scriptures and Israel's God. Effectively, though in a quite different way, many of the Gnostic groups did the same. The outcome of those controversies, in the emerging catholic center, was the conviction that Israel's scriptures, now defined as "the books of the Old Testament," were the church's own, and thereby Israel's history was somehow also the church's history. That conviction brought with it a number of enduring problems. How were those scriptures to be interpreted in light of the novelties of the "New Testament"? What were the implications for the church's life of Paul's rhetorical antitheses between Law and Grace, between "works" and "faith"? We have seen in Parts V and VI how those problems emerged again and again at moments of crisis in the church's life. But those issues, like the ones that plagued Paul in Galatia and Corinth, were internal matters. What of the relation of the church to the continuing existence of the Jewish people, who saw themselves as the rightful owners and interpreters of those same scriptures that the church claimed as its Old Testament?

The internal polemics of the church, together with its defensive stance as a tiny but visible and often despised movement in Greco-Roman cities with strong and established Jewish communities, led it to define Jews and Judaism as the quintessential Other. After Constantine's conversion and the emergence under Theodosius II of a nominally Christian empire, the situation of relative power was reversed and its disparity vastly increased. Now it was the church that threatened the continued existence of the Jewish communities. The church's theological assessment of Israel's future had immediate practical implications. Parts of the New Testament, such as the Gospels of Matthew and John and the Acts of the Apostles, seemed to suggest that the church simply replaced Israel as the chosen people of God. However, this simple supersessionist view of God's plan for the Jews was very hard to square with Paul's assertions in Romans: "Did God reject his people? By no means!" (11: 1). "Did they stumble so as to fall beyond recovery? Not at all!" (11:11). "Israel has experienced a hardening in part until the full number of the Gentiles has come in, and so all Israel will be saved" (11:25f.).

Beginning with Irenaeus in the second century, Christian thinkers struggled to construct a master narrative in which the history of Israel, including Israel

437

in its dispersion between the first and second advents of Christ, was an integral part of the history of the world's salvation. It was Augustine of Hippo who gave that story the grand design that would dominate Western Christian thought through the Middle Ages, and at the heart of Augustine's design was his interpretation of Paul's Letter to the Romans, particularly chapters 9–11. Augustine understood the climax of those chapters, in 11:25–32, to mean that the "fall" of the Jews, by failing to believe in Jesus, was "not in vain, since it profited the Gentiles by salvation," nor was the result of their fall only punishment.[1] The "scattering" of the Jews also served the divine purpose that the prophecies in their scriptures should be known throughout the world and serve as "testimony" concerning the Christ.[2] At the end of the age, they (or some of them) were destined to convert.

The Augustinian outline of salvation history became more brittle in some medieval versions, and the role of the Jews in the cosmic drama more negative, particularly in the age of the Crusades. From time to time popes and other ecclesiastical leaders intervened to restrain acts of aggression against the Jewish communities. These admonitions frequently revert to the Augustinian scheme, but in a form that gave to the Jews a less than happy role. For example, Pope Alexander II writes to the bishops of Spain, ca. 1060:

> We are pleased by the report which we have heard concerning you, that you have protected the Jews living among you, lest they be slain by those who set out to war against the Saracens in Spain. These warriors, moved surely by foolish ignorance and strongly by blind cupidity, wished to bring about the slaughter of those whom divine charity has perhaps predestined for salvation. In the same manner Saint Gregory also admonished those agitated for annihilating them, indicating that it is impious to wish to annihilate those who are protected by the mercy of God, so that, with homeland and liberty lost, in everlasting penitence, damned by the guilt of their ancestors for spilling the blood of the Savior, they live dispersed throughout the various areas of the world.[3]

Thus chapters 9–10 of Romans are understood to declare God's *curse* on the Jews. The promises enunciated in Romans 11 are taken to be eschatological and interpreted as the *conversion* of the Jews at the end of time. In the interim they wander the world, accursed and hated, but under divine protection, like Cain. Luther and his followers notoriously continued and exaggerated this tradition, which distorted Romans 9–10 and placed it under the control of other passages of the New Testament that could be taken with considerably less distortion as anti-Jewish. Protestants subsequently came to see Judaism through the double spectacles of Luther's reading of Paul and Paul's reading of his Jewish-Christian opponents. Through these two distorting lenses, Judaism appeared to most Protestants identical with "narrow legalism," and Paul was identified as the one who delivered Christianity from that legalism. The story of God's dealings with Israel was transformed from *Heilsgeschichte*, the history of salvation, to *Unheilsgeschichte*, its reverse (these terms still appear in German Protestant commentaries on Romans).

The rise of modern historical interpretations of early Christianity, from the eighteenth through the early twentieth centuries, brought with it new attempts to understand Paul against the background of the Judaism that had formed

---

1. *Propositions* 70, trans. by Paula Fredriksen Landes, *Augustine on Romans: Propositions from the Epistle to the Romans, Unfinished Commentary on the Epistle to the Romans,* Texts and Translations: Early Christian Literature Series (Chico, CA: Scholars Press, 1982), 41.
2. *Civ.* 18.46.
3. Translated in Robert Chazan (ed.), *Church, State, and Jew in the Middle Ages* (New York: Behrman House, 1980), 99–100.

him. Because the historical-critical movement was from its outset largely the work of northern European Protestants, however, the Augustinian-Lutheran perspective still controlled the way the questions about Paul's Jewishness were asked. As we saw in Part VI, the peculiar way in which "Judaism" and "Hellenism" were coded blinkered the view of the modernist historians. In that context, there was little incentive for Jewish scholars to read Paul, and those who did inevitably were reacting to an Augustinian-Lutheran Paul. For example, Martin Buber and Leo Baeck, both formed by the same liberal university culture that produced the liberal Protestant debate about Paul between Judaism and Hellenism, were sharply critical of Pauline religion. Buber found in Paul's notion of faith a concept ultimately Greek in origin, utterly different from the *emunah* of Jewish scripture—and of Jesus. Baeck thought Paul was the father of *romantic* religion, ultimately passive and selfish.[4]

In the decades since the end of World War II historical scholarship on Paul's relation to Judaism has undergone sharp revision, for several reasons. Christian scholars, horrified by the Nazi program of extermination of the Jews of Europe, were forced to acknowledge that one of the contributing factors in the modern antisemitism that had fueled the Holocaust had been that tradition of biblical interpretation and the construction of salvation history outlined above. New discoveries, including archaeological and iconographic evidence, required reassessment of the ways in which Jews adapted to the larger culture of the Greco-Roman world. The monolithic and antithetic categories of "Hellenism" and "Judaism" slowly yielded to a much more diverse and nuanced picture of Jews and their neighbors interacting in varied and complex ways. Discovery of new manuscript evidence, including the famous Dead Sea Scrolls, both challenged easy categorizations of Jewish groups and gave new insights into the nuances of Jewish thought, including especially the ways in which biblical texts were being interpreted around the time of Christianity's beginnings. At the same time, formal and historical analysis of long-familiar literature, including the huge corpus of rabbinic legal and midrashic compilations, provided a new basis both for understanding their meanings and functions and for placing them within their historical contexts.[5] The pioneering work of Gershom Scholem recovered for modern readers a strong and varied tradition of Jewish mysticism and showed that its roots reached back deep into antiquity.[6] The time was obviously ripe for re-examining Paul's Jewishness, and both Jewish and Christian scholars took up the task with enthusiasm. The following selections provide a few examples of their work (as does also the essay by Nils Dahl reprinted in Part IX).

4. Martin Buber, *Two Types of Faith*, trans. by Norman P. Goldhawk (New York: Collier Books, 1986); Leo Baeck, "Romantic Religion," in *Judaism and Christianity*, trans. by Walter Kaufmann (New York: Harper Torchbooks, 1958), 189–292. Excerpts from both appeared in the first edition of this work.
5. The work of Jacob Neusner, prodigious in scope and often provocative in style, had revolutionary impact in this area. To name arbitrarily one small, accessible book from his vast list of publications: *From Politics to Piety: The Emergence of Pharisaic Judaism* (2nd ed., 1973, reprinted New York: Ktav, 1979).
6. E.g., Gershom G. Scholem, *Major Trends in Jewish Mysticism* (New York: Schocken, 1961 [1st ed. 1941]); *Jewish Gnosticism, Merkabah Mysticism, and Talmudic Tradition* (New York: Jewish Theological Seminary of America, 1960).

DAVID DAUBE

Pauline Contributions to a Pluralistic Culture (1971)†

As my paper will culminate in a rejection of the accepted thinking concerning the "Pauline privilege," *privilegium Paulinum*, let me remind you that, under this head, a convert to Christianity has the right to divorce a partner who remains unconverted. It is universally believed that Paul in 1 Corinthians 7 in this case relaxed Jesus's teaching of the indissolubility of marriage in the lifetime of the spouses—hence the name of the institution. "There is little evidence of its exercise in the earliest times," says the *Oxford Dictionary of the Christian Church*. No wonder. What Paul advised is pretty much the opposite, really something quite different.

In 1 Corinthians 5:1ff. Paul orders the excommunication of a convert who has married his stepmother—no doubt after his father had died or divorced her. My starting-point is the apostle's emphatic remark (vs. 1) that this kind of incest is avoided even by the heathen.

To appreciate his meaning we must remember the Rabbinic teaching that a proselyte is as a newborn child. Hence he has no relations from before; and as far as his preconversion ties are concerned, in principle the rules of incest do not apply; in principle he may marry his stepmother or indeed his own mother—neither is related to him, a new man. However, the Rabbis feared that a thorough following-out of this doctrine might cause a proselyte to stumble. Suppose he grew up in a culture where marriage with the mother or sister is prohibited. If he finds that his new religion allows him to marry her, he might conclude that it is lax in these matters, that "he has come from a weightier sanctity into a lighter sanctity"; and he might slip back generally into that promiscuity and licentiousness which characterize pagan life. The Rabbis, therefore, modified the principle to this extent that a convert, though really having no preconversion relations, yet must refrain from such degrees as are prohibited by pagan law.

* * *

The Rabbis, I remarked, restricted a proselyte's freedom in order that he should not draw the wrong conclusions and relapse into heathen vice. That is what Paul has in mind when he bids his flock "purge out the old leaven" (vs. 7). "Leaven" is a Rabbinic term for the convert's previous, evil state, ever luring him back. For Eliezer ben Hyrcanus (second half of the first century A.D.) the reason the Pentateuch so many times requests consideration to the convert is to prevent him from "reverting to his leaven". In his actual dealings, this Rabbi was less patient than his contemporary Joshua ben Hananiah: the proselyte Aquila, we are told, was treated harshly by Eliezer and "would have reverted to his leaven" but for Joshua's extreme gentleness.

† From his article in *Jesus and Man's Hope*, ed. by D. G. Miller and D. Y. Hadidian (Pittsburgh: Pittsburgh Theological Seminary, 1971), Vol. II, 223–45. Reprinted by permission of the Pittsburgh Theological Seminary. Daube (1909–1999), an expert on Roman and biblical law, left his native Germany in 1933 to escape the Nazis and went to England, where he earned his doctorate at Cambridge and was appointed Regius Professor of Civil Law at Oxford. He joined the law school faculty at the University of California, Berkeley, in 1970, and is best known to biblical scholars as the author of *The New Testament and Rabbinic Judaism* (1956).

There is indeed a nuance in Paul arising out of his particular situation. The Rabbis were interested in the individual proselyte. The apostle, hoping for a flourishing church at Corinth, pure in the midst of impurity, stresses the possible effect of the wrongdoer's conduct on his fellows: the entire community may go astray—"a little leaven leavens the whole lump" (vs. 6). To use two verbs of his, the Rabbis forbade a convert certain degrees because, though in principle legitimate, they would be the opposite of beneficial, *symphero*, to him. Paul forbids them both for this reason and because they would be the opposite of upbuilding, *oikodomeo*, for the church. It will soon emerge that, in other contexts, the Rabbis, too, weighed up the wider repercussions to be expected from a decision.

I am aware that *symphero* (or the noun belonging to it) may cover what is beneficial to others and *oikodomeo* what is upbuilding for yourself. In 10:33 Paul depicts himself as adjusting to various milieus "not seeking my own benefit but that of many, that they may be saved"; and in 14:4 he holds that "he that speaks in a tongue upbuilds himself, but he that prophesies upbuilds the church". Still, mostly where he distinguishes between the permissible in the abstract or the second-best and elevated Christian choice, he defines the latter as involving *symphero*, your own spiritual welfare, and *oikodomeo*, your contribution to society.

The Hebrew behind *symphero is tobh*, "good". In Sirach we read: "Not everything is good for everyone". Among many feasible courses you must elect that most suited to your individual condition. In 6:12 Paul explains that though in strictness any action is licit—adultery, theft, drunkenness—not any will benefit you. In 7:35 he observes that celibacy, though far from a commandment, is beneficial to a person—at least in certain circumstances. *Symphero* is also met in the Matthean section on the subject: "If the case be so with his wife, it is not beneficial to marry". Here, too, by beneficial is meant what will most advance a man—abstention—in contrast to what he is free to do—marrying. 10:23, towards the end of a disquisition on food offered to idols, opposes to the licit both the beneficial and the upbuilding: we shall see that, according to Paul, it is indeed a man's own salvation and his thought for his fellows which should guide him in this question.

As for *oikodomeo*—in Hebrew *bana*—it occurs in 8:1 and 10:23 in connection with food offered to idols: you must always remember to upbuild the other members of the community. In 14:3f. and 17 Paul finds less merit in the public speech in ecstasy, since it does not upbuild the listeners, than in prophecy, which does.

It is not, then, quite accurate to describe the attitude of those rebuked in chapter 5 as antinomianism. They may, of course, have been antinomians; but in this affair they contended only that their preconversion ties had gone as a result of re-creation. Where they went wrong was in insisting on this principle absolutely, without heeding the harm likely to ensue if it was carried out beyond a certain point.

Once the true nature of this case is grasped, the Epistle gains hugely in thematic unity. Again and again, as here, what Paul is anxious to stop is the making of a fetish of some in itself praiseworthy notion, and especially one peculiar to Christians. That would bring about a rigidity not much better than that he had found entailed by a strict observance of the old law. There is no doctrine (even that of re-creation, for instance) so unconditionally valid that, in practising it, you should not ask at each step whether it is beneficial to yourself and, above all, upbuilding for others or the church as a whole. This overriding importance of the consequences for those around you is summed up in the requirement of constant exercise of *agape*, "love," "charity"—maybe in this area we had better translate "consideration", "considerateness" or "caring for."

The discussion in 8:1 ff. of food offered to idols is closely allied in structure to that of incest. The Christian is not fettered by specific dietary regulations; in principle it does not matter what he eats. Does it follow that he may buy from a pagan, or accept in a pagan home, food which has been, or may have been, dedicated to their gods? Even more extremely, may he take part in temple feasts?

A number of Corinthians said, Yes. A sophisticated Christian would realize that idols were nothings—so the food remained the same whatever heathen invocation had been uttered and at whatever place. However, the advocates of this position, Paul urges, superior though they look, forget about the two limitations to any doctrine. They forget about benefit (9:24–10:23, *symphero* being employed in the last verse). Even the finest mind, if courting temptation, may in the end succumb, find himself back in the mire from which he once escaped. And they forgot about upbuilding, care (8:1–9, 10:23–28, *oikodomeo* appearing in 10:23). To many a simple soul, if he sees his fellow-believer, and especially a highly educated one, take food avowedly dedicated to idols, it will not be clear that this implies utter contempt for them; but, on the contrary, he will infer that there must, after all, be some sense in pagan rites and he will join in to his perdition.

As in chapter 5, the target of the apostle's criticism is a stiff, proud standing on sham knowledge: "We know that we all have knowledge. Knowledge puffs up . . . If any man imagines that he knows anything, he knows nothing as he ought to know" (8:1f.). Freedom mechanically, soullessly exercised can be as deadly as the old Law. As in chapter 5, he is worried not only about the risk to the individual proselyte but also about that which his example spells to others. And as in chapter 5, those he admonishes were not necessarily antinomians *tout court*. All they maintained was that, in view of the utter nothingness of an idol, there was no wrong ever in this particular act, the eating of food devoted to it.

To be sure, the case is not one hundred percent parallel to that of incest. In the matter of food, Paul leaves no doubt that, essentially, it would be desirable to recognize no shackles whatever, to be firm enough in faith not to bother, say, when buying goods in the market, what ceremonies they may have been subjected to. Those to whom such externals matter have not yet reached the heights. If he nevertheless hopes that the "strong" believer will abstain from eating wherever it might be misconstrued by a "weak" one, this is a yielding to the second-best: the latter, in a higher interest, becomes the thing to do. Concession to frailty plays a considerable part in the Rabbinic system. Since the destruction of the Temple, R. Ishmael asserts (first half of the second century A.D.), by rights meat and wine should be banned, but as the majority could not endure this hardship, it will not be imposed.

A fundamental difference between Paul's task from the Rabbinic one which is revealed by this discussion results from his abandonment of the old Law. For the Rabbis, the problem how far a person may go if normal legal restraints are removed arose only within a narrow compass: a convert is as newborn, hence with regard to his previous relations the rules of incest—and a few others affected by the doctrine, inheritance for example—are basically non-operative. Paul faces the problem on a much larger scale. In fact, for him, there is no group and no department of life untouched by it. It is fascinating how in this Epistle, in developing his solutions, he leans on the Rabbinic miniature model. It is partly the pervasive influence of this precedent which accounts for the distinctive flavor of I Corinthians as compared with Romans.

There are numerous variations on the main theme. In 6:8ff., Paul attacks antinomianism proper which would deem wrong-doing irrelevant. He counters it with the same slogan he uses in his discussion of food: "All things are lawful unto me, but not all things are beneficial (*symphero*)." There is no evidence, however, that any Corinthian party actually felt authorized to commit the vices listed. From the tone of the section it is more likely that much objectionable behavior in fact went on and the offenders complacently relied on the saving power of their new religion.

In this warning against immorality, the argument refers only to the individual's salvation; there is no mention of the effect of his actions on others. Conversely, in 14:1ff., the emphasis is heavily on the latter aspect: while ecstatic speech is classed as a great gift, it is rather discouraged in favor of prophecy, which alone of the two upbuilds (*oikodomeo*) the believers and indeed (vss. 23–25) will induce non-believers to join.

The preceding chapter 13 contains the famous praise of *agape*. It is sometimes regarded as an earlier, independent composition by Paul which he decided to insert at this point. In reality, as should be obvious by now, it describes that disposition which, far above the old Law and any new doctrine, furnishes the highest standard for Christian conduct, a standard consistently invoked in this Epistle. (Verse 4, we saw above, employs *physioomai*, recurring five more times in the Epistle: any excellence, if not imbued with love, is empty, "puffs up.") Why does the hymn come just here? In chapter 12 Paul exhorts those with special gifts each to cultivate his variety, at the same time respecting all the others. It would be harsh to go on directly to place one gift, ecstatic speech, below another, prophecy. We must remember that, in this portion of his missive, he has to do with the most zealous, single-minded, valuable members of his church, whose feelings he would strain to spare; and also that possibly in their heathen background ecstatic speech enjoyed particular esteem. To preface chapter 14 by a full exposition of what the truly enlightened Christian—the "man", not the "babe" (vs. 11)—is guided by is an arrangement worthy of the author; in fact, like many another subtlety in the Epistle, an expression of his *agape* towards his flock.

* * *

Paul himself constantly foregoes his due for the sake of his own spiritual welfare as well as the advance of the church and the gaining of converts. 9:1–23 stands in the middle of his advice on food and is intended to illustrate the basic ideas from his own practice. An apostle has the right to material support: yet Paul renounces it since to preach the gospel is his God-imposed task (vs. 16) and acceptance of remuneration might be an obstacle to progress (vs. 12). Indeed (vss. 19–23) though free from all, in order to win over as many as possible he makes himself a servant to all and

accommodates himself to the Jews, to those under the Law, to those outside the Law, to the "weak."

✻   ✻   ✻

The dialectic between the licit, the beneficial and the upbuilding reaches
its climax in the discourse about marriage, chapter 7. First, marriage as
such. Marriage is lawful, not a sin (vss. 28, 36). None the less, ideally, a
person should remain celibate (vss. 1, 8, 26f., 37, 40): this is his most
beneficial state (*symphero* figures in verse 35). Yet again, for those—
doubtless the bulk of the community—who if celibate would succumb to
fornication, marriage is definitely the path to choose (vss. 2, 9, 28, 39): "It
is better to marry than to burn" (vs. 9). Even in this area the ideal must
not become a fetish.

The recommendation of the *pis aller* is couched in the form current in
Rabbinic exposition: "It is better they should transgress in ignorance than
wittingly" Ishmael, "It is better to marry than to burn" Paul. Interestingly,
Paul concentrates on the individual's welfare: genuine celibacy will
enhance it, but sham celibacy will undermine it and is therefore greatly
inferior to marriage. R. Ishmael, when considering a decree against intercourse, gave equal prominence to the communal factor. By rights, he
observed, as the Roman government prevented circumcision and the study
of the Torah, Jews ought to refrain from begetting children. But not only
would the majority not comply (thus falling into willful sin) but such a
course would threaten the existence of the nation. Presumably Paul's conviction that "time is short" (vs. 29) renders the latter peril of less account.

Second, within marriage (vss. 2–5). Marriage is a second-best, though
better than the best for the average, fallible mortal. Once married, it is
your duty to be agreeable to your spouse. Abstention is to be practised only
by consent, for temporary devotion to prayer: undue prolongation might
end in recourse to immoral outlets. You must act, that is, in a manner
conducive to your own contentment and virtue as well as your partner's.
The beneficial and the upbuilding are here inextricably combined.

Paul goes on (vs. 6): "I speak this by way of *syggnome*—permission,
indulgence, concession, Hebrew *reshuth*—not by way of *epitage*—
commandment, duty, Hebrew *miswa* or *hobha*." A technical reference to
a class of rulings, not infrequent in Rabbinism, which make allowance for
human weakness but are not binding on the elite. Exactly what Paul is
saying is not clear. He may be reminding his public that, celibacy being
the ideal, the entire section on marital life is concessive. Or he may be
labelling as a concession his advice against prolongation of continence: a
couple spiritual enough not to have to fear fleshly urges are at liberty to
go on. Chapter 7 presents quite a few ambiguities and obscurities; and it
may be that this reflects some particular involvement on the author's part,
resulting in unease, ambivalence, indecision.

I conclude with a third problem tackled in this chapter: a convert whose
spouse remains an "unbeliever" (vss. 12–16). The Greek is *apistos*, presumably covering an unbelieving Jew as well as a heathen: the mention of
circumcised Christians in the section directly following, vss. 17f., makes
this impression into a near-certainty. How does Paul's approach—the so-
called Pauline Privilege, *privilegium Paulinum*—chime with that to incest
in chapter 5 which latter, in my contention, implies the treatment of a

convert as a new creation? It chimes perfectly. Indeed, it becomes intelligible precisely and only if we bear in mind that strange doctrine. The interpretations so far given are all defective, and the traditional construction of the Privilege will have to be revised.

If one of two spouses converts, the bond, according to Paul, ceases to operate (vs. 15). This cannot possibly, as is generally held, be an indulgence granted by the apostle. Jesus himself had declared marriage indissoluble in the lifetime of one of the partners, a regulation repeated by Paul in the two verses (vss. 10f.) immediately preceding those under review, and, what is more, marked off as the Lord's authoritative charge in contradistinction to his own directions. A contradicting of that charge is unthinkable. What accounts for Paul's position must be something fully within the Jesuanic conception of marriage; it is the nature of conversion as re-creation. The convert is simply not the same person as the preconversion one. Hence his marriage is dissolved; and if the unbeliever goes off, that is that.

In passing—there is much controversy in the literature around this text as to the precise effects on a convert's standing if the partner leaves. Above all, in Paul's opinion, may the convert remarry? The doubts are due entirely to the mistaken assumption that we have before us some discretionary concession of Paul's. There is no real difficulty: of course the believer is free to remarry, "under no bondage"—his previous marriage no longer exists.

However, if the unbeliever is content to stay, you ought not, Paul lays down, to part with him (vss. 12f.). Why not? For one thing, for the sake of peace (vs. 15 at the end). This motive, *mippene darke shalom*, "on account of the ways of peace," is common in Rabbinic extensions to less worthy people within Jewry or to gentiles of privileges to which in strictness only worthy people or Jews are entitled. "A woman may lend a fan or a sieve to another woman though she is suspected of not observing the Sabbatical Year . . . on account of the ways of peace." "The poor of the heathen are supported along with the poor of Israel, the sick of the heathen are visited along with the sick of Israel, on account of the ways of peace." Two passages from Romans are in point. In one, about food, it is a question of accommodation to the "weak" members of the community: "Let us therefore follow after the things which make for peace and things wherewith one may upbuild one another." In the other, Paul is concerned with the behavior of Christians to non-Christians: "As much as lies in you, live peaceably with all men."

In early Rabbinic thought, not surprisingly, the aim of peace with gentiles is often interchangeable with that of eliciting their admiration for the Jewish religion or even winning them over. Simeon ben Shatah (first half of the first century B.C.), though not strictly obliged to do so, returned to a pagan a pearl mistakenly delivered, because "he preferred hearing the Saracene say, Blessed be the God of the Jews, to all the gain of this world." The two ideas of deference for the sake of peace and deference in order to acquire converts are similarly close in first-century Christianity. Paul's injunction in Romans to "live peaceably with all men" is preceded by the recommendation of honesty as a means of attracting unbelievers: "Provide things honest in the sight of all men." In the present case, the motive of peace (vs. 15 at the end) is followed by that of missionizing: by continuing with the unbeliever, you may be the means of saving him (vs. 16). The special influence one member of a family can exercise on another in matters of religious attachment is already known to the Old Testament—where it is mentioned in connection with seduction to idolatry. I Peter expects Christian wives to be so exemplary in their conduct that their non-Christian husbands may join the faith.

It is usual nowadays to see in the clause "God has called us (you) to peace" Paul's reason for allowing the marriage to end. That this would entail sanction of divorce for any deeply divided or even inordinately quarrelsome couple has not escaped notice. It is unnecessary to inspect the tortuous ways in which some commentators have tried to avoid the conclusion, or others have tried to evolve from here a liberal divorce regime. As we have seen, it is not Paul who allows the marriage to end: the marriage is ended because the converted spouse is a new creation. The clause gives Paul's reason for advising against breaking with the unbeliever if he will stay.

Again, the hope Paul expresses in the following verse, that by living on together with the unbeliever you may guide him towards the light, is turned by the prevalent interpretation into its very opposite: let him go since you have no certainty of changing him. This negative attitude to the chance of bringing about a fellow-being's (indeed, in this case, your closest companion's) salvation is grotesquely out of keeping with all that Paul, or any of the leading New Testament figures, stands for. It discourages any extra effort, it advocates callous indifference. I can think of no parallel anywhere in the pertinent sources (whereas the coupling of peace and proselytizing influence, I have just pointed out, is firmly rooted in the missionary thinking of the time). The proper paraphrase is: "For who knows, O wife, you may yet save your husband. Or who knows, O man, you may yet save your wife."

The structure, then, of this little tract is: As a convert you are not to cast off a spouse who remains an unbeliever (vss. 12–14). If he will not stay, that is a different matter: let him go, you are not tied to him (major part of vs. 15). But it is more consonant with God's call if you live on with him, in the hope of saving him (end of vs. 15 and vs. 16). Once more, Paul acknowledges, and wishes his charges to acknowledge, the supremacy of *agape*. Strictly, the convert's marriage is ended, and ended by a supernatural event of the highest order, re-creation, which might easily make him who experiences it proud, unbending, privilege-conscious. Yet he must look further, he must do what upbuilds; which means, if the unbeliever desires that there be no change, that desire is to be respected, even welcomed. It is in the nature of such consideration that its recipient is improved: an unbeliever so treated may attain belief. Paul's self-abnegation with a view to gaining converts will be recalled, as also his preference for prophecy which, unlike ecstatic speech, is adapted to the listener's understanding and, he says, may move gentiles to see the truth. The problem of a mixed marriage, or rather a marriage which becomes mixed, is solved in the spirit pervading the entire Epistle.

* * *

There are, however, two deviations from Jewish practice in vss. 12–14. One is the admission of marriage with a heathen. In these special circumstances, where one spouse converts and the other does not, the convert may, rather should, hold on to the other. Their union is marriage by intercourse—and this is so even if the other is a gentile. For the Rabbis, Paul would be on a par with those priests of whom the Testament of Levi says that they marry gentile women, "purifying them with an unlawful purification."

The second deviation has regard to the role of women. In Judaism, it is invariably the woman who is consecrated to spouse by the man. Paul deems it immaterial whether the convert is a man or a woman. Even if it is a woman, the unbeliever is consecrated [by her spouse]. This is in line with, in the spirit of, the reformed view of marriage proclaimed by Jesus: neither spouse can divorce the other, the husband is as indissolubly tied to the wife as she is to him. Paul's statement in 7:4—"The wife has not power over her body, but the husband; and likewise also, the husband has not power over his body, but his wife"—is not irreconcilable with Jewish tradition though the formulation is peculiarly strong. His extension of consecration is totally untraditional.

*   *   *

This section has a very personally Pauline flavor. It combines the most refined legal analysis with the most imaginative daring—and both are governed by his one great passionately held aim.

Its subsequent history, however, is paradoxical. Christianity soon gave up, and forgot about, that vital presupposition of his teaching: belief in conversion as a real re-creation. As a result of this and a few other developments, the apostle, who had encouraged and justified the staying united with an unbeliever, was understood to introduce the possibility of dissolving a mixed marriage—the Pauline Privilege. Judaism, by adhering to its Law, has preserved the concept of a proselyte as a newborn child, with all its consequences: it is as much part of the Jewish system today as it was at the time of I Corinthians.

BURTON L. VISOTZKY

Trinitarian Testimonies (1988)†

> I am a Jew, born at Tarsus in Cilicia, but brought up in this city at the feet of Gamaliel, educated according to the strict manner of the law of our fathers, being zealous for God as you all are this day. (Acts 22:3)

> Circumcised on the eighth day, of the people of Israel, of the tribe of Benjamin, a Hebrew born of Hebrews; as to the law a Pharisee. (Philippians 3:5)

> Brethren, I am a Pharisee, a son of Pharisees. (Acts 23:6)

---

† This article was originally published in *USQR* 42 (1988): 73–85. Reprinted by permission of the author and the Union Seminary Quarterly Review. Visotzky is the Nathan and Janet Appleman Professor of Midrash and Interreligious Studies at the Jewish Theological Seminary.

I

The self-proclaimed pedigree of the apostle Paul has long tempted scholars into the sin of providing his Gamalielite, Pharisaic background by extensively quoting from Rabbinic literature. Though this phenomenon of "backgrounding" is well known for other parts of the New Testament, it is deemed all the more apt and valid in Pauline studies since the apostle himself, as it were, opened the door to the method by confessing his "yeshiva" training. Raiding Rabbinic literature for Pauline "background" is, at best, a hazardous undertaking—as any careful New Testament scholar is obliged to admit. On one side, there is the temptation to employ the Rabbinic parallels to make the Sages seem very close indeed to Matthew's Pharisees. On the other side, even the best intentioned student of Rabbinic literature will be guilty of some anachronism when citing the Jewish fathers to illustrate Pauline texts composed before the destruction of the Second Temple.

Even if one carefully limits the parallels to the Tannaitic corpus, one is still comparing texts written in the mid-first century with others first redacted (and perhaps only then invented) in the late second and early third centuries. So much the worse when citations are offered from the Talmuds and medieval midrashim. While it is certainly possible that these late Rabbinic texts contain early, even predestruction, traditions, this possibility is at best, difficult to prove. Only very careful exegetes succeed in wending their way through the maze of Rabbinic literature to find appropriate parallels which shed some light on Paul. Even under carefully controlled conditions all that can be offered is background color to the milieu—not the sources of Pauline traditions.

Is it not much more likely that Rabbinic parallels to Paul do not illustrate his Pharasaic background, but rather show some Rabbinic familiarity with Paul? Allow me to carry this logic one step further and suggest that not only do Rabbinic parallels with the New Testament possibly indicate Rabbinic familiarity with the verse in question, but the exegesis of such a Rabbinic passage can be best understood if the NT verse is read within the social context in which the Rabbis heard it. That is to say, proper exegesis of New Testament verses in Rabbinic literature requires an understanding of how that verse was read, interpreted and employed by the church fathers at the time the verse entered the Rabbinic corpus.

In making this argument I do not wish to insist that the study of Rabbinic literature is a fruitless endeavor for students of New Testament. Given careful control of Tannaitic material it can serve a useful purpose of introducing the student to Rabbinic thought a century or more after Paul. To whatever extent current scholarly opinion feels comfortable in making trajectories backward in time, this is a more or less useful tool. My point here is to caution against assuming that a close parallel has given access to Gamalielite, Pharisaic traditions that Paul imbibed while he was yet Saul. Quite the contrary, all those parallels from Rabbinic literature are apt to illuminate is the Rabbinic perception of the patristic interpretation of the Pauline verses. This is particularly the case when the Rabbinic parallels are found in a polemical, probably anti-Christian context. The use of parallels under such circumstances must be considered wholly inadequate as a means of arriving at a critical understanding of a New Testament verse.

II

The temptation to resort to Rabbinic literature to explain Paul rises in direct proportion to the opaqueness of any given passage. Since P. Billerbeck wrote his famous commentary virtually every difficult Pauline text has had the disadvantage of a "Rabbinic exegesis." I focus here on one particular crux, 1 Corinthians 11:3–12, for it illustrates my point about the uses and abuses of Rabbinics for New Testament exegesis. I intend to demonstrate not only that the Rabbinic parallel in question does not provide Pauline "background," but that the Rabbinic text in fact quotes Paul as he was cited by the church fathers in the late fourth century Trinitarian controversy.

The text of 1 Corinthians 11:3–12:

> 3. But I want you to understand that the head of every man is Christ, the head of a woman is her husband, and the head of Christ is God. 4. Any man who prays or prophesies with his head covered dishonors his head, 5. but any woman who prays or prophesies with her head unveiled dishonors her head—it is the same as if her head were shaven. 6. For if a woman will not veil herself, then she should cut off her hair; but if it is disgraceful for a woman to be shorn or shaven, let her wear a veil. 7. For a man ought not to cover his head, since he is the image and glory of God; but woman is the glory of man. 8. For man was not made from woman, but woman from man. 9. Neither was man created for woman, but woman for man. 10. That is why a woman ought to have a veil on her head, because of the angels. 11. Nevertheless, in the Lord woman is not independent of man nor man of woman; 12. for as woman was made from man, so man is now born of woman. And all things are from God.

It is not my concern here to discuss whether Paul is talking about hairstyles or headcoverings, whether he is feminist or chauvinist. It is important to note that this passage contains a blatant contradiction between the vertical hierarchy of men and women in verses 3,7,8,9 and the equality proclaimed in verses 11–12. I am not the first to notice this contradiction, nor am I the first to point out that it mirrors the two creation accounts in Genesis. I may be the first, however, who having pointed out these facts will offer no attempt to harmonize or otherwise resolve them.

I am also not the first to point to a parallel between verses 11–12 and a Rabbinic passage attributed to the mid-third century Sage, R. Simlai,

> In the past, Adam was created from the dust, while Eve was created from Adam. From Adam onward, *In our image, after our likeness* (Genesis 1:26); it is impossible for there to be man independent of woman, nor is it possible for there to be woman independent of man, neither is it possible for both of them to be independent of the Shekinah.

I think the parallel is beyond quibble; the only difficulty is what to make of the parallel. Billerbeck merely lists the text and its Rabbinic citations without extended discussion. This is the standard technique of his commentary which serves as no more than a source book, leaving the student to decide on the meaning of a text as he or she wishes. G. Delling, who five years later chose to explicate the thorny question, *Paulus' Stellung zur Frau und Ehe*, followed Billerbeck's lead by citing the parallel without discussing it. Close to thirty years passed before another scholar linked the texts together on the printed page. J. Jervell cited the Rabbinic passage as not just a parallel, but as an influence on Paul. The question for the scholar to consider, Jervell noted, is just how Paul understood the Rabbinic saying.

Almost a decade later M. Boucher very kindly offered the Rabbinic parallel to show that the rabbis were theoretically just as fair to women as was Paul. Most recently, and most brilliantly, Mary Rose D'Angelo explicated Paul by using the Rabbinic parallel as background. Dr. D'Angelo excelled for she was careful to study the Rabbinic texts as critically as she did the Pauline verses. Her keen insight connected the two strands of the 1 Corinthians passage with the Genesis accounts. By examining the Rabbinic treatment of Genesis in the parallel, Dr. D'Angelo was able to unravel Paul's convoluted and apparently contradictory rhetoric.

Unfortunately, although Dr. D'Angelo had all the correct instincts in her treatment of the Rabbinic passage, carefully weighed the evidence for the dating of the tradition and cited the fullest version of the parallel to be found in any New Testament commentary, she failed methodologically. Although her method brought her, I suspect, to a correct exegesis of Paul, it did so through inadmissible evidence. Nevertheless, she is a careful New Testament scholar, so we must be grateful to her for her perspicacious reading of Paul.

The failure in invoking the Rabbinic parallel was twofold. First, even the lengthy passage Dr. D'Angelo cited was taken out of context. Within the context it is clearly part of an anti-Trinitarian polemic. This being the base, one must suspect that it is the Rabbis quoting the New Testament and not vice versa. Second, for all her care in considering the dating of the saying, the earliest possible date that might have been offered would have been at the end of the first quarter of the second century, some seventy-five years after Paul. However, it is even more likely that the text does not antedate the redaction of the Palestinian Talmud, ca. 425 CE.

III

Let us examine the Rabbinic parallel to 1 Corinthians 11:11. I am assuming that the polemical context of the Rabbinic text and the general earliness of the Pauline passage must lead one to the consideration that the Sages are quoting Paul. In order to prove this point I first analyze the entire text in order to fix a date and redactive context for the saying in question. Exegesis of a smaller portion of the text will establish that 1 Corinthians 11:11 is consciously cited in response to patristic usage of the greater Pauline passage in the Trinitarian controversy. When the Sages wish to debunk the Trinitarian argument in all its late fourth century complexity, they do so by following the church fathers' ground rules—by quoting New Testament texts in support of their argument!

> A. The heretics asked R. Simlai, How many gods created the world? He answered them, Me you're asking? Let's ask Adam, as it is said, *For ask now of the days that are past, which were before you, since the day that God created Adam* . . . (Deuteronomy 4:32). It is not written, since gods created (pl.) Adam, but *since the day that God created (sing.) Adam.*

B. They said to him, But it is written, *In the beginning God created* (Genesis 1:1). He said to them, Is *created* written [as a plural]? What is written here is *created* [in the singular].

C. R. Simlai stated, Every place that the heretics rend [a verse from context to make their point] has the appropriate [textual] response right next to it.

D. They returned to ask him, What of this verse, *Let us make man in our image, after our likeness* (Genesis 1:26). He answered them, It is not written, So God created (pl.) man in his image (pl.), but, *So God created (sing.) man in his own image* (Genesis 1:27). His disciples said to him, Those you pushed off with but a straw, but what shall you answer us?

He told them, In the past, Adam was created from the dust, while Eve was created from Adam. From Adam onward, *In our image, after our likeness* (Genesis 1:26); it is impossible for there to be man independent of woman, nor is it possible for there to be woman independent of man, neither is it possible for both of them to be independent of the Shekinah.

E. They returned to ask him, What of this verse, *The Mighty One, God, the Lord! The Mighty One, God, the Lord! He knows* (Joshua 22: 22). He answered them, It is not written, They know (pl.), but rather, *He knows*.

His disciples said to him, Rabbi, you pushed those off with but a straw, what will you answer us?

He told them, The three are but one name, like one who says: *Basileus, Kaisar, Augustus*.

F. They returned to ask him, What of this verse, *The Mighty One, God, the Lord, speaks and summons the earth* (Psalm 50:1)? He asked them, Is speak (pl.) written? Rather *speaks and summons* (both sing.) is written.

His disciples said to him, Rabbi, those you pushed off with but a straw, what shall you answer us?

He answered them, The three are but one name, like one who says: craftsman, builder, architect.

G. They returned to ask him, What of the verse, *He is a holy (pl.) God* (Joshua 24:19)?

He answered them, It is not written, They are, but *He is a jealous God* (ibid.).

His disciples said to him, Rabbi, those you pushed off with but a straw, what shall you answer us?

R. Yitzhak said, Holy with all types of holiness, as R. Judah said in the name of R. Aha. . . .

H. They returned to ask him, What of the verse, *For what great nation is there that has a God so near (pl.) to it* (Deuteronomy 4:7)?

He answered them, It is not written, Whenever we call upon them, but rather, *whenever we call upon him* (ibid.).

His disciples said to him, Rabbi, those you pushed off with but a straw, what shall you answer us?

He told them, Near in all types of nearness as R. Pinhas quoted R. Judah bar Simon. . . .

I quote the entire passage in its fullest and earliest form, from the Palestinian Talmud. It is not only the earliest redacted, but the only text to retain all of the parts. Later Midrashim merely record those pieces of the pericope that were relevant to the Biblical text being considered in the given Midrash. Thus, Genesis Rabbah only records those sections relevant to Genesis, Midrash Psalms only the section on Psalms, etc.

The segment which quotes Paul (D.) is generally attributed to R. Simlai, although his name does not appear in that specific section. Simlai is cited immediately preceding (C.), offering a maxim about refuting heretics from the very context out of which they have lifted their apparently damaging proof-text. This same maxim is quoted in the Babylonian Talmud in the name of Simlai's contemporary R. Yohanan. There, the comment is connected to his explication of Genesis 1:26.

The quote from 1 Corinthians 11:11 also appears in a debate between R. Akiba and R. Ishmael in Genesis Rabbah 22:2. The form of the debate, however, follows precisely the debates between them found in Genesis Rabbah 53:15 and in Genesis Rabbah 1:14. Each of these instances revolves around proper use of Nahum of Gimzo's Inclusion/Exclusion methodology for resolution of apparently extraneous particles in Biblical Hebrew. In the instance of the Pauline quote, the debate deviates slightly from the prescribed form in that it does not solve the textual difficulty by explicit mention of the Inclusion/Exclusion method. This leads to the conclusion that the text in Genesis Rabbah 22:2 is an editorial construction based upon the loci in Genesis Rabbah 1:14 and 53:15. The quotation from Paul, then, was lifted out of the Palestinian Talmud to provide dialogue for the invented debate. It cannot be considered as genuinely Akiban or Ishmaelian and must be dated at the redaction of Genesis Rabbah, *circa* fifth to sixth century.

We are left, then, with the earliest form of the entire pericope in a document redacted about 425 CE. Still, the name of R. Simlai (fl. mid-third century) appears rather firmly attached to the text in question, even if not absolutely attached to the segment containing the 1 Corinthians quote. It is, after all, paralleled with little change in Genesis Rabbah. But even this much is not secure, for the fact remains that Simlai's name does not appear in the section under discussion. Further, it should be quite clear that the Pauline passage appears as part of a triplet of exchanges (D.E.F.), each of which has an anonymous Rabbi responding to a Biblical plural with a trinity of his own. Genesis Rabbah only excerpts from this triplet. The sections of the Palestinian Talmud (A.B.C.) preceding this grouping of sayings specifically mention R. Simlai. Since he was well known for his debates with heretics, a redactor could have readily slipped the latter grouping of three sayings into a format which would have them appear under R. Simlai's authority. The sayings (G.H.) that follow mention other Sages entirely. This sandwiching of the anonymous dialogues in between two named segments is the work of the Palestinian Talmudic redactor. The era in which he did his work (c. 425 CE) is, then, the only secure date which may be offered for the group of three dialogues (D.E.F.) which include the 1 Corinthians parallel.

The Pauline quotation is part of a group of three discussions among an anonymous Rabbi, his students and his heretics. Yet none of the New Testament scholars who cite the passage as "Pauline background" also cited the two connected parts (E.F.) which follow. Only within the full context can the meaning of these dialogues be apprehended.

IV

To facilitate exegesis of the passage, I will consider the three sections of dialogue in the reverse order from that in the Talmudic pericope. Beginning with the last (F.), first:

> F. They returned to ask him, What of this verse, *The Mighty One, God, the Lord, speaks and summons the earth* (Psalm 50:1)? He asked them, Is speak (pl.) written? Rather *speaks and summons* (both sing.) is written.
> His disciples said to him, Rabbi, those you pushed off with but a straw, what shall you answer us?
> He answered them, The three are but one one name, like one who says: craftsman, builder, architect.

Our Rabbi is approached by a group of heretics with an apparent Trinitarian testimony in hand. What could be better proof of the threefold nature of God than an Old Testament verse listing three differing names for God? Our Rabbi rejects the verse as proof, for it carries singular verbs. This apparently satisfies the heretics, who do not bother to argue that one God with three natures could well employ a singular verb.

The disciples are less pleased with this answer, and say so—the Rabbi has pushed them away with but a straw. The disciples expect a better answer, a private one that perhaps could not be made in public, especially to heretics. How may one refute the Trinitarian testimony? By dismissing the import of the proof-text; the three are but one name. If this satisfies the disciples, the Rabbi has had his little joke on them, for his example offers another trinity in its place: craftsman, builder, architect. These are terms used in the Rabbinic academy to refer to God as creator; they surely should satisfy the heretics as terms appropriate to the Trinity. So, the disciples are pacified by an answer which, if offered to the *minim* would have been initially seized upon as yet another proof. No teacher appreciates it when his debate with heretics is characterized by his pupils as mere straw. Our Rabbi will have his revenge on his insistent disciples when it dawns on them later that his answer was no answer at all.

The middle dialogue (E.) of the three follows much the same pattern. The heretics ask about a verse with the same triple set of names for God and are dismissed with a singular verb. The students object and are mollified by the explanation that the three names refer but to one God, much like the three names for the one Emperor which regularly appeared together on inscriptions. Again, the students have been satisfied by an explanation that leaves the trinity intact and explicates it by invoking royal formula similar to those invoked by the Sages in their parables about God. As in the case considered above, this explanation should at first blush have been taken as a proof by the *minim* had our Rabbi offered it in their presence. Presumably, as before, the aggressive students who demanded a better explanation will realize only too late that they have been had. The text:

> E. They returned to ask him, What of this verse, *The mighty One, God, the Lord! The Mighty One, God, the Lord! He knows* (Joshua 22: 22). He answered them, It is not written, They know (pl.), but rather, *He knows*.

His disciples said to him, Rabbi, you pushed those off with but a straw, what will you answer us?

He told them, The three are but one name, like one who says: *Basileus, Kaisar, Augustus.*

The last segment of this group of three (D.) contains the quotation from 1 Corinthians 11:11. At its simplest level, the response seems to indicate that when God says *Let us make man in our image, after our likeness* (Genesis 1:26), he is talking with Adam and Eve. Although their own creation did not follow the established pattern, from then onwards God, man and woman will all be equal partners in the creation of new humans.

> D. They returned to ask him, What of this verse, *Let us make man in our image, after our likeness* (Genesis 1:26). He answered them, It is not written, So God created (pl.) man in his image (pl.), but, *So God created (sing.) man in his own image* (Genesis 1:27).
> His disciples said to him, Those you pushed off with but a straw, but what shall you answer us?
> He told them, In the past, Adam was created from the dust, while Eve was created from Adam. From Adam onward, *In our image, after our likeness* (Genesis 1:26); it is impossible for there to be man independent of woman, nor is it possible for there to be woman independent of man, neither is it possible for both of them to be independent of the Shekinah.

The pattern established above is followed here as well, though with certain exceptions. First, the verse invoked has both a plural verb *(let us make)* and plural objects *(our likeness, our image)*. Second, though plural, the verse does not explicitly indicate a trinity, merely a plurality. In response to the first problem, our Rabbi does not point to a singular verb, as he has done in the other two cases. Instead, he offers a response which explicates the verse in order to solve the difficulty raised. This approach apparently (but see below) violates the rule suggested by R. Simlai (or R. Yohanan), that the appropriate response to heretics can be found by quoting a verse from the same Scriptural context. As for the second point, about the Trinity, we will see below that Genesis 1:26 had long been a Trinitarian testimony.

Our Rabbi has once more fooled his students. They wanted a better answer—he gave them a trinity (God, Adam, Eve). As an even better joke, he sent them on their way ignorant of the fact that he had satisfied their rigor with a quote from the Apostle Paul.

V

One has to wonder what manner of Rabbi is willing to pull his students' legs by giving aid and comfort to heretics. We must wonder as well, just who these *minim* were, and what was the Trinity they offered testimonies about. A brief excursion into patristic literature will clarify these issues. I say this conscious of the fact that there was very little clarity about the Trinity in the works of the church fathers. Only during the late fourth and early fifth centuries (around the time of the redaction of the Palestinian Talmud) was any type of systematic discussion attempted. There was, therefore, a good deal of confusion, particularly about the status of the third member of the Trinity, the Holy Spirit. Gregory of Nazianzus could thus admit in his Fifth Theological Oration that there were some members of the Church who kept to themselves the opinion that the Holy Spirit was, in fact, to be considered God.

Despite all its confusion, there was a long exegetical tradition linking Genesis 1:26 to the members of the Trinity. As early as the 180's, Irenaeus gave the verse a Trinitarian reading. While he followed the Apostolic Father, Barnabas, in understanding *Let us make* to be God talking to his Word or Son, he also expanded this theology.

> For with Him were always present the Word and Wisdom, the Son and the Spirit, by whom and in whom, freely and spontaneously, He made all things, to whom also He speaks, saying, "Let us make . . ."

Irenaeus makes this point again by reading the plural of Genesis 1:26 as God talking to His hands. He explains,

> Now man is a mixed organization of soul and flesh, who was formed after the likeness of God, and moulded by His hands, that is by the Son and Holy Spirit, to whom also He said, "Let us make man."

Later Christians maintained the assumption that God speaks to the other two members of the Trinity, but at the same time they retreated from explicitly associating the Holy Spirit with the actual creation itself. This seemed to give the Holy Spirit too much power. It was not at all clear that the Spirit should be considered a creator, or for that matter co-equal to the Father and Son as king and royal sovereign. This point was explicitly addressed in the creed of the council of Constantinople in 381 which sought to correct this apprehension about elevating the Spirit. So the creed instructs about the Holy Spirit, "Who with the Father and the Son is together worshipped and together glorified."

I very much doubt that our Rabbi is making an attempt to bring the heretics he debates in line with the creed of Constantinople. Quite the contrary, we see by his taunting answer to his students that if one really wishes to get embroiled in debate about the Trinity, one must attack the heretics at the weak points of their belief. It is not enough merely to trot out Trinitarian testimonies, suggests our Rabbi; if one wishes to accept the divinity of the Trinity, then one must be prepared to accept the Holy Spirit as craftsman, builder and architect of the Universe. One must revere the Spirit as *Basileus, Kaisar, Augustus*. In the privacy of the academy, our Rabbi is not simply having a joke at his students' expense, he is instructing them to engage in *reductio ad absurdum* arguments with the heretics. If you wish to debate heretics, he tells them, then know the details of their beliefs and press them hardest where they are weakest.

Our Rabbi's active involvement in the anti-Trinitarian debate is even more explicitly revealed by his treatment of Genesis 1:26. He responded to the citation by quoting 1 Corinthians. Let us see how the contemporary church fathers understood these verses. In his work, *On The Trinity*, Augustine writes,

> The apostle says that the man is the image of God, and on that account removes the covering from his head, which he warns the woman to use, speaking thus: "For a man indeed ought not to cover

his head, forasmuch as he is the image and glory of God; but the woman is the glory of the man." [1 Corinthians 11:7] What then shall we say to this? If the woman fills up the image of the trinity after the measure of her own person, why is the man still called that image after she has been taken out of his side? . . . But we must notice how that which the apostle says, that not the woman but the man is the image of God, is not contrary to that which is written in Genesis, "God created man: in the image of God created He him; male and female created He them: and He blessed them." [Genesis 1:27–28] . . . How then did the apostle tell us that the man is the image of God, and therefore he is forbidden to cover his head; but the woman is not so, and therefore is commanded to cover hers? . . . The woman together with her own husband is the image of God, so that the whole substance may be one image; but when she is referred separately to her quality of help-meet, which regards the woman herself alone, then she is not the image of God; but as regards the man alone, he is the image of God as fully and completely as when the woman too is joined with him in one.

Leaving Augustine's logic and male chauvinism aside, it should be clear that he specifically makes the connection between the 1 Corinthians passage as a whole and Genesis 1:26–28. If it is not clear from its position in the work, *On the Trinity*, that this juxtaposition of verses has bearing on Augustine's notion of the Trinity, let the following passage make the connection explicit.

Let him believe in the Father, Son and Holy Spirit, one God, alone, great, omnipotent, good, just, merciful, Creator of all things visible and invisible . . . Yet not that the Father Himself is both son and Holy Spirit, or whatever else each is singly called in relation to either of the others; as word, which is not said except of the Son, or gift, which is not said except of the Holy Spirit. On this account also they admit the plural number, as it is written in the Gospel, "I and my Father are one." [John 10: 30]. . . . Sometimes the meaning is altogether latent, as in Genesis [1:26]: "let us make man after our image and likeness." Both *let us make* and *our* is said in the plural, and ought not to be received except as of relatives . . . And God is the Trinity. But because that image of God was not made altogether equal to Him, as being not born of Him, but created by Him . . . there are some who draw this distinction, that they will have the Son to be the image, but man not to be the image, but "after the image." But the apostle refutes them, saying, "For a man indeed ought not to cover his head, forasmuch as he is the image and glory of God." [1 Corinthians 11:7]

Augustine seems to have linked the hierarchy found in 1 Corinthians 11: 7 (also in 1 Corinthians 11:3,8,9) with Genesis 1:26–28 in an attempt to define the Trinity. But what has all his talk about Adam and Eve in God's image to do with the Holy Spirit? An Eastern father, Gregory of Nazianzus, shows the importance of this hierarchy for a proper appreciation of the relationships within the Trinity.

What was Adam? A creature of God. What then was Eve? A fragment of the creature. And what was Seth? The begotten of both. Does it then seem to you that Creature and Fragment and Begotten are the

same thing? Of course it does not. But were not these persons consubstantial? Of course they were. Well then, here it is an acknowledged fact that different persons may have the same substance . . .
did not both Eve and Seth come from the one Adam? And were they
both begotten by him? No; but the one was a fragment of him, and
other was begotten by him. And yet the two were one and the same
thing; both were human beings; no one will deny that. Will you then
give up your contention against the Spirit, that He must be altogether
begotten, or else cannot be consubstantial, or be God; and admit from
human examples the possibility of our position?

Gregory uses the hierarchic relationship of Adam to Eve to make a point
about the relationship between God the Father and the Son. He then
completes the analogy by likening the Spirit to the begotten of both, Seth.
Augustine adapts this model, *mutatis mutandis*, when he cites 1 Corinthians 11:7. The hierarchy of God, Man, Woman is like the relationship of
Father, Son, Spirit. Just as Eve proceeds from God through Adam, so the
Holy Spirit proceeds from the Father through the Son.

Our Rabbi manifestly rejects this argument from Scripture. He is clearly
aware that Genesis has two accounts: one hierarchic, the other egalitarian.
He refers to the former explicitly when he says, "In the past, Adam was
created from the dust, while Eve was created from Adam." By stating the
proposition in these words he informs his students of his awareness that
the account of creation found in Genesis 2 is employed by the church
fathers to explicate the Trinity. He knows that there are those, like Augustine, who impose the relationship of Genesis 2 upon Genesis 1:26. He
signals this awareness not by quoting the appropriate Scriptural response
from the context in Genesis, but by formulating his explication in language
reminiscent of 1 Corinthians 11:7–8, "[Man] is the image and glory of
God; but woman is the glory of man. For man was not made from woman,
but woman from man."

Although the heretics who tangled with our Rabbi may only have known
Genesis 1:26 as a Trinitarian testimony, the importance of setting out this
series of Scriptural models for the relationship of the three members of
the Trinity was clear to the church fathers. The subtle distinctions in the
relationships served to define the role of the Holy Spirit as divine, yet
proceeding from the Father through the Son. To return to Gregory's model,
the Spirit is begotten yet not in the same sense as the Son is begotten.

If He is Unbegotten, there are two Unoriginates. If He is Begotten,
you must make a further subdivision. He is so either by the Father or
by the Son. And, if by the Father, there are two sons and they are
brothers . . . But if by the Son, then such a one will say, we get a
glimpse of a Grandson God, than which nothing could be more
absurd.

Our Rabbi of the Palestinian Talmud knew just how absurd this would
seem. In rejecting the testimony from Genesis 1:26, he was demolishing
an intricately assembled Trinitarian theology. He was sensitive to the adaptation of the Genesis 2 hierarchy in 1 Corinthians 11:7–8 and to its use
in the Trinitarian argument. When the heretics quoted Genesis to him as
a Trinitarian testimony, our Rabbi recognized the unspoken argument
from 1 Corinthians 11:7. As in the other two cases, he refuted a Scriptural

argument using the maxim attributed to R. Simlai, "Every place that the
heretics rend [a verse from context to make their point] has the appropriate
[textual] response right next to it." In this instance, however, he did not
answer by pointing to a singular verb in the Hebrew text but by quoting 1
Corinthians 11:11, a verse that absolutely contradicts the sense of the
earlier verses in that chapter. Just as Genesis has an egalitarian account
of creation as well as the hierarchical one from which the Trinitarian argument had been advanced, so does Paul. Just as the egalitarian model from
Genesis can be used to undermine Scriptural proof of the relationship
between the Holy Spirit and the other members of the Trinity, so too, may
the verses of Paul.

> In the Lord woman is not independent of man nor man of woman;
> for as woman was made from man, so man is now born of woman.
> And all things are from God. Judge for yourselves.
>
> 1 Corinthians 11:11–13

DANIEL BOYARIN

Was Paul an "Anti-Semite"? (1993)†

The supposed conflict between "doing" as such and "faith" as such is simply not present in Galatians. What was at stake was not a way of life
summarized by the word "trust" versus a mode of life summarized by
"requirements," but whether or not the requirement for membership in to
the Israel of God would result in there being "neither Jew nor Greek."
(E. P. Sanders)

One of the crucial passages in Paul for determining (or rather constructing) his posture vis-à-vis the Jewish religion—the Law—is Galatians
3:10–4:7. Many interpreters, particularly of the "Lutheran" school, have
read this passage as if the "curse of the Law" consists of the inability of
human beings to ever meet its demands fully and therefore the irreparable
curse that it places on all. The whole purpose of the Law, on this account,
is to *increase* sin in the world, so that the saving grace of the Cross will be
even more abundant. As can be imagined, such an interpretation of Paul
leads easily to charges that he was rabidly anti-Jewish. Moreover, if such
views are asserted as a theologically correct view of Judaism and its historical role, then the theology is anti-Judaic (and later anti-Semitic). While
there are, of course, passages that *can* be read in support of such a perverse
notion of God—else it would not have achieved such widespread acceptance—, I would like to show (as have several other commentators by now)
that certainly in Galatians this is by no means a necessary construction of
the text. Much more plausible a priori, in my view, would be a conception
(closest to Dunn's) that the ultimate inadequacy of the Law stems from
its ethnic exclusiveness; from the fact that it represents the practices of

† From an article published in *USQR* 47 (1993): 47–80; a slightly revised version was included in
his *A Radical Jew: Paul and the Politics of Identity* (Berkeley: University of California Press, 1994),
136–57, 299–305. Reprinted by permission of the author and the Union Seminary Quarterly
Review. Boyarin is Hermann P. and Sophia Taubman Professor of Talmudic Culture at the University of California, Berkeley.

the Tribe of Israel, and therefore is unsuitable as a way of life and of salvation for the Universal Humanity which Paul seeks to institute. E. P. Sanders's insight here is also very important, namely that this section consists not so much of Paul's critique of the Law but of his explanation of God's purpose in giving the Law, given its inefficacy for salvation.

In the following section I will attempt to show that Paul produces a sort of radical, "heretical" midrash—but midrash nevertheless—in support of his new understandings of Judaism. The very fact, however, that he supports his view with midrash indicates his conviction that he stands in continuity with the Torah and not against it. To be sure, from a "Jewish" point of view, this "continuity" itself constitutes rejection of the Law. The form of Paul's argument itself provides then an elegant analogue for his character; in both we find an entity both inside and outside of Judaism at the same time.

[1.1] *Those who are men of works of Law are under a curse*

"By contrast, those who are men of works of Law are under a curse. For it is written, 'Cursed is everyone who does not uphold everything that is written in the book of the Law, by doing it' (Deut. 27:26). It is, then, obvious that nobody is justified before God by Law, because 'The righteous shall live by faith' (Hab. 2:4). The Law is not by faith, but 'He who does them shall live by them' " (Lev. 18:5).

A proper understanding of these verses of Paul is crucial for any evaluation of his ideology vis-à-vis the Jews, the Torah and Judaism, as many currently held readings end up claiming that Paul significantly distorts Jewish doctrine here. Hans Joachim Schoeps largely based his claim that Paul misunderstood/misrepresented Judaism on this very passage. A reinterpretation of the passage that will not lead to such conclusions is therefore highly important for our general evaluation of Paul on Judaism. In establishing the identity of Paul as a Jewish cultural critic, it is important to demonstrate that he writes *as a Jew*. Showing the thoroughly midrashic character of the main arguments of the Letter is then directly relevant to the descriptive project as a whole. Paul's argument is almost prototypical midrash.

Most interpreters have quite missed the point here in my view. Their interpretations are dependent on theological presuppositions about Paul's relation to the Law as generating sin, a proposition which seems a priori implausible for Paul to have held. Dunn has produced the best arguments against this notion:

> Betz's own reconstruction of Paul's reasoning (the law was given in order to be broken and to generate sin) is hardly obvious from the text (even allowing for 3:19). It would hardly cut much ice with his readers, and on this point Paul could hardly simply assume that his readers shared his presuppositions. . . . Moreover, as Hübner points out, such a theology attributes a very perverse motive on the part of God in giving the law (*Gesetze* 27); it is hard to think that Paul would be unaware of such a corollary or would willingly embrace it.[1]

---

1. James D. G. Dunn, *Jesus, Paul and the Law: Studies in Mark and Galatians* (Louisville, KY: Westminster John Knox, 1990), 234 [Boyarin's note]. * * *

Alternatively, interpretations are based on the notion that one who transgresses even one precept of the Torah is irredeemably cursed—a notion which has no support in Jewish texts of either the first or later centuries.

*　　*　　*

The answer is quite simple when looked at from a midrashic point of view. The verse [Deut. 27:26] reads "Cursed is everyone who does not uphold everything that is written in the book of the Law, by doing it." The words, "by doing it" at the end of the verse are syntactically and semantically superfluous—to check that, just remove them, and you will see that the sense is not harmed. Paul, then, following a very standard midrashic move rereads the verse (or indeed rewrites it syntactically), so that all of its elements will add to the meaning. He does so, in fact, by taking the "by doing it" as modifying the entire phrase "everyone who does not uphold everything that is written in the book of the Law." We could rewrite the verse then as: "Everyone, who [precisely] by *doing* it does not uphold all that is written in the book of the Law, is under a curse"; i.e. by *doing* it, by physical performance, works of the Law, one is *not* upholding all that which is written in the book of the Law, and *that* is the curse, because "all that is written" implies much more than mere doing! The hermeneutical move that Paul makes here is quite similar (although not identical) to that of the Rabbis in the Talmud on Exod. 23:2, who interpreted "After the majority you must not incline to do evil, and you shall not bear witness in a suit to incline after the majority," as meaning, that one *must* follow the majority.

As Stephen Westerholm has concluded in general, "What is crucial to note is that Paul consistently distinguishes between the 'doing' of the law's commands required of those subject to it and the 'fulfilling' of the law by Christians." The end of Galatians provides an important parallel: "For the whole law is fulfilled in one word, 'You shall love your neighbor as yourself' " (5:14). In this verse, Paul speaks of "fulfilling" the Law, not of "doing" it. John Barclay has made the very telling point that πληροῦν and its Hebrew equivalent מלא are never used in Jewish sources in either Hebrew or Greek with reference to the Law. Further, when Paul refers to Jewish observance of the Law he uses φυλάσσω (=keep), ποιέω (=do), and πράσσω (=practice) but not πληροῦν (fulfill). Jews do the Law, but Christians fulfill the Law and even more to the point of this essay, the very notion of fulfillment is a Hellenistically-inspired Pauline innovation in theology, although obviously one for which the way was prepared by the prophetic diatribes against the hypocrisy of bringing sacrifices while ignoring homeless people. It replaces the difference of the doing of *many* material practices with the logos of one ideal fulfillment, just as the difference of Jew and Greek or male and female is also to be replaced by the Ideal One, spiritualized phallus which cannot be circumcised physically but with a "circumcision not made with hands." Thus precisely by dying to the Law according to the flesh, the Christian believer can fulfil the Law of Christ. By crucifying the flesh, together with its passions and desires *and its fleshly practices*, circumcision, the Christian becomes able to walk in the spirit and fulfill the Law of faith working through love. This is the true circumcision which defines the true Jew (Rom. 2:25–29).

This distinction is the clue to understanding the key verse, Gal 3:10, where according to my interpretation Paul argues that those who "do" the Law are not "fulfilling" the Law. I assume that the ἐμμενεῖ (upholding) of the Deuteronomy quotation is semantically (or perhaps theologically) roughly equivalent to e.g. πεπλήρωται (fulfilled) in Galatians 5:14. The Hebrew מקים of the verse certainly means "to fulfill the requirement of" as well as "to preserve." So men of works of the Law, those who hold that works justify and practice accordingly are accursed by the Law itself, because of their misunderstanding of the true import of the Law. It is these to whom Paul will later refer in Romans as, "you who have the written code and circumcision but break the law." This interpretation is supported as well by Paul's own usage in other places, for instance Rom. 3:27, where he explicitly contrasts "doing" which equals "the Law of works," with "The Law of faith."

The next verse is also quite simply understood as a midrashic argument, although from the rabbinic point of view surely a "midrash of lies." Paul wishes to prove that "nobody is justified before God by Law." He first cites the verse of Habbakuk which reads that the "righteous live by faith." It follows from this that those who live by faith are the righteous, i.e. the justified. He then argues that those who live by the Law do not live by faith, since the verse in Leviticus explicitly reads "He who *does them* lives by *them*," i.e. one who does the commandments lives by *them* and not by faith. Since, then, we know from Habbakuk that the righteous live by faith, he who lives by *them* and not by faith (and, thereby, does not *fulfill* the Law) is not righteous—is not justified. Paul has then a perfect proof that "nobody is justified before God by Law." This interpretation obviates Sanders's claim that Paul is here denying the truth of a verse of the Torah. Far from contradicting the Leviticus verse, Paul is confirming its literal truth: One who does them, lives by them. Paul is using methods of interpretation that would not surprise any Pharisee (I suspect) or rabbi, although the results he arrives at would, of course, shock them to their depths. The phrase "does them" in the Leviticus verse is precisely the same as "to do them" in the verse of Deuteronomy, so this argument is a direct sequel to the previous one. Finally, it is highly significant that in the Leviticus context, the Law which one does is specifically marked as that which marks Jews off from Gentiles:

> You shall not act according to the way of life of Egypt in which you lived. And you shall not act according to the way of life of Canaan, into which I will cause you to go, and you shall not live by their laws. You shall do my statutes [משפטים] and keep my laws and live by them. I am the Lord your God. And you shall keep all my laws and all my statutes and do them, which if a man does he will live by them.

Given the whole vector of Paul's argument in Galatians, it is hardly surprising that he would choose this set of verses as his negative example. The word משפטים, "statutes," is a highly marked term for Jewish privilege in having been given the Law, because of its use in the psalm verse: "He has spoken his words to Jacob, his laws and *statutes* to Israel. He has not done so for any other nation, and *statutes*, they do not know" [Ps. 147:16–17]. Therefore, Paul argues, those who do them, and thereby mark themselves off from the Egyptians and the Canaanites, live by them and not by faith, but those who live by faith, which is for all, are righteous. Ergo those who do them are not righteous.

It is not insignificant, moreover, that this verse of Leviticus which Paul has just treated so negatively appears in the context of justification of the laws against incest which appear immediately following it, and it is precisely these which are identified as the "way of life of Egypt and Canaan." This provides, I think, a very elegant account of Paul's sudden panic about libertinism in chapters five and six of Galatians, a much more plausible one than the assumption of a proto-gnostic sect in Galatia. If this was the nature and content of Paul's preaching on his first visit to Corinth as well, it is not entirely surprising that some of the Corinthian Christians "misunderstood" and concluded that Christian freedom consisted of abrogation of the laws against incest as well.

[1.2] Christ has redeemed us from the curse of the Law

"Christ has redeemed us from the curse of the Law by becoming a curse for us, for it is written, 'Cursed is everyone who hangs on a tree.' " (3:13)

"In the context of the letter, he certainly assumes that the Law becomes a curse for those who seek justification before God 'by works of the Law,' because by doing so they deprive themselves of the blessing of Abraham given to 'men of faith.' " Humanity has been enslaved by the "elements of this world," including for Jews, the Law (for the positive role of the law as παιδαγωγός [guardian] see my discussion of 3:24). Christ through his double sacrifice of being born a human, coming under the Law and being crucified has freed Jews from the slavery of the Law and Gentiles from the slavery of the elements of the world. All of this will be developed further in chapter four of the Letter and is prefigured in the present verse.

Once again, the crucial question is how to understand the prooftext that Paul cites, and once again midrashic method provides a possible and, to my mind, very attractive answer. The way to understand this midrash was pointed out by Klein nearly eighty years ago and repeated by Schoeps but needs refining. The important point is that the exegesis is based on a pun, on a double meaning of the Hebrew verbal adjective "taluy" (תלוי=hung). In the older version of this interpretation, the pun was that "hung" also means "elevated," so the reference is to the fact that through the crucifixion Jesus was elevated. While this understanding is certain[ly] in my opinion on the right methodological track, it does not solve the problem of explaining how Paul learns from this verse that "Christ has redeemed us from the curse of the Law," and that is, of course, the crux of the matter. In rabbinic Hebrew, however, the root of תלוי has another sense as well, namely "to suspend," and this usage is attested in the Mishna precisely with a "curse" as its complement." Thus, we find in Mishna Sota 3:4, a statement that the wife who drinks the bitter waters is cursed if she had been guilty of adultery, but "If she had merit, the merit תולה (suspends) [the curse] for her." My suggestion is then that Paul, following accepted midrashic practice, for which the parallels cited in Schoeps are valid, does read the verse as a pun, almost as a visual pun or rhebus on the crucifixion.

Jesus, by being suspended on the cross has suspended the curse, for "He who is hung is a curse of God, and the curse of God is suspended." The entire propositional content of Paul's statement is now supported by the midrashic reading.

[1.3] *The promise of the Spirit through faith*

"That the blessing of Abraham might come upon the Gentiles through Jesus Christ, and that we might receive the promise of the Spirit through faith." (3:14)

Paul here, as elsewhere, spiritualizes and allegorizes the notion of kinship. If, for rabbinic Jews the crucial signifier is actual, physical descent from Abraham, for Paul, it is entry into the faith community of Christ which constitutes descent from Abraham, according to the Spirit. He equates the promise made to Abraham—that Sarah would bear Isaac—to Abraham's spiritual paternity of Jesus, "the seed" to whom the promise was made, and through Jesus of all who believe. Thus the exegetical notion that the blessing is for the descendants of Abraham by the "promise" and not to those who are his descendants "by the flesh" is fulfilled in time by God, through the sending of the Messianic seed through which the promise was made. The fulfillment of the promise is, however, through the participation of the people in the spirit which has been offered them by Christ's crucifixion. The people enter into the spirit by participating in the experience and commitment of the crucifixion and resurrection. Such participation constitutes acceptance of the gift; they thus enter into the descent by the promise, the type of which was the birth of Isaac through the promise and not natural carnal means. Indeed, it is not so much Abraham who is the type of Christ but Isaac. God offers adoption as spiritual children through the sacrifice of his son, but people either accept or reject it. They accept it by allowing the gifts of the spirit into their hearts. If they reject it by going back to the works of the Law, implying thereby that only physical descent or physical adoption into the Jewish family saves, then Christ died on the Cross in vain. As Ferdinand Christian Baur put it so precisely already at the end of the nineteenth century, "According to the [Jerusalem apostles], it is in vain to be a Christian without being a Jew also. According to [Paul], it is in vain to be a Christian if, as a Christian, one chooses to be a Jew as well."

In Galatians Paul supports the connection between the allegorical theory of the Law and christology. The two midrashim together provide the argument. Already the Law itself has informed us of its own dual nature by telling us that anyone who remains with the physical level of "doing the Law" has not fulfilled the Law. This is then followed by the midrashic argument that anyone who does the Law is not living by faith, which alone justifies, and finally, that Christ through his crucifixion has revealed the true meaning of the Law, namely that its material signifier is to be replaced by its spiritual signified. In the next section Paul will turn to the third aspect of the triad, the question of physical descent and genealogy, which he will also read in accord with the allegorical structure.

* * *

[1.5] *Why then the law?*

"Why then the law? It was added because of transgression, until the seed should come to whom the promise had been made; and it was ordained by angels through an intermediary. Now an intermediary is from more than one, but God is one." (3:19–20)

Proper clarification of this and the following passage is crucial to any construal of Paul's theology of Judaism. There seems to me to be not the slightest reason in this text to understand the word χάριν as telic, namely that Paul wishes to say that the Law was given in order to produce transgression, as Betz, following many modern commentators argues. The simplest explanation of the verse is that the Law was given as a temporary and secondary measure, because of the existence of sin in the present age, in order to restrain people from transgressing until the coming of Jesus who is the seed. Thielman has proposed another interpretation which seems to me also to be a distinct possibility. He reads τῶν παραβάσεων χάριν προσετέθη (added because of transgression) as having causal force, not, however, in the sense of preventing transgression, but in the sense of providing an answer to transgression, namely punishment. This helps to make good sense of the συνέγχλεισεν ἡ γραφή (Scripture consigned or confined under sin) of verse 22 below as well.

After hundreds of years and hundreds of interpretations, I believe that Wright has solved the problem of these verses. The "seed" to whom the promise was made is the new one human family of Christ, and it was ordained by angels through an intermediary, Moses. It is the next verse which Wright's reading decisively clarifies. The translation given above follows standard interpretations, none of them successful, which in one way or another find here a logical argument that the Law must have been given by angels and not by God. Wright translates rather, "Now [the mediator] is not a mediator of one, but God is one." Having established above that "one" here means the new unified single family of humanity in Christ, we understand the verse to mean that Moses was not the mediator for this one family of humanity but for only a part of it, for a difference within the sameness, so this cannot be the fulfillment that God looks for, because God is one. The verse becomes on this reading an exact parallel to Paul's argument in Romans 3:20: "Is God the God of the Jews only? Is he not of Gentiles also? Yes, of Gentiles also." As Wright sums up his interpretation:

> The problem of v. 20b can be solved quite easily once 20a is read in this way. Moses is not the mediator of the 'one family,' *but God is one*, and therefore desires one family, as he promised to Abraham. The presupposition of Paul's argument is that, if there is one God—the foundation of all Jewish belief—there must be one people of God. Were there to be two or more 'peoples,' the whole theological scheme would lapse back into some sort of paganism, with each tribe or race possessing its own national deities.[2]

The rabbis, however, did not see it that way, allowing that others could worship God and be saved without joining into one People of God. Once

---

2. N. T. Wright, *The Climax of the Covenant: Christ and the Law in Pauline Theology* (Minneapolis: Fortress, 1992), 170 [Boyarin's note].

more, I think the passion for unity must be ascribed to Paul's Hellenistic Jewish *Weltanschauung*.

The Law is thus demoted in importance vis-à-vis the promise, but whether it was given to prevent or to punish transgression, there is no suggestion here that it has a demonic function nor that these angels are to be understood demonically. It is easy to see, however, how gnostics could find such a meaning here. In any case, the important point is that there is no warrant here to understand that the function of the Law was to produce transgression, in order to increase the scope of the working of God's grace—rather like a doctor making the patient sicker in order to increase the scope of her healing power. Nor do the next verses argue for such an interpretation either.

[1.6] *Is the law then against the promises of God?*

"Is the law then against the promises of God? Certainly not. For if a law had been given which could make alive, then justification would indeed be by the law. But the scripture consigned everything under sin, in order that the promise, by faith in Jesus Christ might be given to those who believe. Before the faith came, we were kept in custody under the Law, confined until the coming faith was to be revealed. Therefore, the Law has been our guardian until Christ, in order that we might be justified by faith. But since the faith has come, we are no longer under a guardian." (3:21–25)

Paul begins this argument with another logical proof. If the Law, as he has just said, is given for the purpose of preventing sin, does it not annul the promise, i.e. does it not substitute itself for the promise and obviate the promise? This seems to me a strong argument against the interpretation of the previous verses that the Law was given to increase sin, in order that the grace of the promise would be necessary, for if that were the case then the question of the Law being against the promise would not arise! Only if the Law is accorded the positive role of confining sin would it be even possible to imagine that it somehow cancels the promise of a "free gift of grace."

* * *

In either case, however, the function of the Law is not to give life. The answer to the question about the Law being against the promises, then, is of course: No it is not. Now comes Paul's proof: If there were a law which could make alive (= justify), then indeed justification would come from the Law and the promise would be nullified. The function of the Law, however, is not to give life. All it does is confine all under sin, or by reason of sin, so that they may continue until the promise is given to those who believe. Therefore, the original premise is proven wrong: The Law does not annul the promise. Paul then explains the positive function of the Law as a pedagogue who makes it possible for people to be justified by faith, and now that his function has been fulfilled, is no longer required.

Accordingly, we need not see the παιδαγωγός in a negative light as Betz implies in order to follow Paul's argument. If the pedagogue is a guide and baby-sitter appropriate for the small child, then we understand Paul's *mashal* perfectly. In the infancy of humanity the pedagogue was necessary because of sin (not to produce sin, a bizarre and near Marcionite notion, which Lutheran theologians refer to as "God's strange work!"), but now with the maturity of the coming [of] the Christ the pedagogue is no longer necessary. If we do not accept the essentially Lutheranizing interpretation of Paul's Law doctrine to the effect that it has never been a way of achieving virtue, then we do not need to render Paul's notion of the Law as a pedagogue so discontinuous with the topos of Law as educator, which, as Betz remarks, was common from Plato on. On the other hand, there may be no doubt that Betz is correct that it is wrong to see here an argument that the Law prepared for the coming of Christ by educating people in that direction. The mashal in the beginning of chapter 4 completely disables such an interpretation. The pedagogue is not a teacher in the sense of one who prepares the child for adulthood but a guardian in the sense of one who keeps him or her out of trouble while waiting for adulthood. This does not, however, translate into such terms as "ugly" or "demonic" that Betz uses, nor to a notion that the pedagogue was sent to increase transgression!

[1.7] *And because you are sons, God has sent the Spirit of his Son into our hearts, crying, 'Abba! Father!'*

"I mean that the heir, as long as he is a child, is no better than a slave, though he is the owner of all the estate; but he is under guardians and trustees until the date set by the father. So with us; when we were children, we were slaves to the elemental spirits of the universe. But when the time had fully come, God set forth his Son, born of woman, born under the law, to redeem those who were under the law, so that we might receive adoption as sons. And because you are sons, God has sent the Spirit of his Son into our hearts, crying, 'Abba! Father!' So through God you are no longer a slave but a son, and if a son then an heir." (4: 1–7)

Paul develops and interweaves here two themes that he has set forth, the metaphor of the pedagogue and the Galatians' memory of their baptism. He conjoins them through the slave-freeman antinomy of the baptismal formula by insisting that the child is alike in status to the slave. Further, the childhood image which has until now only been used to explain the status of the Law, given 430 years after the promise and only temporary, is now used analogously to explain the situation of the Galatians under Paganism. We, all of us, that is I as a Jew and you as Pagans, we were all under the elemental spirits of the universe: You the pagan gods and I the Law. I wonder if Paul is thinking here of Deut. 4:19 which seemingly ordains the stars as the proper worship of "The Nations." Thielman has, once more, made an attractive and simple alternative suggestion. He argues philologically that τὰ στοιχεῖα τοῦ κόσμου (the elements of the world) simply means the world itself, and the reason that Paul uses this "roundabout" term is owing to the fact that στοιχεῖα is also used metaphorically for the "elements" as that which a child learns first in school, thus effectively continuing Paul's figure of a child's education and maturity. But when we had grown up, then God the Father sent forth his son to redeem us born under the Law that we might receive adoption as sons and also you as well. Because you are also sons, at the baptismal ceremony God sent his spirit into our hearts, and we all cried out "Abba! Father."

The explicit citation of the Aramaic alludes, I think, to two things: Jesus's own crying out of "Abba" to God and the traditionary pre-Pauline liturgy of the baptism. Therefore, through God, you (and we) have been recognized as a son, by entering into the spiritual body of the Son, and therefore no longer a slave but an heir. Paul's figure for the condition of Israel under the Law demonstrates, I think, beyond doubt that he does not hold the Law to be demonic or evil, or the commitment to keeping the Law to be contemnable in the way that the variations of the "Lutheran" interpretation of Paul would have it. This "slavery" is the benevolent and beneficial slavery of the child. It is for his own good. Only a fool, however—You foolish Galatians—would prefer to remain in such a state and not grow up into the status of heir. In an unpublished paper, David Henkin has analyzed this text brilliantly. He writes:

> Significantly, the elevation of the Christian to the status of son is not an adoption in the ordinary sense of a superimposition of a natural title on someone who has no natural claim to the title. As the metaphor of the custodian (the *paidagogós*) in the preceding verses implies, the apocalyptic moment is one in which sons (who were always by nature sons, though their contingent historical position obscured this fact) are recognized and redeemed by their rightful father. The reshuffling of the lines of genealogy is presented here as an act of restoration. The historical signifiers that Jewish law prescribed to represent a kind of paternal bond with God are peeled away and sons are recognized by their father by virtue of their faith, which is to say by virtue of the capacity to recognize him as their father.[3]

This, I think then, provides the perfect summation of Paul's theology of Judaism and the Jews. They and their Law had literal value at a certain point in human history, in the childhood of humanity. Now, however, that maturity has come in the guise of the coming of Christ, his crucifixion and rising from the dead, the value of the signifier has been superseded. There is no more role for Israel as such in its concrete sense—except always for the promise of Romans 9–11 that in the end it will not be abandoned but redeemed by coming to faith in Christ. At stake is not Paul's love for Jews. I take very seriously his anguish in the beginning of Romans 9 over his brothers in the flesh. This very anguish, however, is precisely that which signifies that as Jews—that is as the historically understood concrete community of the flesh—Israel has no more role to play in history.

A true parable may help make the point clearer. A Jewish friend of my family's was in the business of importing equipment for chicken farmers. As such, among his major customers, were Anabaptists in Pennsylvania, with whom he became very friendly over a number of years. At one point, at a meal, the wife of his customer became distraught and began to cry. When asked why she was crying, she answered: Because Sidney is such a lovely person, and he is going to go to hell. I have no doubt that her love for Sidney was real—and specific, not merely abstract love for all human

---

3. David M. Henkin, "Faith and Patricide: Paul, Judaism and the Question of Paternity," unpublished paper, Berkeley, CA, Fall 1991 [Boyarin's note].

beings—, just as was Paul's for his Jewish relatives. Nevertheless, it would be hard to claim that this woman valued Sidney, *as a Jew,* and this is my point about Paul. If the only value and promise afforded the Jews, even in Romans 11, is that in the end they will see the error of their ways, one cannot claim that there is a role for Jewish existence in Paul. It has been transcended by that which was its spiritual, allegorical referent always and forever: faith in Jesus Christ and the community of the faithful in which there is no Jew or Greek.

On my reading, then, it is totally inappropriate to think of Paul's thought as anti-Semitic, or even as anti-Judaic (except for perhaps the occasional outbursts of temper and frustration in 1 Thess. 2:14 [if genuine] and Philippians 3). Paul loves his relatives according to the flesh, anguishes over them, and is convinced that in the end they will be saved. This salvation, however, is precisely for those Jews a bitter gospel not a sweet one, because it is conditional precisely on abandoning that to which we hold so dearly, our separate cultural, religious identity, our own fleshy and historical practice, our existence according to the flesh, our Law, our difference. Paul has simply allegorized our difference quite out of existence.

*   *   *

> For it is written that Abraham had two sons, one from the slave woman and one from the free woman. The one from the slave woman was born "according to the flesh," however, while the one from the free woman "through the promise." These things have an allegorical meaning. For they are two covenants: one from Mt. Sinai, giving birth into slavery—this is Hagar. Now Hagar is Mt. Sinai in Arabia, but it also corresponds to the present Jerusalem, for she lives in slavery together with her children. By contrast, the Jerusalem above is free—this is our mother. For it is written, "Rejoice, O barren one who does not bear: break forth and shout, you who are not in travail; for the children of the desolate one are more than the children of the one who has a husband." But you, my brothers, are children of promise, like Isaac. And just as in those days the one born "according to [the] flesh" persecuted the one "according to [the] spirit," so it is today.

We thus see here the political and theological themes of the entire Pauline enterprise in this letter coming together here in one brilliant stroke. All of the antitheses that he has set up until now work together to convince the Galatians that they have but one choice, to remain in the spirit and not recommit themselves to the flesh, to remain in the covenant that was made according to the promise to the one seed of Abraham, the [spiritual] body of the risen Christ and not return to the slavery of the covenant with Sinai, which is the present Jerusalem—that is both the symbolic present Jerusalem as well as the church in Jerusalem by undertaking to fall back into the fleshly hermeneutic of literal interpretation of circumcision. Furthermore, at least in this passage we see how illusory is the contrast between allegory and typology. Because the present Christian situation is to be interpreted spiritually, therefore allegory is the appropriate mode for understanding it. To be sure, it is the historical event of the coming of the Christ, his crucifixion and resurrection which has precipitated the reading, but that very historical event is itself not history but an event that signifies the end—telos, both the finish and the revelation of the meaning—of history.

As a mode of reading events, apocalyptic is, accordingly, structurally homologous to allegory. Allegory, typology, and apocalyptic all equally figure an "end to history." Jesus's birth as a Jew and his transformation in the crucifixion both signifies and effects the transformation/transition from the historical moment to the allegorical one, from the moment of ethnicity to the moment of the universal (spiritual) subject, from natural birth to spiritual rebirth in the promise. That is, it signifies insofar as the allegorical meaning was always already there, and it effects insofar as only at the apocalypse is that meaning revealed in the world. This interpretation, i.e. that the true meaning always existed and only waited for the Christ event in order to be revealed, is strongly supported by Galatians 3:8: "And the scripture, foreseeing that God would justify the Gentiles by faith, preached the gospel beforehand [προευηγγελίσατο] to Abraham, saying, 'In you shall all nations be blessed,'" but "Now before faith came, we were confined under the law, kept under restraint until faith should be revealed" (3:23). The Christ event is thus precisely apocalyptic, in the strictest sense of that term—revelation—; it has revealed the universally true meaning, faith, that always subsisted within and above history, works of the Law.

For Paul allegory is indeed the speaking of the other; it reveals that the particular signifies the universal. We must realize the depth of Paul's understanding of allegory not as a rhetorical device of language but as a revelation of the structure of reality (including-historical reality) itself in order to have an appreciation for this passage and his thought in general. It is not that allegory and typology have been mixed here, but history itself is transformed through this typology into allegory, and Paul's apocalypse is fully realized. Accordingly, interpretations of Paul which focus on his apocalypticism, understanding it as only a version of the general Palestinian Jewish apocalyptic, have also seriously mistaken the thrust of his Gospel in my opinion. It is not only the case that the fulfillment of time has come but more to the point that Paul understands it in a certain, specific way, as the revelation of the inner meaning of outward signs, an inner meaning which is always already there, whether the outward signs are the flesh, the Jews, the Law or the historical Jesus. It seems to me to be a serious hermeneutic error to make one's interpretation of Paul depend on the apocalyptic expectation, which is after all not even mentioned once in Galatians, rather than the apocalyptic fulfillment which has already been realized in the vision of the crucified Christ according to the Spirit, Christ's spirit, Paul's and that of the Galatians. Even J. Christiaan Beker, the most trenchant defender of Paul as apocalyptist, admits that "Galatians threatens to undo what I have posited as the coherent core of Pauline thought, the apocalyptic co-ordinates of the Christ-event that focus on the imminent, cosmic triumph of God." This suggests that as central as expectation of the parousia is for Paul, and Beker's reading is impressive indeed, it is not yet "the coherent core of Pauline thought" but a vitally important element of that thought whose core lies yet elsewhere. The "elsewhere" that I argue for is, of course, the unification of humanity, of which both the realized eschatology of the Cross and the expected eschatology of the parousia are equally vital parts.

                              *   *   *

The upshot of the above discussion is that there is no evidence in Galatians on my reading that Paul's problem with the Law was connected with
the impossibility of keeping the Law fully, nor that the Law was given in
order to increase sin so that grace might abound more fully. The Law was
rather given to the Jews, as a temporary measure for specific historical
reasons, meant to be superseded by its spiritual referent, faith, when the
time would come, which it of course has. Paul's argument is then not anti-
Judaic in the sense that certain interpretations of it would have it be. It is
not a claim that God has rejected the Jews because they were inadequate
in some sense or another, because their keeping of the Law was a striving
against God!, an attempt to force him to justify them, a form of boasting,
self-righteousness and pride, a religion of Sacred Violence or any of the
other variations of this essentially anti-Judaic topos. The Jews as concrete
signifier of the fulfilled spiritual signified, the body of Christ, the Church,
had simply outlived their usefulness. They stood in the world now only as
the sign of something else. They had been allegorized out of real historical
existence, and their concrete, separate existence and cultural difference
were now vestigial, excepting only the faithful promise that in the end God
would keep His promise to them, and they would be redeemed—as Christians. Paul's hermeneutic of the Jews as signifier of the faithful body of
Christians, of the Jews as the literal—κατὰ σάρκα—of which Christians
are the allegorical signified, κατὰ πνεῦμα, even if not the "origin of anti-
Semitism" certainly has effects in the world until this day. In other words,
I argue that while Galatians is not an anti-Judaic text, its theory of the
Jews nevertheless is one that is inimical to Jewish difference, indeed to all
difference as such.

                          ALAN F. SEGAL

        Paul and the Beginning of Jewish Mysticism (1995)†

                              *   *   *

While contemplating Carol Zaleski's material on near-death experiences, I want to say that in a sense all Jewish mystics of this period—and
especially Paul—thought of their experiences as "near death" experiences,
not in a literal sense, but in a figurative sense. They saw their visionary
ascent as an exact parallel to the voyage of the soul to heaven after death.
Indeed, Paul explicitly says that his experience of Christ was like his death,
followed by his rebirth in Christ. It is that identification of the mystic with
the figure in heaven that I want to investigate, so as to show that the
language that Carol mentions in chapter 17 is part of the mystical tradition
of the West.

† From his article in *Death, Ecstasy, and Other Worldly Journeys*, ed. by J. J. Collins and M. Fishbane
  (Albany, NY: SUNY Press, 1995), 95–122. Copyright © 1995 by the State University of New York.
  All rights reserved. Reprinted by permission of the State University of New York. Segal is Ingeborg
  Rennert Professor of Jewish Studies at Barnard College, Columbia University.

Jewish Mysticism

That Jewish mysticism has a history is due to Gershom Scholem. When all the modern Jews were saying that Judaism was a religion of reason, more reasonable than Christianity they thought, hence more able to deal with the modern world, Scholem pointed out that they were forgetting—trying desperately to forget—a lively tradition of Jewish mysticism. That history includes Merkavah mysticism, classical Kabbalah, and Hasidism. Moshe Idel added to and corrected Scholem's history by pointing out the experiential aspect of Jewish mysticism. He noted that altered states of consciousness, ecstasy and not just fanciful cosmology, if you will, was part of Jewish mystical tradition from the beginning.

It is Merkavah mysticism that I want to consider here. But it is clear to me that what we call "Jewish mysticism" grew out of a separate phenomenon, apocalypticism, the tail-end of the prophetic movement that claimed the world is going to end abruptly.

All Jewish mysticism, indeed even the doctrine of resurrection itself, depends on a very peculiar passage in Daniel, chapter 12, the only apocalyptic work accepted into the Hebrew Bible:

> At that time shall arise Michael, the great prince who has charge of your people, And there shall be a time of trouble, such as never has been since there was a nation til that time; but at that time your people shall be delivered, every one whose name shall be found written in the book. And many of those who sleep in the dust of the earth shall awake, some to everlasting life, and some to shame and ever-lasting contempt. And those who are wise shall shine like the brightness of the firmament; and those who turn many to righteousness, like the stars for ever and ever. (Dan. 12:1–3)

We often gloss over the rather peculiar aspects of this prophecy in Daniel. In it, it says that two kinds of people will be resurrected—the very good, and the very bad (not the usual understanding). More interesting to me is the idea that the maskilim, those who are wise, will shine as the stars in heaven, *yazhiru ke'zohar haraqi'a*—this is literally where *Zohar*, the principal book of Jewish mysticism, gets its name. Essentially this document tells us that those who make themselves wise will become stars, but it actually means that the good people on earth will become angels. Angels in heaven and stars are equated. The history of Jewish mysticism is deeply concerned with the experience of becoming a star. But that is precisely what Paul tells us. We must wait to see how this takes place.

I want to underline three aspects of this Jewish mystical spirituality and show how it is fundamental to Paul's experience. The first aspect of the Jewish mystical experience is *angelophany*—the vision of a principal angelic mediator who, like the angel of the Lord in Exodus, carries the name of God or somehow participates in God's divinity. All the passages describing the Glory of the Lord, especially Ezek. 1:26—the human figure on the throne in Ezekiel's vision—are pulled into this angelic figure, making a consistent figure of a principal angelic mediator. This mediator figure can be called a variety of different names—Yahoel, Melchizedek, and even the Son of man—and, as I have tried to show in *Paul the Convert*, it was the figure that Paul saw and with whom he identified the crucified Christ.

So for Paul, the figure was the traditional one except, as he says in 2 Cor., it has the face of Jesus.

The second aspect of this tradition that is important to the study of Paul is *transformation*. In the Jewish mystical tradition, adepts or heroes or patriarchs can be transformed or subsumed into the mediator figure. This is more or less the equivalent of becoming an angel or becoming a star, which is the exact point of Daniel, chapter 12. The most obvious example of this phenomenon, though by no means the only one, is Enoch, who is transformed into the Son of man in 1 Enoch 71. I would submit that what is narrated there is the very experience of being made a star, which is also narrated in Daniel, chapter 12. From a historical point of view, the problem with this tradition is that chapter 71 of Enoch cannot be proven to be pre-Christian. Most scholars believe it to be pre-Christian, but that is not the same thing as proof.

However, this is only the prologue, for Merkavah mysticism involved apocalyptic visions of a violent end to the enemies of God, not quiet contemplation. Also, it was the active desire to journey to heaven and see what was there. One could go to heaven and not only at the end of one's life—some people actually went while alive. This is the third aspect of the tradition I want to highlight here—*ascent*. In fact, the importance of going during one's life, you might say, was to prove that one was going after death. It was a kind of eschatological verification (pace Hick).

Here is an example: In the ninth century, Hai Gaon recounts that the journey to view this divine figure was undertaken by mystics who put their heads between their knees (the posture Elijah assumed when praying for rain in 1 Kings 18:42), reciting repetitious psalms, glossolalic incantations, and mantralike prayers, which are recorded in abundance in the hekhalot literature:

> When he seeks to behold the Merkabah and the palaces of the angels on high, he must follow a certain procedure. He must fast a number of days and place his head between his knees and whisper many hymns and songs whose texts are known from tradition. Then he perceives the chambers as if he saw the seven palaces with his own eyes, and it is as though he entered one palace after another and saw what is there. And there are two *mishnayoth* which the tannaim taught regarding this topic, called *Hekhaloth Rabbati* and *Hekhaloth Zutreti*.

The Gaon is aware of the mystical techniques for heavenly ascent and describes them as "out-of-body" experiences during which the adept ascends to heaven while his body stays on earth. It is even possible that he understands the entire journey as an internal, intrapsychic one, but that is not entirely clear. The hekhaloth texts themselves sometimes mention the transformation of the adept into a heavenly being, whose body becomes fire and whose eyes flash lightening, a theme that is repeated in the Paris Magical Papyrus.

Merkabah and Its Predecessors

Though it would be impractical here to review all the detailed work currently underway on apocalyptic and Merkabah mysticism, its relationship to Christianity and Paul's writing can be briefly summarized. Basically the central issue of Jewish mysticism was the relationship between human beings and an enormous angelic human figure manifesting God. The figure is generally called "God's Glory" or his "Kabod." The relationship was one of absorption, as we shall see.

THE ANGEL OF THE LORD

Let us first see who the figure is. In the Bible, God is sometimes described in human form. In other places, like Exod. 23:21f., an angel is mentioned who has the form of a man and who carries within him or represents "the name of God." The human figure on the divine throne described in different ways in Ezekiel, chapter 1, Daniel, chapter 7, and Exodus, chapter 24, among other places was blended into a consistent picture of a principal mediator figure who, like the angel of the Lord in Exodus, chapter 23, embodied, personified, or carried the name of God, YHWH, the tetragrammaton. We shall see that this figure, greatly elaborated by Jewish tradition, becomes a central metaphor for the Christ in Christianity. To see how, we must trace its history in Judaism.

Several Jewish traditions discuss the *eikon* or image of God as Adam's prelapsarian appearance, an especially glorious and splendid form which humanity lost when Adam sinned, since humanity is described as made in "the image and form of God" in Genesis 1:26: בצלמנו כדמותנו. The same "image and form of God" is thereafter associated with God's human appearance in the Bible or the description of the principal angel of God who carries God's name. Most significantly, the human figure on the Merkabah that Ezekiel describes is called "the appearance of the likeness of the glory of the Lord" (mareh demut ke'vod YHWH). Thus, God's Glory or Kabod can become a technical term for God's human appearances.

It seems likely that this enigmatic human appearance of God, discussed with appropriate self-consciousness in the Bible, is related to the so-called the Son of Man, which is not a proper name. The heavenly Son of Man appears in the vision in Dan. 7:13 in which an Ancient of Days appoints a human figure ("one like a son of man") to execute justice in the destruction of the evil ones. This human figure is best understood as an angel. Later on in Daniel, resurrection is promised both for the faithful dead and for the most heinous villains, who will be resurrected so that they may be sentenced to eternal perdition. *Hamaskilim* (המשכילים) or "those who are wise," apparently the elite of the apocalyptic group, will then shine as the stars in heaven (Dan. 12:3). This scripture essentially states that the leaders will be transformed into angels, since the stars were identified with angels in biblical tradition (e.g., Job 38:7).

The preeminence of this angel is due primarily to the description of the angel of the Lord in Exodus. Exod. 23:20–21 states: "Behold, I send an angel before you, to guard you on the way and to bring you to the place which I have prepared. Give heed to him and hearken to his voice, do not rebel against him, for he will not pardon your transgression; for my name is in him." The Bible expresses the unique status of this angel by means of its participation in the divine name. Thereafter in Exodus 33:18–23, Moses asks to see the Glory (כבוד) of God. In answer, God makes "his goodness" pass in front of him but He cautions, "You cannot see my face; for man shall not see me and live. . . . Behold, there is a place by me where you shall stand upon the rock; and while my glory passes by I will put you in a cleft of the rock, and I will cover you with my hand until I have passed by; then I will take away my hand and you shall see my back; but my face shall not be seen." Yahweh himself, the angel of God, and his Glory (כבוד) are melded together in a peculiar way, which suggested to its readers a deep secret about the ways God manifested himself to humanity.

Let us look at the more philosophical expression of these issues in more detail. The Septuagint, the second century BCE translation of the Hebrew Bible into Greek, identifies the figure on the throne in Ezek. 1:26 with the form (*eidos*) of man. This term has a philosophical history starting in Plato's *Parmenides* 130C, where *eidos* means the *idea* of man. Because of Plato's fortunate use of language, Hellenistic Jews like Philo could reunderstand the phrase "form of man," describing man's resemblance to God in Gen. 1:26 and also occuring in biblical theophanies like Ezek. 1:26, as referring to the Platonic *eidos* or idea of man, which inevitably meant for Platonists the unchanging immortal idea of man that survives death. So for Hellenistic Jewish mystics like Philo, the figure of man on the divine throne described in Genesis, Exodus, Ezekiel, Daniel, and the Psalms (and which formed the basis of the "Son of man" speculation) was also understood as the ideal and immortal man. His immortality and glorious appearance was something Adam possessed in the garden of Eden and lost when he sinned. Paul, as we shall see, uses all these traditions to good advantage. In this form, the traditions are centuries older than Christianity.

In the Hellenistic period many new interpretations of this passage appeared. Foremost among the various names given to this angel in various Jewish sects and conventicles is Yahoel in the first-century apocalyptic work, The Apocalypse of Abraham. The name Yahoel illustrates one interpretation of carrying the divine name, since it is a combination of the tetragrammaton and a suffix denoting angelic stature. Yahoel appears in chapters 10–11, where he is described as the one: "in whom God's ineffable name dwells." Other titles for this figure included Melchizedek, Metatron, Adoil, Eremiel, and preeminently "the Son of Man." For instance, Melchizedek appears at Qumran, in the document called 11QMelch, where he is identified with the "elohim" of Ps. 82:1, thus giving us yet another variation on the theme of carrying the name of God. Metatron is called YHWH hakaton, or YHWH Junior, and sits on a throne equal to God's in 3 Enoch 10:1. Typically, the name of the angel varies from tradition to tradition. Thus, Michael is God's "mediator" and general (archistratēgos, 2 Enoch 33:10, T. Dan. 6:1–5, T. Abr. 1:4, cf. *The Life of Adam and Eve* 14.1–2). Eremiel appears in the Apocalypse of Zephaniah 6:1–15, where he is mistaken for God. In The Ascension of Isaiah 7:2–4, an angel appears whose name cannot be given.

Chief angelic mediators appear all over Jewish literature of the first several centuries. The chief angelic mediator, which we may call by a number of terms—God's vice-regent, His wazir, His regent, or other terms expressing his status as principal angel—is easily distinguished from the plethora of divine creatures, for the principal angel is not only head of the heavenly hosts but sometimes participates in God's own being or divinity.

The rabbis most often call God's principal angel Metatron. The term *Metatron* in rabbinic literature and Jewish mysticism is probably not a proper name but a title adapted from the Greek word metathronos, meaning "one who stands *after* or behind the throne." If so, it represents a rabbinic softening of the more normal Hellenistic term, synthronos, meaning "one who is *with* the throne," sharing enthronement or acting for the properly throned authority. The rabbis would have changed the preposition from one connoting equality (*syn-*, "with") to one connoting inferiority (*meta-*, "after or behind") in order to reduce the heretical implications of calling God's principal helping angel his *synthronos*, his equal regent on the throne.

TRANSFORMATION

Alongside these traditions lies the stranger but more relevant notion to Christianity in some apocalyptic-mystical groups that certain heroes can be transformed into angels as part of their ascension. This may easily be the most puzzling part of the mystic traditions, but, in view of Paul's mysticism, it is the most important to summarize. Amazingly, some patriarchs are exalted as angels. In the Testament of Abraham, chapter 11 (Recension A), Adam is pictured with a terrifying appearance and adorned with glory upon a golden throne. In chapters 12–13 Abel is similarly glorified, acting as judge over creation until the final judgment. Second Enoch 30:8–11 also states that Adam was an angel: "And on earth I assigned him to be a second angel, honored and great and glorious." In the *Prayer of Joseph*, found in Origen's commentary on John 2:31, with a further fragment in *Philocalia* 23:15, Jacob describes himself as "an angel of God and a ruling spirit" and claims to be the "first-born of every living thing," "the first minister before the face of God," "the archangel of the power of the Lord," and the "chief captain among the sons of God."

Another important and rarely mentioned piece of evidence of the antiquity of mystical speculation about the Kabod is from the fragment of the tragedy *Moses* written by Ezekiel the Tragedian. There, in a document of the second century B.C.E. or earlier Moses is depicted as seeing a vision of the throne of God with a figure seated upon it. The figure on the throne is called "*phos gennaios*" (a venerable man), which is a *double entendre* in Greek, since *phos* can mean either "light" or "man" depending on the gender of the noun.

The surviving text of Ezekiel the Tragedian also hints at a transformation of an earthly hero into a divine figure when he relates that the venerable man (*phos gennaios*) handed Moses his sceptre and summoned him to sit upon the throne, placing a diadem on his head. Thereafter the stars bow to him and parade for his inspection. Since, as we have seen, throughout the biblical period the stars are thought to be angels (see, e.g., Job 38:7), there can be no doubt that Moses is here depicted as being leader of the angels and hence above the angels. This enthronement scene with a human figure being exalted as a monarch or divinity in heaven resembles the enthronement of the "Son of man"; the enthronement helps us understand some of the traditions that later appear in Jewish mysticism and may have informed Paul's ecstatic ascent. The identification of Jesus with the manlike appearance of God is both the central characteristic of Christianity and understandable within the context of Jewish mysticism and apocalypticism.

Philo speaks of Moses as being made into a divinity (*eis theon*) in several places (e.g., *Sacrifices* 1–10; *Moses* 1.155–58). In exegeting Moses' receiving the Ten Commandments, Philo envisions an ascent, not merely up the mountain, but to the heavens, possibly describing a mystical identification between this manifestation of God and Moses by suggesting in his *Life of Moses* and *Questions and Answers on Exodus* that Moses attained to a divine nature through contact with the *logos*. In *Questions and Answers on Exodus* 1.29, 1.40, Philo writes that on Sinai Moses was changed into a divinity. In *Life of Moses* 1.155–58, he says that God placed the entire universe into Moses' hands and that all the elements obeyed him as their master; then God rewarded Moses by appointing him a "partner" (*koinonon*) of his own possessions and gave into his hand the world as a portion well fitted for his heir (1.155). In the *Sacrifices of Cain and Abel* 8–10, Philo refers to Deut. 5:31 as proof that certain people are distinguished by God to be stationed "beside himself." Moses is preeminent among these people for his grave is not known, which for Philo apparently means that Moses was transported to heaven.

Much of our evidence is later than Paul. But one apocalyptic mediator clearly predates Paul, and that is the Enoch portrayed in the Enochic literature, now known to be widespread in Judaism through the Dead Sea Scrolls. Enoch is a primeval hero of the Bible whose death is not mentioned. Instead, Gen. 5:18–24 twice relates that Enoch walked with God and then disappeared, for "God took him."

The Parables of Enoch contains several references to angelic transformation. In chapter 39, Enoch ascends to heaven while reciting hymns and blessings as do the Merkabah mystics; there he is overcome with the splendor and glory of the throne rooms. His face changes on account of the vision, which evidently reflects the experience of the prophecy that "those who are wise shall shine as the stars" (Dan. 12:3), because 1 Enoch 62:15 states that the elect shall shine as stars and be clothed with garments of glory.

Most importantly, at the end of The Parables of Enoch, chapters 70–71, Enoch is mystically transformed into the figure of the "son of man" on the throne: "My whole body mollified and my spirit transformed" (1 Enoch 71:1). This is an extraordinarily important event, as it underlines the importance of mystic transformation between the adept and the angelic vice-regent of God, giving a plausible explanation of how the sectarians that produced the visions in Daniel expected to be transformed into stars. Indeed, it is possible to say that 1 Enoch 71 gives us the experience of an adept undergoing the astral transformation prophesied in Dan. 12:3 albeit in the name of a pseudepigraphical hero. And, if that is true, Paul gives us the actual, confessional experience of the same spiritual event, with the Christ substituting for the Son of man. In both cases, the believer is subsumed into the body of a heavenly savior and becomes a kind of star or celestial immortal.

Whatever the intention of the author of Enoch, which may be construed in any number of ways, the relationship to Paul's experience is extremely important. Like Enoch, Paul claims to have gazed on the Glory, whom Paul identifies as the Christ. Like Enoch, Paul understands that he has been transformed into a more divine state, which will be fully realized after his death. Like Enoch, Paul claims that this vision and transformation is somehow a mystical identification. Like Enoch, Paul claims to have received a calling, his special status as intermediary. Paul specifies the meaning of this calling for all believers, a concept absent from the Enoch texts that we have, although it may have been assumed within the original community.

Yet complete surety about the history of this tradition is elusive. Paul does not explicitly call the Christ the "Glory of God." And because the Parables (1 Enoch, chapters 37–71) are missing from the Dead Sea Scrolls, we cannot date them accurately. As opposed to the earlier Enoch material, they *may* date to the first century or later and may be influenced by Christianity, since they are extant only in the Ethiopic Version of Enoch, the official canon of the Ethiopian Christian church. Yet, whatever the date of 1 Enoch chapters 70–71, there is no doubt that the stories of Enoch ascensions in 1 Enoch, chapter 14, antedated Paul and would have influenced any of his conceptions about heavenly journey. Furthermore, as long as the date of 1 Enoch chapters 70–71 cannot be fixed exactly and as long as evidence of the Dead Sea Scrolls remains ambiguous, Paul himself remains the earliest author explicitly expressing transformation in Judaism. If his discussion of transformation can be related to apocalyptic mysticism in Judaism, he also becomes the only Jewish mystic of this period to relate this personal experience confessionally.

The theme of angelic transformation usually accompanies a heavenly journey. It becomes especially important in later Kabbalah, but it is sparsely attested in first-century Judaism. Since we have no rabbinic works that can be firmly dated to the first century, Paul's confessional reports are extremely important, though usually overlooked, as evidence for dating Merkabah mysticism. Thus, Paul provides important information about first-century Judaism and Jewish mysticism, equally important to the use that Jewish texts have found in establishing the meaning of Christian texts. Indeed, Paul's letters may be more important to the history of Judaism than are rabbinic texts for establishing the meaning of Christian scriptures.

Second Enoch, extant only in Slavonic, is a further extension of the Enoch legend, most probably through a Christian recension, since Torah does not figure in the story at all. Yet, the possibility of a Semitic, possibly even a Jewish *Vorlage*, especially in the shorter version, cannot be ruled out. In 2 Enoch 22:7, Enoch is transformed during a face-to-face encounter with the Lord into "one of his glorious ones"—in short, an angel; but note the use of glorification language to characterize angelic status. Immediately afterwards, God decrees: "Let Enoch join in and stand in front of My face forever," thus explaining for us the rabbinic term "Prince of the Presence," which is normally applied to Metatron. Then Enoch is transformed:

> And the LORD said to Michael, "Go, and extract Enoch from [his] earthly clothing. And anoint him with my delightful oil, and put him into the clothes of my glory. And so Michael did, just as the Lord had said to him. He anointed me and he clothed me. And the appearance of that oil is greater than the greatest light, and its ointment is like sweet dew, and its fragrance myrrh; and it is like the rays of the glittering sun. And I looked at myself, and I had become like one of his glorious ones, and there was no observable difference. (2 Enoch 22: 8–10, recension A)

Here, the transformation is affected through a change of clothing. The clothing appears to function as or symbolize Enoch's new immortal flesh for Enoch, as they are immortal clothes emanating from the throne room, not from earth. This is a significant parallel with Paul's future glorification of the mortal body in 2 Cor. 5:1–10. One might even say that Enoch has been put *in* the body of an angel, or that he is *in* the manlike figure in 1 Enoch, chapter 71. This may explain Paul's use of the peculiar terminology *in Christ.*

The Ascension of Isaiah also focuses on ascent and heavenly transformation. In chapters 6 through 11, usually attributed to a Christian hand, the famous theophany of Isaiah, chapter 6, is understood to be a heavenly journey during which the prophet sees God. The prophet is taken through each of the seven heavens, stopping to view the glorious figure seated on the throne of each heaven. When he worships the figure in the fifth heaven, he is explicitly warned not to worship any angel, as the rabbis warn not to commit the crime of assuming "there are two powers in heaven." Instead, Isaiah is told that his throne, garments, and crown await him in heaven (7:22). All those who love the Most High will at their end ascend by the angel of the Holy Spirit (7:23). At each heaven, Isaiah is glorified the more, emphasizing the transformation that occurs as a human travels closer and closer to God (7:24); effectively he becomes one of the angels. According to the other angels, Isaiah's vision is unprecedented; no one else has been vouchsafed such a complete vision of the reward awaiting the good (8:11–13). But Isaiah must return to earth to complete his prophetic commission before he can enjoy the rest that awaits him in heaven.

The climax of the story is angelic transformation, but the stated purpose of the journey in these early apocalyptic texts is usually theodicy—to understand God's justice. The journeys begin after a crisis of human confidence about God's intention to bring justice to the world, while the result of the journey is the discovery that the universe is indeed following God's moral plan. Thus the ancient scriptures about God's providence [are] true and the evil ones who predominate on earth, even oppressing God's saints, will soon receive the punishment that they richly deserve.

In 2 (Syriac) Baruch, the theme of angelic transformation sounds loud and strong. This book is widely believed to have been influenced by Christianity, but it is variously dated from the first century to the third. Second Baruch 51:3ff. portrays a gradual transformation of all believers into angelic creatures, as the process of redemption is fulfilled:

> Also, as for the glory of those who proved to be righteous on account of my law, those who possessed intelligence in their life, and those who planted the root of wisdom in their heart—their splendor will then be glorified by transformations, and the shape of their face will be changed into the light of their beauty so that they may acquire and receive the undying world which is promised to them. . . . When they therefore will see that those over whom they are exalted now will then be more exalted and glorified than they, then both these and those will be changed, these into the splendor of angels and those into startling visions and horrible shapes; . . . For they will live in the heights of that world and they will be like the angels and be equal to the stars. And they will be changed into any shape which they wished, for beauty

to loveliness, and from light to the splendor of glory. . . . And the excellence of the righteous will then be greater than that of the angels.

Here is a true fleshing out of the visions of Daniel. The evil ones are transformed into the terrible beasts of the Daniel vision, while the righteous are explicitly transformed into stars.

In chapters 3–15 of the later Merkabah tract now called 3 Enoch (its Hebrew name is *Sefer Hekhaloth*), the man Enoch is transformed into Metatron. Metatron bears a striking resemblance to Moses in Ezekiel the Tragedian's play. For instance, God makes a throne for Enoch-Metatron in 3 Enoch (10:1). He gives him a special garment of Glory and a royal gown (12:1–3); God makes him ruler over all kingdoms and all heavenly beings (10:3); all the angels of every rank, and the angels of the sun, moon, stars, and planets, fall prostrate when Enoch sits on his throne (14:1–5); he knows the names of all the stars (46:1–2; see Ps. 147:40), God reveals to him all the secrets of heaven and earth so that Enoch knows past, present, and future (10:5, 11:1, cf. 45:1; 48 [D]:7); God calls him YHWH ha-katon, another interpretation of Exod. 23:21 (12:5). Of course, the date of these documents is far too late to be of specific guidance for Paul. Whatever one's scholarly inclination about the dating of Daniel or the earliest son of man traditions, there is no doubt that this angelic figure, the figure that the Bible sometimes calls the Kabod (כבוד) or the principal angel of God, is pre-Christian and is a factor in Paul's description of Christ.

There is adequate evidence, then, that many Jewish mystics and apocalypticists sensed a relationship between the heavenly figure on the throne and important figures in the life of their community. The roots of this tradition are pre-Christian. Furthermore, Jewish scholars have overlooked Christianity as evidence for the existence of these traditions in first-century Judaism. Paul did not have to be a religious innovator to posit an identification between a vindicated hero and the image of the Kabod, the manlike figure in heaven, although the identification of the figure with the risen Christ is obviously a uniquely Christian development.

Paul's experiences are, when seen in this light, not unique so much as characteristic of Jewish mystical thought. Indeed, they give us good evidence that the mystical ascent of adepts to heaven was already known in the first century. Paul is the only Jewish mystic to report his own personal, identifiably confessional mystical experiences in the fifteen hundred years that separate Ezekiel from the rise of Kabbalah.

Paul's Use of Mystical Vocabulary

Paul himself gives the best evidence for the existence of ecstatic journeys to heaven in first-century Judaism, with his report in 2 Corinthians. We begin with heavenly ascent. Although the account of Paul's ecstatic conversion in Acts is a product of Luke's literary genius, Paul gives his own evidence for ecstatic experience. In Galatians, chapter 1, Paul claims that he did not receive the gospel from a human source. And in 2 Cor. 12:1–9, he describes an experience that transcends human ken:

I must boast; there is nothing to be gained by it, but I will go on to visions and revelations of the Lord. I know a man in Christ who fourteen years ago was caught up to the third heaven—whether in the body or out of the body, I do not know, God knows. And I know that this man was caught up into Paradise—whether in the body or out of the body, I do not know, God knows—and he heard things that cannot be told, which man may not utter. On behalf of this man, I will boast, but on my own behalf I will not boast, except of my weaknesses. Though if I wish to boast, I shall not be a fool, for I shall be speaking the truth.

As in Galatians, chapter 1, Paul calls this experience an *apokalypsis* (an apocalypse, a revelation). Just as in Acts and Galatians, chapter 1, the actual vision is not described. Unlike the text [of] Acts and Galatians, chapter 1, however, this passage is a confessional description of a vision, or possibly two different ones, depending on whether the paradise visited in the ascension can be located in the third heaven. Thus, the vision is both mystical and apocalyptic. The vision ought to be seen in the context of first-century Jewish apocalypticism.

Paul's inability to decide whether the voyage took place in the body or out of the body is firm evidence of a mystical ascent and shows that the voyage has not been clearly interiorized as a journey into the self, which later becomes common in Kabbalah. Furthermore, since the rabbis proscribed the discussion of these topics except singly, to mature disciples, and only provided they had experienced it on their own (מבין מדעתו, M. Hag. 2.1), the rabbinic stories interpreting the Merkavah experience often take place while traveling through the wilderness from city to city when such doctrines could easily be discussed in private. This is precisely the scene that Luke picks for Paul's conversion.

It is significant that in 2 Corinthians, chapter 12, when Paul talks about mystical journeys directly, he too adopts a pseudepigraphical stance. He does not admit to the ascent personally. Apart from the needs of his rhetoric, rabbinic rules also forbid public discussion of mystic phenomena. A first century date for this rule would explain why Paul would not divulge his experience *in his own name* at that place. It would also suggest why Jewish mystics consistently picked pseudepigraphical literary conventions to discuss their religious experience, unlocking the mystery behind the entire phenomenon of pseudepigraphical writing. But none of the standard discussions of this incompletely understood phenomenon discuss Paul's confession or the Mishnah here. Again, Paul may be giving us hitherto unrecognized information about Jewish culture in the first century that is unavailable from any other source.

When Paul is not faced with a direct declaration of personal mystical experience, he reveals much about the mystical religion as it was experienced in the first century. Paul himself designates Christ as the image of the Lord in a few places: 2 Cor. 4:4, Col. 1:15 (if it is Pauline), and he mentions the *morphē* [form] of God in Phil. 2:6.

Christ is not explicitly given the title *the Glory of God* in the New Testament. However, there are several New Testament passages in which *doxa* (glory) and, more relevantly, *the* glory is attributed to Christ or the Son. In James 2:1, it is possible that we should translate the text to read "our Lord Jesus Christ, the Glory." Paul himself repeatedly uses the term *glory* to refer to Christ. In Phil. 3:21 Paul speaks of Christ's "Body of Glory" (*soma tes doxes*) to which the believer's body is to be conformed. He thinks of Christ as the Lord of Glory (1 Cor. 2:8). Through the glory of the father, Christ was raised from the dead (Rom. 6:4). God makes known the riches of glory in or through the exalted Christ (Rom. 9:23, Phil. 4:19, see also Eph. 1:18, 3:16, Col. 1:27). The gospel that Paul preaches, which features the death, resurrection, and return of the Christ is called the "gospel of glory" (2 Cor. 4:4, 1 Tim. 1:11, see also Col. 1:27). Other passages bearing on this theme would include 1 Cor. 2:8, describing Christ as "the Lord of Glory," and the doubtfully Pauline Heb. 1:3: "He reflects the Glory of God and bears the very stamp of his nature, upholding the universe by his word of power." In Eph. 1:17 "the God of our Lord Jesus Christ, the Father of the Glory" appears. Some of these references, of course, merely describe the brilliance of vision.

Even more interestingly, Paul describes the "Glory of the Lord" (2 Cor. 3:16–4:6) in the very places where he describes his own conversion, which he also uses as a pattern for experience by which other believers come to be in Christ. As an heir of Christ, the believer shares the glory of Christ (Rom. 8:17), which eclipses any suffering that may have been experienced in the believer's life (Rom. 8:18, 2 Cor. 4:15–17). This exchange of suffering for glory will occur at Christ's coming, according to Col. 3:4. Paul himself talks of the faithful being changed or transformed into the "image of Christ" (Rom. 8:29, 1 Cor. 15:49), which again resembles Ezekiel's language of "the appearance of the likeness of the Glory of the Lord" (Ezek. 1:28, cf. 70). Central to Paul's Christian experience is the transformation of believers at the apocalypse. More importantly, Paul anticipates the technical terminology of the transformation of believers into angels in Jewish mysticism.

Paul's longest discussion of these themes occurs in an unlikely place in 2 Cor. 3:18–4:6. Here he assumes the context rather than explaining it completely:

> And we all, with unveiled face, beholding the glory of the Lord, are being changed into his likeness from one degree of glory to another; for this comes from the Lord who is the Spirit. Therefore, having his ministry by the mercy of God, we do not lose heart. We have renounced disgraceful, underhanded ways; we refuse to practice cunning or to tamper with God's word, but by the open statement of the truth we would commend ourselves to every man's conscience in the sight of God. And even if our gospel is veiled it is veiled only to those who are perishing. In their case, the god of this world has blinded the minds of the unbelievers to keep them from seeing the light of the gospel of the glory of Christ, who is the likeness of God. For what we preach is not ourselves, but Jesus Christ as Lord, with ourselves as your servants for Jesus' sake. For it is the God who said, "Let light shine out of darkness," who has shone in our hearts to give the light of the knowledge of the glory of the Lord in the face of Christ. (2 Cor. 3:18–4:6)

For now, the main point must be the usually unappreciated use of the language of transformation in Paul's works. In 2 Cor. 3:18 Paul says that believers will be changed into Christ's likeness from one degree of glory to another. He refers to Exodus, chapters 33 and 34, where Moses' encounter with the angel of the Lord is narrated. Earlier in that passage, the angel of the Lord is described as carrying the name of God (Exod. 23:21). Moses sees the Glory of the Lord, makes a covenant, receives the commandments upon the two tables of the law and, when he comes down from the mount, the skin of his face shines with light, as the Bible states (Exod. 34:29–35). Moses thereafter must wear a veil, except when he is in the presence of the Lord. Paul assumes that Moses made an ascension to the presence of the Lord, was transformed by that encounter, and that his shining face is a reflection of the encounter.

Thus, Paul's term, "the glory of the Lord" must be taken both as a reference to Christ and as a technical term for the Kabod (כבוד), the human form of God appearing in biblical visions. In 2 Cor. 3:18 Paul says that Christians behold the Glory of the Lord as in a mirror and are transformed into his image. For Paul, as for the earliest Jewish mystics, to be privileged enough to see the Kabod or Glory of God is a prologue to transformation into His image. Paul does not say that all Christians have made the journey literally but compares the experience of knowing Christ to being allowed into the intimate presence of the Lord. However, we know that he has made that journey.

It is very difficult not to read this passage in terms of Paul's later description of the ascension of the man to the third heaven and conclude that Paul's conversion experience also involved his identification of Jesus as the "image" and "glory of God," as the human figure in heaven, and thereafter as Christ, son, and savior. Or at least this is how Paul construes it when he recalls it. In Phil. 2:6, the identification of Jesus with the form of God implies his preexistence. The Christ is depicted as an eternal aspect of divinity that was not proud of its high station but consented to take on the shape of a man and suffer the fate of men, even death on a cross (though many scholars see this phrase as a Pauline addition to the original hymn). This transformation of form from divinity is followed by the converse, the retransformation into God. Because of this obedience God exalted him and bestowed on him the "name which is above every name" (Phil. 2:9). For a Jew this phrase can only mean that Jesus received the divine name Yahweh, the tetragrammaton YHWH, understood as the Greek name *kyrios*, or Lord. We have already seen that sharing in the divine name is a frequent motif of the early Jewish apocalypticism where the principal angelic mediator of God is or carries the name Yahweh, as Exodus, chapter 23, describes the angel of Yahweh. Indeed the implication of the Greek term *morphē*, "form," is that Christ has the form of a divine body identical with the Kabod, the glory, and equivalent also with the *eikon*, for man is made after the *eikon* of God and thus has the divine *morphē* (or in Hebrew, [דמות]). The climax of Paul's confession is that "Jesus Christ is Lord to the glory of God the Father" (Phil. 2:11), meaning that Jesus, the messiah, has received the name Lord in his glorification and that this name, not Jesus' private earthly name, is the one that will cause every knee to bend and every tongue confess.

In paraphrasing this fragment from liturgy, Paul witnesses that the early Christian community directed its prayers to this human figure of divinity along with God (1 Cor. 16:22, Rom. 10:9–12, 1 Cor. 12:3)—all the more striking since the Christians, like the Jews, refuse to give any other god or hero any veneration at all. When the rabbis gain control of the Jewish community they vociferously argue against the worship of any angel and specifically polemicize against the belief that a heavenly figure other than God can forgive sins (b. Sanhedrin 38b), quoting Exod. 23:21 prominently among other scriptures to prove their point. The heresy itself they call believing that there are "two powers in heaven." By this term the rabbis largely (but not exclusively) referred to Christians who, as Paul says, do exactly what the rabbis warn against—worship the second power.

Concomitant with Paul's worship of the divine Christ is transformation. Paul says in Phil. 3:10 "that I may know him and the power of his resurrection and may share his sufferings, becoming like him (*summorphizomenos*) in his death." Later, in Phil. 3:20–21, he says: "But our commonwealth is in heaven, and from it we await a Savior, the Lord Jesus Christ, who will change (*metaskēmatisei*) our lowly body to be like (*summorphon*) his glorious body, by the power which enables him even to subject all things to himself." The body of the believer eventually is to be transformed into the body of Christ.

Paul's depiction of salvation is based on his understanding of Christ's glorification, partaking of early Jewish apocalyptic mysticism for its expression. In Rom. 12:2 Paul's listeners are exhorted to "be transformed" (*metamorphousthe*) [by the] renewing of your minds." In Gal. 4:19 Paul expresses another transformation: "My little children, with whom I am again in travail until Christ be formed (*morphōthē*) in you!" This transformation is to be effected by becoming like him in his death (*summorphizomenos to thanatō autou* [Phil. 3:10]).

Alternatively, Paul can say, as he does in Gal. 1:16 that "God was pleased to reveal His Son in me (*en emoi*)." This is not a simple dative but refers to his having received in him the Spirit, in his case through his conversion. Being *in Christ* in fact appears to mean being united with his heavenly image. The same, however, is available to all Christians through baptism. This is not strange, since apocalyptic and mystical Judaism also promoted *tebilah* (טבילה), ritual immersion or baptism as the central purification ritual preparing for the ascent into God's presence. The Jewish ritual of purification for coming into the divine presence and proselyte baptism has been transformed by Paul's community into a *single* rite of passage, though it does not thereby lose its relationship to its source. Dying and being resurrected along with Christ in baptism is the beginning of the process by which the believer gains the same image of God, his *eikon*, which was made known to humanity when Jesus became the Son of man—that human figure in heaven who brings judgment in the apocalypse described by Daniel.

Paul's conception of the risen body of Christ as the spiritual body (1 Cor. 15:43) at the end of time and as the body of Glory (Phil. 3:21) thus originates in Jewish apocalypticism and mysticism, modified by the unique events of early Christianity. The meaning of Rom. 8:29 can be likewise clarified by Jewish esoteric tradition. There, Paul speaks of God as having "foreordained his elect to be conformed to the image of his Son" (*proōrisen summorphous tēs eikonos tou uiou autou*). Paul uses the genitive here rather than the dative as in Phil. 3:21, softening the identification between believer and savior. But when Paul states that believers conform to the image of his Son, he is not speaking of an agreement of mind or ideas between Jesus and the believers. The word *summorphē* itself suggests a spiritual reformation of the believer's body into the form of the divine image. Paul's language for conversion develops out of mystical Judaism.

Of course, the mystical experience of conversion is not only with the *risen* Christ but with the *crucified* Christ. The most obvious relationship between the believer and Christ is suffering and death (Rom. 7:24, 8:10, 13). By being transformed by Christ, one is not simply made immortal, given the power to remain deathless. Rather, one still experiences death as the Christ did and, like him, survives death for heavenly enthronement. This is a consequence of the Christian's divided state. Although part of the last Adam, living through Spirit, the Christian also belongs to the world of the flesh. As James Dunn has noted: "Suffering was something *all* believers experienced—an unavoidable part of the believer's lot—an aspect of experience as Christians which his converts shared with Paul: Rom 5:3 ('we'); 8:17f ('we'); 2 Cor. 1:16 ('you endure the same sufferings that we suffer'); 8:2; Phil. 1:29f. ('the same conflict which you saw and now hear to be mine'); 1 Thess. 1:6 ('imitators of us and of the Lord'); 2:14 ('imitators of the churches of God in Judea: for you suffered the same things'); 3:3f. ('our lot') 2 Thess. 1:4ff."

Thus, the persecution and suffering of the believers is a sign that the transformation process has begun; it is the way to come to be *in* Christ. Paul is convinced that being united with Christ's crucifixion means not immediate *glorification* but *suffering* for the believers in this interim period. The glorification follows upon the final consummation. The connection between suffering and resurrection has been clear in Jewish martyrology; indeed the connection between death and rebirth was even a prominent part of the mystery religions as well. But the particular way in which Paul makes these connections is explicitly Christian.

Paul's central proclamation is: Jesus is Lord and all who have faith have already undergone a death like his, so will share in his resurrection. As we have seen, this proclamation reflects a baptismal liturgy, implying that baptism provides the moment whereby the believer comes to be "in Christ." Christianity may have been a unique Jewish sect in making baptism a central rather than a preparatory ritual, but some of the mystical imagery comes from its Jewish past.

Paul's letters are the very first witness to Jewish mysticism, in a personal and confessional way. Paul tells us in his own language just what it feels like to be transformed into the Glory of God, to become a star, as it were. Paul is the only Pharisee to leave us his writings and the only Jewish mystic in the first century to do so. And when we look at Paul's writing we discover not so much a systematic theology as the memoirs of a man who has had overwhelming visions which he describes as death in life, bringing him a new life in the body of his savior.

PAULA FREDRIKSEN

[Paul on the Destiny of Israel] (2000)†

I. Paul and Apocalyptic Transparency

Paul describes himself as a Jew learned in the Law, Pharisaic in interpretive orientation (Phil. 3:5), and enthusiastically observant (Gal. 1:14; Phil. 3:6, 'blameless'). Since his experience of the Risen Christ (1 Cor. 15:8), Paul's life had taken an unexpected turn. In the time between that event and the period of the composition of his letters—from roughly 33 to 55 C.E.—Paul had devoted his considerable energies to bringing the good news of Christ's resurrection and impending return to Gentiles, who comprise at least much of the audience of the seven undisputed letters we still have from him.

This revelation convinced Paul that history was in its final act, that he lived and worked within the brief in-between of Christ's resurrection and his triumphant second coming (*Parousia*), when the Lord would descend from heaven to overthrow hostile cosmic powers and finally death itself (1 Cor. 15:26). At that point, the dead would be raised bodily and, together with the living, would be transformed, exchanging 'lowly' bodies for glorious bodies like that of the Risen Christ (Phil. 3:21)—spiritual, imperishable, immortal (1 Cor. 15:44, 54). Until that moment—indeed, in order to achieve that moment—Paul worked strenuously to evangelize the nations, bringing in their 'full number' (*plēroma*, Rom. 11:25) so that they, through the Spirit, might be adopted into the family of God (8:14–23), and Israel itself be finally redeemed.

On a practical level, this meant that Paul expected his Gentiles-in-Christ to conduct themselves in a particular way. They were to eschew 'the works of the flesh,' which Paul enumerates frequently, heatedly, and in detail: 'fornication (*porneia*), impurity, licentiousness, idolatry, sorcery, enmity, strife, jealousy, anger, selfishness, dissension, party spirit, envy, drunkenness, carousing.' Elsewhere, exhorting them, he summarizes their ideal behavior simply as 'fulfilling the Law.' To be 'in Christ' these Gentiles are not to become Jews, that is, receive circumcision and convert—Paul is adamant on this point. Yet, in insisting absolutely that they abandon idols while foreclosing with equal passion their option to convert to Judaism, Paul leads these people to a social no-man's-land: in antiquity, only Jews had the legal right to excuse themselves from the cult that normally expressed responsible participation in the life of a city. Paul has in effect removed these people from their native social map. Through his message, in Christ, they have been relocated: they now stand in the sweep of the coming redemption that God had promised Israel.

Christ provides the vanishing point for Paul's new perspective on Scripture. He accordingly can re-read biblical narrative and deploy scriptural images in ways that would have astounded, indeed sometimes offended, Jews outside the new movement. Sometimes his allegorizing is in service

---

† From "Allegory and Reading God's Book: Paul and Augustine on the Destiny of Israel," in *Interpretation and Allegory*, ed. by Jon Whitman (Leiden: Brill, 2000), 125–49. Reprinted by permission of Brill Academic Publishers. Fredriksen is William Goodwin Aurelio Professor of the Appreciation of Scripture at Boston University.

of a fairly simple point. For example, exhorting his Gentiles in Corinth to seemly behavior, Paul constructs a sustained metaphor around morality and Passover preparations:

> Your boasting is not good. Do you not know that a little leaven leavens the whole lump? Cleanse out the old leaven that you may be a new lump, as you really are unleavened. For Christ, our paschal lamb, has been sacrificed. Let us therefore celebrate the festival, not with the old leaven of malice and evil, but with the unleavened bread of sincerity and truth. (1 Cor. 5:6–8)

'Leaven' as a metaphor for pride is unexceptional. What is interesting here is the image for Christ—the paschal lamb—and the use Paul makes of it. It's late—much too late for the Corinthians to persist in *porneia*. In the language of the metaphor, it's already late in the afternoon just before the Passover feast, and there's still leaven in the house. For all its Christological motivation, then, the metaphor depends on traditionally Jewish elements (leaven, Passover, matzah), *understood* Jewishly, to work.

Later in the letter, Paul obliquely rebukes the Corinthians for not supporting him materially in his evangelizing work. Suddenly he evokes Deuteronomy to drive home his point:

> Do I say this on human authority? Does not the Law say the same? For it is written in the Law of Moses: 'You shall not muzzle an ox when it is treading out the grain' [Dt. 25:4]. Is it for oxen that God is concerned? *Does he not speak entirely for our sake?* (1 Cor. 9:8–10)

Paul explains his invoking Torah by applying agricultural metaphors to the work of his urban apostolate. He has sown spiritual good in his community; it is only right that he should reap some of their material benefits. An apostle is entitled to support, because preaching the gospel is like treading grain, or threshing, or (he continues) serving at the Temple, where the priests get to eat as a result of their service (v. 13). Though he ultimately insists that he would decline such support (v. 15), he makes a vaguely halakhic argument that he is certainly entitled to it. What is of interest here is not the details, but the conviction that mobilizes them: Moses wrote, and God legislated, for the sake of people like Paul. Biblical revelation speaks immediately to present circumstance.

How can Paul be so sure? Because, through Christ's resurrection, he knows that he stands at the end of history, and this knowledge clarifies what preceded. The Exodus narrative, accordingly, also takes on a new transparency:

> I want you to know, brethren, that our fathers were all under a cloud, and all passed through the sea, and all were baptized into Moses in the cloud and in the sea, and all ate the same spiritual food and all drank the same spiritual drink. *For they drank from the spiritual Rock which followed them, and that Rock was Christ* . . . [He then synopsizes their several misadventures with idolatry, *porneia*, insolence and ingratitude, and their subsequent punishment.] Now these things happened to them as a warning, *but they were written down for our instruction, upon whom the end of the ages has come.* (1 Cor. 10:1–11)

The scope of Paul's revision here is much broader, the implications for his construction of the biblical past deeper, than in our preceding example. There, the apostolic present was the *telos* of the biblical past; here, Christ has been retrojected into the biblical past, newly revealed as an actor in Israel's formation. Further, the past event serves to model, and thus interpret, current ones: it provides a *tupos* ('type') of immediate relevance. Thus, while the biblical storyline remains intact—Moses and the tribes still travel from Egypt to Canaan—its fundamental significance has altered. The destruction of those ancient sinners who had drunk of Christ in the desert allows Paul to segue into warnings against those eating and drinking of Christ now who might feel similarly tempted by idolatry and its perennial accompaniment, fornication (vv. 14–22).

In Galatians, his most intemperate letter, Paul pushes this appropriation of the past yet further. Arguing bitterly against fellow apostles (themselves, like Paul, Christian Jews) who urge his Gentiles to convert fully to Judaism, Paul again retrojects Christ as a character into the biblical narrative. Here, however, this retrojection wrenches the biblical past directly into the Christian present. This audacious rescripting has immediate polemical value. Paul can assert to his (confused?) audience that his Judaizing Christian competitors do not even understand the true meaning of their shared foundational myth, the calling of Abraham:

> O foolish Galatians! . . . Did you receive the Spirit by works of the Law, or by hearing with faith? . . . Having begun with the Spirit, are you now ending with the flesh? . . . Scripture, foreseeing that God would justify the Gentiles by faith, preached the gospel beforehand to Abraham, saying, 'In you shall all the nations be blessed' [Gen. 12: 3]. . . . Now the promises were made to Abraham and his offspring [*sperma*]. It does not say, 'And to offsprings,' referring to many; but referring to one, 'And to your offspring,' which is Christ. (Gal. 3:8–16)

Paul weaves antitheses of spirit versus flesh, faith versus the works of the Law, blessing versus curse, into his retelling of God's call and promise to Abraham—a promise, he now urges, that was made not to Abraham's immediate family, nor even to the nation that eventually issued from him, Israel. Redemption and blessing was promised to Abraham and Christ. Gentiles enter into this blessing through the Spirit, by faith, and *not*, urges Paul, through receiving the Law, aligned in his polemic with 'curse' and 'flesh'—precisely where the mark of circumcision would be sealed. The Spirit already enables Gentiles in Christ to cry 'Abba!' (4:6); without any imposition of Law, in freedom, they have been brought into God's household as sons and thus heirs.

To this almost 'midrashic' argument Paul appends a problematic typology (his word is 'allegory') of two wives, two sons, two covenants, and two holy mountains. His earlier terms, especially the antithesis spirit/flesh, polarize this passage, too:

> Tell me, you who desire to be under the Law, do you not hear the Law? For it is written that Abraham had two sons, one by a slave and one by a free woman. But the son of the slave was born according to the flesh, and the son of the free woman through promise. Now this

is an allegory. These women are two covenants. One is from Mount Sinai, bearing children for slavery: she is Hagar. Now Hagar is Mount Sinai in Arabia. She corresponds to the present Jerusalem, for she is in slavery with her children. But the Jerusalem above is free, and she is our mother. For it is written,

> Rejoice, O barren one who does not bear;
> Break forth and shout, you who are not in travail;
> For the children of the desolate one are many more than the children of her that is married. [Isa. 54:1]

Now we, brethren, like Isaac, are children of promise. But as at that time he who was born according to the flesh persecuted him who was born according to the Spirit, so it is now. But what does the scripture say? 'Cast out the slave and her son; for the son of the slave shall not inherit with the son' of the free woman. So, brethren, we are children not of the slave but of the free woman. (Gal. 4:21–31)

Clearly, Paul meant to insult and demean his Christian opponents through this double allegory. Hagar, the first woman, stands both for the Sinai covenant and the earthly Jerusalem. Her children (by implication, Paul's rivals), who persecute the child of the free woman, are slaves: they shall be cast out. But the free woman (Sarah) represents not the flesh or slavery—Paul's code words for Gentile circumcision—but freedom and promise. She is Jerusalem above, the mother of Paul's community. These children, like her son Isaac, though persecuted by Hagar's children, are born of spirit and promise. They shall inherit; they, in Christ, are free (5:1).

Paul's association of circumcision with 'flesh' allows him to conflate the physical act urged by his opponents with other 'works of the flesh' which they, too, would doubtless condemn—*porneia*, idolatry, enmity, and so on (5:19–21). As the Spirit opposes these fleshly works, Paul leaves hanging in the air the implication that the Spirit, on similar moral ground, also condemns circumcision. Again, the polemical context of this letter is quite precise: Paul argues here against rival Christian missionaries, not Jews or Judaism as such. But the force of his re-reading of scriptural history, wherein God's call of Abraham to the Promised Land is a summons to the Pauline mission, seems to disenfranchise much more than his immediate competition. From such a perspective, what value can the Law and circumcision have at all? And if Abraham's blessing goes through Christ to the Gentiles, what then of Israel?

In Romans we find Paul's answer. This letter, in many ways a calmer companion piece to Galatians, is the closest thing we have to a theological position paper from Paul. Written again to a Gentile audience (but one with whom he was not yet personally acquainted), Romans reviews the question of the value of circumcision and of the Law—indeed, the value of being a Jew at all—in light of God's recent revelation of his Son and his concomitant plan to establish Gentile righteousness apart from the Law. Minus the goad of active competition and vituperative polemic, Paul can affirm that Jewishness and circumcision are greatly to be valued (*polu kata panta tropon*, 3:2), that the Law and the prophets bear witness to faith in Jesus Christ (3:21), and that Christians uphold (*histanomen*) the Law through their faith (3:31). Abraham's circumcision is a sign (*sēmeion*) or seal of righteousness by faith (4:11); 'the Law is holy, and the commandment is holy and just and good' (7:13).

Nonetheless, strong tensions charge his discussion. Insisting on the Law's goodness, he still maintains that Jews are no better off than Gentiles, since all are under the power of sin (3:9–20). The Law articulates what sin is, but cannot prevent or absolve it (expiation, rather, is achieved through Christ's blood; 3:25, 5:9). The Law itself, though not sin (7:7), is linked intimately with the powers of flesh, sin, and death (chs. 7–8 passim). What way out of this impasse?

In ch. 6, Paul develops an elaborate conceit around death and baptism. Through baptism, the believer mimetically recapitulates the death and burial of Christ (6:3–4). The correspondences to Christ's experience continue, now linked with resurrection, one already realized, the other still to be fulfilled. The believer, consequent upon this 'dying,' already 'walks in newness of life' and thus does not sin (v. 4); and he or she is assured, through the union in 'death,' of being united with Christ 'in a resurrection like his' (v. 5). Baptism-as-death releases the believer from his own 'sinful body,' thereby ending his servitude to sin (6:6–8) and also to the Law as the calibrator of sin (7:1–6). This extended metaphor continues through the end of chapter 8, where Paul rises to his letter's first eschatological empyrean: the war against sin, death and decay is already won, but not yet; the believer is already an adopted son, but groans while he awaits the redemption of his body; all the hostile forces separating the believer from God have already been overcome and will be overcome in Christ. Between this now and not yet, history hovers over its ultimate caesura: it awaits the redemption of Israel.

Romans 9–11 both describes and explains how God's recent justification of the ungodly in Christ is consistent with his promises to Israel, which are irrevocable (11:28–29; cf. 15:8). Weaving together several paradigmatic examples from Genesis and Exodus of God's control over human history and redemption together with the familiar Hellenistic image of the footrace, Paul holds that Christ is himself the *telos* or goal of the Law with respect to the justification of those who believe (that is, the Gentiles, 10:4). Ultimately, God will bring it about (in Paul's view, very soon) that Israel will acknowledge God's plan so that, with the Gentiles brought in, 'all Israel will be saved' (11:26).

But what prevents that acknowledgement now? Paul answers that God has mysteriously hardened Israel in order to create the opportunity for the Gentiles (hence Israel's 'stumbling,' though not falling, 11:11). It is to this end that he reviews God's sovereign choice of Isaac over Ishmael (9:7), Jacob over Esau (9:10–13), his hardening of Pharaoh's heart: all was done with a view toward the divine 'purpose of election' (v. 11), 'so that my name might be proclaimed in all the earth' (Ex. 9:16; Rom. 9:17). So too God exercises his prerogative in these last days, temporarily hardening Israel as he oversees the final act in the history of redemption.

Leaving biblical history to one side, Paul conjures a prophetic image of divine control: God is (like) a potter, humans (like) clay pots. The potter has an absolute 'right' over the clay (*pēlos*), to shape out of the same lump (*phurama*) whatever sort of vessel he will: man cannot second-guess God's plan. 'Who are you, man, to answer back to God?' (9:20). All will work out in the End, as God has planned (and Paul foresees). 'For God has consigned all men to disobedience, that he may have mercy upon all' (11:32).

Paul's use of extended metaphor and typology, his mobilization of biblical and even halakhic argument in parenetic exhortation, his readings *kata pneuma*, crackling with anger in the heat of controversy—all these rhetorical strategies stand in service of his basic conviction, and thus basic orientation toward biblical interpretation, with which he sums up his letter to the Romans: 'For *whatever was written in former days was written for our instruction*, that by steadfastness and by the encouragement of the scriptures we might have hope' (15:4). His clarity on the impending future enabled and encouraged him to read the biblical past as transparent on the present, its actual matrix of meaning. And that present, itself incandescently eschatological, he construed as consistent with the traditions and convictions of his own people, his 'brothers,' his kinsmen 'according to the flesh' (9:3): 'For Christ became a servant of the circumcised on behalf of God's truthfulness in order to confirm the promises given to the patriarchs, and so that the Gentiles might glorify God for his mercy' (15:8).

But this moment passed. Paul's generation died, and scattered communities very diverse in cultural orientation were left to interpret not only the Scriptures that Paul had interpreted, but also Paul's message itself. The simple passage of time necessarily works changes in any millenarian movement. But given the way that this particular movement was bound up with textual interpretation, in a culture where rhetorical education marked the measure of social and intellectual achievement, we can sense such changes even by glancing at the literary productions of the developing Gentile communities that saw themselves as Paul's heirs. Seeing in Paul himself their warrant to read allegorically, these Christians constructed an evangelical hermeneutic that denied the foundation of Paul's own proclamation: the irrevocable election of Israel and the universality of divine redemption.

*   *   *

PART VIII

Reading Romans

Of all Paul's letters, none has proved to be as highly influential as the one he wrote to the Christ-believers in Rome. One reason is surely its form; far more than any of the other letters, it resembles a theological treatise, and it is easy to understand why it has this appearance. Paul's other letters were written to churches that he had founded, so he could either presuppose his readers' familiarity with his basic views or ask them to remember what he had said on a previous occasion or in an earlier letter. Not so with the letter to Rome. Although in chapter 16 he names more than two dozen Christians whom he knew in the city, he had met all of them elsewhere. He had neither established the Christian community in Rome nor previously visited it nor written to any of its house-churches on a former occasion. Because he can presuppose none of his foundational teaching, he must unfold his gospel more fully than he does in his other letters, and do so in the awareness that both he and his proclamation had become highly controversial in certain Christian circles.

In this chapter we examine two quite different areas in which Paul's thoughts in Romans have influenced later discussions. The first is in the realm of religious experience, where the self-contradiction and human plight articulated in 7:7–25 have often been claimed as essential components of conversion and spiritual renewal. The second is in the political arena, where Paul's statements in 13:1–7 have had an enormous impact on the ways in which subsequent Christians have thought about their government, regardless of whether the latter was ruthlessly persecuting them or they were shamelessly exploiting the state's powers to pursue their own agendas.

Reading Romans 7: Paul and Religious Experience

Inevitably the episode in Paul's career that provokes instant fascination is his conversion. The fact that he never describes it and that he alludes to it only in passing can easily be overlooked, since the reports in Acts more than make up for his reticence. The transition from Pharisaic zealot, persecuting the Jesus sect, to fanatic missionary of that sect, combating continued observance of the law, was obviously cataclysmic. "Paul belongs to that rare class of men whose lives, by a single event, are cut clean in two. He becomes another man, and lives thenceforward in the consciousness that he is another man. . . ."[1] Those figures in the history of Christendom who have themselves experienced a bifurcation of life, whether in becoming Christians or in coming to a new and total awareness of the meaning of Christianity, have naturally found in Paul a prototype. It is not surprising that Augustine, who gave to Western Christianity the first classic of "spiritual autobiography" in his *Confessions*, or that Luther, in his agonies to find peace before the awful justice of God, should find illumination from Paul's experience. It is also not surprising that they should have read their own experiences into Paul's bare allusions.

In the ancient church, Romans 7 seemed to many interpreters to portray the individual's struggle for self-mastery against the corrupting influence of the passions that was the inevitable consequence of life in a body. Paul was thus seen to be addressing one of the most persistent concerns that exercised moral philosophers of his day. Stories of conversion to philosophy in the literature of antiquity characteristically depict the transformation of a dissolute person into a sober model of self-control. The selections from Theodoret's commentary illustrate this way of reading Romans 7, which moves toward that focus on individual experience that characterizes later commentators, though Theodoret is also still very much aware that Paul is telling a larger story, which begins with Adam.

In later interpretations, Paul becomes the exemplar of the "twice-born man." This is true in all those movements within Christianity for which the central issue is how the individual moves from disbelief to faith: in missionary movements, particularly the modern ones that stressed individual conversion rather than Christianization of communities; pietist movements, seeking to leaven dry and rationalistic orthodoxies; "revival" movements and "awakenings" on the American frontier. These movements are particularly fond of this one chapter in Paul's writings, which they treat as the autobiographical "testimony" of a convert, such as one might hear in the course of a revival meeting. Typical, in thought if not in prose, is this statement by James S. Stewart, a Scottish preacher and writer:

> Of Romans 7 and 8 it is surely true to say that nowhere in the literature of personal confession could a nobler fulfilment be found of the Psalmist's injunction, "Let the redeemed of the Lord say so, whom He hath redeemed from the hand of the enemy." *Let the redeemed say so*—and Paul, by disclosing the wretchedness and misery in which Christ had found him, and

1. Wilhelm Wrede, *Paul*, tr. by Edward Lummis (London: P. Green, 1907), 6.

the glory and romance into which Christ had ushered him, is bearing his witness to bowed and burdened spirits everywhere: "This, by God's grace, happened to me, and this, under God, can happen to you." In the service of Christ and of humanity, the man has opened his very heart, and written in his very blood and taken us into the shame and glory of his secret soul; and for this the world stands for ever in his debt.[2]

Romans 7 is part of Paul's discussion of the Jewish law. Read as the confession of a convert, it tended to focus the understanding of conversion upon the problem of moral failure—the problem of the law becomes our inability to obey it. Thus, in the subtle interaction between Paul and his conversionist interpreters, conversion comes to be defined as release from guilt, and guilt comes to be understood more and more in subjective terms. Paul's almost mythical scheme of the history of salvation, in which the law had its special function in the history of Israel "until Christ came" (Gal. 3–4), is transposed into an account of *each individual's* progress toward conversion. The function of the law in this progress is precisely to awaken guilt, to produce that despair of one's own powers that is the reverse side and the negative prerequisite for accepting God's grace. That, of course, was precisely the aspect of Christianity that Nietzsche and George Bernard Shaw found so loathsome (above, Part VI).

In the past four or five decades this introspective reading of Romans 7, with its focus on guilt and its sharp dichotomy between the saved and the unsaved, has come under vigorous attack as a distortion of the historical sense of the text. Among the revisionists are the three whose essays are excerpted here. Krister Stendahl attacks the long tradition, beginning with Augustine, of reading "the introspective conscience of the West" into Paul and particularly those psychologizing interpretations that "modernize" Paul. Paul Meyer, by a close reading of the text, shows that the "pernicious binary language" of conversionist interpretations runs counter to the aim of the whole Letter to Romans, "a single massive argument against the conventional uses of this distinction." Stanley Stowers places Paul's rhetoric in Romans 7:7–25 within the conventions of speech that ancient audiences would have recognized and thus exposes misreadings of the "I" in those verses.

THEODORET OF CYRUS

[Painting the Passions' Domination Prior to Grace] (ca. 445)†

*   *   *

Having said as much, and by reason of his being accorded spiritual grace foreseeing that some heretics would take this as criticism of the Old and consider the Old Law to be from some other god,[1] of necessity he also raises objections and provides solutions. *What then should we say—that the Law is sin?* (7:7) He had cited many things in what was previously said that would have provided those wishing to speak irreverently of the Law with grounds for criticizing the Law had he not adduced the solution

---

2. *A Man in Christ* (London: Hodder & Stoughton, 1935), 102f.
† From Theodoret's commentary on Rom. 7:7–25, tr. by Robert Charles Hill, *Theodoret of Cyrus, Commentary on the Letters of St. Paul* (Brookline: Holy Cross Orthodox Press, 2001), Vol. 1, 82–87. Reprinted by permission of Holy Orthodox Press. Theodoret's interpretation is in certain respects fairly typical of patristic readings of Romans 7, yet there are also distinctive emphases.
1. Marcion, for example.

addressing the questions: *The Law made its appearance with the result that the fall was multiplied*, and *The Law produces wrath*, and *No human being will be justified in his sight by works of the Law*,[2] and statements similar to these. Hence for a solution of these very points he raised the objection. Firstly he proved the question to be blasphemous, using a word of denial, *Far from it*. Then he brings out the utility of the Law: *Yet I would not have known sin except through the Law*. Not only, he is saying, is the Law not a teacher of sin—far from it—but on the contrary it is even an accuser of sin: I would not have known what evil is if it had not taught me. *In fact, I would not have been aware of covetousness if the Law had not said, You shall not covet*. The phrases *I would not have been aware* and *I would not have known* are not completely indicative of ignorance here; rather, they mean, Through the Law I got a more precise grasp of differences arising from nature.

Sin, however, taking occasion from the commandment, gave rise to all kinds of covetousness in me (v.8). He uses every means to show the Law to be free from blame: after saying sins abounded with the imposition of the Law, he is obliged lest anyone suspect the Law to be guilty to give an idea of sin's way of proceeding—namely, sin seized upon the giving of the Law as an occasion for a struggle so as to fight against reason in its greater weakness. *Apart from the Law sin was dead*: with no law to show what had to be done and to forbid what was not to be done, there was no room for sin. He then makes this clear from an example. *I lived at one time apart from the Law* (v.9): before the Fall Adam had no fear of death.[3] *But once the commandment came, sin came to life again, whereas I died* (vv.9–10). As soon as God gave the commandment about the trees, the devil made his approach to the woman in a serpent and employed those deceitful words. She fell for it, noticed the beauty of the fruit and was captivated by the pleasure while at the same time breaking the commandment; immediately she together with Adam became subject to the norm of death, he having been a sharer in the eating. *The commandment that was meant for life proved to be death*. In every way he defends the Law and the commandment, while establishing the evil of sin: the commandment was a source of life (he says), whereas the movement to its opposite produced death. It was appropriate for him to employ the word *proved* so as to bring out that while the Law's purpose is one thing, owing to sin its outcome is another.

Sin, in fact, took occasion from the commandment to deceive me, and through it killed me (v.11). He said the same thing in a different fashion. *And so the Law is holy and the commandment is holy, righteous and good* (v.12). By *Law* he refers to the Mosaic Law, and by *commandment* to that given to Adam. He extolled it with many commendations for the reason that it was the object of much criticism on the part of many: those addicted to sloth and not embracing the hardships of virtue criticize the Lord God for imposing the commandment. If he was unaware of what would happen, they claim, how is he God in not foreseeing the future? Yet if he imposed the commandment while foreseeing the Fall, he himself is responsible for

---

2. Rom. 5:20; 4:15; 3:20.
3. Theodoret does not have a uniform interpretation of the "I" of Rom. 7. Here he says that it refers specifically to Adam (see also the comment on 7:12 below), whereas later (beginning with 7:14) he will take it as descriptive of pre-Christian existence, particularly in its battle with the passions (see on 7:14, 22).

the Fall. They should have realized, however, that the discernment of good and its opposite is proper to those endowed with reason. The wolf is rapacious, for example, the lion carnivorous, and bears and leopards are similar, having no sense of sin or a conscience pricked by their actions. Human beings, on the contrary, even if no one is present during their actions, blush at and feel guilt for their crimes, conscience manufacturing the accusation. How, then, could those in possession of such a nature live a life apart from law? This is surely the reason God gave the commandment, so that they might acknowledge their own nature and fear the lawgiver.

Now, it is possible to recognize also the lawgiver's lovingkindness: the law he imposed was not difficult to practice but actually very easy to observe. He permitted the enjoyment of all the plants, forbidding a share of one only, not out of envy of them in this case (how could he, after all, after giving them authority over everything?) but to instruct them in the limits of service, to teach them to be well-disposed to the Creator, and to provide the rational being with an occasion for exercising that faculty. If, on the contrary, they did not observe the commandment and thus fell under the norm of death, the blame was due not to the one who imposed it but to the one who transgressed it. A physician, after all, in bidding the patient abstain from cold drinks, does so not out of illwill but from concern for health; but if the patient does not keep the command and takes some water, he is the one to suffer harm, whereas the physician is innocent of blame. The Lord God, of course, regaled Adam in person and all his race with care of all kinds. And—to pass over other details and get to the heart of the matter—for the sake of him and his race the Only-begotten Word became man and put an end to the reign of death which had begun with him; he gave a promise of resurrection and made ready the kingdom of heaven, and so he both knew his Fall and prepared in advance the remedy to come. This is surely the reason the divine apostle called the commandment *holy, righteous and good*—*holy* as teaching what is proper, *righteous* as lawfully delivering the sentence on the transgressors, and *good* as making life available to those who keep it.

He next raises the question in turn, *Did the good prove to be death for me?* (v.13), and in turn denies it in his customary way, *Not at all*. He demonstrates the cause of [the] problem: *Rather, it was sin causing death in me by means of the good so that sin might be shown up*. It is lacking in clarity on account of the conciseness; what he means is this, that by means of the good—namely, through the Law and through the commandment—sin is shown to me, that is, evil and wickedness. How is it shown? By causing death: from the fruit I know the tree, and with death before my eyes I hate its mother. Now, the Law is my instructor in this; accordingly, by teaching me this the Law is not evil—sin is, the source of death. Our will's inclination towards worse things brings about sin. *In order that through the commandment sin might prove to be sinful beyond measure*: even if nature lets us see it, nevertheless the Law taught us more clearly the excess of its wickedness. Now, the phrase *might prove* is incomplete: *obviously* is understood, as we said also in what preceded, *Rather, it was sin causing death in me so that sin might be shown up in order that through the commandment sin might prove to be sinful beyond measure*—in other words, in order that through the commandment it might be obvious that sin is sinful (that is, wicked) beyond measure.

Then, like an excellent painter, he depicts the struggle between our nature and sin. *We know that the Law is spiritual* (v.14). Again he extols the Law with commendation; what is more honorable than this title? It was written by the divine Spirit, he is saying; by sharing in this grace blessed Moses composed the Law.[4] *But I am of the flesh, sold into the slavery of sin.* He introduces the human being before grace, beset by passions, using the term *of the flesh* for not yet attaining spiritual assistance. Now, let us take the phrase *sold into the slavery of sin* in the usage of the prophet, "Lo, because of your sins you were sold into slavery."[5] This is his meaning here, too: I threw in my lot with sin, and sold my self into its service.

I mean, what I do I do not understand (v.15). Overcome by pleasure and carried away also by the passion of anger, he has no clear knowledge of sin, whereas at least after the cessation of the passion he has a sense of the evil. *That is to say, what I want I do not do; rather, I do what I detest.* This is the effect of the Law, teaching what is evil and instilling hatred of it in the soul. Of course, the phrases *what I do not want* and *what I detest* imply not compulsion but weakness: we fail, not under the impulse of any compulsion or force; rather, under the spell of pleasure we do what we loath as unlawful. *Now, if I do what I do not want, I concede that the Law is good* (v.16): the very hatred I have for sin I have on receipt from the Law. Consequently I defend the Law, and admit its proper function.

As it is, however, it is no longer I that do it but sin dwelling within me (v.17). This is short on clarity, requiring greater explanation. The body, mortal as it became after the transgression of the commandment, felt the effect of the passions; the course of the present life depends on them. For example, it requires desire, not only for nourishment but also for procreation, agriculture and for the sake of the other trades; where it is lacking, none of them functions. It is also responsible for our practice of virtue: the person with no longing for it shies away from the hardships it involves. It also produces in us the longing for God. So, on the one hand, moderation in desire is an aid to the good, and on the other its excess is productive of intemperance: it causes interference in the marriages of others, hankering after what is improper, brigandage, grave robbing, homicide and other such crimes. This is surely the reason why the God of all linked anger with it, to repress its lack of restraint. Yet this passion also is in need of what restrains its insatiability. Just as, then, we apply heat to what is very cold, and conversely with what is very cold we temper the heat, so in creating us God instilled these two passions, diametrically opposed to one another, and taught us to temper the one with the other. He put the mind in charge of them, you see, like a charioteer with ponies, and imposed the harness of service on them, obliging them to bear it equally. But if at some time it happened that desire slipped out of control, he gave directions for anger to be spurred so that once aroused it might bring the harness level again, whereas if anger experienced the passion of excess, he urges desire in turn to be stimulated, and check anger's excess. The mind, then, when sober and discrete, preserves this style; but should it become negligent and drop the reins, it causes the ponies to bolt, it loses its footing, and with them tumbles into holes and crevices. The divine apostle said as much here, *As*

---

4. Over against the heretics' rejection of the Torah (see note 1 above), Theodoret affirms its divine inspiration as well as its Mosaic composition.
5. Isa. 50:1.

it is, however, it is no longer I that do it but sin dwelling in me, referring by *sin* to the servitude of the mind and the dominance of the passions. He himself does not do it, since he hates what is done; the dominance of the passions has this effect.

I know, in fact, that good does not dwell within me, that is, in my flesh (v.18). He means the control of the passions, which the body turned mortal has brought to the fore and the mind's negligence has augmented. *Willing what is right is within my possibilities, but performing it I cannot reach on*: the zeal for what is right I gained from the Law's teaching, yet I lack strength for its performance, not having any further assistance. *In other words, the good I intend I do not do; instead, the evil I hate is what I perform. Now, if I do what I do not intend, it is no longer I that do it but sin dwelling in me* (vv.19–20). He said the same thing more clearly.

So I find the Law is that when I intend to do what is right (v.21). Here a distinction is required: *evil is close beside me.* Again, owing to the conciseness he put it obscurely; he means, And the Law seems right to me.[6] In other words, I extol what is stated by it as right, and likewise I love what is right and hate what is opposed to it. Yet *evil is close beside me*—that is, sin—through having a body that is subject to death and suffering, and through the soul's indifference and weakness. Then he shows more clearly the struggle between the mind and the passions: *I mean, I delight in God's Law in my inner self* (v.22). By *my inner self* he means the mind. *But I see another law in my members making war against the law of my mind, and holding me a prisoner of the law of sin which is in my members* (v.23). He gives sin the name *law of sin.* Now, it is in force when the body's passions are activated, on the one hand, and on the other when the soul is incapable of checking them owing to the indifference occurring from the outset, and instead forfeits its own freedom and agrees to be enslaved to them. Yet, though enslaved, it hates its slavery, and praises the accuser of the slavery.

The apostle treated of all this so as to show what we were like before grace, and what we became after grace; and as though taking on the viewpoint of those who before grace were beset by sin, as it were finding himself in the midst of the enemy, taken captive and obliged to serve, with no assistance in sight from another quarter, he groans deeply and laments, and shows the Law incapable of helping, saying, *Wretch that I am, who will rescue me from the body of this death? I thank my God through Jesus Christ our Lord* (vv.24–25). Now, he speaks of a *body of death,* as though made subject to death—that is, mortal, the soul being immortal. Our Lord Jesus Christ alone, he is saying, freed us from that harsh domination, undoing death and promising us immortality, an existence free from hardship and grief, and a life without hostility and sin. Of course, we shall receive the enjoyment of these things in the future life, whereas in the present, enjoying the grace of the all-holy Spirit, we are not alone in being drawn up in battle array against the passions, and instead with that to help us we are able to prevail over them.[7]

---

6. Whereas Theodoret takes *nomos* in 7:21 as a reference to the Mosaic Law, most modern scholars think that Paul is referring here to a norm of human experience. See above for Origen's discussion of the multiple meanings of *nomos* in Paul's letters (Part IV, pp. 322–23).

7. Theodoret continues by interpreting Paul's subsequent remarks as the solution to the dilemma that he depicts in 7:14–25.

KRISTER STENDAHL

The Apostle Paul and the Introspective Conscience of the West (1963)†

In the history of Western Christianity—and hence, to a large extent, in the history of Western culture—the Apostle Paul has been hailed as a hero of the introspective conscience. Here was the man who grappled with the problem "I do not do the good I want, but the evil I do not want to do is what I do . . ." (Rom. 7:19). His insights as to a solution of this dilemma have recently been more or less identified, for example, with what Jung referred to as the Individuation Process;[1] but this is only a contemporary twist to the traditional Western way of reading the Pauline letters as documents of human consciousness.

Twenty-five years ago Henry J. Cadbury wrote a stimulating study, "The Peril of Modernizing Jesus" (1937). That book and that very title is a good summary of one of the most important insights of biblical studies in the 20th century. It has ramifications far beyond the field of theology and biblical exegesis. It questions the often tacit presupposition that man remains basically the same through the ages. There is little point in affirming or denying such a presupposition in general terms—much would depend on what the foggy word "basically" could mean. But both the historian and the theologian, both the psychologist and the average reader of the Bible, are well advised to assess how this hypothesis of contemporaneity affects their thinking, and their interpretation of ancient writings.

This problem becomes acute when one tries to picture the function and the manifestation of introspection in the life and writings of the Apostle Paul. It is the more acute since it is exactly at this point that Western interpreters have found the common denominator between Paul and the experiences of man, since Paul's statements about "justification by faith" have been hailed as the answer to the problem which faces the ruthlessly honest man in his practice of introspection. Especially in Protestant Christianity—which, however, at this point has its roots in Augustine and in the piety of the Middle Ages—the Pauline awareness of sin has been interpreted in the light of Luther's struggle with his conscience. But it is exactly at that point that we can discern the most drastic difference between Luther and Paul, between the 16th and the 1st century, and, perhaps, between Eastern and Western Christianity.

A fresh look at the Pauline writings themselves shows that Paul was equipped with what in our eyes must be called a rather "robust" conscience. In Phil. 3 Paul speaks most fully about his life before his Christian calling, and there is no indication that he had had any difficulty in fulfilling the Law. On the contrary, he can say that he had been "flawless" as to the righteous-

† A paper delivered at the Annual Meeting of the American Psychological Association, September 3, 1961; published in HTR 56 (1963): 199–215. An earlier version appeared in SEÅ 25 (1960): 62–77. Reprinted by permission of the Harvard Theological Review. Stendahl served as dean and John Lord O'Brian Professor of Divinity at Harvard Divinity School before becoming Bishop of Stockholm in 1984. Following his retirement from ecclesiastical office, he returned to Harvard, where he is now Mellon Professor of Divinity Emeritus.
1. D. Cox, Jung and St. Paul: A Study of the Doctrine of Justification by Faith and Its Relation to the Concept of Individuation (1959). * * *

ness required by the Law (v.6). His encounter with Jesus Christ—at Damascus, according to Acts 9:1–9—has not changed this fact. It was not to him a restoration of a plagued conscience; when he says that he now forgets what is behind him (Phil. 3:13), he does not think about the shortcomings in his obedience to the Law, but about his glorious achievements as a righteous Jew, achievements which he nevertheless now has learned to consider as "refuse" in the light of his faith in Jesus as the Messiah.

The impossibility of keeping the whole Law is a decisive point in Paul's argumentation in Rom. 2:17–3:20 (cf. 2:1ff.); and also in Gal. 3:10–12 this impossibility is the background for Paul's arguments in favor of a salvation which is open to both Jews and Gentiles in Christ. These and similar Pauline statements have led many interpreters to accuse Paul of misunderstanding or deliberately distorting the Jewish view of Law and Salvation. It is pointed out that for the Jew the Law did not require a static or pedantic perfectionism but supposed a covenant relationship in which there was room for forgiveness and repentance and where God applied the Measure of Grace. Hence Paul should have been wrong in ruling out the Law on the basis that Israel could not achieve the perfect obedience which the Law required. What is forgotten in such a critique of Paul—which is conditioned by the later Western problem of a conscience troubled by the demands of the Law—is that these statements about the impossibility of fulfilling the Law stand side by side with the one just mentioned: "I was blameless as to righteousness—of the Law, that is" (Phil. 3:6). So Paul speaks about his subjective conscience—in full accordance with his Jewish training. But Rom. 2–3 deals with something very different. The actual transgressions in Israel—as a people, not in each and every individual— show that the Jews are not better than the Gentiles, in spite of circumcision and the proud possession of the Law. The "advantage" of the Jews is that they have been entrusted with the Words of God and this advantage cannot be revoked by their disobedience (Rom. 3:1ff.), but for the rest they have no edge on salvation. The Law has not helped. They stand before God as guilty as the Gentiles, and even more so (2:9). All this is said in the light of the new avenue of salvation, which has been opened in Christ, an avenue which is equally open to Jews and Gentiles, since it is not based on the Law, in which the very distinction between the two rests. In such a situation, says Paul, the old covenant, even with its provision for forgiveness and grace, is not a valid alternative any more. The only *metanoia* (repentance/conversion) and the only grace which counts is the one now available in Messiah Jesus. Once this has been seen, it appears that Paul's references to the impossibility of fulfilling the Law is part of a theological and theoretical scriptural argument about the relation between Jews and Gentiles. Judging from Paul's own writings, there is no indication that he had "experienced it in his own conscience" during his time as a Pharisee. It is also striking to note that Paul never urges Jews to find in Christ the answer to the anguish of a plagued conscience.

If that is the case regarding *Paul the Pharisee*, it is, as we shall see, even more important to note that we look in vain for any evidence that *Paul the Christian* has suffered under the burden of conscience concerning personal shortcomings which he would label "sins." The famous formula "simul justus et peccator"—at the same time righteous and sinner—as a description of the status of the Christian may have some foundation in the

Pauline writings, but this formula cannot be substantiated as the center of Paul's conscious attitude toward his personal sins. Apparently, Paul did not have the type of introspective conscience which such a formula seems to presuppose. This is probably one of the reasons why "forgiveness" is the term for salvation which is used least of all in the Pauline writings.

It is most helpful to compare these observations concerning Paul with the great hero of what has been called "Pauline Christianity," i.e., with Martin Luther. In him we find the problem of late medieval piety and theology. Luther's inner struggles presuppose the developed system of Penance and Indulgence, and it is significant that his famous 95 theses take their point of departure from the problem of forgiveness of sins as seen within the framework of Penance: "When our Lord and Master Jesus Christ said: 'Repent (*penitentiam agite*) . . . ,' he wanted the whole life of the faithful to be a repentance (or penance)."

When the period of the European mission had come to an end, the theological and practical center of Penance shifted from Baptism, administered once and for all, to the ever repeated Mass, and already this subtle change in the architecture of the Christian life contributed to a more acute introspection. The manuals for self-examination among the Irish monks and missionaries became a treasured legacy in wide circles of Western Christianity. The Black Death may have been significant in the development of the climate of faith and life. Penetrating self-examination reached a hitherto unknown intensity. For those who took this practice seriously—and they were more numerous than many Protestants are accustomed to think—the pressure was great. It is as one of those—and for them—that Luther carries out his mission as a great pioneer. It is in response to *their* question, "How can I find a gracious God?" that Paul's words about a justification in Christ by faith, and without the works of the Law, appears as the liberating and saving answer. Luther's unrelenting honesty, even to the gates of hell (cf. especially his *De servo arbitrio*, "On the Bondage of the Will"), his refusal to accept the wise and sound consolation from his spiritual directors, these make him into a Christopher Columbus in the world of faith, who finds new and good land on the other side of what was thought to be the abyss.

In these matters Luther was a truly Augustinian monk, since Augustine may well have been one of the first to express the dilemma of the introspective conscience. It has always been a puzzling fact that Paul meant so relatively little for the thinking of the Church during the first 350 years of its history. To be sure, he is honored and quoted but—in the theological perspective of the West—it seems that Paul's great insight into justification by faith was forgotten. It is, however, with Augustine that we find an interpretation of Paul which makes use of what to us is the deeper layer in the thought of the great Apostle. A decisive reason for this state of affairs may well have been that up to the time of Augustine the Church was by and large under the impression that Paul dealt with those issues with which he actually deals: 1) What happens to the Law (the Torah, the actual Law of Moses, not the principle of legalism) when the Messiah has come?—2) What are the ramifications of the Messiah's arrival for the relation between Jews and Gentiles? For Paul had not arrived at his view of the Law by testing and pondering its effect upon his conscience; it was his grappling with the question about the place of the Gentiles in the Church and in the plan of God, with the problem Jews/Gentiles or Jewish Christians/ Gentile Christians, which had driven him to that interpretation of the Law which was to become his in a unique way. These observations agree well with the manner in which both Paul himself and the Acts of the Apostles describe his "conversion" as a call to become the Apostle to and of the Gentiles. This was the task for which he—in the manner of the prophets of old—had been earmarked by God from his mother's womb (Gal. 1:15, cf. Acts 9:15). There is not—as we usually think—first a conversion, and then a call to apostleship; there is only the call to the work among the Gentiles. Hence, it is quite natural that at least one of the centers of gravity in Paul's thought should be how to define the place for Gentiles in the Church, according to the plan of God. Rom. 9–11 is not an appendix to chs. 1–8, but the climax of the letter.

This problem was, however, not a live one after the end of the first century, when Christianity for all practical purposes had a non-Jewish constituency. Yet it was not until Augustine that the Pauline thought about the Law and Justification was applied in a consistent and grand style to a more general and timeless human problem. In that connection we remember that Augustine has often been called "the first modern man." While this is an obvious generalization, it may contain a fair amount of truth. His *Confessiones* are the first great document in the history of the introspective conscience. The Augustinian line leads into the Middle Ages and reaches its climax in the penitential struggle of an Augustinian monk, Martin Luther, and in his interpretation of Paul.

Judging at least from a superficial survey of the preaching of the Churches of the East from olden times to the present, it is striking how their homiletical tradition is either one of doxology or meditative mysticism or exhortation—but it does not deal with the plagued conscience in the way in which one came to do so in the Western Churches.

The problem we are trying to isolate could be expressed in hermeneutical terms somewhat like this: The Reformers' interpretation of Paul rests on an analogism when Pauline statements about Faith and Works, Law and Gospel, Jews and Gentiles are read in the framework of late medieval piety. The Law, the Torah, with its specific requirements of circumcision and food restrictions becomes a general principle of "legalism" in religious matters. Where Paul was concerned about the possibility for Gentiles to be included in the messianic community, his statements are now read as answers to the quest for assurance about man's salvation out of a common human predicament.

This shift in the frame of reference affects the interpretation at many points. A good illustration can be seen in what Luther calls the Second Use of the Law, i.e., its function as a Tutor or Schoolmaster unto Christ. The crucial passage for this understanding of the Law is Gal. 3:24, a passage which the King James Version—in unconscious accord with Western tradition—renders: "Wherefore the law was our schoolmaster (R.V. and A.S.V.: tutor) to bring us unto Christ," but which the Revised Standard Version translates more adequately: "So that the law was our custodian until Christ came." In his extensive argument for the possibility of Gentiles becoming Christians without circumcision etc., Paul states that the Law had not come in until 430 years after the promise to Abraham, and that it was meant to have validity only up to the time of the Messiah (Gal. 3:15–

22). Hence, its function was to serve as a Custodian for the Jews until that time. Once the Messiah had come, and once the faith in Him—not "faith" as a general religious attitude—was available as the decisive ground for salvation, the Law had done its duty as a custodian for the Jews, or as a waiting room with strong locks (vv. 22f.). Hence, it is clear that Paul's problem is how to explain why there is no reason to impose the Law on the Gentiles, who now, in God's good Messianic time, have become partakers in the fulfillment of the promises to Abraham (v. 29).

In the common interpretation of Western Christianity, the matter looks very different. One could even say that Paul's argument has been reversed into saying the opposite to his original intention. Now the Law is the Tutor *unto* Christ. Nobody can attain a true faith in Christ unless his self-righteousness has been crushed by the Law. The function of the Second Use of the Law is to make man see his desperate need for a Savior. In such an interpretation, we note how Paul's distinction between Jews and Gentiles is gone. "*Our* Tutor/Custodian" is now a statement applied to man in general, not "our" in the sense of "I, Paul, and my fellow Jews." Furthermore, the Law is not any more the Law of Moses which requires circumcision etc., and which has become obsolete when faith in the Messiah is a live option—it is the moral imperative as such, in the form of the will of God. And finally, Paul's argument that the Gentiles must not, and should not come to Christ *via* the Law, i.e., *via* circumcision etc., has turned into a statement according to which all men must come to Christ with consciences properly convicted by the Law and its insatiable requirements for righteousness. So drastic is the reinterpretation once the original framework of "Jews and Gentiles" is lost, and the Western problems of conscience become its unchallenged and self-evident substitute.

Thus, the radical difference between a Paul and a Luther at this one point has considerable ramification for the reading of the actual texts. And the line of Luther appears to be the obvious one. This is true not only among those who find themselves more or less dogmatically bound by the confessions of the Reformation. It is equally true about the average student of "all the great books" in a College course, or the agnostic Westerner in general. It is also true in serious New Testament exegesis. Thus, R. Bultmann—in spite of his great familiarity with the history of religions in early Christian times—finds the nucleus of Pauline thought in the problem of "boasting," i.e., in man's need to be utterly convicted in his conscience. Paul's self-understanding in these matters is the existential, and hence, ever valid center of Pauline theology. Such an interpretation is an even more drastic translation and an even more far-reaching generalization of the original Pauline material than that found in the Reformers. But it is worth noting that it is achieved in the prolongation of the same line. This is more obvious since Bultmann makes, candidly and openly, the statement that his existential hermeneutic rests on the presupposition that man is essentially the same through the ages, and that this continuity in the human self-consciousness is the common denominator between the New Testament and any age of human history. This presupposition is stated with the force of an a priori truth.

What in Bultmann rests on a clearly stated hermeneutic principle plays, however, its subtle and distorting role in historians who do not give account of their presuppositions but work within an unquestioned Western framework. P. Volz, in his comprehensive study of Jewish eschatology, uses man's knowledge of his individual salvation in its relation to a troubled conscience as one of the "trenches" in his reconstruction of the Jewish background to the New Testament. But when it comes to the crucial question and he wants to find a passage which would substantiate that this was a conscious problem in those generations of Judaism, he can find only one example in the whole Rabbinic literature which perhaps could illustrate an attitude of a troubled conscience (b. *Ber.* 28b).

To be sure, no one could ever deny that *harmartia*, "sin," is a crucial word in Paul's terminology, especially in his epistle to the Romans. Rom. 1–3 sets out to show that all—both Jews and Gentiles—have sinned and fallen short of the Glory of God (3:19, cf. v. 23). Rom. 3:21–8:39 demonstrates how and in what sense this tragic fact is changed by the arrival of the Messiah.

It is much harder to gage how Paul subjectively experienced the power of sin in his life and, more specifically, how and in what sense he was conscious of actual sins. One point is clear. The Sin with capital S in Paul's past was that he had persecuted the Church of God. This climax of his dedicated obedience to his Jewish faith (Gal. 1:13, Phil. 3:6) was the shameful deed which made him the least worthy of apostleship (1 Cor. 15:9). This motif, which is elaborated dramatically by the author of the Acts of the Apostles (chs. 9, 22 and 26), is well grounded in Paul's own epistles. Similarly, when 1 Timothy states on Paul's account that "Christ Jesus came into the world to save sinners, of whom I am number one" (1:15), this is not an expression of contrition in the present tense, but refers to how Paul in his ignorance had been a blaspheming and violent persecutor, before God in his mercy and grace had revealed to him his true Messiah and made Paul an Apostle and a prototype of sinners' salvation (1:12–16).

Nevertheless, Paul knew that he had made up for this terrible Sin of persecuting the Church, as he says in so many words in 1 Cor. 15:10: ". . . his grace toward me was not in vain; on the contrary, I worked harder than any of them—though it was not I, but the grace of God which is with me."

Thus his call to Apostleship has the same pattern as the more thematic statement that Christ died for us godless ones, while we were yet sinners (Rom. 5:6–11). We note how that statement is only the subsidiary conditional clause in an argument *e majore ad minus*: If now God was so good and powerful that he could justify weak and sinful and rebellious men, how much easier must it not be for him to give in due time the ultimate salvation to those whom he already has justified. Hence, the words about the sinful, the weak and the rebellious have not present-tense meaning, but refer to the past, which is gloriously and gracefully blotted out, as was Paul's enmity to Jesus Christ and his Church.

What then about Paul's consciousness of sins after his conversion? His letters indicate with great clarity that he did not hold to the view that man was free from sin after baptism. His pastoral admonitions show that he had much patience with the sins and weaknesses of Christians. But does he ever intimate that he is aware of any sins of his own which would trouble his conscience? It is actually easier to find statements to the contrary. The tone in Acts 23:1, "Brethren, I have lived before God in all good conscience up to this day" (cf. 24:16), prevails also throughout his letters. Even if we take due note of the fact that the major part of Paul's correspondence contains an apology for his Apostolic ministry—hence it is the antipode to Augustine's Confessions from the point of view of form—the conspicuous absence of reference to an actual consciousness of being a sinner is surprising. To be sure, Paul is aware of a struggle with his "body" (1 Cor. 9: 27), but we note that the tone is one of confidence, not of a plagued conscience.

In Rom. 9:1 and 2 Cor. 1:12 he witnesses to his good conscience. This tone reaches its highest pitch in 2 Cor. 5:10f.: "For we must all appear before the judgment seat of Christ so that each one may receive the retribution for what he has done while in his body, either good or evil. Aware, therefore, of the fear of the Lord, we try to persuade men, but to God it is clear [what we are]; and I hope that it is clear also to your conscience." Here, with the day of reckoning before his eyes, Paul says that the Lord has approved of him, and he hopes that the Corinthians shall have an equally positive impression of him, and of his success in pleasing the Lord (5:9). This robust conscience is not shaken but strengthened by his awareness of a final judgment which has not come yet. And when he writes about the tensions between himself and Apollos and other teachers, he states that "I have nothing on my conscience" (1 Cor. 4:4; N.E.B.—literally "I know nothing with me"; the verb is of the same stem as the word for conscience); to be sure, he adds that this does not settle the case, since "the Lord is my judge," but it is clear from the context that Paul is in little doubt about the final verdict. His warning against a premature verdict is not a plea out of humility or fear, but a plea to the Corinthians not to be too rash in a negative evaluation of Paul.

Thus, we look in vain for a statement in which Paul would speak about himself as an actual sinner. When he speaks about his conscience, he witnesses to his good conscience before men and God. On the other hand, Paul often speaks about his *weakness*, not only ironically as in 2 Cor. 11: 21f. In 2 Cor. 12 we find the proudly humble words, "But He said to me: 'My grace is sufficient to you, for the power is fulfilled in weakness.' I will the more gladly boast of my weakness, that the power of Christ may rest upon me. For the sake of Christ, then, I am content with weaknesses, insults, hardships, persecutions, and calamities; for when I am weak, then I am strong" (vv. 9–10). The weakness which Paul here refers to is clearly without any relation to his sin of his conscience. The "thorn in the flesh" (v. 7) was presumably some physical handicap—some have guessed at epilepsy—which interfered with his effectiveness and, what was more important, with his apostolic authority, as we can see from Gal. 4:13, cf. 1 Cor. 11:30. Sickness was seen as a sign of insufficient spiritual endowment. But there is no indication that Paul ever thought of this and other "weaknesses" as sins for which he was responsible. They were caused by the Enemy or the enemies. His weakness became for him an important facet in his identification with the work of Christ, who had been "crucified in weakness" (2 Cor. 13:4; cf. also 4:10 and Col. 1:24).—In the passage from Rom. 5, mentioned above, we find the only use of the word "weak" as a synonym to "sinner," but there these words helped to describe primarily the power of justification as a past act (and the New English Bible consequently renders it by "powerless"). This is the more clear since the third synonym is "enemy" (v. 10), and points to Paul's past when he had been the enemy of Christ.

Yet there is one Pauline text which the reader must have wondered why we have left unconsidered, especially since it is the passage we mentioned in the beginning as the proof text for Paul's deep insights into the human predicament: "I do not do the good I want, but the evil I do not want to do is what I do" (Rom. 7:19). What could witness more directly to a deep and sensitive introspective conscience? While much attention has been given to the question whether Paul here speaks about a pre-Christian or Christian experience of his, or about man in general, little attention has been drawn to the fact that Paul here is involved in an argument about the Law; he is not primarily concerned about man's or his own cloven ego or predicament. The diatribe style of the chapter helps us to see what Paul is doing. In vv. 7–12 he works out an answer to the semi-rhetorical question: "Is the Law sin?" The answer reads: "Thus the Law is holy, just, and good." This leads to the equally rhetorical question: "Is it then this good (Law) which brought death to me?", and the answer is summarized in v. 25b: "So then, I myself serve the Law of God with my mind, but with my flesh I serve the Law of Sin" (i.e., the Law "weakened by sin" [8:3] leads to death, just as a medicine which is good in itself can cause death in a patient whose organism [flesh] cannot take it).

Such an analysis of the formal structure of Rom. 7 shows that Paul is here involved in an interpretation of the Law, a defense for the holiness and goodness of the Law. In vv. 13–25 he carries out this defense by making a distinction between the Law as such and the Sin (and the Flesh) which has to assume the whole responsibility for the fatal outcome. It is most striking that the "I", the *ego*, is not simply identified with Sin and Flesh. The observation that "I do not do the good I want, but the evil I do not want to do is what I do" does not lead directly over to the exclamation: "Wretched man that I am . . . !", but, on the contrary, to the statement, "Now if I do what I do not want, *then it is not I who do it*, but the sin which dwells in me." The argument is one of acquittal of the ego, not one of utter contrition. Such a line of thought would be impossible if Paul's intention were to describe man's predicament. In Rom. 1–3 the human impasse has been argued, and here every possible excuse has been carefully ruled out. In Rom. 7 the issue is rather to show how in some sense "I gladly agree with the Law of God as far as my inner man is concerned" (v. 22); or, as in v. 25, "I serve the Law of God."

All this makes sense only if the anthropological references in Rom. 7 are seen as means for a very special argument about the holiness and goodness of the Law. The possibility of a distinction between the good Law and the bad Sin is based on the rather trivial observation that every man knows that there is a difference between what he ought to do and what he does. This distinction makes it possible for Paul to blame Sin and Flesh, and to rescue the Law as a good gift of God. "If I now do what I do not want, I agree with the Law [and recognize] that it is good" (v. 16). That is all, but that is what should be proven.

Unfortunately—or fortunately—Paul happened to express this supporting argument so well that what to him and his contemporaries was a common sense observation appeared to later interpreters to be a most penetrating insight into the nature of man and into the nature of sin. This could happen easily once the problem about the nature and intention of

God's Law was not any more as relevant a problem in the sense in which Paul grappled with it. The question about the Law became the incidental framework around the golden truth of Pauline anthropology. This is what happens when one approaches Paul with the Western question of an introspective conscience. This Western interpretation reaches its climax when it appears that even, or especially, the will of man is the center of depravation. And yet, in Rom. 7 Paul had said about that will: "The will (to do the good) is there . . ." (v. 18).

What we have called the Western interpretation has left its mark even in the field of textual reconstruction in this chapter in Romans. In Moffatt's translation of the New Testament the climax of the whole argument about the Law (v. 25b, see above) is placed before the words "wretched man that I am . . ." Such a rearrangement—without any basis in the manuscripts—wants to make this exclamation the dramatic climax of the whole chapter, so that it is quite clear to the reader that Paul here gives the answer to the great problem of human existence. But by such arrangements the structure of Paul's argumentation is destroyed. What was a digression is elevated to the main factor. It should not be denied that Paul is deeply aware of the precarious situation of man in this world, where even the holy Law of God does not help—it actually leads to death. Hence his outburst. But there is no indication that this awareness is related to a subjective conscience struggle. If that were the case, he would have spoken of the "body of sin," but he says "body of death" (v. 25; cf. 1 Cor. 15:56). What dominates this chapter is a theological concern and the awareness that there is a positive solution available here and now by the Holy Spirit about which he speaks in ch. 8. We should not read a trembling and introspective conscience into a text which is so anxious to put the blame on Sin, and that in such a way that not only the Law but the will and mind of man are declared good and are found to be on the side of God.

We may have wasted too much time in trying to demonstrate a fact well known in human history—and especially in the history of religions: that sayings which originally meant one thing later on were interpreted to mean something else, something which was felt to be more relevant to human conditions of later times.

And yet, if our analysis is on the whole correct, it points to a major question in the history of mankind. We should venture to suggest that the West for centuries has wrongly surmised that the biblical writers were grappling with problems which no doubt are ours, but which never entered their consciousness.

For the historian this is of great significance. It could of course always be argued that these ancients unconsciously were up against the same problems as we are—man being the same through the ages. But the historian is rightly anxious to stress the value of having an adequate picture of what these people actually thought that they were saying. He will always be suspicious of any "modernizing," whether it be for apologetic, doctrinal, or psychological purposes.

The theologian would be quite willing to accept and appreciate the obvious deepening of religious and human insight which has taken place in Western thought, and which reached a theological climax with Luther—

and a secular climax with Freud. He could perhaps argue that this Western interpretation and transformation of Pauline thought is a valid and glorious process of theological development. He could even claim that such a development was fostered by elements implicit in the New Testament, and especially in Paul.

The framework of "Sacred History" which we have found to be that of Pauline Theology (cf. our comments on Gal. 3:24 above) opens up a new perspective for systematic theology and practical theology. The Pauline *ephapax* ("once for all", Rom. 6:10) cannot be translated fully and only into something repeated in the life of every individual believer. For Gentiles the Law is *not* the Schoolmaster who leads to Christ; or it is that only by analogy and a secondary one at that. We find ourselves in the new situation where the faith in the Messiah Jesus gives us the right to be called Children of God (1 Jn. 3:1). By way of analogy, one could of course say that in some sense every man has a "legalistic Jew" in his heart. But that *is* an analogy, and should not be smuggled into the texts as their primary or explicit meaning in Paul. If that is done, something happens to the joy and humility of Gentile Christianity.

Thus, the theologian would note that the Pauline original should not be identified with such interpretations. He would try to find ways by which the church—also in the West—could do more justice to other elements of the Pauline original than those catering to the problems raised by introspection. He would be suspicious of a teaching and a preaching which pretended that the only door into the church was that of evermore introspective awareness of sin and guilt. For it appears that the Apostle Paul was a rather good Christian, and yet he seems to have had little such awareness. We note how the bibilical original functions as a critique of inherited presuppositions and an incentive to new thought. Few things are more liberating and creative in modern theology than a clear distinction between the "original" and the "translation" in any age, our own included.

PAUL W. MEYER

The Worm at the Core of the Apple (1990)†

I

First, it is a just principle of interpretation, that we should understand every writer, when this can be done in consonance with the laws of language, as speaking to the purpose which he has immediately before him. There are very many truths of the gospel, and many plain and important truths, which are not taught in this or that passage of Scripture. The question concerning [Romans] chap. vii. 5–25 is not, whether it be true that there is a contest in the breast of Christians,

† This essay appeared in *The Conversation Continues*, ed. by R. T. Fortna and B. R. Gaventa (Nashville: Abingdon, 1990), 62–84. Reprinted by permission of the United Methodist Publishing House. Meyer began his academic career at Yale and later taught at Colgate Rochester, Vanderbilt, and Princeton Theological Seminary, where he is Helen H. P. Manson Professor of New Testament Literature and Exegesis Emeritus.

which might, at least for the most part, be well described by the words there found; but, whether such a view of the subject is congruous with the present design and argument of the apostle.[1]

These words were written over a century and half ago by Moses Stuart, one of America's pioneers in biblical exegesis. If the words bear the unmistakable marks of his time, their point is so contemporary and possesses such undiminished pertinence to theological discourse today that they may still serve as a kind of motto for exegesis. One of the major tasks of exegesis, in our day no less than in earlier ones, is to check the arbitrary exploitation of passages from scripture to score points in theological controversy, to inhibit their use for purposes alien to their original form and function, to prevent their being made simply subservient to the interests of those who use them. One might, of course, ask why such tendencies need to be restrained. Why should anyone not be free to make whatever one wishes of these familiar and fondly held texts? People will be found, after all, to do just that. But if these texts were composed initially to guide, correct, and reform the community's perceptions and understanding, to clarify and restore its identity and direction, and if this role was recognized and conceded to them in the process of canonization by the community that still uses them as scripture, then their own power to shape rather than to be shaped by contemporary interests must be respected. Whatever one may have to say about the failings and inadequacies of actual biblical exegesis in its practice, this continual search to recover and reinstate in the first instance the texts' own integrity must remain its ideal.

In that search, the tools and methods of historical study—defined in the broadest sense as the attempt to understand these texts in their original historical, literary, and cultural contexts—take on growing rather than diminishing significance and urgency. Indeed, one may even redefine the major task of exegesis under discussion here as the purification of all anachronistic understandings from our reading of biblical passages. These anachronisms comprise more than the deliberate uses of texts for purposes that have nothing to do with their original composition. They are even more likely to be the unintended or even well-meaning interpretations that read back into the texts the lexical usages, the debates, the anxieties and designs, and the theological claims of later times in the church's life. It is ironic, but true, and amply documented in the history of biblical interpretation, that one of the major barriers to the recovery of the texts' integrity is often the accumulated freight of the church's own long history of the use of scripture, the sedimentation left behind by its own previous attempts to honor and appeal to these very texts! This surely does not mean that the texts have no integrity of their own. It is the situation and needs of those who take recourse to them that never remain the same. But the task becomes more pressing than ever of distinguishing carefully, in Stuart's words, between what "might, at least for the most part, be well described by the words there found" and what is "congruous with the present design and argument" of the writer. The power of a biblical text to transcend the subsequent tradition in such a way as to perform a regulative function upon it depends on this preservation of its historical distance and priority

---

1. M. Stuart, *A Commentary on the Epistle to the Romans* (3rd ed.; London: Thomas Tegg, 1836), 610 [Meyer's note].

as much as it does on the continuities that bind the biblical materials to the church's life and thought, by virtue of which they remain "the church's book." This in turn requires giving heed in every particular instance to "the purpose which [the writer] has immediately before him."

Recovering that purpose, of course, is just the problem. To recreate the situation that called forth a New Testament text and shaped it requires all the resources and skills the exegete can muster: detailed familiarity with available sources, balanced judgment in their evaluation and use, knowledge of the complex processes by which tradition grows, but above all a sympathetic historical imagination that can use such information in a disciplined projection of the interpreter into another place and time. It requires the ability to sit loose to previous interpretations of a text rather than to let false modesty absolutize these; a willingness to let issues of sometimes immense theological import take on unsuspected and unforeseen contours under the promptings of the text itself and its oft-unnoticed details, sometimes in defiance of what the interpreter or his community has previously held most dear; and a readiness to seek out the critical and reforming intent of the text without the defensive or manipulative reactions that so often distort both historical reconstruction and exegesis.

*   *   *

II

Romans 7 is a showcase of the issues in exegesis that have just been outlined for at least two major reasons. The first is clearly suggested in the passage quoted from Moses Stuart. It is a quality of the text itself: its location at a critical turning point in the general argument of Romans, its susceptibility to a variety of interpretations, and its seeming propensity to evoke from the reader analogy and comparison with one's own apparently similar experiences. These characteristics of this particular text are well-known, and every commentary lays out to some extent the choices with which it confronts the thoughtful reader. Paul's extended use of the first person singular pronoun "I" is one of the features of the text that most notably imparts to it this ostensible multivalence. We need not review here the various proposals that have been made to identify more precisely the antecedent of this pronoun. A fairly strong consensus seems to have emerged that the passage is not autobiographical in any sense that allows it to yield details about Paul's personal life, either before his conversion or after. Paul is employing rather a rhetorical style in which the self functions in a representative way as a type or paradigm for others. At the same time, the pronoun is not used in a purely fictive way, as though Paul were excluding himself from its pattern. The closest parallels in his own letters to this intense and vivid device of casting fundamental religious affirmations involving the self into first person singular language are provided by Gal 2:18–21 and Phil 3:8–14. Both passages follow so closely upon obviously autobiographical references that it is impossible to dismiss all personal nuances from his use of "I." Moreover, the closest formal literary analogies to this style are found in the individual laments and thanksgivings of the Hebrew Psalter and the Qumran hymns. These reinforce the view that Romans 7:7–25 is a theological description, cast in a retrospective and reflective mode, of the destructive power of sin—by one who has himself known it and been delivered from it—and that its antithesis—announced already in the contrasting phrases of v. 6*b*—is provided by Paul in 8:1–11. Yet, the question remains: Who is Paul describing? Who is embraced by this paradigmatic rhetorical style? The answer is not a function of the style itself, but must depend on "the present design and argument of the apostle." In other words, a correct answer cannot simply precede exegesis, but follows it and depends on it.

If one major reason why a consensus in the reading of Romans 7 has been so elusive lies in a certain quality of the text itself, the second lies in the accumulated freight brought to it by its interpreters. The literature on this text seems to offer some particularly striking examples of the anachronistic reading referred to earlier, and it is on these that I should like to focus. The barriers to understanding, thrown up by the legacy of past interpretations, are the hardest ones to identify because they are so intricately interwoven with the positive debts every exegete owes to those who have gone before. Indeed, it is sometimes precisely some insight that once opened up with fresh vitality the force of Paul's gospel that now, taken as self-evident in another situation and frozen into convention, impedes the interpreter's ability to cross the differences of historical space and time in order to approach again that elusive intent of the author. To remove these barriers requires something akin to the paradigm shifts of other disciplines. It can come about only when proposals that may initially seem outlandish can win their way to new acceptance.

III

What would be an example of such an apparent "dogma" that has once appeared in the course of the interpretation of Romans 7:7–25 but now has become an impediment to our understanding of Paul's words?

In one of the most well known and fateful shifts in the history of exegesis, Augustine changed his mind about Romans 7:7–25. In his own words, he at first understood Paul in these verses to be "describing the man who is still under the law and not yet under grace. Long afterwards I learned that these words could also describe the spiritual man and indeed in all probability do so." There had been differences of opinion on these verses before Augustine, but like so much else he wrote and thought, his later view is particularly significant for the influence it has exercised, first, on the Protestant Reformers and then, through them, on subsequent interpretation right up to some of the most recent commentaries. The reasons why the Reformers were so attracted to Augustine's interpretation are complex, and they are not by any means identical with the ones that moved Augustine to alter his view. Nevertheless, on an attentive reading of a few of the key paragraphs, an important element in this line of exegesis emerges quite clearly. A few sentences will suffice.

First, from Martin Luther:

> First, this whole passage clearly reveals disapproval and hatred of the flesh and love for the good and the law. Now such an attitude is not characteristic of a carnal man [*carnalis homo*], for he hates and laughs at the law and follows the inclinations of his flesh.
>
> Yet a spiritual man [*spiritualis*] fights with his flesh and bemoans

the fact that he cannot do as he wills. But a carnal man does not fight
with it but yields and consents to it. Hence, this well-known judgment
of Blessed Augustine: "The will to be righteous is a large part of righteousness."

The first word, then, which proves that a spiritual man is speaking
here is this: *But I am carnal* (Rom. 7:14). Because it is characteristic
of a spiritual and wise man [*spiritualis et sapiens homo*] that he knows
that he is carnal . . . and that he praises the law of God because it is
spiritual.

Certainly no one will declare himself wretched except one who is a
spiritual man. For perfect self-knowledge is perfect humility, and per-
fect humility is perfect wisdom, and perfect wisdom is perfect spiritualness [*perfecta spiritualitas*]. Hence, only a perfectly spiritual man
can say: "Wretched man that I am!"

And then a comment by Philip Melanchthon: "For Paul is speaking here
of the sort of person he was after his conversion. For before his conversion
that conflict did not exist since an ungodly person [*impius*] does not will
from the heart what the law admonishes."

One is naturally drawn to concur with what Luther is doing here. A few
sentences after the last words quoted from him, he moves directly into a
reassertion of his characteristic claim, made familiar in the formula *simul
iustus ac peccator*: "The saints in being righteous are at the same time
sinners." Faced with a "Christianized" society in which every citizen was
also a baptized Christian, Luther was insisting with that formula that
Christian perfection was not to be claimed as a quality of the self in this
life, but belongs to it only by imputation in the gospel's promise of God's
forgiveness. As Wilckens has pointed out, Luther was taking the experience
of confession, the starting point of Christian conversion, out of daily
monastic practice and making it the permanent center of personal piety.
The religious application of Luther's exegesis is explicit and unmistakable:
"Indeed, it is a great consolation to us to learn that such a great apostle
was involved in the same grievings and afflictions in which we find ourselves when we wish to be obedient to God!" Nevertheless, from these last
words one may begin to suspect that the pastoral end has captured and
distorted the exegetical means. The suspicion hardens into certainty when
one notes how Paul's anguished cry in v. 24*a* is turned into an expression
of "perfect spiritualness." If Augustine's exegesis here constitutes a celebrated volte-face, Luther's is a no less notable tour de force. It does not
just water down Paul's language (as do all attempts to make the words of
v. 14*b*, "I am sold under sin," apply to life in Christ). It turns Paul's text
on its head and makes it mean its own opposite. The disparity between
text and interpretation is painfully manifest as well in the "judgment" or
axiom (*sententia*) of Augustine to which Luther appeals: "The will to be
righteous is a large part of righteousness." Not only is there no basis for
such a claim in Romans 7, but also it is altogether un-Pauline and irreconcilable with Paul's argument in chap. 2 (especially vv. 3, 6, 13, 22, 25–
27).

What shall one make of this disparity? Is this a case in which, to paraphrase what Wilckens says about Augustine, Luther has the substance
("Sache") of Paul's theology in his favor, even though he has Paul's text

against him? Is the meaning of Paul's passage to be accessible only at the price of doing such violence to the integrity of the text?

When one looks more closely at these sentences from Luther and Melanchthon, one discovers something else. In v. 14, Paul uses the contrasting terms *pneumatikos* ("spiritual") and *sarkinos* ("fleshly, consisting of flesh" or "belonging to the realm of the flesh") to mark the gulf between *God's* law and the *human* self confronted by it. These adjectives are not used again in this section, although *sarx* ("flesh") reappears by itself in v. 18 and in contrast to *nous* ("mind") in v. 25*b*. But under the influence of Augustine's language, these adjectives have been deflected from Paul's usage and their new meanings have come to dominate the exegesis. They are now made to differentiate two classes of *humans*: the religious person who is righteous, wise, understanding, re-born, perfect in self-knowledge and humility, on the one hand and the irreligious, the ungodly, and the sinner on the other, who is utterly devoid of genuine religious impulse. This is the language of binary opposites, used by triumphalist religion to separate humankind into two groups of people, the saved and the damned. This language has been perpetuated in Protestant commentaries with such generic terms as *regenerate* and *unregenerate*. Such language must have had a certain appeal in the sixteenth century to distinguish the "godly" denizens of Europe from the non-Christian infidels pounding on the eastern gates of Constantinople. So it is not at all surprising that the Reformers, wishing to deflate such natural religious pretension in the apostle's name, should jump to the conclusion that Paul must be describing the tension proper to Christian existence in 7:7–25. He does speak of continuing conflict between flesh and Spirit "in the breast of Christians," to use Moses Stuart's words, most explicitly in the next chapter, in 8:5–8 (compare Gal. 5:16–18). So well-intentioned commentators have continued, with the Reformers, to think that it is the part of true Christian humility and self-knowledge to find that conflict to be "the present design and argument of the apostle," even though there is not a syllable in Romans 7:7–25 about life in Christ, and even though Paul himself has signaled to his reader in both 7:6*b* and 8:1–2 that the rest of chap. 7 is to be understood as the antithesis to chap. 8 and not in simple continuity with it.

The flaw lies in the binary language that has been imposed on Paul's text. The "I" of Romans 7 must be either a "godly" or an "ungodly" person; there is no third possibility. That this reading coerces a false alternative on the text is betrayed by the harsh anachronism that results. It leaves no room for the historical Paul or his kind, the deeply religious Jew devoted to the God of Abraham and Moses. There are complex historical reasons, no doubt, why no living Jew sat in that empty chair at the Reformers' exegetical table. But whatever the reason, this absence permitted the deeper misunderstanding. Like the perfectionist piety that produced it, this binary mode of thinking dismisses with scarcely disguised contempt the religious seriousness of any person outside its own group. Melanchthon's comment is particularly revealing: "An ungodly person [anyone prior to Christian conversion] does not will from the heart what the law admonishes." Its modern counterpart is Cranfield's comment: "A struggle as serious as that which is here described can only take place where the Spirit of God is present and active." The clear assumption here is that the Spirit of God is not at work anywhere outside of the Christian church—even though Paul himself has just stated in unequivocal terms that the (Mosaic!) law is "spiritual"—and so the inference is drawn with Luther and Melanchthon that the "I" of Romans 7 can only refer to the Christian.

But this refusal to take seriously any religious vitality other than Christian, even the apostle's Jewish past, this inability to concede any consequence or substance to a religious existence other than one's own, which breeds that pernicious binary language and feeds on it, has bedeviled the discussion of Romans 7 even among those commentators who have concluded that this section of the letter is to be sharply distinguished from chap. 8 and is Paul's negative description of life under the Mosaic law. They, too, perceive that Paul is saying some positive things about the "inmost self" and the "mind." If Paul is referring here to the unredeemed, one is confronted with what Käsemann identifies as the central hermeneutical quandary of Romans 7: "How can the predicates and capacities of the *redeemed* person be ascribed to the *unredeemed*?" What follows is one of the more opaque sections of Käsemann's magisterial commentary. He simply puts the problem in different words when he asks how it happens that "in some sense the Christian situation of Gal 5:16ff. is here transferred to pre-Christian existence." No reason is given; instead Käsemann insists that the force of Paul's words "sold under sin" must not be compromised by finding something good said about the human will in these verses. Only Wilckens, who singles out Käsemann's formulation of the quandary for quotation and comment, seems to have broken through the tyranny of that false dichotomy. All those positive things said about the "I" in Romans 7 can be taken at their face value because they actually redound to the glory of the *law* and not to the praise of the human self. With that we reach a new stage in our reflections on Romans 7, to which we must return in a moment.

But before we take up the implications of this last move, another observation is needed to conclude the present line of thought. These binary categorizations of religious human beings existed, of course, in Paul's day as well; they were not invented by Luther or by Augustine or by other Christians. Indeed, the depth to which any reading of Paul that clings to such a division between the "godly" and the "ungodly" has misunderstood the apostle is sounded accurately only when one realizes that the whole of Paul's epistle is but a single massive argument against the conventional uses of this distinction. In his own religious tradition the division was between Jew and non-Jew. Paul never erases this historical or cultural distinction completely, but the whole first part of Romans is aimed at showing it to be a distinction without a difference and without consequence. When it comes to accountability before God, possession of the law, around which all the prerogatives of the Jew in 2:17–20 revolve, or non-possession, which defines the Gentile as Gentile (so twice in one verse, 2:14), makes no difference, as circumcision or its absence do not (2:25–29), for there is no favoritism with God (2:11). All have fallen short of God's glory (3:23). Since a right relationship to God cannot be brought about by the fulfilling of any conditions from the side of human beings, or by anything men or women have done or not done (4:4–5; 9:11, 16), but only by God's free and undeserved gift (3:24), the new terms on which God's power to save operates are that both Jew and non-Jew, "the Jew first but also the Greek," relate to God in trust, for only these terms put Jew and Greek on the same footing before God (1:16, the statement of the theme of Romans). The central creed of Judaism, the acknowledgment that God is one, requires that one abandon the notion that God is the patron of one constituency against another (3:27–30). The definition of God's election as his calling of those who were not his people to be "my people" applies equally to both Jew and non-Jew (9:24–26); the cultivated branch and the wild branch belong to God's olive tree on the same terms (11:20–24). Abraham provides the inclusive patriarchal precedent for the way in which God deals with all human beings and the model for the way in which all human beings rightly relate to God—by trusting in what God has promised. God has not changed. In Christ God has done what Abraham trusted God to do: to give life where from a human point of view the only prospect is death (4:11b–12, 19–22). Nowhere in this argument does Paul draw a distinction between Jew and non-Jew that is not aimed at showing that there is no privilege before God on the one side or the other. Nowhere in Romans does Paul draw a distinction between an authentic Jew (2:28–29) and an authentic Christian (4:18–25; 9:24; 15:7–13). "The same God is Lord of all, rich and generous to all who call upon him" (10:12). Nowhere does Paul draw a line through himself, to distinguish the authentic Jew from the non-Jewish Christian in his own person, or through God, to distinguish a God of the one from a God of the other (11:1–5). What Paul has found in Christ is not an alternative God to the God of Abraham and Moses, but God's own gift to restore integrity to obedience to the God of Abraham and Moses.

The problem with human religion rests not with the "ungodly" but with those who separate themselves as the "godly" and in that way seek to establish "a righteousness of their own" (10:3). These "do not submit to God's righteousness," which, since its terms are trust in God, puts all on the same footing. Not a failure to keep and obey the law, but the attempt by those who do keep it and think to have every right to condemn others as "ungodly" to escape their own accountability to God, is what "stores up wrath on the day of wrath when God's righteous judgment will be revealed" (2:3–5). The conclusive demonstration of the power of sin over all, not just the "ungodly" but most especially the "godly" as well, is its power to destroy that inner integrity of trust, to make every genuinely religious person deny that all stand on the same footing before the same God and in that way to blaspheme God's good name. To the extent that Christians for 1,900 years have continued to divide up the world into the "godly" (themselves) and the "ungodly," they have merely remained caught within the very problem that Paul diagnoses in his own religious tradition. Its only remedy is a fresh disclosure of God's righteousness as the undeserved vindication of the unrighteous. Only this eliminates the self-defensiveness Paul calls "enmity" toward God, and by the power of the life-giving Spirit sets men and women on the way to an obedience that the law itself has remained powerless to produce (8:1–11).

IV

We come back to that difficult question of "the present design and argument of the apostle" in Romans 7. If the history of exegesis has imposed on Paul's argument the not uncommon pattern of conventional human religion to separate the "godly" from the "ungodly," what would an interpretation look like that takes its cue from Paul himself and eschews this elitism? Would it provide some relief from the quandaries and anachronisms sketched above? It will be the aim of this final section to explore this possibility.

Due to limitations of space, certain preliminary observations can be noted only briefly. First, the subtleties and complexities of Paul's argument in chaps. 5–8 have rightly led most commentators to abandon as overly simple the thematic proposal that Paul describes the Christian life as freedom from a series of powers: in sequence, freedom from wrath (chap. 5), from sin (chap. 6), from the law (chap. 7), and from death (chap. 8). Instead, the argument advances by cues that it has itself generated, as points require clarification, as potential misunderstandings need to be deflected, and as objections are anticipated. While these movements and turns sometimes have the form of "digressions," they are indispensable stages in the argument, for which rhetorical questions are often the major literary markers.

Second, I take Rom 6:1–7:6 to be one of these larger units, so that 7:1–6 belongs with the preceding more closely than with 7:7–25. The question of 6:1 ("Are we to continue in sin in order that grace might increase?") arose inevitably out of Paul's previous description of the lavish generosity of God's gift in Christ, which the "intruding" law showed to be as undeserved and gracious as it showed the death that otherwise has come upon all since Adam to be deserved and due. Whereas in chap. 5 justification as God's restoration of integrity and righteousness to human life is presented as "a matter of grace" (compare 4:16), 6:1–7:6 reverses the argument to show that God's grace involves a new righteousness and integrity that alter life's previous patterns. Employing the polarities of sin and grace, death and life, and disobedience and obedience that were set up by contrasting Adam and Christ in chap. 5, three separate trains of thought turn aside that essentially libertinistic deduction to answer the question "Why not sin?" (1) An irrevocable death (Christ's) has taken place, in which the destiny of all for whom he died is reshaped. It follows that justification involves a new life of righteousness because it is a death to sin (6:1–14). (2) Justification is a change of controlling allegiance; it sets one free from sin only insofar as it makes one an obedient "slave" to God (6:15–23). (3) Both these aspects of justification are illustrated by an example from the general area of human social law: While living with another man before her husband's death brings upon a married woman the damning epithet of an adulteress, exactly the same action after her husband's death has no such result, and she is free to enter the new relationship. The marriage legislation is not abrogated, but a death has broken its power to condemn (the point resumed in 8:1). Just so, by the death of Christ all those for whom he died have been "vacated" from that power of the law, and a new allegiance and a new productive life have been legitimated for them (7:1–6).

This illustration from everyday legal experience provides one of Paul's most striking definitions of justification, explaining both how a person is put into a completely new situation by the death of another party (Christ) and how that change carries with it new social and moral obligations. It is the quintessential Pauline refutation of all the antinomian constructions that have been laid upon him from his own lifetime (3:8) until now.

Yet, the choice of this very example creates a grave difficulty. While it does not start out as a specific allusion to Mosaic law, its application pertains unmistakably to release from the condemning power that Paul's previous argument has consistently assigned to the Mosaic law, which impartially silences every human attempt to evade God's indictment, imparts to human conduct the dimension of transgression against God, and so discloses the presence and power of sin (3:19–20; 4:15; 5:13, 20). The flow of the argument has progressively confused the roles of the law and the sin it condemns and discloses, so that "dying to sin" in 6:10 has become "being put to death to the law" in Paul's little tableau (7:4), and "being set free from sin" in 6:18 has become a "being vacated from the law" (7:6). The confusion is complete in 7:6a. The grammatical antecedent of the relative clause *en hō kateichometha* ("what bound us" NAB) is the law. Ironically, an illustration initially intended to rebut an antinomian argument has suddenly become itself susceptible to an antinomian interpretation, as if God's law and the demonic power of sin are to be identified.

From that result, Paul "draws back with a kind of horror," and it is to ward off such a misunderstanding that Romans 7:7–12 is written. Verse 12 is Paul's Q.E.D.: the Mosaic law is not demonic and not to be confused with sin, nor is it responsible for producing sin. This demonstration, however, is not carried out by directly defending the goodness of the law but by giving an account of how it has been used by sin. The focus is on the other side of the mistaken confusion: the central protagonist in the whole of 7:7–25—not just in vv. 7–12—the adversary of that "I," is not the law at all but sin as a personified power. Once this is seen, it becomes clear that 7:7–25 advances the main argument of Romans in a variety of ways. In addition to the manifest intention of answering the question in v. 7 and warding off a misunderstanding of the law, this unit forms the first part of an exposition of the contrasts between past and present with which Paul in vv. 5–6 has brought the whole preceding section (6:1–7:6) to its climax. The obsolete quality of life in "what bound us" is depicted and analyzed in 7:7–25 in preparation for the discussion of the eschatological quality of life in 8:1–11. Paul calls the one "letter" and the other "Spirit." This contrasting word-pair has been used earlier in 2:29 to distinguish spurious religious identity from authentic (beginning with the Jew), and its introduction here signals another level of Paul's argument. Chapter 8 forms the second part of the exposition and returns to the theme of what God has done for the restoration of human life by means of the life-giving Spirit; 7:7–25 prepares for that by showing what the law, despite its being God's own holy and good commandment, has not been able to do (8:3), because sin's use of it has produced death instead of life.

Clearly 7:7–25 proceeds in two movements, the first being vv. 7–12. Here the greatest difficulty has been caused by Paul's use of the first person verbs in past tenses, particularly in vv. 8b–9. When was Paul, or anyone else, "once alive apart from law," and when did the commandment "come"? It is useless to look for some point in Paul's own lifetime, so increasingly commentators find in these verses allusion to the story of the Fall in Genesis 3, even though the "commandment" Paul has in mind here is patently the Decalogue (v. 7d). Most of the difficulties disappear if one notices that

Paul is resuming with dramatic juxtaposition and reversal the motifs of death and life in their association with sin already used in 5:12–14. That explains the "epic" use of past tenses here. "In the absence of law" (*chōris nomou*, vv. 8*b*, 9) picks up 5:13; the "entry" (*elthein*, v. 9) of the commandment repeats 5:20, presupposed already by the mention of Moses in 5:14, and thus fits naturally with Paul's quotation from the Decalogue. At the same time, one need not deny the presence of such an echo of the Fall narrative as the "deceived" of v. 11. But clearly the allusion is to the Mosaic Torah, which, as the example of the prohibition of covetousness shows, is not only powerless to prevent what it prohibits but in fact produces the very thing it is supposed to prevent. The climax and center of the whole paragraph is provided in vv. 10*b*-11: "The very commandment that was supposed to lead to life turned out for me to lead to death; for sin, by taking advantage of me through that commandment, tricked me and by using it killed me."

The point of these verses and this section is entirely lost if one understands Paul to be talking only about the "ungodly" Jew who "does not will from the heart what the law admonishes" (Melanchthon), or if one takes the point to be the effect of the *law*. The clear meaning of these sentences is that the effect of *sin* on the genuinely religious person who looks to God's Torah for life has been to produce exactly its opposite, death. This is not because the law has not been obeyed or because there is something demonic about the law. It is not because looking to God's Torah for life is somehow a lower order of human religion. The transcendentally (*kath' hyperbolēn*, v. 13) demonic nature of sin is its power to pervert the highest and best in *all* human piety, typified by the best in Paul's world, his own commitment to God's holy commandment, in such a way as to produce death in place of the promised life.

What these much disputed verses bring to expression is not despair over one's inability to live up to a demanding requirement—such as Luther's experience in the monastery at Erfurt—nor is it the pain of discovering that one has oriented one's life around a lesser surrogate in place of God as one's highest good, which Augustine repeatedly describes in his *Confessions*. It is the realization that one has been deceived by a much more sinister power, capable of making the *best* and the most genuine devotion to the one true God produce, as in the case of God's own commandment in the Decalogue, the very thing it is supposed to vanquish. There is no contradiction between these verses and Paul's claim in Phil. 3:6 that the life he came to count as "loss" was "as to righteousness under the law blameless."

Such a reading of 7:7–12 puts us in a position to take a fresh look at the second movement in the rest of the chapter. The transitional v. 13 does two things. In emphatically repeating first the question of v. 7 and then the substance of the answer in v. 11, but adding two purpose clauses, it makes clear that even when it has been used by sin, the law has remained God's and has continued to serve the divine purpose of disclosing and intensifying sin, attributed to it earlier in the letter. In this way v. 13 rounds out what precedes. At the same time, it begins to shift categories in such a manner as to open up a new level of discussion in the next section. In very much the same way, a change of terms from "life" and "death" to "freedom" and "slavery" marked the break in chap. 6 from vv. 1–11 to vv. 15–23, while vv. 12–14 modulated the transition with language about obedience. This time there is a change from the words for "life" and "death" (both nouns and verbs) that have colored the imagery in 7:8–11 to the vocabulary of "good" and "evil," signaled by the fact that in v. 13 "the good" replaces the law. Of course, this is because Paul has just called the law itself "good." But there is more involved. In a brilliant exegetical observation, Bultmann noticed that "the good" in this new section is equivalent to "life" in the preceding verses. "The object of 'willing' is not the fulfilling of the 'commandments,' but 'life' (zoē). What is really willed in all our doing is 'life,' but what comes out of all our doing is 'death' (thanatos)." "Good" and "evil," then, are not labels for conventional moral values that Paul simply takes for granted. They are "the two eschatological possibilities" of "life" and "death." As a result, "that which is good" (v. 13) is not simply the law itself, but *the good* that the law holds out "to me" (twice in v. 13) in its promise of life, exactly as in v. 10.

This is confirmed by the contrasting verbs that increasingly carry the argument in this next section. They are still in the first person singular of Paul's paradigmatic style, but they shift to the present tense as he describes the self's encounter with the power of sin, the perennial human quandary that is the consequence of that "epic" event of sin's "entry." Since the opposite of "to will" is now "to hate," it is clear that the verbs, too, are not to be understood in any narrowly volitional sense. The "common Greek meaning" of thelein is "to prefer, to want, to desire," and this is retained in the LXX where it often translates ḥāpēṣ "to delight in" (echoed in Paul's synēdomai in v. 22). In v. 15 "the good" becomes "what I want" and in v. 19 "the good that I desire." Its opposite in v. 15 is "what I hate" and in v. 19 "the evil that I do not want." In short, the verbs help to circumscribe "the good" as that which every genuinely religious person longs for. The appeal and attraction and promise of the law, especially since it is God's own instruction, is that it will lead to the life that human beings want and desire more than anything else. When Paul says that he "delights" in God's law in v. 22, he is giving clear expression to the devotion to this law that echoes throughout the Hebrew Psalter (see Ps. 1:2; 119:16). In it the desire to find life and the desire to live by the good that God commands are fully merged, and that desire is the greater the more any religious person realizes that "the good" that amounts to life in this ultimate sense is not available in one's human resources taken by themselves (which is the meaning "my flesh" in v. 18). There is nothing at all in this paragraph to suggest that this longing and desire, exemplified at its highest in the Jewish allegiance to Torah in which Paul was raised from infancy, is either illegitimate or misplaced.

But now something has happened to contradict this expectation. "What a person wants is salvation. What he creates is disaster." What it means to this person to be "sold under sin" is manifested in the discovery that what one in fact "produces" by one's actions is not recognizable, because it is exactly the opposite of what was intended, just what one hoped to avoid in one's reliance on the law (v. 15); katergazesthai ("to bring about, or achieve") has the same meaning throughout vv. 15–20 that it has in v. 13. It is clear that the fault does not lie in the law.

Instead, the self, no longer the agent of its own actions, is controlled by the alien power of sin (vv. 16–17). The thought in these verses is exactly the same as in vv. 10*b*–11, only now it is not the Mosaic Torah but the religious self devoted to it that is powerless to achieve what it longs for, that in fact produces the very thing that it is supposed to avoid. The early chapters of Romans have already unfolded this unexpected power of sin to reverse and subvert the integrity of the relationship all religious persons have to God, both Jews and Greeks (3:9), especially those who know God's commands and judgments (1:31; 2:2) but use that knowledge to exempt themselves from accountability and to deny that all stand on the same footing before God, and so abuse God's goodness and blaspheme God's name (2:4–5, 17–24).

Commentators have made many quite different proposals for understanding the structure of vv. 13–25 in detail. Most suggestions fail in plausibility because they are wedded to prior decisions regarding the subject matter of this section, especially to the effect that Paul is primarily concerned with the malevolent power of the law rather than that of sin, or that he is describing a divided self. Again it was Bultmann who clearly saw that the seemingly impressive parallels to Paul's language that can be found in Greek and Latin literature really have little to do with the purpose his words serve in the present argument. Paul is not talking about the conflict between the rational and the irrational in the human self, nor about two selves at different levels, as though one were under the power of sin and the other not. Both "inmost self" (v. 22) and "members" (v. 23) are but two aspects of the same self that is "sold under sin." The symptom of this enslavement is not simple frustration of good intent, but good intention carried out and then surprised and dumbfounded by the evil it has produced, not despair but the same disillusionment so clearly described in v. 10: What should have effected life has produced death!

Close scrutiny of Paul's verses shows a striking progression that confirms this interpretation. The leading clue is provided by the quite complete and precise parallelism between vv. 15–17 and vv. 18–20, running twice through the same sequence of ideas. Each series begins with an essentially negative proposition introduced with the phrase "We/I know": vv. 14–15*a* ("I don't recognize what I am bringing about, the results of my own actions") and v. 18 ("To desire the good is within my capacity but I cannot bring it about"). In the second place, this is followed each time by a short description of the experience behind this proposition, in almost identical language ("For I do not do what I intend, desire or prefer, but do the very thing I do not want or wish to avoid," vv. 15*b*, 19). In the third place, now in even more striking repetition of linguistic detail, each sequence draws the same conclusion: "If this is my experience, it follows that I am no longer the one producing this result but rather the sin that dwells in me" (vv. 16–17, 20). By their repetition these conclusions forcefully declare what it means to be "fleshly, sold under sin." The parallelism is clearly visible if the two sequences are written out in Greek beside each other in parallel columns * * *. When this is done, two more features become at once apparent: (a) The opening proposition for the second sequence (v. 18) rephrases that of the first (vv. 14–15*a*) in language colored by the intervening verses; and (b) the detail that distinguishes the second sequence and marks its advance over the first is the addition of those "eschatological" categories "good" and "evil" in vv. 18 and 19, expanding the incidental remark in v. 16*b* about the law's being itself "good." This new ingredient continues into v. 21 and provides a bridge to the concluding verses of the chapter.

This conclusion comes in vv. 21–23. The last time the law seriously entered Paul's argument was v. 12, his emphatic repudiation of the suggested identification of the law with sin in v. 7*b*. The place of the law was taken in v. 13 by "the good" (which, incidentally, Paul equates with God's will in 12:2). A brief reminder of 7:12 reappears in v. 14, but it functions only as the foil for its opposite, "I am fleshly, sold under sin," which it has been the main burden of vv. 15–20 to elaborate. There is also a parenthetical remark about the law's goodness in v. 16*b*, but the parallel in v. 20 shows that it can be dropped without loss to the argument—it only anticipates v. 22—and that the real purpose of the conditional clause in v. 16*a* is to serve as a protasis to v. 17. But now that thematic undercurrent of the law bursts to the surface and dominates the discussion in the form of *two* diametrically opposed laws: (a) *ho nomos tou theou* ("the law of God"), vv. 22 and 25*b*, which is also "the law of the mind"—that is, the law I intend to serve, in v. 23; and (b) *heteros nomos* ("a *different* law," not just another law), which is also *ho nomos tēs hamartias* ("the law of sin") "which is in my members," vv. 23 and 25*b*. Verse 22 confesses allegiance and delight in the first. Verse 23 reports the discovery of the second. The contrast could scarcely be sharper. In sum, 7:13–25 culminates with a "cleavage," but it is in the *law* and not in the self.

Attention to this movement toward an antithetical climax helps to solve two perennial difficulties in the exegesis of these verses. One is v. 21, in which commentators struggle both with the meaning of *ho nomos* ("the law") and with the syntax. It strains credulity to read Paul's definite noun in this context as "a law" (RSV) in the sense of a perceived regularity of experience. Serious lexicographical difficulties stand in the way of this translation as well, despite its natural sound in English. It must, instead, refer to the same law that is called a "different" law, or "the law of sin" in v. 23. But what law is that? The polarized duality of "laws" at the end of chap. 7 provides the bridge to chap. 8, and this "different law" must be the same as "the law of sin and death" in 8:2. But the transitional verses in 8:1–2 also serve as a parenthesis with 7:6*b* to enclose the whole of our passage. The phrase "the law of sin and death" in 8:2 can only be intended as a shorthand summary of the whole point of 7:7–25: It is the *law* that has been used by *sin* to produce *death*. But that means that not only the "law of God" (v. 22) but also this "different law" (v. 23) is the Mosaic law! We return to this in a moment.

In the meantime, the problem of the syntax of v. 21 is now also eased. The dative participle and its infinitive have been advanced for emphasis, but they belong syntactically to the *hoti*-clause that is the direct object of *heuriskō*. To take *ton nomon* as an adverbial accusative of respect is not nearly as harsh as is commonly argued if one realizes that the present active *heuriskō* has simply taken the place of the deponential aorist *heurethē* of v. 10, to fit the altered context and its present tenses, but without significant change of meaning. Just as Paul said there, "the law that was supposed to lead to life has turned out for me to lead to death," so also he now opens this final section of chap. 7 by writing, "So then, as far as the (Mosaic) law is concerned, the outcome [of the above experience] is that for me, the very one who wishes to do the good, evil is what I find at hand" (v. 21). He goes on:

> I delight in the law of God . . . but what I see is a quite different law, operative in my members [that aspect of my self that ought to be at God's disposal, 6:13]; it is in conflict with that law of God that I adhere to in my intentions, and keeps me imprisoned to the law that controls me and that is used by sin." (vv. 22–23).

The other celebrated crux of chap. 7 is v. 25b, which has created difficulty both by its position, which has seemed to interrupt or even reverse the natural and logical movement of thought from v. 25a to chap. 8, and by its content, which has seemed to betray an anthropological dualism uncharacteristic of Paul and out of place in this chapter. Here, too, the difficulty disappears once one observes that the load-bearing words in v. 25b are not "mind" and "flesh," even though these have the article, but rather the contrasting datives at the end of each clause, "*God's* law" and "*sin's* law." The verse not only fits the context but also confirms our reading of it. As a summary, it tightens the link with 8:1–4. The same contrast between God and sin reappears in the subject and direct object of 8:3.

The translation of vv. 21–23 we thus arrive at makes "the present design and argument of the apostle" plain. The experience of the demonic power of sin to use the Mosaic law to effect just the opposite of what its devoted adherents expect, even and especially when it is obeyed, manifests not only the sinister nature of sin itself (v. 13) but also how profoundly the religious self is "sold" under it and indeed possessed by it (vv. 14–20). God's own good law takes on a quality and character opposite to that which a person knows to be true, so that the religious self is put in the wretched position of serving sin in its very service of God. Two thousand years of Christian history have shown that in the presence of this power there is no distinction between the "godly" and the "ungodly." As the Latin maxim puts it, *corruptio optimi pessima*, "the worst evil consists in the corruption of the highest good." That is not depicted here simply as a private experience from Paul's Jewish past. It is all part of Paul's explanation of why God sent God's own Son, on behalf of all, to deal with sin as the law could not (8: 3–4). In the end, as Lou Martyn has also argued, the guiding theme of Paul's theology is not the law but Christ. A more adequate penetration of Paul's diagnosis of the condition under which all human religion suffers may lead to a more profound understanding of his gospel.

STANLEY K. STOWERS

[Romans 7:7–25 as Speech-in-Character] (1994)†

Arguments against Gentile Subjection to the Law (7:1–25)

One might reasonably consider Chapter 7 the key to the Western under-standing of Romans, going back to Augustine but with roots also in Origen. Peter Gorday writes, "This entire section of Rom. 7:14–25 is absolutely omnipresent in Augustine's work, and is linked with every other passage in the epistle where the concern is to reinforce the complex interplay of grace and law that Augustine saw in Romans." Romans 7 facilitated the development of a psychologizing interpretation of Paul's statements about sin, law, boasting, and grace. It provided interpreters with a supposed anal-ysis of the human predicament to which Christ was the solution. That reading still dominates the interpretation of Romans.

* * *

Ironically and unfortunately, Romans 7 became a most important text for the Christian understanding of "Jewish religiosity." On this reading, Judaism forms not only the antithesis to Christianity but also the necessary prelude to Christian existence because the supposed archetypical Jewish struggle with pride and lawkeeping occurs on some scale in every person as they seek to do the good.

The editorial tradition has set off chapter 7 as a unit because the section encompasses a discussion of bondage to and freedom from the law. The theme, however, already receives development in 6:14–23. The tradition has also made certain divisions within the chapter. Verses 7–25 stand apart stylistically owing to their special use of the first person singular. Verses 7 and 13 introduce new topics and make transitions in the discourse through the use of rhetorical questions in the form of false conclusions. Thus com-mentators usually treat 7:7–12 and 13–25 as units. Verses 1–6 also have their stylistic peculiarities. Paul first turns to his epistolary audience in 4:23 by using the first person plural. In chapter 6, he reaches a new level of immediacy with the readers by addressing them directly and speaking about their experience. This gradual development in Paul's relation to the literary audience reaches its apex in 7:1 and 4 with the address "brethren." Verses 4–6 also focus intensively on the experience of the readers both under the law, in the life of the flesh, and also free from that bondage in Christ. The rhetoric changes entirely in 7:7–25 as the audience disappears. This section is personal in an entirely different way, as it seems to depict the inner struggle of an individual.

† From chapter nine of his *A Rereading of Romans* (New Haven: Yale University Press, 1994). Reprinted by permission of Yale University Press. The essential elements of Stowers's treatment were presented at a conference in Copenhagen in 1991, with a revised version of his paper pub-lished in *Paul in His Hellenistic Context*, ed. by T. Engberg-Pedersen (Minneapolis: Fortress, 1995), 180–202. In this essay Stowers, who is professor of Religious Studies at Brown University, revives one of the ways in which early Christians read Rom. 7:7–25, viz., as an instance of Paul's use of *prosōpopoiia* or "speech-in-character." The latter was a literary and rhetorical device whereby the writer or speaker assumed the character (*prosōpon*) of another person and uttered words appropriate to that individual or character type. In Stowers's view, Paul is speaking in Romans 7 neither of himself nor of humanity as a whole but as an *akratēs*, someone whose weak will and lack of self-mastery lead to the kinds of deeds delineated in Rom. 1:18–32.

It is necessary first to get behind the Augustinian tradition of reading 7:
7–25 and especially 14–25. When Augustine retrospectively reinterpreted
his conversion in light of the Platonic myth of the soul's falling, alienation
from the Good, and return to it, he created a model of religious experience
that would become characteristic of the West, especially in late medieval
piety and the individualism of Protestantism. So, for instance, the
eighteenth-century conversion of Isaac Backus would not have been possible without Augustine's reinterpretation of Paul and, above all, chapter
7 of Romans:

> As I was mowing alone in the field, August 24th, 1741, all my past
> life was opened plainly before me, and I saw clearly that it had been
> filled up with sin. I went and sat down in the shade of a tree, where
> my prayers and tears, my hearing of the Word of God and striving for
> a better heart, with all my other doings, were set before me in such a
> light that I perceived I could never make myself better, should I live
> ever so long. Divine justice appeared clear in my condemnation, and
> I saw that God had a right to do with me as He would. My soul yielded
> all into His hands, fell at His feet, and was silent and calm before
> Him. And while I sat there, I was enabled by divine light to see the
> perfect righteousness of Christ and the freeness and riches of His
> grace, with such clearness, that my soul was drawn forth to trust Him
> for salvation. And I wondered that others did not also come to Him
> who had enough for all. The Word of God and the promise of His
> grace appeared firmer than a rock, and I was astonished at my unbe-
> lief. My heavy burden was gone, tormenting fears were fled, and my
> joy was unspeakable.[1]

What elements, if any, of the Western theology of conversion and struggle
with sin are attributable to the text read historically in the context of Paul's
time? In what sense is Paul the source for this sort of piety?

A Greek Tradition in 7:14–24

Fortunately, there is a solid place to stand in trying to contextualize
chapter 7 and treat it in a nonanachronistic way: 7:15 and 19 contain a
ubiquitous Greek saying that is central to the Greco-Roman ethic of self-
mastery.

*   *   *

The text remembered as the starting point for this tradition is Euripides'
Medea 1077–80: "I am being overcome by evils. I know that what I am
about to do is evil but passion is stronger than my reasoned reflection and
this is the cause of the worst evils for humans." These words of Euripides'
Medea became the classic text for the long and varied ancient discussion
of *akrasia*, lack of self-mastery. It represents what can be described as the
tragic position in literary depictions and philosophical discussion of "the
will," or self-mastery in moral psychology. The tragic tradition emphasizes
that the good of the human life is vulnerable to luck, conflict of values,
and the passions as structures of perception that allow humans to be
deeply affected by situations and powers they do not control. Tragedy

---

1. Quoted in William G. McLoughlin, *Isaac Backus and the American Pietistic Tradition* (Boston:
Little, Brown, 1967), 14 [Stowers's note].

emphasizes the often evil consequences of these limitations, but it also claims that what is good and beautiful about human life is intrinsically bound to this vulnerability. Just before the text quoted above, Medea, driven by anger and the thought of revenge, determines to follow a terrible plan that includes killing her children. Twice she wavers as she reflects that another course of action would be better (1040–48; 1056–58). Finally, in our text she recognizes how evil her deed will be but says that her desire for revenge is stronger than her reasoned reflections.

The ancients also remembered Phaedra's monologue in Euripides' *Hippolytus* in connection with the failure of self-mastery (377–83):

I do not think people do evil by nature, for many are good
But one must consider that though we know and understand what is good
We don't act on what we know—some through laziness,
Others through preferring pleasure more than goodness.

Not only emotions and drives but other habits of character prevent people from doing the good that they know and recognize.

In the *Protagoras* 352 D, Socrates refers to this view in Euripides as the understanding of the masses: "Most people say that . . . while knowing what is best they do not will to do it although they could do it but instead they do something else. And when I have asked why, they say that those who act this way are acting under pleasure or pain or the power of the things I just mentioned." The other side of the debate was begun by Socrates, who in contrast to the popular view held that akrasia, acting against what one knew was right, was impossible. Plato too, partly under the influence of Socrates and partly for other reasons, opposes the popular view in some of his writing. Plato also opposed the larger tragic perspective. Through ascetic suppression of desire and passion and by valuing the abstract and universal rather than the vulnerable and changeable particular, Plato sought to find a way for humans to become godlike and avoid the limit and vulnerability of human life. Thus in several respects, he sets or anticipates the agenda of the Hellenistic philosophies with which Paul had at least indirect contact. Aristotle, on the other hand, affirmed the tragic and popular view. Book 7 of his *Nicomachean Ethics*, devoted to the discussion of akrasia, distinguishes between lack of self-mastery that is impulsive and lack of self-mastery that is deliberate and fully aware of itself. Later debates focused on whether weakness of will (that is, lack of self-mastery) stemmed from ignorance and false beliefs, the Stoic position, or from inherently rebellious passions, the popular and Platonic position.

The Stoics developed a sophisticated version of the Socratic position that passion and weakness of the will were due to ignorance or false belief. Chrysippus reinterpreted the *Medea* from this perspective: "Medea declared before her infanticide: 'I know what evil I intend to commit, I see it well; but passion is stronger in me than reason.' But this passion is not a sort of foreign power, which wrests dominion from the mind; it is Medea's mind, which in unhealthy agitation chooses the bad. It turns away from itself and from every reasonable reflection. Precisely this conscious turning away from calm reflection and from the mind itself is the essential characteristic of emotion." The early Stoics denied the existence of a distinct, irrational part of the soul, instead arguing for the soul's unity. The passions were disturbed or diseased states of the soul engendered by false beliefs.

To be healthy is to have no contrast in the personality between reason and emotion. What most people think of as reason and emotion harmonize in the healthy person. Chrysippus is said to have studied the *Medea* zealously. Later Stoics showed continued interest in Euripides' tragedy. Paul's nearly exact contemporary Seneca wrote a *Medea* of his own based on Euripides' work. Paul's near contemporary Epictetus has an imaginary interlocutor cite Medea's words to represent the popular view of reason and emotion (*Diss.* 1.28.6–8).

*   *   *

Finally, the famous Medean saying occurs not only in drama and philosophers' debates, but also in such contexts as letters and public orations. The famous parallel to Paul's words in Ovid *Met.* 7.17–21, for example, are the words of Medea dialoguing with herself: "Oh wretched one, drive out these flames that you feel from your maiden breast if you can. If I could, I would be more reasonable. But some strange power holds me back against my will. Desire impels [or "counsels"] me one way, my mind another. I see what is better and approve it, but I follow the worse. Why do you, a royal maiden, burn for a stranger, and think about marriage in a foreign world?"

These texts illustrate how versions of the saying found in 7:15 and 19 played a central role in the Greek moral tradition. The words of Euripides' *Medea* were widely cited in this connection. In philosophy and literature alike the words were variously interpreted in discussions about the roles of the emotions, deliberation, and knowledge of good and evil in moral psychology. Most aspects of Paul's discussion in 7:7–25 can be paralleled with language from this tradition. No one, however, would deny that Paul's text has its own character. In order to get at Paul's use of the tradition it is first necessary to discuss the style and rhetoric of 7:7–25.

The Style and Rhetoric of 7:7–25

Since W. G. Kümmel's monograph, most scholarship on Romans 7 has agreed that the first person singular in 7:7–25 is the fictive "I." The technique dramatically presents a general idea. In Romans 7, the fictive I is not autobiographical, and it does not include Paul. Kümmel based his argument about the fictive I primarily on examples from Paul's letters. Instances such as 1 Cor. 10:29–30 supported Kümmel's case: "For why should my liberty be determined by another man's scruples? If I partake with thankfulness, why am I denounced because of that for which I give thanks?" This is the fictive voice of the strong person who protests against Paul's admonitions about displaying deference to the weak. Kümmel gathered only a few examples of the fictive I from outside the New Testament. Aside from their lateness (some are medieval), the Rabbinic examples lack value because they are narrative texts in the first person and thus not at all parallel.

Fortunately, Paul's rhetoric in chapter 7 can be identified and explained. The texts in question are a type of *prosōpopoiia*, speech-in-character. Both Kümmel and recently Gerd Theissen have concluded that the phenomenon of 7:7–25 was not discussed in ancient rhetoric. Amazingly, Kümmel followed his conclusion with the statement (relegated to a footnote) that the phenomenon in chapter 7 might be related to prosōpopoiia. He defined prosōpopoiia as follows: "where the speaker places a speech in the mouth of another person or where inanimate things can speak."

In contrast to modern interpreters, ancient students of Paul, who were native speakers and had varying levels of Greek education, as a basic reflex recognized speech-in-character in chapter 7. Celsus's polemic against Christianity, the *True Discourse*, extensively employed prosōpopoiia, and Origen's reply to Celsus includes a helpful critique of his prosōpopoiia. Celsus employed a number of different characters and forms of speech-in-character in his polemic. In one instance, he seems to have imitated a child having his first lesson with an orator (*C. Cels.* 1.28). Twice Celsus introduces general types of people: the person who has difficulty seeking God and the fleshly person, and suggests that Christians are like these people (6.66; 7.36.17). Most important, however, Celsus employs an imaginary Jew through major portions of the work who first addresses himself to Jesus, then carries on a dialogue with Jesus that Origen explicitly describes as prosōpopoiia. In another part of the work Celsus has the Jew (or a Jew?) speak to caricatured Christians. In all, Origen explicitly refers to Celsus's prosōpopoiia using either the noun or the verb some twenty-six times.

*   *   *

Toward a Historical Reading with Speech-in-Character

The difficult task of imagining a reading possible for readers in Paul's time must preclude Christian assumptions and readings that make sense only in epochs later than Paul's. The interpreter can neither presuppose the introspective Christian conscience of late antiquity or the middle ages nor assume the much later Christian stereotype of the legalistic Jew who attempts the impossible task of keeping the law. The picture of Paul the Pharisee, who attempted that impossible task, clearly comes from reading the narratives of his conversion in Acts through the lens of later Christian constructions of Judaism and the law. Types and assumptions for reading will have to be those that readers in Paul's time could have made.

The section begins in v. 7 with an abrupt change in voice following a rhetorical question that serves as a transition from Paul's authorial voice, which has previously addressed the readers explicitly described by the letter in 6:1–7:6. This constitutes what the grammarians and rhetoricians described as change of voice (*enallagē* or *metabolē*). These ancient readers would next look for *diaphōnia*, a difference in characterization from the authorial voice. The speaker in 7:7–25 speaks with great personal pathos of coming under the law at some point, learning about his desire and sin, and being unable to do what he wants to do because of enslavement to sin and flesh. If one asks whether Paul gives his readers any clues elsewhere in the letter that this might be his autobiography, the answer is clearly no. And this picture does not fit what he says about himself in other letters. The passage seems to present a distinctive, coherent ethos with a particular life situation. As the handbooks recommend, the person speaks of his happy past before he learned about the law (7:7b-8 and especially 9), his present misery, and his future plight (7:24). Since this tragic characterization also centers on self-reflection and takes the form primarily of a monologue, the passage fits the classic models of speech-in-character. The text portrays emotion, moral-psychological disposition, "inner thoughts," and "complaint" (Quint. 9.2.30–33).

Dividing the character's speech into parts according to the tense reflects different temporal standpoints on the character's life or circumstances. Hermogenes recommends that the order be present, past, and future, and Apthonius's example follows this order. It is clear, however, both from Hermogenes' reasons for this order and from practice that various purposes of the speaker and subjects of characterization could call for different orders of the tenses. Apthonius's example has Niobe speaking in a monologue after discovering the death of her children. She begins in the present tense bemoaning her loss. Then there is a transition to the past—"Woe is me! The misfortune I bear is like that of the one from whom I descended"—in which she explains the origin of her present tragedy. In her final words she reflects on her future fate and on the possibility of receiving help from the gods. Paul also uses all three tenses, although he begins with the past (7:7–11) and moves to the present (7:14–24a, 25) and the future (7:24b).

In accord with a form of the technique discussed in the handbooks, Paul's authorial voice does not explicitly introduce the person. In comparison with the preceding context in 6:1–7:6, in which Paul's voice addresses "brothers," the addressee/s of the voice in 7:7–25 is either ambiguous or only Paul. The explicit audience of the letter addressed in its prescript disappears, as it does in 1:18–4:23, which I have elsewhere argued is also dominated by speech-in-character. At one point (7:25–8:2), again fitting prosōpopoiia, dialogue between the speaker in 7:7–25 and Paul occurs. The characterization of 7:7–25 reads like someone personally witnessing to the statement "when we were in the flesh, our sinful passions worked in our bodily parts through the law (7:5)," after the false conclusion and its rejection in 7:7a, "What shall we say? Is the law sin? By no means!" I find the identity of the speaker at 7:7a unclear: perhaps it is Paul, perhaps the person characterized in what follows, perhaps an anonymous objector.

Tragic characters or newly created characterizations of people in emotionally laden tragic situations were favorite subjects of prosōpopoiia. One finds a remarkable intersection of style and content in Romans 7, an intersection of the techniques of prosōpopoiia and motifs and style of the tragic monologue as mediated by the tradition of moral psychology. As we saw in the tradition of Medea's words, such tragic speeches are often in the form of monologues or soliloquies. They usually employ the first person singular. The tragic speeches were models for the teaching of soliloquy in the *progymnasmata* and rhetoric. Ovid, another near contemporary of Paul, not only wrote a *Medea* but also the *Heroides*, which are letters written by means of prosōpopoiia imagining what legendary women might have written. These include letters from Medea to Jason. When Paul wrote Romans, Ovid's works were popular reading in Rome.

One reason the figure of Medea gained such continuing popularity appears in connection with purity of citizenship and ethnicity ("nationality"). Medea stood for foreigners who corrupted the purity of the citizen body, and her saying about akrasia connoted the moral degeneracy that mixing with foreigners would supposedly bring. I find great irony in the fact that Paul the Jew resonates these allusions back to Greeks and Romans who apparently now see themselves as gentiles, outsiders to Judaism described as immoral foreigners. The figures of Medea and other passion-bound barbarian women from Greek tragedy became important in imperial Rome. As early as Cicero, the type becomes a prominent oratorical slander (*Pro Cael.* 7.18; *Leg. Man.* 8.21). But the theme rose to a height of public consciousness during the struggle between Antony and Octavian and the early years of the empire. The propagandists for Augustus depicted Antony as a man dominated by passionate foreign women and compared Cleopatra to Medea, Omphale, and Semiramis. Niobe, whom we have already seen recommended as a model for prosōpopoiia, paralleled Medea as a type of the degenerate foreign woman. On the doors of the temple to Apollo in Rome, erected as a votive for the victory at Actium, stood the scene of Niobe slaying her children. This not-so-subtle allusion to the defeat of Antony and Cleopatra used Niobe as the paradigm of God's wrath against barbarian hybris. All of this helps us to fathom how the Medean saying might have played in the public consciousness of Paul's time.

Rom. 7:7–25 resembles tragic soliloquy and prosōpopoiia of the person in a tragic situation in several ways. It reveals the conflict of inner thoughts and feelings using the first person singular. The exclamation "wretched man that I am!" (*talaipōros egō anthrōpos*) reads almost as a parody of the tragic outcry. In Seneca's *Medea*, Medea cries "What, wretched woman, have I done?" as she reflects on how her will to do the good has been overpowered by anger. In the *Metamorphoses* (7.18), just before she speaks the famous words about akrasia, Medea calls herself "wretched" (*infelix*). The Vulgate uses the same word to translate *talaipōros* in Rom. 7:24. Just before he introduces the example of Medea, Epictetus uses the fictive I: "Who is more wretched than I?" (2.17.18; cf. 26). In 1.4.23–26, Epictetus says that tragedies in which people say "wretched man that I am" are the depiction of people suffering because they admire external things. The cry of despair "oh wretch that I am" is first made prominent in literature by the tragedians and comedians themselves.

Another important feature that Romans 7 shares with the tragic monologue and the soliloquies of prosōpopoiia is the language of external power for moral and psychological states. I have already discussed the importance of "sin as a power" for traditional readings of Romans, and I have argued that one should not take Paul's language as more than rhetorical and metaphorical except in one regard. Now I can be more specific about the tradition of this rhetoric. Such language is not typical of the Hebrew Bible/Old Testament (for example, the Psalms) or earlier Jewish literature but rather of what scholars often call the fragmented personality of Homer and the Greek poets.

Greek polytheism facilitated expression of the common human dilemma of conflicting goods and obligations. Different gods corresponded to different impulses and demands of human life. So, for example, in the *Hippolytus*, Euripides explores the conflicting demands of Aphrodite, goddess of love, and Artemis, goddess of virginity. As her nurse reflects upon Phaedra's dilemma of knowing what she ought to do but yielding to the power of love, she blames Aphrodite (358–59): "The modest forced against their wills to lust after evils! Aphrodite is no god!" Hippolytus's Phaedra speaks of being unable to subdue the goddess by self-mastering mastery (401). The language of outside powers shows itself in the tradition of Medea's saying and the broader discussion of willing and doing. Plutarch quotes from Euripides' lost *Chrysippus*: "Wretched I am, this evil comes to men from God, when one knows the good but does it not." In Hellenistic and Roman times, philosophers and moralists usually rationalized that language. The powers were not really external but internal. Epictetus said, "When a man does something contrary to his opinion under the compulsion of love, while seeing the better thing but lacking the strength to follow, one might think him worthy of being excused, because he is in the power of something violent, and, in a manner of speaking, godlike" (*Diss.* 4.1.147). I find it no surprise, then, that Rom. 6–7, with part of its subject matter from Greek moral psychology, uses the language of external power.

Thus in 7 one meets a well-known and highly developed kind of rhetoric that was employed by moralists and philosophers to treat the very issues that Paul discusses.

Paul uses prosōpopoiia in chapter 7 to characterize not every human or every human who is not a Christian but rather gentiles, especially those who try to live by works of the law. Paul has already introduced and explained the character depicted in the prosōpopoiia of 7 from a historical point of view in chapter 1.

*   *   *

It is not the later Christian focus on Adam and Eve's moment of disobedience in the garden that stands behind chapters 1 and 7 of Romans, but the story of the gentile peoples as a part of Israel's story. In Romans, this view of gentiles has been Hellenized by a retelling of the narrative in terms of the inner mythology of moral psychology. This was not a unique way of conceptualizing the other in the Greco-Roman world. A most fascinating parallel comes to us through Diodorus of Sicily. He draws on the Egyptian historian Hecataeus of Abdera for the following and precedes the passage with a discussion of how even Egyptian kings had to follow the law (*nomos*):

> And in doing what custom required in these matters, they did not become indignant or take offense in their souls, but rather they believed that they lived a most happy life. For they believed that all other men, in irrationally gratifying their natural passions, do many things which bring them injuries and perils, and that often some who know [*eidotas*] that they are about to sin [*hamartein*] nevertheless do base acts when overpowered by love or hate or some other passion, while they, on the other hand, by virtue of their having followed a manner of life which had been chosen before all others [or "judged superior to all others"] by the wisest of men, fell into the fewest faults. (1.71.3)

Here Egyptians prove superior to all the other peoples because they are able to do what they know is right by following their law rather than be overcome by their passions. Hecataeus characterizes the non-Egyptians with the Medean saying. They know what is right but are not able to do it because of their passions. But how is it that the Egyptians are morally superior in such a basic way? Their superiority results from their having a superior politeia, a better social, political, and cultural constitution. Jewish apologists like Philo and Josephus claimed exactly the same for Judaism: Its superior constitution, the divine law, made Jews typically more self-controlled, just, and humane than non-Jews. Jews could better control their passions.

Not only Jews and Egyptians related moral psychology to culture, but also Greeks and Romans. The Greek equivalent of Jew/gentile is Hellene (Greek)/barbarian. The latter classification was made with far wider criteria of taxonomy than just language. The taxonomic indicators for "barbarian" often included much of what we moderns mean by morals and culture. Even Galen, that sophisticated and most educated Greek in the center of the Roman world, has a Greek view of the other. After citing the famous words of Euripides' Medea about akrasia, Galen writes, "Taught by reason, doubtlessly she knows the greatness of the evils she is about to do, but she says that her anger gets the better of her reason, and therefore she is forcibly led by anger to commit the act. . . . Euripides has used Medea as an example of barbarians and uneducated people, in whom anger is stronger than reason; but among Greeks and educated [read Hellenized] people . . . reason prevails over anger" (*Hippoc. et Plat.* 3.189.20–190.1). Elsewhere (*Hippoc. et. Plat.* 3.214.10–20) Galen explains that children, wild animals, and barbarians are often slaves of their desires (*epithumiai*).

Rom. 1 and 6–7 draw on a Jewish version of a widespread Greco-Roman way of portraying the other. The free adult male of your own people constitutes the norm. As the scale moves away from him, the other becomes less rational and more emotional on the scale of self-mastery. A foreign woman like Medea is doubly dangerous. Jews, Greeks, Romans, and Egyptians all had their own frames of reference, which in Paul's time had been made somewhat ambiguous because of the political dominance of Rome and the cultural dominance of the Greeks. Sexual transgressions and rules of purity and pollution loom large in such conceptions of the other to the extent that the societies are patrilineal or otherwise constructed around lineage and descent. Such societies practice animal or some other form of sacrifice. Since the patrilineal principle of earlier times had been modified and weakened among Greeks, Romans, and Jews, a new order arose that is reflected in the ethic of self-mastery. In Paul's time both codes coexisted and competed. The centrality of the one temple with its hereditary priesthoods, however, reinforced the principles of birth and purity of descent for Jews. The very fact that the Judaism which emerged after the end of the temple so radically moved the focus from ascription by descent to achievement in studying Torah serves as a measure of how important pure blood had been in Paul's time. On the other hand, certain strains of Judaism and Israelite religion that downplayed blood and stressed achievement had always existed. Adaptation to the complexities of the Greco-Roman world made the tension between the two principles even more complex. Thus Paul's talk of gentile immorality, mastery by sexual passions, the theme of works versus adoptive kinship, and his very mission is concerned with working out tensions inherent in Judaism and in similar societies in which purity of birth had been central but achievement had gained a major role.

Ambiguity lay in Paul's own situation. His basic categories for humans are Jew and gentile. He recognizes the dominance of Greek culture in the Roman East by interchanging "gentile" and "Greek." At the same time, however, he views the world from a Greek perspective. The non-Jewish part of humanity, the gentiles, can be divided into two parts, Greeks and barbarians (Rom. 1:13–14). His native language is also Greek. Someone who does not speak Greek is for him a barbarian (1 Cor. 14:11). Whatever Paul's Greekness, and the evidence seems to be that it was great, in his self-conception he has assimilated it to his Jewishness.

If we understand the anachronism of introducing a third term, "Christian," then the persona of Romans 7 can only be a gentile. Some have claimed, however, that it is precisely in 7:1 that Paul turns away from gentiles when he says, "Or are you ignorant, brothers—for I am speaking to those who know the law—that the law rules over a person for as long as he lives?" In fact, 7:1 turns out to be one of the most widely mentioned pieces of evidence for the existence of Jews in the Roman church. The weight of scholarly opinion, however, sees gentiles, who know something about the law, at least included in 7:1. But Paul allows no entry into the discourse for this phantom Jewish audience. If the Roman church was made up of Jews and gentiles, we would never know it from reading Romans. It is most important to pay close attention to Paul's construction of the letter's audience throughout its discourse. As I have shown, 1:18–4:22 lacks explicit recognition of the epistolary audience. There the fiction of imaginary interlocutors takes the place of the epistolary audience, but the first-level readers encoded in the discourse remain gentiles or Greeks. From 4:23 through 6:23, Paul more and more identifies himself with the gentile readers by use of the first person plural. In chapter 6 he addresses them directly with the second person plural, including imperatives. The apex of this development occurs in 7:1–6. Paul addresses his audience as brothers in 7:1 and 4. The last time he did that was at 1:13, where he describes his epistolary audience as gentiles at Rome. The only other places in the letter where Paul addresses his audience so intently are in chapters 9–11, where his own persona both changes and becomes much more vivid. There he shifts from identifying himself with gentiles to identifying himself as a Jew.

All of Paul's rhetoric, including his concern to argue for gentile equality and to argue against gentile judaizing, makes sense if we suppose that Paul's literary audience represents something like those who have traditionally been called godfearers in modern scholarship. From beginning to end, Romans presupposes an audience that consists of gentiles who had or still have a lively interest in Judaism. Such people existed and most likely made up the bulk of the early gentile converts to Christ. Those who know the law in 7:1 were formerly enslaved to their passions and desires while they submitted to the law (7:4–6). Paul supposes that all gentiles are in some sense "under the law" and responsible for teachings that apply to gentiles. The *person* in 7:7–25 whom Paul so carefully constructs by means of prosōpopoiia, however, seems more specific. That person represents those caught between two cultures. Like Medea, he cannot submit to a foreign law because his gentile passions will not allow it. Rom 7:7–25 represents the judaizing gentile's ambiguous status. Neither fully Jew nor fully Greek, he is torn between the passions of an idolator and the law of the one true God.

According to a long, influential line of Western interpretation, Rom. 7 and 8 contrast the Jewish and Christian self-understandings. I believe it a great tragedy that generations of Christians have seen Jews through these dark lenses. The currently most influential commentator has written of 7: 7–13, "First, it is to be maintained under all circumstances that the apostle is speaking of mankind under the law, or specifically of the pious Jew." In a recent study, Gerd Theissen unfortunately falls into this Western reading. He even makes the chapter autobiographical, a description of Paul's struggle as a Pharisee from the later Christian perspective. In this Western reading, the linchpin is usually pride. The human or the Jewish crime is pride. Jews may be outwardly virtuous and good but their good behavior is at the base evil because it is motivated by pride. Again the ghost of Augustine lives on. But Paul says nothing about pride or anxiety or overachievement. These interpreters have to argue that the concepts are hidden but assumed in the concepts of "sin" and "doing the law."

The ten commandments must have been basic to what gentiles who wanted to identify with Judaism were taught. When Paul caricatures the works of the law that a Jewish teacher taught to gentiles, he cites three commandments from the Decalogue (2:21–22). The gentile *persona* in 7: 7 gives the commandment against covetousness as an example of what he was taught. This prohibition was given a special significance by Jews who wanted to show the correspondence of Jewish teaching and the Greco-Roman ethic of self-mastery. The LXX's use of *epithumia* to translate the Hebrew allowed Jews like Philo and the author of 4 Maccabees to claim that the Jewish law agreed with Greek moral psychology in its emphasis on the passions as the source of evil impulses. Furthermore, following the appropriate commandments from the Jewish law was an extraordinarily potent therapy for the ravages of rampant desire. Translations introduce an entirely alien idea when they render *epithumēseis* in 7:7 as "you shall not covet," rather than "you shall not desire," hiding the connections with the motif of gentile desire and Paul's Hellenistic conceptualities.

The dilemma of the gentile who tries to base his life on works of the law appears in 7:8–11. Although the law reveals that desire is sin, it can do little to change the fact that *epithumia* forms a fundamental aspect of his character. The gentile ruled by his God-ordained slavery to the desire arising from passions experiences the law against desire as a deceitful, almost teasing condemnation (7:8–11). Instead of controlling excessive desire, the commandment stimulates desire in accordance with God's punishment and adds a knowledge of God's condemnation. Perhaps Paul thought that the gentile was definitively socialized in one way, the Jew in another or that each carried the characteristics of his ancestors. He definitely believed that lifting a few commandments out of the Jewish politeia could only lead the gentile to a knowledge of his bondage to sin and the penalties of God's wrath. Behind Paul's caricature may lie sociological realities. Gentile godfearers may have aspired to live by certain Jewish teachings, but they still lived in gentile society. Could a gentile living in such circumstances really be expected to forge for himself a life truly pleasing to God? The attendant schizophrenia might even make matters worse.

Rather than merely repeat and elaborate the mythological discourse of Hellenistic moral psychology and its ideology, one must understand the social constructions indicated in such discourse. Paul, of course, employs the Hellenistic discourse and not social analysis. Indeed, the discourse often functions to mask these realities. Romans 7 stands forth as a Jewish Christian adaptation of Greco-Roman discourse about the problem of *akrasia*, in service of an argument against gentiles attempting to gain self-mastery by following the law. Rom. 6–8 uses "sin" in a way similar to the concept of *akolasia*, a set disposition to do wrong. Paul adds the assumption that sin is wrongdoing offensive to God and his law. In Hellenistic moral thought, habitual akrasia becomes *akolasia*. Ancient moralists debated as to whether akrasia, weakness of will or lack of self-mastery, was caused by ignorance and false belief or by passions inherent in human nature. In light of modern study, both approaches vastly oversimplify the problem, but the Stoics had the most sophisticated analysis, attributing akrasia to false beliefs and ignorance. Paul in crucial respects sides with the popular and Platonic view against the Stoics. Knowledge alone cannot cure gentile akrasia. Merely knowing the teachings of the law fails to solve the problem. Using the popular view, Romans explains akrasia in terms of desire arising from passions (similar to our emotions and appetites.).

Again using the popular and Platonic view, Romans 7 divides the person between a true self identified with the mind or rationality and a lower or false self identified with the body or the flesh. According to Paul, the passions and desire reside in the flesh or the body and its parts (Gal. 5:16, 24; Rom. 6:12–13, cf. 1:26–27; 7:5, 18, 22; 8:3). The mind rationally apprehends and wills to do the law (7:22), but since it has been corrupted by the turn to idolatry (1:21–22, 28), the desires of the flesh overcome it. Only a mind renewed by infusion with God's Spirit can enable the gentile to resist the flesh and act according to God's law (8:5–8). Thus the law is not the problem but also not the answer (7:9–13, 16; 8:3a). The problem stems from God withholding his divine Spirit from gentiles who are thus not related to him as children (8:12–30) and cannot master the flesh (8:2–11). God effected gentile redemption from the flesh by making his son the pioneer of the movement from life dominated by the flesh to life dominated by the Spirit. Redeemed gentiles do not leave the body for a spiritual existence but are incorporated into Christ's mode of life by infusion with God's (also called Christ's) life principle (spirit/*pneuma*).

*   *   *

Through Jesus Christ, "who was appointed son of God in power by the holy Spirit" (1:4), God enacted the destiny of others, including the gentile peoples (8:3). Jesus Christ's life figured forth what God had planned for the gentiles and presumably, but on a different track and schedule, for Jews. Christ reversed the curse on the gentiles, which made their flesh weak, being particularly vulnerable to sin (8:3) and not able to do what the law requires (8:4). As the Spirit empowered Jesus Christ, so also the Spirit gives the gentiles a new mind (8:5–6), allowing them to submit to God's law (8:7). Paul does not speak of this new mind as something that eliminates their freedom as agents. Indeed, he exhorts them to cooperate with this power (8:5–8). In Gal. 5:17–21, he describes this new mind as a disposition toward certain social virtues and away from antisocial vices. That text provides a somewhat different description characterizing the new mind as a new set of desires (*epithumiai*), desires of the Spirit. In other words, the new empowerment enables virtues that reverse the state of gentile society described in 1:29–32.

Now enabled to submit to God's law, gentiles are reconciled to God (8:7). As Christ's body was raised by the power of the Spirit to new life (1:4), so also those in Christ will experience new life in their bodies (8:10–11). As Christ was appointed "a son of God" or "the son of God" (Paul's language is ambiguous), so also gentiles in Christ will be designated sons of God. Jesus is the "first born from the dead" (8:29) who "was appointed son of God, coming forth from the [general] resurrection of the dead" (1:3–4). Paul understands Jesus' suffering to have been the beginning of the time of troubles that are a transition to God's redemption of the world. Jesus' resurrection is the first instance of the general resurrection. As fellow heirs with Christ (8:17), Paul's gentile communities will share in the recent turn of events inaugurated by him. They too will share in the sufferings and testing of the period of transition (8:17–25) but will also be glorified as he has been glorified. God planned this boost for the whole world since the beginning of his creation. But he has for a time subjected that creation to decay and futility in order that his ultimate goal of glory might be achieved (8:19–22). The gentile communities that are thus "conformed to the image of his [God's] son" (8:29) have been destined, called, and justified as part of God's plan to reconcile the world.

Paul sums up all that has happened to these gentiles when he explains that they have been "adopted as sons" or have received "sonship." As sons they become heirs of God's promises. Paul has already explained that the redemption of the gentile nations forms part of God's promise to Abraham that he would inherit the world (4:13). Paul conceives of world reconciliation as a kind of ethnic unification. Only Abraham's line has maintained the kinship with God that God intended for all. Through Christ's faithfulness to the patriarchal promises, all of the peoples will now be adopted into the one faithful family. But the principle for the inclusion of the other peoples is not blood or the seed passed down from the patriarch but infusion with the life-giving, creative power (God's Spirit) directly from God. Jews and the other peoples come to share in a principle of kinship prefigured in the miracle of Abraham's and Sarah's fertility and Jesus' resurrection.

Just what this means concretely is notoriously fuzzy. I think it certain, however, that it will not do to make Gal. 3:28 the key and then to construe that text in terms of liberal individualism and the premises of the modern nation-state. The promise that Abraham's seed would inherit the world means that all will be adopted into Abraham's families through the Spirit and that there will be an organization of one government under Christ, who will finally turn things directly over to God. Abraham ends up having many peoples descended from him, all of whom have been infused with a higher level of life. Paul's gentile assemblies seem to be vanguards and beachheads of gentile renewal planted at strategic locations in various parts of the empire. They are in preparation to serve with Christ at his return. The Jewish family of Abraham maintains its integrity. To what extent Greeks, Romans, and others reformed "in Christ" maintain distinct identities remains unclear to me. It may not have been clear to Paul either. After laboring through the eight chapters, Paul has finally explained how the gentile peoples can attain the privileged status of sonship that Israel already has (9:4): They are sons and heirs when they receive the Spirit of Christ and live as communities participating in the paradigmatic narrative of renewal that Jesus Christ has already pioneered. All of this radically reinterprets the goal of self-mastery that drew many gentiles to works from the law.

* * *

Reading Romans 13: Paul's Influence on Political Theory

The New Testament contains no political theory, nor even anything that could be called a political or social ethic for the early Christians. There are only a number of stereotyped or ad hoc admonitions addressed to specific points at which the larger society impinged upon the new sect. Must one pay taxes? Dare one accept dinner invitations from pagans, given the presumption that the meat would have technically been "offered" to some deity? Must a marriage be dissolved if one partner became a Christian and the other refused to convert? Might a Christian sue another Christian before a civil court?

The paucity of general, theoretical statements about the Christian's relationship to the political order is not surprising, because of several obvious factors. First, the church had emerged from the synagogue, and it thus inherited the delicately ambivalent position the Jewish communities occupied in the cities of the eastern Roman provinces. These communities participated in almost all aspects of commercial and civic life, but their intense monotheism made them always a separate, recognizable minority. As a result, they were usually quietistic politically, reluctant to call attention to the community's ambiguous civil status.

Second, the Christian church during New Testament times was numerically insignificant. Moreover, so far as one can tell, most of its members belonged to those strata of society that had little or no political influence and virtually no opportunity for political decision.

Third, the Christians were an eschatological community. They were preoccupied with the events of the end of days which had, they believed, been inaugurated by the death and resurrection of Jesus the Christ. In the first generation, and recurrently among some groups, they anticipated the speedy collapse of the present world order, to be replaced by the visible reign of God. So long as this expectation kept its power, there might be practical need for reaching a *modus vivendi* with the ruling powers, but hardly any impetus for serious discussion of long-range political questions.

Even in the earliest period, however, the Christians could not long evade the necessity of decision about their loyalty and obedience to the imperial authority of Rome. During the decades in which the New Testament books were written, the Jews of Judea and the Galilee fought and lost two wars of national liberation against the Romans. It is true that the two defeats had surprisingly little effect on the Jewish communities outside Roman Palestine and still less direct effect on the Christians. However, Jews of the Diaspora faced their own crises during this period. In 38 CE riots broke out in Alexandria against the large Jewish community there, requiring an urgent delegation by the Jews to Rome to seek redress from the emperor.

Rebuffed by Caligula, they were answered by his successor Claudius, yet Claudius himself issued a decree a few years later expelling Jews from Rome. Toward the end of the reign of the emperor Trajan (115–117), Jews across North Africa and on Cyprus revolted against Rome, for reasons that remain obscure. The revolts and the varying responses to them illustrate in the most graphic manner possible the ambivalence toward the existing political order felt by all Jews. A sect so fundamentally Jewish in its origins and in the structure of its traditions as the early church had inevitably to face the question whether it recognized the Empire's claims. The answers to that question, as represented in the New Testament literature, veer between two poles. One, represented by the apocalyptic imagery of the Revelation of John, identifies the Roman political and religious structures with the classic anti-gods of middle eastern mythology, the dragons of sea and underworld. When in the seer's vision "Babylon," the great city—also pictured as a harlot seated "on seven hills"—is burned, the Christian saints sing, "Hallelujah! The smoke from her goes up for ever and ever" (Rev. 19: 3). At the opposite pole is the quietist position, probably derived from the traditions of the Hellenistic synagogue, which urges that prayers be made "for kings and all those in authority, that we may live peaceful and quiet lives" (1 Tim. 2:1f.), and admonishes:

> Submit yourselves for the Lord's sake to every human authority: whether to the emperor, as the supreme authority, or to governors, who are sent by him to punish those who do wrong and to commend those who do right. (1 Peter 2:13f.)

Paul's letter to Romans contains a more extensive formulation of the same rule. This passage, Romans 13:1–7, was destined to have a central place in the development of Western political thought.

The church, in time, would have to construct a political theory. The world did not end in the first century, nor in the second. The Christian group both spread with incredible rapidity and began to extend its appeal into all classes. Questions such as, May a Christian serve in the army? May a Christian be a school teacher? May a rich person be saved? came to be asked with growing urgency. Direct confrontations with the imperial majesty were provoked by the caesars' acceptance of divine honors and, beginning with Domitian, their use of the imperial cult as a test of political loyalty. By the middle of the third century the church had grown large and strong enough to be perceived as a threat to the established order, and, beginning with the emperor Decius, empire-wide police actions were taken against it. The blood of martyrs, it was said, became the seed of the church. Already in the second century Christians from the educated classes had taken up the task of defending the new religion in public tracts, which were customarily addressed to the emperor. Constantine's Edict of Toleration marked the end of this era of self-defense. And when the converted Constantine himself convened the church's ecumenical council at Nicea in 325, it was evident to all that an era had begun that no New Testament writer could remotely have imagined.

The church had become a power within the Empire. It could use the state's power to suppress its own heretics, and in time it could also affect the political balance of power and even influence the succession of emperors and princes. By the same token, the secular government henceforth was involved in the internal life of the church. The necessity for defining the relationship between the two powers became acute. But even before the fourth century, the necessity for some general theory of the state and of the Christian's obligations toward it had become clear.

In the constantly fluctuating relationship between the church, in its evolving shapes, and the state, in its diverse forms, between the second century and the modern period, Christians have sought again and again to ground their political theory in scripture, or at least to justify their conclusions by proof-texts. There were precious few passages available for this purpose in the New Testament canon. Thus it happened that those few lines of practical admonition, perhaps adapted from the Hellenistic Jewish synagogue, which Paul quoted in Romans 13:1–7, became the kernel of an enormous body of literature. The following essays and excerpts illustrate a few of the main themes in that literature, from the ancient, medieval, and modern periods.

ORIGEN

[Christians and the Governing Authorities] (ca. 246)†

25. Now, then, let us see what the Apostle says additionally in what follows: *Let every soul be subject to the higher authorities.*[1] It does not seem very commendable to me here that what he commands to be subject to the authorities he calls the soul. For he would never have said, Let every spirit be subject to authority, but "every soul." We have already frequently spoken about the difference between them, that sometimes a man is identified through the soul, sometimes through the flesh, sometimes through the spirit. And when man needs to be identified by the better aspect, as one who ought to be understood as spiritual, he is called spirit; when, by his inferior aspect he is identified, he is called soul; and when his lowest aspect is being identified, he is called flesh. On repeated occasions we have furnished proofs for these things from the Scriptures.

(2) Now then, the Apostle is laying down precepts for believers and he wants us to preserve rest and peace in this present life, so far as it depends on us.[2] And indeed, if we are such that, having been united with the Lord, we are one spirit with him,[3] we are said to be subject to the Lord. But if

---

† From Origen's commentary (Book 9, chs. 25–30) on Rom. 13:1–7, tr. by Thomas P. Scheck, *Origen, Commentary on the Epistle to the Romans, Books 6–10* (Washington: Catholic University of America Press, 2002), 222–28. Reprinted by permission of The Catholic University of America Press, Washington, D.C. Origen wrote his commentary on Romans during the reign of Philip the Arabian (244–249), who appears to have been somewhat sympathetic to Christianity and may even have received a letter from Origen (Eusebius, *Hist. eccl.* 6.34, 36). Up to that time, the persecution of Christians had been sporadic and localized, instigated largely by the populace or local officials. But that situation was soon to change, as Origen himself recognized when he wrote his *Against Celsus* (3.15) shortly thereafter. Approximately two years after Origen wrote his commentary, Rome celebrated its first thousand years of existence in 248. This millennial celebration sparked renewed interest in pagan religion, and in 250 Decius, the new Roman emperor, issued an edict that mandated public sacrifice to the state gods. Although the ensuing persecution was brief, it initiated a period of more than sixty years during which several Roman emperors, especially Diocletian, targeted Christians. Origen's exegesis thus antedates Rome's fiercest assault on Christianity.
1. Rom. 13:1.
2. Cf. Rom. 12:18.
3. Cf. 1 Cor. 6:17.

we are not yet that way, but there is still a common soul within us that still possesses something of this world, one that is in someone, a soul shackled by pre-occupations, the Apostle lays down precepts for it and tells it to be subjected to the authorities of the world; for the Lord also said that those who have the inscription of Caesar within themselves should render to Caesar the things that are Caesar's.[4] Peter and John used to have nothing to render to Caesar;[5] for Peter says, "Gold and silver I do not have."[6] He who does not have this has nothing to render to Caesar nor, therefore, what he should subject to the higher authorities. But he who has money or possessions or any worldly preoccupations should listen up: "Let every soul be subject to the higher authorities."

26. *For there is no authority*, he says, *except from God.*[7] Perhaps someone will say: What then? Is even that authority that persecutes God's servants, attacks the faith, and subverts religion, from God? To this we shall briefly respond. There is no one who does not know that even sight is a gift from God to us, as well as hearing and the ability to think. Well then, though we have these things from God, it nevertheless is within our authority to make use of our vision either for good things or evil things.[8] In a similar way we use our hearing, the movement of our hands, and the reflection of thought; and in this the judgment of God is just,[9] because we misuse these things that he has given for good use, for impious and wicked service. So then, all authority has also been given by God "to punish those who are evil but to praise those who are good";[1] just as the same Apostle says in what follows.[2] But the judgment of God will be just[3] in respect to those who govern the authority they have received in accordance with their own impieties and not in accordance with God's laws.

27. This is why he says: *Therefore, whoever resists authority resists the ordinance of God.*[4] Here he is not speaking about those authorities that instigate persecutions against the faith; for in such cases one must say, "It is necessary to obey God rather than men."[5] Instead he is speaking about general authorities, which *are not a terror to the good work but to the evil.*[6] Surely the one who resists them procures condemnation for himself for the quality of his own deeds.

28. *Do you wish, he says, to have no fear of the authority? Do what is good, and you will receive praise from it; for it is God's minister for your good. But if you do what is evil, be afraid; for it does not bear the sword for no reason; for it is the minister of God, the avenger to execute wrath on him who does what is evil.*[7]

---

4. Mt. 22:20–21.
5. Cf. Acts 3:3–5.
6. Acts 3:6.
7. Rom. 13:1.
8. Cf. Origen, *Comm. Rom.* 8.8.6.
9. Cf. 2 Thes. 1:5.
1. 1 Pt. 2:14.
2. Cf. Rom. 13:3–4.
3. Cf. 2 Thes. 1:5.
4. Rom. 13:2.
5. Acts 5:29.
6. Rom. 13:3.
7. Rom. 13:3–4.

(2) Paul troubles [me] by these words, that he calls the secular authority and the worldly judgment a minister of God; and he does this not merely one time, but he even repeats it a second and a third time. I would like to endeavor to ascertain the sense in which a worldly judge is a minister of God. We find it written in the Acts of the Apostles that when the apostles had come together they established decrees that we who have believed in Christ from the Gentiles were obligated to observe, among which are contained: "The apostles and the elders, to the brothers in Antioch and Syria and Cilicia, to all who have believed from among the Gentiles, greetings. Since we have heard that some have gone out from us and are disturbing you in matters that we have not commanded";[8] and after a few things is added, "Therefore, it has pleased the Holy Spirit and us to impose on you no further burden than these essentials, that you abstain from what is sacrificed to idols and from blood and from what is strangled and from fornication; by keeping yourselves from these, you will do well. Farewell."[9] In these precepts, then, in which he says that no further burden is to be imposed upon the Gentile believers except that they should abstain from what is sacrificed to idols and from blood and from strangled things and from fornication, neither murder is prohibited nor adultery nor theft nor homosexuality nor other crimes that are punished by divine and human laws. But if that which he mentioned above alone has to be observed by Christians, it will appear that he has given them license in respect to these other crimes. But observe the ordinance of the Holy Spirit; for indeed since the other crimes are avenged by secular laws and since it was deemed superfluous now to prohibit these things by divine law, since they are adequately punished by human law, he decrees only those things concerning which no human law had spoken about but which seemed to be in agreement with the religion. From this it is clear that the worldly judge fulfills the greatest part of God's law. For all the crimes that God wants to be punished, he has willed that they be punished not through the priests and leaders of the churches, but through the worldly judge. And aware of this, Paul rightly names him a minister of God and an avenger of the one who does what is evil.

(3) But it seems to me that what he says about the authority, "Do what is good and you will receive praise from it," needs to be examined more deeply. For there is no tradition for secular authorities to praise those who fail to become criminals. To be sure they punish those who sin, but there is no custom for them to praise highly those who do not sin. But let us consider whether perhaps Paul, even when he appears to be teaching about moral matters, always refuses to bypass the opportunity to insert something about the mysteries. For he knows that "all who have sinned under the law will be judged through the law."[1] But doubtless that law according to which he lived will convict each one in the judgment. Now we have shown that the Holy Spirit allowed room in many things to human law; therefore, it is certain that on the day of judgment, even on the basis of those laws, the one who has not committed anything against the enacted laws will receive praise in God's presence, when the Lord will say to him, "Well

8. Acts 15:23–24.
9. Acts 15:28–29.
1. Rom. 2:12.

done, good and faithful servant! You have been faithful over a few things; I shall place you over many things."[2]

(4) One should know, however, that "law has not been appointed for the righteous man, but for the unrighteous and insubordinate, for criminals, murderers, for the vile, for perjurers, and others of this sort."[3] For they are the ones who fear the law. But he who does good, i.e., he who does what is good not out of fear of the law but out of love for the good, no longer lives under the law of the letter but under the law of the Spirit.[4]

29. *Therefore, it is necessary to be subject, not only on account of wrath, but also on account of conscience. For it is for this reason that you also pay taxes; for they are God's ministers who are there for this very purpose.*[5] By these things Paul sets the rule for the Church of God not to oppose secular rulers and authorities. Through the quietness and tranquility of life it should practice the work of righteousness and piety.[6] For instance, if we suppose that believers in Christ are not subject to secular authorities, that they do not have to pay taxes, that they are not required to pay out revenues, and that they owe no one fear or honor, would not the weapons of leaders and rulers deservedly turn against them? Would [such Christians] not make them justified persecutors, but themselves guilty? For they would have already seemed to be attacked not because of their faith, but because of rebelliousness. To be sure there would be a case against them that is worthy of death, but it would be a death unworthy of merit.

30. Providing for these things, then, Paul says through his immense wisdom, *Pay to all what is due them; taxes to whom taxes are due; revenue to whom revenue is due; fear to whom fear is due; honor to whom honor is due. You should owe no one anything except that you love one another.*[7] I believe, however, that not even these things that Paul brings forth are without mysteries, customary for his statements. For we have already taught above[8] that every creature and every spirit, whether the good and the upright or even those of a depraved and evil purpose, serves God and presents itself for suitable ministry. For the Apostle has made a pronouncement that applies to all of them together where he said, "Are they not all ministering spirits sent to minister on behalf of those who will receive the inheritance of salvation?"[9]

(2) So then, all spirits minister to the life of human beings, but each, as we have said, according to its own worth and merit; for even they are called ministers by whose ministry the things that pertain to the world are being accomplished. This is also why the Apostle, who had said of himself, "For the world has been crucified to me and I to the world,"[1] also says this: "But we have not received the spirit of this world but the Spirit who is from

---

2. Mt. 25:21.
3. Cf. 1 Tim. 1:9.
4. Cf. Origen, *Comm. Rom.* 4.4.9.
5. Rom. 13:5–6.
6. Cf. Is. 32:17; 1 Tim. 2:5.
7. Rom. 13:7–8.
8. Cf. Origen, *Comm. Rom.* 7.1.2–3.
9. Heb. 1:14.
1. Gal. 6:14.

God."[2] But whoever is still of the world and is mindful of the things that are of the world and seeks the things of the flesh is necessarily subject to the ministers of the world;[3] but he is subjected because of the wrath that he has stored up as a treasure for himself from sins.[4] And it is for this reason it seems to me that he says, "Therefore, it is necessary to be subject, not only because of wrath but also because of conscience."[5] In the conscience too a person is subjected, since he has something in him that will be accused by conscience. Therefore, we pay certain taxes to them, as long as we still live according to the flesh and think on things that belong to the flesh.[6] For if we till the Lord's vineyard and cultivate the true vine, who is Christ,[7] within us, we do not pay taxes from that vineyard to the ministers of the world,[8] but we return fruits in time to the Lord himself.[9] As the Savior himself says in the Gospels, "For he takes the vineyard from the wicked tenants and will give it to other tenants who may return its fruits to him in time."[1]

(3) Moreover, what he says, "Pay to all what is due them; tax to whom tax is due; revenue to whom revenue is due," seems to me to be distinct from what he goes on to say in what follows, "fear to whom fear is due; honor to whom honor is due," even regarding those ministers for whom we have said above taxes and revenue are pertinent.[2] For they exact from us taxes from our land and revenues from our business. And why am I saying, "from us"? Tax was exacted even from our Lord Jesus Christ when he was in the flesh; it was on that account that he claims to pay, not in that he is obligated to, but lest he cause them to stumble.[3] But if he who had nothing in himself that belonged to Caesar[4] and in whom there was nothing of his own possession that the ruler of this world, on arrival, found,[5] though he was free, nevertheless pays tax—for he even went to death in order that he would be "free among the dead"[6]—how much more necessary is it for us to pay out these taxes of the flesh and to pay revenues for our business through diverse trials[7] to the spirits exacting them from us,[8] but only if we do business with the pearls of the kingdom of heaven?[9]

(4) But we ought to refer "fear and honor" more to him who says through the prophet, "Do you not call me Lord and Father? And if I am Lord, where is my fear? And if I am Father, where is my honor?"[1] What he adds later, of course, that we should owe nothing to anyone, is certainly to be referred to the ministers to whom one becomes a debtor when he sins. For on many occasions we have repeatedly shown that sin is a debt. So Paul wants every

2. 1 Cor. 2:12.
3. Cf. Heb. 1:14.
4. Cf. Rom. 2:5.
5. Rom. 13:5.
6. Cf. Rom. 8:5, 12.
7. Cf. Mt. 21:41; Jn. 15:1.
8. Cf. Heb. 1:14.
9. Cf. Mt. 21:41.
1. Mt. 21:41.
2. Cf. Heb. 1:14; Rom. 13:6.
3. Cf. Mt. 17:24–27.
4. Cf. Mt. 22:19, 21.
5. Cf. Jn. 14:30.
6. Cf. Ps. 88:5.
7. Cf. Jas. 1:2.
8. Cf. Heb. 1:14; Rom. 13:7.
9. Cf. Mt. 13:45–46.
1. Mal. 1:6.

debt of sin to be paid and absolutely no debt of sin to remain among us, but for our debt of love to abide and never to cease; for paying this debt even daily and owing it at all times is beneficial to us.

KARL HERMANN SCHELKLE

State and Church in the Patristic Exposition of Romans 13:1–7 (1952)†

It is truly moving to read how Origen, the first expositor of Romans known to us, wrestles with the text Rom. 13:1–7. For him, a witness of the "church of martyrs," the question that immediately arises from Rom. 13:1 is a very difficult one: "Is even that authority from God which persecutes the servants of God, combats the faith, and destroys religion?" Origen replies that we all have our faculties from God, but it is in our power to use them for good or evil. But then it is important for Origen to affirm the inviolable freedom of the person before the state. Again and again his exposition moves toward the demonstration of this freedom. Thus he deduces immediately from v. 1: Paul says that every soul (*omnis anima*) is subject to the authorities. He would never have said that of the spirit (*spiritus*). "If we are united with the Lord, one spirit with him, then we are subject to the Lord. But if we are not thus, but the common soul is still in us, which has something of this world and is united with it through its occupation, then the apostle gives his commandment to that soul, saying that it is subject to the authorities of the world." Only the "animal" and the animal man are subject; the "spiritual" and the spiritual man are free. That is, Origen's exposition makes use of a traditional trichotomous anthropology. Obviously he does not realize that such an interpretation, if carried to its ultimate extension, would dissolve the authority of every government.

Against the obligatory obedience expressed in Rom. 13:2, Origen declares that it is invalid in the face of powers that persecute the faith. Acts 5:29 remains: one must obey God rather than man. Of Rom. 13:3 Origen confesses, "It moves me how, in these words of Paul, he calls the power of this age and the judge of this world God's servants, and that not just once, but repeatedly, two and three times." His solution is that Paul can rightly say this, because "the worldly judge nevertheless does fulfill the greater part of the laws of God. For all the transgressions and crimes that ought to be punished according to God's will are not to be requited by the officials of the church, but by the judges of the world." Thus Origen does recognize and acknowledge the role and value of the state in caring for

---

† "Staat und Kirche in der patristischen Auslegung von Röm 13:1–7" was first published in ZNW 44 (1952–1953): 223–36. Reprinted by permission of Walter De Gruyter, GMBH & Co. Schelkle (1908–1988) was professor of New Testament in the Catholic Faculty of Theology at the University of Tübingen from 1956 until his retirement in 1976. Although Schelkle experienced opposition from both state and church, he lived to enjoy honors from both. He was forbidden to teach in German high schools during the Nazi regime because of "political unfitness." His dissertation (1941) was not published until 1949, and then without the imprimatur of the Church because of objections by the ecclesiastical censor. Yet his subsequent influence in both Catholic and Protestant NT studies was so great that in 1976 Pope John Paul II named him an honorary prelate, and in 1985 the Federal Republic of Germany awarded him the Service Cross First Class.

justice. To be sure, he sees this role chiefly as retributive, the expiation of crime. He does not speak of the positive task of establishing and preserving the order of society. Perhaps the reason lies in the fact that early Christian political theory often finds the origin of the state ultimately in sin. This assumption frequently echoes in the exposition of Romans 13:1–7.

But then Origen, seeking the hidden secrets of Paul's words, is forced into obvious contradiction of the apostle's statement when he says of Rom. 13:3: "Do what is good and you will receive commendation from him— that cannot apply to the powers of this world, but means the commendation and reward which the good and faithful servant will one day receive from God." The servants of God (Rom. 13:4) Origen takes to be God's spirits, which are sent for the service of man and through whose service all things occur in the world. "He who is still of the world, and craves the things of the world, and seeks the things of the flesh, he is necessarily subject to the servants of the world, but subject because of the wrath which he is accumulating for himself because of his sins." For this reason Paul said that one must be subject not only because of wrath, but also for conscience' sake. "For whoever is subject to the world will be accused inwardly by his conscience." To the world's servants "we pay tribute if we live according to the flesh and do that which belongs to the flesh. But if we cultivate the vineyard of the Lord, and tend the true vine in us, which is Christ, then of this vine we pay no tribute to the servants of the world, but in the Lord himself we bring fruit in its time." Origen finally has to divide Rom. 13:7: Give to all what is due, to those to whom you owe it; revenue and taxes—that applies to us, too. Even Christ, who was truly free from the caesars and princes of this world, paid (according to Matt. 17:24ff.) the tax drachma. "How much more must we pay these tributes of the flesh, and, even though our business deals with the pearl of the kingdom of heaven, pay our sales taxes to the powers which demand them from us by manifold temptations." Yet fear and honor, which are demanded in Rom. 13:7 alongside the taxes, are not due to men, but to the one who said through the prophet, If I am the Lord, where is the fear of me? If I am the Father, where is my honor?

Origen adduces Rom. 13:1ff. also in *Contra Celsum* 8.65, where he refers to his commentary on Romans. Here he is answering Celsus, who declares that one ought to serve the demons, "and therefore also the princes and kings that rule over men, since these also did not receive their earthly dignity without demonic power." But Origen says, the Christians despise the favor of kings, if it must be won by sin or by denial of God or by servility, while Rom. 13:1 demonstrates the correct obedience of Christians. He adds, however, that this understanding of the passage is in accord with the simple and customary interpretation, while in his commentary on Romans he treated it extensively from various viewpoints. Does he mean that he himself understands by servants of God and authorities angelic powers, and thus comes himself close to Celsus' doctrine? Origen again appeals to Rom. 13:6 in his homilies on Luke, hom. 23 and 35 (pp. 155 and 215 Rauer). Here, interpreting Rom. 13:6 in terms of angelic powers, he conceives of these ministering angels in mysterious allusions as sentry-demons, who are stationed at the borders of the world to examine those who have died, only allowing them to pass if they can pay good deeds as duty. Otherwise they are thrown into debtors' prison.

Irenaeus also introduces Rom. 13.1–6 when he explains (*Adv. Haer.* 5.24) that Paul "does not say this of the powers of the angels, nor of the invisible princes, as some venture to explain it, but rather of human powers." Thus Irenaeus also was acquainted with an interpretation that understood the "authorities" of Rom. 13:1 as demonic. There can be no doubt that it was understood in that way in Gnostic speculations, for which such things were very important. Irenaeus understood quite well the significance of the matter, and sharply rejected this interpretation.

Romans 13:7 is again used esoterically in the *Pistis Sophia* (ch. 113 Schmidt). When the soul which has received the mysteries of the light has, at its time, left the body, it meets on its upward way the Archons. The soul hands over the secrets to the Archons. "It gives the honor and the glory and the praise of the seal to all those of the place of light—concerning this word, my Lord, you have spoken once through the mouth of our brother Paul: Give tax to whom tax is due, and give fear to whom fear is due, and give praise to whom praise is due, and owe nothing to any other." Here again the powers of Rom. 13:1–7 are demonic powers. Finally Pseudo-Basilius (*Constit. Monast.*, PG 31, 1404A) knows such an interpretation, if only to reject it: "The apostle Paul gives orders to be subject to all governing authorities. These are authorities of the world, not spiritual ones. He makes that evident in the following, since he speaks of tax and tribute, and affirms that whoever offers the slightest resistance to authority opposes God."

Thus there is multiple testimony that in the patristic period the "authorities" of Rom. 13:1 were understood as demons. But what thread of tradition connected the individual witnesses? Did Origen know and adopt the Gnostic exposition, perhaps modifying it and giving it a new basis? Especially the exposition in Origen's commentary on Luke seems related to that in the *Pistis Sophia*. But whom was Pseudo-Basilius opposing—Origen, an Origenism, or gnosis? In any case Celsus, Origen, and Gnosticism together lead us to consider how inclined was the ancient world, pagan as well as Christian, to worship supernatural powers in the governing authority.

Biblical exegesis was never able to ignore the basic affirmation of the state in Paul's teaching. Many fathers, in their explanation of Rom. 13:1–7, speak of it, like Origen, with grave words. Irenaeus does so extensively (*Adv. haer.* 5, 24, 2): Humans, fallen away from God, did every evil without hesitation. They had no fear of God, so at least they must fear the avenging sword. Therefore the government bears the sword as servant of God. And those who demand taxes are servants of God, because the laws restrain unrighteousness. Thus Irenaeus' interpretation draws on the conception of the state's origin after an initial struggle of each against all, a conception known most recently from the Stoa, as well as the biblical tradition of man's original sin. The state is indeed God's creation, but as punishment. To this extent the state had its immediate origin in sin, not in the original human condition. Tertullian (*Scorpiace* 14) reads out of Rom. 13:1–7 the obligation of the Christian to be obedient to all authority, because it exercises divine office. He asserts (*Ad Scapulam* 2), in words that recall Rom. 13:1–7, that for Christians Caesar is installed by God, indeed is the highest human being below God. The apologist Theophilus (*Ad Autolycum* 3.14) confirms the obedience of Christians to the government with the "divine word", namely Rom. 13:1–7 and 1 Tim. 2.1f. Surely the church was correct when, during the time of persecution, it defended itself against the frequent accusation of enmity toward the state by appealing to this saying of Paul as testimony to its true doctrine. The passage is frequently quoted in just this sense in the acts of the martyrs. It is probably historically accurate, in the historically reliable report of the martyrdom of Polycarp (10.2), that Polycarp in his defense before the consul appealed to Rom. 13:1–7 and 1 Pet. 2:13: "We have been taught to render honor, as is proper, to the princes and authorities appointed by God, if it does not hurt us." Paul's sum and defense of his teaching in the *Passio Petri et Pauli* 37, which alludes to Rom. 13:7, is naturally unhistorical, but nevertheless a valid witness to the history of the tradition: "I have taught the merchants to pay taxes to the officials of the state." And in the so-called *Martyrium Romanum* 6.6 (Funk-Diekamp) Ignatius before Trajan clinches the peaceful loyalty of the Christians with Rom. 13.7f. Similarly in a fourth century Syrian martyrology the witness Mar Simon bases his loyalty to the king on Rom. 13.1f. and 1 Tim. 2:2. These verses become an essential element in martyr apologies. Finally Chrysostom actually believed (*Homilies on Romans*, PG 60, 687BC) that Paul had written them for the specific occasion of his own defense, in order "to win unbelieving authorities for the faith and Christians to obedience. A strong rumor was circulating that accused the apostles of rebellion and reforming tendencies, claiming that their whole activity aimed at overthrowing the government."

In the stress of the time of persecution, however, the commentaries sought an escape forbidden by the text. In the third-century *Didascalia* (2, 33, 3 and 34, 1 Funk) the commandment to pay taxes, Rom. 13:7, is applied to the bishops as princes of the church. Of them it says, "Honor them with all honor. They have received from God the power over life and death; to condemn to the death of the eternal fire or to accept and to make alive those who turn and repent. Esteem them as your rulers, heed them as kings and bring them honors and taxes as to kings. For they and their households must live from you." Later the heretics persecuted by the Catholic state would attempt in the same way to transfer Paul's threatening saying from the state to the spiritual power of the church, that is, to their small religious community.

However, after the state becomes Christian, all previous checks on the exposition fall away. Now the state's task is no longer understood merely as the punishment of wickedness. Rather it is understood, even celebrated, as creator and protector of the order and peace of human society. The first to speak expressly of this was Epiphanius of Salamis, in his work against the heresies written 374–377 (*Haer.* 40, 4; 2, 84f. Holl). Not only does the state have the sword, that is, the authority to punish, from God, but "for this reason the governing authorities exist, that everything might exist and be regulated for the well constituted order and government of the entire world according to God's will." In their commentaries on Romans Theodore of Mopsuestia (Staab, *Pauluskommentare aus der griechischen Kirche*, 1933, p. 62), Chrysostom (PG 60, 86E-687A, 488AD), Theodoret (PG 82, 193BC), and Photius (Staab, p. 533) say the same thing. A closer dependence exists among the passages of the Didascalia, Chrysostom, and Photius, with their admonition that the rulers, busy with the care for the common affairs, cannot trouble themselves with their private matters and therefore have a right to demand support by taxes and respect for their office.

Now the interpretation especially emphasizes the obligation of obedience to the state. To be sure, even now it must be admitted that misuse of power is possible. But it is not the government as such that is evil, but the one who misuses governmental authority. The later exegetes repeat what Origen had already said. On Rom. 13:1–7 as on 1 Peter 2:13 Didymus the Blind says (*PG* 39, 1766D): "God gave us the faculties. If we use them for evil, then it is according to our will. Thus men use those offices differently. They are therefore at fault; God is free from all blame." And Chrysostom says (*PG* 60, 689C): "Do not object to me that many misuse their power, but look at the good order of things, and recognize the great wisdom of him who has ordered everything from the beginning." The peace between church and state is complete when Diodorus (Staab, p. 107) expounds from Rom. 13:1 the political theology that the peace of the Roman empire prepared for the coming of the savior: "Since God now put an end to the continuous wars and granted the union of nations and peoples by the message of peaceful life, the apostle acknowledged the plan of God over the kingdom and commanded subjection to the governing authorities. If God has established them, it is godless to disobey them and also for the present life a dangerous madness." Chrysostom says finally (*PG* 60, 698E), "If the apostle gave this commandment then, when the government was still pagan, how much more valid must it be now for the faithful."

Even though the fathers still speak of the possibility that an evil and unjust national power can also produce welfare, their words make it clear that the earlier stress of persecutions is far behind them. These are theoretical discussions. That is the case with Ephraim (*Commentarii in epistolas Pauli ex Armenio translati*, Venice 1893, p. 40), who ponders how every government is established by God: "If one is evil and severe, it is given for punishment of the wicked and for testing of the good. If it is kind and true, it is given out of mercy." Theodoret's exegesis (*PG* 82, 193CD) is similar. And again Severian (Staab, p. 294) admits that it is a hard question, why the kingdoms instituted by God fight against the faithful. But one ought also to consider the good aspects of persecutions: "The virtues of the righteous shine and the corruption of the wicked becomes manifest. The pseudo-pious are exposed; the truly pious are preserved."

From the Latin fathers also we hear the same admonitions. Ambrose (*in Lc.* 4.29) says of Rom. 13:1–4: "The power is not evil, but he who makes evil use of the power. God's order should not displease, but the act of the office-holder." And Pseudo-Augustine (*Quest. Vet. et Novi Test.* 35) explains: "We honor even a pagan who is installed in authority, even if he is unworthy and order is preserved thanks to the devil."

For Origen the clause from Rom. 13:3, "You will receive his approval," is especially hard to bear. His question and solution are expounded likewise by Augustine, looking back on difficult times, in his exposition of Romans (*Propos.* 73, *PL* 35, 2084): "Do what is good, and you will receive his approval—that may disturb many, when they think how Christians have often had to suffer persecution from the authorities. Have they therefore not done good, since they are not only not praised by the authorities, but persecuted and killed? Nevertheless, whether they praise your good deed or persecute you, you shall have praise from them [i.e., on account of them]. Either you will win praise in obedience toward God, or you shall earn the crown through their persecution. Thus they are for you servants of the good, even if for themselves they are servants of evil." And Pelagius (Souter, p. 102) says of Rom. 13:3f.: "The wicked must fear the authorities; the good need fear nothing. If he is killed unjustly, he rejoices. So take my advice, and you will never have to fear. Do what is good, and you will receive his approval." Such an explanation seems to us lightly said; it is far removed from the possibility of putting the statement to serious test.

The state, according to Rom. 13:4, bears the sword. To the question of Comes Studianus Ambrose replies (*Ep.* 25, 1) that while gentleness is perhaps the first commandment for a Christian, yet the state and its officer have also the right of the sword according to Rom. 13:4. And this sword, says his exposition immediately thereafter, is also given to the emperor for the execution of heretics. Pacian appeals to this (*Ep.* 2, 5, *PL* 13, 1061B) against the Novatianists. Augustine affirms it (*C. ep. Parmen.* 1, 10, 16) against the Donatists, as Optatus of Mileve (7, 6) uses Rom. 13:4 to defend Macarius, who had invoked capital punishment against the Donatists. The persecuted Donatists tried to evade this exposition by explaining that the sword was the spiritual power, and meant the right of the church to excommunicate. Augustine (*C. ep. Parmen.* 1, 10, 16) says that certain quite foolish Donatists were of this opinion.

Thus we can also understand Pelagius' interpretation, which at first seems astonishing. He spent the period of the Donatist turmoil temporarily in Africa. His commentary on Romans (Souter, p. 101) mentions the application of Rom. 13:1ff. to the political state in the first place, but under the stress of the times he permits himself to accept a spiritualist application to the church as equally possible. His entire exposition is double throughout. In Rom. 13:1 Paul either turns "against those who think they must use the Christian freedom in such a way, that they show respect to no one and pay no tax. They would suffer punishment certainly more on account of their arrogance than for God's sake. Or the governing authorities could also be taken to mean the ecclesiastical offices." On Rom. 13:4 Pelagius names as the first interpretation that which refers to the right of the state to punish, but as the second: "The priests bear the spiritual sword, with which Peter slew Ananias and Paul slew the magician." And on Rom. 13:5 Pelagius again gives one interpretation pointing to the state but also this: "Not only in order not to anger the priests, but also because honor is due them, as you know, from the righteous." And so further on Rom. 13:7: "The stipends for the priests could also be meant here, which were instituted for them by God," and "Alms too can be designated as 'owed,' for the scripture says: Incline your ear to the poor, and give them what you owe. It is our duty, which we pay to the passers-by, or which we as passers-by pay to those who sit by the road and make their living from it." When pressed, Pelagius takes up again an argument similar to one we read from Origen: "For this reason pay tribute to the kings, for by possessing the world you have willed to be subject." In this way, of course, Paul is entirely disowned, and the church becomes a state within the state.

Nevertheless, in other, more valid ways the indissoluble opposition between the kingdom of the world and the kingdom of God remains open in the exposition of Rom. 13:1–7. Even the later exegesis wants always to preserve the right and freedom of man over against the state. Isidore of Pelusium (*Epist.* 2, 216) already finds in Rom. 13:1ff. that limitation of duty that in later centuries would so often be taught. The duty of obedience exists only toward the God-instituted government. "But if a wicked person has forced his way contrary to law into rulership, then we do not say that he is instituted by God, but God only bears with him in order eventually to requite him, as he did Pharaoh for his malice and Nebuchadnezzar for his coarseness." And Chrysostom (*PG* 60, 686C) achieves his position by distinguishing clearly between person and office of the ruler and separating them. Not every governing person, he says, is instituted by God. Only the institution of the government as such is ordained by God. This distinction recurs in the Romans commentaries of Theodoret (*PG* 62, 193C) and Gennadius (Staab, p. 407), which are dependent upon Chrysostom.

Alternatively, it is declared that the commanded subjection relates only to permitted or secular things, but not when it is a question of a divine commandment. Thus already Polycarp, in the sore straits of his situation, quoted Rom. 13:1 in his defense, but added an essential reservation (*Mart. Polyc.* 10.2): "We have been taught to render honor, as is proper, to the princes and authorities appointed by God, if it does not hurt us." Also another witness, the bishop Mar Simon, had based his loyalty towards the state on Rom. 13:1f. Yet when the judge deduced from there that, if every authority is from God, then the bishop ought to obey the king and to accept the tax that the king demanded, the martyr found his defense in Rom. 13:7: "Our scriptures teach us obedience, but show us also the measure of obedience. For they teach: Pay all of them their dues, taxes to whom taxes are due. But it does not say that we should pay double taxes. The command of the king must correspond to the will of God" (O. Braun, *Akten persischer Martyrer*, pp. 11, 25).

The other fathers say similar things in their exposition. Thus Tertullian (*Scorpiace* 14): "He commands you therefore to be subject to the authorities, not in order to give you an excuse to avoid martyrdom, but to encourage you to live a good life." Another time Tertullian (*De idolis* 15, where the commandment of the apostle refers to Rom. 13:1–7) limits the duty of obedience to state power "by the limits of order, that we may remain free from idolatry."

As a teacher of the "church of martyrs," Hippolytus also has to comment (*Daniel* 3, 23; Bonwetsch, pp. 164f.): "If the authorities compel the faithful to do something contrary to faith, then it is sweeter to die than to obey their command. For when the apostle commands us to be subject to all who exercise authority, he does not speak in favor of our denying our faith and God's commandments, but only that we by fearing authority should do nothing wrong, lest we be punished by them as evildoers." Basilius (*Moralia, PG* 31, 860B) quotes Rom. 13:1f. under the limiting superscript, "That one must be subject to the governing authority, insofar as no commandment of God stands in the way." The same expositions and admonitions recur in the commentaries on Romans of Acacius (Staab, p. 56), Theodore of Mopsuestia (Staab, p. 162), Theodoret (*PG* 82, 194B), and Severian (Staab, p. 224).

Similarly among the Latin fathers Augustine says (*Propos.* 72, *PL* 35, 2083): "The body is subject to the secular government, but not the soul. For by the soul we believe God and that we are called into his kingdom.

With it we are therefore not subject to any man who wants to destroy in us that which God in his kindness has given us for eternal life." The interpolator of Pelagius (Souter, p. 24) remarks, "that one must obey the government in what is right, but not in what is opposed to religion."

The fathers preserve the right of the subjects and limit the power of the rulers further when they hear Rom. 13:3f. as a warning to those in power to exercise their office according to justice and righteousness, and to know that in case of misuse they are threatened with punishment. Thus says Origen (Rufinus; 7, 328 Lommatzsch; cf. *PG* 14, 1227A) on Rom. 13:3f.: "The righteous judgment of God will befall those who use the power committed to them in godlessness and not according to the laws of God." Similarly Irenaeus is certain (*Adv. haer.* 5, 24, 2 and 3), that while the ruling authority executes God's judgment against the wicked, it will even so experience the righteous judgment of God for godlessness and unrighteousness. Basilius (*Moralia*, *PG* 31, 860B) quotes Rom. 13:3f. under the superscript: "That the rulers are responsible to the ordinances of God." Theodore of Mopsuestia (Staab, p. 162) believes that Paul gives here the purpose of the institution of state power; Gennadius (Staab, p. 408) thinks that Paul "at the same time declared what kind of existence must be theirs who are in power."

Origen had to divide Rom. 13.7: the tax belongs to the emperor, but the honor to God. Gregory of Nazianzus adopts this division (*Oratio* 34, 7), for he says, obviously in a reminiscence of Rom. 13.7, that the Christians give to Caesar and to God what belongs to both, "to the one tax, to the other reverence." While others do not make the separation so univocally, the fathers are often inclined to make some kind of break in this verse. Polycarp (*Mart. Polyc.* 10, 2) does attribute honor with Rom. 13.7 to the authorities, but only insofar as rendering it "does not hurt us." Theophilus (*Ad Autolycum* 1, 11), however, uses Rom. 13:1ff. not only to prove the Christians' willing obedience, but also to show that the emperor is installed by God and therefore may not demand divine honors. Tertullian says (*Scorpiace* 14) that Paul "tells how you must be subject to the authorities, by commanding you to pay taxes to whom taxes are due and revenue to whom revenue is due, i.e., to Caesar what is Caesar's and to God what is God's. But man belongs to God alone. Peter also has spoken thus (1 Pet. 2:17), that one must honor the king, yet that he is to be honored as king, if he keeps to his business and stays away from the demand of divine honors." Thus while Tertullian grants taxes to the rulers without further ado, he grants honor only with a reservation which Paul does not expressly state, but which Tertullian attributes to him. Pelagius (Souter, p. 103) brings to his interpretation of Rom. 13:7 an understanding conditioned by his own rejection of state power. He raises against the state the question, "Is it not written that no one but God is to be feared? Indeed! Therefore Paul says, So act that you need fear no one. For the fear of God expels the fear of man. So long as you still have fear (of man), it is necessary that you fear." Rom. 13:7 serves as a provisional commandment and for the imperfect. We are not surprised, of course, that the later fathers, in the time of peace with the state—not to speak of the alliance of caesar and church— attribute the whole of Rom. 13:7 to the rulers without hesitation (so Ambrosiaster 164AB; Chrysostom, *PG* 60, 689D; Theodoret *PG* 82, 196C; Gennadius, Staab, p. 409).

Up to this point, the history of interpretation of Rom. 13:1–7 has showed that the church understood how the gospel revealed the limits and the questionableness of the state. But it also shows that the church lived from the beginning under the temptation to separate itself from the state and then perhaps to make itself into a state. Gennadius (Staab, p. 407) on one occasion explains this possibility with strict accuracy from the "world-alienation" of Christianity: "Those who are filled with the power of the spirit and the spiritual gifts deem everything else to be nothing, whether present, wealth, honor, or state. The form of things seems to them to be passing away. And the letter to Romans itself commanded them to live no more in the flesh, but in the spirit. Therefore now this other admonition of Romans (was necessary)."

Thus from the beginning the fathers point to the danger that poorly informed Christians could, by a false conception of the gospel, become disturbers and opponents of the governmental order. Origen already believed that Paul had foreseen the possibility that Christians would not submit to the earthly authorities, would not pay taxes, would not show respect, and thus could cause a persecution in which they would be in the wrong, so that not the faith, but the rejection of authority would be persecuted. Paul's words, then, are understood as directed against that possibility. Apollinarius (Staab, p. 78) assumes that the revolt of Judas the Galilean, mentioned in Acts, and the terrors accompanying that rebellion were the immediate occasion for Paul's admonition, which wanted to "exclude an imitation of that, as if many wanted to regard it as an act of piety towards God to refuse obedience to the government." Jerome also believes (*in Titum* 3, 1) that Paul was countering the false teaching of Judas the Galilean, who declared that God alone could be called lord. Chrysostom (*PG* 60, 687C) considers that this admonition was important to Paul, as in other letters, in order to show that Christ did not give his laws for the overthrow of governmental order, but for its improvement. Sufficient for the Christians are the enmities which they necessarily encounter because of the truth, without inviting unnecessary dangers.

The fathers warn against the misunderstanding of Christian freedom. Chrysostom (*PG* 60, 687B and 689E) twice mentions, as a possible objection by Christians to the duty of obedience, a speech like this: You humiliate us when you make us, who will someday enjoy the glory of heaven, subject to the government. But Chrysostom answers, You obey not men but God. Another possible remonstrance is, You are destined for great things—so say to yourself that that time has not yet come for you. You are still a stranger and a pilgrim. Chrysostom probably did not invent this response, for Augustine's extensive treatment of Rom. 13:1 (*Propos.* 72, *PL* 35, 2083) is similar: "Let no one pridefully believe, because he has been called in his heart to freedom and has become a Christian, that in the course of this life he need not preserve order. We are indeed called to that kingdom where there is no more authority of this kind. Yet while we are on this path, we must, until we reach that aeon where all this rule and power ceases, comport our life as the order of human affairs demands."

That ecclesiastical temptation becomes evident, however, when a Gregory of Nazianzus regards himself, a church official, as superior to the secular government. In his address to the residents of Nazianzus and to the governor, he admonishes his fellow citizens (*Oratio* 17, 6–9), using Rom.

13:5, to obey the government. Then, however, he limits the power of the secular government and appeals to "Christian freedom" to say to the governor, "We also are rulers; indeed we are such in a higher and more perfect way. Or should perhaps the spirit yield to the flesh and the heavenly to the earthly?" Even the governor must obey the bishop as "a lamb of his flock." He who holds ruling power is God's image. But also the subjects are God's image. True, the ruler has received the sword from Christ—but only to threaten with it, not to draw it! Chrysostom (*PG* 60, 686B) therefore has to say finally that Paul "indicates that this commandment is valid for all, even for priests and monks, not merely for people of the world. In order to emphasize this directive, he places it at the head: Every soul must be subject to the government, whether you are an apostle or an evangelist or a prophet or whatever. For this subjection does no harm to piety." Theodoret (*PG* 82, 193B) repeats that: "Whether one is a priest or a bishop or has taken the monastic vow, he is to obey those who are entrusted with authority." The seriousness of these admonitions must have had good cause. In fact we have heard how the church, both catholic and heretical, sought to evade subjection to the secular power.

The history of interpretation of Rom. 13:1–7 by the fathers is conditioned by the general political history of their times. While it was not easy for the "church of the martyrs" to hear and assimilate the whole word of the apostle, when the church had become the imperial church, it made eager use of it in order to glorify and exalt the state. In the course of this development every possible relationship implied by the duality of church and state is explored and tested in the commentaries. In the exposition one hears often the voice of the church that, conscious of its own higher freedom from the state that oppresses it, opposes the state, whether this be the great church or the small, spiritualist sects. But at other times it is the voice of the church which seems quite unaware of the serious danger that it will become the slave of the all-powerful state. And again it speaks sometimes as the church that is tempted by the desire to be itself a state within the state and lord over the state.

WILFRID PARSONS, S.J.

[Romans 13 and Augustine's Political Thought] (1941)†

* * *

When we approach St. Augustine * * * (354–430 A.D.), we at once enter into a wider and more comprehensive field. Political thought is no longer merely an exegesis of Romans 13. That passage, indeed, still exercises a profound influence, as we shall see, but greater and more revolutionary considerations enter into the field. For the first time, in St. Augustine we

---

† From "The Influence of Romans XIII on Christian Political Thought, II. Augustine to Hincmar," *Theological Studies* 2 (1941), 325–46; the excerpt is from pp. 326–33. All rights reserved. Reprinted by permission. Joseph Wilfrid Parsons, S.J. (1887–1958), taught at the Woodstock School of Theology (professor of Fundamental Theology), at Georgetown University (professor of Political Science and dean of the Graduate School), and the Catholic University of America (professor of Political Philosophy). He was editor-in-chief of the Jesuit periodical *America* from 1925 until 1936, and founded the quarterly *Thought*.

see the Church beginning to entertain two definite convictions concerning this world: 1) that the Church was destined to remain in this world for a long time; and 2) that the Church has a temporal mission as well as a spiritual one, a clear calling to be the creator of a new secular civilization. These two convictions seem to me to be the key to all of St. Augustine's political thought.

Now, naturally, in a paper devoted to only the one aspect of political thought, the continuing influence of St. Paul on it, it cannot be expected to find a detailed and comprehensive outline of the Augustinian political synthesis. It will be necessary, however, to recall certain high points in it.

St. Augustine's thought about the temporal world revolves around four master ideas: Peace, Justice, Order, Law. Without entering into the rather artificial controversy about which of these master ideas is the chief one, we may say that by the mere mention of them our minds are lifted on to a vast plane of contemplation which embraces a new civilization. Thus we will find that St. Augustine at the same time goes both before and after St. Paul's ideas, giving us both a foundation and an application of them.

St. Augustine, consciously or unconsciously, was led, on the occasion of the menace to established order contained in Alaric's sack of Rome in A.D. 410, to bend his powerful mind to the problem of the future fate of mankind if the Roman Empire fell. It is, I think, quite commonly agreed that his solution was the fusion of the natural and the supernatural into one synthesis. To him philosophy and theology were not two separate sciences, but one law of God. Fear of the frightful abyss of Manicheism, out of which he providentially escaped, would naturally lead him to exalt the supernatural, but it did not, as some have always thought, bring him to absorb the natural in the supernatural. Dualism remained for his, as for all Christian thought, the true expression of reality, though many forms of semi-Christian monism have claimed him as their inspirer if not their author.

There are two laws, he teaches, the temporal and the eternal. Both have their origin in God. The greater precepts of justice, which are the same as charity in its largest sense, were given by Christ but the lesser precepts also came from God on Sinai.[1] This Divine law dictates the natural order, both in man and in society and bids it be preserved, forbids it to be disturbed.[2] There are, then, two laws, the eternal and the temporal, and the temporal is derived from the eternal, bringing order among men, through justice.[3] Man, therefore, finds for the changeable fortunes of human life an unchangeable rule of action in this eternal law, and his laws, though varied according to circumstances, will always conform to it.[4]

All of this seems fairly commonplace to us at this late date in the history of the world, but if we project ourselves into his age we can see what a tremendous force he is injecting into society. Followed out, his theory of law, accepted by the Church, will remake the world and will, in fact, create what we call Christendom, a politico-religious order designed to unite mankind, by bending the supernatural to the uses of the temporal state.

It was during thirteen years of his life (413–426) that he worked at that

---

1. *On the Lord's Sermon on the Mount,* cap. I. PL 34, 1231.
2. *Contra Faustum,* XXII, 17. PL 42, 418.
3. Cf. that remarkable passage in the dialogue *De Libero Arbitrio,* I, 6, PL 32, 1129, in which changes of government are justified.
4. *De Vera Religione,* cap. XXXI. PL 34, 148.

general depository of his thought which we call the *City of God*, a sort of scrap book into which he poured his reflections and conclusions about life. All of these reflections concern the Two Cities, the City of God, and the Earthly City, not two separate societies—Church and State—as is sometimes falsely imagined, but two spirits of mind, intermingling with each other in the secular world, and each in its way determining the actions of the State and its citizens, one triumphing for the time, but the other destined to triumph at the end. When the City of God is paramount, "the princes and the subjects serve one another in love, the latter obeying, while the former take thought for all."[5] At the same time, the temporal goods that are sought by the Earthly City are not evil things. On the contrary, "they are good things, and without doubt gifts of God." Men go wrong only when, in their search for temporal felicity, "they so inordinately covet these present goods that they believe them to be the only desirable things, or love them better than those things which are believed to be better."[6]

When St. Augustine approaches the question of the origin of political authority, we find him in full agreement with the Christian thought that preceded him. All men are by nature created equal. It was sin that introduced into the world the necessity of subjecting one man to another.

> He (God) did not intend that His rational creature, who was made in His image, should have dominion over anything but the irrational creation—not man over man, but man over beasts. Hence the just men in primitive times were made shepherds of cattle rather than kings of men, God intending thus to teach us what the relative position of the creature is, and what the desert of sin. . . . By nature, as God first created us, no one is the slave either of man or of sin.[7]

This fundamental assumption will color all that St. Augustine has to say about the teaching of St. Paul on the source and aim of political power. His own exegesis is as follows.[8]

First of all, he brushes aside all those false conclusions from the passage, which, as we have seen, introduced a dangerous anarchism into Christian life and thought. Christian liberty does not exempt man from obedience to his temporal rulers: "Man must not imagine that in the pilgrimage of this life, he may keep his own special order and not be subject to the higher powers to which the temporary administration of temporal affairs has been entrusted."

But then he promptly delves deeper than mere externals, and in the very nature of man, as he is, he finds the real reason why this is so: "We are made of body and soul and as long as we are in this temporal life we must use temporal things for the support of this life. Hence for that part which pertains to this life, we must be subject to the powers; that is, to the men who administer human affairs with some position (*honore*)."

In these words St. Augustine has furnished to the Middle Ages the foundation of the whole grandiose conception of human unity under the Kingdom and the Priesthood, which, as we shall see, was the culmination of Christian political thought. To man, a composite being of body and soul, yet one being, corresponds a twofold government, the Church ruling the

---

5. *De Civitate Dei*, XIX, 28. PL 41, 436.
6. *Ibid.*, XV, 4. PL 41, 440.
7. *Ibid.*, XIX, 15. PL 41, 643. Cf. also *Quaestiones in Genesim*, I, 153. PL 34, 590.
8. *Expositio Quarundam Propositionum ex Epistola ad Romanos*, LXII–LXIV, PL 35, 2083–4.

affairs of the soul and the State ruling the affairs of the body. Christendom, a social being, and a moral person, is but a larger reflection of the physical human person.

Moreover, in these same words St. Augustine has furnished St. Thomas and the Scholastics, when they will have emancipated themselves from the assumption that man is not by nature a political animal, with the reason why that assumption does not hold. The necessity for governments for the affairs of both body and soul does not proceed from the opposition of body and soul which befell man as result of the Fall, as St. Augustine assumed, but dates from creation itself. Man's nature itself demands them, not merely man's fallen nature. It is obvious, however, that St. Augustine, influenced by his predecessors, did not see these two conclusions.

It is not, however, necessary for St. Augustine to have recourse, as did his predecessors, to the words of St. Peter before the Sanhedrin ("We must obey God rather than man.")[9] in order to exempt man from obedience to unjust and sinful commands. He goes on: "But from that part by which we believe in God and are called to His Kingdom, we must not be subject to any man who wishes to overturn in us that which God gave us for eternal life." Faith and morals are not subject to secular government, as the soul is not subject to the body.[1]

> The man who thinks that he must also be subject in such a way as to think that his faith is in the power of him who is exalted to a position of honor in temporal administrations, he falls into a greater error [than to think that he may not pay taxes, etc.] For that proportion is to be observed which the Lord Himself prescribed when He said that we must render to Caesar the things that are Caesar's and to God the things that are God's. For although we are called to that kingdom where there will be an end to all principality and power, let us endure our condition in the due proportion of human affairs, doing nothing with mental reservation, and by this very fact not obeying men so much as God who commands this.

In this last phrase, we are given, as we also saw in St. John Chrysostom, the fundamental reason for civil obedience. It is not subjection of man to man, which would be unworthy of equals, but of man to God. Political allegiance is raised to the level of a Divine service, and that has always remained the only rational justification of civil authority.

Moreover, St. Augustine also implies, in this passage on Romans 13, another consideration which further confirms the rationality of obedience to temporal rulers, and their subjection, in turn, to the eternal law. He makes a distinction between the permanent good and the temporal character of the goods which serve the body in this life. "These things pass away, and hence that subjection is to be placed not in any kind of permanent goods, but in the necessaries of this life." On the other hand, our

---

9. Acts 5:29.
1. Cf. also *Contra Faustum*, XXII, 17 (*PL* 42, 418): "To no one is there any doubt that in the natural order the soul is to come before the body. But in the soul of man is reason, which is not in the beast. Hence, just as the soul should come before the body, so by the law of nature, the reason of the soul itself should come before its other parts which the beast has likewise. And in the reason, which is partly contemplative, partly active, without doubt the contemplative excels. For in this latter is the image of God by which we are transformed through faith to sight. Hence the rational action must obey the rational contemplation."

subjection as to temporary goods is all-inclusive: "It is necessary that we be subject by reason of this life, not resisting when they attempt to deprive us of any of these things over which they have been given power." Here again the lesson was not to be lost on the Middle Ages: the power of the king, while not his own in its origin, is absolute with regard to the things over which he is placed, subject, of course, to the moral law.

In another passage which was destined to be often quoted in the Middle Ages, St. Augustine adds a third consideration by which human rule is fixed in its proper place in a scheme designed by divine Providence. He has told his hearers that they must not obey evil commands:

> Are we puffing you up with pride or telling you to be despisers of well-ordered authority? We do not say this . . . The Apostle himself tells us: 'Let every soul be subject to the higher powers; for there is no power but from God.' But what if he commands what you ought not to do? Here certainly despise the power, fearing the power. Note the hierarchy of human affairs. If the prefect commands, is it not to be done? But if he commands against the will of the proconsul, you do not despise the power, but you choose to obey the higher. Again, if the proconsul commands one thing, and the Emperor another, can you doubt that the proconsul must be despised and the Emperor obeyed? Therefore if the Emperor [commands] one thing and God another, what is your judgment? 'Pay your tribute: do your obeisance to me.' 'Right; but not before an idol. He forbids it in the temple.' 'Who forbids?' 'The higher authority. Pardon me; you threaten prison, He threatens Hell.'[2]

This "hierarchy of human affairs" is the keynote to all that follows in Christian history. In an organic society, when an evil command is resisted, there is really no disobedience; there is merely obedience to the higher powers, as St. Paul enjoined. There is a unity in all being, from the bottom to the top, and at the top is God, above the emperor.

This also solves the old problem of the bad king.

> By bad laws the good are tried and by good laws the evil are corrected. The perverse King Nabuchodonosor passed a savage law that idols were to be adored; the same king, corrected, passed a severe law forbidding the true God to be blasphemed.[3] For in this, kings, as is divinely ordained to them, serve God inasmuch as they are kings if in their kingdom they command what is good, forbid what is bad, not only in what pertains to human society, but also in what pertains to Divine religion."[4]

Even the king, therefore, has the duty to forward the interests of the true religion, for he is also a minister of God. How seriously this was also taken in the Middle Ages, the history of Charlemagne and his successors testifies. St. Augustine himself may not have been aware how greatly he was filling out the whole pattern of the centuries that were to follow, for in his time there must have seemed very little hope of his idealistic principles being carried out, but his great genius, joined to the inspiration of

2. *Sermo LXII*, 8 PL 38, 420.
3. Daniel 3:5–6, 96 [LXX = Dan. 3:5–6, 29 HB].
4. *Contra Cresconium*, III, 51. PL 43, 527.

divine providence, seems to have discerned the outlines of the whole, or nearly the whole, of the Christian commonwealth.

In this plan, the personal character of the actual ruler has very little importance. It is the rule of God that must be discerned in the power even of a tyrant.

> He who gave power to Marius gave it also to Caius Caesar; He who gave it to Augustus, gave it also to Nero; He also who gave it to the most benignant Emperors, the Vespasians, father and son, gave it also to the cruel Domitian. And finally, to avoid having to go over them all, He who gave it to Christian Constantine, gave it also to Apostate Julian, whose gifted mind was deceived by a sacrilegious and detestable curiosity, stimulated by the love of power.[5]

The fullest Christian citizenship, then, in the spirit of St. Paul, consists of obedience to the utmost to the civil authority, out of obedience to God. This is summed up in the following:

> When by Christ's command, you serve a man, you do not serve the man, but Him who commanded you . . . What I have said of master and slave, understand also to be true of powers and kings, of all the exalted stations of the world. Sometimes they are good powers and fear God; sometimes they do not fear God. Julian was an infidel Emperor, an apostate, a wicked man, an idolator; yet Christian soldiers served him, an infidel Emperor. When they came to the accusers of Christ, they acknowledged only Him who was in heaven. If he called upon them at any time to worship idols, to offer incense, they preferred God to Him. But whenever he commanded them to fall into line, to march against this or that nation, they obeyed. They distinguished their eternal from their temporal master. And yet they were, for the sake of their eternal Master, subject to their temporal master.[6]

Now I have not, as I have said, made an attempt to give the whole of St. Augustine's political philosophy in all its details. My purpose was only to trace out the development which he contributed to the crucial passages in St. Paul to the Romans. We can, perhaps, now see both how his doctrine is rooted in that of his predecessors, and how he has developed it to a completely practical pattern for the making of a new civilization under the temporal mission of the Church.

*   *   *

---

5. *De Civitate Dei*, V, 21. *PL* 41, 168. Cf. also *De Natura Boni*, XXXII (*PL* 42, 561) where he tells us that "it is not unjust, that through the wicked (ruler) receiving the power to hurt, the patience of the just be tried, and the iniquity of the wicked be punished." In this passage he had just previously quoted Romans 13, with other similar texts from the OT.
6. *In Psalmum* 124, 7, *PL* 37, 1653. Other passages in which Romans 13 is cited on civil obedience are *Sermo* XIII, 6 (*PL* 38, 109–110); *Sermo* CCCII, 12–44 (*PL* 38, 1390); *Contra Faustum Manichaeum*, XXII, 75 (*PL* 42, 448).

MARTIN LUTHER

[Submission and Resistance] (1523)†

* * *

Formerly I addressed a booklet to the German nobility, setting forth their Christian office and functions. But how they have carried out my suggestions is very plain to see. Hence I must change my tactics and write them, this time, what they should omit and not do. I fear this writing will have just as little effect on them as the former one had—they will by all means remain princes and by no means become Christians. For God Almighty has made our rulers mad. They actually think they have the power to do and command their subjects to do, whatever they please. And the subjects are led astray and believe they are bound to obey them in everything. It has gone so far that the rulers have ordered the people to put away books, and to believe and keep what they prescribe. In this way they presumptuously set themselves in God's place, lord it over men's conscience and faith, and put the Holy Spirit to school according to their mad brains. They let it be known, at the same time, that they are not to be contradicted, but called gracious lords into the bargain.

* * *

I. We must firmly establish secular law and the sword, that no one may doubt that it is in the world by God's will and ordinance. The passages which establish this are the following: Romans 13, "Let every soul be subject to power and authority, for there is no power but from God. The power that is everywhere is ordained of God. He then who resists the power resists God's ordinance. But he who resists God's ordinance shall bring himself under condemnation." Likewise, I Peter 2, "Be subject to every kind of human ordinance, whether to the king as supreme, or to the governors, as to those sent of Him for the punishing of the evil and for the reward of the good."

* * *

III. We must divide all the children of Adam into two classes; the first belong to the kingdom of God, the second to the kingdom of the world. Those belonging to the kingdom of God are all true believers in Christ and are subject to Christ. For Christ is the King and Lord in the kingdom of God, as the second Psalm and all the Scriptures say. For this reason He came into the world, that He might begin God's kingdom and establish it in the world. Therefore He says before Pilate, "My kingdom is not of the world, but whoever is of the truth hears My voice";[1] and continually in the Gospel He refers to the kingdom of God and says, "Amend your ways, the kingdom of God is at hand."[2] Likewise, "Seek first the kingdom of God and

† From "Secular Authority: To What Extent It Should Be Obeyed," tr. by J. J. Schindel in *Works of Martin Luther* (Philadelphia: Muhlenberg, 1930), Vol. 3, 228–73. Reprinted by permission of Augsburg Fortress Press. We have not tried to represent Luther's total argument in the excerpts, but only those elements directly connected with his interpretation of Paul.
1. John 18:36 f.
2. Matt. 3:2.

His righteousness."[3] He also calls the Gospel, a Gospel of the kingdom, for the reason that it teaches, governs, and contains God's kingdom.

Now observe, these people need no secular sword or law. And if all the world were composed of real Christians, that is, true believers, no prince, king, lord, sword, or law would be needed. For what were the use of them, since Christians have in their hearts the Holy Spirit, who instructs them and causes them to wrong no one, to love every one, willingly and cheerfully to suffer injustice and even death from every one. Where every wrong is suffered and every right is done, no quarrel, strife, trial, judge, penalty, law or sword is needed. Therefore, it is not possible for the secular sword and law to find any work to do among Christians, since of themselves they do much more than its laws and doctrines can demand. Just as Paul says in I Timothy 1, "The law is not given for the righteous, but for the unrighteous."[4]

* * *

You ask, Why then did God give to all men so many commandments, and why did Christ teach in the Gospel so many things to be done? Concerning this I have written much in the Postil[5] and elsewhere. To put it as briefly as possible here, Paul says that the law is given for the sake of the unrighteous,[6] that is, that those who are not Christians may through the law be externally restrained from evil deeds, as we shall hear later. Since, however, no one is by nature Christian or pious, but every one sinful and evil, God places the restraints of the law upon them all, so that they may not dare give rein to their desires and commit outward, wicked deeds. In addition, St. Paul gives the law another function in Romans 7 and Galatians 3. It is to teach men to recognize sin, that they may be made humble unto grace and unto faith in Christ. Christ also does this here, when He teaches in Matthew, that we should not resist evil,[7] and thereby glorifies the law and teaches how a real Christian ought to be and must be disposed, as we shall hear further on.

IV. All who are not Christians belong to the kingdom of the world and are under the law. Since few believe and still fewer live a Christian life, do not resist the evil, and themselves do no evil, God has provided for non-Christians a different government outside the Christian estate and God's kingdom, and has subjected them to the sword, so that, even though they would do so, they cannot practice their wickedness, and that, if they do, they may not do it without fear nor in peace and prosperity. Even so a wild, savage beast is fastened with chains and bands, so that it cannot bite and tear as is its wont, although it gladly would do so; whereas a tame and gentle beast does not require this, but without any chains and bands is nevertheless harmless. If it were not so, seeing that the whole world is evil and that among thousands there is scarcely one true Christian, men would devour one another, and no one could preserve wife and child, support himself and serve God; and thus the world would be reduced to chaos. For this reason God has ordained the two governments; the spiritual, which

3. Matt. 6:33.
4. 1 Tim. 1:19.
5. A collection of sermons on the Scripture lessons for the Church Year. Luther's Advent Postil was published in Latin in 1521 and in German in 1522.
6. 1 Tim. 1:9.
7. Matt. 5:39.

by the Holy Spirit under Christ makes Christians and pious people, and the secular, which restrains the unchristian and wicked so that they must needs keep the peace outwardly, even against their will. So Paul interprets the secular sword, Romans 13, and says it is not a terror to good works, but to the evil.[8] And Peter says it is for the punishment of evil doers.[9]

If any one attempted to rule the world by the Gospel, and put aside all secular law and the secular sword, on the plea that all are baptised and Christian, and that according to the Gospel, there is to be among them neither law nor sword, nor necessity for either, pray, what would happen? He would loose the bands and chains of the wild and savage beasts, and let them tear and mangle every one, and at the same time say they were quite tame and gentle creatures; but I would have the proof in my wounds. Just so would the wicked under the name of Christian abuse this freedom of the Gospel, carry on their knavery, and say that they were Christians subject neither to law nor sword, as some are already raving and ranting.

*   *   *

V. But perhaps you will say, Since Christians do not need the secular sword and the law, why does Paul say to all Christians, in Romans 13, "Let all souls be subject to power and authority"?[1] And St. Peter says, "Be subject to every human ordinance,"[2] etc., as quoted above. I answer, as I have said, that Christians, among themselves and by and for themselves, need no law or sword, since it is neither necessary nor profitable for them. Since, however, a true Christian lives and labors on earth not for himself, but for his neighbor, therefore the whole spirit of his life impels him to do even that which he need not do, but which is profitable and necessary for his neighbor. Because the sword is a very great benefit and necessary to the whole world, to preserve peace, to punish sin and to prevent evil, he submits most willingly to the rule of the sword, pays tax, honors those in authority, serves, helps, and does all he can to further the government, that it may be sustained and held in honor and fear. Although he needs none of these things for himself and it is not necessary for him to do them, yet he considers what is for the good and profit of others, as Paul teaches in Ephesians 5.

He serves the State as he performs all other works of love, which he himself does not need. He visits the sick, not that he may be made well; feeds no one because he himself needs food: so he also serves the State not because he needs it, but because others need it—that they may be protected and that the wicked may not become worse. He loses nothing by this, and such service in no way harms him, and yet it is of great profit to the world. If he did not do it, he would be acting not as a Christian but contrary even to love, and would also be setting a bad example to others, who like him would not submit to authority, though they were no Christians. In this way the Gospel would be brought into disrepute, as though it taught rebellion and made self-willed people, unwilling to benefit or serve any one, when in reality it makes a Christian the servant of every

8. Rom. 13:3.
9. 1 Pet. 2:14.
1. Rom. 13:1.
2. 1 Pet. 2:13.

one. Thus in Matthew 17, Christ gave the tribute money that He might not offend them, although He did not need to do it.[3]

Thus you observe in the words of Christ quoted above from Matthew 5 that He indeed teaches that Christians among themselves should have no secular sword nor law. He does not, however, forbid one to serve and obey those who have the secular sword and the law; much rather, since you have no need of them and are not to have them, are you to serve those who have not progressed so far as you and still need them. Although you do not need to have your enemy punished, your weak neighbor does. You should help him, that he may have peace and that his enemy may be curbed; which is not possible unless power and authority are honored and feared. Christ does not say, "Thou shalt not serve the State or be subject to it," but "Thou shalt not resist evil." As though He said, "Take heed that you bear everything, so that you may not need the State to help and serve you and be of profit to you, but that you may on the other hand, help, serve, and be of profit and use to it. I would have you to be far too exalted and noble to have any need of it, but it should have need of you."

[VI]

*   *   *

In this way all the saints wielded the sword from the beginning of the world: Adam and his descendants; Abraham when he rescued Lot, his brother's son, and smote the four kings,[4] though he was a thoroughly evangelical man; Samuel, the holy prophet, slew King Agag,[5] and Elijah the prophets of Baal.[6] So did Moses, Joshua, the children of Israel, Samson, David, and all the kings and princes in the Old Testament. In the same way did Daniel and his associates, Ananias, Asarias and Misael, in Babylon; in the same manner did Joseph in Egypt, and so on.

Should any one advance the argument, that the Old Testament is abolished and avails no more, and that therefore such examples cannot be set before Christians, I answer, That is not correct. For St. Paul says in I Corinthians 10, "They did all eat the same spiritual meat as we, and did drink the same spiritual drink from the rock, which is Christ";[7] that is, they have had the same spirit and faith in Christ as we and were Christians as well as we are. Therefore, wherein they did right, all Christians do right, from the beginning of the world unto the end. For time and external circumstances matter not among Christians. Neither is it true that the Old Testament was abolished in such a way that it need not be kept, or that it would be wrong for any one to keep it in full, as St. Jerome and many more erred in thinking. It is indeed abolished in the sense that we are free to keep it or not to keep it, and it is no longer necessary to keep it on penalty of one's soul, as was formerly the case.

For Paul says in I Corinthians 7 and Galatians 6, that neither uncircumcision nor circumcision avails anything, but a new creature in Christ;[8]

---

3. Matt. 17:27.
4. Gen. 14:15.
5. 1 Sam. 15:33.
6. 1 Kings 18:40.
7. 1 Cor. 10:3–4.
8. 1 Cor. 7:19; Gal. 6:15.

that is, it is not sin to be uncircumcised, as the Jews thought, nor is it sin to be circumcised, as the heathen thought, but either is right and permissible for him who does not think he will be saved by so doing. This is true also of all other parts of the Old Testament; it is not wrong to omit them nor wrong to do them, but all is permissible and good, to do and to leave undone. Nay, if they were necessary or profitable to one's fellow-man for his salvation, it would be necessary to keep them all; for every one is under obligation to do what is for his neighbor's good, whether it be Old or New Testament, Jewish or heathen, as Paul teaches in I Corinthians 12, for love pervades all and transcends all, considers only what is for the profit of others, and does not ask whether it is old or new. Hence, the precedents for the use of the sword also are matters of freedom, and you may follow them or not, but where you see that your neighbor needs it, there love contrains you so that you must needs do what otherwise would be optional and unnecessary for you to do or to leave undone. Only do not suppose that you will grow pious or be saved thereby, as the Jews presumed to be saved by their works, but leave this to faith, which without works makes you a new creature.

*   *   *

Beyond these, we have the clear, definite statement of St. Paul in Romans 13, where he says, "The powers that be are ordained of God"; and again, "The power does not bear the sword in vain, but is the minister of God for thy good, an avenger unto him that doeth evil."[9] Be not so wicked, my friend, as to say, A Christian may not do that which is God's peculiar work, ordinance and creation. Else you must also say, A Christian must not eat, drink or be married, for these are also God's work and ordinance. If it is God's work and creation, it is good, and so good that every one can use it in a Christian and saving way, as Paul says in I Timothy 4, "Every creature of God is good, and nothing to be rejected by the believing and those who know the truth."[1] Among "every creature of God" you must reckon not simply food and drink, clothes and shoes, but also government, citizenship, protection and administration of justice.

In short, since St. Paul here says the power is God's servant, we must admit that it is to be exercised not only by the heathen, but by all men. What else does it mean when it is said it is God's servant except that the power is by its very nature such that one may serve God by it? Now, it should be quite unchristian to say that there is any service of God in which a Christian ought not and dare not take part, when such a service belongs to no one so much as to Christians. It would indeed be good and profitable if all princes were real and good Christians, for the sword and the government, as a special service of God, belong of right to Christians, more than to all other men on earth. Therefore you should cherish the sword or the government, even as the state of matrimony, or husbandry, or any other handiwork which God has instituted. As a man can serve God in the state of matrimony, in husbandry, or at a trade, for the benefit of his fellowman, and must serve Him if necessity demand; just so he can also serve God in the State and should serve Him there, if the necessities of his neighbor

9. Rom. 13:1, 4.
1. 1 Tim. 4:4.

demand it; for the State is God's servant and workman to punish the evil and protect the good. Still it may also be omitted if there is no need for it, just as men are free not to marry and not to farm if there should be no need of marrying and farming.

* * *

* * * Worldly government has laws which extend no farther than to life and property and what is external upon earth. For over the soul God can and will let no one rule but Himself. Therefore, where temporal power presumes to prescribe laws for the soul, it encroaches upon God's government and only misleads and destroys the souls. We desire to make this so clear that every one shall grasp it, and that our junkers, the princes and bishops, may see what fools they are when they seek to coerce the people with their laws and commandments into believing one thing or another.

When a man-made law is imposed upon the soul, in order to make it believe this or that, as that man prescribes, there is certainly no word of God for it. If there is no word of God for it, it is uncertain whether God will have it so, for we cannot be certain that what He does not command pleases Him. Nay, we are sure that it does not please Him, for He desires that our faith be grounded simply and entirely on His divine Word, as He says in Matthew 16, "On this rock will I build my church";[2] and in John 10, "My sheep hear my voice and know me; but the voice of strangers they hear not, but flee from them."[3] It follows from this that the secular power forces souls to eternal death with such an outrageous law, for it compels them to believe as right and certainly pleasing to God what is nevertheless uncertain, nay, what is certainly displeasing to Him, since there is no clear word of God for it. For whoever believes that to be right which is wrong or uncertain denies the truth, which is God Himself, and believes in lies and errors and counts that right which is wrong.

Hence it is the height of folly when they command that one shall believe the Church, the fathers, the councils, though there be no word of God for it. The devil's apostles command such things, not the Church; for the Church commands nothing unless it is sure it is God's Word, as St. Peter says, "If any man speak let him speak as the oracles of God."[4] It will be a very long time, however, before they prove that the statements of the councils are God's Word. Still more foolish is it when they assert that kings and princes and the mass of men believe thus and so. If you please, we are not baptised unto kings, princes, or even unto the mass of men, but unto Christ and unto God himself; neither are we called kings, princes or common folk, but Christians. No one shall and can command the soul, unless he can show it the way to heaven; but this no man can do, only God. Therefore in matters which concern the salvation of souls nothing but God's Word shall be taught and accepted.

* * *

You reply, But Paul said in Romans 13, "Every soul shall be subject to power and authority,"[5] and Peter says, "We should be subject to every

2. Matt. 16:18.
3. John 10:27; 10:5.
4. 1 Pet. 4:11.
5. Rom. 13:1.

ordinance of man."[6] I answer, That is just what I want! These sayings are in my favor. St. Paul speaks of authority and power. Now, you have just heard that no one but God can have authority over souls. Hence Paul cannot be speaking of any obedience except where there can be corresponding authority. From this it follows that he does not speak of faith, and does not say that secular authority should have the right to command faith, but he is speaking of external goods, and that these are to be set in order and controlled on earth. This his words also clearly indicate, when he prescribes the limits to both authority and obedience, and says, "Render to every one his dues, tribute to whom tribute is due, custom to whom custom; honor to whom honor; fear to whom fear."[7] You see, temporal obedience and power apply only externally to tribute, custom, honor and fear. Likewise when he says, "The power is not a terror to good, but to evil works,"[8] he again limits the power, so that it is to have the mastery not over faith or the Word of God, but over evil works.

* * *

Let me illustrate. In Meissen, Bavaria, in the Mark, and other places, the tyrants have issued an order that the New Testaments be delivered to the courts everywhere. In this case their subjects ought not deliver a page or a letter, at risk of their salvation. For whoever does so, delivers Christ into Herod's hands, since they act as murderers of Christ, like Herod. But if their houses are ordered searched and books or goods taken by force, they should suffer it to be done. Outrage is not to be resisted, but endured, yet they should not sanction it, nor serve or obey or follow by moving foot or finger. For such tyrants act as worldly princes should act,—"worldly" princes they are; but the world is God's enemy. Therefore they must also do what is opposed to God, and in accord with the world, that they may by no means lose all honor, but remain worldly princes. Hence do not wonder that they rage and mock at the Gospel; they must live up to their name and title.

* * *

Again you say, Temporal power does not force men to believe, but simply prevents them from being misled by false doctrine; otherwise how could heretics be prevented from preaching? I answer, This the bishops should do, to whom, and not to the princes, such duty is entrusted. Heresy can never be prevented by force. That must be taken hold of in a different way, and must be opposed and dealt with otherwise than with the sword. Here God's Word must strive; if that does not accomplish the end it will remain unaccomplished through secular power, though it fill the world with blood. Heresy is a spiritual matter, which no iron can strike, no fire burn, no water drown. God's Word alone avails here, as Paul says, 2 Corinthians 10, "Our weapons are not carnal, but mighty through God to destroy every counsel and high thing that exalteth itself against the knowledge of God, and to bring into captivity every thought to the obedience of Christ."[9]

* * *

6. 1 Pet. 2:13.
7. Rom. 13:7.
8. Rom. 13:4.
9. 2 Cor. 10:4–5.

JONATHAN MAYHEW

[Romans 13 and the Right of Revolution] (1749)†

* * *

Let us now trace the apostle's reasoning in favor of submission to the *higher powers*, a little more particularly and exactly. For by this it will appear, on one hand, how good and conclusive it is, for submission to those rulers who exercise their power in a proper manner: And, on the other, how weak and trifling and inconnected it is, if it be supposed to be meant by the apostle to show the obligation and duty of obedience to tyrannical, oppressive rulers in common with others of a different character.

The apostle enters upon his subject thus—*Let every soul be subject unto the higher powers; for there is no power but of God: the powers that be, are ordained of God.* Here he urges the duty of obedience from this topic of argument, that civil rulers, as they are supposed to fulfil the pleasure of God, are the ordinance of God. But how is this an argument for obedience to such rulers as do not perform the pleasure of God, by doing good; but the pleasure of the devil, by doing evil; and such as are not, therefore, *God's ministers*, but the devil's! *Whosoever, therefore, resisteth the power, resisteth the ordinance of God; and they that resist, shall receive to themselves damnation.* Here the apostle argues, that those who resist a reasonable and just authority, which is agreeable to the will of God, do really resist the will of God himself; and will, therefore, be punished by him. But how does this prove, that those who resist a lawless, unreasonable power, which is contrary to the will of God, do therein resist the will and ordinance of God? Is resisting those who resist God's will, the same thing with resisting God? Or shall those who do so, *receive to themselves damnation! For rulers are not a terror to good works, but to the evil. Wilt thou then not be afraid of the power? Do that which is good; and thou shalt have praise of the same. For he is the minister of God to thee for good.* Here the apostle argues more explicitly than he had before done, for revering, and submitting to, magistracy, from this consideration, that such as really performed the duty of magistrates, would be enemies only to the evil actions of men, and would befriend and encourage the good; and so be a common blessing to society. But how is this an argument, that we must honor, and submit to, such magistrates as are not enemies to the evil actions of men; but to the good; and such as are not a common blessing, but a common curse, to society!

---

† The seventeenth century in Europe saw a marked tendency toward absolutist governments, a tendency reflected in the exegesis of Romans 13. In England, however, constitutionalist resistance to the divine right of kings culminated in revolution and the execution of Charles I in 1649. No less a propagandist for liberty than John Milton published in that year a defense of the execution, "The Tenure of Kings and Magistrates," which contained his own interpretation of Romans 13. In America a century later, the young minister of the West Church in Boston, Jonathan Mayhew, celebrated the anniversary of Charles' execution by preaching a sermon on Romans 13, "A Discourse concerning Unlimited Submission and Non-Resistance to the Higher Powers: With some Reflections on the Resistance made to King Charles I." While Mayhew was of rather radical theological persuasions, tending toward Unitarianism and Deism, his politics "struck a chord that would become familiar throughout New England in the next decades" (Edmund S. Morgan). The excerpt is from *Puritan Political Ideas*, ed. by Edmund S. Morgan (Indianapolis: Bobbs-Merrill, 1965), 305–13. Copyright © 1965 by The Bobbs-Merrill Company. Reprinted by permission of Hackett Publishing Company, Inc.

But if thou do that which is evil, be afraid: For he is the minister of God, a revenger, to execute wrath upon him that doth evil. Here the apostle argues from the nature and end of magistracy, that such as did evil, (and such only) had reason to be afraid of the *higher powers*; it being part of their office to punish evil doers, no less than to defend and encourage such as do well. But if magistrates are unrighteous; if they are *respecters of persons*; if they are partial in their administration of justice; then those who do well have as much reason to *be afraid*, as those that do evil: there can be no safety for the good, nor any peculiar ground of terror to the unruly and injurious. So that, in this case, the main end of civil government will be frustrated. And what reason is there for submitting to that government, which does by no means answer the design of government? *Wherefore ye must needs be subject not only for wrath, but also for conscience sake*. Here the apostle argues the duty of a chearful and conscientious submission to civil government, from the nature and end of magistracy as he had before laid it down, i.e., as the design of it was to punish evil doers, and to support and encourage such as do well; and as it must, if so exercised, be agreeable to the will of God. But how does what he here says, prove the duty of a chearful and conscientious subjection to those who forfeit the character of rulers? to those who encourage the bad, and discourage the good? The argument here used no more proves it to be a sin to resist such rulers, than it does, to *resist the devil*, that he may *flee from us*. For one is as truly the *minister of God* as the other. *For, for this cause pay you tribute also; for they are God's ministers, attending continually upon this very thing*. Here the apostle argues the duty of paying taxes, from this consideration, that those who perform the duty of rulers, are continually attending upon the public welfare. But how does this argument conclude for paying taxes to such princes as are continually endeavouring to ruin the public? And especially when such payment would facilitate and promote this wicked design! *Render therefore to all their dues; tribute, to whom tribute is due; custom, to whom custom; fear, to whom fear; honor, to whom honor*. Here the apostle sums up what he had been saying concerning the duty of subjects to rulers. And his argument stands thus—"Since magistrates who execute their office well, are common benefactors to society; and may, in that respect, be properly stiled *the ministers and ordinance of God*; and since they are constantly employed in the service of the public; it becomes you to pay them tribute and custom; and to reverence, honor, and submit to, them in the execution of their respective offices." This is apparently good reasoning. But does this argument conclude for the duty of paying tribute, custom, reverence, honor and obedience, to such persons as (although they bear the title of rulers) use all their power to hurt and injure the public? such as are not *God's ministers*, but *satan's*? such as do not take care of, and attend upon, the public interest, but their own, to the ruin of the public? that is, in short, to such as have no natural and just claim at all to tribute, custom, reverence, honor and obedience? It is to be hoped that those who have any regard to the apostle's character as an inspired writer, or even as a man of common understanding, will not represent him as reasoning in such a loose incoherent manner; and drawing conclusions which have not the least relation to his premises. For what can be more absurd than an argument thus framed? "Rulers are, by their office, bound to consult the public welfare and the good of society: therefore you are bound to pay them tribute, to honor, and to submit to them, even when they destroy the public welfare, and are a common pest to society, by acting in direct contradiction to the nature and end of their office."

Thus, upon a careful review of the apostle's reasoning in this passage, it appears that his arguments to enforce submission, are of such a nature, as to conclude only in favour of submission *to such rulers as he himself describes*; i.e. such as rule for the good of society, which is the only end of their institution. Common tyrants, and public oppressors, are not intitled to obedience from their subjects, by virtue of any thing here laid down by the inspired apostle.

I now add, farther, that the apostle's argument is so far from proving it to be the duty of people to obey, and submit to, such rulers as act in contradiction to the public good,[1] and so to the design of their office, that it proves *the direct contrary*. For, please to observe, that if the end of all civil government, be the good of society; if this be the thing that is aimed at in constituting civil rulers; and if the motive and argument for submission to government, be taken from the apparent usefulness of civil authority; it follows, that when no such good end can be answered by submission, there remains no argument or motive to enforce it; if instead of this good end's being brought about by submission, a *contrary end* is brought about, and the ruin and misery of society effected by it, here is a plain and positive reason against submission in all such cases, should they ever happen. And therefore, in such cases, a regard to the public welfare, ought to make us with-hold from our rulers, that obedience and subjection which it would, otherwise, be our duty to render to them. If it be our duty, for example, to obey our king, merely for this reason, that he rules for the public welfare, (which is the only argument the apostle makes use of) it follows, by a parity of reason, that when he turns tyrant, and makes his subjects his prey to devour and to destroy, instead of his charge to defend and cherish, we are bound to throw off our allegiance to him, and to resist; and that according to the tenor of the apostle's argument in this passage. Not to discontinue our allegiance, in this case, would be to join with the sovereign in promoting the slavery and misery of that society, the welfare of which, we ourselves, as well as our sovereign, are indispensably obliged to secure and promote, as far as in us lies. It is true the apostle puts no case of such a tyrannical prince; but by his grounding his argument for submission wholly upon the good of civil society; it is plain he implicitly authorises, and even requires us to make resistance, whenever this shall be necessary to the public safety and happiness. Let me make use of this easy and familiar *similitude* to illustrate the point in hand—Suppose God requires a family of children, to obey their father and not to resist him; and inforces his command with this argument; that the superintendence and care and authority of a just and kind parent, will contribute to the happiness of the whole family; so that they ought to obey him for their own sakes more than for his: Suppose this parent at length runs distracted, and attempts, in his mad fit, to cut all his children's throats: Now, in this case, is not the reason

---

1. This does not intend, their acting so in *a few particular instances*, which the best of rulers may do through mistake, &c. but their acting so *habitually*; and in a manner which plainly shows, that they aim at making themselves great, by the ruin of their subjects.

before assigned, why these children should obey their parent while he continued of a sound mind, namely, *their common good*, a reason equally conclusive for disobeying and resisting him, since he is become delirious, and attempts their ruin? It makes no alteration in the argument, whether this parent, properly speaking, loses his reason; or does, while he retains his understanding, that which is as fatal in its consequences, as any thing he could do, were he really deprived of it. This similitude needs no formal application—

But it ought to be remembred, that if the duty of universal obedience and non-resistance to our king or prince, can be argued from this passage, the same unlimited submission under a republican, or any other form of government; and even to all the subordinate powers in any particular state, can be proved by it as well: which is more than those who alledge it for the mentioned purpose, would be willing should be inferred from it. So that this passage does not answer their purpose; but really overthrows and confutes it. This matter deserves to be more particularly considered.—The advocates for unlimited submission and passive obedience, do, if I mistake not, always speak with reference to kingly or monarchical government, as distinguished from all other forms; and, with reference to submitting to the will of the king, in distinction from all subordinate officers, acting beyond their commission, and the authority which they have received from the crown. It is not pretended that any person besides kings, have a divine right to do what they please, so that no one may resist them, without incurring the guilt of factiousness and rebellion. If any other supreme powers oppress the people, it is generally allowed, that the people may get redress, by resistance, if other methods prove ineffectual. And if any officers in a kingly government, go beyond the limits of that power which they have derived from the crown, (the supposed original source of all power and authority in the state) and attempt, illegally, to take away the properties and lives of their fellow subjects, they may be *forcibly* resisted, at least till application can be made to the crown. But as to the sovereign himself, he may not be resisted in any case; nor any of his officers, while they confine themselves within the bounds which he has prescribed to them. This is, I think, a true sketch of the principles of those who defend the doctrine of passive obedience and non-resistance. Now there is nothing in scripture which supports this scheme of political principles. As to the passage under consideration, the apostle here speaks of civil rulers in *general;* of all persons in *common,* vested with authority for the good of society, without any particular reference to one form of government, more than to another; or to the supreme power in any particular state, more than to subordinate powers. The apostle does not concern himself with the different forms of government.[2] This he supposes left intirely to human pru-

2. The essence of government (I mean *good* government; and this is the *only* government which the apostle treats of in this passage) consists in the *making* and *executing of good laws*—laws attempered to the common felicity of the *governed*. And if this be, *in fact,* done, it is evidently, in it self, a thing of no consequence at all, what the *particular* form of government is;—whether the legislative and executive power be lodged in *one and the same* person, or in *different* persons;—whether in *one* person, whom we call an *absolute monarch;*—whether in a *few,* so as to constitute an *aristocrasy;*—whether in *many,* so as to constitute a *republic;* or whether in *three co-ordinate branches,* in such manner as to make the government *partake* something of *each* of these forms; and to be, at the same time, *essentially different* from them *all.* If the *end* be attained, it is enough. But no form of government seems to be so unlikely to accomplish this *end,* as *absolute monarchy*—

dence and discretion. Now the consequence of this is, that unlimited and passive obedience, is no more enjoined in this passage, under monarchical government; or to the supreme power in any state, than under all other species of government, which answer the end of government; or, to all the subordinate degrees of civil authority, from the highest to the lowest. Those, therefore, who would from this passage infer the guilt of resisting kings, in all cases whatever, though acting ever so contrary to the design of their office, must, if they will be consistent, go much farther, and infer from it the guilt of resistance under all other forms of government; and of resisting *any petty officer* in the state, tho' acting beyond his commission, in the most arbitrary, illegal manner possible. The argument holds equally strong in both cases. All civil rulers, as such, are the *ordinance* and *ministers of God;* and they are all, by the nature of their office, and in their respective spheres and stations, bound to consult the public welfare. With the same reason therefore, that any deny unlimited and passive obedience to be here injoined under a republic or aristocrasy, or any other established form of civil government; or to subordinate powers, acting in an illegal and oppressive manner; (with the same reason) others may deny, that such obedience is enjoined to a king or monarch, or any civil power whatever. For the apostle says nothing that is *peculiar to kings;* what he says, extends equally to *all* other persons whatever, vested with any civil office. They are all, in exactly the same sense, the *ordinance of God;* and the *ministers of God;* and obedience is equally enjoined to be paid to them all. For, as the apostle expresses it, *there is* NO POWER *but of God:* And we are required to *render to* ALL *their* DUES; and not MORE than their DUES. And what these *dues* are, and to *whom* they are to be *rendered*, the apostle *sayeth not;* but leaves to the reason and consciences of men to determine.

Thus it appears, that the common argument, grounded upon this passage, in favor of universal, and passive obedience, really overthrows itself, by proving too much, if it proves any thing at all; namely, that no civil officer is, in any case whatever, to be resisted, though acting in express contradiction to the design of his office; which no man, in his senses, ever did, or can assert.

✳   ✳   ✳

Nor is there any one that has so little pretence to a *divine original,* unless it be in this sense, that God *first* introduced it into, and thereby overturned, the common wealth of *Israel,* as a *curse* upon that people for their *folly* and *wickedness,* particularly in *desiring* such a government. (See I *Sam.* viii. chap.) Just so God, before, sent *Quails* amongst them, as a *plague,* and a *curse,* and not as a *blessing. Numb.* chap. xi.

ERNST KÄSEMANN

Principles of Interpretation of Romans 13 (1961)†

My concern in this lecture is exclusively to initiate a discussion of this passage which has suddenly become so relevant to our contemporary situation. I shall therefore begin by saying something about the problem of Pauline parenesis in general—a matter which is of particular importance for us of all people; I shall then repeat briefly the questions and insights, the formulation of which lay at the root of my article on 'Römer 13:1–7 in unserer Generation' [1959]; and I shall conclude with the interpretation of those textual problems which are decisive ones for our theme.

1. The Understanding of Pauline Parenesis

Over and over again we find difficulties in the way of our understanding of Pauline parenesis simply because we are unable for the most part to discern distinctly its historical and factual presuppositions. Two things above all must be brought out into the clear light of day: just as the New Testament is not the first Christian 'Dogmatic Theology', but (apart from the Gospels) a collection of occasional writings and individual theological tracts, similarly it contains no 'ethic' in our sense, i.e. no logically articulated system designed to be normative for Christian behaviour. It is true that in the New Testament all activity of the Christian is described and evaluated from the perspective of eschatology, as and because the total proclamation is here eschatologically determined. But this does not mean that this activity can be deduced and developed from a master principle.

* * *

In the course of a long development and employing the key principle of scriptural interpretation—the mutual relation of Gospel and Law—we have evolved as it were a mode of dividing up the content in which it seemed obvious that the parenesis should be allotted to the Law. There was, too, a stretching of the concept of law which gave to the divine law the sense of an absolute norm. Parenesis appeared from this standpoint to be the description of moral duties. If an ethical system is really being substituted here for the New Testament exhortations, the error of such a conception emerges with special clarity in the light of Paul's understanding of all activity of the Christian as charismatic, i.e. as the concrete manifestation of self-differentiating *charis* [grace]. As grace endows us, so it puts us also at its disposal by making us willing and able to enter its service— we might say, using the full complex sense of the word, it empowers

† From "Grundsätzliches zur Interpretation von Römer 13," first published in *Unter der Herrschaft Christi* (Beiträge zur evangelishen Theologie 32; Munich: Kaiser, 1961), rp. in *Exegetische Versuche und Besinnungen* (Göttingen: Vandenhoeck & Ruprecht, 1964), Vol. 2, 204–22; tr. by W. J. Montague in *New Testament Questions of Today* (Philadelphia: Fortress, 1969). Reprinted by permission of Vandenhoeck and Ruprecht. During the German Third Reich, Käsemann (1906–1998) was a member of the Confessing Church, organized in opposition to Nazi control of the German churches. In 1937 he was arrested by the Gestapo because of his activities, as pastor in a mining town, on behalf of communist mine workers; after his release he was drafted and served for a time on the eastern front, where he was taken prisoner by Soviet troops. After the war he was professor of New Testament in Mainz, Göttingen, and finally in the Protestant Faculty of Theology at the University of Tübingen, where he taught with distinction from 1959 until he retired in 1971.

[German ermächtigt] us to serve it. Grace and service do not permit themselves to be forcibly divorced. There is no other possible way to preserve grace and to make it real except by persevering in its service.

* * *

This, then, is the connection in which Rom. 13:1–7, too, stands and demands to be treated. It has been frequently maintained that this section does not possess the eschatological ring which normally dominates the Pauline parenesis; and laborious attempts have therefore been made to exhibit connections with the immediate context. These attempts to relieve our verses of the character of a foreign body by clamping them more firmly in their frame have in general not succeeded because of their obviously forced nature. They fail to recognize that the structure of the Pauline parenesis in its detail is built up by co-ordination and not by subordination and deduction, by association of ideas and not by logic. Rom. 13:1–7 is in fact a self-contained passage which as such cannot be directly associated either with the command to love one's enemy in 12:20f. or with the epitomizing demand for love in 13:8–10 or with the eschatological conclusion of the general exhortation in 13:11ff.; much less can it be said to receive its relevance and its theme from any of these. The political authority is neither the adversary of love nor its object. It has to be obeyed, no more and no less, precisely because it is a symbol of the transitory world—a symbol which as such does not in any way point beyond itself to the End. This is the first exegetical acknowledgment, and the premiss of any which may follow, that there can be here no premature connection made between passages which are externally juxtaposed. It is true, however, that our text, and with it the whole parenetical section of this chapter, stands under the sign of the introductory verses 12:1f.—the call to the spiritual worship of God in the everyday life of the world—and is also controlled by the key theme (promulgated in 12:3–6) of charismatic activity. This second indispensable insight for any adequate understanding of the section should also be extremely important for the present analysis: even obedience to earthly authority is regarded by Paul as a fragment of the Christian's worship of God in the secularity of the world and exhibited as having the character of charismatic action. Naturally non-Christians also may render this service in like fashion, grudgingly or enthusiastically or in sober objectivity. Christians are not distinguished from them because they live in another world or because there is any question of their having different tasks laid upon them or of their coming nearer to perfection. But if they are obedient to authority and serve God in this way, they are led and reformed by the grace which leaves no earthly sphere and no ramification of man's inner life without a claim and blessing upon it. In the last resort, therefore, it is not the categorical imperative, a norm, a law or even an obligation which is sovereign over Christians, though even under the rule of grace it is not impossible for the divine word to be 'you must be subject'. In Christ, and concretely in baptism, grace decides our destiny but, according to I Cor. 9:14ff., enables us freely to embrace it. Christians manifest by their doings that the earth, and all that therein is, belongs to the Lord, is not abandoned by him and is blessed in the form in which blessing always and invariably takes under the sovereignty of Christ, i.e. in the form of that free and joyful service of the children of God which is the victorious ensign of the new age planted high in this transitory world.

2. A Critique of Typical Attempts at Interpretation

*   *   *

Almost all the history of the interpretation of our passage, which in essence is divided into four representative types, suffers from its conception of the real problem as lying not in the content of the exhortation as such but in the basis on which it is made—to be specific, in the concept of the divine authorization of the present 'powers that be'.* * *

The traditional catholic construction has continued to influence Protestant exegesis right up to the present. With the intention of providing a foundation for the parenesis, it finds in Romans 13 a doctrine of the State which can more accurately be called a metaphysic of the State. The State, as part of a structure of being comprehending heaven and earth, represents that order of creation, of natural law, which empowers and gives direction to man's earthly being and (as the expression or profile of the 'eternal law') at the same time points him beyond himself and the earthly order to that supernatural order already realized by anticipation in the Church. Correspondingly, the obedience which is due to the State has only one boundary, i.e. the good estate and the authority of the Church. Apart from the fact that the parenesis which determines the text is here being overshadowed by a theological system, there are three kinds of criticism to be levelled against this interpretation. To assume so cavalierly that Paul's main purpose here is to speak of the State is to reduce what he is trying to say to an abstraction. It is certainly true that Paul is dealing with the political powers that be and, because he is concerned with the authority they bear, can talk summarily as if *exousia* and political authority were interchangeable terms. But he has his eye on the circumstances of his own time when he takes as his starting-point the plurality of powers and then speaks personally of the rulers and the ministers of God. He is obviously not thinking primarily or exclusively of the Roman *imperium*, but of all who possess power *de facto*—perhaps therefore of the magistrature also; he is looking not at the nature but at the function of these authorities, i.e. the jurisdiction to which they lay claim and which they exercise. It is a matter of giving them their due respect whenever we encounter them even if it is only in the person of the inspector of taxes. Unlike his later interpreters, the apostle is most at home in the realm of concrete, everyday reality in which there are policemen, writ-servers, magistrates, governors and ultimately, of course, the emperor. It is therefore not necessary for him to theorize as he would have to do if he were propounding a doctrine of the State; he contents himself with the call to obedience and the basis of it, without ranging round the firmament. Thus he goes on to speak not of heavenly and earthly order but of the divine ordinance, the ordaining will of God and not of the 'orders', the immediate concern of metaphysics. Finally, to set up a relation of analogy or a polarizing harmony between the heavenly and the earthly is just what our text does not do. Necessary political obedience is not understood as a sign pointing beyond itself to a completed transaction elsewhere. Rather, it is a piece of Christian worship in this world, justified and fulfilled in itself and needing no sanctioning by a theory which regards it as training for salvation.

A variant of the catholic interpretation is that of conservative Lutheranism. In the succession of Reformation idealism, this variant speaks mostly of the 'magistrate' rather than of the State, and this would be thoroughly in accord with the tenor of the text if we were not far too ready to associate with such a conception the whole burden of legality. Paul is not, however, reflecting on the process by which those powers that be of which he speaks in v. 1b came into existence. For him the man who has asserted himself politically has a God-bestowed function and authority simply as the possessor of power *de facto*. This is why I translate the Greek word *exousia* and its derivatives by power [German *Gewalt*], powers, holders of power: I want to include tyranny and despotism, which in any event reigned supreme over wide stretches of the Roman Empire. It is characteristic of the Lutheran position that it develops on the basis of the Pauline parenesis a theology of 'orders' which speaks now of orders of creation, now of so-called orders of preservation and orders of wrath; and the bearers of political power appear in this scheme of things as the pre-eminent representatives of these orders. If such a view is taken further by speculation, the Catholic metaphysic of the relation of nature and super-nature is apt to be replaced by a theology of history which frequently develops into a salvation history. Support can be found in the mistaken assumption that the predications 'minister, servant of God' were originally sacral terms and have sacral significance in our text also. It is not surprising if, as a logical conclusion, an eschatological function is then ascribed to the political powers that be: they keep the forces of chaos at least within certain definite bounds, thus fulfilling the intention of the divine law, and in both these operations they point beyond themselves to the divine kingdom of perfection, even when they show themselves to be its enemies by overstepping earthly limits. A further immediate critical objection to this kind of interpretation is that the text does not speak of 'orders' but of the 'ordinances' of the divine will and does not move beyond the field of inter-personal relationships into any cosmic dimension. At best then, it provides a springboard for a systematic scheme such as we have outlined but does not reveal it simply by inspection. Whatever may or may not be the theological justification for such a scheme, the exegete as such cannot take on any share of the responsibility for it. On the contrary, he must immediately call attention to further dangers which, as appeared in the Church struggle, are liable to become sinister: this whole approach almost always presupposes the conception of the constitutional State.

* * *

Political power in them [the New Testament texts] has, in general, nothing to do with the forces of chaos but with the individual Christian to whose advantage it functions and with the individual transgressor of its order whom it punishes. Above all, it is not the representative in the political sphere of the divine law: it cannot possibly be this, because the divine law is administered solely by the proclamation of the divine work. Rather, it falls wholly and exclusively into that category of the contingent in which there is also eating and drinking, marriage and slavery and, like these other functions and relationships, becomes the proper object of parenesis. For the contingent is not of no importance for the Christian. It is precisely in everyday life, which is determined by contingency, that his service to God has to be rendered.

Undoubtedly we find it very difficult to do justice and to remain faithful to this kind of demythologization of the contingent, to the sobriety and objectivity on this point which arises out of primitive Christian eschatology. Evidence of this is provided by the sort of interpretation which reads an angelology or demonology into our text, maltreated as it is often enough without this. It proceeds on the assumption that it is possible for Paul's understanding of *exousiai* to include the angelic powers, and maintains that this is always the case when mention is made in a theological context of 'every authority' and of the powers. The final conclusion drawn from this is that our text regards earthly political authority as the instrument of the angelic powers, as the Jewish doctrine of the angels of the nations was still doing at the time. It was not accidental that this thesis played a prominent part in the Church Struggle. At that time men came up against what appeared to be the apostle's overwhelmingly positive valuation of political authority which accorded ill with their own experiences. The comparative study of religion and the outlook it engendered deprived the passage of its sting. An earlier generation, still uninfluenced by the theology of dialectic, would have denied without further ado that it had any theological relevance. As it was no longer possible to do this so lightly, the next move was to bring forward the peculiar ambivalence of the powers: originally bound to the service of God, they have a perpetual tendency towards revolt, and then they become the inspiration behind earthly rebellion. On this view of things Paul has, as it were, only shown us one side of the phenomenon whose obverse is revealed by the Revelation. The interpreter who takes account of both can and indeed must provide a solution in terms of theological dialectic. The question must surely arise as to whether anything is gained by this except an escape road, which may and will lead to a relativization of Scripture in both directions. It seems to me that a dialectical theology argued in this way with the help of a mythology and a theology extracted from a concordance does little credit to its initiators and proves only that it is possible to defend oneself by ingenious harmonization against the ultimate challenge of the text without ever having given this challenge its full weight. But such fruit, plucked unripe from the tree of knowledge, was not bitter enough even yet. The thesis expounded above was patient of being combined with the outlook of the primitive Christian hymns, according to which the heavenly and demonic powers have been subjected to the exalted Christ. By adding the further interpretation that these powers had been made the servants of Christ, these theologians arrived ultimately at the so-called christological foundation of the State. The to-and-fro of argument and counter-argument in the debate, pursued as it was with great passion on all sides, does not need to be repeated yet again. In my opinion the exegetical battle in this matter came to a decisive end when A. Strobel, in his article on Rom. 13,[1] showed conclusively that the Jewish doctrine of the angels of the nations is not to be imported into our text and that, all along the line, the terminology we encounter here has its origin in the vocabulary of secular government in the Hellenistic

1. 'Zum Verständnis vom Röm 13', ZNW 47 (1956): 67–93.

world. We might say that Paul was the first to revive the importance of the usage and phraseology customary in Hellenistic officialdom, by employing them in the service of his theology. This coheres excellently with our other findings: the background here is that of everyday life in the Hellenistic world and this life finds exact verbal expression in the terminology used. For instance, the rationale of the parenesis finds its closest parallel in the sentence in Josephus: 'Sovereignty comes to no man, unless God so orders matters.'[2] If we isolate our own passage, the only voice which echoes in it is that of the synagogue of the Diaspora and its environment. This also explains why eschatology plays no part in it; why what it has to say is based much more on a doctrine of creation. It takes on a Christian imprint solely from its connection with the introduction to the whole parenetic section in 12:1–6.

The only other attempt at interpretation about which I am going to particularize is that represented by Karl Barth and his school. While it is a fact that the theory of angelic powers standing behind the earthly authorities has had some influence on this interpretation its centre of gravity does not lie there. The concern of Barth and his disciples is with the present lordship of Christ over all the world as it is directly and powerfully proclaimed in the primitive Christian hymns. Even the State and the political authorities in general are for the faithful, since the exaltation of Christ, not simply brought into subjection to an abstract divine Creator and Preserver. They are located in the area of christology: admittedly not in the innermost circle in which the community operates, but still in the wider one indicated by the proclamation of Jesus as the Cosmocrator. They, too, must in their special fashion and, even against their will, serve the Christ and those that are his. Conversely, having knowledge of this mystery, those who believe are enabled to assume political responsibility in an unprejudiced, sober and critical spirit—in short, as servants—and thus carry out what may not be the most important part of their service of God in the world, but is nevertheless an indispensable one. Barth's concern is that this is precisely what should happen. Everything else is of interest only as ministering to the necessity and possibility of such a task. The Pauline parenesis is treated as the heart of the passage; and from this standpoint it is heavily underlined and expounded at length with the exegete's eye on the conditions obtaining in contemporary democracies. In New Testament times political responsibility was only a live option for the Christian in rare and exceptional cases and in areas of subordinate jurisdiction. If Paul limits his scope to the requirement of obedience, this corresponds with reality; there was normally no other means of political expression for the stratum of society out of which early Christianity arose. For this reason it is impossible simply to transpose our passage into our modern situation. The fact that this has nevertheless been done in Protestantism for at least a century contributed to the phenomenon of 'passive obedience' and the catastrophes it conjured up. It is a dangerous factor in biblicism, which guards the letter and neglects prophecy, the actualization of the message. None of this should be forgotten when interpreting Romans 13. Exegesis can only be an auxiliary here; it cannot be a substitute for real interpretation, i.e. a

2. Josephus, *Jewish War* II 8.7.

translation into contemporary modes of understanding. I am certainly not saying that free course should be given to a systematic theology which has been arbitrarily imposed on the text, as must inevitably be the case when Barth and his followers give the present passage a christological orientation. It is characteristic of our chapter that any christological, as well as any eschatological, patterning is found wanting. To ignore this is to build castles in the air and to betray oneself in so doing by the christology and cosmology one employs. It is true that the primitive Christian hymns proclaimed that the lordship of Christ had already broken in on the world and the cosmic powers had been brought into subjection. But these hymns originated in the enthusiastic religious life of the community and to this extent it is no accident that they base their message on the myth of the world saviour familiar to us from Vergil's *Fourth Eclogue*. Paul, however, had to fight a life-long battle not only against Judaism but also against enthusiasm. Some fruits of this battle can be seen in his replacement of the pattern of the Incarnation and Exaltation of Christ by the other pattern of the Cross and Resurrection; in his ascription to Christians of a present participation in the Cross but not immediately in the glory of the Resurrection; and in his treatment of the statement that the kingdom and powers of this world have been subjected to Christ, a statement which in I Cor. 15:28 he transposes from the perfect or the present to the future tense, thus refraining from ascribing to Jesus the title of Cosmocrator. These are all ways of fending off enthusiasm. This is not to say that Jesus is not for Paul also the exalted one, and the Kyrios not of the Church only, but also of the world. He is Kyrios, however, in a peculiar hiddenness, so that the assault of grace upon the world is borne forward by the gospel concerning him and by the servanthood of the community, and no corner of our earth is left free from the demand and the promise of that same grace. To speak of Christ's universal sovereignty otherwise than in this relation to the word of preaching and the servanthood of the community can only be to come once again under the spell of enthusiasm and to fall a prey to the same mythology in which primitive Christian enthusiasm found for itself a means of expression. In my view, Barth and his followers do not protect themselves sufficiently against this danger. Earthly institutions and authorities cannot be grounded in christology—only the community of believers and Christian activity.

I have set out in this section the most important types of interpretation of Rom. 13, but have so far not touched upon what is really the latest development. This can best be described by saying that all the positions outlined above are being more or less criticized from within their own camp, and it is becoming clear that modifications and reductions in their claims have to be made. This is happening, under the influence of an exegesis which, here as elsewhere, is pushing back systematic theology. Admittedly, it is not quite so obvious as it might appear that we should applaud this process. For, while on the one hand certain specific fundamental historical findings are gaining general acceptance, on the other, sharp theological contours are becoming blurred. It is becoming continually more difficult to know what is really happening in the guerilla warfare of the specialists, in which there are so many shots fired and so few targets hit, so many issues confused and so few decided. I am not going to develop this point further, but shall attempt in conclusion, only touching lightly on what has been said already, myself to reach something like an interpretation of the most important problems of the text.

3. Necessity and Freedom in Christian Obedience

What does ἀνάγκη ὑποτάσσεσθαι mean? What is the real aim of the apostolic argument for it? Is there any limit to the obedience which is here being demanded? These are the decisive questions thrown up by our text. We may profitably begin with the verb, placed as it is at the beginning of the sentence in a manner which we cannot possibly ignore. Why does Paul not use ὑπακούειν [obey] instead? The many and varied derivatives of the root τασσ- which we encounter in our passage must at least have been intended to make it clear that this is no arbitrary choice. ὑποταγή is the obedience which we owe because it is inherent in some specific τάγμα, i.e. it arises out of given earthly relationships, while ὑπακοή simply designates obedience as an achievement. Paul looks out on a world in which superior and subordinates exist and intends his readers to come to terms with this reality. Just for this reason he can also demand that obedience should be rendered to the subordinate political authorities. Actually our text does offer at this point some foothold for the different variations of that theology of 'the orders' which I delineated above. To dispute this would be to lose the right to criticize this theology from the standpoint of the text. Any serious attempt at interpretation must take up some posture towards the problem even if only to emphasize at once that this approach is not necessarily patient of further development. For Paul himself is not immediately saying any more than that God has so arranged the world from the beginning—at the creation, by all means, if you like—as to make it possible to render him service within it; and this is why he created superiors and subordinates. The questions which arise out of this situation for us, with our demythologized world-view and our prevailing image of political democracy, are not yet felt as questions. Two examples make this clear: the apostle takes the system of slavery in the ancient world for granted and even affirms it on occasions, even though slave revolts were already taking place in his time and, as hinted at in the letter to Philemon, there were in existence armies of runaway slaves and even the theological question as to the relationship of Christian slaves to their Christian masters was already being raised. Paul has so little interest in all this, at least so far as erecting this last case into the sign of a new and better social order is concerned, that, according to the *prima facie* understanding of I Cor. 7:21, he can recommend a slave not to take advantage of a possible release; let alone to strive for it. He bases this on what may rightly be called the provocative axiom 'Every one should remain in the state in which he was called'. The same thing happens when the problem of the equality of the sexes has to be faced, at least in respect to the common life in Christ. Paul continually sets forth the subordination of the woman to the man as self-explanatory and God-ordained and thus remains in this regard within the limits of the conventions both of the classical and the Jewish worlds. The self-explanatory and God-ordained nature of this state of affairs was not in fact so ineluctable as the apostolic decision and the biblical words in question seem to some contemporary theologians, and even to many Church governments, to make it. For, according to the first letter to the Corinthians, at least in those congregations which were under the controlling influence of enthusiasm the question was stirring as to whether, with the invasion of the new age and the reception of women into the Church, female partners in a Christian marriage and the female Christians within a congregation ought not to be exempt from obsolete earthly convention. But, in the face of just such questions as these, Paul holds strictly to tradition, so that we can now summarize the results of this part of our investigation in three propositions:

1. Obviously, the injunction to obedience to the political authorities is connected with the injunctions to slaves and women, indeed, more accurately, runs parallel to them.

2. In this area Paul always acts as the representative of the conservative attitudes of a view of existence we must call patriarchal—a view which, historically borrowed from the synagogue of the diaspora, bases social ordinances on theological principles.

3. Where the apostle is not simply and naively reproducing these attitudes, he is having to sharpen them because in his concrete situation he is confronted with an eschatological enthusiasm. The burden of this is, that in Christ the life-forms of the past have been fundamentally recapitulated and should at least be effective signs within the Christian community of the reality of the new heavenly world. For this reason, such enthusiasm keeps as far aloof as possible from the given realities of political conditions. Paul manages in remarkable fashion to relate to his purpose in a renewed form the opposing positions he captures, even in the context of such a raw encounter with their deep-rooted theological premises and conclusions. It is in the perspective of this encounter that he propagates the slogan ὑποταγή; he seeks to convey thereby that he is harking back to the will of the Creator, acknowledging the reality of superior and subordinate authorities in our world, forcing the Christian to face this reality and designating it the field of his (the Christian's) everyday service of God.

Can we rest content with this historical clarification of the phenomenon? That would mean that the question of the content was irrelevant so far as we were concerned. For while it is quite certain that the Christian community will always from time to time have to reckon with enthusiasm, it is equally certain that it will not, in the circumstances of today, wish to make the field of social order the venue of this confrontation. The Church would be acting in extremely reactionary fashion if she were not to recognize that it is impossible to maintain the apostolic arguments for the subordination of women or for political subjection as they stand, after the argument for slavery has collapsed. Obviously, we can no longer rely solely on the argument from 'my station and its duties' without becoming involved in hopeless contradictions.* * * But is Paul really in the last resort primarily concerned with maintaining respect for existing authorities which doubtless may embody principles of order but may equally preserve principles of disorder or may, in a changed world, become transformed from factors in social order into factors in social injustice? The problem is important enough to justify a digression. I should like to glance here, as I did in my introduction, at I Corinthians, but this time at 11:2ff., where Paul orders that women should be veiled. He makes quite clear the object of this usage, which was probably first introduced by him and was in any case quite foreign to the behaviour pattern of a Greek woman (and for this reason is productive of indignation among the Corinthian enthusiasts); the object is to incorporate into worship itself a sign of the God-willed subordination of the woman to the man. Basically it is a matter not of the custom as such, which could hardly be made the subject of a passionate theological disputation by the two sides; it is more a matter of the problem of Christian freedom, so far as it affects the status of the sexes before God which is now a common and indistinguishable status. In worship least of all—so the Christian women of Corinth may well have argued—ought those distinctions to be adopted which might otherwise be tolerated as the convention and perhaps even the continuing necessity of a transitory world. We ought to be struck by the severity with which Paul reacts against this enlightened and indeed theologically well-founded viewpoint as well as by the unmistakable irritation which drives him to juxtapose the most diverse counter-arguments. We encounter first something like a metaphysic of graded emanations, then, secondly, the creation story; this is followed, thirdly, by what is to our notions a superstitious picture of the presence of lustful angels at Christian worship, fourthly by an order of nature constructed more or less *ad hoc* and, finally, the universal custom of the Pauline congregations. Such an accumulation only succeeds in suggesting to the unprejudiced hearer and reader that no single one of the reasons adduced, thrown together as they are in this odd way, is convincing in itself. This is how a man argues when he is on the defensive, and in any case Paul eventually lost this particular battle. All the more remarkable, therefore, appears the apostle's determination that he will in no circumstances give up the point of principle lying behind the practical issue on which he is being pressed. It is impossible to maintain that he displays a happy touch here. On the contrary, here, if anywhere, we see that the concrete argumentation behind a piece of Pauline parenesis can be problematical; it may neither have a real theological foundation nor be illuminating in its own right. Not only does it make use of traditional attitudes which have already failed to convince their original hearers: sometimes, it does not scruple to dig back into the arsenal of a dubious world-view, even into that of popular superstition. Not until we look clear-sightedly at all this does the question really become a burning one, as to what Paul is really contending for with such determination and yet at the same time with such poor arguments. For neither of these does the preservation of what is traditionally called the 'orders of creation' provide a sufficient motive. The watch-words of the Corinthian enthusiasts, like the letter as a whole, indicate rather that, so far as the custom which forms the *casus belli* here is concerned, the battle for the 'orders of creation' must be considered only as helping to solve the problematic of Christian freedom by providing a paradigm case. The Corinthian watch-word 'freedom', which, considered both in itself and in connection with the specific case at issue, seems to be more enlightened than the Pauline reaction to it, suffers from the basic defect of enthusiastic piety; it takes account of freedom exclusively as freedom from burdensome compulsion. The apostle, on the other hand, is concerned here, as always, with the freedom which knows itself to be called to serve and it is just this freedom which he sees threatened where enthusiasm is rattling at the doors of the existing order and proclaiming its allegedly just claims in the name of the Spirit. The Christian is determined as Christian by service. Spirit ceases to be Holy Spirit if this criterion of Christian existence in the world is obscured, endangered or superseded. It is for the sake of this determining of Christian existence in the world that Paul sets himself so passionately against the separation of creation and new age. The new age is not suspended in mid-air: it takes root on this our earth to which Christ came down. It does not create for itself there an island of the blessed as the Corinthians believe: it creates the possibility of the kind of service which can no longer be universal and alive if it is not carried out in the midst of the old, passing world, thus declaring God's rightful lordship over this earth; that is, preserving the world as divine creation. According to Paul, it is none other than the Spirit who imposes himself on the everyday life of the world as being the locus of our service of God; while emancipation, even when it appeals to the Spirit, prefers to retreat from this everyday life and the possibilities of service that are given with it, and is thus a perversion of Christian freedom.

Now let us return to Romans 13. It seems to me that it is permissible for us to use the method of appraisal applied above without any hesitation in our consideration of this text also. The argumentation on which the parenesis is based is not quite so problematical as in I Cor. 11:2ff., but cannot be said without further qualification to be illuminating. Its brevity, which indicates that it is dealing with familiar material, is enough to mark it as traditional. This is even more true of a certain optimism about political aims which does not merely see in the existing political authorities the divinely constituted servants of the divine will but goes so far as to declare that they are objects of fear only for evil men. The argument is that of the synagogue of the Diaspora which had every reason to be concerned about the integration of its members into the existing set-up. Paul was able to pick up this precise point in his use of traditional material in I Cor. 11. But Rom. 13:1f. shows that his own purpose goes one layer deeper. Certainly he can look at the given realities of the world and say, 'We must be subject'. He can do this because he sees also in these given realities the will of the Creator at work. But equally, the logic of the total theology of the apostle makes it clear that the real basis and the peculiar centre of his gospel do not lie here. The traditional arguments are, to put it in a nutshell, Paul's emergency aids to call the Christian to take his stand before the true God, the Lord of the earth, and thus to call him to the possibility of genuine service in everyday life. Anyone who prefers to live in isolation from the world and its powers is in practice taking away from the world its character as God's creation and is thereby disqualified from serious service. For Christian service must take place on earth and in earth's everyday life; otherwise it becomes fantasy. We have no need arbitrarily to seek out a field in which to serve. It is just the life of everyday which is for us 'the given'; further, it is the same life to which the political powers that be, and even, in certain circumstances, a dictatorship, belong. To acknowledge the given nature of this everyday life, which may possibly wear the colours of dictatorship or slavery—it is just this that is charismatic activity, the possibility of Christian freedom. Finally, it is not the given realities in themselves which move the apostle to argue that 'We must be subject' but the necessity to authenticate Christian existence and the Christian's status in the eyes of the Lord, who stakes his claim to the world by facing it continually, in the person of his servants, with the eschatological token of his lordship—the quality of ταπεινοφροσύνη [humility].

We can now in conclusion take a look at v. 5. What does 'not only to avoid God's wrath, but also for the sake of conscience' mean? * * * Paul is saying no more than 'in the knowledge of the binding summons of God addressed to you'. I am unable to see any compelling reason for regarding v. 5 as a gloss. It is true that v. 6 follows well on v. 4. But v. 5 and v. 6 run parallel to each other, in so far as, corresponding to the argument of the whole section, testimony is borne to the divine ordinance and authority revealed in the existing political power, before attention is paid to the duties which the Christian does actually fulfil. That he does so without question is seen as proof that he has in fact no reason to fear the bearers of political power. Verse 5 does not therefore bring a double motivation to bear—obedience both out of fear and for conscience' sake—but an alternative: others may have grounds to fear the powers that be, the Christian obeys them as one who knows himself to be confronted in their claim with the divine summons and who in his obedience is rendering service to God. There can then, here or elsewhere, be no question of interpreting Christian obedience in action as slavish passive obedience. Christian obedience is never blind; and, indeed, open-eyed obedience, directed by συνείδησις [conscience], must even be critical. For him, God does not dissolve into his own immanence to the extent of being identified with it; rather, he remains Lord of the world and as such calls the Christian into the freedom of son-ship. An obedience which does not breathe this freedom of sonship does not deserve the designation 'Christian'. The transitory is not here being identified with the ultimate, the earthly is not having divine glory ascribed to it, a human claim is not being equated with the divine will, even if the divine will creates the encounter with the human claim. The significance of this for the individual case cannot be laid down beforehand. He who is called to the service of God in the world has always to make sure what the issue is (Phil. 1:9f.); as well as knowledge he needs αἴσθησις, which I should translate as 'the feeling for the actual situation at the time'. We are not exempt from this proviso in our dealings with the political authorities. At this point there opens up before us in principle that whole range of var-iations of practice exemplified in Acts, which stretches from willing subor-dination to martyrdom and from the silent endurance of maltreatment to the appeal to Caesar and the axiom that we ought to obey God rather than man. Christian obedience demonstrates its charismatic nature by its very incapacity to be uniform and conformist. There are for specific cases some-thing like models of the particular attitude required. But no one is robbed of his own power of decision, of the use of his own eyes and his own reason, of the αἴσθησις of Phil. 1:10; nor is the feeling for tact and moral inevita-bility, self-respect and dignity in any way circumscribed.

This brings us to our final question for which, although it does not arise directly out of the exegesis of the passage, our interpretation, taken as a whole, must have some satisfactory answer. Is there anything which might rightly be called a limit to the obedience here being demanded of the Christian and, if so, where is it to be drawn? In a nutshell my answer would be: 'Christian obedience comes to an end at the point where further service becomes impossible—and only there.' That happens incontrovertibly when the suggestion is made to the Christian that he should deny his existence as a Christian and abandon his particular Christian task. On the other hand, that is not the same thing as saying that the Christian has to hold fast inflexibly to certain traditional forms of Christian existence, responsibility and community life. The Lord, who brings upon us new historical situations, does not call us to a conservative or even reactionary attitude, and those who are endowed with *charisma* are able to distinguish between tradition and the opportunity of the hour. Martyrdom for the sake of the traditional form of our service is not enjoined upon us, any more than retreat into 'inward religion' and 'private life'. What we have to do is to authenticate the Christ as the hidden Lord of the world in our doing and in our being. The outward form which corresponds to this content of the hidden Lord of the world may be the narrowing down and straitening of the Church's room for manoeuvre even into the compass of a prison cell or a grave. Sometimes the Lord of the world speaks more audibly out of prison cells and graves than out of the life of churches which congratulate themselves on their concordat with the State. The space his lordship occupies is not identical with our space, the fact that we are hemmed in does not annul the breadth of his word, nor does our death annul his possibilities. A place on earth for us and our institutions is not the ultimate criterion about which our deeds and omissions have to be orientated. The boundary of our service is the point at which we cease to acknowledge Christ as Lord of the world, not the point at which the hiddenness of this Lord as such is demonstrated and made sensible to us. On the contrary it is precisely his hiddenness which, paradoxically enough, defines our service. We ourselves are not permitted to plunge into that most profound hiddenness which still characterizes him today as Lord of the world. We have rather so to bear it both as hallmark and as burden that we do not collapse under its weight into a Christian anonymity. Anonymity cannot be combined with conscientious obedience; we have to resist escape into it and pressure towards it. It is possible to soldier on, or to offer resistance, anonymously, but not to serve.

This raises the problem of the possibility of Christian resistance to the existing political power; it raises, that is, the specific question of participation in revolution. It is clear that this possibility could not yet be considered by Paul, because it is a product of modern democracy. It is equally clear that there cannot be a Christian revolution as such. Earthly revolutions are not to be justified simply by using the name of Christ. The sole consideration is whether, within the framework of modern democracy, that is, as a citizen and acting in full political responsibility, the Christian can rightly take part in a revolution and indeed can manifest his conscientious obedience in this very context. Once again, this question is no more capable of being answered in advance and in general than any other question about our relation to earthly reality. Here we have obviously to create for ourselves and each other a fundamental freedom to make different, and sometimes opposite, decisions. But the presupposition of such different, and even opposite, decisions cannot remain open at both ends; and this is because in both cases the individual decision stands under the sign of the Christian service of God in and for the world. The question of the possible participation of the Christian in a revolution is now framed in sharper terms. Is there such a thing as participation in revolution as an authentication of the service of God in the world? When and where can this be possible—not merely for the citizen of a democratic community in the carrying out of his political responsibility, but for the man who, being such a citizen, yet wills to be, and to remain, a Christian also? My own personal answer would be, that such a possibility could only exist when the possessors of political power are threatening and destroying in a radical way those ties which hold together a political community as a whole in bonds of mutual service. When it becomes impossible any longer to render whole-hearted service within the total context of a common life, but every concrete act of service within the individual's province takes on the character of participation in a common self-destruction—and in my view this possibility became reality for every man with eyes to see in the Third Reich (at least after Stalingrad)—then it also becomes impossible to deny to the Christian his right as a citizen to take part in revolution. Christian obedience in everyday life takes its significance from the fact that we have both the duty and the privilege of service; for this reason, and in the same way, in the conditions of a democracy, Christian obedience can and must end at the point where, because of the nature of the existing political authority, service, though still possible as an act of the individual, is yet robbed of all meaning within the total context of the life of a given community.

It has been my purpose in making these last points to lay bare the issues in this matter of the Christian's conscientious obedience. If my own answer to the question I have posed has not been misleading in its general drift, it may still have been inadequately formulated. But it seems to me necessary that the question should at least be discerned and posed, if we really want to understand Romans 13 not merely in the light of past and present exegesis but as a piece of guidance for ourselves. In this exercise everything will depend on preserving the paradoxical connection of necessity and freedom at the point of their deepest unity—that free man's service which is the good estate of Christian existence in the world.

PART IX

A Sampler of Modern Approaches to Paul and His Letters

The world has been profoundly changed by events and developments of the past century, and these changes have affected biblical scholarship. To begin with, the primary *geographical setting* for research has slowly shifted from Europe to North America and beyond. The unquestioned center was once Germany, but two world wars and their consequences disrupted the educational system that had produced generation after generation of great scholars. Since the end of World War II, the United States and Canada have emerged as major participants in biblical studies. This does not mean that Europe in general or Germany in particular has ceased to produce great scholars, for some of the most significant recent advances have come from scholars born and trained in Europe (such as Jacob Jervell, Ernst Käsemann, and Martin Hengel—see Parts IV and VIII). But two things should be noted in this regard. First, many of Europe's finest scholars came to North America following World War II and trained a whole new generation. Even before that, many Jewish scholars (such as David Daube—see Part VII) fled Europe and settled in England and the Americas, bringing their immense learning and intellectual rigor. There is, of course, a long history of immigration to North and South America, but this type of scholarly transplantation was unprecedented and had an unparalleled impact on the intellectual centers of theological education. That phenomenon continues to occur, though with less frequency, and three of the scholars whose contributions are excerpted below are native Europeans who accepted invitations to teach at North American universities (Nils Dahl, Elisabeth Schüssler Fiorenza, and Hans-Josef Klauck), with another (Peter Lampe) having done so earlier in his career.

Second, while North American scholars are now among the major participants, they are by no means the only ones. Scholarly discussion is much more global than it ever was, and that phenomenon will only increase as the twenty-first century unfolds. To give just one example, the modern state of Israel did not even exist until 1948, yet Israeli scholars now make major contributions, not only to the study of the Hebrew Bible and Second Temple Judaism (as might be expected) but also to the analysis of early Christian literature, and two of their contributions are included in this volume (see the essays by Daniel Schwartz and David Flusser in Part IV).

In addition to the expanding geographical context of critical research, there is now a much greater *diversity among participants*. Cutting-edge biblical scholarship used to be the domain of male European Protestants, especially German Lutherans (such as Adolf von Harnack and Rudolf Bultmann). One only has to compare the contributors to the first (1908–1913) and fourth (1998–2005) editions of the standard German reference work *Religion in Geschichte und Gegenwart* (*RGG = Religion in the Past and Present*) to see the enormous shift that has taken place and how much more inclusive the discussion has become. For example, whereas the first edition of *RGG* only envisioned educated women as potential *readers* of the work, female scholars are among the major *contributors* to the fourth edition. *The Writings of St. Paul* is another reflection of this phenomenon; whereas the first edition had no excerpts from female scholars, the second edition features contributions by seven women (Jouette Bassler, Bernadette Brooten, Paula Fredriksen, Susan Garrett, Margaret M. Mitchell, Elaine Pagels, and Elisabeth Schüssler Fiorenza).

Similarly, Roman Catholic scholars, both male and female, are now at the forefront of academic biblical scholarship, having come into particular prominence in the years following Vatican II. Yet they are as diverse in their approach to early Christian literature as are their Jewish and Protestant colleagues. For instance, Hans-Josef Klauck and Elisabeth Schüssler Fiorenza, to name just two Catholic scholars represented in this volume, approach the New Testament in quite different ways, as the excerpts given below will demonstrate.

The same kind of diversity characterizes the work of contemporary North American biblical scholars. In the United States, a major impetus to this diversification was the GI Bill, which enabled thousands upon thousands of World War II veterans to attend college. No longer were university graduates simply the children of the educated and affluent but now included many who were the first in their families to go to college, much less earn an advanced degree. Those who earned doctorates in Hebrew Bible, New Testament, and related fields were quite diverse economically, racially, and ethnically, and they represented numerous religious traditions. This was especially true during the latter part of the twentieth century, as mainline Protestant churches suffered losses in membership but other religious groups increased in size and strength.

Another aspect of the changing face of biblical scholarship is its *interdisciplinary character*. The American setting for the academic study of the Bible was once the seminary and the religiously affiliated college, institutions that were founded to train ministers, priests, rabbis, and other religious professionals, and to nurture students' personal appropriation of the tradition represented by the institution. Many of these schools remain vital centers of inquiry, but they are no longer the exclusive or even the dominant setting for biblical research. The last half-century has witnessed the establishment and proliferation of departments of religious studies at state universities and private secular colleges, institutions that are committed only to the academic study of the Bible and not to the perpetuation of any particular religious tradition. Furthermore, biblical scholars who work at such institutions are often in daily contact with scholars in the humanities and social sciences. Owing to this greater proximity, they are typically much more aware of various approaches and developments in other fields than were biblical scholars in earlier times, and they have been quick to seize upon the work of scholars in fields as diverse as sociology and rhetoric. Lines of inquiry have thus changed, and this has affected the discipline as a whole. Today, whether the setting is a seminary or a secular classroom, the approach to the biblical text is now highly interdisciplinary.

These new settings, voices, and approaches have affected the ways in which Paul is being read. The following essays are representative of the diverse contemporary approaches to understanding Paul. For a variety of reasons, we begin this sampler of modern approaches with Rudolf Bultmann's classic 1941 essay. Bultmann was the most influential NT scholar of the twentieth century, one of the last products of the great German theological juggernaut. Furthermore, he is a key transitional figure, representing both continuity and change. Trained in the old history-of-religions approach to the Bible, he did his dissertation on Paul's use of the diatribe, a rhetorical and literary device that is still receiving attention as an important feature in some of Paul's letters, especially Romans. Among those who used the diatribe in the Greco-Roman world were the moralists and popular philosophers, such as Seneca and Epictetus, who shared the Christians' interest in moral formation and thus continue to merit the attention of contemporary scholars. Therefore, the essays by Hans-Josef Klauck, Abraham Malherbe, and Margaret Mitchell represent continuing concern with some of the issues that occupied Bultmann's interest and with the methods he used, though each of these scholars' own approach is distinct.

As a student of Johannes Weiss (1863–1914), Bultmann shared his teacher's fascination with Jewish apocalyptic, but he was much more intrigued by the question of how Paul utilized Jewish and Hellenistic myths, adapting them in his proclamation of the gospel. Heavily influenced by the existentialism of Martin Heidegger, he was interested in how Paul's demythologizing (or, more accurately, re-mythologizing) might be instructive for the same hermeneutical endeavor in the modern world. His essay is a vivid reminder of the cultural chasm that separates modern readers from the apostle and his world, and the challenge of avoiding two perennial dangers in interpreting him, the Scylla of modernizing Paul and the Charybdis of archaizing ourselves.

Nils Dahl, like many twentieth-century Lutheran New Testament scholars, studied with Bultmann but was by no means his disciple. A master exegete with catholic interests and a relentless curiosity, Dahl emphasized the Jewishness of early Christianity and explored the manifold ways in which the first Christians interpreted Jesus in light of Jewish scriptures and traditions. This approach entails an examination of the interpretive methods known as midrash, used by scribes and rabbis to draw out the meaning of a sacred text, and the pesher method favored by those at Qumran. The New Testament's interpretation of the Hebrew Bible and its traditions has been a strong interest of modern scholars, and Dahl's essay, printed below, explores the interpretive links between one of the most infamous stories in the Bible—the patriarchal legend of God commanding Abraham to offer his son Isaac as a holocaust— and the crucifixion of Jesus. In Romans 8:32 Paul alludes to this story, known in Jewish tradition as the "Akedah" or "Binding" of Isaac (Gen. 22:9), and Dahl demonstrates in his essay how Paul's depiction of Jesus' death is a midrash on the biblical text.

Archaeological discoveries that yield new evidence can be enormously influential in shaping the discussion of biblical documents and writers. During Bultmann's student days and early career, the discovery of thousands of papyri not only revolutionized the understanding of daily life in ancient Egypt but also revealed the form, function, and vocabulary of the Hellenistic letter. These papyri were particularly exploited for the study of Paul by Adolf Deissmann (1866–1937), who used them *inter alia* to show that Paul's vocabulary represented the Koine Greek of the Greco-Roman period. In a similar way, the discovery in the 1940s of the texts that comprise the Dead Sea Scrolls and the Nag Hammadi library opened up new vistas of understanding in regard to Second Temple Judaism and Gnosticism, and both have been used, with varying degrees of success, in interpreting Paul's letters. Again, modern perspectives on Jewish and Christian pictorial art during the Greco-Roman period were forever changed by the discovery of a Jewish synagogue and Christian church in the Roman frontier town of Dura-Europos (located in modern Syria). The former had frescoed walls depicting both people and animals, and the latter had a baptistery, with the Good Shepherd painted on the canopy wall and scenes inspired by stories from both the Hebrew Bible and New Testament drawn on the baptistery walls. Both buildings had been converted from private homes, the primary setting in which Christians in Paul's day worshiped and celebrated the Eucharist. In addition to making use of these and other discoveries, contemporary scholars are making an increasingly extensive use of epigraphic and demographic evidence to interpret Paul's letters. The relevance of such evidence for understanding the New Testament is shown by Peter Lampe, who uses inscriptions to illumine Romans 16 and the situation that Paul addresses in writing to the Christians in that city.

Deissmann also used the papyri to paint a simple sociological portrait of early Christianity as strictly a movement of the lower classes of society. Making an unfounded terminological distinction between the literary "epistles" of *Hochliteratur* and the simple "letters" used in everyday correspondence, he declared that all of Paul's missives were "letters," written in the medium and with the language that his converts, drawn almost exclusively from the lower classes, could understand. In short, he read Paul's declaration in 1 Corinthians 1:26 that "not many" of the Corinthians were wise, powerful, or of noble birth, to mean that *none* were.

That one-dimensional depiction of Pauline Christians remained the standard view for nearly half a century, until it began to come under vigorous attack from different quarters as a distortion of the evidence. More nuanced literary and rhetorical analyses demonstrated that Paul's letters were quite different from the simple one-sheet papyrus letters that Deissmann had used, and scholars began to invoke both epistolary and rhetorical theory for the study of the apostle's letters. More sophisticated sociological analyses showed that the Pauline communities encompassed not only Jew and Gentile, male and female, slave and free, but also rich and poor, the powerful and the socially impotent. Indeed, most of the individuals whose names we know from his letters seem not to have belonged to the lower classes. For instance, Erastus, the city of Corinth's director of public works (Rom. 16:24), had a position that entailed a certain social prominence, and Aquila and Prisca, though tentmakers like Paul, were sufficiently affluent to live in houses that could accommodate the assembling of a few dozen Christians for worship. Furthermore, many of the issues over which early Christians quarreled had a noteworthy economic aspect. That should have already been clear from Paul's discussion of the Eucharist in 1 Corinthians 11, where he chides the satiated and intoxicated "haves" for shaming the "have-nots." But it also played a role in issues such as the eating of meat, which had a religious, economic, and social significance in Paul's day that it lacks in ours.

One of the pioneers in reopening the sociological investigation of the early Christian movement is Gerd Theissen, one of whose ground-breaking discussions is excerpted below. But recognition of his approach was not instantaneous. On the contrary, Theissen initially had difficulty securing a position in Germany because so many theologians resisted or dismissed this important means of analysis—it was in North America that his proposals first received a positive response and stimulated vigorous dialogue. The rich dividends yielded by sociology ultimately could not be ignored, and this approach is pursued today by many scholars using various social-scientific forms of analysis.

As previously indicated, the last fifty years have witnessed women entering academic life in increasing numbers, and their participation has altered scholarly dialogue in countless salutary ways. Since female New Testament scholars are as diverse as their male counterparts, we offer here excerpts from discussions by two distinguished Pauline scholars. The first is Elisabeth Schüssler Fiorenza, a German-born and trained scholar who has spent most of her career at Harvard. Her 1983 book *In Memory of Her* quickly became a feminist classic that already has been translated into twelve languages. The second is Jouette Bassler, an American who turned to New Testament studies from a career in chemistry and joined a new wave of women attracted to the field as it struggled for a more diverse and open-ended identity in the 1970s. Finally, because issues of gender, sexuality, and ethnicity are important in our own post-modern society, New Testament scholars, female and male alike, have begun to ask questions of early Christian literature that involve these issues. But are our assumptions about these issues the same as Paul's? What, for example, is the relationship between Paul's attitude toward sexuality and his view of the passions? In the final essay in this section Dale Martin explores Paul's view of the relationship between sexual desire and marriage. He challenges the common view that Paul viewed marriage as the appropriate context for the expression of sexual desire and argues that his real goal was the extirpation of desire.

RUDOLF BULTMANN

[Paul's Demythologizing and Ours] (1941)†

The mythology of the New Testament is in essence that of Jewish apoca-lyptic and the Gnostic redemption myths. A common feature of them both is their basic dualism, according to which the present world and its human inhabitants are under the control of daemonic, satanic powers, and stand in need of redemption. Man cannot achieve this redemption by his own efforts; it must come as a gift through a divine intervention. Both types of mythology speak of such an intervention: Jewish apocalyptic of an immi-nent world crisis in which this present aeon will be brought to an end and the new aeon ushered in by the coming of the Messiah, and Gnosticism of a Son of God sent down from the realm of light, entering into this world in the guise of a man, and by his fate and teaching delivering the elect and opening up the way for their return to the heavenly home.

The meaning of these two types of mythology lies once more not in their imagery with its apparent objectivity but in the understanding of human existence which both are trying to express. In other words, they need to be interpreted existentially. A good example of such treatment is to be found in Hans Jonas's book on Gnosticism.[1]

Our task is to produce an existentialist interpretation of the dualistic mythology of the New Testament along similar lines. When, for instance, we read of daemonic powers ruling the world and holding mankind in bondage, does the understanding of human existence which underlies such language offer a solution to the riddle of human life which will be accept-able even to the non-mythological mind of to-day? Of course we must not take this to imply that the New Testament presents us with an anthropol-ogy like that which modern science can give us. It cannot be proved by logic or demonstrated by an appeal to factual evidence. Scientific anthro-pologies always take for granted a definite understanding of existence, which is invariably the consequence of a deliberate decision of the scien-tist, whether he makes it consciously or not. And that is why we have to discover whether the New Testament offers man an understanding of him-self which will challenge him to a genuine existential decision.

Demythologizing in Outline

A. THE CHRISTIAN INTERPRETATION OF BEING

1. Human Existence apart from Faith

What does the New Testament mean when it talks of the "world", of "this world" * * * or of "this aeon"* * *? In speaking thus, the New Tes-tament is in agreement with the Gnostics, for they too speak of "this world", and of the princes, prince, or god of this world; and moreover they

† From "New Testament and Mythology," in *Kerygma and Myth*, ed. by Hans Werner Bartsch, tr. by Reginald H. Fuller (2nd ed.; London: SCM, 1964), 1–44. The essay was first published in 1941. Reprinted by permission of SPCK Publishing. Rudolf Karl Bultmann (1884–1976), profes-sor of New Testament in Giessen, 1920, and Marburg from 1921 until his retirement, was the most influential twentieth-century European scholar of the New Testament.
1. *Gnosis und spätantiker Geist.* I. *Die mythologische Gnosis*, 1934. [Rev. ed., 1964. See the simplified and shortened version. *The Gnostic Religion* (Boston: Beacon, 1963).]

both regard man as the slave of the world and its powers. But there is one significant difference. In the New Testament one of these powers is conspicuously absent—viz., *matter*, the physical, sensual part of man's constitution. Never does the New Testament complain that the soul of man, his authentic self, is imprisoned in a material body: never does it complain of the power of sensuality over the spirit. That is why it never doubts the responsibility of man for his sin. God is always the Creator of the world, including human life in the body. He is also the Judge before whom man must give account. The part played by Satan as the Lord of this world must therefore be limited in a peculiar way, or else, if he is the lord or god of world, "this world" must stand in a peculiar dialectical relation to the world as the creation of God.

"This world" is the world of corruption and death. Clearly, it was not so when it left the hands of the Creator, for it was only in consequence of the fall of Adam that death entered into the world (Rom. 5:12). Hence it is sin, rather than matter as such, which is the cause of corruption and death. The Gnostic conception of the soul as a pure, celestial element imprisoned by some tragic fate in a material body is entirely absent. Death is the wages of sin (Rom. 6:23; cf. 1 Cor. 15:56). True, St Paul seems to agree with the Gnostics as regards the effects which he ascribes to the fall of Adam as the ancestor of the human race. But it is clear that he later returns to the idea of individual responsibility when he says that since Adam death came to all men "for that all sinned" (Rom. 5:12), a statement which stands in formal contradiction to the Adam theory. Perhaps he means to say that with Adam death became possible rather than inevitable. However that may be, there is another idea which St Paul is constantly repeating and which is equally incompatible with the Adam theory, and that is the theory that sin, including death, is derived from the flesh (*sarx*, Rom. 8:13; Gal. 6:8, etc.). But what does he mean by "flesh"? Not the bodily or physical side of human nature, but the sphere of visible, concrete, tangible, and measurable reality, which as such is also the sphere of corruption and death. When a man chooses to live entirely in and for this sphere, or, as St Paul puts it, when he "lives after the flesh", it assumes the shape of a "power". There are indeed many different ways of living after the flesh. There is the crude life of sensual pleasure and there is the refined way of basing one's life on the pride of achievement, on the "works of the law" as St Paul would say. But these distinctions are ultimately immaterial. For "flesh" embraces not only the material things of life, but all human creation and achievement pursued for the sake of some tangible reward, such as for example the fulfilling of the law (Gal. 3:3). It includes every passive quality, and every advantage a man can have, in the sphere of visible, tangible reality (Phil. 3:4ff.).

St Paul sees that the life of man is weighed down by anxiety (* * * 1 Cor. 7:32ff.). Every man focuses his anxiety upon some particular object. The natural man focuses it upon security, and in proportion to his opportunities and his success in the visible sphere he places his "confidence" in the "flesh" (Phil. 3:3f.), and the consciousness of security finds its expression in "glorying" * * *.

Such a pursuit is, however, incongruous with man's real situation, for the fact is that he is not secure at all. Indeed, this is the way in which he loses his true life and becomes the slave of that very sphere which he had hoped to master, and which he hoped would give him security. Whereas hitherto he might have enjoyed the world as God's creation, it has now become "this world", the world in revolt against God. This is the way in which the "powers" which dominate human life come into being, and as such they acquire the character of mythical entities. Since the visible and tangible sphere is essentially transitory, the man who bases his life on it becomes the prisoner and slave of corruption. An illustration of this may be seen in the way our attempts to secure visible security for ourselves bring us into collision with others; we can seek security for ourselves only at their expense. Thus on the one hand we get envy, anger, jealousy, and the like, and on the other compromise, bargainings, and adjustments of conflicting interests. This creates an all-pervasive atmosphere which controls all our judgements; we all pay homage to it and take it for granted. Thus man becomes the slave of anxiety (Rom. 8:15). Everybody tries to hold fast to his own life and property because he has a secret feeling that it is all slipping away from him.

THE LIFE OF FAITH

The authentic life, on the other hand, would be a life based on unseen, intangible realities. Such a life means the abandonment of all self-contrived security. This is what the New Testament means by "life after the Spirit" or "life in faith".

For this life we must have faith in *the grace of God*. It means faith that the unseen, intangible reality actually confronts us as love, opening up our future and signifying not death but life.

The grace of God means *the forgiveness of sin*, and brings deliverance from the bondage of the past. The old quest for visible security, the hankering after tangible realities, and the clinging to transitory objects, is sin, for by it we shut out invisible reality from our lives and refuse God's future which comes to us as a gift. But once we open our hearts to the grace of God, our sins are forgiven; we are released from the past. This is what is meant by "faith": to open ourselves freely to the future. But at the same time faith involves obedience, for faith means turning our backs on self and abandoning all security. It means giving up every attempt to carve out a niche in life for ourselves, surrendering all our self-confidence, and resolving to trust in God alone, in the God who raises the dead (2 Cor. 1:9) and who calls the things that are not into being (Rom. 4:17). It means radical self-commitment to God in the expectation that everything will come from him and nothing from ourselves. Such a life spells deliverance from all worldly, tangible objects, leading to complete detachment from the world and thus to freedom.

This detachment from the world is something quite different from asceticism. It means preserving a distance from the world and dealing with it in a spirit of "as if not" (*hōs mē*, 1 Cor. 7:29–31). The believer is lord of all things (1 Cor. 3:21–3). He enjoys that power (*exousia*) of which the Gnostic boasts, but with the proviso: "All things are lawful for me, but I will not be brought under the power of any" (1 Cor. 6:12; cf. 10:23f.). The believer may "rejoice with them that do rejoice, and weep with them that weep" (Rom. 12:15), but he is no longer in bondage to anything in the world (1 Cor. 7:17–24). Everything in the world has become indifferent and unimportant. "For though I was free from all men, I brought myself under bondage to all" (1 Cor. 9:19–23). "I know how to be abased, and I know also how to abound in everything, and in all things I have learned the secret both to be filled and to be hungry, both to abound and to be in want" (Phil. 4:12). The world has been crucified to him, and he to the world (Gal. 6:14). Moreover, the power of his new life is manifested even in weakness, suffering, and death (2 Cor. 4:7–11; 12:9f.). Just when he realizes that he is nothing in himself, he can have and be all things through God (2 Cor. 12:9f.; 6:8–10).

Now, this is eschatological existence; it means being a "new creature" (2 Cor. 5:17). The eschatology of Jewish apocalyptic and of Gnosticism has been emancipated from its accompanying mythology, in so far as the age of salvation has already dawned for the believer and the life of the future has become a present reality. The fourth gospel carries this process to a logical conclusion by completely eliminating every trace of apocalyptic eschatology. The last judgement is no longer an imminent cosmic event, for it is already taking place in the coming of Jesus and in his summons to believe (John 3:19; 9:39; 12:31). The believer has life here and now, and has passed already from death into life (5:24, etc.). Outwardly everything remains as before, but inwardly his relation to the world has been radically changed. The world has no further claim on him, for faith is the victory which overcometh the world (1 John 5:4).

The eschatology of Gnosticism is similarly transcended. It is not that the believer is given a new nature (*physis*) or that his preexistent nature is emancipated, or that his soul is assured of a journey to heaven. The new life in faith is not an assured possession or endowment, which could lead only to libertinism. Nor is it a possession to be guarded with care and vigilance, which could lead only to asceticism. Life in faith is not a possession at all. It cannot be exclusively expressed in indicative terms; it needs an imperative to complete it. In other words, the decision of faith is never final; it needs constant renewal in every fresh situation. Our freedom does not excuse us from the demand under which we all stand as men, for it is freedom for obedience (Rom. 6:11ff.). To believe means not to have apprehended but to have been apprehended. It means always to be travelling along the road between the "already" and the "not yet", always to be pursuing a goal.

For Gnosticism redemption is a cosmic process in which the redeemed are privileged to participate here and now. Although essentially transcendent, faith must be reduced to an immanent possession. Its outward signs are freedom (*eleutheria*) power (*exousia*), pneumatic phenomena, and above all ecstasy. In the last resort the New Testament knows no phenomena in which transcendent realities become immanent possessions. True, St Paul is familiar with ecstasy (2 Cor. 5:13; 12:1ff.). But he refuses to accept it as a proof of the possession of the Spirit. The New Testament never speaks of the training of the soul in mystical experience or of ecstasy as the culmination of the Christian life. Not psychic phenomena but faith is the hallmark of that life.

Certainly St Paul shares the popular belief of his day that the Spirit manifests itself in miracles, and he attributes abnormal psychic phenomena to its agency. But the enthusiasm of the Corinthians for such things brought home to him their questionable character. So he insists that the gifts of the Spirit must be judged according to their value for "edification", and in so doing he transcends the popular view of the Spirit as an agency that operates like any other natural force. True, he regards the Spirit as a mysterious entity dwelling in man and guaranteeing his resurrection. (Rom. 8:11). He can even speak of the Spirit as if it were a kind of super-natural material (1 Cor. 15:44ff.). Yet in the last resort he clearly means by "Spirit" the possibility of a new life which is opened up by faith. The Spirit does not work like a supernatural force, nor is it the permanent possession of the believer. It is the possibility of a new life which must be appropriated by a deliberate resolve. Hence St Paul's paradoxical injunc-tion: "If we live by the Spirit, by the Spirit also let us walk." (Gal. 5:25). "Being led by the Spirit" (Rom. 8:14) is not an automatic process of nature, but the fulfilment of an imperative: "live after the Spirit, not after the flesh". Imperative and indicative are inseparable. The possession of the Spirit never renders decision superfluous. "I say, Walk by the Spirit and ye shall not fulfil the lust of the flesh" (Gal. 5:16). Thus the concept "Spirit" has been emancipated from mythology.

The Pauline catalogue of the fruits of the Spirit ("love, joy, peace, long-suffering, kindness, goodness, faithfulness, temperance", Gal. 5:22) shows how faith, by detaching man from the world, makes him capable of fellow-ship in community. Now that he is delivered from anxiety and from the frustration which comes from clinging to the tangible realities of the visible world, man is free to enjoy fellowship with others. Hence faith is described as "working through love" (Gal. 5:6). And this means being a new creature (cf. Gal. 5:6 with 6:15).

B. THE EVENT OF REDEMPTION

1. Christian Self-Understanding without Christ?

We have now suggested an existentialist unmythological interpretation of the Christian understanding of Being. But is this interpretation true to the New Testament? We seem to have overlooked one important point, which is that in the New Testament faith is always *faith in Christ*. Faith, in the strict sense of the word, was only there at a certain moment in history. It had to be *revealed; it came* (Gal. 3:23, 25). This might of course be taken as part of the story of man's spiritual evolution. But the New Testament means more than that. It claims that faith only became possible at a definite point in history in consequence of an *event*—viz., the event of Christ. Faith in the sense of obedient self-commitment and inward detachment from the world is only possible when it is faith in Jesus Christ.

Here indeed is the crux of the matter—have we here a remnant of mythology which still requires restatement? In fact it comes to this: can we have a Christian understanding of Being without Christ?

*   *   *

The point at issue is how we understand the fall. Even the philosophers are agreed about the fact of it. But they think that all man needs is to be shown his plight, and that then he will be able to escape from it. In other words, the corruption resulting from the fall does not extend to the core of the human personality. The New Testament, on the other hand, regards the fall as total.

How then, if the fall be total, can man be aware of his plight? He certainly is aware of it, as the philosophers themselves testify. How can man be aware that his fall is total and that it extends to the very core of his personality? As a matter of fact, it is the other way round: it is only because man is a fallen being, only because he knows he is not what he really ought to be and what he would like to be, that he can be aware of his plight. That awareness of his authentic nature is essential to human life, and without it man would not be man. But his authentic nature is not an endowment of creation or a possession at his own disposal. The philosophers would agree thus far, for they also know that man's authentic nature has to be apprehended by a deliberate resolve. But they think that all man needs is to be told about his authentic nature. This nature is what he never realizes, but what at every moment he is capable of realizing—you can because you ought. But the philosophers are confusing a theoretical possibility with an actual one. For, as the New Testament sees it, man has lost that actual possibility, and even his awareness of his authentic manhood is perverted, as is shown by his deluded belief that it is a possession he can command at will.

*   *   *

This means, in the language of the New Testament, that man is a sinner. The self-assertion of which we have spoken is identical with sin. Sin is self-assertion, self-glorying, for "No flesh should glory before God. . . . He that glorieth, let him glory in the Lord" (1 Cor. 1:29, 31; 2 Cor. 10:17). Is that no more than an unnecessary mythologizing of an ontological proposition? Can man as he is perceive that self-assertion involves guilt, and that he is personally responsible to God for it? Is sin a mythological concept or not? The answer will depend on what we make of St Paul's words to the Corinthians: "What hast thou that thou didst not receive? but if thou didst receive it, why dost thou glory, as if thou hadst not received it?" (1 Cor. 4:7). Does this apply to all men alike, or only to Christians? This much at any rate is clear: self-assertion is guilt only if it can be understood as ingratitude. If the radical self-assertion which makes it impossible for man to achieve the authentic life of self-commitment is identical with sin, it must obviously be possible for man to understand his existence altogether as a gift of God. But it is just this radical self-assertion which makes such an understanding impossible. For self-assertion deludes man into thinking that his existence is a prize within his own grasp. How blind man is to his plight is illustrated by that pessimism which regards life as a burden thrust on man against his will, or by the way men talk about the "right to live" or by the way they expect their fair share of good fortune. Man's radical self-assertion then blinds him to the fact of sin, and this is the clearest proof that he is a fallen being. Hence it is no good telling man that he is a sinner. He will only dismiss it as mythology. But it does not follow that he is right.

To talk of sin ceases to be mere mythology when the love of God meets man as a power which embraces and sustains him even in his fallen, self-assertive state. Such a love treats man as if he were other than he is. By so doing, love frees man from himself as he is.

For as a result of his self-assertion man is a totally fallen being. He is capable of knowing that his authentic life consists in self-commitment, but is incapable of realizing it because however hard he tries he still remains what he is, self-assertive man. So in practice authentic life becomes possible only when man is delivered from himself. It is the claim of the New Testament that this is exactly what happened. This is precisely the meaning of that which was wrought in Christ. At the very point where man can do nothing, God steps in and acts—indeed he has acted already—on man's behalf.

St Paul is endeavouring to express this when he speaks of the expiation of sin, or of "righteousness" created as a gift of God rather than as a human achievement. Through Christ, God has reconciled the world to himself, not reckoning to it its trespasses (2 Cor. 5:19). God made Christ to be sin for us, that we through him might stand before God as righteous (2 Cor. 5:21). For everyone who believes, his past life is dead and done with. He is a new creature, and as such he faces each new moment. In short, he has become a free man.

It is quite clear from this that forgiveness of sins is not a juridical concept. It does not mean the remission of punishment. If that were so, man's plight would be as bad as ever. Rather, forgiveness conveys freedom from sin, which hitherto had held man in bondage. But this freedom is not a static quality: it is freedom to *obey*. The indicative implies an imperative. Love is the fulfilment of the law, and therefore the forgiveness of God delivers man from himself and makes him free to devote his life to the service of others (Rom. 13:8–10; Gal. 5:14).

Thus eschatological existence has become possible. God has *acted*, and the world—"this world"—has come to an end. *Man himself has been made new.* "If any man is in Christ, he is a new creature: the old things are passed away; behold, they are become new" (2 Cor. 5:17). * * *

The event of Jesus Christ is therefore the revelation of the love of God. It makes a man free from himself and free to be himself, free to live a life of self-commitment in faith and love. But faith in this sense of the word is possible only where it takes the form of faith in the love of God. Yet such faith is still a subtle form of self-assertion so long as the love of God is merely a piece of wishful thinking. It is only an abstract idea so long as God has not revealed his love. That is why faith for the Christian means faith in Christ, for it is faith in the love of God revealed in Christ. Only those who are loved are capable of loving.

* * *

The classic statement of this self-commitment of God, which is the ground of our own self-commitment, is to be found in Rom. 8:32 "God spared not his Son, but delivered him up for us; how shall he not also with him freely give us all things?" Compare the Johannine text: "God so loved the world, that he gave his only-begotten Son, that whosoever believeth in him should not perish, but have eternal life" (John 3:16). There are also similar texts which speak of Jesus' giving up himself for us: ". . . who gave himself for our sins, that he might deliver us out of this present evil world" (Gal. 1:4); "I have been crucified with Christ; yet I live; and yet no longer I, but Christ liveth in me: and the life which I live in the flesh I live in faith, the faith which is in the Son of God, who loved me and gave himself up for me" (Gal. 2:19f.).

Here then is the crucial distinction between the New Testament and existentialism, between the Christian faith and the natural understanding of Being. The New Testament speaks and faith knows of an act of God through which man becomes capable of self-commitment, capable of faith and love, of his authentic life.

* * *

(A) THE DEMYTHOLOGIZING OF THE EVENT OF JESUS CHRIST

Now, it is beyond question that the New Testament presents the event of Jesus Christ in mythical terms. The problem is whether that is the only possible presentation. Or does the New Testament itself demand a restatement of the event of Jesus Christ in nonmythological terms?

* * *

In the end the crux of the matter lies in the cross and resurrection.

(B) THE CROSS

Is the cross, understood as the event of redemption, exclusively mythical in character, or can it retain its value for salvation without forfeiting its character as history?

* * *

In its redemptive aspect the cross of Christ is no mere mythical event, but a historic (*geschichtlich*) fact originating in the historical (*historisch*) event which is the crucifixion of Jesus. The abiding significance of the cross is that it is the judgement of the world, the judgement and the deliverance of man. So far as this is so, Christ is crucified "for us", not in the sense of any theory of sacrifice or satisfaction. This interpretation of the cross as a permanent fact rather than a mythological event does far more justice to the redemptive significance of the event of the past than any of the traditional interpretations. In the last resort mythological language is only a medium for conveying the significance of the historical (*historisch*) event. The historical (*historisch*) event of the cross has, in the significance peculiar to it, created a new historic (*geschichtlich*) situation. The preaching of the cross as the event of redemption challenges all who hear it to appropriate this significance for themselves, to be willing to be crucified with Christ.

But, it will be asked, is this significance to be discerned in the actual event of past history? Can it, so to speak, be read off from that event? Or does the cross bear this significance because it is the cross of *Christ*? In other words, must we first be convinced of the significance of Christ and believe in him in order to discern the real meaning of the cross? If we are to perceive the real meaning of the cross, must we understand it as the cross of Jesus as a figure of past history? Must we go back to the Jesus of history?

As far as the first preachers of the gospel are concerned this will certainly be the case. For them the cross was the cross of him with whom they had lived in personal intercourse. The cross was an experience of their own lives. It presented them with a question and it disclosed to them its meaning. But for us this personal connection cannot be reproduced. For us the cross cannot disclose its own meaning: it is an event of the past. We can never recover it as an event in our own lives. All we know of it is derived from historical report. But the New Testament does not proclaim Jesus Christ in this way. The meaning of the cross is not disclosed from the life of Jesus as a figure of past history, a life which needs to be reproduced by historical research. On the contrary, Jesus is not proclaimed merely as the crucified; he is also risen from the dead. The cross and the resurrection form an inseparable unity.

(c) THE RESURRECTION

But what of the resurrection? Is it not a mythical event pure and simple? Obviously it is not an event of past history with a self-evident meaning. Can the resurrection narratives and every other mention of the resurrection in the New Testament be understood simply as an attempt to convey the meaning of the cross? Does the New Testament, in asserting that Jesus is risen from the dead, mean that his death is not just an ordinary human death, but the judgement and salvation of the world, depriving death of its power? Does it not express this truth in the affirmation that the Crucified was not holden of death, but rose from the dead?

Yes indeed: the cross and the resurrection form a single, indivisible cosmic event. "He was delivered up for our trespasses, and was raised for our justification" (Rom. 4:25). The cross is not an isolated event, as though it were the end of Jesus, which needed the resurrection subsequently to reverse it. When he suffered death, Jesus was already the Son of God, and his death by itself was the victory over the power of death. St John brings this out most clearly by describing the passion of Jesus as the "hour" in which he is glorified, and by the double meaning he gives to the phrase "lifted up", applying it both to the cross and to Christ's exaltation into glory.

Cross and resurrection form a single, indivisible cosmic event which brings judgement to the world and opens up for men the possibility of authentic life. But if that be so, the resurrection cannot be a miraculous proof capable of demonstration and sufficient to convince the sceptic that the cross really has the cosmic and eschatological significance ascribed to it.

* * *

Yes indeed: the resurrection of Jesus cannot be a miraculous proof by which the sceptic might be compelled to believe in Christ. The difficulty is not simply the incredibility of a mythical event like the resuscitation of a dead person—for that is what the resurrection means, as is shown by the fact that the risen Lord is apprehended by the physical senses. Nor is it merely the impossibility of establishing the objective historicity of the resurrection no matter how many witnesses are cited, as though once it was established it might be believed beyond all question and faith might have its unimpeachable guarantee. No; the real difficulty is that the resurrection is itself an article of faith, and you cannot establish one article of faith by invoking another. You cannot prove the redemptive efficacy of the cross by invoking the resurrection. For the resurrection is an article of faith because it is far more than the resuscitation of a corpse—it is the eschatological event. And so it cannot be a miraculous proof. For, quite apart from its credibility, the bare miracle tells us nothing about the eschatological fact of the destruction of death. Moreover, such a miracle is not otherwise unknown to mythology.

It is however abundantly clear that the New Testament is interested in the resurrection of Christ simply and solely because it is the eschatological event *par excellence*. By it Christ abolished death and brought life and immortality to light (2 Tim. 1:10). This explains why St Paul borrows Gnostic language to clarify the meaning of the resurrection. As in the death of Jesus all have died (2 Cor 5:14f.), so through his resurrection all have been raised from the dead, though naturally this event is spread over a long period of time (1 Cor. 15:21f.). But St Paul does not only say: "In Christ shall all be made alive"; he can also speak of rising again with Christ in the present tense, just as he speaks of our dying with him. Through the sacrament of baptism Christians participate not only in the death of Christ but also in his resurrection. It is not simply that we *shall* walk with him in newness of life and be united with him in his resurrection (Rom. 6:4f.); we are doing so already here and now. "Even so reckon ye yourselves to be dead indeed unto sin, but alive unto God in Jesus Christ" (Rom. 6:11.).

Once again, in everyday life the Christians participate not only in the death of Christ but also in his resurrection. In this resurrection-life they enjoy a freedom, albeit a struggling freedom, from sin (Rom. 6:11ff.). They are able to "cast off the works of darkness", so that the approaching day when the darkness shall vanish is already experienced here and now. "Let us walk honestly as in the day" (Rom. 13:12f.): "we are not of the night, nor of the darkness. . . . Let us, since we are of the day, be sober . . ." (1 Thess. 5:5–8). St Paul seeks to share not only the sufferings of Christ but also "the power of his resurrection" (Phil. 3:10). So he bears about in his body the dying of Jesus, "that the life also of Jesus may be manifested in our body" (2 Cor 4:10f.). Similarly, when the Corinthians demand a proof of his apostolic authority, he solemnly warns them: "Christ is not weak, but is powerful in you: for he was crucified in weakness, yet he liveth in the power of God. For we also are weak in him, but we shall live with him through the power of God toward you" (2 Cor. 13:3f.).

In this way the resurrection is not a mythological event adduced in order to prove the saving efficacy of the cross, but an article of faith just as much as the meaning of the cross itself. Indeed, *faith in the resurrection is really the same thing as faith in the saving efficacy of the cross*, faith in the cross as the cross of Christ. Hence you cannot first believe in Christ and then in the strength of that faith believe in the cross. To believe in Christ means to believe in the cross as the cross of Christ. The saving efficacy of the cross is not derived from the fact that it is the cross of Christ: it is the cross of Christ because it has this saving efficacy. Without that efficacy it is the tragic end of a great man.

*   *   *

The real Easter faith is faith in the word of preaching which brings illumination. If the event of Easter Day is in any sense an historical event additional to the event of the cross, it is nothing else than the rise of faith in the risen Lord, since it was this faith which led to the apostolic preaching. The resurrection itself is not an event of past history. All that historical criticism can establish is the fact that the first disciples came to believe in the resurrection. The historian can perhaps to some extent account for that faith from the personal intimacy which the disciples had enjoyed with Jesus during his earthly life, and so reduce the resurrection appearances to a series of subjective visions. But the historical problem is not of interest to Christian belief in the resurrection. For the historical event of the rise of the Easter faith means for us what it meant for the first disciples—namely, the self-attestation of the risen Lord, the act of God in which the redemptive event of the cross is completed.

NILS ALSTRUP DAHL

[The Atonement and the Akedah] (1969)†

By the atonement, I here understand the death of Jesus interpreted as a divine act of redemption, regardless of the specific terminology used by various writers. The Akedah means what in Christian tradition is called the sacrifice, and in Jewish tradition the binding of Isaac ('*aqedat yiṣḥāq*), as interpreted in the haggadah.[1] Similarities between the atonement and the Akedah have long been observed.

*   *   *

Reactions to the Christian doctrine of the atonement may have stimulated the development of the haggadah, but only as a secondary factor. Much more open is the other problem, namely, to what extent and in which ways the Akedah served as a model for early Christian understanding of the atonement. The number of parallels would be hard to explain without the assumption of some kind of relationship, and yet the New Testament texts are elusive. The few explicit references to the sacrifice of Isaac do not deal with the atonement, and passages that deal with the atonement may be more or less reminiscent of the Akedah but never make the allusion explicit. This is the case even in Romans 8:32, where the formulation "he who did not spare his own Son but gave him up for us all" is obviously reminiscent of Genesis 22, as has been recognized by exegetes from Origen onward. Why did Paul use a phrase drawn from the story of Abraham's sacrifice of his son in order to speak about the death of Christ? An answer to this question would illuminate the way in which the atonement was first related to the Akedah. The results may remain conjectural, but an exploration is worth attempting.

† "The Atonement: An Adequate Reward for the Akedah? (Ro. 8.32)," was first published in *Neotestamentica et Semitica*, ed. by E. Earle Ellis and Max Wilcox (Edinburgh: T & T Clark, 1969), 15–29, and reprinted in two volumes of Dahl's collected essays, *The Crucified Messiah and Other Essays* (Minneapolis: Augsburg, 1974) and *Jesus the Christ* (Minneapolis: Fortress, 1991). Reprinted by permission of Continuum International Publishing Group. Dahl (1911–2001), one of the giants of NT scholarship in the twentieth century, taught at Oslo until joining the faculty at Yale University, where he was Buckingham Professor of New Testament in Yale Divinity School and the Department of Religious Studies from 1965 until his retirement in 1980. Known for his seminal essays and his emphasis upon the earliest years of the Christian movement as a time of intense interpretive activity, Dahl demonstrates here how Jewish traditions about the binding of Isaac in Gen. 22 were applied to the death of Jesus.
1. Heb. *haggadah* (or *aggadah*) refers to rabbinic biblical interpretation (*midrash*) that focuses on narrative content rather than deriving legally binding rules (*halakah*).

* * *

The form of Romans 8:32 is that of a syllogism; if the protasis is valid, the apodosis must follow. Within its present context, the passage reminiscent of Abraham's sacrifice therefore functions as a warrant for the certitude of full salvation. As to its content, the passage runs parallel to Romans 5:8–9 and 5:10, where we have the more regular form for a conclusion a fortiori, with *pollǭ mallon*. The formulations are open to variation, but Paul can assume that there is agreement upon the protasis and, quite likely, that such formulations were familiar to Christians at Rome. The same holds true also for the famous *hilastērion* passage in Romans 3: 24–26, to which the other passages on the atonement refer back. In general, while Paul drew new and radical consequences, his basic affirmations concerning the person of Christ and the event of atonement conform to accepted statements of kerygma, creed, and liturgy.

In his commentary on Romans, O. Michel has argued that Romans 8: 32a is based upon some fixed form of preaching. He finds the use of first person plural to be typical of confessional style and points to the creedlike relative clauses in v. 34 as well as to the analogous passages in Romans 4: 25 and John 3:16. Even the linguistic form favors the assumption that Paul's formulation is based upon tradition. Whereas *ouk epheisato* corresponds to the Septuagint, *tou idiou huiou* does not, but rather is an independent rendering of the Hebrew text. Paul is likely to have commented upon the traditional formula not only by appending the apodosis but also by adding *pantōn* to the current phrase *hyper hēmōn* in the protasis. Thus he stresses a main theme of his letter, at the same time achieving a rhetorical correspondence between *hyper hēmōn pantōn* and *ta panta hēmin*. The latter phrase probably refers to nothing short of the eschatological inheritance promised to Abraham and his offspring. Persons familiar with the Genesis texts and their early Christian interpretation may have realized that Paul's cryptic allusion indicated the possibility of scriptural backing for what he wrote.

If Paul's formulation in Romans 8:32a is not created ad hoc, it is no longer sufficient to assume a loose and not very serious use of biblical phraseology. In recent years a number of scholars, representing various schools, have proved that the New Testament use of Scripture presupposes much more conscientious exegetical work than we were formerly inclined to think. The formulation in Romans 8:32a is likely to go back to some kind of midrashic interpretation. The exegetical pattern must have been one of correspondence: as Abraham did not spare his son, so God did not spare his own Son. The question is how this correspondence was understood. According to a predominant, now somewhat fading mood, one would immediately think of the analogy between type and antitype. And certainly it was possible to find a typological relationship between the "binding of Isaac" and the death of Christ. But typology cannot be made the general principle of early Christian hermeneutics, and the statement in Romans 8:32a relates to the conduct of Abraham and not to the suffering of Isaac. It is unlikely that Abraham's act of obedience was ever considered a typological prefiguration of God's act of love.

The text of Genesis 22:16–17 suggests a different type of correspondence, that of act and reward. "By myself I have sworn, says the LORD, because you have done this, and have not withheld your son, your only son, I will indeed bless you. . . ." A homiletic exposition or paraphrase of this promise may well have been the original context of the passage now found in Romans 8:32a. God rewarded Abraham by corresponding action, not sparing his own Son, but giving him up for us (i.e., the descendants of Abraham), and thus he indeed blessed Abraham and promised to bless all nations in his offspring. A homiletic interpretation of this type is not a pure conjecture. It is attested by Irenaeus: "For Abraham, according to his faith, followed the commandment of the Word of God, and with ready mind gave up his only and beloved son, as a sacrifice to God, in order that God might be pleased to offer His beloved and only Son for all his off-spring, as a sacrifice for our salvation." In the Armenian version the idea of reward is even more explicit; it speaks of Abraham as the one "who also through faith asked God that for the sake of humanity (= philanthropy?) He might reward him for his son." The language used is not derived from Romans 8:32, and the reference to Abraham's offspring points to a Jewish-Christian origin of the paraphrase. Is it conceivable that Irenaeus cites a later version of the haggadah from which Romans 8:32a was drawn?

The passage in Irenaeus does not provide more than late and therefore uncertain evidence in favor of a conjecture that I would have dared to venture even without it: the allusion to Genesis 22 in Romans 8:32a is best explained on the assumption that it is derived from an exposition in which the atonement was understood as an "adequate reward" for the Akedah. Obviously, the adequacy should not be understood in terms of quantitative equivalence but as an exact correspondence of quality. In fact, this is how the rule "measure for measure" was applied both in Judaism and in early Christianity. Some early Jewish adherent of the crucified Messiah may have taken Genesis 22 to imply that God, who judges those who judge and shows mercy upon those who act with mercy, rewarded Abraham's sacrifice by offering up his own Son. If this view was actually held, it would provide a most satisfactory explanation for Paul's otherwise cryptic reference in Romans 8:32. Caution forbids us to postulate that Paul's statement may not be explained otherwise. The conjecture would gain credibility if we could prove (1) that the understanding of the atonement as a reward for the Akedah conforms to some trend in contemporary haggadah, (2) that the hypothesis is supported rather than contradicted by other evidence in Paul's letters, and (3) that it would be in harmony with our general knowledge of pre-Pauline Jewish Christianity. In all three respects I regard the evidence as favorable to the conjecture.

I

In Jewish traditions, Isaac was early regarded as a model for suffering martyrs, but there is little, if any, evidence that he was ever seen as a prototype of the Messiah. In several texts, however, God is said to remember the Akedah and therefore to rescue the descendants of Isaac on various occasions, from the exodus to the resurrection of the dead. Both the daily sacrifices in the temple and the blowing of the shofar at Rosh Hashanah make God recall the Akedah. References in prayers offer features of special interest. The kernel of the tradition may be a simple prayer that God might remember the binding of Isaac to the benefit of Israel. This was often spelled out in terms of an "adequate reward." In the Palestinian Targums a prayer is attributed to Abraham, with the following conclusions: "I have done Thy word with joy and have effected Thy decree. And now, when his [Isaac's] children come into a time of distress (*ăḳtā*), remember the binding (*'aḳēdāh*) of Isaac, their father, and listen to their prayer, and answer them and deliver them from all distress." Here the point of correspondence is that God might listen to Israel's prayers, as Abraham listened to God's word.

A version of the haggadah on the prayer of the patriarch, attributed to Rabbi Johanan, includes a reference to Genesis 21:12, "Through Isaac shall your descendants be named." When God, in spite of this promise, told Abraham to offer Isaac as a burnt offering, Abraham could have made a retort. But he suppressed his impulse and asked God to act likewise: "Whenever Isaac's children enter into distress, and there is no one to act as their advocate, do Thou speak up as their advocate." That is, as Abraham made no retort, so God should make no retort. Another variation of the motif is found in the Zikronoth, part of the additional prayer for Rosh Hashanah: "Consider [literally, 'May there appear before Thee'] the binding with which Abraham our Father bound his son Isaac on the altar, suppressing his compassion in order to do Thy will. So let Thy compassion suppress Thine anger (and remove it) from us." It is not necessary here to discuss the relationship between legends and liturgy or to mention all variants. What is important may best be summarized in Spiegel's statement: "It may be surmised that all these variations originally had one feature in common: a parallelism between Abraham's conduct at the Akedah and the conduct expected in return from God."[2]

The parallelism is also attested outside the Akedah prayers.

* * *

None of this material is older than Paul, but all of it illustrates a tendency (well established in the tannaitic period) to relate the history of Israel to the story of Abraham, including the Akedah, by application of the principle "measure for measure." Yet at the crucial point—Abraham's offering of his son—the principle was not applied in non-Christian Judaism. Only an interpreter who believed the crucified Jesus to be Messiah and Son of God could dare to follow the trend consistently to its bitter end, saying that as Abraham offered up his son, so God offered up his own son for Isaac's children.

II

Apart from Romans 8:32 the clearest Pauline allusion to Genesis 22 is found in Galatians 3:13–14. Verse 14a, "That . . . the blessing of Abraham might come upon the Gentiles," is a paraphrase of Genesis 22:18, "And in your offspring shall all the nations of the earth be blessed." The expression "the blessing of Abraham" is taken from Genesis 28:4, and "in Christ Jesus" has been substituted for "in your offspring." It is also likely that the notion of substitution in verse 13 is related to Genesis 22. Here too there is a conscious interpretation in the background. In Deuteronomy 21:23 it is

---

2. Shalom Spiegel, *The Last Trial* (trans. by Judah Goldin; New York: [Pantheon], 1967). The original essay appeared in *Alexander Marx Jubilee Volume* (New York: [Jewish Theological Seminary], 1950) [Dahl's note].

stated that a hanged man is accursed. This might be taken to exclude faith in a crucified Messiah, but the passage could be turned into an argument in favor of the Christian faith if "a man hanging on a tree" was compared with "a ram caught in a thicket" (Gen. 22:13). Thus the crucified Jesus was understood to be the lamb of sacrifice provided by God. Here there is an element of typology; but the ram, rather than Isaac, is seen as a type of Christ.

The allusions to Genesis 22 in Galatians 3 are all contained in verses 13a–14. These verses must be a fragment of pre-Pauline tradition. By his comment in verse 14b Paul identifies the blessing of Abraham with the Spirit, given as a down payment even to Gentile believers. Thus he makes the fragment bear upon the Galatian controversy but blurs the distinction between "us," the Israelites, and the Gentile nations. Moreover, Paul interprets redemption from the curse of the law to imply freedom from the law itself. The phrase "Christ redeemed us from the curse of the law" by itself suggests no more than liberation from the curse inflicted by transgressions of the law, in analogy with Daniel 9:11. According to the pre-Pauline tradition the Messiah, through his substitutionary death upon the cross, redeemed the Israelites from the curse brought about by their transgressions. As a consequence of Israel's redemption the blessing of Abraham would come upon the Gentiles in Abraham's offspring, the Messiah Jesus. The fragment must be of Jewish-Christian origin. Most likely it is derived from a midrash on Genesis 22.

Without considering possible connections with the Akedah, a number of scholars have argued that Paul makes use of traditional formulations in Romans 3:24–25. Others have proposed that the passage alludes to Genesis 22:8, "God will provide himself the lamb for a burnt offering." It is philologically possible to translate *hon proetheto ho theos hilastērion* as "whom God appointed (designed, purposed) to be an expiation." There is some difficulty in that we have no evidence that *protithesthai* was ever used to render *yir'eh* (Gen. 22:8) or the *y r'h* of 22:14. The twofold theory, that Paul cites a tradition of Jewish-Christian origin in which the atonement was related to the Akedah, would help explain several features in the text of Romans 3:24–26. The use of the term *hilastērion* has its closest analogy in *dia . . . tou hilastēriou (tou) thanatou autōn* (4 Macc. 17:22), where the vicarious death of the Maccabean martyrs is seen as an imitation of Isaac. The blood of Isaac is mentioned as early as Pseudo-Philo; redemption, mostly the prototypical redemption from Egypt, is related to the Akedah. The phrase *en Christǫ Iēsou* may well be of pre-Pauline origin on the assumption that "in Christ Jesus" is a paraphrase of "in your offspring," as in Galatians 3:14a.

Considerable problems have been caused by the phrase *dia tēn paresin tōn progegonotōn hamartēmatōn*. This has often been taken to mean God's tolerant "passing over" sins in the past, but a number of exegetes take *paresis* as a synonym for *aphesis*. They generally assume that *dia* with accusative is in the sense of *dia* with genitive. Thus, the clause would state that God's righteousness was manifested through the forgiveness of past sins. The rare word *paresis* is, however, attested to mean legal nonprosecution, dropping of a case. There is no reason why it should not be used in the same sense in Romans 3:25. The sins were committed in the past, in the generations between Isaac and Christ. That the prosecution was dropped, however, is the negative counterpart of providing for expiation and does not refer to tolerance in the past. I would propose the following translation: "Whom God designed to be an expiation . . . by his blood, in order to manifest his righteousness, because the prosecution of the sins committed in the past was dropped in the forbearance of God, so that his righteousness might be manifested in the present time." This interpretation is favored by the analogy with Romans 8:31ff. There the allusion to the Akedah is followed by the question, "Who shall bring any charge against God's elect?" As God, who did not spare his own Son, is the one who justifies, the case has been dropped, and there will be no prosecution. Somewhat analogous also are the Akedah prayers in which God is asked not to make any retort to the children of Isaac and not to listen to their accusers, but to speak up as their advocate.

   This interpretation also makes clear the meaning of the clause *eis endeixin tēs dikaiosynēs autou* * * *. It does not refer to a justice that requires either punishment or expiation, or to righteousness as a gift of God, or even to God's covenantal faithfulness. The phrase is best understood in analogy with Romans 3:4f., "That thou mayest be justified in thy words. . . ." Providing for an expiation, God manifested his righteousness; that is, he vindicated himself as being righteous, doing what he had said. This he did in spite of Israel's sins in the past, because in divine forbearance he dropped the charge against them. In the original context of the fragment, it would have been clear that the manifestation of God's righteousness especially implied that he kept his oath to Abraham (Gen. 22: 16–18). Thus, the fragments of ancient tradition preserved in Romans 8: 32, Galatians 3:13–14, and Romans 3:25f. concur not merely by using a phraseology vaguely reminiscent of the Akedah but also in interpreting the atonement as the fulfillment of what God promised by a solemn oath to Abraham after the sacrifice of Isaac.

   In the Pauline Epistles all passages reminiscent of the Akedah seem to reproduce traditional phraseology. Paul's own interest in the story of Abraham is focused at other points. The understanding of the atonement as reward for the Akedah might even seem to run contrary to Paul's point of view—indeed, to an extent that would exclude his incorporating fragments of a tradition that expressed this idea. Yet, on closer examination, the theory of dependence is confirmed rather than disproved. Stressing that the atonement excludes the *kauchēsis* (of the Jews), Paul goes on to argue that not even Abraham had anything of which to boast. His reward was given *kata charin* and not *kata opheilēma*. (It is not denied that he was rewarded!) Concentrating upon interpretation of Genesis 15:6, Paul avoids any direct reference to Genesis 22, even where we might have expected one. As it would not have been difficult to argue that the trial was a test of Abraham's faith, Paul may have avoided doing so for the sake of simplicity.

   Paul's use of the ancient Jewish-Christian tradition implies a critical interpretation, sharply formulated in the statement "There is no distinction." Yet Paul did not contradict the old tradition but incorporated it in a new context. He recognized "Jew first" to be a principle of divine economy and reckoned both "the oracles of God" and "the fathers" among the privileges granted to the Israelites. Even when the order was reversed, Gentiles believing the gospel and Jews rejecting it, Paul insisted that the Israelites were "beloved for the sake of their forefathers." At the end of his letter to the Romans, Paul summarized in words that fully conform to the Jewish-Christian interpretation we have been tracing, "Christ became a servant to the circumcised to show God's truthfulness, in order to confirm the promises given to the patriarchs, and in order that the Gentiles might glorify God for his mercy." Both direct and indirect evidence from Paul's letters supports the conjecture that he was familiar with Jewish-Christian interpretation of the promises given to the fathers, especially in Genesis 22:16–18.

III

It has been surmised, and may today be generally accepted, that to the earliest churches in Judea the ministry, death, and resurrection of Jesus were believed to bring redemption to Israel, according to the Scriptures. The effect upon the Gentile nations was considered a further consequence, and an object of eschatological hope rather than of missionary efforts. In this respect my tentative results simply add support to the scant evidence that this really was the case. And if my arguments are correct, they provide information about another important matter: there existed a specifically Jewish-Christian "doctrine of the atonement," more explicit than has often been assumed on the basis of Acts. The death of Jesus upon the cross was interpreted as fulfilling what God had promised Abraham by oath: As Abraham had not withheld his son, so God did not spare his own Son but gave him up for Isaac's descendants. As the sacrifice, provided by God, he expiated their former sins. Vicariously he was made a curse to redeem them from the curse caused by their transgressions of the law, so that even the Gentile nations might be blessed in the offspring of Abraham, the crucified Messiah Jesus. That God in his great mercy rewarded Abraham by acting as the patriarch did at the Akedah would thus seem to be part of fairly coherent early Jewish-Christian theology, in which the crucifixion of Jesus was interpreted in the light of Genesis 22.

The fragments surmised to be contained in Paul's letters to the Romans and the Galatians cannot belong to the very beginnings of Christian doctrine. The interpretation of Genesis 22 presupposes that Jesus was identified not only as the Messiah but was also predicated Son of God, in accordance with 2 Samuel 7:14 and Psalm 2:7. By way of analogy, not only "offspring of David" but also "offspring" of Abraham was taken to refer to Jesus as the Messiah. Yet the interpretation must be early, because it would seem to have been germinal to the phrase "God gave his Son," and possibly to the designations of Jesus as "the only Son" and "the lamb of God."

The use of Genesis 22, attested by the texts we have considered, presupposes some familiarity with haggadic traditions as well as with the biblical text. It is not possible to assume, however, that current ideas about the vicarious suffering of Isaac were simply taken over and applied to the passion of Jesus. Like the biblical story, the New Testament allusions emphasize the conduct of Abraham and the promise of God. If the motifs had been directly transferred from Isaac to Christ, one would have expected more emphasis upon the voluntary submission of the former, as in the haggadah. In many respects it would seem better to regard the early Christian interpretation of Genesis 22 as an independent parallel rather than as derived from Jewish Akedah traditions. What the earliest Jewish Christian traditions presuppose is not so much any special features of the haggadah as the general spiritual climate of Midrash. It cannot be characterized better than in the words of Judah Goldin: "That conviction lies at the heart of Midrash all the time: The Scriptures are not only a record of the past but a prophecy, a foreshadowing and foretelling, of what will come to pass. And if this is the case, text and personal experience are not two autonomous domains. On the contrary, they are reciprocally enlightening: even as the immediate event helps make the age-old text intelligible, so in turn the text reveals the fundamental significance of the recent event or experience."[3] Without alteration this statement might also be applied to early Christian use of Scriptures.

Early Christian use of Scriptures was not differentiated from contemporary Jewish Midrash by some new hermeneutic. The methods of interpretation remained much the same, with variations in branches of the primitive church and Judaism. What caused a basic difference was new events and new experiences. For Judaism, the story of the binding of Isaac provided help in understanding that the God of the fathers allowed the sufferings and death of faithful Jews in the days of Antiochus Epiphanes and later. The same story helped followers of Jesus deal with the scandal of the cross, understanding what had happened as an act of God's love and a manifestation of his righteousness. For centuries the interpretation of Genesis 22 was a part of the controversy between Christians and Jews, and even the common use of scientific methods has not quite brought the controversy to an end. It is interesting, and may be important, to realize that the earliest Christian interpretation antedates the controversy. Close correspondence rather than competition between the Akedah and the atonement was stressed probably to the extent that the redemption by Christ was seen as an adequate reward for the binding of Isaac.

GERD THEISSEN

The Strong and the Weak in Corinth (1975)†

Sociological analysis investigates human social behavior with an eye to those characteristics which are typical and those conditions which transcend individuals. It is interested in what is usual and normal, in what applies to many individuals and many situations. By contrast, what has come down from the past focuses primarily on the unusual or unique. For that reason, evaluating such materials sociologically is often difficult if not impossible. Among the unusual and singular events about which we have some knowledge, however, conflicts play a special role. Here the various customs of social groups collide with one another. In such circumstances

---

3. Ibid., xvi [Dahl's note, citing Goldin's introduction to Spiegel's book].

† The essay "Die Starken und Schwachen in Korinth: Soziologische Analyse eines theologischen Streits" was first published in *EvT* 35 (1975): 155–72, and reprinted in Theissen's *Studien zur Soziologie des Urchristentums* (Tübingen: Mohr-Siebeck, 1979); tr. by John H. Schütz and published in *The Social Setting of Pauline Christianity* (Philadelphia: Fortress, 1982), 121–43. Reprinted by permission of Augsburg Fortress Press. Theissen has been professor of New Testament Theology at the University of Heidelberg since 1980.

the unusual actually sheds light on the ordinary, the dramatic conflict reveals the banal. If ever we can derive information about the social background of our historical traditions, it is through the analysis of such conflicts.

The quarrel between "the strong" and "the weak" in the Corinthian congregation is a matter of just such different customs. The weak avoid all meat sacrificed to idols since it could never be known with certainty that ritual actions had not accompanied the slaughter of the meat. The strong, on the other hand, appeal to their "knowledge": there is only one God; there are no idols and hence "no meat sacrificed to idols" (1 Cor. 8:4ff.).

Paul argues differently. He distinguishes cultic meals in an official setting (8:10) from meals in private houses (10:25ff.). To be sure, his opinion about official cultic meals in a temple is not quite uniform, but the intention is clear. Thus in 8:10ff. he urges the general waiver of a right which he himself would not contest, the right to participate in temple meals with the appropriate mental reservations. In 10:1–22 he goes farther and regards such meals as fundamentally incompatible with the Christian Lord's Supper. This shift in accent could be explained by a situation such as this: anyone who only passively participated in such pagan cultic meals, that is, did so as an invited guest, would eventually face the problem of whether or not he was obliged to extend a reciprocal invitation for the same kind of meal. To do so would make him the initiator of "idol worship." Whether this is the problem cannot be settled here.

What is in any event unmistakable in our text is the fact that from 10:23ff. Paul deals with the problem of private meals. These may be meals eaten at home but involving meat bought in the market—a wholly unproblematic case (10:25–26)—or meals by invitation to others' houses where one is served meat (10:27ff.). Paul has reservations about such meat only if its "sacred" character has been specifically pointed out. Since it would be understood that in a temple only consecrated meat would be offered, he must be referring to a meal in a private setting. It could be said that Paul is inconsistent in distinguishing between public and private behavior and that his position is dependent on the social context of the behavior. He is inclined to go along with the weak where the eating of meat takes on an official character (because of the location, or because of the formula "this is sacred meat") and to go along with the strong when the problem is one of a private setting.

Our task is to analyze the reasons for the opposing attitudes of the weak and the strong. It is doubtless proper to look for theological reasons, on the assumption that at the root of different behavior are to be found different convictions about humanity, the world, and God. Yet the truth of that does not preclude a sociological analysis as well. Convictions and concepts are usually effective only if social groups have invested them with the power to shape behavior. In the case of this conflict it is particularly true that social relationships represent a major theme. Since meals are an important form of social communication and the customs surrounding them are often socially determined there can be no argument, in my opinion, about whether one can or ought to interpret this conflict sociologically. The only argument is about how to do so. Which social factors are responsible for the conflict, religious traditions (whether of Jewish or gentile groups) which have shaped behavior, or class-specific customs and attitudes? It goes without saying that apart from all of this there can be divergent opinions about the significance of sociological analysis for throwing light on the meaning of theological texts. The sociological analysis of a theological quarrel does not, in my opinion, mean reducing it to social factors.

Socio-cultural Factors

To a great extent exegesis has confined itself to these alternatives: either the weak are Jewish Christians or they are gentile Christians. Paul himself, however, seems to have regarded the problem as somewhat more general. He refers to his own behavior as an example of that respect which it is necessary to show the weak, but does so without limiting his behavior to a particular ethnic group: to the Jews he became a Jew, to those outside the Law as one outside the Law, and so forth (9:19–22). This could be a generalization which deliberately goes beyond the concrete context. But at the end of his instructions about meat sacrificed to idols Paul again addresses the strong with these words: "Give no offense to Jews or to Greeks or to the church of God" (10:32). If both Jews and pagans can take offense, then the weak Christians who take offense could themselves have once been either Jews or pagans. Nor do other clues suggest that the weak were an ethnically or socio-culturally homogeneous group.

＊　＊　＊

Socio-cultural customs, traditions and attitudes of various ethnic groups certainly will have been significant in influencing behavior regarding consecrated meat. At the same time, however, it is also conceivable that divergent cultural traditions led to similar rather than divergent behavior. Therefore, we should look for other factors as well.

Socio-economic Factors

Paul himself suggests that we look for the weak among the lower strata. It is hardly an accident that the first chapters of the Corinthian letter already give voice to the distinction between strong and weak, connecting this with the social structure of the Corinthian congregation. In 1:26ff. Paul states that among the Corinthians are not many who are "wise, influential, of noble birth" (author's trans.)—δυνατοί is the term he uses for the influential, the same term he uses for the strong in Rom. 15:1—and he continues: "God chose what is weak in the world to shame the strong." It appears that already here Paul wants to say that it is precisely the weak, people who admittedly lack wisdom, whom God has chosen. And when in 4:10 he draws the contrast with the Corinthians, "We are weak, but you are strong," we may be hearing reverberations of Paul's solidarity with the weak people of Corinth; for in connection with the question of meat sacrificed to idols he expressly repeats the idea that to the weak he himself became weak (9:22). The first Corinthian letter itself, therefore, suggests the hypothesis that the socially weak of 1:26–27 are identical with those who are weak in the face of consecrated meat. This hypothesis can be tested only by looking for class-specific characteristics in what can still be discerned of the behavior of the weak and the strong, that is, behavioral traits which can be correlated with wealth, occupation, and education and thus to a higher or lower social status.

CLASS-SPECIFIC CHARACTERISTICS IN EATING HABITS

We can begin with the commonplace assumption that then, as today, wealthy people could eat meat more often than others. We cannot base our judgment of eating habits in the ancient world on the literary depictions of great banquets (Petronius, *Satyricon* 52ff.; Juvenal, *Satura* 5; Martial, *Epigrammata* III, 60), as if these revels were typical for ordinary people. It must be borne in mind that most such testimonies are produced by a narrow upper stratum and its followers, and that even so, meat was not necessarily a part of such festive meals. When his friend Septicius fails to show up at a meal which the younger Pliny had prepared for him, Pliny writes a letter of reproach (*Epistulae* I, 15) cataloguing the delights which his friend has missed, including lettuce, snails, and eggs. Nothing is said about meat. Pliny, as it happens, lived quite modestly, and perhaps that is why he was left in the lurch at his own table, for he discreetly hints that his friend had preferred to dine where he could get better food than this.

From other sources we learn something about the ordinary person's meal habits. Greek cities, like Rome, had a system of public food distribution. This provisioning included grain, but not meat. Such is the case both for the public distribution of foodstuffs in Samos and for the Roman grain distribution which was regulated by law from the time of Gaius Gracchus. Septimius Severus (193–211 CE) was the first to add to the grain a daily ration of oil, and Aurelian (270–275 CE) subsequently expanded the provisions by allowing the sale of pork and wine at reduced prices. A Roman citizen of lower social status probably had little more available than what he was allowed from the state.

In Greece the great mass of the people were nourished by food made from flour, such as porridge made of barley flour (ἄλφιτα) or bread baked from wheat flour (ἄρτος). That the terms σῖτος and ἄλφιτα could mean simply "sustenance" speaks for itself. In addition, we know from Delos that three stonemasons spent nineteen drachmas and four oboli, or almost two-thirds of their monthly income of thirty drachmas, just for barley flour. Not much was left over for other kinds of food.

The same is true for the Roman situation. From reports that soldiers ate meat only in exceptional circumstances (when no grain was available) it can be concluded that meat did not normally belong to their diet: *ipse exercitusque . . . ita per inopiam et labores fatiscebant, carne pecudum propulsare famem adacti* ("He himself and his army . . . were yet beginning to feel the strain of short rations and hardship—they had been reduced to keeping starvation at bay by a fish diet," Tacitus, *Annales* 14, 24); *usque eo ut complures dies frumento milites caruerint et pecore ex longinquioribus vicis adacto, extremam famem sustentarent* (". . . so much so that for several days the troops were without corn, and staved off the extremity of famine by driving cattle from the more distant hamlets," Caesar, *Bellum Gallicum* 7:17). H. Bolkestein is of the opinion that "the mass of people, in Italy as in Greece, lived primarily on a diet of flour, in earlier times made into porridge (*puls*) and later baked into bread."

On the relationship between social status and meal habits *b. Hullin* 84a is also instructive: "A man having one *maneh* may buy a *litra* of vegetables for his bowl; if ten a *litra* of fish; if fifty *maneh* a *litra* of meat. If someone has a hundred *maneh* he may have a pot cooked for him every day. And how often for the others? From Sabbath eve to Sabbath eve" (that is, once a week).

If in the Corinthian Christian congregation the problem of eating meat became a central point of strife between different groups, that was hardly because of the behavior of Christians of lower social status. Those who scarcely ever eat meat can hardly give offense by eating consecrated meat. For those who lack sufficient money to procure meat in the market, it is a purely theoretical question whether all such meat bought there should be avoided (10:25). To the extent that the conflict originates in the area of private meals it can be explained by the eating habits of various classes. Such instances (10:25ff.), however, do not constitute the real problem. There can be no doubt that Paul is primarily concerned with the problem of cultic meals which take place in an official setting, which means that the matter is more complicated.

From 8:7 it can be inferred that the weak certainly did eat meat, even if they did so with a bad conscience. According to 8:10ff., doing so in a cultic setting is a genuine temptation. In fact, the consumption of meat in a cultic setting is a problem for all citizens and residents of a city, regardless of their social status, since at a celebration open to the public all might participate. Even the lower classes had their chance to eat meat under such circumstances. We can sketch briefly the various kinds of opportunities which might arise.

1. In Greece and Rome meat was publicly distributed to all citizens in connection with extraordinary events such as the celebration of a victory (Plutarch, *Demetrius* 11; Suetonius, *De vita Caesarum* 38) or at a funeral (Livy, VIII, 22, 2, 4; XXXIX 46, 2; XLI 28, 11). More generally, Cicero includes the distribution of meat among the public *beneficientia* by which private individuals seek to win the public's good will (Cicero, *De officiis* II, 52ff.), for example when competing for a municipal office.

2. In addition to such irregular occasions, public sacrificial meals were instituted for particular days. These were sometimes intended for only a limited circle of people, but often they were intended for all the citizens and residents of a city. Xenophon, for example, who instituted a feast at Scillum, expressly states that "all the citizens and men and women of the neighborhood took part in the festival" (πάντες οἱ πολῖται καὶ πρόσχωροι ἄνδρες καὶ γύναικες μετεῖχον τῆς ἑορτῆς, *Anabasis* V, 3, 7ff.). Everyone received flour, bread, wine, and meat. A document for a banquet at Amorgos from the second century C.E. provides that not only all the citizens are to be treated to meat but also all sojourners, strangers, Romans, and women (*IG* XII, 515).

3. More permanent than these bequests were the great religious feasts, frequently involving a distribution of meat to the general populace paid for either by the state or by the contribution of wealthy individual citizens. For example, meat was served in Ath-

ens at the Dionysia and Panathenaea. Was there, perhaps, a public sacrificial meal at the international Isthmian games?

4. Further possibilities for the ceremonial or cultic consumption of meat were provided by the many associations whose bylaws provided for specific feasts. It may be questioned whether in these cases the lower classes always got to eat meat, since the *collegium* of Lanuvium (136 C.E.), for example, provided no meat for its feasts, which were celebrated six times a year (*CIL* XIV 2112 = Dessau, 7212), but only wine, bread, and sardines. This *collegium* included slaves.

5. Finally, there were private invitations to a temple. Those found in Oxyrhynchus are well known, as, for example, "Charemon invites you to a meal at the table of the Lord Serapis in the Serapeum tomorrow, the fifteenth, beginning at 9 o'clock" (*P. Oxy.* I, 110). Whether such invitations could be found among the poor may be questionable, however.

To sum up: Members of the lower classes seldom ate meat in their everyday lives. For that they were largely dependent on public distributions of meat which were always organized around a ceremonial occasion. The community meals of the *collegia* were also religious feasts. As a result, those from the lower classes knew meat almost exclusively as an ingredient in pagan religious celebrations, and the acts of eating meat and worshiping idols must have been much more closely connected for them than for members of the higher strata who were more accustomed to consuming meat routinely. For the poorer classes meat was truly something "special." It belonged to a sacred time segregated from the everyday world. It had a "numinous" character.

Conversion to Christianity brought similar difficulties to both Jewish Christians and gentile Christians of the lower classes. Those who had been pagans must have found it difficult to view meat as something perfectly natural and independent of its ritual setting, while at the same time they were sorely tempted not to miss out on what little bit of meat was offered to them by pagan feasts and institutions. Hence they would eat meat, but with a guilty conscience (8:7). Former Jews who had converted to Christianity had been liberated from Judaism's restrictions. Must it not have been tempting finally to be able to participate in public ceremonies involving meat (8:10)? Yet if they had but little opportunity, now as before, to buy meat which had not been ritually slaughtered, they would not have found it easy to break down the old negative taboos surrounding such meat. On the other hand, we can look for the "less biased" position of the strong among members of the higher classes. Someone accustomed to getting around the positive as well as negative taboos of eating meat could shed any anxiety over demonic infection to the very extent that he has survived eating meat without coming to harm.

SIGNS OF STRATIFICATION WITHIN PATTERNS OF SOCIABILITY

Invitations to sacrificial meals served basically as a means of communication. Families, associations, and cities came together on such occasions and in so doing expressed ceremonially their common membership. This social aspect emerges particularly clearly in Aelius Aristides:

> Moreover, in sacrifices men maintain an especially close fellowship with this god alone. They call him to the sanctuary and install him as both guest of honor and host, so that while some divinities provide portions of their common meals, he is the sole provider of all common meals, holding the rank of symposiarch for those who at anytime are gathered about him. Just as Homer said (*Odyssey* iii, 62) that Athena both poured a libation and completed each request, so he is at one and the same time both participant in libations and the one who receives them, both coming himself to the revelry and inviting to himself the revellers, who because of him dance their dance free from the fear of evil and carry homeward with their crowns a feeling of true well-being, offering a return invitation (*Orationes* 45, 27).

Here we clearly have harmless forms of sociability, the "parties" of the ancient world. The hint about reciprocal invitations at the close marks a connection with the usual obligations of social, and sociable, life.

Restrictions on meat sacrificed to idols were barriers to communication which raised the problem of the relationship of Christians to the society of the ancient world. Originally the debate began over the general problem and only later shifted to the question of eating meat. In 5:9 Paul mentions a lost letter to the Corinthians in which he warned them against contact with the πόρνοις [sexually immoral], the greedy, robbers, and idolaters. That must have been interpreted as his wishing to check every contact with non-Christians. In any event, he corrects himself. He is not referring to contact with non-Christians outside the congregation, but to contact with sinners within it. The relationship of Christians to those outside the community is not to be limited. These relationships, however, cannot have been restricted to casual contact. To the prohibition against contact with Christian sinners Paul specifically adds that one should not even eat with them. From this it follows indirectly that common meals are included among the kinds of contact allowed with non-Christians. Thus even here we encounter the problem raised in 1 Cor. 8–10, but in a somewhat different light. The religious aspect of common meals is touched on, certainly, but contact with idolaters is only mentioned fourth in a list as a special instance of social contact with the world in general. If this social aspect has faded in 1 Cor. 8–10 that is because the debate has there been focused on one issue most accessible to theological argument, the problem of meat sacrificed to idols.

It is perfectly clear, I think, on which side of this conflict the wealthier Christians must have stood. Erastus, the "city treasurer" (Rom. 16:23), could have jeopardized his public position had he rejected all invitations where "consecrated meat" might have been expected. If he is identical with the aedile Erastus known from an inscription, and thus somebody who at one time or another wished to be chosen as overseer for those public places and buildings where such meat was sold, he scarcely could have demonstrated an attitude of reserve about "consecrated meat." Such an attitude would have been wholly inappropriate for his office.

The relationship between high social status and "idolatry" is not ignored by early Christian paraenesis. It is not accidental that the specific vice of the rich, πλεονεξία, "wanting to have more," is closely linked with idolatry and even identified with it (Col. 3:6; Eph. 5:5; cf. 1 Cor. 5:10–11). There are also social reasons for this close association of wealth and idolatry. Those who are wealthy, or want to be, must seek and cultivate contact with pagans. That is clearly stated in Polycarp's letter: "Unless one steers clear of greed he will be tainted by idolatry and judged, as it were, with the pagans" (*Phil.* XI, 2). A greedy person belongs with the pagans. He has numerous social contacts with the pagan world. The Shepherd of Hermas says reproachfully of the wealthy that they live together with the pagans (*Similitudines* VIII, 9, 1). There may have been only a few powerful and well-born in Corinth (1:26), but it is among them that we ought to look for those "gnostics" who, in their contacts with the pagan world, neither could nor did take much notice of their poorer Christian brother's scruples.

It could be objected that according to 10:27ff., both the weak and the strong Christians alike appear in social contact with pagan hosts. The information that this is consecrated meat, however, cannot have come from a Christian. Only a pagan could describe ritually slaughtered meat this way. Respect for this pagan's conscience has a quite different motive from the respect for a Christian brother's conscience in 8:10ff. Thus his conscience is never characterized as "weak," a term which would suggest that it lagged behind the norms appropriate for him. Only "conscience" as such is mentioned. And while in 8:11–13 Christ's death serves as the motive for renouncing a right on the basis of love, this specific Christian motivation is completely missing in 10:27–30. Thus the passage does not presuppose that weak and strong Christians find themselves together as guests at the same meal.

Public and professional duties dictated that Christians of high social status were probably [more] integrated into pagan society than the Christians of more modest circumstances. We may question whether those who belonged to the lower classes might not now be motivated to remain in their pagan clubs in order to participate in the feasts. Paul certainly assumes that the weak also ate meat sacrificed to idols. But it must be remembered that many of these clubs did not offer much more than did the Christian Lord's Supper—bread and wine—while Christians shared meals together far more frequently than perhaps did the members of the *collegium* of Lanuvium, mentioned above, which sponsored six modest public banquets in a year. The lower strata of society found in the congregation full compensation for what they gave up elsewhere. Indeed, they found even more. For while the ancient clubs were largely socially homogeneous, these people had access in the congregation to the upper classes who could use their wealth to serve the congregation and thus to serve the socially weaker. There is also another reason why we must look for the weak among the lower strata. Those who do not have much to lose in the way of "worldly" relationships are more inclined to free themselves of these. In the process a certain *resentiment* may color their negative opinions. Those for whom the world is full of demons and taboos show by their views, which are designed to steer clear of these, how much at heart they are nevertheless attracted to that world.

CLASS-SPECIFIC TRAITS IN THE FORMS OF LEGITIMATION

The strong base their position on their "gnosis." Paul seems to take up some of their arguments: "All of us possess knowledge" (8:1); "an idol has no real existence . . . there is no God but one" (8:4); "all things are lawful" (10:23). The idea of the "weak conscience" (8:7, 10, 12) may have come from them, as well as the argument that "food is meant for the stomach and the stomach for food" (6:13). Unmistakable in all these arguments is the determination to surmount obsolete religious restrictions through "knowledge." Even if the speculative fantasies of later Gnostics cannot be imputed to the Corinthian "gnostics," as they certainly cannot, neither can the parallels between the two be ignored. For a comparable "liberal" position on meat sacrificed to idols the only analogies within Christianity come from Gnostic groups, as may be seen in the following:

Justin on Gnostics in general: "But know that there are many who profess their faith in Jesus and are considered Christians, yet claim there is no harm in their eating meat sacrificed to idols" (*Dialogus cum Tryphone* 35, 1). ". . . Of these some are called Marcionites, some Valentinians, some Basilidians and some Saturnilians" (*Dial.* 35, 6).

Irenaeus on the Valentinians: "For this reason the most perfect among them freely practice everything which is forbidden. . . . For they eat food that was offered to idols with indifference, and they are the first to arrive at any festival party of the gentiles that takes place in honor of the idols, while some of them do not even avoid the murderous spectacle of fights with beasts and single combats, which are hateful to God and man. And some, who immoderately indulge the desires of the flesh, say that they are repaying to the flesh what belongs to the flesh and to the spirit what belongs to the spirit" (*Adversus haereses* I, 6, 3).

Irenaeus on the followers of Basilides: "They despise things sacrificed to idols and think nothing of them, but enjoy them without any anxiety at all. They also enjoy the other (pagan) festivals and all that can be called appetite" (*Adv. haer.* I, 24, 5; cf. Eusebius, *Historia ecclesiastica* IV, 7, 7).

Irenaeus on those descended from Basilides and Carpocrates: "Others . . . taught promiscuous sex and many marriages and claimed that God does not care about their participation in pagan cultic meals" (*Adv. haer.* I, 28, 2).

Irenaeus on the Nicolaitans (cf. Rev. 2:14f; 2:6; Hippolytus, *Adv. haer.* VII, 36): "They live promiscuously. They teach that it is of no significance if one fornicates or eats food sacrificed to pagan gods . . ." (*Adv. haer.* I, 26, 3).

Origen on the Simonians: "Nowhere in the world are Simonians now to be found, although Simon, in order to win a larger following, freed his disciples from the peril of death, which the Christians are taught to prefer, by instructing them to regard pagan worship as a matter of indifference" (*Contra Celsum* VI, 11).

Epiphanius on libertine Gnostics of a much later period: "And whatever we eat, be it meat, vegetables, bread or anything else, we are doing a kindness to created things by collecting the soul from all things and transmitting it with ourselves to the heavenly world. For this reason they eat every kind of meat and say that they do so that we may show mercy to our kind" (*Panarion* XXVI, 9, 2).

It cannot simply be assumed on the basis of these texts that eating meat sacrificed to idols was common to all Gnostic groups. There were also ascetic currents in Gnosticism (cf. Irenaeus, *Adv. haer.* I, 24, 2; Tertullian, *Adv. haer.* I, 14). Eating such meat is not *the* typical, but *one* typical behavior of the Gnostics. Orthodox Christianity rather uniformly forbade eating such consecrated meat. That is confirmed by the one example of doing so which we have from non-Gnostic groups. Lucian reports of Peregrinus that when he was a Christian charismatic he was caught in a lapse from the prohibition: "Then he somehow committed an offense—I believe he was seen eating something which was forbidden . . ." (*De morte Peregrini* 16), following which he lost all influence in the Christian community and became a convert to Cynicism. Thus it seems to be the case that a liberal attitude toward meat sacrificed to idols was to be found only among Gnostic Christians.

The links between the "gnosis" in Corinth and Christian Gnosticism of the second century are a matter of controversy, and with good reason. There is scarcely a direct connection. Yet that simply underlines the problem of how to interpret the obvious analogies. The opinion that in Corinth we are dealing with an incipient Gnosticism is of itself unsatisfactory. Gnosticism's beginnings can be dated much earlier if by that is meant the initial appearance of concepts which play a role in the later Gnostic systems.

What is needed is a sociological-structural perspective to complement the developmental-historical perspective. For example, analogies between Corinthian gnosis and later Gnosticism could be found in the fact that in both instances a typical recasting of Christian faith is evident with its rise into the higher classes. Inferences from Gnosticism to the Corinthian gnosis would then have to be confined to those characteristics which could result from a comparable social situation: intellectual level, soteriology based on knowledge, and elite self-consciousness within the community combined with taking pleasure in contact with the pagan world. Problematic assumptions about the Corinthian gnostics' concepts can thus be left to one side.

a. The Gnostic systems of thought demand a high level of intellect. Their speculations are full of ludicrous systems and logic, and as such were not accessible to simple people. These are set down in numerous books which, in the second century, quite possibly outnumber the writings of orthodox Christians. Basilides will serve as an example of a prolific author. He is said to have written a book of odes (*Muratorian Canon* 83f.), a gospel (Origen, *Homiliae in Lucam 1*), and twenty-four books of gospel commentary (Eusebius, *Hist. eccl.* IV, 7, 7; Clement of Alexandria, *Stromateis* IV, 12, 1). More writings have been preserved from the Valentinians than from all other Gnostic groups. Such an enormous production of books is conceivable only in relatively wealthy circles—and one recalls the wealthy Valentinian Ambrose who could put seven stenographers at Origen's disposal so that his lectures could be copied and published (Eusebius, *Hist. eccl.* VI, 18, 1; 23, 1–2). The Corinthian gnostics, to be sure, did not produce any books, but they did avail themselves of the medium of writing. The community's letter is written entirely from their point of view. Its arguments assume a certain intellectual standard.

b. A soteriology of knowledge, faith in the saving power of discernment, can also be a class-specific factor. Where salvation takes place less through the agency of a deity than through the inner process of "knowledge," the felt need which gives rise to the quest for salvation is also less likely to be rooted in material circumstances. Max Weber has ascribed to the upper classes this kind of hope for salvation: "The success of philosophical salvation doctrines and the propaganda of salvation cults among the lay elite during late Hellenic and Roman times parallels these groups' final turning aside from political partic- ipation." When the educated classes no longer can or will shape the world, they frequently transcend it all the more radically by means of ideas. The transition from being lost to being saved is then regarded as one of gaining "true knowledge." On this score there are compa- rable characteristics in the "knowledge" of Gnosticism and that of the Corinthian gnosis. For the latter, knowledge means recognizing that idols do not really exist, that is, stripping this world's mythically inten- sified appellate agencies of their demands. This might be called demystifying a portion of the world. In later Gnosticism such knowl- edge becomes radicalized so that even the Old Testament's creator God is unmasked as a mythical being to whom this world traces back its restrictive commands and prohibitions.

c. People who understand themselves to be elevated above the "world" also understand themselves to be superior in a very concrete way to those who are imprisoned by it. The division of humankind into three classes encountered in so many Gnostic writings, and espe- cially the differentiation of Christians as either pistics or gnostics, betrays a sharply elitist consciousness in Gnostic circles: normal Christians are only second-rate people. Such rankings may reflect the internal stratification of Hellenistic Christian communities in which— as for example in Rome—Christians of the upper classes frequently separated themselves as Gnostics from the common Christian people. In Corinth there were the beginnings of such a differentiation within the community. Here too the strong were distinguished from the weak, and we even find the terminology of *pneumatikoi* and *sarkikoi* (3:1). Here too some Christians seek to distinguish themselves from others of a lower rank on the basis of "wisdom" and "knowledge."

d. Finally, there is the matter of the relative openness of Gnostics to the culture of antiquity. An example is the reception of pagan mythology and literature among the Naasenes (Hippolytus, *Adv. haer.* V, 6, 3–11, 1). Many of the moral objections raised by the church fathers against Gnostics concern what was but ordinary behavior for that time. Gnostics take part in the pleasures of their day, banquets, theatrical performances, and social life. Many of them were no more strict about sexual morality than was the era itself. They cautioned against seeking martyrdom. In the case of Basilides and Valentinus themselves, however, there can be no denying the earnestness and sympathetic differentiation within their ethical views. C. Andresen is right when he says: "These people belonged to social strata which did not usually find their way into the early catholic communities. The aura of a certain liberality, one that spills over the narrow limits of a community piety anxious for its own traditions, suffuses the testimony to Valentinian and Basilidian Gnosis." It is for just such groups that we have evidence of eating meat sacrificed to idols. This fits with their liberal disposition. It is a mark of broader integration within the society of that day which is at the same time thoroughly comfortable with a radical "theoretical" critique of the world. The world is rejected in a theoretical way in order to profit from it in a practical way—the usual verbal radicalism of the affluent.

The Christian Gnosticism of the second century may have been largely a theology of the upper classes. And even if we may not assume that there were Christians of elevated social status in all Gnostic groups, we may assume that such were to be found in those groups said to eat meat sacrificed to idols, for example the Valentinian and Basilidian Gnostics. It is permissible to make a connection with the Corinthian gnosis since doing so rests not on an inference from the realm of mythic concepts but on the four criteria listed above. In the case of the Corinthian gnostics we also find a certain level of education, the significance of knowledge and wisdom for ethics and salvation, and an elitist self-consciousness within the community which goes hand in hand with a considerable liberalism about associating with the pagan world. In both instances these characteristics taken together point to an elevated social status.

What thus seem probable on the basis of analogy is also independently plausible. Is it not likely that in class-specific conflicts those of higher social standing will appeal to their superior insight? In other instances they were certainly accustomed to play their better insight off against the common man. On the other hand, it seems more reasonable to ascribe superstitious notions of a sort which impede contact with outsiders to the perspective of the lower classes, with their limited experience, than to those whose social status gives them a broader perspective.

CLASS-SPECIFIC TRAITS IN THE FORMS OF COMMUNICATION

First Corinthians is itself a social fact, evidence of communication between Paul and the congregation. From it we learn, first of all, something about the position within the community of those involved in the communication. Indirectly, however, we also get some hints about their general position in society. Three matters are particularly instructive: Paul's informants, those whom he addresses, and his critics.

Paul is told of the problems by a congregational letter which clearly is formulated from the standpoint of the strong. Other opinions are not reflected, the catch phrase "all of us possess knowledge" (8:1) leaving little room for that. The authors write in the conviction that they can represent the community. They comprise the leading circles. Paul is thus informed on the basis of a perspective "from above." It is scarcely an accident that in contrast to this he receives oral information (1:11; 11:18) about problems within the Corinthian community which sees things from below (1:26ff.; 11:20ff.). Might these divergent paths by which information travels have a class-specific character?

Interestingly, Paul also addresses his reply almost exclusively to the strong. Almost all passages in which we find the second person used are directed to them, as for example "Only take care lest this liberty of yours somehow become a stumbling block to the weak" (8:9; cf. 8:10, 11; 10:15, 31). On that basis we can conclude with M. Rauer that the weak have no position of leadership within the congregation.

It is also significant that in his statements addressed to the strong Paul includes a long excursus (9:1–27) in which he appears to have two groups in mind. One group consists of some critics who have attacked him because of his renunciation of support (9:3). The other consists of the strong to whom he represents this posture as a model. Is it not likely that the critics and those whom Paul addresses are partly identical? The critics who reproach Paul because he would not accept material support from them are not likely to have belonged to the materially impoverished, since they are at the moment supporting other missionaries. If these critics of Paul are at least in part identical with the strong, that would confirm their sociological orientation, since renunciation of material privileges is a much more effective example in an exhortation directed to those who are materially privileged.

All of our observations, about forms of eating, sociability, legitimation, and communication, point to the fact that the strong probably belong to the few who are "wise . . . powerful . . . and of noble birth" (1:26). Their more liberal attitude belongs primarily in the upper classes. Naturally, this attitude will have been extended beyond those limits. It is just such Christians of higher social status who bring with them a larger household unit. It is just such Christians who have been influential. But they were unable to win all to their position. There were also the weak, for whom pagan or Jewish traditions still had their influence. Such traditions, however, could be effective only because they undergirded a class-specific attitude.

Finally, we must consider Paul's own position in this conflict between the strong and the weak. It has always been something of an offense to modern exegesis that Paul does not consistently champion the enlightened position of the strong, even though he is in basic agreement with it. If we understand his argument—quite possibly in a way which goes beyond the self-understanding inherent in it—as a plea for consideration of the lower strata by the higher strata, then Paul's alleged inconsistency appears to be quite consistent. For the fact is that for Paul the revaluation of all norms of social rank and dominance—including the dominance of a higher "knowledge" and "wisdom"—proceeds directly from the preaching of the cross (1:18ff.). To be sure, seen from today's perspective it must be emphasized that this revaluation has no "revolutionizing" consequences in the social realm. Paul's recommendation, based on love, that the higher classes accommodate their behavior to the lower classes, only mitigates the tension between the two but allows the differing customs to continue to exist. The factual privileges of status enjoyed by the higher strata are preserved. For example, private meals with consecrated meat continue to be allowed in principle (10:23ff.). Nor is participation in cultic meals excluded in principle. All that is prohibited is disturbing a weak person by doing so. In other words, everything must take place in a very "exclusive" circle. But just those possibilities continue to be available which, as it happens, are more accessible to members of the upper classes. To be sure, the norms for the Christian community are advocated with vigor. But without doubt there is the obvious danger that those who are better off have de facto more possibilities of avoiding the restrictive effects of these norms than do those of the lower classes. The latter come up short—as far as the material side of things is concerned. For it is those very cultic feasts of an official nature, where each can monitor the behavior of the other, but which also would have afforded an opportunity for the lower classes to eat some meat, which are covered by the prohibition against pagan worship. Paul's solution is a compromise. The wishes (or prejudices) of the weak are upheld just as is the knowledge (and social privilege) of the strong. For that very reason it is realistic and practicable. Something comparable is to be found in the solution to a conflict referred to in 1 Cor. 11:17ff. There we find that wealthy Christians can eat their "own" meal privately to their heart's content (11:33–34), but in the congregation they are to be satisfied with the Lord's Supper, with the bread and wine of the fellowship.

These are solutions which are characteristic for the love-patriarchalism of the Pauline letters. This love-patriarchalism allows social inequities to continue but transfuses them with a spirit of concern, of respect, and of personal solicitude. Concern for the conscience of the other person, even when it is a "weak" conscience and obedient to norms now superseded, is certainly one of the congenial characteristics of this love-patriarchalism. This should not be overlooked even if Pauline love-patriarchalism cannot be considered the solution to contemporary social problems. It must be asked critically, however, whether love and knowledge can be joined without restricting knowledge. Was it just cynicism if some of the strong in Corinth believed that under the circumstances they could "edify" the weak by their example (1 Cor. 8:10)? Could they not have believed, with a very clear conscience, that the lower classes should not further curtail their already limited possibilities in life with such religious scruples? For the most part we hear only one side of the argument between Paul and the "gnostics." That should be kept in mind by anyone attributing simply unsocial behavior to the "gnostics." We do not know precisely how they argued their case. The gnostic *Gospel of Philip*, which comes from a later time but is close in spirit to these people, proposes a relationship between love and knowledge in which neither is compromised by the other: "Love, however, builds up. But whoever is free because of knowledge is a slave on account of love for those who cannot yet accept the freedom of knowledge. But knowledge makes them suitable by working to make them free" (110). Perhaps in principle Paul felt not much differently. Perhaps the Corinthian gnostics were even his best "pupils." We ought not to blame Paul because he wanders from this principle. It was being played off against the socially weak. In such a context one can insist on one's right in such a way as to wind up in the wrong.

ELISABETH SCHÜSSLER FIORENZA

[Paul, Women, and the Household Code] (1983)†

*　*　*

Paul's interpretation and adaptation of the baptismal declaration Gal. 3:28 in his letters to the community of Corinth unequivocally affirm the equality and charismatic giftedness of women and men in the Christian

† From *In Memory of Her: A Feminist Theological Reconstruction of Christian Origins* (New York: Crossroad, 1983). The Excerpts are from pp. 235–36, 251–59, and 266–70. Copyright © 1994 by Crossroad Publishing Co. Reprinted by permission. Schüssler Fiorenza, the first woman to be elected president of the Society of Biblical Literature, is the Krister Stendahl Professor of Divinity at Harvard Divinity School.

community. Women as well as men are prophets and leaders of worship in the community. Women as well as men have the call to a marriage-free life. Women as well as men have mutual rights and obligations within the sexual relationships of marriage.

However, in introducing a distinction, between those who are married and those who are not, with respect to missionary work, Paul relegates the former to the cares of this world and ascribes to the latter a special pure and holy state. Therefore, he restricts more severely the active participation of Christian wives in the worship of the community. His use of the virgin-bride metaphor for the church, as well as his figurative characterization of his apostleship as fatherhood, opens the door for a reintroduction of patriarchal values and sexual dualities.

Although he introduces an element of severe tension between the Christian community and the wider society with his emphasis on the marriage-free state of Christians, in his injunctions concerning the worship assembly of the Corinthians he is concerned to reduce this tension as much as possible. Since he wants to prevent "outsiders" from mistaking the Christian assembly as the celebrations of an orgiastic cult, he insists on the "proper" hairstyle for women active in the worship assembly. He then justifies this custom theologically by interpreting it as a symbol of their spiritual power in Christ. Moreover, he silences wives' public speaking, according to traditional Roman sentiment, as being against "law and custom." Similarly, in the case of mixed marriages, he restricts the freedom of Christian partners to separate from their unbelieving spouses by making the separation dependent on the decision of the nonbeliever. Paul's interests in doing so, however, are missionary and not directed against the spiritual freedom and charismatic involvement of women in the community.

Thus Paul's impact on women's leadership in the Christian missionary movement is double-edged. On the one hand he affirms Christian equality and freedom. He opens up a new independent lifestyle for women by encouraging them to remain free of the bondage of marriage. On the other hand, he subordinates women's behavior in marriage and in the worship assembly to the interests of Christian mission, and restricts their rights not only as "pneumatics" but also as "women," for we do not find such explicit restrictions on the behavior of men *qua* men in the worship assembly. The post-Pauline and pseudo-Pauline tradition will draw out these restrictions in order to change the equality in Christ between women and men, slaves and free, into a relationship of subordination in the household which, on the one hand, eliminates women from the leadership of worship and community and, on the other, restricts their ministry to women.

*   *   *

Colossians and the Household Code

Colossians, written by a disciple of Paul, quotes Gal. 3:28 but changes it considerably. Moreover, he balances it out with a household code of patriarchal submission. The relationship of Jews and gentiles was no longer a great problem and concern for the author. The separation between the Jewish and Christian communities probably had already taken place at the time of his writing. In quoting the baptismal formula Colossians mentions Greeks first and elaborates the second member of the pair circumcision and uncircumcision with "barbarian and Scythian," in order to stress that national and cultural differences and inequalities are overcome in the new humanity of Christ. Since Scythians were the proverbial boors of antiquity, it is obvious that the author of Colossians is especially interested in the opposite pair Greek and barbarian. While the third pair of Gal. 3:28—male and female—is not mentioned at all, Col. 3:11 also dissolves the slave-free polarization that defines the social-political stratifications of institutional slavery. Col. 3:11 no longer juxtaposes slave-free as opposite alternatives but adds them to the enumeration and elaboration of those who are uncircumcised: barbarian, Scythian, slave, freeborn.

Although the letter to the Colossians still refers to the baptismal liturgy and theology of the Asian churches, it celebrates not so much the restoration of human equality in the new community but rather "a cosmic event, in which the opposing elements of the universe were reconciled to each other." The so-called enthusiastic theology ascribed to Paul's opponents in Corinth is fully expressed here. Baptism means resurrection and enthronement with Christ in heaven, "stripping away the body of flesh" (2:11), and life in heaven rather than on earth (2:1–4; cf. 2:12, 20). The baptized are delivered from "the dominion of darkness" and transferred into "the kingdom of his beloved son" (1:13). They are "dead to the cosmos," have received a secret mystery (1:26f; 2:2–3), and have the assurance of an inheritance among the "holy ones" in the realm of light. The writer of Colossians agrees with his audience on this theology of exaltation but disagrees with some of the Colossians on how this baptismal "symbolic universe" and drama should be remembered and made effective. While some in the community of Colossae believed that the "removal of the fleshly body" and the "new humanity" in baptism must be realized in ascetic practices and elaborate ritual observances, the author insists on the finality of Christ's reconciliation and unification. The new "angelic religion" and the life in heaven are not to be realized by ascetic and ritual practice but in ethical behavior and communal life. Since they have been raised with Christ, they are to "seek the things that are above," and to set their "minds on the things that are above." They do so "by putting away" anger, wrath, malice, slander, and foul talk and by "putting on" compassion, kindness, lowliness, meekness, and patience, forebearing one another and forgiving each other. Above all, they should "put on love, which binds everything together in perfect harmony" (3:5–17). They should behave wisely to outsiders and be able to answer everyone (4:5f).

This is the context of the household code (3:18–4:1), the first and most precise form of the domestic code in the New Testament. The basic form of this code consists of three pairs of reciprocal exhortations addressing the relationship between wife and husband, children and father, and slaves and masters. In each case, the socially subordinate first member of the pair is exhorted to obedience to the superordinate second. The formal structure of such a household code, then, consists of address (wives), exhortation (submit to your husbands), and motivation (as is fitting in the Lord). The only Christian element in the Colossian code is the addition "in the Lord." However, the author of Colossians quotes the code here, not because he is concerned about the behavior of wives, but that of slaves.

The expansion of the code's third pair, slave-master, indicates that the obedience and acceptance of servitude by Christian slaves are of utmost concern. Colossians asks slaves to fulfill their task with single-mindedness of heart and dedication "as serving the Lord and not men" (3:23). He not only promises eschatological reward for such behavior but also threatens eschatological judgment and punishment for misbehavior (3:24f). The injunction to masters, in turn, is very short and has no Christian component except the reminder that they, too, have a master in heaven. Slave behavior is likened here to the Christian service of the Lord, while the "masters" are likened to the "Master" in heaven. It is obvious that the good behavior of slaves, according to the author, is the concrete realization of Gal. 3:28, insofar as both slaves and freeborn have one Lord in heaven, Christ, and belong to the new humanity, now "hid with Christ in God" (3: 3). There is no question that E. A. Judge is right when he asserts that what we hear in these injunctions is "the voice of the propertied class." We have no way of determining whether "those who are your earthly masters" are only pagan or also Christian masters. The injunction to the masters presupposes that they still have slaves who might or might not have been Christian.

In taking over the Greco-Roman ethic of the patriarchal household code, Colossians not only "spiritualizes" and moralizes the baptismal community understanding expressed in Gal. 3:28 but also makes this Greco-Roman household ethic a part of "Christian" social ethic. However, it is important to keep in mind that such a reinterpretation of the Christian baptismal vision is late—it did not happen before the last third of the first century. Moreover, it is found only in one segment of early Christianity, the post-Pauline tradition, and had no impact on the Jesus traditions. The insistence on equality and mutuality within the Christian community that seems to have been expressed by slaves as well as by women is not due to later "enthusiastic excesses" or to illegitimate agitation for emancipation. The opposite is true. Colossians shows how a so-called "enthusiastic" realized eschatological perspective can produce an insistence on patriarchal behavior as well as an acceptance of the established political-social status quo of inequality and exploitation in the name of Jesus Christ.

In discussing the *Sitz im Leben* of the household code form, exegetes have arrived at different interpretations. While a few scholars think that the demands for the obedience and submission of wives, children, and slaves are genuinely Christian, the majority sees the domestic code as a later Christian adaptation of a Greco-Roman or Jewish-Hellenistic philosophical-theological code. While Dibelius (cf. also Weidinger and Lohse) holds that the household code in Colossians is a slightly Christianized version of a Stoic ethical code, Lohmeyer (and recently Crouch) has stressed the Jewish-Hellenistic origin of the code in an apologetic missionary context. Not Stoicism but oriental Jewish religion provides the background for the code. In adopting the code, Christians followed the example of Hellenistic Judaism and utilized the form of the code developed in Jewish-Hellenistic missionary apologetics.

Most recently scholars have pointed to the treatises on economics and politics that reflect a form already codified by Aristotle and at home in the philosophical schools and morals of the first century C.E. Thraede stresses that the moralists of the early empire sought to formulate an ethics that would find a balance between the absolute traditional demands of subordination and obedience to the *paterfamilias* and the ideals of equality formulated in the Hellenistic age. What comes to the fore in the household code form of the New Testament is the option for "an ethically softened or humanized notion of domination and rule." But while Lührmann stresses the *Sitz im Leben* of the form and of the *topos* in economics with indirect implications for politics, Balch highlights the political context of the teachings about the right order of the house and economics. Both are intertwined because in antiquity the household was economically independent, self-sufficient, hierarchically ordered, and as such the basis of the state. Therefore, the three *topoi*, "concerning the state," "concerning household management," and "concerning marriage," were closely interrelated.

Aristotle, who has decisively influenced Western political philosophy as well as American legal concepts argues against Plato that one must begin the discussion of politics with thoughts about marriage, defined by him as a union of "natural ruler and natural subject." When slaves are added to the family, it can be called a "house." Several households constitute a village and several villages a city-state, or *politeia*:

> The investigation of everything should begin with its smallest parts, and the smallest and primary parts of the household are master and slave, husband and wife, father and children. We ought therefore to examine the proper constitution and character of each of the three relationships, I mean that of mastership, that of marriage and thirdly the progenitive relationship. [*Politics* I.1253b]

It is part of the household science to rule over wife and children as free-born. However, this is not done with the same form of government. Whereas the father rules over his children as a monarch rules, the husband exercises republican government over the wife:

> for the male is by nature better fitted to command than the female . . . and the older and fully developed person than the younger and immature. It is true that in most cases of republican government the ruler and ruled interchange in turn . . . but the male stands in this relationship to the female continuously. The rule of the father over the children on the other hand is that of a king. [*Politics* I.1259b]

Against those who argue that slavery is contrary to nature, Aristotle points to the rule of the soul over the body.

> It is manifest that it is natural and expedient for the body to be governed by the soul and for the emotional part to be governed by the intellect, the part possessing reason, whereas for the two parties to be on equal [*ison*] footing or in the contrary positions is harmful in all cases. . . . Also as between the sexes, the male is by nature superior and the female inferior, the male ruler and the female subject. And the same must also necessarily apply in the case of humankind generally; therefore all human beings that differ as widely as the soul does from the body . . . these are by nature slaves for whom to be governed by this kind of authority is advantageous. [*Politics* I.1254b]

These "natural' differences justify the relationships of domination in household and state.

Hence there are by nature various classes of rulers and ruled. For the free rules the slave, the male the female, the man the child in a different way. And all possess the various parts of the soul but possess them in different ways; for the slave has not got the deliberative part at all, and the female has it but without full authority, while the child has it but in an undeveloped form. [*Politics* I.1260a]

Interestingly enough, Aristotle acknowledges one exception when women can rule with "authority." Usually the relationship between husband and wife is that of "aristocracy" but when the husband controls everything it becomes an "oligarchy," "for he governs in violation of fitness and not in virtue of superiority." "And sometimes when the wife is an heiress, it is she who rules. In these cases, then, authority goes not by virtue but by wealth and power, as in an oligarchy" (*Nicomachean Ethics* VIII.1160b).

Since, however, every household is part of the state, the state is jeopardized if the different forms of household rule are not exercised faithfully.

The freedom in regard to women is detrimental both in regard to the purpose of the *politeia* and in regard to the happiness of the state. For just as man and wife are part of a household, it is clear that the state also is divided nearly in half into its male and female population, so that in all *politeia* in which the position of women is badly regulated one half of the state must be deemed neglected in framing the law. [*Politcs* II.1269b]

Such was the case in Sparta, where women controlled their own wealth. Although the Spartans did attempt to bring their women under the law, they gave up when the women resisted. Therefore, they loved and respected wealth and were under the sway of their women. The women controlled not only many things but also ruled their own rulers! These remarks make it clear that Aristotle knows of a historical state that was differently constituted.

Although the negative influence of Aristotle on Christian anthropology is widely acknowledged today, it is not sufficiently recognized that such an anthropology was rooted in Aristotle's understanding of political rule and domination. Just as he defined the "nature" of slaves with respect to their status as property and to their economic function, so Aristotle defined the "nature" of woman as that of someone who does not have "full authority" to rule, although he is well aware that such rule was an actual historical possibility and reality. The definition of "woman's nature" and "woman's proper sphere" is thus rooted in a certain relation of domination and subordination between man and woman having a concrete political background and purpose. Western misogynism has its root in the rules for the household as the model of the state. A feminist theology therefore must not only analyze the anthropological dualism generated by Western culture and theology, but also uncover its political roots in the patriarchal household of antiquity.

Balch cites considerable evidence that Aristotle's political philosophy was revitalized in neo-Pythagorean and Stoic philosophy. It was also accepted in Hellenistic Judaism, as the writings of Philo and Josephus demonstrate. For instance, Philo stresses the interrelationship between household and state management.

For the future statesman needed first to be trained and practiced in house management, for a house is a city compressed into small dimensions, and a household management may be called a kind of state management [*politeia*]. . . . This shows clearly that the household manager is identical with the statesman. [*Joseph* 38–39]

And he asserts in *Special Laws*:

Organized committees are of two sorts, the greater which we call cities and the smaller which we call households. Both of these have their governors [*prostasian*], the government of the greater is assigned to men, under the name of statesmanship [*politeia*], that of the lesser known as household management to women. A woman then should not be a busybody, meddling with matters outside her household concerns, but should seek a life of seclusion. [III.170f]

Philo insists that Jews are not impious, they respect father and mother, and wives must be in servitude to their husbands. Crouch has argued that the closest parallel to the New Testament domestic code is *Hypothetica* VIIII.7.14:

Any of them whom you attack with inquiries about their ancestral institutions can answer you rapidly and easily. The husband seems competent to transmit knowledge of the laws to his wife, the father to his children, the master to his slaves.

In discussing the *politeia* of Moses and comparing it to that of Romulus, Josephus stresses that Jewish laws do not teach impiety but piety, not the hatred of others but the communal life. They oppose injustice and teach justice, they deter from war and encourage people to work. Therefore, there can be nowhere a greater justice, piety, and harmony than among the Jews. In their marriage laws and the birth and upbringing of children Jews fulfilled the laws of Romulus's *politeia*, which the Romans had imposed on the whole empire. Jewish women were good Roman citizens:

The woman, says the Law, is in all things inferior to the man. Let her accordingly be submissive, not for her humiliation, but that she may be directed, for the authority has been given by God to the man. [*Against Apion* II.201]

Since the Jews were criticized on the ground that Moses, the founder of the Jewish state, had incited a revolt and introduced different marriage and burial laws, Josephus stresses that Jewish wives, unlike Spartan women, are entirely submissive to their husbands. The context of this statement, as for that of Philo, is clearly apologetic. Dionysios of Halicarnassus had in a similar fashion elaborated the position of women in the *politeia* of Romulus:

The law led the women to behave themselves with modesty and great decorum. The law was to this effect that a woman joined to her husband by a holy marriage should share in all his possessions and sacred rites. . . . This law obliged both the married women, as having no other refuge, to conform themselves entirely to the temper of their husbands, and the husbands to rule their wives as necessary and inseparable possessions. Accordingly if a wife was virtuous and in all things obedient to her husband she was the mistress of the house in the same degree as the husband was master of it, and after the death of her husband, she was heir to his property. [*Roman Antiquities* II.25.2]

However, Thraede is correct when he points out that we must not overlook the fact that alongside this Aristotelian ethics of submission and rule, a marriage ethos developed which stressed the harmony between the couples. Plutarch describes the ideal marriage as a copartnership:

It is a lovely thing for a wife to sympathize with her husband's concerns and the husband with the wife's so that, as ropes, by being intertwined, get strength from each other, thus . . . the copartnership may be preserved through the joint action of both. [*Conjugal Precepts* 140e]

Although the wife is clearly the subordinate of the husband, the husband should train her in philosophy and she should respect him as "guide, philosopher and teacher in all that is most lovely and divine." She should not be aggrieved "if like the flute-player, she makes a more impressive sound through a tongue not her own." Therefore, she should always behave with modesty and moderation, appear in public only with her husband, be carefully guarded in her speech, and avoid excessive adornment and luxury. So the neo-Pythagorean Callicratidas advises men to marry virgins in the flower of their youth (usually between 12 and 15 years) because

such virgins are easily fashioned, and are docile and are also naturally well disposed to be instructed by, and to fear and love their husbands.

If the husband, however, wants to be admired and loved, he should

exercise his power so that it might be mingled with pleasure and veneration; pleasure indeed being produced by his fondness, but veneration from doing nothing of a vile or abject nature.

The marriage will be happy if both husband and wife are in accord with each other in prosperous and adverse times. The husband's role is that of a master, teacher, and regulator, the wife's behavior that of prudence, modesty, and respect. Perictione stresses that the wife must venerate the gods by obeying the laws and sacred institutions of her country. She should honor and respect her parents, and live with her husband "legally and socially," especially concerned with performing her duties toward him in "domestic harmony" and being the guardian of his bed,

then she will not only benefit her husband, but also her children, her kindred, her servants, and the whole of her house; in which possessions, friends, citizens, and strangers are contained.

Plutarch also emphasizes that the wife should not only share her husband's friends but also his gods. She must therefore "shut the front door tight upon all queer rituals and outlandish superstitions. For with no god do stealthy and secret rites performed by a woman find any favor" (140d). Thus it is apparent that in antiquity rules of the household are part of economics and politics, as are religious rites and ancestral customs. The well-being of the state and the religious observance of the laws and customs of the patriarchal family are intertwined. Slaves and wives who do not worship the gods of the *paterfamilias* violate not only their household duties but also the laws of the state.

* * *

Ephesians and the Household Code

Ephesians presents the "hope to which Christians are called" (1:18) as the gospel of peace (6:15). Such universal peace was accomplished by Christ's victory over the powers of darkness, a victory which did away with the gulf between Jews and non-Jews. Forgiveness of sin means liberation from the spiritually evil heavenly powers and unification of the two into one "new third race" or into the one family of God. The divine mediator has healed the breach between the world above and the world below, Christ has reconciled Jews and gentiles to a new universal harmony and peace.

The author writes to gentile Christians and reminds them, using Old Testament-Jewish and early Christian traditional materials, that they have received access to the one true God of Israel in Jesus Christ. They who have been sojourners and strangers have become fellow-citizens with the saints and angels. The dividing wall of the Temple, which is here projected into the whole cosmos and into the structure of the universe, is broken down, and a new unified humanity has come into existence in the church. Ephesians reinterprets the cosmic stress of Colossians in terms of ecclesiology. Christ is the head and source of peace for the church. His work as universal peacemaker is now to be carried out by the church, which is his *plērōma*, the sphere of his influence and the force-field of his peacemaking power. The church "embodies" the peace of Christ. Those who are baptized are a new creation (2:10), have put on the new human (4:24; cf. 4:13, the "perfect man"). They have risen with Christ and are seated with him above (2:6). By "grace they have been saved" (2:5c) and have been "sealed with the promised Holy Spirit," the "guarantor" of their "inheritance" (1:13). They are children of God (5:1, 8).

The universal peace of Christ must be manifest in the community of Jew and gentile Christians. They are admonished to "lead a life worthy of your calling to which you have been called" (4:1). They must be eager to preserve

> the unity of the spirit in the bond of peace. There is one body and one Spirit, . . . one Lord, one faith, one baptism, one God and Father of us all. [4:3ff]

The baptismal remembrance of 2:11–22 clearly refers to the pre-Pauline baptismal formula with its opposites, uncircumcision/circumcision. The author expresses in various ways the unification of Jews and gentiles through the death of Christ and their equality in the new community of those baptized into Christ's death and resurrection. Those who once were "far off" have "now been brought near in the blood of Christ" (2:13). Three times the author stresses in 2:14–18 that Christ has made "both one" (*ta amphotera hen*): v. 14 stresses that Christ "our peace" has abolished the enmity between Jews and gentiles; v. 15 names the result of this peacemaking: "That he might create in himself one new human being in place of the two," and v. 16 adds: "and might reconcile us *both* to God in *one* body"; v. 17 repeats again the expression that "those who were far off" and "those who were near" have received peace. Therefore, the author can sum up in v. 18: "For through him we *both* have access in *one* Spirit to the Father." Therefore, the baptized are "members of the household of God" (2:19) which expands into a "holy temple in the Lord," in whom they are built up together as "a dwelling place of God in the Spirit." (2:21f).

The author applies this theological motif of peace and unification to the relationship of gentile and Jewish Christians in the community in order to insist on their unity, equality, and mutuality within the "household of God." He seeks to prevent gentile believers from regarding themselves as superior to Jewish Christians and to encourage them to mutual respect and support of each other. Although there are many similarities between 2:11–22 and 5:21–33 (the admonition to husband and wife), his perception of "making peace in Christ" is quite different here. Whereas wives and slaves are admonished to subordinate themselves and to obey with "fear and trembling," the author does not admonish Jews to subordinate themselves in order to preserve the "peace" of the community; but to live according to their calling. He resorts to a variety of Jewish Christian theologoumena to persuade the gentiles, who seem to be the powerful and decision-making members in the congregation, to preserve the "peace" to be manifested in the body of Christ.

That the author also has the baptismal formula in mind, when elaborating the traditional household code in terms of the Christian community, is apparent from the statement in 6:8c that everyone, slave or free, will receive the same eschatological recompense from the Lord. While the author insists on the mutuality, unity, and equality of uncircumcised and circumcised here and now, he maintains such equality for slaves and free-born only for the eschatological future. Moreover, whereas it was uncertain whether the admonitions of Colossians applied to Christian relationships with pagans, and whereas the advice of 1 Peter clearly was directed to wives married to unbelievers and slaves living in pagan households, Ephesians applies the traditional rules for the household to relationships between Christian couples and Christian slaves and masters, *and thus to the Christian household itself.* That this household is seen in terms of a house church is likely from the introductory section to the traditional household code in 5:18–20, which speaks of the Spirit-filled worship of the Christians. Moreover the whole community is understood as the "household" (2:19), the family (3:15), the house (2:20) of God. The believers are children (5:1, 8; 1:5, sons) of God who have the guarantee of a glorious inheritance (1:4, 18), their father is God (3:14, 4:6; cf. 1:2, 3).

However, it is important to recognize that the author does not develop the patriarchal domination-subordination relationship in terms of the whole community. Although he speaks of those who are apostles, prophets, evangelists, pastors, and teachers for the "equipment of the saints" (4:12), he does not ask the saints to subordinate themselves to them nor does he say that they are the sign of unity. Neither does the author claim that the leaders represent God, the "father" of the household, nor that they are males acting in the name and place of Christ. The church does not, as J. Ernst maintains, receive here "in imitation of the ancient state organizations a social structure which regulates the concrete life in common."

Ephesians elaborates only that some have received these gifts and some have received others "for the upbuilding of the body of Christ." Its enumeration of ministries expands the Pauline catalogue to include evangelists and pastors, but does not restrict it to men.

While the Colossian code clearly was interested in the patriarchally appropriate behavior of slaves, the Ephesian code elaborates upon the relationship of wife and husband in patriarchal marriage. In so doing, the author combines the traditional household code form with the church-body theology and Pauline bride-bridegroom notion found for the first time in 2 Cor. 11:2. The relationship between Christ and the church, expressed in the metaphors of head and body as well as of bridegroom and bride, becomes the paradigm for Christian marriage and vice versa. This theological paradigm reinforces the cultural-patriarchal pattern of subordination, insofar as the relationship between Christ and the church clearly is not a relationship between equals, since the church-bride is totally dependent and subject to her head or bridegroom. Therefore, the general injunction for all members of the Christian community, "Be subject to one another in the fear of Christ," is clearly spelled out for the Christian wife as requiring submission and inequality.

As the church is subordinated to Christ, so the wife has to subject herself to her husband in everything. The phrase "in everything," which in the Colossian code was associated with the obedience of children and slaves, here underlines the subordinate position of the wife (v. 24). 5:22 insists that the submission of the wife to her husband is on a par with her religious submission to Christ, the Lord. The instruction to the wives thus clearly reinforces the patriarchal marriage pattern and justifies it christologically. The instructions to the wife are therefore summed up in the injunction to fear or to respect her husband (v. 33).

However, the patriarchal-societal code is theologically modified in the exhortation to the husband. The negative demand of Colossians that men are not to be harsh with their wives is not repeated here. Instead, the husbands are three times commanded to love their wives (5:25, 28, 33). Jesus' commandment, "to love your neighbor as yourself" (cf. Lev. 19:18) is applied to the marriage relationship of the husband. Moreover, the relationship of Christ to the church becomes the example for the husband. Christ's self-giving love for the church is to be the model for the love relationship of the husband with his wife. Patriarchal domination is thus radically questioned with reference to the paradigmatic love relationship of Christ to the church.

Nevertheless, it must be recognized that this christological modification of the husband's patriarchal position and duties does not have the power, theologically, to transform the patriarchal pattern of the household code, even though this might have been the intention of the author. Instead, Ephesians christologically cements the inferior position of the wife in the marriage relationship. One could say that the exhortations to the husbands spell out what it means to live a marriage relationship as a Christian, while those to the wives insist on the proper social behavior of women. The reason for this theological shortcoming might be the author's interest in clarifying the relationship between Christ and the church, whose unity is his primary concern in the rest of the letter. His interpretation of Gen. 2:24 shows that this is the case. Although early Christian theology used this

Old Testament text for understanding the marriage relationship, the author applies it primarily to the relationship of Christ and the church.

Eph. 5:21–33 thus participates in the trajectory of the patriarchal household-code tradition insofar as it takes over the household-code pattern and reasserts the submission of the wife to the husband as a religious Christian duty. At the same time, it modifies the patriarchal code by replacing patriarchal superordination and domination with the Christian command of love to be lived according to the example of Christ. On the whole, however, the author was not able to "Christianize" the code. The "gospel of peace" has transformed the relationship of gentiles and Jews, but not the social roles of wives and slaves within the household of God. On the contrary, the cultural-social structures of domination are theologized and thereby reinforced. However, it must not be overlooked that the code and its theological legitimation are not descriptive of the actual situation of women and slaves in the communities of Asia Minor. It is exhortative or prescriptive and seeks to establish a Christian behavior that is not yet realized in the life of the Christians in Asia Minor.

JOUETTE M. BASSLER

The Widows' Tale (1984)†

The growing sensitivity in contemporary society to women's issues and roles is shared to some extent by New Testament scholars, who are exploring with increasing frequency the role of women in early Christianity. The Pastoral Epistles are among the most challenging documents to this new quest, not only because of the relatively large number of pertinent texts they contain but also because of their apparent misogynous thrust. This paper is addressed to this challenge as it explores one provocative passage, the advice concerning widows in 1 Tim. 5:3–16, from a perspective that seems to shed additional light on the historical and sociological forces at work in that early community.

Hitherto the questions brought to this text have concerned such issues as the unity of the passage, the tasks and official status of the widows, and the possible connection between the advice tendered here and the heresy problem threatening the church. Rarely has any attention been given to the sociological advantages derived by the widows from membership in their circle. Yet an understanding of these advantages should help us to understand the thrust of the Pastor's remarks. Indeed, the important concept of social freedom for these women may prove to be the key for unlocking the meaning of the widows' actions and the Pastor's response.

I. Introduction

The Christian message was a message of freedom—freedom from the Law, from sin, from death. Beyond these theological dimensions, however, Christian freedom also had a social component. This is nowhere expressed

† This essay was first published in *JBL* 103 (1984): 23–41. Reprinted by permission of the Society of Biblical Literature. Bassler is professor of New Testament at Perkins School of Theology, Southern Methodist University.

more clearly than in Paul's letter to the church at Galatia: "There is neither Jew nor Greek, there is neither slave nor free, there is neither male nor female; for you are all one in Christ Jesus" (Gal. 3:28). Paul here affirms that the hierarchical social patterns of his contemporary culture have no relevance for one's standing within the body of Christ. Jew and Greek are equal, as are slave and master, man and woman.

Though Paul's attention in that letter was directed toward a dissolution of the Jew-Greek dichotomy, it is the last pair that interests us here: "There is neither male nor female." These were extraordinary words for the first century, daring to proclaim and difficult to actualize even within the walls of the church. Indeed, to achieve the equality these words announce, it seems that women turned frequently to celibacy to find freedom from the subservient inequality imposed by the patriarchal marriage structure of that day.

*   *   *

This growing insight into the attraction of celibate equality for women in early Christianity will be shown to provide a useful key for exploring a rather puzzling passage in the deutero-Pauline corpus, the discussion of widows in 1 Tim. 5:3–16. It has been occasionally suggested that some aspect of freedom lies behind this passage, yet the text has never been rigorously examined from this perspective to see what historical, sociological, and exegetical insights it might yield. This approach should allow us to draw together some strands in the Pastoral Epistles in a way that suggests a more complete interpretation of this particular text and of this particular moment in early Christianity. First, however, we need to place this moment in the proper historical context.

II. Historical Context

There have been a vast number of studies of the historical context of early Christianity. An increasing number of these focus on the particular context of the status of women. Though they may differ in details of interpretation, there seems to be general agreement about the overall picture. In the centuries immediately preceding the advent of Christianity, a gradual liberation of women occurred in the Greco-Roman world. Yet this liberation seems to have been somewhat stronger in theory than in practice, and it aroused as much reactionary animosity as support. A brief review of the situation will highlight this.

Beginning perhaps as early as the third or fourth century B.C.E., women began to achieve a greater degree of freedom and control in their lives. Influenced by many factors and proceeding at different rates in different places, there were clear gains for women in legal, economic, and educational fields. Yet the contemporary philosophical schools were not unanimous in their enthusiasm for this new wave of "feminism." The Peripatetics, for example, employed the patriarchal family model to define the nature of the state, thus confirming on several levels the subordinate role of women. The Neo-pythagoreans were rooted in a tradition of an egalitarian acceptance of both male and female adherents, but the Hellenistic resurgence of the sixth-century school responded with some of the most rigorous affirmations of the traditional subordination of women. The

Stoics, with their concept of the common possession of the divine Logos by all rational beings, had the necessary theoretical basis for an egalitarian vision uniting men and women as well as Greeks and barbarians. But if women were included in the vision, they do not seem to have been included in the school, and the practical effects of this theory were thus minimized.

Nevertheless, advances were made. The Epicureans, for example, not only included women in their community, but they included women from diverse social levels and even saw nothing amiss in promoting one of them, a *hetaira*, to presidency of the group. The Cynics, too, whether because of their focus on individual rather than familial or civic values or because of a deliberate desire to flout the current social norms, attracted and accepted women adherents.

The rhetoric and praxis of these philosophical schools, though not overwhelming, seems to have sufficiently eroded traditional expectations to generate a rather widespread and somewhat vituperative response. This negative response seems to have come from many directions, and we are able to hear only its most literary formulations. On the more restrained side, Horace mocked the ostentation of women who lie with philosophical works between their silken pillows, while Epictetus complained about women who misinterpret the philosophers to justify their licentious behavior. Theophrastus was somewhat harsher when he insisted that education would turn women into lazy, talkative busybodies, and Juvenal revealed his own brand of misogyny in his infamous sixth satire.

Even as these voices were being raised in protest against increased participation of women in areas formerly reserved for men, a smaller countermovement developed defending this participation. Yet this apology, even as it affirmed the equal right of women to philosophical schooling, remained somewhat inconsistently wedded to the contemporary conception of the subordinate role of women within the family and the society. Plutarch, for example, encouraged a young husband to teach his wife philosophy since that discipline, better than any other, would protect her from the superstition and gullibility so common to women. This somewhat grudging recognition of a woman's ability and right to participate in her husband's intellectual life was not, however, part of a broader vision of female liberation or equality. The husband remained, in Plutarch's view, the dominant partner in marriage; the wife's role remained one of submission.

The Stoic philosopher Musonius Rufus was much more vigorous and explicit in his defense of woman's right to learn philosophy. Yet even as he defended this right, he defended in the same breath and with equal vigor the prevailing view of the woman's proper, submissive role. Indeed, Musonius claimed that the study of philosophy would nurture this role—hardly a vigorous voice for a liberation movement:

> Yes, but I assure you, some will say, that women who associate with philosophers are bound to be arrogant . . . and presumptuous, in that abandoning their own households and turning to the company of men they practice speeches, talk like sophists, and analyze syllogisms when they should be sitting at home spinning. . . . Above all we ought to see if the study which presents modesty as the greatest good can make them presumptuous, if the study which is a guide to the greatest self-restraint accustoms them to live heedlessly, if what sets forth intem-

perance as the greatest evil does not teach self-control, if what represents management of a household as a virtue does not impel them to manage well their homes. Finally the teachings of philosophy exhort the woman *to be content with her lot* and to work with her hands.[1]

The first-century environment was thus one characterized in part by an increasing freedom for women and in part by reactions to this. The situation is well summarized by Wayne Meeks: "The age brought in all places a heightened awareness of the differentiation of male and female. The traditional social roles were no longer taken for granted but debated, consciously violated by some, vigorously defended by others." * * * Egalitarian hopes might have been aroused by the rhetoric of this period, but few avenues were open to satisfy them. The tombstones and funeral speeches, with their recurring references to domesticity, modesty, and submissiveness, eloquently proclaim the prevailing feminine ideal that stood as a bulwark against real equality.

The message of Christian freedom, especially as it was framed in the baptismal formula of Gal. 3:28, spoke to these egalitarian hopes and seems to have awakened a response. Evidence for this can perhaps be found in the radical attempt by the women of the church at Corinth to symbolize this equality in their dress and hair styles (1 Cor. 11:2–16). The prominent role of women in the Pauline and pre-Pauline mission fields also indicates an enthusiastic appropriation of the message. Indeed, the egalitarian hopes that Christianity aroused could have been an effective aid to proselytizing, for from the beginning women were attracted to the new movement in large numbers.

The Christian response to this egalitarian enthusiasm, however, was increasingly one of restraint. Paul himself, though retaining a sense of the functional equality of all members of the community (1 Cor. 11:11–12), nevertheless delivered some restrictive admonitions to women that arose in part from a practical desire for church order (1 Cor. 14:33b–36) and in part from a theological concern with the eschatological reservations of the Christian message of redemption (1 Cor. 11:2–16).

The early Christian *Haustafeln* also retain the concept of intrinsic equality (1 Pet. 3:7; Eph. 5:21, 6:8–9), yet their emphasis is even more on the obedience and submission of the subordinate members of the community, summoning them to conformity with the expectations of society. This characteristic emphasis has been explained as a cautionary response to the egalitarian enthusiasm of these members. The motivation for such a response may be found in a growing concern for public opinion, which was, as we have seen, profoundly conservative with regard to female equality. Thus the original *communitas* model that seems to lie behind Paul's letters, a model based on equal standing and equal acceptance of all members, was soon eroded by forces of time and public opinion into the patriarchal model of contemporary society in which roles were defined by the dominant-submissive pattern of the extended family.

The Pastoral Epistles climax this movement. We must now turn to these documents to assess the effect of this on the behavior of the widows and the Pastor's response to this behavior.

1. *Or.* 3, "That Women Too Should Study Philosophy," translated by C. E. Lutz, *Musonius Rufus* (New Haven: Yale University, 1947) 43–44; emphasis added.

III. The Pastoral Epistles

SOCIAL PRESSURE, HERESY, AND ETHICS

Before addressing 1 Tim. 5:3–16 and its references to widows, we should review some widely recognized aspects of the Pastoral Epistles that may prove useful to our investigation of this text.

First, the Pastoral Epistles are permeated with a strong concern for the opinion of contemporary society. The advice to bishops (1 Tim. 3:7), young widows (1 Tim. 5:14), young wives (Titus 2:5), young men (Titus 2:8), and slaves (1 Tim. 6:1; Titus 2:10) betrays, for example, an anxiety about the effect of the behavior of these groups of Christians on the reputation of the church. Second, this church was seriously threatened by a heresy problem. Behind the stereotypical accusations of immorality that characterize the polemical style of these letters, the picture emerges of an ascetic (1 Tim. 4:3), gnosticizing (1 Tim. 6:20) group challenging this church and enjoying particular success among women (2 Tim. 3:6–7).

These two factors explain to some extent the third: a rigid hierarchical structure that was coupled with a rather misogynous view was imposed on the community. As a first round of defense against the heresy and a first round of response to outside criticism, the church's hierarchical structure was strengthened and traditional hierarchical values were stressed. Thus we find a concern for the obedient submissiveness of slaves toward their masters (Titus 2:9–10), of children toward their fathers (1 Tim. 3:4), and of women toward their husbands (Titus 2:5) and their ministers (1 Tim. 2:11). Women are admonished to be "sensible, chaste, domestic, kind, and submissive to their husbands" (Titus 2:5), "to adorn themselves modestly and sensibly . . . and to learn in silence with all submissiveness" (1 Tim. 2:9–11). The explicit motivation for this advice, which has been aptly described as "die Stimme der Volksethik [the voice of popular ethics]," is the concern for the opinion of outsiders. Not far beneath the surface, however, lies an equally strong concern to render the somewhat vulnerable women in the congregation immune to the message of the heretics. The net effect of these two concerns is to eliminate the moderating features of earlier *Haustafeln*—the general statements of intrinsic or soteriological equality and the balancing admonitions to the dominant members of the community. Slaves, children and especially wives must be kept submissive, but there is no concern for Christian concessions by masters, fathers, or husbands.

The problem that the church was experiencing with its widows seems to be related to these points. Christianity no longer offered to women the freedom and equality that the movement originally promised. Since the general atmosphere of that time seems to have been one of stirring egalitarian hopes, hopes that were further encouraged by the message of Christian equality, this reversion of an egalitarian movement to the more conservative attitudes of contemporary society probably generated some counterreaction among those most affected by it. The passage studied here, 1 Tim. 5:3–16, seems to provide some evidence of the form this counterreaction took in one early Christian community.

THE WIDOWS

Before we can ask what was wrong with the widows we need to consider the logically anterior question, what is wrong with the text? The primary problem here is the apparent lack of unity in this passage, though it seems to deal with a single issue.

Verses 3–16 are all concerned with widows, and apart from an insistence that the church seek out real widows (ἡ ὄντως χήρα) there is no evidence in the text to suggest that the term shifts in meaning. Thus a clear word pattern is established that points to the unity of this passage. Supporting this is the *inclusio*-frame that the author has supplied. Verse 16 repeats in inverted order the ideas introduced in vv 3–4, using many of the same phrases:

* * *

In spite of this formal evidence supporting the unity of the text, the criteria put forward in it are so numerous and occasionally so contradictory that it seems difficult to maintain that vv. 3–8, 16 and vv. 9–15 refer to the same group, that is, that the true widows (v. 3) are identical to the enrolled (καταλέγειν) widows (v. 9). Verses 3–8 and 16, for example, emphasize the need and piety of the real widow, who is to receive assistance (honor) from the church. Verses 9–15, however, present standards of age (not less than sixty years) and past behavior (wife of one husband, well-attested for good deeds, having brought up children, shown hospitality, washed the feet of the saints, relieved the afflicted) for the widows who are to be enrolled. If one views the passage as a unity and assumes that enrollment was a precondition for financial support, one is left with some nearly untenable conclusions. This would imply, for example, that the church would refuse to render assistance to a widow, regardless of need, if she did not meet a minimum age requirement. Furthermore, under the assumption of unity, a young widow who followed the advice of v. 14 ("I would have younger widows marry") would by this very act of obedience exclude herself from any future assistance should she become widowed again (v. 9). So harsh, indeed so repugnant, are these conclusions that many scholars refuse to equate the enrolled with the real widows, thus preserving the honor of the early church if not the unity of the passage. Thus, while the word pattern and *inclusio*-structure favor a unified interpretation of the passage, its logic seems to point in a different direction. Any interpretation of this text should account for, if not justify, this inconsistent pattern.

If the problems we experience with the text are difficult to penetrate, the problem this early church experienced with the widows is somewhat less opaque. Many of the difficulties presented by the text stem from the fact that the author is not initiating a new benevolence, which would have involved a more careful explication of terms and conditions, but is seeking to limit an existing one. Indeed, this goal unites the content of the two otherwise somewhat disparate halves of the passage, since both seek to exclude various categories and reduce the circle of widows to a minimum. If this portion of the letter accurately reflects historical circumstances, it seems clear that the circle of widows had grown to an unacceptable size, unacceptable both because of the financial strain this placed on the church (v. 16) and because of potential and real abuse of the office (v. 13).

How can we explain this apparently dramatic increase in the number of widows in the community? It may, of course, indicate no more than the mortality rate of this period. If, however, χήρα [widow] is understood in more general terms, the increase in "widows" (women living without a husband) could point instead to a high divorce rate between recently converted Christian women and their pagan husbands. Yet "widow" need not even indicate an earlier marriage. In the context of this passage, the term seems to designate the life of renunciation of the bearer of the title more than her marital history. Since v. 12 * * * seems to suggest a vow of chastity and since the references to marriage * * * of widows (vv. 11, 14) provide no linguistic indication that the author actually had *re*-marriage in mind, it appears that the widows' circle had evolved to the point that chastity, not widowhood, was the determinative feature. It seems necessary to conclude that the factors leading to the increased numbers of widows were not necessarily related to mortality or conversion patterns. Virgins as well as widows were admitted to the circle, but not, as Stählin suggests, to fill up the office. This assumes that the church faced a deficiency of widows, yet the problem here is the opposite, there were too many of them. Virgins, perhaps also converted and divorced women, had joined the widows' circle, swelling its ranks to disturbing proportions. But what had attracted them?

One suggestion has been that the large voluntary association with this group was grounded in the esteem and remuneration accompanying this association. Müller-Bardorff, however, rejects this explanation, claiming that these factors could not have been sufficient to offset the life of renunciation demanded of widows, especially for the younger women. Müller-Bardorff thus seeks a deeper theological grounding and links the popularity of the ideal of renunciation with a radical eschatology that was rooted in ideas akin to those of 1 Cor. 7:25–40. This radical eschatology was then, according to Müller-Bardorff, influenced by a radical dualism, and the blending of these two ideas permitted the ideal to remain alive long after the original eschatological fervor of Christianity had faded. Certainly the Pastoral Epistles show little evidence that this community still had a radical eschatological perspective. However, to assess any hypotheses concerning the popularity of this social group, including those of Ryrie and Müller-Bardorff, it is crucial to consider the sociological advantages that the widows' circle offered to its adherents.

The life demanded of the widows was one of celibacy, yet in the context of the rigid patriarchal norms of contemporary society, norms that this Christian community had embraced, this could have been regarded less as a life of renunciation than as a life of freedom. Pomeroy has noted that in the Greek pantheon, the most liberated goddesses were those not bound to male gods in a permanent relationship. This observation also holds in the mortal realm—and not merely with the vestal virgins whom Pomeroy mentions. The widows of the Pastoral Epistles were, like the vestal virgins, under special restrictions, but, again like the vestals, these restrictions were not those binding ordinary women. Indeed, widows were remarkably free of these ordinary restraints. Freed from the hierarchical dominance of either father or husband, freed from the demands of childbearing and rearing, freed even from pressing economic concerns, the "widows" were granted a degree of freedom usually reserved for the *hetairai*, yet now enhanced by ecclesiastical respectability and esteem. The increased attractiveness of this office may rest as much on the freedom and equality it offered as on the esteem or dualistic influences proposed by Ryrie and Müller-Bardorff. The church was increasingly denying the freedom and equality of the original Christian communities, and thus those women whose attraction to Christianity was enhanced by this promise of equality retreated further into the circle that preserved through its celibate lifestyle a measure of the original promise.

THE CHURCH'S RESPONSE

While the widows' circle may have solved one problem for the women, it was generating at least two problems for the church. First, the lifestyle of the widows seems to have produced a negative reaction in the wider society, which objected to their free and apparently useless behavior (v. 14b). Second, the circle of widows seems to have provided a natural avenue of defection to the heretics, who advocated a similar lifestyle. Indeed, v. 15, with its reference to "straying after Satan," indicates that several widows had already chosen that path.

The response of the Pastor to this was, like the problems themselves, twofold. Since the large number of widows probably exacerbated these problems, the Pastor first attempted to reduce the numbers of this proliferating group. It would have been unthinkable to eliminate entirely a group whose roots reached back to the earliest days of the church (Acts 6:1). This author chose instead to deal with the problem of numbers by recalling the church to a rigid concept of real widows who were entirely without other resources (vv. 3–8, 16). Beyond this, however, there also seems to be evidence of an attempt in vv. 9–15 to develop additional criteria that mold the reduced circle into a type of reverse affirmation of contemporary social norms.

There were a number of religious cults in Greco-Roman society that appealed primarily to women. Two recurrent factors seem to have contributed to their popularity and longevity. They offered, as Pomeroy notes, an emotional outlet for a group whose lives were traditionally rather restricted, yet at the same time they affirmed, either directly or indirectly, the social norms of the larger patriarchal society. Thus the various Fortuna cults explicitly exalted the desired domestic virtues of women: childbearing, marital fidelity, familial bonds, domestic harmony. The Isis cult originally proclaimed an astonishing message of sexual equality and generated thereby an intense and sustained hostile reaction in Greco-Roman society. Only when the cult shifted the emphasis to the traditional ideals of marriage, domesticity, and motherhood did it earn official approbation. At the other extreme the sexual and moral excesses of the Dionysiac cult were remarkably well tolerated by a conservative society. This toleration arose from the fact that these excesses were viewed as the temporary product of religious possession and involved a deliberate and recognizable role reversal. That is, the women engulfed by Dionysiac madness enacted the reverse of the submissive, domestic, nurturing role expected of them, but since this reverse behavior was recognized as the product of religious insanity, the sanity and appropriateness of the traditional behavior was indirectly but clearly affirmed.

The situation in the Pastoral Epistles falls between these extremes (Fortuna cult affirmation and Dionysiac cult reverse affirmation). The basic but potentially objectionable features of the widows' circle were retained— the vow of celibacy and the concomitant liberation of the widows from the patriarchal family structure and responsibilities. Yet even as these features were retained for the widows' circle, criteria were introduced for enroll- ment into that circle that affirmed the very behavior from which the wid- ows themselves were exempt—domesticity, marital fidelity, childbearing, etc. (vv. 9–10). This, then, seems to offer an explanation for the oddly inconsistent criteria proposed for the widows. The rationale for these cri- teria was not exclusively one of locating and honoring the true widows of the community, though the church did not abandon this ideal. Nor do these criteria seem to have been selected with logic and consistency in mind. Rather, the goal here seems to have been the reduction of the offense of this group by accepting only those who, at least in their earlier years, exemplified the domestic virtues expected by contemporary society. Thus a potentially objectionable office has been tamed, for even though the behavior of the widows may continue to deviate from society's expec- tations, the office itself now extols and rewards the expected virtues. Beyond this, the requirement that younger widows marry and bear children (v. 14) not only encourages *them* to conform to society's expectations, but it also has a distinctly anti-ascetic thrust that was probably intended to counter the influence of the heretical camp.

We have covered as much of the social history of this community as this passage allows us to glimpse. Perhaps, however, it is not unreasonable to hypothesize a trajectory of subsequent events. Since the heretical faction, with its message of asceticism, offered a freedom from the patriarchal structure akin to that of the widows' circle, it seems probable that the rate of defections to this group would increase as the church acted to reduce the number of the officially sanctioned "free" women. Those women who first entered the widows' circle to find an actualization of the message of equality are unlikely to have been content with the subordinate lifestyle thrust upon them.

The church thus seems to have been caught in a disastrous feedback loop. The heresy problem combined with social pressure and caused the church to move from a *communitas* structure challenging society's norms to a patriarchal structure embracing them. Increased patriarchalization of the church seems to have led to an increase in the size of the widows' circle, where a degree of freedom from that structure was preserved through the celibate lifestyle. This increase in numbers and its attendant problems was met by a stronger ecclesiastical response reducing the size of the circle and reaffirming through various injunctions the patriarchal norms of society. This in turn probably exacerbated the heresy problem, returning the church to the starting point of the loop. One can only guess at the ultimate outcome for this community.

IV. Conclusion

This paper has attempted to view 1 Tim. 5:3–16 from a particular socio- logical perspective—the perspective of equality and freedom. Viewed from this perspective, certain aspects of this passage and certain aspects of the development of early Christianity seem to come into clearer focus.

Christianity began as an egalitarian movement and precisely this stance of equality fostered its acceptance among fringe groups of society—among slaves and especially among women, who numbered prominently among the first converts. Yet in the Pastoral Epistles we begin to see evidence of what happens when an egalitarian movement becomes less so. As the church moved away from an egalitarian, *communitas* structure to the hierarchical, patriarchal pattern favored by the contemporary society, there seems to have been a rather desperate retrenching attempt by the affected women. The Pastoral Epistles indicate first a retreat into the widows' circle where freedom from the patriarchal structure of society was preserved by a celibate lifestyle. As this circle was narrowed and transformed into a reverse affirmation of traditional norms, we can project a further retreat into a gnosticizing heresy that preserved communal equality if not doctrinal purity.

Several puzzles, however, still remain. One would expect the older women, who had participated longer in the Christian movement and had perhaps experienced the original *communitas* equality, to object most vigorously to the increased patriarchal subordination of their sex, yet they are the ones instructed to teach the traditional feminine values (Titus 2:3). It seems to be consistently the *younger* women who require instruction in these values (Titus 2:4–5) or generate trouble with regard to them (1 Tim. 5:11–15). Can this be explained simply in terms of the increased conservatism that is presumed to accompany increased age? Furthermore, the role or position of the deaconesses, if such they be, in this controversy is far from clear. Are the γυναῖκες [women] mentioned in 1 Tim. 3:11 to be equated with the widows, as some have suggested? If so, does their inclusion in a passage enumerating the requirements for bishop and deacon indicate that they, too, held an ecclesial office? Would this represent a later development of events, or does it need to be worked into the proposed scenario? The paucity of information probably precludes any definitive answers here. Nevertheless, freedom and equality, then as now, seem to be important keys for understanding the response of women to particular religious structures.

ABRAHAM J. MALHERBE

Paul: Hellenistic Philosopher or Christian Pastor? (1986)†

Modern interpreters have operated on the assumption that, like Tennyson's Ulysses, Paul was part of all that he had met, and that to understand him properly, it is necessary to view him in the cultural context in which he lived. As one might expect of him, however, Paul makes it difficult to decide precisely which context, the Jewish or the Greek, we should examine in order to understand his letters better. Born in Tarsus, an important

† This essay was initially published in *AThR* 68 (1986): 3–13 and was rep. in Malherbe's *Paul and the Popular Philosophers* (Minneapolis: Fortress, 1989), 67–77. Reprinted by permission of Augsburg Fortress Press. Malherbe, a native of South Africa, is Buckingham Professor Emeritus of New Testament Criticism and Interpretation at Yale Divinity School.

hellenistic university city of the day, but educated on both the secondary and tertiary levels in Jerusalem (Acts 22:3), he was exposed to both, and interpreters have tended to view him from either a Greek or a Jewish perspective. That Paul claims to have become all things to all people in order to save some (1 Cor. 9:19–23) indicates that he was aware of the need to adapt to particular contexts in which he found himself, and should caution us not to force everything he said or did into one mold. Here I wish to comment on the Greco-Roman side of Paul, without thereby implying that it offers us the keys to unlock all the mysteries surrounding this enigmatic figure.

Modern scholarship was not the first to discover Paul's indebtedness to Greek culture. His letters, even on a superficial level, have many affinities with the popular philosophy of his day, especially as it was represented by Stoicism and Cynicism. It does not surprise us that Tertullian, who was on the side of Jerusalem rather than Athens, referred to Seneca, the Stoic philosopher who served as chaplain to Nero, as "frequently our own" (*An.* 20). Shortly afterward, an anonymous Christian, impressed by the similarities he saw between Paul and Seneca, composed a correspondence that was supposed to have taken place between the two. No wonder, then, that Jerome, one hundred and fifty years after Tertullian, dropped Tertullian's qualifying "frequently," and referred to the Stoic simply as "our own Seneca" (*Jov.* 1.49).

During the last hundred years, New Testament scholars have shown that many aspects of Paul's life and letters are illuminated when they are examined in the light of Greco-Roman culture. There can no longer be any doubt that Paul was thoroughly familiar with the teaching, methods of operation, and style of argumentation of the philosophers of the period, all of which he adopted and adapted to his own purposes. This is not to argue that he was a technical philosopher; neither were his philosophical contemporaries. The philosophers with whom Paul should be compared were not metaphysicians who specialized in systematizing abstractions, but, like Paul, were preachers and teachers who saw their main goal to be the reformation of the lives of people they encountered in a variety of contexts, ranging from the imperial court and the salons of the rich to the street corners.

The points of similarity between Paul and his philosophic competitors may be stressed to the point that he is viewed as a type of hellenistic philosopher. In what follows I propose to note some of the similarities, but then to stress the function to which Paul put what he had received from the moral philosophers. That function is essentially pastoral, and Paul's adoption, and sometimes adaptation, of the philosophical tradition, reveal to us his awareness of the philosophic pastoral methods current in his day. By drawing attention to this function, I wish to sharpen the perspective from which the moral-philosophical material in Paul's letters is to be viewed. I select examples from his practice in establishing and shaping Christian communities, and the ways in which he adapted accepted means of persuasion to nurture his churches.

The Founder of Churches

In his letters, Paul frequently refers to his initial preaching when he founded churches, and to the reception of his message. Equally striking are his references to himself as an example which had either been followed by his converts, of which he reminds his readers, or which he offers for emulation. In thus placing his own person at the very center of his teaching, Paul followed a procedure recommended by philosophers. Seneca illustrates the thinking in advice he gives to his friend Lucilius:

> "Cherish some man of high character, and keep him ever before your eyes, living as if he were watching you, and ordering all your actions as if he beheld them." Such, my dear Lucilius, is the counsel of Epicurus; he has quite properly given us a guardian and attendant. We can get rid of most sins, if we have a witness who stands near us when we are likely to go wrong. The soul should have someone to respect—one by whose authority it may make even its inner shrine more hallowed. Happy is the man who can make others better, not merely when he is in their company, but even when he is in their thoughts! One who can so revere another, will soon be himself worthy of reverence. Choose therefore a Cato; or, if Cato seems too severe a model, choose some Laelius, a gentler spirit. Choose a master whose life, conversation, and soul-expressing face have satisfied you; picture him always to yourself as your protector and your pattern. For we must indeed have someone according to whom we may regulate our characters. (*Ep.* 11.8–10)

Seneca has in mind more than an exemplification of moral virtues that are to be imitated; he is equally interested in the forming of a relationship which would contribute to a sense of security and the continuing spiritual cultivation of the imitator.

The context in which Paul taught was totally different from Nero's court, yet he followed the practice recommended by Seneca. As a maker of tents, Paul plied his trade in a workshop, probably within the setting of a household of artisans, and there offered his practice as an example to be imitated (cf. 2 Thess. 3:6–10). Some philosophers, too, were active in workshops, and took the opportunity to demonstrate their teaching by their practice. Musonius Rufus, another contemporary of Paul, worked the land during his exile, and illustrates how manual labor could be viewed by teachers like himself. He thought a philosopher's students would be benefited "by seeing him at work in the fields, demonstrating by his own labor the lesson which philosophy inculcates—that one should endure hardships, and suffer the pains of labor with his own body, rather than depend on another for sustenance" (frg. 11). Paul, too, thought of manual labor as a hardship (cf. 1 Cor. 4:12), and also required that his converts work with their hands in order to be economically independent (cf. 1 Thess. 4:9–12). Recent investigation has demonstrated that his practice was informed by this Greek context rather than rabbinic custom.

There are, however, sufficient differences between Paul and the philosophers to preclude our viewing him as a slavish, unreflective follower of current practice. While some of the philosophers looked to the practice as an ideal, few actually followed it. Paul not only followed it, but his self-support was an integral part of his understanding of his apostleship. Called by God to be an apostle, he had no other choice than to heed the call, but he exercised his freedom in the manner in which he chose to preach: exultantly to offer the gospel free of charge (1 Cor. 9:15–19). Furthermore, in language one does not find in the philosophers, he describes his manual labor as a demonstration of his self-giving and love for his converts (2 Cor. 11:7–11; cf. 1 Thess. 2:9).

Paul was also more confident than the philosophers when he called on his converts to imitate him, and the nature of that confidence still further distinguishes him from them. Paul did not demand that his converts look to him as a paradigm of what one might accomplish through one's own effort, as the philosophers did. Writing to the Thessalonians, he reminds them of their initial encounter:

> our gospel came to you not only in word, but also in power and in the Holy Spirit and with full conviction. You know what kind of men we proved to be among you for your sake. And you became imitators of us and of the Lord, for you received the word in much affliction, with joy inspired by the Holy Spirit. (1 Thess. 1:5–6)

Philosophers would have drawn attention to their own words and deeds; Paul draws attention to the gospel and the divine role in their conversion. It is only as divine power is exhibited in Paul's ministry that he becomes an example that is to be followed. Finally, Paul differs from the philosophers in his goal to form communities of believers rather than only bring about change in individuals. The communal dimension of self-support is evident in ensuring that within the community some are not burdened with the responsibility to support others (1 Thess. 2:9; cf. 2 Thess. 3:6–10), and that, when Christians in brotherly love work so as not to be dependent on others, they have the respect of outsiders (1 Thess. 4:9–12).

When he first formed churches, therefore, Paul made use of elements from the Greco-Roman philosophical moral tradition, but adapted them to express his theological understanding of his enterprise and to form communities of believers.

The Nurturer of Churches

By the first century A.D., moral philosophers had developed an extensive system of pastoral care which aimed, through character education, at the attainment of virtue and happiness. Paul made use of this tradition as he nurtured the churches he established. His first letter to the Thessalonians illustrates clearly this indebtedness as well as his modification of the tradition.

In 1 Thessalonians 2:1–12, Paul reminds his readers of his pastoral care when he had been with them, and does so in terms used in descriptions of the ideal philosopher. The items that he chooses to mention and the antithetic style he adopts find their counterparts in such descriptions as the one in Dio Chrysostom:

> But to find a man who with purity and without guile speaks with a philosopher's boldness, not for the sake of glory, nor making false pretensions for the sake of gain, but who stands ready out of good will and concern for his fellowman, if need be, to submit to ridicule and the uproar of the mob—to find such a man is not easy, but rather the

good fortune of a very lucky city, so great is the dearth of noble, independent souls, and such the abundance of flatterers, charlatans and
sophists. In my own case I feel that I have chosen that role, not of
my own volition, but by the will of some deity. For when divine providence is at work for men, the gods provide, not only good counsellors
who need no urging, but also words that are appropriate and profitable
to the listener. (*Discourse* 32.11–12)

But, once again, as there are similarities between Paul and such philosophers as Dio, so are there differences.

Basic to the philosophers' approach was the frankness with which they
laid bare the shortcomings of their listeners. Convinced of their own moral
attainment, which gave them the right, indeed the responsibility, to correct
others, they were fearless in their denunciation of moral error. When they
were opposed or reviled, they turned their maltreatment into self-
commendation: their behavior in the face of opposition exhibited their
refusal to give quarter to any sinner, and demonstrated their courage in
continuing in their tasks. Paul uses the same technical language in describing his original preaching in Thessalonica: "though we had already suffered
and been shamefully treated at Philippi, as you know, we waxed bold in
our God to speak to you the gospel of God in the face of great opposition"
(2:2). Here there is nothing of self-attainment, rather an awareness of
God's power. What Paul engaged in was not a philosophical analysis of the
human condition, but preaching God's gospel, and his boldness did not
derive from his own moral freedom, but was engendered by God.

That Paul consciously worked with the philosophical traditions on the
boldness of speech also appears from his use of the image of a wetnurse:
"though we might have made demands as apostles of Christ, yet we were
gentle among you, like a nurse suckling her own children" (2:6–7). In the
first century, some Cynics, viewing the human condition as almost irre-
deemable, held that only the severest speech might have a salutary effect,
and therefore flayed their audiences mercilessly. In response, philosophers
of milder mien insisted that speakers should adapt their speech to the
emotional conditions of their listeners, as nurses did: "When children fall
down," according to Plutarch, "the nurses do not rush up to berate them,
but pick them up, wash them, and straighten their clothes, and after all
this is done, then rebuke and punish them" (*Mor.* 69b–c). Paul uses the
same image, but again distances himself from philosophers like Plutarch
by renouncing personal authority in pastoral care, and stating his reason
for his demeanor: "So, crooning over you, we were ready to share with you
not only the gospel of God but also our own selves, because you had
become very dear to us" (2:8).

The philosophers' concern to adapt their teaching to the conditions of
their listeners is further illustrated by Dio Chrysostom:

But as for himself, the man of whom I speak will strive to preserve
his individuality in seemly fashion and with steadfastness, never
deserting his post of duty, but always honoring and promoting virtue
and prudence and trying to lead men to them, on some occasions
persuading and exhorting them, on others reviling and reproaching
them . . . sometimes taking an individual aside privately, at other
times admonishing them in groups every time he finds a proper occasion, with gentle words at times, at others harsh. (*Discourse* 77/78.38)

Paul followed the same method of modulating his instruction according to individual needs: "you know how, like a father with his children, we exhorted each individual one of you and charged you to lead a life worthy of God, who calls you into his own kingdom and glory" (2:11). Unlike Dio, Paul is not concerned with virtue and prudence, nor does he engage in abuse and reproach. Neither does he share Dio's fear that his individuality or integrity might be compromised, and the eschatological dimension that dominates his work is totally foreign to the philosopher. Nevertheless, the method Paul used was inherited from the philosophers, and he made it part of his own pastoral practice, only now it was informed by a different perception of self and task.

The rapid spread of Christianity should not be taken to mean that the new faith provided a haven from the turmoils of life. On the contrary, as 1 Thessalonians shows, conversion resulted in psychological trauma, discouragement, grief, uncertainty about the implications of the new faith for everyday life, and dislocation from the larger society. These conditions were exacerbated by the shortness of the periods during which Paul remained with his new converts. That the itinerant preacher would list as his chief apostolic hardship "the daily pressure upon me of my anxiety for all the churches" (2 Cor. 11:28) does not, then, surprise us.

Paul prepared his converts for the hardships they would endure, and in this respect shared some things with Seneca. Seneca often writes on the proper, philosophic attitude toward hardships. He reflects two standard arguments from the long tradition of consolation literature.

> What, have you only at this moment learned that death is hanging over your head, at this moment exile, at this moment grief? You were born to these perils. Let us think of everything that can happen as something which will happen. (*Ep.* 24.15)

They will happen because fate so decrees, and we can overcome them by anticipating them (*Ep.* 91.4). Paul evidently followed this advice, for he had told the Thessalonians that they should not be moved by their afflictions: "You yourselves know that this is to be our lot. For when we were with you, we told you beforehand that we were to suffer affliction; just as it has come to pass, and as you know" (3:3–4). Paul, of course, does not ascribe their experiences to impersonal fate; it is God who is in charge of their ultimate destiny, that is, their salvation through the Lord Jesus Christ (5:9). Nor does he desire Stoic impassivity; in fact, he shares their distress and affliction (3:7). What he does share with Seneca is a particular method of pastoral care.

Paul's Continuing Interest

Paul continued the nurture of his churches when he was separated from them. He accomplished this nurture by using intermediaries through whom he maintained contact with the novices in the faith who might otherwise have felt abandoned, and through his letters. A letter was described in antiquity as one half of a dialogue, and was regarded as a substitute for one's presence. Paul was familiar with ancient epistolary theory, especially with its requirement that the style of a letter be appropriate to the occasion and circumstance it addressed. Recent research has demonstrated that Paul with sophistication and originality appropriated philosophical means of persuasion in his own pastoral care. To illustrate how he did so, I again turn to 1 Thessalonians.

As to style, 1 Thessalonians is a paraenetic letter. Paraenesis was a style of exhortation used to influence conduct rather than teach something new. It was, accordingly, used widely by moral philosophers who sought to modify the conduct of their audiences. Paraenesis stressed what was traditional, self-evidently good, and generally applicable. The stylistic devices used therefore sought to confirm the audience or readers in what they already knew by reminding them of it, complimenting them on what they had already accomplished and encouraging them to continue their practice, and offering models of virtue to be imitated. The assumption governing paraenesis was that a friendly relationship, frequently described as that between a father and his children, existed between the exhorter and the exhorted, which would set the tone and justify the advice.

Paul uses this style throughout 1 Thessalonians. He repeatedly impresses his readers with what they already know (1:5; 2:1–2, 5, 11; 3:3–4; 4:2; 5:2), and explicitly calls them to remembrance (2:9; 3:6). In paraenetic style he even says that there is really no need to write to them (4:9; 5:1), but compliments them for already doing what they should, and encourages them to do so more and more (4:1, 10; 5:11). He refers to the examples of the Judean churches (2:14) and the Thessalonians themselves (1:7), and claims that they had already become imitators of himself (1:6). The entire autobiographical sketch in the first three chapters functions as a paraenetic reminder and is paradigmatic. He uses the images of nurse (2:7), father (2:11), and orphan (2:17; RSV, "bereft") to describe his warm relationship with them, and in highly affective language expresses his concern for and identification with them in their tribulations (2:17–3:10).

Paul's use of these stylistic features makes 1 Thessalonians one of the best examples of ancient paraenetic letters. To appreciate Paul's genius, however, it is necessary to move beyond matters of style to the function of the letter, which is essentially pastoral. Paul wrote to a small group of neophyte Christians who were in "tribulation," that is, they were experiencing difficulties in redefining themselves socially, were uncertain about details of the Christian life, and felt abandoned by Paul and isolated in the world. Paul uses the paraenetic style to build their confidence.

His affective language and the images used to describe himself express his sense of the bond he feels with them. His repeated use of the paraenetic "as you know" makes the point that, despite their newness in the faith, they already are possessors of Christian tradition, and his encouragement to continue in what they are doing draws attention to their achievement rather than their shortcomings. As he had modulated his nurture when he was with them, so does he in the letter, where he exhorts (2:12; 4:10), charges (2:12; 4:6), commands (4:2, 11), and beseeches (5:12) them, and offers a basis for their consolation (4:18; 5:11). Paul has clearly used the paraenetic style to create the first Christian pastoral letter, which also happens to be the earliest piece of Christian literature we possess.

The Nurturing Church

Paul thought that, in addition to his own efforts, his congregations' concern for each member was necessary to the nurture of the church. It is striking how a communal concern pervades a letter like 1 Thessalonians. Every item of conduct that Paul takes up in the latter half of the letter is communal in nature. Transgression in marriage is described as fraud of a Christian brother (4:6), social responsibility is inculcated in a context provided by brotherly love (4:9–12), and Paul provides information on the parousia so that the grieving Thessalonians might comfort each other (4: 13–18). He then becomes more explicit:

> Therefore, exhort and build one another up, one on one, as indeed you are doing. But we beseech you, brethren, to respect those who labor among you, who care for you in the Lord, and admonish you, and to esteem them very highly in love because of their work. Be at peace among yourselves. And we exhort you, brethren, admonish the disorderly, comfort the discouraged, help the weak, be patient with all. Beware lest someone repays evil with evil; rather, seek each other's good and that of all. (1 Thess. 5:11–12)

A close comparison of the pastoral care Paul requires of the Thessalonians with his own reveals that theirs is to be an extension of his.

This description of communal soul-care has parallels among certain philosophers. The philosophers who have so far come under consideration in this essay were concerned with individuals rather than communities, but the Epicureans formed communities that in many respects were similar to Christian congregations. They were governed by detailed instructions on how admonition within the community was to be given and received. Recipients of the admonitions were instructed on how to cultivate a proper disposition toward those who did the admonishing, to have the desire to be improved, and on the importance of maintaining harmony. Those delivering the admonition were directed to speak without bitterness, and always to have the goal of benefiting others by taking into consideration the different natures of people and adjusting their admonition accordingly, fully aware that excessive sharpness might result in retaliation.

Paul's directions stress the same elements. His understanding of the Thessalonian community, however, differs radically from the Epicureans' understanding of theirs, and this understanding of Paul's places his comments on the church's pastoral care in a different light. The church of the Thessalonians is "in God" (1:1), that is, it was created by God, who calls them "into his own kingdom and glory" (2:12). It is an eschatological community which Paul hopes he will boast of when Christ returns (2:19), and it will not be destroyed by death (3:11–13; 4:14–15, 17). In the letter, this language, which distinguishes Christians from the Epicureans, "reinforces the sense of uniqueness and solidarity of the community."

Conclusion

I return to the question in the title of this chapter: Was Paul a hellenistic philosopher or a Christian pastor? It may well be the case that, when Paul is viewed as a theologian, the hellenistic elements do not lie at the center of his thinking but provide the means by which he conducts his argument.

But when he and others discuss his ministry, it is extraordinary to what degree the categories and language are derived from the Greeks. The same is also true when Paul is viewed as pastor. Paul is so familiar with the rich Greek traditions of pastoral care, and uses them in so unstudied a fashion, that it would be wrong to think that he only superficially mined the lode for his own purposes. He is more consistent and unconscious in his appropriation of the pastoral tradition than most of his pagan contemporaries. Like Ulysses, he had in fact become part of what he had met. At the same time, his apostolic self-understanding and theology so completely informed his pastoral care that the antithesis in the title is false. As to his method of pastoral care, Paul is at once hellenistic and Christian.

HANS-JOSEF KLAUCK

[The Lord's Supper in the Context of Hellenistic Religious History] (1989)†

Orientation

Meals invested with religious meaning are a universal phenomenon in the history of religions, not restricted to antiquity. To insert the Christian tradition of the Lord's Supper into this panorama is quite difficult, owing to the overwhelming mass of material. It is nevertheless an important and in substance fascinating task.

From the outset it is highly advisable to avoid, as far as possible, certain constricting perspectives and fallacious prejudgments. Here, the research of an earlier generation, the circle of the History-of-Religions School, which traced the origins of the Lord's Supper to Hellenistic mystery cults, can serve as paradigm. In this kind of judgment there is a whole batch of problematic prejudgments, every one of which deserves critical review: (a) belief in a sacramental mediation of salvation has no foothold in the preaching of Jesus and cannot be accounted for from within the cultural world of Palestinian Judaism; (b) a Last Supper of Jesus with his disciples before his death cannot be historically grounded with sufficient certainty, and even if, contrary to expectation, it were to have happened, it would have had no impact on the later practice of the Lord's Supper; (c) available analogies, if there is so much as a single remote relationship in time or place, are always to be analyzed genetically, and in the analysis Christianity is regularly to be assigned the role of the borrower; (d) only altogether original and distinctive elements impose themselves credibly; outside influ-

---

† Klauck wrote his *Habilitationsschrift* (postdoctoral dissertation) on the Lord's Supper in light of the Hellenistic Cult in 1980, which was published in 1982 as *Herrenmahl und hellenistischer Kult* (2nd ed.; Münster: Aschendorff, 1986). This particular essay began as a paper presented at the Cambridge Conference on the Eucharist in 1988. It was first published in German in Klauck's *Gemeinde—Amt—Sakrament* (Würzburg: Echter, 1989), 313–30, and appeared in English as "Presence in the Lord's Supper: 1 Corinthians 11:23–26 in the Context of Hellenistic Religious History," in *One Loaf, One Cup*, ed. by Ben F. Meyer (Macon, GA: Mercer, 1993), 57–74. Reprinted by permission of Mercer University Press. Klauck, a Franciscan who taught previously at Bonn, Würzburg, and Munich, is now Naomi Shenstone Donnelley Professor of New Testament and Early Christian Literature at the University of Chicago.

ences invariably signify a deviation from the pure gospel, which—depending on orientation—is to be derived from the preaching of the historical Jesus or the message of the primitive Christian kerygma.

The manifest misapprehensions that come to expression in this still quite incomplete list have substantially contributed to the undeserved rejection of many accurate and fruitful insights from history-of-religions research. In straightforward dependence on as well as in discriminating development of the older discussion, I would essay a reformulation of the research agenda as follows: (a) analogies of diverse density between the Christian Lord's Supper and non-Christian phenomena cannot seriously be disputed. This means that examination and assessment on various levels—historical, structural, and theological—are a permanent acquisition. But comparison of this kind need not lead to the framing of genetic relationships of dependence. On the contrary, it can just as well allow the distinctive and proper profile of the data in question to come graphically to light. (b) The adoption and adaptation of foreign influences can also be assessed positively, as a sign of Christian faith's assimilative capacity, which is able to fuse diverse elements together. An exclusive fixation on the question of origins—a trait shared, of course, by not a few of the enemies, on principle, of the History-of-Religions School—distracts attention from the processes of reception and inculturation by which what is taken over is reshaped and assimilated. (c) Even if we proceed from the historically plausible premise, which I fully share, that a farewell meal of Jesus with his disciples represents the most important point of departure for the celebration of the Lord's Supper in the primitive Christian communities, the history-of-religions formulation of the state of the question even in its narrower sense as restricted to Hellenism retains its relative validity, be it only in serving to limn the contours of the cultural world in which a Gentile-Christian community adopted the Lord's Supper tradition.

Here numerous points might be added in the context of preliminary methodological remarks and in dialogue with the still to be fully mastered legacy of the History-of-Religions School. To mention only one issue, it is evident that we should not maintain a clean line of division between Hellenism and Judaism. Again, limitation to a single object of comparison—for example, the mystery cults so dear to an earlier generation—can be allowed only on heuristic and technical grounds; and this limitation loses its admissibility, as a consciously and methodically controlled contraction of perspective, as soon as it is invested with absolute claims. Besides, to stay with this example, the question arises whether we know—all that exactly—just what mystery cults and the meals belonging to them actually are. Here it was partly a matter of investigators' having worked with some few standardized premises and without the requisite counter-controls respecting the sources. But a more exactly differentiated approach runs the risk of being overwhelmed by the relevant data. These include, as indispensable context, sacrificial cult generally and the sacrificial meal; the voluntary association and its social meal; the cult of the dead and its cultic meal. On the other hand, early Christian literature, which would have to be examined from the New Testament to, at least, the Didache, Ignatius, and Justin's first apology, offers no fully unified picture, with the result that much depends from the start on selecting and setting up the right levels of comparison.

Time and again since the days of Eichhorn and Heitmüller, 1 Corinthians has shown itself to be the most promising textual base for entry into comparative work. This ties in with the special character of the writing (its themes are dictated by practical problems) and with the specific contour of the Christian community in Corinth (its embeddedness in Hellenistic urban culture). Here too the spectrum of possible points of departure is extremely various. With reference to 1 Cor. 10, the κοινωνία-conceptuality (in my opinion a Hellenistic conceptual resource, which has been brought to bear on the Last Supper tradition) should be investigated. The question of what exactly is meant by "the cup of demons" and "the table of demons" in 10:21, and the question of the extent to which the idea of a demonic infection of food resonates with this, leads back to the most characteristic sphere of Hellenistic history of religions. In 1 Cor. 11 two aspects of the framework of the Last Supper tradition proper merit keener attention: (a) a surprising light falls on the disorders and abuses occurring in the Corinthians' celebration of the Lord's Supper and condemned by Paul, if one brings them into relationship with ancient association-ordinances and with the depictions (partly caricatures) of ancient banquets: (b) at 11:30, it is hardly possible to suppress the alarming suspicion that Paul is tracing physical malady and premature death back to defective behavior at the Lord's Supper. Hence the temptation to speak of "catastrophic taboo-effects" and to compare them with superstitious reactions to certain food regulations in the Gentile world.

In what follows we must be content with more modest aims. We restrict ourselves * * * to the text of 1 Cor. 11:23–26, and select four facets thereof for closer analysis: (1) the transmission-of-tradition terminology in 11:23a; (2) the possible specification of genre as cult aetiology, which is open to correlation with 1 Cor. 11:23b or to correction on the basis of the same text; (3) the sequence of the celebration, 11:25a providing an index to the problem; (4) the double remembrance mandate in 11:24 and 11:25.

* * *

On 1 Corinthians 11:23–26

I. TRANSMISSION-OF-TRADITION TERMS

It has long been recognized that in 1 Cor. 11:23a there exist two terms relating to the transmission of tradition: παραλαμβάνειν (to receive) and παραδιδόναι (hand on, deliver). The latter was already introduced in 11:2, and both recur prominently in 15:3 (cf. also 15:1), functioning to introduce a credo-formula. There are equivalents to these terms in rabbinic terminology: *qbl* (to receive) and *msr* (hand on, deliver). With their help, and in accord with the Pharisaic conception of written Torah and oral tradition operative in unison, chains of tradition take shape that make possible an unbroken line leading written and oral tradition back to their point of origin. One must be clear, however, that the texts adduced as attestations are all to be dated later—some much later—than, for example, 1 Corinthians. This holds first of all for the locus classicus, *Abot* 1:1: "Moses received the Torah on Sinai and delivered it to Joshua, and Joshua delivered it to the elders, and they to the prophets, and the prophets to the men of the great Synagogue." One can partly fill the time gap between

Paul and these texts by appealing to passages like Mark 7:3–4, 13 or Josephus, *Ant* 13.297, where we meet the words παραδιδόναι and παραλαμβάνειν cognates in connection with the oral Torah of the Pharisees. There is already here a Grecising of Pharisaic-rabbinic academic terms, which consequently must be accorded a still earlier origin.

If we go still another step back, we come across a passage in the LXX which clearly presupposes a different frame of reference. In Wisdom 14:15, it is said in the context of a euhemeristic explanation of the fact of heathen polytheism, "And he passed on (παρέδωκεν) to his subordinates secret celebrations and initiations (μυστήρια καὶ τελετάς). Now, that is unmistakably borrowed from the language of the Hellenistic mysteries.

An exclusive derivation of the Pauline terms for transmission-of-tradition from academic rabbinic terminology must be qualified as, at the minimum, one-sided. The abundance and antiquity of attestations drawn from the religious hermeneutic of Hellenism can very well rival the constantly adduced Jewish texts. To choose only a few examples: Plato calls teaching and learning a process of handing on and receiving (*Tht.* 198B: παραδίδοντα . . . παραλαμβάνοντα). In the academic terminology of philosophy both verbs stand for the transmission of authoritative oral teaching, which can also be esoteric secret tradition. A metaphorical use of mystery terminology is discernible in Theon of Smyrna. In the course of a comparison he uses a five-stage model based on the mysteries, the second stage of which represents ἡ τῆς τελετῆς παράδοσις (the handing on of secret initiations) and the fourth stage of which qualifies one for the act of handing on: "What each has received in initiations he can also hand on."

The Latin equivalent of παραδιδόναι is *tradere*. In the *Tusculanae Disputationes* Cicero puts on the lips of one of the speakers, "Remember what is handed on in the mysteries (*quae tradantur mysteriis*), for you indeed belong to the initiated" (*Tusc. Disp.* 1.29). What was handed on in the mysteries could quite concretely be, first of all, certain secret cult objects, as is the case in the mystery-inscription of Andania: "the holy men are to pass on to their successors the case and the books that Mnasistratus (the founder of the cult) has delivered; they should hand on also whatever else was assigned for the mysteries." What might be referred to includes, among other things, the establishment of a cult, instruction in the myth of the mysteries, and the allotting of degrees of initiation.

What emerges from all this? In the matter at hand there is a convergence of academic rabbinic and academic Hellenistic language. The latter exhibits a relationship to the language used in the mysteries. The choice of the terms παραδιδόναι and παραλαμβάνειν in the sphere of Hellenistic Judaism is conditioned by the language both of the mysteries and of philosophical education. With this conceptuality Paul, whether deliberately or not, accommodates the conceptual horizons of the Corinthians. The similarity of Paul's formula, introduced in this way, to mystery myths and mystery formulas must have imposed itself on them, for

> Probably the members of the community had derived from the Greek political system and its laws and from the Hellenistic mystery religions a keen sensitivity for almost magically effective formulas handed on in verbally exact fashion.[1]

1. Paul Neuenzeit, *Das Herrenmahl: Studien zur paulinischen Eucharistieauffassung* (Munich: Kösel, 1960).

2. DEFINITION OF THE GENRE AS "CULTIC AETIOLOGY"

A cultic aetiology serves the grounding and explaining, in narrative form, of a cultic rite, simultaneously reflecting its concrete performance. To make this concrete we shall illustrate it, using the example of the Homeric hymn of Demeter and the mysteries of Eleusis. The goddess Demeter, searching for her daughter Persephone, makes her way into the Eleusinian royal palace. Keeping silence and fasting, she sits on a pelt-covered stool, like the adepts in the μύησις, the first level of initiation. She refuses to drink wine, but asks for a mixed drink called "Kykeon," made of pearl barley, water, and mint. The goddess partakes of it "on account of the sacred practice," or in the translation of Richardson, "for the sake of the rite." We cannot really render "for the sake of the sacred practice" by a single phrase; we can only variously paraphrase it: to establish the rite, to preserve and observe it, to perform and practice it. In the mythical narrative Demeter establishes the rite and, acting at the same time as prototype of all future adepts, she herself performs what she has instituted. Here for once, on the very surface of the text, the aetiological character of the mythical narrative comes to light. A passage of this kind permits the whole narrative-event so to become diaphanous that through it we can see the performance of the mystery ritual.

Ovid, with Eleusis in view, has very beautifully formulated the not always tension-free but doubtless always present homologous relation between myth and rite: "Because the goddess ends her fast as night begins, it is even today at the appearance of the stars that the initiates hold their meal." It is not surprising, then, if some centuries later Clement of Alexandria cites a synthema (roughly, password or watchword) from the Eleusinian mysteries, in which (among other things) the initiate confesses: "I have drunk the mixed drink."

The Last Supper texts of the New Testament, too, although they expressly relate to Jesus' last meal with his disciples, indirectly offer a glimpse of the cultic community's celebration, itself grounded in the initial event. This holds true even to the extent that, as scholarship generally has conceded, liturgical practice has itself exercised an influence on the wording of the text. One need only think of the strong tendencies towards paralleling which are at work in the history of the transmission of "the words of interpretation," and which, finally, in Justin, lead to the extreme short form: "This is my body—this is my blood" (*1 Apol.* 66.3). In this respect there are undeniable analogies to cult aetiologies in Hellenistic forms of religion.

Nevertheless, there exist numerous not inconsiderable reservations respecting the transferal of the genre-designation "cultic aetiology" to a text such as 1 Cor. 11:23–26. Such reservations are in order if, in connection with this designation of genre, which does indeed relate to certain textual phenomena, a negative judgment of historicity is smuggled in and the Last Supper account is classified as a mythical founding legend. In the text itself verse 23b clearly obviates this: "The Lord Jesus on the night he was delivered up. . . ."

An index to the mythical understanding of time is a maxim from late antiquity on the interpretation of myth: "This never happened but is forever extant." Despite its narrative surface structure, the myth does not report historical events, but tells of eternal, changeless being. Language unfolds in chronological sequence what understanding recognizes as time-less unity. 1 Cor. 11:23b is totally different. Here the ritual practice of the community is anchored in history and referred back to a fixed point in the recent, not to say most recent, past. Granted all formal and functional similarities, therein lies an essential difference from the founding legends of the mystery cults.

3. THE SEQUENCE OF THE CELEBRATION

"In the same way also the cup after supper" in 1 Cor. 11:25 signifies that, after eating, a similar act of blessing is performed over the cup as over the bread at the outset. This means that the breaking of the bread and the blessing of the cup frame the full meal as opening rite and closing rite. So it doubtless went at Jesus' farewell meal with his disciples, which exhibited the characteristic sequence of a Jewish festal meal; so it went also in early post-Easter community practice.

Now Gerd Theissen supposes that in Corinth, too, this was still the practice, for otherwise Paul could not have cited the traditional text unchanged. But that leads to a number of other problems. If the rite with the bread stands at the beginning of the meal, followed by the full meal, and the rite with the cup of wine at the end, those who came late would have participated in the cup ritual but not the breaking of the bread. To escape this conclusion one must largely eliminate the temporal aspect from the terms προλαμβάνειν ("anticipate" in 11:21) and ἐκδέχεσθαι ("wait for" one another in 11:33). One must also place the private meal of 11:21 still earlier than the rite with the bread, and limit the full meal for the poor to the bread and wine alone, since the distribution formulas of the Lord's Supper provided for these only and said nothing of the other alimentary elements.

It still seems to me a less forced way of illuminating the situation, if the breaking of the bread and the blessing of the cup, combined in a double rite, took place at the conclusion of the full meal, as in the synoptic tra-dition. (In Mark the gestures and words over the bread and wine follow without discernible interval the notice "while they were eating" in 14:22, and in 14:26 the meal is already finished. Luke, in 22:20, alters the word-ing of 1 Cor. 11:23a ever so slightly, so that the bread and wine rites both take place after the meal.) Paul apparently considers it unnecessary to insert a correction into the sacred text, for his concern is not the liturgical procedure but its theological meaning. He brings the "for you" and the "new covenant" of the words of interpretation into play as critique of the Corinthians' faulty dispositions at the Lord's Supper.

We can further validate this consideration by drawing on an analogy from a Hellenistic model, if at the same time we take up in addition the still disputed question of the relationship between the Lord's Supper in 1 Cor. 11 and the worship service described in 1 Cor. 14. For purposes of comparison we choose the Greek symposium. In its full form it goes like this: It begins, toward evening, with a full meal. A libation marks the tran-sition to the second principal part of the symposium. This is a libation of pure wine offered to the gods of the symposium or to the immortalized founder whose memory a cultic association celebrates with a symposium.

To this is joined the drinking bout, which in its ideal form (not, admittedly, in its normal form) had philosophic discussions and conversation as its main content.

This can already be inferred from Plato's portrayal:

> Afterwards, Socrates, having reclined on the couch and having completed his dinner with the others, and then having offered a drink offering, intoned a hymn to the god and performed the usual customs, finally turning to the drinking bout [*Symp.* 4–5 (176A–E)],

a bout, it should be noted, from which the obligation to drink was lifted, the flute player dismissed, and conversation established as the sole form of entertainment.

In the will, fixed by inscription, of Epicteta of the island of Thera, a libation dedicated to the memory of the foundress together with her husband and two sons, is the point of transition from the meal to the symposium.

It is self-evident that among Christians one proceeded with greater sobriety (cf. the appeals to sobriety in 1 Cor. 15:34; 1 Thess. 5:6–8). But the full meal toward evening in both is roughly the same. In the symposium the transition endowed with religious meaning has its equivalent, on the side of the Lord's Supper, in the double rite of bread and wine, inserted into the center; and in place of philosophic discussion there are the prayers, readings, exhortations, psalms, prophecies, and speaking in tongues of 1 Cor. 14. The pattern, once more, in overview:

SYMPOSIUM	COMMUNITY MEETING	
(1) Festal meal (toward evening)	Full meal (toward evening)	1 Cor. 11:20–22
(2) Libation of pure wine for gods or founders	Twofold rite with bread and wine, harking back to Jesus	1 Cor. 10:16–17 1 Cor. 11:23–26
(3) Drinking bout with conversations, etc.	Worship service with psalms, etc.	1 Cor. 14

4. THE REMEMBRANCE MANDATE

The textual situation may be rapidly summarized as follows: Markan and Matthean tradition contain no remembrance mandate. Luke presents it only once, with the word over the bread (Luke 11:19). Paul has it twice, with the word over the bread and the word over the cup. At first glance this state of affairs elicits the suspicion—by analogy with use of the rule of the shorter as the more original text—that it is a matter of gradual growth, from liturgical practice; that, in other words, the remembrance mandate did not figure in the oldest Last Supper account and in the historical component of the tradition. It is not easily understandable why Markan tradition would have dropped the remembrance mandate. Just at the point at which a liturgical text recedes into the distance of a reported event—as in Mark, in the context of the passion narrative—a founder's mandate would make excellent sense as a historicising effort to ground the community's practice. Whether this point is successfully overturned by the argument that the use of the texts in the celebration of the Lord's Supper effectively replaced the remembrance mandate remains for me somewhat questionable.

Our main attention in any case does not relate to this problematic. It focuses rather on the conceptual horizon to which the remembrance mandate points and against which it takes on profile. With this in mind, here is a rough survey of the history of scholarly opinion.

In his commentary Hans Lietzmann, evidently prompted by Leclerq and with recourse to the material in Laum, compared the formula "in commemoration of me" with the establishment by will of a cultic association to hold regular dinners in memory of its founder. He concluded somewhat tentatively that to a Gentile "converted to Christianity . . . the Lord's Supper would have appeared analogous to such memorial meals."

Joachim Jeremias flatly contradicted this view. Exclusively stressing the Jewish-Palestinian background, he proposed an interpretation of the remembrance mandate which has won little agreement: "Do this, that (God) may remember me (as Messiah, and so bring about his kingdom)."

The more recent investigation of Fritz Chenderlin is relatively close to Jeremias both respecting the preference for the Judaic horizon of comparison and respecting the notion that with the formula or with the fulfillment of what the formula mandated, God was to be reminded of something. He nevertheless makes room for a certain analogy with the Greek meals for the dead and takes account of the transposability of many aspects of the one culture into the other:

> To anyone familiar with Greek ways even to a moderate degree, "memorial" might have suggested a cult to the dead. Such cults occasionally developed into hero worship—an institution that could easily have been seen by Christians as preeminently suited to their own special hero, Christ.[2]

The significance for New Testament tradition of the biblical-Judaic theology of remembrance bound up with the root *zkr*, should by no means be contested or underplayed. On the other hand, however, there should also be kept in mind the simple fact that εἰς ἀνάμνησιν [in/for remembrance] occurs only four times in the LXX, in some notoriously difficult passages, and that there is no passage in the whole of the Old Testament and Jewish material, so far as I know, that would clearly refer to a particular person and to a memorial meal. Just two examples: Epicurus in his will prescribes, in addition to offerings for the dead on behalf of his relatives and the annual celebration of his birthday, that a memorial meal be held on the 20th of each month "in our memory and in memory of Metrodorus." A Roman woman establishes a cultic association and a meetinghouse so that meals be held there regularly in memory of her husband: *ut in memoriam Anici Prisci c(oniugis) sui in ea semper epulentur*.

From a theological perspective this memorial meal is, no doubt, insufficient to interpret the meaning of the Lord's Supper, but neither is it as wholly inappropriate as it is often made out to be. In the background originally stood the belief in the personal presence of the dead one and table-fellowship with him. The meal in his remembrance also bestows partial

---

2. Fritz Chenderlin, *"Do This as My Memorial." The Semantic and Conceptual Background and Value of* Ἀνάμνησις *in 1 Corinthians 11:24–25* (Rome: Biblical Institute Press, 1982) 217; cf. 143–45.

survival on him. In this context the similarity of the Last Supper rites with bread and cup to the mourning rites in Jer. 16:7 deserves mention ("No one shall *break bread* for the mourner to comfort him for the dead, nor shall anyone give him *the cup* of consolation, not even at the death of his father and mother"). Also to be pondered: that against the tendencies to enthusiasm in Corinth, Paul in 1 Cor. 11 would once more inculcate especially the death motif and the bond of the celebration with the historical saving act, the death of Jesus on the cross. Even the motif of comfort, dominant in the meal of mourning and the meal of remembrance, can have a certain function in the Pauline Lord's Supper, for this celebration not only knows the presence of the Lord, it is also painfully conscious of his absence (1 Cor. 11:26: death and parousia).

* * *

PETER LAMPE

The Roman Christians of Romans 16 (1991)†

Was Romans 16 originally addressed to Rome, or was it a separate letter to Ephesus, as has been proposed? I do not want to discuss in detail the problems to which the Ephesus hypothesis leads us, such as: (a) Why does Paul greet only his co-workers Urbanus, Aquila, and Prisca in "Ephesus" (Rom. 16:3, 9), when many others have been staying there? Has the whole group moved? Does Paul forget to greet them? (b) Why was a letter to the Ephesians added to a letter to the Romans? This would be without parallel. It is true, 2 Cor. was comprised of several letters, but these separate letters were not addressed to different churches. (c) We know letters that consisted mainly of greetings. But can we picture *Paul* writing such a letter? (d) Why do the Romans 16 names "Urbanus," "Phlegon," "Persis," and "Asyncritus" not occur in any of the thousands of Ephesian inscriptions, while they do show up on epigraphs in the city of Rome?

I. Romans 16 as an Original Part of the Letter to the Romans

I want to discuss positively the reasons why Romans 16 has to be considered an integral part of the original letter to the Romans.

1. Paul would never have ended a letter with Romans 15:33. Formulations like "the God of peace [with you]" never conclude a letter but precede requests to greet—greetings like the ones in Romans 16! The *de* in Romans 16:1, on the other hand, presupposes a *previous* text. That means: Romans 15 and 16 mutually presuppose each other. Why separate them?

† This essay was initially published in *The Romans Debate*, ed. by Karl P. Donfried (rev. ed.; Peabody: Hendrickson, 1991), 216–30, but it is dependent on his *Die stadtrömischen Christen in den ersten beiden Jahrhunderten* (2nd ed.; Tübingen: Mohr-Siebeck, 1989), 124–53, 301–2, 358. Copyright © 1997, 1991 by Hendrickson Publishers, Inc. Reprinted by permission. All rights reserved. A revised and updated version of this monograph is now available in English; see *From Paul to Valentinus: Christians at Rome in the First Two Centuries* (Minneapolis: Fortress, 2003). Lampe has taught at Union Theological Seminary in Richmond, Virginia, and the Christian-Albrechts University in Kiel, Germany, and he is now professor of New Testament Theology at the University of Heidelberg, where he directs the Heidelberg Archaeological Surface Survey in Phrygia.

2. Textual criticism teaches that no Romans manuscript ever ends with chapter 15. The manuscripts either omit both chapters (15:1–33 and 16:1–23), or they have them both in one block. Therefore, 15:1–16:23 have to be treated as one unit by the textual critic—one block which is addressed to Rome, as 15:22–29 assures.

> There are only two exceptions from this rule. (a) The minuscule 1506 from the year 1320 has chapter 15, but omits 16:1–23. The medieval scribe copied Romans 1–14; 16:25–27; chapter 15, and again 16:25–27. How can this strange arrangement be explained? The genealogical trees (*stemmas*), which have been proposed for the manuscripts of the letter to the Romans agree that the text of minuscule 1506 is a descendant of Marcion's Romans text (Rom. 1–14) and of texts that offer chapters 15 and 16:1–23 as one block *together*. Thus, minuscule 1506 only *seems* to be an exception to the rule. The ancestors of minuscule 1506 assure that Romans 15 and 16:1–23 belong together once we come to the older strata of textual history. (b) P[46] from the year ca. 200 reads chapters 1–14; 15; 16:25–27; 16:1–23. It presents both chapter 15 and 16:1–23, but this time they do not appear in one block. Did P[46] therefore descend from a text which consisted only of 1–14; 15? In other words, Does P[46] suggest this textual history: 1–14; 15 → 1–14; 15; 16:25–27 → 1–14; 15; 16:25–27; 16:1–23 (=P[46])? No. Again, we have to look at the possible *stemmas* that put all manuscripts into a genealogical relation. We know fourteen text types for the letter to the Romans, having the task to put them together into a family tree. If we wanted to put 1–14; 15 at the root of the genealogical tree, an organic plant would not grow. The *stemma* would have several missing pieces, representing the weakest hypothesis. P[46] therefore cannot support the hypothesis that Paul's original letter included only chapters 1–15.

3. Romans 16 shows several unique features when compared to the rest of the Pauline letters. Romans 1–15, on the other hand, offer the unparalleled quality that Paul writes to a church which he has never visited in person, a church which does not belong to his missionary area, but one with which he wants to get acquainted and from which he hopes to start a new missionary project in Spain. In other words, the uncharacteristic features of Romans 16 can be explained *by* the unusual situation of Romans 1–15. Thus, Romans 1–15 and 16 should not be separated.

What do I mean specifically? (a) The ecumenical greeting in Romans 16:16 is unusual for Paul: "All the churches of Christ greet you." This global perspective can be easily explained by the unique situation of Romans 1–15. Paul stands on the door step between east and west. He looks back at his missionary work in the east, leaving behind and summing up (15:19, 23). Making this survey, his eye easily catches "all churches of Christ" in the east. Furthermore, Paul looks ahead (15:22–32). Planning to do missionary work in Spain, he wants the Romans to support him (15:24, 30). But they do not even know him personally. Paul therefore first has to gain their confidence. "All churches" sending greetings through Paul are the best recommendation for Paul himself and for his trustworthiness!

(b) Romans 16:3–16 as a whole is a text of recommendation for Paul himself—and only marginally also for Phoebe (16:1–2). The greetings of Romans 16:3–16 present two peculiarities compared to the other Pauline letters: greetings are sent to individual persons, and the list of greetings is unusually long. Both irregularities can be explained in light of Romans 1–15. Not knowing the Roman church as a whole personally, Paul sends greetings to individuals whom he does know in person. Common friends build a first bridge of confidence between people who do not know each other. Paul wants to signal: See, I already know many of you personally (therefore the long list). And some of these common friends to whom I am connected with love (*agapētos*) have merits (e.g., 16:4, 6) and authority (16:7). They cast some light on myself. Look at these many and honorable personal friends of mine in the midst of your church—and you will find that I, too, am trustworthy. Here we have the hidden message of the unique and long list of personal greetings. The list is a reference for Paul himself! And Paul certainly needed all the recommendations he could get after he and his law-free gospel had become so controversial in the east.

Our interpretation attributes some sense also to the fact that Paul does not greet his personal friends directly but makes the Romans deliver his greetings to them (*aspasasthe*). The greetings send a message to the Roman church as a whole; they are not merely communication between Paul and these individuals.

(c) A last oddity is Timothy's introduction as "my co-worker" (16:21). The eastern churches to which the rest of Paul's letters were addressed knew Timothy. For them this introduction was not necessary, while it makes sense in a letter to the Romans.

4. According to Romans 15:19–29, chapters 1–15 were written in Greece at the end of the so-called third mission journey (Acts 20:1–5). This coincides perfectly with the situation of Romans 16: (a) Romans 16 also was written in Greece; Paul sends off Phoebe from the Corinthian harbor Cenchreae (16:1). (b) The people whom we would expect in Paul's surroundings at the end of the "third mission journey" (Acts 20:4) are exactly those who send greetings in Romans 16:21–23: Timothy, So(si)pater, and Gaius. Both lists, Romans 16:21–23 and Acts 20:4, coincide surprisingly well, although they are source-critically independent from each other.

5. The following material is often quoted in favor of Ephesus as the addressee of Romans 16. I will try to show that it can be understood in a letter to Rome as well. In other words, this material is neutral—it should be left out of the discussion of Rome or Ephesus.

(a) According to Romans 16, Paul knows 26 Christian persons in Rome. Is this strange in a letter to a city where he never has been? Have all these 26 people been in the east? Is 26 an outrageous number? In view of mobility in the Roman Empire, this number is not surprising. Many famous Roman Christians had immigrated to Rome from the east: Aquila, Hermas, Marcion, Valentinus, Justin, many of his students in the Acta Iustini, Tatian, Hippolytus, and the presbyter Anicetus. The fact that the Roman church still spoke predominantly Greek even during the whole second century indicates how high the percentage of eastern immigrants must have been. The Jews, too, were busy travelling back and forth between Rome and the east. On the inscription *CIG* 3920, the craftsman Flavius Zeuxis brags that he sailed 72 times (!) from the east to Italy. Of course, this was exceptional, because it is proudly mentioned on an epitaph. But it shows how vast the possibilities for travel were. Furthermore, many journeys between the east and Rome may even have been forced upon the Christians. It is possible that many of the 26 persons had been expelled from Rome under Claudius and had returned after Claudius' death—just like Aquila and Prisca (Acts 18:2; Rom. 16:3).

No, a number of 26 is not surprising. And for those who still have doubts it may be stated that 26 is only a maximum number. Nothing forces us to assume that Paul actually knew *all* of the 26 personally and that consequently all of them had been in the east for a while. The names of the last ten individuals in verses 14–15 *may* have come to Paul's attention only through narratives told by third persons. Mentioning only the names and no other individual information (vv. 14–15), the greetings for these ten pale in comparison to the ones in verses 3–13. Not even Mary (Maria, 16: 6) needs to be personally acquainted with Paul. The information "she has worked hard among you" presupposes that Paul was told things about her he had not witnessed himself. The same may be true about Tryphaena and Tryphosa (16:12) and about Herodion (16:11), whose Jewish "kinship" may have been reported to Paul by third persons too. Only for the remaining twelve people do we *have* to assume that they saw Paul in person in the east; the comments added to their names leave hardly any room for another interpretation: Prisca, Aquila, Epaenetus, Andronicus, Junia, Urbanus, Rufus and his mother, Ampliatus, Stachys, Persis, and probably also Apelles. Whether 26 or 12 mobile people, a basis for Ephesus as destination can hardly be found in these figures.

(b) The presence of Aquila and Prisca among the addressees has already been explained: After having been expelled from Rome by Claudius (Acts 18:2), they returned to Rome between the times that 1 Corinthians 16:19 and Romans 16:3 were written. In other words, they returned around the year 55/56. This date fits well. Claudius died in the fall of the year 54, which was reason enough to give up finally any remaining timidity to return to Rome.

The craftsman Aquila had already moved at least three times in his life: Pontus—Rome—Corinth—Ephesus (1 Cor. 16:19; the tradition in Acts 18:1–2, cf. 18:18, 26). Why could he not have moved a fourth time? The Christian Aberkios in the second century stayed in Phrygia, in Rome, in Syria, and in Nisibis across the Euphrates. Again, mobility was no problem, especially since Aquila and Prisca were apostolic co-workers (Romans 16: 3). It is easy to imagine that Paul had sent them back to Rome as a "vanguard" for himself, as he had already done with them in Ephesus (Acts 18: 18–21, 24–26; 19:1). It is possible (nothing more) that their return to Rome had been "strategically" planned by Paul. In Rome, they indeed were active again as Paul's "co-workers," assembling even a house-church around them (Rom. 16:3–5). Epaenetus, "the first convert in Asia," may have moved from Ephesus to Rome together with Prisca and Aquila. He is named right after them (Rom. 16:5).

These are only conjectures as to how it could have been. But in our argumentation, they have the function of showing that the Roman addressee of Romans 16 is as conceivable as an Ephesian. In other words, the fact that, for example, the "first convert of Asia" is greeted does not prove anything in favor of an Ephesian addressee. This Asian may easily have moved to Rome together with the people who most likely had converted him: Prisca and Aquila.

Only 2 Timothy 4:19 could be the last branch to hold on to for the defenders of the Ephesus hypothesis: The Pastoral Letters place Paul in Rome while Aquila and Prisca still dwell in Ephesus. Is this a proof for Ephesus? No. It is likely that 2 Timothy 4:19 only presents another example of the historical flaws in the Pastoral Letters; also the next verse (4:20) is historically untenable. Why did the Pastoral Letters place Prisca and Aquila in Ephesus? The author needed some prominent names in Ephesus to support the portrayal of Paul writing from Rome (1:16–17) to Ephesus (1:16–18; 4:13, 19) and sending greetings to people there. In 1 Corinthians 16:19 and Acts 18:26 the author found what he or she wanted: two prominent Christians in Ephesus—Prisca and Aquila. Similarly the Ephesian Tychicus (Acts 20:4; Col. 4:7; Eph. 6:21) was placed fictitiously in Ephesus (2 Tim. 4:12), as was even Mark (2 Tim. 4:11), who had been known to have visited Ephesus (Phlm. 24; Col. 4:10).

(c) Commentators often wonder about the changing of tone in the antiheretical section of Romans 16:17–20a. Contrary to the rest of the letter, Paul suddenly sounds a sharp note. Is Romans 16 therefore not part of the original letter to the Romans? No. The harsh tone is not directed against the Roman church, which is even praised (16:19) like it is in the rest of the letter (1:8; 15:14). The sharp polemic is directed against third persons: against possible heretics not belonging to the Roman church but maybe planning to infiltrate it. Paul may think of his opponents in the east, fearing that they could reach out and influence the Romans' opinion of him. In the rest of the letter, these outside "heretics" were not mentioned directly (except for maybe 15:31). We therefore cannot expect the angry tone in the other Romans passages.

II. The Households of Aristobulus and Narcissus (16:10b, 11b)

Aristobulus and Narcissus are non-Christians: (a) Paul does not send greetings to them but to people in their households. If they were Christians, Paul would also greet these heads of households themselves—similarly to 16:3–5 and probably 16:14, 15. (b) Only a *part* of their households is Christian. Otherwise Paul would have formulated *hoi Aristoboulou* instead of *hoi ek tōn Aristoboulou*. The attribute *tous ontas en kyriō* points in the same direction: those who are Christian—contrary to the others in this household. These Christians were slaves, freedmen, or freedwomen of Aristobulus and Narcissus. There is no means to define their social status more concretely.

Was Aristobulus a member of the royal Herodian family? The least we can say is that he seems to have immigrated to Rome: His name occurs very rarely in the city of Rome. In the event that he had brought his Christian slaves with him from the east, we would be able to identify one channel through which Christianity entered into the capital city of the empire.

III. Women—Men

Romans 16:3–16 name 26 Christian individuals in Rome: 9 women and 17 men. But who is praised for being especially active in the church? More women than men!

* Seven (or six) women:
—Prisca 16:3–4, *synergos* etc.
—Mary 16:6, *polla ekopiasen eis hymas*
—Junia (see below) 16:7, *synaichmalōtoi mou, episēmoi en tois apostolois*
—Tryphaena and
—Tryphosa 16:12, *kopiōsas en kyriō*
—Persis 16:12, *polla ekopiasen en kyriō*
—perhaps also: Rufus' mother 16:13, *mētēr kai emou*
* Five (or three) men:
—Aquila 16:3–4, *synergos* etc.
—Andronicus 16:7, *synaichmalōtoi mou, episēmoi en tois apostolois*
—Urbanus 16:9, *synergos hēmōn*
—perhaps: Apelles 16:10, *dokimos en Christō*
—perhaps: Rufus 16:13, *eklektos en kyriō*

If we were especially picky, we could even state that Andronicus' and Urbanus' activities mentioned took place in the east and not in Rome (*synaichmalōtoi mou, hēmōn*). Mary on the contrary earned special merits in the Roman church (*eis hymas*).

The active part the women took can also be observed in two other instances: (a) *kopiaō* is a technical term describing the labors of a missionary. Paul uses it for himself in Galatians 4:11 and 1 Corinthians 15:10. In Romans 16:3–16 it is used four times—exclusively for women, not for men. (b) Prisca is mentioned *before* her husband Aquila in Romans 16:3; Acts 18:18, 26; and 2 Timothy 4:19. Only 1 Corinthians 16:19 (cf. Acts 18:2) presents the opposite order. Apparently Prisca was even more outstanding in her work for the church than was Aquila.

One woman in our list deserves special attention since she has been mistaken for a man for centuries: Junia. In the majuscules, we cannot distinguish between *Iounian*, an accusative of a feminine "Junia," and *Iounian*, the accusative of a masculine "Junias." Therefore we have to move on to the minuscules. According to Aland's textual critical apparatus, the feminine "Junia" does not appear in the manuscripts. Indeed, most of the medieval scribes of minuscules made Junias a man. But not all, as I discovered recently: Minuscule 33 (9th century) reads the feminine *iounian*. Which reading is to be preferred? Clearly "Junia." "Junia" was a common name in the Roman Empire, while "Junias" did not exist. The modern grammars support a masculine reading by theorizing that "Junias" was a short form of "Junianus," without being able to quote evidence for this assumption. The fathers and mothers of the early church knew better, always identifying Andronicus' companion as the woman Junia. The very first church father coming up with the masculine version was Aegidius of Rome (A.D. 1245–1316). For medieval authors and scribes "Junia" was the "*lectio difficilior.*" They could not picture a woman as an active missionary.

Andronicus and Junia may have travelled together as a married missionary couple, as 1 Corinthians 9:5 reports about other apostles too. The most natural understanding of *episēmoi en tois apostolois* is that they both were outstanding apostles—and not only splendid *in the eyes* of the apostles.

Why would they have been famous only in *their* eyes? The *en* has to be translated as "among" (the apostles) like in 1 Corinthians 15:12 and James 5:13–14, 19.

After having analyzed the women's role in Romans 16, we unfortunately cannot generalize these results. A group of 26 people hardly allows any generalization about the Roman church as a whole. On the contrary, the data that I analyzed in my book about Rome suggest that the women's influence in the Roman church was reduced to a minimum at the latest by the end of the first century. While the 50s of the first century still saw influential church women like Prisca, Junia, Persis, Phoebe, and others, this female influence later survived only in marginal Christian groups which soon were viewed as having the taint of heresy. In 1 Clement 21:7; 1:3, at the end of the first century, the voices of the women were already silenced—otherwise these verses could not have been formulated.

IV. Jewish Christians—Gentile Christians

The names by themselves do not release any information about the persons' Jewish or pagan background. But luckily Paul calls three Roman persons in Romans 16:3–16 "my kins(wo)men": Andronicus, Junia, and Herodion. The term *syngenēs* never occurs in the other Pauline letters. In Romans, however, after chapters 9–11 and especially 9:3, Paul has a *special interest* in emphasizing the Jewish origin of Christians (Rom. 16:7, 11, 21). Why? Paul prays for the salvation of the Jews (10:1). "I ask, has God rejected his people? By no means! I myself am an Israelite" (11:1), and he thus offers a proof that God did not reject the Jews. The "kins(wo)men" in Romans 16 are living proofs of the same grace towards Israel. They and Paul himself are the "remnant at the present time, chosen by grace" (11: 5). "Israel failed to obtain what it sought. But the elect (i.e., Paul and his Christian kins[wo]men) obtained it" (11:7). They are signs of hope that Israel is not yet lost. On the contrary, Israel will be fully included in the salvation one time in the future (11:12, 23, 24, 26, 29, 31, 32).

Having this kind of special theological interest in emphasizing the Jewish kinship of Christians in Romans—and only in Romans—Paul probably applies the term "kins(wo)man" rather consistently to all Jewish Christians he can identify in the group of Romans 16. The list, then, shows that only a small minority of Jewish Christians existed among the 26 persons of this Roman group (15%).

This result is affirmed by two other observations. (a) Several times in Romans Paul presumes that the vast majority in the Roman church is Gentile. These clear and direct statements seem to contradict the impression that much of the contents of Romans could be understood only by people who were trained in Jewish culture. The solution of the paradox is at hand if we assume that most people in the Roman church were of Gentile origin but had lived as sympathizers on the margins of the synagogues before they became Christian.

(b) Only three names of the Romans 16 list occur also in the Jewish inscriptions (*CIJ*) of Rome: "Maria" (Mary) and the typically Latin names "Rufus" and "Julia." Besides these two Latin names, even "Maria" cannot be considered especially Jewish. It is often taken for granted that "Maria/

Mary" equals the semitic *mirjam*. The following epigraphical data, however, suggest that "Maria" in Romans 16 represents the pagan name of a Roman *gens*. "Marius," in the feminine form "Maria," was a Latin *nomen gentile* by which a woman was sufficiently characterized without having to carry a *cognomen*. This Latin-pagan "Maria" occurs approximately 108 times in the city of Rome inscriptions of *CIL* VI. The semitic "Maria" cannot be counted even 20 times in Rome. Thus, chances are good that our Christian Maria was a Gentile—Paul in fact does not call her a "kinswoman," as we saw.

V. *Immigrants—Natives of Rome*

We already saw that *at least* Prisca, Aquila, Epaenetus, Andronicus, Junia, Urbanus, Rufus, his mother, Ampliatus, Stachys, Persis, and Apelles had travelled between the east and Rome. But who was actually of oriental origin? Many of the twelve persons mentioned may have been Romans, having been expelled by Claudius and returning to Rome later. Only four were visibly of oriental birth: Aquila (Pontus), Epaenetus (first convert in Asia), Andronicus, and Junia, who belonged to the first Palestinian apostles and had been Christians already before Paul.

Do we have to give up on our question? A second approach is possible on the basis of the inscriptions in *CIL* VI (computerized concordance) and of Solin's book [*Griechischen Personennamen*] about Greek names in Rome. Which names of our list were rare in the city of Rome, which occurred frequently?

Julia	+ 1400 times
Hermes	640
Rufus	ca. 374
*Junia	+ 250
Prisca/Priscilla	+ 200
Maria	ca. 108
Urbanus	ca. 95
Ampliatus	ca. 80
Tryphaena	47
Tryphosa	29
Nereus	28
*Aquila	ca. 28
*Andronicus	19
Philologus	18
Apelles	15
Stachys	11
Phlegon	7
Persis	3
Hermas	3
*Epaenetus	3
Asynkritos	1

Olympas	0
Patrobas	0, but the name is a shortened version of Patrobius
Patrobius	4
Herodion	0

How does this list coincide with our previous findings? The four oriental persons we found earlier are marked with an asterisk. Three of them, Aquila, Andronicus, and Epaenetus, indeed appear in the lower section (< 29) of the table. Only the oriental Junia ranks high—for good reasons: Her name is not a *cognomen* but a Latin *nomen gentile*, by which a woman was sufficiently identified. Prominent Roman *gentes* included a lot of orientals among their slaves. Being freed, they obtained the name of the *gens*, in this case "Junius/Junia." Our oriental Junia is indeed most likely a freed slave or a descendant of a freed(wo)man of the *gens Junia*.

With three factual orientals occurring in the lower section of the table, chances are good that also the other rare names in the lower section belong to immigrants. Indeed, earlier we had already identified three of them as names of individuals who had at least travelled between the east and Rome: Apelles, Stachys, and Persis.

Thus, about 14 people out of 26 were presumably not born in Rome itself. An oriental origin of the remaining 12 cannot be excluded—but neither can it be indicated. We do not even get a clue about Prisca: Did Aquila meet and start seeing her in Pontus—or in Rome?

Looking at the Roman church of the first and second centuries as a whole, the proportion 14:26 seems a minimal figure. Other data suggest that the proportion of immigrants in the Roman church was much higher than just 54% during this period. The influx of *peregrini* to the church of the capital city was immense—and also had its theological impact.

VI. *Juridical and Social Position*

Which juridical position did the 26 people obtain? Do their *names* release any information about *free birth* or *slave origins*? I am not going to repeat the methodological state of affairs, the five criteria I used, or the many epigraphical data. I just quote the results of my analysis:

1. The names "Urbanus," "Prisca," "Aquila," and "Rufus" do not indicate any affinity to people born into slavery. Surprisingly, this result coincides with three other independent observations. And the reader may decide whether this is mere coincidence or whether a causal relation plays a role: (a) Two of the persons mentioned are married: Aquila and Prisca—apparently both free born. They are also the only ones about whom we have more detailed prosopographical information. (b) Only Aquila, Prisca, and Urbanus are called Paul's "*co-workers*" in Romans 16—nobody else! (c) Rufus' mother was a mother also to Paul (16:13). This fits well to a free matron of a household being hospitable to an apostle.

2. The following people were most probably slaves or freed(wo)men: Nereus, Hermes, Persis, Herodion, Tryphosa, Tryphaena, Ampliatus. Freedwomen or descendants of freed(wo)men were Julia, Junia, and most likely Maria.

3. For the remaining twelve persons, we are not able to make a proba-
bility statement (Asyncritus, Patrobas, Philologus, Andronicus, Olympas,
Apelles, Phlegon, Hermas, Stachys, Epaenetus, also Nereus' sister and
Rufus' mother).

4. Thus, more than two thirds of the people for whom we can make a
probability statement have an affinity to slave origins. The slaves or
freed(wo)men of Narcissus and Aristobulus were not alone in the Romans
16 group. And looking at the first two centuries as a whole, we discover
indeed plenty of Christian slaves and freed(wo)men in Rome.

But to what extent is the two-thirds proportion representative for the
Roman church? Interestingly enough, a similar proportion between freeborn people and persons born into slavery occurs in a variant Roman data
pool; although it is difficult to know whether this is mere coincidence or
not. We do not even know for sure how high the percentage of slaves and
freed(wo)men was in the entire society. The estimations vary between 20%
and 40% slaves. The freed(wo)men counted at least as many on top of the
slave figure, which leaves 20–60% to the freeborn people. However, if we
take the mean average of these figures (30% slaves, 30% freed[wo]men,
40% freeborn), we end up with proportions comparable to the aforemen-
tioned two data pools of the Roman church (63–67% slave-born, 33–37%
freeborn). At some points, the social profile of the church indeed seems
to mirror the profile of the entire society.

To what extent is the juridical status an indicator for the social position?
Many freed(wo)men were rich business people and in a better economic
position than many freeborn. Therefore the juridical status—free birth,
slave, or freed slave—does not necessarily say much about the socioeconomic position of an individual. Only a general direction can be given for
the Romans 16 persons by asking: How did the proportions between
socially elevated persons and lower strata people look in the Roman church
during the first two centuries? The *humiliores* represented the vast majority
in the Roman church—and socially elevated people formed only a minority. This is especially true for the first century. Referring the reader to the
materials in my book, I only select one significant example here: Several
Roman Christians during the first century sold themselves into slavery in
order to finance the support of Christian brothers and sisters. This illustrates the necessity for social action—there were many needy among the
Roman Christians. And it discloses the lack of enough well-to-do Christians supporting these needy.

VII. Divided Nature of the Roman Christianity— House Congregations

During the two first centuries the Christians of the city of Rome met
separately in privately owned locations scattered around the capital city.
Forming a number of house-churches, they had no central worship facility—a lack of central coordination that matched the profile of the separated synagogues in Rome.

With separate pockets of Christians in the city of Rome being prevalent
throughout the first two centuries and even beyond them, Romans 16 must
be read in this light. Indicating the divided nature of Roman Christianity,
Paul does not call it *ekklēsia* anywhere in Romans, not even in 1:7 where

we would expect it according to the other Pauline letters. Only a part is called *ekklēsia*: the house-church around Aquila and Prisca (Rom. 16:5). Besides this first one, four other pockets of Christians in the city of Rome are identified by Romans 16:

—The Christians around Asyncritus, Phlegon, Hermes, Patrobas, and Hermas (16:14).

—The Christians around Philologus, Julia, Olympas, Nereus, and his sister (16:15).

—The Christians in Aristobulus' household (16:10).

—The Christians in Narcissus' household (16:11).

If we assume that the other fourteen individuals in the Romans 16 list belonged to none of these five crystallization points, and that they hardly have belonged to only *one* further circle, the result is at least seven separate groups. The number grew to at least eight when Paul himself started to assemble Christians in his Roman rented lodging (Acts 28:30–31).

Looking at the lack of a central worship place in Rome throughout the centuries, we can hardly avoid the conclusion that these (at least) eight circles also worshipped separately—in separate dwellings somewhere in the different quarters of the city. Thus, probably all eight can be identified as worshipping "house-congregations" or "house-churches." This does not exclude that some of them were also held together by kinship or household-ties.

In the later history of the Roman church, this divided nature helped "heresies" to survive in the capital city for decades. It also prevented the institution of a Roman monarchical bishop until the second half of the second century. Although we are already far beyond Romans 16 with this, it shows again the broader perspectives in which the data of Romans 16 can be integrated.

MARGARET M. MITCHELL

Rhetorical Shorthand in Pauline Argumentation (1994)†

> Paul customarily establishes many things incidentally, and is compact [πυκνός] in his thoughts. . . . He doesn't encompass a few thoughts in many words, but in brevity of words [βραχύτητι ῥημάτων] he sets down a great and manifold idea.[1]

John Chrysostom, the rhetorically trained exegete and orator, made this apt statement about Paul's mode of argumentation in the year 403. In considering the rhetorical functions of 'the gospel' in the Corinthian correspondence, one comes immediately face to face with the phenomenon of Pauline shorthand. Spurred on by this valuable observation of Chrysos-

---

† From an essay published in *Gospel in Paul*, ed. by L. Ann Jervis and Peter Richardson (Sheffield: Sheffield Academic Press, 1994), 63–88. Reprinted by permission of the author. Mitchell is professor of New Testament and Early Christian Literature in the Divinity School of the University of Chicago, where she has taught since 1998.

1. John Chrysostom, *hom. in Heb.* 27.1 [*PG* 63.185]; cf. the similar observation in *hom. in Rom.* 8.28 2 [*PG* 51.166].

tom (who was far closer to the literary culture of Paul than we), and his application of technical terminology (βραχύτης) to Paul's terse expressions, in this essay I shall examine Paul's different ways of accessing the gospel in the Corinthian correspondence in the light of Graeco-Roman techniques of rhetorical shorthand.

1. *Introduction: The Gospel and Rhetorical Shorthand*

The basic structure and content of Paul's gospel is a narrative sequence of events which describes God's salvific acts on behalf of humankind. An extended version of this narrative is found close at hand for our investigation in 1 Cor. 15:3–8: 'Christ died on behalf of our sins according to the Scriptures, he was buried, and he was raised on the third day according to the Scriptures, and he appeared to Kephas, then to the twelve, then to more than five hundred brothers and sisters at one time, of whom most remain alive, but some have died. Then he appeared to James, then to all the apostles. Last of all, as though to one untimely-born, he appeared also to me.' This is the gospel, Paul says, that he handed over to the Corinthians, which he had received. One must exercise caution about assuming that for Paul there was only one formulation of the gospel, or that this was it, but Pauline creedal encapsulations of the gospel do repeatedly contain some central elements, as H. Koester has argued: 'Christ's suffering and death; his sacrifice "for us"; his cross; his being raised from the dead (or rising from the dead); his appearances; his coming again in the future.'[2] We can consider these the basic, well-attested building blocks of 'the gospel' for Paul, which can be expressed and combined in various ways. The resulting composite narrative can be either compacted or expanded, depending on one's literary, rhetorical and theological purposes. One supreme compaction of the narrative is accomplished by the very phrase τὸ εὐαγγέλιον ['the gospel'], which serves as a 'superabbreviation' of the whole, functioning as a title which both characterizes its full contents and interprets its meaning for the hearer. The logic of the gospel title is unitary: no single event in the narrative stands apart from or uninterpreted by the rest. In usage the single phrase τὸ εὐαγγέλιον allows Paul, with great economy and elegance, to insert the entire long narrative of God's plan 'according to the Scriptures' into an argument without repeating the whole. Paul does this often, as for him the gospel is the canon or standard with which all expressions of Christian life or thought are to be compared and assessed.

Though 'the gospel' has received abundant attention in scholarship, especially in regard to its lexical antecedents and cultural influences, the rhetorical functions of 'the gospel', and other means by which Paul brings the gospel into his arguments, have received surprisingly scant attention. My thesis is that Paul does this primarily by effective use of ancient techniques of rhetorical shorthand, which allow him to allude to the gospel and incorporate it into particular argumentative contexts without reciting the whole all over again each time. I shall identify and analyse three forms of rhetorical shorthand by which Paul accesses 'the gospel' in his letters: (1) by τὸ εὐαγγέλιον and synonyms, technical terms or titles which summarize the whole; (2) by brief allusions to a single component of the gospel narra-

---

2. H. Koester, *Ancient Christian Gospels* (Philadelphia: Trinity Press International; London: SCM, 1990), pp. 6–7.

tive; and (3) by metaphorical depictions of the transmission of the gospel. Each of these three techniques is a figure or trope described in ancient rhetorical theory: the first is an instance of βραχυλογία ('brevity'), the second of συνεκδοχή ('synecdoche'), and the third of μεταφορά ('metaphor').

In one sense the phrase τὸ εὐαγγέλιον receives its abbreviative power semantically, because the very term 'good news' (or perhaps merely 'message') points outside of itself to a content and story which must have been told (at least once) for the referent to be clear to the audience. The way Paul uses the phrase absolutely, that is, without any qualifier (as in about half of Pauline usages), shows that he assumes that the audience knows well to what he refers. Yet even the qualified uses of the phrase, such as τὸ εὐαγγέλιον τοῦ θεοῦ ['the gospel of God'] or τὸ εὐαγγέλιον τοῦ Χριστοῦ ['the gospel of Christ'], rely as much upon the hearers' acquaintance with the narrative of events to which they refer. The same is true of such Pauline synonyms for the gospel as τὸ κήρυγμα ('the proclamation') and ὁ λόγος ('the word'), which by their semantic nature summarize some content which must be defined contextually.

But lexical analysis does not sufficiently explain Paul's use τὸ εὐαγγέλιον; in usage it also has a significant, recognizable rhetorical function. To analyse it we turn to ancient rhetorical theory on tropes, forms of 'substitution of one word for another'. The rhetorical figure βραχύτης or βραχυλογία ('brevity'), as described, for example, in the rhetorical handbook *Rhetorica ad Alexandrum*, amply suits Paul's use of τὸ εὐαγγέλιον: 'If you wish to speak briefly, include the whole of an idea in a single word [ὅλον τὸ πρᾶγμα ἑνὶ ὀνόματι περιλαμβάνειν], and that the shortest that is appropriate to the idea' (*Rh. Al.* 22.1434b). Very close to Paul's time, and perhaps even composed at his native Tarsus, is the work Περὶ ἑρμηνείας (*De elocutione*) attributed to Demetrius, in which we find the following statement about rhetorical brevity (ἡ βραχύτης): 'it is a mark of superior skill to compress much thought in a little space [τὸ ἐν ὀλίγῳ πολλὴν διάνοιαν ἠθροῖσθαι], just as seeds contain potentially entire trees' [*Eloc.* 1.9]. τὸ εὐαγγέλιον and a host of synonyms used by Paul in his letters perfectly exemplify such rhetorical brevity.

A second and related rhetorical trope, which is a tremendously flexible argumentative tool in Paul's hands, is συνεκδοχή: 'when the whole is known from a small part or a part from the whole' [*Rh. Her.* 4.33.44]. The grammarian Tryphon, who wrote at Rome during the reign of Augustus, gave a full description of συνεκδοχή in his work Περὶ τρόπων ('On Tropes'). Like other teachers of rhetoric, he gives examples of different types of συνεκδοχή, beginning with the two general categories, ἀπὸ μέρους τὸ ὅλον ['from part to whole'] and ἀπὸ τοῦ ὅλου τὸ μέρος ['from whole to part']. Especially suggestive for Paul's way of accessing 'the gospel' is Tryphon's overall definition of συνεκδοχή, which points out the phrase's necessary participation in a larger context in order for meaning to flow: 'synecdoche is an expression not brought out in full [οὐ κατὰ τὸ πλῆρες ἐξενηνεγμένη], but standing in need of something from the outside which attends to it' [*Trop.* 1.7]. Paul uses συνεκδοχή, this form of shorthand, when he alludes to the entire gospel narrative by reference to only one of its component events, such as when one part, for example, Χριστὸς ἀπέθανεν ('Christ died'), stands for the whole: ὁ λόγος τοῦ σταυροῦ ('the word of the cross').

Συνεκδοχή appears to be a subcategory of the more overarching classification of βραχύτης. We can see this from Tryphon's definition of βραχύτης, which bears much in common with his discussion of συνεκδοχή: 'Brevity is an expression which has more meaning than just what is heard' [*Trop.* 2.9].

He goes on to cite the standard examples of brevity found throughout the tradition of rhetorical education: the utterances of the Delphic oracle, such as γνῶθι σεαυτόν ('know yourself'), and the three word letter of the Lacedaemonians to Philip: Διονύσιος ἐν Κορίνθῳ ('Dionysios is in Corinth'). This is an allusion to the well-known tale of Dionysios II, the tyrant of Syracuse, who inherited the throne of his father, later lost it, and lived out his days as a humble schoolteacher in Corinth. Ps-Demetrius also analyses this famous example in his discussion of βραχύτης, and clarifies precisely our issue:

> For it is felt to be more forcible when thus briefly put * * * than if the Lacedaemonians had said at full length * * * that Dionysius, although once a mighty monarch like yourself, now resides at Corinth in a private station. Once the statement is made in detail * * *, it resembles not a rebuke but a thing narrated * * *; it suggests the expositor * * * rather than the intimidator * * *. The passion and vehemence of the words are enfeebled when thus extended. * * * (*Eloc.* 1.8)

This passage is most important for our study, for it provides an explanation of the dynamics of shorthand references to a narrative in other compositions which is contemporary to Paul. The choice of shorthand is due to the literary/rhetorical genre of the writer. If one is not writing a narrative but something else, as in the Lacedaemonians' case an epistolary rebuke, one will not recite the entire narrative, because that will interfere with the chosen rhetorical genre and purpose, and will take the forcefulness out of the new literary creation. Related to this is the role of the author: if one has a purpose in mind other than being a storyteller, one must abbreviate the narrative in order to accomplish that new purpose. One can abbreviate a narrative by synecdoche, as in the Lacedaemonians' letter, by reference to only one of the events of which it is made up. One chooses the event in each case by reference to the new rhetorical purpose (in this case Dionysios's humble ending is chosen to warn Philip of what can happen to tyrants). Or one could abbreviate a narrative by a brief descriptive title, such as 'Dionysios's demise'.

The above cited passage from *De elocutione* provides an exact analogue to what Paul does. Paul does not write narratives, but letters. Those letters address complex issues in his churches through involved argumentation. By means of the title phrase τὸ εὐαγγέλιον and other partial references to the narrative which suggest the whole, Paul is able to construct new texts which incorporate the authority of the underlying gospel narrative through pointed, carefully chosen shorthand references to it. A third rhetorical figure, μεταφορά (metaphor), 'when a word applying to one thing is transferred to another' [*Rh. Her.* 4.34.45], is also commonly used by Paul. Via metaphor he creates 'vivid mental pictures' which depict the proclamation of the gospel and its effects, and allow Paul to characterize and accent a particular feature of the ongoing history of the gospel which he and his hearers share.

Once the contextual meaning of 'the gospel' was fully established, as by Paul's missionary teaching, it was then possible at a second and later stage of reflection to invoke that known quantity in shorthand, either by a brief phrase, a synecdochical reference, or a metaphorical allusion. Paul used such shorthand references, which served to create and reinforce the social bonds of the group, in service of a variety of specific argumentative purposes: didactic, deliberative, paraenetic, apologetic. As we examine these three types of references to the gospel in the Corinthian correspondence we shall observe how the choices Paul makes in selecting and employing rhetorical shorthand are keyed specifically to his theological and rhetorical purpose in each particular argument.

2. 1 Corinthians

The gospel plays a predominant role throughout Paul's deliberative argument for Christian unity in 1 Corinthians. Paul's purpose for the letter is announced quite clearly in the πρόθεσις, or thesis statement to the argument in the body of the letter, in 1:10. Paul responded to a multiplicity of contacts from the Corinthian church (1:11; 5:1; 7:1; 16:17–18) through his determination that divisiveness in the church was *the* most important problem which he had to address. Throughout the letter Paul urges the Corinthians to seek unity as the course of action most in conformity with the gospel, and offers himself as an example of one who has sought and lived such conformity.

In line with the typology set forth above, Paul draws upon 'the gospel' in three ways in this letter. First, through βραχυλογία Paul uses a variety of shorthand terms and phrases. The exact words εὐαγγέλιον and εὐαγγελίζομαι ['to proclaim the gospel'] occur fully ten times in this long letter (noun 4:15; 9:12, 14, 18, 23; 15:1; verb 1:17; 9:16, 18; 15:1). Other functionally equivalent terms or phrases for the gospel also abound in this letter: τὸ μαρτύριον τοῦ Χριστοῦ ('the testimony of Christ', 1:6; 2:1 v.l.); ὁ λόγος μου ('my word', 2:4; cf. 15:2, and ὁ λόγος τοῦ θεοῦ, 'the word of God' in 14:36); ὁ λόγος τοῦ σταυροῦ ('the word of the cross', 1:18); τὸ κήρυγμα (μου) ('[my] preaching', 1:21; 2:4; 15:14); the verbs κηρύσσω ('to preach', 1:23; 9:27; 15:11, 12) and καταγγέλλω ('to proclaim', 2:1; 9: 14; 11:26); and τὸ μυστήριον (τοῦ θεοῦ) ('the mystery [of God]', 2:1; 4: 1; 13:2; 14:2; 15:51). Secondly, Paul makes terse, synecdochical references to the gospel story in his arguments (1:23; 2:2, 8; 5:7; 6:14, 20; 7:23; 8:11; 11:3, 26; 15:15). Thirdly, Paul includes several most interesting metaphorical depictions of his preaching of the gospel (3:1–2, 6–9, 9–17; 4:1, 15; 9:7, 11, 17). First I shall give a brief sketch of the arguments in 1 Corinthians where the first two types of references come into play, and then treat the metaphorical depictions of gospel preaching altogether.

In the subargument in 1:17–2:5 Paul focuses explicitly on his apostolic preaching of the gospel, using his humble, weak-kneed demeanour as a paradigm of the self-effacement required to counteract the Corinthian divisions which Paul attributes to pride and boastfulness. In this section the term εὐαγγελίζομαι is used only once, in 1:17—the transition verse which introduces the topic—but then the theme is carried forward by synonyms. The first of these, ὁ λόγος τοῦ σταυροῦ ('the word of the cross'), as noted above, is a synecdoche for the gospel narrative in its entirety (including both the death and resurrection of Christ). This synecdoche of the cross for the gospel is named explictly by Paul in 1:23 and 2:2. The idea here is not that Paul preached to the Corinthians a gospel without resurrection (as 15:1–11 shows very clearly), but rather that the whole of the gospel can be alluded to by reference to one of its parts. The choice of which part depends in each case on Paul's particular argument. Here, where Paul seeks to combat Corinthian self-aggrandizement, he turns to the gospel and its preaching as the standard for Christian life and in so doing elevates the foolish, utterly defeated-looking crucifixion to set the 'worldly standards' (which the Corinthians are emulating) on their heads.

The gospel story, as the exemplification of God's paradoxical logic, necessarily entails a whole new re-evaluation of σοφία, δύναμις and εὐγένεια ('wisdom, power and noble birth') which dismantles the 'human' constructs which are still so operative in the Corinthians' lives and dealings with one another. In place of all this, the gospel offers Christ crucified, a new kind of σοφία ('wisdom'), as 1:30 recapitulates. Then three highly compacted terms, δικαιοσύνη, ἁγιασμός and ἀπολύτρωσις ['justification, sanctification, redemption'], make abbreviated reference once again to the crucifixion, and to its salvific consequences for those who have embraced the gospel (cf. 6:11).

Paul will make a synecdochical reference to the gospel by allusion to the single event of the crucifixion also in 1 Cor. 5:7 (τὸ πάσχα ἡμῶν ἐτύθη Χριστός) ['Christ our Passover was sacrificed'] to stress the need for holistic cleansing in the body of Christ of a diseased member, and in 8:11 (ὁ ἀδελφὸς δι' ὃν Χριστὸς ἀπέθανεν) ['the brother for whom Christ died'], where the self-sacrificial death of Christ becomes the basis for Christian ethical decision-making because it defines the relationships with persons who might be affected by one's behaviour. The highly allusive phrase found in 6:20 and 7:23 (τιμῆς ἠγοράσθητε, 'you were bought with a price') encapsulates in two words the meaning of the gospel story for the readers in application to specific sexual and moral decisions which are related to how one lives out one's Christian κλῆσις ('calling').

In ch. 9 Paul provides an explicit discussion of gospel preaching and its rewards, as a part of his overall argument in 5:1–11:1 about the nature and proper exercise of Christian ἐξουσία/ἐλευθερία ('right/freedom'). This chapter is an exemplary argument in which Paul puts himself forward as an example of renunciation of rights for the sake of the greater good: the gaining of others and the success of the gospel. The apostolic standard of behaviour is never to do anything which might constitute a 'hindrance' (ἐγκοπή) to the gospel (9:12), which stands in opposition to how Paul characterizes some Corinthians' exercise of ἐξουσία as a possible 'stumbling block' (πρόσκομμα) to the weak (8:9). It is Paul who freely introduces the topic of his self-support (it is not a Corinthian charge against him) to exemplify the principle μὴ καταχρήσασθαι τῇ ἐξουσίᾳ ἐν τῷ εὐαγγελίῳ, 'not to misuse [one's] rights in the gospel' (9:18; cf. vv. 12, 15).

In vv. 15–18 Paul engages in a complex bit of introspection about his role to preach the gospel, which is occasioned by his clarification of a possible misunderstanding in v. 15: he did not just recite all those proofs for why he should be able to receive support from his churches in order to make it so. Instead, his lack of customary payment is due to the divine call which has entrusted him with this sacred stewardship. Further, he muses, he already has his reward (μίσθος): the gaining (κερδαίνω) of new people for the gospel. The very preaching of the gospel is its own reward, he says, in the hope that he is living in conformity with it, its partner (συγκοινωνὸς αὐτοῦ, 9:23). It is that standard of behaviour which Paul urges, by his example, on the Corinthians. The fuller subargument (5:1–11:1) ends fittingly enough with the call to imitation of Paul, as he imitates Christ, that is, as he lives a life in conformity with the gospel (11:1).

In treating the Corinthian conflict at the eucharist (11:17–34), Paul once again calls on the gospel as the proper standard. After a brief, bitter censure of their divisive behaviour, Paul recites the tradition about the eucharistic words of Jesus (11:23–26). He does not call this τὸ εὐαγγέλιον, though the identical language of tradition in 15:3 (παραλαμβάνω, παραδίδωμι) is suggestive. Nevertheless, where the gospel comes to the fore is in Paul's commentary on the tradition, which begins in v. 26. There Paul uses the technical language for gospel proclamation, and the same synecdochical reference to the crucifixion which was so prominent earlier in the letter: τὸν θάνατον τοῦ κυρίου καταγγέλλετε ('you proclaim the death of the Lord'). Because the eucharist has this signal meaning, the very proclamation of the gospel, Paul's application to the precise situation (v. 27) is to urge the Corinthians to comport themselves worthily (ἀξίως) of it.

Paul also synecdochically alludes to the gospel by reference to the resurrection. In 6:14 (ὁ δὲ θεὸς καὶ τὸν κύριον ἤγειρεν . . .) he stresses the impermanence of the earthly body, and its ultimate fate, resurrection, as assured by the archetype of God's resurrection of the Lord Jesus. An allusion to the resurrection is also likely contained in the early Christian acclamation κύριος Ἰησοῦς ('Jesus is Lord'), which Paul cites in 1 Cor. 12:3 to assure the Corinthians that everyone who recites this fundamental Christian creed is a spiritual person, and not just those who possess more conspicuous, dramatic gifts.

Perhaps the most important text on the gospel in 1 Corinthians, and indeed in all of Paul's letters, is 15:1–11. Here, interestingly, Paul chooses to recite the kerygmatic narrative in full at the outset of the subargument, and not to allude to it by shorthand. Why? The answer lies in Paul's assessment of the nature of this conflict about resurrection—that in denying the resurrection of believers, some members of the Corinthian community have put the very gospel in question (v. 12). We can see this quite clearly in 15:1–2, where Paul introduces the new topic not as ἀνάστασις νεκρῶν ('resurrection of the dead'), but rather as τὸ εὐαγγέλιον. In 1 Corinthians 15 Paul leads not with the problem, but rather with the solution. The gospel is the common principle upon which Paul assumes agreement with his audience (15:11, οὕτως κηρύσσομεν καὶ οὕτως ἐπιστεύσατε, 'thus we preach and thus you believed'), and which contains what he regards as the clear-cut and only answer to the Corinthians' debate about the general resurrection of believers.

So, instead of synecdoche, in this case we get a full recital and even expansion of the gospel that Christ was raised from the dead, the undisputed point from which he will argue for the concomitant resurrection of believers against those who dispute it (15:12). The gospel Paul originally preached perhaps did not say anything concrete about the resurrection of believers, but Paul's consistent hermeneutical principle is that the gospel story is not only about the fate of Christ, but also functions typologically for all human beings who enter into the story through faith and baptism. Thus his inductive argument which follows puts forward the proposition by contraries (15:13): if there is no resurrection of the dead, then Christ has not been raised. In 15:14–15 we have a synecdoche of the gospel (τὸ κήρυγμα ἡμῶν, 'our proclamation') previously explicated in full, but this time by reference, as we should expect, only to the resurrection: ἐμαρτυρήσαμεν κατὰ τοῦ θεοῦ ὅτι ἤγειρεν τὸν Χριστόν ('we testified against God that he raised Christ'). The truthfulness of Paul's κήρυγμα is not and never has been in doubt (15:11). Thus he can argue from that shared premise to his inductive claim that A implies B; that is, the resurrection of Christ implies also the resurrection of all believers. In 15:13–19 Paul stacks up the dire consequences for himself and especially the Corinthians if some are right in denying the resurrection of the dead. Having raised the ante, in 15:20 Paul then returns triumphantly to the gospel premise which he has demonstrated and amplified already in 15:1–11: Νυνὶ δὲ Χριστὸς ἐγήγερται ἐκ νεκρῶν ('Now Christ has been raised from the dead'). The consequence of this is clear: in Christ all shall be brought to new life (v. 22). In 15:23–28 (and also vv. 51–55) Paul provides a fresh narrative of the events of the endtime, an example of the opposite literary tendency from shorthand: an expansion of the gospel narrative to respond to new questions which the gospel has engendered for those who seek to live it out in the present and look toward the future.

The third form of rhetorical shorthand Paul uses in reference to the gospel is metaphor. In 1 Corinthians Paul employs no less than four different metaphors to describe his imparting of the gospel to the Corinthians: planting a field (3:6–9; 9:7 [a vineyard]; also 'sowing spiritual things' in 9:11); laying the foundation of a building (3:9–17); begetting children (4:15, also feeding them, 3:1–2); and stewarding a household (4:1; 9:17). Each of these metaphors alludes to the underlying foundation story of the church at Corinth—one well-known to the Corinthians for they were characters in it—which includes Paul's arrival at Corinth, his preaching of the gospel narrative to them, their reception of it in faith and the consequent birth of the new community. These metaphorical renditions of the tale of the gospel's arrival at Corinth are thus 'stories about a story.' Most of these passages merely allude to a single incident of the fuller narrative, but 3:6 provides the complete narrative sequence: ἐγὼ ἐφύτευσα, ʼΑπολλῶς ἐπότισεν, ἀλλὰ ὁ θεὸς ηὔξανεν ('I planted, Apollos watered, but God made it grow'). The reason for the extended narrative here is that the *sequence* of events (especially Paul's being the first one there) is important to Paul's reading of the history (cf. 3:10–11). Via the metaphorical retellings of the foundation story, either in full or by synecdochical allusion, Paul accents a particular element of the story for use in the present argument:

3:6–9, the abundant growth of the church and the unity of the missionary labourers in the common task;

3:10–17, Paul's singular role in founding the church on the one foundation which is his gospel of Jesus Christ;

4:15 and 3:1–2, the immaturity of the early community and its dependence upon Paul its only father for instruction and correction;

4:1 and 9:17, Paul's sacred and ongoing responsibility for the church
thus established, and his renunciation of all self-concern toward the
execution of that duty.

In terms of rhetorical strategy we see in all these metaphorical depictions
of the preaching of the gospel Paul's wish to ground the Corinthians in
solidarity in the story of their origins as a church (with himself as their
founder), and in the unity of the gospel story which is at the heart of their
common identity and history. Metaphor is a powerful rhetorical tool for
this argumentative purpose as it serves to portray in imaginative terms the
intimate and harmonious relationship between the apostle and his church
which the gospel made possible. We shall see that the breakdown of Paul's
relationship with the Corinthians can be charted by the progressively negative metaphorical identities of the Corinthians in the subsequent letters.

3. 2. *Corinthians*

The considerable literary and historical puzzles of 2 Corinthians are in my
judgment best explained by the five-letter partition theory, which holds
that these individual letters, in the following probable order of composition, have been redacted together to form the canonical letter: 2 Cor. 2:
14–7:4 (minus 6:14–7:1), 2 Cor. 10–13, 2 Cor. 1:1–2:13 and 7:5–16, 2
Cor. 8 and 2 Cor. 9. Because literary context is essential to meaning, our
investigation of the role of the gospel in 2 Corinthians will proceed on a
letter by letter basis. In the letters in 2 Corinthians Paul continues to draw
upon 'the gospel' in the formulation of his arguments, though many of the
arguments here are apologetic in nature, where in 1 Corinthians they were
deliberative.

※   ※   ※

[The last of these letters, 2 Cor. 9], and the entire Corinthian correspondence, ends with a fitting, most paradoxical rhetorical shorthand for
the gospel: Χάρις τῷ θεῷ ἐπὶ τῇ ἀνεκδιηγήτῳ αὐτοῦ δωρεᾷ ('Thanks be
to God for his indescribable gift' v. 15). The actual referent of course
includes the gift of the collection for the saints, but also encompasses the
entirety of God's gifts as told and retold in the gospel. The whole of God's
saving actions in history, the gospel, is hyperbolically declared in this
prayer of thanksgiving to be ἀνεκδιήγητος, 'unnarratable'. Of course this
is literally not true, for that would invalidate Paul's gospel and its preaching, which do indeed narrate God's powerful works in the world. This
'apophatic shorthand' has a most remarkable rhetorical effect which is
much stronger than a recital of the narrative. The declaration of 'inde-
scribability' becomes itself a compact, rhetorical shorthand for the gospel,
the previously described and now assumed narrative of God's saving acts
in Jesus Christ.

4. *Conclusion*

This examination of the Corinthian correspondence has demonstrated that
Paul grounds his arguments solidly upon an underlying gospel narrative,
which he accesses through various forms of rhetorical shorthand—brevity

of expression, synecdoche, and metaphor. Though Paul is thoroughly consistent in his frame of reference—the gospel narrative—his references to it are fluid and flexible. Because these shorthand formulations are geared for each specific argumentative context and purpose, they are essential clues for exegesis, and deserve careful and sustained attention. Paul's punctuated abbreviations unite his readers with himself and one another in a common bond of shared language and assumptions, a task central to the formation of ecclesial self-identity and social cohesion, and at the same time allow for elegant economy of expression in the new literary creations, the letters.

DALE B. MARTIN

Paul without Passion: On Paul's Rejection of Desire in Sex and Marriage (1997)†

Paul was apparently not a very romantic fellow. While most modern Christians consider marriage the proper sphere for the expression of desire (perhaps we should specify *heterosexual* desire), Paul considered marriage a mechanism by which desire could be extinguished. In Paul's view, unlike that of some other ascetic-oriented writers of his day, sex was not so much the problem as desire. And sexual intercourse within the bounds of marriage functioned to keep desire from happening. Sex within marriage was not the expression of desire, proper or improper; rather it was the prophylaxis against desire.

Paul's particular brand of asceticism, the control of desire, is not exactly like other ancient attempts to control it. But a comparison with some of those other attempts shows, in the first place, that Paul was not absolutely peculiar in the ancient world in his belief that sexual desire could and should be completely extirpated, even by means of sexual intercourse if necessary. As other scholars have pointed out, Stoics also advocated sex without desire. In the second place, such a comparison shows that the precise structure of Paul's asceticism—his assumptions about its meanings, his reasons for it, and the ways he believes desire can and ought to be controlled—is different from that of others. This essay will compare Paul's rationality of desire and its avoidance with those of ancient medical writers, on the one hand, and Stoics, on the other. The control of desire was a common concern in the early Roman Empire, at least among many intellectuals, but the logics or rationalities underwriting such control differed among different social groups.

The Extirpation of Desire in Paul's Writings

The key passage that brings out Paul's position is 1 Corinthians 7, which is devoted to the argument that people who are too weak for celibacy should get married, and that people who are strong enough for celibacy

† From "Paul without Passion," first published in *Constructing Early Christian Families*, ed. by Halvor Moxnes (London and New York: Routledge, 1997), 201–15. Copyright © 1997, Routledge. Reprinted by permission of Taylor & Francis Books UK. Martin is Woolsey Professor of Religious Studies at Yale University.

should remain unmarried and chaste. A central point in Paul's argument is an enigmatic statement in which he urges marriage for those who are 'out of control'. They should get married, he says, because 'it is better to marry than to burn' (1 Cor. 7:9). Taking the 'burning' here as a reference to eschatological judgment is possible but not, in the end, compelling. Throughout the chapter Paul is concerned about the here and now of people who are having trouble controlling their sexual desires (7:2, 5, 9, 36). The theme of judgment, though playing a role elsewhere in 1 Corinthians, has not been mentioned in this section and plays little part in Chapter 7. Furthermore, as I have argued elsewhere, conceiving sexual desire as a 'burning' within the body, metaphorically and physically, was so common in Paul's day, as seen in medical, magical, physiological, philosophical, and 'artistic' texts, that it is unimaginable that Graeco-Roman readers would have missed such a reference here. In fact, Paul elsewhere (as I will analyse further below) quite clearly speaks of sexual desire as a burning (Rom. 1:27). Even if we decide that Paul's 'burning' of 1 Corinthians 7 includes a reference to eschatological judgment, we cannot exclude a reference here to sexual passion and desire.

This means, of course, that Paul believed that it was not only possible but preferable, in fact, *necessary* that Christians experience sexual intercourse only within the context of marriage and only in the absence of sexual passion and desire. As remarkable as this may be for modern people, it seems to be the case. Paul can, indeed, use the term 'desire' (*epithymia*) in a morally neutral sense, as when he says that he 'desires' to see someone or do something (Phil. 1:23; 1 Thess. 2:17). But whenever Paul broaches the subject of sex and the desire associated with it, he has nothing good to say about it. In 1 Corinthians 7, for example, Paul nowhere mentions a positive kind of desire as opposed to the 'burning' that he hopes marriage will quench. He says that sex within marriage functions to guard weak Christians from the pollution of *porneia* (7:2); it is a duty Christian spouses owe to one another (7:3); and it protects Christians from Satanic testing (7:5). The romanticism of modern Christian (especially Protestant) attitudes about marriage—that it functions as the 'fulfillment' of divinely created and 'healthy' human sexuality, or at least heterosexuality; that it is the 'normal' outcome of love between a man and a woman; that human beings were practically created *for it*—is strikingly, though not surprisingly, absent. Paul's either/or of 7:9, therefore, should be taken seriously: marriage is the option for weak Christians who cannot otherwise avoid desire.

This complete exclusion of sexual desire is reflected in other Pauline passages. In 1 Thessalonians 4, Paul says that the will of God is the 'holiness' or 'sanctification' of the Thessalonians (*ho hagiasmos*), and the first issue threatening that holiness Paul mentions is *porneia*. Christian men should 'possess' their wives *not* in the passion of desire (*en pathei epithymias*) like the Gentiles who do not know God. As in 1 Corinthians, Paul is concerned about *porneia*, which is taken to be the characteristic sin of the Gentile world 'outside' the closed boundary of the body of Christ. The passion of sexual desire is part of the polluting complex of the cosmos that threatens the Church. The problem of *porneia* is that it is unclean (*akatharsia*: 4:7), as opposed to the holy *pneuma* of God that inhabits the Church. The passion of desire, therefore, is part of the dirty, polluted cosmos in opposition to God. The way to avoid the pollution is for men to possess and control their 'vessels' (their wives) as safe receptacles for their sexual overflow. But the idea that passion could be a part of that process is not entertained; in fact, it is excluded.

This connection of sexual desire with the Gentile world 'out there' is also important for Paul's interpretation of Numbers 11 in 1 Corinthians 10. The people of Israel, according to Paul's reading, pursued a catastrophic path from 'desire' (*epithymia*) to idolatry (v. 7) to *porneia* (v. 8) to 'testing Christ' and subsequent destruction (v. 9). Paul here stands in a long tradition of both Greek and Jewish placements of *epithymia* at the centre of the destructions wrought by the passions. For Paul, as for most Jewish writers on the subject, *epithymia* is linked particularly to idolatry. But for all sorts of writers, Greek, Roman, and Jewish, it was a problem. Moreover, as G. D. Collier has argued, in 1 Corinthians 10 *epithymia* 'is not merely one of the listed sins, but *the source* of sin to be explicated'. What follows in Paul's argument, his warning about idolatry, *porneia*, and rebellion, is simply a 'spelling out' of the passion of desire.

This 'downhill slide' from desire to destruction occurs also in Romans 1, which is again a place where the uncleanness of *porneia*, idolatry, Gentiles, and sexual passion are connected in Paul's argument. Many readers have taken Paul's comments in Romans 1 to refer only to homosexual desire. But this is a tendentious reading prompted by a modern urge to condemn homosexual desire while sparing heterosexual desire. Paul's argument actually does not differentiate between the two kinds of desire, which is understandable when we recognise that desire itself is the problem for Paul, not just what moderns call 'homosexual' desire.

Whereas the sequence in 1 Corinthians 10 was from desire to idolatry to *porneia* to destruction, in Romans 1 the rebellion of idolatry comes first, which merely demonstrates that Paul is less concerned about the *order* of events than the general complex of idolatry, *porneia*, and passion, and their connection to the Gentile world that must be rejected by Christians. Due to their wilful rejection of the true God and preference for idolatry and polytheism, God 'gave up' the Gentiles 'in the desires [*epithymiai*] of their hearts into uncleanness' (1:24). That this reference to *epithymia* includes sexual passion is confirmed by the parallel statement in v. 26, where 'passions of dishonor' express themselves sexually. In v. 27 we have the reference to the 'burning' of the Gentiles' urge (*orexis*) for one another. Here as elsewhere, *epithymia* and *pathos*, when referring to sexual desires, are in a complex of idolatry, *porneia*, pollution, and the Gentile world from which Christians need protection.

Modern Christian interpreters of Paul, often wishing to find some Pauline support for modern notions of romance and marriage, read all these texts as condemning not sexual desire in general but illicit, unnatural, or excessive passions. Paul *must* have had, so the thinking goes, a notion of good, healthy, heterosexual desire; otherwise, why get married at all? Why have sex at all? But I argue that such appeals to what 'must' have been the case just beg the question. The worst historians and cultural anthropologists often appeal to 'common sense' or what 'must' be the case; even good scholars appeal to such arguments when they have no evidence. But all such appeals are problematic. Rather than insisting on what 'must' have been the case based on modern common sense, we would do better to look for structures of plausibility in the ancient world by which the absence of sexual desire would be not only possible but preferable.

Medical and Aristotelian Control of Desire

The medical writers of Paul's day would have found his extreme position puzzling. They also viewed sexual desire as dangerous. They speak of it as a disease, in particular, a disease of burning, and they offer therapies and regimens to control the burning of desire. But they would have considered any absolute avoidance of desire to be impossible. For the medical doctors, the disease of desire sprang from the natural heat of the body, and any body, to be alive at all, had to have some heat. Health was the appropriate balance (dry and moist, hot and cold) of the constituents and dispositions of the body, usually including the body's elements, like the humours. What needed to be kept in balance was debated by doctors and scientists, but they pretty much all agreed that balance was health. * * * A complete quenching of heat would mean death. Furthermore, the doctors were in service to those male heads-of-households who paid the bills, and those men were almost all interested, at least to some degree, in producing babies. According to the dominant theories of sex, the heat of desire was necessary for the concoction of sperm or semen. Some doctors understood semen as the foam from concocted blood and *pneuma*, the most powerful material of the body, that resulted from the natural coming together of these different corporeal elements. Others explained that semen came from the concoction of humours. Still others held that the friction of sex itself caused the foam. In all cases, however, the heat of desire, as either the compulsion towards friction or the friction that led to compulsion, was essential for ejaculation (and for most of the doctors, it seems, both men and women had to produce semen for pregnancy to result). No more heat would mean no more semen and no more progeny. And for a Graeco-Roman householder, that was usually unacceptable.

So doctors taught their patients how to control the heat of desire in themselves, and especially in their wives and daughters. Rufus, who lived perhaps slightly later than Paul, wrote an entire 'Regimen for Virgins' guaranteed to ensure that young girls would not get too hot before they reached marriageable age (12, for Rufus). Soranus, another physician roughly contemporaneous with Paul, believed that the most healthy route for both men and women was the complete avoidance of sex. (He seems to have been in the minority on this.) This did not mean, however, that they could completely avoid the burning of desire. So Soranus gives advice and prescriptions intended to contain and control the disease of desire, the heat of passion.

Physicians weren't the only ones with these beliefs. Plutarch, for example, follows the Aristotelian tradition that says that desires and appetites are placed in the body by nature to assure that the body will get what it needs. There are different kinds of desires, of course. Those that arise from the body and relate to simple urges like that for food or sex are natural and need only be controlled, not extirpated. Only the fantastic and unnatural desires that arise from the mind when undisciplined must be avoided entirely (*De tuenda sanitate praecepta: Mor.* 125B; Aristotle, *Nichoma-*

chean Ethics 3.11.1, 1118b8; 7.2.6, 1146a10). Control and moderation are urged. To be most healthy, one should eat moderately, avoid working to exhaustion, and preserve one's 'spermatic substance' (129F; see also 129E; 125D). Plutarch even criticises those therapists, including perhaps the more strenuous Stoics, who are too rigorous, urging cold baths or periodic fasting on a fixed schedule. Little wonder, then, that Plutarch never advocates either the complete avoidance of sex or the extirpation of desire. As Plutarch says, people ought 'to preserve that natural constitution of our bodies, recognizing that every life has room for both disease and health' (135D; trans. F. C. Babbitt).

The Stoic Control of Desire

In her recent book *The Therapy of Desire* (1994), Martha Nussbaum calls the view I have just outlined the Aristotelian or Peripatetic position. In quite self-conscious opposition to it, according to Nussbaum, were the Stoics. Rather than taking passion or emotion as a natural compulsion that arises out of necessity, the Stoics, in this case Zeno (according to Diogenes Laertius 7.110), took it as irrational and unnatural. Seneca admits that the wise man will experience 'shadows of passion' (*umbras affectuum*), but from passion itself he will be completely free (*De ira* 1.16.7). The Stoics also think of desire as disease, and so they mock the Peripatetics, who would then seem to suggest that one might be content to be just a *little* ill. No, a man with even a slight fever is still sick. If health is what we are after, we will seek complete freedom from the disease of desire, the complete extirpation of the passions (*Ep.* 85.3–4; 116).

Sexual love, Seneca explains, is particularly a state of disorder, as anyone who has experienced it can attest; it is a lack of control, like slavery (*Ep.* 116.5; see also Cicero, *Tusculan Disputations* 35.75; 4.11.25–7). Thus one must learn to have sex without love, without passion, without desire. And one *can* learn this. In fact, the real disagreement, according to Seneca, is about the *ability* of a human being to attain such a free, stable existence without the passions. Critics of the Stoics claim that such a state is against human nature. Seneca claims just the opposite: yes, we can! The real reason, according to Seneca, that Stoic ideas are rejected by other philosophers is because they are too enamoured of their vices. The nature of a human being is to be rational and free. Only with the extirpation of the passions, including sexual desire, can we be free and self-sufficient (see e.g. *Ep.* 116.7).

The Stoics, like Paul, do not think this means an end to marriage or sex. The goal, and they seem to believe it is attainable at least by the wise man, is to have sex without desire. A favourite slogan among later ascetic Christians like Jerome had its origin among the Stoics: 'The man who loves his wife too much is also an adulterer'. The good Stoic will be a good citizen, a member of the community of humanity, and therefore he will marry, have children, participate in society. But he must do all of these things without suffering from *pathos* or *epithymia*. He must completely extirpate desires.

For the question, 'how could or why would a person have sex at all without any compulsion to do so?' the Stoics had an answer, following a lead from Aristotle. They taught that the natural compulsion for intercourse, like that for food, did spring from nature and that human beings shared these impulses with animals (who were not rational beings and therefore could not experience passions or emotions, which are 'misjudgments', and not possible for non-rational beings; see Diogenes Laertius 7.85, 110). But the natural impulse is not *pathos* or *epithymia*; it is *hormê*, which occurs in plants and animals as well as humans. All living beings have an impulse to self-preservation placed there by nature. This includes hunger and an impulse towards self-propagation through sex. Giving in to such an impulse is no more immoral than scratching an itch. But this impulse must not be confused with that harmful and dangerous emotion that people experience when they fall in love or feel as if they can't live without that special someone. The line between 'impulse' and 'desire' is a fine but important one. The wise man may follow the natural, unemotional impulse to propagate, like, say, an impulse to defecate. But to get too involved in it is disgusting and harmful. In fact, it is 'sick'.

The Stoics offered a system of therapy, based on discussion, reasoning, self-questioning, analysis, and critique of conventional beliefs, by which anyone with a strong enough will could learn to control and finally extirpate the passions: grief, pleasure, anger, and desires of all kinds. They claimed to be able to teach people how to live lives of self-control and self-sufficiency. They offered *eudaimonia*, a word difficult to translate but meaning something like well-being, contentedness, happiness, the 'blessed' life. Furthermore, according to Nussbaum, the philosophers (the Stoics and other schools as well) offered their therapy as an alternative to other, perhaps more popular methods of attaining 'the good life', that is, therapies of desire practised by doctors, popular healers, astrologers, priests and other religious leaders, to mention a few.

Desire and Rationality(-ies)

As I hinted at the beginning of this chapter, Nussbaum's account of the Stoics' therapy of desire is important for me because it presents another system of thought in the Graeco-Roman world that advocated, and believed possible, the complete extirpation of sexual desire even within the sexual activities of marriage. What may appear highly improbable and perhaps impossible to modern readers, and to ancient doctors, was quite possible at least to some segment of ancient society. Nussbaum's account is also important because it helps us place Paul's position in relation to other therapies of desire in ancient culture. We have here, to simplify somewhat, three different understandings of desire and its treatment: the physicians', the Stoics', and Paul's.

All three treat desire like a disease and agree that it is dangerous. With the Stoics, Paul shares the belief that the complete extirpation of desire is both possible and preferable, even within sexual relations in marriage. But along with the doctors, Paul would doubtless reject the Stoics' doctrine that complete self-sufficiency is possible, since both Paul and the physicians take the self to be a part of its environment and too constituted by that environment to be able to achieve radical self-sufficiency. The Stoics and the medical writers, however, would share a belief that self-sufficiency is an *ideal* towards which people may strive. Only Paul's position, of these three, takes marriage to be a tool for guarding against desire. And Paul, against both other positions, would certainly reject self-sufficiency as an ideal towards which Christians should strive. This is such an important point that I will return to it later.

What are the more fundamental differences among these three therapies? How or why did these people arrive at these particular differences in understandings and treatments of desire? Nussbaum's answer to such questions is that the philosophical position (and I will concentrate on the Stoics as more important for Paul's position as well as the one given most attention by Nussbaum) differs from all other ancient therapies of desire because it is, well, philosophical. By that she means it is 'rational', it cures the patient by means of discourse rather than drugs, and by critical reasoning rather than miracles or salvation. For Nussbaum, philosophy is basically 'the pursuit of logical validity, intellectual coherence, and truth', and it will deliver 'freedom from the tyranny of custom and convention'. Religious and other therapies depend on dogma, conventional beliefs, or external agents, whether they be divinities, demons, doctors, or drugs. Only philosophy offers a therapy that depends on the rationality of the self; therefore it is *the* rational therapy.

This argument about rationality is difficult to evaluate because, for one thing, Nussbaum actually uses 'rationality' in two different ways in the book. When attempting to define or describe philosophy or rationality, she concentrates on issues of procedure, not the actual content of beliefs. Thus, rationality or reason is the process of seeking truth by questioning; it is dialogical, open-ended with regard to results, free from custom and convention, non-dogmatic. It scrutinises assumptions and the self and is open to self-revision at every point. It avoids prejudice by employing critical thinking and examining every issue from every relevant perspective. This kind of definition, however, is unusable for comparative purposes, as can be seen when one notes the 'question begging' terms that inevitably occur in such definitions. For example, *how* open to any possible end must one be before being accepted as rational? *How* critical must one be of *how many* assumptions? In any actual situation, I would argue, no one can be truly open to *any* possible end nor completely critical of *all* assumptions, given our own contingency and finitude. The parameters of possibility are simply set to some extent. To cite another example, who gets to decide what is or is not a 'relevant' perspective? We would certainly have to admit that no one could consider *all* possible perspectives on an ethical issue, since perspective, as the very mathematical metaphor reveals, is as infinite as the number of possible fractions. These are only examples, but similar question-begging conditions occur in each section where Nussbaum tries to describe 'rationality' by concentrating purely on method in the abstract.

The other way Nussbaum speaks of rationality or reason is more revealing but just as problematic. Throughout the book Nussbaum uses these terms to refer not to a method for arriving at truths but to particular truths themselves. There simply *are* beliefs that are rational, and most of the time Nussbaum makes no attempt to argue *for* the rationality of such beliefs from the ground up. A list of such cases is revealing. Rational positions are those that assume the existence of a stable individual self. Even though human beings live within society and should be part of it, they are individually free beings with free will and capable of free moral agency. Rationality will convince these free agents that they possess universal citizenship and have available to them universal rationality. That is, every human being of all places and times has the ability (at least) to reason alike, and if they would just do so they would arrive at the same truth. Also rational is a belief in the equality of the sexes. Rationality is critical of cultural assumptions, society, and convention. It is naturalistic, which is to say that all things in the universe must be understood to operate by similar mechanisms, the mechanics of 'nature'. Thus rationality may admit a notion of religion or the divine, but only one that would not threaten the freedom of the individual. In fact, a rational belief in divinity (if any is needed) recognises the divine within the human person. The one exception permitted by Nussbaum to this free, stable self, open and visible to itself and subject to its own rule is the presence of the unconscious. But even the unconscious can be accessed and controlled to a great extent by procedures that sound remarkably like modern psychotherapy. The existence of the unconscious therefore offers no real threat to the possibility of a stable, free self.

So whereas rationality sometimes refers to a method for arriving at truth, at other times it refers to actual truths with little or no attention given to the method by which these beliefs came to be accepted as true. There is, though, no contradiction here, because Nussbaum really believes that if human beings—any, anywhere, any time—pursued these methods they would arrive at these truths. In my opinion, this is a 'faith statement' which, although it may be true, can be supported neither by empirical comparative evidence (experience) nor by some abstract argument that uses universal criteria of reasonableness ('rationality'). Indeed, Nussbaum seems to recognise that her position is more akin to faith than knowledge when she admits that someone like Michel Foucault would find her confidence that rationality can make us free, to be an illusion—but, she insists, she still *believes* it.

As my comments reveal, I find this appeal to rationality insufficient for explaining the differences among Paul, the doctors, and the Stoics. I want to argue, rather, that each position is rational in a sense, and that we can see its rationality when we analyse the therapy in light of its different assumptions about the world and the self. Paul's position, for example, would be rejected by both the doctors and the Stoics as hopelessly uneducated and superstitious. As I have shown elsewhere, educated people in the Graeco-Roman world rejected fears of pollution from outside agents as superstition. Rather than following a 'logic of invasion' when thinking about disease, they thought of disease along the lines of a 'logic of imbalance'; disease was the result of an imbalance of the body's normal states and elements. Thus all Paul's concerns in 1 Corinthians that the Church, the body of Christ, might be polluted by idol meat, *porneia*, or desire itself would have appeared ignorant and naive to them. Although the doctors would also have rejected the radical self-sufficiency advocated by the Stoics, they would have assumed that moderate self-sufficiency was a natural ideal. But to accept notions about polluting demons and invading diseases would have posed an unacceptable challenge to the secure, stable, sufficient self that was at least an ideal for upper-class intellectuals in general. Thus their therapies of desire are understandable within the context of their views of the body and the world. And within their system, Paul's fears are irrational.

We can only imagine how Paul would critique their view, especially the more radical Stoic view of self-sufficiency. For rhetorical purposes, Paul can claim self-sufficiency. He tells the Philippians, for instance, that he appreciates their gift but didn't exactly *need* it, since he is *autarkês* and lacks nothing (Phil. 4:11). But this rhetoric carries none of the freight for Paul that it would for the philosophers. Paul readily admits his absolute dependence on God and explicitly rejects the notion that human beings can be self-sufficient: 'Not that we are sufficient (*hikanoi*) of ourselves so that we could consider anything as really ours; rather our sufficiency comes from God' (2 Cor. 3:5–6; note the emphatic placement of 'not' (*ouch*) at the beginning of the sentence). There is no attempt by Paul to establish or protect a stable, secure self. While Christians are 'at home in the body' they are 'away from their home that is the Lord' (2 Cor. 5:6). Even Christ is not thought of as independent and self-sufficient. Note, for example, the thick inter-connections of being in Paul's statement that Christ 'died for all, so that those who live live no longer for themselves but with regard to the one who died and was raised for them' (2 Cor. 5:15). Christ's existence is 'for' others; because of what he did 'for' them, the others no longer live 'for' themselves. Such frank admissions of mutual dependence would be scorned by the Stoics.

Desire, Self-Sufficiency, and Ideology

The Stoics' rejection of the passions is based on their ideal of self-sufficiency and their belief that true well-being could be had only by exercising self-control. The passions threatened the perfect control over their bodies, and indeed, their world, for which they yearned. I would argue, moreover, that of the passions desire was in some ways a special threat because it was a constant signal of need—*in*sufficiency. According to both Aristotelian and early Stoic theory, the 'urge' for food and sex was placed by nature in the body to meet its 'needs'. Desire arose from unnatural confusions surrounding those needs and urges. Desire, therefore, signifies 'lack', and this was a painful confession for Graeco-Roman philosophers. True nobility was a self-sufficient, just like the ancient aristocratic ideal of the self-sufficient household which was capable of growing all its own food, making all its own clothes and utensils, and running its own day-to-day affairs with no interference of any kind. Like the southern American plantation owner of later times, the Graeco-Roman *paterfamilias* nourished an ideal of his own private community. And his body was a microcosm of that self-sufficient community. To recognise that he needed a woman to further his line was something of a shameful surprise, but it was, after all, part of 'nature'. The goal was to fill this lack in such a way as to demonstrate as little lack as possible within himself. Men had many ideological stratagems for getting over what appeared to be an insurmountable lack in nature and their bodies. One example is the Aristotelian theory, eventually rejected by perhaps most doctors, that all the requisite seed for the embryo came from the man, with the woman being only the fertile field in which the important substance was planted. All such theories, in any case, were attempts to minimise the experience of lack, the sign that constantly pointed to the illusion of self-sufficiency.

The entire ideological complex of the self-sufficient man and the stable self is absent in Paul's writings. The reality of 'lack' is recognised all through his letters: Epaphroditus supplies what the Philippians lack (Phil. 2:30); the abundance of the Corinthians supplies what other Christians lack (2 Cor. 8:15); Paul wants to visit the Thessalonians to supply what they are lacking (1 Thess. 3:10). Furthermore, Paul doubtless would have none of that 'moderation' so important to the philosophers. He constantly uses language celebrating both lack and abundance, even 'over-abundance'. The philosophical idea, for example, that too much love is a bad thing would have struck Paul, as it doubtless struck most people in that society, as ridiculous.

But not only would Paul have rejected the *ideal* of self-sufficiency; he also would have believed it absolutely impossible. For Paul, every human being receives its identity by virtue of its place, either in 'this cosmos' or Christ. Christians live by the pneuma of Christ; non-Christians have only the pneuma of 'this world'. Furthermore, every self, even Christian ones, can be threatened by disintegration due to a variety of cosmic forces: the death-dealing of *sarx*, the pollution of *porneia*, even the poison that Christ's body becomes when eaten unworthily. Moreover, however we settle the tricky question of Paul's views on predestination or free will, no one can persuasively argue that Paul would have believed possible the radical kind of free choice so necessary for Stoic doctrine and therapy. Paul can speak of human beings, even Christians, as predestined by God (Rom. 9–11), as hopelessly deluded apart from God's grace and revelation (1 Cor. 2:6–6; 3:18–23), or as hindered by Satan from carrying out their wills (1 Thess. 2:18). Any part of this Pauline complex renders impossible the free will and free moral agency necessary for Stoicism. Thus both the ideal and the possibility of a stable self would be rejected by Paul as illusions.

What started out in this chapter as a comparison of beliefs about desire, sex, and marriage has become an analysis of complex ideological systems. But that is what I believe is necessary for an adequate interpretation of the ancient therapies of desire. Paul's position would doubtless have been rejected by the ancient philosophers and doctors as irrational. But for a modern scholar to be satisfied with that verdict is inadequate. Paul had very good reasons, given his own assumptions about the world and the human self, to fear sexual desire as a polluting force that threatened the health of the Christian's body and Christ's body. His insistence that desire must be excluded entirely, even within sex in marriage, was reasonable—just as reasonable, in fact, as the Stoics' radical position was within their own system, based as it was on a belief in the possibility of a stable self-sufficiency. Both systems, from different rationalities, taught that sexual desire, even within sex, must be extirpated.

One of Martha Nussbaum's goals in writing *The Therapy of Desire* (1994) was to convince modern readers, especially post-religious, liberal Americans, that ancient moral philosophy can provide a method and concepts useful for modern ethics. She finds the Stoics especially appealing, with the proviso that their insistence on complete self-sufficiency and the extirpation of desires is too radical. She would take up, to some extent, the Stoic cause, and she believes that cause to be a good one as long as one adds in a bit of compassion.

I don't believe that's such a good idea, mainly because it either ignores the ancient ideological context and function of their system, or it insists, wrongly I believe, that their therapeutic system can be divorced from the negative aspects of its ideological assumptions. Although Nussbaum begins by noting that ancient philosophy must be studied with a view to society and culture, there is actually very little attention to culture in this book and none to ideology. And that is its problem. In my view, the ancient aristocratic ideal of self-sufficiency was possible only within a context of slavery and exploitation. Indeed, it is hard to imagine the conditions for the rise of that ideal except in a society where a small portion of the population could mask its own great dependence on other human beings by rendering them less human. The extent to which a *paterfamilias* could convince himself that he was or could be self-sufficient was the extent to which he could close his eyes to the thick matrices of economic and social systems on which he unavoidably depended. Self-sufficiency as an ideal requires just such ideological ignorance. The ancient philosophical therapies of desire depend on notions of self-sufficiency and fear of lack; the therapies don't make sense without such presupposed values. And these values are anything but democratic and egalitarian. Of course, from a Christian point of view, and I think this is not just Paul's view, self-sufficiency is neither possible nor desirable. I also find it hard to imagine how a philosopher these days can so confidently *assume* the existence of a stable integrated self capable of exercising free moral agency, given current biomedical and biochemical research, genetic engineering, post-structuralist psychological theories, philosophies of the mind based on artificial intelligence, and studies showing the disintegration of the self through pain and torture.

In the end, I believe the myth of self-sufficiency is especially dangerous for Americans, with our tendency to splendid isolation and self-centredness and our uncanny ability to fail to notice our domination of and dependence on other countries and our own lower class. Americans, 'liberal' and 'conservative' alike, are already far too enamoured of the myth that social problems can be solved by individualism and volunteerism. I understand why a liberal democratic American philosopher like Nussbaum would find 'self-sufficiency' an appealing goal. But I also believe that it plays into the worst aspects of modernist individualism, capitalist ideology, and American lies about the self-saving self.

Is Paul's account of desire, sex, and marriage any better? Not for me, thanks. Given our own probably unshakeable modern assumptions about love, sex, romance, and desire, we perhaps could never wholeheartedly accept the possibility, much less the desirability, of sex without desire. It is significant that no modern Christian church has attempted even to recognise, let alone appropriate, Paul's ethics of sexuality here. And I would not advocate that it do so. Both Nussbaum's advocacy of ancient philosophy and some Christians' belief that our sexual ethics should come rather simplistically 'from the Bible' are just different forms of Classicism, which in my view is nostalgic and self-deluding. I do not understand why modern persons would want to ground their own therapies of desire on either the ancient philosophers or Paul. I suppose I'm too much a post-modernist to find real Classicism alluring, whether in art, architecture, or morality.

Epilogue

WAYNE A. MEEKS

The Christian Proteus†

The significance of Paul for the development of European and American religious traditions can hardly be overestimated, however difficult it may be to describe the precise nature of his influence. Sydney Ahlstrom, the great historian of American religion, once wrote:

> Just as the European philosophical tradition, in Whitehead's famous phrase, consists of a series of footnotes to Plato, so Christian theology is a series of footnotes to St. Paul.[1]

That is not an overstatement, but it must be qualified by the reminder that footnotes can express many things: rejection, for instance, or bafflement, as well as agreement and expansion. Harnack was more judicious when he suggested, "One might write a history of dogma as a history of the Pauline *reactions* in the Church, and in doing so would touch on all the *turning points* of the history."[2] The history of Paulinism, as we have seen, contains a peculiar ambivalence. The "most holy apostle" of the sacred traditions is at the same time, again and again, "the apostle of the heretics." There is singular irony in the fact that the great system builders of Christian doctrine quarried their choicest propositions from Paul's letters, only to have later generations discover that they had thus built time-bombs into the structure that would, in a moment of crisis, bring the whole tower of syllogisms crashing down. Paul has become the foe of all authoritative systems. "Paulinism has proved to be a ferment in the history of dogma, a basis it has never been."[3]

The ferment of Paulinism has affected not only the history of dogma, but also broader realms of religious and cultural history, even political history, as the variety of interpretive essays collected in this volume illustrates. The more recent of these essays also make clear that the ferment has by no means subsided. As we look back over this diverse array of reactions to the apostle, a new question arises, which was not so urgent in earlier centuries as it has become in our time. Where among these multiple pictures of Paul and his influence is the real Paul to be found? Or is the

---

† I wrote "The Christian Proteus" for the first edition; I have shortened and revised it for the present edition.
1. Sydney E. Ahlstrom, *Theology in America: The Major Protestant Voices from Puritanism to Neo-Orthodoxy* (Indianapolis: Bobbs-Merrill, 1967), 23.
2. Adolf von Harnack, *History of Dogma*, vol.1, translated by Neil Buchanan (New York: Dover, 1961), 136, italics added.
3. Ibid.

question itself, when posed against this history of "strong misreadings" (as the literary critic Harold Bloom might call them), not itself naive? Do the methods of modern historical research enable us to nail down the identity of any figure of the past—and are not our own identities fatefully intertwined with the attempt?

It is easy enough to see in some of the images of Paul that we have surveyed the results of willful distortion or, more often, of unconscious imposition of preconceptions. As we reconsider our own and our contemporaries' attempts to make sense of the man behind those images, we are apt to lament the paucity of information, or the failure of imagination, or the excess of imagination where information is wanting. But none of these factors nor all of them together quite suffice to explain the most persistent perplexity. There is no figure in the first generation of Christianity about whom we know so much as about Paul—and precisely at the points where he reveals most about himself we are most puzzled. The polar tendencies of the interpretations of Paul may suggest that there is something polar in the person being interpreted. He once wrote about himself:

> Free from all, to all I became a slave, that I might win over the greater number. I became to the Jews as a Jew, that I might win over Jews; to people under law, as one under law, though I'm not myself under law, that I might win those under law. To people without law, I became as one without law, though I am not without God's law but rather, belonging to Christ, standing within the law. To the weak I became weak, that I might win over the weak. To all people I became all things, that I might by all means save some—and I do it all for the sake of the gospel . . . .[4]

This rhetorical statement is no mere admission of tactical disguises. The conditions that Paul lists are not superficial customs that the missionary could adopt in order to gain a better hearing with a given cultural group. Rather, each goes to the heart of that group's identity, either in its own eyes or in those of others. For the Jewish Christians in Galatia, to be "under the law" was a prerequisite for salvation; for the Corinthian spirituals, to be free from the law was the sign of exalted status. "The weak" were those whose consciences were still torn by anxieties over religious taboos, and who tried to impose their own scrupulosity on the liberty of the strong-minded, who in turn disdained the weak. In each case Paul vigorously opposed the condition named, when it threatened to fragment the vibrant but vulnerable little groups that he called "the holy ones" and "God's town meeting." Yet here he tells us that he could himself adopt each of these conditions (though the "as" in three of the cases is not to be overlooked) when that served his purpose to gain adherents to "the gospel."[5]

4. 1 Cor. 9:19–23, my trans.
5. For ways Paul's self-designation as "enslaved leader" might have been heard by his contemporaries, see Dale B. Martin, *Slavery as Salvation: The Metaphor of Slavery in Pauline Christianity* (New Haven: Yale University Press, 1990). On philosophical dimensions of his argument, Abraham J. Malherbe, "Determinism and Free Will in Paul: The Argument of 1 Corinthians 8 and 9," in *Paul in His Hellenistic Context*, edited by Troels Engberg-Pedersen (Minneapolis: Fortress Press, 1995), 231–55. On the rhetorical function of 1 Cor. 9:19–23 in the argument of the whole letter, Margaret Mary Mitchell, *Paul and the Rhetoric of Reconciliation: An Exegetical Investigation of the Language and Composition of 1 Corinthians* (Louisville: Westminster/John Knox, 1992). On ethical implications of Paul's strategy, see Wayne A. Meeks, "The Polyphonic Ethics of the Apostle Paul," in *In Search of the Early Christians: Selected Essays*, edited by Allen R. Hilton and H. Gregory Snyder (New Haven; London: Yale University Press, 2002), 196–209. For insight into ways ancient

Clearly then, Paul's adaptation to the positions of the contending parties did not involve his capitulation to them. Rather, when he became "as one under the law," it was only in order to insist to those under the law that Christ had replaced the law as the way to reconciliation with God. When he became "as a lawless one," it was to insist that "we must all still stand before the tribunal of Christ." The Paul who was "all things to all people" was the same man who could shout down the compromising Peter at Antioch (Gal. 2:11–14) and hurl anathemas at angels and men who might dare to deviate from "his gospel" (Gal. 1:8 f.). Polemics were just as important in Paul's missionary and pastoral methods as were apologetics. He veered from one side to another not only in order to approach different audiences, but in order to *resist* different points of view that he thought inimical to the peace and unity of the faithful.

Consequently anyone who wishes to understand Paul must recognize the large part that the objections of his opponents and the misunderstandings of his allies and friends played in shaping his literary bequest. We never see pure Pauline thought being developed at leisure by its own inner logic; rather we see Paul always thinking under pressure, usually in the heat of immediate controversy. It would be an illusion to suppose that the "real" Paul could be filtered out of this disconcerting ebb and flow by the proper logical analysis or psychoanalytic theory. The real Paul is to be found precisely in the dialectic of his apparent inconsistencies. Paul is the Christian Proteus.

Homer's Proteus was a demigod, a *daimōn* of the sea who could assume any form he chose. When Menelaos and his men seized him, hoping to learn from the Old Man the way of escape to their distant homeland,

> First he turned into a great bearded lion,
>   and then to a serpent, then to a leopard, then to a
>   great boar,
> and he turned into fluid water, to a tree with towering
>   branches. . . . [6]

Only when the captors had clung undaunted to the many-formed daimon, compelling him to resume again his human shape, did he answer their questions—and then not until *he* had questioned *them*.

As we look back over the history of readings and misreadings of the Pauline letters, we see that believers, critics, and historians alike have failed to immobilize the Christian Proteus. Therein lies the first of the troubling questions he puts to us, but therein also may be hidden a hopeful sign, yet another lesson to be learned from the enigmatic apostle. The question goes to the heart of our confidence, as modern men and women, that we, better than all who went before us, can know the meaning of the past. Our vaunted objectivity, the universality of our reasoning, the efficacy of our methods are all in question. The aim of the modernist project that, beginning in the eighteenth century, came to dominate the writing of history in the nineteenth and twentieth centuries, was to free ourselves, by

---

readers would have heard Paul's "condescension," Margaret M. Mitchell, "Pauline Accommodation and 'Condescension' (συγκατάβασις): 1 Cor 9:19–23 and the History of Influence," in *Paul Beyond the Judaism/Hellenism Divide*, edited by Troels Engberg-Pedersen (Louisville, KY: Westminster John Knox, 2001), 197–214, 298–309.

6. *Ody.* 4.456–8, tr. by Richmond Lattimore, *The Odyssey of Homer* (New York: Harper, 1967).

the sheer power of our rationality and the austerity of our method, from traditions and dogmas and the institutions that sustained and lived by them. Thus, by seeing the past as it really was, we thought to find a secure starting place for knowing and valuing. Instead, we found texts and lives that are always open to interpretation. We discovered meaning to be dependent always on context. We found identity to be a social process. And we learned that we could not avoid involving ourselves whenever we attempted to assess historical events and personages in any non-trivial way.

The resultant instability of our knowledge owes as much to the successes of modern historiography as to its failures. If what we learned is not what we set out to learn, it is nevertheless not unimportant. On the one hand, we have made significant strides toward having the ability to read Paul in the specific context of life in the eastern Roman provinces of the first century. On the other, the history of the reception of Paul's letters and of his story impresses upon us both the malleability of their meaning and the unending variety of ways that readers have injected their own identities into the process of interpretation. Modernist historiography has succeeded in defamiliarizing the past—things then were not as they are now. Potentially this defamiliarization of things we thought we owned as *our* past can have the salutary effect of challenging our own provincialism as moderns. Our common sense is called into question as a cultural construct, like the different common sense of the ancients. And that sobering experience could open us to what is perhaps the most frightening and hopeful lesson the historic Paul could teach us: how a person could dare, propelled by the most profound loyalty to a tradition ancient, wonderful, and all-encompassing, to overleap that tradition's boundaries, to alter it radically in the name of an event wholly new and for the sake of those whom the tradition had hitherto defined as alien.

Paul was a Jew. But what kind of Jew was he? And when he had that prophetic vision that he describes variously as a "revelation," as "seeing the Lord Jesus," as being "appointed"—like the classical prophets of Israel—for a special task, was he "converted"? Did he join—or found—a new "religion"? Did he become "a Christian"? Slowly we have come to see these categories as anachronisms, and the question of Paul's Jewishness has become both much more complicated and more urgent. It is a question that touches not only on matters central to the identity of Christianity (a name absent from Paul's vocabulary) but also to the identity of Judaism. The essays in Parts VI and VII above illustrate both dimensions of the debate, and also suggest how fraught its terms have been with the history of polemics not only between Jews and Christians but also within each community.

In the mid-nineteenth century, in certain German academic circles, the terms "Judaism" and "Hellenism" became code words for two fundamentally opposed types of culture (see the Introduction to Part VI). According to a widespread construction of intellectual history, the collision between those two cultures, in the period between Alexander the Great and the end of the Roman Empire, produced those patterns of belief and practice that would guide the evolution of modern Western civilization. Theologians took up the schema with enthusiasm, and, with many variations and often opposite conclusions, it dominated twentieth-century reconstructions of early Christian history. Only very recently has the artificiality of the construction become apparent and its distorting effects on our understanding of ancient Judaism and ancient Christianity—and of Paul—begun to be dismantled.[7] We are now forced to recognize that there was no single "Judaism" in antiquity. Jews living in different parts of the early Roman Empire—Judaea and the Galilee, the Greek-speaking Diaspora in cities of the eastern provinces, the Latin colonies, villages and towns—adapted in many different ways to the challenges of Roman and Greek structures of power and styles of living, balancing accommodation and identity in ways analogous to many other ethnic communities, with endless local variations, some uniquely shaped by Israel's traditions, scriptures, and customs. And of this variety of ways of being Jewish, no one was "normative"—"normative Judaism" is an invention of modern scholarship, exaggerating the unity of the rabbinic establishment and projecting its eventual dominance back into a time when it had scarcely begun to take form as one alternative among many.[8] Attempts to define Paul by that template, whether by forcing him into the "normative" mold or by seeing him as a rebel against it, are therefore misleading. On the other hand, placing Paul's writings on our new, vastly more complicated and puzzling map of ways people found to live as Jews in the Greco-Roman world not only illuminates what Paul and the new converts to whom he wrote were doing and saying, it also sheds light on some of those other kinds of Jewishness. Certainly Paul was an unusual Jew, but his uniqueness was not absolute.

It is equally clear that Paul was at home in the Roman and "Hellenistic" world. Indeed his life and writings constitute a parade instance of the failure of the Judaism-versus-Hellenism antithesis by which last century's scholarship tried to define him and to explain the evolution of early Christianity. Even as some scholars were busy showing the Jewishness of Paul's method of scriptural interpretation, for example, or of his beliefs about God's actions in the end time, by comparing his writings with all kinds of Jewish documents, others were demonstrating the importance of comparing Greek and Roman literature. Topics discussed in the popular philosophical schools, standard forms of Greek letter-writing, tropes and whole topics and argumentative patterns taught in Greek rhetoric—all these and more appear in Paul's letters and would have signaled to a competent first-century audience ways the writer meant to be heard. Moreover, a generation of labor by social historians has vastly extended our understanding of everyday life in the Roman provinces and thus of the social forms of the Pauline communities and the social force of the letters by Paul and his disciples.

Not least among the things we learn from the attempt to lay hold of the protean apostle is that earliest Christianity was itself a polymorphous movement, often taking shape only in the forge of conflict. In this new millenium, when the future of Christianity and its relationship to Western culture have become almost as uncertain and paradoxical as they were before Constantine, a more accurate understanding of that crucial and complex first period of expansion may provide useful insight into our own

---

7. See Troels Engberg-Pedersen, ed., *Paul Beyond the Judaism/Hellenism Divide* (Louisville, KY: Westminster John Knox, 2001), especially chaps. 1–3.
8. The term "normative Judaism" was introduced by the Harvard historian of religions George Foot Moore in his classic work, *Judaism in the First Centuries of the Christian Era: The Age of the Tannaim* (Cambridge, MA: Harvard University Press, 1927), 1:125–6.

cultural flux. If so, the study of Paul and his context will have a central place. He embodies some elements that are peculiarly expressive of the Christian center: the dialectical character of his fundamental assertions; his waging of controversy for the sake of peace; his affirmation of the world in the name of what transcends and relativizes it; his speaking harsh truth for the sake of love; his exercise of severe discipline for the protection of freedom; his insistence that the power of God is experienced and transmitted only in weakness. One of his rhetorical catalogues of circumstances could stand as the superscription over the history of the Christian movement at its best:

> But we hold this treasure in earthenware pots, so it will be apparent that the transcendent power is God's and doesn't come from us. Afflicted in every way, yet not hemmed in; baffled, yet not despairing; persecuted, yet not abandoned; brought down, but not destroyed; always carrying around the death of Jesus in the body, in order that the life of Jesus may also become visible in our body. (2 Cor. 4:7–10, my trans.)

Selected Bibliography

This is intended as a working bibliography for undergraduate and beginning seminary students. It is therefore very brief and limited to works in English, except for section I, which will guide the advanced student into a broader range of scholarly literature. Works that have been excerpted above are not included here.

I. BIBLIOGRAPHIES AND REVIEWS OF RESEARCH

Mills, Watson E. *Bibliographies for Biblical Research: New Testament Series*, Vols. 5–15 (Lewiston, NY: Mellen, 1996–2002). Bibliographies for Acts-Philemon.
Baird, William. *History of New Testament Research* (2 vols., Minneapolis: Fortress, 1992–2003).
Plevnik, Joseph. *What Are They Saying about Paul?* (New York: Paulist, 1986).
Hübner, Hans. "Paulusforschung seit 1945: Ein kritischer Literaturbericht." In *Aufstieg und Niedergang der römischen Welt* II.25.4 (1987): 2649–2840.
Merk, Otto. "Paulus-Forschung 1936–1985." In *Theologische Rundschau* 53 (1988): 1–81.
Powell, Mark Allan. *What Are They Saying about Acts?* (New York: Paulist, 1991).
Riches, John K. "Recent Study of Paul." In *A Century of New Testament Study* (Cambridge: Lutterworth, 1993), 125–49.
Martin, Ralph P. *A Hymn of Christ: Philippians 2:5–11 in Recent Interpretation and in the Setting of Early Christian Worship* (Downers Grove, IL: Inter Varsity, 1997).
Harding, Mark. *What Are They Saying about the Pastoral Epistles?* (New York: Paulist, 2001).
Koperski, Veronica. *What Are They Saying about Paul and the Law?* (New York: Paulist, 2001).
To keep abreast of new publications, the database maintained by the American Theological Library Association and available on-line through subscribing libraries, is invaluable (ATLA Religion Database with ATLASerials).

II. PAUL'S LIFE AND THOUGHT

A. General Treatments and Collections of Essays

Barrett, C. K. *Essays on Paul* (Philadelphia: Westminster, 1982), *Paul: An Introduction to His Thought* (Louisville: Westminster John Knox, 1994), and *On Paul: Aspects of His Life, Work, and Influence in the Early Church* (London: T & T Clark, 2003).
Bassler, Jouette (ed.). *Pauline Theology, Volume I: Thessalonians, Philippians, Galatians, Philemon* (Minneapolis: Fortress, 1991).
Becker, Jürgen. *Paul: Apostle to the Gentiles*, tr. by O. C. Dean, Jr. (Louisville: Westminster John Knox, 1993).
Beker, J. Christiaan. *Paul the Apostle: The Triumph of God in Life and Thought* (Philadelphia: Fortress, 1980), and *Paul's Apocalyptic Gospel* (Philadelphia: Fortress, 1982).
Bruce, F. F. *Paul: Apostle of the Heart Set Free* (Grand Rapids: Eerdmans, 1977).
Dahl, Nils Alstrup. *Studies in Paul* (Minneapolis: Augsburg, 1971).
Davies, W. D. *Paul and Rabbinic Judaism* (4th ed.; Philadelphia: Fortress, 1980).
Dunn, James D. G. *The Theology of Paul the Apostle* (Grand Rapids: Eerdmans, 1998), *The Cambridge Companion to St. Paul* (Cambridge: Cambridge University Press, 2003), and *The New Perspective on Paul* (Tübingen: Mohr-Siebeck, 2005).
Fitzmyer, Joseph A., S.J. *Paul and His Theology: A Brief Sketch* (2nd ed.; Englewood Cliffs, NJ: Prentice-Hall, 1989), and *According to Paul: Studies in the Theology of the Apostle* (New York: Paulist, 1993).
Hay, David M. (ed.). *Pauline Theology, Volume II: 1 & 2 Corinthians* (Minneapolis: Fortress, 1993), and Hay and E. Elizabeth Johnson (eds.). *Pauline Theology, Volume III: Romans* (Minneapolis: Fortress, 1995).
Johnson, E. Elizabeth, and David M. Hay (eds.). *Pauline Theology, Volume IV: Looking Back, Pressing On* (Atlanta: Scholars, 1997).
Käsemann, Ernst. *Perspectives on Paul*, tr. by Margaret Kohl (Philadelphia: Fortress, 1971).
Keck, Leander E. *Paul and His Letters* (2nd ed., Philadelphia: Fortress, 1988).
Lambrecht, Jan. *Pauline Studies: Collected Essays* (Leuven: Leuven University Press, 1994).
Levine, Amy-Jill (ed.). *A Feminist Companion to the Deutero-Pauline Epistles* (Cleveland: Pilgrim, 2003), and *A Feminist Companion to Paul* (Cleveland: Pilgrim, 2004).

Malherbe, Abraham J. *Paul and the Thessalonians* (Philadelphia: Fortress, 1987).

Meeks, Wayne A. *The First Urban Christians: The Social World of the Apostle Paul* (2nd ed.; New Haven: Yale University Press, 2003), and *In Search of the Early Christians*, ed. by A. R. Hilton and H. G. Snyder (New Haven: Yale University Press, 2002).

Murphy-O'Connor, Jerome. *Paul: A Critical Life* (Oxford: Clarendon, 1996).

Neyrey, Jerome H. *Paul, in Other Words: A Cultural Reading of His Letters* (Louisville: Westminster John Knox, 1990).

Schnelle, Udo. *Apostle Paul: His Life and Theology* (Grand Rapids: Eerdmans, 2005).

Stendahl, Krister. *Paul among Jews and Gentiles* (Philadelphia: Fortress, 1977).

B. Chronology

Darr, John. "Chronologies of Paul." In *Paul's Faith and the Power of the Gospel*, by Daniel Patte (Philadelphia: Fortress, 1983), 352–60. Gives useful charts comparing different chronologies for Paul's life and letters. The charts are reprinted in Fred O. Francis and J. Paul Sampley, *Pauline Parallels* (2nd ed., Philadelphia: Fortress, 1984).

Jewett, Robert. *A Chronology of Paul's Life* (Philadelphia: Fortress, 1979).

Knox, John. *Chapters in a Life of Paul*, with an introduction by Douglas R. A. Hare (rev. ed., Macon, GA: Mercer University Press, 1987).

Lüdemann, Gerd. *Paul, Apostle to the Gentiles: Studies in Chronology*, tr. by F. Stanley Jones, with a foreword by John Knox (Philadelphia: Fortress, 1984).

C. Miscellaneous Topics

Deming, Will. *Paul on Marriage and Celibacy* (2nd ed.; Grand Rapids: Eerdmans, 2004).

Dunn, James D. G. (ed.). *Paul and the Mosaic Law* (Tübingen: Mohr-Siebeck, 1996).

Engberg-Pedersen, Troels (ed.). *Paul in His Hellenistic Context* (Minneapolis: Fortress, 1995), and *Paul beyond the Judaism/Hellenism Divide* (Louisville: Westminster John Knox, 2001), and *Paul and the Stoics* (Louisville: Westminster John Knox, 2000).

Fee, Gordon D. *God's Empowering Presence: The Holy Spirit in the Letters of Paul* (Peabody, MA: Hendrickson, 1994).

Furnish, Victor Paul. *Theology and Ethics in Paul* (Nashville: Abingdon, 1968), and *The Moral Teaching of Paul* (2nd ed.; Nashville: Abingdon, 1985).

Hays, Richard B. *Echoes of Scripture in the Letters of Paul* (New Haven: Yale University Press, 1989), and *The Moral Vision of the New Testament* (San Francisco: HarperCollins, 1996).

Hengel, Martin. *The Pre-Christian Paul* (Philadelphia: Fortress, 1991), and (with Anna Maria Schwemer), *Paul between Damascus and Antioch: The Unknown Years* (Louisville: Westminster John Knox, 1997).

Hock, Ronald F. *The Social Context of Paul's Ministry: Tentmaking and Apostleship* (Philadelphia: Fortress, 1980).

Jewett, Robert. *Saint Paul at the Movies: The Apostle's Dialogue with American Culture* (Louisville: Westminster John Knox, 1993), and *Saint Paul Returns to the Movies: Triumph over Shame* (Grand Rapids: Eerdmans, 1998).

Meeks, Wayne A. *The Moral World of the First Christians* (Philadelphia: Westminster, 1986), and *The Origins of Christian Morality: The First Two Centuries* (New Haven: Yale University Press, 1993).

Mitchell, Margaret M. *Paul and the Rhetoric of Reconciliation* (Tübingen: Mohr-Siebeck, 1991; Louisville: Westminster John Knox, 1992).

Rosner, Brian S. (ed.). *Understanding Paul's Ethics: Twentieth Century Approaches* (Grand Rapids: Eerdmans, and Carlisle, UK: Paternoster, 1995).

Sampley, J. Paul (ed.). *Paul in the Greco-Roman World* (Harrisburg, PA: Trinity, 2003), and *Walking between the Times: Paul's Moral Reasoning* (Minneapolis: Fortress, 1991).

Sanders, E. P. *Paul and Palestinian Judaism* (Philadelphia: Fortress, 1977), and *Paul, the Law, and the Jewish People* (Philadelphia: Fortress, 1983).

Sumney, Jerry L. *Identifying Paul's Opponents: The Question of Method in 2 Corinthians* (Sheffield: Sheffield Academic Press, 1990), and *'Servants of Satan', 'False Brothers' and Other Opponents of Paul* (Sheffield: Sheffield Academic Press, 1999).

Wansink, Craig S. *Chained in Christ: The Experience and Rhetoric of Paul's Imprisonments* (Sheffield: Sheffield Academic Press, 1996).

III. JEWISH PERSPECTIVES ON PAUL

Baeck, Leo. "The Faith of Paul," and "Romatic Religion," tr. by Walter Kaufmann in *Judaism and Christianity* (Philadelphia: Jewish Publication Society, 1960), 139–68, 189–292. See also J. Louis Martyn. "Leo Baeck's Reading of Paul." In *Theological Issues in the Letters of Paul* (Nashville: Abingdon, 1997), 47–69.

Boyarin, Daniel. *A Radical Jew: Paul and the Politics of Identity* (Berkeley: University of California Press, 1994).

Schoeps, Hans Joachim. *Paul: The Theology of the Apostle in the Light of Jewish Religious History*, tr. by Harold Knight (Philadelphia: Westminster, 1961).

Segal, Alan F. *Paul the Convert: The Apostolate and Apostasy of Saul the Pharisee* (New Haven: Yale University Press, 1990).

IV. STYLE, LANGUAGE, AND FORM OF LETTERS

Aune, David E. *The New Testament in its Literary Environment* (Philadelphia: Westminster, 1987), esp. 158–225 (letters), and idem, (ed.), *Greco-Roman Literature and the New Testament* (Atlanta: Scholars, 1988), esp. 71–84 (diatribe) and 85–106 (ancient Greek letters).
Francis, Fred O., and J. Paul Sampley. *Pauline Parallels* (2nd ed., Philadelphia: Fortress, 1984).
Stirewalt, M. Luther, Jr. *Paul, the Letter Writer* (Grand Rapids: Eerdmans, 2003).

V. INDIVIDUAL LETTERS

The best commentaries are published as part of a series, though most series are notoriously uneven in quality. For advanced students with knowledge of Greek, the most useful are *The Anchor Bible, Hermeneia, The International Critical Commentary, The New International Greek Testament Commentary,* and *Word Biblical Commentary.* Less technical are *Abingdon New Testament Commentaries, Augsburg Commentaries on the New Testament, Black's (Harper's) New Testament Commentaries, Interpretation, The New International Commentary on the New Testament, The New Interpreter's Bible, The New Testament Library, Reading the New Testament,* and *Sacra Pagina.*

Useful information can also be found in one-volume biblical commentaries, such as Raymond E. Brown, Joseph A. Fitzmyer, and Roland E. Murphy (eds.), *The New Jerome Biblical Commentary* (Englewood Cliffs: Prentice-Hall, 1990), the *HarperCollins Bible Commentary,* ed. by James L. Mays et al. with the Society of Biblical Literature (San Francisco: HarperSanFrancisco, 2000), and two that pay particular attention to feminist concerns: Elisabeth Schüssler Fiorenza (ed.), *Searching the Scriptures* (2 vols., New York: Crossroad, 1993–94), and Carol A. Newsom and Sharon H. Ringe (eds.), *Women's Bible Commentary: Expanded Edition* (Louisville: Westminster John Knox, 1998).

Helpful treatments of Paul and his letters can often be found in Bible dictionaries. The best is *The Anchor Bible Dictionary* (5 vols.), edited by David Noel Freedman. For a conservative dictionary devoted to Paul, see Gerald F. Hawthorne and Ralph P. Martin (eds.), *Dictionary of Paul and His Letters* (Downers Grove: InterVarsity, 1993). The best website for finding internet resources on virtually anything related to early Christianity is *The New Testament Gateway,* available at the following URL address: http://www.ntgateway.com.

VI. EARLY INFLUENCE AND INTERPRETATION

A. General Treatments

Babcock, William S. (ed.). *Paul and the Legacies of Paul* (Dallas: SMU Press, 1990).
Wiles, M. F. *The Divine Apostle: The Interpretation of St. Paul's Epistles in the Early Church* (Cambridge: Cambridge University Press, 1967).

B. Paulinism and the New Testament

Beker, J. Christiaan. *Heirs of Paul: Paul's Legacy in the New Testament and in the Church Today* (Minneapolis: Fortress, 1991).
Kroedel, Gerhard (ed.). *The Deutero-Pauline Letters* (rev. ed., Minneapolis: Fortress, 1993).
Lentz, J. C. *Luke's Portrait of Paul* (Cambridge: Cambridge University Press, 1993).
Vielhauer, Phillip. "On the 'Paulinism' of Acts." In *Studies in Luke-Acts,* ed. by Leander E. Keck and J. Louis Martyn (Nashville: Abingdon, 1966), 33–50.

C. Paul and the Ancient Church

Ancient Christian Commentary on Scripture: New Testament, edited by Thomas C. Oden (Downers Grove: InterVarsity, 1999–). [Excerpts of comments on Paul's letters and other NT books by various pre-Nicene and post-Nicene Christian writers.]
Augustine: *Augustine on Romans,* tr. by Paula Fredriksen Landes (Chico, CA: Scholars, 1982).
John Chrysostom: *Homilies on the Acts of the Apostles* and *Homilies on Paul's Letters,* in Series 1, Vols. 11–13 of *A Select Library of the Nicene and Post-Nicene Fathers of the Christian Church,* edited by Philip Schaff (rp. Grand Rapids: Eerdmans, 1979), and *In Praise of St. Paul,* tr. by Margaret M. Mitchell, *The Heavenly Trumpet* (Tübingen: Mohr-Siebeck, 2000; Louisville: Westminster John Knox, 2000), 440–87.
Origen: *Origen, Commentary on the Epistle to the Romans,* tr. by Thomas P. Scheck (2 vols.; Washington: Catholic University of America Press, 2001).
Pelagius: *Pelagius' Commentary on St. Paul's Epistle to the Romans,* tr. by Theodore de Bruyn (Oxford: Oxford University Press, 1993).
Theodore of Mopsuestia: *The Commentaries on the Minor Epistles of Paul,* tr. by Rowan A. Greer (Atlanta: Society of Biblical Literature, forthcoming).
Theodoret: *Theodoret of Cyrus, Commentary on the Letters of St. Paul,* tr. by Robert Charles Hill (2 vols.; Brookline, MA: Holy Cross Orthodox Press, 2001).
Victorinus: *Marius Victorinus' Commentary on Galatians,* tr. by S. A. Cooper (Oxford: Oxford University Press, 2005), and *Commentary on Ephesians,* tr. by S. A. Cooper, *Metaphysics and Morals in Marius Victorinus' Commentary on the Letter to the Ephesians* (New York: Peter Lang, 1995), 43–114.

Name Index

Abraham, 15, 16–17, 18, 68–69, 241, 328–29, 463, 603–10 *passim*
Acherusian Lake, 155
Acts of Phileas, 319
Acts of the Scillitan Martyrs, 319, 342
Adam, 42, 43, 70–71, 294, 360–61, 416
Agabus, 181
Agrippa, 183–84
Ahlstrom, Sydney, 689
Alexander, 126, 135, 308
Alexandria, 341, 343, 539
Ambrosiaster, 213, 229, 309, 336–37, 360–62
Ananias, 175
Antioch, 176, 325, 342
Apollos, 21, 24, 26, 137, 171
Aquila, 62, 85, 135, 659–69 *passim*
Arabia, 13, 18, 426
Archippus, 113
Aristarchus, 113
Aristotle, 527, 626–28
Asia, 47
Asia Minor, 341, 343
Augustine, 339, 365–78, 438, 455–56, 503–4, 550–51

Backus, Isaac, 526
Baeck, Leo, 439
Bar Jesus, 204–9
Barnabas, 13, 455
Barth, Karl, 356–57, 390–93
Basilides/Basilideans, 341–42, 343, 345, 349–51, 618, 620
Bassler, Jouette M., 592, 634–43
Baur, Ferdinand Christian, 325*n*, 399–408, 463
Beatty, Chester, 113, 124
Belial, 53

Bloom, Harold, 690
Boyarin, Daniel, 458–70
Brooten, Bernadette J., 338–40
Buber, Martin, 439
Bultmann, Rudolf, 274, 505, 521, 522, 590, 593–603
Bunyan, John, 416–18

Cadbury, Henry J., 501
Caelestius, 356
Caesarea, 88, 95, 182–83
Caligula, 540
Callicratidas, 630
Calvin, John, 416
Campenhausen, Hans von, 303, 346
Carpocrates/Carpocratians, 294, 341, 343
Cassianus, Julius, 341
Cephas, *see* Peter, St.
Chloe, 21, 23
Chrysostom, Dio, 22, 646–48
Chrysostom, John, 54, 216–22, 294, 339, 549, 550, 552, 554, 669
Claudius, 62, 540
Clement of Alexandria, 93*n*, 213, 216, 293, 338–39
Clement of Rome, 224–25
Constantine, 540
Corinth, 21
Crescens, 134

Dahl, Nils Alstrup, 591, 603–10
Damascus, 59, 175–76, 184, 427
D'Angelo, Mary Rose, 450
Daniel, 479
Daube, David, 440–47
David, 69, 79, 157
Deissmann, Adolf, 591
Demas, 134, 308, 309
Dibelius, Martin, 242–43

699

Subject Index